Choices in Relationships

An Introduction to Marriage and the Family · TENTH EDITION

David Knox
East Carolina University

Caroline Schacht
East Carolina University

WADSWORTH
CENGAGE Learning

Australia • Brazil • Japan • Korea • Mexico • Singapore • Spain • United Kingdom • United States

WADSWORTH
CENGAGE Learning

Choices in Relationships: An Introduction to Marriage and the Family, **Tenth Edition**
David Knox and Caroline Schacht

Senior Acquisitions Editor: Chris Caldeira

Developmental Editor: Melanie Cregger

Assistant Editor: Melanie Cregger

Editorial Assistant: Rachael Krapf

Media Editor: Lauren Keyes

Marketing Manager: Andrew Keay

Marketing Assistant: Jillian Myers

Marketing Communications Manager:
Laura Localio

Content Project Manager: Cheri Palmer

Creative Director: Rob Hugel

Art Director: Caryl Gorska

Print Buyer: Judy Inouye

Rights Acquisitions Account Manager, Text:
Bob Kauser

Rights Acquisitions Account Manager, Image:
Leitha Etheridge-Sims

Production Service: Macmillan Publishing
Solutions

Text Designer: Lou Ann Thesing

Photo Researcher: Pre-PressPMG

Copy Editor: Heather McElwain

Illustrator: Macmillan Publishing Solutions

Cover Designer: RHDG

Cover Image: Getty Images/Digital Vision

Compositor: Macmillan Publishing Solutions

For product information and technology assistance, contact us at
Cengage Learning Customer & Sales Support, 1-800-354-9706
For permission to use material from this text or product,
submit all requests online at **www.cengage.com/permissions**
Further permissions questions can be e-mailed to
permissionrequest@cengage.com

Library of Congress Control Number: 2009926708

Student Edition:
ISBN-13: 978-0-495-80843-5

ISBN-10: 0-495-80843-1

Loose-leaf Edition:
ISBN-13: 978-0-495-80925-8

ISBN-10: 0-495-80925-X

Wadsworth
10 Davis Drive
Belmont, CA 94002-3098
USA

Cengage Learning is a leading provider of customized learning solutions with office locations around the globe, including Singapore, the United Kingdom, Australia, Mexico, Brazil, and Japan. Locate your local office at **www.cengage.com/global**

Cengage Learning products are represented in Canada by Nelson Education, Ltd.

To learn more about Wadsworth, visit **www.cengage.com/Wadsworth**

Purchase any of our products at your local college store or at our preferred online store **www.ichapters.com**

Printed in the United States of America
1 2 3 4 5 6 7 13 12 11 10 09

To Jack Turner

Contents in Brief

Contents

CHAPTER *3*

Gender 76

CHAPTER *4*

Communication 107

CHAPTER *10*

Planning Children and Contraception 309

CHAPTER *11*

Parenting 351

CHAPTER *17*

Relationships in the Later Years 551

EPILOGUE

The Future of Marriage and the Family 586

SPECIAL TOPIC *1*

Sexual Anatomy and Physiology 588

SPECIAL
TOPIC *2*

Sexual Dysfunctions 595

SPECIAL
TOPIC *3*

Human Immunodeficiency Virus and Other Sexually Transmitted Infections 602

SPECIAL
TOPIC *4*

Careers in Marriage and the Family 610

SPECIAL
TOPIC *5*

Resources and Organizations 614

Preface

The title of this text is *Choices in Relationships* because of an important, enduring fact: The choices we make in our relationships have consequences for the happiness, health, and well-being of ourselves, our partners, our marriage, our parents, and our children. By making deliberate informed choices, everyone wins. Not to take our relationship choices seriously is to limit our ability to enjoy fulfilling emotional relationships—the only game in town.

New to the Tenth Edition: Chapter-by-Chapter Changes

In addition to new research, a new feature "What If?" has been added to each chapter. These encourage critical thinking of relationship issues. In addition, examples of new content added to each chapter include the following:

Chapter 1 Choices in Relationships: An Introduction

Decision making styles of college students

Global influences on choices

Media influences on choices

Social organization as theoretical framework

Game theory as theoretical framework

Transpersonal as theoretical framework

Chapter 2 Love

The difference between love, lust, and infatuation

The neurobiology of love

Romantic love in marriage in four countries

Types of jealousy

Interview with person practicing polyamory

Effect of romantic love on personal happiness

Chapter 3 Gender

Gender differences in views of romantic relationships

Gender roles in Latino families

Self-Assessment: *Beliefs about Women's Scale*

Research Application: *Traditional wife? College men who want one*

Effect of female circumcision on the sexuality of wives

Self-immolation of Afghan women

Chapter 4 Communication

Lying in "monogamous" relationships

Cheating in "monogamous" relationships

Meaning and importance of touch as a principle of communication

Research Application: *Cell phone use and romantic partner reaction*

Use of "soft" emotions rather than "hard" emotions when communicating with a partner

Chapter 5 Singlehood, Hanging Out, Hooking Up, and Cohabitation

Research Application: *"Hey Big Boy!"—Women who initiate relationships with men*

Individuals delaying marriage longer

Legal blurring of the married and unmarried

Hispanic rite of passage—Quinceñera

Alternatives to Marriage Project

Living apart together

Internet—meeting a partner online and after

Children during cohabitation?

Chapter 6 Mate Selection

Research Application: *Becoming involved with someone on the rebound? How fast should you run?*

Searching for homogamy: An in-class exercise

Black and white dating relationships compared

Helen Fisher's personality types and mate selection

Marriage to escape debt or gain access to a partner's health benefits

Optimism as a personality quality predictive of happy relationships

Chapter 7 Marriage Relationships

Hispanic families

Canadian families

The wedding night

Unique Features of the Text

Choices in Relationships has several unique features that are a part of every chapter.

Self-Assessment Scales

Each chapter features one or more self-assessment scales, which allow students to measure a particular aspect of themselves or their relationships. Examples include the "Love Attitudes Scale," "Supportive Communication Scale," and "Involved Couple's Inventory."

What If?

To personalize the focus of choices in relationships, we present a new feature whereby we present two "what ifs?" in each chapter. Examples include "What if you have made a commitment to marry someone but feel it is a mistake?" or "What if you are in love with two people at the same time?" and "What if an old lover contacts you?"

Research Application

To emphasize that *Choices in Relationships* is not merely a self-help book but a college textbook, we present a research application section in every chapter and specify how new research may be applied to one's interpersonal relationships. Examples of new research applications to this edition include "Cell Phone Use and Romantic Partner Reaction," "Hey Big Boy!—Women Who Initiate Relationships with Men," and "Becoming Involved with Someone on the Rebound—How Fast Should You Run?"

Personal Choices

An enduring popular feature of the text is that of personal choices—detailed discussions of personal choice dilemmas. Examples include "Who is the Best Person for You to Marry?" "Should I Get Involved in a Long-Distance Relationship?" and "Deciding to Have Intercourse with a New Partner."

Social Policies

The Obama administration has emphasized the need for "social policies that work." In each chapter, we review social policies relevant to marriage and the family—abstinence or comprehensive sex education in the public school system, marriage education in public schools, and mediation before litigation in divorce proceedings.

Diversity in the United States

These paragraphs reveal racial, religious, same-sex, economic and educational differences in regard to relationship phenomena. For example, Kurdek (2008) compared relationship quality of cohabitants over a ten-year period of both partners from 95 lesbian, 92 gay male, and 226 heterosexual couples living without children, and both partners from 312 heterosexual couples living with children. Lesbian couples showed the highest levels of relationship quality averaged over all assessments.

Diversity in Other Countries

To reveal courtship, marriage, and family patterns in other societies, "Diversity in Other Countries" paragraphs are presented throughout the text. For example, research by Lucas et al. (2008) examined 2,000 couples in Britain, Turkey, China, and the United States and found that romantic love and spousal support functioned similarly for all couples. Other research shows differences from the United States—for example, living together before marriage in Italy is virtually nonexistent, but is expected in Sweden.

Data—National and International

To replace speculation and guessing with facts, we provide data from national samples as well as data from around the world. For example, divorce rates in the United States are not soaring but have stabilized. The United States is not alone in having a relatively high divorce rate.

Summary

The chapter summaries include questions and answers, with each question highlighting a major section in the chapter.

Key Terms

Boldfaced type indicates key terms used in the text, listed at the end of each chapter, and defined in the glossary at the end of the text.

Web Links

The Internet is an enormous relationship resource. Internet addresses are provided at the end of each chapter. These have been checked at the time of publication to ensure that they are "live."

Supplements and Resources

The tenth edition of *Choices in Relationships* is accompanied by a wide array of supplements prepared for both the instructors and students. Some new resources have been created specifically to accompany the tenth edition, and all of the continuing supplements have been thoroughly revised and updated.

Supplements for the Instructor

Instructor's Resource Manual with Test Bank   This manual provides instructors with learning objectives, a list of major concepts and terms (with page references), detailed lecture outlines, extensive student projects and classroom activities, current InfoTrac® College Edition articles, current movie and video suggestions for use of media in the classroom, Internet exercises, and self-assessment handouts for each chapter. Also included is a concise user guide for InfoTrac College Edition and a table of contents for the *ABC® News* Marriage and Family Video Series. The Test Bank contains fifty multiple-choice questions, ten true-false questions, ten short answer and discussion questions, and five essay questions per chapter. Objective test items are also provided for the Special Topics sections. The Test Bank items are also available electronically on PowerLecture with JoinIn™ and ExamView®.

PowerLecture with JoinIn™ and ExamView®   This easy-to-use, one-stop digital library and presentation tool includes preassembled Microsoft® PowerPoint® lecture slides with graphics from the text, making it easy for you to assemble, edit, publish, and present custom lectures for your course. The PowerLecture CD-ROM also includes video-based polling and quiz questions that can be used with the JoinIn on TurningPoint personal response system. PowerLecture also features ExamView testing software, which includes all the test items from the printed Test Bank in electronic format, enabling you to create customized tests of up to 250 items that can be delivered in print or online.

Classroom Activities for Marriage and Family   Made up of contributions by instructors who teach the course, this book will add new life to your lectures. It includes group exercises, lecture ideas, and homework assignments.

***ABC News* Marriage and Family Video Series, Volumes I–II**   This series illustrates how the principles that students learn in the classroom apply to the stories they see on television with the *ABC News* Marriage and Family Video Series, an exclusive series jointly created by Wadsworth and ABC. Each volume consists of approximately forty-five minutes of footage originally broadcast on ABC and selected specifically to illustrate concepts relevant to the marriage and the family course. The videos are broken into short two- to five-minute segments, perfect for classroom use as lecture launchers or to illustrate key concepts. An annotated table of contents accompanies each video with descriptions of the segments. Special adoption conditions apply. Topics include living together versus marriage, the aftermath of sperm donation, and the effect of war on marriage.

Supplements for the Student

Study Guide   Each chapter of the Study Guide includes learning objectives, key terms (with page references), a detailed chapter outline, current InfoTrac College Edition exercises, Internet exercises, and a personal application section. Students can test and apply their knowledge of concepts with chapter practice tests, including twenty multiple-choice questions, ten true-false questions, ten completion questions, five short-answer questions, and five essay questions all with page references. The Study Guide includes practice test items for not only each of the chapters but the Special Topics sections of the text as well.

Relationship Skills Exercises   This new supplement, full of assessments and questionnaires, will encourage students to think more reflectively on important topics related to marriage, such as finances and intimacy. Assignments can be completed in class or at home, alone or with a partner.

Online Resources

The Companion Website for *Choices in Relationships: An Introduction to Marriage and the Family,* Tenth Edition   The book's companion site includes chapter-specific resources for instructors and students. For instructors, the site offers a password-protected instructor's manual, Microsoft PowerPoint presentation slides, and more. For students, there are a multitude of text-specific study aids: tutorial practice quizzes that can be scored and e-mailed to the instructor, Web links, InfoTrac College Edition exercises, flash cards, MicroCase® Online data exercises, crossword puzzles, Virtual Explorations, and much more!

InfoTrac College Edition   Give your students anytime, anywhere access to reliable resources with InfoTrac College Edition, the online library. This fully searchable database offers full-text articles from thousands of diverse sources, such as academic journals, newsletters, and up-to-the-minute periodicals including *Time, Newsweek, Science, Forbes,* and *USA Today.* The incredible depth and breadth of material—available twenty-four hours a day from any computer with Internet access—makes conducting research so easy, your students will want to use it to enhance their work in every course! Through InfoTrac College Edition's InfoWrite®, students now also have instant access to critical thinking and paper writing tools. Both adopters and their students receive unlimited access for four months.

Acknowledgments

Texts are always a collaborative and collective product. This tenth edition reflects the commitment and vision of Chris Caldeira. We thank Chris for her state-of-the-art content guidance throughout this new edition. We would also like to thank Melanie Cregger, our developmental editor who was always prompt in moving the revision forward; Andrew Keay, the marketing manager; Lauren Keyes, the media editor; Cheri Palmer, the production project manager; Leitha Etheridge-Sims, the image permissions manager; Bob Kauser, the text permissions manager; and Jill Traut, the project manager at Macmillan Publishing Solutions. All were superb, and we appreciate their professionalism and attention to detail. We would also like to thank Charla Blumell for updating the information on contraception and sexually transmitted diseases.

Reviewers for the Tenth Edition

Kim Farmer, Martin Community College; Susan Schuller Friedman, California State University Los Angeles; Christina Hawkey, Arizona Western College; Jane A. Nielsen, College of Charleston; Patricia J. Sawyer, Middlesex Community College; Kathleen Wells, University of Arizona South

Reviewers for the Previous Editions

Grace Auyang, University of Cincinnati; Rosemary Bahr, Eastern New Mexico University; Von Bakanic, College of Charleston; Mary Beaubien, Youngstown State University; Sampson Lee Blair, Arizona State University; Mary Blair-Loy, Washington State University; David Daniel Bogumil, Wright State University; Elisabeth O. Burgess, Georgia State University; Craig Campbell, Weber State University; Michael Capece, University of South Florida; Lynn Christie, Baldwin-Wallace College; Laura Cobb, Purdue University and Illinois State University; Jean Cobbs, Virginia State University; Donna Crossman, Ohio State University; Karen Dawes, Wake Technical Community College; Susan Brown Donahue, Pearl River Community College; Doug Dowell, Heartland Community College; John Engel, University of Hawaii; Mary Ann Gallagher, El Camino College; Shawn Gardner, Genesee Community College; Ted Greenstein, North Carolina State University; Heidi Goar, St. Cloud State University; Norman Goodman, State University of New York at Stony Brook; Jerry Ann Harrel-Smith, California State University, Northridge; Gerald Harris, University of Houston; Rudy Harris, Des Moines Area Community College; Terry Hatkoff, California State University, Northridge; Sheldon Helfing, College of the Canyons; Tonya Hilligoss, Sacramento City College; Rick Jenks, Indiana University; Richard Jolliff, El Camino College; Diane Keithly, Louisiana State University; Steve Long, Northern Iowa Area Community College; Patricia B. Maxwell, University of Hawaii; Carol May, Illinois Central College; Tina Mougouris, San Jacinto College; Lloyd Pickering, University of Montevallo; Scott Potter, Marion Technical College; Janice Purk, Mansfield University; Cherylon Robinson, University of Texas at San Antonio; Cynthia Schmiege, University of Idaho; Eileen Shiff, Paradise Valley Community College; Scott Smith, Stanly Community College Beverly Stiles; Tommy Smith, Auburn University; Beverly Stiles, Midwestern State University; Dawood H. Sultan, Louisiana State University; Elsie Takeguchi, Sacramento City College; Myrna Thompson, Southside Virginia Community College; Teresa Tsushima, Iowa State University; Janice Weber-Breaux, University of Southwestern Louisiana; Loreen Wolfer, University of Scranton

We love the study, writing, and teaching of marriage and the family and recognize that no one has a corner on relationships. We welcome your insights, stories, and suggestions for improvement in the next edition of this text. We are also available to respond to questions about your own interpersonal issues. We check our e-mail frequently and invite you to e-mail us.

David Knox, e-mail: *Knoxd@ecu.edu*
Caroline Schacht, e-mail: *Schachtc@ecu.edu*

About the Authors

David Knox, Ph.D., is Professor of Sociology at East Carolina University, where he teaches courtship and marriage, marriage and the family, and sociology of human sexuality. He is a marriage and family therapist and the author or coauthor of ten books and seventy professional articles. He and Caroline Schacht are married.

Caroline Schacht, M.A. in Sociology and M.A. in Family Relations, is instructor of sociology at East Carolina University and teaches courtship and marriage, introduction to sociology, and the sociology of food. Her clinical work includes marriage and family relationships. She is also a divorce mediator and the coauthor of several books, including *Understanding Social Problems* (Wadsworth 2010).

Nobody can go back and start a new beginning, but anyone can start today and make a new ending.

Maria Robinson, author

Choices in Relationships: An Introduction

Contents

True or False?

1. College students today (Generation Yers) are in no hurry to find "the one," to marry, and to have children.

2. In a study of college students on decision making, most viewed their predominant pattern in making decisions as "being irresponsible" rather than "being in control."

3. Most individuals regard pets as family members.

4. High school students who take a marriage education course can identify an unhealthy relationship and are more realistic about relationships and marriage.

5. The social exchange framework is the most common theoretical framework used in empirical studies of marriage and the family.

Answers: **1.** T **2.** F **3.** T **4.** T **5.** T

Of all the rocks upon which we build our lives, we are reminded today that family is the most important.

Barack Obama

When Wilbur and Orville Wright (of the famous Wright brothers) reviewed the progress of previous "experts" about how to fly, they noticed a preoccupation with getting the machines off the ground with little attention to controlling the craft once in flight. Our focus in this text is not only those choices that help to launch a loving relationship but also those choices that help to ensure a long-lasting, durable flight.

We encourage a proactive approach of taking charge of your life and making wise relationship choices. The World Health Organization defines *health* as a state of complete physical, mental, and social well-being, and not merely the absence of disease or infirmity. This definition underscores the importance of social relationships as an important element in our individual and national health. Making the right choices in our relationships, including marriage and family relationships, is critical to our health, happiness, and sense of well-being. Our times of greatest elation and sadness are in reference to our love relationships.

Choices in Relationships—View of the Text

The central theme of this text is choices in relationships. Although we have over a hundred such choices to make, among the most important are whether to marry, who to marry, when to marry, whether to have children, whether to remain emotionally and sexually faithful to one's partner, and whether to use a condom. Though structural and cultural influences are operative, a choices framework emphasizes that individuals have some control over their relationship destiny by making deliberate choices to initiate, respond to, nurture, or terminate intimate relationships.

Facts about Choices in Relationships

The facts to keep in mind when making relationship choices include the following.

Not To Decide Is To Decide Not making a decision is a decision by default. If you are sexually active and decide not to use a condom, you have made a decision to increase your risk for contracting a sexually transmissible infection, including HIV. If you don't make a deliberate choice to end a relationship that is unfulfilling, abusive, or going nowhere, you have made a choice to continue in that relationship and have little chance of getting into a more positive and satisfying relationship. If

Authors

If these individuals do not decide to become committed to each other and to work on their relationship, they have decided to drift, which means they may not end up together—not to decide is to decide.

you don't make a decision to be faithful to your partner, you have made a decision to be vulnerable to cheating.

If we don't change the direction we are headed, we will end up where we are going.

Chinese Proverb

Some Choices Require Correction   Some of our choices, although appearing correct at the time that we make them, turn out to be disasters. Once we realize that a choice is having consistently negative consequences, we need to stop defending the old choice, reverse the position, make new choices, and move forward. Otherwise, one remains consistently locked into continued negative outcomes of "bad" choices. For example, choosing a partner who was loving and kind but who turns out to be abusive and dangerous requires correcting that choice. To stay in the abusive relationship will have predictable disastrous consequences—to make the decision to disengage and to move on opens the opportunity for a loving relationship with another partner. In the meantime, living alone may be a better alternative than living in a relationship in which you are abused and may end up

What if You Have Made a Commitment to Marry but Feel It Is a Mistake?

WHAT IF?

We know three individuals who reported the following: "On my wedding day, I knew it was a mistake to marry this person." Although all had their own reasons for going through with marrying, the basic reason was social pressure. All three are now divorced and clearly regret marrying. The take-home message is to "listen to your senses" and to act accordingly. To avoid acting on the feelings that the relationship is doomed may be to delay the inevitable. The price of ending a marriage, particularly with children, is much higher than ending a relationship before marriage.

The Relationship Involvement Scale

This scale is designed to assess the level of your involvement in a current relationship. Please read each statement carefully, and write the number next to the statement that reflects your level of disagreement to agreement, using the following scale.

1	2	3	4	5	6	7
Strongly Disagree						Strongly Agree

_____ 1. I have told my friends that I love my partner.

_____ 2. My partner and I have discussed our future together.

_____ 3. I have told my partner that I want to marry him/her.

_____ 4. I feel happier when I am with my partner.

_____ 5. Being together is very important to me.

_____ 6. I cannot imagine a future with anyone other than my partner.

_____ 7. I feel that no one else can meet my needs as well as my partner.

_____ 8. When talking about my partner and me, I tend to use the words "us," "we," and "our."

_____ 9. I depend on my partner to help me with many things in life.

_____ 10. I want to stay in this relationship no matter how hard times become in the future.

Scoring

Add the numbers you assigned to each item. A 1 reflects the least involvement and a 7 reflects the most involvement. The lower your total score (10 is the lowest possible score), the lower your level of involvement; the higher your total score (70), the greater your level of involvement. A score of 40 places you at the midpoint between a very uninvolved and very involved relationship.

Other Students Who Completed the Scale

Valdosta State University. The participants were 31 male and 86 female undergraduate psychology students haphazardly selected from Valdosta State University. They received course credit for their participation. These participants ranged in age from 18 to 59 with a mean age of 20.25 (SD = 4.52). The ethnic background of the sample included 70.9% white, 23.9% Black, 1.7% Hispanic, and 3.4% from other ethnic backgrounds. The college classification level of the sample included 46.2% freshmen, 36.8% sophomores, 14.5% juniors, and 2.6% seniors.

East Carolina University. Also included in the sample were 60 male and 129 female undergraduate students haphazardly selected from East Carolina University. These participants ranged in age from 18 to 43 with a mean age of 20.40 (SD 5 3.58). The ethnic background of the sample included 76.2% white, 14.3% Black, 0.5% Hispanic, 1.6% Asian, 2.6% American Indian, and 4.8% from other ethnic backgrounds. The college classification level of the sample included 40.7% freshmen, 19.0% sophomores, 19.6% juniors, and 20.6% seniors. All participants were treated in accordance with the ethical guidelines of the American Psychological Association (1992).

Scores of Participants

When students from both universities were combined, the average score of the men was 50.06 (SD = 14.07) and the average score of the women was 52.93 (SD = 15.53), reflecting moderate involvement for both sexes. There was no significant difference between men and women in level of involvement. However, there was a significant difference (p < .05) between whites and non-whites, with whites reporting greater relationship involvement (M = 53.37; SD = 14.97) than non-whites (M = 48.33; SD = 15.14).

In addition, there was a significant difference between the level of relationship involvement of seniors compared with juniors (p < .05) and freshmen (p < .01). Seniors reported more relationship involvement (M = 57.74; SD = 12.70) than did juniors (M = 51.57; SD 5 15.37) or freshmen (M = 50.31; SD = 15.33).

Source

"The Relationship Involvement Scale" 2004 by Mark Whatley, Ph.D., Department of Psychology, Valdosta State University, Valdosta, Georgia 31698-0100. Used by permission. Other uses of this scale by written permission of Dr. Whatley only (mwhatley@valdosta.edu). Information on the reliability and validity of this scale is available from Dr. Whatley.

Life is the sum of all of your choices.

Albert Camus, French author and philosopher

dead. Other examples of making corrections involve ending dead or loveless relationships (perhaps after investing time and effort to improve the relationship or love feelings), changing jobs or career, and changing friends.

Choices Involve Trade-Offs By making one choice, you relinquish others. Every relationship choice you make will have a downside and an upside. If you decide to stay in a relationship that becomes a long-distance relationship, you are continuing involvement in a relationship that is obviously important to you. However, you may spend a lot of time alone when you could be discovering new relationships. If you decide to marry, you will give up your freedom to pursue other emotional and/or sexual relationships, and you will also give up some of your control over how you spend your money—but you may also get a wonderful companion with whom to share life. The Relationship Involvement Scale (see the Self-Assessment section) will help you identify the level of your involvement in your current relationship.

Chapter 1 Choices in Relationships: An Introduction

Choices Include Selecting a Positive or Negative View As Thomas Edison progressed toward inventing the light bulb, he said, "I have not failed. I have found ten thousand ways that won't work." In spite of an unfortunate event in your life, you can choose to see the bright side. Regardless of your circumstances, you can choose to view a situation in positive terms. A breakup with a partner you have loved can be viewed as the end of your happiness or an opportunity to become involved in a new, more fulfilling relationship. The discovery of your partner cheating on you can be viewed as the end of the relationship or an opportunity to examine your relationship, to open up communication channels with your partner, and to develop a stronger relationship. Finally, discovering that one is infertile can be viewed as a catastrophe or as a challenge to face adversity with one's partner. One's point of view does make a difference—it is the one thing we have control over.

We choose our joys and sorrows long before we experience them.

Kahlil Gibran, Lebanese-American author

Choices Involve Different Decision-Making Styles Allen et al. (2008) identified four patterns in the decision-making process of 148 college students. These patterns and the percentage using each pattern included (1) "I am in control" (45 percent), (2) "I am experimenting and learning" (33 percent), (3) "I am struggling but growing" (14 percent), and (4) "I have been irresponsible" (3 percent). Of those who reported that they were in control, about a third (34 percent) said that they were "taking it slow," and about 11 percent reported that they were "waiting it out." Men were more likely to report that they were "in control." Hence, these college students could conceptualize their decision-making style; they knew what they were doing. Of note, only 3 percent labeled themselves as being irresponsible.

Choices Produce Ambivalence Choosing among options and trade-offs often creates ambivalence—conflicting feelings that produce uncertainty or indecisiveness as to a course of action to take. There are two forms of ambivalence: sequential and simultaneous. In **sequential ambivalence**, the individual experiences one wish and then another. For example, a person may vacillate between wanting to stay in a less-than-fulfilling relationship or to end it. In **simultaneous ambivalence**, the person experiences two conflicting wishes at the same time. For example, the individual may feel both the desire to stay with the partner and the desire to break up at the same time. The latter dilemma is reflected in the saying, "You can't live with them, and you can't live without them." Some anxiety about choices is normative and should be embraced.

Most Choices Are Revocable; Some Are Not Most choices can be changed. For example, a person who has chosen to be sexually active with multiple partners can later decide to be monogamous or to abstain from sexual relations. Individuals who have in the past chosen to emphasize career, money, or advancement over marriage and family can choose to prioritize relationships over economic and career-climbing behaviors. People who have been unfaithful in the past can elect to be emotionally and sexually committed to a new partner.

Other choices are less revocable. For example, backing out of the role of spouse is much easier than backing out of the role of parent. Whereas the law permits disengagement from the role of spouse (formal divorce decree), the law ties parents to dependent offspring (for example, through child support). Hence, the decision to have a child is usually irrevocable. Choosing to have unprotected sex can also result in a lifetime of coping with sexually transmitted infections.

Choices of Generation Y Those in **Generation Y** (typically born between 1979 and 1984) are the children of the baby boomers. About 40 million of them, these Generation Yers (also known as the Millennial or Internet Generation) have been the focus of their parents' attention. They have been nurtured, coddled, and scheduled into day-care centers for getting ahead. The result is a generation of high self-esteem, self-absorbed individuals who believe they "are the best." Unlike their parents who believe in paying one's dues, getting credentials, and sacrifice through hard work to achieve economic stability, Generation Yers focus on fun, enjoyment, and flexibility. They might choose a summer job at the beach if it buys a burger and a room with six friends over an internship at IBM that smacks of the corporate America sellout. Generation Yers know college graduates who work at McDonald's, so they may wonder, *why bother?* and instead, seek innovative ways of drifting through life; they may continue to live with their parents, live communally, or get food by "dumpster diving." In effect, they are the generation of immediate gratification; they focus only on the here and now. The need for social security is too far off, and health care is available, so they say, "for free at the local hospital emergency room."

Generation Yers are also relaxed about relationship choices. Rather than pair-bond, they "hang out," "hook up," and "live together." They are in no hurry to find "the one," to marry, or to begin a family. To be sure, not all youth fit this characterization. Some have internalized their parents' values, and are focused on education, credentials, a stable job, a retirement plan, and health care. They may view education as the ticket to a good job and expect their college to provide a credential they can market. However, increasingly, Generation Yers are taking their time getting to the altar and focusing on education, career, and enjoying their freedom in the meantime (Generation Y Data 2007).

Choices Are Influenced by the Stage in the Family Life Cycle   The choices a person makes tend to be individualistic or familistic, depending on the stage of the family life cycle that the person is in. Before marriage, individualism characterizes the thinking and choices of most individuals. Individuals need only be concerned with their own needs. Most people delay marriage in favor of completing school, becoming established in a career, and enjoying the freedom of singlehood.

Once married, and particularly after having children, the person's familistic values and choices ensue as the needs of a spouse and children begin to influence. Evidence of familistic choices is reflected in the fact that spouses with children are less likely to divorce than spouses without children.

Making Wise Choices is Facilitated by Learning Decision-Making Skills   Choices occur at the individual, couple, and family level. Deciding to transfer to another school or take a job out of state may involve all three levels, whereas the decision to lose weight is more likely to be an individual decision. Regardless of the level, the steps in decision making include setting aside enough time to evaluate the issues involved in making a choice, identifying alternative courses of action, carefully weighing the consequences for each choice, and being attentive to your own inner voice ("Listen to your senses"). The goal of most people is to make relationship choices that result in the most positive and least negative consequences.

We asked our students to identify their "best" and "worst" relationship choices (see Table 1.1)

Table 1.1   "Best" and "Worst" Choices Identified by University Students

Best Choice	Worst Choice
Waiting to have sex until I was older and involved.	Cheating on my partner.
Ending a relationship with someone I did not love.	Getting involved with someone on the rebound.
Insisting on using a condom with a new partner.	Making decisions about sex when drunk.
Ending a relationship with an abusive partner.	Staying in a relationship I knew was dead.
Forgiving my partner and getting over cheating.	Changing schools to be near my partner.
Getting out of a relationship with an alcoholic.	Not going after someone I really wanted.

Buddy Marterre, photographer

One's choice of a spouse is socially constrained—less than 1 percent of all marriages consist of a black and a white spouse.

Global, Structural/Cultural, and Media Influences on Choices

Choices are influenced by global, structural/cultural, and media factors. This section reviews the ways in which globalization, social structure, and culture impact choices in relationships. Although a major theme of this book is the importance of taking active control of your life in making relationship choices, it is important to be aware that the social world in which you live restricts and channels such choices. For example, enormous social disapproval for marrying someone of another race is part of the reason that 95 percent of all individuals in the United States marry someone of the same race.

Globalization Families exist in the context of world globalization. Economic, political, and religious happenings throughout the world affect what happens in your marriage and family in the United States. When the price of oil per barrel increases in the Middle East, gasoline costs more, leaving fewer dollars to spend on other items. When the stock market in Hong Kong drops 500 points, Wall Street reacts, and U.S. stocks drop. The politics of the Middle East (for example, terrorist or nuclear threats from Iran) impact Homeland Security measures so that getting through airport security to board a plane may take longer. The outbreak of Swine Flu in Mexico affects other countries.

The country in which you live also affects your happiness and well-being. For example, in a study, citizens of thirteen countries were asked to indicate their level of life satisfaction on a scale from 1 (dissatisfied) to 10 (satisfied): citizens in Switzerland averaged 8.3, those in Zimbabwe averaged 3.3, and those in the United States averaged 7.4 (Veenhoven 2007). The Internet, CNN, and mass communications provide global awareness so that families are no longer isolated units.

Social Structure The social structure of a society consists of institutions, social groups, statuses, and roles.

1. Institutions. The largest elements of society are social **institutions**, which may be defined as established and enduring patterns of social relationships. In addition to the family, major institutions of society include the economy, education, and religion. Institutions affect individual decision making. For example,

The greatest tragedy in life is not failing to reach your goals. The great tragedy lies in having no goals to reach.

Benjamin Mays, former president of Morehouse College

you live in a capitalistic society where economic security is valued—the number-one value held by college students (Pryor et al. 2008). In effect, the more time you spend focused on obtaining money, the less time you have for relationships. You are now involved in the educational institution that will impact your choice of a mate (college-educated people tend to select and marry one another). Religion also affects sexual and relationship choices (for example, religion may result in delaying first intercourse, not using a condom or marrying someone of the same faith). The family is a universal institution. Spouses who "believe in the institution of the family" are highly committed to maintaining their marriage and do not regard divorce as an option.

2. *Social groups.* Institutions are made up of social groups, defined as two or more people who share a common identity, interact, and form a social relationship. Most individuals spend their day going between social groups. You may awaken in the context (social group) of a roommate, partner, or spouse. From there you go to class with other students, lunch with friends, work with the boss, and talk on the phone to your parents. So, within twenty-four hours you have been in at least five social groups. These social groups have varying influences on your choices. Your roommate influences who you have in your room for how long, your friends may want to eat at a particular place, your boss will assign you certain duties, and your parents may want you to come home for the weekend.

Your interpersonal choices are influenced mostly by your partner and peers (for example, your sexual values, use of condoms, and the amount of alcohol you consume). Thus, selecting a partner and peers carefully is important. Falstaff, one of Shakespeare's characters, said, "Company, villainous company, hath been the spoil of me."

The age of the partner you select to become romantically involved with is influenced by social context. If you are a woman, your parents and peers will probably approve of you dating and marrying "someone a little older." Likewise, if you are a guy, your parents and peers will probably approve of you dating and marrying someone "a little younger."

Tables 1.2 and 1.3 reflect how these social influences restrict who you end up dating and marrying. East Carolina University has a student body of 27,000 students. Notice how being a freshmen or senior impacts the number of available partners for women and men. These figures are based on the **mating gradient**, that women tend to date and to marry men who are older and vice versa.

Social groups may be categorized as primary or secondary. **Primary groups**, which tend to involve small numbers of individuals, are characterized by

Table 1.2 Men Available to Women at ECU—Example of Social Constraint on Potential Partner of 27,000 Students at ECU, 10,800 Are Men

Female	Total Men	Uninvolved Men
Freshmen	10,800 Freshmen through seniors	5,400
Sophomore	8,100 Sophomores through seniors	4,050
Junior	5,400 Juniors through seniors	2,700
Senior	2,700 *Only* seniors	1,350

Note: As the woman moves from freshmen to senior status, the number of men available to her decreases annually (mating gradient). Hence, as a freshmen coed at ECU, there are 5,400 men who do not have girlfriends whom she can date. By her senior year, there are only 1,350 available men because only seniors will likely date her (freshmen males will think she is too old).

Table 1.3 Women Available to Men at ECU—Example of Social Influences on Who One Can Date of 27,000 Students at ECU, 16,200 Are Women

Male	Total Women	Uninvolved Women
Freshmen	4,050 Only freshmen	2,025
Sophomore	8,100 Freshmen plus sophomores	4,050
Junior	12,150 Freshmen, sophomores, and juniors	6,075
Senior	16,200 All undergraduates	8,100

Note: As the male moves from freshmen to senior status, the number of women available to him increases annually (mating gradient). Hence, as a first-year male student, there are only 2,025 freshmen coeds who don't have boyfriends that are potential dates (senior females are not likely to date a freshmen male). By his senior year, there are over 8,000 potential dates because all unattached females are available to a senior male.

interaction that is intimate and informal. Parents are members of one's primary group and may exercise enormous influence over one's mate choice. Lehmiller and Agnew (2007) found that romantically involved couples that perceived that their parents and friends did not approve of their relationship were more likely to break up than couples that viewed approval from these social networks.

Although parents may register direct disapproval, influence may also be less direct in how they influence the mate choices of their children; by living in the "right" neighborhood, joining a particular church, and enrolling their children in a college or university, parents influence the context in which their children are likely to meet and select a "suitable" marriage partner.

In contrast to primary groups, **secondary groups** may involve small or large numbers of individuals and are characterized by interaction that is impersonal and formal. Being in a context of classmates, coworkers, or fellow students in the library are examples of secondary groups. Members of secondary groups have much less influence over one's relationship choices than members of one's primary groups.

Most people regard primary groups as crucial for their personal happiness and feel adrift if they have only secondary relationships. Indeed, in the absence of close primary ties, they may seek meaning in secondary group relationships. Comedian George Carlin said that his "fans were his family" because he was in a different town performing more than half the weekends a year, implying he had no "real" family.

3. Statuses. Just as institutions consist of social groups, social groups consist of statuses. A **status** is a position a person occupies within a social group. The statuses we occupy largely define our social identity. The statuses in a family may consist of mother, father, child, sibling, stepparent, and so on. In discussing family issues, we refer to statuses such as teenager, cohabitant, and spouse. Statuses are relevant to choices in that many choices can significantly change one's status. Making decisions that change one's status from single person to spouse to divorced person can influence how people feel about themselves and how others treat them.

4. Roles. Every status is associated with many **roles**, or sets of rights, obligations, and expectations associated with a status. Our social statuses identify who we are; our roles identify what we are expected to do. Roles guide our behavior and allow us to predict the behavior of others. Spouses adopt a set of obligations

I don't want to spend my life jaded, waiting . . . to wake up one day and find that I let all these years go by . . . wasted.

Carrie Underwood, *Wasted*

and expectations associated with their status. By doing so, they are better able to influence and predict each other's behavior.

Because individuals occupy a number of statuses and roles simultaneously, they may experience role conflict. For example, the role of the parent may conflict with the role of the spouse, employee, or student. If your child needs to be driven to the math tutor, your spouse needs to be picked up at the airport, your employer wants you to work late, and you have a final exam all at the same time, you are experiencing role conflict.

Culture   Just as social structure refers to the parts of society, culture refers to the meanings and ways of living that characterize people in a society. Two central elements of culture are beliefs and values.

1. *Beliefs.* **Beliefs** refer to definitions and explanations about what is true. The beliefs of an individual or couple influence the choices they make. Dual-earner couples that believe that young children flourish best with a full-time parent in the home make different child-care decisions than do couples who believe that day care offers opportunities for enrichment. If a person believes that children are best served by being reared with two parents, the decision regarding what to do about a premarital pregnancy or an unhappy marriage will differ from a decision made by a person who believes that single-parent families can provide an enriching context for rearing children.

2. *Values.* **Values** are standards regarding what is good and bad, right and wrong, desirable and undesirable. Values influence choices. **Individualism** involves making decisions that are more often based on what serves the individual's rather than the family's interests (**familism**). Americans are characteristically individualistic, whereas Hispanics are characteristically familistic. **Collectivism** emphasizes doing what is best for the group (not specific to the family group); this is characteristic of traditional Chinese families.

Those who remain single, who live together, who seek a childfree lifestyle, and who divorce are more likely to be operating from an individualistic philosophical perspective than those who marry, do not live together before marriage, rear children, and stay married (a familistic value). Collectivistic values would be illustrated by an Asian child on a swim team who would work for the good of the team, not for personal acclaim.

These elements of social structure and culture play a central role in making interpersonal choices and decisions. One of the goals of this text is to encourage awareness of how powerful social structure and culture are in influencing decision making. Sociologists refer to this awareness as the **sociological imagination** (or sociological mindfulness). For example, though most people in the United States assume that they are free to select their own sex partner, this choice (or lack of it) is in fact heavily influenced by structural and cultural factors. Most people date, have sex with, and marry a person of the same racial background. Structural forces influencing race relations include segregation in housing, religion, and education. The fact that African Americans and European Americans live in different neighborhoods, worship in different churches, and often attend different schools makes meeting a person of a different race unlikely. When such encounters occur, prejudices and bias may influence these interactions so that individuals are hardly "free" to act as they choose. Hence, cultural values (transmitted by and through parents and peers) generally do not support or promote mixed racial interaction, relationship formation, and marriage. In a study of college students, DeCuzzi et al. (2006) found that both European Americans and African Americans tended to view their respective groups more positively. Consider the last three relationships in which you were involved, the level of racial similarity, and the structural and cultural influences on those relationships.

Media Pescosolido et al. (2008) emphasized that "individuals do not come to social interaction devoid of affect and motivation and that all social interactions take place in a context in which organizations, media and larger cultures structure normative expectations which create the possibility of marking 'difference'" (p. 431). Media in all of its forms (television, Internet, movies, print) influences how we think about and make our relationship choices. Media exposure colors the "acceptability" of cohabitation, abortion, same-sex relationships, divorce, single-parent families, and so on. For example, Vogel et al. (2008) noted that the greater the television exposure, the lower the willingness to seek therapy.

Diversity in the United States

People develop and maintain gay and lesbian relationships in the context of disapproving institutions (most religions disapprove of homosexuality) and primary groups (family members often react with shock and grief when their child "comes out"). In addition, although the status terms in marriage are husband and wife, gay and lesbian individuals struggle with which term to use (lover, partner, significant other, companion, spouse, life mate, and so on). As well, their roles as partners in the relationship are not socially scripted.

Other Influences on Relationship Choices

Aside from structural and cultural influences on relationship choices, other influences include family of origin (the family in which you were reared), unconscious motivations, habit patterns, individual personality, and previous experiences.

To dare is to lose one's footing momentarily. Not to dare is to lose oneself.

Soren Kierkegaard, philosopher

1. *Family of origin.* Your family of origin is a major influence on your subsequent choices and relationships. Over half (55.9 percent) of 658 undergraduates at a southeastern university (a random sample phone interview) reported that they were "very close" to their family, and almost another third (31.2 percent) reported that they were "somewhat close" (Bristol and Farmer 2005). Such closeness may translate into the desire for parental approval for one's choice of partner. In addition, Busby et al. (2005) analyzed data on 6,744 individuals in regard to the impact of their family of orientation on their current relationship functioning; they found that the quality of the parents' relationship was strongly related to the quality of their own relationship. The happiness of one's family of origin may vary by sex. Dotson-Blake et al. (2009) analyzed data from 288 undergraduate and graduate students and found that 57 percent of males compared to 45 percent of females viewed their parents' marriage as "excellent."

2. *Unconscious motivations.* Unconscious processes are operative in our choices. A person reared in a lower-class home without adequate food and shelter may become overly concerned about the accumulation of money and may make all decisions in reference to obtaining, holding, or hoarding economic resources.

3. *Habits.* Habit patterns also influence choices. People who are accustomed to and enjoy spending a great deal of time alone may be reluctant to make a commitment to live with people who make demands on their time. A person who has workaholic tendencies is unlikely to allocate enough time to a relationship to make it flourish. Alcohol abuse is associated with a higher number of sexual partners and not using condoms to avoid pregnancy and contraction of sexually transmitted infections.

4. *Personality.* One's personality (for example, introverted, extroverted; passive, assertive) also influences choices. For example, people who are assertive are more likely than those who are passive to initiate conversations with someone they are attracted to at a party. People who are very quiet and withdrawn may never choose to initiate a conversation even though they are attracted to someone. People with a bipolar disorder who are manic one part of the semester (or relationship) and depressed the other part are likely to make different choices when each phase is operative.

5. *Relationships and life experiences.* Current and past relationship experiences also influence one's perceptions and choices. Individuals in a current relationship are more likely to hold relativistic sexual values (choose intercourse

over abstinence). Similarly, people who have been cheated on in a previous relationship are vulnerable to not trusting a new partner.

The life of Ann Landers illustrates how life experience changes one's views and choices. After Landers's death, her only child, Margo Howard (2003), noted that her mother was once against premarital intercourse, divorce, and involvement with a married man. However, when Margo told her that unmarried youth were having intercourse, Landers shifted her focus to the use of contraception. When Margo divorced, Landers began to say that ending an unfulfilling marriage is an option. When Landers was divorced and fell in love with a married man, she said that you can't control who you fall in love with.

The effect of one relationship on another is illustrated by the life of Chet Baker, legendary trumpet player. His biographer details Baker's innocent love for a woman who dumped him to marry his buddy. ". . . [T]hat woman to whom he had opened his heart and who turned out to be a liar and a phony, permanently marred his attitude toward love. In future relationships he would veer between a need for mothering and paranoid mistrust" (Gavin 2003, 28).

In spite of the numerous influences on choices, the theme of this text is to not let destiny direct you but to make deliberate choices. See the Personal Choices section for examples of taking charge of your life.

PERSONAL CHOICES

Relationship Choices—Deliberately or by Default?

It is a myth that we can avoid making relationship decisions, because not to make a decision is to make a decision by default. Some examples follow:

- If we don't make a decision to pursue a relationship with a particular person, we have made a decision (by default) to let that person drift out of our life.
- If we don't decide to do the things that are necessary to keep or improve the relationships we have, we have made a decision to let these relationships slowly disintegrate.
- If we don't make a decision to be faithful to our partner or spouse, we have made a decision to be open to situations and relationships in which we are vulnerable to being unfaithful.
- If we don't make a decision to avoid having intercourse early in a new relationship, we have made a decision to let intercourse occur at any time.
- If we are sexually active and don't make a decision to use birth control or a condom, we have made a decision to expose ourselves to risk for pregnancy or a sexually transmitted infection.
- If we don't make a decision to break up with an abusive partner or spouse, we have made a decision to continue the relationship.

Throughout the text, as we discuss various relationship choices, consider that you automatically make a choice by being inactive—that not to make a choice is to make one. We encourage a proactive style whereby you make deliberate relationship choices.

Having emphasized that making choices in relationships is the theme of this text and having reviewed the mechanisms operative in those choices, we turn to where many relationship choices are made—marriage and family.

Marriage

All of us were born into a family and will end up in a family (however one defines this concept) of our own. "Raising a family" remains one of the top values in life (superseded only by "being well off financially") for undergraduates. In a nationwide study of 240,000 undergraduates in 340 colleges and universities, 76 percent identified this as an essential objective (77 percent for financial success) (Pryor et al. 2008). In a smaller study of 1,319 undergraduates, a "happy marriage" was the top value in life (over financial security and "having a career I love"; Knox and Zusman 2009). Clearly, relationships and family life are important values.

National Data

Over 95 percent of U.S. adult women (96.3 percent) and men (96 percent) aged 65 and older have married at least once (*Statistical Abstract of the United States, 2009*, Table 33).

Traditionally, **marriage** has been viewed as a legal relationship that binds a man and a woman together for reproduction and the subsequent physical and emotional care and socialization of children. Each society works out its own details of what marriage is. In the United States, marriage is a legal contract between a heterosexual couple and the state in which they reside that specifies economic cooperation and encourages sexual fidelity (we discuss gay marriage later in the chapter). The fine print and implied factors implicit during a wedding ceremony include the following elements.

Facts do not cease to exist because they are ignored.

Aldous Huxley, philosopher

Elements of Marriage

Several elements comprise the meaning of marriage in the United States.

Legal Contract Marriage in our society is a legal contract into which two people of different sexes and legal age (usually eighteen or older) may enter when they are not already married to someone else. The marriage license certifies that a legally empowered representative of the state married the individuals, often with two witnesses present.

Under the laws of the state, the license means that spouses will jointly own all future property acquired and that each will share in the estate of the other. In most states, whatever the deceased spouse owns is legally transferred to the surviving spouse at the time of death. In the event of divorce and unless the couple had a prenuptial agreement, the property is usually divided equally regardless of the contribution of each partner. The license also implies the expectation of sexual fidelity in the marriage. Though less frequent because of no-fault divorce, infidelity is a legal ground for both divorce and alimony in some states.

The marriage license is also an economic license that entitles a spouse to receive payment for medical bills by a health insurance company if the partner is insured, to collect Social Security benefits at the death of the other spouse, and to inherit from the estate of the deceased. One of the goals of gay rights advocates who seek the legalization of marriage between homosexuals is that the couple will have the same rights and benefits as heterosexuals.

Though the courts are reconsidering the definition of what constitutes a "family," the law is currently designed to protect spouses, not lovers or cohabitants. An exception is **common-law marriage**, in which a heterosexual couple cohabit and present themselves as married; they will be regarded as legally married in those states that recognize such marriages. Common-law marriages exist in ten states and the District of Columbia (Google "common law marriage states").

Emotional Relationship Most people in the United States regard being in love with the person they marry as an important reason for staying married. Almost

Marriage in the United States begins with an intense love the individuals feel for each other.

half (47.9 percent) of 1,319 undergraduates reported that they would divorce if they no longer loved their spouse (Knox and Zusman 2009). This emphasis on love is not shared throughout the world. Individuals in other cultures (for example, India and Iran) do not require love feelings to marry—love is expected to follow, not precede, marriage. In these countries, parental approval and similarity of religion, culture, and education are considered more important criteria for marriage than love.

Sexual Monogamy   Marital partners expect sexual fidelity. Over two-thirds (68 percent) of 1,319 undergraduates agreed, "I would divorce a spouse who had an affair," and a similar percentage (69 percent) agreed that they would end a relationship with a partner who cheated on them (Knox and Zusman 2009).

Legal Responsibility for Children   Although individuals marry for love and companionship, one of the most important reasons for the existence of marriage from the viewpoint of society is to legally bond a male and a female for the nurture and support of any children they may have. In our society, child rearing is the primary responsibility of the family, not the state.

Marriage is a relatively stable relationship that helps to ensure that children will have adequate care and protection, will be socialized for productive roles in society, and will not become the burden of those who did not conceive them. Even at divorce, the legal obligation of the noncustodial father to the child is maintained through child-support payments.

Announcement/Ceremony   The legal bonding of a couple is often preceded by an announcement in the local newspaper and a formal ceremony in a church or synagogue.

Such a ceremony reflects the cultural importance of the event. Telling parents, siblings, and friends about wedding plans helps to verify the commitment of the partners and also helps to marshal the social and economic support to launch the couple into marital orbit. Most people in our society decide to marry, and the benefits of doing so are enormous. When married people are

Table 1.4 Benefits of Marriage and the Liabilities of Singlehood

Male	Benefits of Marriage	Liabilities of Singlehood
Health	Spouses have fewer hospital admissions, see a physician more regularly, and are "sick" less often.	Single people are hospitalized more often, have fewer medical checkups, and are "sick" more often.
Longevity	Spouses live longer than single people.	Single people die sooner than married people.
Happiness	Spouses report being happier than single people.	Single people report less happiness than married people.
Sexual satisfaction	Spouses report being more satisfied with their sex lives, both physically and emotionally.	Single people report being less satisfied with their sex lives, both physically and emotionally.
Money	Spouses have more economic resources than single people.	Single people have fewer economic resources than married people.
Lower expenses	Two can live more cheaply together than separately.	Cost is greater for two singles than one couple.
Drug use	Spouses have lower rates of drug use and abuse.	Single people have higher rates of drug use and abuse.
Connectedness	Spouses are connected to more individuals who provide a support system—partner, in-laws, etc.	Single people have fewer individuals upon whom they can rely for help.
Children	Rates of high school dropouts, teen pregnancies, and poverty are lower among children reared in two-parent homes.	Rates of high school dropouts, teen pregnancies, and poverty are higher among children reared by single parents.
History	Spouses develop a shared history across time with significant others.	Single people may lack continuity and commitment across time with significant others.
Crime	Spouses are less likely to be involved in crime.	Single people are more likely to be involved in crime.
Loneliness	Spouses are less likely to report loneliness.	Single people are more likely to report being lonely.

compared with singles, the differences are strikingly in favor of the married (see Table 1.4.).

Types of Marriage

Although we think of marriage in the United States as involving one man and one woman, other societies view marriage differently. **Polygamy** is a form of marriage involving more than two spouses. Polygamy occurs "throughout the world . . . and is found on all continents and among adherents of all world religions" (Zeitzen 2008, 8). There are three forms of polygamy: polygyny, polyandry, and pantagamy.

Polygyny **Polygyny** involves one husband and two or more wives and is practiced illegally in the United States by some religious fundamentalist groups. These groups are primarily in Arizona, New Mexico, and Utah (as well as Canada), and have splintered off from the Church of Jesus Christ of Latter-day Saints (commonly known as the Mormon Church). To be clear, the Mormon Church does not practice or condone polygyny. The group that split off represents only about 5 percent of Mormons in Utah and is called the Fundamentalist Church of Jesus Christ of the Latter-day Saints (FLDS). Members of the group feel that the practice of polygyny is God's will. Although illegal, polygynous individuals are rarely prosecuted for several reasons:

1. *One legal marriage; many religious marriages*—in effect, a man will legally marry one wife and bring other wives into the unit via a religious ceremony.

There is no law against a husband living with several women and their children in the same house as long as he is only legally married to one of them.

2. *Population*—Mormons outnumber non-Mormons, representing 70 percent of the population in Utah (there is limited public momentum for prosecuting Mormons).

3. *Prosecution witness*—the absence of finding someone willing to testify for the prosecution makes mounting a case difficult.

4. *Prosecution priorities*—local prosecutors elect to spend available resources on organized crime and drug trafficking rather than on illegal civil relationships.

5. *Jail space*—there is no jail space for housing the hundreds of individuals if convicted.

In spite of the tolerance toward polygyny in Utah, there are some abuses. Some former wives in plural marriages report (a) living in poverty (it is difficult for one man to financially support fifteen wives), (b) nonconsent (some existing wives resent their husbands taking new wives), and (c) child sex abuse (some children as young as 14 are made "new wives"). Warren Steed Jeffs, a former president of FLDS, was charged in Arizona with child sex abuse for arranging the marriage of a teenager to an older married man. In 2007, he was found guilty of two counts of rape as an accomplice and sentenced to ten years to life, and has begun serving his sentence at the Utah State Prison.

Although the items on the previous list may be factors in explaining why polygynous individuals are rarely prosecuted, Hall (2009) has provided an alternative explanation:

> *It is important to note that in many, if not almost all, of these unions only the first wife is legally married to the husband and the other wives are comparable to cohabiting women (in their minds "spiritual wives"). Hence, there is technically no bigamy to prosecute. In addition, pockets of these groups are known to exist in several locations across the country, yet are not being aggressively prosecuted by the local governments (including where there is little LDS influence.) It seems that religion may be less of a factor in the lack of prosecution than other considerations. A primary one is that people in general don't have a stomach for taking kids away from parents or taking parents away from their children and locking them up—unless there is clear danger involved. This is particularly true in that our society is becoming increasingly open to "nontraditional" (kind of an ironic term in this sense) relationship forms among adults. There have been a couple of raids in the past (1953 in Arizona and Texas in 2008), and there was clear national backlash against what was perceived as overly-aggressive breaking up of families.*

There is some concern that, because the wives in the FLDS community have limited education, job skills, and contact with the outside community, they are disadvantaged in extricating themselves if they wanted to. Tapestry Against Polygamy is an organization that has helped women break free from bigamous marriages.

Polygyny among fundamentalist Mormons serves a religious function in that large earthly families are believed to result in large heavenly families. Notice that polygynous sex is only a means to accomplish another goal—large families. See http://www.absalom.com/mormon/polygamy/faq.htm for more information.

It is often assumed that polygyny exists to satisfy the sexual desires of the man, that the women are treated like slaves, and that jealousy among the wives is common. In most polygynous societies, however, polygyny has a political and economic rather than a sexual function. Polygyny is a means of providing many male heirs to continue the family line. In addition, a man with many wives can produce a greater number of children for domestic or farm labor. Wives are not treated like slaves (although women have less status than men in general), all

Marriage Education in Public Schools

Social policies are purposive courses of action that individuals or groups of individuals take regarding a particular issue or problem of concern (Moen and Coltrane 2005). The U.S. government actively supports and encourages marriage via its National Health Marriage Resource Center (see website listing at end of chapter). In addition, public schools are a major source for socialization of values and skills in our youth. With almost half of new marriages ending in divorce, politicians ask whether social policies designed to educate youth about the realities of marriage might be beneficial in promoting marital quality and stability. Might students profit from education about marriage, before they get married, if such relationship skill training is made mandatory in the school curriculum? Of students enrolled in a marriage education course, 100 percent noted that they wished to have happy marriages and relationships, 59 percent feared divorce, and 47 percent reported they were having actual trouble in current or past relationships (Nielsen et al. 2004).

The philosophy behind premarital education is that building a fence at the top of a cliff is better than putting an ambulance at the bottom. Over 2,000 public schools nationwide offer such a course. In Florida, all public high school seniors are required to take a marriage and relationship skills course. Baeder et al. (2007) studied the effectiveness of a marriage education program called "Love U2: Increasing Your Relationship Smarts" with an economically, geographically, and racially diverse sample of 340 high school students. The researchers found participants were more able to identify unhealthy relationship patterns and to become more realistic about relationships and marriages.

McGeorge and Carlson (2006) compared couples exposed to an eight-week premarital education course with those not exposed and found greater readiness for marriage among those who had premarital education. Kirby (2005) also found that, in a pre- and posttest of over 1,000 married couples, those who took a marriage education course scored significantly higher on marital satisfaction after completing the course.

The federal government has a stake in marriage education programs. One motivation is economic because divorce often leads to poverty. Hence, to the degree that people enter marriages that turn out to be stable, there is greater economic stability for the family and less drain on social services for single-parent mothers.

Another motivation for marriage education courses is control of content. The School Textbook Marriage Protection Act, considered in the House education committee in Arkansas, would require that marriage textbooks define marriage as between one man and one woman (*Education Daily* 2005).

There is also opposition to marriage education programs. Opponents question using school time for relationship courses. Teachers are already seen as overworked, and an additional course on marriage seems to press the system to the breaking point. In addition, some teachers lack the training to provide relationship courses. Although training teachers would stretch already-thin budgets, many schools already have programs in family and consumer sciences, and teachers in these programs are trained in teaching about marriage and the family. A related concern with teaching about marriage and the family in high school is the fear on the part of some parents that the course content may be too liberal. Some parents who oppose teaching sex education in the public schools fear that such courses lead to increased sexual activity.

Your Opinion?

1. To what degree do you believe marriage education belongs in the public school system?
2. How should marriage be defined?
3. Should marriage be encouraged by the federal government?

Sources

Baeder, F. A., J. L. Kerpelman, D. G. Schramm, B. Higginbotham, and A. Paulk. 2007. Impact of relationship education on adolescents of diverse backgrounds. *Family Relations* 56:291–304.

Education Daily. 2005. House bill to define marriage in textbooks heads back to education committee. 38(16):4.

Kirby, J. S. 2005. A study of the marital satisfaction levels of participants in a marriage education course. Dissertation Abstracts, International A: *The Humanities and Social Sciences* 66(4):1513-A.

McGeorge, C., and T. Carlson. 2006. Premarital education: An assessment of program efficacy. *Contemporary Family therapy: An International Journal* 28:165–90.

Moen, P., and S. Coltrane. 2005. Families, theories, and social policy. In *Sourcebook of family theory & research*, ed. Vern L. Bengtson, Alan C. Acock, Katherine R. Allen, Peggye Dilworth-Anderson, and David M. Klein, 543–56. Thousand Oaks, CA: Sage Publications.

Nielsen, A., W. Pinsof, C. Rampage, A. H. Solomon, and S. Goldstein. 2004. Marriage 101: An integrated academic and experiential undergraduate marriage education course. *Family Relations* 53:485–94.

household work is evenly distributed among the wives, and each wife is given her own house or own sleeping quarters. Jealousy is minimal because the husband often has a rotational system for conjugal visits, which ensures that each wife has equal access to sexual encounters.

Polyandry The Buddhist Tibetans foster yet another brand of polygamy, referred to as **polyandry**, in which one wife has two or more (up to five) husbands. These husbands, who may be brothers, pool their resources to support one wife. Polyandry is a much less common form of polygamy than polygyny. The major reason for polyandry is economic. A family that cannot afford wives or marriages for each of its sons may find a wife for the eldest son only. Polyandry allows the younger brothers to also have sexual access to the one wife or marriage that the family is able to afford.

Polyamory **Polyamory** (also known as **open relationships**) is a lifestyle in which two lovers do not forbid one another from having other lovers. By agreement, each partner may have numerous other emotional and sexual relationships. Some (about 20 percent) of the 100 members of Twin Oaks Intentional Community in Louisa, Virginia, are polyamorous in that each partner may have several emotional or physical relationships with others at the same time. Although not legally married, these adults view themselves as emotionally bonded to each other and may even rear children together. Polyamory is not swinging, as polyamorous lovers are concerned about enduring, intimate relationships that include sex (Tupelo and Freeman, 2008). We discuss polyamory in greater detail in Chapter 2 on love.

Pantagamy **Pantagamy** describes a group marriage in which each member of the group is "married" to the others. Pantagamy is a more formal arrangement than polyamory and is reflected in communes (for example, Oneida) of the nineteenth and twentieth centuries. Pantagamy is, of course, illegal in the United States.

Our culture emphasizes monogamous marriage and values stable marriages. One expression of this value is the concern for marriage education (see the Social Policy feature on page 17).

Family

Most people who marry choose to have children and become a family. However, the definition of what constitutes a family is sometimes unclear. This section examines how families are defined, their numerous types, and how marriages and families have changed in the past fifty years.

Definitions of Family

The U.S. Census Bureau defines **family** as a group of two or more people related by blood, marriage, or adoption. This definition has been challenged because it does not include foster families or long-term couples (heterosexual or homosexual) that live together. The answer to "who is family?" is important because access to resources such as health care, social security, and retirement benefits is involved. Cohabitants are typically not viewed as "family" and are not accorded health benefits, social security, and retirement benefits of the partner. Indeed, the "live-in partner" or a partner who is gay (although a long-term significant other) may not be allowed to see the beloved in the hospital, which limits visitation to "family only." Nevertheless, the definition of who counts as family is being challenged. In some cases, families are being defined by function rather than by structure—what is the level of emotional and financial commitment and interdependence? How long have they lived together? Do the partners view themselves as a family?

Friends sometimes become family. Due to mobility, spouses may live several states away from their respective families. Although they may visit their families for holidays, they often develop close friendships with others on whom they rely locally for emotional and physical support on a daily basis.

Sociologically, a family is defined as a kinship system of all relatives living together or recognized as a social unit, including adopted people. The family is regarded as the basic social institution because of its important functions of procreation and socialization, and because it is found in some form in all societies. Henley-Walters et al. (2002) studied family life in different cultures and noted that in many respects,

> *the experience of living in a family is the same in all cultures. For example, relationships between spouses and parents and children are negotiated; most relationships within families are hierarchical; the work of the home is primarily the responsibility of the wife; . . . destructive conflict between spouses or parents and children is damaging to children . . . . (p. 449)*

Same-sex couples (for example, Rosie O'Donnell, her partner, and their children, as well as Ellen DeGeneres and her partner) certainly define themselves as family. Massachusetts, Connecticut, Maine, Vermont and Iowa recognize marriages between same-sex individuals. Short of marriage, New Jersey recognizes committed gay relationships as **civil unions**.

Although other states typically do not recognize same-sex marriages or civil unions (and thus people moving from these states to another state lose the privileges associated with marriage), over twenty-four cities and countries (including Canada) recognize some form of domestic partnership. In addition, some corporations, such as Disney, are recognizing the legitimacy of such relationships by providing medical coverage for partners of employees. **Domestic partnerships** are considered an alternative to marriage by some individuals and tend to reflect more egalitarian relationships than those between traditional husbands and wives.

As an aside, some individuals view their pets as part of their family. In a Harris Poll survey of 2,455 adults, 88 percent regarded their pets as family members—more women (93 percent) than men (84 percent), and more dog owners (93 percent) over cat owners (89 percent). Two-thirds of pet owners buy holiday presents for their pets (Harris Poll 2007). Some pet owners buy accident insurance—Progressive© car insurance covers pets. Custody battles have been fought and financial trusts have been set up for pets, and lawsuits against veterinarians have been filed over pets that did not make it out of surgery (Parker 2005).

Pets are routinely included in "family" photos.

Authors

You will either step forward into growth or you will step back into safety.

Abraham Maslow, psychologist

National Data

Based on a survey of 1,000 registered voters age 18 and older, 69 percent considered family pets as a "member of the family"; 19 percent considered them property; and 8 percent considered them both family members and property (Best Friends Survey 2006). According to the Humane Society of the United States, Americans have 71 million household pets: 88 million cats and 75 million dogs (Ward 2007).

Types of Families

There are various types of families.

Family of Origin   Also referred to as the **family of orientation**, this is the family into which you were born or the family in which you were reared. It involves you, your parents, and your siblings. When you go to your parents' home for the holidays, you return to your **family of origin**. Your experiences in your family of origin have an impact on subsequent outcome behavior. For example, if you are born into a family on welfare, you are less likely to attend college than if your parents are both educated and affluent.

Novilla et al. (2006) emphasized the important role the family of orientation plays in health promotion. Children learn the importance of a healthy diet, exercise, moderate alcohol use, and so on, from their family of orientation and may duplicate these patterns in their own families.

Siblings represent an important part of one's family of origin. Indeed, a team of researchers (Meinhold et al. 2006) noted that the relationship with one's siblings, particularly sister–sister relationships, represent the most enduring relationship in a person's lifetime. Sisters who lived near one another and who did not have children reported the greatest amount of intimacy and contact.

Family of Procreation   The **family of procreation** represents the family that you will begin when you marry and have children. Of U.S. citizens living in the United States, 96.3 percent marry and establish their own family of procreation (*Statistical Abstract of the United States, 2009*, Table 33). Across the life cycle, individuals move from the family of orientation to the family of procreation.

Nuclear Family   The **nuclear family** refers to either a family of origin or a family of procreation. In practice, this means that your nuclear family consists of you, your parents, and your siblings; or you, your spouse, and your children. Generally, one-parent households are not referred to as nuclear families. They are binuclear

The relationship these brothers have with each other is likely to be the most enduring relationship of their lives (longer than with their parents, spouses, or children).

Authors

families if both parents are involved in the child's life, or single-parent families if one parent is involved in the child's life and the other parent is totally out of the picture.

Sociologist George Peter Murdock (1949) emphasized that the nuclear family is a "universal social grouping" found in all of the 250 societies he studied. Not only does it channel sexual energy between two adult partners who reproduce, but also these partners cooperate in the care for and socialization of offspring to be productive members of society. "This universal social structure, produced through cultural evolution in every human society, as presumably the only feasible adjustment to a series of basic needs, forms a crucial part of the environment in which every individual grows to maturity" (p. 11). Neyer and Lang (2003) emphasized that closeness to one's kinship members continues throughout one's life and found some evidence for "blood being thicker than water" (p. 310).

Traditional, Modern, and Postmodern Family Silverstein and Auerbach (2005) distinguished between three central concepts of the family. The **traditional family** is the two-parent nuclear family, with the husband as breadwinner and wife as homemaker. The **modern family** is the dual-earner family, where both spouses work outside the home. **Postmodern families** represent a departure from these models, such as lesbian or gay couples and mothers who are single by choice, which emphasizes that a healthy family need not be heterosexual or include two parents.

Binuclear Family A **binuclear family** is a family in which the members live in two separate households. This family type is created when the parents of the children divorce and live separately, setting up two separate units, with the children remaining a part of each unit. Each of these units may also change again when the parents remarry and bring additional children into the respective units (**blended family**). Hence, the children may go from a nuclear family with both parents, to a binuclear unit with parents living in separate homes, to a blended family when parents remarry and bring additional children into the respective units.

Extended Family The **extended family** includes not only the nuclear family but other relatives as well. These relatives include grandparents, aunts, uncles, and cousins. An example of an extended family living together would be a husband and wife, their children, and the husband's parents (the children's grandparents).

> ### Diversity in Other Countries
>
> Kenyan families reflect great diversity. Of 80 million people who live in Kenya, Africa, 80 percent live in rural areas and 20 percent in urban areas. In all, forty-two ethnic groups live in different parts of the country. A "family" in Kenya may mean one nuclear family or networks of related households living very close to one another or at great distances (Odero 2004).

> ### Diversity in Other Countries
>
> Asians are more likely than Anglo-Americans to live with their extended families. Among Asians, the status of the elderly in the extended family derives from religion. Confucian philosophy, for example, prescribes that all relationships are of the super ordinate–subordinate type—husband-wife, parent-child, and teacher-pupil. For traditional Asians to abandon their elderly rather than include them in larger family units would be unthinkable. However, commitment to the elderly may be changing as a result of the Westernization of Asian countries such as China, Japan, and Korea.
>
> In addition to being concerned for the elderly, Asians are socialized to subordinate themselves to the group. Familism (what is best for the group), collectivism (what is best for the larger group), and group identity are valued over independence and individualism (what is best for the individual). Divorce is not prevalent because Asians are discouraged from bringing negative social attention to the family.

Differences between Marriage and Family

The concepts of marriage and the family are often used in tandem. Marriage can be thought of as a set of social processes that lead to the establishment of family. Indeed, every society or culture has mechanisms (from "free" dating to arranged marriages) of guiding their youth into permanent emotionally, legally, or socially

Table 1.5 Differences between Marriage and the Family in the United States

Marriage	Family
Usually initiated by a formal ceremony	Formal ceremony not essential
Involves two people	Usually involves more than two people
Ages of the individuals tend to be similar	Individuals represent more than one generation
Individuals usually choose each other	Members are born or adopted into the family
Ends when spouse dies or is divorced	Continues beyond the life of the individual
Sex between spouses is expected and approved	Sex between near kin is neither expected nor approved
Requires a license	No license needed to become a parent
Procreation expected	Consequence of procreation
Spouses are focused on each other	Focus changes with addition of children
Spouses can voluntarily withdraw from marriage via divorce	Parents cannot divorce themselves from obligations to children
Money in unit is spent on the couple	Money is used for the needs of children
Recreation revolves around adults	Recreation revolves around children

Reprinted by permission of Dr. Lee Axelson.

bonded heterosexual relationships that are designed to result in procreation and care of offspring. Although the concepts of marriage and the family are closely related, they are distinct. Sociologist Dr. Lee Axelson identifies some of these differences in Table 1.5.

Changes in Marriage and the Family

Whatever family we experience today was different previously and will change yet again. A look back at some changes in marriage and the family follow.

The Industrial Revolution and Family Change

The Industrial Revolution refers to the social and economic changes that occurred when machines and factories, rather than human labor, became the dominant mode for the production of goods. Industrialization occurred in the United States during the early- and mid-1800s and represents one of the most profound influences on the family.

Before industrialization, families functioned as an economic unit that produced goods and services for its own consumption. Parents and children worked together in or near the home to meet the survival needs of the family. As the United States became industrialized, more men and women left the home to sell their labor for wages. The family was no longer a self-sufficient unit that determined its work hours. Rather, employers determined where and when family members would work. Whereas children in preindustrialized America worked on farms and contributed to the economic survival of the family, children in industrialized America became economic liabilities rather than assets. Child labor laws and mandatory education removed children from the labor force and lengthened their dependence on parental support. Eventually, both parents had to work away from the home to support their children. The dual-income family had begun.

During the Industrial Revolution, urbanization occurred as cities were built around factories and families moved to the city to work in the factories. Living space in cities was crowded and expensive, which contributed to a decline in the birthrate and thus smaller families. The development of transportation systems during the Industrial Revolution made it possible for family members to travel to work sites away from the home and to move away from extended kin. With increased mobility, many extended families became separated into smaller nuclear family units consisting of parents and their children. As a result of parents leaving the home to earn wages and the absence of extended kin in or near the family household, children had less adult supervision and moral guidance. Unsupervised children roamed the streets, increasing the potential for crime and delinquency.

Industrialization also affected the role of the father in the family. Employment outside the home removed men from playing a primary role in child care and in other domestic activities. The contribution men made to the household became primarily economic.

Finally, the advent of industrialization, urbanization, and mobility is associated with the demise of familism and the rise of individualism. When family members functioned together as an economic unit, they were dependent on one another for survival and were concerned about what was good for the family. This familistic focus on the needs of the family has since shifted to a focus on self-fulfillment—individualism. Families from familistic cultures such as China who immigrate to the United States soon discover that their norms, roles, and values begin to alter in reference to the industrialized, urbanized, individualistic patterns and thinking. Individualism and the quest for personal fulfillment are thought to have contributed to high divorce rates, absent fathers, and parents spending less time with their children.

Hence, although the family is sometimes blamed for juvenile delinquency, violence, and divorce, it is more accurate to emphasize changing social norms and conditions of which the family is a part. When industrialization takes parents out of the home so that they can no longer be constant nurturers and supervisors, the likelihood of aberrant acts by children and adolescents increases. One explanation for school violence is that absent, career-focused parents have failed to provide close supervision for their children.

Changes in the Last Half-Century

Enormous changes have occurred in marriage and the family in the last fifty years. Among changes, divorce has replaced death as the endpoint for the majority of marriages, marriage and intimate relations have become legitimate objects of scientific study, feminism and changes in gender roles in marriage have risen, and remarriages have declined (Amato et al. 2007). Other changes include a delay in age at marriage, increased acceptance of singlehood, cohabitation, and childfree marriages. Even the definition of what constitutes a family is being revised, with some emphasizing that durable emotional bonds between individuals is the core of "family," whereas others insist on a more legalistic view, emphasizing connections by blood marriage or adoption mechanisms. Table 1.6 reflects some of the changes evident in 2010.

In spite of the persistent and dramatic changes in marriage and the family, marriage and the family continue to be resilient. Using this **marriage-resilience perspective**, changes in the institution of marriage are not viewed negatively nor are they indicative that marriage is in a state of decline. Indeed, these changes are thought to have "few negative consequences for adults, children, or the wider society" (Amato et al. 2007, 6).

Families amid a Context of Terrorism

Prior to September 11, 2001, with the exception of Timothy McVeigh bombing the federal building in Oklahoma in 1995, terrorism was thought to exist mostly in foreign countries. Today, husbands, wives, parents, and children live under a new cloud of terror anxiety with "threat levels," "airport security measures," and "new terrorist bombing reports" as part of the evening news. Richman et al.

Table 1.6 Changes in Marriages and Families—1950 and 2010

	1950	2010
Family Relationship Values	Strong values for marriage and the family. Individuals who wanted to remain single or childless were considered deviant, even pathological. Husband and wife should not be separated by jobs or careers.	Individuals who remain single or childfree experience social understanding and sometimes encouragement. Single and childfree people are no longer considered deviant or pathological but are seen as self-actuating individuals with strong job or career commitments. Husbands and wives can be separated for reasons of job or career and live in a commuter marriage. Married women in large numbers have left the role of full-time mother and housewife to join the labor market.
Gender Roles	Rigid gender roles, with men earning income and wives staying at home, taking care of children.	Fluid gender roles, with most wives in workforce, even after birth of children. Part-time work is the modal choice for married women.
Sexual Values	Marriage was regarded as the only appropriate context for intercourse in middle-class America. Living together was unacceptable, and a child born out of wedlock was stigmatized. Virginity was sometimes exchanged for marital commitment.	For many, concerns about safer sex have taken precedence over the marital context for sex. Virginity is no longer exchanged for anything. Living together is regarded as not only acceptable but sometimes preferable to marriage. For some, unmarried single parenthood is regarded as a lifestyle option. It is certainly less stigmatized.
Homogamous Mating	Strong social pressure existed to date and marry within one's own racial, ethnic, religious, and social class group. Emotional and legal attachments were heavily influenced by obligation to parents and kin.	Dating and mating have become more heterogamous, with more freedom to select a partner outside one's own racial, ethnic, religious, and social class group. Attachments are more often by choice.
Cultural Silence on Intimate Relationships	Intimate relationships were not an appropriate subject for the media.	Talk shows, interviews, and magazine surveys are open about sexuality and relationships behind closed doors.
Divorce	Society strongly disapproved of divorce. Familistic values encouraged spouses to stay married for the children. Strong legal constraints kept couples together. Marriage was forever.	Divorce has replaced death as the endpoint of a majority of marriages. Less stigma is associated with divorce. Individualistic values lead spouses to seek personal happiness. No-fault divorce allows for easy divorce. Marriage is tenuous. Increasing numbers of children are being reared in single-parent households apart from other relatives.
Familism versus Individualism	Families were focused on the needs of children. Mothers stayed home to ensure that the needs of their children were met. Adult concerns were less important.	Adult agenda of work and recreation has taken on increased importance, with less attention being given to children. Children are viewed as more sophisticated and capable of thinking as adults, which frees adults to pursue their own interests. Day care is used regularly.
Homosexuality	Same-sex emotional and sexual relationships were a culturally hidden phenomenon. Gay relationships were not socially recognized.	Gay relationships are increasingly a culturally open phenomenon. Some definitions of the family include same-sex partners. Domestic partnerships are increasingly given legal status in some states. Same-sex marriage is a hot social and political issue. More states legalizing same-sex marriage.
Scientific Scrutiny	Aside from Kinsey, few studies were conducted on intimate relationships.	Acceptance of scientific study of marriage and intimate relationships.
Family Housing	Husbands and wives lived in same house.	Husbands and wives may "live apart together" (LAT), which means that, although they are emotionally and economically connected, they (by choice) maintain two households, houses, condos, or apartments. They may be separated for reasons of career, or mutually desire the freedom and independence of having a separate domicile.

(2008) assessed the effects of the terrorist attacks of September 11, 2001, on subsequent mental health among participants in a Midwestern town study. The researchers revealed higher stress and alcohol consumption levels two and four years after the attacks, even after controlling for sociodemographic characteristics and pre-September 11 distress and drinking patterns and concluded that the 9/11 attacks continue to have a negative effect on the health of the American population. Military families, who have always lived with an increased sense of vulnerability, are a first line of defense against terrorism. These families are featured in Chapter 7 on Marriage Relationships.

Theoretical Frameworks for Viewing Marriage and the Family

Although we emphasize choices in relationships as the framework for viewing marriage and the family, other conceptual theoretical frameworks are helpful in understanding the context of relationship decisions. All **theoretical frameworks** are the same in that they provide a set of interrelated principles designed to explain a particular phenomenon and provide a point of view. In essence, theories are explanations.

Social Exchange Framework

In a review of 673 empirical articles, exchange theory was most common among those using a theoretical perspective (Taylor and Bagd 2005). The **social exchange framework** views interaction in terms of cost and profit.

The social exchange framework also operates from a premise of **utilitarianism—** that individuals rationally weigh the rewards and costs associated with behavioral choices. Each interaction between spouses, parents, and children can be understood in terms of each individual's seeking the most benefits at the least cost so as to have the highest "profit" and avoid a "loss" (White and Klein 2002). Both men and women marry because they perceive more benefits than costs for doing

These spouses are not only exchanging companionship but also food.

Authors

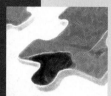
What if Your Partner Is a "Taker" Rather than a "Giver"?

In complementary relationships where one is a "giver" and the other a "taker," the needs of the respective partners may be met. However, where a giver expects a high rate of exchange, a taker will be unacceptable and the relationship will not last. Can a taker become a giver? Yes. But the taker has learned to expect a high rate of exchange (giving very little to get a great deal back), which the giver must cut back on. In effect, the giver must teach the taker that more is required. In general, win-win relationships, those in which each partner derives satisfaction from the ratio of exchanged positives, are desirable. Exploitive or lopsided relationships where one is the giver to the point of abuse are never healthy.

Both optimists and pessimists contribute to our society. The optimist invents the airplane and the pessimist the parachute.

G. B. Stern, British novelist

so. Similarly, those who remain single or who divorce perceive fewer benefits and more costs for marriage. Foster (2008) confirmed that narcissists require a high profit margin in relationships they stay in. We examine how the social exchange framework is operative in mate selection later in the text.

A social exchange view of marital roles emphasizes that spouses negotiate the division of labor on the basis of exchange. For example, a man participates in child care in exchange for his wife earning an income, which relieves him of the total financial responsibility. Social exchange theorists also emphasize that power in relationships is the ability to influence, and avoid being influenced by, the partner.

The various bases of power, such as money, the need for a partner, and brute force, may be expressed in various ways, including withholding resources, decreasing investment in the relationship, and violence.

Family Life Course Development Framework

The **family life course development** framework is the second most frequently used theory in empirical family studies (Taylor and Bagd 2005), and emphasizes the important role transitions that occur in different periods of life and in different social contexts. For example, young married couples become young parents, which changes the interaction between the couple. As spouses age and retire, their new roles impact not only each of them but also their partners.

The family life course developmental framework has a basis in sociology (for example, role transitions), whereas the **family life cycle** has a basis in psychology, with its emphasis on developmental tasks at different ages and stages. If developmental tasks at one stage are not accomplished, functioning in subsequent stages will be impaired. For example, one of the developmental tasks of early marriage is to emotionally and financially separate from one's family of origin. If such separation does not take place, independence as individuals and as a couple is impaired.

The family life course development framework may help to identify the choices with which many individuals are confronted throughout life. Each family stage presents choices. For example, never-married people are choosing partners; newly married people are making choices about careers and when to begin a family; soon-to-be-divorced people are making decisions about custody, child support, and division of property; and remarried people are making choices with regard to stepchildren and ex-spouses. Grandparents are making choices about how much child care to which they want to commit, and widows or widowers are concerned with where to live (with children, a friend, alone, or in a retirement home).

Structural-Functional Framework

The **structural-functional framework** emphasizes how marriage and family contribute to society. Just as the human body is made up of different parts that work together for the good of the individual, society is made up of different institutions (family, education, economics, and so on) that work together for the good of society. **Functionalists** view the family as an institution with values, norms, and activities meant to provide stability for the larger society. Such stability is dependent on families performing various functions for society.

First, families serve to replenish society with socialized members. Because our society cannot continue to exist without new members, we must have some way of ensuring a continuing supply. However, just having new members is not enough. We need socialized members—those who can speak our language and know the norms and roles of our society. So-called **feral** (meaning wild, not domesticated) children are those who are thought to have been reared by animals. Newton (2002) details nine such children, the most famous of which was Peter the Wild Boy found in the Germanic woods at the age of 12 and brought to London in 1726. He could not speak; growling and howling were his modes of expression. He lived until the age of 70 and never learned to talk. Feral children emphasize that social interaction and family context make us human.

Real-life Genie is a young girl who was discovered in the 1970s who had been kept in isolation in one room in her California home for twelve years by her abusive father (James 2008). She could barely walk and could not talk. Although provided intensive therapy at UCLA and the object of thousands of dollars of funded research, Genie progressed only briefly. Today, she is in her early fifties, institutionalized, and speechless. Her story illustrates the need for socialization; the legal bond of marriage and the obligation to nurture and socialize offspring help to ensure that this socialization will occur.

Second, marriage and the family promote the emotional stability of the respective spouses. Society cannot provide enough counselors to help us whenever we have problems. Marriage ideally provides in-residence counselors who are loving and caring partners with whom people share their most difficult experiences.

Children also need people to love them and to give them a sense of belonging. This need can be fulfilled in a variety of family contexts (two-parent families, single-parent families, extended families). The affective function of the family is one of its major offerings. No other institution focuses so completely on meeting the emotional needs of its members as marriage and the family.

Third, families provide economic support for their members. Although modern families are no longer self-sufficient economic units, they provide food, shelter, and clothing for their members. One need only consider the homeless in our society to be reminded of this important function of the family.

In addition to the primary functions of replacement, emotional stability, and economic support, other functions of the family include the following:

- *Physical care*—families provide the primary care for their infants, children, and aging parents. Other agencies (neonatal units, day care centers, assisted-living residences) may help, but the family remains the primary and recurring caretaker. Spouses are also concerned about the physical health of one another by encouraging the partner to take medications and to see the doctor.

- *Regulation of sexual behavior*—spouses are expected to confine their sexual behavior to each other, which reduces the risk of having children who do not have socially and legally bonded parents, and of contracting or spreading sexually transmitted infections.
- *Status placement*—being born in a family provides social placement of the individual in society. One's family of origin largely determines one's social class, religious affiliation, and future occupation. Prince William, the son of Prince Charles and the late Princess Diana, was automatically in the upper class and destined to be in politics by virtue of being born into a political family.
- *Social control*—spouses in high-quality, durable marriages provide social control for each other that results in less criminal behavior. Parole boards often note that the best guarantee that a person released from prison will not return to prison is a spouse who expects the partner to get a job and avoid criminal behavior and who reinforces these goals.

Conflict Framework

Conflict framework views individuals in relationships as competing for valuable resources. Conflict theorists recognize that family members have different goals and values that result in conflict. Conflict is inevitable between social groups (such as parents and children). Conflict theory provides a lens through which to view these differences. Whereas functionalists look at family practices as good for the whole, conflict theorists recognize that not all family decisions are good for every member of the family. Indeed, some activities that are good for one member are not good for others. For example, a woman who has devoted her life to staying home and taking care of the children may decide to return to school or to seek full-time employment. This may be a good decision for her personally, but her husband and children may not like it. Similarly, divorce may have a positive outcome for spouses in turmoil but a negative outcome for children, whose standard of living and access to the noncustodial parent are likely to decrease.

Conflict theorists also view conflict not as good or bad but as a natural and normal part of relationships. They regard conflict as necessary for change and growth of individuals, marriages, and families. Cohabitation relationships, marriages, and families all have the potential for conflict. Cohabitants are in conflict about commitment to marry, spouses are in conflict about the division of labor, and parents are in conflict with their children over rules such as curfew, chores, and homework. These three units may also be in conflict with other systems. For example, cohabitants are in conflict with the economic institution for health benefits for their partners. Similarly, employed parents are in conflict with their employers for flexible work hours, maternity or paternity benefits, and day-care or eldercare facilities.

Karl Marx emphasized that conflict emanates from struggles over scarce resources and for power. Though Marxist theorists viewed these sources in terms of the conflict between the owners of the means of production (bourgeoisie) and the workers (proletariat), they are also relevant to conflicts within relationships. The first of these concepts, conflict over scarce resources, reflects the fact that spouses, parents, and children compete for scarce resources such as time, affection, and space. Spouses may fight with each other over how much time should be allocated to one's job, friends, or hobbies. Parents are sometimes in conflict with each other over who will do what housework or child care. Children are in conflict with their parents and with one another over time, affection, what programs to watch on television, and money.

Conflict theory is also helpful in understanding choices in relationships with regard to mate selection and jealousy. Unmarried individuals in search of a partner are in competition with other unmarried individuals for the scarce resources of a desirable mate. Such conflict is particularly evident in the case of older women in competition for men. At age 85 and older, there are twice as many women (3.9 million) as there are men (1.9 million) (*Statistical Abstract of the United States, 2009,* Table 10). Jealousy is also sometimes about scarce resources. People fear that their "one and only" will be stolen by someone else who has no partner.

Conflict theorists also emphasize conflict over power in relationships. Premarital partners, spouses, parents, and teenagers also use power to control one another. The reluctance of some courtship partners to make a marital commitment is an expression of wanting to maintain their autonomy because marriage implies a relinquishment of power from each partner to the other. Spouse abuse is sometimes the expression of one partner trying to control the other through fear, intimidation, or force. Divorce may also illustrate control. The person who executes the divorce is often the person with the least interest in the relationship. Having the least interest gives that person power in the relationship. Parents and adolescents are also in a continuous struggle over power. Parents attempt to use privileges and resources as power tactics to bring compliance in their adolescent. However, adolescents may use the threat of suicide as their ultimate power ploy to bring their parents under control.

Symbolic Interaction Framework

Symbolic interaction framework views marriages and families as symbolic worlds in which the various members give meaning to each other's behavior. Human behavior can be understood only by the meaning attributed to behavior (White and Klein 2002). Herbert Blumer (1969) used the term *symbolic interaction* to refer to the process of interpersonal interaction. Concepts inherent in this framework include the definition of the situation, the looking-glass self, and the self-fulfilling prophecy.

Definition of the Situation   Two people who have just spotted each other at a party are constantly defining the situation and responding to those definitions. Is the glance from the other person (1) an invitation to approach, (2) an approach, or (3) a misinterpretation—the other person was looking at someone behind the person? The definition a person arrives at will affect subsequent interaction.

Looking-Glass Self   The image people have of themselves is a reflection of what other people tell them about themselves (Cooley 1964). People may develop an idea of who they are by the way others act toward them. If no one looks at or speaks to them, they will begin to feel unsettled, according to Cooley. Similarly, family members constantly hold up social mirrors for one another into which the respective members look for definitions of self.

The importance of the family (and other caregivers) as an influence on the development and maintenance of a positive self-concept cannot be overemphasized (Brown et al. 2009). Orson Welles, known especially for his film *Citizen Kane,* once said that he was taught that he was wonderful and that everything he did was perfect. He never suffered from a negative self-concept. Cole Porter, known for creating such memorable songs as "I Get a Kick out of You," had a mother who held up social mirrors offering nothing but praise and adoration. Because children spend their formative years surrounded by their family, the self-concept they develop in that setting is important to their feelings about themselves and their positive interaction with others.

G. H. Mead (1934) believed that people are not passive sponges but evaluate the perceived appraisals of others, accepting some opinions and not others. Although some parents teach their children that they are worthless, they may eventually overcome the definition.

Your assumptions are your windows on the world. Scrub them off every once in a while or the light won't come through.

Alan Alda, at his daughter's commencement address

Self-Fulfilling Prophecy   Once people define situations and the behaviors in which they are expected to engage, they are able to behave toward one another in predictable ways. Such predictability of behavior also tends to exert influence on subsequent behavior. If you feel that your partner expects you to be faithful, your behavior is likely to conform to these expectations. The expectations thus create a self-fulfilling prophecy.

Symbolic interactionism as a theoretical framework helps to explain various choices in relationships. Individuals who decide to marry have defined their situation as a committed reciprocal love relationship. This choice is supported by the belief that the partners will view each other positively (looking-glass self) and be faithful spouses and cooperative parents (self-fulfilling prophecies).

Later we will discuss the negative emotion of violence. Turner (2007) noted how symbolic interactionism may be used to explain the dynamics of intense emotions (such as violence). He suggested that extreme violence (which depends on intense negative emotions) has its genesis when negative emotions about the self and identity are repressed. All of this happens through the manipulation of symbols (negative self-reference statements) inside one's head.

Family Systems Framework

Systems theory is the most recent of all the theories for understanding family interaction (White and Klein 2002). The **family systems framework** views each member of the family as part of a system and the family as a unit that develops norms of interacting, which may be explicit (for example, parents specify chores for the children) or implied (for example, spouses expect fidelity from each other). These rules serve various functions, such as allocating the resources (money for vacation), specifying the division of power (who decides how money is spent), and defining closeness and distance between systems (seeing or avoiding parents or grandparents).

Rules are most efficient if they are flexible. For example, they should be adjusted over time in response to children's growing competence. A rule about not leaving the yard when playing may be appropriate for a 4-year-old but inappropriate for a 15-year-old. The rules and individuals can be understood only by recognizing that "all parts of the system are interconnected" (White and Klein 2002, 122).

Family members also develop boundaries that define the individual and the group and separate one system or subsystem from another. A boundary is a "border between the system and its environment that affects the flow of information and energy between the environment and the system" (White and Klein 2002, 124). A boundary may be physical, such as a closed bedroom door, or social, such as expectations that family problems will not be aired in public. Boundaries may also be emotional, such as communication, which maintains closeness or distance in a relationship. Some family systems are cold and abusive; others are warm and nurturing.

In addition to rules and boundaries, family systems have roles (leader, follower, scapegoat) for the respective family members. These roles may be shared by more than one person or may shift from person to person during an interaction or across time. In healthy families, individuals are allowed to alternate roles rather than being locked into one role. In problem families, one family member is often allocated the role of scapegoat, or the cause of all the family's problems (for example, an alcoholic spouse).

Family systems may be open, in that they are open to information and interaction with the outside world, or closed, in that they feel threatened by such contact. The Amish have closed family systems and minimize contact with the outside world. Some communes also encourage minimal outside exposure. Twin Oaks Intentional Community of Louisa, Virginia, does not permit any of its almost 100 members to own or keep televisions in their rooms. Exposure to the negative drumbeat of the evening news is seen as harmful.

Social Organization Framework

The family is a social organization that exists and interacts amid other social organizations where there is mutual influence (Zusman et al. 2009). The following are some examples:

1. Societies. The society in which the family exists affects the family. Some families in Iraq live in terror and fear in the context of a politically unstable country. Families in Cuba are not free to travel wherever they would like. Families in China are encouraged to be small (the one-child family policy). Families also affect society. With 61 percent of wives in the United States working outside the home, the need for fast food restaurants and day-care centers increases so that Burger King provides food for the family and KinderCare takes care of the children during the day.

2. Communities. Families affect communities or towns where people live. Every year, over one million divorces impact the legal system (domestic courts are jammed), housing (increased need for single-parent housing), and economic resources (divorced females with children do not receive adequate child support and need money from social services) needed from the community.

3. Associations. Schools, churches, and hospitals are associations that help parents teach their children basic educational skills, instill moral principles, and provide health care. Indeed, the college or university you are attending will increase your intellectual skills and economic independence so that you can become a freestanding adult in our society as you leave the nest.

Feminist Framework

Although a **feminist framework** views marriage and family as contexts of inequality and oppression, there are eleven feminist perspectives, including lesbian feminism (oppressive heterosexuality and men's domination of social spaces), psychoanalytic feminism (cultural domination of men's phallic-oriented ideas and repressed emotions), and standpoint feminism (neglect of women's perspective and experiences in the production of knowledge) (Lorber 1998). Regardless of which feminist framework is being discussed, all feminist frameworks have the themes of inequality and oppression. According to feminist theory, gender structures our experiences (for example, women and men will experience life differently because there are different expectations for the respective genders) (White and Klein 2002). Feminists seek equality in their relationships with their partners.

Human Ecological Framework

Human ecology framework is the study of **ecosystems**, or the interaction of families with their environment. Individuals, couples, and families are dependent on the environment for air, food, and water, and on other human beings for social interaction (White and Klein 2002). The well-being of individuals and families cannot be considered apart from the well-being of the ecosystem. This framework emphasizes the importance of examining families within multiple contexts. For example, nutrition and housing are important to the functioning of families. If a family does not have enough to eat or adequate housing, it will not be able to function at an optimal level. Judkins and Presser (2005) noted that wives engaged in more environmentally sustainable domestic labor than did their husbands (for example, wives would spend more time sorting cans and bottles to be thrown away in different containers).

To let earth continue warming would be deeply immoral.

Al Gore, former vice president

Transpersonal Psychology Framework

Transpersonal psychology focuses on the transpersonal aspects of body, mind, and spirit and how these interact with and strengthen the family. Key concepts include mysticism, spirituality, consciousness, and ultimate potential. The Institute of Transpersonal Psychology in Palo Alto, California, features a curriculum with six areas of inquiry—the intellectual, emotional, spiritual, physical, social, and creative aspects of life. In effect, the transpersonal framework emphasizes the uniqueness of each family member in its "transpersonal" dimension. All members are not just filling social roles but have their own life experiences that are processing.

Game Framework

Game theory views marriage and family relationships not as recreational contexts but as a way to describe behavior as unique patterns of interaction. All games have several concepts. These concepts and examples in reference to marriage and family follow (Hagerty 1970):

1. *Goals—the reason for the game.* All games have goals. The goal of football is to score more points. The goal of marriage (for some) is to maximize one's happiness, enhance financial security, and/or to procreate.

2. *Expectations—perceived outcomes for playing the game.* Expectations are different from goals. Although a football team may have the goal of winning, they may have the expectation of losing if they are playing last year's Super Bowl champ. Similarly, although individuals may have the goal of a happy and durable marriage, they may expect that their own marriage is not immune to divorce if their parents were unhappy and divorced.

3. *Roles—behavior assigned to individual positions of those playing the game.* The various roles in football include the quarterback, center, and kicker. In marriage, the roles are husband, wife, children, and in-laws.

4. *Rules—guidelines for how the game is played.* In football, the penalty for an offensive player holding a defensive player is ten yards. In marriage, a spouse may not greet an old partner with a prolonged hug and kiss without the penalty of disapproval from the spouse. Rules in marriage may include how late a spouse can be, how much a spouse can spend without consulting the other, and what to disclose to those outside the marriage.

5. *Values—standards of achievement.* Steroid use is supposed to be contrary to the values of playing football. In marriage, examples of values may include saying a blessing at meals, fidelity, and staying out of debt.

6. *Language—unique terminology of a game.* In football, "Hail Mary pass," "fourth down conversion," and "punt" are examples. In marriage, spouses may call each other "honey bun," "sweetie," and "mamma/daddy."

7. *Strategies—behaviors designed to maximize one's advantage in playing the game.* In football, the strategy may be to "run the wishbone," which allows the offensive team options of running or passing each time the offensive team has the football. In marriage, a husband may cook his wife's favorite meal before asking if his mother can visit for a month. A wife may encourage her husband to go fishing with his buddy before bringing up that she would like to go to the beach for a week with her girlfriends.

8. *Rituals—patterned behaviors surrounding a game.* In football, the national anthem is played before a game is played. Players representing each team also meet midfield to toss a coin to determine which team gets the ball first. In marriage, going to church on Sunday morning, going to the beach for a week in the summer, and having black-eyed peas on New Year's Day are example of rituals.

9. *Artifacts—concrete symbols that the game exists.* In football, **artifacts** include the football, helmets, and goalposts. In marriage, wedding rings and photographs on the mantle are examples.

10. *Myths—beliefs that perpetuate the game.* In football, the myths include that "sports build character," "the best team wins," and "it's not whether you win or lose but how you play the game." In marriage, myths include, "there is only one true love," "love conquers all," and "children are the bright flowers in the marital garden."

The major theoretical frameworks for viewing marriage and the family are summarized in Table 1.7.

Table 1.7 Theoretical Frameworks for Marriage and the Family

Theory	Description	Concepts	Level of Analysis	Strengths	Weaknesses
Social Exchange	In their relationships, individuals seek to maximize their benefits and minimize their costs.	Benefits Costs Profit Loss	Individual Couple Family	Provides explanations of human behavior based on outcome.	Assumes that people always act rationally and all behavior is calculated.
Family Life Course Development	All families have a life course that is composed of all the stages and events that have occurred within the family.	Stages Transitions Timing	Institution Individual Couple Family	Families are seen as dynamic rather than static. Useful in working with families who are facing transitions in their life courses.	Difficult to adequately test the theory through research.
Structural-Functional	The family has several important functions within society; within the family, individual members have certain functions.	Structure Function	Institution	Emphasizes the relation of family to society, noting how families affect and are affected by the larger society.	Families with non-traditional structures (single-parent, same-sex couples) are seen as dysfunctional.
Conflict	Conflict in relationships is inevitable, due to competition over resources and power.	Conflict Resources Power	Institution	Views conflict as a normal part of relationships and as necessary for change and growth.	Sees all relationships as conflictual, and does not acknowledge cooperation.
Symbolic Interaction	People communicate through symbols and interpret the words and actions of others.	Definition of the situation Looking-glass self Self-fulfilling prophecy	Couple	Emphasizes the perceptions of individuals, not just objective reality or the viewpoint of outsiders.	Ignores the larger social interaction context and minimizes the influence of external forces.
Family Systems	The family is a system of interrelated parts that function together to maintain the unit.	Subsystem Roles Rules Boundaries Open system Closed system	Couple Family	Very useful in working with families who are having serious problems (violence, alcoholism). Describes the effect family members have on each other.	Based on work with systems, troubled families, and may not apply to nonproblem families.
Social Organization	Family interacts with other social contexts and social organizations.	Societies Communities Associations	Institution Micro	Demonstrates interaction and effects of various social contexts.	Various linkages overlap.
Feminism	Women's experience is central and different from man's experience of social reality.	Inequality Power Oppression	Institution Individual Couple Family	Exposes inequality and oppression as explanations for frustrations women experience.	Multiple branches of feminism may inhibit central accomplishment of increased equality.
Human Ecological	Families interact with and are interdependent with their environment.	Ecosystem Interdependence Environment	Institution Individual Couple Family	Can be applied to families of different structures and ethnic or racial backgrounds.	Scope of the theory may be too broad.
Transpersonal Psychology	Family members have transcendent, spiritual, religious, meditative aspects of their being.	Mysticism Spirituality Consciousness Ultimate potential	Micro	Emphasizes transcendent aspects of family members.	Various linkages overlap. Not differentiated from humanistic psychology.
Game Theory	Marriage and family involve unique patterns of interaction.	Goals Rules Values Language Rituals Myths	Micro	Easy to conceptualize because it's similar to a recreational game.	Game is dynamic so rules, rituals, and language are constantly changing with time.

Evaluating Research in Marriage and the Family

"New Research Study" is a frequent headline in popular magazines (such as *Cosmopolitan, Glamour, Redbook*) promising accurate information about "hooking up," "what women want," "what men want," or other relationship, marriage, and family issues. As you read such articles, as well as the research in such texts as this, be alert to their potential flaws. Following a list of steps in the research process, we present some specific issues to keep in mind when evaluating research.

Steps in the Research Process

Several steps are used in conducting research.

1. *Identify the topic or focus of research.* Select a focus about which you are passionate. For example, are you interested in studying cohabitation of college students? Give your projected study a title in the form of a question—"Do People Who Cohabit before Marriage Have Happier Marriages Than Those Who Do Not?"

2. *Review the literature.* Go online to the various databases of your college or university and read research that has already been published on cohabitation. Not only will this prevent you from "reinventing the wheel" (you might find a research study has already been conducted on exactly what you want to study), but it will give you ideas for your study.

3. *Develop hypotheses.* A **hypothesis** is a suggested explanation for a phenomenon. For example, you might suggest that cohabitation results in greater marital happiness and less divorce because the partners have a chance to "test-drive" each other.

4. *Decide on a method of data collection.* To test your hypothesis, do you want to interview college students, give them a questionnaire, or ask them to complete an online questionnaire? Of course, you will also need to develop a list of questions for your interview or survey questionnaire.

5. *Get IRB approval.* To ensure the protection of people who agree to be interviewed or who complete questionnaires, researchers must submit a summary

All research must be critically evaluated.

of their proposed research to the Institutional Review Board (IRB) of their institution who reviews the research to ensure that the project is consistent with research ethics and poses no undue harm to participants. Important considerations include collecting data from individuals who are told that their participation is completely voluntary, that maintains their anonymity, and that is confidential.

6. *Collect and analyze data.* There are various statistical packages designed to analyze data to discover if your hypotheses are true or false.

7. *Write up and publish results.* Writing up and submitting your findings for publication is important so that your study becomes part of the literature in cohabitation.

Specific Issues in Evaluating Research Quality
The following numerous issues need to be considered in evaluating research.

Sample   Some of the research on marriage and the family is based on random samples. In a **random sample**, each individual in the population has an equal chance of being included in the sample. Random sampling involves randomly selecting individuals from an identified population. That population often does not include the homeless or people living on military bases. Studies that use random samples are based on the assumption that the individuals studied are similar to and therefore representative of the population that the researcher is interested in.

Because of the trouble and expense of obtaining random samples, most researchers study subjects to whom they have convenient access. This often means students in the researchers' classes. The result is an overabundance of research on "convenience" samples consisting of white, Protestant, middle-class college students. Because college students cannot be assumed to be similar in their attitudes, feelings, and behaviors to their noncollege peers or older adults, research based on college students cannot be generalized beyond the base population. To provide a balance, this text includes data that reflects people of different ages, marital statuses, racial backgrounds, lifestyles, religions, and social classes. When presenting only data on college student samples, it is important not to generalize the findings too broadly.

In addition to having a random sample, having a large sample is important. The American Council on Education and University of California (Pryor et al. 2008) collected a national sample of 240,580 first-semester undergraduates at 340 colleges and universities throughout the United States; the sample was designed to reflect the responses of 1.4 million first-time, full-time students entering four-year colleges and universities. If only fifty college students had been in the sample, the results would have been less valuable in terms of generalizing beyond that sample. Similarly, Corra et al. (2009) analyzed national data collected over a thirty-year period from the 1972–2002 General Social Survey (GSS) to discover the influence of sex (male or female) and race (white or black) on the level of reported marital happiness. This is an enormous set of random samples and gives validity to the findings.

Be alert to the sample size of the research you read. Most studies are based on small samples. In addition, considerable research has been conducted on college students, leaving us to wonder about the attitudes, values, and behaviors of noncollege students.

Control Groups   In an example of a study that concludes that an abortion (or any independent variable) is associated with negative outcomes (or any dependent variable), the study must necessarily include two groups: (1) women who have had an abortion, and (2) women who have not had an abortion. The latter would serve as a **control group**—the group not exposed to the independent variable you are studying (**experimental group**). Hence, if you find that women in both groups in your study develop negative attitudes toward sex, you know that abortion cannot be the cause. Be alert to the existence of a control group, which is usually *not* included in research studies.

Age and Cohort Effects   In some research designs, different cohorts or age groups are observed and/or tested at one point in time. One problem that plagues such research is the difficulty—even impossibility—of discerning whether observed differences between the subjects studied are due to the research variable of interest, cohort differences, or some variable associated with the passage of time (for example, biological aging).

A good illustration of this problem is found in research on changes in marital satisfaction over the course of the family life cycle. In such studies, researchers may compare the levels of marital happiness reported by couples that have been married for different lengths of time. For example, a researcher may compare the marital happiness of two groups of people—those who have been married for fifty years and those who have been married for five years. However, differences between these two groups may be due to (1) differences in age (age effect), (2) the different historical time period that the two groups have lived through (cohort effect), or (3) being married different lengths of time (research variable). Keeping these issues in mind when you read studies on marital satisfaction over time is helpful.

Terminology   In addition to being alert to potential shortcomings in sampling and control groups, you should consider how the phenomenon being researched is defined. For example, if you are conducting research on living together, how would you define this term?, How many people, of what sex, spending what amount of time, in what place, engaging in what behaviors will constitute your definition? Indeed, researchers have used more than twenty definitions of what constitutes living together.

What about other terms? Considerable research has been conducted on marital success, but how is the term to be defined? What is meant by marital satisfaction, commitment, interpersonal violence, and sexual fulfillment? Before reading too far in a research study, be alert to the definitions of the terms being used. Exactly what is the researcher trying to measure?

Researcher Bias   Although one of the goals of scientific studies is to gather data objectively, it may be impossible for researchers to be totally objective. Researchers are human and have values, attitudes, and beliefs that may influence their research methods and findings. It may be important to know what the researcher's bias is to evaluate the findings. For example, a researcher who does not support abortion rights may conduct research that focuses only on the negative effects of abortion. Similarly, researchers funded by corporations who have a vested interest in having their products endorsed are also suspect. Thomas (2007) investigated the toy industry and noted that some researchers are funded by corporations that make them celebrities when their research supports outcomes conducive to selling products to infants and toddlers. In 2008, Dr. Eric Westman of Duke University compared the Atkins diet with two other diets and found the Atkins diet superior in terms of patients keeping weight off. However, the Robert C. and Veronica Atkins Foundation funded the study. Similarly, in 2008, the makers of Crestor (AstraZeneca) funded a study that showed the cholesterol-lowering statin drug resulted in big reductions in heart attacks, strokes, and deaths in people with so-called healthy cholesterol levels. Should we be suspicious?

Time Lag   Typically, a two-year lag exists between the time a study is completed and the study's appearance in a professional journal. Because textbook production takes even longer than getting an article printed in a professional journal, they do not always present the most current research, especially on topics in flux. In addition, even though a study may have been published recently, the data on which the study was based may be old. Be aware that the research you read in this or any other text may not reflect the most current, cutting-edge research.

Distortion and Deception Our society is no stranger to distortion and deception—weapons of mass destruction? Writers at the prestigious *New York Times* have been fired after they were discovered to have fabricated articles. Chemists at the University of Utah reported that they had discovered "cold fusion." "They hadn't, it turned out. . . ." (Lemonick 2006, 43).

Distortion and deception, deliberate or not, also exist in marriage and family research. Marriage is a very private relationship that happens behind closed doors; individual interviewees and respondents to questionnaires have been socialized not to reveal the intimate details of their lives to strangers. Hence, they are prone to distort, omit, or exaggerate information, perhaps unconsciously, to cover up what they may feel is no one else's business. Thus, researchers sometimes obtain inaccurate information.

Marriage and family researchers know more about what people say they do than about what they actually do. An unintentional and probably more common form of distortion is inaccurate recall. Sometimes researchers ask respondents to recall details of their relationships that occurred years ago. Time tends to blur some memories, and respondents may relate not what actually happened, but rather what they remember to have happened, or, worse, what they wish had happened.

Other Research Problems Nonresponse on surveys and the discrepancy between attitudes and behaviors are other research problems. With regard to nonresponse, not all individuals who complete questionnaires or agree to participate in an interview are willing to provide information about such personal issues as date rape and partner abuse. Such individuals leave the questionnaire blank or tell the interviewer they would rather not respond. Others respond but give only socially desirable answers. The implications for research are that data gatherers do not know the nature or extent to which something may be a problem because people are reluctant to provide accurate information. Computer-administered self-interviewing (CASI) has been suggested as a way of collecting sensitive information (for example, sexual). However, a study by Testa et al. (2005) comparing CASI and self-administered mailed questionnaires found that the latter had a higher response rate with greater disclosure of sensitive information.

The discrepancy between people's attitudes and their behavior is another cause for concern about the validity of research data. It is sometimes assumed that, if people have a certain attitude (for example, a belief that extramarital sex is wrong), then their behavior will be consistent with that attitude (avoidance of extramarital sex). However, this assumption is not always accurate. People do indeed say one thing and do another. This potential discrepancy should be kept in mind when reading research on various attitudes.

Finally, most research reflects information that volunteers provide. However, volunteers may not represent nonvolunteers when they are completing surveys. In view of the research cautions identified here, you might ask, "Why bother to report the findings?" The quality of some family science research is excellent. For example, articles published in *Journal of Marriage and the Family* (among other journals) reflect the high level of methodologically sound articles that are being published. Even less sophisticated journals provide useful information on marital, family, and other relationship data. Table 1.8 summarizes potential inadequacies of any research study.

Table 1.8 Potential Research Problems in Marriage and Family

Weakness	Consequences	Example
Sample not random	Cannot generalize findings	Opinions of college students do not reflect opinions of other adults.
No control group	Inaccurate conclusions	Study on the effect of divorce on children needs control group of children whose parents are still together.
Age differences between groups of respondents	Inaccurate conclusions	Effect may be due to passage of time or to cohort differences.
Unclear terminology	Inability to measure what is not clearly defined	What is living together, marital happiness, sexual fulfillment, good communication, quality time?
Researcher bias	Slanted conclusions	A researcher studying the value of a product (e.g. The Atkins Diet) should not be funded by the organization being studied.
Time lag	Outdated conclusions	Often-quoted Kinsey sex research is over fifty years old.
Distortion	Invalid conclusions	Research subjects exaggerate, omit information, and/or recall facts or events inaccurately. Respondents may remember what they wish had happened.

SUMMARY

What is the view/theme of this text?

A central theme of this text is to encourage you to be proactive—to make conscious, deliberate relationship choices to enhance your own well-being and the well-being of those in your intimate groups. Although there are over a hundred such choices, among the most important are whether to marry, who to marry, when to marry, whether to have children, whether to remain emotionally and sexually faithful to one's partner, and whether to use a condom. Though global, structural, cultural, and media influences are operative, a choices framework emphasizes that individuals have some control over their relationship destiny by making considered choices to initiate, respond to, nurture, or terminate intimate relationships. Important issues to keep in mind about a choices framework for viewing marriage and the family are that (1) not to decide is to decide, (2) some choices require correcting, (3) all choices involve trade-offs, (4) choices include selecting a positive or negative view, (5) making choices produces ambivalence, and (6) some choices are not revocable. Generation Yers (born in the early 1980s) are relaxed about relationship choices. Rather than pair bond, they "hang out," "hook up," and "live together." They are in no hurry to find "the one," to marry, and to begin a family.

What is marriage?

Marriage is a system of binding a man and a woman together for the reproduction, care (physical and emotional), and socialization of offspring. Marriage in the United States is a legal contract between a heterosexual couple and the state in which they reside that regulates their economic and sexual relationship. Other elements of marriage involve emotion, sexual monogamy, and a formal ceremony. The federal government supports marriage education in the public school system with the intention of reducing divorce (which is costly to both individuals and society). The various types of marriage are polygyny, polyandry, and pantagamy. Polyamory is a lifestyle of multiple emotional and sexual relationships between individuals who may or may not be married.

What is family?

The U.S. Census Bureau defines family as a group of two or more people related by blood, marriage, or adoption. In recognition of the diversity of families, the definition of family is increasingly becoming two adult partners whose interdependent relationship is long-term and characterized by an emotional and financial commitment. Types of family include nuclear, extended, and blended. The traditional family is the two-parent nuclear family with the husband as breadwinner and wife as homemaker. The modern family is the dual-earner family where both spouses work outside the home. Postmodern families represent a departure from these models, such as lesbian and gay couples and single mothers by choice, which emphasizes that a healthy family need not be heterosexual or include two parents.

How do the concepts of marriage and the family differ?

Marriage involves a license; having a child does not. Marriage ends when one person dies or the couple divorce; relationships between the family members of parent and child continue. Marriages involve spouses who are expected to have sex with each other; families involve parents and children, and sex between them is prohibited.

How have marriage and the family changed?

The advent of industrialization, urbanization, and mobility involved the demise of familism and the rise of individualism. When family members functioned together as an economic unit, they were dependent on one another for survival and were concerned about what was good for the family. This familistic focus on the needs of the family has since shifted to a focus on self-fulfillment—individualism.

Other changes have occurred in the last fifty years: divorce has replaced death as the endpoint for the majority of marriages, marriage and intimate relations have emerged as legitimate objects of scientific study, feminism and changes in gender roles in marriage have risen, the age at marriage has increased, some spouses may now live apart together (LAT), and the acceptance of singlehood, cohabitation, and childfree marriages has increased.

Families today continue to be affected by the terrorism of 9/11. In one study of the subsequent mental health among participants in a Midwestern town, the researchers revealed higher stress and alcohol consumption levels two and four years after the attacks, even after controlling for socio demographic characteristics and pre-September 11 distress and drinking patterns.

What are the theoretical frameworks for viewing marriage and the family?

Theoretical frameworks provide a set of interrelated principles designed to explain a particular phenomenon and provide a point of view. Those used to study the family include the (1) social exchange framework (spouses exchange resources, and decisions are made on the basis of perceived profit and loss), (2) structural-functional framework (how the family functions to serve society), (3) conflict framework (family members are in conflict over scarce resources of time and money), (4) symbolic interaction framework (symbolic worlds in which the various family members give meaning to each other's behavior), (5) family systems framework (each member of the family is part of a system and the family as a unit develops norms of interaction), (6) social organization framework (the ways in which the family interfaces or interacts with other social organizations), (7) family life course development framework (the stages and process of how families change over time), (8) feminist framework (inequality and oppression), (9) human ecological framework (individuals, couples, and families are dependent on the environment for air, food, and water, and on other human beings for social interaction), (10) transpersonal psychology framework (focuses on transpersonal aspects of body, mind, and spirit and how these strengthen the family), and (11) game framework (marriage and family have characteristics similar to a game as in goals, roles, myths, and so on). The framework used in most empirical family studies is the social exchange framework.

What are steps in the research process and caveats to be kept in mind?

Steps in the research process include identifying a topic, reviewing the literature, deciding on methods and data collection procedures, ensuring protection of subjects, analyzing the data, and submitting the results to a journal for publication.

Caveats that are factors to be used in evaluating research include a random sample (the respondents providing the data reflect those who were not in the sample), a control group (the group not subjected to the experimental design for a basis of comparison), terminology (the phenomenon being studied should be objectively defined), researcher bias (present in all studies), time lag (takes two years from study to print), and distortion or deception (although rare, some researchers distort their data). Few studies avoid all research problems.

KEY TERMS

artifacts	family life cycle	marriage-resilience perspective	simultaneous ambivalence
beliefs	family of orientation	mating gradient	social exchange framework
binuclear family	family of origin	modern family	social organization framework
blended family	family of procreation	nuclear family	sociological imagination
civil union	family systems framework	open relationship	status
collectivism	feminist framework	pantagamy	structural-functional framework
common-law marriage	feral children	polyamory	symbolic interaction
conflict framework	functionalists	polyandry	framework
control group	game theory	polygamy	theoretical framework
domestic partnership	Generation Y	polygyny	traditional family
ecosystem	human ecology framework	postmodern family	transpersonal psychology
experimental group	hypothesis	primary group	framework
extended family	individualism	random sample	utilitarianism
familism	institution	role	values
family	IRB approval	secondary group	
family life course development	marriage	sequential ambivalence	

The Companion Website for *Choices in Relationships: An Introduction to Marriage and the Family,* Tenth Edition

www.cengage.com/sociology/knox

Supplement your review of this chapter by going to the Companion Website to take one of the tutorial quizzes, use the flash cards to master key terms, or check out the many other study aids, like crossword puzzles and self-assessments. You'll also find special features such as General Social Survey (GSS) data, Census data, and other resources to help you with that special project or to do some research on your own.

WEB LINKS

Gilder Lehrman Institute of American History—History of the Family
http://www.digitalhistory.uh.edu/historyonline/familyhistory.cfm

National Center for Health Statistics
http://www.cdc.gov/nchs/

National Council on Family Relations
http://www.ncfr.org/

National Healthy Marriage Resource Center
http://twoofus.org/index.aspx

National Marriage Project
http://marriage.rutgers.edu/

National Survey of Families and Households
http://www.ssc.wisc.edu/nsfh/home.htm

The Institute of Transpersonal Psychology
http://www.itp.edu/

U.S. Census Bureau
http://www.census.gov/

REFERENCES

Allen, K. R., E. K. Husser, D. J. Stone, and C. E. Jordal. 2008. Agency and error in young adults' stories of sexual decision making. *Family Relations* 57:517–29.

Amato, P. R., A. Booth, D. R. Johnson, and S. F. Rogers. 2007. *Alone together: How marriage in America is changing.* Cambridge, Massachusetts: Harvard University Press.

Best Friends Survey. 2006. All in the family. *USA Today*, June 21, A1.

Blumer, H. G. 1969. The methodological position of symbolic interaction. In *Symbolic interactionism: Perspective and method.* Englewood Cliffs, NJ: Prentice-Hall.

Bristol, K., and B. Farmer 2005. Sexuality among southeastern university students: A survey. Unpublished data, East Carolina University, Greenville, NC.

Brown, G. L., S. C. Mangelsdorf, C. Neff, S. J. Schoppe-Sullivan, and C. A. Frosch. 2009. Young children's self-concepts: Associations with child temperament, mothers' and fathers' parenting, and triadic family interaction. *Merrill-Palmer Quarterly* 55:207.

Busby, D. M., B. Gardner, C. Brandt, and N. Taniguchi. 2005. The family of origin parachute model: Landing safely in adult romantic relationships. *Family Relations* 54:254–64.

Cooley, C. H. 1964. *Human nature and the social order.* New York: Schocken.

Corra, M., S. Carter, J. S. Carter, and D. Knox. 2009. Trends in marital happiness by sex and race, 1973–2006. *Journal of Family Issues* (in press).

DeCuzzi, A., D. Knox, and M. Zusman. 2006. Racial differences in perceptions of women and men. *College Student Journal* 40:343–49.

Dotson-Blake, K., D. Knox, and A. Holman. Forthcoming. College student rank/gender/race and attitudes toward therapy.

Foster, J. D. 2008. Incorporating personality into the investment model: Probing commitment processes across individual differences in narcissism. *Journal of Social and Personal Relationships* 25:211–23.

Gavin, J. 2003. *Deep in a dream: The long night of Chet Baker.* New York: Welcome Rain.

Generation Y Data. 2007. http://www.docuticker.com/wp-content/uploads/2007/09/factsheet_geny.htm.

Hagerty, E. L. 1970. Game theory. Lecture notes recorded by David Knox.

Hall, S. 2009. Personal communication.

Harris Poll. 2007. Pets as family members. www.harrispollonline.com (retrieved December 11, 2007).

Henley-Walters, L., W. Warzywoda-Kruszynska, and T. Gurko. 2002. Cross-cultural studies of families: Hidden differences. *Journal of Comparative Family Studies* 33:433–50.

Howard, Margo. 2003. *A life in letters: Ann Landers's letters to her only child.* New York: Warner.

James, S. D. 2008. Wild child speechless after tortured life. *ABC News,* May 7.

Judkins, B., and L. Presser. 2005. Gender asymmetry in the division of eco-friendly domestic labor. Paper, Society of Social Problems, Philadelphia, PA, August.

Knox, D., and M. E. Zusman. 2009. Relationship and sexual behaviors of a sample of 1319 university students. Unpublished data collected for this text. Department of Sociology, East Carolina University, Greenville, NC.

Lehmiller, J. J., and C. R. Agnew. 2007. Perceived marginalization and the prediction of romantic relationship stability. *Journal of Marriage and Family* 69:1036–49

Lemonick, M. D. 2006. The rise and fall of the cloning king. *Time,* January 6, 40–43.

Lorber, J. 1998. *Gender inequality: Feminist theories and politics.* Los Angeles, CA: Roxbury.

Mead, G. H. 1934. *Mind, self, and society.* Chicago: University of Chicago Press.

Meinhold, J. L., A. Acock, and A. Walker. 2006. The influence of life transition statuses on sibling intimacy and contact in early adulthood. Paper presented at the Annual Meeting of the National Council on Family Relations in Orlando in November 2005.

Murdock, G. P. 1949. *Social structure.* New York: Free Press.

Newton, N. 2002. *Savage girls and wild boys: A history of feral children.* New York: Thomas Dunne Books/St. Martin's Press.

Neyer, F. J., and F. R. Lang. 2003. Blood is thicker than water: Kinship orientation across adulthood. *Journal of Personality and Social Psychology* 84:310–21.

Novilla, M., B. Lelinneth, M. D. Barnes, N. G. De La Cruz, P. N. Williams, and J. Rogers. 2006. Public health perspectives on the family. *Family and Community Health* 29:28–42.

Odero, D. R. 2004. Families in Kenya. *Family Focus* 49:f14–f15.

Parker, L. 2005. When pets die at the vet, grieving owners call lawyers. *USA Today,* March 15, A1.

Pescosolido, B. A., J. K. Martin, A. Lang, and S. Olafsdottir. 2008. Rethinking theoretical approaches to stigma: A Framework Integrating Normative Influences on Stigma (FINIS). *Social Science & Medicine* 67:431–51

Pryor, J. H., S. Hurtado, L. DeAngelo, J. Sharkness, L. C. Romero, W. K. Korn, and S. Trans. 2008. *The American freshmen: National Norms for fall 2008.* Los Angeles: Higher Education Research Institute, UCLA.

Richman, J. A., L. Cloninger, and K. M. Rospenda. 2008. Macrolevel stressors, terrorism, and mental health outcomes: Broadening the stress paradigm. *American Journal of Public Health* 98:323–30.

Silverstein, L. B., and C. F. Auerbach. 2005. (Post) modern families. In *Families in global perspective,* ed. Jaipaul L. Roopnarine and U. P. Gielen, 33–48. Boston, MA. Pearson Education.

Statistical Abstract of the United States, 2009, 128th ed. Washington, DC: U.S. Bureau of the Census.

Taylor, A. C., and A. Bagd. 2005. The lack of explicit theory in family research: The case analysis of the *Journal of Marriage and the Family 1990–1999.* In *Sourcebook of family theory & research,* ed. Vern

L. Bengtson, Alan C. Acock, Katherine R. Allen, Peggye Dilworth-Anderson, and David M. Klein, 22–25. Thousand Oaks, CA: Sage Publications.

Testa, M., J. A. Livingston, and C. VanZile-Tamsen. 2005. The impact of questionnaire administration mode on response rate and reporting of consensual and nonconsensual sexual behavior. *Psychology of Women Quarterly* 29:345–52.

Thomas, S. G. 2007. *Buy buy baby: How consumer culture manipulates parents and harms young minds.* Boston: Houghton Mifflin.

Tupelo, A., and E. Freeman. 2008. Polyamory. Presentation to Sociology of Human Sexuality class, Department of Sociology, East Carolina University, Greenville, NC. October.

Turner, J. H. 2007. Self, emotions, and extreme violence: Extending symbolic interactionist theorizing. *Symbolic Interaction* 30:501–31.

Veenhoven, R. 2007. Quality-of-life-research. In *21st century sociology: A reference handbook*, ed. Clifton D. Bryant and Dennis L. Peck, 54–62. Thousand Oaks, California: Sage Publications.

Vogel, D. L., D. A. Gentile, and S. A. Kaplan. 2008. The influence of television on willingness to seek therapy. *Journal of Clinical Psychology* 64:276–81.

Ward, S. 2007. Celebrating animals. *USA Today*, June 22, A.

White, J. M., and D. M. Klein. 2002. *Family theories*, 2d ed. Thousand Oaks, CA: Sage Publications.

Zeitzen, M. K. 2008. *Polygamy: A cross-cultural analysis.* Oxford: Berg.

Zusman, M. E., D. Knox, and T. Gardner. 2009. *The social context view of sociology.* Durham, North Carolina: Carolina Academic Press.

*I'm a movement by myself.
But I'm a force when we're
together.
I'm good all by myself.
But baby, you make me better.
You make me better.
You plus me, it equals better
math.*

From "Make Me Better"
by Fabolous Timbo

Love

Contents

True or False?

1. Most college students report that love would see them through any relationship difficulty.

2. The most common love style of college students is that of treating love as a game and having fun.

3. Heavy women who lose weight are more likely to become involved in a romantic relationship.

4. Couples who married after "love at first sight" have lower quality relationships than those whose relationship developed more gradually.

5. As an index of more liberal relationships among today's college youth, most undergraduates report they would feel good about their partner having an emotional or sexual relationship with someone else.

Answers: **1.** T **2.** F **3.** T **4.** F **5.** F

I got within feet of her and I got goofy. I couldn't talk. She's sunshine. She sure is. She completes my life like no other woman I've met.

Brad Pitt of his relationship with Gwyneth Paltrow (before he met Angelina Jolie)

David Levy (2007) is an artificial intelligence expert who predicts that individuals will have romantic relationships with robots by 2050. He emphasizes that the technology will reach a level of sophistication so that robots can simulate emotions, personality, and consciousness. They will be able to talk to you, make you laugh, and tell you that they love you as though they mean it…and you won't be able to tell the difference. In an interview, Levy noted, "robots need only simulate human intelligence and emotions to the point that they are absolutely convincing. If you can't tell whether the thing is man or machine, what difference does it make? You'll treat it as if it were alive" (Lanham 2008, 16).

In the meantime, the rest of us will work out our love relationships with "real humans." J. H. Newman, cardinal and philosopher, noted that we tend to fear less that life will end but, rather, that life will never begin. His point targets the importance of love in one's life that provides an unparalleled richness, meaning, and happiness. Demir (2008) emphasized that involvement in a romantic relationship moves one to a new level of happiness independent of one's personality. In other words, although some individuals have personalities that tend to be happy anyway, love moves them to an even higher level.

We are also reminded that young lovers note that nothing is like being in love. The late trumpet player Chet Baker also noted the value of love in one's life—"I don't think life is really worth all the pain and effort and struggling if you don't have somebody that you love very much" (Gavin 2003, 349). When asked what word best characterizes her relationship with her husband Jay Leno, Mavis Leno said, "Joy. I don't' just love Jay—I'm madly in love. And I say this as someone who didn't think the state could persist" (Burford 2005, 174).

For many, being in love is a prerequisite for remaining married. Falling out of love paves the way for divorce. Almost half (47.9 percent) of 1,319 university students reported that they would divorce their spouse if they fell out of love. Lovers affect each other. Schoebi (2008) identified hard (angry) and soft (depressed) emotions and the degree to which the emotions of one spouse affected another. When one spouse was experiencing hard emotions, the partner tended to mirror those, particularly when feeling interpersonal insecurity.

Love is very much a part of student life. More than half (57.8 percent) of 1,319 undergraduates reported that they were emotionally involved with one person, engaged, or married (Knox and Zusman 2009).

Chapter 2 Love

This chapter is concerned with the nature of love (both ancient and modern views), various theories of the origin of love, how love develops in a new relationship, and problems associated with love. Because jealousy in love relationships is common, we also examine its causes and consequences.

Ways of Conceptualizing Love

Love is elusive and incapable of being defined by those caught in its spell. Love is often confused with lust and infatuation (Jefson 2006). Love is about deep, abiding feelings; **lust** is about sexual desire; and **infatuation** is about emotional feelings based on little actual exposure to the love object. In the following section, we look at the various ways of conceptualizing love.

Love Styles

Theorist John Lee (1973; 1988) identified a number of styles of love that describe the way lovers relate to each other. Keep in mind that the same individual may view love in more than one way at a time or may view love in different ways at different times. These love styles are also independent of one's sexual orientation—no one love style is characteristic of heterosexuals or homosexuals.

1. *Ludic.* Country-and-western singer George Strait's song "*She'll Leave You with a Smile*" reflects involvement with a ludic lover: "You're gonna give her all your heart/Then she'll tear your world apart./You're gonna cry a little while/Still she'll leave you with a smile." The ludic lover views love as a game, refuses to become dependent on any one person, and does not encourage another's intimacy. Two essential skills of the ludic lover are to juggle several partners at the same time and to manage each relationship so that no one partner is seen too often.

These strategies help to ensure that the relationship does not deepen into an all-consuming love. Don Juan represented the classic ludic lover. "Love 'em and leave 'em" is the motto of the ludic lover. Tzeng et al. (2003) found that, whereas men were more likely than women to be ludic lovers, ludic love characterized the love style of college students the least.

In a study (Paul et al. 2000) of "hookups" between college students, certain love styles were characteristic of students who hooked up. Distinguishing features of those who had noncoital hookups were a ludic love style and high concern for personal safety. These individuals may have been participating in collegiate cultural expectations by engaging in "playful" sexual exploration but refraining from intercourse out of their concern for personal safety. Indeed, those who engaged in coital hookups were also characterized by ludic love styles that included heavy drinking. The researchers worried that the combination of ludic orientation (motivated by the thrill of the game) and alcohol intoxication might be a precursor to sexual experiences that were forced or unwanted by a partner.

The **ludic love style** is sometimes characterized as manipulative and uncaring. However, ludic lovers may also be compassionate and very protective of another's feelings. For example, some uninvolved, soon-to-graduate seniors avoid involvement with anyone new and become ludic lovers so as not to encourage anyone.

2. *Pragma.* The **pragma love style** is the love of the pragmatic—that which is logical and rational. Pragma lovers assess their partners on the basis of assets and liabilities. Economic security may be regarded as very important. Pragma lovers do not become involved with interracial, long-distance, or age-discrepant partners because logic argues against doing so. Bulcroft et al. (2000) noted that,

The love of this couple is eros, characterized by romance and passion, the type reported as most prevalent among college students.

Well, love is insanity. The ancient Greeks knew that. It is the taking over of a rational and lucid mind by delusion and self-destruction. You lose yourself, you have no power over yourself, you can't even think straight.

Marilyn French, author

increasingly, individuals are becoming more pragmatic about their love choices.

3. Eros. Just the opposite of the pragmatic love style, the **eros love style** is one of passion and romance. Intensity of both emotional and sexual feelings dictates one's love involvements. Research varies on the degree to which passion characterizes most relationships. Tzeng et al. (2003) assessed the love styles of more than 700 college students and found that eros was the most common love style of women and men. Similarly, a *Redbook* (2005) survey found that 6 percent of 700 readers reported that "passionate" best described their relationship. Hendrick et al. (1988) found that couples who were more romantically and passionately in love were more likely to remain together than couples that avoided intimacy by playing games with each other.

4. Mania. The person with **mania love style** feels intense emotion and sexual passion but is out of control. The person is possessive, dependent, and "must have" the beloved. People who are extremely jealous and controlling reflect manic love. "If I can't have you, no one else will" is sometimes the mantra of the manic lover. Stalking is an expression of love gone wild. O. J. Simpson once said, "If I killed her, it would be because I loved her… right?"

5. Storge. The **storge love style** is a calm, soothing, nonsexual love devoid of intense passion. Respect, friendship, commitment, and familiarity are characteristics that help to define the relationship. The partners care deeply about each other but not in a romantic or lustful sense. Their love is also more likely to endure than fleeting romance. One's grandparents who have been married fifty years and who still love and enjoy each other are likely to have a storge type of love.

6. Agape. One of the forms of love identified by the ancient Greeks, the **agape love style** involves selflessness and giving, without expecting anything in return. These nurturing and caring partners are concerned only about the welfare and growth of each other. The love parents have for their children is often described as agape love.

International Data

Data from a survey of 641 young adults at three international universities indicated that young American adults are the most romantic, followed by Turkish students, with Indians having the lowest romanticism scores (*Medora et al. 2002*).

Diversity in Other Countries

Love among Chinese couples is of the storge variety. Pimentel (2000) studied a large representative sample of married couples in urban China and found that "Chinese couples have what Westerners might characterize as a relatively unromantic vision of love, more like companionship." The words most often accompanying remarks about love were "respect," "mutual understanding," and "support." Expressions of passion, of "sparks flying," or similar phrases, were not noted.

Romantic versus Realistic Love

Love may also be described as being on a continuum from romanticism to realism. For some people, love is romantic; for others, it is realistic. **Romantic love** is characterized by such beliefs as "love at first sight," and "If I were really in love, I would marry someone I had known for only a short time." Regarding these beliefs, 26.2 percent of 1,319 undergraduates reported that they had experienced love at first sight; a similar percentage

The Love Attitudes Scale

This scale is designed to assess the degree to which you are romantic or realistic in your attitudes toward love. There are no right or wrong answers.

Directions

After reading each sentence carefully, circle the number that best represents the degree to which you agree or disagree with the sentence.

1	2	3	4	5
Strongly agree	Mildly agree	Undecided	Mildly disagree	Strongly disagree

	SA	MA	U	MD	SD
1. Love doesn't make sense. It just is.	1	2	3	4	5
2. When you fall "head over heels" in love, it's sure to be the real thing.	1	2	3	4	5
3. To be in love with someone you would like to marry but can't is a tragedy.	1	2	3	4	5
4. When love hits, you know it.	1	2	3	4	5
5. Common interests are really unimportant; as long as each of you is truly in love, you will adjust.	1	2	3	4	5
6. It doesn't matter if you marry after you have known your partner for only a short time as long as you know you are in love.	1	2	3	4	5
7. If you are going to love a person, you will "know" after a short time.	1	2	3	4	5
8. As long as two people love each other, the educational differences they have really do not matter.	1	2	3	4	5
9. You can love someone even though you do not like any of that person's friends.	1	2	3	4	5
10. When you are in love, you are usually in a daze.	1	2	3	4	5
11. Love "at first sight" is often the deepest and most enduring type of love.	1	2	3	4	5
12. When you are in love, it really does not matter what your partner does because you will love him or her anyway.	1	2	3	4	5
13. As long as you really love a person, you will be able to solve the problems you have with the person.	1	2	3	4	5
14. Usually you can really love and be happy with only one or two people in the world.	1	2	3	4	5
15. Regardless of other factors, if you truly love another person, that is a good enough reason to marry that person.	1	2	3	4	5
16. It is necessary to be in love with the one you marry to be happy.	1	2	3	4	5
17. Love is more of a feeling than a relationship.	1	2	3	4	5
18. People should not get married unless they are in love.	1	2	3	4	5
19. Most people truly love only once during their lives.	1	2	3	4	5
20. Somewhere there is an ideal mate for most people.	1	2	3	4	5
21. In most cases, you will "know it" when you meet the right partner.	1	2	3	4	5
22. Jealousy usually varies directly with love; that is, the more you are in love, the greater your tendency to become jealous will be.	1	2	3	4	5
23. When you are in love, you are motivated by what you feel rather than by what you think.	1	2	3	4	5
24. Love is best described as an exciting rather than a calm thing.	1	2	3	4	5
25. Most divorces probably result from falling out of love rather than failing to adjust.	1	2	3	4	5
26. When you are in love, your judgment is usually not too clear.	1	2	3	4	5
27. Love comes only once in a lifetime.	1	2	3	4	5
28. Love is often a violent and uncontrollable emotion.	1	2	3	4	5
29. When selecting a marriage partner, differences in social class and religion are of small importance compared with love.	1	2	3	4	5
30. No matter what anyone says, love cannot be understood.	1	2	3	4	5

Scoring

Add the numbers you circled. 1 (strongly agree) is the most romantic response and 5 (strongly disagree) is the most realistic response. The lower your total score (30 is the lowest possible score), the more romantic your attitudes toward love. The higher your total score (150 is the highest possible score), the more realistic your attitudes toward love. A score of 90 places you at the midpoint between being an extreme romantic and an extreme realist. Both men and women undergraduates typically score above 90, with men scoring closer to 90 than women.

A team of researchers (Medora et al. 2002) gave the scale to 641 young adults at three international universities in America, Turkey, and India. Female respondents in all three cultures had higher romanticism scores than male respondents (reflecting their higher value for, desire for, and thoughts about marriage). When the scores were compared by culture, American young adults were the most romantic, followed by Turkish students, with Indians having the lowest romanticism scores.

Reference

Medora, N. P., J. H. Larson, N. Hortacsu, and P. Dave. 2002. Perceived attitudes towards romanticism: A cross-cultural study of American, Asian-Indian, and Turkish young adults. *Journal of Comparative Family Studies* 33:155–78.

Source

Knox, D. "Conceptions of Love at Three Developmental Levels" Dissertation, Florida State University, 1969. Permission to use the scale for research available from David Knox at davidknox2@prodigy.net or by contacting Dr. Knox, Department of Sociology, East Carolina University, Greenville, NC 27858.

Jealousy is all the fun you think they had.

Erica Jong, American writer

(26 percent) reported that they would marry quickly if they were in love (Knox and Zusman 2009). Men were significantly more likely than women to believe in love at first sight (32.3 percent versus 24.3 percent). One explanation is that men must be visually attracted to young, healthy females to inseminate them. This biologically based reproductive attraction is interpreted as a love attraction so that the male feels immediately drawn to the female, but he may actually see an egg needing fertilization. Dotson-Blake et al. (2008) found further evidence that males are more romantic than females in that men were significantly more likely (85 percent versus 73 percent) than women to believe that they could solve any relationship problem as long as they were in love.

In regard to love at first sight, Barelds and Barelds-Dijkstra (2007) studied the relationships of 137 married couples or cohabitants (together for an average of twenty-five years) and found that those who fell in love at first sight had similar relationship quality to those couples who came to know each other more gradually. Huston et al. (2001) found that, after two years of marriage, the couples that had fallen in love more slowly were just as happy as couples that fell in love at first sight.

The symptoms of romantic love include drastic mood swings, palpitations of the heart, and intrusive thoughts about the partner. F. Scott Fitzgerald immortalized the concept of romantic obsession in *The Great Gatsby*. Of Daisy Buchanan, he wrote, "She was the first girl I ever loved and I have faithfully avoided seeing her . . . to keep that illusion perfect." He actually was writing about a real-life true love, Ginevra King, whom he had met when she was 16; she eventually married another man (West 2005).

Infatuation is sometimes regarded as synonymous with romantic love. Infatuation comes from the same root word as *fatuous*, meaning "silly" or "foolish," and refers to a state of passion or attraction that is not based on reason. Infatuation is characterized by the tendency to idealize the love partner. People who are

This photo not only illustrates romantic (young couple) and conjugal love (older couple) but also the importance of social approval of one's mate choice. The parents are meeting the boyfriend of their daughter for the first time. They were very pleased with their daughter's choice for a husband, and the couple married within a year of this meeting.

Authors

infatuated magnify their lovers' positive qualities ("My partner is always happy") and overlook or minimize their negative qualities ("My partner doesn't have a problem with alcohol; he just likes to have a good time").

In contrast to romantic love is realistic love. Realistic love is also known as conjugal love. **Conjugal (married) love** is less emotional, passionate, and exciting than romantic love and is characterized by companionship, calmness, comfort, and security. The Love Attitudes Scale provides a way for you to assess the degree to which you tend to be romantic or realistic (conjugal) in your view of love. When you determine your score from the Love Attitudes Scale, be aware that your tendency to be a romantic or a realist is neither good nor bad. Both romantics and realists can be happy individuals and successful relationship partners.

To be in love is merely to be in a state of perceptual anesthesia—to mistake an ordinary young man for a Greek god or an ordinary young woman for a goddess.

H. L. Mencken, *Prejudices*

PERSONAL CHOICES

Do You Make Relationship Choices with Your Heart or Head?

Lovers are frequently confronted with the need to make decisions about their relationships, but they are divided on whether to let their heart or head rule in such decisions. Some evidence suggests that the heart rules. Almost 60 percent (59.6 percent) of 1,319 undergraduates agreed with the statement, "I make relationship decisions more with my heart than my head" (Knox and Zusman 2009), suggesting that the heart tends to rule in relationship matters. We asked students in our classes on marriage and family to fill in the details about deciding with their heart or head. Some of their answers follow:

Heart

Those who relied on their hearts for making decisions (women more than men) felt that emotions were more important than logic and that listening to their heart made them happier. One woman said:

In deciding on a mate, my heart would rule because my heart has reasons to cry and my head doesn't. My heart knows what I want, what would make me most happy. My head tells me what is best for me. But I would rather have something that makes me happy than something that is good for me.

Some men also agreed that the heart should rule. One said:

I went with my heart in a situation, and I'm glad I did. I had been dating a girl for two years when I decided she was not the one I wanted and that my present girlfriend was. My heart was saying to go for the one I loved, but my head was telling me not to because if I broke up with the first girl, it would hurt her, her parents, and my parents. But I decided I had to make myself happy and went with the feelings in my heart and started dating the girl who is now my fiancée.

Relying on one's emotions does not always have a positive outcome, as the following experience illustrates:

Last semester, I was dating a guy I felt more for than he did for me. Despite that, I wanted to spend any opportunity I could with him when he asked me to go somewhere with him. One day he had no classes, and he asked me to go to the park by the river for a picnic. I had four classes that day and exams in two of them. I let my heart rule and went with him. Nothing ever came of the relationship and I didn't do well in those classes.

Head

In contrast to making relationship decisions with one's heart, 12 percent of 1,319 undergraduates previously surveyed reported that they made such decisions with their head (Knox and Zusman 2009). Some student comments about making relationship decisions rationally follow from a class on marriage and family:

I have sought love, first, because it brings ecstasy—ecstasy so great that I would often have sacrificed all the rest of life for a few hours of this joy. I have sought it, next, because it relieves loneliness, that terrible loneliness in which one shivering consciousness looks over the rim of the world into the cold unfathomable lifeless abyss.

Bertrand Russell, philosopher

In deciding on a mate, I feel my head should rule because you have to choose someone that you can get along with after the new wears off. If you follow your heart solely, you may not look deep enough into a person to see what it is that you really like. Is it just a pretty face or a nice body? Or is it deeper than that, such as common interests and values? After the new wears off, it's the person inside the body that you're going to have to live with. The "heart" sometimes can fog up this picture of the true person and distort reality into a fairy tale.

Another student said:

Love is blind and can play tricks on you. Two years ago, I fell in love with a man who I later found out was married. Although my heart had learned to love this man, my mind knew the consequences and told me to stop seeing him. My heart said, "Maybe he'll leave her for me," but my mind said, "If he cheated on her, he'll cheat on you." I got out and am glad that I listened to my head.

Some individuals feel that both the head and the heart should rule when making relationship decisions.

When you really love someone, your heart rules in most of the situations. But if you don't keep your head in some matters, then you risk losing the love that you feel in your heart. I think that we should find a way to let our heads and hearts work together.

There is an adage, "Don't wait until you find the person you can live with; wait and find the person that you can't live without!" Upon hearing this quote, one of our students said, "I think both are important. I want my head to let me know it 'feels' right."

Triangular View of Love

Sternberg (1986) developed the "triangular" view of love, consisting of three basic elements: intimacy, passion, and commitment. The presence or absence of these three elements creates various types of love experienced between individuals, regardless of their sexual orientation. These various types include:

1. *Nonlove*—the absence of intimacy, passion, and commitment. Two strangers looking at each other from afar have a nonlove.

2. *Liking*—intimacy without passion or commitment. A new friendship may be described in these terms of the partners liking each other.

3. *Infatuation*—passion without intimacy or commitment. Two people flirting with each other in a bar may be infatuated with each other.

4. *Romantic love*—intimacy and passion without commitment. Love at first sight reflects this type of love.

5. *Conjugal love (also known as companionate love)*—intimacy and commitment without passion. A couple that has been married for fifty years is said to illustrate conjugal love.

6. *Fatuous love*—passion and commitment without intimacy. Couples who are passionately wild about each other and talk of the future but do not have an intimate connection with each other have a fatuous love.

7. *Empty love*—commitment without passion or intimacy. A couple who stay together for social and legal reasons but who have no spark or emotional sharing between them have an empty love.

8. *Consummate love*—combination of intimacy, passion, and commitment; Sternberg's view of the ultimate, all-consuming love.

Individuals bring different combinations of the elements of intimacy, passion, and commitment (the triangle) to the table of love. One lover may bring a

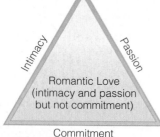

Figure 2.1
Romantic love is characterized by eros–intimacy and passion and is the type reported as most prevalent among college students.

Chapter 2 Love

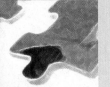

What if You Fall out of Love with the Person You Had Planned to Marry?

WHAT IF?

In a sample of 1,319 undergraduate students, 47.9 percent agreed that, "I would divorce my spouse if I no longer loved him or her" (Knox and Zusman 2009). Although Asians sometimes view love as a feeling that may follow marriage, Americans have been socialized to expect being in love with their spouse-to-be, and to feel embarrassed about and to hide it if they are not. Although falling in love with someone after marriage is more than possible, one might be very cautious in proceeding with a wedding because such an enormous value is placed on love in U.S. society. To do so is to run the risk of being in a "loveless" marriage that may make one vulnerable to "falling in love" outside the marriage.

predominance of passion, with some intimacy but no commitment (romantic love), whereas the other person brings commitment but no passion or intimacy (empty love). The triangular theory of love allows lovers to see the degree to which they are matched in terms of passion, intimacy, and commitment in their relationship (see Figure 2.1).

A common class exercise among professors who teach about marriage and the family is to randomly ask class members to identify one word they most closely associate with love. Invariably, students identify different words (commitment, feeling, trust, altruism, and so on), suggesting great variability in the way we think about love. Indeed, just the words "I love you" have different meanings, depending on whether they are said by a man or a woman. In a study of 147 undergraduates (72 percent female, 28 percent male), men (more than women) reported that saying "I love you" was a ploy to get a partner to have sex, whereas women (more than men) reported that saying "I love you" was a reflection of their feelings, independent of a specific motive (Brantley et al. 2002).

Give me a little more time and our love will surely grow.

Anonymous

Love in Social and Historical Context

Though we think of love as an individual experience, the society in which we live exercises considerable control over our love object or choice and conceptualizes it in various ways.

Social Control of Love

The ultimate social control of love is **arranged marriage**. Parents arrange 80 percent of marriages in China, India, and Indonesia (three countries representing 40 percent of the world's population). The parents select the mate for their child in an effort to prevent any potential love relationship from forming with the "wrong" person and to ensure that the child marries the "right" person. Such a person must belong to the desired social class and have the economic resources that the parents desire. Marriage is regarded as the linking of two families; the love feelings of the respective partners are irrelevant. Love is expected to follow marriage, not precede it.

An arranged marriage illustrates social control of love. The marriage of this Indian couple was arranged by the parents of the respective spouses.

I have loved to the point of madness;
That which is called madness,
That which to me,
Is the only sensible way to love.

F. Sagan, philosopher

In an arranged marriage, the couple may get a fifteen-minute meeting, followed in a few months by a wedding. However, love marriages—where the individuals meet, fall in love, and then convince and cajole their parents to approve of a wedding—are slowly becoming more common in Eastern societies (Jones 2006). Similarly, to accommodate the needs of traditional parents in a small village in Western Turkey who want to arrange the marriage of their children but appear "modern," anthropologist Hart (2007) observed that they now allow a period of time for the couple to develop romantic love feelings for each other.

America is a country that prides itself on the value of individualism. We proclaim that we are free to make our own choices. Not so fast, however. Love may be blind, but it knows what color a person's skin is. The data are clear—potential spouses seem to see and select people of similar color, as more than 95 percent of people marry someone of their own racial background (*Statistical Abstract of the United States, 2009*, Table 59). Hence, parents and peers may approve of their offsprings' and friends' love choice when the partner is of the same race and disapprove of the selection when the partner is not. These approval and disapproval mechanisms illustrate social control of love.

National Data

Fewer than 1 percent of the almost 60 million married couples in the United States include an African American spouse and a white spouse (*Statistical Abstract of the United States, 2009*, Table 59).

Another example of the social control of love is that individuals attracted to someone of the same sex quickly feel the social and cultural disapproval of this attraction. Although we discuss same-sex relationships later in the text, these relationships are challenged by the lack of institutional support. Even though Massachusetts and Connecticut permit same-sex marriage, these couples are no longer "married" once they cross the border into another state. Nevertheless, regardless of the law, same-sex love is common. Diamond (2003) emphasized that individuals are biologically wired and capable of falling in love and establishing intense emotional bonds with members of their own or

Love in Black and White

To what degree are African American and white adolescent experiences with love similar or different?

Sample and Methods

To find out, a team of researchers analyzed data collected during interviews with adolescents in grades 7 through 11 at more than 80 high schools. The sample consisted of 575 African American girls, 379 African American boys, 1,528 white girls, and 985 white boys. Each of these respondents reported having a "current" or "recent" relationship. The data are part of Add Health, a longitudinal study of a nationally representative sample of adolescents.

Selected Findings and Conclusions

1. *European Americans valued romantic love relationships more than African Americans.* When the respondents were asked, "How much would you like to have a romantic relationship in the next year?" they selected a number on a continuum from 1 to 7 (the higher the number, the greater the importance):

White respondents, compared with African American respondents, rated having a romantic relationship in the next year as significantly more important (mean = 3.47 and 3.24, respectively). Interestingly, a similar percentage (36 percent of European Americans and 34 percent of African Americans) reported current involvement in a love relationship.

2. *European Americans engaged in more romantic behaviors than African Americans.* When "romantic behaviors" were defined as "told other people that we were a couple," "went out together alone," "kissed," "held hands," "gave each other presents," "told each other we loved each other," and "thought of ourselves as a couple," white adolescents, on average, reported significantly more romantic behaviors with the current partner than did African American teens.

3. *African Americans were less likely to report involvement in an exclusive relationship.* Although more than 90 percent of both European Americans and African Americans reported current involvement in only one relationship, African American respondents were less likely than white respondents to report exclusive involvement in their current relationship (94 percent versus 98 percent).

4. *African Americans were less likely to report intimate self-disclosure than European Americans.* Self-disclosure was identified in terms of telling a partner about a problem. Females, older individuals, and those who had been in a relationship for a considerable amount of time were also more likely to self-disclose than males, younger adolescents, and those who had known each other for only a short period of time.

5. *African Americans reported longer current relationships and more inclusion of sexual intercourse.* The duration of African American relationships was about a month longer than those of white respondents. African Americans also more often reported the inclusion of sexual intercourse in their current relationships, a circumstance that might be related to the fact that sexual involvement increases with relationship duration.

What are the implications of this study? One, love remains an important experience for adolescents, even as young as the seventh grade. Two, although there are statistically "significant" differences in some of the variables studied, the actual experienced differences may be irrelevant. For example, the mean scores of 3.47 and 3.24, respectively, for European Americans and African Americans on a scale of 1 to 7 (reflecting the importance of wanting to be involved in a love relationship) may actually reflect more similarities than differences between the races. Other findings reflect the similarity of the races, rather than the differences (for example, more than 90 percent of both races reported exclusive involvement in a relationship).

Source

Giordano, P. C., W. D. Manning, and M. A. Longmore. 2005. The romantic relationships of African-American and white adolescents. *The Sociological Quarterly* 46:545–68.

---

opposite sex (hence, one's partners for love desire and for sexual desire can be different).

Because romantic love is such a powerful emotion and marriage such an important relationship, mate selection is not left to chance in connecting an outsider into an existing family. Parents inadvertently influence the mate choice of their children by moving to certain neighborhoods, joining certain churches, and enrolling their children in certain schools. Doing so increases the chance that their offspring will "hang out" with, fall in love with, and

When lovers are agreed, not even their parents can control them.

Bai Xingqian, Tang Dynasty
The Little Book of Chinese Proverbs

Madathil and Benshoff (2008) compared the importance attributed to love of Asian and Indian couples living in the United States who had arranged marriages versus American couples who selected their own partners. The researchers found greater importance attributed to love by Asian and Indian couples than American couples. One explanation is the greater joy of Asian and Indian couples in being less restricted by culture than American couples who take freedom to love and choice of their mate as a given.

marry people who are similar in race, education, and social class. Although twenty-first-century parents normally do not have large estates and are not concerned about the transfer of wealth, they usually want their offspring to meet someone who will "fit in" and with whom they will feel comfortable. Peers exert a similar influence on homogenous mating by approving or disapproving certain partners. Their motive is similar to that of parents—they want to feel comfortable around the people their peers bring with them to social encounters. Both parents and peers are influential, as most offspring and friends end up falling in love with and marrying people of the same race, education, and social class.

Social approval of one's partner is normally important for a love relationship to proceed on course. Even the engagement of Prince Charles to Camilla Parker Bowles received the "blessing" of Queen Elizabeth, and 70 percent of Britons either approved of it or did not care (Soriano 2005).

Partners also use love to control each other. Fehr and Harasymchuk (2005) noted that a comment expressing dissatisfaction by a romantic partner has considerably more negative emotional impact than a similar comment by a friend. In effect, we give considerable credence to what our love partner thinks of us, and we get upset when they criticize us.

The social control of love may also occur in the workplace (see the Social Policy section).

Ancient Views of Love

Many of our present-day notions of love stem from early Buddhist, Greek, and Hebrew writings.

Buddhist Conception of Love   The Buddhists conceived of two types of love—an "unfortunate" kind of love (self-love) and a "good" kind of love (creative spiritual attainment). Love that represents creative spiritual attainment was described as "love of detachment," not in the sense of withdrawal from the emotional concerns of others but in the sense of accepting people as they are and not requiring them to be different from their present selves as the price of friendly affection. To a Buddhist, the best love is one in which you accept others as they are without requiring them to be like you.

Greek and Hebrew Conceptions of Love   Three concepts of love introduced by the Greeks and reflected in the New Testament are phileo, agape, and eros. *Phileo* refers to love based on friendship and can exist between family members, friends, and lovers. The city of Philadelphia was named after this phileo type of love. Another variation of phileo love is *philanthropia,* the Greek word meaning "love of humankind."

Agape refers to a love based on a concern for the well-being of others. Agape is spiritual, not sexual, in nature. This type of love is altruistic and requires nothing in return. "Whatever I can do to make your life happy" is the motto of the agape lover, even if this means giving up the beloved to someone else. Such love is not always reciprocal.

Eros refers to sexual love. This type of love seeks self-gratification and sexual expression. In Greek mythology, Eros was the god of love and the son of Aphrodite. Plato described "true" eros as sexual love that existed between two men. According to Plato's conception of eros, homosexual love was the highest form of love because it existed independent of the procreative instinct and free from the bonds of matrimony. Also, women had low status and were uneducated and were therefore not considered ideal partners for men. By implication, love and marriage were separate.

Love in the Workplace

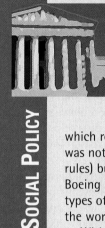

Working together is a context under which many love relationships begin. Although such beginnings are often between peers, sometimes a love relationship develops between individuals occupying different status positions. Such was the case of Harry Stonecipher (a 68-year-old married man and head of Boeing) and a female employee, which resulted in Stonecipher being fired. His dismissal was not because of the affair (there were no company rules) but because of the negative publicity he brought to Boeing when his steamy e-mails became public. These types of love relationships are sometimes problematic in the workplace.

With an increase of women in the workforce, an increase in the age at first marriage, and longer work hours, the workplace has become a common place for romantic relationships to develop. More future spouses may meet at work than in school, social, or neighborhood settings.

Pros and Cons of Office Romances

The energy that both fuels and results from intense love feelings can also fuel productivity on the job. If the co-workers eventually marry or enter a nonmarital but committed, long-term relationship, they may be more satisfied with and committed to their jobs than spouses whose partners work elsewhere. Working at the same location enables married couples to commute together, go to company-sponsored events together, and talk shop together.

Recognizing the potential benefits of increased job satisfaction, morale, productivity, creativity, and commitment, some companies even look favorably upon love relationships among employees. Prior to the economic downturn following 9/11, Apple Computer, in Cupertino, California, encouraged socializing among employees by sponsoring get-togethers every Friday afternoon with beer, wine, food, and, on occasion, live bands. The company also had ski clubs, volleyball clubs, and Frisbee clubs, providing employees with opportunities to meet and interact socially. Some companies hire two employees who are married, reflecting a focus on the value of each employee to the firm rather than on their love relationship outside work.

However, workplace romances can also be problematic for the individuals involved as well as for their employers. When a workplace romance involves a supervisor/subordinate relationship, other employees might make claims of favoritism or differential treatment. In a typical differential-treatment allegation, an employee (usually a woman) claims that the company denied her a job benefit because her supervisor favored a female coworker—who happens to be the supervisor's girlfriend.

If a workplace relationship breaks up, it may be difficult to continue to work in the same environment (and others at work may experience the fallout). A breakup that is less than amicable may result in efforts by partners to sabotage each other's work relationships and performance, incidents of workplace violence, harassment, and/or allegations of sexual harassment. In a survey the Society for Human Resource Management and CareerJournal.com conducted of 1,221 human-resource managers, 81 percent of human resource professionals and 76 percent of executives saw office romances as "dangerous" (Franklin 2002). Raso (2008) noted that such love relationships may also become a problem because coworkers do not want to be subjected to the open display of a roller coaster love affair at work.

Workplace Policies on Intimate Relationships

Some companies such as Disney, Universal, and Columbia have "anti-fraternization" clauses that impose a cap on workers talking about private issues or sending personal e-mails. Some British firms have "love contracts" that require workers to tell their managers if they are involved with anyone from the office. Although these restrictions are rare, they seem to have the desired effect of curtailing office romances (Cooper 2003).

Most companies (Wal-Mart is an example) do not prohibit romantic relationships among employees. However, the company may have a policy prohibiting open displays of affection between employees in the workplace and romantic relationships between supervisor and subordinate. Most companies have no policy regarding love relationships at work and generally regard romances between coworkers as "none of their business." There are some exceptions to the general permissive policies regarding workplace romances. Many companies have written policies prohibiting intimate relationships when one member of the couple is in a direct supervisory position over the other. These policies may be enforced by transferring or dismissing employees who are discovered in romantic relationships.

Your Opinion?

1. To what degree do you believe corporations should develop policies in regard to workplace romances?
2. What are the advantages and disadvantages of a workplace romance for a business?
3. What are the advantages and disadvantages for individuals involved in a workplace romance?
4. How might an office romance of peers affect coworkers?

Sources

Cooper, C. 2003. Office affairs are hard work. *The Australian*, March 5.

Franklin, R. 2002. Office romances: Conduct unbecoming? *Business Week Online*, February 14, 1.

Raso, R. 2008. How to handle workplace romance, foster interpersonal skills. *Nursing Management* 39:56–57.

Love in Medieval Europe—from Economics to Romance

Love in the 1100s was a concept influenced by economic, political, and family structure. In medieval Europe, land and wealth were owned by kings controlling geographical regions—kingdoms. When so much wealth and power were at stake, love was not to be trusted as the mechanism for choosing spouses for royal offspring. Rather, marriages of the sons and daughters of the aristocracy were arranged with the heirs of other states with whom an alliance was sought. Love was not tied to marriage but was conceptualized as an adoration of physical beauty (often between a knight and his beloved) and as spiritual and romantic, even between people not married or of the same sex. Hence, romantic love had its origin in extramarital love and was not expected between spouses (Trachman and Bluestone 2005).

The presence of kingdoms and estates and the patrimonial households declined with the English revolutions of 1642 and 1688 and the French Revolution of 1789. No longer did aristocratic families hold power; the power was transferred to individuals through parliaments or other national bodies. Even today, English monarchs are figureheads, with parliament handling the real business of international diplomacy. Because wealth and power were no longer in the hands of individual aristocrats, the need to control mate selection decreased and the role of love changed. Marriage became less of a political and business arrangement and more of a mutually desired emotional union. Just as bureaucratic structure held together partners in medieval society, a new mechanism—love—would now provide the emotional and social bonding.

Hence, love in medieval times changed from a feeling irrelevant to marriage—because individuals (representing aristocratic families) were to marry even though they were not in love—to a feeling that bonded a woman and a man together for marriage.

Love in Colonial America

Love in colonial America was similar to that in medieval times. Marriage was regarded as a business arrangement between the fathers of the respective families (Dugan 2005). An interested suitor would approach the father of a girl to express his desire to court his daughter. The fathers would generally confer on the amount of the **dowry**, which included the money and/or valuables the girl's father would pay the boy's father. Because unmarried women were stigmatized, marrying them off was desirable; thus, the dowry was an added inducement for a boy to marry the girl. Fathers could deny their daughters a dowry if the daughters were unwilling to marry the man their father chose. Love was not totally absent, however; sometimes a girl could persuade her father to tell the suitor she was not interested.

Theories on the Origins of Love

Various theories have been suggested with regard to the origins of love.

Evolutionary Theory

Gillath et al. (2008) provided evidence that sexual interest and arousal are associated with motives to form and maintain a close relationship, to fall in love. They suggested these motives are hardwired to ensure a stable relationship for producing offspring. Although these motives are subject to distraction of new sexual opportunities, they nevertheless suggest a broader relationship motivation to sex. In effect, love has an evolutionary purpose by providing a bonding mechanism between the parents during the time their offspring are dependent infants. Love's strongest bonding lasts about four years, the time when children are most dependent and when two parents can cooperate in handling their new infant. "If a woman was carrying the equivalent of a twelve-pound bowling ball in one arm and a pile of sticks in the other, it was ecologically critical to pair up with a mate to rear the young," observed anthropologist Helen Fisher (Toufexis 1993). The "four-year itch" is Fisher's term for the time at which parents with one child are most likely to divorce—the time when the woman can more easily survive without parenting help from the male. If the couple has a second child, doing so resets the clock, and "the seven-year itch" is the next most vulnerable time.

Learning Theory

Unlike evolutionary theory, which views the experience of love as innate, learning theory emphasizes that love feelings develop in response to certain behaviors in which a partner engages. Individuals in a new relationship who look at each other, smile at each other, compliment each other, touch each other endearingly, do things for each other, and do enjoyable things together are engaging in behaviors that make love feelings develop easily. In effect, love can be viewed as a feeling that results from a high frequency of positive behavior and a low frequency of negative behavior. One high-frequency behavior is positive labeling whereby the partners flood each other with positive statements. We asked one of our students who reported that she was deliriously in love to identify the positive statements her partner had said to her. She kept a list for a week, which included:

Angel, Sweetie, Cinderella, Sleeping Beauty.

You understand me so well.

Precious jewel, Sugar bear, Snow White, Honey.

You are my best friend.

I never thought you were out there.

You know me better than anyone in my whole life.

You're always safe in my arms.

I would sell my guitar for you if you need money.

People who "fall out of love" may note the high frequency of negatives on the part of their partner and the low frequency of positives. People who say, "this is not the person I married," are saying the ratio of positives to negatives has changed dramatically.

Cunningham et al. (2005) used the term **social allergy** to refer to being annoyed and disgusted by a repeated behavior on the part of the partner. Examples are uncouth habits (for example, picking one's teeth), inconsiderate acts (not offering to get something from the kitchen when going one's self), intrusive behaviors (opening one's mail or e-mail or checking one's cell phone to see the listing on speed-dial), and norm violations (drinking out of someone else's glass). The researchers found that these types of behaviors increased over time and were associated with both decreased relationship satisfaction and termination of the relationship.

Sociological Theory

Almost fifty years ago, Ira Reiss (1960) suggested the wheel model as an explanation for how love develops. Basically, the wheel has four stages—rapport, self-revelation, mutual dependency, and fulfillment of personality needs. In the rapport stage, each partner has the feeling of having known the partner before, feels comfortable with the partner, and wants to deepen the relationship.

Such desire leads to self-revelation or self-disclosure, whereby each reveals intimate thoughts to the other about one's self, the partner, and the relationship. Such revelations deepen the relationship because it is assumed that the confidences are shared only with special people, and each partner feels special when listening to the revelations of the other.

As the level of self-disclosure becomes more intimate, a feeling of mutual dependency develops. Each partner is happiest in the presence of the other and

When two people are under the influence of the most violent, most insane, most delusive, and most transient of passions, they are required to swear that they will remain in that exalted, abnormal, and exhausting condition continuously until death do them part.

George B. Shaw, Irish dramatist

begins to depend on the other for creating the context of these euphoric feelings. "I am happiest when I am with you" is the theme of this stage.

The feeling of mutual dependency involves the fulfillment of personality needs. The desires to love and be loved, to trust and be trusted, and to support and be supported are met in the developing love relationship.

Psychosexual Theory

According to psychosexual theory, love results from blocked biological sexual desires. In the sexually repressive mood of his time, Sigmund Freud (1905/1938) referred to love as "aim-inhibited sex." Love was viewed as a function of the sexual desire a person was not allowed to express because of social restraints. In Freud's era, people would meet, fall in love, get married, and have sex. Freud felt that the socially required delay from first meeting to having sex resulted in the development of "love feelings." By extrapolation, Freud's theory of love suggests that love dies with marriage (access to one's sexual partner).

Biochemical Theory

There may be a biochemical basis for love feelings. **Oxytocin** is a hormone that encourages contractions during childbirth and endears the mother to the suckling infant. It has been referred to as the "cuddle chemical" because of its significance in bonding. Later in life, oxytocin seems operative in the development of love feelings between lovers during sexual arousal. Oxytocin may be responsible for the fact that more women than men prefer to continue cuddling after intercourse.

Phenylethylamine (PEA) is a natural, amphetamine-like substance that makes lovers feel euphoric and energized. The high that they report feeling just by being with each other is from the PEA that the brain releases in their bloodstream. The natural chemical high associated with love may explain why the intensity of passionate love decreases over time. As with any amphetamine, the body builds up a tolerance to PEA, and it takes more and more to produce the special kick. Hence, lovers develop a tolerance for each other. "Love junkies" are those who go from one love affair to the next in rapid succession to maintain the high. Alternatively, some lovers break up and get back together frequently as a way of making the relationship new again and keeping the high going.

Zeki (2007) emphasized the neurobiology of love in that both romantic love and maternal love are linked to the perpetuation of the species. Romantic love bonds the male and female together to reproduce, take care of, and socialize new societal members, whereas maternal love ensures that the mother will prioritize the care of her baby over other needs. Because of the social functions of these love states, neurobiologists have learned via brain imaging techniques that both types of attachment activate regions of the brain that access the brain's reward system (areas rich in oxytocin and vasopressin receptors). At the same time, negative cognitions or emotions about these relationships are shut down to allow the positive to predominate. No wonder both lovers and mothers seem very happy and focused. They are on a biological mission, and the reward center of their brain keeps them on track.

Meyer (2007) noted that taking selective serotonin reuptake inhibitor (SSRI) medications commonly used for depression and anxiety can affect relationship satisfaction (for example, blunt emotions and decrease sexual interest); Meyer also emphasized the importance of checking with one's physician. In some cases, other medications can be used to block these negative side effects.

Attachment Theory

The attachment theory of love emphasizes that a primary motivation in life is to be connected with other people. Monteoliva et al. (2005) confirmed that the attachment style an individual has with one's parents is associated with the quality of one's later romantic relationships. Specifically, a secure emotional attachment

Table 2.1 Love Theories and Criticisms

Theory	Criticism
Evolutionary—love is the social glue that bonds parents with dependent children and spouses with each other to care for offspring.	This assumption that women and children need men for survival is not necessarily true today. Women can have and rear children without male partners.
Learning—positive experiences create love feelings.	This does not account for (1) why some people will share positive experiences yet will not fall in love, and (2) why some people stay in love despite negative behavior.
Psychosexual—love results from blocked biological drive.	This does not account for people who report intense love feelings yet are having sex regularly.
Sociological—the wheel theory whereby love develops from rapport, self-revelation, mutual dependency, and personality need fulfillment.	Not all people are capable of rapport, revealing one's self, and so on.
Biochemical—love is chemical. Oxytocin is an amphetamine-like chemical that bonds mother to child and produces a giddy high in young lovers.	This does not specify how much of what chemicals result in the feeling of love. Chemicals alone cannot create the state of love; cognitions are also important.
Attachment—primary motivation in life is to be connected to others. Children bond with parents and spouses to each other.	Not all people feel the need to be emotionally attached to others. Some prefer to be detached.

with loving adults as a child is associated with later involvement in a satisfying, loving, communicative relationship. This finding was true regardless of ethnic or racial background. People who evidence a secure attachment to a love partner also report higher levels of commitment and dedication (Pistole and Vocaturo 2000). Hence, the benefits of a secure love attachment are enormous.

One form of family therapy is "emotionally focused family therapy" (EFFT), which emphasizes intensifying the emotional bonds between family members on the premise that such emotional connectedness creates a context for resolving family problems (Furrow et al. 2005). Attachment theory has its basis in the work of Rene Spitz and Harry Harlow. The former emphasized the importance of infants being held and nurtured for their physical and emotional development. Dr. Harlow studied infant rhesus monkeys and found that they preferred soft motherlike dummies that offered no food over dummies that provided a food source but were made of wire and were less pleasant to the touch.

Each of the theories of love presented in this section has critics (see Table 2.1).

How Love Develops in a New Relationship

Various social, physical, psychological, physiological, and cognitive conditions affect the development of love relationships.

Social Conditions for Love

Love is a social label given to an internal feeling. Our society promotes love through popular music (see the quote that opens this chapter), movies (*Twilight*), and novels (Harlequin romances). These media convey the message that love is an experience to pursue, enjoy, and maintain. People who fall out of love are encouraged to try again: "love is lovelier the second time you fall." Unlike people reared in Eastern cultures, Americans grow up in a context to turn on their radar for love.

Body Type Condition for Love

The probability of being involved in a love relationship is influenced by approximating the cultural ideal of physical appearance. Halpern et al. (2005)

analyzed data on a nationally representative sample of 5,487 African American, white, and Hispanic adolescent females and found that, for each one-point increase in body mass index (BMI), the probability of involvement in a romantic relationship dropped by 6 percent. Hence, to the degree that a woman approximates the cultural ideal of being trim and "not being fat," she increases the chance of attracting a partner and becoming involved in a romantic love relationship. One of our former students dropped from 225 pounds to 125 pounds and noted, "You wouldn't believe the dramatic difference in the way guys noticed and talked to me [between] when I was beefed up and when I was trim. I was engaged within three months of getting the weight off and am now married."

Ambwani and Strauss (2007) found that body image has an effect on sexual relations and that relationships affect their self-image. Hence, women who felt positively about their body were more likely to report having sexual relations with a partner. The fact that they were in a relationship was associated with positive feelings about themselves.

Psychological Conditions for Love

Two psychological conditions associated with the development of healthy love relationships are high self-esteem and self-disclosure.

Self-Esteem   High self-esteem is important for defining success (Bianchi and Povilavicius 2006). High self-esteem is also important for developing healthy love relationships because it enables individuals to feel worthy of being loved. Feeling good about yourself allows you to believe that others are capable of loving you. Individuals with low self-esteem doubt that someone else can love and accept them (DeHart et al. 2002). Having high self-esteem provides other benefits:

1. It allows one to be open and honest with others about both strengths and weaknesses.

2. It allows one to feel generally equal to others.

3. It allows one to take responsibility for one's own feelings, ideas, mistakes, and failings.

4. It allows for the acceptance of both strengths and weaknesses in one's self and others.

5. It allows one to validate one's self and not to expect the partner to do this.

6. It permits one to feel empathy—a very important skill in relationships.

7. It allows separateness and interdependence, as opposed to fusion and dependence.

Positive physiological outcomes also follow from high self-esteem. People who feel good about themselves are less likely to develop ulcers and are likely to cope with anxiety better than those who don't. In contrast, low self-esteem has devastating consequences for individuals and the relationships in which they become involved. Not feeling loved as a child and, worse, feeling rejected and abandoned creates the context for the development of a negative self-concept and mistrust of others. People who have never felt loved and wanted may require constant affirmation from a partner as to their worth, and may cling desperately to that person out of fear of being abandoned. Such dependence (the modern term is *codependency*) may also encourage staying in unhealthy relationships (for example, abusive and alcoholic relationships) because the person may feel "this is all I deserve." Fuller and Warner (2000) studied 257 college students and observed that women had higher codependency scores than men. Codependency was also associated with being reared in families that were stressful and alcoholic.

One characteristic of individuals with low self-esteem is that they may love too much and be addicted to unhealthy love relationships. Petrie et al. (1992) studied fifty-two women who reported that they were involved in unhealthy love relationships in which they had selected men with problems (such as alcohol or other drug addiction) that they attempted to solve at the expense of neglecting themselves. "Their preoccupation with correcting the problems of others may be an attempt to achieve self-esteem," the researchers noted (p. 17). "I know I can help this man" is the motif of these women.

Although having positive feelings about one's self when entering into a love relationship is helpful, sometimes these develop after one becomes involved in the relationship. "I've always felt like an ugly duckling," said one woman. "But once I fell in love with him and him with me, I felt very different. I felt very good about myself then because I knew that I was somebody that someone else loved." High self-esteem, then, is not necessarily a prerequisite for falling in love. People who have low self-esteem may fall in love with someone else as a result of feeling deficient. The love they perceive the other person has for them may compensate for the perceived deficiency and improve their self-esteem. This phenomenon can happen with two individuals with low self-esteem—love can elevate the self concepts of both of them.

Self-Disclosure Disclosing one's self is necessary if one is to love—to feel invested in another (Radmacher and Azmitia 2006). Ross (2006) identified eight dimensions of self-disclosure: (1) background and history, (2) feelings toward the partner, (3) feelings toward self, (4) feelings about one's body, (5) attitudes toward social issues, (6) tastes and interests, (7) money and work, and (8) feelings about friends. Disclosed feelings about the partner included "how much I like the partner," "my feelings about our sexual relationship," "how much I trust my partner," "things I dislike about my partner," and "my thoughts about the future of our relationship"—all of which were associated with relationship satisfaction. Of interest in Ross's findings is that disclosing one's tastes and interests was negatively associated with relationship satisfaction. By telling a partner too much detail about what one likes, partners may discover something that turns them off and lowers relationship satisfaction.

Kito (2005) examined the self-disclosure patterns of 145 college students (both American and Japanese) and found that self-disclosure was higher in romantic relationships than in friendships and that Americans were more disclosing than the Japanese. The researcher also found that disclosure was higher in same-sex friendships than in cross-sex friendships.

It is not easy for some people to let others know who they are, what they feel, or what they think. They may fear that, if others really know them, they will be rejected as a friend or lover. To guard against this possibility, they may protect themselves and their relationships by allowing only limited information about their past behaviors and present thoughts and feelings. Some people keep others at a distance—they do not want psychological intimacy. Audrey Hepburn, Academy Award-winning screen actress of the 1950s, is said to have been wary of being close. Stanley Donen, with whom she was involved in the making of three movies, noted:

I longed to get closer, to get behind whatever was the invisible, but decidedly present barrier between her and the rest of us, but I never got to the deepest part of Audrey. I don't mean to imply that I thought she was playing a game with me. But she always kept a little of herself in reserve, which was hers alone, and I couldn't ever find out what it was, let alone share it with her. She was the pot of gold at the end of the rainbow. (Spoto 2006, 251)

Trust is the condition under which people are most willing to disclose themselves. When people trust someone, they tend to feel that whatever feelings or information they share will not be judged and will be kept safe with that person. If trust is betrayed, people may become bitterly resentful and vow never to disclose themselves again. One woman said, "After I told my partner that I had had

And think not you can Direct the course of love, For love, If it finds you worthy, Directs your course.

Kahlil Gibran, philosopher

an abortion, he told me that I was a murderer and he never wanted to see me again. I was devastated and felt I had made a mistake telling him about my past. You can bet I'll be careful before I disclose myself to someone else" (personal communication).

Gallmeier et al. (1997) studied the communication patterns of 360 undergraduates at two universities and found that women were significantly more likely to disclose information about themselves. Specific areas of disclosure included previous love relationships, what they wanted for the future of the relationship, and what their partners did that they did not like.

Physiological and Cognitive Conditions for Love

Physiological and cognitive variables are also operative in the development of love. The individual must be physiologically aroused and interpret this stirred-up state as love (Walster and Walster 1978).

Suppose, for example, that Dan is afraid of flying, but his fear is not particularly extreme and he doesn't like to admit it to himself. This fear, however, does cause him to be physiologically aroused. Suppose that Dan takes a flight and finds himself sitting next to Judy on the plane. With heart racing, palms sweating, and breathing labored, Dan chats with Judy as the plane takes off. Suddenly, Dan discovers that he finds Judy terribly attractive, and he begins to try to figure out ways that he can continue seeing her after the flight is over. What accounts for Dan's sudden surge of interest in Judy? Is Judy really that appealing to him, or has he taken the physiological arousal of fear and mislabeled it as attraction? (Brehm 1992, 44)

Although most people who develop love feelings are not aroused in this way, they may be aroused or anxious about other issues (being excited at a party or feeling apprehensive about meeting someone), and may mislabel these feelings as those of attraction when they meet someone.

In the absence of one's cognitive functioning, love feelings are impossible. Individuals with brain cancer who have had the front part of their brain (between the eyebrows) removed are incapable of love. Indeed, emotions are not present in them at all (Ackerman 1994). The social, physical, psychological, physiological, and cognitive conditions are not the only factors important for the development of love feelings. The timing must also be right. There are only certain times in life (for example, when educational and career goals are met or within sight) when people seek a love relationship. When those times occur, a person is likely to fall in love with another person who is there and who is also seeking a love relationship. Hence, many love pairings exist because each of the individuals is available to the other at the right time—not because they are particularly suited for each other.

Love as a Context for Problems

Though love may bring great joy, it also creates a context for problems. Four such problems are simultaneous loves, involvement in an abusive relationship, making risky or dangerous choices, and the emergence of stalking.

Destruction of Existing Relationships

Sometimes the development of one love relationship is at the expense of another. A student in our classes noted that when she was 16, she fell in love with a person at work who was 25. Her parents were adamant in their disapproval and threatened to terminate the relationship with their daughter if she continued to see this man. The student noted that she initially continued to see her lover and to keep their relationship hidden. However, eventually she decided that giving up her family was not worth the relationship, so she stopped seeing him

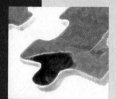

What if You Are in Love with Two People at the Same Time?

Because you are probably not in a polyamorous relationship (in which multiple loves are encouraged), one answer to the dilemma is to let the clock run. Most love relationships do not have a steady course. Time has a way of changing them. If you maintain both relationships, one is likely to emerge as more powerful, and you will have your answer. Alternatively, if you feel "guilty" for having two loves, you may make the conscious choice to spend your time and attention with one partner and let the other relationship go in terms of actual time spent with the partner. Although you can have emotions for two people at the same time, you cannot be with more than one person at a time. The person with whom you choose to spend your time is likely to be the person you love "a little bit more" and with whom your love feelings are likely to increase. Indeed, Lundstrom and Jones-Gotman (2009) noted that being romantically in love with one partner helps one to deflect the development of love with a potential new partner.

permanently. Others in the same situation would end the relationship with their parents and continue the relationship with their beloved. Choosing to end a relationship with one's parents is a downside of love.

Simultaneous Loves

For all the wonder of love, awareness that one's partner is in love with or having sex with someone else can create heartbreak. As we will discuss in the section on jealousy later in the chapter, multiple involvements are not a problem for some individuals or couples (for example, in compersion or polyamorous relationships). However, most people are not comfortable knowing their partner has other emotional or sexual relationships. Only 2.2 percent of 1,317 undergraduates agreed: "I can feel good about my partner having an emotional/sexual relationship with someone else" (Knox and Zusman 2009). In a study on "undesirable marriage forms," 91.2 percent of 111 undergraduates reported that they would "never participate" in a "group marriage" (Billingham et al. 2005). Hence, for most individuals, simultaneous lovers are viewed as a problem.

Abusive Relationships

Another problem associated with love is being in love with someone who may be emotionally or physically abusive (see Johnson 2005). Almost a third (31.6 percent) of 1,319 undergraduates reported that they had been involved in an emotionally abusive relationship with a partner (10.7 percent reported previous involvement in a physically abusive relationship) (Knox and Zusman 2009). Someone who criticizes you (for example, "you're ugly, stupid, pitiful"), is dishonest with you (is sexually unfaithful, for instance), or physically harms you will create a context of interpersonal misery for you. Nevertheless, you might love and feel emotionally drawn to that person.

Most marriage therapists suggest examining why you love and continue to stay with such a person. Do you feel that you deserve this treatment because you are "no good" or that you would not be able to find a better alternative (low self-concept)? Do you feel you would rather be with a person who treats you badly than be alone (fear of the unknown)? Or do you hang on because you look forward to a better tomorrow (hope)?

The sun's gone dim, and
The moon's turned black;
For I loved him, and
He didn't love back.

Dorothy Parker
Sunset Gun

Another explanation for why some people with abusive partners continue to be in love is that the abuse is only one part of the relationship. When such partners are not being abusive, they may be kind, loving, and passionate. Shackelford et al. (2005) analyzed data on 1,461 men and found that they often used "mate-retention behaviors," such as giving flowers or gifts to entice a partner to stay in the relationship, which can become even more abusive.

The presence of these mate-retention behaviors, which happen every now and then (a periodic reinforcement), keeps the love feelings alive. Love stops when insufficient positive behaviors counteract the extent of the abusive behaviors. One abused partner said, "when he started abusing my kids, that was it."

Stalking: When Loves Goes Mad

In the name of love, people have stalked their beloved. **Stalking** is defined as a repeated malicious pursuit that threatens the safety of the victim. It may involve following a victim; threats of physical harm to the victim, one's self, or another person; or restricting the behavior of the victim, including kidnapping or home invasion. The most common stalking behavior (which is also prohibited by stalking laws) is unwanted "obsessional following" (Meloy and Fisher 2005). Stalking behaviors typically cause great distress or fear and impact the emotional well-being and social and work activities of the victim.

Who are the stalkers? Most often (in 85 percent of cases), men are stalkers and women are their victims. Two primary reasons for stalking are rejection by a sexual intimate (hence the male has been in a previous emotional or sexual relationship with the woman and obsessively tries to win her back) or rejection by a stranger with whom the stalker is infatuated and who fails to return romantic overtures. The stalking of celebrity females (for example, Jodie Foster) sometimes becomes visible in the media. The two most common emotions of the stalker are anger (over being rejected) and jealousy (at being replaced) (Meloy and Fischer 2005). Exercising a great deal of control in an existing relationship is predictive that the controlling partner will become a stalker when the other partner ends the relationship (King 2003). For the 15 percent of stalkers who are women, the most common victim is another woman. These may be partners in lesbian relationships that have ended. The stalker feels rejected and wants to renew the relationship.

Stalkers are obsessional and very controlling. Obsessional thinking is their most common cognitive trait (Meloy and Fisher 2005). They are typically mentally ill and have one or more personality disorders involving paranoid, antisocial, or obsessive-compulsive behaviors. Reid (2005) and Meloy and Fischer (2005) noted a neurobiological component in the stalker. Meloy and Fischer (2005) identified three primary brain systems involved in stalking: sex drive, whereby the individual is motivated to achieve sexual gratification; attraction, whereby the individual is driven to emotionally connect with a specific mating partner; and attachment, whereby the individual is motivated to experience a secure relationship with a long-term partner. In effect, the stalker feels a barrier in access to the beloved (physically and emotionally), which intensifies the drive to be with the rejecting partner (referred to as abandonment rage). Indeed, brain activity can be observed with magnetic resonance imaging (MRI) that reveals differences between a person who is happily in love and a person who is the "spurned or unrequited stalker" (Meloy and Fischer 2005, 1,475).

Although various coping strategies have been identified, additional research is needed on how to manage unwanted attention. A survey of young adults suggested the following general coping categories (Spitzberg and Cupach 1998):

1. Make a direct statement to the person ("I am not interested in dating you, my feelings about you will not change, and I know that you will respect my decision and direct your attention elsewhere") (Regan 2000, 266).

2. Seek protection through formal channels (for example, police, court restraining order).

3. Avoid the perpetrator (ignore, don't walk with or talk to, hang up if the person calls).

4. Use informal coping methods (for example, telephone caller identification and advice from others).

Direct statements and actions that unequivocally communicate lack of interest are probably the most effective types of intervention.

Unrequited or Unfulfilling Love Relationships

It is not unusual for lovers to vary in the intensity of their love for each other. The interesting question is whether being the person who loves more in a relationship is better than the person who loves less. The person who loves more may suffer more anguish. Such was the case of Jack Twist (in the now-classic *Brokeback Mountain*), who was hurt that his love interest, Ennis Del Mar, would not make time for them to continue their clandestine meetings on Brokeback Mountain.

Love as a Context for Risky, Dangerous, or Questionable Choices

Plato said that "love is a grave mental illness," and some research suggests that individuals in love make risky, dangerous, or questionable decisions. In a study on "what I did for love," college students reported that "driving drunk," "dropping out of school to be with my partner," and "having sex without protection" were among the more dubious choices they had made while they were under the spell of love (Knox et al. 1998). Similarly, a team of researchers examined the relationship between having a romantic love partner and engaging in minor acts of delinquency (for example, smoking cigarettes, getting drunk, skipping school); they found that females were particularly influenced by their "delinquent" boyfriends (Haynie et al. 2005). Their data source was the National Longitudinal Study of Adolescent Health. Furthermore, researchers have found that women who are "romantically in love" are less likely to use condoms with their partners. Doing so isn't regarded as very romantic, and they elect not to inject realism into a love context (East et al. 2007).

Jealousy in Relationships

Jealousy can be defined as an emotional response to a perceived or real threat to an important or valued relationship. People experiencing jealousy fear being abandoned and feel anger toward the partner or the perceived competition (Guerrero et al. 2005). As Buss (2000) emphasized, "Jealousy is an adaptive emotion, forged over millions of years. . . . It evolved as a primary defense against threats of infidelity and abandonment" (p. 56). People become jealous when they fear replacement. Although jealousy does not occur in all cultures (polyandrous societies value cooperation, not sexual exclusivity; Cassidy and Lee 1989), it does occur in our society and among both heterosexuals and homosexuals.

Of 1,319 university students, 41.7 percent reported, "I am a jealous person" (Knox and Zusman 2009). In another study, 185 students gave information about their experience with jealousy (Knox et al. 1999). On a continuum of 0 ("no jealousy") to 10 ("extreme jealousy"), with 5 representing "average jealousy," these students reported feeling jealous at a mean level of 5.3 in their current or last relationship. Students who had been dating a partner for a year or less were significantly more likely to report higher levels of jealousy (mean = 4.7) than those who had dated 13 months or more (mean = 3.3). Hence, jealously is more likely to occur early in a couple's relationship.

Types of Jealousy

Barelds-Dijkstra and Barelds (2007) identified three types of jealousy as reactive jealousy, anxious jealousy, and possessive jealousy. **Reactive jealousy** consists of feelings that are a reaction to something the partner is doing (for example, coming home late every night). **Anxious jealousy** is obsessive ruminations about the partners alleged infidelity that make one's life a miserable emotional torment. **Possessive jealousy** involves an attack at the partner or the alleged person to whom the partner is showing attention. The motive suggested for the presumed murder by O.J. Simpson of Nicole Brown was possessive jealousy—another man (Ron Goldman) was with her at the time of the murder.

Causes of Jealousy

Jealousy can be triggered by external or internal factors.

External Causes   External factors refer to behaviors a partner engages in that are interpreted as (1) an emotional and/or sexual interest in someone (or something) else, or (2) a lack of emotional and/or sexual interest in the primary partner. In the study of 185 students previously referred to, the respondents identified "actually talking to a previous partner" (34 percent) and "talking about a previous partner" (19 percent) as the most common sources of their jealousy. Also, men were more likely than women to report feeling jealous when their partner talked to a previous partner, whereas women were more likely than men to report feeling jealous when their partner danced with someone else.

Internal Causes   Jealousy may also exist even when no external behavior indicates the partner is involved or interested in an **extradyadic relationship**—an emotional or sexual involvement between a member of a pair and someone other than the partner. Internal causes of jealousy refer to characteristics of individuals that predispose them to jealous feelings, independent of their partner's behavior. Examples include being mistrustful, having low self-esteem, being highly involved in and dependent on the relationship, and having no perceived alternative partners available (Pines 1992). The following are explanations of these internal causes of jealousy:

1. *Mistrust.* If an individual has been deceived or cheated on in a previous relationship, that individual may learn to be mistrustful in subsequent relationships. Such mistrust may manifest itself in jealousy. Mistrust and jealousy may be intertwined. Tilley and Brackley (2005) examined the factors involved for men convicted of assaulting a female and suggested that both jealousy and mistrust may have been involved in aggression against a female.

2. *Low self-esteem.* Individuals who have low self-esteem tend to be jealous because they lack a sense of self-worth and hence find it difficult to believe anyone can value and love them (Khanchandani 2005). Feelings of worthlessness may contribute to suspicions that someone else is valued more.

3. *Anxiety.* In general, individuals who experience higher levels of anxiety also display more jealousy (Khanchandani 2005).

4. *Lack of perceived alternatives.* Individuals who have no alternative person or who feel inadequate in attracting others may be particularly vulnerable to jealousy. They feel that, if they do not keep the person they have, they will be alone.

5. *Insecurity.* Individuals who feel insecure in a relationship with their partner may experience higher levels of jealousy. Khanchandani (2005) found that individuals who had been in relationships for a shorter time, who were in less committed relationships, and who were less satisfied with their relationships were more likely to be jealous.

Consequences of Jealousy

Jealousy can have both desirable and undesirable consequences.

Desirable Outcomes Barelds-Dijkstra and Barelds (2007) studied 961 couples and found that reactive jealousy is associated with a positive effect on the relationship. Not only may reactive jealousy signify that the partner is cared for (the implied message is "I love you and don't want to lose you to someone else"), but also the partner may learn that the development of other romantic and sexual relationships is unacceptable.

One wife said:

> When I started spending extra time with this guy at the office, my husband got jealous and told me he thought I was getting in over my head and asked me to cut back on the relationship because it was "tearing him up." I felt he really loved me when he told me this, and I chose to stop having lunch with the guy at work. (personal communication)

The researchers noted that making the partner jealous may also have the positive function of assessing the partner's commitment and of alerting the partner that one could leave for greener mating pastures. Hence, one partner may deliberately evoke jealousy to solidify commitment and ward off being taken for granted. In addition, sexual passion may be reignited if one partner perceives that another would take the love object away. That people want what others want is an adage that may underlie the evocation of jealousy.

Undesirable Outcomes Shakespeare referred to jealousy as the "green-eyed monster," suggesting that it sometimes leads to undesirable outcomes for relationships. Anxious jealousy with its obsessive ruminations about the partner's alleged infidelity can make an individual miserable, and such jealousy spills over into one's evaluation or experience of the relationship as negative. If the anxious jealousy results in repeated unwarranted accusations, a partner can tire of such attacks and end the relationship.

In its extreme form, jealousy may have devastating consequences. In the name of love, people have stalked or shot the beloved and killed themselves in reaction to rejected love. Barelds-Dijkstra and Barelds (2007) noted that possessive jealousy involves an attack on a partner or an alleged person to whom the partner is showing attention. Possessive jealousy definitely may have negative consequences for a relationship. The next section details the different ways women and men cope with jealousy.

Gender Differences in Coping with Jealousy

Jealousy is a theme of popular movies and part of our cultural language. Defined as "one's emotional reaction to the perception that one's love relationship may end because of a third party," jealousy was the topic of a study of 291 undergraduates where 51.9 percent "agreed" or "strongly agreed" that "jealousy is normal" (Knox et al. 2007).

Analysis of the data on women's and men's reactions to jealousy revealed four significant differences:

1. Food. Women were significantly more likely than men to report that they turned to food when they felt jealous: 30.3 percent of women, in contrast to 22 percent of men, said that they "always, often, or sometimes" looked to food when they felt jealous.

2. Alcohol. Men were significantly more likely than women to report that they drank alcohol or used drugs when they felt jealous: 46.9 percent of men, in contrast to 27.1 percent of women, said that they "always, often, or sometimes" would drink or use drugs to make the pain of jealousy go away.

3. Friends. Women were significantly more likely than men to report that they turned to friends when they felt jealous: 37.9 percent of women, in contrast to 13.5 percent of men, said that they "always" turned to friends for support when feeling jealous.

This couple has a polyamorous relationship. Both partners have emotional and sexual relationships with others and both encourage the other to have multiple relationships.

Authors

4. *Nonbelief that "jealousy shows love."* Women were significantly more likely than men to disagree or to strongly disagree that "jealousy shows how much your partner loves you": 63.2 percent of women, in contrast to 42.6 percent of men, disagreed with the statement. This difference may be related to the fact that more often jealous and abusive males victimize women.

Coping Strategies Implications of the data may be relevant to women who may be alert to the "extra urge" to eat in reaction to jealousy, and turn instead to vigorous exercise as a way of reducing stress. Not only might exercise better reduce the stress; it will do so without adding pounds, which could lead to further self-deprecation and depression. Similarly, men might consider talking with a buddy rather than turning to the bottle; strengthening friendships would be more productive than risking a hangover or a fatal car wreck.

Compersion and Polyamory

Compersion denotes a situation in which an individual feels positive about a partner's emotional and sexual enjoyment with another person, and is sometimes thought of as the opposite of jealousy. **Polyamory** means multiple loves (poly = many; amorous = love); polyamorous relationships may be heterosexual or homosexual (Bettinger 2005). People in polyamorous relationships agree that they will have emotional or sexual relationships with others and seek to rid themselves of jealous feelings and to increase their level of compersion. To feel happy for a partner who delights in the attention and affection of—and sexual involvement with—another person is the goal of polyamorous couples.

Embracing polyamory and compersion has both advantages and disadvantages (Tupelo and Freeman 2008). Advantages of polyamory include greater variety in one's emotional and sexual life; the avoidance of hidden affairs and the attendant feelings of deception, mistrust, or betrayal; and the opportunity to have different needs met by different people. Of the latter advantage, one polyamorous partner interviewed by Sheff (2006) said the following:

> I have one partner with whom I enjoy movies/books, another with whom I fish, another with whom I cook, and still another with whom I play the guitar. Each of these partners does not have the other three interests, which I dearly love and enjoy, so polyamory allows one to enjoy different things with different people.

Sheff (2006) also noted, "The vast majority of polyamorists espouse gender equality." One polyamorous woman she interviewed said the following:

> Women with multiple lovers are usually called sluts, bitches, very derogatory, very demeaning in sexual context. Whereas men who have multiple lovers—they're studs, they're playboys, they're glorified names, where with a woman it's very demeaning. So to be a woman and have multiple partners, it's been very empowering and claiming some of that back, saying I have just as much right to be a sexual person with many lovers as men do . . . without the shame and the guilt. . . .

The disadvantages of polyamory involve having to manage one's feelings of jealousy, greater exposure of one's self and partners to human immunodeficiency virus and other sexually transmitted infections, and limited time with each partner. Of the latter, one polyamorous partner said, "With three relationships and a full-time job, I just don't have much time to spend with each partner so I'm frustrated about who I'll be with next. And managing the feelings of the other partners who want to spend time with me is a challenge." More information about the various nuances of polyamory is presented in the following section. We are discussing polyamory in the chapter on love rather than sexuality because polyamory is as much about emotional intimacy as sexuality.

A Short Primer on Polyamory*

This very brief and incomplete discussion focuses on polyamory, a relationship style in which people openly conduct sexual relationships with multiple partners. Polyamory is more emotionally intimate than swinging and offers the possibility of greater gender equality than polygyny because both men and women can have more than one partner. These relationships have a number of different elements that include (but are not limited to) levels of sexual exclusivity, numbers of people involved, and various degrees of emotional intimacy between partners.

Sexual Exclusivity　Many community members use the term *polyamory*, or more commonly "poly," as an umbrella term to encompass both polyamory and polyfidelity. Those in *polyamorous* relationships generally have sexually and (ideally) emotionally intimate extradyadic relationships, with no promise of sexual exclusivity. **Polyfidelity** differs from polyamory in that *polyfideles* (the term for someone who practices polyfidelity) expect their partners to remain sexually exclusive within a group that is larger than two people, though some polyfidelitous groups have members who do not have sex with one another. Almost all polyfideles see each other as family members, regardless of the degree of sexual contact within their relationships. Not all polys in a relationship have sex with each other, and I call those who are emotionally intimate but not sexually connected *polyaffective*.

Polygeometry　The number of people involved in poly relationships varies and can include open couples, vees, triads, quads, and moresomes. As the number of people involved in a relationship rises, the relationships become rarer and potentially less stable. The most common form is the *open couple*, usually composed of two people who often are in a long-term relationship, cohabitate (some married, others unmarried), and have extradyadic sexual relationships. **Vees** are three-person relationships in which one member is sexually connected to each of the other two. The relationship between the two nonlovers can range from strangers (who are aware of and cordial with each other), to casual friends, to enemies. A *triad*, commonly understood as a *ménage à trois*, generally includes three sexually involved adults. Sometimes triads begin as threesomes, but more often they form when a single joins an open couple or a larger group loses members. *Quads*, as the name implies, are groups of four adults most commonly formed when two couples join, although sometimes they develop when a triad adds a fourth or a moresome loses members. Quads are notoriously unstable, frequently losing someone to poly-style divorce. *Moresomes*, groups with five or more adult members, are larger, more fragile, and more complicated than quads.

Emotional Intimacy　Polys frequently use the terms *primary*, *secondary*, and *tertiary* to describe their varied levels of intimacy. *Primary* partners—sometimes corresponding to the larger cultural conception of a spouse—usually have long-term relationships,

*This section was written for this text by Dr. Elizabeth Sheff, Department of Sociology, Georgia State University, Atlanta, Georgia. Dr. Sheff conducted more than forty interviews with people involved in polyamory.

joint finances, and sometimes have children; cohabitate; and make major life decisions together. *Secondary* partners tend to keep their lives more separate than primary partners, frequently maintain separate finances and residences, may have less intense emotional connections than primaries, and usually discuss major life decisions, though they generally do not make those decisions jointly. *Tertiary* relationships are often less emotionally intimate, sometimes with long-distance or more casual partners. Some tertiary relationships closely resemble swinging. Some poly families have *spice*, the poly word for more than one spouse.

My 20+ Years of Experience with Polyamory: An Interview with Paxus Starr**

What was your motivation to become polyamorous?

There are two different theories about the polyamory relationship model. Some people (including myself) think it is a choice, others (like my lover Shana) think it is genetically predisposed, like the conventional wisdom around being homosexual. Your question assumes the former position. Be aware that some don't think this question is appropriate. I choose polyamory because it felt more emotionally honest than being in a monogamous relationship and having strong attractions to other people and not acting on them (which sometimes caused resentments).

When did you decide to become polyamorous?

Over twenty years ago.

How many women are you involved with? Is this a typical amount?

This question needs clarification since "involved" is not defined. You probably mean "having sex with," but even this is a poor question. I've had a romantic relationship with a woman named Jana in Slovakia; we don't see each other very often, we have had a sexual relationship off and on over our many years of connection. I don't know if we will be sexual again when I go back to Europe. Does she "count"?

The definition of lover I use is someone who inspires me to write a love letter to them. I have a close relationship with a woman named Kat who founded Twin Oaks, the intentional community I live in. She is not interested in a sexual relationship with me, but I am without doubt in my mind involved with her.

I don't reveal the number of regular sexual relationships I have, because I find that people outside a poly lifestyle have no capacity to understand what the number means. I am happy to describe specific relationships in my life—but the sexual aspects are dynamic, largely independent of level of commitment, and as private as the practices of monogamous people. I am certain I have had more sexually intimate relationships than most poly people.

What's it like to live in a polyamorous community? What are the main differences from a monogamous household/neighborhood?

I don't live in a polyamorous community. Twin Oaks is more monogamous (15 percent) than poly. The community is tolerant of poly, just like it is of Islam, veganism, queer culture, and homeschooling. It is a community which embraces diversity.

My son has two dads. What is the difference between his reality and that of a kid of a single mom? When he was asked (he is now 5) about what he thought about having two dads, he said "I guess I lucked out." Between his three parents and other caregivers, my son, Willow, spends almost all his time with people who really want to be with him.

**Interview conducted by Emily Richey.

Have you ever had any acceptance issues from your parents or peers because of your choice to be polyamorous?

My parents are not accepting of my lifestyle; almost all my friends are.

What do you find are the main advantages to being polyamorous?

It improves your skill at processing emotions, because you have to make it work. It makes you more transparent and honest, because if you are not, it more quickly spins out of control. There is more sex, which is great. You don't feel like you need to get all your physical or emotional needs met by a single person. It is great for having interesting conversations with people. It angers dogmatic moralists and religious fanatics, which I enjoy. It is a model for a different, and I believe, better society (not that everyone must choose this lifestyle, but those who do get lots from it including personal growth).

What do you find are the main disadvantages to being polyamorous?

Stereotypes and prejudices people have about what poly is and means. The disconnection with my parents over it.

Do you have a main belief system/religion? If so what?

I am culturally pagan and spiritually atheist. I am an anarchist and a heretic.

Does your practice of polyamory ever get confused with the Mormon polygamy and, if so, how does it make you feel?

No one I have ever spoken with has made the mistake of confusing these things. The Mormons actually believe in multiple marriages but only for males. This makes me feel sorry for them.

On a daily basis, how do you manage seeing/interacting with the various women you are involved with?

The answer to that question is basically the same as the identical question with the phrase "romantically involved" replaced with "friends."

I don't think I have significantly more sex than many monogamous people. Just like healthy monogamous relationships, there is a sexual connection between myself and my physical intimates when we both feel like that is what we want. There is no rigid schedule as to when I am going to see a certain lover. There is not a fixed person I sleep with every Tuesday night. I very often see Hawina (Willow's mom) with Willow, but this has more to do with us being co-parents than being romantically involved (which we are).

I sometimes schedule dates with lovers; I also leave free time in my schedule so I can do things spontaneously.

How would your relationships change if children were involved?

Children are involved. Having a child was one of the smartest things I have done in my life (I was much less sure of this before we decided to try to have a child). Having three parents for a single child allows the parents unusually full lifestyles, and Willow still gets good care.

SUMMARY

What are some ways that love has been described?

Love remains an elusive and variable phenomenon. Researchers have conceptualized love as a continuum from romanticism to realism, as a triangle consisting of three basic elements (intimacy, passion, and commitment), and as a style (from playful ludic love to obsessive and dangerous or manic love).

How has love expressed itself in various social and historical contexts?

The society in which we live exercises considerable control over our love object or choice and conceptualizes it in various ways. Love may be blind, but it knows what color a person's skin is. Because romantic love is such a powerful emotion and marriage such an important relationship, mate selection is not left to chance when connecting an outsider with an existing family and peer network. Parents inadvertently influence the mate choice of their children by moving to certain neighborhoods, joining certain churches, and enrolling their children in certain schools. Doing so increases the chance that their offspring will "hang out" with, fall in love with, and marry people who are similar in race, education, and social class.

In the 1100s in Europe, love was not expected between spouses but existed primarily between the unmarried, such as a knight and his beloved. Marriage was an economic and political arrangement that linked two families. As aristocratic families declined after the French Revolution, love became an emotion to bind a woman and man together to bear and rear children. Previously, Buddhists, Greeks, and Hebrews had their own views of love. Love in colonial America was also tightly controlled.

What are the various theories of love?

Theories of love include evolutionary (love provides the social glue needed to bond parents with their dependent children and spouses with each other to care for their dependent offspring), learning (positive experiences create love feelings), sociological (Reiss's "wheel" theory), psychosexual (love results from a blocked biological drive), and biochemical (love involves feelings produced by biochemical events). For example, the neurobiology of love emphasizes that, because romantic love and maternal love are linked to the perpetuation of the species, biological wiring locks in the bonding of the male and female to rear offspring and to ensure the bonding of the mother to the infant. Finally, attachment theory focuses on the fact that a primary motivation in life is to be connected with other people.

How does love develop in a new relationship?

Love occurs under certain conditions. Social conditions include a society that promotes the pursuit of love, peers who enjoy it, and a set of norms that link love and marriage. Psychological conditions involve high self-esteem and a willingness to disclose one's self to others. Physiological and cognitive conditions imply that the individual experiences a stirred-up state and labels it "love."

How is love a context for problems?

Love sometimes provides a context for problems in that a young person in love will lie to parents and become distant from them so as to be with the lover. Also, lovers experience problems such as being in love with two people at the same time, being in love with someone who is abusive, and making risky, dangerous, or questionable choices while in love (for example, not using a condom) or reacting to a former lover who has become a stalker.

How do jealousy and love interface?

Jealousy is an emotional response to a perceived or real threat to a valued relationship. Types of jealousy are reactive (partner shows interest in another), anxious (ruminations about partner's unfaithfulness), and possessive (striking back at a partner or another). Jealous feelings may have both internal and external causes and may have both positive and negative consequences for a couple's relationship. Compersion is the opposite of jealousy and involves feeling positive about a partner's emotional and physical relationship with another person. Polyamory ("many loves") is an arrangement whereby lovers agree to have numerous emotional and/or sexual relationships with others at the same time, and each person is aware of every relationship. Polyamorous lovers note both the difficulties of this arrangement (coping with feelings of jealousy) and the advantages (not having to lie about being interested in others).

KEY TERMS

agape love style
anxious jealousy
arranged marriage
compersion
conjugal (married) love
dowry

eros love style
extradyadic relationship
infatuation
jealousy
ludic love style
lust

mania love style
oxytocin
polyamory
polyfidelity
possessive jealousy
pragma love style

reactive jealousy
romantic love
social allergy
stalking
storge love style
vees

The Companion Website for *Choices in Relationships: An Introduction to Marriage and the Family,* Tenth Edition

www.cengage.com/sociology/knox

Supplement your review of this chapter by going to the Companion Website to take one of the tutorial quizzes, use the flash cards to master key terms, or check out the many other study aids, like crossword puzzles and self-assessments. You'll also find special features such as General Social Survey (GSS) data, Census data, and other resources to help you with that special project or to do some research on your own.

WEBLINKS

Love and Relationships Center
http://health.discovery.com/centers/loverelationships/loverelationships.html

Love Quotes
http://library.lovingyou.com/quotes/

The Polyamory Society
http://www.polyamorysociety.org/

Third Age
http://www.thirdage.com/romance/

REFERENCES

Ackerman, D. 1994. *A natural history of love.* New York: Random House.

Ambwani, S., and J. Strauss. 2007. Love thyself before loving others? A qualitative and quantitative analysis of gender differences in body image and romantic love. *Sex Roles* 56:13–22.

Barelds, D. P., and P. Barelds-Dijkstra. 2007. Love at first sight or friends first? Ties among partner personality trait similarity, relationship onset, relationship quality, and love. *Journal of Social and Personal Relationships* 24:479–96.

Barelds-Dijkstra, D. P. H., and P. Barelds. 2007. Relations between different types of jealousy and self and partner perceptions of relationship quality. *Clinical Psychology & Psychotherapy* 14:176–88.

Bettinger, M. 2005. Polyamory and gay men: A family systems approach. *Journal of GLBT Family Studies* 1:97–116.

Bianchi, A. J., and L. Povilavicius. 2006. Cultural meanings versus academic meaning of self-esteem. Paper presented for Southern Sociological Society, New Orleans, LA, March 24.

Billingham, R. E., P. B. Perera, and N. A. Ehlers. 2005. College women's rankings of the most undesirable marriage and family forms. *College Student Journal* 39:749–53.

Brantley, A., D. Knox, and M. E. Zusman. 2002. When and why gender differences in saying "I love you" among college students. *College Student Journal* 36:614–15.

Brehm, S. S. 1992. *Intimate relationships,* 2nd ed. New York: McGraw-Hill.

Bulcroft, R., K. Bulcroft, K. Bradley, and C. Simpson. 2000. The management and production of risk in romantic relationships: A postmodern paradox. *Journal of Family History* 25:63–92.

Burford, M. 2005. The un-Hollywood wife. In *The Oprah Magazine Book,* 174. Birmingham, Alabama: Oxmoor House.

Buss, D. M. 2000. Prescription for passion. *Psychology Today* May/June, 54–61.

Cassidy, M. L., and G. Lee. 1989. The study of polyandry: A critique and synthesis. *Journal of Comparative Family Studies* 20:1–11.

Coontz, S. 2005. *Marriage, a history: How love conquered marriage.* New York: Penguin Books.

Cunningham, M. R., S. R. Shamblen, A. P. Barbee, and L. K. Ault. 2005. Social allergies in romantic relationships: Behavioral repetition, emotional sensitization, and dissatisfaction in dating couples. *Personal Relationships* 12:273–95.

DeHart, T., S. L. Murray, B. W. Pelham, and P. Rose. 2002. The regulation of dependency in parent-child relationships. *Journal of Experimental Social Psychology* 39:59–67.

Demir, M. 2008. Sweetheart, you really make me happy: Romantic relationship quality and personality as predictors of happiness among emerging adults. *Journal of Happiness Studies* 9:257–77.

Diamond, L. M. 2003. What does sexual orientation orient? A biobehavioral model distinguishing romantic love and sexual desire. *Psychological Review* 110:173–92.

Dotson-Blake, K., D. Knox, and A. Holman. 2008. College student attitudes toward marriage, family, and sex therapy. Unpublished data from 288 undergraduate/graduate students. East Carolina University, Greenville, NC.

Dugan, J. 2005. Colonial America. http://www.suite101.com/article.cfm/colonial_america_retired/61531/1 (retrieved on December 12).

East, L., D. Jackson, L. O'Brien, and K. Peters. 2007. Use of the male condom by heterosexual adolescents and young people: Literature review. *Journal of Advanced Nursing* 59:103–10.

Fehr, B., and C. Harasymchuk. 2005. The experience of emotion in close relationships: Toward and integration of the emotion-in-relationships and interpersonal script models. *Personal Relationships* 12:181–96.

Freud, S. 1905/1938. Three contributions to the theory of sex. In *The basic writings of Sigmund Freud*, ed. A. A. Brill. New York: Random House.

Fuller, J. A., and R. M. Warner. 2000. Family stressors as predictors of codependency. *Genetic, Social, and General Psychology Monographs* 126:5–22.

Furrow, J. L., B. Bradley, and S. M. Johnson. 2005. Emotionally focused family therapy with stepfamilies. In *Sourcebook of family theory & research*, ed. Vern L. Bengtson, Alan C. Acock, Katherine R. Allen, Peggye Dilworth-Anderson, and David M. Klein, 220–22. Thousand Oaks, CA: Sage Publications.

Gallmeier, C. P., M. E. Zusman, D. Knox, and L. Gibson. 1997. Can we talk? Gender differences in disclosure patterns and expectations. *Free Inquiry in Creative Sociology* 25:219–25.

Gavin, J. 2003. *Deep in a dream: The long night of Chet Baker*. New York: Welcome Rain.

Gillath, O., M. Mikulincer, G. E. Birnbaum, and P. R. Shaver. 2008. When sex primes love: Subliminal sexual priming motivates relationship goal pursuit. *Personality and Social Psychology Bulletin* 34:1057–73.

Giordano, P. C., W. D. Manning, and M. A. Longmore. 2005. The romantic relationships of African-American and White adolescents. *The Sociological Quarterly* 46:545–68.

Guerrero, L. K., M. R. Trost, and S. M. Yoshimura. 2005. Romantic jealousy: Emotions and communicative responses. *Personal Relationships* 12:233–52.

Halpern, C. T., R. B. King, S. G. Oslak, and J. R. Udry. 2005. Body mass index, dieting, romance, and sexual activity in adolescent girls: Relationships over time. *Journal of Research on Adolescence* 15:535–59.

Hart, K. 2007. Love by arrangement: The ambiguity of "spousal choice" in a Turkish village. *Journal of the Royal Anthropological Institute* 13:345–63.

Haynie, D. L., P. C. Giordano, W. D. Manning, and M. A. Longmore. 2005. Adolescent romantic relationships and delinquency involvement. *Criminology* 43:177–210.

Hendrick, S. S., C. Hendrick, and N. L. Adler. 1988. Romantic relationships: Love, satisfaction, and staying together. *Journal of Personality and Social Psychology* 54:980–88.

Huston, T. L., J. P. Caughlin, R. M. Houts, S. E. Smith, and L. J. George. 2001. The connubial crucible: Newlywed years as predictors of marital delight, distress, and divorce. *Journal of Personality and Social Psychology* 80:237–52.

Jefson, C. 2006. Candy hearts: Messages about love, lust, and infatuation. *Journal of School Health* 76:117–22.

Johnson, S. 2005. *When "I love you" turns violent: Recognizing and confronting dangerous relationships*. New York: New Horizon Press.

Jones, D. 2006. One of USA's exports: Love, American style. *USA Today*, February 14, 1B.

Khanchandani, L. 2005. Jealousy during dating among college women. Paper presented at Third Annual East Carolina University Undergraduate Research and Creative Activities Symposium, Greenville, NC, April 8.

King, P. A. 2003. Stalking: A control factor. Paper presented at 73rd Annual Meeting of the Eastern Sociological Society, Philadelphia, February 28.

Kito, M. 2005. Self-disclosure in romantic relationships and friendships among American and Japanese college students. *Journal of Social Psychology* 145:127–40.

Knox, D., R. Breed, and M. Zusman. 2007. College men and jealousy. *College Student Journal* 41:494–98.

Knox, D., and M. E. Zusman. 2009. Relationship and sexual behaviors of a sample of 1,319 university students. Unpublished data. Department of Sociology, East Carolina University, Greenville, NC.

Knox, D., M. E. Zusman, L. Mabon, and L. Shivar. 1999. Jealousy in college student relationships. *College Student Journal* 33:328–29.

Knox, D., M. Zusman, and W. Nieves. 1998. What I did for love: Risky behavior of college students in love. *College Student Journal* 32:203–05.

Lanham, F. 2008. Programmed for love—An interview with David Levy. *Houston Chronicle*, December 15.

Lee, J. A. 1973. *The colors of love: An exploration of the ways of loving*. Don Mills, Ontario: New Press.

———. 1988. Love-styles. In *The psychology of love*, ed. R. Sternberg and M. Barnes, 38–67. New Haven, CN: Yale University Press.

Levy, D. 2007. *Love and sex with robots: The evolution of human-robot relationships*. New York: Harper Collins.

Lucas, T., M. R. Parkhill, C. A. Wendorf, and E. O. Imamoglu. 2008. Cultural and evolutionary components of marital satisfaction. *Journal of Cross-Cultural Psychology* 39:109–29.

Lundstrom, J. N., and M. Jones-Gotman. 2009. Romantic love modulates women's identification of men's body odors *Hormones and Behavior* 55:280–95.

Madathil, J., and J. M. Benshoff. 2008. Importance of marital characteristics and marital satisfaction: A comparison of Asian Indians in arranged marriages and Americans in marriages of choice. *Family Journal* 16:222–32.

Medora, N. P., J. H. Larson, N. Hortacsu, and P. Dave. 2002. Perceived attitudes towards romanticism: A cross-cultural study of American, Asian-Indian, and Turkish young adults. *Journal of Comparative Family Studies* 33:155–78.

Meloy, J. R., and H. Fisher. 2005. Some thoughts on the neurobiology of stalking. *Journal of Forensic Science* 50:1472–80.

Meyer, D. 2007. Selective serotonin reuptake inhibitors and their effects on relationship satisfaction. *The Family Journal* 15:392–97.

Monteoliva, A., J. Garcia-Martinez, and A. Miguel. 2005. Adult attachment style and its effect on the quality of romantic relationships in Spanish students. *Journal of Social Psychology* 145:745–47.

Paul, E. L., B. McManus, and A. Hayes. 2000. "Hookups": Characteristics and correlates of college students' spontaneous and anonymous sexual experiences. *Journal of Sex Research* 37:76–88.

Petrie, J., J. A. Giordano, and C. S. Roberts. 1992. Characteristics of women who love too much. *Affilia: Journal of Women and Social Work* 7:7–20.

Pimentel, E. E. 2000. Just how do I love thee? Marital relations in urban China. *Journal of Marriage and the Family* 62:32–47.

Pines, A. M. 1992. *Romantic jealousy: Understanding and conquering the shadow of love.* New York: St. Martin's Press.

Pistole, M. C., and L. C. Vocaturo. 2000. Attachment and commitment in college students' romantic relationships. *Journal of College Student Development* 40:710–20.

Radmacher, K., and M. Azmitia. 2006. Are there gendered pathways to intimacy in early adolescents' and emerging adults' friendships? *Journal of Adolescent Research* 21:415–48.

Redbook. 2005. Survey on "Description of Relationship with a Partner." August, 14.

Regan, P. 2000. Love relationships. In *Psychological perspectives on human sexuality,* ed. L. T. Szuchman and F. Muscarella, 232–82. New York: Wiley.

Reid, M. J. 2005. Some thoughts on the neurobiology of stalking. *Journal of Forensic Sciences* 50:1472–80.

Reiss, I. L. 1960. Toward a sociology of the heterosexual love relationship. *Journal of Marriage and Family Living* 22:139–45.

Ross, C. B. 2006. An exploration of eight dimensions of self-disclosure on relationship. Paper for Southern Sociological Society, New Orleans, LA. March 24.

Schoebi, D. 2008 The coregulation of daily affect in marital relationships. *Journal of Family Psychology* 22:595–604.

Shackelford, T. K., A. T. Goetz, D. M. Buss, H. A. Euler, and S. Hoier. 2005. When we hurt the ones we love: Predicting violence against women from men's mate retention. *Personal Relationships* 12:447–63.

Sheff, E. 2006. The reluctant polyamorist: Conducting auto-ethnographic research in a sexualized setting. In *Sex matters: The sexuality and society reader,* ed. M. Stombler, D. Baunach, E. Burgess, D. Donnelly, and W. Simonds. New York: Pearson Allyn & Bacon.

Soriano, C. G. 2005. Prince Charles and Camilla to wed. *USA Today,* A1.

Spitzberg, B. H., and W. R. Cupach, eds. 1998. *The dark side of close relationships.* Mahway, N.J.: Erlbaum.

Spoto, D. 2006. *Enchantment: The life of Audrey Hepburn.* New York: Harmony Books.

Statistical Abstract of the United States, 2009, 128th ed. Washington, DC: U.S. Bureau of the Census.

Sternberg, R. J. 1986. A triangular theory of love. *Psychological Review* 93:119–35.

Tilley, D. S., and M. Brackley. 2005. Men who batter intimate partners: A grounded theory study of the development of male violence in intimate partner relationships. *Issues in Mental Health Nursing* 26:281–97.

Toufexis, A. 1993. The right chemistry. *Time,* February 15, 49–51.

Trachman, M., and C. Bluestone. 2005. What's love got to do with it? *College Teaching* 53:131–36.

Tupelo, A., and E. Freeman 2008. Polyamory and compersion. Presentation, Courtship and Marriage class, Department of Sociology, East Carolina University, Fall.

Tzeng, O. C. S., K. Wooldridge, and K. Campbell. 2003. Faith love: A psychological construct in intimate relations. *Journal of the Indiana Academy of the Social Sciences* 7:11–20.

Walster, E., and G. W. Walster. 1978. *A new look at love.* Reading, MA: Addison-Wesley.

West III, J. L. W. 2005. *The perfect hour.* New York: Random House.

Zeki, S. 2007. The neurobiology of love. *Febs Letters* 581:2575–79.

Woman wants monogamy;
Man delights in novelty.
Love is woman's moon and sun;
Man has other forms of fun.
Woman lives but in her lord;
Count to ten, and man is bored.
With this the gist and sum of it;
What earthly good can come of it?

Dorothy Parker
Poet, theater critic

Gender

Authors

Contents

True or False?

1. If you had been blind since age 3 and suddenly were able to "see," you would immediately be able to recognize a woman or a man when you saw one.

2. Women are more likely than men to believe that love is more important than factors like age and race in choosing a mate.

3. In a study comparing wives who had been circumcised with those who had not, both groups reported similar levels of sexual desire and capacity for orgasm.

4. Undergraduate men who want a wife to stay home and take care of the family (not earn an income) are virtually nonexistent. Less than 10 percent in one study expressed such a preference.

5. College males who want to marry a traditional wife (one who stays home to take care of children) believe that the marriage will suffer if she works outside the home.

Answers: **1.** F   **2.** T   **3.** F   **4.** F   **5.** T

Mike May was blinded at age 3 due to a chemical explosion. Years later, after he had married and had children, he was offered the possibility of sight again (through stem cell technology). It worked. However, Mike had to learn to "see"; he could not distinguish between women and men. His wife, Jennifer, went with him to a coffee shop and taught him what to look for to discover whether a person was a woman or a man. For a woman, she taught him to look for:

> *Swinging hips* ("Women walk with a bounce; men don't.")
> *Purses* ("Men don't carry things over their shoulders, at least in the United States.")
> *Tight pants* ("Women sometimes paint them on; men's are more baggy.")
> *Bellies* ("Women show them a lot these days. Men almost never do.")
> *Jewelry* ("Some men might wear necklaces, but very few wear shiny bracelets.")
> (Kurson 2007, 191–92)

Although Jennifer detailed a current cultural list of symbolic behavior that helps to differentiate the sexes, sociologists note that one of the defining moments in an individual's life is when the sex of a fetus (in the case of an ultrasound) or infant (in the case of a birth) is announced. "It's a boy" or "It's a girl" immediately summons an onslaught of cultural programming affecting the color of the nursery (for example, blue for a boy and pink for a girl), name of the baby (there are few gender-free names such as Chris), occupational choices (in spite of Nancy Pelosi and Hillary Clinton, few women are in politics), and Jennifer's list of symbolic behaviors. In this chapter, we examine variations in gender roles and the way they express themselves in various relationships. We begin by looking at the terms used to discuss gender issues.

> *Here's all you have to know about men and women: women are crazy, men are stupid. And the main reason women are crazy is that men are stupid.*
>
> George Carlin, comedian

Terminology of Gender Roles

In common usage, the terms *sex* and *gender* are often interchangeable, but sociologists, family or consumer science educators, human development specialists, and health educators do not find these terms synonymous. After clarifying the distinction between *sex* and *gender*, we discuss other relevant terminology, including *gender identity*, *gender role*, and *gender role ideology*.

Sex

Sex refers to the biological distinction between females and males. Hence, to be assigned as a female or male, several factors are used to determine the biological sex of an individual:

- *Chromosomes:* XX for females; XY for males
- *Gonads:* Ovaries for females; testes for males
- *Hormones:* Greater proportion of estrogen and progesterone than testosterone in females; greater proportion of testosterone than estrogen and progesterone in males
- *Internal sex organs:* Fallopian tubes, uterus, and vagina for females; epididymis, vas deferens, and seminal vesicles for males
- *External genitals:* Vulva for females; penis and scrotum for males

Even though we commonly think of biological sex as consisting of two dichotomous categories (female and male), biological sex exists on a continuum. Sometimes not all of the items identified are found neatly in one person (who would be labeled as a female or a male). Rather, items typically associated with females or males might be found together in one person, resulting in mixed or ambiguous genitals; such persons are called **hermaphrodites** or **intersexed individuals**. Indeed, the genitals in these intersexed (or middlesexed) individuals (about 2 percent of all births) are not clearly male or female (Crawley et al. 2008). **Intersex development** refers to congenital variations in the reproductive system, sometimes resulting in ambiguous genitals. Even if chromosomal makeup is XX or XY, too much or too little of the wrong kind of hormone during gestation can also cause variations in sex development. Although intersexed people currently prefer the term *intersexed* or *middlesexed,* intersex conditions that may result from hormonal abnormalities are referred to as *hermaphroditism* and *pseudohermaphroditism* in the medical literature. **True hermaphroditism** is an extremely rare condition in which individuals are born with both ovarian and testicular tissue. More common than hermaphroditism is **pseudohermaphroditism**, which refers to a condition in which an individual is born with gonads matching the sex chromosomes, but with genitals either ambiguous or resembling those of the other sex. Meyer-Bahlburg (2005) suggested that the genesis of the ambiguity may be the brain anatomy, whereby the wiring is different for those with gender identity disorder (GID). Genetics, hormones, and brain mechanisms might all underlie neuroanatomic changes inducing intersexuality.

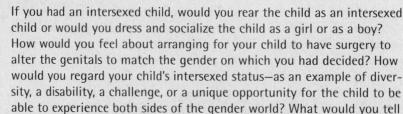

WHAT IF?

What if You Have a Child Who Is Intersexed?

If you had an intersexed child, would you rear the child as an intersexed child or would you dress and socialize the child as a girl or as a boy? How would you feel about arranging for your child to have surgery to alter the genitals to match the gender on which you had decided? How would you regard your child's intersexed status—as an example of diversity, a disability, a challenge, or a unique opportunity for the child to be able to experience both sides of the gender world? What would you tell your child about the intersex "condition"? Do you think acceptance of an intersexed child would vary by gender of the parent (for example, would mothers be more accepting than fathers)? How would you respond to your spouse who did not accept your intersexed child?

The Beliefs about Women Scale (BAWS)

The following statements describe different attitudes toward men and women. There are no right or wrong answers, only opinions. Indicate how much you agree or disagree with each statement, using the following scale: (A) strongly disagree, (B) slightly disagree, (C) neither agree nor disagree, (D) slightly agree, or (E) strongly agree.

_____ **1.** Women are more passive than men.

_____ **2.** Women are less career-motivated than men.

_____ **3.** Women don't generally like to be active in their sexual relationships.

_____ **4.** Women are more concerned about their physical appearance than are men.

_____ **5.** Women comply more often than men.

_____ **6.** Women care as much as men do about developing a job or career.

_____ **7.** Most women don't like to express their sexuality.

_____ **8.** Men are as conceited about their appearance as are women.

_____ **9.** Men are as submissive as women.

_____ **10.** Women are as skillful in business-related activities as are men.

_____ **11.** Most women want their partner to take the initiative in their sexual relationships.

_____ **12.** Women spend more time attending to their physical appearance than men do.

_____ **13.** Women tend to give up more easily than men.

_____ **14.** Women dislike being in leadership positions more than men.

_____ **15.** Women are as interested in sex as are men.

_____ **16.** Women pay more attention to their looks than most men do.

_____ **17.** Women are more easily influenced than men.

_____ **18.** Women don't like responsibility as much as men.

_____ **19.** Women's sexual desires are less intense than men's.

_____ **20.** Women gain more status from their physical appearance than do men.

The Beliefs about Women Scale (BAWS) consists of fifteen separate subscales; only four are used here. The items for these four subscales and coding instructions are as follows:

1. Women are more passive than men (items 1, 5, 9, 13, 17).

2. Women are interested in careers less than men (items 2, 6, 10, 14, 18).

3. Women are less sexual than men (items 3, 7, 11, 15, 19).

4. Women are more appearance conscious than men (items 4, 8, 12, 16, 20).

Score the items as follows: strongly agree = +2; slightly agree = +1; neither agree nor disagree = 0; slightly disagree = −1; strongly disagree = −2.

Scores range from 0 to 40; subscale scores range from 0 to 10. The higher your score, the more traditional your gender beliefs about men and women.

Source

William E. Snell, Jr., PhD. 1997. College of Liberal Arts, Department of Psychology, Southeast Missouri State University. Reprinted with permission. Contact Dr. Snell for further use: wesnell@semo.edu.

Gender

Gender refers to the social and psychological characteristics associated with being female or male. For example, women see themselves (and men agree) as moody and easily embarrassed; men see themselves (and women agree) as competitive, sarcastic, and sexual (Knox et al. 2004). In popular usage, gender is dichotomized as an either/or concept (feminine or masculine). Each gender has some characteristics of the other. However, gender may also be viewed as existing along a continuum of femininity and masculinity.

The Self-Assessment of this chapter examines various beliefs about women.

There is an ongoing controversy about whether gender differences are innate as opposed to learned or socially determined. Just as sexual orientation may be best explained as an interaction of biological and social or psychological variables, gender differences may also be seen as a consequence of both biological and social or psychological influences. For example, Irvolino et al. (2005) studied the genetic and environmental effects on the sex-typed behavior of 3,999 3- to 4-year-old twin and nontwin sibling pairs and concluded that their gender

Women and cats will do as they please, and men and dogs should relax and get used to the idea.

Robert A. Heinlein, author

role behavior was a function of both genetic inheritance (for example, chromosomes and hormones) and social factors (for example, male/female models such as parents, siblings, peers).

Whereas some researchers emphasize an interaction of the biological and social, others emphasize a biological imperative as the basis of gender role behavior. As evidence for the latter, the late John Money, psychologist and former director of the now-defunct Gender Identity Clinic at Johns Hopkins University School of Medicine, encouraged the parents of a boy (Bruce) to rear him as a girl (Brenda) because of a botched circumcision that rendered the infant without a penis. Money argued that social mirrors dictate one's gender identity, and thus, if the parents treated the child as a girl (for example, name, dress, toys), the child would adopt the role of a girl and later that of a woman. The child was castrated and sex reassignment began.

However, the experiment failed miserably; the child as an adult (David Reimer—his real name) reported that he never felt comfortable in the role of a girl and had always viewed himself as a boy. He later married and adopted his wife's two children. In the book *As Nature Made Him: The Boy Who Was Raised as a Girl* (Colapinto 2000), David worked with a writer to tell his story. His courageous decision to make his poignant personal story public has shed light on scientific debate on the "nature/nurture" question. In the past, David's situation was used as a textbook example of how "nurture" is the more important influence in gender identity, if a reassignment is done early enough. Today, his case makes the point that one's biological wiring dictates gender outcome (ibid.). Indeed, David Reimer noted in a television interview, "I was scammed," referring to the absurdity of trying to rear him as a girl. Distraught with the ordeal of his upbringing and beset with financial difficulties, he committed suicide in May 2004 via a gunshot to the head.

Although the story of David Reimer is a landmark in terms of the power of biology in determining gender identity, other research supports the critical role of biology. Cohen-Kettenis (2005) emphasized that biological influences in the form of androgens in the prenatal brain are very much at work in creating one's gender identity.

Nevertheless, **socialization** (the process through which we learn attitudes, values, beliefs, and behaviors appropriate to the social positions we occupy) does impact gender role behaviors, and social scientists tend to emphasize the role of social influences in gender differences. Although her research is controversial, Margaret Mead (1935) focused on the role of social learning in the development of gender roles in her study of three cultures.

She visited three New Guinea tribes in the early 1930s, and observed that the Arapesh socialized both men and women to be feminine, by Western standards. The Arapesh people were taught to be cooperative and responsive to the needs of others. In contrast, the Tchambuli were known for dominant women and submissive men—just the opposite of our society. Both of these societies were unlike the Mundugumor, which socialized only ruthless, aggressive, "masculine" personalities. The inescapable conclusion of this cross-cultural study is that human beings are products of their social and cultural environment and that gender roles are learned. As Peoples observed, "cultures construct gender in different ways" (2001, 18). Indeed, the very terms we use to describe various body parts of women and men carry notions of power and use. A penis is a "probe" (active) whereas a vagina is a "hole" (to be filled) (Crawley et al. 2008).

Gender Identity

Gender identity is the psychological state of viewing oneself as a girl or a boy, and later as a woman or a man. Such identity is largely learned and is a reflection of society's conceptions of femininity and masculinity.

Chapter 3 Gender

Some individuals experience **gender dysphoria**, a condition in which one's gender identity does not match one's biological sex. An example of gender dysphoria is transsexualism (discussed in the next section).

Transgenderism

The word **transgender** is a generic term for a person of one biological sex who displays characteristics of the other sex. **Cross-dresser** is a broad term for individuals who may dress or present themselves in the gender of the opposite sex. Some cross-dressers are heterosexual adult males who enjoy dressing and presenting themselves as women.

Cross-dressers may also be women who dress as men and present themselves as men. Some cross-dressers are bisexual or homosexual. Another term for cross-dresser is **transvestite,** although the latter term is commonly associated with homosexual men who dress provocatively as women to attract men—sometimes as sexual customers.

Transsexuals are people with the biological and anatomical sex of one gender (for example, male) but the self-concept of the opposite sex (that is, female). "I am a woman trapped in a man's body" reflects the feelings of the male-to-female transsexual, who may take hormones to develop breasts and reduce facial hair and may have surgery to artificially construct a vagina. Such a person lives full-time as a woman.

The female-to-male transsexual is one who is a biological and anatomical female but feels "I am a man trapped in a female's body." This person may take male hormones to grow facial hair and deepen her voice and may have surgery to create an artificial penis. This person lives full-time as a man. Thomas Beatie, born a biological woman, viewed himself as a man and transitioned from living as a woman to living as a man. His wife could not have children so Tom agreed to be artificially inseminated (because he had ovaries), became pregnant, and delivered a child in the summer of 2008. The media referred to him as "The Pregnant Man"; they asked him, if he gave birth to the child, could he be the father? Technically, Oregon law defines birth as an expulsion or extraction from the mother so Tom is the technical mother. However, the new parents could petition the courts and have "him" declared as the father and his wife as the mother (Heller 2008).

Individuals need not take hormones or have surgery to be regarded as transsexuals. The distinguishing variable is living full-time in the role of the gender opposite one's biological sex. A man or woman who presents full-time as the opposite gender is a transsexual by definition. Table 3.1 may help to keep the categories clear.

Some transsexuals prefer the term **transgenderist**, which refers to individuals who live in a gender role that does not match their biological sex but who have no desire to surgically alter their genitalia (as do people who are transsexual). Another variation is the she-male, a person who looks like and has the breasts of a woman yet has the genitalia and reproductive system of a male.

This cross-dresser is a biological male who enjoys dressing in the clothes of a woman.

Briannolan/istockphoto.com

This transsexual is a biological man who has the self-concept of a woman and prefers to always be dressed as a woman.

Authors

The old-fashioned girls would take two drinks and go out like a light; now they take two drinks—and out goes the light.

Steve Allen, late-night talk show host

Gender Roles

Gender roles are the social norms that dictate what is socially regarded as appropriate female and male behavior. All societies have expectations of how boys and girls, men and women "should" behave. Gender roles influence women and men in virtually every sphere of life, including family and occupation. One prevalent norm in family life is that women end up devoting more time to child rearing and child care. Lareau and Weininger (2008) studied the division of labor of parents getting their children to various leisure activities and found that traditional gender roles were the norm and that mothers "are the ones who must satisfy these demands" (p. 450). The sheer number of activities forces some mothers to cut back. One mother said:

> *I know that all these things are good for my child and they develop all those things but time-wise, I just don't have time for all that stuff. I mean I have to live up to my label as the meanest Mom in the world and I try to do a real good job of it [laughs]. I told her she could be either on soccer or softball. She'll be on one of them. (p. 450)*

Walzer (2008) noted that marriage is a place where men and women "do gender" in the sense that roles tend to be identified as breadwinning, housework, parenting, and emotional expression and are gender-differentiated. She also noted that divorce generates "redoing" gender in the sense that it changes the expectations for masculine and feminine behavior in families (for example, women become breadwinners, men become single parents, and so on).

The term **sex roles** is often confused with and used interchangeably with the term *gender roles*. However, whereas gender roles are socially defined and can be enacted by either women or men, sex roles are defined by biological constraints and can be enacted by members of one biological sex only—for example, wet nurse, sperm donor, childbearer.

How Undergraduate Women View Men

McNeely et al. (2004) assessed how a sample of 326 undergraduates viewed men. She compared women's and men's views and found that women were significantly more likely to believe that all men cheat on their partners at least once, that a man will not call when he says he will, that men prefer to cohabit with a woman rather than marry her, that they think about sex more than women, and that they have poorer communication skills than women. These views include that men are more sex-focused than women and less likely to be faithful.

Table 3.1	Transgender Categories		
Category	**Biological Sex**	**Sexual Orientation**	**Most Usual Case**
Cross-dresser	Either	Either	Male heterosexual dresses as woman
Transvestite	Male	Homosexual	Homosexual male dresses as woman
Transsexual	Either	Either	Heterosexual male in woman's body who wants surgery

Men are socialized to hunt for food to feed the family.

How Undergraduate Men View Women

McNeely et al. (2005) also assessed how 326 undergraduates viewed women. They compared men's and women's agreement with various beliefs about women and found several significant differences. Table 3.2 reflects the percentage differences and suggests that, indeed, what men think about women is very different from what women think about themselves.

A man is never so weak as when a woman is telling him how strong he is.

Anonymous

Gender Differences in Viewing Romantic Relationships

Abowitz et al. (2009) also assessed the respective gender views of romantic relationships of the same 326 undergraduates previously mentioned and found that men were significantly more likely to believe that bars are good places to meet a potential partner, that cohabitation improves marriage, that men control relationships, and that people will "cheat" if they feel they will not be caught. In contrast, women were significantly more likely to believe that love is more important than factors like age and race in choosing a mate, that couples stop "trying" after they marry, and that women know when their men are lying.

Table 3.2   Gender Differences in Beliefs about Women (N = 326)

Beliefs about Women	% Men Believing	% Women Believing
Unmarried women aged 30+ years are unhappy or depressed	16.3%	6.2%
Women assume men are mind readers	55.4%	40.8%
Women are controlling	58.2%	36.4%
Red-haired women are fiery and saucy	23.7%	9.2%
Women want marriage, not cohabitation	84.0%	68.2%
Women love money	16.7%	3.5%
Women are possessive	52.1%	32.9%
Women are manipulative	58.3%	33.3%

McNeely, A., D. Knox, and M.E. Zusman. 2005. College student beliefs about women: Some gender differences. *College Student Journal* 39:769–74. Used by permission of *College Student Journal.*

Traditional Wife?: College Men Who Want One

When the young lovers (Christy and Raoul) of *The Phantom of the Opera* are finally alone, Raoul sings his song of love and protection:

> *No more talk of darkness, forget these wide-eyed fears.*

> *I'm here, nothing can harm you; my words will warm and calm you.*

> *Let me be your shelter, let me be your life . . .*

Christy responds with:

> *Promise me everything you say is true, that's all I ask of you.*

This scene reflects the traditional relationship where the man is the protector and the woman is being taken care of. Like the lovers in *Phantom*, some university students also seek a traditional relationship whereby the wife stays at home and the husband is the breadwinner. This research focused on the degree to which undergraduate men at a large southeastern university sought a traditional wife and the various background characteristics of these men.

Methods

The data were taken from a larger nonrandom sample of 1,027 undergraduates at a large southeastern university. Of these undergraduates, 335 men or 30.8 percent agreed with the statement, "I prefer to marry a traditional wife who sees her role as staying home and rearing children." In contrast, 69.2 percent of the undergraduate men disagreed with the statement.

Cross-classification was conducted to determine any relationships, with chi-square utilized to assess statistical significance.

Findings and Discussion

Analysis of the data revealed the following five statistically significant differences in regard to the characteristics of those who wanted a traditional wife in contrast to those who did not:

1. **Financial security valued over happiness.** Almost three-fourths (73.6 percent) of the men who valued financial security wanted a traditional wife compared to 42.8 percent who wanted happiness over money.

Two factors may explain this association: One reason men who valued financial security sought a traditional wife could be the belief that a man would be better able to earn money and to focus on his career if he had a traditional wife who supported them (for example, prepared meals and took care of the children). Indeed, career wives often say that they need a "wife" to take care of them (for example, have dinner ready, take care of the children, do the grocery shopping, take care of laundry, and so on).

A second reason men who valued financial security sought a traditional wife may be that a traditional wife might actually be very cost-effective. Sefton (1998) calculated that the value of the stay-at-home mother in terms of what it would cost to pay for all services that she provides (domestic cleaning, laundry, meal planning and preparation, shopping, providing transportation to child's activities, taking the children to the doctor, and running errands) and, adjusting for changes in the consumer price index, the figure was $47,982 in 2009.

What is most beautiful in virile men is something feminine; what is most beautiful in feminine women is something masculine.

Susan Sontag, novelist

Gender Role Ideology

Gender role ideology refers to beliefs about the proper role relationships between women and men in any given society. Where there is gender equality, there is enhanced relationship satisfaction (Walker and Luszcz 2009). Egalitarian wives are also most happy with their marriages if their husbands share both the work and the emotions of managing the home and caring for the children (Wilcox and Nock 2006).

In spite of the rhetoric regarding the entrenchment of egalitarian interaction between women and men in the United States, there is evidence of traditional gender roles in mate selection with men in the role of initiating relationships. When 692 undergraduate females at a large southeastern university were asked if they had ever asked a new guy to go out, 60.1 percent responded, "no" (Ross et al., forthcoming). In another study, thirty percent of the female respondents reported a preference of marrying a traditional man (one who saw his role as provider and who was supportive of his wife staying home to rear children) (McGinty et al. 2006). Some undergraduate men also prefer a traditional wife (see Research Application).

2. A wife's higher income believed to weaken the marriage. Of the respondents who believed that a woman's higher income weakens one's marriage, 61.9 percent wanted a nontraditional wife. Indeed, men preferring a traditional wife may have felt that a wife earning more money threatened their masculinity, head of the household, and chief breadwinner roles.

3. Belief that children turn out better when one parent stays home. Men who believed that children benefit from staying at home with their mother were significantly (p < .001) more likely than those who rejected this belief to want to marry a traditional woman. Of the respondents who believed that children turn out better when one parent stays home, 51.3 percent preferred a traditional wife.

4. Religion. Of the male respondents who viewed themselves as "religious," 33.6 percent reported a preference for marrying a traditional woman who wanted to stay home and rear children. In contrast, 18.6 percent of those who did not regard themselves as religious reported a preference for a traditional wife.

5. Divorce not considered an option. The undergraduates who did not believe divorce to be an option were 25.9 percent more likely to prefer a traditional wife than men who regarded divorce as an alternative. Being against divorce and having a traditional family with only one breadwinner (the husband) are both traditional values.

Implications

The study has three implications. The finding that men who want a traditional wife value money over happiness has implications for the professions they choose. Men who seek such a wife will tend to seek those professions such as business, medicine, engineering, and those associated with high incomes. Similarly, men who are not intent on seeking a traditional wife are more likely to seek those professions such as elementary school education, art, social work, and those associated with relatively low incomes.

A second implication is in reference to the finding that men who seek a traditional wife tend to believe that the marriage will be weakened by a wife's earning a high income. Such men may have a need to be in control because money is considered power. These women might be sensitive to the need of such a husband to exercise control in the relationship.

A third implication is in reference to the finding that men who seek a traditional wife believe that children benefit from the wife staying at home. Such a belief reveals that men may view parenting as the primary responsibility of the mother with a limited role for the father. Indeed, these men may view earning money as their role with little interest in hands-on parenting. This view may be consistent with the traditional wife's view. Or she may reject this view and want a more involved father.

Sources

Denton, M. L. 2004. Gender and marital decision making: Negotiating religious ideology and practice. *Social Forces* 82:1151–80.

Sefton, B. W. 1998. The market value of the stay-at-home mother. *Mothering* 86:26–29.

Source: Adapted from Zusman, M., and D. Knox. 2007. Paper presented at the Annual Conference of the Indiana Academy of Social Sciences.

Traditional American gender role ideology has perpetuated and reflected patriarchal male dominance and male bias in almost every sphere of life. Even our language reflects this male bias. For example, the words *man* and *mankind* have traditionally been used to refer to all humans. There has been a growing trend away from using male-biased language. Dictionaries have begun to replace *chairman* with *chairperson* and *mankind* with *humankind*.

A man is a person who will pay two dollars for a one-dollar item he wants. A woman will pay one dollar for a two-dollar item she doesn't want.

William Binger, farmer

Theories of Gender Role Development

Various theories attempt to explain why women and men exhibit different characteristics and behaviors.

Biosocial

In the discussion of gender at the beginning of the chapter, we noted the profound influence of biology on one's gender. **Biosocial theory** emphasizes that social behaviors (for example, gender roles) are biologically based and have an evolutionary survival function. For example, women tend to select and mate with men whom they deem will provide the maximum parental investment in their offspring. The term **parental investment** refers to any investment by a parent that increases the offspring's chance of surviving and thus increases reproductive success. Parental investments require time and energy. Women have a great deal of parental investment in their offspring (including nine months of gestation), and they tend to mate with men who have high status, economic resources, and a willingness to share those economic resources.

The biosocial explanation (also referred to as **sociobiology**) for mate selection is extremely controversial. Critics argue that women may show concern for the earning capacity of a potential mate because they have been systematically denied access to similar economic resources, and selecting a mate with these resources is one of their remaining options. In addition, it is argued that both women and men, when selecting a mate, think more about their partners as companions than as future parents of their offspring.

Social Learning

Derived from the school of behavioral psychology, the social learning theory emphasizes the roles of reward and punishment in explaining how a child learns gender role behavior. This is in contrast to the biological explanation for gender roles. For example, consider two young brothers who enjoy playing "lady"; each of them puts on a dress, wears high-heeled shoes, and carries a pocketbook. Their father came home early one day and angrily demanded, "Take those clothes off and never put them on again. Those things are for women." The boys were punished for "playing lady" but rewarded with their father's approval for playing cowboys, with plastic guns and "Bang! You're dead!" dialogue.

Reward and punishment alone are not sufficient to account for the way in which children learn gender roles. Another way children learn is when parents or peers offer direct instruction (for example, "girls wear dresses" or "a man stands up and shakes hands"). In addition, many of society's gender rules are learned through modeling. In modeling, children observe and imitate another's behavior. Gender role models include parents, peers, siblings, and characters portrayed in the media.

The impact of modeling on the development of gender role behavior is controversial. For example, a modeling perspective implies that children will tend to imitate the parent of the same sex, but children in all cultures are usually reared mainly by women. Yet this persistent female model does not seem to interfere with the male's development of the behavior that is considered appropriate for his gender. One explanation suggests that boys learn early that our society generally grants boys and men more status and privileges than girls and women. Therefore, boys devalue the feminine and emphasize the masculine aspects of themselves.

Identification

Freud was one of the first researchers to study gender role development. He suggested that children acquire the characteristics and behaviors of their same-sex parent through a process of identification. Girls identify with their mothers; boys identify with their fathers. For example, girls are more likely to become involved in taking care of children because they see women as the primary caregivers of young children. In effect, they identify with their mothers and will see their own primary identity and role as those of a mother. Likewise, boys will observe their fathers and engage in similar behaviors to lock in their own gender identity. The classic example is the son who observes his father shaving and wants to do likewise (be a man too).

Cognitive-Developmental

The cognitive-developmental theory of gender role development reflects a blend of biological and social learning views. According to this theory, the biological readiness of the child, in terms of cognitive development, influences how the child responds to gender cues in the environment (Kohlberg 1966). For example, gender discrimination (the ability to identify social and psychological characteristics associated with being female or male) begins at about age 30 months. However, at this age, children do not view gender as a permanent characteristic. Thus, even though young children may define people who wear long hair as girls and those who never wear dresses as boys, they also believe they can change their gender by altering their hair or changing clothes.

Not until age 6 or 7 do children view gender as permanent (Kohlberg 1966; 1969). In Kohlberg's view, this cognitive understanding involves the development of a specific mental ability to grasp the idea that certain basic characteristics of people do not change. Once children learn the concept of gender permanence, they seek to become competent and proper members of their gender group. For example, a child standing on the edge of a school playground may observe one group of children jumping rope while another group is playing football. That child's gender identity as either a girl or a boy connects with the observed gender-typed behavior, and the child joins one of the two groups. Once in the group, the child seeks to develop behaviors that are socially defined as gender-appropriate.

Anyone who limits her vision to memories of yesterday is already dead.

Lillie Langtry, feminist

Agents of Socialization

Three of the four theories discussed in the preceding section emphasize that gender roles are learned through interaction with the environment. Indeed, though biology may provide a basis for one's gender identity, cultural influences in the form of various socialization agents (parents, peers, religion, and the media) shape the individual toward various gender roles. These powerful influences in large part dictate what people think, feel, and do in their roles as man or woman. In the next section, we look at the different sources influencing gender socialization.

Family

The family is a gendered institution with female and male roles highly structured by gender. The names parents assign to their children, the clothes they dress them in, and the toys they buy them all reflect gender. Parents may also be stricter on female children—determining the age they are allowed to leave the house at night, the time of curfew and using directives such as "call your mamma when you get to the party."

The importance of the father in the family was noted in Pollack's (2001) study of adolescent boys. "America's boys are crying out for a new gender revolution that does for them what the last forty years of feminism has tried to do for girls and women," he stated (p. 18). This new revolution will depend on fathers who teach their sons that feelings and relationships are important. How equipped do you feel today's fathers are to provide these new models for their sons?

Siblings also influence gender role learning. As noted in Chapter 1, the relationship with one's sibling (particularly in sister-sister relationships) is likely to be the most enduring of all relationships (Meinhold et al. 2006). Also, growing up in a family of all sisters or all brothers intensifies social learning experiences toward femininity or masculinity. A male reared with five sisters and a single-parent mother is likely to reflect more feminine characteristics than a male reared in a home with six brothers and a stay-at-home dad.

Race/Ethnicity

The race and ethnicity of one's family also influence gender roles. Although African American families are often stereotyped as being matriarchal, the more common pattern of authority in these families is egalitarian (Taylor 2002). Both President Barack and First Lady Michelle Obama have law degrees from Harvard, and their relationship appears to be very egalitarian.

The fact that African American women have increased economic independence provides a powerful role model for young African American women. A similar situation exists among Hispanics, who represent the fastest-growing segment of the U.S. population. Mexican American marriages have great variability, but where the Hispanic woman works outside the home, her power may increase inside the home. However, because Hispanic men are much more likely to be in the labor force than Hispanic women, traditional role relationships in the family are more likely to be the norm.

Peers

Though parents are usually the first socializing agents that influence a child's gender role development, peers become increasingly important during the school years. Haynie and Osgood (2005) analyzed data from the National Longitudinal Study of Adolescents reflecting responses from adolescents in grades 7 through 12 at 132 schools over an eleven-year period and confirmed the influence of peers in delinquent behavior. If friends drank, smoked cigarettes, skipped school without an excuse, and became involved in serious fights, then the adolescents had an increased likelihood that they would also engage in delinquent acts. Regarding gender, the gender role messages from adolescent peers are primarily traditional. Boys are expected to play sports and be career-oriented. Female adolescents are under tremendous pressure to be physically attractive and thin, popular, and achievement-oriented. Female achievements may be traditional (cheerleading) or nontraditional (sports or academics). Adolescent females are sometimes in conflict because high academic success may be viewed as being less than feminine.

Peers also influence gender roles throughout the family life cycle. In Chapter 1, we discussed the family life cycle and noted the various developmental tasks throughout the cycle. With each new stage, role changes are made and one's peers influence those role changes. For example, when a couple moves from being childfree to being parents, peers who are also parents quickly socialize them into the role of parent and the attendant responsibilities.

National Data

Based on interviews with 35,000 Americans age 18 and older, 56 percent of adults in the United States say that religion is "very important" in their lives; 82 percent report religion is "somewhat" important (Pew Research 2008).

Religion

Religion remains a potentially important influence in the lives of university students. Of a sample of 1,319 undergraduates at a large southeastern university, 54.8 percent viewed themselves as "religious" (Knox and Zusman 2009). Because women (particularly white women) are "socialized to be submissive, passive, and nurturing," they may be predisposed to greater levels of religion and religious influence (Miller and Stark 2002). Such exposure includes a traditional framing of gender roles. Male dominance is indisputable in the hierarchy of religious organizations, where power and status have been accorded mostly to men. Mormons, particularly, adhere to traditional roles in marriage where men are regarded as the undisputed head of the household.

The Roman Catholic Church does not have female clergy, and men dominate the nineteen top positions in the U.S. dioceses. Popular books marketed to the Christian right also emphasize traditional gender roles. Denton (2004) found that conservative Protestants are committed to the ideology that the husband is the head of the family. However, this implies "taking spiritual leadership" and may not imply dominance in marital decision making (p. 1,174).

Education

The educational institution serves as an additional socialization agent for gender role ideology. However, such an effect must be considered in the context of the society or culture in which the "school" exists and of the school itself. Schools are basic cultures of transmission in that they make deliberate efforts to reproduce the culture from one generation to the next. Sumsion (2005) noted that even having male teachers in the lower grades does not seem to disrupt traditional gender stereotypes that young children have.

Economy

The economy of the society influences the roles of the individuals in the society. The economy is a very gendered institution. **Occupational sex segregation** denotes the fact that women and men are employed in gender-segregated occupations, that is, occupations in which workers are either primarily male or female (for example, men may work as mechanical or electrical engineers and women as flight attendants). Female-dominated occupations tend to require less education, have lower status, and pay lower salaries than male-dominated occupations. If men typically occupy a role, it tends to pay more. For example, the job of child-care attendant requires more education than the job of animal shelter attendant. However, animal shelter attendants are more likely to be male and earn more than child-care attendants, who are more likely to be female.

PERSONAL CHOICES

Do You Want a Nontraditional Occupational Role?

The concentration of women in certain occupations and men in others is referred to as occupational sex segregation. Although women perform nontraditional work as coal miners, construction workers, steelworkers, tractor-truck drivers, subway conductors, firefighters, and harness-horse track race drivers, less than 2 percent occupy these blue-collar jobs. Similarly, although men can work as preschool and kindergarten teachers, less than 3 percent do (Crawley, Foley, and Shehan 2008). However, some work, traditionally occupied by one gender, is sometimes selected by the other gender. Some men want to be nurses and librarians; some women want to be lawyers and physicians. Increasingly, occupations are becoming less segregated on the basis of gender, and social acceptance of nontraditional career choices has increased. The U.S. government is committed to opening occupations to both genders.

The trend continues; women now fly jet aircraft on military combat missions and study at the previously all-male West Point and Virginia Military Institute. However, only 15 percent and 3 percent, respectively, of the cadets at West Point and Virginia Military Institute are female. Even when women enter male-dominated professions like law, they tend to remain at the lower levels of practice due to the priority they give to their families (Bacik and Drew 2006). Traditional occupational choices are also still sometimes operative. In a study of medical students at two Dutch medical schools, women were more likely to select pediatrics and psychiatry whereas men were more likely to select surgery and internal medicine (Soethout et al. 2008).

Choosing nontraditional occupational roles may have benefits both for individuals and for society. On the individual level, women and men can make career choices on the basis of their personal talents and interests rather than on the basis of arbitrary social restrictions regarding who can and cannot have a particular job or career. Because traditional male occupations generally pay higher than traditional female occupations, women who make nontraditional career choices can gain access to higher-paying and higher-status jobs.

On the societal level, an increase in nontraditional career choices reduces gender-based occupational segregation, thereby contributing to social equality among women and men. In addition, women and men who enter nontraditional occupations may contribute greatly to the field that they enter. For example, such traditionally male-dominated fields as politics, science, and technology may benefit greatly from the increased involvement of women. Similarly, among preschool and kindergarten teachers (98 percent of whom are female), there are not enough male role models for their students.

Sources

Bacik, I., and E. Drew. 2006. Struggling with juggling: Gender and work/life balance in the legal professions. *Women's Studies in International Forum* 29:136–146.

Crawley, S. L. , L. J. Foley, and C. L. Shehan. 2008. *Gendering bodies*. Boston: Rowman and Littlefield.

Soethout, M. B., M. W. Heymans, and O. Th. J. Ten Cate. 2008. Career preference and medical students' biographical characteristics and academic achievement. *Medical Teacher* 30:E15–E28.

Mass Media

Mass media, such as movies, television, magazines, newspapers, books, music, and computer games, both reflect and shape gender roles. Media images of women and men typically conform to traditional gender stereotypes, and media portrayals depicting the exploitation, victimization, and sexual objectification of women are common. Observe the array of magazine covers at any newsstand. Compare the number of provocative females with males. Similarly, notice the traditional gender role scripting in popular television programs. Kim et al. (2007) identified the gender or sexual scripting of twenty-five prime-time television shows and found evidence of the traditional scripting (for example, men are dominant and "need sex"; women are passive and valued for their bodies).

Rivadeneyraa and Lebob (2008) studied ninth grade students and found that watching "romantic" television (for example, soaps, Lifetime movies) was associated with having more traditional gender role attitudes in dating situations. However, watching nonromantic television dramas and thinking television was realistic was related to having less traditional dating role attitudes.

Self-help parenting books are also biased toward traditional gender roles. A team of researchers conducted a content analysis of six of the best-selling self-help books for parents and found that 82 percent were wrought with stereotypical gender role messages (Krafchick et al. 2005).

The cumulative effects of family, peers, religion, education, the economy, and mass media perpetuate gender stereotypes. Each agent of socialization reinforces gender roles that are learned from other agents of socialization, thereby creating a gender role system that is deeply embedded in our culture.

Gender Roles in Other Societies

Because culture largely influences gender roles, individuals reared in different societies typically display the gender role patterns of those societies. The following subsections discuss how gender roles differ in Latin America, Spain, Afghanistan under the Taliban, the Caribbean, Greece, Sweden, and East and South Africa.

Gender Roles in Latino/Hispanic Families

Although there is no one Latino/Hispanic family and the gender roles differ across families, there seems to be a drift toward less role rigidity. Royo-Vela et al. (2008) emphasized that, although the traditional family model in Spain calls for men as providers and women as homemakers and mothers, a new feminine culture and a social reality is moving steadily toward gender equality and complementariness between genders.

Parra-Cardona et al. (2008) compared the gender role views of sixty-four foreign and U.S.-born parents who identified themselves as Latino or Hispanic. They found that foreign-born parents tended to regard the role of the man as provider and the role of the woman as primary caretaker and the main source of emotional nurturance for children and the family. However, 30 percent of foreign-born parents "expressed the need to challenge predetermined gender roles." One father felt that mothers are often blamed for the outcome of their children when fathers should be more involved. ". . . . [I]t's the mother who gets blamed for [this] because we say 'Where were you?, What were you doing?, Did you spoil them too much?' . . . I think we should not delegate so much on the mother" (p. 165).

U.S.-born Latinos were even more (half) egalitarian. A mother expressed, "I grew up in a family in which girls were supposed to do the cleaning and the cooking . . . boys were supposed to take care of the garbage and fixed the bicycles . . . I got divorced because my ex-husband was like that" (p. 167). A U.S.-born Latino reported that her husband not only participated in domestic chores but remained attentive to her personal needs: "My husband is really involved with the children . . . He also cooks and cleans . . . He goes to all my OBGYN appointments . . . No matter what I ask from him, he always says to me 'all right, I'm here'" (p. 168).

Finally a male talked about his interpretation of "machismo," which is usually associated with negative stereotypes. "Being a macho . . . a lot of people take the macho thing the wrong way . . . Being a macho is about being a man . . . being strong for your family . . . not giving up when you feel down . . . to know what you are doing . . . being a man about it" (p. 169).

Gender Roles in Afghanistan under the Taliban

Because of the war on terrorism and the war in Iraq, Afghanistan is very much in the news. It is a country about the size of Texas, with an estimated population of 32 million. The Taliban reached the peak of their dominance there in 1996. The Revolutionary Association of the Women of Afghanistan (RAWA) compiled an "abbreviated" list of restrictions against women (including "creating noise when they walk" and "wearing white socks"). The life for many women and children was often cruel, demeaning, and fatal. Some women drank household bleach rather than continue to endure their plight. They were not allowed to go to school or work and thus were completely dependent economically. Indeed, they were required to stay in the house, to paint the windows black, and to leave the house only if they were fully clothed (wearing a burka) and accompanied by a male relative. Some could not afford burkas and had no living male relatives. According to Skaine, "There are two places for women: one is the husband's bed and the other is the graveyard" (2002, 64). One mother reported that the Taliban came to her house, dragged her 19-year-old daughter from it, and drove away with her. "They sell them," she lamented (p. 116).

Although the plight of Afghan women may seem horrible to an outsider, some Afghan women who are thoroughly socialized in the culture and tradition may not feel oppressed but rather are accepting of their role. They may feel love, protection, and security inside the context of their marriage and family. Some may relish tradition and be against those who wish to change their sacred traditions.

Nevertheless, subsequent to 9/11, the United States attacked the Taliban in Afghanistan with the goal of removing them; in doing so, it improved the lives of Afghan women. However, the role of women in Afghanistan, particularly in the rural areas, has typically been one of submissiveness. "Most of the women in rural areas (which comprise over 80 percent of Afghanistan) have never had the opportunity to get out of their own little house, little village, little province" (Consolatore 2002, 13).

Some men spend a lifetime in an attempt to comprehend the complexities of women. Others pre-occupy themselves with somewhat simpler tasks, such as understanding the theory of relativity!

Albert Einstein, brilliant Nobel Prize winner in physics

Hence, outside of Kabul, Afghan women go uneducated, become child brides, produce children, and rarely expect their daughters' lives to be different. The patriarchal social structure and the absence of a centralized and modernized state in Afghanistan predict that changes will be limited for Afghan women (Moghadam 2002). In spite of some changes, **self-immolation** continues "at a steady rate" (Raj et al. 2008). Over 100 Afghan women (Raj et al. 2008) set themselves on fire as a means of escaping their mistreatment and to use the only voice they have in protest (public suicide).

Gender Roles in Caribbean Families

For spring break, college students sometimes go to the Bahamas, Jamaica, or other English-speaking islands in the Caribbean (for example, Barbados, Trinidad, Guyana) and may wonder about the family patterns and role relationships of the people they encounter. The natives of the Caribbean represent more than 30 million, with a majority being of African ancestry. Their family patterns are diverse but are often characterized by women and their children as the primary family unit—the fathers of these children rarely live in the home (29 percent in St. Kitts and 55 percent in Jamaica) (Roopnarine et al. 2005). Hence, men may have children with different women and be psychologically and physically absent from their children's lives. When they do live with a woman, traditional division of labor prevails, with women taking care of domestic and child-care tasks.

About half of all female household heads have never been married. Women view motherhood, not marriage, as the symbol of their womanhood. Hence, their focus is on taking care of their children and the children of others. Caribbean fathers vary from showing negligible levels of involvement with their children (e.g. in Belize) to showing levels comparable to those in other societies (e.g. in Trinidad and Guyana) (ibid.).

Gender Roles in Greek Families

Greek families reflect predictable roles for a father, mother, children, and married couple. Although adherence to traditional values is changing, it is doing so slowly. The father is regarded as the head of the household, economic provider, and disciplinarian of the children. The mother takes care of the children, is the go-between for them and the father, and supervises them carefully. Indeed, the "first goal in life is to be a good mother" (Georgas et al. 2005, 213). Greek parents are to teach their children to behave properly and to support them financially. In addition, they are to "be involved in the private lives of their married children" (ibid.).

The role of the children is to do as they are told, to be seen and not heard, to respect their parents, and to take care of them when they are old. They are to "keep no secrets" from their parents and to respect their grandparents as well.

Role relationships within the marriage are also traditional, with the wife being responsible for food preparation and cleaning. While in the home of a Greek couple, I [Knox] got up after dinner and started taking dinner plates to the kitchen. The husband politely said, "Sit down, that is woman's work." I looked at the wife, who smiled and said, "We are Greek," emphasizing they both were very firm in their traditional roles.

Gender Roles in Swedish Families

The Swedish government is strongly concerned with equality between women and men. In 1974, Sweden became the first country in the world to introduce a system that enables mothers and fathers to share parental leave (paid by the government) from their jobs in any way they choose. Furthermore, Swedish law states that employers may not penalize the careers of working parents because they have used parental rights. By encouraging fathers to participate more in child rearing, the government aims to provide more opportunities for women to pursue other roles. Women hold about one-quarter of the seats in the Parliament of Sweden. However, few Swedish women are in high-status positions in business, and governmental efforts to reduce gender inequality are weak compared with the power of tradition.

Gender Roles in East and South African Families

Africa is a diverse continent with more than fifty nations. The cultures range from Islamic and Arab cultures of northern Africa to industrial and European influences in South Africa. In some parts of East Africa (for example, in Kenya), gender roles are in flux.

Meredith Kennedy (2007) has lived in East Africa and makes the following observations of gender roles:

> *The roles of men and women in most African societies tend to be very separate and proscribed, with most authority and power in the men's domain. For instance, Maasai wives of East Africa do not travel much, since when a husband comes home he expects to find his wife (or wives) waiting for him with a gourd of sour milk. If she is not, he has the right to beat her when she shows up. As attempts are made to soften these boundaries and equalize the roles, the impacts are very visible and cause a lot of reverberations throughout these communal societies. Many African women who believe in and desire better lives will not call themselves "feminists" for fear of social censure. Change for people whose lives are based on tradition and "fitting in" can be very traumatic.*
>
> *Similarly, young East African men (for example, Kenyans) view white American coeds who visit their country as students to be very forward and available for sex. These perceptions are sometimes due to the way female students dress and require an adjustment of female dress to avoid inaccurate perceptions.*

In South Africa, where more than 75 percent of the racial population is African and around 10 percent are white, the African family is also known for its traditional role relationships and patriarchy. African men were socialized by the Dutch with firm patriarchal norms and adopted this style in their own families. In addition, women were subordinate to men "within a wider kinship system, with the chief as the controlling male. An unequal division of labor according to age and sex prevailed, and this system was exacerbated by the absence of men from the home because of migrant labor" (Pretorius 2005, 372). Gold had been discovered in 1870, and young men were recruited to work the mines while living in single quarters (separated from their families).

Consequences of Traditional Gender Role Socialization

This section discusses different consequences, both negative and positive, for women and men, of traditional female and male socialization in the United States.

Consequences of Traditional Female Role Socialization

Table 3.3 summarizes some of the negative and positive consequences of being socialized as a woman in U.S. society. Each consequence may or may not be true for a specific woman. For example, although women in general have less education and income, a particular woman may have more education and a higher income than a particular man.

As the traveler who has once been from home is wiser than he who has never left his own doorstep, so a knowledge of one other culture should sharpen our ability to scrutinize more steadily, to appreciate more lovingly, our own.

Margaret Mead, anthropologist

Table 3.3 Consequences of Traditional Female Role Socialization

Negative Consequences	Positive Consequences
Less education/income (more dependent)	Longer life
Feminization of poverty	Stronger relationship focus
Higher STD/HIV infection risk	Keep relationships on track
Negative body image	Bonding with children
Less marital satisfaction	Identity not tied to job

Table 3.4 Women's and Men's Median Income with Similar Education

	Bachelor's	Master's	Doctoral Degree
Men	$54,403	$67,425	$90,511
Women	$35,094	$46,250	$61,091

Source: *Statistical Abstract of the United States, 2009*. 128th ed. Washington, DC: U.S. Bureau of the Census, Table 680.

Negative Consequences of Traditional Female Role Socialization   There are several negative consequences of being socialized as a woman in our society.

1. *Less Income.* Although women now earn 46 percent of PhDs (Welch 2008), they have lower academic rank (Probert 2005) and earn less money. The lower academic rank is because women give priority to the care of their children and family (Aissen and Houvouras 2006). In addition, women tend to be more concerned about the nonmonetary aspects of work. In a study of 102 seniors and 504 alumni from a mid-sized Midwestern public university that rated forty-eight job characteristics, women gave significantly higher ratings to family life accommodations, pleasant working conditions, travel, and interpersonal relationships. Women still earn about two-thirds of what men earn, even when the level of educational achievement is identical (see Table 3.4). Their visibility in the ranks of high corporate America is also still low. Of Fortune 500 companies, women run only thirteen as CEO. Angela Braly is one of them. She heads WellPoint and earns 9.1 million annually (Fortune 500 2008).

With divorce being a nearly 45 percent probability for marriages begun in the 2000s, the likelihood of being a widow for seven or more years, and the almost certain loss of her parenting role midway through her life, a woman without education and employment skills is often left high and dry. As one widowed mother of four said, "The shock of realizing you have children to support and no skills to do it is a worse shock than learning that your husband is dead." In the words of a divorced, 40-year-old mother of three, "If young women think it can't happen to them, they are foolish."

2. *Feminization of Poverty.* Another reason many women are relegated to a lower income status is the **feminization of poverty.** This term refers to the disproportionate percentage of poverty experienced by women living alone or with their children. Single mothers are particularly associated with poverty.

When head-of-household women are compared with married-couple households, the median income is $28,829 versus $69,404 (*Statistical Abstract of the United States, 2009*, Table 677). The process is cyclical—poverty contributes to teenage pregnancy because teens have limited supervision and few alternatives to parenthood. (The median income for head-of-household men is $41,844.)

Such early childbearing interferes with educational advancement and restricts women's earning capacity, which keeps them in poverty. Their offspring are born into poverty, and the cycle begins anew.

Even if they get a job, women tend to be employed fewer hours than men, and they earn less money, even when they work full-time. Not only is discrimination in the labor force operating against women, but women also usually make their families a priority over their employment, which translates into less income. Such prioritization is based on the patriarchal family, which ensures that women stay economically dependent on men and are relegated to domestic roles. Such dependence limits the choices of many women.

Low pay for women is also related to the fact that they tend to work in occupations that pay relatively low incomes. Indeed, women's lack of economic power stems from the relative dispensability of women's labor (it is easy to replace) and how work is organized (men control positions of power). Women also live longer than men, and poverty is associated with being elderly (Lipsitz 2005).

When women move into certain occupations, such as teaching, there is a tendency in the marketplace to segregate these occupations from men's, and the result is a concentration of women in lower-paid occupations. The salaries of women in these occupational roles increase at slower rates. For example, salaries in the elementary and secondary teaching profession, which is predominately female, have not kept pace with inflation.

Conflict theorists assert that men are in more powerful roles than women and use this power to dictate incomes and salaries of women and "female professions." Functionalists also note that keeping salaries low for women keeps women dependent and in child-care roles so as to keep equilibrium in the family. Hence, for both conflict and structural reasons, poverty is primarily a feminine issue. One of the consequences of being a woman is to have an increased chance of feeling economic strain throughout life.

3. *Higher Risk for Sexually Transmitted Infections.* Gender roles influence a woman's vulnerability to sexually transmitted infection and HIV, not only because women receive more bodily fluids from men, who have a greater number of partners (and are therefore more likely to be infected), but also because some women feel limited power to influence their partners to wear condoms.

4. *Negative Body Image.* There are more than 3,800 beauty pageants annually in the United States. The effect for many women who do not match the cultural ideal is to have a negative body image. Although women are becoming less likely to view themselves as overweight, the obsession of even females of normal weight to mirror the cultural ideal is strong (Neighbors et al. 2008).

Women also live in a society that devalues them in a larger sense. Their lives and experiences are not taken as seriously. **Sexism** is defined as an attitude, action, or institutional structure that subordinates or discriminates against individuals or groups because of their sex. Sexism against women reflects the tradition of male dominance and presumed male superiority in American society. It is reflected in the fact that women are rarely found in power positions in our society. In the 111th Congress, only 75 of the 435 members of the House of Representatives are women. Seventeen women and eighty-three men are serving as senators. A signal of change emerged when Democrat Nancy Pelosi became Speaker of the House in 2007. And, Hillary Clinton was a close second to Barack Obama in becoming the Democratic candidate for the presidency.

5. *Less Marital Satisfaction.* Corra et al. (2009) analyzed General Social Survey data over a thirty-year period (1972–2002), controlled for socioeconomic factors such as income and education, and found that women reported less marital satisfaction than men. Similarly, twice as many husbands as wives among 105 late-life couples (average age, 69 years) reported that they had "no disappointments in the marriage" (15 percent versus 7 percent), suggesting greater dissatisfaction among wives (Henry et al. 2005). The lower marital satisfaction of wives is attributed to power differentials in the marriage. Traditional husbands expect to be dominant, which translates into their earning an income and the expectation that the wife not only will earn an income but also will take care of the house and children. The latter expectation results in a feeling of unfairness. Analysis of other large national samples has yielded the same finding of lower marital satisfaction among wives (Faulkner et al. 2005).

We come in different sizes so get over it.

Rosie O'Donnell

Female Genital Alteration

Female genital alteration, more commonly known as FGC (female genital cutting) or female circumcision, involves cutting off the clitoris (**clitoridectomy**) or excising (partially or totally) the labia minora. "World-wide about 130 million women have undergone FGC. In the USA, more than 168,000 females have had or are at risk for this procedure and the number may be increasing as the admission ceiling for African refugees is raised. Federal law criminalizes the performance of FGC on females under 18 in the USA; however, the procedure is not unknown in this country. More commonly, young women are sent back to their country of origin for the procedure. Over 90 percent of women from Djibouti, Egypt, Eritrea, Ethiopia, Mali, Sierra Leone, Somalia, and Northern Sudan have had the procedure" (Nicoletti 2007).

The practice of FGC is not confined to a particular religion. The reasons for the practice include:

a. Sociological/cultural—parents believe that female circumcision makes their daughters lose their desire for sex, which helps them maintain their virginity and helps to ensure their marriageability and fidelity to their husbands. Hence, the "circumcised" female is seen as one whom males will desire as a wife. FGC is seen as a "rite of passage" that initiates a girl into womanhood and increases her bonding and social cohesion with other females.

b. Hygiene/aesthetics—female genitalia are considered dirty and unsightly so that their removal promotes hygiene and provides aesthetic appeal.

c. Religion—some Muslim communities practice FGC in the belief that the Islamic faith demands it. But it is not mentioned in the Qur'an.

d. Myths: FGC is thought to enhance fertility and promote child survival (Nicoletti 2007).

Elnashar and Abdelhady (2007) compared the sexuality of married women who had been circumcised with those who had not. The researchers found statistically significant differences such that the former were more likely to report pain during intercourse, loss of libido, and failure to orgasm. The wives who had been circumcised also reported more physical complaints, anxiety, and phobias.

Changing a country's deeply held beliefs and values concerning this practice cannot be achieved by denigration. More effective approaches to discouraging the practice include the following:

1. Respect the beliefs and values of countries that practice female genital operations. Calling the practice "genital mutilation" and "a barbaric practice" and referring to it as a form of "child abuse" and "torture" convey disregard for the beliefs and values of the cultures where it is practiced. In essence, we might adopt a culturally relativistic point of view (without moral acceptance of the practice).

2. Remember that genital operations are arranged and paid for by loving parents who deeply believe that the surgeries are for their daughters' welfare.

3. It is important to be culturally sensitive to the meaning of being a woman. Indeed, genital cutting is mixed up with how a woman sees herself; thus Westerners are becoming involved in her identity when attempting to alter long-held historical practices (James and Robertson 2002).

Your Opinion?

1. To what degree do you feel the United States should become involved in the practice of female genital alterations of U.S. citizens?

2. To what degree can you regard the practice from the view of traditional parents and daughters?

3. How could not having the operation be a liability and a benefit for the woman whose culture supports the practice?

Sources

Elnashar, A., and R. Abdelhady. 2007. The impact of female genital cutting on health of newly married women. *International Journal of Gynecology & Obstetrics* 97:238–44.

James, S. M., and C. C. Robertson, eds. 2002. *Genital cutting and transnational sisterhood: Disputing U.S. polemics.* Urbana, IL: University of Illinois Press.

Nicoletti, A. 2007. Female genital cutting. *Journal of Pediatric & Adolescent Gynecology* 20:261–62.

Heaven help the American-born boy with a talent for ballet.

Camille Paglia, feminist

Before ending this section on negative consequences of being socialized as a woman, look at the Social Policy feature on female genital alteration. This is more of an issue for females born in some African, Middle Eastern, and Asian countries than for women in the United States. However, the practice continues even here.

Positive Consequences of Traditional Female Role Socialization   We have discussed the negative consequences of being born and socialized as a woman. However, there are also decided benefits.

National Data

Females born in the year 2010 are expected to live to the age of 80.8, in contrast to men, who are expected to live to the age of 75.7 (*Statistical Abstract of the United States, 2009*, Table 100).

1. *Longer Life Expectancy.* Women have a longer life expectancy than men. It is not clear if their greater longevity is related to biological or to social factors.

2. *Stronger Relationship Focus.* Women continue to prioritize family relationships over work relationships (Stone 2007). Female family members, in contrast to male family members, are viewed as more nurturing and responsive (Monin et al. 2008).

3. *Keep Relationships on Track.* Because women evidence more concern for relationships, they are more likely to be motivated to keep them on track and to initiate conversation when there is a problem. In a study of 203 undergraduates, two-thirds of the women, in contrast to 60 percent of the men, reported that they were likely to start a discussion about a problem in their relationship (Knox et al. 1998). Ingram et al. (2008) also noted that, of 300,000 crisis calls to a national hotline over a five-year period, women were more likely than men to call by a two-to-one margin.

4. *Bonding with Children.* Another advantage of being socialized as a woman is the potential to have a closer bond with children. In general, women tend to be more emotionally bonded with their children than men do. Although the new cultural image of the father is of one who engages emotionally with his children, many fathers continue to be content for their wives to take care of their children, with the result that mothers, not fathers, become more emotionally bonded with their children.

Consequences of Traditional Male Role Socialization

Male socialization in American society is associated with its own set of consequences. Both the negative and positive consequences are summarized in Table 3.5. As with women, each consequence may or may not be true for a specific man.

Negative Consequences of Traditional Male Role Socialization   There are several negative consequences associated with being socialized as a man in U.S. society.

National Data

Seventy percent of men, compared with 65.3 percent of women, were in the civilian workforce in 2007 (*Statistical Abstract of the United States, 2009*, Table 576).

1. *Identity Synonymous with Occupation.* Ask men who they are, and many will tell you what they do. Society tends to equate a man's identity with his occupational role. Male socialization toward greater involvement in the labor force is evident in governmental statistics (see National Data above).

Maume (2006) analyzed national data on taking vacation time and found that men were much less likely to do so. They cited fear that doing so would affect their job or career performance evaluation. Women, on the other hand, were much more likely to use all of their vacation time. However, the "work equals identity" equation for men may be changing. Increasingly, as women are more present in the labor force and become co-providers, men become co-nurturers and co-homemakers. In addition, more stay-at-home dads and fathers are seeking full custody in divorce litigation. These changes challenge cultural notions of masculinity.

That men work more and play less may translate into fewer friendships and relationships. In a study of 377 university students, 25.9 percent of the men

Table 3.5 Consequences of Traditional Male Role Socialization

Negative Consequences	Positive Consequences
Identity tied to work role	Higher income and occupational status
Limited emotionality	More positive self-concept
Fear of intimacy; more lonely	Less job discrimination
Disadvantaged in getting custody	Freedom of movement; more partners to select from; more normative to initiate relationships
Shorter life	Happier marriage

compared to 16.7 percent of the women reported feeling a "deep sense of loneliness" (Vail-Smith et al. 2007). Similarly, Grief (2006) reported that a quarter of 386 adult men reported that they did not have enough friends. Grief also suggested some possible reasons for men having few friends—homophobia, lack of role models, fear of being vulnerable, and competition between men. McPherson et al. (2006) also found that men reported fewer confidantes than women.

2. *Limited Expression of Emotions.* Some men feel caught between society's expectations that they be competitive, aggressive, and unemotional and their own desire to be more cooperative, passive, and emotional. Indeed, men see themselves as less emotional and loving than women (Hill 2007), and are pressured to disavow any expression that could be interpreted as feminine (for example, be emotional). Indeed, 55 percent of the soldiers serving in Iraq or Afghanistan reported that they feared they would appear "weak" if they expressed feelings of fear or symptoms of post-traumatic stress disorder (Thompson 2008). In addition, Cordova et al. (2005) studied a sample of husbands and wives, and confirmed that the men were less able to express their emotions than the women. Notice that men are repeatedly told to "prove their manhood" (which implies not being emotional), whereas women in our culture have no dictum "to 'prove their womanhood'"—the phrase itself sounds ridiculous (Kimmel 2001, 33). Indeed, men today are encouraged to shed their traditional masculinity, with the result that they will "live longer, happier, and healthier lives, lives characterized by close and caring relationships with children, with women, and with other men" (Kimmel 2006, 187).

3. *Fear of Intimacy.* Men may be socialized to withhold information about themselves that encourages the development of intimacy. Giordano et al. (2005) analyzed data from the National Longitudinal Study of Adolescent Health, consisting of more than 9,000 interviews, and found that adolescent boys reported less willingness to disclose than adolescent girls.

4. *Custody Disadvantages.* Courts are sometimes biased against divorced men who want custody of their children. Because divorced fathers are typically regarded as career-focused and uninvolved in child care, some are relegated to seeing their children on a limited basis, such as every other weekend or four evenings a month.

5. *Shorter Life Expectancy.* Men typically die five years sooner (at age 76) than women (*Statistical Abstract of the United States, 2009*, Table 100). One explanation is that the traditional male role emphasizes achievement, competition, and suppression of feelings, all of which may produce stress. Not only is stress itself harmful to physical health, but it may lead to compensatory behaviors such as smoking, alcohol and other drug abuse, and dangerous risk-taking behavior (all of which is higher in males).

In sum, the traditional male gender role is hazardous to men's physical health. However, as women have begun to experience many of the same stresses and behaviors as men, their susceptibility to stress-related diseases has increased. For example, since the 1950s, male smoking has declined whereas female smoking has increased, resulting in an increased incidence of lung cancer in women.

Benefits of Traditional Male Socialization   As a result of higher status and power in society, men tend to have a more positive self-concept and greater confidence in themselves. In a sample of 288, 48 percent of undergraduate/graduate men, in contrast to 30 percent of undergraduate women agreed that "we determine whatever happens to us, and nothing is predestined" (Dotson-Blake et al. 2008). Men also enjoy higher incomes and an easier climb up the good-old-boy corporate ladder; they are rarely stalked or targets of sexual harassment. Other benefits are the following:

1. *Freedom of Movement.* Men typically have no fear of going anywhere, anytime. Their freedom of movement is unlimited. Unlike women, who are taught to fear rape and to be aware of their surroundings, walk in well-lit places, and not walk alone after dark, men are oblivious to these fears and perceptions. They can be alone in public and be anxiety-free about something ominous happening to them.

2. *Greater Available Pool of Potential Partners.* Because of the mating gradient (men marry "down" in age and education whereas women marry "up"), men tend to marry younger women so that a 35-year-old man may view women from 20 years to 40 years as possible mates. However, a woman of age 35 is more likely to view men her same age or older as potential mates. As she ages, fewer men are available; less so for men.

Table 3.6   Effects of Gender Role Socialization on Relationship Choices

Women

1. A woman who is not socialized to pursue advanced education (which often translates into less income) may feel pressure to stay in an unhappy relationship with someone on whom she is economically dependent.

2. Women who are socialized to play a passive role and not initiate relationships are limiting interactions that could develop into valued relationships.

3. Women who are socialized to accept that they are less valuable and important than men are less likely to seek or achieve egalitarian relationships with men.

4. Women who internalize society's standards of beauty and view their worth in terms of their age and appearance are likely to feel bad about themselves as they age. Their negative self-concept, more than their age or appearance, may interfere with their relationships.

5. Women who are socialized to accept that they are solely responsible for taking care of their parents, children, and husband are likely to experience role overload. Potentially, this could result in feelings of resentment in their relationships.

6. Women who are socialized to emphasize the importance of relationships in their lives will continue to seek relationships that are emotionally satisfying.

Men

1. Men who are socialized to define themselves more in terms of their occupational success and income and less in terms of positive individual qualities leave their self-esteem and masculinity vulnerable should they become unemployed or work in a low-status job.

2. Men who are socialized to restrict their experience and expression of emotions are denied the opportunity to discover the rewards of emotional interpersonal sharing.

3. Men who are socialized to believe it is not their role to participate in domestic activities (child rearing, food preparation, house cleaning) will not develop competencies in these life skills. Potential partners often view domestic skills as desirable qualities.

4. Heterosexual men who focus on cultural definitions of female beauty overlook potential partners who might not fit the cultural beauty ideal but who would nevertheless be good life companions.

5. Men who are socialized to view women who initiate relationships in negative ways are restricted in their relationship opportunities.

6. Men who are socialized to be in control of relationship encounters may alienate their partners, who may desire equal influence in relationships.

3. *Norm of Initiating a Relationship.* Men are advantaged because traditional norms allow men to be aggressive in initiating relationships with women. In contrast, women are less often aggressive in initiating a relationship. In a study of 1,027 undergraduates, 61.1 percent of the female respondents reported that they had not "asked a guy to go out" (Ross et al., forthcoming).

We have been discussing the respective ways in which traditional gender role socialization affects women and men. Table 3.6 on page 99 summarizes twelve implications that traditional gender role socialization has for the relationships of women and men.

Changing Gender Roles

Imagine a society in which women and men each develop characteristics, lifestyles, and values that are independent of gender role stereotypes. Characteristics such as strength, independence, logical thinking, and aggressiveness are no longer associated with maleness, just as passivity, dependence, emotions, intuitiveness, and nurturance are no longer associated with femaleness. Both sexes are considered equal, and women and men may pursue the same occupational, political, and domestic roles. Some gender scholars have suggested that people in such a society would be neither feminine nor masculine but would be described as androgynous. The next subsections discuss androgyny, gender role transcendence, and gender postmodernism.

Androgyny

Androgyny typically refers to being neither male nor female but a blend of both traits. Two forms of androgyny are described here:

1. Physiological androgyny refers to intersexed individuals, discussed earlier in the chapter. The genitals are neither clearly male nor female, and there is a mixing of "female" and "male" chromosomes and hormones.

2. Behavioral androgyny refers to the blending or reversal of traditional male and female behavior, so that a biological male may be very passive, gentle, and nurturing and a biological female may be very assertive, rough, and selfish. Identifying an androgynous individual as male or female may be difficult.

Androgyny may also imply flexibility of traits; for example, an androgynous individual may be emotional in one situation, logical in another, assertive in another, and so forth. Ward (2001) classified 311 (159 male, 152 female) undergraduates at the National University of Singapore as androgynous (33.8 percent men and 16.0 percent women), feminine (11.0 percent men and 39.6 percent women), masculine (35.7 percent men and 13.9 percent women), and undifferentiated (19.5 percent men and 30.6 percent women). Peters (2005) emphasized that the blending of genders is inevitable.

Cheng (2005) found that androgynous individuals have a broad coping repertoire and are much more able to cope with stress. As evidence, Moore et al. (2005) found that androgynous individuals with Parkinson's disease were not only better able to cope with their disease but also reported having a better quality of life than those with the same disease who expressed the characteristics of one gender only. Similarly, androgynous individuals reported much less likelihood of having an eating disorder (Hepp et al. 2005).

Woodhill and Samuels (2003) emphasized the need to differentiate between positive and negative androgyny. **Positive androgyny** is devoid of the negative traits associated with masculinity (aggression, hard-heartedness, indifference, selfishness, showing off, and vindictiveness). Antisocial behavior has also been associated with masculinity (Ma 2005). Negative aspects of femininity include being passive, submissive, temperamental, and fragile. The researchers also found that positive androgyny is associated with psychological health and well-being.

Gender Role Transcendence

Beyond the concept of androgyny is that of gender role transcendence. We associate many aspects of our world, including colors, foods, social or occupational roles, and personality traits, with either masculinity or femininity. The concept of **gender role transcendence** involves abandoning gender schema (for example, becoming "gender aschematic" [Bem 1983]) so that personality traits, social or occupational roles, and other aspects of our lives become divorced from gender categories. However, such transcendence is not equal for women and men. Although females are becoming more masculine, in part because our society values whatever is masculine, men are not becoming more feminine. Indeed, adolescent boys may be described as very gender-entrenched.

Beyond gender role transcendence is gender postmodernism.

Gender Postmodernism

Mirchandani (2005) emphasized that empirical postmodernism can help us see into the future. Such a view would abandon the notion that the genders are natural and focus on the social construction of individuals in a gender-fluid society. Monro (2000) previously noted that people would no longer be categorized as male or female but be recognized as capable of many identities—"a third sex" (p. 37). A new conceptualization of "trans" people calls for new social structures, "based on the principles of equality, diversity and the right to self determination" (p. 42). No longer would our society telegraph transphobia but embrace pluralization "as an indication of social evolution, allowing greater choice and means of self-expression concerning gender" (p. 42).

This woman enjoys both her femininity and masculinity.

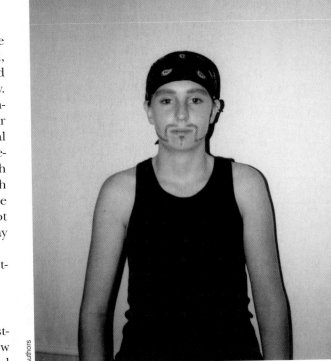

Authors

What if Your Spouse Were a Cross-Dresser?

WHAT IF?

What if your spouse were androgynous to the point of wanting to cross-dress? Although most cross-dressers are men who enjoy dressing as a woman, a smaller percentage of women enjoy dressing as a man. Some spouses are accepting of this cross-dressing, even to the extent of being comfortable in public with them when the spouse is cross-dressed, or shopping with the partner for other-gender clothes; other spouses require the cross-dressing partner to only cross-dress at home and when the spouse is not at home. Still other spouses say this is "too weird for me" and file for divorce. How would you react if you discovered a drawerful of other-sex clothes?

SUMMARY

What are the important terms related to gender?

Sex refers to the biological distinction between females and males. One's biological sex is identified on the basis of one's chromosomes, gonads, hormones, internal sex organs, and external genitals, and exists on a continuum rather than being a dichotomy. *Gender* refers to the social and psychological characteristics often associated with being female or male. Other terms related to gender include *gender identity* (one's self-concept as a girl or boy), *gender role* (social norms of what a girl or boy "should" do), *gender role ideology* (how women and men "should" interact), *transgender* (expressing characteristics different from one's biological sex), and *transgenderism* (living in a role other than one of the person's biological sex).

What theories explain gender role development?

Biosocial theory emphasizes that social behaviors (for example, gender roles) are biologically based and have an evolutionary survival function. Traditionally, women stayed in the nest or gathered food nearby, whereas men traveled far to find food. Such a conceptualization focuses on the division of labor between women and men as functional for the survival of the species. Social learning theory emphasizes the roles of reward and punishment in explaining how children learn gender role behavior. Identification theory says that children acquire the characteristics and behaviors of their same-sex parent through a process of identification. Boys identify with their fathers; girls identify with their mothers. Cognitive-developmental theory emphasizes biological readiness, in terms of cognitive development, of the child's responses to gender cues in the environment. Once children learn the concept of gender permanence, they seek to become competent and proper members of their gender group.

What are the various agents of socialization?

Various socialization influences include parents and siblings (representing different races and ethnicities), peers, religion, the economy, education, and mass media. These shape individuals toward various gender roles and influence what people think, feel, and do in their roles as woman or man. For example, the family is a gendered institution with female and male roles highly structured by gender. The names parents assign to their children, the clothes they dress them in, and the toys they buy them all reflect gender. Parents may also be stricter on female children, determining the age they are allowed to leave the house at night, time of curfew, and directives such as "call your mamma when you get to the party."

How are gender roles expressed in other societies?

Although there is no one Latino or Hispanic family and the gender roles differ across families, there seems to be a drift from the male provider or family homemaker toward less role rigidity. However, foreign-born Latino or Hispanic parents tend to regard the role of the man as provider and the role of the woman as primary caretaker and the main source of emotional nurturance for children and the family.

Women under Taliban rule in Afghanistan have been very oppressed. Some women drank household bleach rather than continue to endure their plight. They were not allowed to go to school or work and thus were completely dependent economically.

In the Caribbean, family patterns are diverse but are often characterized by women and their children as the primary family unit, with men often not living in the home.

What are the consequences of traditional gender role socialization?

Traditional female role socialization may result in negative outcomes such as less education, less income, negative body image, and lower marital satisfaction but positive outcomes such as a longer life, a stronger relationship focus, keeping relationships on track, and a closer emotional bond with children. Traditional male role socialization may result in the fusion of self and occupation, a more limited expression of emotion, disadvantages in child custody disputes, and a shorter life but higher income, greater freedom of movement, a greater available pool of potential partners, and greater acceptance in initiating relationships. The Research Application for the chapter revealed that about 30 percent of college men in one study reported their preference for marrying a traditional wife (one who would stay at home to take care of children). These men believe that a wife's working outside the home weakens the marriage.

How are gender roles changing?

Androgyny refers to a blend of traits that are stereotypically associated with both masculinity and femininity. It may also imply flexibility of traits; for example, an androgynous individual may be emotional in one situation, logical in another, assertive in another, and so forth. The concept of gender role transcendence involves abandoning gender schema (for example, becoming "gender aschematic"), so that personality traits, social and occupational roles, and other aspects of our lives become divorced from gender categories. However, such transcendence is not equal for women and men. Although females are becoming more masculine partly because our society values whatever is masculine, men are not becoming more feminine.

KEY TERMS

androgyny	gender identity	occupational sex segregation	socialization
biosocial theory	gender role ideology	parental investment	sociobiology
clitoridectomy	gender role transcendence	positive androgyny	transgender
cross-dresser	gender roles	pseudohermaphroditism	transgenderism
female genital alteration	hermaphrodites	self-immolation	transgenderist
feminization of poverty	intersex development	sex	transsexual
gender	intersexed (middlesexed)	sex roles	transvestite
gender dysphoria	individuals	sexism	true hermaphroditism

The Companion Website for *Choices in Relationships: An Introduction to Marriage and the Family,* Tenth Edition

www.cengage.com/sociology/knox

Supplement your review of this chapter by going to the Companion Website to take one of the tutorial quizzes, use the flash cards to master key terms, or check out the many other study aids, like crossword puzzles and self-assessments. You'll also find special features such as General Social Survey (GSS) data, Census data, and other resources to help you with that special project or to do some research on your own.

WEB LINKS

Androgyny
http://www.lilithgallery.com/feminist/males_crying.html

Equal Employment Opportunity Commission
http://www.eeoc.gov/

Female Genital Alteration/Cutting
http://www.womenshealth.gov/faq/fgc.htm

Intersexed Individuals
http://www.notjustskin.org/en/intersex.html
http://www.isna.org/

American Men's Studies Association
http://www.mensstudies.org/

National Organization for Women (NOW)
http://www.now.org/

Transgender Forum
http://www.tgforum.com/

Transsexuality
http://www.transsexual.org/

Abowitz, D. A., D. Knox, M. Zusman, and A. McNeely. 2009. Beliefs about romantic relationships: Gender differences among undergraduates. *College Student Journal* 43:276–284.

Aissen, K., and S. Houvouras. 2006. Family first: Negotiating motherhood and doctoral studies. Southern Sociological Society, New Orleans, March 24.

Bacik, I., and E. Drew. 2006. Struggling with juggling: Gender and work/life balance in the legal professions. *Women's Studies in International Forum* 29:136–46.

Bem, S. L. 1983. Gender schema theory and its implications for child development: Raising gender-aschematic children in a gender-schematic society. *Signs* 8:596–616.

Cheng, C. 2005. Processes underlying gender-role flexibility: Do androgynous individuals know more or know how to cope? *Journal of Personality* 73:645–74.

Cohen-Kettenis, P. T. 2005. Gender change in 46, XY persons with 5[alpha]-reductase-2 deficiency and 17[beta]-hydroxysteroid dehydrogenase-3 deficiency. *Archives of Sexual Behavior* 34:399–411.

Colapinto, J. 2000. *As nature made him: The boy who was raised as a girl.* New York: Harper Collins.

Consolatore, D. 2002. What next for the women of Afghanistan? *The Humanist* 62:10–15.

Cordova, J. V., C. B. Gee, and L. Z. Warren. 2005. Emotional skillfulness in marriage: Intimacy as a mediator of the relationship between emotional skillfulness and marital satisfaction. *Journal of Social & Clinical Psychology* 24:218–35.

Corra, M., J. S. Carter, and D. Knox. 2006. Marital happiness by sex and race: A second look. Paper, Annual Meeting of the American Sociological Association, New York, August.

Crawley, S. L. , L. J. Foley, and C. L. Shehan. 2008. *Gendering bodies.* Boston: Rowman and Littlefield.

Denton, M. L. 2004. Gender and marital decision making: Negotiating religious ideology and practice. *Social Forces* 82:1151–80.

Dotson-Blake, K., D. Knox, and A. Holman 2008. College student attitudes toward marriage, family, and sex therapy. Unpublished data from 288 undergraduate/graduate students. East Carolina University, Greenville, NC.

Faulkner, R., A. M. Davey, and A. Davey. 2005. Gender-related predictors of change in marital satis-faction and marital conflict. *American Journal of Family Therapy* 33:61–83.

Fortune 500 in 2008 http://money.cnn.com/galleries/2008/fortune/0804/gallery.500_women_ceos.fortune/index.html.

Georgas, J., T. Bafiti, K. Mylonas, and L. Papademou. 2005. Families in Greece. In *Families in global perspective,* ed. J. L. Roopnaraine and U. P. Gielen, 207–24. Boston: Pearson Allyn & Bacon.

Giordano, P. C., W. D. Manning, and M. A. Longmore. 2005. The romantic relationships of African-American and white adolescents. *The Sociological Quarterly* 46:545–68.

Grief, G. L. 2006. Male friendships: Implications from research for family therapy. *Family Therapy* 33:1–15.

Haynie, D. L., and D. W. Osgood. 2005. Reconsidering peers and delinquency: How do peers matters? *Social Forces* 84:1109–30.

Heller, N. 2008. Will the transgender dad be a father? What goes on the birth certificate? http://www.slate.com/id/2193475/ (accessed June 13, 2008).

Henry, R. G., R. B. Miller, and R. Giarrusso. 2005. Difficulties, disagreements, and disappointments in late-life marriages. *International Journal of Aging & Human Development* 61:243–65.

Hepp, U., A. Spindler, and G. Milos. 2005. Eating disorder symptomalogy and gender role orientation. *International Journal of Eating Disorders* 37:227–33.

Hill, D. B. 2007. Differences and similarities in men's and women's sexual self-schemas. *Journal of Sex Research* 44:135–44.

Ingram, S., J. L. Ringle, K. Hallstrom, D. E. Schill, et al. 2008. Coping with crisis across the lifespan: The role of a telephone hotline. *Journal of Child and Family Studies* 17:663–75.

Irvolino, A. C., M. Hines, S. E. Golombok, J. Rust, and R. Plomin. 2005. Genetic and environmen-tal influences on sex-typed behavior during the preschool years. *Child Development* 76:826–40.

Kennedy, M. 2007. Gender role observations of East Africa. Written exclusively for this text.

Kilmartin, C., T. Smith, A. Green, H. Heinzen, M. Kuchler, and D. Kolar. 2008. A real time social norms intervention to reduce male sexism. *Journal Sex Roles* 59: 264–73.

Kim, J. L., C. L. Sorsoli, K. Collins, B. A. Zylbergold, D. Schooler, and D. L. Tolman. 2007. From sex to sexuality: Exposing the heterosexual script on primetime network television. *Journal of Sex Research.* 44:145–57.

Kimmel, M. S. 2001. Masculinity as homophobia: Fear, shame, and silence in the construction of gender identity. In *Men and masculinity: A text reader,* ed. T. F. Cohen, 29–41. Belmont, CA: Wadsworth.

Kimmel, M. S. 2006. *Manhood in America: A cultural history.* New York: Oxford University Press.

Knox, D., S. Hatfield, and M. E. Zusman. 1998. College student discussion of relationship prob-lems. *College Student Journal* 32:19–21.

Knox, D., and M. E. Zusman. 2009. Relationship and sexual behaviors of a sample of 1,319 univer-sity students. Unpublished data collected for this text. Department of Sociology, East Carolina University, Greenville, NC.

Knox, D., M. E. Zusman, and H. R. Thompson. 2004. Emotional perceptions of self and others: Stereotypes and data. *College Student Journal* 38:130–42.

Kohlberg, L. 1966. A cognitive-developmental analysis of children's sex-role concepts and attitudes. In *The development of sex differences,* ed. E. E. Macoby. Stanford, CA: Stanford University Press.

———. 1969. State and sequence: The cognitive developmental approach to socialization. In *Handbook of socialization theory and research,* ed. D. A. Goslin, 347–480. Chicago: Rand McNally.

Krafchick, J. L., T. S. Zimmerman, S. A. Haddock, and J. H. Banning. 2005. Best-selling books advising parents about gender: A feminist analysis. *Family Relations* 54:84–101.

Kurson, R. 2007. *Crashing through: A true story of risk, adventure, and the man who dared to see.* New York: Random House.

Lareau, A., and E. B. Weininger. 2008. Time, work, and family life: Reconceptualizing gendered time patterns through the case of children's organized activities. *Sociological Forum* 23:419–54.

Lipsitz, L. A. 2005. The elderly people of post-soviet Ukraine: Medical, social, and economic challenges. *Journal of the American Geriatrics Society* 53:2,216–20.

Ma, M.K. 2005. The relation of gender-role classifications to the prosocial and antisocial behavior of Chinese adolescents. *Journal of Genetic Psychology* 166:189–201.

Maume, D. J. 2006. Gender differences in taking vacation time. *Work and Occupations* 33:161–90.

McGinty, K., D. Knox, and M. E. Zusman. 2006. Research report on undergraduate women who prefer a traditional man. Unpublished research created for this text.

McNeely, A., D. Knox, and M. E. Zusman. 2004. Beliefs about men: Gender differences among college students. Poster for Annual Meeting of the Southern Sociological Society, Atlanta, April 16–17.

McNeely, A., D. Knox, and M. E. Zusman. 2005. College student beliefs about women: Some gender differences. *College Student Journal* 39:769–74.

McPherson, M., L. Smith-Lovin, and M. E. Brashears. 2006. Social isolation in America, 1985–2004. *American Sociological Review* 71:353–75.

Mead, M. 1935. *Sex and temperament in three primitive societies.* New York: William Morrow.

Meinhold, J. L., A. Acock, and A. Walker. 2006. The influence of life transition statuses on sibling intimacy and contact in early adulthood. Presented at the National Council on Family Relations Annual meeting in Orlando in 2005.

Meyer-Bahlburg, H. F. L. 2005. Introduction: Gender dysphoria and gender change in persons with intersexuality. *Archives of Sexual Behavior* 34:371–74.

Miller, A. S., and R. Stark. 2002. Gender and religiousness: Can socialization explanations be saved? *American Journal of Sociology* 107:1399–423.

Mirchandani, R. 2005. Postmodernism and sociology: From the epistemological to the empirical. *Sociological Theory* 23:86–115.

Moghadam, V. M. 2002. Patriarchy, the Taliban, and the politics of public space in Afghanistan. *Women's Studies International Forum* 25:19–31.

Monin, J. K., M. S. Clark, and E. P. Lemay. 2008. Communal responsiveness in relationships with female versus male family members. *Journal Sex Roles* 59:176–88.

Monro, S. 2000. Theorizing transgender diversity: Towards a social model of health. *Sexual and Relationship Therapy* 15:33–42.

Moore, O., S. Kreitler, M. Ehrenfeld, and N. Giladi. 2005. Quality of life and gender identity in Parkinson's disease. *Journal of Neural Transmission* 112:1511–22.

Neighbors, L., J. Sobal, C. Liff, and D. Amiraian. 2008. Weighing weight: Trends in body weight evaluation among young adults, 1990 and 2005. *Journal of Sex Roles* 59:68–80.

Parra-Cardona, J. R., D. Córdova, Jr., K. Holtrop, F. A. Villarruel, and E. Wieling. 2008. Shared ancestry, evolving stories: Similar and contrasting life experiences described by foreign born and U.S. born Latino parents. *Family Process* 47:157–73.

Peoples, J. G. 2001.The cultural construction of gender and manhood. In *Men and masculinity: A text reader,* ed. T. F. Cohen, 9–18. Belmont, CA: Wadsworth.

Peters, J. K. 2005. Gender remembered: The ghost of "unisex" past, present, and future. *Women's Studies* 34:67–83.

Pew Research. 2008 The U.S. religious landscape survey. Pew Forum on Religion & Public Life. http://pewresearch.org/pubs/743/united-states-religion.

Pollack, W. S. (with T. Shuster). 2001. *Real boys' voices.* New York: Penguin Books.

Pretorius, E. 2005. Family life in South Africa. In *Families in global perspective,* ed. J. L. Roopnaraine and U. P. Gielen, 363–80. Boston: Pearson Allyn & Bacon.

Probert, B. 2005. "I Just Couldn't Fit It In": Gender and unequal outcomes in academic careers. *Gender, Work & Organization* 12:50–73.

Raj, A., C. Gomez, and J. G. Silverman. 2008. Driven to a fiery death: The tragedy of self-immolation in Afghanistan. *The New England Journal of Medicine* 358:2201–17.

Rivadeneyraa, R., and M. J. Lebob. 2008. The association between television-viewing behaviors and adolescent dating role attitudes and behaviors. *Journal of Adolescence* 31:291–305.

Roopnarine, J. L., P. Bynoe, R. Singh, and R. Simon. 2005. Caribbean families in English-speaking countries. In *Families in global perspective,* ed. J. L. Roopnaraine and U. P. Gielen, 311–29. Boston: Pearson Allyn & Bacon.

Ross, C., D. Knox, and M. Zusman. Forthcoming. "Hey Big Boy": Characteristics of university women who initiate relationships with men. *College Student Journal.*

Royo-Vela, M., J. Aldas-Manzano, I. Kuster, and N. Vila. 2008. Adaptation of marketing activities to cultural and social context: Gender role portrayals and sexism in Spanish commercials. *Sex Roles* 58:379–91.

Skaine, R. 2002. *The women of Afghanistan under the Taliban.* Jefferson, NC: McFarland.

Statistical Abstract of the United States, 2009. 128th ed. Washington, DC: U.S. Bureau of the Census.

Stone, P. 2007. *Opting out?* Berkley: University of California Press.

Sumsion, J. 2005. Male teachers in early childhood education: Issues and case study. *Early Childhood Research Quarterly* 20:109–23.

Taylor, R. L. 2002. Black American families. In *Minority families in the United States: A multicultural perspective,* ed. Ronald L. Taylor, 19–47. Upper Saddle River, NJ: Prentice Hall.

Thompson, M. 2008. America's medicated army. *Time,* July 16, 38–42.

Vail-Smith, K., D. Knox, and M. Zusman. 2007. The lonely college male. *International Journal of Men's Health* 6:273–79.

Walker, R. B., and M. A. Luszcz. 2009. The health and relationship dynamics of late-life couples: a systematic review of the literature. *Ageing and Society* 29:455–81.

Walzer, S. 2008. Redoing gender through divorce. *Journal of Social and Personal Relationships.* 25:5–21.

Ward, C. A. 2001. Models and measurement of psychological androgyny: A cross-cultural extension of theory and research. *Sex Roles: A Journal of Research* 43:529–52.

Welch, V. 2008. *Doctorate recipients from United States universities: Selected Tables 2007.* Chicago: National Opinion Research Center.

Wilcox, W. B., and S. L. Nock. 2006. What's love got to do with it? Equality, equity, commitment and marital quality. *Social Forces* 84:1321–45.

Woodhill, B. M., and C. A. Samuels. 2003. Positive and negative androgyny and their relationship with psychological health and well-being. *Sex Roles* 48:555–65.

An argument is always about what has been made more important than the relationship.

Hugh Prather, counselor

Communication

Contents

1. Before marriage, partners in relationships are focused on "I" issues ("Why don't you spend time with me?"); after marriage, the focus becomes "we" issues ("What about the children?").

2. Mothers and fathers have the same communication styles with their daughters and sons.

3. In a study of 1,341 undergraduates, almost one-third of the men and 20 percent of the women in "monogamous" relationships reported that they have had oral, vaginal, or anal sex with a partner outside their "monogamous" relationship.

4. The "nonverbal" part of communication is more important than the "verbal" part.

5. One's physiological makeup may enhance or impede one's potential to learn communication skills.

Answers: **1.** T **2.** F **3.** T **4.** T **5.** T

While women speak a language of connection and intimacy, men speak a language of status and independence—in effect they speak different genderlects.

Deborah Tannen, *You Just Don't Understand*

Philosopher Arthur Schopenhauer noted the delicate movements of two porcupines huddling together on a cold winter night. They need each other for warmth but must avoid the pain of quills pricking their delicate skin. They continually move and adjust so as to achieve the maximum amount of warmth with the least amount of sticking. So it is in relationships, individuals are constantly seeking the warmth of the emotional relationship yet must be careful to avoid painful conflict.

"Good communication" is regarded as the primary factor responsible for a good relationship. It provides a way for individuals to find that balance between warmth and pain. Individuals report that communication confirms the quality of their relationship ("We can talk all night about anything and everything") or condemns their relationship ("We have nothing to say to each other; we are getting a divorce"). Couples before marriage also have different content themes than couples who are married. Knobloch (2008) noted that people before marriage are focused on individual issues (for example, "Why don't you spend more leisure time with me?") in contrast to married people who couch issues in the context of "we" (for example, "How will we rear our children?"). In this chapter, we examine various issues related to communication and identify some communication principles and skills. We begin by looking at the nature of interpersonal communication.

The Nature of Interpersonal Communication

Communication can be defined as the process of exchanging information and feelings between two or more people. Communication is both verbal and nonverbal. Although most communication is focused on verbal content, most (estimated to be as high as 80 percent) interpersonal communication is nonverbal. **Nonverbal communication** is the "message about the message," the gestures, eye contact, body posture, tone, volume, and rapidity of speech. Even though a person says, "I love you and am faithful to you," crossed arms and lack of eye

Supportive Communication Scale

This scale is designed to assess the degree to which partners experience supportive communication in their relationships. After reading each item, circle the number that best approximates your answer.

0 = strongly disagree (SD)
1 = disagree (D)
2 = undecided (UN)
3 = agree (A)
4 = strongly agree (SA)

		SD	D	UN	A	SA
1.	My partner listens to me when I need someone to talk to.	0	1	2	3	4
2.	My partner helps me clarify my thoughts.	0	1	2	3	4
3.	I can state my feelings without my partner getting defensive.	0	1	2	3	4
4.	When it comes to having a serious discussion, it seems we have little in common (reverse scored).	0	1	2	3	4
5.	I feel put down in a serious conversation with my partner (reverse scored).	0	1	2	3	4
6.	I feel discussing some things with my partner is useless (reverse scored).	0	1	2	3	4
7.	My partner and I understand each other completely.	0	1	2	3	4
8.	We have an endless number of things to talk about.	0	1	2	3	4

Scoring

Look at the numbers you circled. Reverse score the numbers for questions 4, 5, and 6. For example, if you circled a 0, give yourself a 4; if you circled a 3, give yourself a 1, and so on. Add the numbers and divide by 8, the total number of items. The lowest possible score would be 0, reflecting the complete absence of supportive communication; the highest score would be 4, reflecting complete supportive communication. The average score of 94 male partners who took the scale was 3.01; the average score of 94 female partners was 3.07. Thirty-nine percent of the couples were married, 38 percent were single, and 23 percent were living together. The average age was just over 24.

Source

Sprecher, S., S. Metts, B. Burelson, E. Hatfield, and A. Thompson. 1995. Domains of expressive interaction in intimate relationships: Associations with satisfaction and commitment. *Family Relations* 44:203–10. Copyright © 1995 by the National Council on Family Relations.

---

contact will convey a very different meaning than the same words accompanied by a tender embrace and sustained eye-to-eye contact. Bos et al. (2007) found that the greater the congruence between verbal and nonverbal communication, the better. Indeed, when the two are congruent, a person experiences fewer stressful events and lowered depression.

We tend to assign more importance to nonverbal cues than verbal cues (Preston 2005). In effect, we like to hear sweet words but we feel more confident when we see behavior that supports the words. "Show me the money, honey" is a phrase that reflects a partner's focus on behavior rather than words.

One of the by-products of communication is the feeling of intimacy. Individuals differ in their capacity for intimacy. Jane Fonda noted in her autobiography that, "danger lies in intimacy and that far away is safe" (Fonda 2005, 34). She noted that if she tried to be close with her father, he would erupt into an angry rage so that she learned to smile, act happy, and never try to connect or become emotionally intimate with her father for fear of him turning his rage on her.

Having a supportive communicative partner, one who listens and is engaged is a plus for any relationship. The above Self-Assessment allows you to assess the degree to which your relationship is characterized by supportive communication.

Do not worry if others do not understand you. Worry if you do not understand them.

Confucius

Diversity in Other Countries

The culture in which one is reared will influence the meaning of various words. An American woman was dating a man from Iceland. When she asked him, "Would you like to go out to dinner?" he responded, "Yes, maybe." She felt confused by this response and was uncertain whether he wanted to eat out. It was not until she visited his home in Iceland and asked his mother, "Would you like me to set the table?"—to which his mother replied, "Yes, maybe"—that she discovered that "Yes, maybe" means "Yes, definitely."

Conflicts in Relationships

Conflict can be defined as the process of interaction that results when the behavior of one person interferes with the behavior of another. A professor in a marriage and family class said, "If you haven't had a conflict with your partner, you haven't been going together long enough." This section explores the inevitability, desirability, sources, and styles of conflict in relationships.

Inevitability of Conflict

If you are alone this Saturday evening from six o'clock until midnight, you are assured of six conflict-free hours. However, if you plan to be with your partner, roommate, or spouse during that time, the potential for conflict exists. Whether you eat out, where you eat, where you go after dinner, and how long you stay must be negotiated. Although it may be relatively easy for you and your companion to agree on the evening agenda, marriage involves the meshing of desires on an array of issues for potentially sixty years or more. Indeed, conflict is inevitable in any intimate relationship. DeMaria (2005) studied 129 married

"Hold the Phone!"—Cell Phone Use and Partner Reaction*

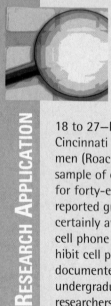

RESEARCH APPLICATION

Cell phones are as common as coffee shops before the recession. It is almost impossible to walk across campus without seeing someone chatting on a cell phone. Kroski (2008) reported that nine out of ten college students in the United States own a cell phone, with Generation Yers—those age 18 to 27—leading the pack. Indeed, the University of Cincinnati provides a free cell phone to incoming freshmen (Roach 2006). Stam and Stanton (2004) asked a sample of college students to give up their cell phones for forty-eight hours and revealed that the students reported great distress in doing so. University faculty are certainly aware of (and sometimes annoyed by) student cell phone use as some have developed policies to prohibit cell phone use in class (Campbell 2006). This study documented the cell phone use among a sample of undergraduates at a large southeastern university. The researchers were particularly interested in gender and racial differences and the degree to which students viewed the use of a cell phone by a partner as a problem.

Methodology and Sample
The study was on responses from 995 undergraduates who answered "yes" or "no" to the question, "I use a cell phone regularly" (from a larger questionnaire of 100 items): 93.8 percent checked "yes" and 6.2 percent checked "no." In comparing men and women and white and black respondents, cross-classification was

conducted to determine any relationships with chi-square utilized to assess statistical significance. The majority of the respondents (67.4 percent) were female, with male participants representing only 32.6 percent of the sample. The median age was 19.

Findings and Discussion
Analysis of the data revealed both gender and racial differences in regard to cell phone usage.

1. *Gender Differences in Use.* Females were more likely than males to report using a cell phone regularly (95 percent versus 91.2 percent) ($p < .03$). Explanations for this finding include that cell phones are technological devices designed to connect people and that females are more relationship-oriented than males. In addition, cell phones may serve as a safety device. Because parents typically fear for the physical safety of their daughters more than sons (in terms of potential sexual assault), they may be more insistent that the former rather than the latter carry a cell phone with them at all times.

2. *Racial Differences in Use.* Whites were more likely than blacks to report using a cell phone regularly (95.1 percent versus 87.7 percent) ($p < .001$). Cell phones are expensive, and some consider them a luxury. Because whites typically have more economic resources than blacks, it comes as no surprise that they would both own and use cell phones more. Per capita, money income of whites and blacks is

couples who signed up for a communication and marriage education workshop presumably designed for couples who were already functioning well and who were there for a "relationship tune-up." Analysis of the data revealed that the couples were highly distressed, conflicted, devitalized, and lacked communication skills. Hence, one need not be on the verge of divorce in the office of a marriage counselor to profit from learning effective communication skills. Conflict in regard to communication may also occur when two lovers are talking and one answers a cell phone call and begins to talk (see the Research Application on page 110).

The person who angers you conquers you.

Elizabeth Kenny, nurse/health administrator in Australia

Benefits of Conflict

Conflict can be healthy and productive for a couple's relationship. Ignoring an issue may result in the partners becoming increasingly resentful and dissatisfied with the relationship. Indeed, not talking about a concern can do more damage to a relationship than bringing up the issue and discussing it (Campbell 2005). Couples in trouble are not those who disagree but those who never discuss their disagreements.

$27, 821 and $17,902, respectively (*Statistical Abstract of the United States, 2009*, Table 682).

3. *Racial Differences in Reactions to Use by Romantic Partner.* Blacks were twice as likely as whites to be annoyed by their partner using a cell phone when the two were together. When asked to disagree or agree to the statement, "I would not be bothered if my partner talked on a cell phone when we are together," 25.1 percent of blacks compared to 12.8 percent of whites disagreed (p < .001). One explanation may be that, as noted earlier, black people are less likely to own and to use a cell phone. Hence, when two black individuals are together, the one not using the cell phone may view the other person as having access to more resources. Hence, one may feel jealous and irritated that the partner has technology that may not be affordable to the other. When two whites are together, both are more likely to afford a cell phone so that the economic differential is not operative. Further research is needed to confirm if this interpretation is accurate.

Black females were also more likely to be upset by their romantic partners' cell phone use than white females. Although the number of black females in the sample was too low to provide a definitive conclusion on this issue, one interpretation suggested by a black female follows:

> *Honestly, I believe blacks are less tolerant than whites when their partners use a cell phone in their*

presence because it is seen by the black woman as an act of disrespect. There is an expectation of how quality time should be spent, and the cell phone completely interrupts that time.

Sources

Aoki, K., and E. J. Downes. 2003. An analysis of young people's use of and attitudes toward cell phones. *Telematics and Informatics* 20:349–64.

Ashforth, B. E., G. E. Kreiner, and M. Fugate. 2000. All in a day's work: Boundaries and micro role transitions. *Academy of Management Review* 25:472–91.

Campbell, S. W. 2006. Perceptions of mobile phones in college classrooms: Ringing, cheating, and classroom policies. *Communication Education* 55:280–94.

Chesley, N. 2005. Blurring boundaries? Linking technology use, spillover, individual distress and family satisfaction. *Journal of Marriage and the Family* 67:1237–48.

Roach, R. 2006. University of Cincinnati offers free cell phones to incoming freshmen. *Diverse Issues in Higher Education* 23:31.

Stam, K. R., and J. M. Stanton. 2004. Examining personal and cultural assumptions about information technology using a technology abstinence exercise. *Journal of Information Systems Education* 15:87–97.

Statistical Abstract of the United States, 2009. 128th ed. Washington, DC: U.S. Bureau of the Census.

*Adapted from Beaver, T., D. Knox, and M. Zusman. 2009. "Hold the Phone!" Cell phone use and romantic partner reaction. Poster, Eastern Sociological Society, Baltimore, March.

By the time you swear you're his,
Shivering and sighing,
And he vows his passion is
Infinite, undying—
Lady, make a note of this:
One of you is lying.

Dorothy Parker, American writer/poet

Sources of Conflict

Conflict has numerous sources, some of which are easily recognized, whereas others are hidden inside the web of marital interaction.

1. Behavior. Stanley et al. (2002) noted that money was the issue over which a national sample of couples reported that they argued the most. The behavioral expression of a money issue might include how the partner spends money (excessively), the lack of communication about spending (for example, does not consult the partner), and the target (for example, items considered unnecessary by the partner). However, marital conflict is not limited to behavioral money issues. Stanley et al. (2002) found that remarried couples argued most about the children (for example, rules for and discipline of). In a sample of 105 older married couples (average age, 69), the most often reported behavior problem was related to leisure activities (Henry et al. 2005). One 67-year-old wife noted, "My spouse watches too much football and after 48 years, I get upset" (p. 249).

2. Cognitions and perceptions. Aside from your partner's actual behavior, your cognitions and perceptions of a behavior can be a source of satisfaction or dissatisfaction. One husband complained that his wife "had boxes of coupons everywhere and always kept the house a wreck." The wife made the husband aware that she saved $100 on their grocery bill every week and asked him to view the boxes and the mess as "saving money." He changed his view and the clutter ceased to be a problem.

3. Value differences. Because you and your partner have had different socialization experiences, you may also have different values—about religion (one feels religion is a central part of life; the other does not), money (one feels uncomfortable being in debt; the other has the buy-now-pay-later philosophy), in-laws (one feels responsible for parents when they are old; the other does not), and children (number, timing, discipline). The effect of value differences depends less on the degree of the difference than on the degree of rigidity with which each partner holds values. Dogmatic and rigid thinkers, feeling threatened by value disagreement, may try to eliminate alternative views and thus produce more conflict. Partners who recognize the inevitability of difference may consider the positives of an alternative view and move toward acceptance.

Spouses who have fun together have fewer conflicts because they value each other's companionship and don't want to interrupt the positive interaction (see opening quote of chapter).

Authors

Chapter 4 Communication

When both partners do this, the relationship takes priority and the value differences suddenly become less important.

4. *Inconsistent rules.* Partners in all relationships develop a set of rules to help them function smoothly. These unwritten but mutually understood rules include what time you are supposed to be home after work, whether you should call if you are going to be late, how often you can see friends alone, and when and how to make love. Conflict results when the partners disagree on the rules or when inconsistent rules develop in the relationship. For example, one wife expected her husband to take a second job so they could afford a new car, but she also expected him to spend more time at home with the family.

5. *Leadership ambiguity.* Unless a couple has an understanding about which partner will make decisions in which area (for example, the wife may make decisions about money management, and the husband may make decisions about rearing the children), unnecessary conflict may result. Whereas some couples may want to discuss certain issues, others may want to develop a clear specification of roles.

Styles of Conflict

Spouses develop various styles of conflict. If you were watching a videotape of various spouses disagreeing over the same issue, you would notice at least six styles of conflict. These styles have been described by Greeff and De Bruyne (2000) as the following:

Competing Style The partners are both assertive and uncooperative. Both try to force their way on the other so that there is a winner and a loser. A couple arguing over whether to discipline a child with a spanking or time-out would resolve the argument with the dominant partner's forcing a decision.

Collaborating Style The respective partners are both assertive and cooperative. Both partners express their views and cooperate to find a solution. A spanking, time-out, or just talking to the child might resolve the previous issue, but both partners would be satisfied with the resolution.

Compromising Style Here there would be an intermediate solution: both partners would find a middle ground they could live with—perhaps spanking the child for serious infractions such as playing with matches in the house and imposing a time-out for talking back.

Avoiding Style The partners are neither assertive nor cooperative. They would avoid a confrontation and let either parent control the disciplining of the child. Thus the child might be both spanked and put in time-out. Marchand and Hock (2000) noted that depressed spouses were particularly likely to use avoidance as a conflict-resolution strategy.

Accommodating Style The respective partners are not assertive in their positions, but each accommodates to the other's point of view. Each attempts to soothe the other and to avoid conflict. Although the goal of this style is to rise above the conflict and keep harmony in the relationship, fundamental feelings about the "rightness" of one's own approach may be maintained.

Parallel Style Both partners deny, ignore, and retreat from addressing a problem issue. "Don't talk about it, and it will go away" is the theme of this conflict style. Gaps begin to develop in the relationship; neither partner feels free to talk, and both believe that they are misunderstood. They eventually become involved in separate activities rather than spending time together.

Greeff and De Bruyne (2000) studied fifty-seven couples who had been married at least ten years and found that the collaborating style was associated with

Force is all-conquering, but its victories are short-lived.

Abraham Lincoln

the highest level of marital and spousal satisfaction. The competitive style, used by either partner, was associated with the lowest level of marital satisfaction. Regardless of the style of conflict, partners who say positive things to each other at a ratio of 5:1 (positives to negatives) seem to stay together (Gottman 1994).

Principles and Techniques of Effective Communication

People who want effective communication in their relationship follow various principles and techniques, including the following:

1. *Make communication a priority.* Communicating effectively implies making communication an important priority in a couple's relationship. When communication is a priority, partners make time for it to occur in a setting without interruptions: they are alone; they do not answer the phone; and they turn the television off. Making communication a priority results in the exchange of more information between partners, which increases the knowledge each partner has about the other.

Negative relationship outcomes occur when partners do not prioritize communication with each other but are passionately and obsessively interacting with others via the Internet. Seguin-Levesque et al. (2003) found that the use of the Internet is not destructive per se but the obsessive passion of involvement with the Internet.

2. *Establish and maintain eye contact.* Shakespeare noted that a person's eyes are the "mirrors to the soul." Partners who look at each other when they are talking not only communicate an interest in each other but also are able to gain information about the partner's feelings and responses to what is being said. Not looking at your partner may be interpreted as lack of interest and prevents you from observing nonverbal cues.

3. *Ask open-ended questions.* When your goal is to find out your partner's thoughts and feelings about an issue, using **open-ended questions** is best. Such questions (for example, "How do you feel about me?") encourage your partner to give an answer that contains a lot of information. **Closed-ended questions** (for example, "Do you love me?"), which elicit a one-word answer such as *yes* or *no*, do not provide the opportunity for the partner to express a range of thoughts and feelings.

"Honey, when you say we can't communicate...
what exactly do you mean?"

4. *Use reflective listening.* Effective communication requires being a good listener. One of the skills of a good listener is the ability to use the technique of **reflective listening**, which involves paraphrasing or restating what the person has said to you while being sensitive to what the partner is feeling. For example, suppose you ask your partner, "How was your day?" and your partner responds, "I felt exploited today at work because I went in early and stayed late and a memo from my new boss said that future bonuses would be eliminated because of a company takeover." Listening to what your partner is both saying and feeling, you might respond, "You feel frustrated because you really worked hard and felt unappreciated . . . and it's going to get worse."

Reflective listening serves the following functions: (1) it creates the feeling for speakers that they are being listened to and are being understood; and (2) it increases the accuracy of the listener's understanding of what the speaker is saying. If a reflective statement does not accurately reflect what a speaker thinks and feels, the speaker can correct the inaccuracy by restating the thoughts and feelings.

An important quality of reflective statements is that they are nonjudgmental. For example, suppose two lovers are arguing about spending time with their respective friends and one says, "I'd like to spend one night each week with my friends and not feel guilty about it." The partner may respond by making a statement that is judgmental (critical or evaluative), such as those exemplified in Table 4.1. Judgmental responses serve to punish or criticize people for what they think, feel, or want and often result in frustration and resentment.

Table 4.1 also provides several examples of nonjudgmental reflective statements.

5. *Use "I" statements.* **"I" statements** focus on the feelings and thoughts of the communicator without making a judgment on others. Because "I" statements are a clear and nonthreatening way of expressing what you want and how you feel, they are likely to result in a positive change in the listener's behavior.

In contrast, **"you" statements** blame or criticize the listener and often result in increasing negative feelings and behavior in the relationship. For example, suppose you are angry with your partner for being late. Rather than say, "You are always late and irresponsible" (which is a "you" statement), you might respond with, "I get upset when you are late and will feel better if you call me when you will be delayed." The latter focuses on your feelings and a desirable future behavior rather than blaming the partner for being late.

6. *Touch.* Hertenstein et al. (2007) identified the various meanings of touch such as conveying emotion, attachment, bonding, compliance, power, and intimacy. The researchers also emphasized the importance of using touch as a

Marriage is like life in this—that it is a field of battle and not a bed of roses.

Robert Louis Stevenson

Table 4.1 Judgmental and Nonjudgmental Responses to A Partner's Saying, "I'd Like to Spend One Evening a Week with my Friends"

Nonjudgmental, Reflective Statements	Judgmental Statements
You value your friends and want to maintain good relationships with them.	You only think about what you want.
You think it is healthy for us to be with our friends some of the time.	Your friends are more important to you than I am.
You really enjoy your friends and want to spend some time with them.	You just want a night out so that you can meet someone new.
You think it is important that we not abandon our friends just because we are involved.	You just want to get away so you can drink.
You think that our being apart one night each week will make us even closer.	You are selfish.

Regarding touch, this couple notes that, "We can't keep our hands off each other."

My wife said I don't listen—at least I think that's what she said.

Laurence Peter, *Humorist*

mechanism of nonverbal communication to emphasize one's point or meaning.

7. Use "soft" emotions. Sanford (2007) identified "hard" emotions (for example, angry or aggravated) or "soft" emotions (sad or hurt) displayed during conflict. The use of hard emotions resulted in an escalation of negative communication, whereas the display of "soft" emotions resulted in more benign communication and an increased feeling regarding the importance of resolving interpersonal conflict.

8. *Avoid negative expressivity.* Rayer and Volling (2005) studied the levels of emotional expressivity (both positive and negative) and found that negative expressivity had a strong impact on marital love and conflict. Because intimate partners are capable of hurting each other so intensely, be careful how you criticize or communicate disapproval to your partner.

9. *Say positive things about your partner.* A team of researchers found that emotional expressiveness was strongly related to marital adjustment, particularly when coupled with the suppression of negative statements (Ingoldsby et al. 2005).

People like to hear others say positive things about them. These positive statements may be in the form of compliments (for example, "You look terrific!") or appreciation ("Thanks for putting gas in the car"). Gable et al. (2003) asked fifty-eight heterosexual dating couples to monitor their interaction with one another. The respondents observed that they were overwhelmingly positive, at a five-to-one ratio.

10. *Tell your partner what you want.* Focus on what you want rather than on what you don't want. Rather than say, "You always leave the bathroom a wreck," an alternative might be "Please hang up your towel after you take a shower." Rather than say, "You never call me when you are going to be late," say "Please call me when you are going to be late."

11. *Stay focused on the issue.* **Branching** refers to going out on different limbs of an issue rather than staying focused on the issue. If you are discussing the overdrawn checkbook, stay focused on the checkbook. To remind your partner that he or she is equally irresponsible when it comes to getting things repaired or doing housework is to get off the issue of the checkbook. Stay focused.

12. *Make specific resolutions to disagreements.* To prevent the same issues or problems from recurring, agreeing on what each partner will do in similar circumstances in the future is important. For example, if going to a party together results in one partner's drinking too much and drifting off with someone else, what needs to be done in the future to ensure an enjoyable evening together? In this example, a specific resolution would be to decide how many drinks the partner will have within a given time period.

13. *Give congruent messages.* **Congruent messages** are those in which the verbal and nonverbal behaviors match. A person who says, "Okay, you're right" and smiles while embracing the partner is communicating a congruent message.

In contrast, the same words accompanied by leaving the room and slamming the door communicate a very different message. Walther et al. (2005) compared affect in online and face-to-face interaction and found few differences.

14. *Share power.* One of the greatest sources of dissatisfaction in a relationship is a power imbalance and conflict over power (Kurdek 1994). **Power** is the ability to impose one's will on the partner and to avoid being influenced by the partner. Expressions of power are numerous and include the following:

Withdrawal (not speaking to the partner)

Guilt induction ("How could you ask me to do this?")

Being pleasant ("Kiss me and help me move the sofa.")

Negotiation ("We can go to the movie if we study for a couple of hours before we go.")

Deception (running up credit card debts of which the partner is unaware)

Blackmail ("I'll find someone else if you won't have sex with me.")

Physical abuse or verbal threats ("I'll kill you if you leave.")

Criticism ("I can't think of anything good about you.")

In general, the spouse with the more prestigious occupation, higher income, and more education exerts the greater influence on family decisions. Indeed, Dunbar and Burgoon (2005) noted that, the greater the perception of one's own power, the more dominant one was in conversation with the partner.

However, power may also take the form of love and sex. The person in the relationship who loves less and who needs sex less has enormous power over the partner who is very much in love and who is dependent on the partner for sex. This pattern reflects the principle of least interest we discussed earlier in the text.

15. *Keep the process of communication going.* Communication includes both content (verbal and nonverbal information) and process (interaction). It is important not to allow difficult content to shut down the communication process (Turner 2005). To ensure that the process continues, the partners should focus on the fact that sharing information is essential and reinforce each other for keeping the process alive. For example, if your partner tells you something that you do that bothers him or her, it is important to thank him or her for telling you that rather than becoming defensive. In this way, your partner's feelings about you stay out in the open rather than hidden behind a wall of resentment. Otherwise, if you punish such disclosure because you don't like the content, subsequent disclosure will stop.

Although effective communication skills can be learned, Robbins (2005) noted that physiological capacities may enhance or impede the acquisition of these skills. She noted that people with attention-deficit/hyperactivity disorder (ADHD) might have deficiencies in basic communication and social skills. Being able to communicate effectively is valuable. Rosof (2005) found that positive couple communication is related to feelings of individual fulfillment in an intimate relationship. Not only is a relationship enhanced by healthy communication, but also the individuals involved in the relationship benefit.

Self-Disclosure, Honesty, and Lying

Shakespeare noted in Macbeth that "the false face must hide what the false heart doth know," suggesting that withholding and dishonesty may affect the way one feels about one's self and relationships with others. All of us make choices, consciously or unconsciously, about the degree to which we disclose, are honest, and/or lie.

Self-Disclosure in Intimate Relationships

One aspect of intimacy in relationships is self-disclosure, which involves revealing personal information and feelings about oneself to another person. McKenna et al. (2002) found that a positive function of meeting online is that people were better able to express themselves and disclose on the Internet than in person. Gibbs et al. (2006) also noted that people seeking a partner on the Internet were more honest about their disclosures if they had the goal of a long-term relationship.

Relationships become more stable when individuals disclose themselves—their formative years, previous relationships (positive and negative), experiences of elation and sadness or depression, and goals (achieved and thwarted). We noted in the discussion of love in Chapter 2 that self-disclosure is a psychological condition necessary for the development of love. To the degree that you disclose yourself to another, you invest yourself in and feel closer to that person. People who disclose nothing are investing nothing and remain aloof. One way to encourage disclosure in one's partner is to make disclosures about one's own life and then ask about the partner's life. Patford (2000) found that the higher the level of disclosure, the more committed the spouses were to each other.

Honesty in Intimate Relationships

Lying is pervasive in American society. Presidential candidate John Edwards repeatedly lied about his affair with Rielle Hunter, a member of his campaign staff, until he was caught meeting her at a hotel. Investment consultant Bernie Madoff lied to 4,800 clients over twenty-five years and stole over $50 billion from them. Baseball hitter Alex Rodriguez ("A-Rod") lied to investigators about steroid use. Politicians routinely lie to citizens ("Lobbyists can't buy my vote"), and citizens lie to the government (via cheating on taxes). Teachers lie to students ("The test will be easy"), and students lie to teachers ("I studied all night"). Parents lie to their children ("It won't hurt"), and children lie to their parents about where they have been, whom they were with, and what they did. Dating partners lie to each other ("I've had a couple of previous sex partners"), women lie to men ("I had an orgasm"), and men lie to women ("I'll call"). The price of lying is high—distrust and alienation. A student in class wrote:

> At this moment in my life I do not have any love relationship. I find college dating to be very hard. The guys here lie to you about anything and you wouldn't know the truth. I find it's mostly about sex here and having a good time before you really have to get serious. That is fine, but that is just not what I am all about.

In addition to lying to gain sexual access is the behavior of cheating—having sex with someone else while involved in a relationship with a romantic partner. When 1,319 undergraduates were asked if they had cheated on a partner they were involved with, 37.4 percent responded that they had done so (Knox and Zusman 2009). McAlister et al. (2005) noted that extradyadic activity (defined as kissing or "sexual activity") among young adults who were dating could be predicted. Those young adults who had a high number of previous sexual partners, who were impulsive, who were not satisfied in their current relationship, and who had attractive alternatives were more vulnerable to being unfaithful.

Forms of Dishonesty and Deception

Dishonesty and deception take various forms. In addition to telling an outright lie, people may exaggerate the truth, pretend, conceal the truth, or withhold information. Regarding the latter, in virtually every relationship, partners may not share things with each other about themselves or their past. We often withhold information or keep secrets in our intimate relationships for what we believe are good reasons—we believe that we are protecting our partners from

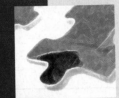
What if an Old Lover Contacts You?

Partners may differ in terms of how they would respond to an old lover who contacts them. Although some may not respond at all to an e-mail or letter, others may e-mail, call, and meet without the current partner's knowledge. Still others may make the partner aware of the contact and negotiate an outcome. One scenario is to meet the person in a public place with a time frame (for example, lunch at McDonalds). Another is that the old lover may be made aware of the new relationship and given the choice to meet the partner (for example, come to the apartment for lunch). To increase the security and strength of the new relationship, include the current partner in what is happening with the "old love surfacing." To keep the contact with the old love secret is to invite escalation of the relationship, deception, and eventual relationship disaster.

anxiety or hurt feelings, protecting ourselves from criticism and rejection, and protecting our relationships from conflict and disintegration. Finkenauer and Hazam (2000) found that happy relationships depend on withholding information. The researchers contend, "Nobody wants to be criticized (for example, 'You're really fat') or talk about topics that are known to be conflictive (for example, 'You should not have spent that much money')." Ennis et al. (2008) noted three types of lies: (1) self-centered to protect one's self ("I didn't do it."); (2) oriented to protect another ("Your hair looks good today."); or (3) altruistic to protect a third party ("She didn't do it.").

> *Marriage is one long conversation chequered by disputes.*
>
> Robert Louis Stevenson, novelist and poet

PERSONAL CHOICES

How Much Do I Tell My Partner about My Past?
Because of the fear of HIV infection and other sexually transmitted infections (STIs), some partners want to know the details of each other's previous sex life, including how many partners they have had sex with and in what contexts. Those who are asked will need to decide whether to disclose the requested information, which may include one's sexual orientation, present or past sexually transmitted diseases, and any sexual proclivities or preferences the partner might find bizarre (for example, bondage and discipline). Ample evidence suggests that individuals are sometimes dishonest with regard to the sexual information they provide to their partners. We have noted that "number of previous sexual partners" is the most frequent lie undergraduates report telling each other.

In deciding whether or not to talk honestly about your past to your partner, you may want to consider the following questions: How important is it to your partner to know about your past? Do you want your partner to tell you (honestly) about her or his past?

Lying in College Student Relationships
Lying is epidemic in college student relationships. In response to the statement, "I have lied to a person I was involved with," 77 percent of 1,319 undergraduates reported "yes" (Knox and Zusman 2009). Almost one in four (23.9 percent) of 1,319 reported having lied to a partner about their previous number of sexual partners (ibid.).

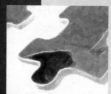
What if You Discover Your Partner Is Cheating on You?

Because cheating does occur, to deny that this will ever happen in one's own relationship may be unrealistic. Reactions will vary from immediate termination of the relationship forever, to taking a break from the relationship, to revenge by cheating also. One scenario is to discuss the dishonesty with the partner to discover any relationship deficits that may be corrected. Another is to discuss the acceptability of the behavior in terms of frequency. Does everyone make a mistake sometimes and this is to be overlooked, or is the dishonesty of a chronic variety that will continue? Most individuals are devastated to discover a betrayal but find a way to continue the relationship. This reaction is functional only if the dishonesty is not chronic. To be so is to take advantage of the forgiveness of the partner and to permanently infuse the relationship with distrust and deceit—a recipe for disaster.

The person who forgives, ends the quarrel.

Nixon Waterman, author

Even in "monogamous" relationships, there is considerable lying. Vail-Smith et al. (forthcoming) found that 27.2 percent of the males and 19.8 percent of the females of 1,341 undergraduates reported having oral, vaginal, or anal sex outside of a relationship that their partner considered monogamous. People most likely to cheat in these "monogamous" relationships were men over the age of 20, those who were binge drinkers, members of a fraternity, male NCAA athletes, and those who reported that they were "nonreligious." The data suggest a need for people in "committed" relationships to reconsider their risk of sexually transmitted infections and to protect themselves via condom usage.

In addition, one of the ways in which college students deceive their partners is by failing to disclose that they have an STI. Approximately 25 percent of college students will contract an STI while they are in college (Purkett 2009). Because the potential to harm an unsuspecting partner is considerable, should we have a national social policy regarding such disclosure?

Gender Differences in Communication

Numerous jokes address the differences between how women and men communicate. One anonymous quote on the Internet follows:

> When a woman says, "Sure . . . go ahead," what she means is "I don't want you to." When a woman says, "I'm sorry," what she means is "You'll be sorry." When a woman says, "I'll be ready in a minute," what she means is "Kick off your shoes and start watching a football game on TV."

Women and men differ in their approach to and patterns of communication. Women are more communicative about relationship issues, view a situation emotionally, and initiate discussions about relationship problems. Deborah Tannen (1990; 2006) is a specialist in communication. She observed that, to women, conversations are negotiations for closeness in which they try "to seek and give confirmations and support, and to reach consensus" (1990, 25). A woman's goal is to preserve intimacy and avoid isolation. To men, conversations are about winning and achieving the upper hand.

Should One Partner Disclose Human Immunodeficiency Virus (HIV)/Sexually Transmitted Infection (STI) Status to Another?

An estimated 25 percent of undergraduates report that they have or have had an STI. Individuals often struggle over whether or how to tell a partner if they have an STI, including HIV infection. If a person in a committed relationship acquires an STI, then that individual, or the partner, may have been unfaithful and have had sex with someone outside the relationship. Thus, disclosure about an STI may also mean confessing one's own infidelity or confronting the partner about the possible infidelity. (However, the infection may have occurred prior to the current relationship but gone undetected.) Individuals who have an STI and who are beginning a new relationship face a different set of concerns. Will their new partner view them negatively? Will they want to continue the relationship? One Internet ad began, "I have herpes—Now that that is out of the way. . . ."

Although telling a partner about having an STI may be difficult and embarrassing, avoiding disclosure or lying about having an STI represents a serious ethical violation. The responsibility to inform a partner that one has an STI—before having sex with that partner—is a moral one. But there are also legal reasons for disclosing one's sexual health condition to a partner. If you have an STI and you do not tell your partner, you may be liable for damages if you transmit it to your partner. Ayres and Baker (2004) proposed a new crime, reckless sexual conduct, of which a person would be guilty for not using a condom the first time of intercourse with a person. The penalty for the perpetrator would be three months in prison.

Khalsa (2006) noted that reporting HIV infection and acquired immunodeficiency syndrome (AIDS) is mandatory in most states, although partner notification laws vary from state to state. New York has a strong partner notification law that requires health care providers to either notify any partners the infected person names or to forward the information about partners to the Department of Health, where public health officers notify the partners that they have been exposed to an STI and to schedule an appointment for STI testing. The privacy of the infected individual is protected by not revealing names to the partner being notified of potential infection. In cases where the infected person refuses to identify partners, standard partner notification laws require doctors to undertake notification without cooperation if they know of the sexual partner or spouse.

Your Opinion?

1. What percentage of undergraduates (who knowingly has an STI) would have sex with another undergraduate and not tell the partner?
2. What do you think the penalty should be for deliberately exposing a person to an STI?
3. What partner notification law do you recommend?

Sources

Ayres, I., and K. Baker. 2004. A separate crime of reckless sex. *Yale Law School, Public Law Working Paper No. 80.*

Khalsa, A. M. 2006. Preventive counseling, screening, and therapy for the patient with newly diagnosed HIV infection. *American Family Physician* 73:271–80.

PERSONAL CHOICES

How Close Do You Want to Be?

Individuals differ in their capacity for and interest in an emotionally close and disclosing relationship. These preferences may vary over time; the partners may want closeness at some times and distance at other times. Individuals frequently choose partners according to an "emotional fit"—agreement about the amount of closeness they desire in their relationship. Haas and Stafford (2005) noted that one of the ways both heterosexual and homosexual couples maintain emotional closeness is through task sharing. Alexandrov (2005) found a link between couple attachment and marital quality.

In addition to emotional closeness, some partners prefer a pattern of physical presence and complete togetherness (the current buzzword is *codependency*), in which they spend all of their leisure and discretionary time. Others enjoy time alone and time with other friends and do not want to feel burdened by the demands of a partner with high companionship needs. Partners might consider their own choices and those of their partners in regard to emotional and spatial closeness.

Women also tend to approach a situation emotionally. A husband might react to a seriously ill child by putting pressure on the wife to be mature about the situation (for example, stop crying) and by encouraging stoicism (asking her not to feel sorry for herself). Wives, on the other hand, want their husbands to be more emotional (by asking them to cry to show that they really care that their child is ill). Mothers and fathers also speak differently to their children. Shinn and O'Brien (2008) observed the interactions between parents and their third grade children and found that mothers used more affiliative (relationship) speech than fathers, and fathers used more assertive speech than mothers. No sex differences in children's speech were found, suggesting that these differences do not emerge until later.

Women disclose more in their relationships than men do (Gallmeier et al. 1997). In this study of 360 undergraduates, women were more likely to disclose information about previous love relationships, previous sexual relationships, their love feelings for the partner, and what they wanted for the future of the relationship. They also wanted their partners to reciprocate their (the women's) disclosure, but such disclosure was not forthcoming. Punyanunt-Carter (2006) confirmed that female college students are more likely to disclose than are male college students.

Behringer (2005) found that in spite of the fact that women and men may have different communication foci, they both value openness, honesty, respect, humor, and resolution as principal components of good communication. They also each endeavor to create a common reality. Hence, although spouses may be on different pages, they are reading the same book.

Theories Applied to Relationship Communication

Symbolic interactionism and social exchange are theories that help to explain the communication process.

Symbolic Interactionism

Interactionists examine the process of communication between two actors in terms of the meanings each attaches to the actions of the other. Definition of the situation, the looking-glass self, and taking the role of the other (discussed in Chapter 1) are all relevant to understanding how partners communicate. With regard to resolving a conflict over how to spend the semester break (for example, vacation alone or go to see parents), the respective partners must negotiate their definitions of the situation (is it about their time together as a couple or their loyalty to their parents?). The looking-glass self involves looking at each other and seeing the reflected image of someone who is loved and cared for and someone with whom a productive resolution is sought. Taking the role of the other involves each partner's understanding the other's logic and feelings about how to spend the break.

Social Exchange

Exchange theorists suggest that the partners' communication can be described as a ratio of rewards to costs. Rewards are positive exchanges, such as compliments, compromises, and agreements. Costs refer to negative exchanges, such as critical remarks, complaints, and attacks. When the rewards are high and the costs are low, the outcome is likely to be positive for both partners (profit). When the costs are high and the rewards low, neither may be satisfied with the outcome (loss).

When discussing how to spend the semester break, the partners are continually in the process of exchange—not only in the words they use but also in the way they use them. If the communication is to continue, both partners need to feel acknowledged for their points of view and to feel a sense of legitimacy and respect. Communication in abusive relationships is characterized by the parties criticizing and denigrating each other, which usually results in a shutdown of the communication process.

Make all of your relationships win win.

Jack Turner, clinical psychologist

Fighting Fair: Seven Steps in Conflict Resolution

When a disagreement ensues, it is important to establish rules for fighting that will leave the partners and their relationship undamaged after the disagreement. Such guidelines for fair fighting include not calling each other names, not bringing up past misdeeds, not attacking each other, and not beginning a heated discussion late at night. In some cases, a good night's sleep has a way of altering how a situation is viewed and may even result in the problem no longer being an issue.

Fighting fairly also involves keeping the interaction focused, respective, and moving toward a win-win outcome. If recurring issues are not discussed and resolved, conflict may create tension and distance in the relationship, with the result that the partners stop talking, stop spending time together, and stop being intimate. A conflictual, unsatisfactory marriage is similar to divorce in terms of its impact on the diminished psychological, social, and physical well-being of the partners (Hetherington 2003). Developing and using skills for fair fighting and conflict resolution are critical for the maintenance of a good relationship. Resolving issues via communication is not easy. Rhoades et al. (2009) noted that relationship partners who decided to live together to test their relationship noted that communication was difficult or negative.

Howard Markman is head of the Center for Marital and Family Studies at the University of Denver. He and his colleagues have been studying 150 couples at yearly intervals (beginning before marriage) to determine those factors most responsible for marital success. They have found that communication skills that reflect the ability to handle conflict, which they call "constructive arguing," are the single biggest predictor of marital success over time (Marano 1992). According to Markman, "Many people believe that the causes of marital problems are the differences between people and problem areas such as money, sex, children. However, our findings indicate it is not the differences that are important, but how these differences and problems are handled, particularly early in marriage" (Marano 1992, 53). The following sections identify fair fighting and steps for resolving interpersonal conflict.

Address Recurring, Disturbing Issues

Addressing issues in a relationship is important. As noted earlier, couples who stack resentments rather than discuss conflictual issues do no service to their relationship. Indeed, the healthiest response to feeling upset about a partner's behavior is to engage the partner in a discussion about the behavior. Not to do so is to let the negative feelings fester, which will result in emotional and physical withdrawal from the relationship. For example, Pam is jealous that Mark spends more time with other people at parties than with her. "When we go someplace together," she blurts out, "he drops me to disappear with someone else for two hours." Her jealousy is spreading to other areas of their relationship. "When we are walking down the street and he turns his head to look at another woman, I get furious." If Pam and Mark don't discuss her feelings about Mark's behavior, their relationship may deteriorate as a result of a negative response cycle: He looks at another woman and she gets angry; he gets angry at her getting angry and finds that he is even more attracted to other women; she gets angrier because he escalates his looking at other women, and so on.

To bring the matter up, Pam might say, "I feel jealous when you spend more time with other women at parties than with me. I need some help in dealing with these feelings." By expressing her concern in this way, she has identified the problem from her perspective and asked her partner's cooperation in handling it.

When discussing difficult relationship issues, it is important to avoid attacking, blaming, or being negative. Such reactions reduce the motivation of the partner to talk about an issue and thus reduce the probability of a positive outcome.

Using good timing in discussing difficult issues with your partner is also important. In general, it is best to discuss issues or conflicts when (1) you are alone with your partner in private rather than in public, (2) you and your partner have ample time to talk, and (3) you and your partner are rested and feeling generally good (avoid discussing conflict issues when one of you is tired, upset, or under unusual stress).

Identify New Desired Behaviors

Dealing with conflict is more likely to result in resolution if the partners focus on what they *want* rather than what they *don't want*. For example, rather than tell Mark she doesn't want him to spend so much time with other women at parties, Pam might tell him that she wants him to spend more time with her at parties.

Identify Perceptions to Change

Rather than change behavior, changing one's perception of a behavior may be easier and quicker. Rather than expect one's partner to always be "on time," it may be easier to drop the expectation that one's partner be on time and to stop being mad about something that doesn't matter. Pam might also decide that it does not matter that Mark looks at and talks to other women. If she feels secure in his love for her, the behavior is inconsequential.

Summarize Your Partner's Perspective

We often assume that we know what our partner thinks and why he or she does things. Sometimes we are wrong. Rather than assume how our partner thinks and feels about a particular issue, we might ask open-ended questions in an effort to learn our partner's thoughts and feelings about a particular situation.

Pam's words to Mark might be, "What is it like for you when we go to parties?" and "How do you feel about my jealousy?" Once your partner has shared thoughts about an issue with you, summarizing your partner's perspective in a nonjudgmental way is important. After Mark has told Pam how he feels about their being at parties together, she can summarize his perspective by saying, "You feel that I cling to you more than I should, and you would like me to let you wander around without feeling like you're making me angry." (She may not agree with his view, but she knows exactly what it is—and Mark knows that she knows.) In addition, Mark should summarize Pam's view—"You enjoy our being together and prefer that we hang relatively close to each other when we go to parties. You do not want me off in a corner talking to another girl or dancing."

Generate Alternative Win-Win Solutions

Looking for win-win solutions to conflicts is imperative. Solutions in which one person wins means that one person is not getting needs met. As a result, the person who loses may develop feelings of resentment, anger, hurt, and hostility toward the winner and may even look for ways to get even. In this way, the winner is also a loser. In intimate relationships, one winner really means two losers.

Authors

This couple notes, "We are both artists and specialize in metal sculpting so we feel it is easy to stay connected and keep our communication channels open and clear."

Generating win-win solutions to interpersonal conflict often requires **brainstorming.** The technique of brainstorming involves suggesting as many alternatives as possible without evaluating them. Brainstorming is crucial to conflict resolution because it shifts the partners' focus from criticizing each other's perspective to working together to develop alternative solutions.

With our colleagues (Knox et al. 1995), we studied the degree to which 200 college students who were involved in ongoing relationships were involved in win-win, win-lose, and lose-lose relationships. Descriptions of the various relationships follow:

Win-win relationships are those in which conflict is resolved so that each partner derives benefits from the resolution. For example, suppose a couple have a limited amount of money and disagree on whether to spend it on eating out or on seeing a current movie. One possible win-win solution might be for the couple to eat a relatively inexpensive dinner and rent a movie.

An example of a **win-lose solution** would be for one of the partners to get what he or she wanted (eat out or go to a movie), with the other partner getting nothing of what he or she wanted. Caughlin and Ramey (2005) studied demand-and-withdraw patterns in parent–adolescent dyads and found that the demand on the part of one of them was usually met by withdrawal on the part of the other partner. Such demand may reflect a win-lose interaction.

A **lose-lose solution** is one in which both partners get nothing that they want—in the scenario presented, the partners would neither go out to eat nor see a movie and would be mad at each other.

More than three-quarters (77.1 percent) of the students reported being involved in a win-win relationship, with men and women reporting similar percentages. Of the respondents, 20 percent were involved in win-lose relationships. Only 2 percent reported that they were involved in lose-lose relationships. Of the students in win-win relationships, 85 percent reported that they expected to continue their relationship, in contrast to only 15 percent of students in win-lose relationships. No student in a lose-lose relationship expected the relationship to last.

What power has love but forgiveness?
In other words
by its intervention
what has been done
can be undone.
What good is it otherwise?
William Carlos Williams, American poet

After a number of solutions are generated, each solution should be evaluated and the best one selected. In evaluating solutions to conflicts, it may be helpful to ask the following questions:

1. Does the solution satisfy both individuals? (Is it a win-win solution?)

2. Is the solution specific? Does it specify exactly who is to do what, how, and when?

3. Is the solution realistic? Can both parties realistically follow through with what they have agreed to do?

4. Does the solution prevent the problem from recurring?

5. Does the solution specify what is to happen if the problem recurs?

Kurdek (1995) emphasized that conflict-resolution styles that stress agreement, compromise, and humor are associated with marital satisfaction, whereas conflict engagement, withdrawal, and defensiveness styles are associated with lower marital satisfaction. In his own study of 155 married couples, the style in which the wife engaged the husband in conflict and the husband withdrew was particularly associated with low marital satisfaction for both spouses.

Communicating effectively and creating a context of win-win in one's relationship contributes to a high-quality marital relationship, which is good for one's health (see the Research Application).

Forgive

Too little emphasis is placed on forgiveness as an emotional behavior that can move a couple from a deadlock to resolution. Forgiveness requires acknowledging to one's self and the partner that either can make a mistake and that the focus should be on moving beyond the transgression, mistake, accident, or whatever . . . to "let it go." It takes more energy to hold on to resentment than to move beyond it. One reason some people do not forgive a partner for a transgression is that one can use the fault to control the relationship. "I wasn't going to let him forget," said one woman of her husband's infidelity.

Gordon et al. (2005) emphasized that forgiveness is one of the important factors in a couple's recovery from infidelity on the part of one or both partners. Toussaint and Webb (2005) noted that women and men are equally forgiving. Day and Maltby (2005) found that individuals who are not capable of forgiveness tend to withdraw from social relationships and to become more lonely and/or socially isolated. We discuss forgiveness and infidelity in Chapter 14.

Be Alert to Defense Mechanisms

Effective conflict resolution is sometimes blocked by **defense mechanisms—** unconscious techniques that function to protect individuals from anxiety and to minimize emotional hurt. The following paragraphs discuss some common defense mechanisms.

Escapism is the simultaneous denial of and withdrawal from a problem. The usual form of escape is avoidance. The spouse becomes "busy" and "doesn't have time" to think about or deal with the problem, or the partner may escape into recreation, sleep, alcohol, marijuana, or work. Denying and withdrawing from problems in relationships offer no possibility for confronting and resolving the problems.

Rationalization is the cognitive justification for one's own behavior that unconsciously conceals one's true motives. For example, one wife complained that her husband spent too much time at the health club in the evenings. The underlying reason for the husband's going to the health club was to escape an unsatisfying home life. However, the idea that he was in a dead marriage was too painful and difficult for the husband to face, so he rationalized to himself and his wife that he spent so much time at the health club because he made a lot of important business contacts there. Thus, the husband concealed his own true motives from himself (and his wife).

Marital Quality—Keep It High for Good Health

Spouses who do not communicate effectively to reduce the stress in their relationship end up in a poor-quality marriage. Research has shown that "among the married, those in distressed marriages are in poorer health than those in nondistressed marriages . . . and individuals in low-quality marriages exhibit an even greater health risk than do divorced individuals" (Umberson et al. 2006, 1). To better understand the relationship between marriage and physical health, researchers conducted a study that attempts to answer the following questions: How do positive and negative aspects of marital quality affect physical health, and do these effects vary with age or gender?

Sample and Methods

Researchers used three waves of data from the Americans' Changing Lives (ACL) panel survey of U.S. adults (collected in 1986, 1989, and 1994) and found 1,049 individuals who were continuously married across the eight-year period (1986–1994). Data from the ACL survey were obtained in ninety-minute face-to-face interviews with respondents. In addition to looking at respondents' demographic variables, such as age, sex, education, race, and income, the researchers were interested in the degree to which respondents had positive and negative marital experiences and how respondents rated their physical health.

Positive marital experience was measured by respondents' answers to four questions: (1) How satisfied are you with your marriage? (2) How much does your husband/wife make you feel loved and cared for? (3) How much is he/she willing to listen when you need to talk about your worries or problems? and (4) Can you share your very private feelings and concerns with your spouse?

Negative marital experience was measured by asking respondents two questions: (1) How often do you feel bothered or upset by your marriage? and (2) How often would you say the two of you typically have unpleasant disagreements or conflicts? Self-rated physical health was measured by asking respondents the following question: Would you say your health in general is excellent, good, fair, or poor?

Selected Findings and Conclusions

Statistical analysis revealed that marital quality tended to diminish over time: positive marital experiences generally decreased over the eight-year period, and negative marital experiences increased. Not surprisingly, self-rated health also diminished over time.

The study also revealed that negative marital experiences were more important to the health of older individuals than to younger ones. The researchers explained that "the adverse effects of negative experiences may become apparent only at older ages either because they take a cumulative toll on health or because health status becomes more vulnerable to stress at older ages" (Umberson et al. 2006, 8). Regarding gender differences, this study found that the effects of marital quality on self-rated health are similar for men and women across the life course.

What are the practical lessons of this study? The researchers suggest the following:

1. Unhappily married individuals have yet another reason to identify marital difficulties and seek to improve marital quality: their very health may depend on it.
2. Moreover, there is no reason for clinicians and policy makers to think that marital quality is less important for older couples. In fact, the negative aspects of marriage appear to become more consequential for health as individuals age (Umberson et al. 2006, 13).

Source

Umberson, D., K. Williams, D. A. Powers, H. Liu, and B. Needham. 2006. You make me sick: Marital quality and health over the life course. *Journal of Health and Social Behavior* 47(March):1–16. Used by permission of Wiley-Blackwell.

Projection occurs when one spouse unconsciously attributes individual feelings, attitudes, or desires to the partner. For example, the wife who desires to have an affair may accuse her husband of being unfaithful to her. Projection may be seen in such statements as "You spend too much money" (projection for "I spend too much money") and "You want to break up" (projection for "I want to break up"). Projection interferes with conflict resolution by creating a mood of hostility and defensiveness in both partners. The issues to be resolved in the relationship remain unchanged and become more difficult to discuss.

Displacement involves shifting your feelings, thoughts, or behaviors from the person who evokes them onto someone else. The wife who is turned down for a promotion and the husband who is driven to exhaustion by his boss may

Some think it's holding on that makes one strong; sometimes it's letting go.

Sylvia Robinson, singer/songwriter

direct their hostilities (displace them) onto each other rather than toward their respective employers. Similarly, spouses who are angry at each other may displace this anger onto someone else, such as the children.

By knowing about defense mechanisms and their negative impact on resolving conflict, you can be alert to them in your own relationships. When a conflict continues without resolution, one or more defense mechanisms may be operating.

When Silence Is Golden

Even in the midst of a heated quarrel, some words should never be spoken. To do so is to destroy the relationship forever. William Berle, adopted son of comedian Milton Berle, recalled being in an argument with his dad who lashed out at him, "Oh yeah? Well, I did make one mistake and that was twenty-seven years ago when we adopted you . . . how do you like that you little prick!" (Berle and Lewis 1999, 188). The son recalled being devastated and walking into the next room to take out a pistol to kill himself. Luckily, a knock on the door interrupted his plan.

PERSONAL CHOICES

Should Parents Argue in Front of the Children?

Parents may disagree about whether to argue in front of their children. One parent may feel that it is best to argue behind closed doors so as not to upset their children, but the other may feel that exposing children to the reality of relationships is best. This includes seeing parents argue and, hopefully, negotiating win–win solutions. Most therapists agree that being open is best. Children need to know that relationships involve conflict and learn how to resolve it. In the absence of such exposure, children may have an unrealistic view of relationships.

SUMMARY

What is the nature of interpersonal communication?

Communication is the exchange of information and feelings by two individuals. It involves both verbal and nonverbal messages. The nonverbal part of a message often carries more weight than the verbal part.

What are various issues related to conflict in relationships?

Conflict is both inevitable and desirable. Unless individuals confront and resolve issues over which they disagree, one or both may become resentful and withdraw from the relationship. Conflict may result from one partner's doing something the other does not like, having different perceptions, or having different values. Sometimes it is easier for one partner to view a situation differently or alter a value than for the other partner to change the behavior causing the distress.

What are some principles and techniques of effective communication?

Some basic principles and techniques of effective communication include making communication a priority, maintaining eye contact, asking open-ended questions, using reflective listening, using "I" statements, complimenting each other, and sharing power. Partners must also be alert to keeping the dialogue (process) going even when they don't like what is being said (content).

How are relationships affected by self-disclosure, dishonesty, and lying?

The levels of self-disclosure and honesty influence intimacy in relationships. High levels of self-disclosure are associated with increased intimacy. Most individuals value honesty in their relationships. Honest communication is associated with trust and intimacy.

If you are patient in one moment of anger, you will escape a hundred days of sorrow.

Chinese Proverb

Despite the importance of honesty in relationships, deception occurs frequently in interpersonal relationships. Partners sometimes lie to each other about previous sexual relationships, how they feel about each other, and how they experience each other sexually. Telling lies is not the only form of dishonesty. People exaggerate, minimize, tell partial truths, pretend, and engage in self-deception. Almost 80 percent of undergraduates in one study reported that they had lied to a partner they were involved with. Almost a third of undergraduate men and 20 percent of undergraduate women in "monogamous" relationships reported that they had had oral, vaginal, or anal intercourse with another partner. Partners may withhold information or keep secrets to protect themselves and/or to preserve the relationship. However, the more intimate the relationship, the greater our desire to share our most personal and private selves with our partner and the greater the emotional consequences of not sharing. In intimate relationships, keeping secrets can block opportunities for healing, resolution, self-acceptance, and a deeper intimacy with your partner.

What are gender differences in communication?

Men and women tend to focus on different content in their conversations. Men tend to focus on activities, information, logic, and negotiation and "to achieve and maintain the upper hand." To women, communication focuses on emotion, relationships, interaction, and maintaining closeness. A woman's goal is to preserve intimacy and avoid isolation. Women are also more likely than men to initiate discussion of relationship problems, and women disclose more than men.

How are interactionist and exchange theories applied to relationship communication?

Symbolic interactionists examine the process of communication between two actors in terms of the meanings each attaches to the actions of the other. Definition of the situation, the looking-glass self, and taking the role of the other are all relevant to understanding how partners communicate.

Exchange theorists suggest that the partners' communication can be described as a ratio of rewards to costs. Rewards are positive exchanges, such as compliments, compromises, and agreements. Costs refer to negative exchanges, such as critical remarks, complaints, and attacks. When the rewards are high and the costs are low, the outcome is likely to be positive for both partners (profit). When the costs are high and the rewards low, neither may be satisfied with the outcome (loss).

What are examples of fighting fair to resolve conflict?

The sequence of resolving conflict includes deciding to address recurring issues rather than suppressing them, asking the partner for help in resolving issues, finding out the partner's point of view, summarizing in a nonjudgmental way the partner's perspective, and finding alternative win-win solutions. Defense mechanisms that interfere with conflict resolution include escapism, rationalization, projection, and displacement.

KEY TERMS

accommodating style of conflict	competing style of conflict	"I" statements	rationalization
avoiding style of conflict	compromising style of conflict	lose-lose solution	reflective listening
brainstorming	conflict	nonverbal communication	win-lose solution
branching	congruent message	open-ended questions	win-win relationships
closed-ended questions	defense mechanisms	parallel style of conflict	"you" statements
collaborating style of conflict	displacement	power	
communication	escapism	projection	

The Companion Website for *Choices in Relationships: An Introduction to Marriage and the Family,* Tenth Edition

www.cengage.com/sociology/knox

Supplement your review of this chapter by going to the Companion Website to take one of the tutorial quizzes, use the flash cards to master key terms, or check out the many other study aids, like crossword puzzles and self-assessments. You'll also find special features such as General Social Survey (GSS) data, Census data, and other resources to help you with that special project or to do some research on your own.

WEB LINKS

Department of Communication Resources
http://communication.ucsd.edu/resources/commlinks .html

Guidelines on Effective Communication, Healthy Relationships & Successful Living
http://www.drnadig.com/

Association for Couples in Marriage Enrichment
http://www.bettermarriages.org/

Episcopal Marriage Encounter
http://www.episcopalme.com/

REFERENCES

Alexandrov, E. Q. 2005. Couple attachment and the quality of marital relationships. *Attachment and Human Development* 7:123–52.

Behringer, A. M. 2005. Bridging the gap between Mars and Venus: A study of communication meanings in marriage. *Dissertation Abstracts International, A: The Humanities and Social Sciences* 65:4007A–8A.

Berle, W., with B. Lewis 1999. *My father uncle Miltie.* New York: Barricade Books, Inc.

Bos, E. H., A. L. Bouhuys, E. Geerts, T.W. D. P. Van Os, and J. Ormel. 2007. Stressful life events as a link between problems in nonverbal communication and recurrence of depression *Journal of Affective Disorders* 97:161–69.

Campbell, S. 2005. *Seven keys to authentic communication and relationship satisfaction.* New York: New World Library.

Caughlin, J. P. and M. B. Ramey. 2005. The demand/withdraw pattern of communication in parent-adolescent dyads. *Personal Relationships* 12:337–55.

Day, L., and J. Maltby. 2005. Forgiveness. *Journal of Psychology* 139:553–55.

DeMaria, R. M. 2005. Distressed couples and marriage education. *Family Relations* 54:242–53.

Dunbar, N. E., and J. K. Burgoon. 2005. Perceptions of power and interactional dominance in interpersonal relationships. *Journal of Social and Personal Relationships* 22:207–33.

Ennis, E., A. Vrij, and C. Chance. 2008. Individual differences and lying in everyday life. *Journal of Social and Personal Relationships* 25:105–118.

Finkenauer, C., and H. Hazam. 2000. Disclosure and secrecy in marriage: Do both contribute to marital satisfaction? *Journal of Social and Personal Relationships* 17:245–63.

Fonda, J. 2005. *My life, so far.* New York: Random House.

Gable, S. L., H. T. Reis, and G. Downey. 2003. He said, she said: A Quasi-Signal detection analysis of daily interactions between close relationship partners. *Psychological Science* 14:100–05.

Gallmeier, C. P., M. E. Zusman, D. Knox, and L. Gibson. 1997. Can we talk? Gender differences in disclosure patterns and expectations. *Free Inquiry in Creative Sociology* 25:129–225.

Gibbs, J. L., N. B. Ellison, and R. D. Heino. 2006. Self-presentation in online personals: The role of anticipated future interaction, self-disclosure, and perceived success in Internet dating. *Communication Research* 33:152–177.

Gordon, K. C., D. H. Baucom, and D. K. Snyder. 2005. Treating couples recovering from infidelity: An integrative approach. *Journal of Clinical Psychology* 61:1393–405.

Gottman, John. 1994. *Why marriages succeed or fail.* New York: Simon & Schuster.

Greeff, A. P., and T. De Bruyne. 2000. Conflict management style and marital satisfaction. *Journal of Sex and Marital Satisfaction* 26:321–34.

Haas, S. M., and L. Stafford. 2005. Maintenance behaviors in same-sex and marital relationships: A matched sample comparison. *Journal of Family Communication* 5:43–60.

Henry, R. G., R. B. Miller, and R. Giarrusso. 2005. Difficulties, disagreements, and disappointments in late-life marriages. *International Journal of Aging & Human Development* 61:243–65.

Hertenstein, M. J., M. J. Hertenstein, J. M. Verkamp, A. M. Kerestes, and R. M. Holmes. 2007. The communicative functions of touch in humans, nonhuman primates, and rats: A review and synthesis of the empirical research. *Genetic Social and General Psychology Monographs* 132:5–94.

Hetherington, E. M. 2003. Intimate pathways: Changing patterns in close personal relationships across time. *Family Relations* 52:318–31.

Ingoldsby, B. B., G. T. Horlacher, P. L. Schvaneveldt, and M. Matthews. 2005. Emotional expressiveness and marital adjustment in Ecuador. *Marriage and Family Review* 38:25–44.

Knobloch, L. K. 2008. The content of relational uncertainty within marriage. *Journal of Social and Personal Relationships* 25:467–95.

Knox, D. and Zusman, M. E. 2009. Relationship and sexual behaviors of a sample of 1,319 university students. Unpublished data collected for this text. Department of Sociology, East Carolina University, Greenville, NC.

Knox, D., C. Schacht, J. Turner, and P. Norris. 1995. College students' preference for win-win relationships. *College Student Journal* 29:44–46.

Kurdek, L. A. 1994. Areas of conflict for gay, lesbian, and heterosexual couples: What couples argue about influences relationship satisfaction. *Journal of Marriage and the Family* 56:923–34.

———. 1995. Predicting change in marital satisfaction from husbands' and wives' conflict resolution styles. *Journal of Marriage and the Family* 57:153–64.

Marano, H. E. 1992. The reinvention of marriage. *Psychology Today*. January/February, 49.

Marchand, J. F., and E. Hock. 2000. Avoidance and attacking conflict-resolution strategies among married couples: Relations to depressive symptoms and marital satisfaction. *Family Relations* 49:201–06.

McAlister, A. R., N. Pachana, and C. J. Jackson. 2005. Predictors of young dating adults' inclination to engage in extra dyadic sexual activities: A multi-perspective study. *British Journal of Psychology* 96:331–50.

McKenna, K. Y. A., A. S. Green, and M. E. J. Gleason. 2002. Relationship formation on the Internet: What's the big attraction? *Journal of Social Issues* 58:9–22.

Patford, J. L. 2000. Partners and cross-sex friends: A preliminary study of the way marital and de facto partnerships affect verbal intimacy with cross-sex friends. *Journal of Family Studies* 6:106–19.

Preston, P. 2005. Nonverbal communication: Do you really say what you mean? *Journal of Healthcare Management* 50:83–87.

Punyanunt-Carter, N. N. 2006. An analysis of college students' self-disclosure behaviors. *College Student Journal* 40:329–31.

Purkett, T. 2009. Sexually transmitted infections. Presentation to Courtship and Marriage class, Spring.

Rayer, A. J., and B. L. Volling. 2005. The role of husbands' and wives' emotional expressivity in the marital relationship. *Sex Roles: A Journal of Research* 52:577–88.

Rhoades, G. K., S. M. Stanley, and H. J. Markman. 2009. Couples' reasons for cohabitation: Associations with individual well-being and relationship quality. *Journal of Family Issues* 30:233–46.

Robbins, C. A. 2005. ADHD couple and family relationships: Enhancing communication and understanding through Imago Relationship Therapy. *Journal of Clinical Psychology* 61:565–78.

Rosof, F. 2005. An investigation of the therapeutic role of communication in couple relationships. Dissertation, Union Institute US. Dissertation Abstract International, Section B, Vol. 25 (8-B):4302.

Sanford, K. 2007. Hard and soft emotion during conflict: Investigating married couples and other relationships *Personal Relationships* 14:65–90.

Seguin-Levesque, C., M. L. N. Laliberte, L. G. Pelletier, C. Blanchard, and R. J. Vallerand. 2003. Harmonious and obsessive passion for the Internet: Their associations with the couple's relationship. *Journal of Applied Social Psychology* 33:197–221.

Shinn, L. K., and M. O'Brien 2008. Parent-child conversational styles in middle childhood: Gender and social class differences. *Sex Roles* 59:61–69.

Stanley, S. M., H. J. Markman, and S. W. Whitton. 2002. Communication, conflict, and commitment: Insights on the foundations of relationship success from a national survey. *Interpersonal Relations* 41:659–66.

Tannen, D. 1990. *You just don't understand: Women and men in conversation*. London: Virago.

Tannen, D. 2006. *You're wearing that? Understanding mothers and daughters in conversation*. New York: Random House.

Toussaint, L., and J. R. Webb. 2005. Gender differences in the relationship between empathy and forgiveness. *Journal of Social Psychology* 145:673–85.

Turner, A. J. 2005. Communication basics. Personal communication.

Vail-Smith, K., L. MacKenzie, and D. Knox. Forthcoming. The illusion of safety in "monogamous" undergraduates. *American Journal of Health Behavior* 34.

Walther, J. B., T. Loh, and L. Granka 2005. Let me count the ways: The interchange of verbal and nonverbal cues in computer mediated and face to face affinity. *Journal of Language and Social Psychology* 34:36–65.

Marriage has become a more optional and less permanent part of adult life now than in the past.

Paul Amato et al., *Alone Together: How Marriage in America is Changing*

Singlehood, Hanging Out, Hooking Up, and Cohabitation

Contents

True or False?

1. American youth are unique in their delay in getting married; youth in France, Germany, and Italy are beginning to get married earlier.

2. African Americans are much more likely to delay marriage than European Americans.

3. Singlehood has become the new norm, with 60 percent of American adults electing never to marry.

4. In general, people who live together and then marry are more likely to get divorced than those who don't live together before marriage.

5. Over half of women who cohabit end up getting married to their partner.

Answers: **1.** F **2.** T **3.** F **4.** T **5.** F

---

*T*he Best Years of Our Lives is the title of an Oscar-winning movie of the 1940s. It captures the perception of a time when life is exiting, full, and relatively problem-free. Just as marriage is stereotyped as a prison via the stereotypical ball and chain, singlehood and the years before marriage are thought of as some of "the best years of our lives."

To keep the "best years of life" (singlehood) going, individuals are delaying marriage. Concerns about launching one's career, paying off debts, and enjoying the freedom of singlehood (which implies avoiding expectations of either a spouse or a child) have propelled a pattern adopted by today's youth to put off marriage in a ten-year float from the late teens to the late twenties.

Young American adults are not alone: individuals in France, Germany, and Italy are engaging in a similar pattern of delaying marriage. In the meantime, the process of courtship has evolved, with various labels and patterns, including "hanging out" (undergraduates rarely use the term *dating*), "hooking up" (the new term for "one-night stand"), and "pairing off," which may include cohabitation as a prelude to marriage. We begin with examining singlehood versus marriage.

Never before have so many people lived alone.

Stephanie Coontz, family historian

Singlehood

In this section, we discuss how social movements have increased the acceptance of singlehood, the various categories of single people, the choice to be permanently unmarried, the human immunodeficiency virus (HIV) infection risk associated with this choice, and the fact that more people are delaying marriage.

Individuals Are Delaying Marriage Longer

American adults are more likely to live alone today than in the past. The proportion of households consisting of one person living alone increased from 30.1 percent in 2005 to 31.1 percent in 2007 (*Statistical Abstract of the United States, 2009*, Table 61). In part, this is due to the fact that American women and men are staying single longer (see Figure 5.1).

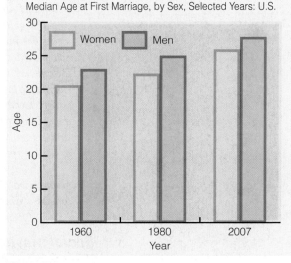

Figure 5.1

Median Age at First Marriage in America in Selected Years, by Sex

Source: U.S. Census Bureau. 2006. *America's Families and Living Arrangements: 2006.* Table MS-2 Estimated Median Age at First Marriage, by Sex (updated for 2007). http://www.census.gov.

Table 5.1   Reasons to Remain Single

Benefits of Singlehood	Limitations of Marriage
Freedom to do as one wishes	Restricted by spouse or children
Variety of lovers	One sexual partner
Spontaneous lifestyle	Routine, predictable lifestyle
Close friends of both sexes	Pressure to avoid close other-sex friendships
Responsible for one person only	Responsible for spouse and children
Spend money as one wishes	Expenditures influenced by needs of spouse and children
Freedom to move as career dictates	Restrictions on career mobility
Avoid being controlled by spouse	Potential to be controlled by spouse
Avoid emotional and financial stress of divorce	Possibility of divorce

Whether you marry or stay single you will regret it.

Socrates, Greek philosopher

Whether today's individuals are embracing singlehood forever or just delaying marriage is unknown. We won't know until they reach their seventies, which is the age by which more than 95 percent typically marry. Indeed, Gloria Steinem, the ardent feminist, who once spoke of marriage as a prison, married when she was 66. We do know, however, that people are opting for singlehood longer than in the past (Vanderkam 2006). Table 5.1 lists the standard reasons people give for remaining single. The primary advantage of remaining single is freedom and control over one's life. Once a decision has been made to involve another in one's life, one's choices become vulnerable to the influence of that other person. The person who chooses to remain single may view the needs and influence of another person as things to avoid.

Some people do not set out to be single but drift into singlehood longer than they anticipated—and discover that they like it. Meredith Kennedy (shown in the photo on page 135) is a never-married veterinarian who has found that singlehood works very well for her. She writes:

> As a little girl, I always assumed I'd grow up to be swept off my feet, get married, and live happily ever after. Then I hit my 20s, became acquainted with reality, and discovered that I had a lot of growing up to do. I'm still working on it now, in my late 30s.
>
> I've gotten a lot out of my relationships with men over the years, some serious and some not so serious, and they've all left their impression on me. But gradually I've moved away from considering myself "between boyfriends" to getting very comfortable with being alone, and finding myself good company. The thought of remaining single for the rest of my life doesn't bother me, and the freedom that comes with it is very precious. I've worked and traveled all over the world, and my schedule is my own. I don't think this could have come about with the responsibilities of marriage and a family, and the time and space I have as a single woman have allowed me to really explore who I am in this life.
>
> It's not always easy to explain why I'm single in a culture that expects women to get married and to have children, but the freedom and independence I have allow me to lead a unique and interesting life.

Social Movements and the Acceptance of Singlehood

Though more than 95 percent of American adults eventually marry (*Statistical Abstract of the United States, 2009*, Table 56) and only 5 percent of a sample of 1,293 adolescents predicted that they would never marry (Manning et al. 2007), more people are delaying marriage and enjoying singlehood. The acceptance of singlehood as a lifestyle can be attributed to social movements—the sexual revolution, the women's movement, and the gay liberation movement.

Chapter 5 Singlehood, Hanging Out, Hooking Up, and Cohabitation

This never-married woman has traveled the world and is seen here on a camel in Kenya.

The sexual revolution involved openness about sexuality and permitted intercourse outside the context of marriage. No longer did people feel compelled to wait until marriage for involvement in a sexual relationship. Hence, the sequence changed from dating, love, maybe intercourse with a future spouse, and then marriage and parenthood to "hanging out," "hooking up" with numerous partners, maybe living together (in one or more relationships), marriage, and children.

The women's movement emphasized equality in education, employment, and income for women. As a result, rather than get married and depend on a husband for income, women earned higher degrees, sought career opportunities, and earned their own income. This economic independence brought with it independence of choice. Women could afford to remain single or to leave an unfulfilling or abusive relationship.

The gay liberation movement, with its push for recognition of same-sex marriage, has increased the visibility of gay people and relationships. Though some gay people still marry heterosexuals to provide a traditional social front, the gay liberation movement has provided support for a lifestyle consistent with one's sexual orientation. This includes rejecting traditional heterosexual marriage. Today, some gay pair-bonded couples regard themselves as married even though they are not legally wed. Some gay couples have formal wedding ceremonies in which they exchange rings and vows of love and commitment.

In effect, there is a new wave of youth who feel that their commitment is to themselves in early adulthood and to marriage in their late twenties and thirties, if at all. The increased acceptance of singlehood translates into staying in school or getting a job, establishing oneself in a career, and becoming economically and emotionally independent from one's parents. The old pattern was to leap from high school into marriage. The new pattern of these Generaton Yers (discussed in Chapter 1) is to wait until after college, become established in a career, and enjoy themselves. A few (less than 5 percent of American adults) opt for remaining single forever.

The value young adults attach to singlehood may vary by race. Brewster (2006) interviewed forty African American men 18 to 25 years of age in New York City. These men dated numerous women and some maintained serious relationships with multiple women simultaneously. These men "have redefined family for themselves, and marriage is not included in the definition" (p. 32).

My strong objection is to the notion that there's one kind of relationship that's best for everyone.

Judith Stacey, Sociologist

Ferguson (2000) studied sixty-two never-married Chinese American and Japanese American women and found that 40 percent expressed some regret at not being married. However, for most of these women, their regret was primarily about not having children and not about never marrying. Instead, most of these never-married women were happy with the decisions they made and were living rich and fulfilling lives. Most were economically successful, immersed in a community of friends and family, and actively involved in their work or community projects (p. 155).

A never married person cresting 35 was asked, "Do you ever think of getting married?" The person replied, "I worry."

Anonymous

Alternatives to Marriage Project

According to the mission statement identified on the website of the Alternatives to Marriage Project (http://www.unmarried.org/aboutus.php), the emphasis of the Alternatives to Marriage Project (ATMP) is to advocate "for equality and fairness for unmarried people, including people who are single, choose not to marry, cannot marry, or live together before marriage." The nonprofit organization is not against marriage but provides support and information for the unmarried and "fights discrimination on the basis of marital status. . . . We believe that marriage is only one of many acceptable family forms, and that society should recognize and support healthy relationships in all their diversity."

The Alternatives to Marriage Project is open to everyone, "including singles, couples, married people, individuals in relationships with more than two people, and people of all genders and sexual orientations. We welcome our married supporters, who are among the many friends, relatives, and allies of unmarried people."

Legal Blurring of the Married and Unmarried

The legal distinction between married and unmarried couples is blurring. Whether it is called the deregulation of marriage or the deinstitutionalization of marriage, the result is the same—more of the privileges previously reserved for the married and now available to unmarried and/or same-sex couples. As noted earlier, domestic partnership conveys rights and privileges (for example, health benefits for a partner) previously available only to married people.

PERSONAL CHOICES

Is Singlehood for You?

Singlehood is not a one-dimensional concept. Whereas some are committed to singlehood, others enjoy it for now but intend to eventually marry, and still others are conflicted about it. There are many styles of singlehood from which to choose. As a single person, you may devote your time and energy to career, travel, privacy, heterosexual or homosexual relationships, living together, communal living, or a combination of these experiences over time. An essential difference between traditional marriage and singlehood is the personal, legal, and social freedom to do as you wish. Although singlehood offers freedom, issues such as loneliness, less money, and establishing an identity sometimes challenge single people.

1. *Loneliness.* For some singles, being alone is a desirable and enjoyable experience. "The major advantage of being single," said one 49-year-old artist, "is that I don't have to deal with another person all the time. I like my privacy. I have my animals, my painting studio, and I am really very content." In an American Association of Retired Persons (AARP) survey of single women aged 40 to 69, 93 percent noted that their "independence" was important for their quality of life (and that this overshadowed the occasional feelings of loneliness) (Mahoney 2006). Henry David Thoreau, who never married, spent two years alone on fourteen acres bordering Walden Pond in Massachusetts. He said of his experience, "I love to be alone. I have never found the companion that was so companionable as solitude."

Nevertheless, some singles are lonely. In the AARP study of single women, 28 percent reported that they had felt lonely occasionally in the past two weeks or most of the time (13 percent of married women reported these same feelings) (Mahoney 2006). Some research suggests that single men may be lonelier than single women. In a study of 377 undergraduates, 25.9 percent of the men compared to 16.7 percent of the women agreed that they felt a "deep sense of loneliness" (Knox et al. 2007).

2. *Less money.* Married couples who combine their incomes usually have more income than single people living alone. The median income of a married couple is $69,716, compared with $47,076 for a male householder with no wife and $31,816 for a female householder with no husband (*Statistical Abstract of the United States, 2009*, Table 670). In addition, debt can be a serious issue. The average female aged 45 to 59 carries $11,414 in revolving debt; divorced women and those between the ages of 45 and 49 are the least likely to pay off their credit cards (Mahoney 2006).

3. *Social Identity.* Single people must establish a social identity—a role—that helps to define who they are and what they do, independent of the role of spouse. Couples eat together, sleep together, party together, and cooperate economically. They mesh their lives into a cooperative relationship that gives them the respective identity of being a spouse. On the basis of their spousal roles, we can predict what they will be doing most of the time. For example, at noon on Sunday, they are most likely to be having lunch together. Not only can we predict what they will be doing, but their roles as spouses tell them what they will be doing—interacting with each other.

Single people find other roles and avenues to identity. A meaningful career is the avenue most singles pursue. A career provides structure, relationships with others, and a strong sense of identity ("I am a veterinarian—I love my work," said Meredith Kennedy).

4. *Children.* Some individuals want to have a child but not a spouse. We will examine this issue in Chapter 11 in a section on Single Mothers by Choice. There are no data on single men seeking the role of parent. Although some custodial divorced men are single fathers, this is not the same as never having married and having a child.

In evaluating the single lifestyle, to what degree, if any, do you feel that loneliness is or would be a problem for you? What is your social identity, your work role satisfaction? What are your emotional and structural needs of "marriage"? For children? The old idea that you can't be happy unless you are married is no longer credible. Whereas marriage will be the first option for some, it will be the last option for others. As one 76-year-old single person by choice said, "A spouse would have to be very special to be better than no spouse at all."

Sources

Knox, D., K. Vail-Smith, and M. Zusman. 2007. The lonely college male. *International Journal of Men's Health* 6:273–79.

Mahoney, S. 2006. The secret lives of single women—lifestyles, dating and romance: A study of midlife singles. *AARP: The Magazine* May/June, 62–69.

Statistical Abstract of the United States, 2009. 128th ed. Washington, DC: U.S. Bureau of the Census, Table 56.

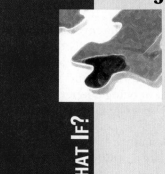

WHAT IF?

What if You Are Afraid of Being Alone and Just Settle for Someone?

Fear of loneliness is a powerful motivator to pair-bond with anyone who may be available. It is possible to blend your life with the person who is available and have a good life? A larger question is your level of attraction ("chemistry") and similarity. If you don't feel attracted to the person and have nothing in common, the ending may be sad because these are basic prerequisites for an enjoyable and enduring relationship.

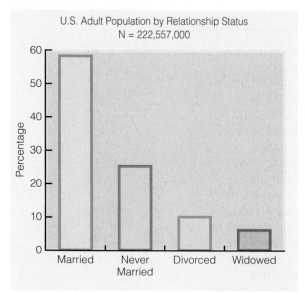

Figure 5.2
U.S. Adult Population by Relationship Status
Source: *Statistical Abstract of the United States, 2009*. 128th ed. Washington, DC: U.S. Bureau of the Census, Table 56.

Categories of Singles

The term **singlehood** is most often associated with young unmarried individuals. However, there are three categories of single people: the never-married, the divorced, and the widowed. See Figure 5.2 for the distribution of the American adult population by relationship status.

Never-Married Singles

Kevin Eubanks (*Tonight Show* music director), Oprah Winfrey, Diane Keaton, and Drew Carey are examples of heterosexuals who have never married. Nevertheless, it is rare for people to remain single their entire life. One reason is stigma. DePaulo (2006) asked 950 undergraduate college students to describe single people. In contrast to married people, who were described as "happy, loving, stable," single people were described as "lonely, unhappy, and insecure."

National Data

By age 75, only 3.4 percent of American women and 3.7 percent of American men have never married (*Statistical Abstract of the United States, 2009*, Table 56). Between the ages of 25 and 29, 57.6 percent of males and 43.4 percent of females are not married (Table 56).

Though the never-married singles consist mostly of those who want to marry someday, these individuals are increasingly comfortable delaying marriage to pursue educational and career opportunities. Others, such as African American women who have never married, note a lack of potential marriage partners. Educated black women report a particularly difficult time finding eligible men from which to choose.

National Data

Among adults 18 years and older, about 39 percent of black women and 42 percent of black men have never married, in contrast to about 19.1 percent of white women and 26.5 percent of white men (*Statistical Abstract of the United States, 2009*, Table 55).

As noted in the national data, there is a great racial divide in terms of remaining single. In her article, "Marriage is for White People," Jones (2006, B5) notes:

Sex, love, and childbearing have become a la carte choices rather than a package deal that comes with marriage. Moreover, in an era of brothers on the "down low," the spread of sexually transmitted diseases and the decline of the stable blue-collar jobs that black men used to hold, linking one's fate to a man makes marriage a risky business for a black woman.

In spite of the viability of singlehood as a lifestyle, stereotypes remain, as never-married people are viewed as desperate or swingers. Indeed, a cultural norm still disapproves of singlehood as a lifelong lifestyle. In an episode of *Sex and the City*, the character of Carrie felt the pressure to marry and said, "When did being alone become the modern-day equivalent of being a leper?" Indeed, a major theme of *Sex and the City: The Movie* was Carrie's escape from being single and her marriage to Big.

Jessica Donn (2005) emphasized that, because mature "adulthood" implies that one is married, single people are left to negotiate a positive identity outside of marriage. She studied the subjective well-being of 171 self-identified heterosexual, never-married singles (40 men and 131 women), aged 35 to 45 years, who were not currently living with a romantic partner. Results revealed that women participants reported higher life satisfaction and positive affect than men. Donn hypothesized that having social connections and close friendships (greater frequency of social contact, more close friends, someone to turn to in times of distress, and greater reciprocity with a confidant) was the variable associated with higher subjective well-being for both women and men (but women evidenced greater connectedness). Other findings included that relationships, career, older age, and avoiding thoughts of old age contributed to a sense of well-being for never-married men. For women, financial security, relationships, achievement, and control over their environment contributed to a sense of well-being.

Sharp and Ganong (2007) interviewed thirty-two white never-married college-educated women ages 28 to 34 who revealed a sense of uncertainty about their lives. One reported:

> *Like all or nothing, it is either—you assume it [your life] is either going to be great or horrible. You just have to get better at accepting the fact that you don't know, it is probably somewhere in between and you are just going to have to wait and see.*

Although some were despondent that they would ever meet a man and have children, others (particularly when they became older) reminded themselves of the advantages of being single: freedom, financial independence, ability to travel, and so on. However, the overriding theme of these respondents was that they were "running out of time to marry and to have children." The researchers emphasized the enormous cultural expectation to follow age-graded life transitions and to stay on time and on course. People outside the norm struggle with managing their difference, with varying degrees of success. See Table 5.2 for the issues involved in being a single woman.

When single and married people are compared, married people report being happier. Lucas et al. (2003) analyzed data from a fifteen-year longitudinal study of more than 24,000 individuals and found that married people were happier than single people and hypothesized that marriage may draw people who are already more satisfied than average (for example, unhappy people may be less in demand as marriage partners). Wienke and Hill (2009) also compared single people with married people and cohabitants (both heterosexual and homosexual) and found that single people were less happy regardless of sexual orientation.

Divorced Singles

Divorced people are also regarded as single. For many of divorced people, the return to singlehood is not an easy transition. Knox and Corte (2007) studied a sample of people going through divorce, many of whom reported their unhappiness and a desire to reunite with their partner.

National Data

There were 13.2 million divorced females and 9.6 million divorced males in the United States in 2007 (*Statistical Abstract of the United States, 2009*, Table 55).

Most divorced individuals have children. Most of these are single mothers, but increasingly, single fathers have sole custody of their children. Most single parents prioritize their roles of "single parent" as a parent first and as a single adult second. One newly divorced single parent said, "My kids come first. I don't have time for anything else now." We discuss the topic of single parenthood in greater detail in Chapter 10 on planning children.

Divorced people tend to die earlier than married people. On the basis of a study of 44,000 deaths, Hemstrom (1996) observed that, "on the whole, marriage protects both men and women from the higher mortality rates experienced by unmarried groups" (p. 376). One explanation is the protective aspect of marriage. "The protection against diseases and mortality that marriage provides may take the form of easier access to social support, social control, and

Table 5.2 A Never-Married Single Woman's View of Singlehood

A never-married woman, 40 years of age, spoke to our marriage and family class about her experience as a single woman. The following is from the outline she developed and the points she made about each topic.

Stereotypes about Never-Married Women

Various assumptions are made about the never-married woman and why she is single. These include the following:

Unattractive—She's either overweight or homely, or else she would have a man.

Lesbian—She has no real interest in men and marriage because she is homosexual.

Workaholic—She's career-driven and doesn't make time for relationships.

Poor interpersonal skills—She has no social skills, and she embarrasses men.

History of abuse—She has been turned off to men by the sexual abuse of, for example, her father, a relative, or a date.

Negative previous relationships—She's been rejected again and again and can't hold a man.

Man-hater—Deep down, she hates men.

Frigid—She hates sex and avoids men and intimacy.

Promiscuous—She is indiscriminate in her sexuality so that no man respects or wants her.

Too picky—She always finds something wrong with each partner and is never satisfied.

Too weird—She would win the Miss Weird contest, and no man wants her.

Positive Aspects of Being Single

1. Freedom to define self in reference to own accomplishments, not in terms of attachments (for example, spouse).
2. Freedom to pursue own personal and career goals and advance without the time restrictions posed by a spouse and children.
3. Freedom to come and go as you please and to do what you want, when you want.
4. Freedom to establish relationships with members of both sexes at desired level of intensity.
5. Freedom to travel and explore new cultures, ideas, values.

Negative Aspects of Being Single

1. Increased extended-family responsibilities. The unmarried sibling is assumed to have the time to care for elderly parents.
2. Increased job expectations. The single employee does not have marital or family obligations and consequently can be expected to work at night, on weekends, and holidays.
3. Isolation. Too much time alone does not allow others to give feedback such as "Are you drinking too much?" "Have you had a checkup lately?" or "Are you working too much?"
4. Decreased privacy. Others assume the single person is always at home and always available. They may call late at night or drop in whenever they feel like it. They tend to ask personal questions freely.
5. Less safety. A single woman living alone is more vulnerable than a married woman with a man in the house.
6. Feeling different. Many work-related events are for couples, husbands, and wives. A single woman sticks out.
7. Lower income. Single women have much lower incomes than married couples.
8. Less psychological intimacy. The single woman does not have an emotionally intimate partner at the end of the day.
9. Negotiation skills lie dormant. Because single people do not negotiate issues with someone on a regular basis, they may become deficient in compromise and negotiation skills.
10. Patterns become entrenched. Because no other person is around to express preferences, the single person may establish a very repetitive lifestyle.

Maximizing One's Life as a Single Person

1. Frank discussion. Talk with parents about your commitment to and enjoyment of the single lifestyle and request that they drop marriage references. Talk with siblings about joint responsibility for aging parents and your willingness to do your part. Talk with employers about spreading workload among all workers, not just those who are unmarried and childfree.
2. Relationships. Develop and nurture close relationships with parents, siblings, extended family, and friends to have a strong and continuing support system.
3. Participate in social activities. Go to social events with or without a friend. Avoid becoming a social isolate.
4. Be cautious. Be selective in sharing personal information such as your name, address, and phone number.
5. Money. Pursue education to maximize income; set up a retirement plan.
6. Health. Exercise, have regular checkups, and eat healthy food. Take care of yourself.

integration, which leads to risk avoidance, healthier lifestyles, and reduced vulnerability" (p. 375). Married people also look out for the health of the other. Spouses often prod each other to "go to the doctor," "have that rash on your skin looked at," and "remember to take your medication." Single people often have no one in their life to nudge them toward regular health maintenance.

Widowed Singles

Although divorced people often choose to return to singlehood, widowed people are forced into singlehood. The stereotype of the widow and widower is utter loneliness, even though there are compensations (for example, escape from an unhappy marriage, social security). Ha (2008) compared widowed people with married couples and found the former less likely to have a confidant, but they received greater support from children, friends, and relatives. Hence, widowed people may have a broader array of relationships than married people.

Nevertheless, widowhood is a difficult time for most individuals. Widowed men, in contrast to widowed women, may feel particularly disconnected from their children (Kalmijn 2007).

National Data

There were 11.2 million widowed females and 2.7 widowed males in the United States in 2007 (*Statistical Abstract of the United States, 2009*, Table 55). Widowed people represent 6.2 percent of the U.S. adult population (Table 55).

In a study conducted by the American Association of Retired Persons (AARP), most widows were between the ages of 40 and 69. Almost a third (31 percent) were in an exclusive relationship and another 32 percent were dating nonexclusively. Of the remaining 37 percent, only 13 percent reported that they were actively looking; 10 percent said that they had no desire to date; and the rest said they were open to meeting someone but not obsessive about it (Mahoney 2006).

Singlehood and HIV Infection Risk

Individuals who are not married or not living with someone are at greater risk for contracting human immunodeficiency virus (HIV) and other sexually transmitted infections (STIs). Though women typically report having had fewer sexual partners than men, the men they have sex with have usually had multiple sexual partners. Hence, women are more likely to get infected from men than men are from women. In addition to the social reason for increased risk of infection, there is a biological reason—sperm that may be HIV-infected is deposited into the woman's body.

Intentional Communities

Although single people often live in apartments, condominiums, or single-family houses, living in an intentional community (previously called a commune) is an alternative. Less than 10 percent (7 percent) of 1,319 undergraduates at a large southeastern university agreed, "Someday, I would like to live in an intentional community [a commune]" (Knox and Zusman 2009). Intentional communities are not just for single or young people. Married people and seniors also embrace communal living. Blue Heron Farm, for example, is home to a collective of individuals, ages 20 to 70, who live in ten houses (Yeoman 2006). The range of intentional community alternatives may be explored via the Cohousing Association

"Hey Big Boy!": Women who Initiate Relationships with Men*

Mae West, film actress of the 1930s and '40s, is remembered for being very forward with men. Two classic phrases of hers are "Is that a pistol in your pocket or are you glad to see me?" and "Why don't you come up and see me sometime, I'm home every night?" As a woman who went after what she wanted, West was not alone—then or now. There have always been women not bound by traditional gender role restrictions. This study was concerned with women who initiate relationships with men—women who, like Mae West, have ventured beyond the traditional gender role expectations of the passive female.

Sample and Methodology

Data for this study consisted of 692 undergraduate women who answered "yes" or "no" on a questionnaire to the question, "I have asked a new guy to go out with me"—a nontraditional gender role behavior.

Findings and Discussion

Of the 692 women surveyed, 39.1 percent reported that they had asked a new guy out on a date; 60.9 percent had not done so. Analysis of the data revealed ten statistically significant findings in regard to the characteristics of those women who had initiated a relationship with a man and those who had not done so.

1. *Nonbeliever in "one true love."* Of the women who asked men out, 42.3 percent did not believe in "one true love" in contrast to 31.7 percent who believed in one true love—a statistically significant difference ($p < .01$). These assertive women felt they had a menu of men from which to choose.

2. *Experienced "love at first sight."* Of the women who had asked a man out, 45.7 percent had experienced falling in love at first sight in contrast to 28.2 percent who had not had this experience. Hence, women who let a man know they were interested in him were likely to have already had a "sighting" of a man with whom they fell in love.

3. *Sought partner on the Internet.* Only a small number (59 of 692; 8.5 percent) of women reported that they had searched for a partner using the Internet. However, 54.2 percent of those who had done so (in contrast to

only 37.5 percent who had not used the Internet to search for a partner) reported that they had asked a man to go out ($p < .02$). Because both seeking a partner on the Internet and asking a partner to go out verbally are reflective of nontraditional gender role behavior, these women were clearly in charge of their lives and moved the relationship forward rather than waiting for the man to make the first move.

4. *Nonreligious.* Respondents who were not religious were more likely to ask a guy out than those who were religious (74.6 percent versus 64.2 percent; $p < .001$). This finding comes as no surprise, as previous research suggests that being nonreligious is associated with having nontraditional values or roles (McCready and McCready 1973; Miller and Stark 2002).

5. *Nontraditional sexual values.* Consistent with the idea that women who had asked a guy out were also nonreligious (a nontraditional value) is the finding that these same women tended to have nontraditional sexual values. Of those women who had initiated a relationship with a guy, 44.4 percent reported having a hedonistic sexual value ("If it feels good, do it) compared to 25.7 percent who regarded themselves as having absolutist sexual values ("Wait until marriage to have intercourse"). Hence, women with nontraditional sexual values were much more likely to be aggressive in initiating a new relationship with a man.

6. *Open to cohabitation.* Of the women who reported that they had asked a man to go out, 44.6 percent reported that they would cohabit with a man compared to 26.0 percent who would not cohabit. This finding is supported by the research of Michael et al. (1994), who confirmed that cohabitating men and women are more likely to have nontraditional sexual values.

7. *White.* Over forty percent (41.4 percent) of the white women, compared to 28.2 percent of the black women, in the sample reported that they had asked a guy out. This finding is not surprising in that black people are traditionally more conservative than white people in religion (Sherkat 2002) and sexual values (Michael et al. 1994).

8. *Sexually faithful.* Women who had asked a guy out were more likely to report having been faithful in

---

Home life is no more natural to us than a cage to a cockatoo.

George B. Shaw, Irish dramatist

of the United States (www.cohousing.org) and the Federation of Egalitarian Communities (www.thefec.org). In the next section, we describe one such intentional community.

Twin Oaks: An Alternative Context for Living

Twin Oaks is a community of ninety adults and fifteen children living together on 450 acres of land in Louisa, Virginia (about forty-five minutes east of Charlottesville and one hour west of Richmond). The **commune** (an older term now replaced by the newer term), now known as an **intentional community** previous relationships than women who had not asked a guy out (44.5 percent versus 34.8 percent; p > .02). One explanation for this finding is that the act of their initiating a relationship may reflect the strong positive value these women placed on the relationship with the person they pursued and that the value of sexual fidelity is consistent with not wanting to jeopardize a valued relationship.

Previous research also confirms that people in high-quality, happy relationships are less likely to have affairs (Treas and Giesen 2000). Extramarital sex lowers marital satisfaction and contributes to relationship breakdown (Previti and Amato 2004).

9. *Involvement in "friends with benefits" relationship.* Women who have been in a "friends with benefits" relationship (had sex with a friend in a nonromantic, uncommitted relationship) were more likely to have asked a guy out than women who had not been involved in such a relationship (47.6 percent versus 30.4 percent; p < .001). Because involvement in a FWB relationship may be considered a "deviant" relationship, particularly for the woman because it is a context of sex without commitment, we might expect less traditional women to be attracted to the relationship and to be open to other nontraditional behaviors such as asking guys out.

10. *Used birth control last intercourse.* Women who reported that they had used some form of birth control (other than withdrawal) the last time they had intercourse were more likely to have asked a guy out than women who had used no method of contraception their last intercourse experience (44 percent versus 27.9 percent; p < .006). Similar to the previously used rationale, women initiators sometimes reflected a great deal of selectivity in with whom they choose to have sex. Consistent with such deliberate thinking about intercourse was the decision to protect the relationship from an unwanted pregnancy.

Implications

Analysis of these data revealed that 39.1 percent of the undergraduate women at a large southeastern university had asked a guy to go out (a nontraditional gender role behavior). There are implications of this finding for both women and men. Women who feel uncomfortable asking a man out, who fear rejection for doing so, or who lack the social skills to do so ("Hey big boy! ...Wanna get a pizza?") may be less likely to find the man who will be whisked away by women who have such comfort, overcome their fear of rejection, and who make their interest in a partner known.

The implication of this study for men is not to be surprised when a woman makes a direct request to go out—relationship norms are changing. For some men, this comes as a welcome trend in that they feel burdened that they must always be the first one to indicate interest in a partner and to move the relationship forward. Men might also reevaluate their negative stereotypical notions of women who initiate relationships ("they are loose") and be reminded that the women in this study who had asked men out were *more* likely to have been faithful in previous relationships than those who had not.

Sources

McCready, W., and N. McCready. 1973. "Socialization and the Persistence of Religion." In *The Persistence of Religion*, ed. M. Sussman and S. Steinmetz, 58–68. New York: Macmillan.

Michael, R. T., J. H. Gagnon, E. O. Laumann, and G. Kolata. 1994. *Sex In America: A Definitive Survey*. Boston, MA: Little, Brown and Company.

Miller, A. S., and R. Stark. 2002. "Gender and Religiousness: Can Socialization Explanations Be Saved?" *American Journal of Sociology* 107:1399–1423.

Previti, D., and P. R. Amato. 2004. "Is Infidelity a Cause or Consequence of Poor Marital Quality?" *Journal of Social and Personal Relationships* 21:217–30.

Sherkat, D. E. 2002. "African American Religious Affiliation in the Late 20th Century: Cohort Variations and Patterns of Switching, 1973–1998." *Journal of the Scientific Study of Religion* 41:485–93.

Treas, J., and D. Giesen. 2000. "Sexual Infidelity among Married and Cohabiting Americans." *Journal of Marriage and Family* 62:48–60.

*Study abridged from C. Ross, D. Knox, and M. Zusman. 2008. "Hey Big Boy": Characteristics of university women who initiate relationships with men. Poster, Southern Sociological Society Annual Meeting, April, Richmond, VA.

(comprising a group of people who choose to live together on the basis of a set of shared values), was founded in 1967, and is one of the oldest nonreligious intentional communities in the United States.

The membership is 55 percent male and 45 percent female. Most of the members are white, but there is a wide range of racial, ethnic, and social class backgrounds. Members include gay, straight, bisexual, and transgender people; most are single never-married adults, but there are married couples and families. Sexual values range from celibate to monogamous to polyamorous (about 25 percent of the community are involved in more than one emotional or sexual relationship at the same time). The age range of the members is newborn to 78, with an average age of 40.

The average length of stay for current members is over seven years. There are no officially sanctioned religious beliefs at Twin Oaks—it is not a "spiritual" community, although its members represent various religious values (Jewish, Christian, pagan, atheist, and so on). The core values of the community are nonviolence (no guns, low tolerance for violence of any kind in the community, no parental use of violence against children), egalitarianism (no leader, with everyone having equal political power and the same access to resources), and environmental sustainability (the community endeavors to live off the land, growing its own food and heating its buildings with wood from the forest).

Another core value is income sharing. All the members work together to support everyone in the community instead of working individually to support themselves. Money earned from the three community businesses (weaving hammocks, making tofu, and writing indexes for books) is used to provide food and other basic needs for all members. No one needs to work outside the community. Each member works in the community in a combination of income-producing and domestic jobs. An hour of cooking or gardening receives the same credit as an hour of fixing computers or business management. No matter what work one chooses to do, each member's commitment to the community is forty-two hours of work a week. This includes preparing meals, taking care of children, cleaning bathrooms, and maintaining buildings—activities not considered in the typical mainstream forty-hour workweek.

The community places high value on actively creating a "homegrown" culture. Members provide a large amount of their own entertainment, products, and services. They create homemade furniture, present theatrical and musical performances, and enjoy innovative community holidays such as Validation Day (a distant relative of Valentine's Day, minus the commercialism). The community also encourages participation in activism outside the community. Many members are activists for peace and justice, feminism, and ecological organizations. (This section is based on information provided by Kate Adamson and Ezra Freeman, members of Twin Oaks, and is used with their permission.)

Undergraduate Interest in Finding a Partner

Many college students are not involved in an emotional relationship but are looking for a partner. In a sample of 1,319 undergraduates, 23.1 percent reported that they were not dating and not involved with anyone (Knox and Zusman 2009). In a sample of 377 first-year students at the same university, 57 percent of the men and 43 percent of the women reported that finding a girlfriend or boyfriend was important (Knox et al. 2007). Indeed, all societies have a way of moving women and men from same-sex groups into pair-bonded legal relationships for the reproduction and socialization of children.

Ways of Finding a Partner

One of the unique qualities of the college or university environment is that it provides a context in which to meet thousands of potential partners of similar age, education, and social class. This context will likely never recur following graduation. Although people often meet through friends or on their own in school, work, or recreation contexts, an increasing number are open to a range of alternatives, from hanging out to the Internet.

Hanging Out

The term *hanging out* has made its way into the professional literature (Harcourt 2005; Thomas 2005). **Hanging out**, also referred to as getting together, refers to going out in groups where the agenda is to meet others and have fun. The individuals may watch television, rent a video, go to a club or party, and/or eat out. Hanging out may be considered "testing the waters," as a possible prelude to more serious sexual involvement and commitment (Luff and Hoffman 2006). Of 1,319 undergraduates, 93.4 percent reported that "hanging out for me is basically about meeting people and having fun" (Knox and Zusman 2009). Hanging out may occur in group settings such as at a bar, a sorority or fraternity party, or a small gathering of friends that keeps expanding. Friends may introduce individuals, or they may meet someone "cold," as in initiating a conversation. There is usually no agenda beyond meeting and having fun. Of the 1,319 respondents, only 4 percent said that hanging out was about beginning a relationship that may lead to marriage (Knox and Zusman 2009).

Hooking Up

Hooking up is also a term that has entered the social science literature and has become the focus of research. **Hooking up** is defined as a one-time sexual encounter in which there are generally no expectations of seeing one another again. The nature of the sexual expression may be making out, oral sex, and/or sexual intercourse. The term is also used to denote getting together periodically for a sexual encounter, with no strings attached (Luff and Hoffman 2006). Renshaw (2005) wrote his dissertation on hooking up and noted that hooking up involves playful or nonserious interaction where one's body and the context of alcohol move the encounter to a sexual ending.

In a sample of 1,319 undergraduates, 29 percent reported that they had "hooked up" (had oral sex or sexual intercourse) the first time they met someone. As a hypothetical question, when respondents were asked if they were to "hook up" with the right person, and felt good about the interaction would they have oral or sexual intercourse with a person they just met, 32.4 percent responded "yes" (Knox and Zusman 2009).

Bogle (2008) interviewed fifty-seven college students and alumni at two universities in the eastern United States about their experiences with dating and sex. She found that hooking up had become the *primary* means for heterosexuals to get together on campus. About half (47 percent) of hookups start at a party and involve alcohol, with men averaging five drinks and women three drinks (England and Thomas 2006). The sexual behaviors that were reported to occur during a hookup included kissing and nongenital touching (34 percent), hand stimulation of genitals (19 percent), oral sex (22 percent), and intercourse (23 percent) (England and Thomas 2006).

Researchers (Bogle 2008; Eshbaugh and Gute 2008) note that, although hooking up may be an exciting sexual adventure, it is fraught with feelings of regret. Some of the women in their studies were particularly disheartened to discover that hooking up usually did not result in the development of a relationship that went beyond a one-night encounter. Eshbaugh and Gute (2008) examined hooking up as a predictor of sexual regret in 152 sexually active college women and identified two sexual behaviors that were particularly predictive of participants' regret: (a) engaging in sexual intercourse with someone once and only once, and (b) engaging in intercourse with someone known for less than twenty-four hours. Noncoital hookups (performing and receiving oral sex) were not significantly related to regret. Indeed, Bogle (2002; 2008) noted three outcomes of hooking up. In the first, previously described, nothing results from the first-night sexual encounter. In the second, the college students will

The problem with hooking up is the lack of trust. The defining characteristic of hooking up is the ability to unhook at any time—it is the context of lack of commitment that has become the norm. Hookups are sex without love.

Laura Stepp, *Unhooked*

repeatedly hook up with each other on subsequent occasions of "hanging out." However, a low level of commitment characterizes this type of relationship, in that each person is still open to hooking up with someone else. A third outcome of hooking up, and the least likely, is that the two people begin going out or spending time together in an exclusive relationship. Hence, hooking up is most often a sexual adventure that rarely results in the development of a relationship. Stepp (2007) interviewed two groups of high school and one group of college students and discovered the same outcome in most relationships involving hooking up—they rarely end with the couple becoming a monogamous pair. However, there are exceptions. When 1,319 undergraduates were presented with the statement "People who 'hook up' and have sex the first night don't end up in a stable relationship," 16.7 percent disagreed (Knox and Zusman 2009).

Renshaw (2005) noted that hooking up is becoming normative and replacing contemporary patterns of dating. He suggested that it is "shrouded in deception," "contains individual health risks associated with sex," and "may also threaten traditional conceptions of marriage and family."

The Internet—Meeting Online and After

"We could never let anyone know how we really met," remarked a couple who had met on the Internet. "People who meet online are stigmatized as desperate losers." As more individuals use the Internet, such stigmatization is changing. Almost three-fourths (74 percent) of single Americans have used the Internet to find a romantic partner, and 15 percent report that they know someone who met their spouse or significant other online (Madden and Lenhart 2006). Yahoo.com claims over 375 million visits to their online dating site each month (Whitty et al. 2007).

Online meetings will continue to increase as people delay getting married and move beyond contexts where hundreds or thousands of potential partners are available (the undergraduate coed classroom filled with same-age potential mates is rarely equaled in the workplace after college). The profiles that individuals construct or provide for others to view reflect impression management, presenting an image that is perceived to be what the target audience wants. In this regard, men tend to emphasize their status characteristics (for example,

This couple met on the Internet and are now married.

Chapter 5 Singlehood, Hanging Out, Hooking Up, and Cohabitation

income, education, career), whereas women tend to emphasize their youth, trim body, and beauty (Spitzberg and Cupach 2007).

The attraction of online dating is its efficiency. It takes time and effort to meet someone at a coffee shop for an hour, only to discover that the person has habits (for example, does or doesn't smoke) or values (too religious or too agnostic) that would eliminate them as a potential partner. Match.com features 8 million profiles that can be scanned at one's leisure. For noncollege people who are busy in their job or career, the Internet offers the chance to meet someone outside their immediate social circle. "There are only six guys in my office," noted one Internet user. "Four are married and the other two are alcoholics. I don't go to church and don't like bars so the Internet has become my guy store."

More than 1,000 Internet sites are designed for the purpose of meeting a partner online (Jerin and Dolinsky 2007). Over $500 million are spent on these sites (Stringfield 2008). Right Mate at Heartchoice.com is one of them and offers not only a way to meet others but a free "Right Mate Checkup" to evaluate whether the person is right for you. Some websites exist to target specific interests such as black singles (BlackPlanet.com), Jewish singles (Jdate.com), and gay people (Gay.com). In one study on online dating, women received an average of fifty-five replies compared to men who reported receiving thirty-nine replies. Younger women (average age of 35), attractive women, and those who wrote longer profiles were more successful in generating replies (Whitty 2007).

In addition to the efficiency of meeting someone online, other advantages include the opportunity to develop a relationship with another on the basis of content independent of visual distraction. The Internet also allows one to avoid noisy, smoky bars and to try on new identities. Defining identity as an understanding of who one is, Yurchisin et al. (2005) interviewed individuals who had used an Internet dating service in the past year and found that some posted a profile of who they wanted to be rather than who they were. For example, a respondent reported wanting to be more athletic so she checked various recreational activities she didn't currently engage in but wanted to. The Internet is also a place for people to "try out" a gay identity if they are very uncomfortable doing so in real life, around people they know. The disadvantages of online meeting include deception; the potential to fall in love too quickly as a result of intense mutual disclosure; not being able to assess "chemistry" or to observe nonverbal cues and gestures or how a person interacts with your friends or family; and the tendency to move too quickly (from e-mail to phone to meeting to first date) to marriage, without spending much time to get to know each other. Of the respondents in the previously mentioned Internet study, 40 percent reported that they had lied online. Men tend to lie about their economic status, and women tend to lie about their physical appearance, weight, or age. Other lies include marital status (Gibbs et al. 2006). Kassem Saleh was married yet maintained fifty simultaneous online relationships with other women. He allegedly wrote intoxicating love letters, many of which were cut and paste jobs to various women. He made marriage proposals to several and some bought wedding gowns in anticipation of the wedding (Albright 2007). Although Saleh is an "Internet guy," it is important to keep in mind that people not on the Internet may also be very deceptive and cunning. To suggest that the Internet is the only place where deceivers lurk is to turn a blind eye to those people met through traditional channels.

McGinty (2006) noted the importance of using Internet dating sites safely, including not giving out home or business phone numbers or addresses, always meeting the person in one's own town with a friend, and not posting photos that are "too revealing," as these can be copied and posted elsewhere. She recommends being open and honest: "Let them know who you are and who you are looking for," she suggests.

The Internet may also be used to find out information about a partner. Argali.com can be used to find out where the Internet mystery person lives, Zabasearch.com for how long the person has lived there, and Zoominfo.com for where the person works. The person's birth date can be found at Birthdatabase.com. Women might want to see if any red flags have been posted on the Internet at Dontdatehimgirl.com.

For individuals who learn about each other online, what is it like to finally meet? First, they tend to meet each other relatively quickly; often, after three e-mail exchanges, they will move to a phone call and set up a time to meet during that phone call (McKenna 2007). When they do meet, Baker (2007) is clear: "If they have presented themselves accurately and honestly online, they encounter few or minor surprises at the first meeting offline or later on in further encounters" (p. 108). About 7 percent end up marrying someone they met online (Albright 2007).

Internet Partners: The Downside

Although most Internet exchanges or relationships are positive, it is important to be cautious of meeting someone online. See the website WildXAngel (the address is in the Weblinks at the end of this chapter) for horror stories of online dating. Although the Internet is a good place to meet new people, it also allows someone you rejected or an old lover to monitor your online behavior. Most sites note when you have been online last, so if you reject someone online by saying, "I'm really not ready for a relationship," that same person can log on and see that you are still looking. Some individuals become obsessed with a person they meet online and turn into a cyberstalker when rejected. This will be discussed in Chapter 13 on violence and abuse.

Video Chatting

Video chatting moves beyond communicating by typewritten words and allows potential partners to see each other while chatting online. One of the largest online communities with downloadable software is iSpQ ("Eye Speak," http://www.ispq.com/), which enables people to visually meet with others all over the world. Hodge (2003) noted, "Unlike conventional chat rooms, iSpQ does not have a running dialogue or conversation for anyone to view. Video chatting allows users to have personal or private conversations with another user. Hence an individual can not only write information but see the person with whom he or she is interacting online." Half of the respondents in Hodge's study of video chat users reported "meeting people and having fun" as their motivation for video chatting.

Speed-Dating: The Eight-Minute Date

Dating innovations that involve the concept of speed include the eight-minute date. The website http://www.8minutedating.com/ identifies these "Eight-Minute Dating Events" throughout the country, where a person has eight one-on-one dates that last eight minutes each. If both parties are interested in seeing each other again, the organizer provides contact information so that the individuals can set up another date. Speed-dating is cost-effective because it allows daters to meet face-to-face without burning up a whole evening. Adams et al. (2008) interviewed participants who had experienced speed-dating to assess how they conceptualized the event. They found that women were more likely to view speed-dating as an investment of time and energy to find someone (58 percent versus 25 percent), whereas men were more likely to see the event as one of exploration (for example, see how flexible a person was) (75 percent versus 17 percent). Wilson et al. (2006) collected data on nineteen young men who had three-minute social exchanges with nineteen young women and found that those partners who wanted to see each other again had more in common than those who did not want to see each other again. Common interests were assessed using the compatibility quotient (CQ).

These individuals are on a "speed-date" where they have only a few minutes to evaluate each other before a bell rings and they move to a new table.

Authors

International Dating

Go to google.com and type in "international brides," and you will see an array of sites dedicated to finding foreign women for Americans. Not listed is Ivan Thompson, who specializes in finding Mexican women for his American clients. As documented in the movie *Cupid Cowboy* (Ohayon 2005), Ivan takes males (one at a time) to Mexico (Torreón is his favorite place). For $3,000, Ivan places an ad in a local newspaper for a young (age 20 to 35), trim (less than 130 pounds), single woman "interested in meeting an American male for romance and eventual marriage" and waits in a hotel for the phone to ring. They then meet and interview "candidates" in the hotel lobby. Ivan says his work is done when his client finds a woman he likes.

Advertising for a partner is not unusual. Jagger (2005) conducted a content analysis of 1,094 advertisements and found that young men and older women were the most likely to advertise for a partner. The researcher also noted a trend in women seeking younger men.

Diversity in Other Countries

Matchmakers and astrologers were the precursors to Match.com and eHarmony. Prior to 1950, Chinese parents arranged for the marriages of their children with the help of a professional matchmaker. The matchmaker was "usually an elderly woman who knew the birthday, temperament, and appearance of every unmarried man and woman in her community" (Xia and Zhou 2003, 231). This woman would visit parents with children who were ready for marriage and propose specific individuals, usually of similar social and economic status. If the parents liked a man the matchmaker was proposing for their daughter, the matchmaker would meet with the man's parents and alert them of the family's interest in their son marrying the daughter. If the parents agreed, a Chinese astrologer would be consulted to see if their signs of the zodiac were compatible. If the signs were off, the marriage would be too, and the families would have no further contact.

If you are looking for love on the Internet, you better look here first.

Lisa, founder of Wildxangel.com

Functions of Involvement with a Partner

Meeting and becoming involved with someone has at least seven functions: (1) confirmation of a social self; (2) recreation; (3) companionship, intimacy, and sex; (4) anticipatory socialization; (5) status achievement; (6) mate selection; and (7) health enhancement.

1. *Confirmation of a social self.* In Chapter 1, we noted that symbolic interactionists emphasize the development of the self. Parents are usually the first social mirrors in which we see ourselves and receive feedback about who we are; new partners continue the process. When we are hanging out with a person, we are continually trying to assess how that person sees us: Does the person like me? Will the person want to be with me again? When the person gives us positive feedback through speech and gesture, we feel good about ourselves and tend to view ourselves in positive terms. Hanging out provides a context for the confirmation of a strong self-concept in terms of how we perceive our effect on other people.

2. Recreation. The focus of hanging out and pairing off is fun. Reality television programs such as *Next, Blind Date, Elimidate,* and *The Bachelor* always use recreational activities as a context to help participants interact; being a fun person seems to be a criterion for being selected. The couples may make only small talk and learn very little about each other—what seems important is not that they have common interests, values, or goals but that they "have fun."

3. Companionship, intimacy, and sex. Beyond fun, major motivations for finding a new person and pairing off are companionship, intimacy, and sex. The impersonal environment of a large university makes a secure relationship very appealing. "My last two years have been the happiest ever," remarked a senior in interior design. "But it's because of the involvement with my partner. During my freshman and sophomore years, I felt alone. Now I feel loved, needed, and secure."

4. Anticipatory socialization. Before puberty, boys and girls interact primarily with same-sex peers. A fifth grader may be laughed at if showing an interest in someone of the other sex. Even when boy-girl interaction becomes the norm at puberty, neither sex may know what is expected of the other. Meeting a new partner and hanging out provides the first opportunity for individuals to learn how to interact with other-sex partners. Though the manifest function of hanging out is to teach partners how to negotiate differences (for example, how much sex and how soon), the latent function is to help them learn the skills necessary to maintain long-term relationships (empathy, communication, and negotiation, for example). In effect, pairing off involves a form of socialization that anticipates a more permanent union in one's life. Individuals may also try out different role patterns, like dominance or passivity, and try to assess the feel and comfort level of each.

5. Status achievement. Being involved with someone is usually associated with more status than being unattached and alone. Some may seek such involvement because of the associated higher status. Others may become involved for peer acceptance and conformity to gender roles, not for emotional reasons. Though the practice is becoming less common, some gay people may pair off with someone of the other sex so as to provide a heterosexual cover for their sexual orientation.

6. Mate selection. Finally, pairing off may eventually lead to marriage, which remains a major goal in our society (Pryor et al. 2008). Selecting a mate has

Married couples may also find themselves in a long-distance relationship. President Barack Obama and his wife Michelle were separated for a year and a half while he campaigned for the presidency.

Chapter 5 Singlehood, Hanging Out, Hooking Up, and Cohabitation

become big business. B. Dalton, one of the largest bookstore chains in the United States, carries about 200 titles on relationships, about 50 of which are specifically geared toward finding a mate.

7. Health enhancement. In Chapter 1, we reviewed the benefits of marriage. Not the least of marital benefits is health. Specifically, there is a direct relationship between getting married for the first time and the cessation of smoking (Weden and Kimbro 2007).

PERSONAL CHOICES

Should I Get Involved in a Long-Distance Relationship?

About a third of university students will become involved in a long-distance relationship (Cameron and Ross 2007). These result when couples in a relationship part due to one of them going away to school, to a job, or to a military deployment. Alternatively, individuals may meet online and discover that great distances separate them. Career commitments may also involve being separated from one's partner. Michelle Obama noted that Barack was "away for a couple of years during the campaign for the presidency but called home very night." After the election, when Obama was asked how things had changed, he replied, "I sleep in my own bed at night."

The primary advantages of long-distance relationships include: positive labeling ("even though we are separated, we care about each other enough to maintain our relationship"), keeping the relationship "high" because constant togetherness does not dull it, having time to devote to school or a career, and having a lot of one's own personal time and space. People suited for such relationships have developed their own autonomy or independence for the times they are apart, have a focus for their time such as school or a job, have developed open communication with their partner to talk about the difficulty of being separated, and have learned to trust each other because they spend a lot of time away from each other. Another advantage is that the partner may actually look better from afar than up close. One respondent noted that he and his partner could not wait to live together after they had been separated—but "when we did, I found out I liked her better when she wasn't there."

The primary disadvantages of long-distance relationships include being frustrated over not being able to be with the partner, loneliness, feeling as though one is missing out on other activities and relationships, missing physical intimacy, and spending a lot of money on phone calls or travel.

Knox et al. (2002) analyzed a sample of 438 undergraduates at a large southeastern university on their attitudes and involvement in a long-distance relationship (LDR)—defined as being separated from a love partner by at least 200 miles for a period of not less than three months. The median number of miles these LDR respondents had been separated was 300 to 399 (about a six-hour drive), and the median length of time they were separated was five months. Of the total sample, 20 percent were currently involved in an LDR, and 37 percent had been previously.

Being separated is associated with stress, depression, relationship unhappiness, and breaking up (Cameron and Ross 2007). In the Knox et al. (2002) study, one in five (21.5 percent) broke up, and another one in five (20 percent) said that the separation made their relationship worse. Only 18 percent reported that the separation improved their relationship (other responses included a mixed effect for 33 percent and no effect for 9 percent).

Does absence make the heart grow fonder for the beloved? Most of those who have not been separated seemed to think so. But 40 percent of those who had experienced an LDR believed that "out of sight, out of mind" was a more accurate characterization (Knox et al. 2002). One respondent said, "I got tired of being lonely, and the women around me started looking good." However, Guldner (2003) noted that LDRs are no more likely to end because of infidelity than those relationships in which the partners lived in the same town. In this regard, he noted that the quality of the relationship and personality of the individuals were more important factors than distance.

For couples who have the goal of maintaining their relationship and not letting the distance break them, some specific things to do include:

1. *Maintain daily contact.* In the Knox et al. (2002) study previously mentioned, actual contact between the lovers during the period of separation was limited. Only 11 percent reported seeing each other weekly, and 16 percent reported that they never saw each other. However, 77 percent reported talking with each other by phone several times each week (22 percent daily), and 53 percent e-mailed the partner several times each week (18 percent daily). Some partners maintain daily contact by web cams. One student reported the following:

> We get to see each other every day, in real time, whenever we want to. Because the connection doesn't interfere with the telephone, we stay connected 24 hours a day. It has been a big help in keeping our relationship going strong. If we need to talk about an important issue, we can do it face-to-face without worrying about time or money. Also, because we can't physically be together, this device has helped our personal lives as well. We can see each other whenever we want in whatever way that we want. We have been together for over a year, and during that year we have been connected by the web cams for over eleven months. Technology has certainly helped our relationship last!

2. *Enjoy or use the time when apart.* While separated, it is important to remain busy with study, friends, work, sports, and personal projects. Doing so will make the time pass faster.

3. *Avoid conflictual phone conversations.* Talking on the phone should involve the typical sharing of events. When the need to discuss a difficult topic arises, the phone is not the best place for such a discussion. Rather, it may be wiser to wait and have the discussion face-to-face. If you decide to settle a disagreement over the phone, stick to it until you have a solution acceptable to both of you.

4. *Stay monogamous.* Agreeing not to be open to other relationships is crucial to maintaining a long-distance relationship. This translates into not being open to others while apart. Individuals who say, "Let's date others to see if we are really meant to be together," often discover that they are capable of being attracted to and becoming involved with numerous "others." Such other involvements usually predict the end of an LDR. Lydon et al. (1997) studied sixty-nine undergraduates who were involved in LDRs and found that "moral commitment" predicted the survival of the relationships. Individuals committed to maintaining their relationships are often successful in doing so.

5. *Other strategies.* Researchers at the University of Pittsburgh revealed that partners who were separated from each other reported preserving, smelling, and wearing the clothes of a sexual partner. Over half the men and almost 90 percent of the women had deliberately smelled their partner's blouse or shirt to feel a sense of closeness with the partner from whom they were separated (Gardiner 2005). Maguire (2007) noted that those who cope successfully with long-distance relationships report less stress and depression, and feel that they will end up together again.

Sources

Cameron, J. J., and M. Ross. 2007. In times of uncertainty: Predicting the survival of long-distance relationships. *The Journal of Social Psychology* 147:581–604.

Gardiner, D. 2005. A sniff of your sweetie. *Psychology Today* 38:31–2.

Guldner, G. T. 2003. *Long Distance Relationships: The Complete Guide.* Corona, CA: JFMilne Publications.

Knox, D., M. Zusman, V. Daniels, and A. Brantley. 2002. Absence makes the heart grow fonder? Long-distance dating relationships among college students. *College Student Journal* 36:365–67.

Lydon, J., T. Pierce, and S. O'Regan. 1997. Coping with moral commitment to long-distance dating relationships. *Journal of Personality and Social Psychology* 73:104–13.

Maguire, K. C. 2007. "Will It Ever End?": A (re)examination of uncertainty in college student long-distance dating relationships. *Communication Quarterly* 55:415–27.

Dating after Divorce

Over 2 million Americans get divorced each year. As evidenced by the fact that more than three-quarters of divorced people remarry within five years, most divorced people are open to a new relationship. But this single-again population differs from those becoming involved for the first time.

1. *Internet for New Partner.* Aside from traditional ways to meet new partners (through friends, at work, at health or exercise clubs, religious services) the Internet has become a valuable tool for divorced people in finding someone new. Divorced people are very busy. With full-time jobs and single parenthood, they can have little time for traditional dating. The Internet provides a quick way to sift through hundreds of people in one's spare time and start up an e-mail relationship on the home computer. Then, if the person looks and "feels right," the couple can set up a time to meet. One researcher studied the profiles of people on the Internet and found that the more attractive the photograph on one's profile, the greater the number of responses (de Vries et al. 2007).

2. *Older population.* Divorced individuals are, on the average, ten years older than people in the marriage market who have never been married before. Hence, divorced people tend to be in their mid- to late thirties. Widows and widowers are usually 40 and 30 years older, respectively (hence, around ages 65 and 55), when they begin to date the second time around. Most divorced people date and marry others who are divorced.

3. *Fewer potential partners.* Most men and women who are dating the second time around find fewer partners from whom to choose than when they were dating before their first marriage. The large pool of never-married people (25 percent of the population) and currently married people (56 percent of the population) is usually not considered an option (*Statistical Abstract of the United States, 2009,* Table 55). Most divorced people (10 percent of the population) date and marry others who have also been married before.

4. *Increased HIV risk.* The older unmarried people are, the greater the likelihood that they have had multiple sexual partners, which is associated with increased risk of contracting HIV and other STIs. Therefore, individuals entering the dating market for the second time are advised to *always* use a condom and to assume that one's partner has been sexually active and is at risk.

5. *Children.* More than half of the divorced people who are dating again have children from a previous marriage. How these children feel about their parents dating, how the partners feel about each other's children, and how the partners' children feel about each other are challenging issues. Deciding whether to have intercourse when one's children are in the house, when a new partner should be introduced to the children, and what the children should call the new partner are other issues familiar to parents dating for the second time.

6. *Ex-spouse issues.* Ex-spouses may be uncomfortable with their former partner's involvement in a new relationship. They may not only create anxiety on the part of their former spouse but may also directly attack the new partner. Dealing with an ex-spouse may be challenging. Ties to an ex-spouse, in the form of child support or alimony, and phone calls may also have an influence on the new dating relationship. Some individuals remain psychologically and sexually involved with their exes. In other cases, if the divorce was bitter, partners may be preoccupied or frustrated in their attempts to cope with a harassing ex-spouse (and feel emotionally distant).

7. *Brief courtship.* Divorced people who are dating again tend to have a shorter courtship period than people married for the first time. In a study of 248 individuals who remarried, the median length of courtship was nine

months, as opposed to seventeen months the first time around (O'Flaherty and Eells 1988). A shorter courtship may mean that sexual decisions are confronted more quickly—timing of first intercourse, discussing the use of condoms and contraceptives, and clarifying whether the relationship is to be monogamous. People who have been previously divorced or widowed derive a new sense of well-being for spending time with or becoming involved with a new partner. Caution may be prudent because the old rules still apply. Knowing a partner at least two years before marrying that person is predictive of a happier and more durable relationship than marriage after a short courtship. Divorced people pursuing a new relationship might consider slowing down their relationship.

Aside from the various issues to keep in mind regarding a new partner, Krumrei et al. (2007) studied unhappiness and maladjustment of divorced people in twenty-one studies in reference to social relationships. Divorced people who had a network of relationships reported higher levels of positive adjustment. One take-home message is that dating again and creating a new network of friendships and relationships is functional for one's divorce adjustment.

Cultural and Historical Background of Dating

Any consideration of current patterns of pairing off must take into account a historical view. Contemporary patterns of hanging out in the United States today are radically different from courtship and dating in other cultures and times.

Traditional Chinese "Dating" Norms

The freedom with which American partners today select each other on the basis of love is a relatively recent phenomenon. At most times and in most cultures, parents arranged marriages more often. Love feelings between the partners, if they existed, were given either no or limited consideration. In traditional China, **blind marriages**, wherein the bride and groom were prevented from seeing each other for the first time until their wedding day, were the norm. The marriage of two individuals was seen as the linking of two families. The influence of parents in the mate selection of offspring in China today is decreasing (such arranged marriages are no longer the norm).

Quinceñera, Hispanic Rite of Passage

The fiesta of **quinceñera** is a rite of passage for 15-year-old Latina/Hispanic girls. The word *quinceñera* comes from the Spanish quince meaning "fifteen" and from años, which means "years." The event marks the time when young girls emerge from childhood into womanhood and when young men may show interest in them as future wives and mothers. A family priest in the church performs the quinceñera ceremony that both the girl's family and surrounding community attend, and the girl's baptismal godparents oversee the spiritual celebration.

Dating during the Puritan Era in the United States

Although less strict than traditional courtship norms among the Chinese, the European marriage patterns brought to America were conservative. Puritans who settled on the coast of New England in the seventeenth century were radical Protestants who had seceded from the Church of England. They valued marriage and fidelity, as reflected in a very rigid pattern of courtship.

Bundling, also called *tarrying*, was a courtship custom commonly practiced among the Puritans. In this custom, the would-be groom sleeps in the girl's bed in her parents' home. But there were rules to restrict sexual contact. Both

These 15-year-old Hispanic girls are experiencing their *quinceñera*, which will change the way men relate to them and their parents.

Ed Andrieski/AP Photo

partners had to be fully clothed, and a board was placed between them. In addition, the young girl might be encased in a type of long laundry bag up to her armpits, her clothes might be sewn together at strategic points, and her parents might sleep in the same room.

The justifications for bundling were convenience and economics. Aside from meeting at church, bundling was one of the few opportunities a couple had to get together to talk and learn about each other. Because heavy work demands consumed daylight hours, night became the only time for courtship. How did the bed become the courtship arena? New England winters were cold. Firewood, oil for lamps, and candles were in short supply. By talking in bed, the young couple could come to know each other without wasting valuable sources of energy. Although bundling flourished in the middle of the eighteenth century, it provoked a great deal of controversy. By about 1800, the custom had virtually disappeared.

Effects of the Industrial Revolution on Dating

The transition from a courtship system controlled by parents to the relative freedom of mate selection experienced today occurred in response to a number of social changes. The most basic change was the Industrial Revolution, which began in England in the middle of the eighteenth century. In the past, the "good husband" was evaluated primarily in terms of being an economic provider. The "good wife" was valued for her domestic aptitude—her ability to spin yarn, make clothes, cook meals, preserve food, and care for children. Commercial industries had developed to provide these services, and women transferred their activities in these areas from the home to the factory. The result was that women had more frequent contact with men.

Women's involvement in factory work decreased parental control because parents were unable to dictate the extent to which their offspring could interact with those they met at work. Hence, values in mate selection shifted from the parents to the children. Contemporary mates are more likely to be selected on the basis of personal qualities, particularly for love and companionship, than for either utilitarian or economic reasons.

Changes in Dating in the Past Fifty Years

The Industrial Revolution had a profound effect on courtship patterns, but these patterns have continued to change in the past fifty years. The changes include an increase in the age at marriage. Marrying at age 29 rather than 22 provides more time and opportunity to date more people.

The dating pool today also includes an increasing number of individuals in their thirties who have been married before. These individuals often have children, which changes the nature of a date from two adults going to a movie alone to renting a movie and babysitting in the apartment or home of one of the partners.

As we will note later in this chapter, cohabitation has become more normative. For some couples, the sequence of dating, falling in love, and getting married has been replaced by dating, falling in love, and living together. Such a sequence results in the marriage of couples that are more relationship-savvy than those who dated and married out of high school.

Not only do individuals now date more partners and live together more often, but also gender role relationships have become more egalitarian. Though the double standard still exists, women today are more likely than women in the 1950s to ask men out, to have sex with them without requiring a commitment, and to postpone marriage until meeting their own educational and career goals. Women no longer feel desperate to marry but consider marriage one of many goals they have for themselves.

Unlike during the 1950s, both sexes today are aware of and somewhat cautious of becoming HIV-infected. Sex has become potentially deadly, and condoms are being used more frequently. The 1950s fear of asking a druggist for a condom has been replaced by the confidence and mundaneness of buying condoms along with one's groceries.

Finally, couples of today are more aware of the impermanence of marriage. However, most couples continue to feel that divorce will not happen to them, and they remain committed to domestic goals. Over three-quarters (76 percent) of all first-year college students in the United States reported that "raising a family" was "an essential or very important goal" for them (Pryor et al. 2008).

To assess the relationship with your partner at this time, complete the Relationships Dynamics in the Self-Assessment section.

Cohabitation

Cohabitation, also known as living together, is becoming more normative. In a sample of 1,293 adolescents, 75 percent regarded living together as an option before marriage (Manning et al. 2007). Of 1,319 undergraduates at a large southeastern university, 71.9 percent reported that they would live with a partner they were not married to, and 16 percent were or had already done so (Knox and Zusman 2009). Reasons for the increase in cohabitation include career or educational commitments; increased tolerance of society, parents, and peers; improved birth control technology; desire for a stable emotional and sexual relationship without legal ties; and greater disregard for convention. Twenge (2006) surveyed university students and found that 62 percent paid little attention to social conventions. Cohabitants also regard living together as a vaccination against divorce. Later, we will review studies emphasizing that this hope is more often an illusion.

Diversity in Other Countries

Over 90 percent of first marriages in Sweden are preceded by cohabitation; however, only 12 percent of first marriages in Italy are preceded by cohabitation (Kiernan 2000).

Relationships Dynamics Scale

Please answer each of the following questions in terms of your relationship with your "mate" if married, or your "partner" if dating or engaged. We recommend that you answer these questions by yourself (not with your partner), using the ranges following for your own reflection.

Use the following three-point scale to rate how often you and your mate or partner experience the following:

1 = almost never
2 = once in a while
3 = frequently

1 2 3 Little arguments escalate into ugly fights with accusations, criticisms, name-calling, or bringing up past hurts.

1 2 3 My partner criticizes or belittles my opinions, feelings, or desires.

1 2 3 My partner seems to view my words or actions more negatively that I mean them to be.

1 2 3 When we have a problem to solve, it is like we are on opposite teams.

1 2 3 I hold back from telling my partner what I really think and feel.

1 2 3 I think seriously about what it would be like to date or marry someone else.

1 2 3 I feel lonely in this relationship.

1 2 3 When we argue, one of us withdraws (that is, doesn't want to talk about it anymore; or leaves the scene).

Who tends to withdraw more when there is an argument?

Male
Female
Both Equally
Neither Tend to Withdraw

Where Are You in Your Marriage

We devised these questions based on seventeen years of research at the University of Denver on the kinds of communication and conflict management patterns that predict if a relationship is headed for trouble. We have recently completed a nationwide, random phone survey using these questions. The average score was 11 on this scale. Although you should not take a higher score to mean that your relationship is somehow destined to fail, higher scores can mean that your relationship may be in greater danger unless changes are made. (These ranges are based only on your individual ratings—not a couple total.)

8 to 12 "Green Light"

If you scored in the 8 to 12 range, your relationship is probably in good or even great shape *at this time,* but we emphasize "*at this time*" because relationships don't stand still. In the next twelve months, you'll either have a stronger, happier relationship, or you could head in the other direction.

To think about it another way, it's like you are traveling along and have come to a green light. There is no need to stop, but it is probably a great time to work on making your relationship all it can be.

13 to 17 "Yellow Light"

If you scored in the 13 to 17 range, it's like you are coming to a "yellow light." You need to be cautious. Although you may be happy now in your relationship, your score reveals warning signs of patterns you don't want to let get worse. You'll want to take action to protect and improve what you have. Spending time to strengthen your relationship now could be the best thing you could do for your future together.

18 to 24 "Red Light"

Finally, if you scored in the 18 to 24 range, this is like approaching a red light. Stop, and think about where the two of you are headed. Your score indicates the presence of patterns that could put your relationship at significant risk. You may be heading for trouble—or already be there. But there is *good news.* You can stop and learn ways to improve your relationship now!

1. *We wrote these items based on understanding of many key studies in the field.* The content or themes behind the questions are based on numerous in-depth studies on how people think and act in their marriages. These kinds of dynamics have been compared with patterns on many other key variables, such as satisfaction, commitment, problem intensity, and so on. Because the kinds of methods researchers can use in their laboratories are quite complex, this actual measure is far simpler than many of the methods we and others use to study marriages over time. However, the themes are based on many solid studies. Caution is warranted in interpreting scores.

2. *The discussion of the Relationships Dynamics Scale gives rough guidelines for interpreting the meaning of the scores.* The ranges we suggest for the measure are based on results from a nationwide, random phone survey of 947 people (85 percent married) in January 1996. These ranges are meant as a rough guideline for helping couples assess the degree to which they are experiencing key danger signs in their marriages. The measure as you have it here powerfully discriminated between those doing well in their marriages or relationships and those who were not doing well on a host of other dimensions (thoughts of divorce, low satisfaction, low sense of friendship in the relationship, lower dedication, and so on). Couples scoring more highly on these items are truly more likely to be experiencing problems (or, based on other research, are more likely to experience problems in the future).

3. *This measure in and of itself should not be taken as a predictor of couples who are going to fail in their marriages.* No couple should be told they will "not make it" based on a higher score. That would not be in keeping with our intention in developing this scale or with the meaning one could take from it for any one couple. Although the items are based on studies that assess such things as the likelihood of a marriage working out, we would hate for any one person to take this and assume the worst about their future based on a high score. Rather, we believe that the measure can be used to motivate high- and moderately high-scoring people to take a serious look at where their relationships are heading—and take steps to turn such negative patterns around for the better.

Source

Stanley S. M., and H. J. Markman. 1997. *Marriage and Family: A Brief Introduction.* Reprinted with permission of PREP, Inc.

Note

For more information on constructive tools for strong marriages, or for questions about the measure and the meaning of it, please write to us at PREP, Inc., P. O. Box 102530, Denver, Colorado 80250-2530.

National Data

There are 6 million unmarried-couple households in the United States (*Statistical Abstract of the United States, 2009*, Table 62).

Almost 60 percent of women (59 percent) have lived together before age 24. Most of these relationships were short-lived, with 20 percent resulting in marriage (Schoen et al. 2007). People who live together before marriage are more likely to be high school dropouts than college graduates (60 percent versus 37 percent), to have been married, to be less religious or traditional, and to be supportive of egalitarian gender roles (Baxter 2005). Indeed, compared to married people, cohabitant couples are more likely to include men who perform household chores (Davis et al. 2007). Cohabitants are also less likely to be getting economic support from their parents (Eggebeen 2005).

Same-Sex Cohabitation and Race

Although U.S. Census Bureau surveys do not ask about sexual orientation or gender identity, same-sex cohabiting couples may identify themselves as "unmarried partners." Those couples in which both partners are men or both are women are considered to be same-sex couples or households for purposes of research. Of the six million unmarried partner households, 7 percent consist of two males; 6 percent consist of two females (*Statistical Abstract of the United States, 2009*, Table 62). Of these 779,867 households, we might estimate that about 13 percent or about 100,000 (101,382) are black couples. These couples must cope with both heterosexism and racism.

Definitions of Cohabitation

Research has used more than twenty definitions of cohabitation (also referred to as **living together**). These various definitions involve variables such as duration of the relationship, frequency of overnight visits, emotional or sexual nature of the relationship, and sex of the partners. Most research on cohabitation has been conducted on heterosexual live-in couples. Even partners in relationships may view the meaning of their cohabitation differently, with women viewing it more as a sign of a committed relationship moving toward marriage and men viewing it as an alternative to marriage or as a test to see whether future commitment is something to pursue. We define cohabitation as two unrelated adults involved in an emotional and sexual relationship who sleep overnight in the same residence on a regular basis. The terms used to describe live-in couples include cohabitants and **POSSLQs** (people of the opposite sex sharing living quarters), the latter term used by the U.S. Census Bureau.

Eight Types of Cohabitation Relationships

There are various types of cohabitation:

1. *Here and now*. These new partners have an affectionate relationship and are focused on the here and now, not the future of the relationship. Only a small proportion of people living together report that the "here and now" type characterizes their relationship (Jamieson et al. 2002). Rhoades et al. (2009) studied a sample of 240 cohabiting heterosexual couples and found that wanting to spend more time together was one of the top motivations for living together.

2. *Testers*. These couples are involved in a relationship and want to assess whether they have a future together. As in the case of here-and-now cohabitants, only a small proportion of cohabitants characterize themselves as "testers" (Jamieson et al. 2002). Rhoades et al. (2009) found that those who were motivated to

Diversity in Other Countries

Dolbik-Vorobei (2005) noted that university student attitudes in Russia are increasingly accepting of cohabitation and of intercourse out of marriage as long as "close spiritual relations" have been established between the partners.

Chapter 5 Singlehood, Hanging Out, Hooking Up, and Cohabitation

live together to test their relationship (in contrast to spending more time together) reported more negative couple communication, more aggression, and lower relationship adjustment.

   3. Engaged. These couples are in love and are planning to marry. Although not all cohabitants consider marriage their goal, most view themselves as committed to each other (Jamieson et al. 2002). Oppenheimer (2003) studied a national sample of cohabitants and found that cohabiting European Americans were much more likely to marry their partner than cohabiting African Americans—51 percent versus 22 percent. Dush et al. (2005) compared people in marriage; people in cohabiting, steady dating, and casual dating relationships; and people who dated infrequently or not at all. They found that individuals in a happy relationship, independent of the nature of the relationship, reported higher subjective well-being. In addition, the more committed the relationship, the higher the subjective well-being. Hence, for cohabiting people who define their relationships as involved, committed, or engaged, we would expect higher levels of subjective well-being.

   4. Money savers. These couples live together primarily out of economic convenience. They are open to the possibility of a future together but regard such a possibility as unlikely.

   5. Pension partners. This type is a variation of the money savers category. These individuals are older, have been married before, still derive benefits from their previous relationships, and are living with someone new. Getting married would mean giving up their pension benefits from the previous marriage. An example is a widow from the war in Afghanistan who was given military benefits due to a spouse's death. If remarried, the widow forfeits both health and pension benefits, but now lives with a new partner and continues to get benefits from the previous marriage.

   6. Security blanket cohabiters. Some of the individuals in these cohabitation relationships are drawn to each other out of a need for security rather than mutual attraction.

   7. Rebellious cohabiters. Some couples use cohabitation as a way of making a statement to their parents that they are independent and can make their own choices. Their cohabitation is more about rebelling from parents than being drawn to each other.

   8. Marriage never (cohabitants forever). These couples feel that a real relationship is a commitment of the heart, not a legal document. Living together provides both companionship and sex without the responsibilities of marriage. Skinner et al. (2002) found that individuals in long-term cohabiting relationships scored the lowest in terms of relationship satisfaction when compared with married and remarried couples. The "marriage never" couples are rare (celebrities Johnny Depp and Vanessa Paradis, Goldie Hawn and Kurt Russell, and Susan Sarandon and Tim Robbins are examples of couples who live together, have children, and have opted not to marry).

There are various reasons and motivations for living together as a permanent alternative to marriage. Some may have been married before and don't want the entanglements of another marriage. Others feel that the real bond between two people is (or should be) emotional. They contend that many couples stay together because of the legal contract, even though they do not love each other any longer. "If you're staying married because of the contract," said one partner, "you're staying for the wrong reason." Some couples feel that they are "married" in their hearts and souls and don't need or want the law to interfere with what they feel is a private act of commitment. For most couples, living together is a short-lived experience. About 55 percent will marry and 40 percent will break up within five years of beginning cohabitation (Smock 2000). Some couples who view their living together as "permanent" seek to have it defined as a **domestic partnership** (see the following Social Policy box).

Domestic Partnerships

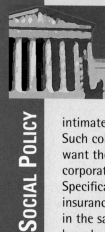

Although same-sex partners find little recognition, protection, and benefits for their relationship in terms of legal marriage, there is greater acceptance when their relationship is viewed in terms of a domestic partnership. Domestic partnerships involve two adults who have chosen to share each other's lives in an intimate and committed relationship of mutual caring. Such cohabitants, both heterosexual and homosexual, want their employers, whether governmental or corporate, to afford them the same rights as spouses. Specifically, employed people who pay for health insurance would like their domestic partner to be covered in the same way that one's spouse would be. Employers have been reluctant to legitimize domestic partners as qualifying for benefits because of the additional expense. One reason for the reluctance is the fear that a higher proportion of partners may be HIV-infected, which would involve considerable medical costs.

Aside from the economic issue, fundamentalist religious groups have criticized domestic partner benefits as eroding family values by giving nonmarital couples the same rights as married couples. California and New Jersey lead the way in domestic partner benefits, with the law providing rights and responsibilities in areas as varied as child custody, legal claims, housing protections, bereavement leave, and state government benefits.

To receive benefits, domestic partners must register, which involves signing an affidavit of domestic partnership verifying that they are a nonmarried, cohabiting couple 18 years of age or older and unrelated by blood close enough to bar marriage in the state of residence. Other criteria typically used to define a domestic partnership include that the individuals must be jointly responsible for debts to third parties, they must live in the same residence, they must be financially interdependent, and they must intend to remain in the intimate committed relationship

indefinitely. Should they terminate their domestic partnership, they are required to file notice of such termination.

The right to be defined as the next of kin may or may not be included in a state's domestic partnership guidelines. In Washington State, Charlene Strong and Kate Fleming (same-sex partners for ten years) enjoyed their life together but had not registered as domestic partners. So when Kate was rushed to the trauma center in Harborview Medical Center in Seattle, Charlene was stopped by a social worker from entering Kate's room because she was not "family." Kate died. Charlene, devastated, testified before the Washington State legislature and had the law changed so that same-sex relationships were included in the category of domestic partnerships.

Domestic partnerships offer a middle ground between those states that want to give full legal recognition to same-sex marriages and those that deny any legitimacy to same-sex unions. Such relationships also include long-term, committed heterosexuals who are not married. Rothblum et al. (2008) compared couples in same-sex marriages, domestic partnerships, and civil unions and found few differences.

Your Opinion?

1. To what degree do you believe benefits should be given to domestic partners?
2. What criteria should be required for a couple to be regarded as domestic partners?
3. How can abuses of those claiming to be domestic partners be eliminated?

Sources

Rothblum, E. D., K. F. Balsam, and S. E. Solomon. 2008. Comparison of same-sex couples who were married in Massachusetts, had domestic partnerships in California, or had civil unions in Vermont. *Journal of Family Issues* 29:48–63. © 2008 by SAGE PUBLICATIONS. Reprinted by Permission of SAGE Publications.

Consequences of Cohabitation

Although living together before marriage does not ensure a happy, stable marriage, it has some potential advantages.

Advantages of Cohabitation Many unmarried couples who live together report that it is an enjoyable, maturing experience. Other potential benefits of living together include the following:

1. *Sense of well-being.* Compared to uninvolved individuals or those involved but not living together, cohabitants are likely to report a sense of well-being (particularly if the partners see a future together). They are in love, the relationship is new, and the disenchantment that frequently occurs in long-term relationships has not had time to surface. One student reported, "We have had to make some adjustments in terms of moving all our stuff into one place, but we very much enjoy our life together." Although young cohabitants report high levels of enjoyment compared to single people, cohabitants in midlife who have

This couple has lived together with no marriage plans, but has remained friends.

never married when compared to married spouses, report lower levels of relational and subjective well-being. However, those who have been married before and are currently cohabitating do not evidence lower levels of relational or personal well-being when compared to married people (Hansen et al. 2007).

2. *Delayed marriage.* Another advantage of living together is remaining unmarried—and the longer one waits to marry, the better. Being older at the time of marriage is predictive of marital happiness and stability, just as being young (particularly 18 years and younger) is associated with marital unhappiness and divorce. Hence, if a young couple who have known each other for a short time is faced with the choice of living together or getting married, their delaying marriage while they live together seems to be the better choice. Also, if they break up, the split will not go on their "record" as would a divorce.

3. *Knowledge about self and partner.* Living with an intimate partner provides couples with an opportunity for learning more about themselves and their partner. For example, individuals in a living together relationship may find that their role expectations are more (or less) traditional than they had previously thought. Learning more about one's partner is a major advantage of living together. A person's values (calling parents daily), habits (leaving the lights on), and relationship expectations (how emotionally close or distant) are sometimes more fully revealed when living together than in a traditional dating context.

4. *Safety.* Particularly for females, living together provides a higher level of safety not enjoyed by single females who live alone. Of course, living with a roommate or group of friends would provide a similar margin of safety.

Disadvantages of Cohabitation There is a downside for individuals and couples who live together.

1. *Feeling used or tricked.* We have mentioned that women are more prone than men to view cohabitation as reflective of a more committed relationship. When expectations differ, the more invested partner may feel used or tricked if the relationship does not progress

Diversity in Other Countries

Iceland is a homogeneous country of 250,000 descendants of the Vikings. Their sexual norms include early protected intercourse (at age 14), nonmarital parenthood, and living together before marriage. Indeed, a wedding photo often includes not only the couple but also the children they have already had. One American woman who was involved with an Icelander noted, "My parents were upset with me because Ollie and I were thinking about living together, but his parents were upset that we were not already living together" (personal communication).

toward marriage. One partner said, "I always felt we would be getting married, but it turns out that he never saw a future for us."

2. *Problems with parents.* Some cohabiting couples must contend with parents who disapprove of or do not fully accept their living arrangement. For example, cohabitants sometimes report that, when visiting their parents' homes, they are required to sleep in separate beds in separate rooms. Some cohabitants who have parents with traditional values respect these values, and sleeping in separate rooms is not a problem. Other cohabitants feel resentful of parents who require them to sleep separately. Some parents express their disapproval of their child's cohabiting by cutting off communication, as well as economic support, from their child. Other parents display lack of acceptance of cohabitation in more subtle ways. One woman who had lived with her partner for two years said that her partner's parents would not include her in the family's annual photo portrait. Emotionally, she felt very much a part of her partner's family and was deeply hurt that she was not included in the family portrait. Still other parents are completely supportive of their children's cohabiting and support their doing so. "I'd rather my kid live together than get married and, besides, it is safer for her and she's happier," said one father.

3. *Economic disadvantages.* Some economic liabilities exist for those who live together instead of getting married. In the Social Policy section on domestic partnerships, we noted that cohabitants typically do not benefit from their partner's health insurance, Social Security, or retirement benefits. In most cases, only spouses qualify for such payoffs.

Given that most relationships in which people live together are not long-term and that breaking up is not uncommon, cohabitants might develop a written and signed legal agreement should they purchase a house, car, or other costly items together. The written agreement should include a description of the item, to whom it belongs, how it will be paid for, and what will happen to the item if the relationship terminates. Purchasing real estate together may require a separate agreement, which should include how the mortgage, property taxes, and repairs will be shared. The agreement should also specify who gets the house if the partners break up and how the value of the departing partner's share will be determined.

If the couple have children, another agreement may be helpful in defining custody, visitation, and support issues in the event the couple terminates the relationship. Such an arrangement may take some of the romance out of the cohabitation relationship, but it can save a great deal of frustration should the partners decide to go their separate ways.

In addition, couples who live together instead of marrying can protect themselves from some of the economic disadvantages of living together by specifying their wishes in wills; otherwise, their belongings will go to next of kin or to the state. They should also own property through joint tenancy with rights of survivorship.

This means that ownership of the entire property will revert to one partner if the other partner dies. In addition, the couple should save for retirement, because live-in companions may not access Social Security benefits, and some company pension plans bar employees from naming anyone other than a spouse as the beneficiary.

4. *Effects on children.* About 40 percent of children will spend some time in a home where the adults are cohabiting. In addition to being disadvantaged in terms of parental income and education, they are likely to experience more disruptions in family structure. Raley et al. (2005) analyzed data on children who lived with cohabiting mothers (from the National Survey of Families and Households) and found that these children fared exceptionally poorly and sometimes were significantly worse off than were children who lived with divorced or remarried mothers. The researchers reasoned that the instability associated with cohabitation may account for why these children do less well.

The stereotype of cohabitants is the young college couple. This unmarried couple (the individuals are previously divorced) are in their fifties and have been living together for five years.

5. *Other issues.* Over a million cohabitants are over the age of 50. When compared to married people, they report more depressive symptoms independent of their economic resources, social support, and physical health (Brown et al. 2005). These middle-aged individuals may possibly prefer to be married and their unhappiness reflects that preference.

Having Children while Cohabitating?
Sassler and Cunningham (2008) interviewed twenty-five never-married women who were cohabiting with their heterosexual partners. Most (two-thirds) reported

What if Your Partner Wants to Live Together and You Do Not?

WHAT IF?

It is not unusual that partners in love have different values and goals for the relationship. Wanting to live together as well as not wanting to do so are equally valid positions.

However, the costs to the person who is asked to go against a value is greater than the cost of not having one's preference. The consequence of going against one's values is to continually feel uncomfortable while cohabiting and to risk blaming the other person if something goes wrong. Win-lose decisions and relationships are never a good idea.

that they wanted to be married before having a child. Indeed, none of the respondents planned on having a child in the near future and none were actively trying to conceive. However, some noted that marriage made no difference. One respondent noted.

> *I don't see a reason to get married if you don't want to get married. Everyone, everyone is so traditional, which is really silly because it's not a traditional world anymore. Like when, like when my sister had her baby. I mean, she was concerned about. . ."* I wonder what they are going to think if I don't have a husband?" I mean, who cares? Who cares if you don't have a husband? What does marriage have to do with anything? (p. 13)

PERSONAL CHOICES

Will Living Together Ensure a Happy, Durable Marriage?

Couples who live together before marrying assume that doing so will increase their chances of having a happy and durable marriage relationship. In a *USA Today* poll, 49 percent believed that living together before marriage decreases the chance of divorce (Jayson 2008). But will it? The answer is, "It depends." For women who have only one cohabitation experience with the man they marry, there is no increased risk of divorce. However, if a woman is a serial cohabitant, there is an increased risk (Teachman 2003).

Because people commonly have more than one cohabitation experience, the term **cohabitation effect** applies. This means that those who have multiple cohabitation experiences prior to marriage are more likely to end up in marriages characterized by violence, lower levels of happiness, lower levels of positive communication, depression, you name it (Cohan and Kleinbaum 2002; Booth et al. 2008).

In the meantime, cohabitation relationships are no match for married relationships. Hansen et al. (2007) compared Norway cohabitants (who had never been married) in midlife with spouses in midlife and found cohabitants less happy, less close, and more conflictual. When the cohabitation relationship breaks, it gets worse. Williams et al. (2008) noted the psychological distress is particularly acute for single mothers. The message to single mothers was to stay single or get married (living together had a high chance of negative consequences).

What is it about serial cohabitation relationships that predict negatively for future marital happiness and durability? One explanation is that cohabitants tend to be people who are willing to violate social norms by living together before marriage. Once they marry, they may be more willing to break another social norm and divorce if they are unhappy than are unhappily married people who tend to conform to social norms and have no history of unconventional behavior. A second explanation is that, because cohabitants are less committed to the relationship than married people, this may translate into withdrawing from conflict by terminating the relationship rather than communicating about the problems and resolving them because the stakes are higher (White et al. 2004). Whatever the reason, cohabitants should not assume that cohabitation will make them happier spouses or insulate them from divorce.

Not all researchers have found negative effects of cohabitation on relationships. Skinner et al. (2002) compared those who had cohabited and married and those who married but did not cohabit and found no distinguishing characteristics. They concluded, "cohabiting couples may not be stigmatized if there is an expectation that marriage will occur." In addition, Musick (2005) examined national longitudinal data on married people and cohabiting couples and found few differences between the two groups on the variable of well-being the first three years. However, after three years, married people reported higher levels of well-being. The researcher suggested that "institutional commitment adds value to relationships" (p. 104).

Sources

Booth, A., E. Rustenbach, and S. McHale. 2008. Early family transitions and depressive symptom changes from adolescence to early adulthood. *Journal of Marriage and Family* 70:3–14.

Cohan, C. L., and S. Kleinbaum. 2002. Toward a greater understanding of the cohabitation effect: Premarital cohabitation and marital communication. *Journal of Marriage and the Family* 64:180–92.

Hansen, T., T. Moum, and A. Shapiro. 2007. Relational and individual well-being among cohabitors and married individuals in midlife: Recent trends from Norway *Journal of Family Issues* 28:910–33.

Jayson, S. 2008. Poll: Cohabitation is healthy. *USA Today*, July 29, 6D.

Musick, K. 2005. Does marriage make people happier? Marriage, cohabitation, and trajectories in well-being. In *Sourcebook of Family Theory and Research*, ed. Vern L. Bengtson, Alan C. Acock, Katherine R. Allen, Peggye Dilworth-Anderson, and David M. Klein, 103–04. Thousand Oaks, CA: Sage Publications.

Skinner, K. B., S. J. Bahr, D. R. Crane, and V. R. A. Call. 2002. Cohabitation, marriage, and remarriage. *Journal of Family Issues* 23:74–90.

Teachman, J. 2003. Premarital sex, premarital cohabitation, and the risk of subsequent marital disruption among women. *Journal of Marriage and the Family* 65:444–55.

White, A. M., F. S. Christopher, and T. K. Poop. 2004. Cohabitation and the early years of marriage. Poster session, National Council on Family Relations, November, Orlando, FL.

Whitty, M. T., A. J. Baker, and J. A. Inman, eds. 2007. *Online matchmaking*. New York: Palgrave Macmillan.

Williams, K., S. Sassler, and L. M. Nicholson. 2008. For better or worse? The consequences of marriage and cohabitation for single mothers. *Social Forces* 86:1481–1512.

Legal Aspects of Living Together

In recent years, the courts and legal system have become increasingly involved in relationships in which couples live together. Some of the legal issues concerning cohabiting partners include common-law marriage, palimony, child support, and child inheritance. Lesbian and gay couples also confront legal issues when they live together.

Technically, cohabitation is against the law in some states. For example, in North Carolina, cohabitation is a misdemeanor punishable by a fine not to exceed $500, imprisonment for not more than six months, or both. Most law enforcement officials view cohabitation as a victimless crime and feel that the general public can be better served by concentrating upon the crimes that do real damage to citizens and their property.

Common-Law Marriage   The concept of **common-law marriage** dates to a time when couples who wanted to be married did not have easy or convenient access to legal authorities (who could formally sanction their relationship so that they would have the benefits of legal marriage). Thus, if the couple lived together, defined themselves as husband and wife, and wanted other people to view them as a married couple, they would be considered married in the eyes of the law.

Despite the assumption by some that heterosexual couples who live together a long time have a common-law marriage, only eleven jurisdictions recognize such marriages. In ten states (Alabama, Colorado, Idaho, Iowa, Kansas, Rhode Island, South Carolina, Montana, Pennsylvania, and Texas) and the District of Columbia, a heterosexual couple may be considered married if they are legally competent to marry, if the partners agree that they are married, and if they present themselves to the public as a married couple. A ceremony or compliance with legal formalities is not required.

In common-law states, individuals who live together and who prove that they were married "by common law" may inherit from each other or receive alimony and property in the case of relationship termination. They may also receive health and Social Security benefits, as would other spouses who have a marriage license. In states not recognizing common-law marriages, the individuals who live together are not entitled to benefits traditionally afforded married individuals.

More than three-quarters of the states have passed laws prohibiting the recognition of common-law marriages within their borders.

Palimony A takeoff on the word *alimony*, **palimony** refers to the amount of money one "pal" who lives with another "pal" may have to pay if the partners end their relationship. In 2005, for instance, comedian Bill Maher was the target of a $9 million palimony suit by ex-girlfriend Coco Johnsen. In 2007, Candace Cabbil sued NBA star Latrell Sprewell for $200 million, claiming that he broke their long-term cohabitation agreement. Cabbil also alleged that Sprewell had fathered four of her children.

Avellar and Smock (2005) compared the economic well-being of cohabitants who ended their relationship. Whereas the economic standing of the cohabiting man declined moderately, that of the former cohabiting woman declined steeply, leaving a substantial proportion of women in poverty (and even more so for African American and Hispanic women).

Child Support Heterosexual individuals who conceive children are responsible for those children whether they are living together or married. In most cases, the custody of young children will be given to the mother, and the father will be required to pay child support. In effect, living together is irrelevant with regard to parental obligations. However, a woman who agrees to have a child with her lesbian partner cannot be forced to pay child support if the couple breaks up. In 2005, the Massachusetts Supreme Judicial Court ruled that their informal agreement to have a child together did not constitute an enforceable contract.

Couples who live together or who have children together should be aware that laws traditionally applying only to married couples are now being applied to many unwed relationships. Palimony, distribution of property, and child support payments are all possibilities once two people cohabit or parent a child.

Child Inheritance Children born to cohabitants who view themselves as spouses and who live in common-law states are regarded as legitimate and can inherit from their parents. However, children born to cohabitants who do not present themselves as married or who do not live in common-law states are also able to inherit. A biological link between the parent and the offspring is all that needs to be established.

Living Apart Together

A new lifestyle and family form has emerged called living apart together (Hess 2009). The premise is that individuals are socialized to believe that "more is better" . . . that the more time they spend together, including moving in together, the better. In effect, loving and committed couples automatically assume that they will marry or live together in one residence and that to do otherwise or to have "spaces in their togetherness," to quote Gibran, would suggest that they do not "really" love each other and aren't "really" committed to each other.

National Data

In an MSNBC poll of 63,823 respondents, 44 percent of spouses reported that, although they loved their spouse, they would consider living apart because they liked having their own space; 46 percent said "no" (they would not live apart); and 9.9 percent didn't know (MSNBC Poll 2007).

The definition of **living apart together (LAT)** is a committed couple who does not live in the same home (and others such as children or elderly parents may live in those respective homes). Three criteria must be met for a couple to be defined as an LAT couple: (1) they must define themselves as a committed couple; (2) others must define the partners as a couple; and (3) they must live in separate domiciles. The lifestyle of living apart together involves partners in loving and committed relationships (married or unmarried) identifying their independent needs in terms of the degree to which they want time and space away from each other. People living apart together exist on a continuum from partners who have separate bedrooms and baths in the same house to those who live in a separate place (apartment, condo, house) in the same or different cities. LAT couples are not those couples who are forced by their career or military assignment to live separately. Rather, LAT partners choose to live in separate domiciles.

This new lifestyle or family form has been identified as a new social phenomenon in several Western European countries (for example, France, Sweden, Norway), as well as in the United States (Lara 2005). Couples choose this pattern for a number of reasons, including the desire to maintain some level of independence, to enjoy their time alone, to keep their relationship exciting, and so on.

Advantages of LAT

The benefits of LAT relationships include the following:

1. Space and privacy. Having two places enables each partner to have a separate space to read, watch TV, talk on the phone, or whatever. This not only provides a measure of privacy for the individuals, but also as a couple. When the couple has overnight guests, the guests can stay in one place while the partners stay in the other place. This arrangement gives guests ample space and the couple private space and time apart from the guests.

2. Career or work space. Some individuals work at home and need a controlled quiet space to work on projects, talk on the phone, concentrate on their work, and so on, without the presence of someone else. The LAT arrangement is particularly appealing to musicians for practicing, artists to spread out their materials, and authors for quiet (Hemingway had his own wing of the house).

3. Variable sleep needs. Although some partners enjoy going to bed at the same time and sleeping in the same bed, others like to go to bed at radically different times and to sleep in separate beds or rooms. The LAT arrangement allows for partners to have their own sleep needs or schedules met without interfering with a partner. A frequent comment from LAT partners is, "My partner thrashes throughout the night and kicks me, not to speak of the wheezing and teeth grinding, so to get a good night's sleep, I need to sleep somewhere else."

4. Allergies. Individuals who have cat or dog allergies may need to live in a separate antiseptic environment from their partner who loves animals and won't live without them. "He likes his dog on the couch," said one woman.

5. Variable social needs. Partners differ in terms of their need for social contact with friends, siblings, and parents. The LAT arrangement allows for the partner who enjoys frequent time with others to satisfy that need without subjecting the other to the presence of a lot of people in one's life space. One wife from a family of seven children enjoyed both her siblings and parents being around. The LAT arrangement allowed her to continue to enjoy her family at no expense to her husband who was upstairs in another condo.

6. Blended family needs. A variation of the previous item is a blended family in which remarried spouses with children from previous relationships sometimes find it easier to separate out the living space of their children. The happy "Brady Bunch" on TV is often not mirrored in reality. In reality, a married couple may live in a duplex with each spouse having their own kids live with them.

7. Keeping the relationship exciting. Zen Buddhists remind us of the necessity to be in touch with polarities, to have a perspective where we can see and appreciate the larger picture—without the darkness, we cannot fully appreciate the light. The two are inextricably part of a whole. This is the same with relationships; time apart from our beloved can make time together feel more precious.

Whenever I date a guy, I think, is this the man I want my children to spend their weekends with?

Rita Rudner, comedian

The term **satiation** is a well-established psychological principle. Basically, satiation means that a stimulus loses its value with repeated exposure. Just as we tire of eating the same food, listening to the same music, or watching the same movie twice, so satiation is relevant to relationships. Indeed, couples who are in a long-distance dating relationship know the joy of "missing" each other and the excitement of being with each other again. Similarly, individuals in a LAT relationship help to ensure that they will not "satiate" on each other but maintain some of the excitement in seeing or being with each other.

8. *Self-expression and comfort.* Partners often have very different tastes in furniture, home décor, music, and temperature. With two separate places, each can arrange and furnish their respective homes according to their own individual preferences. The respective partner can also set the heat or air conditioning according to their own preferences, and play whatever music they like.

9. *Cleanliness or orderliness.* Separate residences allow each partner to maintain the desired level of cleanliness and orderliness without arguing about it. Some individuals like their living space to be as clean as a cockpit. Others simply don't care.

10. *Elder care.* One partner may be taking care of an elderly parent in the parents' house or in his or her own house. Either way, the partners may have a preference not to live in the same house as a couple with a parent. An LAT relationship allows for the partner taking care of the elderly parent to do so and a place for the couple to be alone.

11. *Maintaining one's lifetime residence.* Some retirees, widows, and widowers meet, fall in love, and want to enjoy each other's companionship. However, they don't want to move out of their own house. The LAT arrangement allows each partner to maintain a separate residence but to enjoy the new relationship.

12. *Leaving inheritances to children from previous marriages.* Having separate residences allows respective partners to leave their family home or residential property to their children from their first marriage without displacing their surviving spouse.

Disadvantages of LAT

There are also disadvantages to the LAT lifestyle.

1. *Stigma or disapproval.* Because the norm that married couples move in together is firmly entrenched, couples who do not do so are suspect. "People who love each other want to be together. . . . those who live apart don't really want a life together" is the traditional perception of people involved in a living together relationship.

2. *Cost.* Certainly, maintaining two separate living arrangements can be more expensive than two people living in one domicile. But there are ways LAT couples manage their lifestyle. Some live in two condominiums that are cheaper than two houses. Others are willing to set up their housing out of high-priced real estate arrears. One partner said, "We can simply drive twenty miles out of town where the price of housing drops 50 percent so we can afford a duplex. We have our separation and it didn't cost us a fortune."

3. *Inconvenience.* Unless the partners live in a duplex or two units in the same condominium, going between the two places to share meals or be together can be inconvenient.

4. *Lack of shared history.* Because the adults are living in separate quarters, a lot of what goes on in each house does not become a part of the life history of the other. For example, children in one place don't benefit as much from the other adult who lives in another domicile most of the time.

5. *Waking up alone.* Although some LAT partners sleep together overnight, others say goodnight and sleep in separate beds or houses. A potential disadvantage is waking up and beginning the day alone without the early-morning connection with one's beloved.

SUMMARY

What are the attractions of singlehood and the social movements that created it?

An increasing percentage of people are delaying marriage. Between the ages of 25 and 29, 57.6 percent of males and 43.4 percent of females are not married. The Alternatives to Marriage Project is designed to give visibility and credibility to the status of being unmarried. The primary attraction of singlehood is the freedom to do as one chooses. As a result of the sexual revolution, the women's movement, and the gay liberation movement, there is increased social approval of being unmarried. Single people are those who never married as well as those who are divorced or widowed.

To what degree are undergraduates interested in finding a partner?

About a quarter of university students in one study reported that they were not involved with anyone. More than half of the men and about four in ten women reported that they were looking for a partner.

How do university students go about finding a partner?

Besides the traditional way of meeting people at work or school or through friends and going on a date, couples today may also "hang out," which may lead to "hooking up." Internet dating, video dating, and speed-dating are new forms for finding each other.

What issues do divorced people face when they start dating again?

Divorced people are older and select from an older, more limited population with a higher chance of having a sexually transmitted infection (STI). Most have children from a previous marriage and are dealing with an ex-spouse.

What is the cultural and historical background of dating?

The freedom with which American partners today select each other on the basis of love is a relatively recent phenomenon. At most times and in most cultures, parents often arranged marriages. Unlike during the 1950s, both sexes today are aware of and somewhat cautious of becoming HIV/STI-infected. Sex has become potentially deadly, and condoms are being used more frequently. Couples of today are also more aware of the impermanence of marriage.

What is cohabitation like among today's youth?

Cohabitation, also known as living together, is becoming a "normative life experience," with almost 60 percent of American women reporting that they had cohabited before marriage. Reasons for an increase in living together include a delay of marriage for educational or career commitments, fear of marriage, increased tolerance of society for living together, and a desire to avoid the legal entanglements of marriage. Types of relationships in which couples live together include the here-and-now, testers (testing the relationship), engaged couples (planning to marry), and cohabitants forever (never planning to marry). Most people who live together eventually marry but not necessarily to each other.

Domestic partners are two adults who have chosen to share each other's lives in an intimate and committed relationship of mutual caring. Such cohabitants, both heterosexual and homosexual, want their employers, whether governmental or corporate, to afford them the same rights as spouses. Only about 10 percent of firms recognize domestic partners and offer them benefits.

Although living together before marriage does not ensure a happy, stable marriage, it has some potential advantages. These include a sense of well-being, delayed marriage, learning about yourself and your partner, and being able to disengage with minimal legal hassle. Disadvantages include feeling exploited, feeling guilty about lying to parents, and not having the same economic benefits as those who are married. Social Security and retirement benefits are paid to spouses, not live-in partners.

What are the pros and cons of "living apart together"?

A new lifestyle and family form is living apart together (LAT), which means that monogamous committed partners—whether married or not—carve out varying degrees of physical space between them. People living apart together exist on a continuum from partners who have separate bedrooms and baths in the same house to those who live in separate places (apartment, condo, house) in the same or different cities. Couples choose this pattern for a number of reasons, including the desire to maintain some level of independence, to enjoy their time alone, to keep their relationship exciting, and so on.

Advantages to involvement in an LAT relationship include space and privacy, sleeping without being cramped or dealing with snoring, not living with animals if there is an allergy, having family or friends over without interfering with a partner's life space, and keeping the relationship exciting. Disadvantages include being confronted with stigma or disapproval, cost, inconvenience, and waking up alone.

KEY TERMS

blind marriage	commune	living apart together (LAT)	satiation
bundling	domestic partnership	living together	singlehood
cohabitation	hanging out	palimony	
cohabitation effect	hooking up	POSSLQ	
common-law marriage	intentional community	quinceñera	

The Companion Website for *Choices in Relationships: An Introduction to Marriage and the Family,* Tenth Edition
www.cengage.com/sociology/knox

Supplement your review of this chapter by going to the Companion Website to take one of the tutorial quizzes, use the flash cards to master key terms, or check out the many other study aids, like crossword puzzles and self-assessments. You'll also find special features such as General Social Survey (GSS) data, Census data, and other resources to help you with that special project or to do some research on your own.

WEB LINKS

Alternatives to Marriage Project
http://www.unmarried.org/

Right Mate at Heartchoice
http://www.heartchoice.com/rightmate/

Single Dad
http://www.singledad.com/

Single Fathers
http://www.singlefather.org/

8minuteDating
http://www.8minutedating.com/

WildXAngel
http://www.wildxangel.com/

Independent Women's Forum
http://www.happinessonline.org/
BeFaithfulToYourSexualPartner/p17.htm

REFERENCES

Adams, M. et al. 2008. Rhetoric of alternative dating: Investment versus exploration. Southern Sociological Society, Richmond, VA, April.

Albright, J. M. 2007. How do I love thee and thee and thee?: Self-presentation, deception, and multiple relationships online. In *Online Matchmaking,* ed. M. T. Whitty, A. J. Baker, and J. A. Inman, 81–93. New York: Palgrave Macmillan.

Avellar, S., and P. J. Smock. 2005. The economic consequences of the dissolution of cohabiting unions. *Journal of Marriage and the Family* 67:315–27.

Baker, A. J. 2007. Expressing emotion in text: Email communication of online couples. In *Online Matchmaking,* ed. M. T. Whitty, A. J. Baker, and J. A. Inman, 97–111. New York: Palgrave Macmillan.

Baxter, J. 2005. To marry or not to marry: Marital status and the household division of labor. *Journal of Family Issues* 26:300–21.

Bogle, K. A. 2002. From dating to hooking up: Sexual behavior on the college campus. Paper presented at the Annual Meeting of the Society for the Study of Social Problems, Summer.

Bogle, K. A. 2008 *Hooking up: Sex, dating, and relationships on campus.* New York: New York University Press.

Brewster, C. D. D. 2006. African American male perspective on sex, dating, and marriage. *The Journal of Sex Research* 43:32–33.

Brown, S. L., J. R. Bulanda, and G. R. Lee. 2005. The significance of nonmarital cohabitation: Marital status and mental health benefits among middle-aged and older adults. *Journals of Gerontology Series B—Psychological Sciences and Social Sciences,* 60(1):S21–S29.

Cohan, C. L., and S. Kleinbaum. 2002. Toward a greater understanding of the cohabitation effect: Premarital cohabitation and marital communication. *Journal of Marriage and the Family* 64:180–92.

Davis, S. N., T. N. Greenstein, and J. P. Gerteisen Marks. 2007. Effects of union type on division of household labor. *Journal of Family Issues* 28:1246–72.

de Vries, J. M. A., L. Swenson, and R. P. Walsh. 2007. Hot picture or great self-description: Predicting mediated dating success with parental investment theory. *Marriage & Family Review* 42:7–23

DePaulo, B. 2006. *Singled out: How singles are stereotyped, stigmatized, and ignored, and still live happily ever after.* New York: St. Martin's Press.

Dolbik-Vorobei, T. A. 2005. What college students think about problems of marriage and having children. *Russian Education and Society* 47:47–58.

Donn, J. 2005. Adult development and well-being of midlife never-married singles. Unpublished dissertation. Miami University, Oxford, Ohio.

Dush, C., M. Kamp, and P. R. Amato. 2005. Consequences of relationship status and quality for subjective well-being. *Journal of Social and Personal Relationships* 22:607–27.

Eggebeen, D. J. 2005. Cohabitation and exchanges of support. *Social Forces* 83:1097–110.

England, P., and R. J. Thomas. 2006. The decline of the date and the rise of the college hook up. In *Family in transition,* 14th ed., ed. A. S. Skolnick and J. H. Skolnick, 151–62. Boston: Pearson Allyn & Bacon.

Eshbaugh, E. M., and G. Gute. Hookups and sexual regret among college women. *The Journal of Social Psychology* 148:77–87.

Ferguson, S. J. 2000. Challenging traditional marriage: Never married Chinese American and Japanese American women. *Gender and Society* 14:136–59.

Gibbs, J. L., N. B. Ellison, and R. D. Heino. 2006. Self-presentation in online personals: The role of anticipated future interaction, self-disclosure, and perceived success in Internet dating. *Communication Research* 33:152–77.

Guldner, G. T. 2003. *Long distance relationships: The complete guide.* Corona, CA: JFMilne Publications.

Ha, J. H. 2008. Changes in support from confidants, children, and friends following widowhood. *Journal of Marriage and Family* 70:306–29.

Hansen, T., T. Moum, and A. Shapiro. 2007. Relational and individual well-being among cohabitors and married individuals in midlife. *Journal of Family Issues* 28:910–33.

Harcourt, W. 2005. Gender and community in the social construction of the Internet/Hanging out in the virtual pub: Masculinities and relationships online. *Signs: Journal of Women in Culture and Society* 30:1,981–84.

Hemstrom, O. 1996. Is marriage dissolution linked to differences in mortality risks for men and women? *Journal of Marriage and the Family* 58:366–78.

Hess, J. 2009. Personal communication. Appreciation is expressed to Judye Hess for the development of this section. For more information about Judye Hess, see http://www.psychotherapist.com/judyehess/.

Hodge, A. 2003. Video chatting and the males who do it. Paper presented at the 73rd Annual Meeting of the Eastern Sociological Association, Philadelphia, February 28.

Jagger, E. 2005. Is thirty the new sixty? Dating, age and gender in postmodern consumer society. *Sociology* 9:89–106.

Jamieson, L., M. Anderson, D. McCrone, F. Bechhofer, R. Stewart, and Y. Li. 2002. Cohabitation and commitment: Partnership plans of young men and women. *The Sociological Review* 50:356–77.

Jayson, S. 2008. Poll: Cohabitation is healthy. *USA Today,* July 29, 6D.

Jerin, R. A., and B. Dolinsky. 2007. Cyber-victimization and online dating. In *Online Matchmaking,* ed. M. T. Whitty, A. J. Baker, and J. A. Inman, 147–56. New York: Palgrave Macmillan.

Jones, J. 2006. Marriage is for white people. *The Washington Post,* March 26, B3–B4.

Kalmijn, M. 2007. Gender differences in the effects of divorce, widowhood and remarriage on intergenerational support: Does marriage protect fathers? *Social Forces* 85:1079–85.

Kiernan, K. 2000. European perspectives on union formation. In *The ties that bind,* ed. L. J. Waite, 40–58. New York: Aldine de Gruyter.

Knox, D., and U. Corte. 2007. "Work it out/See a counselor": Advice from spouses in the separation process. *Journal of Divorce and Remarriage* 48:79–90.

Knox, D., and M. E. Zusman. 2009. Relationship and sexual behaviors of a sample of 1319 university students. Unpublished data collected for this text. Department of Sociology, East Carolina University, Greenville, NC.

Knox, D., M. Zusman, V. Daniels, and A. Brantley. 2002. Absence makes the heart grow fonder? Long-distance dating relationships among college students. *College Student Journal* 36:365–67.

Krumrei, E., C. Coit, S. Martin, W. Fogo, and A. Mahoney. 2007. Post-divorce adjustment and social relationships: A meta-analytic review. *Journal of Divorce & Remarriage* 46:145–56.

Lara, Adair. 2005. "One for the price of two: Some couples find their marriages thrive when they share separate quarters." *San Francisco Chronicle,* June 29. http://www.sfgate.com/cgi-bin/article.cgi?file=/c/a/2005/06/29/HOG7HDEB7B1.DTL.

Lucas, R. E., A. E. Clark, Y. Georgellis, and E. Diener. 2003. Reexamining adaptation and the set point model of happiness: Reactions to changes in marital status. *Journal of Personality and Social Psychology* 84:527–39.

Luff, T., and K. Hoffman. 2006. College dating patterns: Cultural and structural influences. Roundtable presentation, Southern Sociological Society, New Orleans, LA, March 24.

Lydon, J., T. Pierce, and S. O'Regan. 1997. Coping with moral commitment to long-distance dating relationships. *Journal of Personality and Social Psychology* 73:104–13.

Madden, M., and A. Lenhart 2006. *Online dating.* Washington, DC: Pew Internet & American Life Project.

Mahoney, S. 2006. The secret lives of single women—lifestyles, dating and romance: A study of midlife singles. *AARP: The Magazine* May/June, 62–69.

Manning, W. D., M.A. Longmore, and P. C. Giordano. 2007. The changing institution of marriage: Adolescents' expectations to cohabit and to marry *Journal of Marriage and Family* 69:559–75.

McGinty, C. 2006. Internet dating. Presentation to courtship and marriage class, East Carolina University, Greenville, NC.

McKenna, K. Y. A. 2007. A progressive affair: Online dating to real world mating. In *Online Matchmaking,* ed. M. T. Whitty, A. J. Baker, and J. A. Inman, 112–24. New York: Palgrave Macmillan.

MSNBC Poll. 2007. Living apart together poll. November 1. http://www.msnbc.msn.com/id/21473532/.

O'Flaherty, K. M., and L. W. Eells. 1988. Courtship behavior of the remarried. *Journal of Marriage and the Family* 50:499–506.

Ohayon, M. 2005. *Cowboy Amor* (video released in 2005).

Oppenheimer, V. K. 2003. Cohabiting and marriage during young men's career-development process. *Demography* 40:127–49.

Pryor, J. H., S. Hurtado, L. DeAngelo, J. Sharkness, L. C. Romero, W. K. Korn, and S. Trans. 2008. *The American freshmen: National Norms for fall 2008.* Los Angeles: Higher Education Research Institute, UCLA.

Raley, R. K., M. L. Frisco, and E. Wildsmith. 2005. Maternal cohabitation and educational success. *Sociology of Education* 78:144–164.

Renshaw, S. W. 2005. "Swing Dance" and "Closing Time": Two ethnographies in popular culture. Dissertation Abstracts International. A: *The Humanities and Social Sciences* 25:4355A–56A.

Rhoades, G. K., S. M. Stanley, and H. J. Markman. 2009. Couples' reasons for cohabitation: Associations with individual well-being and relationship quality. *Journal of Family Issues* 30:233–46.

Sassler, S., and A. Cunningham. 2008. How cohabitors view childrearing. *Sociological Perspectives* 51:3–29.

Schoen, R., N. S. Landale, and K. Daniels. 2007. Family transitions in young adulthood. *Demography* 44:807–30.

Sharp, E. A., and L. Ganong. 2007. Living in the gray: Women's experiences of missing the marital transition *Journal of Marriage and Family* 69:831–844.

Skinner, K. B., S. J. Bahr, D. R. Crane, and V. R. A. Call. 2002. Cohabitation, marriage, and remarriage. *Journal of Family Issues* 23:74–90.

Smock, P. J. 2000. Cohabitation in the United States: An appraisal of research themes, findings, and implications. *Annual Review of Sociology* 26:1–20.

Spitzberg, B. H., and W. R. Cupach. 2007. Cyberstalking as (mis)matchmaking. In *Online matchmaking,* ed. M. T. Whitty, A. J. Baker, and J. A. Inman, 127–46. New York: Palgrave Macmillan.

Statistical Abstract of the United States, 2009. 128th ed. Washington, DC: U.S. Bureau of the Census.

Stepp, L. S. 2007 *Unhooked: How young women pursue sex, delay love, and lose at both.* Riverhead, New York: Riverhead Publishing Co.

Stringfield, M. D. 2008. Online dating. Unpublished paper, East Carolina University.

Thomas, M. E. 2005. Girls, consumption space and the contradictions of hanging out in the city. *Social and Cultural Geography* 6:587–605.

Twenge, J. 2006. *Generation me.* New York: Free Press.

Vanderkam, L. 2006. Love (or not) in an iPod world. *USA Today,* February 14, 13A.

Weden, M., and R. T. Kimbro. 2007. Racial and ethnic differences in the timing of first marriage and smoking cessation. *Journal of Marriage and Family* 69:878–87.

Whitty, M. T. 2007. The art of selling one's 'self' on an online dating site: The BAR approach. In *Online matchmaking,* ed. M. T. Whitty, A. J. Baker, and J. A. Inman, 37–69. New York: Palgrave Macmillan.

Wienke, C., and G. J. Hill. 2009. Does the "Marriage Benefit" extend to partners in gay and lesbian relationships?: Evidence from a random sample of sexually active adults. *Journal of Family Issues* 30:259–73.

Wilson, G. D., J. M. Cousins, and B. Fink. 2006. The CQ as a predictor of speed-date outcomes. *Sexual & Relationship Therapy* 21:163–69.

Xia, Y. R., and Z. G. Zhou 2003. The transition of courtship, mate selection, and marriage in China. In *Mate Selection across Cultures,* ed. R. R. Hamon and B. B. Ingoldsby, 231–46. Thousand Oaks, CA: Sage Publications.

Yeoman, B. 2006. Rethinking the commune. *AARP: The Magazine* March/April, 88–97.

Yurchisin, J., K. Watchravesrighkan, and D. M. Brown. 2005. An exploration of identity re-creation in the context of Internet dating. *Social Behavior and Personality: An International Journal* 33:735–50.

Chapter 5 Singlehood, Hanging Out, Hooking Up, and Cohabitation

We clicked right away . . . by the end of the first date it was over . . . I was sold.

Michelle Obama, First Lady

Mate Selection

Contents

True or False?

1. Opposites attract, and couples who are characterized by being different have more exciting, happier, and durable relationships than those who are more similar to each other.

2. College students are just as open to marrying someone of another race as they are to dating someone of another race.

3. Similarity of attachment to each other is the variable most predictive of relationship quality.

4. A narcissist is a high risk as a durable marriage partner.

5. One study on rebound relationships asked, "how fast should you run?" in terms of getting involved with a person on the rebound and concluded with the answer "as fast as you can."

Answers: **1.** F **2.** F **3.** T **4.** T **5.** T

Not to know is bad. Not to wish to know is worse.

African proverb

Lee Iacocca, the former president of both Chrysler and Ford corporations is noted for his insistence on taking action. *"Get all the education you can, but then, by God, do something! Don't just stand there. Make something happen."* In terms of mate selection, this same movement to action is necessary. After gathering the facts on you, your partner, and your relationship and checking with your senses and feelings, make the hard choices. Get out of a relationship that is going nowhere and get into a relationship going somewhere. "Don't just stand there . . . do something." Otherwise, others will make choices for you, and you will get to the end of someone else's life.

The data are clear. Marriage is a major lifetime goal for most people. Even though individuals today are delaying marriage to complete their educations, establish themselves in a career, pay off their debts, and/or enjoy their friends and freedom, more than 95 percent of American adults end up getting married by age 75 (*Statistical Abstract of the United States, 2009,* Table 56). Indeed, 94.8 percent of 1,319 undergraduates at a large southeastern university agreed, "Someday, I want to marry" (Knox and Zusman 2009). No other choice in life is as important as your choice of a marriage partner. Your day-to-day happiness, health, and economic well-being will be significantly influenced by the partner with whom you choose to share your life. Most have high hopes and even believe in the perfect mate. An anonymous comic said, "I married Miss Right. . . . I just didn't know her first name was Always." In this chapter, we examine the cultural factors and pressures that influence the choice of one's mate, the tendency for individuals to select a partner with similar characteristics, and the effect of psychological factors on mate selection.

Because the heart of this text is about making wise choices in relationships, this chapter examines cultural, sociological, and psychological filters involved in mate selection (see Figure 6.1). We begin by looking at the cultural factors that are operative.

Cultural Aspects of Mate Selection

Individuals are not free to marry whomever they please. Indeed, university students routinely assert, "I can marry whomever I want!" Hardly. Rather, their culture and society radically restrict and influence their choice. The best example

Cultural Filters		
For two people to consider marriage to each other,		
Endogamous factors (same race, age)	and ↓ must be met. ↓	Exogamous factors (not blood-related)
After the cultural prerequisites have been satisfied, sociological and psychological filters become operative.		

Sociological Filters		
Propinquity = the tendency to select a mate from among those who live, work, or go to school nearby.		
Homogamy = the tendency to select a mate similar to oneself with regard to the following:		
	Race	Physical appearance
	Education	Body clock compatibility
	Social class	Religion
	Age	Marital status
	Intelligence	Interpersonal values

Psychological Filters
Complementary needs
Reward-cost ratio for profit
Parental characteristics
Desired personality characteristics

Figure 6.1
Cultural, Sociological, and Psychological Filters involved in Mate Selection

of mate choice being culturally and socially controlled is the fact that *less than 1 percent* of people marry someone outside their race (*Statistical Abstract of the United States, 2009*, Table 59). Homosexual people are also not free to marry whomever they choose. Indeed, although Massachusetts Connecticut, Iowa, New Hampshire, and Maine recognize same-sex marriage, federal law does not, reflecting wide societal disapproval.

Independent of the sexual orientation of the partners, endogamy and exogamy are two forms of cultural pressure operative in mate selection.

Above the neck and below the neck—together at last! One stop shopping. You want sex, romance, laughs, shared values, intellectual stimulation, companionship, eroticism, friendship. You want it all, and he seemed to have it all.

Jane Fonda of Ted Turner in courtship

Endogamy

Endogamy is the cultural expectation to select a marriage partner within one's own social group, such as in the same race, religion, and social class. **Endogamous pressures** involve social approval and encouragement to select a partner within your own group (for example, someone of your own race and religion) and disapproval for selecting someone outside your own group. The pressure toward an endogamous mate choice is especially strong when race is concerned. Love may be blind, but it knows the color of one's partner. Over 95 percent of individuals end up selecting someone of the same race to marry.

Exogamy

In addition to the cultural pressure to marry within one's social group, there is also the cultural expectation that one will marry outside the family group. This expectation is known as **exogamy**. **Exogamous pressures**

Diversity in Other Countries

In most cultures, mate selection has rarely been left to chance, and parents have been involved in the selection of their offspring's partner. However, who picks the best mate: parents or the individual? India is made up of twenty-nine states, reflecting a range of languages, dialects, and religions. Most (82 percent) are Hindu, followed in prevalence by Muslims (12 percent). Because the culture is largely collectivistic or familistic (focusing on family unity and loyalty) rather than individualistic (focusing on personal interests and freedom), most Indian youth see parents as better able to select a lifetime marital partner and defer to their judgment (Medora 2003, 227). Love is seen as that which follows rather than precedes marriage. A stable companion rather than an intense love interest is the focus of courtship.

If you would marry wisely, marry your equal.

Ovid

involve social approval and encouragement to select a partner outside one's own group (for example, someone outside of your own family).

Incest taboos are universal; as well, children are not permitted to marry the parent of the other sex in any society. In the United States, siblings and (in some states) first cousins are also prohibited from marrying each other. The reason for such restrictions is fear of genetic defects in children whose parents are too closely related.

Once cultural factors have determined the general **pool of eligibles** (the population from which a person selects an appropriate mate), individual mate choice becomes more operative. However, even when individuals feel that they are making their own choices, social influences are still operative.

Sociological Factors Operative in Mate Selection

Numerous sociological factors are at work in bringing two people together who eventually marry.

Homogamy: Twelve Factors

Whereas endogamy is a concept that refers to cultural pressure, **homogamy** refers to individual initiative toward sameness or "likes attract." The **homogamy theory of mate selection** states that we tend to be attracted to and become involved with those who are similar to ourselves in such characteristics as age, race, religion, and social class. In general, the more couples have in common, the higher the reported relationship satisfaction and the more durable the relationship (Clarkwest 2007; Amato et al. 2007).

Race As noted above, **racial homogamy** operates strongly in selecting a live-in or marital partner (with greater homogamy for marital partners). In a national survey, more than eight in ten American adults (83 percent) agree that "it's all right for blacks and whites to date," up from 48 percent in 1987 (Pew Research Center 2007). Among younger people—those born since 1977—94 percent say it is all right for black people and white people to date. Over a third (36.4 percent) of 1,319 undergraduates reported that they had dated someone of another race. However, 44.2 percent reported that marrying someone of the same race was important for them (Knox and Zusman 2009).

Although homogamy states that similar individuals are more comfortable with each other, racism is also operative. In their book on *Two-Faced Racism*, Picca and Feagin (2007) found that three-fourths of the 9,000 journal entries of college students included reports of racist remarks on campus. The researchers pointed out that, although college students commonly say "I'm not prejudiced" in a public context, racist comments are sometimes made when they are alone (backstage) with their friends. One journal entry follows:

> *On Thursday . . . my friend Megan (a white female) went on her first date with Steve. As their conversation began they discussed typical first date topics like family, friends, home, etc. Somehow Megan began talking about how squirrels in the Bronx are black and so people call them "squiggers." When Steve did not laugh Megan wondered why he did not think it was funny. As the conversation progressed and Steve began to talk about his family, he revealed to Megan that his dad is black and mom is white. Right then, Megan realized why Steve did not find her joke to be so*

Although most undergraduates are open to dating outside their race, marrying someone of another race is rare for them.

funny. Megan felt horrible. Without realizing it, Megan hurt someone that appeared to be just as white as she was . . . (p. 195)

Racism, in the form of residential segregation, is also alive. Vesselinov (2008) noted that "gated" communities is yet another form of residential segregation and that "little has changed in segregation levels despite antidiscriminatory legislation and efforts by various groups, social movements, and federal and local institutions" (p. 553).

Although a greater number of white people are available to black people for marriage, black mothers and white fathers have different roles in the respective black and white communities, in terms of setting the norms of interracial relationships. Hence, the black mother who approves of her son's or daughter's interracial relationship may be less likely to be overruled than the white mother (the white husband may be more disapproving than the black husband). Race may also affect one's perceptions. In a study of racial perceptions among college students, DeCuzzi et al. (2006) found that, although both races tended to view women and men of their own and the other race positively, there was a pronounced tendency to view women and men of their own race more positively and members of the other race more negatively.

National Data

Of the almost 60 million married couples in the United States, less than 1 percent (0.007 percent) consists of a black spouse and white spouse. Those consisting of a Hispanic and a non-Hispanic spouse represent 3.6 percent (*Statistical Abstract of the United States, 2009*, Table 59).

Hohmann-Marriott and Amato (2008) found that individuals (both men and women) in interethnic (includes interracial relationships such as Hispanic-white, black-Hispanic, and black-white) marriages and cohabitation relationships have lower quality relationships than those in same-ethnic relationships. Lower relationship quality was defined in terms of reporting less satisfaction, more problems, higher conflict, and lower commitment to the relationship.

Similarly, Bratter and King (2008) analyzed national data and found higher divorce rates among interracial couples (compared to same-race couples). They also found race and gender variation. Compared to white couples, white female/

Married in haste, we may repent in leisure.

William Congreve, playwright

black male and white female/Asian male marriages were more prone to divorce; meanwhile, those involving nonwhite females and white males and Hispanics and non-Hispanic people had similar or lower risks of divorce.

Age Most individuals select someone who is relatively close in age. Men tend to select women three to five years younger than themselves. The result is the "**marriage squeeze**," which is the imbalance of the ratio of marriageable-aged men to marriageable-aged women. In effect, women have fewer partners to select from because men choose from not only their same age group but also those younger than themselves. One 40-year-old recently divorced woman said, "What chance do I have with all these guys looking at all these younger women?"

Education **Educational homogamy** (selecting a cohabitant or marital partner with similar education) also operates strongly in selecting a live-in and marital partner (with greater homogamy for marital partners) (Kalmijn and Flap 2001). Not only does college provide an opportunity to meet, date, live with, and marry another college student, but it also increases one's chance that only a college-educated partner becomes acceptable as a potential cohabitant or spouse. The very pursuit of education becomes a value to be shared. However, Lewis and Oppenheimer (2000) observed that, when people of similar education are not available, women are particularly likely to marry someone with less education. The older the woman, the more likely she is to marry a partner with less education. In effect, the number of educated, eligible males may decrease as she ages.

Open-Mindedness People vary in the degree to which they are **open-minded** (an openness to understanding alternative points of view, values, and behaviors). Homogamous pairings in regard to homogamy are those that reflect partners who are relatively open or closed to new points of view, behaviors, and experiences. For example, an evangelical may not be open to people of alternative religions. The Self-Assessment section on the next page allows you to assess your open-mindedness. You might ask your partner to take the same assessment and compare your scores and views.

Social Class You have been reared in a particular social class that reflects your parents' occupations, incomes, and educations as well as your residence, language, and values (see Table 6.1). If you were brought up in a home in which both parents were physicians, you probably lived in a large house in a nice residential area—summer vacations and a college education were givens. Alternatively, if your parents dropped out of high school and worked a "blue-collar" job, your home would be smaller and in a less expensive part of town, and your opportunities would be more limited (for example, education). Social class affects one's comfort in interacting with others—we tend to feel more comfortable with others from our same social class.

Diversity in Other Countries

The social class of one's family may have an effect on one's selection of a mate. Middle- and upper-class individuals in Ecuador and Latin America typically have longer courtships, engagements, and wedding ceremonies than those from lower socioeconomic backgrounds—hence, the respective families of the bride and groom want considerable involvement. In contrast, individuals from lower socioeconomic families are more likely to pair bond in their teens, to cohabit, and to experience an out-of-marriage pregnancy and childbirth (Schvaneveldt 2003).

The **mating gradient** refers to the tendency for husbands to be more advanced than their wives with regard to age, education, and occupational success. Indeed, husbands are typically older than their wives, have more advanced education, and earn higher incomes (*Statistical Abstract of the United States, 2009*, Table 679).

Physical Appearance Homogamy is operative in regard to physical appearance in that people tend to become involved with those who are similar in degree of physical attractiveness. However, a partner's attractiveness may be a more important consideration for

Open-Mindedness Scale

The purpose of this scale is to assess the degree to which you are open-minded. Open-mindedness is one's receptiveness to arguments, ideas, suggestions, and opinions. As such, someone who is open-minded typically does not prejudge or have preconceptions of others and is receptive and tolerant of new information. After reading each statement, select the number that best reflects your answer, using the following scale:

1	2	3	4	5	6	7
Strongly Disagree						Strongly Agree

_____ 1. I am an open-minded person.

_____ 2. I like diversity of thoughts and ideas.

_____ 3. I think knowledge of different viewpoints is the only way to find the truth.

_____ 4. I have often changed my mind about something after reading more about it.

_____ 5. I consider more than one point of view before taking a stand on an issue.

_____ 6. It really bothers me if someone makes fun of another person's idea.

_____ 7. I am willing to explore a different point of view even if I do not agree with it.

_____ 8. I am willing to really listen to any point of view.

_____ 9. I evaluate information on the basis of its merit rather than my emotional reaction to it.

_____ 10. I try to read about both sides of an issue before I form an opinion.

Scoring

Selecting a 1 reflects the least open-mindedness; selecting a 7 reflects the greatest open-mindedness. Add the numbers you assigned to each item. The lower your total score (10 is the lowest possible score), the more closed-minded you are; the higher your total score (70 is the highest possible score), the greater your open-mindedness. A score of 40 places you at the midpoint between being very closed-minded and very open-minded.

Scores of Other Students Who Completed the Scale

The scale was completed by 44 male and 81 female students at Valdosta State University. They received course credit for their participation. Their ages ranged from 18 to 46 years, with a mean age of 20.50 (standard deviation [SD] = 4.00). The racial and ethnic background of the sample included 64.0 percent white, 29.6 percent black, 1.6 percent Hispanic, and 4.8 percent other. The college classification level of the sample included 61.6 percent freshmen, 27.2 percent sophomores, 8.0 percent juniors, 1.6 percent seniors, and 0.8 percent postbaccalaureate students. Male participants had higher open-mindedness scores (mean [M] = 57.55; SD = 6.85) than did female participants (M = 54.58; SD = 7.75; $p < .05$). Freshman had lower open-mindedness scores (M = 54.01; SD = 7.50) than did upper-classmen (M = 58.04; SD = 6.94; $p = .05$). There were no significant differences in regard to race.

Source

"Open-Mindedness Scale" 2006 by Mark Whatley, Ph.D., Department of Psychology, Valdosta State University, Valdosta, Georgia 31698-0100. Used by permission. Other uses of this scale by written permission of Dr. Whatley only (mwhatley@valdosta.edu). Information on the reliability and validity of this scale is available from Dr. Whatley.

---

men than for women. In a study of homogamous preferences in mate selection, men and women rated physical appearance an average of 7.7 and 6.8 (out of 10) in importance, respectively (Knox et al. 1997).

Marital Status   Never-married people tend to select other never-married people as marriage partners, divorced people tend to select other divorced people, and widowed people tend to select other widowed people. Similar marital status may be more important to women than to men. In the study of homogamous preferences in mate selection, women and men rated similarity of marital status an average of 7.2 and 6.3 (out of 10) in importance, respectively (Knox et al. 1997).

Religion/Spirituality   Most adults in the United States tend to be affiliated with a religion. Only 11 percent of two national samples reported no religious affiliation (Amato et al. 2007). **Religion** may be broadly defined as a specific fundamental set of beliefs (in reference to a supreme being, and so on) and practices generally agreed upon by a number of people or sects. Similarly, some individuals view themselves as "not religious" but "spiritual," with spirituality defined as belief in the spirit as the seat of the moral or religious nature that guides one's decisions

Education is what you have left over after you have forgotten everything you have learned.

Anonymous

Table 6.1 112 Million U.S. Family Households by Social Class*

Class Identification	Percentage of Population	Household Income	Education/Occupation	Lifestyle	Example
Upper Class (4%)					
Upper-upper class (old money capitalists)	1%	$500,000	Prestigious schools/ wealth passed down	Large, spacious homes in lush residential areas	Kennedy
Lower-upper class (nouveau riche)	3%	$250,000	Prestigious schools/ investors in or owners of large corporations	(same as above)	Bill Gates, Donlald Trump
Middle Class (45%)					
Upper-middle class	26%	$75,000– $250,000	Postgraduate degrees/ physicians, lawyers, managers of large corporations	Nice homes, nice neighborhoods, send children to state universities	Your physician
Lower-middle class	19%	$50,000– $75,000	College degrees/nurses, elementary or high school teachers	Modest homes, older cars	High school English teacher
Working Class	26%	$25,000– $50,000	High school diploma/ Waitresses, mechanics	Home in lower-income suburb; children get job after high school	Employee at fast food restaurant
Working Poor	15%	Below poverty line of $22,050 for family of three	Some high school/ service jobs	Live in poorest of housing; barely able to pay rent or buy food	Janitor
Underclass	10%	—	Unemployed/ unemployable; survive via public assistance, begging, hustling, or illegal behavior (e.g., selling drugs)	Homeless; contact with mainstream society is via criminal justice system	Bag lady

*Appreciation is expressed to Arunas Juska, PhD, for his assistance in the development of this table. Estimates of percentage in each class are in reference to household incomes as published in *Statistical Abstract of the United States, 2009, Table 684.*

It is better to be looked over, than to be overlooked.

Mae West, actress of the 1930s

and behavior. Because religious or spiritual views reflect, in large part, who the person is, they have an enormous impact on one's attraction to a partner, the level of emotional engagement with that partner, and the durability of the relationship and marital happiness (Swenson et al. 2005).

Religious homogamy is operative in that people of similar religion or spiritual philosophy tend to seek out each other. Over 40 percent of 1,319 undergraduates agreed that "It is important that I marry someone of my same religion." Exactly half reported that they had dated someone of another religion (Knox and Zusman 2009).

The phrase "the couple that prays together, stays together" is more than just a cliché. However, it should also be pointed out that religion could serve as a divisive force. For example, when one partner becomes "born again" or "saved," the relationship can be dramatically altered and eventually terminated unless the other partner shares the experience. A former rock-and-roller, hard-drinking, drug-taking wife noted that, when her husband "got saved," it was the end of their marriage. "He gave our money to the church as the 'tithe' when we couldn't even pay the light bill," she said. "And when he told me I could no longer wear pants or lipstick or have a beer, I left." Another example of how religious disharmony has a negative effect on relationships is the marriage of Ted Turner and Jane Fonda. Soon after she became a "Christian" and was "saved," she and Turner split up. In an interview, Fonda noted that she feared telling her husband about her religious conversion because she knew it would be the end of their eight-year marriage.

Attachment   Individuals who report similar levels of attachment to each other report high levels of relationship satisfaction. This is the conclusion of Luo and Klohnen (2005), who studied 291 newlyweds to assess the degree to which similarity affected marital quality. Indeed, similarity of attachment was *the* variable most predictive of relationship quality.

Personality   Helen Fisher (2009) analyzed data from over 28,000 heterosexual members of chemistry.com. She observed a tendency for certain personality types to select other personality types. For example, "explorers" (curious, creative, adventurous, sexual) were attracted to other "explorers," and "builders" (calm, loyal, traditional) were attracted to other "builders." These pairings are an obvious example of homogamy—like seeking like.

Economic Values, Money Management, and Debt   Individuals vary in the degree to which they have money, spend money, and save. Some have very limited resources and are careful about all spending. Others have significant resources and buy whatever they want. Some are deeply in debt whereas others have no debt. Of 1,319 undergraduates, 9 percent noted that they owed more than a thousand dollars on a credit card (Knox and Zusman 2009). Some carry significant educational debt. The median debt for those with a bachelor's degree was $19,300 (Chu 2007). Money becomes an issue in mate selection in that different economic backgrounds, values, and spending patterns are predictable conflict issues. One undergraduate noted, "There is no way I would get involved with/marry this person as they don't know how to handle money."

Homogamy operates almost without awareness. This couple reports, "we love each other"... but they are also of the same race, age, education, social class, and religious background.

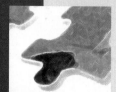
There is small choice in rotten apples.

William Shakespeare

Psychological Factors Operative in Mate Selection

Psychologists have focused on complementary needs, exchanges, parental characteristics, and personality types with regard to mate selection.

Complementary-Needs Theory

"In spite of the Women's Movement and a lot of assertive friends, I am a shy and dependent person," remarked a transfer student. "My need for dependency is met by Warren, who is the dominant, protective type." The tendency for a submissive person to become involved with a dominant person (one who likes to control the behavior of others) is an example of attraction based on complementary needs.

Complementary-needs theory states that we tend to select mates whose needs are opposite and complementary to our own. Partners can also be drawn to each other on the basis of nurturance versus receptivity. These complementary needs suggest that one person likes to give and take care of another, whereas the other likes to be the benefactor of such care. Other examples of complementary needs may involve responsibility versus irresponsibility, peacemaker versus troublemaker, and disorder versus order. Helen Fisher (2009), referred to previously, also found evidence of complementary needs in her study of 28,000 participants looking for a partner on chemistry.com. In terms of personality, "directors" (analytical, decisive, focused) sought "negotiators" (introspective, verbal, intuitive) and vice versa.

The idea that mate selection is based on complementary needs was suggested by Winch (1955), who noted that needs can be complementary if they are different (for example, dominant and submissive) or if the partners have the same need at different levels of intensity.

As an example of the latter, two individuals may have a complementary relationship if they both want to pursue graduate studies but want to earn different degrees. The partners will complement each other if, for instance, one is comfortable with aspiring to a master's degree and approves of the other's commitment to earning a doctorate.

Winch's theory of complementary needs, commonly referred to as "opposites attract," is based on the observation of twenty-five undergraduate married couples at Northwestern University. Other researchers who have not been able to replicate Winch's study have criticized the findings (Saint 1994). Two researchers said, "It would now appear that Winch's findings may have been an artifact of either his methodology or his sample of married people" (Meyer and Pepper 1977). Singer Carly Simon said of her former husband, James Taylor:

> *Our needs are different; it seemed impossible to stay together. James needs a lot more space around him—aloneness, remoteness, more privacy. I need more closeness, more communication. He's more abstract in our relationship. I'm more concrete. He's more of a . . . poet, and I'm more of a . . . reporter.* (White 1990, 525)

Three questions can be raised about the theory of complementary needs:

1. *Couldn't personality needs be met just as easily outside the couple's relationship as through mate selection?* For example, couldn't a person who has the need to be dominant find such fulfillment in a job that involved an authoritative role, such as being a supervisor?

2. *What is a complementary need as opposed to a similar value?* For example, is the desire to achieve at different levels a complementary need or a shared value?

3. *Don't people change as they age?* Could dependent people grow and develop self-confidence so that they might no longer need to be involved with a dominant person? Indeed, such a person might no longer enjoy interacting with a dominant person.

Exchange Theory

Exchange theory emphasizes that mate selection is based on assessing who offers the greatest rewards at the lowest cost. The following five concepts help to explain the exchange process in mate selection:

1. *Rewards.* Rewards are the behaviors (your partner looking at you with the eyes of love), words (saying "I love you"), resources (being beautiful or handsome, having a car, condo, and money), and services (cooking for you, typing for you) your partner provides that you value and that influence you to continue the relationship. Increasingly, men are interested in women who offer "financial independence." In a study of Internet ads placed by women, the woman who described herself as "financially independent . . . successful and ambitious" produced 50 percent more responses than the next most popular ad, in which the woman described herself as "lovely . . . very attractive and slim" (Strassberg and Holty 2003).

2. *Costs.* Costs are the unpleasant aspects of a relationship. A woman identified the costs associated with being involved with her partner: "He abuses drugs, doesn't have a job, and lives nine hours away." The costs her partner associated with being involved with this woman included "she nags me," "she doesn't like sex," and "she wants her mother to live with us if we marry." Ingoldsby et al. (2003) assessed the degree to which various characteristics were associated with reducing one's attractiveness on the marriage market. The most undesirable traits were not being heterosexual, having alcohol or drug problems, having a sexually transmitted disease, and being lazy.

3. *Profit.* Profit occurs when the rewards exceed the costs. Unless the couple previously referred to derive a profit from staying together, they are likely to end their relationship and seek someone else with whom there is a higher profit margin.

4. *Loss.* Loss occurs when the costs exceed the rewards.

5. *Alternative.* Is another person currently available who offers a higher profit margin?

Before you run in double harness, look well to the other horse.

Ovid

Most people have definite ideas about what they are looking for in a mate. For example, Xie et al. (2003) found that men with good incomes were much more likely to marry than men with no or low incomes. The currency used in the marriage market consists of the socially valued characteristics of the people involved, such as age, physical characteristics, and economic status. In our free choice system of mate selection, we typically get as much in return for our social attributes as we have to offer or trade. An unattractive, drug-abusing high school dropout with no job has little to offer an attractive, drug-free, college student who has just been accepted to graduate school.

Once you identify a person who offers you a good exchange for what you have to offer, other bargains are made about the conditions of your continued relationship. Waller and Hill (1951) observed that the person who has the least interest in continuing the relationship could control the relationship. This **principle of least interest** is illustrated by the woman who said, "He wants to date me more than I want to date him, so we end up going where I want to go and doing what I want to do." In this case, the woman trades her company for the man's acquiescence to her recreational choices. In effect, the person with the least interest controls the relationship.

Parental Characteristics   Whereas the complementary-needs and exchange theories of mate selection are relatively recent, Freud suggested that the choice of a love object in adulthood represents a shift in libidinal energy from the first love objects—the parents. **Role theory of mate selection** (also known as **modeling theory of mate selection**) emphasizes that a son or daughter models after the parent of the same sex by selecting a partner similar to the one the parent selected.

This means that a man looks for a wife who has similar characteristics to those of his mother and that a woman looks for a husband who is very similar to her father.

Searching for Homogamy: An In-Class Exercise

"Searching for Homogamy" is a way for students to "see" the courtship process in class. Six students participated in the in-class exercise, whereby one man interviewed five women, selected one, and went out on a "real" date with his

These students are playing the "Searching for Homogamy" game whereby the male is finding which of four females he has the most in common with.

Authors

selection (Knox and McGinty 2009). (Alternative versions of the exercise include one women selecting from five men or same-sex partners selecting each other.) Lecture and discussion of the "dating/mate selection process" preceded the exercise; the in-class exercise reflected traditional gender roles in society, the high probability of being rejected, and how homogamy operates in the selection of a partner.

Marry yourself.

Jack Wright, sociologist

The participants were recruited from the class. Participants had to be able to take rejection (each female participant has an 80 percent chance of being rejected), uninvolved in a current relationship, and open to dating or involvement with people of any racial, ethnic, or religious background. No extra credit was awarded for playing the game. The first six people who e-mailed their instructor (and specified agreement to the terms) were included in the game. (The format involves a man selecting from among women because there were never enough volunteers in past classes for one woman to select from five men, and gay individuals did not volunteer.)

Rules of the game included the following:

1. Participants became involved in a question-and-answer session in front of the class, during which the "dater" asked each of five potential dates two questions. One question was generated by the dater and another by class members or the instructor. Each date candidate also asked the dater one question and may have been rejected before he made his selection. The dater ultimately selected the woman he would like to take out on a real date.

2. The couple went out to dinner the following weekend (both paid their own way). They agreed to no alcohol and no sex.

3. Both participants reported to the class about their experience on the date. Each did so alone, while the other waited outside the classroom.

Advantages reported by students included "fun," "seeing guys answer questions asked by girls," and "learning how to ask questions." Disadvantages included the game didn't last long enough, some of the questions could get too personal, and no one liked to be rejected.

Desired Personality Characteristics for a Potential Mate

In a study of 700 undergraduates, both men and women reported that the personality characteristics of being warm, kind, and open and having a sense of humor were very important to them in selecting a romantic or sexual partner. Indeed, these intrinsic personality characteristics were rated as more important than physical attractiveness or wealth (extrinsic characteristics) (Sprecher and Regan 2002). Similarly, adolescents wanted intrinsic qualities such as intelligence and humor in a romantic partner but looked for physical appearance and high sex drive in a casual partner (no gender-related differences in responses were found) (Regan and Joshi 2003). Sometimes what individuals say they want and actually select may be different. Bogg and Ray (2006) noted that, although women in one study said that they consistently preferred to date and marry men who were egalitarian, it was not unusual for them to select ultramasculine men who were sometimes dominant, mysterious, and rebellious.

Assad et. al. (2007) studied the personality quality of optimism and found that optimistic individuals tended to be involved in satisfying and happy romantic relationships, and a substantial portion of this association was mediated by willingness to be a cooperative problem solver. Hence, selecting a person who is optimistic seems to predict well for the future of the relationship.

In another study, women were significantly more likely than men to identify "having a good job" and "being well-educated" as important attributes in a future mate, whereas significantly more men than women wanted their spouse to be physically attractive (Medora et al. 2002). Toro-Morn and Sprecher (2003) noted that both American and Chinese undergraduate women identified characteristics associated with status (earning potential, wealth) more than physical attractiveness.

The behavior that 60 percent of a national sample of adult single women reported as the most serious fault of a man was his being "too controlling" (Edwards 2000). Women are also attracted to men who have good manners. In a study of 398 undergraduates, women were significantly more likely than men to report that they wanted to "date or be involved with [only] someone who had good manners," that "manners are very important," and that "the more well mannered the person, the more I like the person" (Zusman et al. 2003). Twenge (2006) noted that good manners are being displayed less often.

Personality Characteristics of Partners to Avoid

Researchers have identified several personality factors predictive of relationships that either do not endure or are unfulfilling (Foster 2008; Wilson and Cousins 2005). Potential partners who are observed to consistently display these characteristics might be avoided.

1. *Narcissism.* Foster (2008) observed that individuals high on narcissism view relationships in terms of what they get out of them. When satisfactions wane and alternatives are present, narcissists are the first to go. Because all relationships have difficult times, a narcissist is a high risk for a durable marriage partner.

2. *Disagreeableness or low positives.* Gattis et al. (2004) studied 132 distressed couples seeking treatment and found that the personality characteristics of "low agreeableness" and "low positive expressions" were associated with their not getting along. Hence, partners who always find something to argue about and who find few opportunities to make positive observations or expressions should be considered with caution.

3. *Poor impulse control.* People who have poor impulse control have little self-restraint and may be prone to aggression and violence (Snyder and Regts 1990). Lack of impulse control is also problematic in relationships because such people are less likely to consider the consequences of their actions. For example, to some people, having an affair might seem harmless but it will have devastating consequences for the partners and their relationship in most cases.

4. *Hypersensitivity.* Hypersensitivity to perceived criticism involves getting hurt easily. Any negative statement or criticism is received with a greater impact than a partner intended. The disadvantage of such hypersensitivity is that a partner may learn not to give feedback for fear of hurting the hypersensitive partner. Such lack of feedback to the hypersensitive partner blocks information about what the person does that upsets the other and what could be done to make things better. Hence, the hypersensitive one has no way of learning that something is wrong, and the partner has no way of alerting the hypersensitive partner. The result is a relationship in which the partners can't talk about what is wrong, so the potential for change is limited (ibid.).

5. *Inflated ego.* An exaggerated sense of oneself is another way of saying a person has a big ego and always wants things to be his or her way. A person with an inflated sense of self may be less likely to consider the other person's opinion in negotiating a conflict and prefer to dictate an outcome. Such disrespect for the partner can be damaging to the relationship (Snyder and Regts 1990).

6. *Perfectionism.* Individuals who are perfectionists may require perfection of themselves and others. This attitude is associated with relationship problems (Haring et al. 2003).

7. *Insecurity.* Feelings of insecurity also compromise marital happiness. Researchers studied the personality trait of attachment and its effect on marriage in 157 couples at two-time intervals and found that "insecure participants reported more difficulties in their relationships. . . [I]n contrast, secure participants reported greater feelings of intimacy in the relationship at both assessments" (Crowell et al. 2002).

Traditional Husband? University Women Who Want One

A theme permeating the media in regard to relationships is that of equality. Women presumably seek a "modern" relationship in which the spouse is equal in terms of career status and division of labor. But do they? To what degree do women seek traditional husbands who view their primary role as provider and who are supportive of their wife staying at home to rear the children? This study sought to identify the degree to which undergraduate women at a large southeastern university seek a traditional husband and to identify the various background characteristics of these women.

Sample and Methods

To find out, researchers analyzed data from a sample of 692 undergraduate women at a large southeastern university who answered "yes" (30.9 percent) or "no" (69.1 percent) to the yes-or-no statement, "As a female, I prefer to marry a traditional man who will be the provider and be supportive of my staying at home to rear the children." The sample of respondents was 80.8 percent white and 19.2 percent black, and the median age was 19 years. Of the respondents, 50.7 percent were first-year students; 24.6 percent, sophomores; 14.6 percent, juniors; and 10.0 percent, seniors. In regard to current relationships, 43.4 percent were not dating anyone or were casually dating different people, whereas 56.6 percent were emotionally committed or involved.

Selected Findings and Conclusions

As noted, 30.9 percent of the 692 undergraduate women surveyed reported that they wanted to marry a traditional husband; 69.1 percent did not want to do so. Analysis of the data revealed the following five statistically significant findings in regard to the characteristics of the undergraduate women who wanted a traditional husband versus those who did not:

1. *Valued happy marriage over financial security or career.* Indicating their top three values, 40.8 percent of the women in this sample identified "having a happy marriage" in life, followed by "financial security" (27.1 percent) and "having a career I love" (17 percent). This finding came as no surprise, as we would expect women who prefer to marry a traditional man to value a happy marriage first and a career last. What did come as a surprise was that only 17 percent of these women valued having a career as their top priority. Is the women's movement, with its emphasis on financial independence, losing support from women who reevaluate being married to a man who makes a good income and

takes care of his wife and children financially? Are feminists discovering that emphasizing a career leaves them empty? Did these undergraduate women have mothers who were devoted to their careers, did they feel cheated and abandoned by their mothers when they were growing up, and have they vowed to stay at home and take care of their own children?

2. *Believed children turn out better in a traditional family.* One might expect women who preferred a traditional husband to be motivated by the desire to stay at home to rear their children and to believe that doing so would be beneficial to their children. Analysis of the data revealed this expectation to be true in that 52.7 percent of the women answered "yes" to the statement "Children turn out better when one parent stays home to take care of them"; in comparison, 12.4 percent answered "no."

3. *Against cohabitation.* A final characteristic of being conservative and having traditional values, as evidenced by the women in this sample, is their reluctance to cohabit. Of those preferring a traditional husband, 38.3 percent reported that they would not live with a man before marriage, compared with 27.6 percent who reported they would.

4. *White.* Of the women who preferred a traditional husband, 33.4 percent were white, compared with 18.6 percent who self-identified as black. Hence, white women were 14.8 percent more likely to prefer a traditional, provider husband than black women. This finding may say more about black women than white women. Because black women tend to have more education than black men and are more likely to come from matriarchal (female-dominated) homes, they may feel less need to have a man take care of them.

This research study has two implications for mate selection: (1) although most undergraduate women in this sample preferred a "modern" man, 30 percent did not and were explicit about wanting a traditional partner to earn the income and be supportive of their desire to stay home and rear children; and (2) women who are looking for a traditional man have other traditional values: they are focused on a happy relationship rather than money, they feel that children flourish best with a stay-at-home mother, and they are against cohabitation.

Source

McGinty, K., D. Knox, and M. E. Zusman. 2006. *Traditional husband? University women who want one.* Research study conducted for this text. Greenville, NC: Department of Sociology, East Carolina University.

Table 6.2   Personality Types Problematic in a Potential Partner

Type	Characteristics	Impact on Partner
Paranoid	Suspicious, distrustful, thin-skinned, defensive	Partners may be accused of everything.
Schizoid	Cold, aloof, solitary, reclusive	Partners may feel that they can never "connect" and that the person is not capable of returning love.
Borderline	Moody, unstable, volatile, unreliable, suicidal, impulsive	Partners will never know what their Jekyll-and-Hyde partner will be like, which could be dangerous.
Antisocial	Deceptive, untrustworthy, conscienceless, remorseless	Such a partner could cheat on, lie, or steal from a partner and not feel guilty.
Narcissistic	Egotistical, demanding, greedy, selfish	Such a person views partners only in terms of their value. Don't expect such a partner to see anything from your point of view; expect such a person to bail in tough times.
Dependent	Helpless, weak, clingy, insecure	Such a person will demand a partner's full time and attention, and other interests will incite jealousy.
Obsessive-compulsive	Rigid, inflexible	Such a person has rigid ideas about how a partner should think and behave and may try to impose them on the partner.

8. *Controlled.* Individuals who are controlled by their parents, grandparents, former partner, child, or whomever compromise the marriage relationship because their allegiance is external to the couple's relationship. Unless the person is able to break free of such control, the ability to make independent decisions will be thwarted, which will both frustrate the spouse and challenge the marriage.

In addition to personality characteristics, Table 6.2 reflects some particularly troublesome personality types and how they may impact you negatively.

PERSONAL CHOICES

Who Is the Best Person for You to Marry?

Although no perfect mate exists, some individuals are more suited as a marriage partner than others. As we have seen in this chapter, people who have a big ego, poor impulse control, and an oversensitivity to criticism and who are anxious and neurotic should be considered with great caution.

Equally as important as avoiding someone with problematic personality characteristics is selecting someone with whom you have a great deal in common. "Marry someone just like you" may be a worthy guideline in selecting a marriage partner. Homogamous matings with regard to race, education, age, values, religion, social class, and marital status (for example, never-married people marry never-married people; divorced people with children marry those with similar experience) are more likely to result in more durable, satisfying relationships. "Marry your best friend" is another worthy guideline for selecting the person you marry.

Finally, marrying someone with whom you have a relationship of equality and respect is associated with marital happiness. Relationships in which one partner is exploited or intimidated engender negative feelings of resentment and distance. One man said, "I want a co-chair, not a committee member, for a mate." He was saying that he wanted a partner to whom he related as an equal.

Sociobiological Factors Operative in Mate Selection

In contrast to cultural, sociological, and psychological aspects of mate selection, which reflect a social learning assumption, the sociobiological perspective suggests that biological or genetic factors may be operative in mate selection.

Definition of Sociobiology

Sociobiology suggests a biological basis for all social behavior—including mate selection. Based on Charles Darwin's theory of natural selection, which states that the strongest of the species survive, sociobiology holds that men and women select each other as mates on the basis of their innate concern for producing offspring who are most capable of surviving.

According to sociobiologists, men look for a young, healthy, attractive, sexually conservative woman who will produce healthy children and invest in taking care of the children. Women, in contrast, look for an ambitious man with good economic capacity who will invest his resources in her children. Earlier in this chapter, we provided data supporting the idea that men seek attractive women and women seek ambitious, financially successful men.

Diversity in the United States

Among the Hopi Indians, when a couple think of getting married, the potential bride's family prepares food and takes it to the potential groom's family. If his family members accept the food and approve of the union, they reciprocate by giving food (usually meat) to her family—and the engagement is on.

Criticisms of the Sociobiological Perspective

The sociobiological explanation for mate selection is controversial. Critics argue that women may show concern for the earning capacity of men because women have been systematically denied access to similar economic resources, and selecting a mate with these resources is one of their remaining options. In addition, it is argued that both women and men, when selecting a mate, think about their partners more as companions than as future parents of their offspring.

Engagement

Engagement moves the relationship of a couple from a private love-focused experience to a public, parent-involved experience. Family and friends are invited to enjoy the happiness and commitment of the individuals to a future marriage. Unlike casual dating, **engagement** is a time in which the partners are emotionally committed, are sexually monogamous, and are focused on wedding preparations. The engagement period is the last opportunity before marriage to systematically examine the relationship, ask each other specific questions, find out about the partner's parents and family background, and participate in marriage education or counseling.

Asking Specific Questions

Because partners might hesitate to ask for or reveal information that they feel will be met with disapproval during casual dating, the engagement is a time to be specific about the other partner's thoughts, feelings, values, goals, and expectations. The **Involved Couple's Inventory** is designed to help individuals in committed relationships learn more about each other by asking specific

Involved Couple's Inventory

The following questions are designed to increase your knowledge of how you and your partner think and feel about a variety of issues. Assume that you and your partner have considered getting married. Each partner should ask the other the following questions:

Partner Feelings and Issues

1. If you could change one thing about me, what would it be?

2. On a scale of 0 to 10, how well do you feel I respond to criticism or suggestions for improvement?

3. What would you like me to say or not say that would make you happier?

4. What do you think of yourself? Describe yourself with three adjectives.

5. What do you think of me? Describe me with three adjectives.

6. What do you like best about me?

7. On a scale of 0 to 10, how jealous do you think I am? How do you feel about my level of jealousy?

8. How do you feel about me emotionally?

9. To what degree do you feel we each need to develop and maintain outside relationships so as not to focus all of our interpersonal expectations on each other? Does this include other-sex individuals?

10. Do you have any history of abuse or violence, either as an abused child or adult or as the abuser in an adult relationship?

11. If we could not get along, would you be willing to see a marriage counselor? Would you see a sex therapist if we were having sexual problems?

12. What is your feeling about prenuptial agreements?

13. Suppose I insisted on your signing a prenuptial agreement?

14. To what degree do you enjoy getting and giving a massage?

15. How important is it to you that we massage each other regularly?

16. On a scale of 0 to 10, how emotionally close do you want us to be?

17. How many intense love relationships have you had, and to what degree are these individuals still a part of your life in terms of seeing them or having e-mail or phone contact?

18. Have you been in a live-in relationship with anyone before? Are you open to our living together? What would be your understanding of the meaning of our living together? Would we be "finding out more about each other" or would we be "committed to marriage"?

19. What do you want for the future of our relationship? Do you want us to marry? When?

20. On a ten-point scale (0 = very unhappy and 10 = very happy), how happy are you in general? How happy are you about us?

21. How depressed have you been? What made you feel depressed?

Feelings about Parents and Family

1. How do you feel about your mother? Your father? Your siblings?

2. On a ten-point scale, how close are you to your mom, dad, and each of your siblings?

3. How close were your family members to one another? On a ten-point scale, what value do you place on the opinions or values of your parents?

4. How often do you have contact with your father or mother? How often do you want to visit your parents and/or siblings? How often would you want them to visit us? Do you want to spend holidays alone or with your parents or mine?

5. What do you like and dislike most about each of your parents?

6. What do you like and dislike about my parents?

7. What is your feeling about living near our parents? How would you feel about my parents living with us? How do you feel about our parents living with us when they are old and cannot take care of themselves?

8. How do your parents get along? Rate their marriage on a scale of 0 to 10 (0 = unhappy, 10 = happy).

9. To what degree do your parents take vacations alone together? What are your expectations of our taking vacations alone or with others?

10. To what degree did members of your family consult one another on their decisions? To what degree do you expect me to consult you on the decisions that I make?

11. Who was the dominant person in your family? Who had more power? Who do you regard as the dominant partner in our relationship? How do you feel about this power distribution?

12. What "problems" has your family experienced? Is there any history of mental illness, alcoholism, drug abuse, suicide, or other such problems?

13. What did your mother and father do to earn an income? How were their role responsibilities divided in terms of

having income, taking care of the children, and managing the household? To what degree do you want a job and role similar to that of the same-sex parent?

Social Issues, Religion, and Children

1. How do you feel about Obama as President? How do you feel about America being in Afghanistan?

2. What are your feelings about women's rights, racial equality, and homosexuality?

3. To what degree do you regard yourself as a religious or spiritual person? What do you think about religion, a Supreme Being, prayer, and life after death?

4. Do you go to religious services? Where? How often? Do you pray? How often? What do you pray about? When we are married, how often would you want to go to religious services? In what religion would you want our children to be reared? What responsibility would you take to ensure that our children had the religious training you wanted them to have?

5. How do you feel about abortion? Under what conditions, if any, do you feel abortion is justified?

6. How do you feel about children? How many do you want? When do you want the first child? At what intervals would you want to have additional children? What do you see as your responsibility in caring for the children—changing diapers, feeding, bathing, playing with them, and taking them to lessons and activities? To what degree do you regard these responsibilities as mine?

7. Suppose I did not want to have children or couldn't have them. How would you feel? How do you feel about artificial insemination, surrogate motherhood, in vitro fertilization, and adoption?

8. To your knowledge, can you have children? Are there any genetic problems in your family history that would prevent us from having normal children? How healthy (mentally and physically) are you? How often have you seen a physician in the last three years? What medications have you taken or do you currently take? What are these medications for? Have you seen a therapist, psychologist, or psychiatrist? What for?

9. How should children be disciplined? Do you want our children to go to public or private schools?

10. How often do you think we should go out alone without our children? If we had to decide between the two of us going on a cruise to the Bahamas alone or taking the children camping for a week, what would you choose?

11. What are your expectations of me regarding religious participation with you and our children?

Sex

1. How much sexual intimacy do you feel is appropriate in casual dating, involved dating, and engagement?

2. Does "having sex" mean having sexual intercourse? If a couple has experienced oral sex only, have they "had sex"?

3. What sexual behaviors do you most and least enjoy? How often do you want to have intercourse? How do you want me to turn you down when I don't want to have sex? How do you want me to approach you for sex? How do you feel about just being physical together—hugging, rubbing, holding, but not having intercourse?

4. By what method of stimulation do you experience an orgasm most easily?

5. What do you think about masturbation, oral sex, homosexuality, sadism and masochism (S & M), and anal sex?

6. What type of contraception do you suggest? Why? If that method does not prove satisfactory, what method would you suggest next?

7. What are your values regarding extramarital sex? If I had an affair, would you want me to tell you? Why? If I told you about the affair, what would you do? Why?

8. How often do you view pornographic videos or pornography on the Internet?

9. How important is our using a condom to you?

10. Do you want me to be tested for human immunodeficiency virus (HIV)? Are you willing to be tested?

11. What sexually transmitted infections (STIs) have you had?

12. How much do you want to know about my sexual behavior with previous partners?

13. How many "friends with benefits" relationships have you been in? What is your interest in our having such a relationship?

14. How much do you trust me in terms of my being faithful or monogamous with you?

15. How open do you want our relationship to be in terms of having emotional or sexual involvement with others, while keeping our relationship primary?

16. What things have you done that you are ashamed of?

17. What emotional, psychological, or physical health problems do you have? What issues do you struggle with?

18. What are your feelings about your sexual adequacy? What sexual problems do you or have you had?

19. Give me an example of your favorite sexual fantasy.

Careers and Money

1. What kind of job or career will you have? What are your feelings about working in the evening versus being home with the family? Where will your work require that we live? How often do you feel we will be moving? How much travel will your job require?

2. To what degree did your parents agree on how to deal with money? Who was in charge of spending, and who was in charge of saving? Did working, or earning the bigger portion of the income, connect to control over money?

3. What are your feelings about a joint versus a separate checking account? Which of us do you want to pay the bills? How much money do you think we will have left over each month? How much of this do you think we should save?

4. When we disagree over whether to buy something, how do you suggest we resolve our conflict?

5. What jobs or work experience have you had? If we end up having careers in different cities, how do you feel about being involved in a commuter marriage?

6. What is your preference for where we live? Do you want to live in an apartment or a house? What are your needs for a car, television, cable service, phone plan, entertainment devices, and so on? What are your feelings about us living in two separate places, the "living apart together" idea whereby we can have a better relationship if we give each other some space and have plenty of room?

7. How do you feel about my having a career? Do you expect me to earn an income? If so, how much annually? To what degree do you feel it is your responsibility to cook, clean, and take care of the children? How do you feel about putting young children or infants in day-care centers? When the children are sick and one of us has to stay home, who will that be?

8. To what degree do you want me to account to you for the money I spend? How much money, if any, do you feel each of us should have to spend each week as we wish without first checking with the other partner? What percentage of income, if any, do you think we should give to charity each year?

9. What assets or debts will you bring into the marriage?

10. How much child support or alimony do you get or pay each month? Tell me about your divorce.

11. In your will, what percentage of your assets, holdings, and retirement will you leave to me versus anybody else (siblings, children of a previous relationship, and so on)?

12. May I read your divorce settlement agreement? When?

Recreation and Leisure

1. What is your idea of the kinds of parties or social gatherings you would like for us to go to together?

2. What is your preference in terms of us hanging out with others in a group versus being alone?

3. What is your favorite recreational interest? How much time do you spend enjoying this interest? How important is it for you that I share this recreational interest with you?

4. What do you like to watch on television? How often do you watch television and for what periods of time?

5. What are the amount and frequency of your current use of alcohol and other drugs (for example, marijuana, cocaine, crack, speed)? What, if any, have been your previous alcohol and other drug behaviors and frequencies? What are your expectations of me regarding the use of alcohol and other drugs?

6. Where did you vacation with your parents? Where will you want us to go? How will we travel? How much money do you feel we should spend on vacations each year?

Relationships with Friends and Coworkers

1. How do you feel about my three closest same-sex friends?

2. How do you feel about my spending time with my friends or coworkers, such as one evening a week?

3. How do you feel about my spending time with friends of the opposite sex?

4. What do you regard as appropriate and inappropriate affectional behaviors with opposite-sex friends?

Remarriage Questions

1. How and why did your first marriage end? What are your feelings about your former spouse now? What are the feelings of your former spouse toward you? How much "trouble" do you feel your former spouse will want to cause us? What relationship do you want with your former spouse?

2. Do you want your children from a previous marriage to live with us? What are your emotional and financial expectations of me in regard to your children? What are your feelings about my children living with us? Do you want us to have additional children? How many? When?

3. When your children are with us, who will be responsible for their food preparation, care, discipline, and driving them to activities?

4. Suppose your children do not like me and vice versa. How will you handle this? Suppose they are against our getting married?

5. Suppose our respective children do not like one another. How will you handle this?

It would be unusual if you agreed with each other on all of your answers to the previous questions. You might view the differences as challenges and then find out the degree to which the differences are important for your relationship. You might need to explore ways of minimizing the negative impact of those differences on your relationship. It is not possible to have a relationship with someone in which there is total agreement. Disagreement is inevitable; the issue becomes how you and your partner manage the differences.

Note

This self-assessment is intended to be thought-provoking and fun. It is not intended to be used as a clinical or diagnostic instrument.

questions. Other couples use technology to find out information about their potential partners.

Visiting Your Partner's Parents

Seize the opportunity to discover the family environment in which your partner was reared and consider the implications for your subsequent marriage. When visiting your partner's parents, observe their standard of living and the way they interact and relate (for example, level of affection, verbal and nonverbal behavior, marital roles) with one another. How does their standard of living compare with that of your own family? How does the emotional closeness (or distance) of your partner's family compare with that of your family? Such comparisons are significant because both you and your partner will reflect your respective family or origins. "This is the way we did it in my family" is a phrase you will hear your partner say from time to time. If you want to know how your partner is likely to treat you in the future, observe the way your partner's parent of the same sex treats and interacts with his or her spouse. If you want to know what your partner may be like in the future, look at your partner's parent of the same sex. There is a tendency for a man to become like his father and a woman to become like her mother. Your partner's parent of the same sex and their marital relationship is the model of a spouse and a marriage relationship your partner is likely to duplicate in the way the partner relates to you.

Premarital Education Programs

Various **premarital education programs** (also known as premarital prevention programs, premarital counseling, premarital therapy, and marriage preparation), both academic and religious, are formal systematized experiences designed to provide information to individuals and to couples about how to have a good relationship. About 30 percent of couples getting married become involved in some type of premarital education. The greatest predictor of whether a couple will become involved in a premarital education program is the desire and commitment of the female to do so. In effect, she ensures that she and her partner become involved in such a program. A second important predictor is the presence of problems in the relationship of the couple about to marry (Duncan et al. 2007).

Premarital education programs are valuable in that they not only help partners assess the degree to which they are compatible with each other but they may also provide a context to discuss some specific relationship issues. Carroll and Doherty (2003) conducted a review of the various outcome studies of these programs and found that the average participant in a premarital prevention program experienced about a 30 percent increase in measures of outcome success. Specifically, people who attended a premarriage education program were more likely than nonparticipants to experience immediate and short-term gains in interpersonal skills and overall relationship quality. Busby et al. (2007) noted that structured premarital programs such as RELATE (google The Relate Institute) were more effective than giving the couple a workbook or participating in a therapist-led program. The greatest value of premarital education programs is that they provide a context for individuals to discuss relationship issues that they may have avoided.

Prenuptial Agreement

Presidential candidate John McCain has a prenuptial agreement with his wife Cindy. She is heiress to a beer fortune estimated to be $100 million. Britney

Spears and Kevin Federline had a prenuptial agreement whereby he was awarded only $300,000 of over $100 million in assets. Paul McCartney and Heather Mills did not have a prenuptial agreement. She was awarded almost $50 million. Some couples, particularly those with considerable assets or those in subsequent marriages, might consider discussing and signing a prenuptial agreement. To reduce the chance that the agreement will later be challenged, each partner should hire an attorney (months before the wedding) to develop and/or review the agreement.

The primary purpose of a **prenuptial agreement** (also referred to as a premarital agreement, marriage contract, or antenuptial contract) is to specify how property will be divided if the marriage ends in divorce or when it ends by the death of one partner. In effect, the value of what you take into the marriage is the amount you are allowed to take out of the marriage. For example, if you bring $250,000 into the marriage and buy the marital home with this amount, your ex-spouse is not automatically entitled to half the house at divorce. Some agreements may also contain clauses of no spousal support (alimony) if the marriage ends in divorce (but some states prohibit waiving alimony). See Appendix C for an example of a prenuptial agreement developed by a husband and wife who had both been married before and had assets and children.

Reasons for a prenuptial agreement include the following.

1. *Protecting assets for children from a prior relationship.* People who are in their middle or later years, who have considerable assets, who have been married before, and who have children are often concerned that money and property be kept separate in a second marriage so that the assets at divorce or death go to the children. Some children encourage their remarrying parent to draw up a prenuptial agreement with the new partner so that their (the offspring's) inheritance, house, or whatever will not automatically go to the new spouse upon the death of their parent.

2. *Protecting business associates.* A spouse's business associate may want a member of a firm or partnership to draw up a prenuptial agreement with a soon-to-be-spouse to protect the firm from intrusion by the spouse if the marriage does not work out.

Prenuptial contracts have a value beyond the legal implications. Their greatest value may be that they facilitate the partners discussing with each other their expectations of the relationship. In the absence of such an agreement, many couples may never discuss the issues they may later face.

There are also disadvantages of signing a prenuptial agreement. They are often legally challenged ("My partner forced me to sign it or call off the wedding"), and not all issues can be foreseen (for example, who gets the time-share vacation property or the pets?).

Prenuptial agreements also are not very romantic ("I love you, but sign here and see what you get if you don't please me.") and may serve as a self-fulfilling prophecy ("We were already thinking about divorce."). Indeed, 22.8 percent of 1,319 undergraduates agreed "I would not marry someone who required me to sign a prenuptial agreement" and 21.97 percent feel that couples who have a prenuptial agreement are more likely to get divorced (Knox and Zusman 2009). Prenuptial contracts are almost nonexistent in first marriages and are still rare in second marriages. Whether or not signing a prenuptial agreement is a good idea depends on the circumstances. Some individuals who do sign an agreement later regret it. Sherry, then a never-married 22-year-old, signed such an agreement:

Paul was adamant about my signing the premarriage agreement. He said he loved me but would never consider marrying me unless I signed a prenuptial

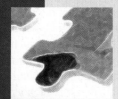
What if My Partner Insists That I Sign a Prenuptial Agreement?

Prenuptial agreements become a problem when one partner has assets to protect and the other has no assets. What begins as an idyllic love relationship with the implied "I love you and want to spend my life with you" turns out to be "if we end up getting divorced, I want to limit what you can get." Shades of distrust cloud the garden love affair. Option one is to sign the prenuptial agreement. As noted earlier, John McCain (Republican presidential candidate) signed a prenuptial agreement with his wife Cindy so as to protect her $100 million fortune. Option two is to delay signing the agreement, which may result in the person with the assets dropping the requirement or the person being willing to sign the agreement. In this option, the relationship continues. Option three is to refuse to sign the agreement and end the relationship.

agreement stating that he would never be responsible for alimony in case of a divorce. I was so much in love, it didn't seem to matter. I didn't realize that basically he was and is a selfish person. Now, five years later after our divorce, I live in a mobile home and he lives in a big house overlooking the lake with his new wife.

The husband viewed it differently. He was glad that she had signed the agreement and that his economic liability to his former wife was limited. He could afford the new house by the lake with his new wife because he was not sending money to Sherry. Billionaire Donald Trump attributed his economic survival of his two divorces to prenuptial agreements with his ex-wives.

Couples who decide to develop a prenuptial agreement need separate attorneys to look out for their respective interests. The laws regulating marriage and divorce vary by state, and only attorneys in those states can help ensure that the document drawn up will be honored. Individuals may not waive child support or dictate child custody. Full disclosure of assets is also important. If one partner hides assets, the prenuptial can be thrown out of court. One husband recommended that the issue of the premarital agreement should be brought up and that it be signed a minimum of six months before the wedding. "This gives the issue time to settle rather than being an explosive emotional issue if it is brought up a few weeks before the wedding." Indeed, as noted previously, if a prenuptial agreement is signed within two weeks of the wedding, that is grounds enough for the agreement to be thrown out of court because it is assumed that the document was executed under pressure.

Although individuals are deciding whether to have a prenuptial agreement, states are deciding whether to increase marriage license requirements, this chapter's social policy issue.

Increasing Requirements for a Marriage License

Should marriage licenses be obtained so easily? Should couples be required, or at least encouraged, to participate in premarital education before saying "I do"? Given the high rate of divorce today, policy makers and family scholars are considering this issue. Although evidence of long-term effectiveness of premarital education remains elusive (Carroll and Doherty 2003), some believe that "mandatory counseling will promote marital stability" (Licata 2002, 518).

Several states have proposed legislation requiring premarital education. For example, an Oklahoma statute provides that parties who complete a premarital education program pay a reduced fee for their marriage license. Also, in Lenawee County, Michigan, local civil servants and clergy have made a pact: they will not marry a couple unless that couple has attended marriage education classes. Other states that are considering policies to require or encourage premarital education include Arizona, Illinois, Iowa, Maryland, Minnesota, Mississippi, Missouri, Oregon, and Washington.

Proposed policies include not only mandating premarital education and lowering marriage license fees for those who attend courses but also imposing delays on issuing marriage licenses for those who refuse premarital education. However, "no state mandates premarital counseling as a prerequisite to obtaining a license" (Licata 2002, 525).

Traditionally, most Protestant pastors and Catholic priests require premarital counseling before they will perform marriage ceremonies. Couples who do not want to participate in premarital education can simply get married in secular ceremonies (justices of the peace).

Advocates of mandatory premarital education emphasize that such courses reduce marital discord. However, questions remain about who will offer what courses and whether couples will take the content of such courses seriously. Indeed, people contemplating marriage are often narcotized with love and would doubtless not take any such instruction seriously. Love myths such as "divorce is something that happens to other people" and "our love will overcome any obstacles" work against the serious consideration of such courses.

Your Opinion?

1. To what degree do you believe premarital education should be required before the state issues a marriage license?
2. How effective do you feel such programs are for people in a hurry to marry?
3. How receptive do you feel individuals in love are to marriage education?

Sources

Carroll, J. S., and W. J. Doherty. 2003. Evaluating the effectiveness of premarital prevention programs: A meta-analytic review of outcome research. *Family Relations* 52:105–08.

Licata, N. 2002. Should premarital counseling be mandatory as a requisite to obtaining a marriage license? *Family Court Review* 40:518–32.

Consider Calling Off the Wedding If . . .

"No matter how far you have gone on the wrong road, turn back" is a Turkish proverb. If your engagement is characterized by the following factors, consider prolonging your engagement and delaying your marriage at least until the most distressing issues have been resolved. Alternatively, break the engagement (which happens in 30 percent of formal engagements). Indeed, rather than defend a course of action that does not feel right, stop and reverse directions. Breaking an engagement has fewer negative consequences and is less stigmatized than ending a marriage (which is stigmatized and called a divorce).

Age 18 or Younger

The strongest predictor of getting divorced is getting married during the teen years. Individuals who marry at age 18 or younger have three times the risk of divorce than those who delay marriage into their late twenties or early thirties. Teenagers may be more at risk for marrying to escape an unhappy home and may be more likely to engage in impulsive decision making and behavior. Early marriage is also associated with an end to one's education, social isolation from peer networks, early pregnancy or parenting, and locking one's self into a low income.

Research by Meehan and Negy (2003) on being married while in college revealed higher marital distress among spouses who were also students. In addition, when married college students were compared with single college students, the married students reported more difficulty adjusting to the demands of higher education. The researchers conclude that "these findings suggest that individuals opting to attend college while being married are at risk for compromising their marital happiness and may be jeopardizing their education" (p. 688). Hence, waiting until one is older and through college not only may result in a less stressful marriage but may also be associated with less economic stress.

National Data

The median annual incomes of women who complete high school, college, and graduate school (master's level) are $17,546, $35,094, and $46,250, respectively. The corresponding salaries for men are $31,009, $54,403, and $67,425 (*Statistical Abstract of the United States, 2009*, Table 680).

Known Partner Less Than Two Years

Of 1,319 undergraduates, 26 percent agreed, "If I were really in love, I would marry someone I had known for only a short time" (Knox and Zusman 2009). Impulsive marriages in which the partners have known each other for less than a month are associated with a higher-than-average divorce rate. Indeed, partners who date each other for at least two years (twenty-five months to be exact) before getting married report the highest level of marital satisfaction and are less likely to divorce (Huston et al. 2001). Nevertheless, Dr. Carl Ridley (2009) observed, "I am not sure it is about time but more about attending to self and other needs, desires, preferences and then assessing if one's potential partner can meet these needs or be willing to negotiate so that mutual needs are met. For some, this takes lots of time and for others, not very long."

A short courtship does not allow partners to learn about each other's background, values, and goals and does not permit time to observe and scrutinize each other's behavior in a variety of settings (for example, with one's close friends, parents, or siblings). Indeed, some individuals may be more prone to fall in love at first sight and to want to hurry the partner into a committed love relationship *before* the partner can find out about who they really are ("Let the buyer beware!"). If your partner is pressuring you to marry after dating for a short time and your senses tell you that this is too fast, tell you partner you need to slow the relationship down and don't want to get married now.

To increase the knowledge you and your partner have about each other, find out the answers from each other identified in the Involved Couple's Inventory, take a five-day "primitive" camping trip, take a fifteen-mile hike together, wallpaper a small room together, or spend several days together when one partner is sick. If the couple plans to have children, they may want to take care of a 6-month-old together for a weekend. Time should also be spent with each other's friends.

Abusive Relationship

As we will discuss in Chapter 13, Violence and Abuse in Relationships, partners who emotionally and/or physically abuse their partners while dating and living together continue these behaviors in marriage. Abusive lovers become abusive spouses, with predictable negative outcomes. Though extricating oneself from an abusive relationship is difficult before the wedding, it becomes even more difficult after marriage and even more difficult once the couple has children.

One characteristic of an abusive partner is their attempt to systematically detach their intended spouse from all other relationships ("I don't want you spending time with your family and friends—you should be here with me."). This is a serious flag of impending relationship doom, should not be overlooked, and one should seek the exit ramp as soon as possible.

Numerous Significant Differences

Relentless conflict often arises from numerous significant differences. Though all spouses are different from each other in some ways, those who have numerous differences in key areas such as race, religion, social class, education, values, and goals are less likely to report being happy and to have durable relationships. Skowron (2000) found that the less couples had in common, the more their marital distress. People who report the greatest degree of satisfaction in durable relationships have a great deal in common (Wilson and Cousins 2005).

On-and-Off Relationship

A roller-coaster premarital relationship is predictive of a marital relationship that will follow the same pattern. Partners who break up and get back together several times have developed a pattern in which the dissatisfactions in the relationship become so frustrating that separation becomes the antidote for relief. In courtship, separations are of less social significance than marital separations. "Breaking up" in courtship is called "divorce" in marriage. Couples who routinely break up and get back together should examine the issues that continue to recur in their relationship and attempt to resolve them.

Dramatic Parental Disapproval

A parent recalled, "I knew when I met the guy it wouldn't work out. I told my daughter and pleaded that she not marry him. She did, and they divorced." Although parental and in-law dissatisfaction is rare (Amato et al. [2007] found that 13 percent of parents disapprove of the partner their son or daughter plans to marry), such parental predictions (whether positive or negative) often come true. If the predictions are negative, they sometimes contribute to stress and conflict once the couple marries.

Even though parents who reject the commitment choice of their offspring are often regarded as uninformed and unfair, their opinions should not be taken lightly. The parents' own experience in marriage and their intimate knowledge of their offspring combine to put them in a unique position to assess how their child might get along with a particular mate. If the parents of either partner disapprove of the marital choice, the partners should try to evaluate these concerns objectively. The insights might prove valuable. The value of parental approval is illustrated in a study of Chinese marriages. Pimentel (2000) found that higher marital quality was associated with parents' approving of the mate choice of their offspring.

Low Sexual Satisfaction

Sexual satisfaction is linked to relationship satisfaction, love, and commitment. Sprecher (2002) followed 101 dating couples across time and found that low sexual satisfaction (for both women and men) was related to reporting low relationship quality, less love, lower commitment, and breaking up. Hence, couples who are dissatisfied with their sexual relationship might explore ways of improving it (alone or through counseling) or consider the impact of such dissatisfaction on the future of their relationship.

Basically it is time to end a relationship when the gain or advantages of staying together no longer outweigh the pain and disadvantages of staying—the pain of leaving is less than the pain of staying. Of course, all relationships go through periods of time when the disadvantages outweigh the benefits, so one should not bail out without careful consideration.

Does Race Matter in Quality of Dating Relationships?

Do black and white couples who are dating report the same relationship quality? In a word, "no" with blacks reporting less satisfaction.

Kurdek (2008) compared 111 black dating heterosexual couples with 535 white dating heterosexual couples and found that black people reported less harmonious relationships, less commitment, less dependence on the relationship, and more ineffective arguing. The researcher noted that the differences were small, but did exist. There was also a greater difference in regard to females. For example, black females were less satisfied with their relationships than white females. One explanation may be that black males provide fewer economic benefits and may have less often had fathers as models for strong involved relationships.

Marrying for the Wrong Reason

Some of the following reasons for getting married are more questionable than others.

Rebound

A rebound marriage results when people marry someone immediately after another person has ended a relationship with them. It is a frantic attempt on their part to reestablish their desirability in their own eyes and in the eyes of the partner who dropped them. One man said, "After she told me she wouldn't marry me, I became desperate. I called up an old girlfriend to see if I could get the relationship going again. We were married within a month. I know it was foolish, but I was very hurt and couldn't stop myself." To marry on the rebound is questionable because the marriage is made in reference to the previous partner and not to the partner being married. In reality, people who engage in rebound marriage are using the person they intend to marry to establish themselves as a "winner" in a previous relationship.

To avoid the negative consequences of marrying on the rebound, wait until the negative memories of a past relationship have been replaced by positive aspects of a current relationship. In other words, marry when the satisfactions of being with the current partner outweigh any feelings of revenge. This normally takes between twelve and eighteen months. In addition, be careful about getting involved in a relationship with someone who is recently divorced or just emerged from a painful ending of a previous relationship (see Research Application page 200).

Escape

A person might marry to escape an unhappy home situation in which the parents are oppressive, overbearing, conflictual, alcoholic, and/or abusive. One woman said, "I couldn't wait to get away from home. Ever since my parents divorced, my mother has been drinking and watching me like a hawk. 'Be home early, don't drink, and watch out for those horrible men,' she would always say. I admit it. I married the first guy that would have me. Marriage was my ticket out of there."

Marriage for escape is a bad idea. It is far better to continue the relationship with the partner until mutual love and respect, rather than the desire to escape an unhappy situation, which can become the dominant force propelling you toward marriage. In this way, you can evaluate the marital relationship in terms of its own potential and not solely as an alternative to an unhappy situation.

Become Involved with Someone on the Rebound? How Fast Should You Run?

Analysis of survey data from 1,002 undergraduates at a large southeastern university revealed differences between the 535 or 53.4 percent who had become involved in a new relationship (while on the rebound from a previous love relationship), compared to 316 or 31.5 percent who had not become involved in a new relationship while on the rebound. A profile of the rebounder included the following characteristics:

1. **Rebounders were love seekers.**

Love seekers were defined as those who reported falling in love at first sight. Exactly three-fourths of those who *had* experienced love at first sight had become involved on the rebound compared to 55.5 percent who *had not* experienced love at first sight ($p < .001$). Hence, individuals who experienced love at first sight were 19.5 percent more likely to become involved on the rebound.

We also defined individuals as love seekers if they had looked for a partner on the Internet. Over three-fourths (77.4 percent) of those who had looked for a partner on the Internet had become involved in a love relationship on the rebound compared to 61.1 percent who had not looked for an Internet partner ($p < .002$). In effect, those looking on the Internet were 16.3 percent more likely to become involved on the rebound.

Finally, we defined individuals as love seekers if they would marry someone with whom they were in love for only a short time. Over three-fourths (76.7 percent) of those had become involved in a love relationship on the rebound compared to 57 percent who would not marry quickly even if they were in love ($p < .001$). Indeed, the "quick to marry if in love" were 19.7 percent more likely to become involved on the rebound.

The profile of the rebounder that emerged is of someone who feels a void in life and seeks to fill that void as soon as possible. Believing in love at first sight, using the Internet to find a partner, and being willing to marry quickly all reflect a sense of urgency and impatience. One coed in our classes advised against dating on the rebound: "I got dumped and immediately sought a new relationship to ease the pain. I got sexually involved very quickly in the new relationship and it never moved beyond that. I should have healed first before putting myself back on the market."

2. **Rebounders were deceptive.**

Individuals were defined as deceptive if they reported that they had been dishonest with a previous partner. Almost three-fourths (72.3 percent) of those who had been dishonest in a previous relationship had become involved in a love relationship on the rebound compared to 44.8 percent who had not been dishonest ($p < .001$). In effect, those who had been dishonest were 27.5 percent more likely to become involved on the rebound.

Individuals were also defined as deceptive if they reported that they had cheated on a partner with whom they were involved. Almost eighty percent (79.3 percent) of those who had cheated on a partner had become involved on the rebound compared to 51.6 percent who had not cheated ($p < .001$). Hence, those who cheated were 27.7 percent more likely to become involved in a relationship on the rebound. One student in our classes who was dating someone on the rebound said, "He always wanted to just hang around the dorm and never wanted to take me out in public. I later found out he was dating and having sex with six girls."

3. **Rebounders were hedonistic risk takers.**

Individuals were defined as hedonistic who selected "hedonism" to the statement, "The sexual value that best describes me is 'If it feels good, do it. Being in love or married doesn't matter.'" Almost three-quarters (73 percent) of undergraduates who reported that they were a hedonist had been in a rebound relationship compared to 60.7 percent who were "relativists" (people who felt intercourse with a new person depended on the situation—for example, whether or not they were in love), and 59.6 percent who were "absolutists" (people who didn't believe in intercourse until marriage) ($p < .009$). Hence, hedonists were more likely to become involved on the rebound than those who were relativists or absolutists.

Risk takers were defined as those who reported that they had not used a condom to prevent STIs the last time they had intercourse. Over two-thirds (69.4 percent) of those who reported not using a condom the last time they had intercourse (risk takers) also reported having become involved in a rebound relationship compared to 61.3 percent who did use a condom ($p < .03$). Hence, those who did not use a condom at last intercourse were 8.1 percent more likely to become involved on the rebound.

To summarize, the profile of someone who engages in a relationship on the rebound is one who is impatient for a new love, deceptive, hedonistic, and who does not practice safe sex. Caution about becoming involved with someone on the rebound may be warranted. One answer to the question, "How fast should you run?" may be "as fast as you can."

Source

Knox, D. and M. Zusman. 2009. Become involved with someone on the rebound?: How fast should you run? *College Student Journal* 43: 99–104.

Unplanned Pregnancy

Getting married just because a partner becomes pregnant is usually a bad idea. Indeed, the decision of whether to marry should be kept separate from of a pregnancy. Adoption, abortion, single parenthood, and unmarried parenthood (the couple can remain together as an unmarried couple and have the baby) are all alternatives to simply deciding to marry if a partner becomes pregnant. Avoiding feelings of being trapped or later feeling that the marriage might not have happened without the pregnancy are a couple of reasons for not rushing into marriage because of pregnancy. Couples who marry when the woman becomes pregnant have an increased chance of divorce.

Psychological Blackmail

Some individuals get married because their partner takes the position that "I can't live without you" or "I will commit suicide if you leave me." Because the person fears that the partner may commit suicide, the partner agrees to the wedding. The problem with such a marriage is that one partner has learned to manipulate the relationship to get control. Use of such power often creates resentment in the other partner, who feels trapped in the marriage. Escaping from the marriage becomes even more difficult. One way of coping with a psychological blackmail situation is to encourage the person to go with you to a therapist to "discuss the relationship." Once inside the therapy room, you can tell the counselor that you feel pressured to get married because of the suicide threat. Counselors are trained to respond to such a situation.

Insurance Benefits

In a poll conducted by the Kaiser Family Foundation, a health policy research group, 7 percent of adults said someone in their household had married in the past year to gain access to insurance. "For today's couples, 'in sickness and in health' may seem less a lover's troth than an actuarial contract. They marry for better or worse, for richer or poorer, for co-pays and deductibles" (Sack 2008). Although selecting a partner who has resources (which may include health insurance) is not unusual, selecting a partner for health benefits is yet another matter. Both parties might be cautious if the alliance is more about "benefits" than the relationship.

Pity

Some partners marry because they feel guilty about terminating a relationship with someone whom they pity. The fiancé of one woman got drunk one Halloween evening and began to light fireworks on the roof of his fraternity house. As he was running away from a Roman candle he had just ignited, he tripped and fell off the roof. He landed on his head and was in a coma for three weeks. A year after the accident, his speech and muscle coordination were still adversely affected. The woman said she did not love him anymore but felt guilty about terminating the relationship now that he had become physically afflicted.

She was ambivalent. She felt marrying her fiancé was her duty, but her feelings were no longer love feelings. Pity may also have a social basis. For example, a partner may fail to achieve a lifetime career goal (for example, the partner may flunk out of medical school). Regardless of the reason, if one partner loses a limb, becomes brain damaged, or fails in the pursuit of a major goal, keeping the issue of pity separate from the advisability of the marriage is important. The decision to marry should be based on factors other than pity for the partner.

Filling a Void

A former student in our classes noted that her father died of cancer. She acknowledged that his death created a vacuum, which she felt driven to fill immediately by getting married so that she would have a man in her life.

Getting in a rush to marry when things are not right is a mistake. This coed opted out of an engagement rather than move ahead with a relationship that did not feel right.

Authors

Because she was focused on filling the void, she had paid little attention to the personality characteristics of or her relationship with the man who had asked to marry her.

She reported that she discovered on her wedding night that her new husband had several other girlfriends whom he had no intention of giving up. The marriage was annulled.

In deciding whether to continue or terminate a relationship, listen to what your senses tell you ("Does it feel right?"), listen to your heart ("Do you love this person or do you question whether you love this person?"), and evaluate your similarities ("Are we similar in terms of core values, goals, view of life?"). Also, be realistic. It would be unusual if none of these factors applied to you. Indeed, most people have some negative and some positive indicators before they marry.

SUMMARY

What are the cultural factors that influence mate selection?

Two types of cultural influences in mate selection are endogamy (to marry someone inside one's own social group—race, religion, social class) and exogamy (to marry someone outside one's own family).

What are the sociological factors that influence mate selection?

Sociological aspects of mate selection involve homogamy—"like attracts like" or the tendency to be attracted to people similar to one's self. Variables include race, age, religion, education, social class, personal appearance, attachment, personality, and open-mindedness. Couples who have a lot in common are more likely to have a happy and durable relationship.

What are the psychological factors operative in mate selection?

Psychological aspects of mate selection include complementary needs, exchange theory, and parental characteristics. Complementary-needs theory suggests that people select others who have characteristics opposite to their own. For example, a highly disciplined, well-organized individual might select a free-and-easy, worry-about-nothing mate. Most researchers find little evidence for complementary-needs theory.

Exchange theory suggests that one individual selects another on the basis of rewards and costs. As long as an individual derives more profit from a relationship with one partner than with another, the relationship will continue. Exchange concepts influence who dates whom, the conditions of the dating relationship, and the decision to marry. Parental characteristics theory suggests that individuals select a partner similar to the opposite-sex parent.

Personality characteristics of a potential mate desired by both men and women include being warm, kind, and open and having a sense of humor. Negative personality characteristics to avoid in a potential mate include disagreeableness or expressing few positives, poor impulse control, hypersensitivity to criticism, inflated ego, neurosis (perfectionism) or insecurity, and control by someone else (for example, parents). Paranoid, schizoid, and borderline personalities are also to be avoided.

What are the sociobiological factors operative in mate selection?

The sociobiological view of mate selection suggests that men and women select each other on the basis of their biological capacity to produce and support healthy offspring. Men seek young women with healthy bodies, and women seek ambitious men who will provide economic support for their offspring. There is considerable controversy about the validity of this theory.

What factors should be considered when becoming engaged?

The engagement period is the time to ask specific questions about the partner's values, goals, and marital agenda, to visit each other's parents to assess parental models, and to consider involvement in premarital educational programs and/or counseling. Negative reasons for getting married include being on the rebound, escaping from an unhappy home life, psychological blackmail, and pity.

Some couples (particularly those with children from previous marriages) decide to write a prenuptial agreement to specify who gets what and the extent of spousal support in the event of a divorce. To be valid, the document should be developed by an attorney in accordance with the laws of the state in which the partners reside. Last-minute prenuptial agreements put enormous emotional strain on the couple and are often considered invalid by the courts. Discussing a prenuptial agreement six months in advance is recommended.

What factors suggest you might consider calling off the wedding?

Factors suggesting that a couple may not be ready for marriage include being in their teens, having known each other less than two years, and having a relationship characterized by significant differences and/or dramatic parental disapproval. Some research suggests that partners with the greatest number of similarities in values, goals, and common interests are most likely to have happy and durable marriages.

KEY TERMS

complementary-needs theory	exogamy	modeling theory of mate selection	racial homogamy
educational homogamy	homogamy	selection	religion
endogamous pressures	homogamy theory of mate selection	open-minded	religious homogamy
endogamy	selection	pool of eligibles	role theory of mate selection
engagement	Involved Couple's Inventory	premarital education programs	sociobiology
exchange theory	marriage squeeze	prenuptial agreement	status
exogamous pressures	mating gradient	principle of least interest	

The Companion Website for *Choices in Relationships: An Introduction to Marriage and the Family,* Tenth Edition

www.cengage.com/sociology/knox

Supplement your review of this chapter by going to the Companion Website to take one of the tutorial quizzes, use the flash cards to master key terms, or check out the many other study aids, like crossword puzzles and self-assessments. You'll also find special features such as General Social Survey (GSS) data, Census data, and other resources to help you with that special project or to do some research on your own.

WEB LINKS

PAIR Project

www.utexas.edu/research/pair

RightMate

http://www.heartchoice.com/rightmate/

REFERENCES

Amato, P. R., A. Booth, D. R. Johnson, and S. F. Rogers. 2007. *Alone together: How marriage in America is changing.* Cambridge, Massachusetts: Harvard University Press.

Assad, K. K., M. B. Donnellan, and R. D. Conger. 2007. Optimism: An enduring resource for romantic relationships. *Journal of Personality and Social Psychology* 93:285–96.

Bogg, R. A., and J. M. Ray. 2006. The heterosexual appeal of socially marginal men. *Deviant Behavior* 27:457–77.

Bratter, J. L., and R. B. King. 2008. "But Will It Last?": Marital instability among interracial and same-race couples. *Family Relations* 57:160–71.

Busby, D. M., D. C. Ivey, S. M. Harris, and C. Ates. 2007. Self-directed, therapist-directed, and assessment-based interventions for premarital couples *Family Relations* 56: 279–90.

Carroll, J. S., and W. J. Doherty. 2003. Evaluating the effectiveness of premarital prevention programs: A meta-analytic review of outcome research. *Family Relations* 52:105–18.

Chu, K. 2007. As higher education costs rise, so do debt loads. *USA Today*, May 25, 3B

Clarkwest, A. 2007. Spousal dissimilarity, race, and marital dissolution. *Journal of Marriage and the Family* 69:639–53.

Crowell, J. A., D. Treboux, and E. Waters. 2002. Stability of attachment representations: The transition to marriage. *Developmental Psychology* 38:467–79.

DeCuzzi, A., D. Knox, and M. Zusman. 2006. Racial differences in perceptions of women and men. *College Student Journal* 40:343–49.

Duncan, S. F., T. B. Holman, and C. Yang. 2007. Factors associated with involvement in marriage preparation programs. *Family Relations* 56:270–78.

Edwards, T. M. 2000. Flying solo. *Time* August 28, 47–53.

Fisher, H. 2009. *Why him? Why her?* New York: Henry Holt and Company.

Foster, J. D. 2008. Incorporating personality into the investment model: Probing commitment processes across individual differences in narcissism. *Journal of Social and Personal Relationships* 25:211–23.

Gattis, K. S., S. Berns, L. E. Simpson, and A. Christensen. 2004. Birds of a feather or strange birds? Ties among personality dimensions, similarity, and marital quality. *Journal of Family Psychology* 18:564–78.

Haring, M., P. L. Hewitt, and G. L. Flett. 2003. Perfectionism, coping, and quality of relationships. *Journal of Marriage and the Family* 65:143–59.

Hohmann-Marriott, B. E., and P. Amato. 2008. Relationship quality in interethnic marriages and cohabitation. *Social Forces* 87:825–55.

Huston, T. L., J. P. Caughlin, R. M. Houts, S. E. Smith, and L. J. George. 2001. The connubial crucible: Newlywed years as predictors of marital delight, distress, and divorce. *Journal of Personality and Social Psychology* 80:237–52.

Ingoldsby, B., P. Schvaneveldt, and C. Uribe. 2003. Perceptions of acceptable mate attributes in Ecuador. *Journal of Comparative Family Studies* 34:171–86.

Kalmijn, M., and H. Flap. 2001. Assortative meeting and mating: Unintended consequences of organized settings for partner choices. *Social Forces* 79:1289–312.

Knox, D. and K. McGinty. 2009. Searching for homogamy: An in class exercise. *College Student Journal* 43:243–247.

Knox, D., and Zusman, M. E. 2009. Relationship and sexual behaviors of a sample of 1,319 university students. Unpublished data collected for this text. Greenville, NC: Department of Sociology, East Carolina University.

Knox, D., M. E. Zusman, and W. Nieves. 1997. College students' homogamous preferences for a date and mate. *College Student Journal* 31:445–48.

Kurdek, L. A. 2008. Differences between partners from Black and White heterosexual dating couples in a path model of relationship commitment. *Journal of Social and Personal Relationships* 25:51–70.

Lewis, S. K., and V. K. Oppenheimer. 2000. Educational assortative mating across marriage markets: Non-Hispanic whites in the United States. *Demography* 37:29–40.

Licata, N. 2002. Should premarital counseling be mandatory as a requisite to obtaining a marriage license? *Family Court Review* 40:518–32.

Luo, S. H., and E. C. Klohnen. 2005. Assortative mating and marital quality in newlyweds: A couple-centered approach. *Journal of Personality and Social Psychology* 88:304–26.

Medora, N. P. 2003. Mate selection in contemporary India: Love marriages versus arranged marriages. In *Mate Selection Across Cultures*, ed. R. R. Hamon and B. B. Ingoldsby, 209–30. Thousand Oaks, California: Sage Publications.

Medora, N. P., J. H. Larson, N. Hortacsu, and P. Dave. 2002. Perceived attitudes towards romanticism: A cross-cultural study of American, Asian-Indian, and Turkish young adults. *Journal of Comparative Family Studies* 33:155–78.

Meehan, D., and C. Negy. 2003. Undergraduate students' adaptation to college: Does being married make a difference? *Journal of College Student Development* 44:670–90.

Meyer, J. P., and S. Pepper. 1977. Need compatibility and marital adjustment in young married couples. *Journal of Personality and Social Psychology* 35:331–42.

Pew Research Center. 2007. Trends in political values and core attitudes: 1987-2007. Washington DC: Pew Research Center for People & the Press.

Picca, L. H., and J. R. Feagin. 2007. *Two-faced racism.* New York: Routledge.

Pimentel, E. E. 2000. Just how do I love thee? Marital relations in urban China. *Journal of Marriage and the Family* 62:32–47.

Regan, P. C., and A. Joshi. 2003. Ideal partner preferences among adolescents. *Social Behavior and Personality* 31:13–20.

Ridley, C. 2009. Personal communication with retired professor from University of Arizona in 2009.

Sack, K. 2008. Health benefits inspire rush to marry, or divorce. *The New York Times*, August 12.

Saint, D. J. 1994. Complementarity in marital relationships. *Journal of Social Psychology* 134:701–4.

Schvaneveldt, P. L. 2003. Mate selection preferences and practices in Ecuador and Latin America. In *Mate selection across cultures*, ed. R. R. Hamon and B. B. Ingoldsby, 43–59. Thousand Oaks, California: Sage Publications.

Skowron, E. A. 2000. The role of differentiation of self in marital adjustment. *Journal of Counseling Psychology* 47:229–37.

Snyder, D. K., and J. M. Regts. 1990. Personality correlates of marital dissatisfaction: A comparison of psychiatric, maritally distressed, and nonclinic samples. *Journal of Sex and Marital Therapy* 90:34–43.

Sprecher, S. 2002. Sexual satisfaction in premarital relationships: Associations with satisfaction, love, commitment, and stability. *Journal of Sex Research* 39:190–96.

Sprecher, S., and P. C. Regan. 2002. Liking some things (in some people) more than others: Partner preferences in romantic relationships and friendships. *Journal of Social and Personal Relationships* 19:463–81.

Statistical abstract of the United States, 2009. 128th ed. Washington, DC: U.S. Bureau of the Census.

Strassberg, D. S., and S. Holty. 2003. An experimental study of women's Internet personal ads. *Archives of Sexual Behavior* 32:253–61.

Swenson, D., J. G. Pankhurst, and S. K. Houseknecht. 2005. Links between families and religion. In *Sourcebook of family theory & research*, ed. V. L. Bengtson, A. C. Acock, K. R. Allen, P. Dilworth-Anderson, and D. M. Klein, 530–33. Thousand Oaks, California: Sage Publications.

Toro-Morn, M., and S. Sprecher. 2003. A cross-cultural comparison of mate preferences among university students: The United States versus the People's Republic of China (PRC). *Journal of Comparative Family Studies* 34:151–62.

Twenge, J. 2006. *Generation me.* New York: Free Press.

Vesselinov, E. 2008. Members only: Gated communities and residential segregation in the metropolitan United States. *Sociological Forum* 23:536–55.

Waller, W., and R. Hill. 1951. *The family: A dynamic interpretation.* New York: Holt, Rinehart and Winston.

White, T. 1990. *Rock lives.* New York: Henry Holt and Co.

Wilson, G. D., and J. M. Cousins. 2005. Measurement of partner compatibility: Further validation and refinement of the CQ test. *Sexual and Relationship Therapy* 20:421–29.

Winch, R. F. 1955. The theory of complementary needs in mate selection: Final results on the test of the general hypothesis. *American Sociological Review* 20:552–55.

Xie, Y., J. M. Raymo, K. Govette, and A. Thornton. 2003. Economic potential and entry into marriage and cohabitation. *Demography* 40:351–64.

Zusman, M. E., J. Gescheidler, D. Knox, and K. McGinty. 2003. Dating manners among college students. *Journal of Indiana Academy of Social Sciences* 7:28–32.

Courtship is like looking at the beautiful photos in a seed catalogue.
Marriage is what actually comes up in your garden.

Anonymous

Marriage Relationships

True or False?

1. Couples who have the same friends are likely to have a higher-quality relationship than those where the friends of the respective partners get along with the partner.

2. In a study of 1,001 married adults, the feature the highest percentage reported that they missed most about being single was "living by my own rules."

3. The stereotypes about in-law relationships are true—most spouses report that they do not get along with their in-laws.

4. Grooms report more delight on their wedding night than brides.

5. Spouses who are close in age are happier than spouses who have a lot of years difference between them.

Answers: **1.** T   **2.** T   **3.** F   **4.** T   **5.** F

Jay Leno's wife, Mavis, was asked the secret of their enduring marriage. She replied:

> One of my beliefs about a happy relationship—whether it's a marriage, a friendship, or a business—is that you let people go their own way. I always want to communicate to Jay that as far as I'm concerned, he can do any damn thing he wants and it's OK with me. Within reasonable limits, you have to mind your own business. If Jay's schedule becomes grueling, I'll just say, "How are you feeling? Don't you think you should cut yourself some slack?" (Burford 2005, 174)

Although the secret of a happy relationship is one thing to Mavis Leno, it is something else to another spouse. "Religion," "monogamy," "children," and so on, are the "secrets" for other couples. The title of this chapter, with plural "relationships" confirms that marriages are different. *Diversity* is the term that best describes relationships, marriages, and families today. No longer is there a one-size-fits-all cultural norm of what a relationship, marriage, or family should be. Rather, individuals, couples, and families select their own path. In this chapter, we review the diversity of relationships. We begin with looking at some of the different reasons people marry.

Keep thy eyes wide open before marriage, and half shut afterwards.

Ben Franklin, statesman

Motivations for and Functions of Marriage

In this section, we discuss both why people marry and the functions that getting married serve for society.

Individual Motivations for Marriage

We have defined marriage as a legal contract between two heterosexual adults that regulates their economic and sexual interaction. However, individuals in the United States tend to think of marriage in more personal than legal terms. The following are some of the reasons people give for getting married.

Love   Many couples view marriage as the ultimate expression of their love for each other—the desire to spend their lives together in a secure, legal, committed relationship. In U.S. society, love is expected to precede marriage—thus, only couples in love consider marriage. Those not in love would be ashamed to admit it.

These spouses love being together and sharing their love of fishing.

Authors

Personal Fulfillment We marry because we feel a sense of personal fulfillment in doing so. We were born into a family (family of origin) and want to create a family of our own (family of procreation). We remain optimistic that our marriage will be a good one. Even if our parents divorced or we have friends who have done so, we feel that our relationship will be different.

Companionship Talk show host Oprah Winfrey once said that lots of people want to ride in her limo, but what she wants is someone who will take the bus when the limo breaks down. One of the motivations for marriage is to enter a structured relationship with a genuine companion, a person who will take the bus with you when the limo breaks down.

Although marriage does not ensure it, companionship is the greatest expected benefit of marriage in the United States. Coontz (2000) noted that it has become "the legitimate goal of marriage" (p. 11). Eating meals together is one of the most frequent normative behaviors of spouses. Indeed, although spouses may eat lunch apart, dinner together becomes an expected behavior. **Commensality** is eating with others, and one of the issues spouses negotiate is "who eats with us" (Sobal et al. 2002).

Parenthood Most people want to have children. In response to the statement, "Someday, I want to have children," 91.7 percent of 1,319 undergraduates at a large southeastern university responded, "yes" (Knox and Zusman 2009). The amount of time parents spend in rearing their children has increased. Sayer et al. (2004) documented that, contrary to conventional wisdom, both mothers and fathers report spending greater amounts of time in child-care activities in the late 1990s than in the "family-oriented" 1960s.

Although some people are willing to have children outside marriage (in a cohabiting relationship or in no relationship at all), most Americans prefer to have children in a marital context. Previously, a strong norm existed in our society (particularly for white people) that individuals should be married before they have children. This norm has relaxed, with more individuals willing to have children without being married. An Australian survey revealed that women who elect to remain childfree are viewed more negatively than women who express a desire to have children (Rowland 2006).

Economic Security Married people report higher household incomes than do unmarried people. Indeed, national data from the Health and Retirement Survey revealed that individuals who were not continuously married had significantly lower wealth than those who remained married throughout the life course. Remarriage offsets the negative effect of marital dissolution (Wilmoth and Koso 2002).

Although individuals may be drawn to marriage for the preceding reasons on a conscious level, unconscious motivations may also be operative. Individuals reared in a happy family of origin may seek to duplicate this perceived state of warmth, affection, and sharing. Alternatively, individuals reared in unhappy, abusive, drug-dependent families may inadvertently seek to re-create a similar family because that is what they are familiar with. In addition, individuals are motivated to marry because of the fear of being alone, to better themselves economically, to avoid birth out of wedlock, and to prove that someone wants them.

Just as most individuals want to marry (regardless of the motivation), most parents want their children to marry. If their children do not marry too young and if they marry someone they approve of, parents feel some relief from the economic responsibility of parenting, anticipate that marriage will have a positive, settling effect on their offspring, and look forward to the possibility of grandchildren.

Societal Functions of Marriage

As noted in Chapter 1, important societal functions of marriage are to bind a male and female together who will reproduce, provide physical care for their dependent young, and socialize them to be productive members of society who will replace those who die (Murdock 1949). Marriage helps protect children by giving the state legal leverage to force parents to be responsible to their offspring whether or not they stay married. If couples did not have children, the state would have no interest in regulating marriage.

Additional functions include regulating sexual behavior (spouses have less exposure to sexually transmitted infections [STIs] than singles) and stabilizing adult personalities by providing a companion and "in-house" counselor. In the past, marriage and family have served protective, educational, recreational, economic, and religious functions.

However, as these functions have gradually been taken over by police or legal systems, schools, the entertainment industry, workplace, and church or synagogue, only the companionship-intimacy function has remained virtually unchanged.

The emotional support each spouse derives from the other in the marital relationship remains one of the strongest and most basic functions of marriage (Coontz 2000). In today's social world, which consists mainly of impersonal, secondary relationships, living in a context of mutual emotional support may be particularly important. Indeed, the companionship and intimacy needs of contemporary U.S. marriage have become so strong that many couples consider divorce when they no longer feel "in love" with their partner. Of 1,319 undergraduates, 47.9 percent reported that they would divorce their spouse if they no longer loved the spouse (Knox and Zusman 2009).

The very nature of the marriage relationship has also changed from being very traditional or male-dominated to being very modern or egalitarian. A summary of these differences is presented in Table 7.1. Keep in mind that these are stereotypical marriages and that only a small percentage of today's modern marriages have all the traditional or egalitarian characteristics that are listed.

The honeymoon is over when the kiss that was a temptation becomes an obligation.

Anonymous

Table 7.1 Traditional versus Egalitarian Marriages

Traditional Marriage	Egalitarian Marriage
There is limited expectation of husband to meet emotional needs of wife and children.	Husband is expected to meet emotional needs of wife and to be involved with children.
Wife is not expected to earn income.	Wife is expected to earn income.
Emphasis is on ritual and roles.	Emphasis is on companionship.
Couples do not live together before marriage.	Couples may live together before marriage.
Wife takes husband's last name.	Wife may keep her maiden name.
Husband is dominant; wife is submissive.	Neither spouse is dominant.
Roles for husband and wife are rigid.	Roles for spouses are flexible.
Husband initiates sex; wife complies.	Either spouse initiates sex.
Wife takes care of children.	Parents share child rearing.
Education is important for husband, not for wife.	Education is important for both spouses.
Husband's career decides family residence.	Career of either spouse determines family residence.

Happy marriages begin when we marry the ones we love, and they blossom when we love the ones we marry.

Tom Mullen, *A Very Good Marriage*

Marriage as a Commitment

Marriage represents a multilevel commitment—person-to-person, family-to-family, and couple-to-state.

Person-to-Person Commitment

Commitment is the intent to maintain a relationship. Behavioral indexes of commitment (928 of them) were identified by 248 people who were committed to someone. These behaviors were then coded into ten major categories and included providing affection, providing support, maintaining integrity, sharing companionship, making an effort to communicate, showing respect, creating a relational future, creating a positive relational atmosphere, working on relationship problems together, and expressing commitment (Weigel and Ballard-Reisch 2002). Glover et al. (2006) noted that being committed to another was associated with relationship satisfaction and feeling predisposed toward caregiving for the partner.

What if My Partner Is Not as Interested in the Relationship as I Am?

WHAT IF?

Both partners in a relationship rarely have the same level of interest, involvement, and desire for the future. These differences are due to personality, previous relationships, and the rebound effect. In regard to personality, some individuals forge ahead and want to escalate new relationships whereas others are very cautious. As for previous relationships, people who have been betrayed in a former relationship are slow to reengage. The rebound effect is that people who have been recently dumped are often quick to reengage. Unless the different levels of interest are dramatic such that one is unsure whether to remain in the relationship at all, one option is to continue the relationship to give time for one partner to catch up while the other partner slows down so that the partners are closer in their walk together.

Family-to-Family Commitment

Whereas love is private, marriage is public. Marriage is the second of three times that one's name can be expected to appear in the local newspaper. When individuals marry, the parents and extended kin also become enmeshed. In many societies (for example, Kenya), the families arrange for the marriage of their offspring, and the groom is expected to pay for his new bride. How much is a bride worth? In some parts of rural Kenya, premarital negotiations include the determination of **bride wealth**—this is the amount of money a prospective groom will pay to the parents of his bride-to-be. Such a payment is not seen as "buying the woman" but compensating the parents for the loss of labor from their daughter. Forms of payment include livestock ("I am worth many cows," said one Kenyan woman), food, and/or money. The man who raises the bride wealth also demonstrates not only that he is ready to care for a wife and children but also that he has the resources to do so (Wilson et al. 2003).

Marriage also involves commitments by each of the marriage partners to the family members of the spouse. Married couples are often expected to divide their holiday visits between both sets of parents.

Couple-to-State Commitment

In addition to making person-to-person and family-to-family commitments, spouses become legally committed to each other according to the laws of the state in which they reside. This means they cannot arbitrarily decide to terminate their own marital agreement.

Just as the state says who can marry (not close relatives, the insane, or the mentally deficient) and when (usually at age 18 or older), legal procedures must be instituted if the spouses want to divorce. The state's interest is that a couple stays married, have children, and take care of them. Should they divorce, the state will dictate how the parenting is to continue, both physically and economically.

Social policies designed to strengthen marriage through divorce law reform reflect the value the state places on stable, committed relationships (see the following Social Policy).

Cold Feet?

Having cold feet about getting married is not unusual. The following are examples of persons who "knew" they were doing the wrong thing the closer they got to the wedding:

> "I knew the day of the wedding that I did not want to marry. I told my dad, and he said, 'Be a man.' I went through with the marriage and regretted it ever since." (This person divorced after twenty-five years of marriage.)

> "I said 'Holy Jesus' just before I walked down the aisle with my dad. He said, 'What's the matter, honey?' I couldn't tell him, went through with the wedding and later divorced." (This person divorced after twelve years.)

> "I never really believed I was getting married till I saw my name in the paper that I was soon to be married. It scared me. I called it off after the announcements had been sent out and we had been to see the preacher. It was a real mess. She kept the ring."

Marriage as a Rite of Passage

A **rite of passage** is an event that marks the transition from one social status to another. Starting school, getting a driver's license, and graduating from high school or college are events that mark major transitions in status (to student, to driver, and to graduate). The wedding itself is another rite of passage that marks

The kind of marriage you make depends upon the kind of person you are. If you are a happy, well-adjusted person, the chances are your marriage will be a happy one.

Evelyn Duvall and Reuben Hill, *When You Marry*

Strengthening Marriage through Divorce Law Reform

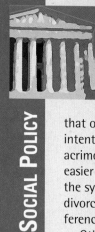

Some family scholars and policy makers advocate strengthening marriage by reforming divorce laws to make divorce harder to obtain. Because California became the first state to implement "no-fault" divorce laws in 1969, every state has passed similar laws allowing couples to divorce without proving in court that one spouse was at fault for the marital breakup. The intent of no-fault divorce legislation was to minimize the acrimony and legal costs involved in divorce, making it easier for unhappy spouses to get out of a marriage. Under the system of no-fault divorce, a partner who wanted a divorce could get one, usually by citing irreconcilable differences, even if their spouse did not want a divorce.

Other states believe the no-fault system has gone too far and have taken measures designed to make breaking up harder to do by requiring proof of fault (such as infidelity, physical or mental abuse, drug or alcohol abuse, and desertion) or extending the waiting period required before granting a divorce. In most divorce law reform proposals, no-fault divorces would still be available to couples who mutually agree to end their marriages.

Opponents argue that divorce law reform measures would increase acrimony between divorcing spouses (which harms the children as well as the adults involved), increase the legal costs of getting a divorce (which leaves less money to support any children), and delay court decisions on child support, custody, and distribution of assets. In addition, critics point out that ending no-fault divorce would add countless court cases to the dockets of an already overloaded court system. Efforts to repeal no-fault divorce laws in many state legislatures have largely failed.

The Louisiana legislature became the first in the nation to pass a law (in 1997) creating a new kind of marriage contract that would permit divorce only in narrow circumstances. Under the Louisiana law, couples can voluntarily choose between two types of marriage contracts: (1) the standard contract that allows a no-fault divorce, or (2) a **covenant marriage** that permits divorce only under conditions of fault (such as abuse, adultery, or imprisonment on a felony) or after a marital separation of more than two years. Couples who choose a covenant marriage are also required to get premarital counseling from a clergy member or another counselor. These couples view a covenant marriage as emphasizing the seriousness of marriage and their commitment to it. One spouse involved in a covenant marriage said, "A lot of people think marriage is something you can take back to Wal-Mart for a refund if it breaks" (Brown 2008).

The goal of a state offering a covenant marriage is to show the positive public regard for marriage and the disregard for single-parent families. Leah Ward Sears, Chief Justice of the Georgia Supreme Court, emphasized the value of the family for our society and the importance of a renewed commitment to marriage (Sears 2007). Covenant marriage is a unique way to begin married life, but there has been no rush on the part of couples to seek these marriages. Fewer than 3 percent of couples who marry in Louisiana have chosen to take on the extra restrictions of marriage by covenant (Licata 2002). Arizona and Arkansas are two other states that offer covenant marriages, which are primarily promoted through evangelical churches.

Your Opinion?

1. To what degree do you believe the government can legislate "successful" marriage relationships?
2. How has no-fault divorce gone too far?
3. Why do you feel that covenant marriage is an idea that has not caught on?

Sources

Brown, M. 2008. The state of our unions. *Redbook*, June 38.

Licata, N. 2002. Should premarital counseling be mandatory as a requisite to obtaining a marriage license? *Family Court Review* 40:518–32.

Sears, L. W. 2007. The "marriage gap": A case for strengthening marriage in the 21st century. *New York University Law Review* 82:1243–53.

Love is an obsessive delusion that is cured by marriage.

Karl Bowman

the transition from fiancé to spouse. Preceding the wedding is the traditional bachelor party for the soon-to-be groom. What is new on the cultural landscape is the bachelorette party (sometimes more wild than the bachelor party), which conveys the message of equality and that great changes are ahead (Montemurro 2006).

Weddings

The wedding is a rite of passage that is both religious and civil. To the Catholic Church, marriage is a sacrament that implies that the union is both sacred and indissoluble. According to Jewish and most Protestant faiths, marriage is a special bond between the husband and wife sanctified by God, but divorce and remarriage are permitted. Wedding ceremonies still reflect traditional cultural definitions of women as property. For example, the father of the bride usually walks the bride down the aisle and "hands her over to the new husband." In some cultures, the bride is not even present at the time of the actual marriage. For example, in the upper-middle-class Muslim Egyptian wedding, the actual marriage contract

Chapter 7 Marriage Relationships

signing occurs when the bride is in another room with her mother and sisters. The father of the bride and the new husband sign the actual marriage contract (identifying who is marrying whom, the families they come from, and the names of the two witnesses). The father will then place his hand on the hand of the groom, and the maa'zun, the official presiding, will declare that the marriage has occurred (Sherif-Trask 2003).

Blakely (2008) noted that weddings are increasingly becoming outsourced, commercialized events. The latest wedding expense is to have the wedding webcast so that family and friends afar can actually see and hear the wedding vows in real time. One such website is http://www.webcastmywedding.net/, where the would-be bride and groom can arrange the details. That marriage is a public experience is emphasized by weddings in which the couple invites family and friends of both parties to participate. The wedding is a time for the respective families to learn how to cooperate with each other for the benefit of the couple. Conflicts over number of bridesmaids and ushers, number of guests to invite, and place of the wedding are not uncommon. Though some families harmoniously negotiate all differences, others become so adamant about their preferences that the prospective bride and groom elope to escape or avoid the conflict. However, most families recognize the importance of the event in the life of their daughter or son and try to be helpful and nonconflictual as seen in *Second Chance Harvey*.

To obtain a marriage license, some states require the partners to have blood tests to certify that neither has an STI. The document is then taken to the county courthouse, where the couple applies for a marriage license. Two-thirds of states require a waiting period between the issuance of the license and the wedding. A member of the clergy marries 80 percent of couples; the other 20 percent (primarily in remarriages) go to a justice of the peace, judge, or magistrate.

Brides often wear traditional **artifacts** (concrete symbols that reflect existence of an event): something old, new, borrowed, and blue. The "**old**" **wedding artifact** is something that represents the durability of the impending marriage (for example, an heirloom gold locket). The "**new**" **wedding artifact,** perhaps in the form of new, unlaundered undergarments, emphasizes the new life to begin. The "**borrowed**" **wedding artifact** is something that has already been worn by a currently happy bride (for example, a wedding veil). The "**blue**" **wedding artifact** represents fidelity (for example, those dressed in blue or in blue ribbons have lovers true). When the bride throws her floral bouquet, it signifies the end of girlhood; the rice thrown by the guests at the newly married couple signifies fertility.

Couples now commonly have weddings that are neither religious nor traditional. In the exchange of vows, neither partner may promise to obey the other, and the couple's relationship may be spelled out by the partners rather than by tradition. Vows often include the couple's feelings about equality, individualism, humanism, and openness to change. In 2009, the average wedding for a couple getting married for the first time is estimated to be $30,000 (www.theknot.com).

Ways in which couples lower the cost of their wedding include marrying any day but Saturday, or marrying off-season (not June), off-locale (in Mexico or a Caribbean Island where fewer guests will attend), and, as mentioned previously, broadcasting their wedding ceremony live over the Internet (http://www.liveinternetweddings.com/). The latter means that the couple can get married in Hawaii and have their ceremony beamed back to the states where well-wishers can see the wedding without leaving home.

Honeymoons

Traditionally, another rite of passage follows immediately after the wedding—the **honeymoon** (the time following the wedding whereby the couple become isolated to recover from the wedding and to solidify their new status change from lovers to spouses).

Getting married for the sex is like buying a 747 for the free peanuts.

Jeff Foxworthy

Diversity in Other Countries

In contemporary Japanese weddings, it is not unusual for the father to openly weep at the wedding of his daughter. Because the daughter will leave her family and move in with her husband, fathers often "spend more time with a daughter than a son as the child grows up, in anticipation of her marrying and leaving his family" (Murray and Kimura 2003, 263). At the end of the wedding reception, the newlyweds may present their parents with flowers, "including the bride giving one to her father to show her sense of appreciation" (p. 263).

Wedding traditions vary widely throughout the world. In this photo essay, we look at Jewish weddings, Hindu Indian weddings, and Islamic Turkish weddings.

JEWISH WEDDINGS

In a traditional Jewish wedding, the bride and groom do not see each other for a week before the wedding, and they both fast on the day of the wedding until after the ceremony. Before the ceremony, while the bride is being veiled, the groom signs the *ketubah*, which is a Jewish premarital contract stating that the husband commits to provide food, clothing, and sexual relations to his wife, and that he will pay a specified sum of money if he divorces her. The groom and bride may not engage in marital relations unless the groom and two witnesses have signed the *ketubah*.

Dan Porges/Peter Arnold Inc.

The wedding ceremony takes place underneath a *chuppah*— a cloth canopy supported by four poles, symbolizing the home the couple will build. The groom enters the chuppah first, then the bride enters, approaches the groom, and circles him seven times, symbolizing the seven days of creation.

Mario Tama/Getty Images

Buccina Studios/Getty Images

The ceremony ends with the groom smashing a glass (or a small symbolic piece of glass) with his right foot, to symbolize the destruction of the Temple. At this point, the guests shout "mazel tov!" which literally means "good fortune" and also means "congratulations."

HINDU INDIAN WEDDINGS

About 13 percent of the world's population is Hindu. In India, where most Hindus live, parents or a matchmaker arrange most marriages. Weddings vary according to the wealth and ▶

Photosindia.com/SuperStock

status of the couple. Traditionally, some of the prayers of a Hindu wedding are recited at least partially in Sanskrit—the classical language of India. Hindu weddings are very festive and can last several days. Prior to the wedding ceremony, there is music and dancing and other pre-ceremony activities such as fireworks and throwing flowers. The groom arrives at the wedding riding a decorated horse or elephant. The bride wears a colorful sari and has elaborate henna applied to her feet, hands, and perhaps face.

JASON EDWARDS/National Geographic Stock

The Hindu Indian wedding ceremony takes place under a decorated canopy called a *mandap*. The ceremony lasts for about two hours, during which the Brahmin priests intone Sanskrit chants to various Hindu deities and throw grains of rice on the couple and into a small sacred fire that is supposed to be sustained and nurtured through a couple's entire marriage, with oblations offered into the fire each day.

ISLAMIC TURKISH WEDDING

About one in five people in the world is Muslim; they follow the religion of Islam. Prior to the traditional Islamic Turkish wedding, a bride attends a henna ceremony at the home of the bride's in-laws. The groom sends the henna paste, which is placed on the bride's palms and on the palms of other women from both families who attend. Prior to the wedding, the bride's father or brother puts a red belt around the bride's waist to symbolize the bride's virginity.

Yavuz Arslan/Peter Arnold Inc.

After a fifteen-minute civil marriage ceremony at the municipality's wedding hall, the couple and parents receive presents and congratulations from guests outside the wedding hall entrance. A wedding reception with food and drink may be held on the evening of the marriage ceremony. If a reception is held, it may be a small dinner party at a restaurant or at the home of the groom's parents or a big event with a couple hundred guests at a hotel. If the families are conservative, male and female guests may not sit together, but are seated in different parts of the same hall.

Images & Stories/Alamy

The Wedding Night

There is considerable interest about a couple's wedding night. Stereotypes are that they are wonderful or disastrous. What are the data?

Sample

This sample consisted of 95 spouses, 75 percent women and 25 percent men. Over three-fourths had been married once, with 20 percent in their second marriages. The respondents were asked to report on their "most recent wedding night." Over 80 percent (81.1 percent) were virgins on their wedding night.

Findings

The questionnaire was designed to assess the quality of the wedding night experience, the best and worst experiences, and some recommendations.

1. *Rating.* When asked the question, "On a scale of one to ten with zero being awful and ten being 'wonderful', what number would you select to -describe you wedding night experience?," the average was 6.81 when we looked at all marriages. Grooms reported more positive experiences than brides, 7.19 to 6.68, respectively. When second marriages were the focus, the average was 8.4.
2. *Summaries.* When asked to "summarize your wedding night experience" some of the comments were:
   a. "We only went away for 1 night as the next day was Christmas. I was 17, it was lots of fun, we ate out, and had a great night."
   b. "It was a fulfilling, happy occasion, knowing that I was starting a new chapter in life."
   c. "It was a disaster. He was thinking about his old girlfriend and wishing he had married her."
   d. "We had an amazing night. It was so hard to keep our hands off each other."
   e. "It was so wonderful but we were tired. It could have been better."
3. *Best part.* When asked to identify "the best part of the wedding night," 29.7 percent listed "just being with my new partner"; 17.8 percent listed "sex"; 10.5 percent said "nothing"; and 9.4 percent listed the "reception."
4. *Worst part.* When asked to identify the "worst part of the wedding night," 23.1 percent listed "accommodations and the partner's demeanor"; 21 percent said "being so tired"; 9.4 percent said the "end of celebration"; 8.4 percent said "nothing"; 6.3 percent listed "sex"; and 3.1 percent listed "pain."
5. *Change.* To the question, "If you could replay your wedding night, what would you change?" 34.7 percent of respondents answered, "nothing"; 18.9 percent responded "not be tired"; 14.7 percent listed "different time/place"; and 9.5 percent listed "different person."

The data suggest that the wedding nights for these respondents were mostly positive experiences. Recommendations were to plan weddings early in the day so that the reception is over early. Also, the couple might plan to spend the first night a short drive from the reception. Avoid leaving a reception at 11:00 p.m. and driving four hours. Many newlyweds suggested staying in a hotel close to the reception and flying to a honeymoon destination late the following afternoon. Also, avoid an early-morning flight the day after your wedding.

Source

This research is based on unpublished data collected for this text. Appreciation is expressed to Kelly Woody for distribution of the questionnaires (that were mailed to us) and to Emily Richey who tabulated the data.

What if My Partner and I Disagree over Various Wedding Issues?

Wedding issues over which partners may disagree include number of guests, place, and time. Although some couples will decide to let the wife's preferences prevail, other couples will negotiate each item. The details of the resolution are not important. What is important is that the partners negotiate their different wedding preferences in a way that leaves both parties satisfied (for example, there is a win-win outcome).

The functions of the honeymoon are both personal and social. The personal function is to provide a period of recuperation from the usually exhausting demands of preparing for and being involved in a wedding ceremony and reception. The social function is to provide a time for the couple to be alone to solidify the change in their identity from that of an unmarried to a married couple. Now that they are married, their sexual expression and childbearing with each other achieves full social approval and legitimacy.

Changes after Marriage

After the wedding and honeymoon, the new spouses begin to experience changes in their legal, personal, and marital relationship.

Legal Changes

Unless the partners have signed a prenuptial agreement specifying that their earnings and property will remain separate, after the wedding, each spouse becomes part owner of what the other earns in income and accumulates in property. Although the laws on domestic relations differ from state to state, courts typically award to each spouse half of the assets accumulated during the marriage (even though one of the partners may have contributed a smaller proportion).

For example, if a couple buys a house together, even though one spouse invested more money in the initial purchase, the other will likely be awarded half of the value of the house if they divorce. (Having children complicates the distribution of assets because the house is often awarded to the custodial parent.) In the case of death of the spouse, the remaining spouse is legally entitled to inherit between one-third and one-half of the partner's estate, unless a will specifies otherwise.

Personal Changes

New spouses experience an array of personal changes in their lives. One initial consequence of getting married may be an enhanced self-concept. Parents and close friends usually arrange their schedules to participate in your wedding and give gifts to express their approval of you and your marriage. In addition, the strong evidence that your spouse approves of you and is willing to spend a lifetime with you also tells you that you are a desirable person.

Married people also begin adopting new values and behaviors consistent with the married role. Although new spouses often vow that "marriage won't change me," it does. For example, rather than stay out all night at a party, which is not uncommon for single people who may be looking for a partner, spouses (who are already paired off) tend to go home early. Their roles of spouse, employee, and parent result in their adopting more regular, alcohol- and drug-free hours.

Friendship Changes

Marriage also affects relationships with friends of the same and other sex. Less time will be spent with friends because of the new role demands as a spouse. More time will be spent with other married couples who will become powerful influences on the new couple's relationship. Indeed, to the degree that married couples have the *same* friends is the degree the marital quality of the couple will be high.

What spouses give up in friendships, they gain in developing an intimate relationship with each other. However, abandoning one's friends after marriage may be problematic because one's spouse cannot be expected to satisfy all of one's social needs. Because many marriages end in divorce, friendships that have been maintained throughout the marriage can become a vital source of support for a person adjusting to a divorce.

Is "Partner's Night Out" a Good Idea?

Although spouses may want to spend time together, they may also want to spend time with their friends—shopping, having a drink, fishing, golfing, seeing a movie, or whatever. Some spouses have a flexible policy based on trust with each other. Other spouses are very suspicious of each other. One husband said, "I didn't want her going out to bars with her girlfriends after we were married. You never know what someone will do when they get three drinks in them." For "partner's night out" to have a positive impact on the couple's relationship, it is important that the partners maintain emotional and sexual fidelity to each other, that each partner have a night out, and that the partners spend some nights alone with each other. Friendships can enhance a marriage relationship by making the individual partners happier, but friendships cannot replace the marriage relationship. Spouses must spend time alone to nurture their relationship.

Marital Changes

A happily married couple of forty-five years spoke to our class and began their presentation with, "Marriage is one of life's biggest disappointments." They spoke of the difference between all the hype and cultural ideal of what marriage is supposed to be . . . and the reality. One effect of getting married is **disenchantment**—the transition from a state of newness and high expectation to a state of mundaneness tempered by reality. It may not happen in the first few weeks or months of marriage, but it is almost inevitable. Whereas courtship is the anticipation of a life together, marriage is the day-to-day reality of that life together—and reality does not always fit the dream. "Moonlight and roses become daylight and dishes" is an old adage reflecting the realities of marriage. Disenchantment after marriage is also related to partners shifting their focus away from each other to work or children; each partner usually gives and gets less attention in marriage than in courtship. Most college students do not anticipate a nosedive toward disenchantment; of 1,319 respondents, 17.3 percent agreed that "most couples become disenchanted with marriage within five years." Only 1.4 percent "strongly agreed" (Knox and Zusman 2009).

A couple will experience other changes when they marry, as the following details:

1. Experiencing loss of freedom. Single people do as they please. They make up their own rules and answer to no one. Marriage changes that as the expectations of the spouse impact the freedom of the individual. In a study of 1,001 married adults, although 41 percent said that they missed "nothing" about the single life, 26 percent reported that they most missed not being able to live by their own rules (Cadden and Merrill 2007).

2. Feeling more responsibility. Single people are responsible for themselves. Spouses are responsible for the needs of each other and sometimes resent it. One wife said she loved when her husband went out of town on business because she then did not feel the responsibility to cook for him. One husband said that he felt burdened by having to help his wife care for her aging parents. In the study of 1,001 married adults referred to previously, 25 percent reported that having less responsibility was what they missed most about being single.

Courtship is the anticipation of a life together. Marriage is the reality. Numerous changes await this couple.

3. *Missing alone time.* Aside from the few spouses who live apart, most live together. They wake up together, eat their evening meals together, and go to bed together. Each may feel too much togetherness. "This altogether, togetherness thing is something I don't like," said one spouse. In the study referred to previously, 24 percent reported that "having time alone for myself" was what they missed most about being single (Cadden and Merrill 2007). One wife said, "My best time of the day is at night when everybody else is asleep."

4. *Change in how money is spent.* Entertainment expenses in courtship become allocated to living expenses and setting up a household together. In the same study, 17 percent reported that they missed managing their own money most (Cadden and Merrill 2007).

5. *Discovering that one's mate is different from one's date.* Courtship is a context of deception. Marriage is one of reality. Spouses sometimes say, "He (she) is not the person I married." Jay Leno once quipped that, "It doesn't matter who you marry since you will wake up to find that you have married someone else."

6. *Sexual changes.* The sexual relationship of the couple also undergoes changes with marriage. First, because spouses are more sexually faithful to each other than are dating partners or cohabitants (Treas and Giesen 2000), their number of sexual partners will decline dramatically. Second, the frequency with which they have sex with each other decreases. One wife said the following:

> *The urgency to have sex disappears after you're married. After a while you discover that your husband isn't going to vanish back to his apartment at midnight. He's going to be with you all night, every night. You don't have to have sex every minute because you know you've got plenty of time. Also, you've got work and children and other responsibilities, so sex takes a lower priority than before you were married.*

Although married couples may have intercourse less frequently than they did before marriage, marital sex is still the most satisfying of all sexual contexts. Of married people in a national sample, 85 percent reported that they experienced extreme physical pleasure and extreme emotional satisfaction with their spouses. In contrast, 54 percent of individuals who were not married or not living with anyone said that they experienced extreme physical pleasure with their partners, and 30 percent said that they were extremely emotionally satisfied (Michael et al. 1994). Fisher and McNulty (2008) studied seventy-two couples just after their weddings and found that high sexual satisfaction was associated with high marital satisfaction one year later.

7. *Power changes.* The distribution of power changes after marriage and across time. The way wives and husbands perceive and interact with each other continues to change throughout the course of the marriage. Two researchers studied 238 spouses who had been married more than thirty years and observed that (across time) men changed from being patriarchal to collaborating with their wives and that women changed from deferring to their husbands' authority to challenging that authority (Huyck and Gutmann 1992). In effect, men tend to lose power and women gain power. However, such power changes may not always occur. In abusive relationships, abusive partners may increase the display of power because they fear the partner will try to escape from being controlled.

Parents and In-Law Changes

Marriage affects relationships with parents. Time spent with parents and extended kin radically increases when a couple has children. Indeed, a major difference between couples with and without children is the amount of time they spend with relatives. Parents and kin rally to help with the newborn and are typically there for birthdays and family celebrations.

Emotional separation from one's parents is an important developmental task in building a successful marriage. When choices must be made between

No joy shall equal the delights of our wedding night. These shall never be forgotten no matter how old we may grow.

Zhang Heng's poem of a bride to her husband, Han Dynasty

The Little Book of Chinese Proverbs

one's parents and one's spouse, more long-term positive consequences for the married couple are associated with choosing the spouse over the parents. However, such choices become more complicated and difficult when one's parents are old, ill, or widowed.

Only a minority of spouses (3 percent to 4 percent) report that they do not get along with their in-laws (Amato et al. 2007). Nuner (2004) interviewed twenty-three daughters-in-law married between five and ten years (with no previous marriages and at least one child from the marriage) and found that most reported positive relationships with their mothers-in-law. The evaluation by the daughters depended on the role of the mothers-in-law within the family (for example, mothers-in-law as grandmothers were perceived more positively). Mother-son relationships were described by the daughters-in-law to be close, "mama's boy," polite, or distant.

The behavior in-laws engage in affects how their children and their spouses like and perceive them. Morr Serewicz and Canary (2008) investigated newlyweds' perceptions of private disclosures received from their in-laws and found that, when these were positive (for example, the in-law talked positively about family members), the spouse perceived the in-law positively. Conversely, when the in-law talked negatively about family members or told negative stories, the spouse viewed the in-law negatively.

PERSONAL CHOICES

Should a Married Couple Have Their Parents Live with Them?

This question is more often asked by individualized Westernized couples who live in isolated nuclear units. Asian couples reared in extended-family contexts expect to take care of their parents and consider it an honor to do so. As the parents of American spouses age, a decision must often be made by the spouses about whether to have the parents live with them. Usually the person involved is the mother of either spouse because the father is more likely to die first. One wife said, "We didn't have a choice. His mother is 82 and has Alzheimer's disease. We couldn't afford to put her in a nursing home at $5,200 a month, and she couldn't stay by herself. So we took her in. It's been a real strain on our marriage, since I end up taking care of her all day. I can't even leave her alone to go to the grocery store."

Some elderly people have resources for nursing home care, or their married children can afford such care. However, even in these circumstances, some spouses decide to have their parents live with them. "I couldn't live with myself if I knew my mother was propped up in a wheelchair eating Cheerios when I could be taking care of her," said one daughter.

When spouses disagree about parents in the home, the result can be devastating. According to one wife, "I told my husband that Mother was going to live with us. He told me she wasn't and that he would leave if she did. She moved in, and he moved out (we were divorced). Five months later, my mother died."

Financial Changes

An old joke about money in marriage says that "two can live as cheaply as one as long as one doesn't eat." The reality behind the joke is that marriage involves the need for spouses to discuss and negotiate how they are going to get and spend money in their relationship. Some spouses bring considerable debt into the marriage. In a sample of 1,319 undergraduates, 8.9 percent reported that they owed "over a thousand dollars on one or more credit cards" (Knox and Zusman 2009). Dew (2008) also observed that debt was associated with marital dissatisfaction. Spouses who were in debt reported spending less leisure time together and arguing more about money. We will discuss more about debt in Chapter 12 on Family and the Economy.

Diversity in Marriage

The tragedies of September 11, 2001, emphasized the need to understand other cultures and an appreciation for military families who make personal sacrifices for the larger societal good. In this section, we review Hispanic, Canadian, Muslim American, Amish and Mennonite, and military families. We also look at other examples of family diversity: interracial, interreligious, cross-national, and age-discrepant.

Hispanic Families

The "pan ethnic" term *Hispanic* refers to both immigrants and U.S. natives with an ancestry to one of twenty Spanish-speaking countries in Latin America and the Caribbean (Landale and Oropesa 2007). Of the estimated 45 million Hispanics who represent 15 percent of the U.S. population by 2010 (and 25 percent by 2050), most (65 percent) are from Mexico, 17 percent are from Central or South America (Latino), 8 percent are Puerto Rican, and 4 percent are Cuban (*Statistical Abstract of the United States, 2009,* Table 38). Hispanic families vary not only by where they are from but by whether they were born in the United States. About 40 percent of U.S. Hispanics are foreign-born and immigrated here, 32 percent have parents who were born in the United States, and 28 percent were born here of parents who were foreign-born.

Great variability exists among Hispanic families. Although it is sometimes assumed that immigrant Hispanic families come from rural impoverished Mexico where family patterns are traditional and unchanging, immigrants may also come from economically developed urbanized areas in Latin America (Argentina, Uruguay, and Chile), where family patterns include later family formation, low fertility, and nuclear family forms.

Nevertheless, Hispanics tend to have higher rates of marriage, early marriage, higher fertility, nonmarital child rearing, and prevalence of female householder. They also have two micro family factors: male power and strong familistic values.

1. *Male power.* The husband and father is the head of the family in most Hispanic families. The children and wife respect him as the source of authority in the family. The wife assumes the complementary role where her focus is taking care of the home and children. As more Hispanic wives work outside the home, these role relationships will become more egalitarian. As noted in Chapter 3, half of the U.S.-born Latino sample in Parra-Cardona et al. (2008) sample reported egalitarian values. Not only might the husband cook and clean, he might look after the children.

2. *Strong familistic values.* The family is the most valued social unit in the society—not only the parents and children but also the extended family. Hispanic families have a moral responsibility to help family members with money, health, or transportation needs. Children are also taught to respect their parents as well as the elderly. Indeed, elderly parents may live with the Hispanic family where children may address their grandparents in a formal way. Spanish remains the language spoken in the home as a way of preserving family bonds. Mogro-Wilson (2008) studied alcohol abuse among Latino adolescents and found that adolescents from families who spoke Spanish in the home had lower rates of alcohol abuse than families speaking English at home.

Even family patterns may be changing with generational differences of assimilation. For example, foreign-born people tend to bring their traditional values with them. However, these may erode over time. "With respect to family patterns, a key question is whether some of the strengths of Hispanic families are eroded as they spend more time in the United States. Several patterns suggest that this is indeed the case. For example, levels of divorce, nonmarital childbearing, and female family headship increase across generations, while the prevalence of family extension declines" (Landale and Oropesa 2007, 400).

Of all the peoples whom I have studied, from city dwellers to cliff dwellers, I always find that at least 50 percent would prefer to have at least one jungle between themselves and their mothers-in-law.

Margaret Mead, anthropologist

What about marital happiness or divorce risk of Hispanic families compared to white and black families? Using data from the National Survey of Families and Households (N = 6,231), Mexican Americans and white people have similar levels of marital quality, whereas black people report poorer marital quality than these two groups (Bulanda and Brown 2007). Strong familistic values and the fact that Hispanic wives are less of an economic threat to their husband's provider role are influential in this finding.

Canadian Families

Although Canada stretches from coast to coast, its population of 33 million is roughly only 10 percent of the U.S. population of over 300 million. Although much of marriage and family life in Canada is similar to that in the United States, some of the differences include the following:

1. *Language.* Canada is officially bilingual with both English and French being spoken there. The owner of a bed-and-breakfast on Prince Edward Island noted, "I need to brush up on my French since a lot of our guests speak French."

2. *Definition of family.* Although only thirteen states in America recognize common-law marriages, common-law couples with or without children are officially included in the definition of "family" (along with married couples with and without children and single parents).

3. *Same-sex relationships.* Although three of the ten Canadian provinces (Quebec, British Columbia, and Ontario) have legalized same-sex marriage, national court rulings provide greater protection for same-sex relationships than in the United States. In Canada, individuals in same-sex couple relationships have the right to inherit from each other, the right to each other's pension benefits, and are protected under the law from discrimination based on sexual orientation.

4. *Children.* "Not so soon, not so many" is the norm for having children in Canada. Families are slightly smaller, and children are born later. A stronger patrilineal norm is operative—women usually take the husband's last name, live where the husband works, and the children are given the last name of the father.

5. *Government programs for families.* Quebec offers universal access to childcare centers for a low fee, medical costs are covered by the state, and parental leave for up to a year is paid for at the rate of employment insurance.

6. *Divorce.* Canada has half the divorce rate of the United States. A strong Catholic religious presence is the most likely explanation for a lower divorce rate. One also gets the sense that Canadian spouses have a rural mentality and take their relationships more seriously (Harvey 2005).

Muslim American Families

Although Islam (the religious foundation for Muslim families in sixty nations) is the third-largest religion in North America, 9/11 resulted in an increased awareness that Muslim families are part of American demographics. These families hardly represent the extremists responsible for terrorism, but more than 5.8 million adults in the United States and 1.3 billion worldwide self-identify with the Islamic religion (there are now more Muslims than Christians in the world). The three largest American Muslim groups in the United States are African Americans, Arabs, and South Asians (for example, from Pakistan, Bangladesh, Afghanistan, and India).

The five "pillars" of Islam provide the basis for the values and perspectives of its followers: (1) faith (there is no god but Allah—One True God—and Muhammad is His Messenger); (2) prayer (five times a day); (3) alms (giving 2.5 percent annually of one's wealth to other Muslims in need, such as a Muslim orphanage); (4) fasting for the month of Ramadan (the ninth of the month in the Islamic lunar year); and (5) going for Hajj (pilgrimage) to Mecca (in Saudi Arabia, where Kasbah is located) once in one's life if physically and financially possible. Although

Muslims vary in devoutness and practice, this discussion will focus on Muslim families in America who attempt to maintain their traditions based on the *Qur'an* (the holy book of Islam) and the *Hadith* (teachings of Prophet Mohammad).

Islamic tradition emphasizes close family ties with the nuclear and extended family, social activities with family members, and respect for the authority of the elderly and parents. Religion and family are strong sources of a Muslim's personal identity. Following one's religious and family codes results in a strong sense of emotional and social support. Breaking from one's religion and family comes at a great cost because alternatives are perceived as limited. Parents of Muslim children who are reared in America struggle to maintain traditional values while allowing their children (particularly sons) to pursue higher education and professional training.

One of the striking features of Muslim American families is the strong influence parents have over the behavior of their children. Because the families control the property and economic resources and generally provide total financial support to the children, and because the offspring may not be able to find adequate work outside the family system, they generally acquiesce to parents' wishes. Such acquiescence does not imply the nonexistence of genuine love and affection children may have for their parents, however. Table 7.2 details the various practices, values, and beliefs involved in Muslim family life.

Table 7.2 Core Values of Muslim American Families

Courtship. In Muslim American families, courtship is tightly controlled. Intimate mixing of sexes is against Islamic teaching. Therefore, mixed-sex gatherings of children, teens, and young adults do not occur unless in the presence of adults. At such gatherings, there is "separate seating" next to one's same-sex peers. "Dating" in the sense of being alone with a partner to explore romance and sex is prohibited and contrary to the Muslim idea that marriage is between two families.

Mate Choice. Offspring are taught early to consider marrying only a person who shares their religion and culture and to defer to their parents and kin, whose experience qualifies them to guide the choice of a mate. Offspring (particularly women) are expected to marry another Muslim (for example, marriage to a cousin on either parent's side is permissible and not unusual). A man may marry outside of Islam only to a Christian or Jewish woman (who is not required to convert to Islam) as long as the partner agrees to rear children in the Islamic traditions. In the usual case, the parents of one Muslim family contact parents of another Muslim family for their respective offspring to meet. They may go off alone for a brief time to talk, but their time alone is limited and elders are not far away. Each has the right of refusal. In effect their only "choice" is to reject a preselected choice. Parents prefer to select a son-in-law whose education and financial resources are equal to or higher than their own and who has close family ties to the girl's family.

The ideal daughter-in-law is one who is integrated into the parent's family (she knows her husband's parents) and who accepts the norm of patrilocal residence (she expects to live near her husband's parents). Independent dating or mate selection is prohibited. A Muslim daughter who sees men without supervision (or who continually rejects the marriage choices her parents offer) can be ostracized by her family, and, in some cases, have her support cut off and inheritance withdrawn. Her chances for marriage to a Muslim may be lost because she may be regarded as morally depraved or promiscuous and will not be accepted by the family of a Muslim man. The threat of losing marriageability is a frightening prospect for young Muslim women and bears a strong force of social control over her behavior. Singlehood for both women and men is viewed as unnatural and abnormal.

Love. Because marriage is generally seen as a merging of two families and the individuals getting married are allowed to be alone together for only infrequent, brief periods, love is expected to follow, not precede marriage. Hence, romantic love in the American sense is nonexistent. For Muslims, the selection and approval by parents or kin and satisfactory financial circumstances are the necessary ingredients of a successful marriage.

Sexual behavior. Holding hands, kissing, and sexual intercourse are strictly forbidden before marriage. Indeed, the *Qur'an* implores individuals to "not go near fornication, as it is immoral and an evil way" (XVII:32). This translates into daughters avoiding provocative dress—no lipstick, makeup, tank tops, short dresses, or high heels—and dancing (except for the pleasure of her husband). Sexual behavior after marriage allows only for penile vaginal penetration (which is procreative). Mutual manual stimulation and oral and anal sex are prohibited (these are nonprocreative acts). Adultery in traditional Muslim countries (such as Pakistan) by married adults is punishable by being publicly stoned to death. Adultery committed by unmarried adults is punishable by flogging in public. However, there must be a confession of four eyewitnesses, so "catching" the adulterer is rare.

(Continued)

Table 7.2 Core Values of Muslim American Families (*Continued*)

Marriage. The ceremony involves two male witnesses for the bridegroom, a guardian (vakil) for the bride, and a payment by the husband of a dowry for the marriage to be valid. The dowry (also known as mehr) is an amount of money or property the husband gives to the wife at the time of the wedding (or that he promises to give her on demand). It symbolizes respect for the woman and becomes her property to spend as she wishes and remains hers even in the case of divorce. Indeed, it provides a sense of security should the marriage fail.

Gender roles. Equality between husbands and wives is emphasized. Although fathers, husbands, and sons are in the role of protector or guardian of daughters, wives, and sisters, the teachings of the Prophet Mohammad specify protections and rights for women. They can keep their own name; inherit (although one-half as much as sons); own, buy, sell, or inherit property; refuse a marriage proposal; initiate a divorce; and be awarded custody of the children in case of divorce. The husband is obligated to provide for his wife and children. The wife is expected to be responsible for child care, maintain her chastity, and manage the household. She may be employed if she wants or in the event of financial necessity but not in jobs such as waitressing, which might involve short dresses or alcohol.

Rearing children. Children are highly valued, loved, and indulged. Parents tightly regulate and monitor their children's leisure activities (after-school activities, mixed parties, television, and playing cards are prohibited), particularly their daughters', and ensure that they spend as much time with other family members or other Muslims. Such restrictions are also designed to prohibit the development of a love relationship with a non-Muslim. This value is held so strongly that some families send their daughters to school in the homeland or move the whole family back home during the child's adolescence or young adulthood. *Communication* is the key word for parent-child relationships in the Muslim American home. Parents always make themselves available to their children and keep a close watch on them. Parents also show Islamic values to their children by their behavior, not just by what they say. Girls are also kept busy performing domestic chores (washing dishes, cooking, cleaning the house, and watching younger siblings). Boys are usually spared such chores and are given more freedom. Sisters and brothers may feel that they live in separate worlds.

Elderly. Children are expected to respect and be kind and dutiful toward their parents. Sons are specifically obligated financially and otherwise to take care of their elderly parents in need (daughters are not as they receive only one-half the inheritance share of a son). Other Muslims will look down on a son if he fails in his responsibility to take care of his parents. Most sons will take their parents into their home or put them in an apartment nearby. A nursing home for the Muslim elderly is a rare exception in the United States. Many elderly Muslims have financial resources and require only frequent visits and help with some chores.

Alcohol. All Muslims (men, women, young, old) are prohibited from consuming alcohol or alcoholic products (for example, even some cough syrups). Also, producing, buying, selling, or giving or receiving alcohol are sins. The worst nightmare for Muslim parents is if their young adult children drink wine or any alcoholic beverage.

Birth Control. Although Muslims may limit the number of children in a family by *coitus interruptus*, birth control is not generally accepted. Any birth control method that is known to interrupt pregnancy after fertilization is prohibited.

Abortion. Abortion is allowed only to save the life of a mother.

Divorce. Although spouses are expected to stay together unless doing so becomes intolerable, either spouse may request divorce. A wife may divorce because of her husband's impotence, refusal to provide economic subsistence or clothing, change of religion, or infectious disease. A husband may divorce his wife for several reasons, such as infidelity, cultural incompatibility, persistent refusal to abide by Shariah (Islamic jurisprudence), or chronic complaints in spite of his sincere efforts to fulfill her legitimate needs. Custody and care of the children usually go to the husband, who is responsible for the expenses of child rearing, even if the wife is willing to do it.

This table was developed for this text with the assistance of Dr. Saeed Dar, a Muslim and professor of pharmacology and toxicology, East Carolina University School of Medicine. Dr. Dar has lectured on Muslim family values as well as Islamic sexuality.

Amish and Mennonite Families*

The Amish became the focus of media attention in 2006, when a lone gunman entered an Amish school and shot ten female students (five later died). The response of the Amish was compassion and forgiveness for the assailant. A cultural question arose, "Who are these Amish?" In the sixteenth century, Martin

*Based on the authors visit to the Amish community in Lancaster County, Pennsylvania as well as the following: A. M. Denlinger. 1993. *Real people: Amish and Mennonites in Lancaster County, Pennsylvania.* 4th ed. Scottdale, PA: Herald Press; M. Good, and P. Good. 1995. *Twenty most asked questions about the Amish and Mennonites.* Intercourse, PA: Good Books; and R. Koehn. 1996. *A threefold cord.* Moundridge, KS: Gospel Publishers. Appreciation is also expressed to Merlin and Edith Nichols, members of the Church of God in Christ—Mennonite in Ayden, North Carolina, for their assistance in the development of this section.

Luther broke from the Catholic Church in what is known as the Protestant Reformation. Around the same time, the Anabaptist movement emphasized a return to the simplicity of faith and practice as seen in the early Christian church. They believed that adult, not infant, baptism was preferable (the adult could make decisions; the child could not). Indeed, at age 16, Amish youth are released from the church and its rules. **Rumspringa**, a traditional rite of passage, describes this period that lasts from a few months to years during which adolescents are allowed to leave home and experience "the world," including music, TV, drugs, sex, whatever. The custom is based on the Amish belief that only informed adults can "accept Christ" and be baptized. Over 90 percent of adolescents return to the Amish for baptism. Rumspringa is the subject of the film *The Devil's Playground* by director Lucy Walker.

The name Mennonite came from Menno Simons of Holland, who was a leader of the Anabaptist movement in 1536, and the group became known as the Mennonites. In 1693, a Mennonite elder named Jacob Amman felt the church was losing its purity and broke off to form the Amish sect. The Amish (the smaller of the two groups) are known as the right wing—the more conservative—of the two groups. Although the Amish or Mennonite have great variations in the values and behaviors of specific families or groups, the Amish are less likely to use electricity and cars. However, both groups see themselves as attempting to be separate from the world of individualism, materialism, and secularism in favor of being more familistic, simplistic, and spiritual.

Today, about 200,000 Amish live in twenty-two states, Mexico, and Canada. Between 16,000 and 18,000 Old Order Amish live in Lancaster County, Pennsylvania. There are over 1 million Mennonite church members in sixty countries. The Mennonite Church USA is one of nearly twenty formally organized groups of Mennonites in North America. For example, the Church of God in Christ—Mennonite is one such group of 20,000. Some general beliefs of this group regarding courtship, marriage, and the family include:

1. *Endogamy.* Church members are expected to marry someone of their own faith. Among the Amish, marriage to a member outside the faith is forbidden. Because the community is "closed" to outsiders and because "families" know each other, eligible offspring are known to everyone. Mennonites are also encouraged to marry someone of their faith and, in practice, typically meet someone within their church or community.

2. *Courtship.* The Amish couple typically meets at one of the youth sings at church. The boy will then take the girl home, meet her parents (whom he no doubt knows because of the small community), and ask if he can return to see her again. Such meetings typically occur in the living room of the girl's home with other family members nearby. When the couple is ready to marry, the deacon publishes their intent about two weeks before the wedding in November (when harvest is over). The ceremony takes place in the bride's home and is followed by an array of food for the wedding guests. The couple does not take a honeymoon but visits extended family throughout the winter and set up their own place in the spring.

Among the Church of God in Christ—Mennonite, a boy who is interested in a particular girl he has seen at church is expected to pray to God and seek spiritual guidance that she is "the one." If he feels God is leading him to this "sister" as his mate, he approaches his minister who further prays with him for God's direction. If the two feel that God encourages this union, the minister will approach the girl's parents and alert them of the boy's interest. If the parents approve, the minister takes the proposal to the girl. If she is interested and feels that God is leading her to marry this man, the wedding, involving a very holy ceremony of commitment whereby the individual lives are bound together into one strong cord, will soon follow in the church. The church membership brings gifts to the couple. After the wedding ceremony, food is served on the grounds and the couple opens their gifts. Notice that no "courtship" precedes the wedding, and there is very little time between the mutual acknowledgment of interest and the wedding.

3. *Marital roles.* Amish and Mennonite roles are clear and distinct, with the man being the spiritual leader of the family and his wife complementing (that is, submitting to) his role or leadership. The role of the man is to work the farm and be the provider; the role of the woman is to take care of the home, cook, sew, and so on. Women are not encouraged to work outside the home. Indeed, Mennonite women who feel that outside work would be more interesting than taking care of the home, "should reject all such thoughts at once" and recognize that homemaking is a "privilege" (Koehn 1996, 30).

4. *Children.* Both groups emphasize large families, with family life the focus of adults. Children are educated in parochial schools until the eighth grade. Public schools are seen as secular and are considered to encourage impure values. Children are encouraged to work on the farm and not look to education and careers in mainstream society.

5. *Elderly.* Both the Amish and Mennonite treat their elderly with respect and regard aging as honorable. The elderly are rarely put in nursing homes, and are instead cared for by their children in their (offspring's) own home. It is not unusual to see a new rooms added to a home to accommodate the needs of the parents.

6. *Divorce.* Both Amish and Mennonites strongly discourage divorce, resulting in very low divorce rates. Marital conflict is seen as an individual problem that can be resolved by getting one's spiritual life in order, which will have a positive impact on the marriage. Hence, when a couple have a disagreement, the resolution is to work on one's own relationship with God, and when this is "fixed," the marriage problem will disappear.

Military Families

Although Barack Obama has pledged to draw down the troops in Iraq, newspaper headlines, nightly television news, and presidential news conferences remind us that America is still at war and that individuals and families are coping with danger and the sacrifices of deployments in Iraq, Afghanistan, and other peacekeeping and humanitarian operations. Approximately 1.4 million are active-duty military personnel. Another 1.1 million are in the military reserve and 375,000 in the National Guard (*Statistical Abstract of the United States, 2009,* Tables 493, 499,

There are over 10 million military personnel—their lives are not their own because they are duty-bound to respond to the needs of their country.

Chapter 7 Marriage Relationships

501). About 60 percent of military personnel are married and/or have children (NCFR Policy Brief 2004).

There are three main types of military marriages. One, those in which the soldier falls in love with a high school sweetheart, marries the person, and subsequently joins the military. A second type of military marriage consists of those who meet and marry after one of them has signed up for the military. This is a typical marriage where the partners fall in love on the job and one or both of them happens to be the military. The final and least common military marriage is known as a contract marriage in which a person will marry a civilian to get more money and benefits from the government. For example, a soldier might decide to marry a platonic friend and split the money from the additional housing allowance (which is sometimes a relatively small amount of money and varies depending on geographical location and rank). Other times, the military member keeps the extra money and the civilian will take the benefit of health insurance. Often, in these types of military marriages, the couple does not reside together. There is no emotional connection because the marriage is mercenary. Contract military marriages are not common but they do exist.

Of Americans in a national sample, 60 percent report that they have a family member, close friend, or office worker in Iraq (Page 2006). When accounting for spouses, children, and other dependents, there are actually more family members of active duty military personnel than there are military members themselves (Martin and McClure 2000; Military Family Resource Center 2003). Spouses of military members play an important role in the readiness and retention of the active-duty force and, thus, factors that affect the well-being of military spouses are important to study when looking at military families (Easterling 2005). It is also important to note that, although military and civilian families have many similarities, there are also some unique aspects of military families.

Some ways in which military families are unique include:

1. *Traditional sex roles.* Although both men and women are members of the military service, the military has considerably more men than women (Caforio 2003). In the typical military family, the husband is deployed (sent away) and the wife is expected to "understand" his military obligations and to take care of the family in his absence. Her duties include paying the bills, keeping up the family home, and taking care of the children; a military wife must often play the role of both spouses due to the demands of her husband's military career and obligations. The wife often has to sacrifice her career to follow (or stay behind in the case of deployment) and support her husband in his fulfillment of military duties (Easterling 2005).

In the case of wives or mothers who are deployed, the rare husband is able to switch roles and become Mr. Mom. One military career wife said of her husband, whom she left behind when she was deployed, "What a joke. He found out what taking care of kids and running a family was really like and he was awful. He fed the kids SpaghettiOs for the entire time I was deployed."

There are also circumstances in which both parents are military members, and this can blur traditional sex roles because the woman has already deviated from a traditional "woman's job." Military families in which both spouses are military personnel are rare.

2. *Loss of control—deployment.* Military families have little control over their lives as the specter of deployment is ever-present. Where one of the spouses will be next week and for how long are beyond the control of the spouses and parents. Saleska (2004) interviewed wives of Air Force men (enlisted and officers) who emphasized the difficulty of being faced with the constant possibility that their husbands could leave immediately for an indeterminate period of time. Once gone, they may be relegated to a ten-minute phone call every two weeks. The needs of the military (referred to as a "greedy institution") come first, and military personnel are expected to be obedient and to do whatever is necessary to comply and get through the ordeal. "You can't believe what it's like to have an empty chair at the dinner table sprung on you and not know where he is or when he'll be back," one respondent said.

Compounding the loss of control is the fear of being captured, imprisoned, shot, killed by a suicide bomber, or beheaded. Not only may deployed soldiers have such fears, but their spouses, parents, and children may look at the evening news in stark terror and fear that their beloved will be the next to die. Sleeplessness, irritability, and depression may result in those who are left behind to carry on their jobs and parenting. Children may also become anxious and depressed over the absence of their deployed parent, who more often is the father (Cozza et al. 2005).

According to a 2008 survey of military wives, some of the most-reported negative feelings during the deployment of their husbands included loneliness, fear, and sadness. They may go extended periods of time without communicating with their partner and are often in constant worry over the well-being of their deployed spouse. On the positive side, wives of deployed husbands report feelings of independence and strength. They are the sole family member available to take care of the house and children, and they rise to the challenge. The challenges of coping with deployment are enormous.

3. *Infidelity.* Although most spouses are faithful to each other, the context of separation from each other for months (sometimes years) at a time increases the vulnerability of both spouses to infidelity. The double standard may also be operative, whereby "men are expected to have other women when they are away" and "women are expected to remain faithful and be understanding." Separated spouses try to bridge the time they are apart with e-mails and phone calls (when possible), but sometimes the loneliness becomes more difficult than anticipated. One enlisted husband said that he returned home after a year-and-a-half deployment to be confronted with the fact that his wife had become involved with someone else. "I absolutely couldn't believe it," he noted. "In retrospect, I think the separation was more difficult for her than it was for me."

4. *Frequent moves and separation from extended family or close friends.* Because military couples are often required to move to a new town, parents no longer have doting grandparents available to help them rear their children. As well, although other military families become a community of support for each other, the consistency of such support may be lacking. "We moved seven states away from my parents to a town in North Dakota," said one wife. "It was dreadful."

This child is sleeping in the bathtub because his bed is in the truck—his military parents are moving again.

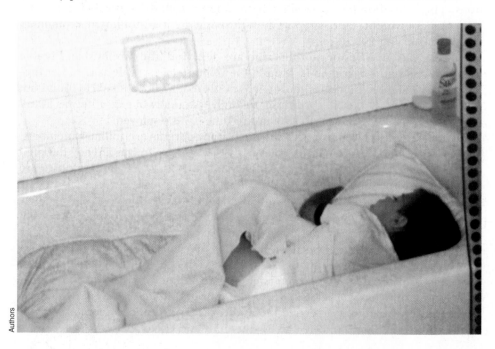

Authors

Chapter 7 Marriage Relationships

Similar to being separated from parents and siblings is the separation from one's lifelong friends. Although new friendships and new supportive relationships develop within the military community to which the family moves, the relationships are sometimes tenuous and temporary as the new families move on. The result is the absence of a stable, predictable social structure of support, which may result in a feeling of alienation and not belonging in either the military or the civilian community. The more frequent the moves, the more difficult the transition and the more likely the alienation of new military spouses. "A higher divorce rate among military families is no surprise," notes Donald Wolfe (2006), who is a marriage and family counselor who specializes in military marriages. Among military marriages, white people are as likely to divorce as black people (Lindquist 2004).

5. *Divorce among military families.* There is conflicting research on whether or not military marriages are more likely to end in divorce than are civilian marriages, like most people assume. Preliminary findings in one study indicate that military men are actually less likely to divorce than civilian men. However, military women who marry are more likely to divorce. This indicates that incentives for military men to remain married are greater than are those for military women (Pollard et al., n.d.). Additionally, a study concentrating on military families suggests that military divorce rates are not significantly increasing, even with the wars that have begun since 2001 (Karney and Crown 2007).

6. *Employment of spouses.* Well-documented research indicates that employment is beneficial to one's well-being. Military spouses, however, are at a disadvantage when it comes to finding and maintaining careers or even finding a job they can enjoy. Employers in military communities are often hesitant to hire military spouses because they know the demands that are placed on them in the absence of the deployed military member can be enormous. They are also aware of frequent moves that military families make and may be reluctant to hire employees for what may be a relatively short amount of time. The result is a disadvantaged wife who has no job and must put her career on hold. Military spouses, when they do find employment, are often underemployed, which can lead to low levels of job satisfaction. They also make less, on average, than their civilian counterparts with similar characteristics. All of these factors can contribute to distress among military spouses (Easterling 2005).

7. *Resilient military families.* In spite of these difficulties, there are also enormous benefits to being involved in the military, such as having a stable job (one may get demoted but it is much more difficult to get "fired") and having one's medical bills paid for. In addition, most military families are amazingly resilient. Not only do they anticipate and expect mobilization and deployment as part of their military obligation, they respond with pride. Indeed, some reenlist eagerly and volunteer to return to military life even when retired. One military captain stationed at Fort Bragg, in Fayetteville, North Carolina, noted, "It is part of being an American to defend your country. Somebody's got to do it and I've always been willing to do my part." He and his wife made a presentation in our classes. She said, "I'm proud that he cares for our country and I support his decision to return to Afghanistan to help as needed. And most military wives that I know feel the same way."

Although military families face great challenges and obstacles, many adopt the philosophy of "whatever doesn't kill us makes us stronger." Facing deployments and frequent moves often forces a military couple to learn to rely on themselves as well as each other. They make it through difficult life events, unique to their lifestyle, which can make day-to-day challenges seem trivial. The strength that is developed within a military marriage through all the challenges they face has the potential to build a strong, resilient marriage.

The wife/mother and child have experienced four deployments of their marine husband/father. "It isn't easy but we know how to do this," says the mother.

Authors

Interracial Marriages

Interracial marriages may involve many combinations, including American white, American black, Indian, Chinese, Japanese, Korean, Mexican, Malaysian, and Hindu mates. Of a sample of 1,319 undergraduates at a southeastern university, 44.2 percent agreed that "It is important to me that I marry someone of my same race" (Knox and Zusman 2009). However, actual interracial marriages are rare in the United States—fewer than 5 percent of all marriages in the United States are interracial. Of these, fewer than 1 percent are of a black person and a white person (*Statistical Abstract of the United States, 2009,* Table 59). Examples of African American men who are married to Caucasian women are Tiger Woods and Charles Barkley. Segregation in religion (the races worship in separate churches), housing (white and black neighborhoods), and education (white and black colleges), not to speak of parental and peer endogamous pressure to marry within one's own race, are factors that help to explain the low percentage of interracial black and white marriages.

The spouses in black and white couples are more likely to have been married before, to be age-discrepant, to live far away from their families of orientation, to have been reared in racially tolerant homes, and to have educations beyond high school. Some may also belong to religions that encourage interracial unions. The Baha'i religion, which has more than 6 million members worldwide and 84,000 in the United States, teaches that God is particularly pleased with interracial unions. Finally, interracial spouses may tend to seek contexts of diversity. "I have been reared in a military family, been everywhere and met people of different races and nationalities throughout my life. I seek diversity," noted one student.

Kennedy (2003) identified three reactions to a black-white couple who cross racial lines to marry: (1) approval (increases racial open-mindedness, decreases social segregation), (2) indifference (interracial marriage is seen as a private choice), and (3) disapproval (reflects racial disloyalty, impedes perpetuation of black culture). As Kennedy notes, "The argument that intermarriage is destructive of racial solidarity has been the principal basis of black opposition" (p. 115). There is also the concern for the biracial identity of offspring of mixed-race parents. Although most mixed-race parents identify their child as having minority race status, there is a trend toward identifying their child as multiracial. Obama is of multiracial heritage with a black father and a white mother.

Interracial partners sometimes experience negative reactions to their relationship. Black people partnered with white people have their blackness and racial identity challenged by other black people. White people partnered with black people may lose their white status and have their awareness of whiteness heightened more than ever before. At the same time, one partner is not given full status as a member of the other partner's race (Hill and Thomas 2000). Gaines and Leaver (2002) also note that the pairing of a black male and a white female is regarded as "less appropriate" than that of a white male and a black female. In the former, the black male "often is perceived as attaining higher social status (i.e., the white woman is viewed as the black man's 'prize,' stolen from the more deserving white man)" (p. 68). In the latter, when a white male pairs with a black female, "no fundamental change in power within the American social structure

Attitudes toward Interracial Dating Scale

Interracial dating or marrying is the dating or marrying of two people from different races. The purpose of this survey is to gain a better understanding of what people think and feel about interracial relationships. Please read each item carefully, and in each space, score your response using the following scale. There are no right or wrong answers to any of these statements.

1	2	3	4	5	6	7
Strongly Disagree						Strongly Agree

_____ **1.** I believe that interracial couples date outside their race to get attention.

_____ **2.** I feel that interracial couples have little in common.

_____ **3.** When I see an interracial couple, I find myself evaluating them negatively.

_____ **4.** People date outside their own race because they feel inferior.

_____ **5.** Dating interracially shows a lack of respect for one's own race.

_____ **6.** I would be upset with a family member who dated outside our race.

_____ **7.** I would be upset with a close friend who dated outside our race.

_____ **8.** I feel uneasy around an interracial couple.

_____ **9.** People of different races should associate only in nondating settings.

_____ **10.** I am offended when I see an interracial couple.

_____ **11.** Interracial couples are more likely to have low self-esteem.

_____ **12.** Interracial dating interferes with my fundamental beliefs.

_____ **13.** People should date only within their race.

_____ **14.** I dislike seeing interracial couples together.

_____ **15.** I would not pursue a relationship with someone of a different race, regardless of my feelings for that person.

_____ **16.** Interracial dating interferes with my concept of cultural identity.

_____ **17.** I support dating between people with the same skin color, but not with a different skin color.

_____ **18.** I can imagine myself in a long-term relationship with someone of another race.

_____ **19.** As long as the people involved love each other, I do not have a problem with interracial dating.

_____ **20.** I think interracial dating is a good thing.

Scoring

First, reverse the scores for items 18, 19, and 20 by switching them to the opposite side of the spectrum. For example, if you selected 7 for item 18, replace it with a 1; if you selected 3, replace it with a 5, and so on. Next, add your scores and divide by 20. Possible final scores range from 1 to 7, with 1 representing the most positive attitudes toward interracial dating and 7 representing the most negative attitudes toward interracial dating.

Norms

The norming sample was based upon 113 male and 200 female students attending Valdosta State University. The participants completing the Attitudes toward Interracial Dating Scale (IRDS) received no compensation for their participation. All participants were U.S. citizens. The average age was 23.02 years (standard deviation [SD] = 5.09), and participants ranged in age from 18 to 50 years. The ethnic composition of the sample was 62.9 percent white, 32.6 percent black, 1 percent Asian, 0.6 percent Hispanic, and 2.2 percent other. The classification of the sample was 9.3 percent freshmen, 16.3 percent sophomores, 29.1 percent juniors, 37.1 percent seniors, and 2.9 percent graduate students. The average score on the IRDS was 2.88 (SD = 1.48), and scores ranged from 1.00 to 6.60, suggesting very positive views of interracial dating. Men scored an average of 2.97 (SD=1.58), and women, 2.84 (SD = 1.42). There were no significant differences between the responses of women and men.

Source

"Attitudes Toward Interracial Dating Scale," 2004 by Mark Whatley, Ph.D., Department of Psychology, Valdosta State University, Valdosta, Georgia 31698-0100. Used by permission. Other uses of this scale by written permission of Dr. Whatley only (mwhatley@valdosta.edu). Information on the reliability and validity of this scale is available from Dr. Whatley.

is perceived as taking place" (p. 68). Interracial marriages are also more likely to dissolve than same-race marriages (Fu 2006). Disapproval of cross-racial relationships begins early. Kreaer (2008) studied adolescents who were dating cross-racially—they reported disapproval from peers.

Black-white interracial marriages are likely to increase—slowly. Not only has white prejudice against African Americans in general declined, but also segregation in school, at work, and in housing has decreased, permitting greater contact between the races. The above Self-Assessment allows you to assess your openness to involvement in an interracial relationship.

There is not a black America and a white America and Latino America and Asian America; there's the United States of America.

President Barack Obama

Interreligious Marriages

National Data

Of married couples in the United States, 37 percent have an interreligious marriage (Pew Research 2008).

Although religion may be a central focus of some individuals and their marriage, Americans in general have become more secular, and religion has become less influential as a criterion for selecting a partner as a result. In a survey of 1,319 undergraduates, only 40.2 percent reported that marrying someone of the same religion was important for them (Knox and Zusman 2009).

Are people in interreligious marriages less satisfied with their marriages than those who marry someone of the same faith? The answer depends on a number of factors. First, people in marriages in which one or both spouses profess "no religion" tend to report lower levels of marital satisfaction than those in which at least one spouse has a religious tie. People with no religion are often more liberal and less bound by traditional societal norms and values; they feel less constrained to stay married for reasons of social propriety.

The impact of a mixed religious marriage may also depend more on the devoutness of the partners than on the fact that the partners are of different religions. If both spouses are devout in their religious beliefs, they may expect some problems in the relationship (although not necessarily). Less problematic is the relationship in which one spouse is devout but the partner is not. If neither spouse in an interfaith marriage is devout, problems regarding religious differences may be minimal or nonexistent. In their marriage vows, one interfaith couple who married (he Christian, she Jewish) said that they viewed their different religions as an opportunity to strengthen their connections to their respective faiths and to each other. "Our marriage ceremony seeks to celebrate both the Jewish and Christian traditions, just as we plan to in our life together."

Cross-National Marriages

Of 1,319 undergraduates, 60.4 percent reported that they would be willing to marry someone from another country (Knox and Zusman 2009). The opportunity to meet someone from another country is increasing as more than 600,000 foreign students are studying at American colleges and universities. Because not enough Americans are going into math and engineering, these foreign students are wanted because they may find the cure for cancer or invent a vaccine for HIV (Marklein 2008).

National Data

Approximately 600,000 foreign students are enrolled at more than 2,500 colleges and universities in the United States. Most (60 percent) are from Asia (*Statistical Abstract of the United States, 2009*, Table 273).

Because American students take classes with foreign students, there is the opportunity for dating and romance between the two groups, which may lead to marriage. Some people from foreign countries marry an American citizen to gain citizenship in the United States, but immigration laws now require the marriage to last two years before citizenship is granted. If the marriage ends before two years, the foreigner must prove good faith (that the marriage was not just to gain entry into the country) or will be asked to leave the country.

When the international student is male, more likely than not his cultural mores will prevail and will clash strongly with his American bride's expectations, especially if the couple should return to his country. One female American student described her experience of marriage to a Pakistani, who violated his parents' wishes by not marrying the bride they had chosen for him in childhood. The marriage produced two children before the four of them returned to Pakistan.

The woman felt that her in-laws did not accept her and were hostile toward her. The in-laws also imposed their religious beliefs on her children and took control of their upbringing. When this situation became intolerable, the woman wanted to return to the United States. Because the children were viewed as being "owned" by their father, she was not allowed to take them with her and was banned from even seeing them. Like many international students, the husband was from a wealthy, high-status family, and the woman was powerless to fight the family. The woman has not seen her children in six years.

Cultural differences do not necessarily cause stress in cross-national marriage; the degree of cultural difference is not necessarily related to degree of stress. Much of the stress is related to society's intolerance of cross-national marriages, as manifested in attitudes of friends and family. Japan and Korea place an extraordinarily high value on racial purity. At the other extreme is the racial tolerance evident in Hawaii, where a high level of out-group marriage is normative.

Age-Discrepant Relationships and Marriages

Although people in most pairings are of similar age, sometimes the partners are considerably different in age. In marriage, these are referred to as ADMs (age-dissimilar marriages) and are in contrast to ASMs (age-similar marriages). ADMs are also known as **May-December marriages.** Typically, the woman is in the spring of her youth (May) whereas the man is in the later years of his life (December). There have been a number of May-December celebrity marriages, including that of Celine Dion, who is twenty-six years younger than René Angelil (in 2011, aged 42 and 68). Larry King is also twenty-six years older than his seventh wife, Shawn (in 2010 he was 75). Michael Douglas is twenty-five years older than his wife, Catherine Zeta Jones, and Ellen DeGeneres is fifteen years older than Portia de Rossi, her partner (they "married" in 2008).

One might assume that these marriages are less happy because the spouses were born into such different age contexts. Research shows otherwise. Barnes and Patrick (2004) compared thirty-five ADMs (in which spouses were fourteen or more years apart) and thirty-five ASMs (in which spouses were less than five

This age-discrepant couple (twenty years difference) reports that, "our age difference is no big deal"—they love each other.

years apart) and found no difference in reported marital satisfaction between the two groups. As is true in other research, wives reported lower marital satisfaction and more household responsibilities in both groups.

Perhaps the greatest example of a May-December marriage that "worked" is of Oona Chaplin, wife of Charles Chaplin. She married him when she was age 18 (he was age 54). Their May-December alliance was expected to last the requisite six months, but they remained together and raised eight children.

Although less common, some age-discrepant relationships are those in which the woman is older than her partner. Mary Tyler Moore (married twenty-five years) is eighteen years older than her husband, Robert Levine. Demi Moore is sixteen years older than husband Ashton Kutcher (she was 40 and he was 27 at the time of the wedding). Valerie Gibson (2002) is the author of *Cougar: A Guide for Older Women Dating Younger Men.* She noted that the current use of the term **cougars** refers to "women, usually in their 30s and 40s, who are financially stable and mentally independent and looking for a younger man to have fun with." Gibson noted that one-third of women between the ages of 40 and 60 are dating younger men. Financially independent women need not select a man in reference to his breadwinning capabilities. Instead, these "cougars" are looking for men, not to marry but to enjoy. The downside of such relationships comes if the man gets serious and wants to have children, which may spell the end of the relationship.

Marriage Quality

A successful marriage is the goal of most couples. But what is successful marriage and what are the characteristics?

Definition and Characteristics of Successful Marriages

Marital success is measured in terms of marital stability and marital happiness. Stability refers to how long the spouses have been married and how permanent they view their relationship, whereas marital happiness refers to more subjective aspects of the relationship.

In describing marital success, researchers have used the terms *satisfaction, quality, adjustment, lack of distress,* and *integration.* Marital success is often measured by asking spouses how happy they are, how often they spend their free time together, how often they agree about various issues, how easily they resolve conflict, how sexually satisfied they are, and how often they have considered separation or divorce. The degree to which the spouses enjoy each other's companionship is another variable of marital success. Not all couples, even those recently married, achieve high-quality marriages. In a national sample comparing married people with unmarried people, Princeton Survey Research Associates International found that 43 percent of the spouses reported that they were "very happy," compared with 24 percent of unmarried people (Stuckey and Gonzalez 2006).

Corra et al. (forthcoming) analyzed data collected over a thirty-year period, from the 1972 to 2002 General Social Surveys, to discover the influence of sex (male or female) and race (white or black) on the level of reported marital happiness. Findings indicated greater levels of marital happiness among males and white people than among females and black people. The researchers suggested that males make fewer accommodations in marriage and that white people are not burdened with racism and have less economic stress. Amato et al. 2007 also reported less marital happiness and more marital problems among wives than husbands.Wallerstein and Blakeslee (1995) studied fifty financially secure couples in stable (from ten to forty years), happy marriages with at least one child.

These couples defined marital happiness as feeling respected and cherished. They also regarded their marriages as works in progress that needed continued attention to avoid becoming stale. No couple said that they were happy all the time. Rather, a good marriage is a process. Billingsley et al. (1995) interviewed thirty happily married couples who had been wed an average of thirty-two years and had an average of 2.5 children. They found various characteristics associated with couples who stay together and who enjoy each other. These qualities appear to be the same for both husbands and wives (Amato et al. 2007). Based on these studies of couples in stable, happy relationships, the following twelve characteristics emerge:

1. *Personal and emotional commitment to stay married.* Divorce was not considered an option. The spouses were committed to each other for personal reasons rather than societal pressure. In addition, the spouses were committed to maintain the marriage out of emotional rather than economic need (DeOllos 2005).

2. *Common interests.* The spouses talked of sharing interests, values, goals, children, and the desire to be together.

3. *Communication.* Gottman and Carrere (2000) studied the communication patterns of couples over an eleven-year period and emphasized that those spouses who stay together are five times more likely to lace their arguments with positives ("I'm sorry I hurt your feelings") and to consciously choose to say things to each other that nurture the relationship rather than destroy it. Successful spouses also feel comfortable telling each other what they want and not being defensive at feedback from the partner.

4. *Religiosity.* A strong religious orientation provided the couples with social, spiritual, and emotional support from church members and with moral guidance in working out problems (DeOllos 2005). People with no religious affiliation report more marital problems and are more likely to divorce (Amato et al. 2007).

5. *Trust.* Trust in the partner provided a stable floor of security for the respective partners and their relationship. Neither partner feared that the other partner would leave or become involved in another relationship. "She can't take him anywhere he doesn't want to go" is a phrase from a country-and-western song that reflects the trust that one's partner will be faithful.

6. *Not materialistic.* Being nonmaterialistic was a characteristic of these happily married couples. Although the couples may have lived in nice houses and had expensive toys (for example, a boat and camper), they were tied to nothing. "You can have my things, but don't take away my people," is a phrase from one husband reflecting his feelings about his family.

7. *Role models.* The couples spoke of positive role models in their parents. Good marriages beget good marriages—good marriages run in families. It is said that the best gift you can give your children is a good marriage.

8. *Sexual desire.* Wilson and Cousins (2005) confirmed that partners' similar rankings of sexual desire as important in predicting long-term relationship success. Earlier, we noted the superiority of marital sex over sex in other relationship contexts in terms of both emotion and physical pleasure.

9. *Equitable relationships.* Amato et al. (2007) observed that the decline in traditional gender attitudes and the increase in egalitarian decision making is related to increased happiness in today's couples.

10. *Absence of negative attributions.* Spouses who do not attribute negative motives to their partner's behavior report higher levels of marital satisfaction than spouses who ruminate about negative motives. Dowd et al. (2005) studied 127 husbands and 132 wives and found that the absence of negative attributions was associated with higher marital quality.

11. *Forgiveness.* At some time in all marriages, each spouse engages in behavior that may hurt the partner. Forgiveness rather than harboring resentment

A little girl asked if m-i-r-a-g-e spelled marriage and was quickly told "Yes."

Anonymous

allows spouses to move forward. Spouses who do not "drop the lowest test score" (a metaphor of academics) find that they inadvertently create a failing marriage in which they then must live. McNulty (2008) noted the value of forgiveness particularly when married to partners who rarely behaved negatively.

12. Economic security. Although money does not buy happiness, having a stable, secure economic floor is associated with marital quality (Amato et al. 2007). North et al. (2008) examined the role of income and social support in predicting concurrent happiness and change in happiness among 274 married adults across a ten-year period. They found that income had a small, positive impact on happiness, which diminished as income increased. In contrast, family social support, as reflected in cohesion, expressiveness, and low conflict showed a substantial, positive association with concurrent happiness, particularly when income was low.

Theoretical Views of Marital Happiness and Success

Interactionists, developmentalists, exchange theorists, and functionalists view marital happiness and success differently. Symbolic interactionists emphasize the subjective nature of marital happiness and point out that the definition of the situation is critical.

A happy marriage exists only when spouses define the verbal and nonverbal behavior of their partner as positive, and only when they label themselves as being in love. Hence, marital happiness is not defined by the existence of eight or more specific criteria but is subjectively defined by the respective partners.

Family developmental theorists emphasize the developmental tasks that must be accomplished to enable a couple to have a happy marriage. Wallerstein and Blakeslee (1995) identified several of these tasks, including separating emotionally from one's parents, building a sense of "we-ness," establishing an imaginative and pleasurable sex life, and making the relationship safe for expressing differences.

Exchange theorists focus on the exchange of behavior of a kind and at a rate that is mutually satisfactory to both spouses. When spouses exchange positive behaviors at a high rate, they are more likely to feel marital happiness than when the exchange is characterized by high-frequency negative behavior (Turner 2005).

Structural functionalists see marital happiness as contributing to marital stability, which is functional for society. When two parents are in love and happy, the likelihood that they will stay together to provide physical care and emotional nurturing for their offspring is increased. Furthermore, when spouses take care of their own children, society is not burdened with having to pay for the children's care through welfare payments, paying foster parents, or paying for institutional management (group homes) when all else fails. Happy marriages also involve limiting sex to each other. In their national sex survey, Michael and colleagues reported, "[H]appiness is clearly linked to having just one partner—which may not be too surprising since that is the situation that society smiles upon" (1994, 130). Fewer cases of HIV also mean lower medical bills for society. Similarly, marriage is associated with improved health (Stack and Eshleman 1998) because spouses monitor each other's health and encourage or facilitate medical treatment as indicated.

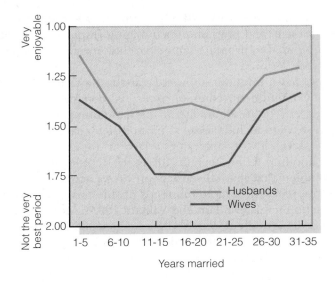

Figure 7.1

Source: Caroline O. Vaillant and George E. Vaillant. 1993. Is the U-curve of marital satisfaction an illusion? A 40-year study of marriage. *Journal of Marriage and the Family* 55:237, Figure 6. Copyright © 1993. Reprinted by permission of Wiley-Blackwell.

Marital Happiness across the Family Life Cycle

Although a successful marriage is one in which the partners are happy and in love across time, spouses report that some periods are happier than others. Figure 7.1 provides a retrospective of marriage by fifty-two white college-educated husbands and wives over a period of thirty-five years together. The couples reported the most enjoyment with their relationship in the beginning, followed by less enjoyment during the child-bearing stages, and a return to feeling more satisfied after the children left home. Corra et al. (forthcoming) found a similar curvilinear relationship in their analysis of survey data covering a period of thirty years. Whiteman et al. (2007) also observed decreases in marital satisfaction and love, as well as increases in conflict, as the couple's offspring reached puberty and an improvement when their children were 18 to 20—the time children typically leave home for college.

Plagnol and Easterlin (2008) conceptualized happiness as the ratio of aspirations and attainments in the areas of family life and material goods. They studied 47,000 women and men and found that up to age 48, women are happier than men in both domains. After age 48, a shift causes women to become less satisfied with family life (their children are gone) and material goods (some are divorced and have fewer economic resources). In contrast, men become more satisfied with family life (the empty nest is less of a problem) and finances (men typically have more economic resources than women, whether married or divorced). Individuals who are black and/or with lower education report less happiness.

The Value of Marriage Education Programs

A team of researchers (Macomber et al. 2005) evaluated the numerous programs designed to strengthen marriage available in American society. They found an incredible diversity of programs offered through a variety of settings (for example, churches, mental health clinics), focused on a variety of populations (for example, couples, parents), by personnel with a range of academic training (from none to PhD). The lack of systematic content, control groups, and follow-ups makes evaluating the myriad programs impossible, so their value remains an open question. DeMaria (2005) also confirmed the lack of data as to the effectiveness of marriage education programs.

Nevertheless, Congress passed legislation in 2005 (Deficit Reduction Act), including $750 million for a five-year program to fund marriage education programs such as marriage skills training, high school education programs on the value of marriage, and programs encouraging responsible fatherhood. The funds may not be used to promote same-sex relationships or marriage (Healthy Marriage Initiative 2006).

What can we learn from our knowledge about the characteristics of successful marriages? Commitment, common interests, communication skills, and a nonmaterialistic view of life all are factors in maintaining a successful marriage. Couples might strive to include these as part of their relationships.

As noted, durability is only one criterion for a successful marriage. Satisfaction is another. Researchers in the early 1990s analyzed cross-sectional data and concluded that marital satisfaction drops across time, reaches a low point during the years the couple has teens in the house, and then returns to preteen satisfaction levels (Vaillant and Vaillant 1993). More recently, researchers have studied longitudinal data and found that marital satisfaction consistently drops across time (with the steepest declines in the early and later years) (Vanlaningham et al. 2001).

Healthy Marriage Resource Center

The Healthy Marriage Resource Center has been set up in Washington, DC, as a result of a $4.5 million grant from the U.S. Department of Health and Human Services Administration for Children and Families (ACF) to The National Council on Family Relations of Minneapolis, Minnesota. The goal of the center is to collect and disseminate information on the skills and knowledge to build and sustain healthy marriages. An annual Marriage Summit is also held to advise the center and discuss the state of marriage. The primary method of exposure to knowledge about healthy marriage is via the web (http://www.healthymarriageinfo.org/). Individuals interested in national and regional events related to healthy marriages can use an online map that will direct them to healthy marriage opportunities in their area.

SUMMARY

What are individual motivations and societal functions of marriage?

Individuals' motives for marriage include personal fulfillment, companionship, legitimacy of parenthood, and emotional and financial security. Societal functions include continuing to provide society with socialized members, regulating sexual behavior, and stabilizing adult personalities.

What are three levels of commitment in marriage?

Marriage involves a commitment—person-to-person, family-to-family, and couple-to-state.

What are two rites of passage associated with marriage?

The wedding is a rite of passage signifying the change from the role of fiancé to the role of spouse. Women, more than men, are more invested in preparation for the wedding, the wedding is more for the bride's family, and women prefer a traditional wedding. Most spouses report a positive wedding night experience with exhaustion from the wedding or reception being a problem. The honeymoon is a time of personal recuperation and making the transition to the new role of spouse.

What changes might a person anticipate after marriage?

Changes after the wedding are legal (each becomes part owner of all income and property accumulated during the marriage), personal (enhanced self-concept), social (less time with friends), economic (money spent on entertainment in courtship is diverted to living expenses and setting up a household), sexual (less frequency), and parental (improved relationship with parents).

What are examples of diversity in marriage relationships?

Hispanic families tend to marry earlier, and have higher rates of marriage and higher fertility. Male power and strong familistic values also characterize Hispanic families. Canadian families are unique in that they exist in a bilingual (English and French) country, may be common-law with full legal recognition, and have half the divorce rate of marriages in the United States. Same-sex relationships in Canada also have greater approval and government protection, including legal marriage in three provinces. In Muslim American families, norms involve no premarital sex, close monitoring of children, and intense nurturing of the parental-child bond. Military families cope with deployment, the double standard, and limited income. Amish and Mennonite families represent a system where courtship, marriage, and family patterns are tightly controlled. The result is a very low divorce rate. Mixed marriages include interracial, interreligious, and age-discrepant. When age-discrepant and age-similar marriages are compared, there are no differences in regard to marital happiness.

What are the characteristics associated with successful marriages?

Marital success is defined in terms of both quality and durability. Characteristics associated with marital success include commitment, common interests, communication, religiosity, trust, and nonmaterialism, and having positive role models, low stress levels, and sexual desire. Marriage education programs are designed to improve marriage. There are few empirical studies on marriage education programs.

KEY TERMS

artifact	commensality	disenchantment	"new" wedding artifact
"blue" wedding artifact	commitment	honeymoon	"old" wedding artifact
"borrowed" wedding artifact	cougar	marital success	rite of passage
bride wealth	covenant marriage	May-December marriage	rumspringa

The Companion Website for *Choices in Relationships: An Introduction to Marriage and the Family,* Tenth Edition
www.cengage.com/sociology/knox

Supplement your review of this chapter by going to the Companion Website to take one of the tutorial quizzes, use the flash cards to master key terms, or check out the many other study aids, like crossword puzzles and self-assessments. You'll also find special features such as General Social Survey (GSS) data, Census data, and other resources to help you with that special project or to do some research on your own.

WEB LINKS

American Marriage
http://www.heartchoice.com/marriage/

Bridal Registry
http://www.theknot.com

Brides and Grooms
http://www.bridesandgrooms.com/

The Castle
http://www.castlemcculloch.com

Facts about Marriage
http://www.cdc.gov/nchs/fastats/marriage.htm

National Healthy Marriage Resource Center
http://www.healthymarriageinfo.org/

Marriage Builders
http://marriagebuilders.com/

Military Marriages
http://www.defenselink.mil/ (The Department of Defense website)

http://www.nmfa.org/ (The National Military Family Association)

Project Everlasting
http://www.projecteverlasting.com/

Smart Marriages
http://www.smartmarriages.com/

Traditional Korean Marriage
http://www.lifeinkorea.com/culture/marriage/marriage.cfm

Wedding Channel
http://www.weddingchannel.com/home.html

Wedding Webcasts
http://www.webcastmywedding.net/

http://www.liveinternetweddings.com/

REFERENCES

Amato, P. R., A. Booth, D. R. Johnson, and S. F. Rogers. 2007. *Alone together: How marriage in America is changing.* Cambridge, Massachusetts: Harvard University Press.

Barnes, K. And J. Patrick. 2004. Examining age-congruency and marital satisfaction. *The Gerontologist* 44:185–87.

Billingsley, S., M. Lim, and G. Jennings. 1995. Themes of long-term, satisfied marriages consummated between 1952–1967. *Family Perspective* 29:283–95.

Blakely, K. 2008. Busy brides and the business of family life. *Journal of Family Issues* 29:639–43.

Brunsma, D. L. 2005. Interracial families and the racial identification of mixed-race children: Evidence from the early childhood longitudinal study. *Social Forces* 84:1131–57.

Bulanda, J. R., and S. L. Brown. 2007. Race-ethnic differences in marital quality and divorce *Social Science Research* 36:945–59.

Burford, M. 2005. The un-Hollywood wife. In *The Oprah Magazine Book,* 174. Birmingham, Alabama: Oxmoor House.

Cadden, M., and D Merrill 2007. What married people miss most (based on *Reader's Digest* study of 1,001 married adults). *USA Today,* D1.

Caforio, G. 2003. *Handbook on the sociology of the military.* New York: Kluwer Academic.

Coontz, S. 2000. Marriage: Then and now. *Phi Kappa Phi Journal* 80:16–20.

Corra, M., S. Carter, J. S. Carter, and D. Knox. Forthcoming. Trends in marital happiness by sex and race, 1973–2006. *Journal of Family Issues.*

Cozza, S. J., R. S. Chun, and J. A. Polo. 2005. Military families and children during operation Iraqi freedom. *Psychiatric Quarterly* 76:371–78.

DeMaria, R. M. 2005. Distressed couples and marriage education. *Family Relations* 54:242–53.

DeOllos, I. Y. 2005. Predicting marital success or failure: Burgess and beyond. In *Sourcebook of family theory and research,* ed. Vern L. Bengtson, Alan C. Acock, Katherine R. Allen, Peggye Dilworth-Anderson, and David M. Klein, 134–36. Thousand Oaks, CA: Sage Publications.

Dew, J. 2008. Debt change and marital satisfaction change in recently married couples *Family Relations* 57:60–71.

Dowd, D. A., M. J. Means, J. F. Pope, and J. H. Humphries. 2005. Attributions and marital satisfaction: The mediated effects of self-disclosure. *Journal of Family and Consumer Sciences* 97:22–27.

Easterling, B. A. 2005. *The invisible side of military careers: An examination of employment and well-being among military spouses.* MA Thesis, University of North Florida.

Fisher, T. D., and J. K. McNulty. 2008. Neuroticism and marital satisfaction: The mediating role played by the sexual relationship. *Journal of Family Psychology* 22:112–23.

Fu, X. 2006. Impact of socioeconomic status on inter-racial mate selection and divorce. *Social Science Journal* 43:239–58.

Gaines, S. O., Jr., and J. Leaver. 2002. Interracial relationships. In *Inappropriate relationships: The unconventional, the disapproved, and the forbidden,* ed. R. Goodwin and D. Cramer, 65–78. Mahwah, NJ: Lawrence Erlbaum.

Gibson, V. 2002. *Cougar: A guide for older women dating younger men.* Boston, MA: Firefly Books.

Glover, K. R., M. Phelps, A. Sean Burleson, and A. Dessie. 2006. Friends or lovers: Understanding the cognitive underpinnings of the transition from affiliation to care-giving in romantic relationships. 4th Annual ECU Research and Creative Activities Symposium, April 21, East Carolina University, Greenville, NC.

Gottman, J., and S. Carrere. 2000. Welcome to the love lab. *Psychology Today,* September/October, 42.

Harvey, C. D. H. 2005. Families in Canada. In *Handbook of world families,* ed Bert N. Adams and Jan Trost, 539–59. Thousand Oaks, CA: Sage Publications.

Healthy Marriage Initiative. 2006. http://www.acf.hhs.gov/healthymarriage/about/mission.html (accessed Feb. 21, 2006).

Hill, M. R., and V. Thomas. 2000. Strategies for racial identity development: Narratives of black and white women in interracial partner relationships. *Family Relations* 49:193–200.

Huyck, M. H., and D. L. Gutmann. 1992. Thirty something years of marriage: Understanding experiences of women and men in enduring family relationships. *Family Perspective* 26:249–65.

Karney, B. R., and J. S. Crown. 2007. *Families under stress: An assessment of data, theory, and research on marriage and divorce in the military.* Rand Corporation: National Defense Research Institute; Prepared for the Office of the Secretary of Defense. http://www.rand.org/pubs/monographs/2007/RAND_MG599.pdf (accessed November 18, 2008).

Kennedy, R. 2003. *Interracial intimacies.* New York: Pantheon.

Knox, D., and Zusman, M. E. 2009. Relationship and sexual behaviors of a sample of 1,319 university students. Data collected for this text. Department of Sociology, East Carolina University, Greenville, NC.

Kreaer, D. A. 2008. Guarded borders: Adolescent interracial romance and peer trouble at school. *Social Forces* 87:887–910.

Landale, N. S., and R. S. Oropesa. 2007. Hispanic families: Stability and change. *Annual Review of Sociology* 33:381–405.

Licata, N. 2002. Should premarital counseling be mandatory as a requisite to obtaining a marriage license? *Family Court Review* 40:518–32.

Lindquist, J. H. 2004. When race makes no difference: Marriage and the military. *Social Forces* 83:731–57.

Macomber, J. E., J. Murray, and M. Stagner. 2005. Investigation of programs to strengthen and support healthy marriages. http://www.urban.org/url.cfm?ID=411141.

Madathil, J., and J. M. Benshoff. 2008. Importance of marital characteristics and marital satisfaction: A comparison of Asian Indians in arranged marriages and Americans in marriages of choice. *Family Journal* 16:222–32.

Marklein, M. B. 2008. High mark for foreign students here. *USA Today,* November 17, 4D.

Chapter 7 Marriage Relationships

Martin, J. A., and P. McClure. 2000. Today's active duty military family: The evolving challenges of military family life. In *The military family: A practice guide for human service providers*, ed. J. A. Martin, L. N. Rosen, and L. R. Sparacino, 3–24. Connecticut: Praeger Publishers.

McNulty, J. K. 2008. Forgiveness in marriage: Putting the benefits into context. *Journal of Family Psychology* 22:171–83.

Michael, R. T., J. H. Gagnon, E. O. Laumann, and G. Kolata. 1994. *Sex in America: A definitive survey*. Boston: Little, Brown.

Military Family Resource Center. 2003. Active Duty Families in *2003 Demographics Report*. www.mfrc-dodqol.org/pdffiles/demo2003/SectionIIIActiveDutyFamilies.pdf (accessed January 30, 2005).

Mogro-Wilson, C. 2008. The influence of parental warmth and control on Latino adolescent alcohol use. *Hispanic Journal of Behavioral Sciences* 30:89–95.

Montemurro, B. 2006. *Something old, something bold*. New Brunswick, NJ: Rutgers University Press.

Morr Serewicz, M. C., and D. J. Canary. 2008. Assessments of disclosure from the in-laws: Links among disclosure topics, family privacy orientations, and relational quality. *Journal of Social and Personal Relationships* 25:333–57.

Murdock, G. P. 1949. *Social structure*. New York: Free Press.

Murray, C. I., and N. Kimura. 2003. Multiplicity of paths to couple formation in Japan. In *Mate selection across cultures* ed. R. R. Hamon and B. B. Ingoldsby, 247–68. Thousand Oaks, CA: Sage Publications.

NCFR Policy Brief. 2004. *Building strong communities for military families*. Minneapolis, MN: National Council on Family Relations.

North, R. J., C. J. Holahan, R. H. Moos, and R. C. Cronkite. 2008. Family support, family income, and happiness: A 10-year perspective. *Journal of Family Psychology* 22:475–83.

Nuner, J. E. 2004. A qualitative study of mother-in-law/daughter-in-law relationships. *Dissertation Abstracts International, A: The Humanities and Social Sciences*, 65(August): 712A–13A.

Page, S. 2006. War has hurt USA. *USA Today*, March 17, A1.

Parra-Cardona, J. R., D. Córdova, Jr., K. Holtrop, F. A. Villarruel, and E. Wieling. 2008. Shared ancestry, evolving stories: Similar and contrasting life experiences described by foreign born and U.S. born Latino parents. *Family Process* 47:157–73.

Pew Research—Pew Forum on Religion and Public Life. 2008. The U.S. religious landscape survey. http://pewresearch.org/pubs/743/united-states-religion.

Pimentel, E. E. 2000. Just how do I love thee? Marital relations in urban China. *Journal of Marriage and the Family* 62:32–47.

Plagnol, A. C., and R. A. Easterlin. 2008. Aspirations, attainments, and satisfaction: Life cycle differences between American women and men. *Journal of Happiness Studies*. Published online July 2008.

Pollard, M., B. Karney, and D. Loughran. n.d. Comparing Rates of Marriage and Divorce in Civilian, Military, and Veteran Populations. http://paa2008.princeton.edu/download.aspx?submissionId=81696 (accessed November 18, 2008).

Rowland, I. 2006. Choosing to have children or choosing to be childfree: Australian students' attitudes towards the decisions of heterosexual and lesbian women. *Australian Psychologist* 41:55–59.

Saleska, S. 2004. Exploratory study of problems and stresses dependent military spouses experience. Paper presented at the Second Annual East Carolina University Research and Scholarship Day, March 26, Greenville, NC.

Sayer, L. C., S. M. Bianchi, and J. P. Robinson. 2004. Are parents investing less in children? Trends in mothers' and father's time with children. *American Journal of Sociology* 110:1–43.

Sherif-Trask, B. 2003. Love, courtship, and marriage from a cross-cultural perspective: The upper middle class Egyptian example. In *Mate Selection Across Cultures* ed. R. R. Hamon and B. B. Ingoldsby, 121–36. Thousand Oaks, CA: Sage Publications.

Sobal, J., C. F. Bove, and B. S. Rauschenbach. 2002. Commensal careers at entry into marriage: Establishing commensal units and managing commensal circles. *Sociological Review* 50:378–97.

Stack, S., and J. R. Eshleman. 1998. Marital happiness: A 17-nation study. *Journal of Marriage and the Family* 60:527–36.

Statistical Abstract of the United States, 2009. 128th ed. Washington, DC: U.S. Bureau of the Census.

Stuckey, D., and A. Gonzalez. 2006. Princeton Survey Research Associates Poll on marriage happiness. *USA Today* March 7, 1A.

Treas, J., and D. Giesen. 2000. Sexual infidelity among married and cohabiting Americans. *Journal of Marriage and the Family* 62:48–60.

Turner, A. J. 2005. Personal communication, Huntsville, Alabama, September.

Vaillant, C. O., and G. E. Vaillant. 1993. Is the U-curve of marital satisfaction an illusion? A 40-year study of marriage. *Journal of Marriage and the Family* 55:230–39.

Vanlaningham, J., D. R. Johnson, and P. Amato. 2001. Marital happiness, marital duration, and the U-shaped curve: Evidence from a five-year wave panel study. *Social Forces* 79:1313–41.

Wallerstein, J., and S. Blakeslee. 1995. *The good marriage*. Boston: Houghton-Mifflin.

Weigel, D. J., and D. S. Ballard-Reisch. 2002. Investigating the behavioral indicators of relational commitment. *Journal of Social and Personal Relationships* 19:403–23.

Whiteman, S. D., S. M. McHale, and A. C. Crouter. 2007. Longitudinal changes in marital relationships: The role of offspring's pubertal development. *Journal of Marriage and Family* 69:1005–20.

Wilmoth, J., and G. Koso. 2002. Does marital history matter? Marital status and wealth outcomes among preretirement adults. *Journal of Marriage and the Family* 64:254–68.

Wilson, G., and J. Cousins. 2005. Measurement of partner compatibility; further validation and refinement of the CQ test. *Sexual and Relationship Therapy* 20:421–29.

Wilson, S. M., L. W. Ngige, and L. J. Trollinger. 2003. Kamba and Maasai paths to marriage in Kenya. In *Mate selection across cultures*, ed. R. R. Hamon and B. B. Ingoldsby, 95–117. Thousand Oaks, CA: Sage Publications.

Wolfe, D. 2006. Personal communication. Jacksonville, NC: Camp LeJune Military Base.

Homophobia alienates mothers and fathers from their sons and daughters, friend from friend, neighbor from neighbor, Americans from one another.

Byrne Fone, Homophobia: A History

Same-Sex Couples and Families

Contents

True or False?

1. Lesbian couples report higher relationship satisfaction than gay male and heterosexual couples.

2. Physical abuse is much more common than psychological abuse in male same-sex relationships.

3. Love feelings are more likely than sexual feelings to be both same and other sex directed.

4. Children reared by same-sex parents do not fare as well as children who have two heterosexual parents.

5. Lesbians and bisexuals have the same sexually transmitted infection rates.

Answers: **1.** T **2.** F **3.** T **4.** F **5.** F

We were vacationing in central Mexico and stayed at a bed-and-breakfast in a town west of Mexico City. We befriended a young Mexican male who worked in the office who was responsible for helping guests with various issues such as touring surrounding cities and sites, identifying places in town to eat, and so on. We were also interested to know his perception of the acceptance of homosexual people as a male who was reared in central Mexico. "Their life is over," he said, "the parents will disown them and the mother will be blamed that the child turned out this way." He also gave an example of a hate crime in the area in which a young gay male was found dead . . . his penis had been cut off and stuffed in his mouth with a note on him that said, "this will happen to you if you are gay." The police did nothing.

The police/judicial system looking the other way for the murder of homosexuals has also occurred in the United States. Harvey Milk (portrayed by Sean Penn who won the best actor academy award for his role in the 2008 *MILK*) was the first openly gay man elected to any substantial political office anywhere and was assassinated point blank in 1978 by Dan White (a political rival). Although premeditated murder carries the death penalty in California, White was convicted of voluntary manslaughter which resulted in a lesser sentence.

In the United States, homosexuality remains a subject over which there continues to be wide differences of approval. In 2007, Senator Larry Craig (R-Idaho) lost his job in the wake of a homosexual scandal in the Minneapolis-St. Paul International Airport men's room after he pleaded guilty to misconduct. In regard to "marriage," although some states grant "marriage" licenses to gay couples (for example, Massachusetts, Connecticut), others have overturned a state supreme court decision upholding gay marriage (for example, California's Proposition 8) and defined marriage as the exclusive union between a woman and a man. Hate crimes against homosexuals are not uncommon. Worldwide, approval differences are considerable, with the Netherlands, Spain, Belgium, Norway, and South Africa granting equal marriage rights to same-sex couples, whereas intense discrimination is the norm in other countries (for example, Pakistan and Kenya).

In this chapter, we discuss same-sex couples and families—relationships that are, in many ways, similar to heterosexual ones. A major difference, however, is that gay and lesbian couples and families are subjected to **prejudice** and **discrimination**. Although other minority groups also experience prejudice and discrimination, only minorities of sexual orientation are denied federal legal marital status and the benefits and responsibilities that go along with marriage (which we discuss later in this chapter). Also, gay couples are sometimes rejected

To discriminate against our sisters and brothers who are lesbian or gay on grounds of their sexual orientation for me is as totally unacceptable and unjust as Apartheid ever was.

Archbishop Desmond Tutu

by their own parents, siblings, and other family members. One father told his son, "I'd rather have a dead son than a gay son."

Homosexual behavior has existed throughout human history and in most (perhaps all) human societies (Kirkpatrick 2000). In this chapter, we focus on Western views of sexual diversity that define **sexual orientation** as a classification of individuals as heterosexual, bisexual, or homosexual, based on their emotional, cognitive, and sexual attractions and self-identity. **Heterosexuality** refers to the predominance of emotional and sexual attraction to individuals of the opposite sex. **Homosexuality** refers to the predominance of emotional and sexual attraction to individuals of the same sex, and **bisexuality** is emotional and sexual attraction to members of both sexes. The term **lesbian** refers to homosexual women; **gay** can refer to either homosexual women or homosexual men. Lesbians, gays, and bisexuals, sometimes referred to collectively as the **lesbigay population**, are considered part of a larger population referred to as the transgendered community. **Transgendered** individuals are those who express their masculinity and femininity in nontraditional ways consistent with their biological sex. For example, a biological male is not expected to wear a dress. Transgendered individuals include not only homosexuals and bisexuals but also cross-dressers, transvestites, and transsexuals (see Chapter 3 on Gender). Because much of the current literature on the lesbigay population includes other members of the transgendered community, the terms **LGBT** or **GLBT** are often used to refer collectively to lesbians, gays, bisexuals, and transgendered individuals.

Prevalence of Homosexuality, Bisexuality, and Same-Sex Couples

Before looking at prevalence data concerning homosexuality and bisexuality in the United States, it is important to understand the ways in which identifying or classifying individuals as heterosexual, homosexual, gay, lesbian, or bisexual can be problematic.

This couple has been together twenty-nine years.

Authors

Problems Associated with Identifying and Classifying Sexual Orientation

The classification of individuals into sexual orientation categories (for example, heterosexual, homosexual, bisexual) is problematic for a number of reasons (Savin-Williams 2006). First, because of the social stigma associated with non-heterosexual identities, many individuals conceal or falsely portray their sexual-orientation identities to avoid prejudice and discrimination.

Second, not all people who are sexually attracted to or have had sexual relations with individuals of the same sex view themselves as homosexual or bisexual. A final difficulty in labeling a person's sexual orientation is that an individual's sexual attractions, behavior, and identity may change across time. For example, in a longitudinal study of 156 lesbian, gay, and bisexual youth, 57 percent consistently identified as gay or lesbian and 15 percent consistently identified as bisexual over a one-year period, but 18 percent transitioned from bisexual to lesbian or gay (Rosario et al. 2006).

Early research on sexual behavior by Kinsey and his colleagues (1948; 1953) found that, although 37 percent of men and 13 percent of women had had at least one same-sex sexual experience since adolescence, few of the individuals reported exclusive homosexual behavior. These data led Kinsey to conclude that most people are not exclusively heterosexual or homosexual. Rather, Kinsey suggested an individual's sexual orientation may have both heterosexual and homosexual elements. In other words, Kinsey suggested that heterosexuality and homosexuality represent two ends of a sexual-orientation continuum and that most individuals are neither entirely homosexual nor entirely heterosexual, but fall somewhere along this continuum.

The Heterosexual-Homosexual Rating Scale that Kinsey et al. (1953) developed allows individuals to identify their sexual orientation on a continuum. Individuals with ratings of 0 or 1 are entirely or largely heterosexual; 2, 3, or 4 are more bisexual; and 5 or 6 are largely or entirely homosexual (see Figure 8.1). Very few individuals are exclusively a 0 or 6, prompting Kinsey to believe that most individuals are bisexual.

Sexual-orientation classification is also complicated by the fact that sexual behavior, attraction, love, desire, and sexual-orientation identity do not always match. For example, "research conducted across different cultures and historical periods (including present-day Western culture) has found that many individuals develop passionate infatuations with same-gender partners in the absence of same-gender sexual desires . . . whereas others experience same-gender sexual desires that never manifest themselves in romantic passion or attachment" (Diamond 2003, 173).

Bisexuality immediately doubles your chance for a date on Saturday nights.

Woody Allen, director

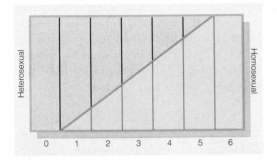

Based on both psychologic reactions and overt experience, individuals rate as follows:
0. Exclusively heterosexual with no homosexual
1. Predominantly heterosexual, only incidentally homosexual
2. Predominantly heterosexual, but more than incidentally homosexual
3. Equally heterosexual and homosexual
4. Predominantly homosexual, but more than incidentally heterosexual
5. Predominantly homosexual, but incidentally heterosexual
6. Exclusively homosexual

Figure 8.1
The Heterosexual-Homosexual Rating Scale
Source: *Sexual Behavior in the Human Male,* W.B. Saunders, 1948. Reprinted by permission of the Kinsey Institute for Research in Sex, Gender, and Reproduction, Inc.

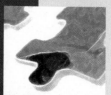
What if I Am Attracted to Someone of the Same Sex?

As noted elsewhere in this chapter, one's sexual orientation is fluid. Although most people tend to be attracted to opposite-sex people most of the time, it is not uncommon to find one's self attracted to someone of the same sex. This is particularly true in regard to emotional attraction that has no sexual orientation barrier (Diamond 2003). Such attractions are usually suppressed because of the cultural heterosexual bias. Where there are physical attractions as well, the person has a harder time diverting them. Gay people typically say that sex with an opposite-sex partner was "OK but nothing like the explosive feelings I felt with a same-sex partner." What one does with these feelings depends on the strength of the feelings, the imperative to "be true to one's self," and the social context. Although some deny or suppress the feelings or attractions, others explore them.

The world is not divided into sheep and goats. Not all things are black nor all things white. It is a fundamental of taxonomy that nature rarely deals with discrete categories. Only the human mind invents categories and tries to force facts into separated pigeon-holes. The living world is a continuum in each and every one of its aspects. The sooner we learn this concerning sexual behavior the sooner we shall reach a sound understanding of the realities of sex.

Alfred Kinsey, *Sexual Behavior in the Human Male*

Consider the findings of a national study of U.S. adults that investigated (1) sexual attraction to individuals of the same sex, (2) sexual behavior with people of the same sex, and (3) homosexual self-identification (Michael et al. 1994). This survey found that 4 percent of women and 6 percent of men said that they are sexually attracted to individuals of the same sex, and 4 percent of women and 5 percent of men reported that they had had sexual relations with a same-sex partner after age 18. What these data tell us is that "those who acknowledge homosexual sexual desires may be far more numerous than those who actually act on those desires" (Black et al. 2000, 140).

Prevalence of Homosexuality, Heterosexuality, and Bisexuality

Despite the difficulties inherent in categorizing individuals' sexual orientation, recent data reveal the prevalence of individuals in the United States who identify as lesbian, gay, or bisexual. In a national survey by Michael et al. (1994), fewer than 2 percent of women and 3 percent of the men identified themselves as homosexual or bisexual. Berg and Lein (2006) estimated that 7 percent of males and 4 percent of females were not heterosexual. A 2004 national poll showed that about 5 percent of U.S. high school students identified themselves as lesbian or gay (Curtis 2004). Tao (2008) analyzed U.S. women ages 15 to 44 and found that 1.6 percent and 4 percent, respectively, self-identified as being lesbian and bisexual. Whether women are lesbian or bisexual is relevant to rates of sexually transmitted infections (STIs). Bisexual women were more likely to report having an STI than lesbian women (16 percent to 4.5 percent). In a university sample of 1,319 students, .09 percent, .06 percent, and 1.7 percent reported that they were lesbian, gay male, or bisexual, respectively (Knox and Zusman 2009).

National Data

According to the previously cited research, estimates of the U.S. lesbigay population range from about 2 percent to 7 percent of the U.S. adult population. An easy-to-remember percentage is 5 percent (with a higher percentage of gay men than gay women and a higher percentage of bisexuals than gays), which translates into 15 million gay individuals in the United States (population of over 300 million) and 875,000 *gay college students (of 17.5 million total college students in the United States).*

Prevalence of Same-Sex Couple Households

Although U.S. Census surveys do not ask about sexual orientation or gender identity, same-sex cohabiting couples may identify themselves as "unmarried partners." Those couples in which both partners are men or both are women are considered to be same-sex couples or households for purposes of research. In 2006, there were 800,000 unmarried same-sex couple households (*Statistical Abstract of the United States: 2009.* Table 62).

Carpenter and Gates (2008) analyzed data in California and noted that, although 62 percent of heterosexual couples cohabit, about 40 percent of gay males and about 60 percent of lesbians cohabit. Same-sex couples are more likely to live in metropolitan areas than in rural areas. However, the largest proportional increases in the number of same-sex couples self-reporting in 2000 versus 1990 came in rural, sparsely populated states.

Why are data on the numbers of GLBT individuals and couples in the United States relevant? The primary reason is that census numbers on the prevalence of GLBT individuals and couples can influence laws and policies that affect gay individuals and their families. In anticipation of the 2000 census, the National Gay and Lesbian Task Force Policy Institute and the Institute for Gay and Lesbian Strategic Studies conducted a public education campaign urging people to "out" themselves on the 2000 census. The slogan was, "The more we are counted, the more we count" (Bradford et al. 2002, 3). "The fact that the Census documents the actual presence of same-sex couples in nearly every state legislative and U.S. Congressional district means anti-gay legislators can no longer assert that they have no gay and lesbian constituents" (p. 8).

> *The question is not what family form or marriage arrangement we would prefer in the abstract but how can we help people in a wide variety of committed relationships.*
>
> Stephanie Coontz, family historian

Origins of Sexual-Orientation Diversity

Much of the biomedical and psychological research on sexual orientation attempts to identify one or more "causes" of sexual-orientation diversity. The driving question behind this research is, "Is sexual orientation inborn or is it learned or acquired from environmental influences?" Although a number of factors have been correlated with sexual orientation, including genetics, gender role behavior in childhood, and fraternal birth order, no single theory can explain diversity in sexual orientation.

Beliefs about What "Causes" Homosexuality

Aside from what "causes" homosexuality, social scientists are interested in what people believe about the "causes" of homosexuality. Most gay people believe that homosexuality is an inherited, inborn trait. In a national study of homosexual men, 90 percent reported that they believed that they were born with their homosexual orientation; only 4 percent believed that environmental factors were the sole cause (Lever 1994).

Individuals who believe that homosexuality is genetically determined tend to be more accepting of homosexuality and are more likely to be in favor of equal rights for lesbians and gays (Tyagart 2002). In contrast, "those who believe homosexuals choose their sexual orientation are far less tolerant of gays and lesbians and more likely to feel that homosexuality should be illegal than those who think sexual orientation is not a matter of personal choice" (Rosin and Morin 1999, 8).

Although the terms *sexual preference* and *sexual orientation* are often used interchangeably, the term *sexual orientation* avoids the implication that homosexuality, heterosexuality, and bisexuality are determined. Hence, those who believe that sexual orientation is inborn more often use the term *sexual orientation*, and those who think that individuals choose their sexual orientation use *sexual preference* more often.

Can Homosexuals Change Their Sexual Orientation?

Individuals who believe that homosexual people choose their sexual orientation tend to think that homosexuals can and should change their sexual orientation. Various forms of **reparative therapy** or **conversion therapy** are dedicated to changing homosexuals' sexual orientation. Some religious organizations sponsor "ex-gay ministries," which claim to "cure" homosexuals and transform them into heterosexuals by encouraging them to ask for "forgiveness for their sinful lifestyle," through prayer and other forms of "therapy." Serovich et al. (2008) reviewed twenty-eight empirically based, peer-reviewed articles and found them methodologically problematic, which threatens the validity of interpreting available data on this topic.

Parelli (2007) attended private as well as group therapy sessions to change his sexual orientation from homosexuality to heterosexuality. It did not work. In retrospect, he identified seven reasons for the failure of reparative therapy. In effect, he noted that these therapies focus on outward behavioral change and do not acknowledge the inner yearnings:

> *By my mid-forties, I was experiencing a chronic need for appropriately affectionate male touch. It was so acute I could think of nothing else. Every cell of my body seemed relationally isolated and emotionally starved. Life was so completely and fatally ebbing out of my being that my internal life-saving system kicked in and put out a high-alert call for help. I desperately needed to be held by loving, human, male arms.* (p. 32)

Critics of reparative therapy and ex-gay ministries take a different approach: "It is not gay men and lesbians who need to change . . . but negative attitudes and discrimination against gay people that need to be abolished" (Besen 2000, 7). The National Association for the Research and Therapy of Homosexuality (NARTH) has been influential in moving public opinion from "gays are sick" to "society is judgmental." The American Psychiatric Association, the American Psychological Association, the American Academy of Pediatrics, the American Counseling Association, the National Association of School Psychologists, the National Association of Social Workers, and the American Medical Association agree that homosexuality is not a mental disorder and needs no cure—that efforts to change sexual orientation do not work and may, in fact, be harmful (Human Rights Campaign 2000; Potok 2005). An extensive review of the ex-gay movement concludes, "There is a growing body of evidence that conversion therapy not only does not work, but also can be extremely harmful, resulting in depression, social isolation from family and friends, low self-esteem, internalized homophobia, and even attempted suicide" (Cianciotto and Cahill 2006, 77). According to the American Psychiatric Association, "clinical experience suggests that any person who seeks conversion therapy may be doing so because of social bias that has resulted in internalized homophobia, and that gay men and lesbians who have accepted their sexual orientation are better adjusted than those who have not done so" (quoted by Holthouse 2005, 14).

Close scrutiny of reports of "successful" reparative therapy reveal that (1) many claims come from organizations with an ideological perspective on sexual orientation rather than from unbiased researchers, (2) the treatments and their outcomes are poorly documented, and (3) the length of time that clients are followed after treatment is too short for definitive claims to be made about treatment success (Human Rights Campaign 2000). Indeed, at least thirteen ministries of Exodus International—the largest ex-gay ministry network—have closed because their directors reverted to homosexuality (Fone 2000). Michael Bussy, who helped start Exodus International in 1976, said, "After dealing with hundreds of people, I have not met one who went from gay to straight. Even if you manage to alter someone's sexual behavior, you cannot change their true sexual orientation" (quoted by Holthouse 2005, 14). Michael Bussy worked to help "convert" gay people for three years, until he and another male Exodus employee fell in love and left the organization.

Chapter 8 Same-Sex Couples and Families

Heterosexism, Homonegativity, Homophobia, and Biphobia

When I was in the military they gave me a medal for killing two men and a discharge for loving one.

Epitaph of Leonard P. Matlovich

The United States, along with many other countries throughout the world, is predominantly heterosexist. **Heterosexism** refers to "the institutional and societal reinforcement of heterosexuality as the privileged and powerful norm." Heterosexism is based on the belief that heterosexuality is superior to homosexuality. Of 1,319 undergraduates, 41.5 percent agreed, "It is better to be heterosexual than homosexual" (Knox and Zusman 2009). Heterosexism results in prejudice and discrimination against homosexual and bisexual people. Prejudice refers to negative attitudes, whereas discrimination refers to behavior that denies equality of treatment for individuals or groups. Before reading further, you may wish to complete the Self-Assessment feature on page 250, which assesses behaviors toward individuals perceived to be homosexual.

Homonegativity and Homophobia

The term **homophobia** is commonly used to refer to negative attitudes and emotions toward homosexuality and those who engage in it. Homophobia is not necessarily a clinical phobia (that is, one involving a compelling desire to avoid the feared object despite recognizing that the fear is unreasonable). Other terms that refer to negative attitudes and emotions toward homosexuality include **homonegativity** and **antigay bias**.

International Data

The percentage of residents in various countries who believe that "homosexuality should be accepted by society" include the following: 83 percent in Czech Republic; 69 percent in Canada; 54 percent in Japan; 51 percent in the United States; 33 percent in South Africa; 9 percent in Pakistan; and 1 percent in Kenya (Pew Research Center 2008).

The Sex Information and Education Council of the United States states that "individuals have the right to accept, acknowledge, and live in accordance with their sexual orientation, be they bisexual, heterosexual, gay or lesbian. The legal system should guarantee the civil rights and protection of all people, regardless of sexual orientation" (SIECUS, 2009, retrieved March 23). Nevertheless, negative attitudes toward homosexuality are reflected in the high percentage of the U.S. population who disapprove of homosexuality. According to national surveys by the Gallup Organization, 51 percent of Americans say that homosexuality should be considered an acceptable alternative lifestyle (Saad 2005). Although attitudes toward homosexuality have become more positive, there continues to be more support for same-sex civil unions or domestic partnerships than for same-sex marriage (Avery et al. 2007). In general, individuals who are more likely to have negative attitudes toward homosexuality and to oppose gay rights are those who (1) are men, older, and less educated; (2) attend religious services; (3) live in the South or Midwest; (4) reside in small rural towns; and (5) have had limited contact with someone who is gay or lesbian (Herek 2002; Curtis 2003; Loftus 2001; Page 2003; Mohipp and Morry 2004). Jenkins et al. (2009) found no significant difference between black and white students in reported levels of homophobia in a sample of 551 Midwestern college students.

Negative social meanings associated with homosexuality can affect the self-concepts of LGBT individuals. **Internalized homophobia**—a sense of personal failure and self-hatred among lesbians and gay men resulting from social rejection and stigmatization—has been linked to increased risk for depression, substance abuse and addiction, anxiety, and suicidal thoughts (Bobbe 2002; Gilman et al. 2001).

The Self-Report of Behavior Scale (Revised)

This questionnaire is designed to examine which of the following statements most closely describes your behavior during past encounters with people you thought were homosexuals. Rate each of the following self-statements as honestly as possible by choosing the frequency that best describes your behavior: Never = 1; Rarely = 2; Occasionally = 3; Frequently = 4; Always = 5.

_____ 1. I have spread negative talk about someone because I suspected that the person was gay.

_____ 2. I have participated in playing jokes on someone because I suspected that the person was gay.

_____ 3. I have changed roommates and/or rooms because I suspected my roommate was gay.

_____ 4. I have warned people who I thought were gay and who were a little too friendly with me to keep away from me.

_____ 5. I have attended antigay protests.

_____ 6. I have been rude to someone because I thought that the person was gay.

_____ 7. I have changed seat locations because I suspected the person sitting next to me was gay.

_____ 8. I have had to force myself to keep from hitting someone because the person was gay and very near me.

_____ 9. When someone I thought to be gay has walked toward me as if to start a conversation, I have deliberately changed directions and walked away to avoid the person.

_____ 10. I have stared at a gay person in such a manner as to convey my disapproval of the person being too close to me.

_____ 11. I have been with a group in which one (or more) person(s) yelled insulting comments to a gay person or group of gay people.

_____ 12. I have changed my normal behavior in a restroom because a person I believed to be gay was in there at the same time.

_____ 13. When a gay person has checked me out, I have verbally threatened the person.

_____ 14. I have participated in damaging someone's property because the person was gay.

_____ 15. I have physically hit or pushed someone I thought was gay because the person brushed against me when passing by.

_____ 16. Within the past few months, I have told a joke that made fun of gay people.

_____ 17. I have gotten into a physical fight with a gay person because I thought the person had been making moves on me.

_____ 18. I have refused to work on school and/or work projects with a partner I thought was gay.

_____ 19. I have written graffiti about gay people or homosexuality.

_____ 20. When a gay person has been near me, I have moved away to put more distance between us.

Scoring

The Self-Report of Behavior Scale (SBS-R) is scored by totaling the number of points endorsed on all items, yielding a range from 20 to 100 total points. The higher the score, the more negative the attitudes toward homosexuals.

Comparison Data

Sunita Patel (1989) originally developed the Self-Report of Behavior Scale in her thesis research in her clinical psychology master's program at East Carolina University. College men (from a university campus and from a military base) were the original participants (Patel et al. 1995). The scale was revised by Shartra Sylivant (1992), who used it with a coed high school student population, and by Tristan Roderick (1994), who involved college students to assess its psychometric properties. The scale was found to have high internal consistency. Two factors were identified: a passive avoidance of homosexuals and active or aggressive reactions.

In a study by Roderick et al. (1998), the mean score for 182 college women was 24.76. The mean score for 84 men was significantly higher, at 31.60. A similar-sex difference, although with higher (more negative) scores, was found in Sylivant's high school sample (with a mean of 33.74 for the young women, and 44.40 for the young men).

The following table provides detail for the scores of the college students in Roderick's sample (from a mid-sized state university in the southeast):

	N	Mean	Standard Deviation
Women	182	24.76	7.68
Men	84	31.60	10.36
Total	266	26.91	9.16

Sources

Patel, S. 1989. Homophobia: Personality, emotional, and behavioral correlates. Master's thesis, East Carolina University.

Patel, S., T. E. Long, S. L. McCammon, and K. L. Wuensch. 1995. Personality and emotional correlates of self reported antigay behaviors. *Journal of Interpersonal Violence* 10:354–66.

Roderick, T. 1994. Homonegativity: An analysis of the SBS-R. Master's thesis, East Carolina University.

Roderick, T., S. L. McCammon, T. E. Long, and L. J. Allred. 1998. Behavioral aspects of homonegativity. *Journal of Homosexuality* 36:79–88.

Sylivant, S. 1992. The cognitive, affective, and behavioral components of adolescent homonegativity. Master's thesis, East Carolina University.

The SBS-R is reprinted by the permission of the students and faculty who participated in its development: S. Patel, S. L. McCammon, T. E. Long, L. J. Allred, K. Wuensch, T. Roderick, and S. Sylivant.

Biphobia

Just as the term *homophobia* is used to refer to negative attitudes toward homosexuality, gay men, and lesbians, **biphobia** (also referred to as **binegativity**) refers to a parallel set of negative attitudes toward bisexuality and those identified as bisexual. Although heterosexuals often reject both homosexual- and bisexual-identified individuals, bisexual-identified women and men also face rejection from many homosexual individuals. Thus, bisexuals experience "double discrimination."

Some negative attitudes toward bisexual individuals "are based on the belief that bisexual individuals are really lesbian or gay individuals who are in transition or in denial about their true sexual orientation" (Israel and Mohr 2004, 121). According to this view, bisexual people lack the courage to come out as lesbian or gay, or they are trying to maintain heterosexual privilege. Negative attitudes toward bisexuality are also based on the negative stereotype of bisexuals as incapable of or unwilling to be monogamous. In a review of research on bisexuality, Israel and Mohr (2004) state that, "although bisexual individuals are more likely to value nonmonogamy as an ideal compared to lesbian, gay, and heterosexual individuals, research clearly indicates that some bisexual-identified individuals prefer monogamous relationships" (p. 122). Given the cultural bias against being gay, gay individuals must be careful about "coming out" (see the following Personal Choices section).

> *In itself, homosexuality is as limiting as heterosexuality: the ideal should be to be capable of loving a woman or a man; either, a human being, without feeling fear, restraint, or obligation.*
>
> Simone de Beauvoir, French writer and feminist, 1908–1986

PERSONAL CHOICES

Are the Benefits of "Coming Out" Worth the Risks?

In a society where heterosexuality is expected and considered the norm, heterosexuals do not have to choose whether or not to tell others that they are heterosexual. However, decisions about **"coming out,"** or being open and honest about one's sexual orientation and identity (particularly to one's parents—Heatherington and Lavner 2008), are some of the most difficult and important choices that gay, lesbian, and bisexual individuals face. Choices about coming out include whether to come out to others, who to come out to, and when and how to come out.

Risks of Coming Out

Whether GLBT individuals come out is influenced by the degree to which they are tired of hiding their sexual orientation, the degree to which they feel more "honest" about being open, their assessment of the risks of coming out, and their prediction of how others will respond. Some of the risks involved in coming out include disapproval and rejection by parents and other family members; harassment and discrimination at school; discrimination and harassment in the workplace; and hate crime victimization.

1. *Parental and family members' reactions.* When GLBT individuals come out to their parents, parental reactions range from "I already knew you were gay and I'm glad that you feel ready to be open with me about it" to "get out of this house, you are no longer welcome here." Mary Cheney reported that, when she told her father, former Vice President Dick Cheney, that she is a lesbian, his response was, "You're my daughter and I love you and I just want you to be happy" (quoted in Walsh 2006, 27). When Reverend Mel White—a closeted gay Christian man who was nearly driven to suicide after two decades of struggling to save his marriage and his soul with "reparative therapies"—finally came out to his mother, her response was, "I'd rather see you at the bottom of that swimming pool, drowned, than to hear this" (White 2005, 28).

According to *The Resource Guide to Coming Out* (Human Rights Campaign 2004), "many parents are shocked when their children say they are gay, lesbian, or bisexual. Some parents react in ways that hurt. Some cry. Some get angry. Some ask where they went wrong as a parent. Some call it a sin. Some insist it's a phase. Others try to send their child to counselors or therapists who attempt to change gay people into heterosexuals . . ." (p. 24).

I know my roommate is gay. I just wish he would tell me. It would make it easier for me to come out to him.

University student

Because black people are more likely than white people to view homosexual relations as "always wrong," African Americans who are gay or lesbian are more likely to face disapproval from their families (and straight friends) than are white lesbians and gays (Lewis 2003). The result is that African Americans are more likely to stay closeted—not let their parents know of their homosexuality (Grov et al. 2006).

The Resource Guide notes, however, that "for many parents it's very hard to completely reject their children" and that it takes time for parents to adjust—sometimes months, sometimes years. In some families with a GLBT member, the "gay issue" is not openly discussed, even though family members may know or suspect that a loved one is gay, lesbian, or bisexual. One gay male student explained, "My parents know I live with my 'friend' Christopher, and they have invited Christopher to our family holiday gatherings and family vacations. I am sure my parents know that I'm gay. . . . We just don't talk about it" (personal communication).

Parents and other family members can learn more about homosexuality from the local chapter of Parents, Families, and Friends of Lesbians and Gays (PFLAG) and from books and online resources, such as those found at Human Rights Campaign's National Coming Out Project (http://www.hrc.org/).

2. *Harassment and discrimination at school.* In a national survey of students aged 13 to 18 years, 65 percent of LGBT students reported that they had been verbally harassed, 16 percent physically harassed, and 8 percent physically assaulted because of their sexual orientation (Harris Interactive and GLSEN 2005). "Students who openly identify as lesbian, gay, bisexual, and transgender (LGBT) have a more acute problem with being harassed at school" (p. 4). This survey found that LGBT students are over three times more likely than non-LGBT students to report that they feel unsafe at school (20 percent versus 6 percent). Only eight states and the District of Columbia have statewide policies that prohibit antigay harassment in public schools (Snorton 2005).

A study of GLBT college students, faculty, and staff or administrators found that 51 percent had concealed their sexual orientation or gender identity to avoid intimidation (Rankin 2003). The same study found that in the previous year 36 percent of undergraduates experienced harassment in the form of derogatory remarks, verbal threats, antigay graffiti, threats of physical violence, denial of services, and physical assault.

3. *Discrimination and harassment at the workplace.* The 2005 Workplace Fairness Survey found that 39 percent of lesbian and gay employees reported experiencing some form of discrimination or harassment in the workplace (Lambda Legal and Deloitte Financial Advisory Services, LLP 2006). Although 88 percent of U.S. adults support equal employment rights for gays and lesbians, firing, declining to hire or promote, or otherwise discriminating against an employee because of sexual orientation was legal in thirty-three states as of March 2006 (National Gay and Lesbian Task Force 2006; Saad 2005).

4. *Hate crime victimization.* Another risk of coming out is that of being victimized by antigay hate crimes—crimes against individuals or their property that are based on bias against the victim because of their perceived sexual orientation. Such crimes include verbal threats and intimidation, vandalism, sexual assault and rape, physical assault, and murder.

Benefits of Coming Out

Given the risks of coming out, some GBLT individuals (not surprisingly) never come out, live a life of repressed feelings, and deny who they are to others and (sometimes) to themselves. However, according to the Human Rights Campaign, "most people come out because, sooner or later, they can't stand hiding who they are any more. Once they've come out, most people acknowledge that it feels much better to be open and honest than to conceal such an integral part of themselves" (2004, 16). Political gay activist Harvey Milk emphasized the importance of coming out.

In addition to the benefits for individuals who choose to come out, there are also benefits for the entire GLBT population. Research has found that, in general, heterosexuals have more positive attitudes toward gays and lesbians if they have had prior contact with or know someone who is gay (Mohipp and Morry 2004). One woman describes how her brother's coming out changed her views on homosexuality (Yvonne 2004):

> I was raised in a devout born-again Christian family . . . to believe that homosexuality was evil and a perversion. When I was growing up, I used to wonder if any of the kids at my school could be gay. I couldn't imagine it could be so. As it happens, there was a gay individual even closer than I imagined. My brother Tommy came out of the closet in the early 1990s. After he came out, I had to confront my own denial about the fact that, in my heart of hearts, I had always known that Tommy was gay.
>
> Over the years, his partner Rod has come to be a loved and cherished member of our family, and we have all had to confront the prejudices and stereotypes we have held onto for so long about sexual orientation. It seems to me that coming out of the closet is the greatest weapon that gays and lesbians have. If my own brother had never come out, my family would never have been forced to confront the deep-seated prejudices we were raised with. . . . I am still a Christian, but my husband (who also has a gay brother) and I attend a church that truly puts the teachings of Christ into practice—teachings about love, tolerance and inclusivity. As a Christian who grew up with a gay family member, I know that the propaganda put forth by the religious right on this issue is founded in fear, hatred, and prejudice. None of these are values taught by Jesus!

Cheryl Jacques, a Massachusetts state senator who came out publicly in the *Boston Globe*, recognizes that coming out is a risk. But she suggests the following:

> Coming out is a risk worth taking because it is one of the most powerful things any of us can do. I've yet to meet anyone who regretted the decision to live life truthfully. . . . That's why while coming out may be just one step in the life of a gay, lesbian, bisexual or transgender person, it contributes to a giant leap for all GLBT people. (Human Rights Campaign 2004, 4)

Gay, Lesbian, Bisexual, and Mixed-Orientation Relationships

Research suggests that gay and lesbian couples tend to be more similar than different from heterosexual couples (Kurdek 2005; 2006). However, there are some unique aspects of intimate relationships involving gay, lesbian, and bisexual individuals. In this section, we note the similarities as well as differences between heterosexual, gay male, and lesbian relationships in regard to relationship satisfaction, conflict and conflict resolution, and monogamy and sexuality. We also look at relationship issues involving bisexual individuals and mixed-orientation couples.

Relationship Satisfaction

For both heterosexual and LGBT partners, relationship satisfaction tends to be high in the beginning of the relationship and decreases over time. In a review of literature on lesbian and gay couples, Kurdek (1994) concluded, "The most striking finding regarding the factors linked to relationship satisfaction is that

One of the most visible lesbian couples in America is that of Ellen DeGeneres and her partner, Portia de Rossi.

Mark Savage/Corbis

they seem to be the same for lesbian couples, gay couples, and heterosexual couples" (p. 251). These factors include having equal power and control, being emotionally expressive, perceiving many attractions and few alternatives to the relationship, placing a high value on attachment, and sharing decision making. Kurdek (2008) compared relationship quality of cohabitants over a ten-year period of both partners from 95 lesbian, 92 gay male, and 226 heterosexual couples living without children, and both partners from 312 heterosexual couples living with children. Lesbian couples showed the highest levels of relationship quality averaged over all assessments.

Researchers who studied relationship quality among same-sex couples noted that, "in trying to create satisfying and long-lasting intimate relationships, LGBT individuals face all of the same challenges faced by heterosexual couples, as well as a number of distinctive concerns" (Otis et al. 2006, 86). These concerns include if, when, and how to disclose their relationships to others and how to develop healthy intimate relationships in the absence of same-sex relationship models.

In one review of research on gay and lesbian relationships, we concluded that the main difference between heterosexual and nonheterosexual relationships is that, "Whereas heterosexuals enjoy many social and institutional supports for their relationships, gay and lesbian couples are the object of prejudice and discrimination" (Peplau et al. 1996, 268). Both gay male and lesbian couples must cope with the stress created by antigay prejudice and discrimination and by "internalized homophobia" or negative self-image and low self-esteem due to being a member of a stigmatized group. Not surprisingly, higher levels of such stress are associated with lower reported levels of relationship quality among LGBT couples (Otis et al. 2006).

Despite the stresses and lack of social and institutional support LGBT individuals experience, gay men and lesbians experience relationship satisfaction at a level that is at least equal to that reported by married heterosexual spouses (Kurdek 2005). Partners of the same sex enjoy the comfort of having a shared gender perspective, which is often accompanied by a sense of equality in the relationship. For example, contrary to stereotypical beliefs, same-sex couples (male or female) typically do not assign "husband" and "wife" roles in the division of household labor; as well, they are more likely than heterosexual couples to achieve a fair distribution of household labor and at the same time accommodate the different interests, abilities, and work schedules of each partner (Kurdek 2005). In contrast, division of household labor among heterosexual couples tends to be unequal, with wives doing the majority of such tasks.

Same-sex relationships are not without abuse. Bartholomew et al. 2008 studied violence in a random sample of 284 gay and bisexual men and found that almost all reported psychological abuse, more than a third reported physical abuse, and 10 percent reported being forced to have sex. Abuse in gay relationships is less likely to be reported to the police because some gays do not want to be "outed."

What if My Partner Is Attracted to Someone of the Same Sex?

Earlier we discussed the "what if one discovers an attraction to a same-sex individual?" Although rare, it may also happen to one's partner and the same information applies—sexuality is fluid, emotional and physical attraction occurs, and the factors that determine what a person will do are determined by the strength of the attraction, the imperative to "be one's self," and the social context one lives in. People make different choices in deciding what to do. Although some will develop a dual life, others will suppress their orientation, and still others will alter their lifestyles from straight to gay. An example of the latter is a female who had been involved in an emotional and sexual relationship with a male but found herself attracted to a woman at a summer camp. She noted that the strength of her feelings were beyond what she could deny. She told her boyfriend who responded, "we can work this out," which meant that he wanted her to "come to her senses and give up this gay nonsense." She did not, broke with the boyfriend, and is now involved with her girlfriend.

Conflict and Conflict Resolution

All couples experience conflict in their relationships, and gay and lesbian couples tend to disagree about the same issues that heterosexual couples argue about. In one study, partners from same-sex and heterosexual couples identified the same sources of most conflict in their relationships: finances, affection, sex, being overly critical, driving style, and household tasks (Kurdek 2004).

However, same-sex couples and heterosexual couples tend to differ in how they resolve conflict. In a study in which researchers videotaped gay, lesbian, and heterosexual couples discussing problems in their relationships, gay and lesbian partners began their discussions more positively and maintained a more positive tone throughout the discussion than did partners in heterosexual marriages (Gottman et al. 2003). Other research has found that, compared with heterosexual married spouses, same-sex partners resolve conflict more positively, argue more effectively, and are more likely to suggest possible solutions and compromises (Kurdek 2004). One explanation for the more positive conflict resolution among same-sex couples is that they value equality more and are more likely to have equal power and status in the relationship than are heterosexual couples (Gottman et al. 2003).

Monogamy and Sexuality

Like many heterosexual women, most gay women value stable, monogamous relationships that are emotionally as well as sexually satisfying. Gay and heterosexual women in U.S. society are taught that sexual expression should occur in the context of emotional or romantic involvement.

A common stereotype of gay men is that they prefer casual sexual relationships with multiple partners versus monogamous long-term relationships. However, although most gay men report having more casual sex than heterosexual men (Mathy 2007), most gay men prefer long-term relationships, and sex outside of the primary relationship is usually infrequent and not emotionally involving (Green et al. 1996).

The degree to which gay males engage in casual sexual relationships is better explained by the fact that they are male than by the fact that they are gay. In this regard, gay and straight men have a lot in common: they both tend to have fewer barriers to engaging in casual sex than do women (heterosexual or lesbian). One way that gay men meet partners is through the Internet. Ogilvie et al. (2008) surveyed men who have sex with men (MSM) who found partners using the Internet; he noted that they were more likely to have had ten sexual partners in the last year and to agree with the statement, "I think most guys in relationships have condom-free sex."

Such nonuse of condoms results in the high rate of human immunodeficiency virus (HIV) infection and acquired immunodeficiency syndrome (AIDS). Although most worldwide HIV infections occur through heterosexual transmission, male-to-male sexual contact is the most common mode of HIV transmission in the United States (Centers for Disease Control and Prevention 2005). Women who have sex exclusively with other women have a much lower rate of HIV infection than do men (both gay and straight) and women who have sex with men. Many gay men have lost a love partner to HIV infection or AIDS; some have experienced multiple losses. Those still in relationships with partners who are HIV-positive experience profound changes, such as developing a sense of urgency to "speed up" their relationship because they may not have much time left together (Palmer and Bor 2001).

Relationships of Bisexuals

Individuals who identify as bisexual have the ability to form intimate relationships with both sexes. However, research has found that the majority of bisexual women and men tend toward primary relationships with the other sex (McLean 2004). Contrary to the common myth that bisexuals are, by definition, nonmonogamous, some bisexuals prefer monogamous relationships (especially in light of the widespread concern about HIV). In another study of sixty bisexual women and men, 25 percent of the men and 35 percent of the women were in exclusive relationships; 60 percent of the men and 53 percent of the women were in "open" relationships in which both partners agreed to allow each other to have sexual and or emotional relationships with others, often under specific conditions or rules about how this would occur (McLean 2004). In these "open" relationships, nonmonogamy was not the same as infidelity, and the former did not imply dishonesty. The researcher concluded:

> *Despite the stereotypes that claim that bisexuals are deceitful, unfaithful, and untrustworthy in relationships, most of the bisexual men and women I interviewed demonstrated a significant commitment to the principles of trust, honesty, and communication in their intimate relationships and made considerable effort to ensure both theirs and their partner's needs and desires were catered for within the relationship.* (McLean 2004, 96)

Monogamous bisexual women and men find that their erotic attractions can be satisfied through fantasy and their affectional needs through nonsexual friendships (Paul 1996). Even in a monogamous relationship, "the partner of a bisexual person may feel that a bisexual person's decision to continue to identify as bisexual . . . is somehow a withholding of full commitment to the relationship. The bisexual person may be perceived as holding onto the possibility of other relationships by maintaining a bisexual identity and, therefore, not fully committed to the relationship" (Ochs 1996, 234). However, this perception overlooks the fact that one's identity is separate from one's choices about relationship involvement or monogamy. Ochs notes that "a heterosexual's ability to establish and maintain a committed relationship with one person is not assumed to falter, even though the person retains a sexual identity as 'heterosexual' and may even admit to feeling attractions to other people despite her or his committed status" (p. 234).

Mixed-Orientation Relationships

Mixed-orientation couples are those in which one partner is heterosexual and the other partner is gay, lesbian, or bisexual. Up to 2 million gay, lesbian, or bisexual people in the United States have been in heterosexual marriages at some point (Buxton 2004). Some lesbigay individuals do not develop same-sex attractions and feelings until after they have been married. Others deny, hide, or repress their same-sex desires.

In a study of twenty gay or bisexual men who had disclosed their sexual orientation to their wives, most of the men did not intentionally mislead or deceive their future wives with regard to their sexuality. Rather, they did not fully grasp their feelings toward men, although they had a vague sense of their same-sex attraction (Pearcey 2004). The majority of the men in this study (14 of 20) attempted to stay married after disclosure of their sexual orientation to their wives, and nearly half (9 of 20) stayed married for at least three years.

Although gay and lesbian spouses in heterosexual marriages are not sexually attracted to their spouses, they may nevertheless love them. However, that is little consolation to spouses, who upon learning that their husband or wife is gay, lesbian, or bisexual, often react with shock, disbelief, and anger. The Straight Spouse Network (http://www.ssnetwk.org) provides support to heterosexual spouses or partners, current or former, of GLBT mates.

Legal Recognition and Support of Same-Sex Couples and Families

As current divorce rates of heterosexuals suggest (4 in 10 marriages end in divorce), maintaining long-term relationships is challenging. However, the challenge is even greater for same-sex couples who lack the many social supports and legal benefits of marriage. A leading researcher and scholar on LGBT issues noted, "perhaps what is most impressive about gay and lesbian couples is . . . that they manage to endure without the benefits of institutionalized supports" (Kurdek 2005, 253). In this section, we discuss laws and policies designed to provide institutionalized support for same-sex couples and families.

Decriminalization of Sodomy

In the United States, a 2003 Supreme Court decision in *Lawrence v. Texas* invalidated state laws that criminalized **sodomy**—oral and anal sexual acts. The ruling, which found that sodomy laws were discriminatory and unconstitutional, removed the stigma and criminal branding that sodomy laws have long placed on GLBT individuals. Prior to this historic ruling, sodomy was illegal in thirteen states. Sodomy laws, which carried penalties ranging from a $200 fine to twenty years of imprisonment, were usually not used against heterosexuals but were used primarily against gay men and lesbians. Same-sex sexual behavior is still considered a criminal act in many countries throughout the world.

International Data

In more than eighty countries, sexual activity between consenting adults of the same sex is illegal; in nine countries, individuals found guilty of engaging in same-sex sexual behavior may receive the death penalty (International Gay and Lesbian Human Rights Commission 2003). In China, there is enormous pressure for the male to marry and to produce children. The result is that gay individuals live in loveless relationships for the sake of family (Johnson 2007).

Registered Partnerships, Civil Unions, and Domestic Partnerships

Aside from same-sex marriage (which we discuss later), other forms of legal recognition of same-sex couples exist in a number of countries throughout the world at the national, state, and/or local level. In addition, some workplaces recognize same-sex couples for the purposes of employee benefits. Legal recognition of same-sex couples, also referred to as registered partnerships, **civil unions**, or **domestic partnerships**, conveys most but not all the rights and responsibilities of marriage. Carpenter and Gates (2008) analyzed data in California and noted that half of partnered lesbians are officially registered.

International Data

Federally recognized registered partnerships, civil unions, or domestic partnerships for same-sex couples are available in Croatia, Denmark, Finland, France, Germany, Iceland, Israel, New Zealand, Norway, Portugal, Slovenia, Sweden, Switzerland, and the United Kingdom (Human Rights Campaign, n.d.). A number of other countries recognize same-sex couples for the purposes of immigration policy.

State and Local Legal Recognition of Same-Sex Couples   There is no federal recognition of same-sex couples in the United States. However, a number of U.S. states allow same-sex couples legal status that entitles them to many of the same rights and responsibilities as married opposite-sex couples (see Table 8.1). For example, in New Jersey, same-sex couples can apply for a civil union license, which entitles them to all the rights and responsibilities available under state law to married couples. Unlike marriage for heterosexual couples, the rights of partners in same-sex civil unions are not recognized by U.S. federal law, so they do not have the federal protections that go along with civil marriage, and their legal status is not recognized in other states. (Vermont recognized same sex marriage in 2009.)

Three states—Hawaii, California, and New Jersey—have enacted laws that provide varying degrees of protection for domestic partners. The rights and responsibilities granted to domestic partners vary from place to place but may include coverage under a partner's health and pension plan, rights of inheritance

Table 8.1   States that Recognize Same-Sex Relationships

State	Same-Sex Relationship Recognition
California	California has a domestic partner registry that confers almost all the state-level spousal rights and responsibilities to registered domestic partners.
Connecticut	Connecticut grants same-sex marriage licenses to residents.
Hawaii	Hawaii offers "reciprocal beneficiary" status to same-sex registered couples
Iowa	Iowa grants same-sex marriage licenses to residents.
Maine	Maine grants same-sex marriage licenses to residents.
Massachusetts	Massachusetts grants same-sex marriage licenses only to residents. The license is not valid if the couple moves to another state.
New Hampshire	New Hampshire grants same-sex marriage licenses to residents.
New Jersey	New Jersey offers same-sex civil unions.
New York	Recognizes same-sex marriages from couples legally married outside the United States.
Vermont	Vermont grants same-sex marriage licenses to residents.

Source: Human Rights Campaign (2006), updated in 2009; Luther (2006).

and community property, tax benefits, access to housing for married students, child custody and child and spousal support obligations, and mutual responsibility for debts. The California law (the Domestic Partnership Rights and Responsibilities Act of 2003) provides the broadest array of protections, including eligibility for family leave, other employment and health benefits, the right to sue for wrongful death of partner or inherit from partner as next of kin, and access to the stepparent adoption process (National Gay and Lesbian Task Force 2005–2006). Ten states and the District of Columbia, as well as several dozen U.S. municipalities, offer domestic partner benefits to the same-sex partners of public employees.

Recognition of Same-Sex Couples in the Workplace In 1991, the Lotus Development Corporation became the first major American firm to extend domestic partner recognition to gay and lesbian employees. By the end of 2004, the Human Rights Campaign (2005) identified 8,250 employers that provided domestic partner health insurance benefits to their employees—an increase of 13 percent from the previous year. The percentage of Fortune 500 companies that offered health benefits to employees' domestic partners nearly doubled from 25 percent in 2000 to 49 percent in March 2006 (Luther 2006). However, even when companies offer domestic partner benefits to same-sex partners of employees, these benefits are usually taxed as income by the federal government, whereas spousal benefits are not.

International Data

In 2001, the Netherlands became the first country in the world to offer full legal marriage to same-sex couples. Same-sex married couples and opposite-sex married couples in the Netherlands are treated identically, with two exceptions. Unlike other-sex marriages, same-sex couples married in the Netherlands are unlikely to have their marriages recognized as fully legal abroad. Regarding children, parental rights will not automatically be granted to the nonbiological spouse in gay couples. To become a fully legal parent, the spouse of the biological parent must adopt the child. In 2003, Belgium passed a law allowing same-sex marriages but disallowing any adoptions. In June 2005, Spain became the third country to legalize same-sex marriage; shortly thereafter, Canada became the fourth, and South Africa became the fifth.

Anyone who wishes to examine the 20 years of peer-reviewed studies on the emotional, cognitive and behavioral outcomes of children of gay and lesbian parents will find not one shred of evidence that children are harmed by their parents' sexual orientation.

Carol Trust, executive director, National Association of Social Workers

**"Same-sex marriage is nothing new.
We've been having the same sex for 25 years."**

Same-Sex Marriage

In 2009, Iowa, Vermont, Maine, and New Hampshire approved gay marriage (following Connecticut in 2008). In 2004, Massachusetts became the first U.S. state to offer civil marriage licenses to same-sex couples. In the first year after the court order went into effect, more than 5,000 same-sex couples were married in Massachusetts (Johnston 2005). Porche and Purvin (2008) interviewed four lesbian and five gay male same-sex couples in Massachusetts who had been together twenty years or more. Seven of the nine couples married soon after same-sex marriage was enacted in Massachusetts. The two who did not marry reaffirmed and maintained their commitment. These data emphasize the value these couples placed on having their relationship sanctioned by the state and culture. (However, unlike marriages between a man and a woman, the same-sex marriages in Massachusetts are not recognized in other states, nor does the federal government recognize them.)

Attorney Robert Zaleski (2007) coined the term **garriage.** "The 'g' is borrowed from the word gay and connotes the same-sex status of the committed couple. And let the new verb be 'garry,' which would be conjugated in identical fashion with the verb 'marry,' thereby enabling these words to be used interchangeably in conversation." Zaleski also emphasized that the word *garriage* allows heterosexual couples to maintain their uniqueness as it does to gay couples.

Anti-Gay Marriage Legislation   In a national survey, 32 percent of U.S. adults support gay marriage, whereas 59 percent are opposed (Pew Research Center 2008). In a national study of first year freshmen in colleges and universities throughout the United States, 72.4% were in favor of same sex marriage (Pryor et al. 2008). Where disapproval exists, the primary reason is morality. Gay marriage is viewed as "immoral, a sin, against the Bible." However, support for gay marriage varies by age; about half of young adults (18 to 29) in the same survey support gay marriage. A higher percentage of U.S. adults (41 percent) are in favor of equal legal rights for gay relationships (Pew Research Center 2008).

In 1996, Congress passed and former President Clinton signed the **Defense of Marriage Act** (DOMA), which states that marriage is a "legal union between one man and one woman" and denies federal recognition of same-sex marriage. In effect, this law allows states to either recognize or not recognize same-sex marriages performed in other states. As of March 2006, thirty-six states have banned gay marriage either through statute or a state constitutional amendment, and seventeen states have passed broader antigay family measures that ban other forms of partner recognition in addition to marriage, such as domestic partnerships and civil unions. These broader measures, known as "Super DOMAs," potentially endanger employer-provided domestic partner benefits, joint and second-parent adoptions, health care decision-making proxies, or any policy or document that recognizes the existence of a same-sex partnership (Cahill and Slater 2004). Some of these "Super DOMAs" ban partner recognition for unmarried heterosexual couples as well.

At the federal level, there are efforts to amend the U.S. Constitution to define marriage as being between a man and a woman. The Federal Marriage Amendment did not pass in 2004 in the Senate or the House, but supporters vowed to continue the fight. The Federal Marriage Amendment was reintroduced and voted on in 2006, and although it garnered more support than in 2004, it failed to reach the two-thirds majority vote necessary for proposal as an amendment. If it had passed, the constitutional amendment would have denied marriage and likely civil union and domestic partnership rights to same-sex couples (LAWbriefs 2005). Such an amendment would also hurt the children in same-sex couple families. Dr. Kathleen Moltz, an assistant professor at Wayne State University School of Medicine, testified against the passage of an antigay constitutional amendment before a United States Senate Judiciary Committee, expressing her fears about how such an amendment would affect her family:

> *I don't know what harm . . . a constitutional amendment might cause. I fear that families like mine, with young children, will lose health benefits; will be denied common decencies like hospital visitation when tragedy strikes; will lack the ability to provide support for one another in old age. I fear that my loving, innocent children will face hatred and insults implicitly sanctioned by a law that brands their family as unequal. I know that these sweet children have already been shunned and excluded by people claiming to represent values of decency and compassion. I also know what such an amendment will not do. It will not help couples who are struggling to stay married. It will not assist any impoverished families struggling to make ends meet or to obtain health care for sick children. It will not keep children with their parents when their parents see divorce as their only option. It will not help any single American citizen to live life with more decency, compassion or morality.* (Moltz 2005)

Arguments in Favor of Same-Sex Marriage   Advocates of same-sex marriage argue that banning or refusing to recognize same-sex marriages granted in other states is a violation of civil rights that denies same-sex couples the many legal and financial benefits that are granted to heterosexual married couples. Rights and benefits that married spouses have include the following:

- The right to inherit from a spouse who dies without a will;
- No inheritance taxes between spouses;
- The right to make crucial medical decisions for a partner and to take care of a seriously ill partner or parent of a partner under current provisions in the federal Family and Medical Leave Act;
- Social Security survivor benefits; and
- Health insurance coverage under a spouse's insurance plan.

Other rights bestowed on married (or once-married) partners include assumption of a spouse's pension, bereavement leave, burial determination, domestic violence protection, reduced-rate memberships, divorce protections (such as equitable division of assets and visitation of partner's children), automatic housing lease transfer, and immunity from testifying against a spouse. As noted earlier, same-sex couples are taxed on employer-provided insurance benefits for domestic partners, whereas married spouses receive those benefits tax-free. Finally, unlike seventeen other countries that recognize same-sex couples for immigration purposes, the United States does not recognize same-sex couples in granting immigration status because such couples are not considered "spouses." Another argument for same-sex marriage is that it would promote relationship stability among gay and lesbian couples. "To the extent that marriage provides status, institutional support, and legitimacy, gay and lesbian couples, if allowed to marry, would likely experience greater relationship stability" (Amato 2004, 963). Indeed, same-sex relationships, like cohabitation relationships, end at a higher rate than marriage relationships (Wagner 2006).

Recognized marriage, argues Amato, would be beneficial to the children of same-sex parents. Without legal recognition of same-sex families, children living in gay- and lesbian-headed households are denied a range of securities that protect children of heterosexual married couples. These include the right to get health insurance coverage and Social Security survivor benefits from a nonbiological parent. In some cases, children in same-sex households lack the automatic right to continue living with their nonbiological parent should their biological mother or father die (Tobias and Cahill 2003). It is ironic that the same pro-marriage groups that stress that children are better off in married-couple families disregard the benefits of same-sex marriage to children.

Opponents of gay marriage sometimes suggest that gay marriage leads to declining marriage rates, increased divorce rates, and increased nonmarital births. However, data in Scandinavia reflects that these trends were in place ten years before Scandinavian adopted registered partnership laws, liberalized alternatives to marriage (such as cohabitation), and expanded exit options (such as no-fault divorce) (Pinello 2008).

Finally, there are religious-based arguments in support of same-sex marriage. Although many religious leaders teach that homosexuality is sinful and prohibited by God, some religious groups, such as the Quakers and the United Church of Christ (UCC), accept homosexuality, and other groups have made reforms toward increased acceptance of lesbians and gays. In 2005, the UCC became the largest Christian denomination to endorse same-sex marriages. In a sermon titled, "The Christian Case for Gay Marriage," Jack McKinney (2004) interprets Luke 4: "Jesus is saying that one of the most fundamental religious tasks is to stand with those who have been excluded and marginalized. . . . [Jesus] is determined to stand with them, to name them beloved of God, and to dedicate his life to seeing them empowered." McKinney goes on to ask, "Since when has it been immoral for two people to commit themselves to a relationship of mutual love and caring? No, the true immorality around gay marriage rests with the heterosexual majority that denies gays and lesbians more than 1,000 federal rights that come with marriage."

Arguments Against Same-Sex Marriage   Whereas advocates of same-sex marriage argue that they will not be regarded as legitimate families by the larger society so long as same-sex couples cannot be legally married, opponents do not want to legitimize same-sex couples and families. Opponents of same-sex marriage who view homosexuality as unnatural, sick, and/or immoral do not want their children to view homosexuality as socially acceptable.

Opponents of same-sex marriage commonly argue that such marriages would subvert the stability and integrity of the heterosexual family. However, Sullivan (1997) suggests that homosexuals are already part of heterosexual families:

> [Homosexuals] are sons and daughters, brothers and sisters, even mothers and fathers, of heterosexuals. The distinction between "families" and "homosexuals" is, to begin with, empirically false; and the stability of existing families is closely linked to how homosexuals are treated within them. (p. 147)

Many opponents of same-sex marriage base their opposition on their religious views. In a Pew Research Center national poll, the majority of Catholics and Protestants opposed legalizing same-sex marriage, whereas the majority of secular respondents favored it (Green 2004). However, churches have the right to deny marriage for gay people in their congregations. Legal marriage is a contract between the spouses and the state; marriage is a civil option that does not require religious sanctioning.

In previous years, opponents of gay marriage have pointed to public opinion polls that suggested that the majority of Americans are against same-sex marriage. However, public opposition to same-sex marriage is decreasing. We previously noted that a 2008 Pew Research Center national poll found that 59 percent of U.S. adults oppose legalizing gay marriage, down from 63 percent in 2004 (Pew Research Center 2006). We also noted that support for gay marriage is higher among young adults.

GLBT Parenting Issues

National Data

Nearly one-quarter of all same-gender couples are raising children; 34.3 percent of lesbian couples are raising children, and 22.3 percent of gay male couples are raising children (compared with 45.6 percent of married heterosexual and 43.1 *percent* of unmarried heterosexual couples raising children) (Pawelski et al., 2006). Over half (54 percent) of U.S. adults feel that same-sex parents can be good parents (Pew Research Center 2008).

Of the more than 600,000 same-sex-couple households identified in the 2000 census, 162,000 had one or more children living in the household. This is a low estimate of children who have gay or lesbian parents, as it does not count children in same-sex households who did not identify their relationship in the census, those headed by gay or lesbian single parents, or those whose gay parent does not have physical custody but is still actively involved in the child's life.

National Data

Estimates of the number of U.S. children with gay or lesbian parents range from 1 to 14 million (Howard 2006).

Many gay and lesbian individuals and couples have children from prior heterosexual relationships or marriages. Up to 2 million gay, lesbian, or bisexual people in the United States have been in heterosexual marriages at some point (Buxton 2005). Some of these individuals married as a "cover" for their homosexuality; others discovered their interest in same-sex relationships after they married. Children with mixed-orientation parents may be raised by a gay or lesbian parent, a gay or lesbian stepparent, a heterosexual parent, and a heterosexual stepparent.

A gay or lesbian individual or couple may have children through the use of assisted reproductive technology, including donor insemination, in vitro fertilization, and surrogate mothers. Others adopt or become foster parents.

Less commonly, some gay fathers are part of an emergent family form known as the hetero-gay family. In a hetero-gay family, a heterosexual mother and gay father conceive and raise a child together but reside separately.

Antigay views concerning gay parenting include the belief that homosexual individuals are unfit to be parents and that children of lesbians and gays will not develop normally and/or that they will become homosexual. As the following section suggests, research findings paint a more positive picture of the development and well-being of children with gay or lesbian parents.

Development and Well-Being of Children with Gay or Lesbian Parents

A growing body of research on gay and lesbian parenting supports the conclusion that children of gay and lesbian parents are just as likely to flourish as are children of heterosexual parents. Crowl et al. (2008) reviewed nineteen studies on the developmental outcomes and quality of parent-child relationships among children raised by gay and lesbian parents. As previously stated, results confirmed previous studies that children raised by same-sex parents fare equally well to children raised by heterosexual parents. For example, one study compared a national sample of forty-four adolescents

Diversity in the United States

Female same-sex couples in which both partners are Hispanic are raising children at over twice the rate of white, non-Hispanic female same-sex couples (66 percent versus 32 percent). Male same-sex couples in which both partners are Hispanic are raising children at more than three times the rate of white, non-Hispanic male couples (58 percent versus 19 percent) (Cianciotto 2005).

The data on gay parents reveals that gay parents provide a healthy, nurturing, and loving context in which children thrive.

AFP/Getty Images

parented by same-sex couples -with forty-four adolescents parented by opposite-sex couples (Wainwright et al. 2004). On an array of assessments, the study showed that the personal, family, and school adjustment of adolescents living with same-sex parents did not differ from that of adolescents living with opposite-sex parents. Self-esteem, depressive symptoms and anxiety, academic achievement, trouble in school, quality of family relationships, and romantic relationships were similar in the two groups of adolescents. Regardless of family type, adolescents were more likely to show positive adjustment when they perceived more caring from adults and when parents described having close relationships with them. Thus, the qualities of adolescent-parent relationships rather than the sexual orientation of the parents were significantly associated with adolescent adjustment.

In another study, researchers examined the quality of parent-child relationships and the socioemotional and gender development of a sample of 7-year-old children with lesbian parents, compared with 7-year-olds from two-parent heterosexual families and with single heterosexual mothers (Golombok et al. 2003). No significant differences between lesbian mothers and heterosexual mothers were found for most of the parenting variables assessed, although lesbian mothers reported smacking their children less and playing more frequently with their children than did heterosexual mothers. No significant differences were found in psychiatric disorders or gender development of the children in lesbian families versus heterosexual families. The findings also suggest that having two parents is associated with more positive outcomes for children's psychological well-being, but the gender of the parents is not relevant.

In addition, the American Psychological Association (2004) noted that "results of research suggest that lesbian and gay parents are as likely as heterosexual parents to provide supportive and healthy environments for their children" and that "the adjustment, development, and psychological well-being of children [are] unrelated to parental sexual orientation and that the children of lesbian and gay parents are as likely as those of heterosexual parents to flourish." Indeed, Pro-Family Pediatricians cheered when a proposal to ban gay marriage was defeated. "Our duty as pediatricians is to see that all children have the same security and protection regardless of the sexual orientation of their parents. Denying legal rights to same-sex couples injures their children," noted Asch-Goodkin (2006, 2)

Discrimination in Child Custody, Visitation, Adoption, and Foster Care

A student in one of our classes reported that, after she divorced her husband, she became involved in a lesbian relationship. She explained that she would like to be open about her relationship to her family and friends, but she was afraid that if her ex-husband found out that she was in a lesbian relationship, he might take her to court and try to get custody of their children. Although several respected national organizations—including the American Academy of Pediatrics, the Child Welfare League of America, the American Bar Association, the American Medical Association, the American Psychological

Should We Prohibit Adoption by Lesbian and Gay Couples?

According to the U.S. Children's Bureau, 119,000 children in the U.S. child welfare system were waiting to be adopted in 2003, only 20,000 of whom were in pre-adoptive homes (Howard 2006). Thousands of these children will never be adopted and will never have stable, permanent homes and families. Most adoptive parents want infants or young children, yet two-thirds of children waiting to be adopted are over 5 years old. A report by the Evan B. Donaldson Adoption Institute concludes that "laws and policies that preclude adoption by gay or lesbian parents disadvantage the tens of thousands of children mired in the foster care system who need permanent, loving homes" and that "adoption by gays and lesbians holds promise as an avenue for achieving permanency for many of the waiting children in foster care" (pp. 2, 3).

As noted earlier in this chapter, Crowl et al. (2008) reviewed nineteen studies on the quality of parent-child relationships among children raised by gay and lesbian parents and found that children raised by same-sex parents fare equally well to children raised by heterosexual parents. A study of adoptive parents showed no significant differences between gay and lesbian adoptive parents and heterosexual adoptive parents on measures of family functioning and child behavior problems (Erich et al. 2005). Despite this and other research that finds positive outcomes for children raised by gay or lesbian parents, and despite the support for gay adoption by

child advocacy organizations, placing children for adoption with gay or lesbian parents remains controversial. A 2006 poll reveals that 46 percent of U.S. adults support gay adoption, up from 38 percent in 1999 (Pew Research Center 2006). Although public support for gay adoption has increased in recent years, fewer than half of U.S. adults reported support for gay adoption in 2006.

At the time of this writing, efforts are under way in sixteen states to ban gay adoption (Stone 2006). Social policies that prohibit LGBT individuals and couples from adopting children result in fewer children being adopted. What happens to children who are not adopted? The thousands of children who "age out" of the foster care system annually experience high rates of homelessness, incarceration, early pregnancy, failure to graduate from high school, unemployment, and poverty (Howard 2006). Essentially, social policies that prohibit gay adoption are policies that deny thousands of children the opportunity to have a nurturing family.

Your Opinion?

1. Do you believe children who grow up with same-sex parents are disadvantaged?
2. Do you believe that children without homes should be prohibited by law from being adopted by lesbian or gay individuals or couples?
3. If you were a 6-year-old child with no family, would you rather remain in an institutional setting or be adopted by a gay or lesbian couple?

Association, the American Psychiatric Association, and the National Association of Social Workers—have gone on record in support of treating gays and lesbians without prejudice in parenting and adoption decisions (Howard 2006; Landis 1999), lesbian and gay parents are often discriminated against in child custody, visitation, adoption, and foster care.

Some court judges are biased against lesbian and gay parents in custody and visitation disputes. For example, in 1999, the Mississippi Supreme Court denied custody of a teenage boy to his gay father and instead awarded custody to his heterosexual mother who remarried into a home "wracked with domestic violence and excessive drinking" (Custody and Visitation 2000, 1).

Gay and lesbian individuals and couples who want to adopt children can do so through adoption agencies or through the foster care system in at least twenty-two states and the District of Columbia. However, Florida and Mississippi forbid adoption by gay and lesbian people, Utah forbids adoption by any unmarried couple (which includes all same-sex couples), and Arkansas prohibits lesbians and gay men from serving as foster parents (National Gay and Lesbian Task Force 2004). This chapter's Social Policy section asks whether gay and lesbian individuals and couples should be prohibited from adopting.

Most adoptions by gay people are second-parent adoptions. A **second-parent adoption** (also called co-parent adoption) is a legal procedure that allows individuals to adopt their partner's biological or adoptive child without terminating the first parent's legal status as parent. Second-parent adoption gives children in same-sex families the security of having two legal parents. Second-parent adoption potentially benefits a child by:

- Placing legal responsibility on the parent to support the child;
- Allowing the child to live with the legal parent in the event that the biological (or original adoptive) parent dies or becomes incapacitated;
- Enabling the child to inherit and receive Social Security benefits from the legal parent;
- Enabling the child to receive health insurance benefits from the parent's employer; and
- Giving the legal parent standing to petition for custody or visitation in the event that the parents break up. (Clunis and Green 2003)

However, in four states (Colorado, Nebraska, Ohio, and Wisconsin), court rulings have decided that the state adoption law does not allow for second-parent adoption by members of same-sex couples, and it is unclear whether the state adoption laws in twenty-two states allows second-parent adoption (National Gay and Lesbian Task Force 2005b). Second-parent adoption is not possible when a parent in a same-sex relationship has a child from a previous heterosexual marriage or relationship, unless the former spouse or partner is willing to give up parental rights. Although "third-parent" adoptions have been granted in a small number of jurisdictions, this option is not widely available (National Center for Lesbian Rights 2003).

Effects of Antigay Bias and Discrimination on Heterosexuals

As a junior and senior at Homewood-Flossmoor High School in the suburbs of Chicago, Myka Held played a key role in leading a campaign to promote tolerance of gay and lesbian students. The campaign involved selling gay-friendly T-shirts to students and teachers and having as many people as possible wear the T-shirts to school on a designated day. The T-shirts, made by Duke University, say, "gay? fine by me." "I think it's really important for gay people out there to know that there are straight people who support them," Ms. Held said (quoted in Puccinelli 2005, 20). "I have always supported equal rights for every person and have been disgusted by discrimination and prejudice. As a young Jewish woman, I believe it is my duty to stand up and support minority groups. . . . In my mind, fighting for gay rights is a proxy for fighting for every person's rights" (Held 2005). Myka Held's T-shirt campaign illustrates that fighting prejudice and discrimination against sexual-orientation minorities is an issue not just for lesbians, gays, and bisexuals but also for all those who value fairness and respect for human beings in all their diversity.

The antigay and heterosexist social climate of our society is often viewed in terms of how it victimizes the gay population. However, heterosexuals are also victimized by heterosexism and antigay prejudice and discrimination. Some of these effects follow:

1. *Heterosexual victims of hate crimes.* As discussed earlier in this chapter, extreme homophobia contributes to instances of violence against homosexuals—acts known as hate crimes. Hate crimes are crimes of perception, meaning that victims of antigay hate crimes may not be homosexual; they may just be perceived as being homosexual. The National Coalition of Anti-Violence Programs (2005) reported that, in 2004, 192 heterosexual individuals in the United States were victims of antigay hate crimes, representing 9 percent of all antigay hate crime victims.

2. *Concern, fear, and grief over well-being of gay or lesbian family members and friends.* Many heterosexual family members and friends of homosexual people experience concern, fear, and grief over the mistreatment of their gay or lesbian

friends and/or family members. For example, heterosexual parents who have a gay or lesbian teenager often worry about how the harassment, ridicule, rejection, and violence experienced at school might affect their gay or lesbian child. Will their child drop out of school, as one-fourth of gay youth do (Chase 2000), to escape the harassment, violence, and alienation they endure there? Will the gay or lesbian child respond to the antigay victimization by turning to drugs or alcohol or by committing suicide? Such fears are not unfounded: lesbian, gay, and bisexual youth who report high levels of victimization at school also have higher levels of substance use and suicidal thoughts than heterosexual peers who report high levels of at-school victimization (Bontempo and D'Augelli 2002). A survey of youths' risk behavior conducted by the Massachusetts Department of Education in 1999, revealed that 30 percent of gay teens had attempted suicide in the previous year, compared with 7 percent of their straight peers (Platt 2001).

Meyer et al. (2008) studied the lifetime prevalence of mental disorders and suicide attempts of a diverse group of lesbian, gay, and bisexual individuals and found higher rates of substance abuse among bisexual people than lesbians and gay men. Also, Latino respondents attempted suicide more often than white respondents.

Heterosexual individuals also worry about the ways in which their gay, lesbian, and bisexual family members and friends could be discriminated against in the workplace.

To heterosexuals who have lesbian and gay family members and friends, lack of family protections such as health insurance and rights of survivorship for same-sex couples can also be cause for concern. Finally, heterosexuals live with the painful awareness that their gay or lesbian family member or friend is a potential victim of antigay hate crime. Imagine the lifelong grief experienced by heterosexual family members and friends of hate crime murder victims, such as Matthew Shepard, a 21-year-old college student who was brutally beaten to death in 1998, for no apparent reason other than he was gay.

National Data

As of March 2006, only seventeen states had laws banning discrimination based on sexual orientation (National Gay and Lesbian Task Force 2006).

3. *Restriction of intimacy and self-expression.* Because of the antigay social climate, heterosexual individuals, especially males, are hindered in their own self-expression and intimacy in same-sex relationships. "The threat of victimization (i.e., antigay violence) . . . causes many heterosexuals to conform to gender roles and to restrict their expressions of (nonsexual) physical affection for members of their own sex" (Garnets et al. 1990, 380). Homophobic epithets frighten youth who do not conform to gender role expectations, leading some youth to avoid activities—such as arts for boys, athletics for girls—that they might otherwise enjoy and benefit from (Gay, Lesbian, and Straight Education Network 2000). A male student in our class revealed that he always wanted to work with young children and had majored in early childhood education. His peers teased him relentlessly about his choice of majors, questioning both his masculinity and his heterosexuality. Eventually, this student changed his major to psychology, which his peers viewed as an acceptable major for a heterosexual male.

4. *Dysfunctional sexual behavior.* Some cases of rape and sexual assault are related to homophobia and compulsory heterosexuality. For example, college men who participate in gang rape, also known as "pulling train," entice each other into the act "by implying that those who do not participate are unmanly or homosexual" (Sanday 1995, 399). Homonegativity also encourages early sexual activity among adolescent men. Adolescent male virgins are often teased by their male peers, who say things like "You mean you don't do it with girls yet? What are you, a fag or something?" Not wanting to be labeled and stigmatized as a "fag," some adolescent boys "prove" their heterosexuality by having sex with girls.

5. *School shootings.* Antigay harassment has also been a factor in many of the school shootings in recent years. In March 2001, 15-year-old Charles Andrew Williams fired more than thirty rounds in a San Diego suburban high school, killing two and injuring thirteen others. A woman who knew Williams reported that the students had teased him and called him gay (Dozetos 2001). According to the Gay, Lesbian, and Straight Education Network (GLSEN), Williams's story is not unusual. Referring to a study of harassment of U.S. students that was commissioned by the American Association of University Women, a GLSEN report concluded, "For boys, no other type of harassment provoked as strong a reaction on average; boys in this study would be less upset about physical abuse than they would be if someone called them gay" (Dozetos 2001).

6. *Loss of rights for individuals in unmarried relationships.* The passage of state constitutional amendments that prohibit same-sex marriage can also result in denial of rights and protections to opposite-sex unmarried couples. For example, in 2005, Judge Stuart Friedman of Cuyahoga County (Ohio) agreed that a man who was charged with assaulting his girlfriend could not be charged with a domestic violence felony because the Ohio state constitutional amendment granted no such protections to unmarried couples (Human Rights Campaign 2005). As discussed earlier, some antigay marriage measures also threaten the provision of domestic partnership benefits to unmarried heterosexual couples.

Changing Attitudes toward Same-Sex Couples and Families

Over the past few decades, attitudes toward the morality of homosexuality have become more accepting, and support for protecting civil rights of gay and lesbian individuals has increased (Loftus 2001). Part of the explanation for these changing attitudes is the increasing levels of education in the U.S. population, because individuals with more education tend to be more liberal in their attitudes toward homosexuality. Increased contact between homosexual and heterosexual people and positive depictions of gay and lesbian individuals and couples in the media also contribute to increased acceptance of homosexuality and same-sex relationships.

Increased Contact between Homosexuals and Heterosexuals

Greater acceptance of homosexuality may be due to increased personal contact between heterosexual and openly gay individuals, as more gay and lesbian Americans are coming out to their families, friends, and coworkers. Psychologist Gordon Allport's (1954) "contact hypothesis" asserts that contact between groups is necessary for the reduction of prejudice. Recent research has found that, in general, heterosexual individuals have more favorable attitudes toward gay men and lesbian women if they have had prior contact with or know someone who is gay or lesbian (Mohipp and Morry 2004). Contact with openly gay individuals reduces negative stereotypes and ignorance and increases support for gay and lesbian equality (Wilcox and Wolpert 2000).

Beaver and Knox (2010) analyzed data from 436 self-identified heterosexual women, 47.9 percent of whom reported having kissed someone of the same sex. When these women were compared with those who had not engaged in same-sex kissing behavior, those who had kissed a woman of the same sex were significantly (p < .000) more in favor of same-sex marriage, to agree that gay individuals should be allowed to adopt children, and to agree that gay individuals should be allowed to have their own children. Previous same-sex kissing behavior was also significantly related to not feeling that homosexuality was immoral or to not hating gay people.

Polls of U.S. adults find that 56 percent of respondents say they have a friend or acquaintance who is gay or lesbian; 32 percent say they work with someone who is gay or lesbian; and 23 percent say that someone in their family is gay or lesbian (Newport 2002). A national poll of U.S. high school students showed that 16 percent of students have a gay or lesbian person in their family and 72 percent know someone who is gay or lesbian (Curtis 2004).

Gays and Lesbians in the Media

Another explanation for the increasing acceptance of gay and lesbian individuals is their positive depiction in the popular media. One study found that college students reported lower levels of antigay prejudice after watching television shows such as *Six Feet Under* and *Queer Eye for the Straight Guy* with prominent homosexual characters (Schiappa et al. 2005).

In 1998, Ellen DeGeneres came out on her sitcom *Ellen*, and, by 2006, many television viewers had seen gay and lesbian characters in television shows such as *Will and Grace, Buffy the Vampire Slayer, The Sopranos,* and those mentioned earlier. In 2009, Sean Penn won best actor for his role as Harvey Milk in *MILK*, the story of the first homosexual man elected to a visible political office in 1977. The 2006 HBO documentary, *All Aboard! Rosie's Family Cruise,* provided viewers with positive images of the love and care between same-sex couples and their children.

Aging

When compared to heterosexual individuals, unique problems befall gay couples as they age together (Cahill 2007). When a heterosexual spouse dies, the partner is entitled to Social Security benefits. When a gay male or lesbian partner dies (even though the couple may have been in an exclusive relationship for fifty years)—no Social Security benefits are available. Likewise, the remaining partner does not automatically inherit or become the beneficiary of a pension or retirement plan of a corporation. Health benefits available for one partner may also be available only to a spouse, leaving all partners not meeting this legal definition, without benefits.

The Global Fight for Same-Sex Equality

The struggle that LGBT individuals, couples, and families face for acceptance and equal rights is worldwide. In 1996, South Africa became the first country in the world to include in its constitution a clause banning discrimination based on sexual orientation. Fiji, Canada, Ecuador, and Portugal also have constitutions that ban discrimination based on sexual orientation. In 2009, President Obama signed a United Nations resolution decriminalizing homosexuality, joining sixty-six other nations whose leaders have endorsed the resolution. Former President G. W. Bush had refused to sign the statement during his presidency.

Human rights treaties and transnational social movement organizations have increasingly asserted the rights of people to engage in same-sex relations. International organizations such as Amnesty International, which resolved in 1991 to defend those imprisoned for homosexuality, the International Lesbian and Gay Association (founded in 1978), and the International Gay and Lesbian Human Rights Commission (founded in 1990) continue to fight antigay prejudice and discrimination. The United Nations Commission on Human Rights has proposed the Resolution on Sexual Orientation and Human Rights. This landmark resolution recognizes the existence of discrimination based on sexual orientation around the world, affirms that such discrimination is a violation of human rights, and calls on all governments to promote and protect the human rights of all people, regardless of their sexual orientation (International Gay and Lesbian Human Rights Commission 2004).

In the United States, advancements in gay rights include the Supreme Court's 2003 decriminalization of sodomy, the growing adoption of nondiscrimination policies covering sexual orientation, the increased recognition of domestic partnerships, the state civil union rights and responsibilities offered to same-sex couples in Connecticut, Iowa, Maine, Vermont, Massachusetts, and New Hampshire ruling that same-sex marriage is allowable under the state constitution. However, these victories for LGBT individuals and families fuel the backlash against them by groups who are determined to maintain traditional notions of family and gender. Often, this determination is rooted in and derives its strength from uncompromising religious ideology. Despite the worldwide movement toward increased acceptance and protection of homosexual individuals, the status and rights of lesbians and gays and their families in the United States continue to be some of the most divisive issues in U.S. society.

SUMMARY

How prevalent are homosexuality/bisexuality and same-sex households and families?

Estimates of the lesbigay population in the United States range from about 2 percent to 5 percent of the total U.S. population, with more lesbians than gay males and more bisexual than gay individuals. The 2000 census revealed that about 1 in 9 (or 594,000) unmarried-partner households in the United States involved partners of the same sex. About one-fifth (22.3 percent) of gay male couples and one-third (34.3 percent) of lesbian couples have children in the home.

Can homosexuals change their sexual orientation?

Some individuals who believe that homosexuals choose their sexual orientation think that homosexual people can and should change their sexual orientation. Various forms of reparative therapy or conversion therapy are dedicated to changing homosexuals' sexual orientation. However, the American Psychiatric Association, the American Psychological Association, the American Academy of Pediatrics, the American Counseling Association, the National Association of School Psychologists, the National Association of Social Workers, and the American Medical Association agree that homosexuality is not a mental disorder and needs no cure—that efforts to change sexual orientation do not work and may, in fact, be harmful. These organizations also support the notion that societal reaction to homosexuals rather "curing homosexuality" is a more appropriate focus.

Who tends to have more negative views toward homosexuality?

In general, individuals who are more likely to have negative attitudes toward homosexuality and to oppose gay rights are older, attend religious services, are less educated, live in the South or Midwest, and reside in small rural towns. In addition, black people are more likely than white people to view homosexual relations as "always wrong." Heterosexual women who have kissed other women are less homophobic, more likely to approve same-sex marriage, and more likely to approve same-sex adoption. Countries with the lowest percentage of adults approving homosexuality are Kenya (1 percent) and South Africa (33 percent); those countries with the highest percentage of approval are Czech Republic (83 percent) and Canada (69 percent). About half (51 percent) of U.S. adults approve.

How are gay and lesbian couples different from heterosexual couples?

Research suggests that gay and lesbian couples tend to be more similar to than different from heterosexual couples. Both gay and straight couples tend to value long-term monogamous relationships. For both heterosexual and same-sex partners, relationship satisfaction tends to be high in the beginning of the relationship and decreases over time, and the factors linked to relationship satisfaction (such as equal power and control and being emotionally expressive) are the same for same-sex and heterosexual couples. Gay and lesbian couples also tend to disagree about the same issues that heterosexual couples argue about.

Same-sex couples' relationships are different from heterosexual relationships in that same-sex couples have more concern about when and how to disclose their relationships to others. Same-sex couples are also more likely than heterosexual couples to achieve a fair distribution of household labor and to argue more effectively and resolve conflict in a positive way. Most significantly, whereas heterosexuals enjoy many social and institutional supports for their relationships, gay and lesbian couples face prejudice and discrimination.

What forms of legal recognition of same-sex couples exist in the United States and in other countries?

Connecticut, Iowa, Maine, Vermont, Massachusetts, and New Hampshire are the only states in which same-sex couples can be legally married (although these marriages are not recognized by the federal government or in other states). Same-sex couples can also be legally married in the Netherlands, Belgium, Spain, and Canada.

In a number of countries throughout the world at the national, state, and/or local level, other forms of legal recognition of same-sex couples exist that include registered partnerships, civil unions, and domestic partnerships, which convey most but not all the rights and responsibilities of marriage. Some workplaces also recognize domestic partnerships of their employees for the purposes of benefits such as health insurance coverage and family leave.

What does research on gay and lesbian parenting conclude?

A growing body of credible, scientific research on gay and lesbian parenting concludes that children raised by gay and lesbian parents adjust positively and their families function well. Lesbian and gay parents are as likely as heterosexual parents to provide supportive and healthy environments for their children, and the children of lesbian and gay parents are as likely as those of heterosexual parents to flourish. Some research suggests that children raised by lesbigay parents develop in less gender-stereotypical ways, are more open to homoerotic relationships, contend with the social stigma of having gay parents, and have more empathy for social diversity than children of opposite-sex parents. There is no credible social science evidence that gay parenting negatively affects the well-being of children.

In what ways are heterosexual individuals victimized by heterosexism and antigay prejudice and discrimination?

Heterosexual individuals may be victims of antigay hate crimes if they are just perceived as gay. Many heterosexual family members and friends of homosexuals experience concern, fear, and grief over the mistreatment of and discrimination toward their gay or lesbian friends and/or family members. Because of the antigay social climate, heterosexuals, especially males, are hindered in their own self-expression and intimacy in same-sex relationships. Homophobia has also been linked to some cases of rape and sexual assault by males who are trying to prove they are not gay. Antigay harassment has been a factor in many of the school shootings in recent years. Finally, the passage of state constitutional amendments that prohibit same-sex marriage can also result in denial of rights and protections to opposite-sex unmarried couples.

How have attitudes toward homosexuality and same-sex relationships changed in recent decades?

Over the past few decades, attitudes toward the morality of homosexuality have become slightly more accepting, and support for protecting civil rights of gays and lesbians has increased. In the United States, increased acceptance of homosexuality has resulted from increasing levels of education in the U.S. population (individuals with more education tend to be more liberal in their attitudes toward homosexuality), increased contact between homosexual and heterosexual individuals (as a result of more gays and lesbians "coming out"), and positive depictions of gay and lesbian individuals and couples in the media.

KEY TERMS

antigay bias	Defense of Marriage Act	heterosexuality	LGBT
binegativity	discrimination	homonegativity	prejudice
biphobia	domestic partnerships	homophobia	reparative therapy
bisexuality	garriage	homosexuality	second-parent adoption
civil unions	gay	internalized homophobia	sexual orientation
coming out	GLBT	lesbian	sodomy
conversion therapy	heterosexism	lesbigay population	transgendered

The Companion Website for *Choices in Relationships: An Introduction to Marriage and the Family,* Tenth Edition

www.cengage.com/sociology/knox

Supplement your review of this chapter by going to the Companion Website to take one of the tutorial quizzes, use the flash cards to master key terms, or check out the many other study aids, like crossword puzzles and self-assessments. You'll also find special features such as General Social Survey (GSS) data, Census data, and other resources to help you with that special project or to do some research on your own.

WEB LINKS

Advocate (Online Newspaper for LGBT News)
http://www.advocate.com/

Bisexual Resource Center
http://www.biresource.org

Children of Lesbians & Gays Everywhere (COLAGE)
http://www.colage.org

Gay and Lesbian Support Groups for Parents
http://www.gayparentmag.com/29181.html

Human Rights Campaign
http://www.hrc.org

National Gay and Lesbian Task Force
http://www.ngltf.org

Other Sheep (Christian organization for empowering sexual minorities)
http://www.othersheepexecsite.com/
http://www.othersheep.org/

PFLAG (Parents, Families, and Friends of Lesbians and Gays)
http://www.pflag.org

PlanetOut (Online News Source)
http://www.planetout.com

Same-sex Relationships
http://www.alternet.org/sex/

Straight Spouse Network
http://www.ssnetwk.org

REFERENCES

Allport, G. W. 1954. *The nature of prejudice.* Cambridge, MA: Addison-Wesley.

Amato, Paul R. 2004. Tension between institutional and individual views of marriage. *Journal of Marriage and Family* 66:959–65.

American Psychological Association. 2004. *Sexual Orientation, Parents, & Children.* APA Policy Statement on Sexual Orientation, Parents, & Children. APA Online. http://www.apa.org.

Andersson, G., T. Noack, A. Seierstad, and H. Weedon-Fekjaer. 2006. The demographics of same-sex marriages in Norway and Sweden. *Demography* 43:79–98.

Asch-Goodkin, J. 2006. An unsuccessful attempt to adopt a constitutional amendment that bans gay marriage. *Contemporary Pediatrics* 23:14–15.

Avery, A., J. Chase, L. Johansson, S. Litvak, D. Montero, and M. Wydra. 2007. America's changing attitudes toward homosexuality, civil unions, and same-gender marriages. *Social Work* 52:71–79.

Bartholomew, K., K. V. Regan, M. A. White, and D. Oram. 2008. Patterns of abuse in male same-sex relationships. *Violence and Victims* 23:617–37.

Beaver, T., and D. Knox. 2010. "I Kissed a Woman and I Think Gays are Great": Data on Attitudes of Heterosexual Women toward Homosexuality who Report Having Kissed another Woman. Poster at Southern Sociological Association's Annual Meeting, Atlanta.

Berg, N., and D. Lein. 2006. Same-sex behaviour: U.S. frequency estimates from survey data with simultaneous misreporting and non-response. *Applied Economics* 39:757–70.

Besen, W. 2000. Introduction. In *Feeling free: Personal stories—How love and self-acceptance saved us from "ex-gay" ministries.* Washington, DC: Human Rights Campaign Foundation, 7.

Black, D., G. Gates, S. Sanders, and L. Taylor. 2000. Demographics of the gay and lesbian population in the United States: Evidence from available systematic data sources. *Demography* 37:139–54.

Bobbe, J. 2002. Treatment with lesbian alcoholics: Healing shame and internalized homophobia for ongoing sobriety. *Health and Social Work* 27:218–23.

Bontempo, D. E., and A. R. D'Augelli. 2002. Effects of at-school victimization and sexual orientation on lesbian, gay, or bisexual youths' health risk behavior. *Journal of Adolescent Health* 30:364–74.

Bradford, J., K. Barrett, and J. A. Honnold. 2002. *The 2000 census and same-sex households: A user's guide.* New York: National Gay and Lesbian Task Force Policy Institute, Survey and Evaluation Research Laboratory, and Fenway Institute. http://www.thetaskforce.org.

Buxton, A. P. 2004. Paths and pitfalls: How heterosexual spouses cope when their husbands or wives come out. *Journal of Couple and Relationship Therapy* 3.

Buxton, A. 2005. A family matter: When a spouse comes out as gay, lesbian, or bisexual. *Journal of GLBT Family Studies* 1:49–70.

Cahill, S. 2007. The coming GLBT senior boom. *Gay & Lesbian Review Worldwide* 13:19–21.

Cahill, S., and S. Slater. 2004. *Marriage: Legal protections for families and children. Policy brief.* Washington, DC: National Gay and Lesbian Task Force Policy Institute.

Carpenter, C. and G. J. Gates. 2008. Gay and lesbian partnership: Evidence from California. *Demography* 45:573–691.

Centers for Disease Control and Prevention. 2005. *HIV/AIDS Surveillance Report* 2004, Vol. 16. http://www.cdc.gov.

Chase, B. 2000. NEA president Bob Chase's historic speech from 2000 GLSEN Conference. http://www.glsen.org.

Cianciotto, J. 2005. Hispanic and Latino same-sex couple households in the U.S.: A report from the 2000 Census. National Gay and Lesbian Task Force Policy Institute. http:www.ngltf.org.

Cianciotto, J., and S. Cahill. 2006. Youth in the crosshairs: The third wave of ex-gay activism. National Gay and Lesbian Task Force Policy Institute. http:www.thetaskforce.org.

Clunis, D. M., and G. Dorsey Green. 2003. *The lesbian parenting book,* 2nd ed. Emeryville, CA: Seal Press.

Crowl, A., S. Ahn, and J. Baker. 2008. A meta-analysis of developmental outcomes for children of same-sex and heterosexual parents. *Journal of GLBT Family Studies* 4:385–407.

Curtis, C. 2003. Poll: U.S. public is 50–50 on gay marriage. *PlanetOut* (October 7). http://www.planetout.com.

Curtis, C. 2004. Poll: 1 in 20 High school students is gay. *PlanetOut.* http://www.planetout.com.

Custody and Visitation. 2000. *Human Rights Campaign FamilyNet.* http://familynet.hrc.org.

Diamond, L. M. 2003. What does sexual orientation orient? A biobehavioral model distinguishing romantic love and sexual desire. *Psychological Review* 110:173–92.

Dozetos, B. 2001. School shooter taunted as 'gay.' *PlanetOut* (March 7). http:www.planetout.com.

Erich, S., P. Leung, and P. Kindle. 2005. A Comparative analysis of adoptive family functioning with gay, lesbian, and heterosexual parents and their children. *Journal of GLBT Family Studies* 1:43–60.

Fone, B. 2000. *Homophobia: A history.* New York: Henry Holt.

Garnets, L., G. M. Herek, and B. Levy. 1990. Violence and victimization of lesbians and gay men: Mental health consequences. *Journal of Interpersonal Violence* 5:366–83.

Gay, Lesbian, and Straight Education Network. 2000. Homophobia 101: Teaching respect for all. Gay, Lesbian, and Straight Education Network. http:www.glsen.org.

Gilman, S. E., S. D. Cochran, V. M. Mays, M. Hughes, D. Ostrow, and R. C. Kessler. 2001. Risk of psychiatric disorders among individuals reporting same-sex sexual partners in the National Comorbidity Survey. *American Journal of Public Health* 91:933–39.

Golombok, S., B. Perry, A. Burston, C. Murray, J. Money-Somers, M. Stevens, and J. Golding. 2003. Children with lesbian parents: A community study. *Developmental Psychology* 39:20–33.

Gottman, J. M., R. W. Levenson, C. Swanson, K. Swanson, R. Tyson, and D. Yoshimoto. 2003. Observing gay, lesbian, and heterosexual couples' relationships: Mathematical modeling of conflict interaction. *Journal of Homosexuality* 45:65–91.

Green, J. C. 2004. The American religious landscape and political attitudes: a baseline for 2004. Pew Forum on Religion and Public Life. http://pewforum.org.

Green, R. J., J. Bettinger, and E. Sacks. 1996. Are lesbian couples fused and gay male couples disengaged? In *Lesbians and gays in couples and families,* ed. J. Laird and R. J. Green, 185–230. San Francisco: Jossey-Bass.

Grov, C., D. S. Bimbi, J. E. Nanin, and J. T. Parsons. 2006. Race, ethnicity, gender and generational factors associated with the coming-out process among gay, lesbian, and bisexual individuals. *The Journal of Sex Research* 43:115–22.

Harris Interactive and GLSEN. 2005. *From teasing to torment: School climate in America.* New York: GLSEN (Gay, Lesbian, and Straight Education Network).

Heatherington, L., and J. A. Lavner. 2008. Coming to terms with coming out: Review and recommendations for family systems-focused research. *Journal of Family Psychology* 22:329–43.

Held, Myka. 2005. Mix it up: T-shirts and activism. (March 16). http://www.tolerance.org/teens.

Herek, G. M. 2002. Heterosexuals' attitudes toward bisexual men and women in the United States. *The Journal of Sex Research* 39:264–74.

Holthouse, D. 2005. Curious cures. *Intelligence Report* 117 (Spring):14.

Howard, J. 2006. *Expanding resources for children: Is adoption by gays and lesbians part of the answer for boys and girls who need homes?* New York: Evan B. Donaldson Adoption Institute.

Human Rights Campaign. 2000. *Feeling free: Personal stories—How love and self-acceptance saved us from "ex-gay" ministries.* Washington, DC: Human Rights Campaign Foundation.

Human Rights Campaign. 2004. *Resource guide to coming out.* Washington, DC: Human Rights Campaign Foundation.

Human Rights Campaign. 2005. *The state of the workplace for lesbian, gay, bisexual, and transgendered Americans,* 2004. Washington, DC: Human Rights Campaign. http://www.hrc.org.

International Gay and Lesbian Human Rights Commission. 2004 (January 30). IGLHRC calls for global mobilization to help pass the United Nations Resolution on Sexual Orientation and Human Rights. http://www.iglhrc.org.

———. 2003. Where You Can Marry: Global Summary of Registered Partnership, Domestic Partnership and Marriage Laws. http://www.iglhrc.org.

Israel, T., and J. J. Mohr. 2004. Attitudes toward bisexual women and men: Current research, future directions. In *Current research on bisexuality*, ed. R. C. Fox, 117–34. New York: Harrington Park Press.

Jenkins, M., E. G. Lambert, and D. N. Baker. 2009. The attitudes of Black and White college students toward gays and lesbians. *Journal of Black Studies*. 39: 589–601

Johnson, T. 2007. Attitudes toward homosexuality relax in China, but pressures remain. *Knight Ridder* (Washington bureau), January 31.

Johnston, E. 2005. Massachusetts releases data on same-sex marriages. *PlanetOut* (May 5). http://www.planetout.com.

Kinsey, A. C., W. B. Pomeroy, and C. E. Martin. 1948. *Sexual behavior in the human male*. Philadelphia: Saunders.

Kinsey, A. C., W. B. Pomeroy, C. E. Martin, and P. H. Gebhard. 1953. *Sexual behavior in the human female*. Philadelphia: Saunders.

Kirkpatrick, R. C. 2000. The evolution of human sexual behavior. *Current Anthropology* 41:385–414.

Knox, D., and M. E. Zusman. 2009. Relationship and sexual behaviors of a sample of 1,319 university students. Unpublished data collected for this text. Department of Sociology, East Carolina University, Greenville, NC.

Kurdek, L. A. 2008. Change in relationship quality for partners from lesbian, gay male, and heterosexual couples. *Journal of Family Psychology* 22:701–11.

_____. 2005. What do we know about gay and lesbian couples? Current Directions in *Psychological Science* 14:251–54.

_____. 2004. Gay men and lesbians: The family context. In *Handbook of contemporary families: Considering the past, contemplating the future*, ed. M. Coleman and L. H. Ganong, 96–115. Thousand Oaks, CA: Sage Publications.

_____. 1994. Conflict resolution styles in gay, lesbian, heterosexual nonparent, and heterosexual parent couples. *Journal of Marriage and the Family* 56:705–22.

Lambda Legal and Deloitte Financial Advisory Services LLP. 2006. 2005 Workplace Fairness Survey (April). http:www.lambdalegal.org.

Landis, D. 1999. Mississippi Supreme Court made a tragic mistake in denying custody to gay father, experts say. American Civil Liberties Union News (February 17). http://www.aclu.org.

LAWbriefs. 2005. Recent developments in sexual orientation and gender identity law. LAWbriefs 7(April):1.

Lever, J. 1994. The 1994 Advocate survey of sexuality and relationships: The men. *The Advocate* August 23, 16–24.

Lewis, G. B. 2003. Black-white differences in attitudes toward homosexuality and gay rights. *Public Opinion Quarterly* 67:59–78.

Loftus, J. 2001. America's liberalization in attitudes toward homosexuality, 1973 to 1998. *American Sociological Review* 66:762–82.

Luther, S. 2006. Domestic partner benefits. Human Rights Campaign (March). http://www.hrc.org.

Mathy, R. M. 2007. Sexual orientation moderates online sexual activity. In *Online Matchmaking* ed. M. T. Whitty, A. J. Baker, and J. A. Inman, 159–77. New Work: Paulgrave Macmillan.

McKinney, J. 2004. *The Christian case for gay marriage*. Pullen Memorial Baptist Church (February 8). http://www.pullen.org.

McLean, K. 2004. Negotiating (non)monogamy: Bisexuality and intimate relationships. In *Current research on bisexuality*, ed. R. C. Fox, 82–97. New York: Harrington Park Press.

Meyer, I. H., J. Dietrich and S. Schwartz. 2008. Lifetime prevalence of mental disorders and suicide attempts in diverse lesbian, gay, and bisexual populations. *American Journal of Public Health* 98:1004–03.

Michael, R. T., J. H. Gagnon, E. O. Laumann, and G. Kolata. 1994. *Sex in America: A definitive survey*. Boston: Little, Brown.

Mohipp, C., and M. M. Morry. 2004. Relationship of symbolic beliefs and prior contact to heterosexuals' attitudes toward gay men and lesbian women. *Canadian Journal of Behavioral Science* 36:36–44.

Moltz, K. 2005. Testimony of Kathleen Moltz, given before the United States Senate Judiciary Committee, Subcommittee on the Constitution, Civil Rights and Property Rights. Human Rights Campaign (April 13). http://www.hrc.org.

National Center for Lesbian Rights. 2003. Second-parent adoptions: A snapshot of current law. http://www.nclrights.org.

National Coalition of Anti-Violence Programs. 2005. *2004 National hate crimes report: Anti-lesbian, gay, bisexual and transgender violence in 2004*. New York: National Coalition of Anti-Violence Programs.

National Gay and Lesbian Task Force. 2004. Anti-Gay parenting laws in the U.S. National Gay and Lesbian Task Force (June). http://www.thetaskforce.org.

National Gay and Lesbian Task Force. 2005a. The Issues: Seniors. National Gay and Lesbian Task Force. http://www.thetaskforce.org.

National Gay and Lesbian Task Force. 2005b. Second-parent adoption in the U.S. National Gay and Lesbian Task Force. http://www.thetaskforce.org.

National Gay and Lesbian Task Force. 2005–2006. Marriage and partnership recognition. http://www.thetaskforce.org.

National Gay and Lesbian Task Force. 2006. State nondiscrimination laws in the U.S. (as of March 2006). http:www.thetaskforce.com.

Newport, F. 2002. In-depth analysis: Homosexuality. Gallup Organization (September). http://www.gallup.com.

Ochs, R. 1996. Biphobia: It goes more than two ways. In *Bisexuality: The psychology and politics of an invisible minority*, ed. B. A. Firestein, 217–39. Thousand Oaks, CA: Sage.

Ogilvie, G. S., D. L. Taylor, T. Trussler, R. Marchand, M. Gilbert, A. Moniruzzaman, and M. L. Rekart. 2008. Seeking sexual partners on the Internet: A marker for risky sexual behaviour in men who have sex with men. *Canadian Journal of Public Health* 99:185–89.

Otis, M. D., S. S. Rostosky, E. D. B. Riggle, and R. Hamrin. 2006. Stress and relationship quality in same-sex couples. *Journal of Social and Personal Relationships* 23:81–99.

Page, S. 2003. Gay rights tough to sharpen into political "wedge issue." *USA Today*, July 28, 10A.

Palmer, R., and R. Bor. 2001. The challenges to intimacy and sexual relationships for gay men in HIV serodiscordant relationships: A pilot study. *Journal of Marital and Family Therapy* 27:419–31.

Parelli, S. 2007. Why ex-gay therapy doesn't work. *The Gay & Lesbian Review Worldwide* 14:29–32.

Paul, J. P. 1996. Bisexuality: Exploring/exploding the boundaries. In *The lives of lesbians, gays, and bisexuals: Children to adults*, ed. R. Savin-Williams and K. M. Cohen, 436–61. Fort Worth, TX: Harcourt Brace.

Pawelski, J. G., E. C. Perrin, J. M. Foy, C. E. Allen, J. E. Crawford, M. Del Monte, M. Kaufman, J. D. Klein, K. Smith, S. Springer, J. L. Tanner, and D. L. Vickers. 2006. The effects of marriage, civil union, and domestic partnership laws on the health and well-being of children *Pediatrics* 118:349–55.

Pearcey, M. 2004. Gay and bisexual married men's attitudes and experiences: Homophobia, reasons for marriage, and self-identity. *Journal of GLBT Family Studies* 1:21–42.

Peplau, L. A., R. C. Veniegas, and S. N. Campbell. 1996. Gay and lesbian relationships. In *The lives of lesbians, gays, and bisexuals: Children to adults*, ed. R. C. Savin-Williams and K. M. Cohen, 250–73. Fort Worth, TX: Harcourt Brace.

Pew Research Center. 2006. Less opposition to gay marriage, adoption and military service (March 22). http://people-press.org.

Pew Research Center. 2008. Gay Marriage Opposed. http://pewforum.org/docs/index.php?DocID=39 (accessed November 16).

Pinello, D. R. 2008. Gay marriage: For better or for worse? What we've learned from the evidence. *Law & Society Review* 42:227–30.

Platt, L. 2001. Not your father's high school club. *American Prospect* 12:A37–39.

Porche, M. V., and D. M. Purvin. 2008. "Never in Our Lifetime": Legal marriage for same-sex couples in long-term relationships. *Family Relations* 57:144–59.

Potok, M. 2005. Vilification and violence. *Intelligence Report* 117(Spring):1.

Pryor, J. H., S. Hurtado, L. DeAngelo, J. Sharkness, L. C. Romero, W. K. Korn, and S. Trans. 2008. *The American freshmen: National Norms for fall 2008*. Los Angeles: Higher Education Research Institute, UCLA.

Puccinelli, M. 2005. Students support, decry gays with t-shirts. CBS 2 Chicago (April 19). http://cbs2chicago.com.

Rankin, S. R. 2003. Campus climate for gay, lesbian, bisexual, and transgendered people: A national perspective. New York: National Gay and Lesbian Task Force Policy Institute. http://www.thetaskforce.org.

Rosario, M., E. W. Schrimshaw, J. Hunter, and L. Braun. 2006. Sexual identity development among lesbian, gay, and bisexual youth: Consistency and change over time. *Journal of Sex Research* 43:46–58.

Rosin, H., and R. Morin. 1999. In one area, Americans still draw a line on acceptability. *Washington Post National Weekly Edition* 16(January 11):8.

Saad, L. 2005. Gay rights attitudes a mixed bag. Gallup Organization (May 20). http://www.gallup.com.

Sanday, P. R. 1995. Pulling train. In *Race, class, and gender in the United States*, 3rd ed., ed. P. S. Rothenberg, 396–402. New York: St. Martin's Press.

Savin-Williams, R. C. 2006. Who's gay? Does it matter? Current Directions in *Psychological Science* 15:40–44.

Schiappa, E., P. B. Gregg, and D. E. Hewes. 2005. The parasocial contact hypothesis. *Communication Monographs* 72:92–115.

Serovich, J. M., S. M. Craft, P. Toviessi, R. Gangamma, et al. 2008. A systematic review of the research base on sexual reorientation therapies. *Journal of Marital and Family Therapy* 34:227–39.

SIECUS (Sexuality Information and Education Council of the United States). 2009. Facts. Retrieved March 23, http://www.dianedew.com/siecus.htm

Snorton, R. 2005. GLSEN's 2004 State of the States Report is the first objective analysis of statewide safe schools policies (April 1). http://www.glsen.org.

Stone, A. 2006. Drives to ban gay adoption up in 16 states. *USA Today*, February 20. http://www.usatoday.com.

Sullivan, A. 1997. The conservative case. In *Same sex marriage: Pro and con*, ed. A. Sullivan, 146–54. New York: Vintage Books.

Tao, G. 2008. Sexual orientation and related viral sexually transmitted disease rates among U.S. women aged 15 to 44 years. *American Journal of Public Health* 98:1007–10.

Tobias, S., and S. Cahill. 2003. School lunches, the Wright brothers, and gay families. National Gay and Lesbian Task Force. http://www.thetaskforce.org.

Tyagart, C. E. 2002. Legal rights to homosexuals in areas of domestic partnerships and marriages: Public support and genetic causation attribution. *Educational Research* Quarterly 25:20–29.

Wagner, C. G. 2006. Homosexual relationships. *Futurist* 40:6.

Wainwright, J., Russell, S. T., and Patterson, C. J. 2004. Psychosocial adjustment, school outcomes, and romantic relationships of adolescents with same-sex parents. *Child Development* 75:1886–98.

Walsh, K. T. 2006. And now it's her turn. *U.S. News & World Report* (May 15):27.

White, M. 2005. A thorn in their side. *Intelligence Report* 117(Spring):27–30.

Wilcox, C., and R. Wolpert. 2000. Gay rights in the public sphere: Public opinion on gay and lesbian equality. In *The Politics of Gay Rights*, ed. C. A. Rimmerman, K. D. Wald, and C. Wilcox, 409–32. Chicago: University of Chicago Press.

Yvonne. 2004. Devout Christian finds a reason to stand up for equality. Human Rights Campaign (December 1). http://www.hrc.org.

Zaleski, R. M. 2007. What's in a name? (equal treatment for gay couples) (New Jersey) *New Jersey Law Journal*, March 30.

Money, it turned out, was exactly like sex, you thought of nothing else if you didn't have it and thought of other things if you did.

James Arthur Baldwin, writer

Sexuality in Relationships

Contents

Authors

True or False?

1. "Being horny" is the top reason students report engaging in sexual behavior.

2. Having an orgasm via masturbation is similar to having an orgasm with a partner in terms of positive mood feelings and less stress.

3. People who French kiss with multiple partners are at increased risk of meningitis.

4. Undergraduate men evidence more interest in experimental, risky sex than undergraduate women.

5. Single individuals report more satisfying sex lives than married people.

Answers: **1.** F   **2.** F   **3.** T   **4.** T   **5.** F

The lyrics to the classic song, "Hold Me, Thrill Me, Kiss Me" (made famous by Mel Carter) begin with, "They told me be sensible with your new love. Don't be fooled thinking this is the last you'll find. But they never stood in the dark alone with you love. . . . when you take me in your arms and drive me slowly out of my mind." Being driven out of one's mind in the dark with one's beloved is one of the delights of being involved in a relationship. Indeed, sexuality is a major relationship aspect and the subject of this chapter. We begin by discussing the sexual values lovers bring to the encounter.

A kiss can be a comma, a question mark or an exclamation point.

Mistinguette, French actress

Sexual Values

The following are some examples of choices (reflecting sexual values) with which individuals in a new relationship are confronted:

How much sex/how soon in a relationship is appropriate?

Do you require a condom for vaginal or anal intercourse?

Do you require a condom and/or dental dam (vaginal barrier) for oral sex?

Before having sex with someone do you require that they have been recently tested for sexually transmitted infections (STIs) and the human immunodeficiency virus (HIV)?

Do you tell your partner the *actual* number of previous sexual partners?

Do you tell your partner your sexual fantasies?

Do you reveal to your partner previous or current same-sex behavior or interests?

Sexual values are moral guidelines for making sexual choices in nonmarital, marital, heterosexual, and homosexual relationships. Attitudes and values sometimes predict sexual behavior. One's sexual values may be identical to one's sexual choices. For example, a person who values abstinence until marriage may choose to remain a virgin until marriage. One's behavior does not always correspond with one's values. Some who express a value of waiting until marriage have intercourse before marriage. One explanation for the discrepancy between values and behavior is that a person may engage in a sexual behavior, then decide the behavior was wrong, and adopt a sexual value against it.

Alternative Sexual Values

There are at least three sexual value perspectives that guide choices in sexual behavior: absolutism, relativism, and hedonism. People sometimes have different sexual values at different stages of the family life cycle. For example, elderly individuals are more likely to be absolutist, whereas those in the middle years are more likely to be relativistic. Young unmarried adults are more likely than the elderly to be hedonistic.

Absolutism

Absolutism refers to a belief system based on unconditional allegiance to the authority of science, law, tradition, or religion. A religious absolutist makes sexual choices on the basis of moral considerations. To make the correct moral choice is to comply with God's will, and to not comply is a sin. A legalistic absolutist makes sexual decisions on the basis of a set of laws. People who are guided by absolutism in their sexual choices have a clear notion of what is right and wrong.

The official creeds of fundamentalist Christian and Islamic religions encourage absolutist sexual values. Intercourse is solely for procreation, and any sexual acts that do not lead to procreation (masturbation, oral sex, homosexuality) are immoral and regarded as sins against God, Allah, self, and community. Waiting until marriage to have intercourse is also an absolutist sexual value. This value is often promoted in the public schools (see Social Policy).

"True Love Waits" is an international campaign designed to challenge teenagers and college students to remain sexually abstinent until marriage. Under this program, created and sponsored by the Baptist Sunday School Board, young people are asked to agree to the absolutist position and sign a commitment to the following: "Believing that true love waits, I make a commitment to God, myself, my family, my friends, my future mate, and my future children to be sexually abstinent from this day until the day I enter a biblical marriage relationship" (True Love Waits 2008, http://www.lifeway.com/tlw/students/join.asp).

How effective are these "True Love Waits" and "virginity pledge" programs in delaying sexual behavior until marriage? Data from the National Longitudinal Study of Adolescent Health revealed that, although youth who took the pledge were more likely than other youth to experience a later "sexual debut," had fewer partners, and married earlier, most eventually engaged in premarital sex, were less likely to use a condom when they first had intercourse, and were more likely to substitute oral and/or anal sex in the place of vaginal sex. There was no significant difference in the occurrence of STIs between "pledgers" and "nonpledgers" (Brucker and Bearman 2005). The researchers speculated that the emphasis on virginity may have encouraged the pledgers to engage in non-coital (nonintercourse) sexual activities (for example, oral sex), which still exposed them to STIs and to be less likely to seek testing and treatment for STIs. Similarly, Hollander (2006) collected national data on two waves of adolescents. Half of those who had taken the virginity pledge reported no such commitment a year later. Males and black individuals were particularly likely to retract their pledge.

A similar cultural ritual to encourage and celebrate virginity until one's wedding day is the "Father-Daughter Purity Ball." Over 4,000 such events occur annually that involve fathers and daughters as young as 4 years old taking mutual pledges to be pure. Fathers promise to protect their daughters and as well to be faithful and shun pornography themselves. Daughters promise to be pure, which implies the value of absolutism (Gibbs 2008).

Diversity in Other Countries

Absolutism is still a viable sexual value in the Hai Duong Province of Vietnam. In a survey of 800 married respondents, 40 percent of the husbands and 70 percent of the wives reported that premarital intercourse was not acceptable. People most likely to have absolutist values were female, had less education, and were from rural areas (Ghuman 2005).

Abstinence Sex Education in the Public Schools

Sexuality education was introduced in the American public school system in the late nineteenth century with the goal of combating STIs (sexually transmitted infections) and instilling sexual morality (typically understood as abstinence until marriage). Over time, the abstinence agenda became more formalized.

In the Bush administration, only sex education programs that emphasized or promoted abstinence were eligible to qualify for federal funding. Those that also discussed contraception and other means of pregnancy protection, referred to as **comprehensive programs**, were not eligible. A study of 1,284 parents of children in the public schools in California revealed that 89 percent preferred a comprehensive sex education program (Constantine et al. 2007).

Expressing his view on abstinence education, Barack Obama (2008) said, "We want to make sure that, even as we are teaching responsible sexuality and we are teaching abstinence to children, that we are also making sure that they've got enough understanding about contraception that they don't end up having much more severe problems because of a dumb mistake." Clearly, abstinence education will be reviewed by the new administration.

To what degree does exposure to abstinence-only sex education programs result in delay of first intercourse? Bristol (2006) conducted a phone survey of 472 university students and found that the type of sex education program they experienced in high school (abstinence versus comprehensive) was unrelated to age at first intercourse. Abel and Greco (2008) examined pre- and posttest scores of students enrolled in an abstinence sex education program and concluded that they had no way to know if exposure to the program actually changed the participants' behavior. Hollander (2008) reported data from the National Survey of Family Growth, which suggested that the comprehensive sex education approach is having more of an effect in reducing pregnancy than the abstinence-only strategy. The teenage survey respondents who had had comprehensive sex education were less likely than those who had had no formal sex education to report involvement in a pregnancy; the same was not true for participants who had received abstinence-only instruction.

Santelli et al. (2006) noted that, although federal support of abstinence-only programs has grown rapidly since 1996, "the evaluations of such programs find little evidence of efficacy in delaying initiation of sexual intercourse." Lindberg and Singh (2008) analyzed national data from a representative sample of single women (6,493 women age 20 to 44) in regard to their sexual behavior and found that 90 percent were sexually experienced, with 70 percent currently being sexually active. The researchers concluded that government policies encouraging adult women to have sex only within marriage appear out of touch with the reality of the sexual behavior of single women.

Your Opinion?

1. To what degree do you support abstinence education in public schools?
2. Should condoms be made available for students already having sex?
3. Should parents control the content of sex education in public schools?

Sources

Abel, E. M., and M. Greco. 2008. A preliminary evaluation of an abstinence-oriented empowerment program for public school youth. *Research on Social Work Practice* 18:223–35.

Bristol, K. 2006. The influence of community factors on sex education program effectiveness. Sociology Honors Thesis, East Carolina University, Greenville, NC.

Constantine, N. A., P. Jerman, and A. X. Huang. 2007. California parents' preferences and beliefs regarding school-based sex education policy. *Perspectives on Sexual and Reproductive Health* 39:167–76.

Hollander, D. 2008. Sex education: What works? Perspectives on *Sexual and Reproductive Health* 40:64–65.

Lindberg, L. D., and S. Singh. 2008. Sexual behavior of single adult American women. *Perspectives on Sexual and Reproductive Health* 40:27–34.

Obama, B. 2008. Presentation at the Democratic Compassion Forum at Messiah College, April 13.

Santelli, J., M. A. Ott, M. Lyon, J. Rogers, and D. Summers. 2006. Abstinence-only education policies and programs: A position paper of the Society for Adolescent Medicine. *Journal of Adolescent Health* 38:83–87.

Some individuals do value virginity. Among a sample of undergraduates, 13 percent of 783 undergraduates at a southeastern university selected absolutism as their primary sexual value (Richey et al. 2009). Black individuals were significantly (p < .009) more likely than white individuals to select absolutism as their sexual value (20.6 percent versus 12.1 percent). The fact that significantly more black than white students reported, "I am very religious" (24.2 percent versus 10 percent) helps to account for the fact that black individuals adhered to a more absolutist position. However, Davidson et al. (2008) noted that the conservative sexual values among black individuals may not translate into conservative

Lead us not into temptation. Just tell us where it is, and we'll find it.

Sam Levenson, writer

Over 4,000 Father-Daughter Purity Balls occur annually and involve fathers and daughters as young as 4 years old taking mutual pledges to be pure.

Rick Wilking/Reuters/Corbis

Don't mistake pleasures for happiness. They are a different breed of dog.

Josh Billings, humorist

sexual behavior (see section on Racial Differences in Sex Attitudes and Behaviors of Undergraduates later in chapter).

Some individuals still define themselves as virgins even though they have engaged in oral sex. Of 1,319 university students, 74.2 percent agreed that, "If you have oral sex, you are still a virgin." Hence, according to these undergraduates, having oral sex with someone is not really having sex (Knox and Zusman 2009).

In her paper "Like a Virgin . . . Again?" Carpenter (2003) discussed the concept of **secondary virginity**—the conscious decision of a sexually active person to refrain from intimate encounters for a specified period of time. Secondary virginity closely resembles a pattern scholars have called "regretful" nonvirginity, the chief difference being the adoption of the label *virgin* by the nonvirgin in question. Secondary virginity may be a result of physically painful, emotionally distressing, or romantically disappointing sexual encounters. Of sixty-one young adults Carpenter interviewed, more than half (women more than men) believed that a person could, under some circumstances, be a virgin more than once. Fifteen people contended that people could resume their virginity in an emotional, psychological, or spiritual sense. Terence Duluca, a 27-year-old, heterosexual, white, Roman Catholic, explained:

There is a different feeling when you love somebody and when you just care about somebody. So I would have to say if you feel that way, then I guess you could be a virgin again. Christians get born all the time again, so. . . . When there's true love involved, yes, I believe that.

A subcategory of absolutism is **asceticism**. Ascetics believe that giving in to carnal lust is unnecessary and attempt to rise above the pursuit of sensual pleasure into a life of self-discipline and self-denial. Accordingly, spiritual life is viewed as the highest good, and self-denial helps one to achieve it. Catholic priests, monks, nuns, and some other celibate people have adopted the sexual value of asceticism.

Sexual values may have a cultural basis. This Hmong couple has the value of absolutism.

Relativism

Relativism is a value system emphasizing that sexual decisions should be made in the context of a particular situation. Whereas absolutists might feel that having intercourse is wrong for unmarried people, relativists might feel that the moral correctness of sex outside marriage depends on the particular situation. For example, a relativist might feel that in some situations, sex between casual dating partners is wrong (such as when one individual pressures the other into having sex or lies to persuade the other to have sex). However, in other cases—when there is no deception or coercion and the dating partners are practicing "safer sex"—intercourse between casual dating partners may be viewed as acceptable.

Of 783 undergraduates, 62 percent selected "relativism" as their prevailing sexual value. Most of these undergraduates felt that sexual intercourse was justified if they were in a secure, mutual love relationship (Richey et al. 2009). As expected, women were more likely to be relativists than men (72 percent versus 52 percent).

Sexual values and choices that are based on relativism often consider the degree of love, commitment, and relationship involvement as important factors. In a study

Relativism is the sexual value that most college students hold.

I think men talk to women so they can sleep with them and women sleep with men so they can talk to them.

Jay McInerney

designed to assess "turn-ons" and "turn-offs" in sexual arousal, women spoke of "feeling desired versus feeling used" by the partner. "Many women talked about how their arousal was increased with partners who seemed particularly interested in them as individual women, rather than someone that they just wanted to have sex with" (Graham et al. 2004).

A disadvantage of relativism as a sexual value is the difficulty of making sexual decisions on a relativistic case-by-case basis. The statement "I don't know what's right anymore" reflects the uncertainty of a relativistic view. Once a person decides that mutual love is the context justifying intercourse, how often and how soon is it appropriate for the person to fall in love? Can love develop after some alcohol and two hours of conversation? How does one know that love feelings are genuine? The freedom that relativism brings to sexual decision making requires responsibility, maturity, and judgment. In some cases, individuals may convince themselves that they are in love so that they will not feel guilty about having intercourse. Though one may feel "in love," "secure," and "committed" at the time first intercourse occurs, only 17 percent of all first intercourse experiences that women reported are with the person they eventually marry (Raley, 2000).

Absolutists and relativists have different views on whether or not two unmarried people should have intercourse. Whereas an absolutist would say that having intercourse is wrong for unmarried people and right for married people, a relativist would say, "It depends on the situation." Suppose, for example, that a married couple do not love each other and intercourse is an abusive, exploitative act. Suppose also that an unmarried couple love each other and their intercourse experience is an expression of mutual affection and respect. A relativist might conclude that, in this particular situation, having intercourse is "more right" for the unmarried couple than the married couple. Students who become involved in a "friends with benefits" relationship reflect a specific expression of relativism.

Friends with Benefits

Friends with benefits is becoming part of the relational sexual landscape of youth. **Friends with benefits** (FWB) is a relationship of nonromantic friends who also have a sexual relationship. Of 1,319 undergraduates, 47.1 percent reported that they have been in an FWB relationship (Knox and Zusman 2009). Puentes et al. (2008) analyzed data from 1,013 undergraduates (over half of which reported experience with a "friends with benefits" relationship), and compared the background characteristics of participants with nonparticipants in such a relationship. Findings revealed that participants were significantly more likely to be males, casual daters, hedonists, nonromantics, jealous, black, juniors or seniors, those who have had sex without love, and those who regard "financial security" as their top value. The friends with benefits relationship is primarily sexual and engaged in by nonromantic hedonists who have a pragmatic view of relationships.

In a smaller sample of 170 undergraduates at the same university, 57.3 percent of these undergraduates reported that they were or had been involved in an FWB relationship. There were no significant differences between the percentages of women and men reporting involvement in an FWB relationship. This is one of the few studies finding no difference in sexual behavior between women and men (for example, one would expect men to have more FWB relationships than women). However, the percentages of women and men were very similar in their reported rates of FWB involvement—57.1 percent and 57.9 percent, respectively. Is a new sexual equality operative in FWB relationships? (McGinty et al. 2007) Analysis of the data revealed other significant differences between female and male college students in regard to various aspects of the FWB relationship.

1. *Women were more emotionally involved.* Women were significantly more likely than men (62.5 percent versus 38.1 percent) to view their current FWB relationship as an emotional relationship. In addition, women were significantly more likely than men to be perceived as being more emotionally involved in the FWB relationship. Of the men, 43.5 percent, compared with 13.6 percent of the women, reported "my partner is more emotionally involved than I am."

2. Men were more sexually focused. As might be expected from the first finding, men were significantly more likely than women to agree with the statement, "I wish we had sex more often than we do" (43.5 percent versus 13.6 percent).

3. Men were more polyamorous. With polyamory defined as desiring to be involved in more than one emotional or sexual relationship at the same time, men were significantly more likely than women to agree that "I would like to have more than one FWB relationship going on at the same time" (34.8 percent versus 4.5 percent). Serial FWB relationships may already be occurring. Of the men, 52.2 percent, compared with 24.6 percent of women, reported that they had been involved in more than one FWB relationship. Hughes et al. (2005) studied 143 undergraduates in FWB relationships and noted that a ludic, playful, noncommittal love characterized them.

Hedonism

Hedonism is the belief that the ultimate value and motivation for human actions lie in the pursuit of pleasure and the avoidance of pain. The hedonistic value is reflected in the statement, "If it feels good, do it." Hedonism assumes that sexual desire, like hunger and thirst, is an appropriate appetite and its expression is legitimate. Of 1,319 undergraduates, 29 percent reported that they had hooked up (had oral or sexual intercourse) the first time they met someone (Knox and Zusman 2009).

Of 783 undergraduates, 24.6 percent selected "hedonism" as their primary sexual value. Men were significantly ($p < .001$) more likely than women to select hedonism as their sexual value (36.7 percent versus 12.5 percent). In addition, hedonists were more likely to report having "hooked up," to have been in a friends with benefits relationship, and to be open to living together (Richey et al. 2009).

Sexual Double Standard

The **sexual double standard**—the view that encourages and accepts sexual expression of men more than women—is reflected in Table 9.1. As noted previously, men were about three times more hedonistic than women (Richey et al. 2009). Acceptance of the double standard is evident in that hedonistic men are thought of as "studs" but hedonistic women as "sluts."

The sexual double standard is also evident in that there is lower disapproval of men having higher numbers of sexual partners but high disapproval of women for having the same number of sexual partners as men. In a recent study, England and Thomas (2006) noted that the double standard was operative in hooking up. Women who hooked up too often with too many men and had sex too easily were vulnerable to getting bad reputations. Men who did the same thing got a bad

We're women; we have double standards to live up to.

Ally McBeal, fictional TV character

Table 9.1 Sexual Value by Sex of Respondent

Respondents	Absolutism	Relativism	Hedonism
Male students	11.6%	51.8%	36.7%
Female students	15.1%	72.4%	12.5%

Source: E. Richey, D. Knox, and M. E. Zusman. 2009. Sexual values of 783 undergraduates. *College Student Journal* 43:175–80.

reputation among women, but with fewer stigmas. In addition, men gained status among other men for their exploits; women were quieter. Similarly, women who looked at pornography (in contrast to men who viewed pornography) were viewed as "loose" (19.4 percent versus 4.5 percent) (O'Reilly et al. 2007).

Kim et al. (2007) found evidence for the double standard in their review of twenty-five prime-time television programs. In addition, Greene and Faulkner (2005) studied 689 heterosexual couples and found that women were disadvantaged in negotiating sexual issues with their partners, particularly when their traditional gender roles were operative.

PERSONAL CHOICES

Deciding to Have Intercourse with a New Partner

The following are issues you might consider in making the decision to have sex with a new partner:

1. *Personal consequences.* How do you predict you will feel about yourself after you have had intercourse with a new partner? An increasing percentage of college students are relativists and feel that the outcome will be positive if they are in love. The following quote is from a student in our classes:

> I believe intercourse before marriage is OK under certain circumstances. I believe that when a person falls in love with another and the relationship is stable, it is then appropriate. This should be thought about very carefully for a long time, so as not to regret engaging in intercourse.

Those who are not in love and have sex in a casual context often report sexual regret about their decision. Following is another quote from a student:

> I viewed sex as a new toy—something to try as frequently as possible. I did my share of sleeping around, and all it did for me was to give me a total loss of self-respect and a bad reputation. Besides, guys talk. I have heard rumors that I have slept with guys that I have never slept with.

The effect intercourse will have on you personally will be influenced by your personal values, your religious values, and the emotional involvement with your partner. Some people prefer to wait until they are married to have intercourse and feel that this is the best course for future marital stability and happiness. There is often, but not necessarily, a religious basis for this value.

Strong personal and religious values against nonmarital intercourse may result in guilt and regret following an intercourse experience. In a sample of 270 undergraduates who had had intercourse, 71.9 percent regretted their decision to do so at least once (for example, they may have had intercourse more than once or with multiple partners and reported regret at least once). The most cited reason for these students' regret was going against their own morals (37 percent) (Oswalt et al. 2005). Similarly, in a sample of first-year students at a large southeastern university, one-third regretted their sexual activity in high school, and almost half reported that they had made changes in their sexual behavior: engaging in less sexual behavior, with fewer partners (Doub 2006).

2. *Partner consequences.* Because a basic moral principle is to do no harm to others, it is important to consider the effect of intercourse on your partner. Whereas intercourse may be a pleasurable experience with positive consequences for you, your partner may react differently. What is your partner's religious background, and what are your partner's sexual values? A highly religious person with absolutist sexual values will typically have a very different reaction to sexual intercourse than a person with low religiosity and relativistic or hedonistic sexual values. In the study of 270 undergraduates previously referred to, 23 percent (more women than men) reported regret due to

pressure from the partner (Oswalt et al. 2005). Anderson et al. (2005) also noted that university women might use varying tactics (sexy dancing, verbal intimidation, and alcohol) to pressure a man to have sex.

3. *Relationship consequences.* What is the effect of intercourse on a couple's relationship? One's personal reaction to having intercourse may spill over into the relationship. Individuals might predict how they feel having intercourse will affect their relationship before including it in their relationship.

4. *Contraception.* Another potential consequence of intercourse is pregnancy. Once a couple decides to have intercourse, a separate decision must be made as to whether intercourse should result in pregnancy. Most sexually active undergraduates do not want children. People who want to avoid pregnancy must choose and plan to use a contraceptive method. However, many do not. In a study of almost 73,000 pregnancies, 45 percent were unintended (Naimi et al. 2003).

5. *HIV and other sexually transmissible infections.* Engaging in casual sex has potentially fatal consequences. Avoiding HIV infection and other STIs is an important consideration in deciding whether to have intercourse in a new relationship. The increase in the number of people having more partners results in the rapid spread of the bacteria and viruses responsible for numerous varieties of STIs. However, in a sample of 1,319 undergraduates, 24.8 percent reported that they had used a condom the last time they had intercourse (Knox and Zusman 2009).

Serovich and Mosack (2003) reported that only 37 percent of men with HIV infection told a casual partner of their positive HIV status. Those who did so reported, "I thought [my partner] had a right to know." Although depending on a person's integrity is laudable, it may not be wise. Indeed, a condom should be used routinely to help protect one from contracting a STI.

6. *Influence of alcohol and other drugs.* A final consideration with regard to the decision to have intercourse in a new relationship is to be aware of the influence of alcohol and other drugs on such a decision. Of students who reported regretting having had intercourse, 31.9 percent noted that alcohol was involved in their decision to have intercourse (Oswalt et al., 2005). A new term has emerged to describe these pregnancies: **alcohol-exposed pregnancy** (AEP) (Ingersoll et al. 2005).

7. *OK to change decision about including intercourse in a relationship.* Although most couples who include intercourse in their relationship continue the pattern, some decide to omit it from their sexual agenda. One coed said, "Since I did not want to go on the pill and would be frantic if I got pregnant, we decided the stress was not worth having intercourse. While we do have oral sex, we don't even think about having intercourse any more. I must say, that a side benefit is that our relationship has become more emotionally close and we are less 'sex focused.'"

Sources

Anderson, P. B., A. P. Kontos, H. Tanigoshi, and C. Struckman-Johnson. 2005. An examination of sexual strategies used by urban southern and rural Midwestern university women. *Journal of Sex Research* 42:335–41.

Ingersoll, K. S., S. D. Ceperich, M. D. Nettleman, K. Karanda, S. Brocksen, and B. A. Johnson. 2005. Reducing alcohol-exposed pregnancy risk in college women: Initial outcomes of a clinical trial of a motivational intervention. *Journal of Substance Abuse Treatment* 29:173–80.

Knox, D., and M. E. Zusman. 2009. Relationship and sexual behaviors of a sample of 1,319 university students. Unpublished data collected for this text. Department of Sociology, East Carolina University, Greenville, NC.

Naimi, T. S., L. E. Lipscomb, R. D. Brewer, and B. C. Gilbert. 2003. Binge drinking in the preconception period and the risk of unintended pregnancy: Implications for women and their children. *Pediatrics* 111:1136–41.

Oswalt, S. B., K. A. Cameron, and J. J. Koob. 2005. Sexual regret in college students. *Archives of Sexual Behavior* 34:663–69.

Serovich, J. M., and K. E. Mosack. 2003. Reasons for HIV disclosure or nondisclosure to casual sexual partners. *AIDS Education and Prevention* 15:70–81.

Sources of Sexual Values

The sources of one's sexual values are numerous and include one's school, religion, and family, as well as technology, television, social movements, and the Internet. Halstead (2005) emphasized that schools play a powerful role in shaping a child's sexual values. Previously we noted that public schools in the United States promote absolutist sexual values through abstinence education and that the effectiveness of these programs has been questioned.

Religion is also an important influence. More than 45 percent of 657 undergraduates at a large southeastern university (assessed via random digit dialing) reported that religion had been influential on their sexual choices: "very influential" for 26.9 percent and "somewhat influential" for 18.4 percent (Bristol and Farmer 2005). Bersamin et al. (2008) studied the effects of parental attitudes, practices, and television viewing behavior on adolescent sexual behaviors in a sample of 887 adolescents. They found that adolescents reporting greater parental disapproval and limits on their television viewing were less likely to initiate both oral sex and sexual intercourse. The researchers emphasized that parental attitudes and watching TV together can delay potentially risky adolescent sexual behaviors. Similarly, more than 40 percent of 657 undergraduates at a large southeastern university (assessed via random digit dialing) reported that their parents had been influential in their sexual choices: "very influential" for 17.5 percent and "somewhat influential" for 24.7 percent (Bristol and Farmer 2005). Similarly, among 918 university students, "mom" was identified as the most influential source of sexual information.

Siblings are also influential. Kornreich et al. (2003) found that girls who had older brothers held more conservative sexual values. "Those with older brothers in the home may be socialized more strongly to adhere to these traditional standards in line with power dynamics believed to shape and reinforce more submissive gender roles for girls and women" (p. 197).

Reproductive technologies such as birth control pills, the morning-after pill, and condoms influence sexual values by affecting the consequences of behavior. Being able to reduce the risk of pregnancy and HIV infection with the pill and condoms allows one to consider a different value system than if these methods of protection did not exist.

The media is also a source of sexual values. A television advertisement shows an affectionate couple with minimal clothes on in a context where sex could occur. "Be ready for the moment" is the phrase of the announcer, and Levitra, the new quick-start Viagra, is the product for sale. The advertiser uses sex to get the attention of the viewer and punches in the product.

However, as a source of sexual values and responsible treatments of contraception, condom usage, abstinence, and consequences of sexual behavior, television is woefully inadequate. Indeed, viewers learn that sex is romantic and exciting but learn nothing about discussing the need for contraception or HIV and STI protection. With few exceptions, viewers are inundated with role models who engage in casual sex without protection.

Social movements such as the women's movement affect sexual values by empowering women with an egalitarian view of sexuality. This translates into encouraging women to be more assertive about their own sexual needs and giving them the option to experience sex in a variety of contexts (for example, without love or commitment) without self-deprecation. The net effect is a potential increase in the frequency of recreational, hedonistic sex. The gay liberation movement has also been influential in encouraging values that are accepting of sexual diversity.

Another influence on sexual values is the Internet; its sexual content is extensive. The Internet features erotic photos, videos, and "live" sex acts and stripping by webcam sex artists. Individuals can exchange nude photos, have explicit sex dialogue, arrange to have "phone sex" or meet in person, or find a prostitute.

Sexual Behaviors

We have been discussing the various sources of sexual values. We now focus on what people report that they do sexually. Some individuals are **asexual**—absence of sexual behavior with a partner and one's self (masturbation). About 4 percent of females and 11 percent of males reported being asexual in the last twelve months (DeLamater and Hasday 2007). In contrast, most individuals report engaging in various sexual behaviors. The following discussion includes kissing, masturbation, oral sex, vaginal intercourse, and anal sex and ends with an examination of gender differences in sexual behavior.

Kissing

Kissing has been the subject of literature and science. The meanings of a kiss are variable—love, approval, hello, goodbye, or as a remedy for a child's hurt knee. There is also a kiss for luck, a stolen kiss, and a kiss to seal one's marriage vows. Kisses have been used to denote hierarchy. In the Middle Ages, only peers kissed on the lips, a person of lower status kissed someone of higher status on the hand, and a person of low status showed great differential of status by kissing on the foot. Kissing has a negative connotation in the "kiss of death," which reflects the kiss Judas gave Jesus as he was about to betray him. Kissing may be an aggressive act as some do not want to be kissed (Gross et al. 2005). Kissing, particularly French kissing, may be very dangerous. Individuals who engage in French kissing with multiple partners face a fourfold risk of contracting meningococcal disease, a bacterial infection that may lead to meningitis, swelling of the brain and spinal cord (Gross 2006).

Although the origin of kissing is unknown, one theory posits that kissing is associated with parents putting food into their offspring's mouth . . . the bird pushes food down the throat of a chick in the nest. Some adult birds also exchange food by mouth during courtship. Anthropologists note that some cultures (for example, Eskimos, Polynesians) promote meeting someone by rubbing noses. Kissing is not too far a leap from rubbing noses.

The way a person kisses reflects the person's country, culture, and society. The French kiss each other once on each cheek or three times in the same region. Greeks tend to kiss on the mouth, regardless of the sex of the person. Eskimos, we have noted, rub noses. The Chinese rarely kiss in public.

Where kissing is normative (for example, the United States), it is thought of as being a behavior of youth (O'Donnell et al. 2006). However, Ginsberg et al. (2005) studied 179 females over the age of 60 and found that 59 percent reported kissing daily to at least once a month. On the other end of the continuum is an almost absence of kissing. Schuster et al. (2005) found that parents who had contracted HIV were reluctant to kiss their children; not only did they fear giving their children HIV, they also feared contracting an illness from them.

Masturbation

Masturbation involves stimulating one's own body with the goal of experiencing pleasurable sexual sensations. Of 1,319 undergraduates at a large southeastern university, 62.2 percent reported having masturbated (Knox and Zusman 2009).

Kiss—to a young girl, faith; to a married woman, hope; to an old maid, charity.

V. P. Skipper

Previous research on masturbation among college students revealed that being male, hedonistic, nonreligious, and cohabitants were characteristic of people who have masturbated (O'Reilly et al. 2006). Alternative terms for masturbation include *autoeroticism, self-pleasuring, solo sex,* and *sex without a partner.* An appreciation of the benefits of masturbation has now replaced various myths about it (for example, it causes blindness). Most health care providers and therapists today regard masturbation as a normal and healthy sexual behavior. Furthermore, masturbation has become known as a form of safe sex in that it involves no risk of transmitting diseases (such as HIV) or producing unintended pregnancy. Masturbation is also associated with orgasm during intercourse. In a study by Thomsen and Chang (2000), 292 university undergraduates reported whether they had ever masturbated and whether they had an orgasm during their first intercourse experience. The researchers found that the strongest single predictor of orgasm and emotional satisfaction with first intercourse was previous masturbation.

Oral Sex

In a sample of 1,319 undergraduates, 77.7 percent reported that they had given or received (84.3 percent) oral sex (Knox and Zusman 2009). **Fellatio** is oral stimulation of the man's genitals by his partner. In many states, legal statutes regard fellatio as a "crime against nature." "Nature" in this case refers to reproduction, and the "crime" is sex that does not produce babies. Nevertheless, most men have experienced fellatio.

Cunnilingus is oral stimulation of the woman's genitals by her partner. With regard to their most recent sexual event, 20 percent of women reported that their partner performed cunnilingus on them the last time they had sex. Women who were neither married nor living with a partner reported the highest frequency of cunnilingus as their most recent sexual event (26 percent, noncohabiting; 22 percent, cohabiting; 17 percent, married) (Michael et al. 1994).

African Americans typically have lower rates of oral sex than white people. Gagnon (2004) noted:

> *I think that these differences are mostly the result of education and religion—but there may be other factors relating to the symbolic meanings of oral sex in Western cultures. As a result of the economic and racial oppression of African Americans, potential threats to men's power and masculinity are often more present when African American men have sex. There is always the threat of symbolic subordination when men perform oral sex, particularly if it is not identified by the woman as masculinity enhancing and it is not reciprocated. This is a parallel to the symbolic subordination of women when they perform unreciprocated oral sex. However, if the men will not do it, then the women will not either, since they view fellatio without reciprocation as simply servicing the man.*

We noted earlier that, increasingly, youth who have oral sex regard themselves as virgins, believing that only sexual intercourse constitutes "having sex." As noted previously, of 1,319 university students, 74.2 percent agreed that, "If you have oral sex, you are still a virgin." Dotson-Blake et al. (2009) developed a profile of those most likely to believe that "oral sex is sex": they tended to be first-year students, white, nonreligious, and hedonistic in sexual values with experience in hooking up, oral sex, and cohabitation.

One researcher found that, among her respondents, "overwhelmingly, oral sex is seen as foreplay, rather than sex, even among those abstaining from intercourse" (Hertzog 2004).

 Diversity in Other Countries

More than a thousand high school students (1,368) in the United Kingdom revealed their expectations regarding oral sex. Of the sexually experienced males, 48.9 percent expected oral sex during a sexual experience; 46.5 percent of the sexually experienced females expected oral sex. However, only 14 percent of the males and 29 percent of the females reported that they believed it was important to use a condom during fellatio (Stone et al. 2006).

Table 9.2 Virginity by Academic Rank

	Female (N = 944)	Male (N = 349)
Freshmen	23.0%	21.2%
Sophomore	18.3%	16.9%
Junior	7.6%	16.4%
Senior	3.2%	10.0%

Source: D. Knox and M. E. Zusman. 2009. Relationship and sexual behaviors of a sample of 1,319 university students. Unpublished data collected for this text. Department of Sociology, East Carolina University, Greenville, NC.

There is the mistaken belief that only intercourse carries the risk of contracting a STI. However, STIs as well as HIV can be contracted orally. A team of researchers confirmed that a person may contract not only the herpes virus from oral sex but also HIV (Mbopi-Keou et al. 2005). Use of a condom or dental dam, a flat latex device that is held over the vaginal area, is recommended.

A kiss is something which you cannot give without taking, and cannot take without giving.

Anonymous

Vaginal Intercourse

Vaginal intercourse, or **coitus**, refers to the sexual union of a man and woman by insertion of the penis into the vagina. In a study of 1,319 undergraduates, 81.3 percent reported that they had had sexual intercourse (Knox and Zusman 2009). In regard to university students, each academic year, there are fewer virgins. Table 9.2 shows the percentage of 1,293 female and male university students at each academic level who agreed with the statement, "I have never had sexual intercourse."

Meston and Buss (2007) surveyed 1,549 university students and identified 237 reasons for having sexual intercourse. The top reasons included: (1) pure attraction to the other person in general; (2) physical pleasure; (3) expression of love; (4) feelings of being desired by the other; (5) escalation of the depth of the relationship; (6) curiosity for new experiences; (7) special occasion for celebration; (8) mere opportunity; and (9) seemingly uncontrollable circumstances. Indeed, twenty of the twenty-five top reasons were remarkably similar for women and men.

Sexual Behavior and Well-Being

How does sexual behavior affect one's mood and stress level? Are the effects similar with and without a partner? Burleson et al. (2007) reported the effect of physical affection and sexual behavior on one's mood and stress level. Fifty-eight women (median age 47.6) kept a record for thirty-six weeks. Results revealed that experiencing affection and sex with a partner on one day predicted lower negative mood, higher positive mood, and lower stress the following day. The prediction did not hold for individuals who had an orgasm without a partner.

First Intercourse

Kaestle et al. (2002) noted that females who are involved with an older partner are more likely to report having had intercourse. Data from 1,975 females revealed that if a 17-year-old female was romantically involved with a partner six years older, the female was twice as likely to report having had intercourse as was a female with a partner the same age.

A team of researchers (Else-Quest et al. 2005) examined data from the National Health and Social Life Survey on the outcome of the respondent's first vaginal intercourse. The first experience was premarital for 82.9 percent of the respondents, at an average age of 17.7 years. The relationship status of the respondent was not associated with later psychological or physical health outcomes. However, if the first was "prepubertal, forced, with a blood relative or stranger, or the result of peer pressure, drugs, or alcohol, poorer psychological

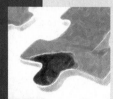

What if My Partner Does Not Like Sex?

Sex is an important part of a couple's relationship, particularly in new relationships. However, individuals vary in their interest in, capacity for, and preference for different sexual behaviors. Although some need sex daily, are orgasmic, and enjoy a range of sexual behaviors, others never think of sex, have never had an orgasm, and want to get any sexual behavior over with as soon as possible. When two people of widely divergent views on sex end up in the same relationship, clear communication and choices are necessary. The person who has no interest must decide if developing an interest is a goal and be open to learning about masturbation and sexual fantasy. Where becoming interested in sex is not a goal, the partner must decide the degree to which this is an issue. Some will be pleased the partner has no interest because this means no sexual demands, whereas others will bolt. Openness about one's sexual feelings and hard choices will help resolve the dilemma.

Masturbation—it's sex with someone I love.

Woody Allen, film producer/director

and physical outcomes were consistently reported in later life" (p. 102). The takeaway message of this research is to delay first intercourse, which might best occur with a partner in an emotional relationship where no pressure, alcohol, or drugs are involved.

Anal Sex

Of 1,319 undergraduates (96.2 percent heterosexual), 24.1 percent reported that they had engaged in anal sex (Knox and Zusman 2009). The greatest danger of anal sex is that the rectum might tear, in which case blood contact can occur; STIs (including HIV infection) may then be transmitted. Gay men are particularly vulnerable. Wolitski (2005) emphasized that **barebacking** (intentional unprotected anal sex) is a significant threat to the health of gay, bisexual, and other men who have sex with men (MSM). Partners who use a condom during anal intercourse reduce their risk of not only HIV infection but also other STIs. Pain (physical as well as psychological) may also occur; 14 percent of 404 men who have sex with men reported experiencing **anodyspareunia**—frequent, severe pain during receptive anal sex (Damon and Simon Rosser 2005).

Table 9.3 Sexual Behaviors of 1,319 Undergraduates*

Percent Ever Having Experienced**

Received Oral Sex = 84%
Sexual Intercourse = 81%
Given Oral Sex = 78%
Masturbation = 62%
Anal Sex = 24%

Source: D. Knox and Zusman, M. E. 2009. Relationship and sexual behaviors of a sample of 1,319 university students. Unpublished data collected for this text. Department of Sociology, East Carolina University, Greenville, NC

**Demographics
Gender = 73% female, 27% male
Class = 42% freshmen, 35% sophomore, 13% junior, 10% senior
Race = 74% white, 17% black, 3% Asian, 2% Hispanic, 2% biracial
Age = 20.1 average age

Chapter 9 Sexuality in Relationships

Attitudes toward Premarital Sex Scale

Premarital sex is defined as engaging in sexual intercourse prior to marriage. The purpose of this survey is to assess your thoughts and feelings about intercourse before marriage. Read each item carefully and consider how you feel about each statement. There are no right or wrong answers to any of these statements, so please give your honest reactions and opinions. Please respond by using the following scale:

1	2	3	4	5	6	7
Strongly Disagree						Strongly Agree

_____ 1. I believe that premarital sex is healthy.

_____ 2. There in nothing wrong with premarital sex.

_____ 3. People who have premarital sex develop happier marriages.

_____ 4. Premarital sex is acceptable in a long-term relationship.

_____ 5. Having sexual partners before marriage is natural.

_____ 6. Premarital sex can serve as a stress reliever.

_____ 7. Premarital sex has nothing to do with morals.

_____ 8. Premarital sex is acceptable if you are engaged to the person.

_____ 9. Premarital sex is a problem among young adults.

_____ 10. Premarital sex puts unnecessary stress on relationships.

Scoring

Selecting a 1 reflects the most negative attitude toward premarital sex; selecting a 7 reflects the most positive attitude toward premarital sex.

Before adding the numbers you assigned to each item, change the scores for items #9 and #10 as follows: replace a score of 1 with a 7; 2 with a 6; 3 with a 5; 4 with a 4; 5 with a 3; 6 with a 2; and 7 with a 1. After changing these numbers, add your ten scores. The lower your total score (10 is the lowest possible score), the less accepting you are of premarital sex; the higher your total score (70 is the highest possible score), the greater your acceptance of premarital sex. A score of 40 places you at the midpoint between being very disapproving of premarital sex and very accepting of premarital sex.

Scores of Other Students Who Completed the Scale

The scale was completed by 252 student volunteers at Valdosta State University. The mean score of the students was 40.81 (standard deviation [SD] = 13.20), reflecting that the students were virtually at the midpoint between a very negative and a very positive attitude toward premarital sex. For the 124 males and 128 females in the total sample, the mean scores were 42.06 (SD = 12.93) and 39.60 (SD = 13.39), respectively (not statistically significant). In regard to race, 59.5 percent of the sample was white and 40.5 percent was nonwhite (35.3 percent black, 2.4 percent Hispanic, 1.6 percent Asian, 0.4 percent American Indian, and 0.8 percent other). The mean scores of whites, blacks, and nonwhites were 41.64 (SD = 13.38), 38.46 (SD = 13.19), and 39.59 (SD = 12.90) (not statistically significant). Finally, regarding year in college, 8.3 percent were freshmen, 17.1 percent sophomores, 28.6 percent juniors, 43.3 percent seniors, and 2.8 percent graduate students. Freshman and sophomores reported more positive attitudes toward premarital sex (mean = 44.81; SD = 13.39) than did juniors (mean = 40.32; SD = 12.58) or seniors and graduate students (mean = 38.91; SD = 13.10) ($p = .05$).

Source

"Attitudes toward Premarital Sex Scale" 2006 by Mark Whatley, Ph.D., Department of Psychology, Valdosta State University, Valdosta, Georgia 31698-0100. Used by permission. Other uses of this scale by written permission of Dr. Whatley only (mwhatley@valdosta.edu). Information on the reliability and validity of this scale is available from Dr. Whatley.

Cybersex

Cybersex is "any consensual, computer mediated, participatory sexual experience involving two or more individuals" (Hamman 2007, 34). In effect, this means that the individuals are typing or sending text about what they are doing to the other sexually (or doing to themselves—for example, masturbation). Or, they are writing sex stories with the goal of arousal. Hamman noted that, "increasing numbers of teenagers and young people will have their first sexual experiences, the ones that will shape their sex lives forever, online" (p. 38).

Internet use also varies by whether the user is male or female. Males are more likely than females to meet a partner for sex online. Similarly, Internet use varies by sexual orientation with gay and bisexual males more likely than heterosexual males to meet a partner for sex online. Bisexual females are more likely than gay females and heterosexual females to meet a partner for sex online (Mathy 2007).

All of these sources of sexual values combine to provide an attitude toward premarital sex. The above Self-Assessment allows you to assess your sexual values.

Clinton lied. A man might forget where he parks or where he lives, but he never forgets oral sex, no matter how bad it is.

Barbara Bush, wife of former President George H. W. Bush

Gender Differences in Sexuality

Gender differences exist in what men and women believe about sex as well as what they do. In this section, we examine these differences as well as how pheromones impact sexual behavior.

Gender Differences in Sexual Beliefs

Knox et al. (2008) analyzed data from 326 undergraduates to discover gender differences in beliefs about sex. Men were more likely to think that oral sex is not sex, that cybersex is not cheating, that men can't tell if a woman is faking orgasm, and that sex frequency drops in marriage. Meanwhile, women tended to believe that oral sex is sex, that cybersex is cheating, that faking orgasm does occur, and that sex frequency stays high in marriage. Little wonder there is frustration and disappointment between men and women as they include sexuality into their relationship.

Gender Differences in Sexual Behavior

In national data based on interviews with 3,432 adults, women reported having fewer sexual partners than men (2 percent versus 5 percent reported having had five or more sexual partners in the previous year), and reported having orgasm during intercourse less often (29 percent versus 75 percent) (Michael et al. 1994, 102, 128, 156). In a more recent analysis of the responses of 5,385 males and 1,038 females who completed a questionnaire online, males were significantly more likely than females to report frequenting strip clubs, paying for sex, having anonymous sex with strangers, and having casual sexual relations (Mathy 2007).

Pornography use is also higher among males. In a study of 305 undergraduates, 31.7 percent of the men (in contrast to 3.8 percent of the women) reported viewing pornography three to five times a week (O'Reilly et al. 2007).

Men and women also differ in their motivations for sexual intercourse, with men viewing sex more casually (Lenton and Bryan 2005). Earlier, we noted that undergraduate men (in comparison with undergraduate women) were almost three times more likely to report being hedonistic in their sexual values.

Sociobiologists explain males' more casual attitude toward sex, engaging in sex with multiple partners, and being hedonistic as biologically based (that is, due to higher testosterone levels). Social learning theorists, on the other hand, emphasize that the media and peers socialize men to think about and to seek sexual experiences. Men are also accorded social approval and called "studs" for their sexual exploits. Women, on the other hand, are more often punished and labeled "sluts" if they have many sexual partners. Because **social scripts** guide sexual behavior, what individuals think, do, and experience is a reflection of what they have learned (Simon and Gagnon 1998). These scripts operate at the cultural (for example, societal norms for broad sexual conduct—women should not be promiscuous), interpersonal (for example, sexual desires translated into strategies—man should be aggressive in sexual encounters), and intrapsychic (for example, sexual dialogues with self that elicit and sustain arousal—"this will be erotic") levels (DeLamater and Hasday 2007). There are also differences in the perceptions of foreplay and intercourse. Miller and Byers (2004) compared the reported duration of actual foreplay (men = 13 minutes; women = 11 minutes) and desired foreplay (men = 18 minutes; women = 19 minutes), and the reported duration of actual intercourse (men = 8 minutes; women = 7 minutes) and desired intercourse (men = 18 minutes; women = 14 minutes) of heterosexual men and women in long-term relationships with each other. These findings suggested that both men and women underestimated their partner's desires for the duration of both foreplay and intercourse; also, they had similar preferences for duration of foreplay, but men wanted longer intercourse than women.

What Happens in Vegas: Sexual Desires Absent Social Constraints

RESEARCH APPLICATION

"What happens in Vegas, stays in Vegas" is a phrase used to promote tourism to the "Sin City." Individuals are encouraged to come and act out their wildest fantasies without discovery or consequences. This "play with impunity" ploy is working. Tourism in Vegas is flourishing. To handle the over 23 million flying into Vegas annually, a new terminal is to open in 2011.

Sample

The data for this research consisted of 268 undergraduates at a large southeastern university who answered a 56-item questionnaire designed to identify what sexual behaviors men and women would engage in if they could be assured that they would be discovered by no one and that their sexual decisions would result in no negative consequences. Demographics of the respondents included 26.5 percent male and 73.5 percent female. The median age of the respondents was 19 (range 17 to 40). Almost all (88 percent) were never married and not living together.

Findings

Several significant findings emerged. The percentage of men and women responding, the significance level, and a discussion of each finding, follows. (Sexual behaviors are ranked from those receiving the highest percentage to the lowest percentage of interest.)

1. *Sex on a secluded beach.* The most prominent desire of both men and women was to have sex on a secluded beach. Over 80 percent of the men and over 70 percent of women reported they would be interested in this sexual scenario (men = 82 percent; women = 74 percent). The difference between the genders was statistically significant ($p < .03$).

2. *Sex in a threesome.* Over 70 percent of the men, in contrast to less than 30 percent of the women, reported they would be interested in having sex in a threesome (men = 71 percent; women = 28 percent; gender difference = $p < .001$).

3. *Sex in public with a chance of getting caught.* Almost 70 percent of the men, in contrast to almost 50 percent of the women, reported they would be interested in having sex in a public place with a chance of getting caught (men = 69 percent; women = 48 percent; gender difference = $p < .001$).

4. *Sex with someone of another race.* Almost 70 percent of the men, in contrast to almost 50 percent of the women, reported they would be interested in having sex with someone of another race (men = 68 percent; women = 46 percent; gender difference = $p < .001$).

5. *Going to a nude beach.* Almost 60 percent of the men, in contrast to slightly over 40 percent of the women, reported they would be interested in going to a nude beach (men = 59 percent; women = 41 percent; gender difference = $p < .001$).

6. *Sex with a married person.* Over 40 percent (44 percent) of the men, in contrast to 20 percent of the women, reported they would be interested in having sex with a married person. The difference between the genders was $p < .001$.

7. *Forced to have sex.* Almost 30 percent of the men, in contrast to slightly less than 20 percent of the women, reported they would like to be forced to have sex (men = 26 percent; women = 19 percent; gender difference = $p < .05$).

8. *Sex with a prostitute.* Slightly less than a quarter (24 percent) of the men, in contrast to 11 percent of the women, reported they would be interested in having sex with a prostitute. The difference between the genders was $p < .001$.

9. *Forcing someone to have sex.* Almost 20 percent of the men, in contrast to just over 10 percent of the women, reported they would be interested in forcing someone to have sex (men = 18 percent; women = 14 percent; gender difference = $p < .05$).

Discussion

The overall data of this sample emphasize that most of the undergraduates reported *no* interest in engaging in a variety of sexual behavior even if there were no consequences in terms of discovery or STDs. In spite of the assumption that college youth are unprincipled sex addicts who will jump at the chance to do anything, the researchers found a group of undergraduates who were rather mainstream.

Of those who evidenced an interest in moving beyond traditional sexual norms, there were numerous statistically significant gender differences. On all variables, men (more than women) reported higher levels of interest in erotic (sex on the beach), experimental (threesome), risky (public sex), taboo (mixed-race sex or sex with married person), voyeuristic (nude beach), paid (prostitute), and forced sex (by others or on others). Previous researchers have also found men considerably more sex-focused.

Source

Adapted from D. Knox, P. Groom, and M. Zusman. (2008). What Happens in Vegas: Sexual Desires Absent Social Constraints (abridged), *Psychology Journal* 5:40–50.

Sexual satisfaction reported by men and women seems to be equal, at least among the French. In a representative sample of 1,002 French respondents (483 men and 519 women) aged 35 years, 83 percent reported relative or full satisfaction with their sex life (Colson et al. 2006).

Mood states typically affect both men and women equally (Lykins et al. 2006). In a study of 663 female college students and 399 college men, the researchers found that individuals who were depressed were less likely to be interested in engaging in sexual behavior. However, this was not always the case, as about 10 percent of women and a higher percentage of men reported that they were interested in engaging in sexual behavior in spite of a negative mood state.

Finally, gender differences may also be influenced by ethnic background. Eisenman and Dantzker (2006) surveyed 128 men and 199 women at a Texas-Mexico border university and found that the genders differed significantly on twenty-six of thirty-eight items. For example, women were less permissive and had more negative attitudes than men in regard to oral sex, premarital intercourse, and masturbation.

Pheromones and Sexual Behavior

The term *pheromone* comes from the Greek words *pherein*, meaning "to carry," and *hormon*, meaning to "excite." Pheromones are "chemical messengers that are emitted into the environment from the body, where they can then activate specific physiological or behavioral responses in other individuals of the same species" (Grammer et al. 2005, 136). Pheromones are produced primarily by the apocrine glands located in the armpits and pubic region. The functions of pheromones include opposite-sex attractants, same-sex repellents, and mother-infant bonding.

Pheromones typically operate without the person's awareness; researchers disagree about whether pheromones do in fact influence human sociosexual behaviors. Although Levin (2004) reviewed the literature on chemical messengers in attraction, the strongest evidence for the effect of hormones on sexual behavior is that thirty-eight male volunteers who applied a male hormone to their aftershave lotion reported significant increases in sexual intercourse and sleeping next to a partner when compared with men who had a placebo in their aftershave lotion (Cutler et al. 1998).

Racial Differences in Sex Attitudes and Behaviors of Undergraduates

Davidson et al. (2008) surveyed 1,915 undergraduate women and 1,111 undergraduate men at four universities and found that race was the most influential factor differentiating the sexual attitudes and behavior of the sample. When black people were compared with white people, the former had more permissive attitudes and were more likely to approve of sexual intercourse with casual, occasional, and regular dating partners. Black people also experienced sexual intercourse earlier and with more lifetime partners. Uecker (2008) confirmed that sexual behavior of black people is inconsistent with their close affiliation with religion. One explanation is that the churches attended by black people are often reluctant to address sexual issues.

This couple is involved in a stable, committed relationship. When compared to white people, black people typically have intercourse the first time when they are younger, and they have more lifetime sexual partners.

Sexuality in Relationships

Why don't women blink during foreplay? There isn't time.
Anonymous

Sexuality occurs in a social context that influences its frequency and perceived quality.

Sexual Relationships among Never-Married Individuals

Never-married individuals and those not living together report more sexual partners than those who are married or living together. In one study, 9 percent of never-married individuals and those not living together reported having had five or more sexual partners in the previous twelve months; 1 percent of married people and 5 percent of cohabitants reported the same. However, unmarried individuals, when compared with married individuals and cohabitants, reported the lowest level of sexual satisfaction. One-third of a national sample of people who were not married and not living with anyone reported that they were emotionally satisfied with their sexual relationships. In contrast, 85 percent of the married and pair-bonded individuals reported emotional satisfaction in their sexual relationships. Hence, although never-married individuals have more sexual partners, they are less emotionally satisfied (Michael et al. 1994).

Sexual Relationships among Married Individuals

Marital sex is distinctive for its social legitimacy, declining frequency, and satisfaction (both physical and emotional).

1. *Social legitimacy.* In our society, marital intercourse is the most legitimate form of sexual behavior. Homosexual, premarital, and extramarital intercourse do not have as high a level of social approval as does marital sex. It is not only okay to have intercourse when married, it is expected. People assume that married couples make love and that something is wrong if they do not.

2. *Declining frequency.* Sexual intercourse between spouses occurs about six times a month, which declines in frequency as spouses age. Pregnancy also decreases the frequency of sexual intercourse. In addition to biological changes due to aging and pregnancy, satiation also contributes to the declining frequency

My message to the businessman of this country when they go abroad on business is that there is one thing above all they can take with them to stop them catching AIDS, and that is the wife.

Edwina Currie, former member British Parliament

of intercourse between spouses and partners in long-term relationships. Psychologists use the term **satiation** to mean that repeated exposure to a stimulus results in the loss of its ability to reinforce. For example, the first time you listen to a new CD, you derive considerable enjoyment and satisfaction from it. You may play it over and over during the first few days. After a week or so, listening to the same music is no longer new and does not give you the same level of enjoyment that it first did. So it is with intercourse. The thousandth time that a person has intercourse with the same partner is not as new and exciting as the first few times.

3. *Satisfaction (emotional and physical).* Despite declining frequency and less satisfaction over time (Liu 2003), marital sex remains a richly satisfying experience. Contrary to the popular belief that unattached singles have the best sex, the married and pair-bonded adults enjoy the most satisfying sexual relationships. In a national sample, 88 percent of married people said they received great physical pleasure from their sexual lives, and almost 85 percent said they received great emotional satisfaction (Michael et al. 1994). Individuals least likely to report being physically and emotionally pleased in their sexual relationships are those who are not married, not living with anyone, or not in a stable relationship with one person (ibid.).

Sexual Relationships among Divorced Individuals

Of the almost 2 million people getting divorced, most will have intercourse within one year of being separated from their spouses. The meanings of intercourse for separated or divorced individuals vary. For many, intercourse is a way to reestablish—indeed, repair—their crippled self-esteem. Questions like, "What did I do wrong?" "Am I a failure?" and "Is there anybody out there who will love me again?" loom in the minds of divorced people. One way to feel loved, at least temporarily, is through sex. Being held by another and being told that it feels good give people some evidence that they are desirable. Because divorced people may be particularly vulnerable, they may reach for sexual encounters as if for a lifeboat. "I felt that, as long as someone was having sex with me, I wasn't dead and I did matter," said one recently divorced person.

National Data

When asked whether intercourse was occurring less frequently than desired, 38 percent of cohabiting, 49 percent of married, 60 percent of widowed, 65 percent of single, and 74 percent of divorced people answered "yes." Hence, those most dissatisfied with frequency of intercourse are the divorced, and those most satisfied are cohabitants (*Dunn et al. 2000, 145*).

Because divorced individuals are usually in their thirties or older, they may not be as sensitized to the danger of contracting HIV as people in their twenties. Divorced individuals should always use a condom to lessen the risk of STI, including HIV infection, and AIDS.

Safe Sex: Avoiding Sexually Transmitted Infections

The Student Sexual Risks Scale (SSRS) on page 298 allows you to assess the degree to which you are at risk for contracting an STI, including HIV infection.

One of the negative consequences of sexual behavior is the risk of contracting a sexually transmitted infection (STI). Also known as sexually transmitted disease, or *STD*, **STI** refers to the general category of sexually transmitted infections such as chlamydia, genital herpes, gonorrhea, and syphilis. The most lethal of all STIs is that due to human immunodeficiency virus (**HIV**), which attacks the immune system and can lead to autoimmune deficiency syndrome **(AIDS)**. Because the consequences of contracting HIV are the most severe, we focus on HIV here. In Chapter 19 on Special Topics, we discuss other STIs.

Transmission of HIV and High-Risk Behaviors

HIV can be transmitted in several ways.

1. *Sexual contact.* HIV is found in several body fluids of infected individuals, including blood, semen, and vaginal secretions. During sexual contact with an infected individual, the virus enters a person's bloodstream through the rectum, vagina, penis (an uncircumcised penis is at greater risk because of the greater retention of the partner's fluids), and possibly the mouth during oral sex. Saliva, sweat, and tears are not body fluids through which HIV is transmitted.

2. *Intravenous drug use.* Drug users who are infected with HIV can transmit the virus to other drug users with whom they share needles, syringes, and other drug-related implements.

3. *Blood transfusions.* HIV can be acquired by receiving HIV-infected blood or blood products. Currently, all blood donors are screened, and blood is not accepted from high-risk individuals. Blood that is accepted from donors is tested for the presence of HIV. However, prior to 1985, donor blood was not tested for HIV. Individuals who received blood or blood products prior to 1985, may have been infected with HIV.

4. *Mother-child transmission.* A pregnant woman infected with HIV has a 40 percent chance of transmitting the virus through the placenta to her unborn child. These babies will initially test positive for HIV as a consequence of having the antibodies from their mother's bloodstream. However, azidothymidine (AZT, alternatively called zidovudine or ZVD) taken by the mother twelve weeks before birth seems to reduce the chance of transmission of HIV to her baby by two-thirds. HIV may also be transmitted, although rarely, from mother to infant through breast-feeding.

5. *Organ or tissue transplants and donor semen.* Receiving transplant organs and tissues, as well as receiving semen for artificial insemination, could involve risk of contracting HIV if the donors have not been tested for HIV. Such testing is essential, and recipients should insist on knowing the HIV status of the organ, tissue, or semen donor.

6. *Other methods of transmission.* For health care professionals, HIV can also be transmitted through contact with amniotic fluid surrounding a fetus, synovial

What if I Fear My Partner Has Given Me an STI?

Because most college students report having had numerous sexual partners (around fourteen for men and seven for women in our classes), it is not unlikely that either partner may have an STI and infect the other. Infecting one's partner is, of course, not necessarily reflective of being unfaithful to the current partner. Nevertheless, coping with an STI can be challenging for both the individual and for the newly infected partner. Most decide to avoid the blame game and weather the issue together.

WHAT IF?

Student Sexual Risks Scale

Safer sex means sexual activity that reduces the risk of transmitting STIs, including the AIDS virus. Using condoms is an example of safer sex. Unsafe, risky, or unprotected sex refers to sex without a condom, or to other sexual activity that might increase the risk of transmitting the AIDS virus. For each of the following items, check the response that best characterizes your option.

A = Agree
U = Undecided
D = Disagree

                                      A   U   D

____ 1. If my partner wanted me to have unprotected sex, I would probably give in.

____ 2. The proper use of a condom could enhance sexual pleasure.

____ 3. I may have had sex with someone who was at risk for HIV/AIDS.

____ 4. If I were going to have sex, I would take precautions to reduce my risk for HIV/AIDS.

____ 5. Condoms ruin the natural sex act.

____ 6. When I think that one of my friends might have sex on a date, I remind my friend to take a condom.

____ 7. I am at risk for HIV/AIDS.

____ 8. I would try to use a condom when I had sex.

____ 9. Condoms interfere with romance.

____ 10. My friends talk a lot about safer sex.

____ 11. If my partner wanted me to participate in risky sex and I said that we needed to be safer, we would still probably end up having unsafe sex.

____ 12. Generally, I am in favor of using condoms.

____ 13. I would avoid using condoms if at all possible.

____ 14. If a friend knew that I might have sex on a date, the friend would ask me whether I was carrying a condom.

____ 15. There is a possibility that I have HIV/AIDS.

____ 16. If I had a date, I would probably not drink alcohol or use drugs.

____ 17. Safer sex reduces the mental pleasure of sex.

____ 18. If I thought that one of my friends had sex on a date, I would ask the friend if he or she used a condom.

____ 19. The idea of using a condom doesn't appeal to me.

____ 20. Safer sex is a habit for me.

____ 21. If a friend knew that I had sex on a date, the friend wouldn't care whether I had used a condom or not.

____ 22. If my partner wanted me to participate in risky sex and I suggested a lower-risk alternative, we would have the safer sex instead.

____ 23. The sensory aspects of condoms (smell, touch, and so on) make them unpleasant.

____ 24. I intend to follow "safer sex" guidelines within the next year.

____ 25. With condoms, you can't really give yourself over to your partner.

____ 26. I am determined to practice safer sex.

____ 27. If my partner wanted me to have unprotected sex and I made some excuse to use a condom, we would still end up having unprotected sex.

fluid surrounding bone joints, and cerebrospinal fluid surrounding the brain and spinal cord.

STI Transmission—The Illusion of Safety in a "Monogamous" Relationship

Most individuals in a serious "monogamous" relationship assume that they are at zero risk for contracting an STI from their partner. Vail-Smith et al. (2010)

_____ 28. If I had sex and I told my friends that I did not use condoms, they would be angry or disappointed.

_____ 29. I think safer sex would get boring fast.

_____ 30. My sexual experiences do not put me at risk for HIV/AIDS.

_____ 31. Condoms are irritating.

_____ 32. My friends and I encourage each other before dates to practice safer sex.

_____ 33. When I socialize, I usually drink alcohol or use drugs.

_____ 34. If I were going to have sex in the next year, I would use condoms.

_____ 35. If a sexual partner didn't want to use condoms, we would have sex without using condoms.

_____ 36. People can get the same pleasure from safer sex as from unprotected sex.

_____ 37. Using condoms interrupts sex play.

_____ 38. Using condoms is a hassle.

Scoring (to be read after completing the previous scale)

Begin by giving yourself 80 points. Subtract one point for every undecided response. Subtract two points every time that you disagreed with odd-numbered items or with item number 38. Subtract two points every time you agreed with even-numbered items 2 through 36.

Interpreting Your Score

Research shows that students who make higher scores on the SSRS are more likely to engage in risky sexual activities, such as having multiple sex partners and failing to consistently use condoms during sex. In contrast, students who practice safer sex tend to endorse more positive attitudes toward safer sex, and tend to have peer networks that encourage safer sexual practices. These students usually plan on making sexual activity safer, and they feel confident in their ability to negotiate safer sex, even when a dating partner may press for riskier sex. Students who practice safer sex often refrain from using alcohol or drugs, which may impede

negotiation of safer sex, and often report having engaged in lower-risk activities in the past. How do you measure up?

(Below 15) Lower Risk

Congratulations! Your score on the SSRS indicates that, relative to other students, your thoughts and behaviors are more supportive of safer sex. Is there any room for improvement in your score? If so, you may want to examine items for which you lost points and try to build safer sexual strengths in those areas. You can help protect others from HIV by educating your peers about making sexual activity safer. (Of 200 students surveyed by DeHart and Berkimer, 16 percent were in this category.)

(15 to 37) Average Risk

Your score on the SSRS is about average in comparison with those of other college students. Though it is good that you don't fall into the higher-risk category, be aware that "average" people can get HIV, too. In fact, a recent study indicated that the rate of HIV among college students is ten times that in the general heterosexual population. Thus, you may want to enhance your sexual safety by figuring out where you lost points and work toward safer sexual strengths in those areas. (Of 200 students surveyed by DeHart and Berkimer, 68 percent were in this category.)

(38 and Above) Higher Risk

Relative to other students, your score on the SSRS indicates that your thoughts and behaviors are less supportive of safer sex. Such high scores tend to be associated with greater HIV-risk behavior. Rather than simply giving in to riskier attitudes and behaviors, you may want to empower yourself and reduce your risk by critically examining areas for improvement. On which items did you lose points? Think about how you can strengthen your sexual safety in these areas. Reading more about safer sex can help, and sometimes colleges and health clinics offer courses or workshops on safer sex. You can get more information about resources in your area by contacting the Center on Disease Control's HIV/AIDS Information Line at 1-800-342-2437. (Of 200 students surveyed by DeHart and Birkimer, 16 percent were in this category.)

Source

DeHart, D. D. and J. C. Birkimer. 1997. The Student Sexual Risks Scale (modification of SRS for popular use; facilitates student self-administration, scoring, and normative interpretation). Developed specifically for this text by Dana D. DeHart, College of Social work at the University of South Carolina; John C. Birkimer, University of Louisville. Used by permission of Dana DeHart.

analyzed data from 1,341 undergraduates at a large southeastern university and found that 27.2 percent of the males and 19.8 percent (almost one in five) females reported having oral, vaginal, or anal sex outside of a relationship that their partner considered monogamous. People most likely to cheat were men over the age of 20, those who were binge drinkers, members of a fraternity, male college athletes, or nonreligious people. These data suggest the need for educational efforts to encourage undergraduates in committed relationships to reconsider their STI risk and to protect themselves via condom usage.

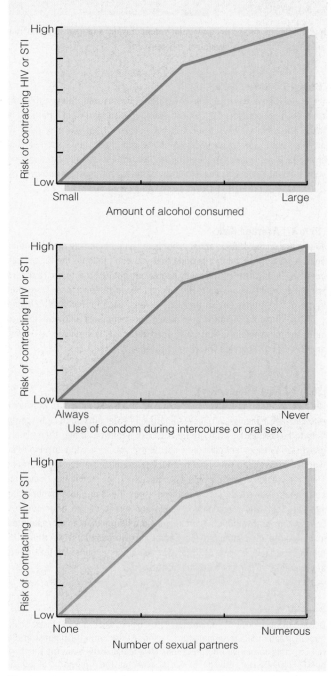

Figure 9.1
Risk of Contracting an STI, as Related to Alcohol, Condom Use, and Number of Partners

Prevention of HIV and STI Transmission

The safest relationship context for avoiding an STI (including HIV) is marriage, with cohabitation a close second (Hattori and Dodoo 2007). Of course, the best way to avoid getting an STI is to avoid sexual contact or to have contact only with partners who are not infected. This means restricting your sexual contacts to those who limit their relationships to one person. The person most likely to get an STI has sexual relations with a number of partners or with a partner who has a variety of partners. Even if you are in a mutually monogamous relationship, you may be at risk for acquiring or transmitting an STI. This is because health officials suggest that when you have sex with someone, you are having sex (in a sense) with everyone that person has had sexual contact with in the past ten years.

Condoms should be used for vaginal, anal, and oral sex and should never be reused. However, in a sample of 1,319 undergraduates, only 24.8 percent reported that they always used a condom before having intercourse (Knox and Zusman 2009). Feeling that the partner is disease-free, having had too much alcohol, and believing that "getting an STI won't happen to me" are reasons individuals do not use a condom. Some partners are also forced to have sex or do not feel free to negotiate the use of a condom in their sexual relationship (Heintz and Melendez 2006).

Using the condom properly is also important. Putting on a latex or polyurethane condom before the penis touches the partner's body makes passing STIs from one person to another difficult (natural membrane condoms do not block the transmission of STIs). Care should also be taken to withdraw the penis while it is erect to prevent fluid from leaking from the base of the condom into the partner's genital area. If a woman is receiving oral sex, she should wear a dental dam, which will prevent direct contact between the genital area and her partner's mouth.

Sexuality in an age of HIV and STIs demands talking about safer sex issues with a new potential sexual partner. Bringing up the issue of condom use should be perceived as caring for oneself, the partner, and the relationship rather than as a sign of distrust. Some individuals routinely have a condom available, and it is a "given" in any sexual encounter. Figure 9.1 illustrates that one is more likely to contract an STI through high alcohol use, low condom use, and having sex with multiple partners.

Sexual Fulfillment: Some Prerequisites

There are several prerequisites for having a good sexual relationship.

Self-Knowledge, Self-Esteem, and Health

Sexual fulfillment involves knowledge about yourself and your body. Such information not only makes it easier for you to experience pleasure but also allows you to give accurate information to a partner about pleasing you. It is not possible to teach a partner what you don't know about yourself.

Sexual fulfillment also implies having a positive self-concept. To the degree that you have positive feelings about yourself and your body, you will regard yourself as a person someone else would enjoy touching, being close to, and making love with. If you do not like yourself or your body, you might wonder why anyone else would.

Effective sexual functioning also requires good physical and mental health. This means regular exercise, good nutrition, lack of disease, and lack of fatigue. Performance in all areas of life does not have to diminish with age—particularly if people take care of themselves physically (see Chapter 17 on Relationships in the Later Years).

Good health also implies being aware that some drugs may interfere with sexual performance. Alcohol is the drug most frequently used by American adults. Although a moderate amount of alcohol can help a person become aroused through a lowering of inhibitions, too much alcohol can slow the physiological processes and deaden the senses. Shakespeare may have said it best: "It [alcohol] provokes the desire, but it takes away the performance" (*Macbeth*, act 2, scene 3). The result of an excessive intake of alcohol for women is a reduced chance of orgasm; for men, overindulgence results in a reduced chance of attaining an erection.

The reactions to marijuana are less predictable than the reactions to alcohol. Though some individuals report a short-term enhancement effect, others say that marijuana just makes them sleepy. In men, chronic use may decrease sex drive because marijuana may lower testosterone levels.

A Good Relationship, Positive Motives

A guideline among therapists who work with couples who have sexual problems is to treat the relationship before focusing on the sexual issue. The sexual relationship is part of the larger relationship between the partners, and what happens outside the bedroom in day-to-day interaction has a tremendous influence on what happens inside the bedroom. The statement, "I can't fight with you all day and want to have sex with you at night" illustrates the social context of the sexual experience.

Women most valued a partner who was open to discussing sex, who was knowledgeable about sex, who clearly communicated his desires, who was physically attractive, and who paid her compliments during sex. Being easily sexually aroused and being uninhibited were also important.

Sexual interaction communicates how the partners are feeling and acts as a barometer for the relationship. Each partner brings to a sexual encounter, sometimes unconsciously, a motive (pleasure, reconciliation, procreation, duty), a psychological state (love, hostility, boredom, excitement), and a physical state (tense, exhausted, relaxed, turned on). The combination of these factors will change from one encounter to another. Tonight a wife may feel aroused and loving and seek pleasure, but her husband may feel exhausted and hostile and have sex only out of a sense of duty. Tomorrow night, both partners may feel relaxed and have sex as a means of expressing their love for each other.

One's motives for a sexual encounter are related to the outcome. Impett et al. (2005) found that, when individuals have intercourse out of the desire to enhance personal and interpersonal or relationship pleasure, the personal and interpersonal effect on well-being is very positive. However, when sexual motives were to avoid conflict, the personal and interpersonal effects did not result in similar positive outcomes. In a study of 1,002 French adults, sexuality was more synonymous with pleasure (44.0 percent) and love (42.1 percent) than with procreation, children, or motherhood (7.8 percent) (Colson et al. 2006).

An Equal Relationship

Laumann et al. (2006) surveyed 27,500 individuals in twenty-nine countries and found that reported sexual satisfaction was higher where men and women were considered equal. Austria topped the list, with 71 percent reporting sexual satisfaction; only 25.7 percent of those surveyed in Japan reported sexual satisfaction. The United States was among those countries in which a high percentage of the respondents reported sexual satisfaction.

Open Sexual Communication and Feedback

Sexually fulfilled partners are comfortable expressing what they enjoy and do not enjoy in the sexual experience. Unless both partners communicate their needs, preferences, and expectations to each other, neither is ever sure what the other wants. In essence, the Golden Rule ("Do unto others as you would have them do unto you") is *not* helpful, because what you like may not be the same as what your partner wants. A classic example of the uncertain lover is the man who picks up a copy of *The Erotic Lover* in a bookstore and leafs through the pages until the topic on how to please a woman catches his eye. He reads that women enjoy having their breasts stimulated by their partner's tongue and teeth. Later that night in bed, he rolls over and begins to nibble on his partner's breasts. Meanwhile, she wonders what has possessed him and is unsure what to make of this new (possibly unpleasant) behavior.

Sexually fulfilled partners take the guesswork out of their relationship by communicating preferences and giving feedback. This means using what some therapists call the touch-and-ask rule. Each touch and caress may include the question, "How does that feel?" It is then the partner's responsibility to give feedback. If the caress does not feel good, the partner should say what does feel good.

Guiding and moving the partner's hand or body are also ways of giving feedback. What women and men want each other to know about sexuality is presented in Table 9.4.

Having Realistic Expectations

To achieve sexual fulfillment, expectations must be realistic. A couple's sexual needs, preferences, and expectations may not coincide. It is unrealistic to assume that your partner will want to have sex with the same frequency and in the same way that you do on all occasions. It may also be unrealistic to expect the level of sexual interest and frequency of sexual interaction in long-term relationships to remain consistently high.

Sexual fulfillment means not asking things of the sexual relationship that it cannot deliver. Failure to develop realistic expectations will result in frustration and resentment. One's health, feelings about the partner, age, and previous sexual experiences (including child sexual abuse, rape, and so on) will have an effect on one's sexuality and one's sexual relationship.

Avoiding Spectatoring

One of the obstacles to sexual functioning (we discuss sexual dysfunctions in detail at the end of this chapter) is **spectatoring**, which involves mentally observing your sexual performance and that of your partner. When the researchers in one extensive study observed how individuals actually behave during sexual intercourse, they reported a tendency for sexually dysfunctional partners to act as spectators by mentally observing their own and their partners' sexual performance. For example, the man would focus on whether he was having an erection, how complete it was, and whether it would last. He might also watch to see whether his partner was having an orgasm (Masters and Johnson 1970).

Spectatoring, as Masters and Johnson conceived it, interferes with each partner's sexual enjoyment because it creates anxiety about performance, and anxiety blocks performance. A man who worries about getting an erection reduces his chance of doing so. A woman who is anxious about achieving an orgasm probably will not. The desirable alternative to spectatoring is to relax, focus on and enjoy your own pleasure, and permit yourself to be sexually responsive.

Table 9.4 What Women and Men Want Each Other to Know about Sexuality

What Women Want Men to Know about Sex

Women tend to like a loving, gentle, patient, tender, and understanding partner. Rough sexual play can hurt and be a turnoff.

It does not impress women to hear about other women in the man's past.

If men knew what it is like to be pregnant, they would not be so apathetic about birth control.

Most women want more caressing, gentleness, kissing, and talking before and after intercourse.

Some women are sexually attracted to other women, not to men.

Sometimes the woman wants sex even if the man does not. Sometimes she wants to be aggressive without being made to feel that she shouldn't be.

Intercourse can be enjoyable without orgasm.

Many women do not have an orgasm from penetration only; they need direct stimulation of their clitoris by their partner's tongue or finger.

Men should be interested in fulfilling their partner's sexual needs.

Most women prefer to have sex in a monogamous love relationship.

When a woman says "no," she means it.

Women do not want men to expect sex every time they are alone with their partner.

Many women enjoy sex in the morning, not just at night.

Sex is *not* everything.

Women need to be lubricated before penetration.

Men should know more about menstruation.

Many women are no more inhibited about sex than men are.

Women do not like men to roll over, go to sleep, or leave right after orgasm.

Intercourse is more of a love relationship than a sex act for some women.

The woman should not always be expected to supply a method of contraception. It is also the man's responsibility.

Men should always have a condom with them and initiate putting it on.

What Men Want Women to Know about Sex

Men do not always want to be the dominant partner; women should be aggressive.

Men want women to enjoy sex totally and not be inhibited.

Men enjoy tender and passionate kissing.

Men really enjoy fellatio and want women to initiate it.

Women need to know a man's erogenous zones.

Men enjoy giving oral sex; it is not bad and unpleasant.

Many men enjoy a lot of romantic foreplay and slow, aggressive sex.

Men cannot keep up intercourse forever. Most men tire more easily than women.

Looks are not everything.

Women should know how to enjoy sex in different ways and different positions.

Women should not expect a man to get a second erection right away.

Many men enjoy sex in the morning.

Pulling the hair on a man's body can hurt.

Many men enjoy sex in a caring, loving, exclusive relationship.

It is frustrating to stop sex play once it has started.

Women should know that not all men are out to have intercourse with them. Some men like to talk and become friends.

Spectatoring is not limited to sexually dysfunctional couples and is not necessarily associated with psychopathology. It is a reaction to the concern that the performance of one's sexual partner is consistent with expectations. We all probably have engaged in spectatoring to some degree. When such spectatoring is continuous, performance is impaired.

Table 9.5 Common Sexual Myths

Masturbation is sick.

Women who love sex are sluts.

Sex education makes children promiscuous.

Sexual behavior usually ends after age 60.

People who enjoy pornography end up committing sexual crimes.

Most "normal" women have orgasms from penile thrusting alone.

Extramarital sex always destroys a marriage.

Extramarital sex will strengthen a marriage.

Simultaneous orgasm with one's partner is the ultimate sexual experience.

My partner should enjoy the same things that I do sexually.

A man cannot have an orgasm unless he has an erection.

Most people know a lot of accurate information about sex.

Using a condom ensures that you won't get HIV.

Most women prefer a partner with a large penis.

Few women masturbate.

Women secretly want to be raped.

An erection is necessary for good sex.

An orgasm is necessary for good sex.

Debunking Sexual Myths

Sexual fulfillment also means not being victim to sexual myths. Some of the more common myths include that sex equals intercourse and orgasm, that women who love sex don't have values, and that the double standard is dead. Another common sexual myth is that the elderly have no interest in sex. Beckman et al. (2006) examined the sexual interests and needs of 563 70-year-olds and found that 95 percent reported the continuation of such interests and needs as they aged. Almost 70 percent (69 percent) of the married men and 57 percent of the married women reported continued sexual behavior. Nobre et al. (2006) noted that belief in sexual myths makes one vulnerable to sexual dysfunctions. Table 9.5 presents some other sexual myths.

SUMMARY

What are sexual values?

Sexual values are moral guidelines for making sexual choices in nonmarital, marital, heterosexual, and homosexual relationships.

What are alternative sexual values?

Three sexual values are absolutism (rightness is defined by official code of morality), relativism (rightness depends on the situation—who does what, with whom, in what context), and hedonism ("if it feels good, do it"). Relativism is the sexual value most college students hold, with women being more relativistic than men and men being more hedonistic than women. Black people report having more absolutist values. Under the Bush administration, this value was taught in the public school system if the school wanted federal funds. There is no evidence that these abstinence-based sex education programs are effective in stopping unmarried youth from having sex. Half of those who take the "virginity pledge" withdraw the pledge within one year (male and black individuals most likely). About three-fourths of college students believe that if they have oral sex, they are still virgins. About half of undergraduates reported involvement in a "friends with benefits" relationship. Women are more likely to focus on the "friendship" aspect, men on the "benefits" (sex) aspect.

What is the sexual double standard?

The sexual double standard is the view that encourages and accepts sexual expression of men more than women. For example, men may have more sexual partners than women without being stigmatized. The double standard is also reflected in movies.

What are sources of sexual values?

The sources of sexual values include one's school, family, and religion as well as technology, television, social movements, and the Internet.

What are various sexual behaviors?

Some individuals are asexual—having an absence of sexual behavior with a partner and one's self (masturbation). About 4 percent of females and 11 percent of males report being asexual in the last twelve months.

Kissing involves various meanings including love, approval, hello, goodbye, or as an ointment such as when a parent kisses the hurt knee of a child, and so on. French kissing may be dangerous by increasing risk of a bacterial infection that may lead to meningitis. Masturbation involves stimulating one's own body with the goal of experiencing pleasurable sexual sensations. Fellatio is oral stimulation of the man's genitals by his partner. In many states, legal statutes regard fellatio as a "crime against nature," in that the sex does not produce babies. Cunnilingus is oral stimulation of the woman's genitals by her partner. Increasingly, youth who have oral sex regard themselves as virgins, believing that only sexual intercourse constitutes "having sex." Vaginal intercourse, or coitus, refers to the sexual union of a man and woman by insertion of the penis into the vagina. The top reasons for intercourse include: (1) pure attraction to the other person in general; (2) physical pleasure; (3) expression of love; (4) feelings of desire by the other; (5) escalation of the depth of the relationship.

Anal (not vaginal) intercourse is the sexual behavior associated with the highest risk of HIV infection. The potential for the rectum to tear and blood contact to occur presents the greatest danger. AIDS is lethal. Partners who use a condom during anal intercourse reduce their risk of not only HIV infection but also other STIs.

Sexual behavior with a partner is associated with feelings of well-being. Indeed, experiencing affection and sex with a partner on one day predicted lower negative mood, higher positive mood, and lower stress the following day.

Cybersex is "any consensual, computer mediated, participatory sexual experience involving two or more individuals" (Hamman 2007, 34). Men are more likely to engage in cybersex behavior.

What are gender differences in sexuality?

Gender differences in sexual beliefs include that men are more likely than women to believe that oral sex is not sex, that cybersex is not cheating, that men can't tell if a woman is faking orgasm, and that sex frequency drops in marriage. In regard to sexual behavior, men are more likely than females to report frequenting strip clubs, paying for sex, having anonymous sex with strangers, having casual sexual relations, and having more sexual partners. When asked what they would do in a "Vegas" context where no one would know what they did, males were more likely than females to identify a range of sexual behaviors they would engage in.

How do pheromones affect sexual behavior?

Pheromones are chemical messengers emitted from the body that activate physiological and behavioral responses. The functions of pheromones include opposite-sex attractants, same-sex repellents, and mother-infant bonding. Researchers disagree about whether pheromones do in fact influence human sociosexual behaviors. In one study, men who applied a male hormone to their aftershave lotion reported significant increases in sexual intercourse and sleeping next to a partner in comparison with men who had a placebo in their aftershave lotion.

What are the sexual relationships of never-married, married, and divorced people?

Never-married and noncohabiting individuals report more sexual partners than those who are married or living with a partner. Marital sex is distinctive for its social legitimacy, declining frequency, and satisfaction (both physical and emotional). Divorced individuals have a lot of sexual partners but are the least sexually fulfilled.

How does one avoid contracting or transmitting STIs?

The best way to avoid getting an STI is to avoid sexual contact or to have contact only with partners who are not infected. This means restricting your sexual contacts to those who limit their relationships to one person. The person most likely to get an STI has sexual relations with a number of partners or with a partner who has a variety of partners. Even if you are in a mutually monogamous relationship, you may be at risk for acquiring an STI, as 30 percent of male undergraduate students and 20 percent of female undergraduate students in "monogamous" relationships reported having oral, vaginal, or anal sex with another partner outside of the monogamous relationship.

What are the prerequisites of sexual fulfillment?

Fulfilling sexual relationships involve self-knowledge, self-esteem, health, a good nonsexual relationship, open sexual communication, safer sex practices, and making love with, not to, one's partner. Other variables include realistic expectations ("my partner will not always want what I want") and not buying into sexual myths ("masturbation is sick").

KEY TERMS

absolutism	barebacking	friends with benefits	secondary virginity
AIDS	coitus	hedonism	sexual double standard
alcohol-exposed pregnancy	comprehensive program	HIV	sexual values
anodyspareunia	cunnilingus	masturbation	social script
asceticism	cybersex	relativism	spectatoring
asexual	fellatio	satiation	STI (sexually transmitted infection)

The Companion Website for *Choices in Relationships: An Introduction to Marriage and the Family*, Tenth Edition
www.cengage.com/sociology/knox

Supplement your review of this chapter by going to the Companion Website to take one of the tutorial quizzes, use the flash cards to master key terms, or check out the many other study aids, like crossword puzzles and self-assessments. You'll also find special features such as General Social Survey (GSS) data, Census data, and other resources to help you with that special project or to do some research on your own.

WEB LINKS

Body Health: A Multimedia AIDS and HIV Information Resource
http://www.thebody.com

Centers for Disease Control and Prevention (CDC)
http://www.cdc.gov

Go Ask Alice: Sexuality
http://www.goaskalice.columbia.edu/

Sex Ed 101
http://www.libidoh.com/

Sexual Intimacy
http://www.heartchoice.com/sex_intimacy/

Sexual Health Network
http://www.sexualhealth.com/

Sexuality Information and Education Council of the United States (SIECUS)
http://www.siecus.org

REFERENCES

Beckman, N. M., M. Waern, I. Skoog, and The Sahlgrenska Academy at Goteborg University, Sweden. 2006. Determinants of sexuality in 70 year olds. *The Journal of Sex Research* 43:2–3.
Bersamin, M., M. Todd, D. A. Fisher, D. L. Hill, J. W. Grube, and S. Walker. 2008. Parenting practices and adolescent sexual behavior: A longitudinal study. *Journal of Marriage and Family* 70: 97–112.

Bristol, K., and B. Farmer. 2005. *Sexuality among Southeastern university students: A survey.* Unpublished data. Greenville, NC: East Carolina University.

Brucker, H., and P. Bearman 2005. After the promise: The STD consequences of adolescent virginity pledges. *Journal of Adolescent Health* 36:271–78.

Burleson, M. H., W. R. Trevathan, and M. Todd. 2007. In the mood for love or vice versa? Exploring the relations among sexual activity, physical affection, affect, and stress in the daily lives of mid-aged women *Archives of Sexual Behavior* 36:357–68.

Carpenter, L. M. 2003. Like a virgin . . . again? Understanding secondary virginity in context. Paper presented at the 73rd Annual Meeting of the Eastern Sociological Society, Philadelphia, February 28.

Centers for Disease Control and Prevention. 2004. *HIV/AIDS Surveillance Report 2004.* Vol 16. Atlanta: U.S. Department of Health and Human Services, Centers for Disease Control and Prevention.

Cheung, M. W., P. W. Wong, K. Y. Liu, S. Y. Fan, and T. Lam. 2008. A study of sexual satisfaction and frequency of sex among Hong Kong Chinese couples. *Journal of Sex Research* 45:129–39.

Colson, M., A. Lemaire, P. Pinton, K. Hamidi, and P. Klein. 2006. Sexual behaviors and mental perception, satisfaction, and expectations of sex life in men and women in France. *The Journal of Sexual Medicine* 3:121–31.

Cutler, W. B., E. Friedmann, and N. L. McCoy. 1998. Pheromonal influences on sociosexual behavior in men. *Archives of Sexual Behavior* 27:1–13.

Damon, W., and B. R. Simon Rosser. 2005. Anodyspareunia in men who have sex with men: Prevalence, predictors, consequences and the development of DSM diagnostic criteria. *Journal of Sex & Marital Therapy* 31:129–41.

Davidson, J. K., Sr., N. B. Moore, J. R. Earle, and R. Davis. 2008. Sexual attitudes and behavior at four universities: Do region, race, and/or religion matter? *Adolescence* 43:189–223.

DeLamater, J., and M. Hasday. 2007 The sociology of sexuality. In *21st century sociology: A reference handbook,* ed. Clifton D. Bryant and Dennis L. Peck, 254–64. Thousand Oaks, California: Sage.

Dolbik-Vorobei, T. A. 2005. What college students think about problems of marriage and having children. *Russian Education and Society* 47:47–58.

Dotson-Blake, K., D. Knox, and M. Zusman. Forthcoming. Oral sex and still a virgin?: A profile of undergraduates who agree.

Doub, L. J. 2006. Adolescent sexual behaviors and attitudes: A retrospective report. 4th Annual ECU Research and Creative Activities Symposium, April 21, East Carolina University, Greenville, NC.

Dunn, K. M., P. R. Croft, and G. I. Hackett. 2000. Satisfaction in the sex life of a general population sample. *Journal of Sex and Marital Therapy* 26:141–51.

Eisenman, R., and M. L. Dantzker. 2006. Gender and ethnic differences in sexual attitudes at a Hispanic-serving university. *The Journal of General Psychology* 133:153–63.

Else-Quest, N. M., J. S. Hyde, and J. D. DeLamater. 2005. Context counts: Long-term sequelae of premarital intercourse of abstinence. *Journal of Sex Research* 42:102–12.

England, P., and R. J. Thomas. 2006. The decline of the date and the rise of the college hook up. In *Family in transition,* 14th ed., ed. A.S. Skolnick and J. H. Skolnick, 151–62. Boston: Pearson Allyn & Bacon.

Gagnon, J. (2004) Personal communication.

Ghuman, S. 2005. Attitudes about sex and marital sexual behavior in Hai Duong Province, Vietnam. *Studies in Family Planning* 36:95–106.

Gibbs, N. 2008. The pursuit of purity. *Time,* July 28, 46–49.

Ginsberg, T. B., S. C. Pomerantz, and V. K. Freeley. 2005. Sexuality in older adults: behaviours and frequencies. *Age and Ageing* 34:475–86.

Graham, C. A., S. A. Sanders, R. R. Milhausen, and K. R. McBride. 2004. Turning on and turning off: A focus group study of the factors that affect women's sexual arousal. *Archives of Sexual Behavior* 33:527–38.

Grammer, K., F. Bernard, and N. Neave. 2005. Human pheromones and sexual attraction. *European Journal of Obstetrics & Gynecology and Reproductive Biology* 118:135–42.

Greene, K. and S. Faulkner. 2005. Gender, belief in the sexual double standard, and sexual talk in heterosexual dating relationships. *Sex Roles* 53:239–51.

Gross, A. M., A. Winslett, M. Roberts, and C. L. Gohm. 2005. Heterosexual risk behaviors among urban young adolescents. *Violence Against Women* 12:288–301.

Gross, K. 2006. Teenage kissing may increase meningococcal risk. *Youth Studies Australia* 25:5–6.

Halstead, M. J. 2005. Teaching about love. *British Journal of Educational Studies* 53:290–305.

Hamman, R. 2007. Cyberorgasms: Ten years on and not enough learned. In *Online Matchmaking* ed. M. T. Whitty, A. J. Baker, and J. A. Inman, 31–39. New Work: Paulgrave Macmillan.

Hattori, M. K., and F. N. Dodoo. 2007. Cohabitation, marriage and sexual monogamy in Nairobi's slums. *Social Science and Medicine* 64:1067–72.

Heintz, A. J., and R. M. Melendez. 2006. Intimate partner violence and HIV/STD risk among lesbian, gay, bisexual and transgender individuals. *Journal of Interpersonal Violence* 21:193–208.

Hertzog, 2004. Negotiating the gray area: Women reflecting on the "sex talk" and abstinence. Poster session at the National Council on Family Relations, November. Orlando, Florida.

Hollander, D. 2006. Many teenagers who say they have taken a Virginity Pledge retract that statement after having intercourse. *Perspectives on Sexual and Reproductive Health* 38:168–73.

Hughes, M., K. Morrison, and K. J. Asada. 2005. What's love got to do with it? Exploring the impact of maintenance rules, love attitudes, and network support on friends with benefits relationships. *Western Journal of Communication* 69:49–66.

Impett, E. A., L. A. Peplau, and S. L. Gable. 2005. Approach and avoidance sexual motives: Implications for personal and interpersonal well-being. *Personal Relationships* 12:465–82.

Kaestle, C. E., D. E. Morisky, and D. J. Wiley. 2002. Sexual intercourse and the age difference between adolescent females and their romantic partners. *Perspectives on Sexual and Reproductive Health* 34:304–30.

Kim, J. L., C. L. Sorsoli, K. Collins, B. A. Zylbergold, D. Schooler, and D. L. Tolman. 2007. From sex to sexuality: Exposing the heterosexual script on primetime network television. *Journal of Sex Research* 44:145–57.

Knox, D., and Zusman, M. E. 2009. Relationship and sexual behaviors of a sample of 1,319 university students. Unpublished data collected for this text. Department of Sociology, East Carolina University, Greenville, NC.

Knox, D., M. Zusman, and A. McNeely. 2008. University student beliefs about sex: Men vs. women *College Student Journal* 42:181–85.

Kornreich, J. L., K. D. Hern, G. Rodriguez, and L. F. O'Sullivan. 2003. Sibling influence, gender roles, and the sexual socialization of urban early adolescent girls. *Journal of Sex Research* 40:101–10.

Laumann, E. O., A. Nicolosi, D. B. Glasser, A. Paik, C. Gingell, E. Moreira, and T. Wang. 2005. Sexual problems among women and men aged 40–80: Prevalence and correlates identified in the Global Study of Sexual Attitudes and Behaviors. *International Journal of Impotence Research* 17:39–57.

Laumann, E. O., A. Paik, D. B. Glasser, J.-H. Kang, T. Wang, B. Levinson, E. D. Moreira, Jr., A. Nicolosi, and C. Gingell. 2006. A cross-national study of subjective sexual well-being among older women and men: Findings from the global study of sexual attitudes and behaviors. *Archives of Sexual Behavior* (April).

Lenton, A. P., and A. Bryan. 2005. An affair to remember: The role of sexual scripts in perceptions of sexual intent. *Personal Relationships* 12:483–98.

Levin, R. 2004. Smells and tastes: their putative influence on sexual activity in humans. *Sexual & Relationship Therapy* 19:451–62.

Liu, C. 2003. Does quality of marital sex decline with duration? *Archives of Sexual Behavior* 32:55–60.

Lykins, A. D., E. Janssen, and C. A. Graham. 2006. The relationship between negative mood and sexuality in heterosexual college women and men. *The Journal of Sex Research* 43:136–44.

Masters, W. H., and V. E. Johnson. 1970. *Human sexual inadequacy.* Boston: Little, Brown.

Mathy, R. M. 2007. Sexual orientation moderates online sexual activity. In *Online Matchmaking* ed. M. T. Whitty, A. J. Baker, and J. A. Inman, 159–77. New Work: Paulgrave Macmillan.

Mbopi-Keou, F. X, R. E. Mbu, H. Gonsu Kamga, G. C. M. Kalla, M. Monny Lobe, C. G. Teo, R. J. Leke, P. M. Ndumbe, and L. Belec. 2005. Interactions between human immunodeficiency virus and herpes viruses within the oral mucosa. *Clinical Microbiology and Infection* 11:83–85.

McGinty, K., D. Knox, and M. Zusman. 2007. Friends with benefits: Women want "friends," men want "benefits." *College Student Journal* 41:1128–31.

Meston, C. M., and D. M.Buss. 2007. Why humans have sex. *Archives of Sexual Behavior* 36:477–507.

Michael, R. T., J. H. Gagnon, E. O. Laumann, and G. Kolata. 1994. *Sex in America.* Boston: Little, Brown.

Miller, S. A., and E. S. Byers. 2004. Actual and desired duration of foreplay and intercourse: Discordant and misperceptions within heterosexual couples. *The Journal of Sex Research* 41:301–09.

Naimi, T. S., L. E. Lipscomb, R. D. Brewer, and B. C. Gilbert. 2003. Binge drinking in the preconception period and the risk of unintended pregnancy: Implications for women and their children. *Pediatrics* 111:1136–41.

Nobre, P. J., and J. Pinto-Gouveia. 2006. Dysfunctional sexual beliefs as vulnerability factors for sexual dysfunction. *The Journal of Sex Research* 43:68–74.

O'Donnell, L., A. Stueve, R. W. Simmons, K. Dash, G. Agronick, and V. JeanBaptiste. 2006. Heterosexual risk behaviors among urban young adolescents. *The Journal of Early Adolescence* 26:87–98.

O'Reilly, S., D. Knox, and M. Zusman. 2006. "I have never masturbated": 973 college students who said "yes" or "no." Paper presented at the annual Meeting Southern Sociological Society, March. New Orleans.

O'Reilly, S., D. Knox, and M. Zusman. 2007. College student attitudes toward pornography use. *College Student Journal* 41:402–06.

Puentes, J., D. Knox, and M. Zusman. 2008. Participants in "Friends with Benefits" relationships. *College Student Journal* 42:176–80.

Raley, R. K. 2000. Recent trends and differentials in marriage and cohabitation: The United States. In *The ties that bind,* ed. L. J. Waite, 19–39. New York: Aldine de Gruyter.

Richey, E., D. Knox, and M. Zusman. 2009. Sexual values of 783 undergraduates. *College Student Journal* 43:175–80.

Rose, S. 2005. Going too far? Sex, sin and social policy. *Social Forces* 84:1207–32.

Sakalh-Ugurlu, N., and P. Glick. 2003. Ambivalent sexism and attitudes toward women who engage in premarital sex in Turkey. *Journal of Sex Research* 40:296–302.

Schuster, M. A., M. K. Beckett, R. Corona, and A. J. Zhou. 2005. Hugs and kisses: HIV Infected parents' fears about contagion and the effects on parent-child interaction in a nationally representative sample. *Archives of Pediatrics & Adolescent Medicine* 159:173–80.

Simon, W., and J. Gagnon. 1998. Psychosexual development. *Society* 35:60–68.

Stone, N., B. Hatherall, R. Ingham, and J. McEachron. 2006. Oral sex and condom use among young people in the United Kingdom. *Perspectives on Sexual and Reproductive Health* 38:6–13.

Thomsen, D., and I. J. Chang. 2000. Predictors of satisfaction with first intercourse: A new perspective for sexuality education. Poster at the 62nd Annual Conference of the National Council on Family Relations, Minneapolis, November.

True Love Waits. 2006. http://www.lifeway.com/tlw/students/join.asp (accessed January 14, 2006).

Uecker, J. E. 2008. Religion, pledging, and the premarital sexual behavior of married young adults. *Journal of Marriage and the Family* 70:728–44.

Vail-Smith, K., D. Knox, and L. M. Whetstone. 2010. The illusion of safety in "monogamous" relationships. *American Journal of Health Behavior.*

Wolitski, R. J. 2005. The emergence of barebacking among gay and bisexual men in the United States: A public health perspective. *Journal of Gay & Lesbian Psychotherapy* 9:9–34.

Chapter 9 Sexuality in Relationships

Making the decision to have a child—it's momentous. It is to decide forever to have your heart walking around outside your body.

Elizabeth Stone, *author*

Planning Children and Contraception

Contents

True or False?

1. The majority of undergraduates no longer want to have children.

2. The fertility rate in Canada, Europe, Japan, and Korea has fallen below the replacement level.

3. Genetic testing has now advanced so that the full range of potential diseases and their certainty can be predicted.

4. Postabortion attitudes of men are typically those of regret because they were against the abortion.

5. Having an abortion has more negative consequences than birthing a child from an unplanned pregnancy.

Answers: **1.** F **2.** T **3.** F **4.** F **5.** F

Love is all fun and games until someone loses an eye or gets pregnant.

Unknown

A husband noted that the reason he and his wife have six children is that he is deaf. When the couple goes to bed, his wife asks, "Do you want to go to sleep or what?" He would always ask, "What?"

The cultural message on having children is mixed. Although young married individuals are encouraged to "have fun and travel before they begin their family" and to "strap on their seat belts when their children become teenagers," spouses are also told that "marriage has no real meaning without children" and "aren't they precious?" In spite of these dichotomous messages, having children continues to be a major goal of college students. In a nonrandom sample of 1,319 undergraduates at a large southeastern university, 91 percent agreed, "Someday I want to have children" (Knox and Zusman 2009).

Planning children, or failing to do so, is a major societal issue. Planning when to become pregnant has benefits for both the mother and the child. Having several children at short intervals increases the chances of premature birth, infectious disease, and death of the mother or the baby. Would-be parents can minimize such risks by planning fewer children with longer intervals in between. Women who plan their pregnancies can also modify their behaviors and seek preconception care from a health care practitioner to maximize their chances of having healthy pregnancies and babies. For example, women planning pregnancies can make sure they eat properly and avoid alcohol and other substances (such as cigarettes) that could harm developing fetuses. Partners who plan their children also benefit from family planning by pacing the financial demands of their offspring. Having children four years apart helps to avoid having more than one child in college at the same time. Conscientious family planning will also help to reduce the number of unwanted pregnancies. Schwarz et al. (2008) asked 192 women how they would feel if they learned they were pregnant. Of them, 9 percent reported that they would feel like they were dying, and 28 percent said they would trade time from the end of their life.

International Data

Worldwide, 80 million unintended pregnancies occur each year (38 percent of all pregnancies). These pregnancies result in 42 million induced abortions and 34 million unintended births (Speidel et al. 2008).

Your choices in regard to children and contraception have important effects on your happiness, lifestyle, and resources. These choices, in large part, are influenced by social and cultural factors that may operate without your awareness. We now discuss these influences.

Do You Want to Have Children?

Nothing you do for children is ever wasted. They seem not to notice us, hovering, averting our eyes, and they seldom offer thanks, but what we do for them is never wasted.

Garrison Keillor, storyteller, humorist

National Data

Marital births increased from 2,611,000 in 2005 to 2,624,000 in 2006, or an increase of 13,000. Nonmarital births increased from 1,527,000 to 1,642,000, or an increase of 117,000. For the first time in thirty-five years, the rate of births to American women averages out to a level at which the population will reproduce itself by births alone, without counting any population growth fueled by the arrival of new immigrants (Martin 2008).

Beyond a biological drive to reproduce, societies socialize their members to have children. This section examines the social influences that motivate individuals to have children, the lifestyle changes that result from such a choice, and the costs of rearing children.

Social Influences Motivating Individuals to Have Children

Our society tends to encourage childbearing, an attitude known as **pronatalism**. Our family, friends, religion, and government help to develop positive attitudes toward parenthood. Cultural observances also function to reinforce these attitudes.

Family Our experience of being reared in families encourages us to have families of our own. Our parents are our models. They married; we marry. They had children; we have children. Some parents exert a much more active influence. "I'm 73 and don't have much time. Will I ever see a grandchild?" asked the mother of an only child.

Friends Our friends who have children influence us to do likewise. After sharing an enjoyable weekend with friends who had a little girl, one husband wrote to the host and hostess, "Lucy and I are always affected by Karen—she is such a good child to have around. We haven't made up our minds yet, but our desire to have a child of our own always increases after we leave your home." This couple became parents sixteen months later.

Religion Religion is a powerful influence on the decision to have children. Catholics are taught that having children is the basic purpose of marriage and gives meaning to the union. Mormonism and Judaism also have a strong family orientation.

Race Although Hispanics have the highest fertility rate, their numbers are not sufficient to account for the fact that fertility rates for the United States are increasing (Martin 2008).

Government The tax structures that our federal and state governments impose support parenthood. Married couples without children pay higher taxes than couples with children, although the reduction in taxes is not sufficient to offset the cost of rearing a child and is not large enough to be a primary inducement to have children.

Economy Times of affluence are associated with a high birth rate. Postwar expansion of the 1950s resulted in the oft-noted "baby boom" generation. Similarly, couples are less likely to decide to have a child during economically depressed times. In addition, the necessity of two wage earners in our postindustrial economy is associated with a reduction in the number of children.

Diversity in Other Countries

Most other wealthy countries, from Canada, to Europe, to Japan, to Korea, have seen their fertility fall well below replacement level. (Our closest European counterpart is France, which has seen its fertility rate rise from 1.66 percent in 1993 to 1.98 percent in 2007) (Martin 2008).

Diversity in Other Countries

In China and Korea, the eldest son is expected to take care of his aging parents by earning money for them and by marrying and bringing his wife into their home to physically care for his parents. The wife's parents need their own son and daughter-in-law to provide old age insurance. Beyond its value in providing economic security and old age insurance, having numerous children is regarded as a symbol of virility for a man, a source of prestige for a woman, and a sign of good fortune for the couple. In modern societies, having large numbers of children is less valued.

How Old Is Too Old to Have a Child?

Rajo Devi was age 70 when she gave birth to a baby girl in Calcutta in 2008. Her pregnancy was the result of in vitro fertilization. Jaci Dalenberg, of Wooster, Ohio, was 56, when she gave birth to triplets in 2008. She carried the babies as a surrogate for her daughter, Kim Coseno. Hence, Jaci gave birth to her own grandchildren. The two identical twins and their sister were born October 11, at Cleveland Clinic's Hillcrest Hospital. Jaci is thought to be the oldest woman in America to give birth to twins. Talk show host Larry King had a child at the age of 65. Births to older parents are becoming more common, and questions are now being asked about the appropriateness of elderly individuals becoming parents. Should social policies on this issue be developed?

There are advantages and disadvantages of having a child as an elderly parent. The primary developmental advantage for the child of retirement-aged parents is the attention the parents can devote to their offspring. Not distracted by their careers, these parents have more time and interest to nurture, play with, and teach their children. Although they may have less energy, their experience and knowledge are doubtless better.

The primary disadvantage of having a child in the later years is that the parents are likely to die before, or early in, the child's adult life. Larry King will need to live until he is in his mid-eighties to experience the high school graduation and marriage of his son.

There are also medical concerns for both the mother and the baby during pregnancy in later life. They include an increased risk of morbidity (chronic illness and disease) and mortality (death) for the mother. These risks are typically a function of chronic disorders that go along with aging, such as diabetes, hypertension, and cardiac disease. Stillbirths, miscarriages, ectopic pregnancies, multiple births, and congenital malformations are also more frequent for women with advancing age. However, prenatal testing can identify some potential problems such as the risk of Down syndrome, and any chromosome abnormality and negative neonatal outcomes are not inevitable. Because an older woman can usually have a healthy baby, government regulations on the age at which a woman can become pregnant are not likely.

Age of the father may also be an issue in older parenting. Auger and Jouannet (2005) observed that a higher rate of miscarriages has been related to older fathers, and several studies have suggested that older fathers are at the origin of several diseases in the newborn. However, Romkens et al. (2005) reviewed both the medical and psychological literature of older men (age 50 years and up) having children and concluded that there are no medical or psychosocial data-based justifications to support an age limit for men having children. Given the lack of scientific support and the cultural norm that older men may fertilize younger women, governmental regulations on age limits for parenting are unlikely.

Your Opinion?

1. How old do you think is "too old" to begin being a parent?
2. Do you think the government should attempt to restrict people from having a biological child in their fifties?
3. Who do you feel benefits most and least from having a child in later life?

Sources

Auger, J., and P. Jouannet. 2005. Age and male fertility: biological factors. *Review of Epidemiology et de Sante Publique* 53:225–35.

Romkens, M., B. Gordijn, C. M. Verhaak, E. J. H. Meuleman, and D. D. M. Braat. 2005. No arguments to support an age limit for men entering an in vitro fertilization or intracytoplasmic sperm injection programme. *Nederlands Tijdschrift Voor Geneeskunde* 149:992–95.

He changed everything, but in the most wonderful way. Everything that should matter, matters. He's absolutely the center of my life.

Angelina Jolie, on her adopted son, Maddox

Cultural Observances   Our society reaffirms its approval of parents every year by identifying special days for Mom and Dad. Each year on Mother's Day and Father's Day (and now Grandparents' Day), parenthood is celebrated across the nation with cards, gifts, and embraces. People choosing not to have children have no cultural counterpart (for example, Childfree Day). In addition to influencing individuals to have children, society and culture also influence feelings about the age parents should be when they have children. Recently, couples have been having children at later ages. Is this a good idea? The above Social Policy discusses this issue.

Individual Motivations for Having Children

Individual motivations, as well as social influences, play an important role in the decision to have children. Some of these are conscious, as in the desire to love and to be loved by one's own child, companionship, and the desire to be personally fulfilled as an adult by having a child. Some also want to recapture their own childhood and youth by having a child. Unconscious motivations for parenthood

This father was 58 when his daughter was born. They are celebrating her twentieth birthday. He had another child, a son, when he was 62.

may also be operative. Examples include wanting a child to avoid career tracking and to gain the acceptance and approval of one's parents and peers. Teenagers sometimes want to have a child to have someone to love them. Later in the chapter we detail teenage motherhood as a major social issue.

Lifestyle Changes and Economic Costs of Parenthood

Although becoming a parent has numerous potential positive outcomes, parenting also has drawbacks. Every parent knows that parenthood involves difficulties as well as joys. Some of the difficulties associated with parenthood are discussed next.

Children have never been very good at listening to their elders, but they have never failed to imitate them.

James Baldwin, author

Lifestyle Changes Becoming a parent often involves changes in lifestyle. Daily living routines become focused around the needs of the children. Living arrangements change to provide space for another person in the household. Some parents change their work schedule to allow them to be home more. Food shopping and menus change to accommodate the appetites of children. A major lifestyle change is the loss of freedom of activity and flexibility in one's personal schedule. Lifestyle changes are particularly dramatic for women. The time and effort required to be pregnant and rear children often compete with the time and energy needed to finish one's education. Building a career is also negatively impacted by the birth of children. Parents learn quickly that being both involved, on-the-spot parents and climbing the career ladder are difficult. The careers of women may suffer most.

Financial Costs Meeting the financial obligations of parenthood is difficult for many parents. The costs begin with prenatal care and continue at childbirth. For an uncomplicated vaginal delivery, with a two-day hospital stay, the cost may total $10,000, whereas a cesarean section birth may cost $14,000. The annual cost of a child less than 2 years old for middle-income parents ($45,800 to $77,100)— which includes housing ($4,010), food ($1,280), transportation ($1,390), clothing ($410), health care ($780), child care ($2,000), and miscellaneous ($1,090)—is $10,960. For a 15- to 17-year-old, the cost is $12,030 (*Statistical Abstract of the United States*, 2009, Table 667). These costs do not include the wages lost when a parent drops out of the workforce to provide child care.

Undergraduate Gender Differences in Attitudes toward Children*

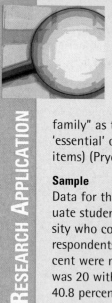

Although undergraduate life includes parties, alcohol, and sex, the larger personal agenda of pair-bonding, procreation, and socialization of one's offspring remains a major life goal. Indeed, 75.5 percent of 240,000 plus freshmen in 340 colleges and universities identified "raising a family" as the most important "objective considered 'essential' or 'very important'" (from a list of twenty items) (Pryor et al. 2008).

Sample

Data for the study involved a sample of 293 undergraduate student volunteers at a large southeastern university who completed a fifty-item questionnaire. Of the respondents, 73.4 percent were female, and 26.6 percent were male. The median age of the respondents was 20 with a range of 17 to 46. Of the respondents, 40.8 percent were freshmen, 20.5 percent sophomores, 17.5 percent juniors, and 21.2 percent seniors. Racial background of the respondents was 82 percent white people and 17.9 percent black people (respondent self-identified as African American Black, African Black, or Caribbean Black). In comparing the responses of women and men, cross-classification was conducted to determine any relationships with chi-square utilized to assess statistical significance.

Findings

Analysis of the data revealed the following ten statistically significant gender differences in regard to attitudes toward children:

1. *Females were more likely to feel having children is important* (94.3 percent versus 90.5 percent) (p < .007). This finding is consistent with previous research. Indeed, De Marneffe (2004) emphasized that women "naturally" have the desire to care for children and that this is one of life's great pleasures. She suggested that the desire to nurture is a biological imperative and crucial to the survival of the species.

2. *Females were more likely to view children as providing a reason to live* (40.1 percent versus 23.2 percent) (p < .008).

3. *Females were more likely to enjoy being around toddlers or young children* (93.2 percent versus 74.1 percent) (p < .001).

4. *Females were more likely to have taken care of an infant.* The pro-child value females have is related to the fact that they have almost three times the experience of taking care of an infant than a male. Almost 60 percent of the female respondents, compared to less than a fourth of male respondents (59.7 percent versus 23.1 percent) (p < .000) reported that they had taken care of an infant.

5. *Females were less likely to be annoyed by crying babies.* In response to the statement, "crying babies drive me crazy," 32.4 percent of the female respondents compared to 56.2 percent (p < .004) of the male respondents agreed.

6. *Females were more likely to view "wanting children" as an important criteria for a mate* (91.7 percent versus 70.5 percent) (p < .001).

7. *Females were less likely to marry a man who did not want children.* Consistent with the previous finding, females were more likely to eliminate from consideration marrying a person who could not or would not have children (44.3 percent versus 21.5 percent) (p < .007).

8. *Females were more likely to divorce a spouse if the spouse turned against children.* Were a marriage to occur with the woman assuming that her husband wanted children and she were to find out that he had changed his mind, she would divorce him. Almost three times as many female as male (29.5 percent versus 10.8 percent) respondents agreed that they would divorce their spouse if "I was married and my spouse turned against having children."

9. *Females were more likely to consider adoption if the spouse were sterile* (89.3 percent versus 76.2 percent) (p < .001).

Home is the place where boys and girls first learn how to limit their wishes, abide by rules, and consider the rights and needs of others.

Sidonie Gruenberg, author

Most parents value their children attending college. See the website at the end of this chapter in regard to the College Cost Calculator. The price varies depending on whether a child attends to a public or private college. The annual cost for a child attending a four-year public college in the state of residence is around $14,203 (including tuition, board, dorm); for a private college the cost is around $40,000 annually (*Statistical Abstract of the United States, 2009*, Table 282). Collegeboard.com will identify the cost of a specific college.

In spite of the costs children incur, most people look forward to having children. The Self-Assessment section on page 316 allows you to assess the degree to which you value having children.

10. *Females were more likely to be open to having a child of either sex.* Although spouses tend to prefer having two children (one of each sex) (Overington 2006), if they could have only one child, 46.2 percent of the female respondents compared to 33.8 percent of the male respondents reported that they could "care less" whether they had a male or female child.

Theoretical Explanation for the Findings

Both sociobiology and biosocial theoretical perspectives are helpful in explaining the findings of this study. The data emphasized that women evidenced significantly more interest in having children, in selecting a mate who wanted children, and in divorcing a husband who turned against children. Sociobiology (social behavior can be explained on the basis of biology) emphasizes the fact that women carrying their babies to term and providing milk for their survival are a reflection of a biological genetic wiring that predisposes women to greater interest in having a baby and in bonding with them. Indeed the species demands that at least one parent take responsibility for ensuring the survival of the species. That men do not have such a biological link but more often derive their reward from social approval for economic productivity in the workplace may help to explain the discrepancy in female and male attitudes and behaviors.

The biosocial theoretical framework emphasizes the interaction of one's biological or genetic inheritance with one's social environment to explain and predict human behavior (Ingoldsby et al. 2004). Borgerhoff Mulder and McCabe (2006) noted that, although sociobiology is sometimes dismissed as purely genetic determinism, the biosocial perspective is not merely genetics but also interested in the environmental and social context. Hence, although human behavior can be explained as having an evolutionary function, it operates in a social context. In effect, women may not only have the genetic wiring for motherhood but are more likely to experience the social rewards from parents and peers for acknowledging and acting on this biological imperative.

Implications

One, traditional gender roles with the female more focused on children may be a genetically wired and culturally supported norm. Women who move into demanding career roles may continue to be challenged by the need to balance career and family. The reluctance some women feel when they leave their baby at a day-care center and the tug they feel at work to return to pick up their baby may have its origin in evolutionary biology. This dilemma was a consistent theme in Pamela Stone's book on *Opting Out* (2007).

Two, egalitarian gender role relationships may be more of an illusion than a reality. As long as women prioritize children, their nurturing and child-care behavior will follow. Because males are less likely to prioritize children, their lack of commitment in this area often translates into less involvement.

Three, the finding that females are more likely to "care less" whether their baby is a boy or a girl reflects the value that children are valued per se. In contrast, men may be more likely to value a child if it is a male because this may be connected to issues of masculinity.

Sources

Borgerhoff Mulder, M., and C. McCabe. 2006. Whatever happened to human sociobiology? *Anthropology* 22:21–22.

De Marneffe, D. 2004. *Maternal desire: On children, love, and the inner life.* New York: Little, Brown, and Company.

Ingoldsby, B. B., S. R. Smith, and J. E. Miller. 2004. *Exploring family theories.* Los Angeles, CA: Roxbury Publishing Co.

Overington, C. 2006. Desire for children of each sex grows families. *Australasian Business Intelligence*, May 28.

Pryor, J. H., S. Hurtado, L. DeAngelo, J. Sharkness, L. C. Romero, W. K. Korn, and S. Trans. 2008. *The American freshmen: National Norms for fall 2008.* Los Angeles: Higher Education Research Institute, UCLA.

Stone, P. 2007. *Opting out? Why women really quit careers and head home.* Berkeley: University of California Press.

Note: Abridged from B. Bragg, D. Knox, and M. Zusman. 2008. *The Little ones: Gender differences in attitudes toward children among university students.* Poster, Southern Sociological Society, April, Richmond, VA.

How Many Children Do You Want?

Before you were conceived I wanted you
Before you were born I loved you
Before you were here an hour I would die for you
This is the miracle of life.

Maureen Hawkins

National Data

U.S. women annually have an estimated 6.4 million pregnancies, of which 4.1 million ended in live births, 1.2 million were terminated by abortions, and 1.1 million ended in fetal losses (Hollander 2008a).

Procreative liberty is the freedom to decide whether or not to have children. More women are deciding not to have children or to have fewer children.

Attitudes toward Parenthood Scale

The purpose of this survey is to assess your attitudes toward the role of parenthood. Please read each item carefully and consider what you believe and feel about parenthood. There are no right or wrong answers to any of these statements. After reading each statement, select the number that best reflects your answer, using the following scale:

1	2	3	4	5	6	7
Strongly Disagree						Strongly Agree

_____ 1. Parents should be involved in their children's school.

_____ 2. I think children add joy to a parent's life.

_____ 3. Parents attending functions such as sporting events and recitals of their children help build their child socially.

_____ 4. Parents are responsible for providing a healthy environment for their children.

_____ 5. When you become a parent, your children become your top priority.

_____ 6. Parenting is a job.

_____ 7. I feel that spending quality time with children is an important aspect of child rearing.

_____ 8. Mothers and fathers should share equal responsibilities in raising children.

_____ 9. The formal education of children should begin at as early an age as possible.

Scoring

After assigning a number to each item, add the numbers and divide by 9. The higher the number (7 is the highest possible), the more positive your view and the stronger your commitment to the role of parenthood. The lower the number (1 is the lowest possible), the more negative your view and the weaker your commitment to parenthood.

Norms

Norms for the scale are based upon twenty-two male and seventy-two female students attending Valdosta State University. The scores ranged from 3.89 to 7.00, and the average was 6.36 (standard deviation [SD] = 0.65); hence, the respondents had very positive views. There was no significant difference between male participants' attitudes toward parenthood (mean [M] = 6.15; SD = 0.70) and female participants' attitudes (M = 6.42; SD = 0.63). There were also no significant differences between ethnicities.

The average age of participants completing the Attitudes Toward Parenthood Scale was 22.09 years (SD = 3.85), and their ages ranged from 18 to 39. The ethnic composition of the sample was 73.4 percent white, 22.3 percent black, 2.1 percent Asian, 1.1 percent American Indian, and 1.1 percent other. The classification of the sample was 20.2 percent freshmen, 6.4 percent sophomores, 22.3 percent juniors, 47.9 percent seniors, and 3.2 percent graduate students.

Source

"Attitudes Toward Parenthood Scale," 2004 by Mark Whatley, Ph.D., Department of Psychology, Valdosta State University, Valdosta, Georgia 31698-0100. Used by permission. Other uses of this scale by written permission of Dr. Whatley only (mwhatley@valdosta.edu). Information on the reliability and validity of this scale is available from Dr. Whatley.

> There never was a child so lovely, but his mother was glad to get him asleep.
>
> Ralph Waldo Emerson, poet

Childfree Marriage?

National Data

Census data reveal that more women ages 40 to 44 are opting to remain childfree—20 percent in 2006, in contrast to 10 percent thirty years ago. Those who decide to have children want fewer children (Kornblum 2008).

Koropeckyj-Cox and Pendell (2007a) examined attitudes about childlessness in the United States. They used a national sample and found that college-educated, white females had the most favorable attitudes toward childlessness. Those who were most negative were not college-educated, were black, male, and held conservative religious beliefs. In general, there seems to be an acceptance of childlessness, not an endorsement of the lifestyle. The data reflecting adults in a national study revealed that 55.9 percent of females compared to 48.1 percent of males disagreed that "People who have never had children have empty lives." Hence, a stigma is still associated with not having children, and men buy into this more than women (Koropeckyj-Cox and Pendell 2007b).

When a couple does not have children, is it by choice or because of infertility? Aside from infertility, typical reasons couples give for not having children include the freedom to spend their time and money as they choose, to enjoy their partner without interference, to continue in school or pursue their career, to avoid health problems associated with pregnancy, and to avoid passing on genetic disorders to a new generation.

Some people simply do not like children. Aspects of our society reflect **antinatalism** (a perspective against children). Indeed, there is a continuous fight for corporations to implement or enforce any family policies (from family leaves to flex time to on-site day care). Profit and money—not children—are priorities. In addition, although people are generally tolerant of their own children, they often exhibit antinatalistic behavior in reference to the children of others. Notice the unwillingness of some individuals to sit next to a child on an airplane.

One Child?

Some couples have an only child because they want the experience of parenthood without children markedly interfering with their lifestyle and careers. Still others have an only child because of the difficulty in pregnancy or birthing the child. "I threw up every day for nine months including on the delivery table." Another said, "I was torn up giving birth to my child." "It took two years for my body to recover. Once is enough for me." There are also those who have only one child because they can't get pregnant a second time. Couples in China typically have one child due to China's One Child Policy—there are penalties for having more than one.

Two Children?

The most preferred family size in the United States (for non-Hispanic white women) is the two-child family (1.9 to be exact!). Reasons for this preference include feeling that a family is "not complete" without two children, having a companion for the first child, having a child of each sex, and repeating the positive experience of parenthood enjoyed with their first child. Some couples may not want to "put all their eggs in one basket." They may fear that, if they have only one child and that child dies or turns out to be disappointing, they will not have another opportunity to enjoy parenting.

For most women, including women who want to have children, contraception is not an option; it is a basic health care necessity.

Louise Slaughter, Congresswoman from New York

Both the child and parents benefit from only one child in a family. The child benefits by focused parental attention (emotional and economic), and the parents have the experience of being a parent without being overwhelmed by its demands. In this photo, the implied message of this interaction between parent and young adult is the importance of keeping one's eye on the ball (apple).

Authors

Families with babies and families without are so sorry for each other.

Ed Howe, country town philosopher

Three Children?

Religion is a strong influence in the number of children a couple have. Twenty percent of Mormons and 15 percent of Muslims have at least three children (Pew Research 2008). In addition to religious influences, couples are more likely to have a third child, and to do so quickly, if they already have two girls rather than two boys. They are least likely to bear a third child if they already have a boy and a girl. Some individuals may want three children because they enjoy children and feel that "three is better than two." In some instances, a couple that has two children may simply want another child because they enjoy parenting and have the resources to do so.

Having a third child creates a "middle child." This child is sometimes neglected because parents of three children may focus more on the "baby" and the firstborn than on the child in between. However, an advantage to being a middle child is the chance to experience both a younger and an older sibling. Each additional child also has a negative effect on the existing children by reducing the amount of parental time available to existing children. The economic resources for each child are also affected for each subsequent child.

Hispanics are more likely to want larger families than are white or African American people. Larger families have complex interactional patterns and different values. The addition of each subsequent child dramatically increases the possible relationships in the family. For example, in a one-child family, four interpersonal relationships are possible: mother-father, mother-child, father-child, and father-mother-child. In a family of four, eleven relationships are possible; in a family of five, 26; and in a family of six, 57.

Four Children—New Standard for the Affluent?

Smith (2007) noted that, among affluent couples, four children may be the new norm. Fueled by competitive career moms who have opted out of the workforce and who find themselves in suburbia surrounded by other moms with resources and time on their hands, having a large family is being reconsidered. A pattern has begun called **competitive birthing**, where "keeping up with the Joneses" now means having the same number of kids. Subsequent research will need to confirm that the pattern is widespread.

PERSONAL CHOICES

Is Genetic Testing for You?

Because each of us may have flawed genes that carry increased risk for diseases such as cancer and Alzheimer's, the question of whether to have a genetic test before becoming pregnant becomes relevant. The test involves giving a blood sample. The advantage is the knowledge of what defective genes you may have and what diseases you may pass to your children. The disadvantage is stress or anxiety (for example, what do you do with the information?) as well as discrimination from certain health insurance companies (who may deny coverage). The validity of the test is also problematic. Hunter et al. (2008) warned, ". . . even the ardent proponents of genomic susceptibility testing would agree that for most diseases, we are still at the early stages of identifying the full list of susceptibility-associated variants" (p. 106). Because no treatment may be available if the test results are positive, the knowledge that they might pass diseases to their children can be devastating to a couple. Finally, genetic testing is expensive, ranging from $200 to $2,400. The National Society of Genetic Counselors (http://www.nsgc.org) offers information about genetic testing.

Teenage Motherhood

National Data

In 2007, there were 1.7 million births to unmarried women, most of whom were teenagers. One in four births in the United States is to unmarried women. The rate has risen 26 percent since 2002 (Cohn 2009).

Reasons for these teenagers having a child include not being socialized as to the importance of contraception, having limited parental supervision, and perceiving few alternatives to parenthood. Indeed, motherhood may be one of the only remaining meaningful roles available to them. In addition, some teenagers feel lonely and unloved and have a baby to create a sense of being needed and wanted. In contrast, in Sweden, eligibility requirements for welfare payments make it almost necessary to complete an education and get a job before becoming a parent.

Problems Associated with Teenage Motherhood

Teenage parenthood is associated with various negative consequences, including the following:

1. ***Stigmatization and marginalization.*** Wilson and Huntington (2006) noted that, because teen mothers resist the typical life trajectory of their middle-class peers, they are stigmatized and marginalized. In effect, they are a threat to societal goals of economic growth through higher education and increased female workforce participation. In spite of such stigmatization and marginalization, McDermott and Graham (2005) noted the resilient behaviors of teen mothers: they invest in the "good" mother identity, maintain kin relations, and prioritize the mother-child dyad in their life. Rolfe (2008) interviewed thirty-three young women who were mothers before the age of 21 and discovered three themes of their experience of teenage motherhood—as "hardship and reward," "growing up and responsibility," and "doing things differently." The researcher noted that the respondents were "active in negotiating and constructing their own identities as mothers, careers and women" (p. 299).

2. ***Poverty among single teen mothers and their children.*** Many teen mothers are unwed. Livermore and Powers (2006) studied a sample of 336 unwed mothers and found them plagued with financial stress; almost 20 percent had difficulty providing food for them and their children (18.5 percent), had their electricity cut off for nonpayment (19.7 percent), and had no medical care for their children (18.2 percent). Almost half (47 percent) reported experiencing "one or more financial stressors" (p. 6).

3. ***Poor health habits.*** Teenage unmarried mothers are less likely to seek prenatal care and more likely than older and married women to smoke, drink alcohol, and take other drugs. These factors have an adverse effect on the health of the baby. Indeed, babies born to unmarried teenage mothers are more likely to have low birth weights (less than five pounds, five ounces) and to be born prematurely. Children of teenage unmarried mothers are also more likely to be developmentally delayed. These outcomes are largely a result of the association between teenage unmarried childbearing and persistent poverty.

4. ***Lower academic achievement.*** Poor academic achievement is both a contributing factor and a potential outcome of teenage parenthood. Some studies note that between 30 percent and 70 percent of teen mothers drop out of high school before graduation (the schools may push them out and/or they may no longer feel motivated). Mollborn (2007) confirmed that teen parenthood diminished the chance that the mother would complete high school.

Baby Think It Over: Evaluation of an Infant Simulation Intervention for Adolescent Pregnancy Prevention

Baby Think It Over (BTIO) is a pregnancy-prevention intervention in which adolescents take care of a realistic, life-sized computerized infant simulation doll to gain an understanding of the amount of time and effort involved in taking care of an infant and how an infant's needs might affect their daily lives and the lives of their family and significant others. Diane de Anda (2006) conducted research to evaluate the effects of participation in a BTIO intervention on adolescent participants' attitudes toward pregnancy and parenthood. The following is a description of her research methods and findings:

Sample and Methods

The sample consisted of 353 predominantly ninth grade and Latino students at a Los Angeles County high school (140 male, 204 female, 9 unreported genders). For two and a half days, these students were responsible for taking care of a realistic, life-sized computerized infant simulator. The infant simulator is programmed to cry at random intervals, typically between eight and twelve times in twenty-four hours, with crying periods lasting typically between ten and fifteen minutes. The "baby" stops crying only when the adolescent "attends" to the doll by inserting a key into a slot in the infant simulator's back until it stops crying. The key is attached to a bracelet, which is worn by the participant. The bracelets are designed so that an attempt to remove the bracelet is detectable. In certain situations, such as when a participant had a test in another class, another student with a key or the health class teacher who had extra keys was permitted to "babysit" a participant's infant simulator.

The infant simulator recorded data, including the amount of time the participant took to "attend" to the infant (insert the key) and any instances of "rough handling," such as dropping or hitting the doll. Students whose infant simulator recorded neglect and rough handling received a private counseling session with the health class teacher and were required to take a parenting class.

In addition to taking care of a computerized infant simulator, participants attended presentations and group discussions on such topics as the high incidence of adolescent pregnancy in the community, the factors that increase risk of adolescent pregnancy, and the costs of adolescent pregnancy and parenthood, with emphasis on the limitation of education and career opportunities and achievement. The health class teacher also offered a pregnancy-prevention education program in preparation for taking care of the infant simulator and a debriefing discussion period after everyone in the class had taken care of the infant simulator for two and a half days.

The Baby Think It Over intervention in this study had seven major objectives. The first four intended to increase the degree to which the adolescent recognized that (1) caring for a baby affects an adolescent's academic and social life; (2) other family members are affected by having an adolescent with a baby in the family; (3) there are emotional risks for each parent in having a baby during adolescence; and (4) there are family and cultural values related to having a baby during adolescence. In addition, the intervention aimed to increase the number of adolescents planning to postpone parenthood until (5) a later age (for the majority, until graduation from high school), (6) until education and career goals were met, or (7) until after marriage.

Zachry (2005) interviewed nineteen mothers and noted that, although all dropped out of school, each evidenced a new appreciation for education as a way of providing a better future for their child. Wendy, one of the mothers, said, "I want to better my education for my kids, and myself . . . because I'm their role model. And they're only gonna learn from what they see from me" (p. 2566).

Although it is assumed that children of teen mothers do poorly in school, Levine et al. 2007 provided longitudinal data and noted no causal relationship between having a teenager as a mother and doing poorly on academic tests. Hence, dire predictions for youngsters of teen mothers might be revised.

Baby Think It Over is an intervention program aimed at giving adolescent females a realistic view of parenting (see the Research Application section above and on the next page).

Diversity in Other Countries

The teenage birth rate in the United States, as measured by births per thousand teenagers, is nine times that of teens in the Netherlands (Fiejoo 2006). Teens in countries such as France and Germany are as sexually active as U.S. teenagers, but the former grow up in a society that promotes responsible contraceptive use. In the Netherlands, for example, individuals are taught to use both the pill and the condom (an approach called "double Dutch") for prevention of pregnancy and sexually transmitted infections (STIs).

Data were collected through written surveys. The adolescents who participated in this research completed the surveys prior to the BTIO intervention. Survey responses obtained after the BTIO intervention provided posttest data.

Findings and Discussion

Statistical tests conducted on the data as well as the participants' self-report data revealed that the BTIO intervention was effective in changing perceptions of the time and effort involved in caring for an infant and in recognizing the significant effect having a baby has on all aspects of one's life. For example, significant gains from pretest to posttest were found on objectives 1, 2, and 3, suggesting that the BTIO intervention increases the degree to which adolescents recognize that caring for a baby affects their academic and social life; that other family members are affected by having an adolescent with a baby in the family; and that there are emotional risks for each parent in having a baby during adolescence. Self-report data indicated that more than half of participants agreed that BTIO changed their perceptions of what having a baby would be like. The most frequently cited reason was that taking care of a baby was much harder than they previously had thought. Nearly two-thirds reported that BTIO helped change their minds about using birth control.

To add to the data detailed in the previous study, we provided the same experience for fifteen students in our classes. The results were similar to those of adolescents. The following is part of the write-up of two of our students:

The whole idea of the electronic baby was to see if I was ready to be a mother. I am sad to say that I failed the test. I am not ready to be a mother. This whole experience was extremely difficult for me because I am a full-time student and I work. It was really hard to get the things that I needed to get done. Suddenly, I couldn't just think about myself but I also had a little one to think about.

The baby seemed to cry a lot, even if I had just changed her, she still cried. The experience really hit me when I had to wake up four and five times in the night to feed and to change the baby. I learned that when the baby sleeps, I need to sleep as well. I also learned that if I had to take care of the baby by myself, I just couldn't do it. What is sad is that single moms do it every day. If I had a supportive boyfriend or husband to help, the whole idea of having a baby wouldn't be so bad. But my boyfriend told me to call him when the project was over and I had given the baby back.

De Anda (2006) further suggests that a comprehensive program that covers birth control methods (as well as abstinence) and that provides access to contraception "would provide adolescents with the knowledge and skills needed to actualize their intentions and the opportunity for choice in the means to accomplish this" (p. 33).

Source

"Baby Think It Over: Simulation Intervention for Adolescent Pregnancy Prevention" by Diane de Anda. *Health and Social Work.* 31(1): 26-35, 2006. Copyrighted material reprinted with permission from the National Association of Social Workers, Inc.

The *Baby Think It Over* (BTIO) infant simulator cited in the study, Standard Baby, is a discontinued model. Realityworks, Inc., the company that developed BTIO, currently produces more sophisticated and realistic infant simulators using wireless technology called *RealCare® Baby II* and *RealCare® Baby II-plus* (for more information, see www.realityworks.com).

Infertility

Infertility is defined as the inability to achieve a pregnancy after at least one year of regular sexual relations without birth control, or the inability to carry a pregnancy to a live birth. Different types of infertility include the following:

1. *Primary infertility.* The woman has never conceived even though she wants to and has had regular sexual relations for the past twelve months.

2. *Secondary infertility.* The woman has previously conceived but is currently unable to do so even though she wants to and has had regular sexual relations for the past twelve months.

3. *Pregnancy wastage.* The woman has been able to conceive but has been unable to produce a live birth.

There is also an epidemic of infertility in this country. There are more women who have put off childbearing in favor of their professional lives.

Iris Chang, historian

This student was assigned to keep the electronic baby for a week but had turned it in early. She said, "I couldn't sleep or do my school work, and my boyfriend told me to call him when the project was over."

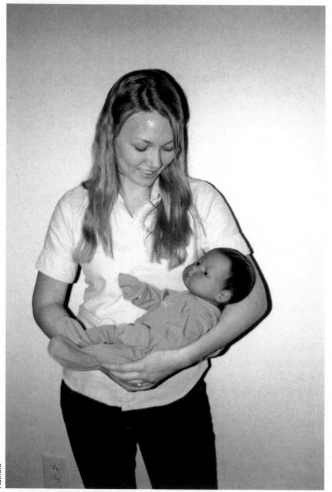

Authors

Between 17 percent and 26 percent of all couples of reproductive age in industrialized societies are involuntarily childless. Half of these couples seek treatment for their infertility (Schmidt 2006). Infertility risks increase with age: 4.1 percent of 15- to 24-year-olds versus 13.1 percent of 25- to 34-year-olds versus 21.4 percent of 35- to 44-year-olds suffer from infertility (Sinclair and Pressinger 2008). The take-home message for women is that to delay getting pregnant is to delay the chance of getting pregnant.

Causes of Infertility

Although popular usage does not differentiate between the terms *fertilization* and the *beginning of pregnancy*, **fertilization** or **conception** refers to the fusion of the egg and sperm, whereas **pregnancy** is not considered to begin until five to seven days later, when the fertilized egg is implanted (typically in the uterine wall). Hence, not all fertilizations result in a pregnancy. An estimated 30 percent to 40 percent of conceptions are lost prior to or during implantation. Forty percent of infertility problems are attributed to the woman, 40 percent to the man, and 20 percent to both of them. Some of the more common causes of infertility in men include low sperm production, poor semen motility, effects of STIs (such as chlamydia, gonorrhea, and syphilis), and interference with passage of sperm through the genital ducts due to an enlarged prostate. The causes of infertility in women include blocked fallopian tubes, endocrine imbalance that prevents ovulation, dysfunctional ovaries, chemically hostile cervical mucus that may kill sperm, and effects of STIs.

An at-home fertility kit, **Fertell**, allows women to measure the level of their follicle-stimulating hormone on the

What if Your Partner Is Infertile—Would You Marry the Partner?

WHAT IF?

Given that most individuals report an interest in having children, to learn of a partner's infertility may be met with the decision to end the relationship. One woman told her infertile partner, "I love you but having my own baby is part of my being a woman and a life goal . . . and I fear if I don't have a child, I might feel that I missed an important experience and come to resent you." For others, as long as the partner is willing to adopt, there is no consideration to ending the relationship. Still others reevaluate the positives of not having children and opt to marry and be childfree. Any option is acceptable. What is important is to carefully assess one's own needs for having a biological child or to adopt a child and make these preferences known to the partner.

third day of their menstrual cycles. An abnormally high level means that egg quality is low. The test takes thirty minutes and involves a urine stick. The same kit allows men to measure the concentration of motile sperm. Men provide a sample of sperm (for example, via masturbation) that swim through a solution similar to cervical mucus. This procedure takes about eighty minutes. Fertell has been approved by the Food and Drug Administration (FDA), no prescription is necessary, and costs around $100.

Being infertile (for the woman) may have a negative lifetime effect. Wirtberg et al. (2007) interviewed fourteen Swedish women twenty years after their infertility treatment and found that childlessness had had a major impact on all the women's lives and remained a major life theme. The effects were both personal (sad) and interpersonal (half were separated and all reported negative effects on their sex lives). The effects of childlessness were especially increased at the time the study was conducted, as the women's peer group was entering the "grandparent phase." The researchers noted that infertility has lifetime consequences for the individual woman and her relationships.

Assisted Reproductive Technology

A number of technological innovations are available to assist women and couples in becoming pregnant. These include hormonal therapy, artificial insemination, ovum transfer, in vitro fertilization, gamete intrafallopian transfer, and zygote intrafallopian transfer.

Hormone Therapy   Drug therapies are often used to treat hormonal imbalances, induce ovulation, and correct problems in the luteal phase of the menstrual cycle. Frequently used drugs include Clomid, Pergonal, and human chorionic gonadotropin (HCG), a hormone extracted from human placenta. These drugs stimulate the ovary to ripen and release an egg. Although they are fairly effective in stimulating ovulation, hyperstimulation can occur, which may result in permanent damage to the ovaries.

Hormone therapy also increases the likelihood that multiple eggs will be released, resulting in multiple births. The increase in triplets and higher order multiple births over the past decade in the United States is largely attributed to the increased use of ovulation-inducing drugs for treating infertility. Infants of higher order multiple births are at greater risk of having low birth weight and their mortality rates are higher. Mortality rates have improved for these babies, but these low birth-weight survivors may need extensive neonatal medical and social services.

Artificial Insemination   When the sperm of the male partner are low in count or motility, sperm from several ejaculations may be pooled and placed directly into the cervix. This procedure is known as *artificial insemination by husband* (AIH). When sperm from someone other than the woman's partner are used to fertilize a woman, the technique is referred to as *artificial insemination by donor* (AID).

National Data

There are 60,000 births annually from donor inseminations with a minimum of one million children being born since the 1950s (Berger and Paul 2008).

Lesbians who want to become pregnant may use sperm from a friend or from a sperm bank (some sperm banks cater exclusively to lesbians). Regardless of the source of the sperm, it should be screened for genetic abnormalities and STIs, quarantined for 180 days, and retested for human immunodeficiency virus (HIV); also, the donor should be younger than 50 to diminish hazards related to aging. These precautions are not routinely taken—let the buyer beware.

How do children from donor sperm feel about their fathers? A team of researchers (Scheib et al. 2005) studied twenty-nine individuals (41 percent from lesbian couples, 38 percent from single women, and 21 percent from heterosexual couples) and found that most (75 percent) always knew about their origin and were comfortable with it. All but one reported a neutral to positive impact with the birth mother. Most (80 percent) indicated a moderate interest in learning more about the donor. No youths reported wanting money, and only 7 percent reported wanting a father-child relationship. Berger and Paul (2008) studied the effects of disclosing or not disclosing to the child that he or she is from a donor sperm. The results were inconclusive but favored disclosure.

Artificial Insemination of a Surrogate Mother In some instances, artificial insemination does not help a woman get pregnant. (Her fallopian tubes may be blocked, or her cervical mucus may be hostile to sperm.) The couple that still wants a child and has decided against adoption may consider parenthood through a surrogate mother. There are two types of surrogate mothers. One is the contracted surrogate mother who supplies the egg, is impregnated with the male partner's sperm, carries the child to term, and gives the baby to the man and his partner. A second type is the surrogate mother who carries to term a baby to whom she is not genetically related (a fertilized egg from the "infertile couple" who can't carry a baby to term is implanted in her uterus). As with AID, the motivation of the prospective parents is to have a child that is genetically related to at least one of them. For the surrogate mother, the primary motivation is to help childless couples achieve their aspirations of parenthood and to make money. Although some American women are willing to "rent their wombs," women in India have also begun to provide this service. For $5,000, an Indian wife who already has a child will carry a baby to term for an infertile couple (for a fraction of the cost of an American surrogate).

California is one of twelve states in which entering into an arrangement with a surrogate mother is legal. The fee to the surrogate mother is $20,000 to $25,000. Other fees (travel, hospital, lawyers, and so on) can run the figure to as high as $125,000. Surrogate mothers typically have their own children, making giving up a child that they carried easier. For information about the legality of surrogacy in your state, see http://www.surrogacy.com/legals/map.html.

In Vitro Fertilization About 2 million couples cannot have a baby because the woman's fallopian tubes are blocked or damaged, preventing the passage of eggs to the uterus. In some cases, blocked tubes can be opened via laser surgery or by inflating a tiny balloon within the clogged passage. When these procedures are not successful (or when the woman decides to avoid invasive tests and exploratory surgery), *in vitro* (meaning "in glass") *fertilization* (IVF), also known as test-tube fertilization, is an alternative.

Using a laparoscope (a narrow, telescope-like instrument inserted through an incision just below the woman's naval to view tubes and ovaries), the physician is able to see a mature egg as it is released from the woman's ovary. The time of release can be predicted accurately within two hours. When the egg emerges, the physician uses an aspirator to remove the egg, placing it in a small tube containing stabilizing fluid. The egg is taken to the laboratory, put in a culture petri dish, kept at a certain temperature-acidity level, and surrounded by sperm from the woman's partner (or donor). After one of these sperm fertilizes the egg, the egg divides and is implanted by the physician in the wall of the woman's uterus. Usually, several eggs are implanted in the hope one will survive. Usually, several eggs are implanted in the hope one will survive. This was the case of Nadya Suleman, who ended up giving birth to eight babies. Eight embryos were transferred in 2008, at Duke University's in vitro fertilization program into her body with the thought that some would not survive . . . all did (Rochman 2009).

Some couples want to ensure the sex of their baby. In a procedure called "family balancing" because couples that already have several children of one sex often use it, the eggs of a woman are fertilized and the sex of the embryos three and eight days old is identified. Only those of the desired sex are then implanted in the woman's uterus.

Alternatively, the Y chromosome of the male sperm can be identified and implanted. The procedure is accurate 75 percent of the time for producing a boy baby and 90 percent of the time for a girl baby. The Genetics and IVF Institute, in Fairfax, Virginia, specializes in the sperm sorting technique.

Occasionally, some fertilized eggs are frozen and implanted at a later time, if necessary. This procedure is known as **cryopreservation**. Separated or divorced couples may disagree over who owns the frozen embryos, and the legal system is still wrestling with the fate of their unused embryos, sperm, or ova after a divorce or death.

Ovum Transfer In conjunction with in vitro fertilization is ovum transfer, also referred to as embryo transfer. In this procedure, an egg is donated, fertilized in vitro with the husband's sperm, and then transferred to his wife. Alternatively, a physician places the sperm of the male partner in a surrogate woman. After about five days, her uterus is flushed out (endometrial lavage), and the contents are analyzed under a microscope to identify the presence of a fertilized ovum.

The fertilized ovum is then inserted into the uterus of the otherwise infertile partner. Although the embryo can also be frozen and implanted at another time, fresh embryos are more likely to result in successful implantation. Infertile couples that opt for ovum transfer do so because the baby will be biologically related to at least one of them (the father) and the partner will have the experience of pregnancy and childbirth. As noted earlier, the surrogate woman participates out of her desire to help an infertile couple or to make money.

Other Reproductive Technologies A major problem with in vitro fertilization is that only about 15 percent to 20 percent of the fertilized eggs will implant on the uterine wall. To improve this implant percentage (to between 40 percent and 50 percent), physicians place the egg and the sperm directly into the fallopian tube, where they meet and fertilize. Then the fertilized egg travels down into the uterus and implants.

Because the term for sperm and egg together is *gamete*, this procedure is called *gamete intrafallopian transfer*, or GIFT. This procedure, as well as in vitro fertilization, is not without psychological costs to the couple.

Gestational surrogacy, another technique, involves fertilization in vitro of a woman's ovum and transfer to a surrogate. Trigametic IVF also involves the use of sperm in which the genetic material of another person has been inserted. This technique allows lesbian couples to have a child genetically related to both women. Infertile couples hoping to get pregnant through one of the more than 400 in vitro fertilization clinics should make informed choices by asking questions such as, "What is the center's pregnancy rate for women with a similar diagnosis?"

What percentage of these women has a live birth? According to the Centers for Disease Control and Prevention, the typical success rate (live birth) for infertile couples who seek help in one of the 400 fertility clinics is 28 percent (Lee 2006). Beginning assisted-reproductive technology as early after infertility is suspected is important. Wang et al. (2008) analyzed data on 36,412 patients to assess success of actual births for infertile women using assisted-reproductive technology and found that, for women age 30 and above, each additional year in age was associated with an 11 percent reduction in the chance of achieving pregnancy and a 13 percent reduction in the chance of a live delivery. If women aged 35 years or older would have had their first treatment one year earlier, 15 percent more live deliveries would be expected.

Finally, Hammarberg et al. (2008) studied 166 women who had conceived through assisted-reproductive technology to identify any differences in birthing. They did find that ART participants were more likely to have a cesarean birth (51 percent versus 25 percent) and to report disappointment with the birth event when compared with those who had a vaginal birth.

Adoption

Angelina Jolie and Brad Pitt are celebrities who have given national visibility to adopting children. They are not alone in their desire to adopt children. The various routes to adoption are public (children from the child welfare system), private agency (children placed with nonrelatives through agencies), independent adoption (children placed directly by birth parents or through an intermediary such as a physician or attorney), kinship (children placed in a family member's home), and stepparent (children adopted by a spouse). Motives for adopting a child include wanting a child because of an inability to have a biological child (infertility), a desire to give an otherwise unwanted child a permanent loving home, or a desire to avoid contributing to overpopulation by having more biological children. Some couples may seek adoption for all of these motives. Adoption is actually quite rare, with less than 5 percent of couples adopting; 15 percent of these adoptions will be children from other countries.

Demographic Characteristics of People Seeking to Adopt a Child

Whereas demographic characteristics of those who typically adopt are white, educated, and high-income, adoptees are being increasingly placed in nontraditional families including with older, gay, and single individuals. Sixteen states have taken steps to ban adoption by gay couples on the grounds that, because "marriage" is "heterosexual marriage," children do not belong in homosexual relationships (Stone 2006). Leung et al. (2005) compared children adopted or reared by gay or lesbian and heterosexual parents. They found no negative effects when the adoptive parents were gay or lesbian. Approval for adoption by same-sex couples is evident in the population, as half of the respondents in surveys in the United States report approval of same-sex adoptions (Maill and March 2005).

Characteristics of Children Available for Adoption

Adoptees in the highest demand are healthy, white infants. Those who are older, of a racial or ethnic group different from that of the adoptive parents, of a sibling group, or with physical or developmental disabilities have been difficult to place. Flower Kim (2003) noted that, because the waiting period for a healthy white infant is from five to ten years, couples are increasingly open to cross-racial adoptions. Of the 1.6 million adopted children younger than 18 living in U.S. households, the percentages adopted from other countries are as follows: 24 percent from Korea; 11 percent from China; 10 percent from Russia; and 9 percent from Mexico. International or cross-racial adoptions may complicate the adoptive child's identity. Children adopted after infancy may also experience developmental delays, attachment disturbances, and post-traumatic stress disorder (Nickman et al. 2005). Baden and Wiley (2007) reviewed the literature on adoptees as adults and found that the mental health of most was on par with those who were not adopted. However, a small subset of the population showed concerns that may warrant therapeutic intervention.

Costs of Adoption

Adopting from the U.S. foster care system is generally the least expensive type of adoption, usually involving little or no cost, and states often provide subsidies to adoptive parents. However, a couple can become foster care parents to a child

Some parents adopt children internationally. This little girl is in an orphanage in Mexico.

and become emotionally bonded with the child, and the birth parents can reappear and request their child back.

Stepparent and kinship adoptions are also inexpensive and have less risk of the child being withdrawn. Agency and private adoptions can range from $5,000 to $40,000 or more, depending on travel expenses, birth mother expenses, and requirements in the state. International adoptions can range from $7,000 to $30,000 (see http://costs.adoption.com/).

Transracial Adoption

Transracial adoption is defined as the practice of adopting children of a race different from that of the parents—for example, a white couple adopting a Korean or African American child. In a study on transracial adoption attitudes of college students (using the following Attitudes toward Transracial Adoption Scale), the scores of the 188 respondents reflected overwhelmingly positive attitudes toward transracial adoption. Overall, women, people willing to adopt a child at all, interracially experienced daters, and those open to interracial dating were more willing to adopt transracially than were men, people rejecting adoption as an optional route to parenthood, people with no previous interracial dating experience, and people closed to interracial dating (Ross et al. 2003).

Ethiopia has become a unique country from which to adopt a child. Not only is the adoption time shorter (four months) and less expensive, but the children there are also psychologically very healthy. "You don't hear crying babies [in the orphanages]. . . . they are picked up immediately" (Gross and Conners 2007, A16). In addition, "adoption families are encouraged to meet birth families and visit the villages where the children are raised . . ." (ibid.). Ethiopian adoptions have received considerable visibility in the United States due to the involvement of celebrity Angelina Jolie who adopted there.

Transracial adoptions are controversial. Wolters et al. (forthcoming) analyzed data from 1,027 undergraduates at a large undergraduate university and found that females were 17.5 percent more supportive of transracial adoption than males ($p < .001$). Black females were the most favorable toward transracial adoption, whereas white males were the least favorable. Kennedy (2003) noted, "Whites who seek to adopt black children are widely regarded with suspicion. Are they ideologues, more interested in making a political point than in actually being parents?" (p. 447). Another controversy is whether it is beneficial for

Attitudes toward Transracial Adoption Scale

Transracial adoption is the adoption of children of a race other than that of the adoptive parents. Please read each item carefully and consider what you believe about each statement. There are no right or wrong answers to any of these statements, so please give your honest reaction and opinion. After reading each statement, select the number that best reflects your answer, using the following scale:

1	2	3	4	5	6	7
Strongly Disagree						Strongly Agree

_____ 1. Transracial adoption can interfere with a child's well-being.

_____ 2. Transracial adoption should not be allowed.

_____ 3. I would never adopt a child of another race.

_____ 4. I think that transracial adoption is unfair to the children.

_____ 5. I believe that adopting parents should adopt a child within their own race.

_____ 6. Only same-race couples should be allowed to adopt.

_____ 7. Biracial couples are not well prepared to raise children.

_____ 8. Transracially adopted children need to choose one culture over another.

_____ 9. Transracially adopted children feel as though they are not part of the family they live in.

_____ 10. Transracial adoption should occur only between certain races.

_____ 11. I am against transracial adoption.

_____ 12. A person has to be desperate to adopt a child of another race.

_____ 13. Children adopted by parents of a different race have more difficulty developing socially than children adopted by foster parents of the same race.

_____ 14. Members of multiracial families do not get along well.

_____ 15. Transracial adoption results in "cultural genocide."

Scoring

After assigning a number to each item, add the numbers and divide by 15. The lower the score (1 is the lowest possible), the more positive one's view of transracial adoptions. The higher the score (7 is the highest possible), the more negative one's view of transracial adoptions. The norming sample was based upon thirty-four male and sixty-nine female students attending Valdosta State University. The average score was 2.27 (SD = 1.15), suggesting a generally positive view of transracial adoption by the respondents, and scores ranged from 1.00 to 6.60.

The average age of participants completing the scale was 22.22 years (SD = 4.23), and ages ranged from 18 to 48. The ethnic composition of the sample was 74.8 percent white, 20.4 percent black, 1.9 percent Asian, 1.0 percent Hispanic, 1.0 percent American Indian, and one person of non-indicated ethnicity. The classification of the sample was 15.5 percent freshmen, 6.8 percent sophomores, 32.0 percent juniors, 42.7 percent seniors, and 2.9 percent graduate students.

Source

"Attitudes Toward Transracial Adoption Scale," 2004 by Mark Whatley, Ph.D., Department of Psychology, Valdosta State University, Valdosta, Georgia 31698-0100. Used by permission. Other uses of this scale by written permission of Dr. Whatley only (mwhatley@valdosta.edu). Information on the reliability and validity of this scale is available from Dr. Whatley.

children to be adopted by parents of the same racial background. In regard to the adoption of African American children by same-race parents, the National Association of Black Social Workers (NABSW) passed a resolution against transracial adoptions, citing that such adoptions prevented black children from developing a positive sense of themselves "that would be necessary to cope with racism and prejudice that would eventually occur" (Hollingsworth 1997, 44).

The counterargument is that healthy self-concepts, an appreciation for one's racial heritage, and coping with racism or prejudice can be learned in a variety of contexts. Legal restrictions on transracial adoptions have disappeared, and social approval for transracial adoptions is increasing. However, a substantial number of studies conclude that "same-race placements are preferable and that special measures should be taken to facilitate such placements, even if it means delaying some adoptions" (Kennedy 2003, 469).

One 26-year-old black female was asked how she felt about being reared by white parents and replied, "Again, they are my family and I love them, but I am black. I have to deal with my reality as a black woman" (Simon and Roorda 2000, 41). A black man reared in a white home advised white parents considering a transracial adoption, "Make sure they have the influence of blacks in their lives; even if they have to go out and make friends with black families—it's a must" (p. 25). Indeed, Huh and Reid (2000) found that positive adjustment by adoptees was associated with participation in the cultural activities of the race of the parents who adopted them. Thomas and Tessler (2007) found that American parents intent on keeping the Chinese cultural heritage of their adopted child alive take specific steps (for example, establish friendships with Chinese adults and families).

Open versus Closed Adoptions

Another controversy is whether adopted children should be allowed to obtain information about their biological parents. Surveys in both Canada and the United States reveal that about three-fourths of the respondents approve of some form of open adoption and of giving adult adoptees unlimited access to confidential information about their birth parents (Maill and March 2005). In general, there are considerable benefits for having an open adoption—the biological parent has the opportunity to stay involved in the child's life. Adoptees learn early that they are adopted and who their biological parents are. Birth parents are more likely to avoid regret and to be able to stay in contact with their child. Adoptive parents have information about the genetic background of their adopted child. Ge et al. (2008) studied birth mothers and adoptive parents and found that increased openness between the two sets of parents was positively associated with greater satisfaction for both birth mothers and adoptive parents.

Foster Parenting

Some individuals seek the role of parent via foster parenting. A **foster parent**, also known as a family caregiver, is neither a biological nor an adoptive parent but is a person who takes care of and fosters a child taken into custody. A foster parent has made a contract with the state for the service, has judicial status, and is reimbursed by the state. Foster parents are screened for previous arrest records and child abuse and neglect. Foster parents are licensed by the state; some states require a "foster parent orientation" program. Rhode Island, for example, provides a twenty-seven-hour course. Brown (2008) asked sixty-three foster parents what they needed to allow them to have a successful foster parenting experience. They reported that they needed the right personality (for example, patience and nurturance), information about the foster child, a good relationship with the fostering agency, linkages to other foster families, and supportive immediate and extended families. Other research has found the need for formal foster parent organizations.

Children placed in foster care have typically been removed from parents who are abusive, who are substance abusers, and/or who are mentally incompetent. Although foster parents are paid for taking care of children in their home, they are also motivated by love of children. The goal of placing children in foster care is to remove them from a negative family context, improve that context, and return them, or find a more permanent home than foster care. Some couples become foster parents in hopes of being able to adopt a child that is placed in their custody.

Due to tighter restrictions on foreign adoptions (for example, it typically takes three years to complete a foreign adoption; China excludes people seeking to adopt who are unmarried, obese, and over age 50) and due to the limited number of domestic infants, more couples are considering adoption of a foster child. Tax credits are available for up to $11,650 for adopting a special needs child (Block 2008).

Contraception*

Once individuals have decided on whether and when they want children, they need to make a choice about contraception. Pregnancy prevention, STI prevention, opinion of partner, ease of use, and cost are among the factors considered in selecting contraception (Delavande 2008).

In a study of 1,319 undergraduates at a southeastern university, 62.1 percent reported that the last time they had sexual intercourse, they used a form of birth control (other than withdrawal). Forty-four percent used a condom to prevent contracting an STI (Knox and Zusman 2009). Even when contraception is used, Speidel et al. (2008) noted that 9 percent of pill users, 17 percent of condom users, and 5 percent of injectable users become pregnant during the first year of typical use. All contraceptive practices have one of two common purposes: to prevent the male sperm from fertilizing the female egg or to keep the fertilized egg from implanting itself in the uterus. About five to seven days after fertilization, pregnancy begins. Although the fertilized egg will not develop into a human unless it implants on the uterine wall, pro-life supporters believe that conception has already occurred.

Hormonal Contraceptives

Hormonal methods of contraception currently available to women include "the pill," Norplant, Depo-Provera, NuvaRing, and Ortho Evra.

Oral Contraceptive Agents (Birth Control Pills) Birth control pills are the most commonly used method of all the nonsurgical forms of contraception. Although almost 10 percent of women who take the pill still become pregnant in the first year of use, it remains a desirable birth control option.

Oral contraceptives are available in basically two types: the combination pill, which contains varying levels of estrogen and progestin, and the minipill, which is progestin only. Combination pills work by raising the natural level of hormones in a woman's body, inhibiting ovulation, creating an environment where sperm cannot easily reach the egg, and hampering implantation of a fertilized egg.

The second type of birth control pill, the minipill, contains the same progesterone-like hormone found in the combination pill but does not contain estrogen. Progestin-only pills are taken every day, with no hormone-free interval. As with the combination pill, the progestin in the minipill provides a hostile environment for sperm and does not allow implantation of a fertilized egg in the uterus, but unlike the combination pill, the minipill does not always inhibit ovulation. For this reason, the minipill is somewhat less effective than other types of birth control pills. The minipill has also been associated with a higher incidence of irregular bleeding. Neither the combination pill nor the minipill should be taken unless prescribed by a health care provider who has detailed information about the woman's medical history. Contraindications—reasons for not prescribing birth control pills—include hypertension, impaired liver function, known or suspected tumors that are estrogen-dependent, undiagnosed abnormal genital bleeding, pregnancy at the time of the examination, and history of poor blood circulation or blood clotting. The major complications associated with taking oral contraceptives are blood clots and high blood pressure. Also, the risk of heart attack is increased for those who smoke or have other risk factors for heart disease. The risk of cancer from using hormonal contraception is actually lower (Walling 2008).

If they smoke, women older than 35 should generally use other forms of contraception. Although the long-term negative consequences of taking birth

*Appreciation is expressed to Charla Blumell, MA, PhD candidate, a health education specialist for her assistance in the development of this section.

control pills are still the subject of research, short-term negative effects are experienced by 25 percent of all women who use them. These side effects include increased susceptibility to vaginal infections, nausea, slight weight gain, vaginal bleeding between periods, breast tenderness, headaches, and mood changes (some women become depressed and experience a loss of sexual desire). Women should also be aware of situations in which the pill is not effective, such as the first month of use, with certain prescription medications, and when pills are missed. On the positive side, pill use reduces the incidence of ectopic pregnancy and offers noncontraceptive benefits, such as reduced incidence of ovarian and endometrial cancers, pelvic inflammatory disease, anemia, and benign breast disease.

Finally, women should be aware that pill use is associated with an increased incidence of chlamydia and gonorrhea. One reason for the association of pill use and a higher incidence of STIs is that sexually active women who use the pill sometimes erroneously feel that they are also protected from contracting STIs because they are protected from becoming pregnant. The pill provides no protection against STIs; the only methods that provide some protection against STIs are the male and female condoms.

Despite the widespread use of birth control pills, many women prefer a method that is longer acting and does not require daily action. Research continues toward identifying safe, effective hormonal contraceptive delivery methods that are more convenient. One recent hormonal contraceptive is Seasonale®, which reduces the number of periods a woman experiences from thirteen to four per year. This hormonal contraceptive manages the menstrual cycles by skipping the hormone-free week and limiting women's menstrual periods to once every three months. However, unexpected menstrual bleeding occurs four times as often with this extended-cycle regimen, and women who use Seasonale are four times as likely to discontinue use in the first twenty-six weeks as a result (Wilson and Kudis 2005). Two other similar hormonal contraceptives are Seasonique® (also an extended-cycle regime) and Lybrel® (a continuous-cycle regime) that is taken orally every day with no hormone-free week.

Norplant   **Norplant** is a system of rod-shaped silicone implants that are inserted under the skin in the upper inner arm and provide timed-release progestin into a woman's system for contraception. A common side effect is irregular menstrual bleeding. **Implanon®** is a newer type of implant that is not available everywhere. It also is a progestin-only method that provides three years of pregnancy protection, in contrast with Norplant that provides five.

Depo-Provera®   Also known as "Depo" and "the shot," **Depo-Provera** is a synthetic compound similar to progesterone that is injected into the woman's arm or buttock and protects against pregnancy for three months by preventing ovulation. Side effects of Depo-Provera include menstrual spotting, irregular bleeding, and some heavy bleeding the first few months of use, although eight of ten women using Depo-Provera will eventually experience amenorrhea, or the absence of a menstrual period. Mood changes, headaches, dizziness, and fatigue have also been observed. Some women report a weight gain of five to ten pounds.

Also, after the injections are stopped, it takes an average of eighteen months before the woman will become pregnant at the same rate as women who have not used Depo-Provera. Slightly fewer than 3 percent of American women report using the injectable contraceptive. Most fear the side effects or are just satisfied with their current contraceptive method.

Recent research has shown that prolonged use of Depo-Provera is associated with significant loss of bone density, which may not be completely reversible after discontinuing use. A "black box" warning highlights this information. Depo-Provera should be used only as a long-term contraceptive method (longer than two years) if other methods are inadequate.

Vaginal Rings **NuvaRing**, which is a soft, flexible, transparent ring approximately two inches in diameter that is worn inside the vagina, provides month-long pregnancy protection. NuvaRing has two major advantages. First, because the hormones are delivered locally rather than systemically, very low levels are administered (the lowest of any of the hormonal contraceptives). Second, unlike oral contraceptives, with which the hormone levels rise and fall depending on when the pill is taken, the hormone level from the NuvaRing remains constant. The NuvaRing is a highly effective contraceptive when used according to the labeling. Out of a hundred women using NuvaRing for a year, one or two will become pregnant. This method is self-administered.

NuvaRing is inserted into the vagina and is designed to release hormones that are absorbed by the woman's body for three weeks. The ring is then removed for a week, at which time the menstrual cycle will occur; afterward, the ring is replaced with a new ring. Side effects of NuvaRing are similar to those of the birth control pill.

Transdermal Applications **Ortho Evra** is a contraceptive transdermal patch that delivers hormones to a woman's body through skin absorption. The contraceptive patch is worn on the buttocks, abdomen, upper torso (excluding the breasts), or on the outside of the upper arm for three weeks and is changed on a weekly basis. The fourth week is patch-free and the time when the menstrual cycle will occur. Under no circumstances should a woman allow more than seven days to lapse without wearing a patch.

Ortho Evra provides pregnancy protection and has side effects similar to those of the pill. Ortho Evra simply offers a different delivery method of the hormones needed to prevent pregnancy from occurring. In clinical trials, the contraceptive patch was found to keep its adhesiveness even through showers, workouts, and water activities, such as swimming. However, the FDA approved updating the labeling of Ortho Evra to warn users and health care providers that this product exposes women to about 60 percent more estrogen than most birth control pills and it may be less effective for women who weigh more than 198 pounds. In general, increased estrogen exposure may increase the risk of blood clots.

Male Hormonal Methods Because of dissatisfaction with the few contraceptive options available to men, research and development are occurring in this area.

Numerous studies have found that administration of testosterone to men markedly reduces sperm count and is a very efficient and well-tolerated method of contraception. Combinations with progestogens or with gonadotropin-releasing hormone antagonists are even more effective and suggest that hormonal contraception in men is feasible and may be as effective as the currently used methods (Amory et al. 2006). Several promising male products under development rely on MENT™, a synthetic steroid that resembles testosterone. In contrast to testosterone, however, MENT does not have the effect of enlarging the prostate. A MENT implant and MENT transdermal gel and patch formulation are being developed for contraception.

Male Condom

Condoms are thin sheaths made of latex, polyurethane, or natural membranes. Latex condoms, which can be used only with water-based lubricants, historically have been more popular. They are also less likely to slip off and have a much lower chance of breakage. However, the polyurethane condom, which is thinner but just as durable as latex, is growing in popularity.

Polyurethane condoms can be used with oil-based lubricants, are an option for some people who have latex-sensitive allergies, provide some protection against

HIV and other STIs, and allow for greater sensitivity during intercourse. Condoms made of natural membranes (sheep intestinal lining) are not recommended because they are not effective in preventing transmission of HIV or other STIs.

The condom works by being rolled over and down the shaft of the erect penis before intercourse. When the man ejaculates, sperm are caught inside the condom. When used in combination with a spermicidal lubricant that is placed on the inside of the reservoir tip of the condom as well as a spermicidal (sperm-killing) agent that the woman inserts into her vagina, the condom is a highly effective contraceptive. Care should be taken to *avoid* using nonoxynol-9 (N-9) as a contraceptive lubricant because it has been shown to provide no protection against STIs or HIV. N-9 products, such as condoms that have N-9 as a lubricant, should not be used rectally because doing so could *increase* one's risk of getting HIV or other STIs.

Like any contraceptive, the condom is effective only when used properly. Practice putting the male condom on reduces the chance of the condom breaking or coming off during intercourse. A recent study found that the male condom breakage rate fell from 7 percent among first-time users to 2 percent among those who had used the method at least fifteen times; the slippage rate dropped from 3 percent to 0.4 percent (Hollander 2005).

The condom should be placed on the penis early enough to avoid any seminal leakage into the vagina. In addition, polyurethane or latex condoms with a reservoir tip are preferable, as they are less likely to break. Even when a condom has a reservoir tip, air should be squeezed out of the tip as it is being placed on the penis to reduce the chance of breaking during ejaculation. However, such breakage does occur. Finally, the penis should be withdrawn from the vagina immediately after ejaculation, before it returns to its flaccid state. If the penis is not withdrawn and the erection subsides, semen may leak from the base of the condom into the vaginal lips. Alternatively, when the erection subsides, the condom will come off when the man withdraws his penis if he does not hold onto the condom. Either way, the sperm will begin to travel up the vagina to the uterus and fertilization may occur.

In addition to furnishing extra protection, spermicides also provide lubrication, which permits easy entrance of the condom-covered penis into the vagina. If no spermicide is used and the condom is not of the prelubricated variety, a sterile lubricant (such as K-Y Jelly) may be needed. Vaseline or other kinds of petroleum jelly should not be used with condoms because vaginal infections and/or condom breakage may result. Though condoms should also be checked for visible damage and for the date of expiration, this is rarely done. Three-fourths of the respondents in Lane's (2003) study did not check for damage, and 61 percent did not check the date of expiration.

Female Condom

The **female condom** resembles the male condom except that it fits in the woman's vagina to protect her from pregnancy, HIV infection, and other STIs. The female condom is a lubricated, polyurethane adaptation of the male version. It is about six inches long and has flexible rings at both ends. It is inserted like a diaphragm, with the inner ring fitting behind the pubic bone against the cervix; the outer ring remains outside the body and encircles the labial area. Like the male version, the female condom is not reusable. Female condoms have been approved by the FDA and are being marketed under the brand names Femidom and Reality. The one-size-fits-all device is available without a prescription.

The female condom is durable and may not tear as easily as latex male condoms. Some women may encounter some difficulty with first attempts to insert the female condom. A major advantage of the female condom is that, like the male counterpart, it helps protect against transmission of HIV and other STIs, giving women an option for protection if their partner refuses to wear a condom.

Placement may occur up to eight hours before use, allowing greater spontaneity. Women who have had an STI are more likely to use the female condom. If women have instruction and training in the use of the female condom, including a chance to practice the method, this increases its use. Women who had a chance to practice skills on a pelvic model were more likely to rate the method favorably, use it, and use it correctly.

There are problems with the female condom, however. London (2003) found in a study of 2,232 female condom uses that slippage occurred in 10 percent of the cases and that women may have been exposed to semen in one in five uses. Problems also occur when there is a large disparity between the size of the woman's vagina and the size of her partner's penis and when intercourse is very active. The female condom is also very expensive in comparison with other non-reusable barrier methods.

Vaginal Spermicides

A **spermicide** is a chemical that kills sperm. Vaginal spermicides come in several forms, including foam, cream, jelly, film, and suppository. Only spermicides without N-9 should be used. Spermicidal creams or gels should be used with a diaphragm. Spermicidal foams, creams, gels, suppositories, and films may be used alone or with a condom.

Spermicides must be applied before the penis enters the vagina no more than twenty minutes before intercourse (appropriate applicators are included when the product is purchased). Foam is effective immediately, but suppositories, creams, and jellies require a few minutes to allow the product to melt and spread inside the vagina (package instructions describe the exact time required). Each time intercourse is repeated, more spermicide must be applied. Spermicide must be left in place for at least six to eight hours after intercourse; douching or rinsing the vagina should not be done during this period.

Spermicides are advantageous in that they are available without a prescription or medical examination. They also do not manipulate the woman's hormonal system and have few side effects such as urinary tract infections that young women may develop. It was believed that a major noncontraceptive benefit of some spermicides is that they offer some protection against STIs. However, spermicides are not recommended for STI or HIV protection.

Contraceptive Sponge

The Today contraceptive sponge is a disk-shaped polyurethane device containing the spermicide N-9. This small device, which has a 72 percent to 86 percent effectiveness rate, is dampened with water to activate the spermicide and then inserted into the vagina before intercourse.

The sponge protects for repeated acts of intercourse for twenty-four hours without the need for supplying additional spermicide. It cannot be removed for at least six hours after intercourse, but it should not be left in place for more than thirty hours. Possible side effects that may occur with use include irritation, allergic reactions, or difficulty with removal; the risk of toxic shock syndrome, a rare but serious infection, is greater when the device is kept in place longer than recommended. The sponge provides no protection from STIs. The Today sponge was taken off the market for eleven years due to manufacturing concerns. National distribution has resumed (http://www.todaysponge.com/).

Intrauterine Device (IUD)

Although not technically a barrier method, the **intrauterine device** (IUD) is a structural device that prevents implantation. A physician inserts it into the uterus to prevent the fertilized egg from implanting on the uterine wall or to dislodge the fertilized egg if it has already implanted. Two common IUDs sold in the United States are ParaGard Copper T 380A and the Progestasert Progesterone T.

The Copper T is partly wrapped in copper and can remain in the uterus for ten years. The Progesterone T contains a supply of progestin, which it continuously releases into the uterus in small amounts; after a year, the supply runs out and a new IUD must be inserted. The Copper T has a lower failure rate than the Progesterone T.

Although there is risk of perforation of the uterus, Hollander (2008a) noted that the American College of Obstetricians and Gynecologists' Committee on Adolescent Health Care has come out strongly in favor of providing IUDs to adolescents. The organization states, "health care providers should strongly encourage young women who are appropriate candidates to use this method." Speidel et al. (2008) also noted that long-acting reversible contraception (LARC) methods, including intrauterine contraceptives and implants, have a proven record of very high effectiveness, many years of effectiveness, convenience, cost effectiveness, suitability for a wide variety of women and, in general, high user satisfaction

National Data

IUDs and implants account for only about 2 percent of contraceptive use in the United States (Speidel et al. 2008).

Diaphragm

The **diaphragm** is a shallow rubber dome attached to a flexible, circular steel spring. Varying in diameter from two to four inches, the diaphragm covers the cervix and prevents sperm from moving beyond the vagina into the uterus. This device should always be used with a spermicidal jelly or cream.

To obtain a diaphragm, a woman must have an internal pelvic examination by a physician or nurse practitioner, who will select the appropriate size and instruct the woman on how to insert the diaphragm. The woman will be told to apply spermicidal cream or jelly on the inside of the diaphragm and around the rim before inserting it into the vagina (no more than two hours before intercourse).

The diaphragm must also be left in place for six to eight hours after intercourse to permit any lingering sperm to be killed by the spermicidal agent. After the birth of a child, a miscarriage, abdominal surgery, or the gain or loss of ten pounds, a woman who uses a diaphragm should consult her physician or health practitioner to ensure a continued good fit. In any case, the diaphragm should be checked every two years for fit.

A major advantage of the diaphragm is that it does not interfere with the woman's hormonal system and has few, if any, side effects. Also, for those couples who feel that menstruation diminishes their capacity to enjoy intercourse, the diaphragm may be used to catch the menstrual flow for a brief time. On the negative side, some women feel that using the diaphragm with spermicidal gel is messy and a nuisance, and using a spermicide may possibly produce an allergic reaction. Furthermore, some partners feel that spermicides make oral genital contact less enjoyable. Finally, if the diaphragm does not fit properly or is left in place too long (more than twenty-four hours), pregnancy or toxic shock syndrome can result.

Cervical Cap

The **cervical cap** is a thimble-shaped contraceptive device made of rubber or polyethylene that fits tightly over the cervix and is held in place by suction. Like the diaphragm, the cervical cap, which is used in conjunction with spermicidal cream or jelly, prevents sperm from entering the uterus. The cervical cap cannot be used during menstruation, because the suction cannot be maintained. The effectiveness, problems, risks, and advantages are similar to those of the diaphragm.

Natural Family Planning

Also referred to as **periodic abstinence**, rhythm method, and fertility awareness, **natural family planning** involves refraining from sexual intercourse during the seven to ten days each month when the woman is thought to be fertile. Women who use natural family planning must know their time of ovulation and avoid intercourse just before, during, and immediately after that time. Calculating the fertile period involves knowing when ovulation has occurred. This is usually the fourteenth day (plus or minus two days) before the onset of the next menstrual period. Numerous "home ovulation kits" are available without a prescription in a pharmacy; these allow women to identify twelve to twenty-six hours in advance when they will ovulate (by testing their urine). Another method of identifying when ovulation has occurred is by observing an increase in the basal body temperature and a sticky cervical mucus. Calculating the time of ovulation may also be used as a method of becoming pregnant because it helps the couple to know when the woman is fertile.

Nonmethods: Withdrawal and Douching

Because withdrawal and douching are not effective in preventing pregnancy, we call them "nonmethods" of birth control. Also known as **coitus interruptus, withdrawal** is the practice whereby the man withdraws his penis from the vagina before he ejaculates. The advantages of coitus interruptus are that it requires no devices or chemicals, and it is always available. The disadvantages of withdrawal are that it does not provide protection from STIs, it may interrupt the sexual response cycle and diminish the pleasure for the couple, and it is very ineffective in preventing pregnancy.

Withdrawal is not a reliable form of contraception for two reasons. First, a man can unknowingly emit a small amount of pre-ejaculatory fluid, which may contain sperm. One drop can contain millions of sperm. In addition, the man may lack the self-control to withdraw his penis before ejaculation, or he may delay his withdrawal too long and inadvertently ejaculate some semen near the vaginal opening of his partner. Sperm deposited there can live in the moist vaginal lips and make their way up the vagina.

Though some women believe that douching is an effective form of contraception, it is not. Douching refers to rinsing or cleansing the vaginal canal. After intercourse, the woman fills a syringe with water, any of a variety of solutions that can be purchased over the counter, or a spermicidal agent and flushes (so she assumes) the sperm from her vagina. In some cases, however, the fluid will actually force sperm up through the cervix. In other cases, a large number of sperm may already have passed through the cervix to the uterus, so the douche may do little good.

Sperm may be found in the cervical mucus within ninety seconds after ejaculation. In effect, douching does little to deter conception and may even encourage it. In addition, douching is associated with an increased risk for pelvic inflammatory disease and ectopic pregnancy.

Emergency Contraception

National Data

Based on a national sample of 7,643 women aged 15 to 44, 4 percent of those who had ever had sex with a man reported having used emergency contraception (Kavanaugh and Schwarz 2008).

Also called postcoital contraception, **emergency contraception** (EC) refers to various types of morning-after pills that are used primarily in three circumstances: when a woman has unprotected intercourse, when a contraceptive method fails (such as condom breakage or slippage), and when a woman is raped. EC methods should be used in emergencies for those times when unprotected intercourse has occurred, and medication can be taken within seventy-two hours of exposure. Plan B, an emergency contraceptive, is now available over the counter for someone who is age 18 or above.

Combined Estrogen-Progesterone The most common morning-after pills are the combined estrogen-progesterone oral contraceptives routinely taken to prevent pregnancy. In higher doses, they serve to prevent ovulation, fertilization of the egg, or transportation of the egg to the uterus. They may also make the uterine lining inhospitable to implantation. Known as the "Yuzpe method" after the physician who proposed it, this method involves ingesting a certain number of tablets of combined estrogen-progesterone. *These pills must be taken within seventy-two hours of unprotected intercourse to be effective.*

Common side effects of combined estrogen-progesterone EC pills (sold under the trade names Preven and Plan B) include nausea, vomiting, headaches, and breast tenderness, although some women also experience abdominal pain, headache, and dizziness. Side effects subside within a day or two after treatment is completed.

Postcoital IUD Insertion of a copper IUD within five to seven days after ovulation in a cycle when unprotected intercourse has occurred is very effective for preventing pregnancy. This option, however, is used much less frequently than hormonal treatment because women who need EC often are not appropriate IUD candidates. Women who have chlamydia or gonorrhea when an IUD is inserted are at higher risk of developing pelvic inflammatory disease; therefore, testing is recommended prior to insertion.

Mifepristone (RU-486) **Mifepristone**, also known as **RU-486**, is a synthetic steroid that effectively inhibits implantation of a fertilized egg by making the endometrium unsuitable for implantation. The so-called abortion pill, approved by the FDA in the United States in 2000, is marketed under the name Mifeprex and can be given to induce abortion within seven weeks of pregnancy. Side effects of RU-486 are usually very severe and may include cramping, nausea, vomiting, and

What if the Condom Breaks—Do You Seek Emergency Contraception?

WHAT IF?

For couples using a condom for the first time, the condom will break about 7 percent of the time. Alternative responses include nothing ("I'm not going to worry about it") to worrying but doing nothing ("I hope I don't get pregnant") to worrying and doing something—seeking emergency contraception. "Rather be safe than sorry" requires immediate action because the sooner the EC (emergency contraception) pills are taken, the lower the risk of pregnancy—twelve hours is best, seventy-two is the latest. The medication is available over the counter—no prescription is necessary (and no pregnancy test is required). Although the side effects (nausea, vomiting, and so on) may occur, they will be over in a couple of days and the risk of being pregnant is minimal.

breast tenderness. Potential serious adverse effects include the possibility of hemorrhage and infection. The pregnancy rate associated with RU-486 is low, which suggests that RU-486 is an effective means of EC. More than 90 percent of U.S. women who tried RU-486 would recommend it to others and choose it over surgery again. Its use remains controversial. To be clear, an abortion is not a method of contraception because conception has already occurred. An abortion simply prevents conception, fertilization, and development to progressing toward a normal pregnancy.

Effectiveness of Various Contraceptives

In Table 10.1, we present data on the effectiveness of various contraceptive methods in preventing pregnancy and protecting against STIs. Table 10.1 also describes the benefits, disadvantages, and costs of various methods of contraception. Also included in the chart is the obvious and most effective form of birth control: abstinence. Its cost is the lowest, it is 100 percent effective for pregnancy prevention, and it also eliminates the risk of HIV and other STIs from intercourse. Abstinence can be practiced for a week, a month, several years, until marriage, or until someone finds the "right" sexual partner.

Sterilization

Unlike the temporary and reversible methods of contraception already discussed, **sterilization** is a permanent surgical procedure that prevents reproduction. Sterilization may be a contraceptive method of choice when the woman should not have more children for health reasons or when individuals are certain about their desire to have no more children or to remain child-free. Most couples complete their intended childbearing in their late twenties or early thirties, leaving more than fifteen years of continued risk of unwanted pregnancy. Because of the risk of pill use at older ages and the lower reliability of alternative birth control methods, sterilization has become the most popular method of contraception among married women who have completed their families.

Slightly more than half of all sterilizations are performed on women. Although male sterilization is easier and safer than female sterilization, women feel more certain they will not get pregnant if they are sterilized. "I'm the one that ends up being pregnant and having the baby," said one woman. "So I want to make sure that I never get pregnant again."

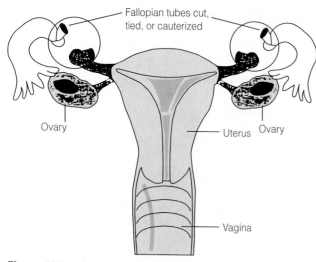

Figure 10.1
Female Sterilization: Tubal Sterilization

Female Sterilization   Although a woman may be sterilized by removal of her ovaries (**oophorectomy**) or uterus (**hysterectomy**), these operations are not normally undertaken for the sole purpose of sterilization because the ovaries produce important hormones (as well as eggs) and because both procedures carry the risks of major surgery. Sometimes, however, another medical problem requires hysterectomy.

The usual procedures of female sterilization are the salpingectomy and a variant of it, the laparoscopy. **Salpingectomy,** also known as tubal ligation or tying the tubes (see Figure 10.1), is often performed under a general anesthetic while the woman is in the hospital just after she has delivered a baby. An incision is made in the lower abdomen, just above the pubic line, and the fallopian tubes are brought into view one at a time. A part of each tube is cut out, and the ends are tied, clamped, or cauterized (burned). The operation takes about thirty minutes.

Table 10.1 Methods of Contraception and Sexually Transmitted Infection Protection

Method	Typical Use[1] Effectiveness Rates	STI Protection	Benefits	Disadvantages	Cost[2]
Oral contraceptive, combined or progestin-only pills ("the pill")	92%	No	High effectiveness rate; 24-hour protection; menstrual regulation	Daily administration; side effects possible; medication interactions	$10–60 per month
Implanon® (one rod, three-year implant)	99.95%	No	High effectiveness rate; long-term protection	Menstrual changes; side effects possible	$150–200, not including implantation fees
Depo-Provera® (three-month injection)	97%	No	High effectiveness rate; no estrogen; Privacy of use	Can seriously impact bone density; short-term use recommended unless other methods are inadequate; side effects likely	$45–75 per injection
Ortho Evra® (transdermal patch)	92%	No	Same as oral contraceptives except maintenance is weekly, not daily	Visibility; side effects possible; 60% more hormone exposure than pills	$15–32 per month
NuvaRing® (vaginal ring)	92%	No	Lower dosage than other hormonal methods	Must be comfortable with body for insertion	$15–48 per month
Male condom	85%	Yes	Few or no side effects; easy to purchase and use	Can interrupt spontaneity	$2–10 a box
Female condom	79%	Yes	Few or no side effects; easy to purchase	Decreased sensation; insertion takes practice	$4–10 a box
Spermicide	71%	No	Many forms to choose; easy to purchase and use	Can cause irritation and be messy	$8–18 per box, tube, or can
Today® Sponge[3]	68–84%	No	Few side effects; effective for 24 hours after insertion	Spermicide irritation possible	$3–5 per sponge
Diaphragm, Lea's Shield, and cervical cap[3]	68–84%	No	Few side effects; can be inserted within two hours before intercourse	Can be messy; increased risk of vaginal or urinary tract infections	$50–200 plus spermicide
Intrauterine device (IUD): Mirena	98.2–99%	No	Little maintenance; longer-term protection	Risk of pelvic inflammatory disease increased; chance of expulsion	$200–400
Withdrawal	73%	No	Requires little planning; always available	Pre-ejaculatory fluid can contain sperm	$0
Periodic abstinence (also called natural family planning or fertility awareness)	75%	No	No side effects; accepted in all religions or cultures	Requires a lot of planning; need ability to interpret fertility signs	$0
Emergency contraception	75%	No	Provides an option after intercourse has occurred	Must be taken within 72 hours; side effects likely	$10–32
Abstinence	100%	Yes	No risk of pregnancy or STDs	Partners both have to agree to abstain	$0
Sterilization	99.5% (Female) 99.85% (Male)	No	Long-term; complications are rare	May not be reversible	$250–5,000

[1]Effectiveness rates are listed as percentages of women not experiencing an unintended pregnancy during the first year of typical use. Typical use refers to use under real-life conditions. Perfect use effectiveness rates are higher.
[2]Costs may vary.
[3]Lower percentages apply to parous women (women who have given birth). Higher rates apply to nulliparous women (women who have never given birth).
Source: Charla Blumell, MA Ed, Certified Health Education Specialist

A less expensive and quicker (about fifteen minutes) form of salpingectomy, which is performed on an outpatient basis, is the **laparoscopy**. Often using local anesthesia, the surgeon inserts a small, lighted viewing instrument (laparoscope) through the woman's abdominal wall just below the navel, through which the uterus and the fallopian tubes can be seen. The surgeon then makes another small incision in the lower abdomen and inserts a special pair of forceps that carry electricity to cauterize the tubes. The laparoscope and the forceps are then withdrawn, the small wounds are closed with a single stitch, and small bandages are placed over the closed incisions. (Laparoscopy is also known as "the Band-Aid operation.") As an alternative to reaching the fallopian tubes through an opening below the navel, the surgeon may make a small incision in the back of the vaginal barrel (vaginal tubal ligation).

Essure is a permanent sterilization procedure that requires no cutting and only a local anesthetic in a half-hour procedure that blocks the fallopian tubes. Women typically may return home within forty-five minutes (and to work the next day).

These procedures for female sterilization are greater than 95 percent effective, but sometimes they have complications. In rare cases, a blood vessel in the abdomen is torn open during the sterilization and bleeds into the abdominal cavity. When this happens, another operation is necessary to tie the bleeding vessel closed. Occasionally, injury occurs to the small or large intestine, which may cause nausea, vomiting, and loss of appetite. The fact that death may result, if only rarely, is a reminder that female sterilization is surgery and, like all surgery, involves some risks. In addition, although some female sterilizations may be reversed, a woman should become sterilized only if she does not want to have a biological child.

Male Sterilization   **Vasectomies** are the most frequent form of male sterilization. They are usually performed in the physician's office under a local anesthetic. In this operation the physician makes two small incisions, one on either side of the scrotum, so that a small portion of each vas deferens (the sperm-carrying ducts) can be cut out and tied closed. Sperm are still produced in the testicles, but because there is no tube to the penis, they remain in the epididymis and eventually dissolve.

The procedure takes about fifteen minutes. The man can leave the physician's office within a short time. Because sperm do not disappear from the ejaculate immediately after a vasectomy (some remain in the vas deferens above the severed portion), a couple should use another method of contraception until the man has had about twenty ejaculations. In about 1 percent of the cases, the vas deferens grows back and the man becomes fertile again.

A vasectomy does not affect the man's desire for sex, ability to have an erection or an orgasm, amount of ejaculate (sperm account for only a minute portion of the seminal fluid), health, or chance of prostate cancer. Although a vasectomy may be reversed in some instances, a man should get a vasectomy only if he does not want to have a biological child.

Talking with a Partner about Contraception

Having a conversation about birth control is a good way to begin sharing responsibility for it; one can learn of the partner's interest in participating in the choice and use of a contraceptive method. Men can also share responsibility by purchasing and using condoms, paying for medical visits and the pharmacy bill, reminding his partner to use the method, assisting with insertion of barrier methods, checking contraceptive supplies, and having a vasectomy if that is an appropriate option. However, in addition, women need to take steps to protect themselves from unwanted pregnancy and from exposure to STIs.

Abortion

An abortion may be either an **induced abortion**, which is the deliberate termination of a pregnancy through chemical or surgical means, or a **spontaneous abortion (miscarriage)**, which is the unintended termination of a pregnancy. In this text, however, we will use the term *abortion* to refer to induced abortion. In general, abortion is legal in the United States but had been challenged under the Bush administration. Specifically, federal funding was withheld if an aid group offered abortion or abortion advice. However, the election of Obama restored approval from the administration for abortion. Obama said that denying such aid undermined "safe and effective voluntary family planning in developing countries."

Incidence of Abortion

National Data

The number of abortions performed in the United States in 2005 was 1,206,200. This is 8 percent fewer than in 2000 (Jones 2008).

Table 10.2 reflects the abortion rates and the number of abortions in the United States for selected years. **Abortion rate** refers to the number of abortions per thousand women aged 15 to 44; **abortion ratio** refers to the number of abortions per thousand live births. Whether looking at the rate, ratio, or actual number, abortions are decreasing. Reasons for the decrease in abortions include increased access to contraceptives, a reduced rate of unintended pregnancies, and more supportive attitudes toward women becoming single parents. In addition, part of the decline may be due to an increase in restrictive abortion policies, such as those requiring parental consent and parental notification. **Parental consent** means that a woman needs permission from a parent to get an abortion if under a certain age, usually 18. **Parental notification** means that a woman has to tell a parent she is getting an abortion if she is under a certain age, usually 18, but she doesn't need parental permission. Laws vary by states. See Table 10.3 for Parental Consent by State on page 343 or call National Abortion Federation Hotline at 1-800-772-9100 for laws in your state.

The Self-Assessment on pg 342 provides a way for you to assess your abortion views.

International Data

Gomperts et al. (2008) noted that Women on Web is a service that uses telemedicine to help women access mifepristone and misoprostol in countries with no safe care for termination of pregnancy (TOP). Research shows that the outcome of such care is in the same range as TOP provided in outpatient settings.

Table 10.2 Abortion Rate and Numbers for Selected Years

Year	Rate	Numbers
	Number of abortions per 1,000 women aged 15 to 44	Number of abortions per year
2000	21.3	1,312,990
2004	19.7	1,222,100
2005	19.4	1,206,200

Source: *Statistical Abstract of the United States, 2009,* 128th ed. Washington, DC. U.S. Bureau of the Census, Table 99.

Abortion Attitude Scale

This is not a test. There are no wrong or right answers to any of the statements, so just answer as honestly as you can. The statements ask your feelings about legal abortion (the voluntary removal of a human fetus from the mother during the first three months of pregnancy by a qualified medical person). Tell how you feel about each statement by circling only one response. Use the following scale for your answers:

Strongly Agree	Slightly Agree	Slightly Disagree	Strongly Agree	Disagree
5	4	3	2	1

_____ 1. The Supreme Court should strike down legal abortions in the United States.

_____ 2. Abortion is a good way of solving an unwanted pregnancy.

_____ 3. A mother should feel obligated to bear a child she has conceived.

_____ 4. Abortion is wrong no matter what the circumstances are.

_____ 5. A fetus is not a person until it can live outside its mother's body.

_____ 6. The decision to have an abortion should be the pregnant mother's.

_____ 7. Every conceived child has the right to be born.

_____ 8. A pregnant female not wanting to have a child should be encouraged to have an abortion.

_____ 9. Abortion should be considered killing a person.

_____ 10. People should not look down on those who choose to have abortions.

_____ 11. Abortion should be an available alternative for unmarried pregnant teenagers.

_____ 12. People should not have the power over the life or death of a fetus.

_____ 13. Unwanted children should not be brought into the world.

_____ 14. A fetus should be considered a person at the moment of conception.

Scoring and Interpretation

As its name indicates, this scale was developed to measure attitudes toward abortion. Sloan (1983) developed the scale by for use with high school and college students. To compute your score, first reverse the point scale for items 1, 3, 4, 7, 9, 12, and 14. For example, if you selected a 5 for item one, this becomes a 0; if you selected a 1, this becomes a 4. After reversing the scores on the seven items specified, add the numbers you circled for all the items. Sloan provided the following categories for interpreting the results:

70–56	Strong proabortion
54–44	Moderate proabortion
43–27	Unsure
26–16	Moderate pro-life
15–0	Strong pro-life

Reliability and Validity

The Abortion Attitude Scale was administered to high school and college students, Right to Life group members, and abortion service personnel. Sloan (1983) reported a high total test estimate of reliability (0.92). Construct validity was supported in that the mean score for Right to Life members was 16.2; the mean score for abortion service personnel was 55.6; and other groups' scores fell between these values.

Source

"Abortion Attitude Scale" by L. A Sloan. _Journal of Health Education_ Vol. 14, No. 3, May/June 1983. The Journal of Health Education is a publication of the American Allegiance for Health, Physical Education, Recreation and Dance, 1900 Association Drive, Reston, VA 20191. Reprinted by permission.

Republicans are against abortion until their daughter needs one; Democrats are for abortion until their daughter wants one.

Grace McGarvie,
political science teacher

Reasons for an Abortion

A team of researchers (Finer et al. 2005) surveyed 1,209 women who reported having had an abortion. The most frequently cited reasons were that having a child would interfere with a woman's education, work, or ability to care for dependents (74 percent); that she could not afford a baby now (73 percent); and that she did not want to be a single mother or was having relationship problems (48 percent). Nearly four in ten women said they had completed their childbearing, and almost one-third of the women were not ready to have a child. Fewer than 1 percent said their parents' or partner's desire for them to have an abortion was the most important reason.

Abortions performed to protect the life or health of the woman are called **therapeutic abortions.** However, there is disagreement over this definition. Garrett et al. (2001) noted, "Some physicians argue that an abortion is therapeutic if it prevents or alleviates a serious physical or mental illness, or even if it alleviates temporary emotional upsets. In short, the health of the pregnant woman is given such a broad definition that a very large number of abortions can be classified as therapeutic" (p. 218).

Table 10.3 Parental Consent by State

State	Status	Comments	State	Status	Comments
Alabama	PC		Montana	NONE	PN stopped by court
Alaska	NONE	PN law stopped by court	Nebraska	PN	
			Nevada	NONE	PN stopped by court
Arizona	PC		New Hampshire	NONE	
Arkansas	PC		New Jersey	NONE	PN law stopped by court
California	NONE	PC law stopped by court	New Mexico	NONE	PC law stopped by court
Colorado	PN				
Connecticut	NONE		New York	NONE	
Delaware	PN	Applies only to girls under 16 years old; notice may also be to grandparent or counselor; doctor can bypass	North Carolina	PC	Also allows consent of grandparent instead
			North Dakota	PC2	
			Ohio	PC	
			Oklahoma	PN and PC	Law requiring both started November 2006
Washington	NONE		Oregon	NONE	
Florida	PN		Pennsylvania	PC	
Georgia	PN		Rhode Island	PC	
Hawaii	NONE		South Carolina	PC	Women under 17 years old; also allows for consent of grandparent
Idaho	PC	PC law is back as of March 2007			
Illinois	NONE	PN law stopped by court	South Dakota	PN	
			Tennessee	PC	
Indiana	PC		Texas	PC	Law enacted by Gov. George W. Bush in October 1999
Iowa	PN	Also allows consent of grandparent instead			
Kansas	PN		Utah	PN and PC	
Kentucky	PC		Virginia	PC	Also allows consent of grandparent instead
Louisiana	PC				
Maine	NONE		Vermont	NONE	
Maryland	PN	Doctor can bypass	Washington	NONE	
Massachusetts	PC		West Virginia	PN	Doctor can bypass
Michigan	PC		Wisconsin	PC	Also allows other family members over 25 to consent; doctor can bypass
Minnesota	PN2				
Mississippi	PC2				
Missouri	PC				
			Wyoming	PC	

Key

PC = Parental Consent

PN = Parental Notification

NONE = No PC or PN are required now

2 = Both parents required

Source: Coalition for Positive Sexuality. downloaded May 2009.

Some women with multifetal pregnancies (a common outcome of the use of fertility drugs) may have a procedure called *transabdominal first-trimester selective termination*. In this procedure, the lives of some fetuses are terminated to increase the chance of survival for the others or to minimize the health risks associated with multifetal pregnancy for the woman. For example, a woman carrying five fetuses may elect to abort three of them to minimize the health risks of the other two.

Pro-Life and Pro-Choice Abortion Positions

A dichotomy of attitudes toward abortion is reflected in two opposing groups of abortion activists. Individuals and groups who oppose abortion are commonly referred to as "pro-life" or "antiabortion."

Pro-Life Of 657 undergraduates in a random sample at a large southeastern university, 40 percent reported that they were pro-life in regard to their feelings about abortion (Bristol and Farmer 2005). Pro-life groups favor abortion policies or a complete ban on abortion. They essentially believe the following:

The unborn fetus has a right to live and that right should be protected.

Abortion is a violent and immoral solution to unintended pregnancy.

The life of an unborn fetus is sacred and should be protected, even at the cost of individual difficulties for the pregnant woman.

Individuals who are over the age of 44, female, mothers of three or more children, married to white-collar workers, affiliated with a religion, and Catholic are most likely to be pro-life (Begue 2001). Pro-life individuals emphasize the sanctity of human life and the moral obligation to protect it. The unborn fetus cannot protect itself so is literally dependent on others for life. Naomi Judd noted that if she had had an abortion she would have deprived the world of one of its greatest singers—Wynonna Judd.

In a large, nonrandom sample, 60.1 percent of 1,319 undergraduates at a southeastern university reported that, "abortion is acceptable under certain conditions" (Knox and Zusman 2009). Pro-choice advocates support the legal availability of abortion for all women. They essentially believe the following:

Freedom of choice is a central value—the woman has a right to determine what happens to her own body.

Those who must personally bear the burden of their moral choices ought to have the right to make these choices.

Procreation choices must be free of governmental control.

People most likely to be pro-choice are female, are mothers of one or two children, have some college education, are employed, and have annual income of more than $50,000. Although many self-proclaimed feminists and women's organizations, such as the National Organization for Women (NOW), have been active in promoting abortion rights, not all feminists are pro-choice.

Physical Effects of Abortion

Part of the debate over abortion is related to the presumed effects of abortion. In regard to the physical effects, legal abortions, performed under safe medical conditions, are safer than continuing the pregnancy. The earlier in the pregnancy the abortion is performed, the safer it is. Vacuum aspiration, a frequently used method in early pregnancy, does not increase the risks to future childbearing. However, late-term abortions do increase the risks of subsequent miscarriages, premature deliveries, and babies of low birth weight.

Postabortion complications include the possibility of incomplete abortion, which occurs when the initial procedure misses the fetus and the procedure must be repeated. Other possible complications include uterine infection; excessive bleeding; perforation or laceration of the uterus, bowel, or adjacent organs; and an adverse reaction to a medication or anesthetic. After having an abortion, women are advised to expect bleeding (usually not heavy) for up to two weeks and to return to their health care provider thirty days after the abortion to check that all is well.

Psychological Effects of Abortion

Of equal concern are the psychological effects of abortion. The American Psychological Association reviewed all outcome studies on the mental health effects of abortion and concluded, "Based on our comprehensive review and evaluation of the empirical literature published in peer-reviewed journals since 1989, this Task Force on Mental Health and Abortion concludes that the most methodologically sound research indicates that among women who have a single, legal, first-trimester abortion of an unplanned pregnancy for nontherapeutic reasons, the relative risks of mental health problems are no greater than the risks among women who deliver an unplanned pregnancy" (Major et al. 2008, 71). Steinberg and Russo (2008) also looked at national data and did not find a significant relationship between first pregnancy abortion and subsequent rates of generalized anxiety disorder, social anxiety, or post-traumatic stress disorder.

Postabortion Attitudes of Men

Researchers Kero and Lalos (2004) conducted interviews with men four and twelve months after their partners had had an abortion. Overwhelmingly, the men (at both time periods) were happy with the decision of their partners to have an abortion. More than half accompanied their partner to the abortion clinic (which they found less than welcoming); about a third were not using contraception a year later.

PERSONAL CHOICES

Should You Have an Abortion?

The decision to have an abortion continues to be a complex one. Women who are faced with the issue may benefit by considering the following guidelines:

   1. *Consider all the alternatives available to you, realizing that no alternative may be all good or all bad.* As you consider each alternative, think about both the short-term and the long-term consequences of each course of action.

   2. *Obtain information about each alternative course of action.* Inform yourself about the medical, financial, and legal aspects of abortion, childbearing, parenting, and placing the baby up for adoption.

   3. *Talk with trusted family members, friends, or unbiased counselors.* Consider talking with the man who participated in the pregnancy. If possible, also talk with women who have had abortions as well as with women who have kept and reared a baby or placed a baby for adoption. If you feel that someone is pressuring you in your decision making, look for help elsewhere.

   4. *Consider your own personal and moral commitments in life.* Understand your feelings, values, and beliefs concerning the fetus and weigh those against the circumstances surrounding your pregnancy.

SUMMARY

Why do people have children?

Worldwide, 80 million unintended pregnancies occur each year (38 percent of all pregnancies). These pregnancies result in 42 million induced abortions and 34 million unintended births. Having children continues to be a major goal of most college students (women more than men). Social influences to have a child include family, friends, religion, government, favorable economic conditions, and cultural observances. The reasons people give for having children include love and companionship with one's own offspring, the desire to be personally fulfilled as an adult by having a child, and the desire to recapture one's youth.

Having a child (particularly for women) reduces one's educational and career advancement. The cost for housing, food, transportation, clothing, health care, and child care for a child up to age 2 is over $10,000 annually.

How many children do people have?

About 20 percent of women aged 40 to 44 do not have children. Whether these women will remain childfree or eventually have children is unknown. Reasons that spouses elect a childfree marriage include the freedom to spend their time and money as they choose, to enjoy their partner without interference, to pursue a career, to avoid health problems associated with pregnancy, and to avoid passing on genetic disorders to a new generation.

The most preferred type of family in the United States is the two-child family (1.9 children to be exact). Some of the factors in a couple's decision to have more than one child are the desire to repeat a good experience, the feeling that two children provide companionship for each other, and the desire to have a child of each sex.

Are teen mothers disadvantaged?

There are 1.7 million births annually to teenage mothers and this number is rising. The teenage birthrate in the United States, as measured by births per thousand teenagers, is nine times that of teens in the Netherlands. The reason is openness in sexuality and contraception in France, Germany, and other European countries in contrast to abstinence thinking in the United States (for example, "Don't tell a teen about contraception and they won't have sex"). Teens in the United States also view motherhood as one of the only viable roles open to them. Consequences associated with teenage motherhood include poverty, alcohol or drug abuse, babies with lower birth weights, and lower academic achievement.

What are the causes of infertility?

Infertility is defined as the inability to achieve a pregnancy after at least one year of regular sexual relations without birth control, or the inability to carry a pregnancy to a live birth. Forty percent of infertility problems are attributed to the woman, 40 percent to the man, and 20 percent to both of them. The causes of infertility in women include blocked fallopian tubes, endocrine imbalance that prevents ovulation, dysfunctional ovaries, chemically hostile cervical mucus that may kill sperm, and effects of STIs. The psychological reaction to infertility is often depression over having to give up a lifetime goal. Some of the more common causes of infertility in men include low sperm production, poor semen motility, effects of STIs (such as chlamydia, gonorrhea, and syphilis), and interference with passage of sperm through the genital ducts due to an enlarged prostate.

A number of technological innovations are available to assist women and couples in becoming pregnant. These include hormonal therapy, artificial insemination, ovum transfer, in vitro fertilization, gamete intrafallopian transfer, and zygote intrafallopian transfer. Being infertile (for the woman) may have a negative lifetime effect, both personal and interpersonal (half the women in one study were separated or reported a negative effect on their sex lives).

Why do people adopt?

Motives for adoption include a couple's inability to have a biological child (infertility), their desire to give an otherwise unwanted child a permanent loving home, or their desire to avoid contributing to overpopulation by having more biological children. Adoption is actually quite rare, with less than 5 percent of couple adopting; 15 percent of these adoptions will be children from other countries.

Whereas demographic characteristics of those who typically adopt are white, educated, and of high income, adoptees are increasingly being placed in nontraditional families including with older, gay, and single individuals; it is recognized that these individuals may also be white, educated, and of high income. Most college students are open to transracial adoption.

Some individuals seek the role of parent via foster parenting. A foster parent, also known as a family caregiver, is a person who, either alone or with a spouse, takes care of and fosters a child taken into custody in home. A foster parent has made a contract with the state for the service, has judicial status, and is reimbursed by the state.

What are various methods of contraception?

The primary methods of contraception include hormonal methods (Depo-Provera®, NuvaRing®, and Ortho Evra®), which prevent ovulation; the IUD, which prevents implantation of the fertilized egg; condoms and diaphragms, which are barrier methods; and vaginal spermicides and the rhythm method. These and numerous new methods vary in effectiveness and safety.

Sterilization is a surgical procedure that prevents fertilization, usually by blocking the passage of eggs or sperm through the fallopian tubes or vas deferens, respectively. The procedure for female sterilization is called salpingectomy, or tubal ligation. Laparoscopy is another method of tubal ligation. The most frequent form of male sterilization is vasectomy.

What are the types of and motives for an abortion?

An abortion may be either an induced abortion, which is the deliberate termination of a pregnancy through chemical or surgical means, or a spontaneous abortion (miscarriage), which is the unintended termination of a pregnancy. The most frequently cited reasons for induced abortion were that having a child would interfere with a woman's education, work, or ability to care for dependents (74 percent); that she could not afford a baby now (73 percent); and that she did not want to be a single mother or was having relationship problems (48 percent). Nearly four in ten women said they had completed their childbearing, and almost one-third of the women were not ready to have a child. Less than 1 percent said their parents' or partner's desire for them to have an abortion was the most important reason. In regard to the psychological effects of abortion, the American Psychological Association reviewed the literature and concluded that "among women who have a single, legal, first-trimester abortion of an unplanned pregnancy for nontherapeutic reasons, the relative risks of mental health problems are no greater than the risks among women who deliver an unplanned pregnancy."

KEY TERMS

abortion rate	female condom	miscarriage	procreative liberty
abortion ratio	Fertell	natural family planning	RU-486
antinatalism	fertilization	Norplant	salpingectomy
cervical cap	foster parent	NuvaRing®	spermicide
coitus interruptus	hysterectomy	oophorectomy	spontaneous abortion
competitive birthing	Implanon	Ortho Evra®	sterilization
conception	induced abortion	parental consent	therapeutic abortion
cryopreservation	infertility	parental notification	transracial adoption
Depo-Provera®	intrauterine device	periodic abstinence	vasectomy
diaphragm	laparoscopy	pregnancy	withdrawal
emergency contraception	Mifepristone	pronatalism	

The Companion Website for *Choices in Relationships: An Introduction to Marriage and the Family*, Tenth Edition
www.cengage.com/sociology/knox

Supplement your review of this chapter by going to the Companion Website to take one of the tutorial quizzes, use the flash cards to master key terms, or check out the many other study aids, like crossword puzzles and self-assessments. You'll also find special features such as General Social Survey (GSS) data, Census data, and other resources to help you with that special project or to do some research on your own.

REFERENCES

Amory, J., S. Page, and W. Bremner. 2006. Drug insight: recent advances in male hormonal contraception. *Nature Clinical Practice Endocrinology & Metabolism* 2:32–41.

Baden, A. L., and M. O. Wiley. 2007. Counseling adopted persons in adulthood: Integrating practice and research. *Counseling Psychologist* 35:868–79.

Begue, L. 2001. Social judgment of abortion: A black-sheep effect in a Catholic sheepfold. *Journal of Social Psychology* 141:640–50.

Berger, R., and M. Paul. 2008, Family secrets and family functioning: The case of donor assistance. *Family Process* 47:553–66.

Block, S. 2008. Adopting domestically can lower hurdles to claiming tax credit. *USA Today*, August 19, 3B.

Bristol, K., and B. Farmer. 2005. *Sexuality among southeastern university students: a survey.* Unpublished data, East Carolina University, Greenville, NC.

Brown, J. D. 2008. Foster parents' perceptions of factors needed for successful foster placements. *Journal of Child and Family Studies* 17:538–55.

Chatterjee, P. 2005. Doctors' group proposes one-child policy for India. *Lancet* 365:1609.

Cohn, D. 2009. Public has split verdict on increased level of unmarried motherhood. Pew Research Center. March 19. http://pewresearch.org/pubs/1158/out-of-wedlock-births-public-sees-costly-to-society-splits-on-morality (retrieved April 1, 2009).

Delavande, A. 2008. Pill, patch, or shot? Subjective expectations and birth control choice. *International Economic Review* 49:999–1012.

Fiejoo, A. N. 2006. Adolescent sexual health in the U.S. and Europe: Why the difference? Updated article originally written by S. Alford and A. N. Fiejoo. Published by Youth Advocates, 2000. http://www.advocatesforyouth.org/PUBLICATIONS/factsheet/fsest.pdf (retrieved on February 22, 2006).

Finer, L. B., L. F. Frohwirth, L. A. Dauphinne, S. Singh, and A. M. Moore. 2005. Reasons U.S. women have abortions: quantitative and qualitative reasons. *Perspectives on Sexual and Reproductive Health* 37:110–18.

Flower Kim, K. M. 2003. We are family. Paper presented at the 73rd Annual Meeting of the Eastern Sociological Society, February 27, Philadelphia.

Food and Drug Administration. 2005. FDA updates labeling for Ortho Evra contraceptive patch. FDA Publication No. P05-90. Washington, DC: FDA News. Retrieved from http://www.fda.gov/bbs/topics/news/2005/NEW01262.html.

Garrett, T. M., H. W. Baillie, and R. M. Garrett. 2001. *Health care ethics,* 4th ed. Upper Saddle River, NJ: Prentice Hall.

Ge, X., M. N. Natsuaki, D. Martin, J. M. Neiderhiser, D. S. Shaw, L. Scaramella, J. B. Reid, and D. Reiss. 2008. Bridging the divide: Openness in adoption and post adoption psychosocial adjustment among birth and adoptive parents issue: Public health perspectives on family interventions. American Psychological Association. Sage Periodicals Press.

Gomperts, R. J., K. Jelinska, S. Davies, K. Gemzell-Danielsson, G. Kleiverda. 2008. Using telemedicine for termination of pregnancy with mifepristone and misoprostol in settings where there is no access to safe services. *BJOG* 115:1171–82.

Gross, J., and W. Connors. 2007. Ethopia, Open doors for foreign adoptions. *The New York Times*, June 4, A1.

Hammarberg, K., J. R. W. Fisher, and H. J. Rowe. 2008. Women's experiences of childbirth and post-natal healthcare after assisted conception. *Human Reproduction* 23:1567–74.

Hollander, D. 2005. Failure rates of male and female condoms fall with use. *International Family Planning Perspectives* 31(2).

Hollander, D. 2008a. IUDs for teenagers? *Perspectives on Sexual and Reproductive Health* 40:5–6.

Hollander, D. 2008b. New pregnancy data out. *Perspectives on Sexual and Reproductive Health.* 40: 65–67.

Hollingsworth, L. D. 1997. Same race adoption among African Americans: A ten-year empirical review. *African American Research Perspectives* 13:44–49.

Huh, N. S., and W. J. Reid. 2000. Intercountry, transracial adoption and ethnic identity: a Korean example. *International Social Work* 43:75–87.

Hunter, D. J., M. J. Khoury, and J. M. Drazen. 2008. Letting the genome out of the bottle—Will we get our wish? *The New England Journal of Medicine* 358:105–08.

Jones, R. K., M. R. S. Zolna, S. K. Henshaw, and L. B. Finer. 2005. Abortion in the United States: Incidence and access to services, 2005. *Perspectives on Sexual and Reproductive Health* 40:6–17.

Kavanaugh, M. L., and E. B. Schwarz. 2008. Counseling about and use of emergency contraception in the United States. *Perspectives on Sexual and Reproductive Health* 40:81–87.

Kennedy, R. 2003. *Interracial intimacies.* New York: Pantheon.

Kero, A., and A. Lalos. 2004. Reactions and reflections in men, 4 and 12 months post-abortion. *Journal of Psychosomatic Obstetrics and Gynecology* 25:135–43.

Knox, D., and M. E. Zusman. 2009. Relationship and sexual behaviors of a sample of 1,319 university students. Unpublished data collected for this text. Department of Sociology, East Carolina University, Greenville, NC.

Kornblum, J. 2008. More women 40 to 44 remaining childless. Census Report. *USA Today,* August 19, 12B.

Koropeckyj-Cox, T., and G. Pendell. 2007a. Attitudes about childlessness in the United States: Correlates of positive, neutral, and negative responses. *Journal of Family Issues* 28:1054–82.

Koropeckyi-Cox, T., and G. Pendell. 2007b. The gender gap in attitudes about childlessness in the United States. *Journal of Marriage and Family* 69:899–915.

Lane, T. 2003. High proportion of college men using condoms report errors and problems. *Perspectives on Sexual and Reproductive Health* 35:50–52.

Lee, D. 2006 Device brings hope for fertility clinics. http://www.indystar.com/apps/pbcs.dll/ article?AID=/20060221/BUSINESS/602210365/1003 (retrieved February 22, 2006).

Leung, P., S. Erich, and H. Kanenberg. 2005. A comparison of family functioning in gay/lesbian, heterosexual and special needs adoptions. *Children and Youth Services Review* 27:1031–44.

Levine, J. A., C. R. Emery, and H. Pollack. 2007. The well-being of children born to teen mothers. *Journal of Marriage and Family* 69:105–22.

Livermore, M. M., and R. S. Powers. 2006. Unfulfilled plans and financial stress: unwed mothers and unemployment. *Journal of Human Behavior in the Social Environment* 13:1–17.

London, S. 2003. Method-related problems account for most failures of the female condom. *Perspectives on Sexual and Reproductive Health* 35:193–99.

Maill, C. E., and K. March. 2005. Social support for changes in adoption practice: gay adoption, open adoption, birth reunions, and the release of confidential identifying information. *Families in Society* 86:83–92.

Major, B., M. Appelbaum, and C. West. 2008. Report of the APA task force on mental health and abortion. August 13.

Martin, S. 2008. Recent changes in fertility rates in the United States: What do they tell us about American's changing families? Report for Council on Contemporary Families. http://www .contemporaryfamilies.org/subtemplate.php?t=briefingPapers&ext=changesinfertility (retrieved August 10, 2008).

McDermott, E., and H. Graham. 2005. Resilient young mothering: social inequalities, late modernity and the problem if teenage motherhood. *Journal of Youth Studies* 8:59–79.

Mollborn, S. 2007. Making the best of a bad situation: Material resources and teenage parenthood. *Journal of Marriage and Family* 69:92–104.

Nickman, S. L., A. A. Rosenfeld, P. Fine, J. C. MacIntyre, D. J. Pilowsky, R. Howe, A. Dereyn, M. Gonzales, L. Forsythe, and S. A. Sveda. 2005. Children in adoptive families: overview and update. *Journal of the American Academy of Child and Adolescent Psychiatry* 44:987–95.

Pew Research. 2008. The U.S. religious landscape survey. Pew Forum on Religion & Public Life. http://pewresearch.org/pubs/743/united-states-religion.

Rochman, B. 2009 The ethics of octuplets. *Time.* February 16, 43–44.

Rolfe, A. 2008. "You've got to grow up when you've got a kid": Marginalized young women's accounts of motherhood. *Journal of Community & Applied Social Psychology* 18:299–312.

Ross, R., D. Knox, M. Whatley, and J. N. Jahangardi. 2003. Transracial adoption: some college student data. Paper presented at the 73rd Annual Meeting of the Eastern Sociological Society, Philadelphia.

Scheib, J. E., M. Riordan, and S. Rubin 2005. Adolescents with open-identity sperm donors: reports from 12–17 year olds. *Human Reproduction* 20:239–52.

Schmidt, L. 2006. Psychosocial burden of infertility and assisted reproduction. *The Lancet* 367:379–81.

Schwarz, E. B., R. Smith, J. Steinauer, M. F. Reeves, and A. B. Caughey. 2008. Measuring the effects of unintended pregnancy on women's quality of life. *Contraception* 78:204–10.

Simon, R. J., and R. M. Roorda. 2000. *In their own voices: Transracial adoptees tell their stories.* New York: Columbia University Press.

Sinclair, W., and R. W. Pressinger. 2008. Infertility statistics. http://www.yourfuturehealth.com/ resources_statistics.htm#infertility (retrieved August 16).

Smith, T. 2007. Four kids is the new standard. National Public Radio, August 5.

Speidel, J. J., C. C. Harper, and W. C. Shields. 2008. The potential of long-acting reversible contraception to decrease unintended pregnancy. *Contraception* 78:197–270.

Statistical Abstract of the United States, 2009. 128th ed. Washington, DC. U.S. Bureau of the Census.

Steinberg, J. R., and N. F. Russo. 2008. Abortion and anxiety: What's the relationship? *Social Science & Medicine* 67:238–42.

Stone, A. 2006. Drives to ban gay adoption heat up. *USA Today*, February 21, A1.

Tanturri, M. L., and L. *Mencarini*. 2008. Childless or childfree? Paths to voluntary childlessness in Italy. *Population and Development Review* 34:51–71.

Thomas, K. A., and R. C. Tessler. 2007. Bicultural socialization among adoptive families: Where there is a will, There is a way. *Journal of Family Issues* 28:1189–1219.

Walling, A. D. 2008. Oral contraception is associated with reduced overall cancer risk. *American Family Physician* 77:1597–99.

Wang, Y. A., D. Healy, D. Black and E. A. Sullivan. 2008 Age-specific success rate for women undertaking their first assisted reproduction technology treatment using their own oocytes in Australia, 2002–2005. *Human Reproduction* 23: 1533-1639

Wilson, H., and A. Huntington. 2006. Deviant mothers: the construction of teenage motherhood in contemporary discourse. *Journal of Social Policy* 35:59–76.

Wilson, S. A., and H. A. Kudis 2005. Ethinyl estradiol/levinorgestrol (Seasonale) for oral contraception. *American Family Physician* 71(8):1581–86.

Wirtberg I., A. Möller, L. Hogström, S. E. Tronstad, and A. Lalos. 2007. Life 20 years after unsuccessful infertility treatment. *Human Reproduction* 22:598–604.

Wolters, J., D. Knox, and M. Zusman. Forthcoming. Male and female attitudes toward transracial adoption. *Journal of Indiana Academy of Social Sciences*.

Zachry, E. M. 2005. Getting my education: teen mothers' experiences in school before and after motherhood. *Teachers College Record* 107:2566–98.

What the vast majority of American children need is to stop being pampered, stop being indulged, stop being chauffeured, stop being catered to. In the final analysis it is not what you do for your children but what you have taught them to do for themselves that will make them successful human beings.

Ann Landers, columnist

Parenting

Contents

True or False?

1. Today's parents note that one of the biggest difficulties in rearing their children is societal influences.

2. Parents (whether married or divorced) in high conflict relationships tend to have children who report high conflict and low quality in their own romantic relationships.

3. African American adult children are more likely than white adult children to believe that their mothers supported their relationship with their father.

4. Parents who elect not to medicate their children with attention-deficit/hyperactivity disorder (ADHD) avoid having their children labeled negatively.

5. Contact with nature may be as important as good nutrition and adequate sleep for children.

Answers: **1.** T   **2.** T   **3.** T   **4.** F   **5.** T

A happy family is but an earlier heaven.

George Bernard Shaw, playwright

There is a story of Picasso's mother who was most ambitious for him. She told him if he were to become a soldier that he would be a general and if he were to be a monk he would end up as the pope. But alas, he became a painter and ended up Picasso. Such is the enormous influence of parents (Fadiman 1985, 451). Although there are guidelines for effective parenting (and we will review them in this chapter), a number of influential factors (for example, genetics, peers, health, economics) are beyond our control. Nevertheless, our focus in this chapter is on wise parenting choices, with the goal of facilitating happy, economically independent, socially contributing members to our society. We begin by looking at the various roles of parenting.

Roles Involved in Parenting

Although finding one definition of **parenting** is difficult, there is general agreement about the various roles parents play in the lives of their children. New parents assume at least seven roles:

1. *Caregiver.* A major role of parents is the physical care of their children. From the moment of birth, when infants draw their first breath, parents stand ready to provide nourishment (milk), cleanliness (diapers), and temperature control (warm blanket). The need for such sustained care continues and becomes an accepted and anticipated role of parents. Parents who excuse themselves early from a party because they "need to check on the baby" are alerting the hostess of their commitment to the role of caregiver.

2. *Emotional resource.* Beyond providing physical care, parents are sensitive to the emotional needs of children in terms of their need to belong, to be loved, and to develop positive self-concepts. In hugging, holding, and kissing an infant, parents not only express their love for the infant but also reflect an awareness that such display of emotion is good for the child's sense of self-worth. Kouros et al. (2008) found that children exhibit increased emotional insecurity when their parents are in conflict or depression. The family context is the emotional context for children. Strife or depression in this context does occur without a negative effect on the children.

3. *Teacher.* All parents think they have a philosophy of life or set of principles their children will benefit from. Parents later discover that their children may not be interested in their religion or philosophy—indeed, they may rebel against it.

This possibility does not deter them from their role as teacher. Children are forever learning from their parents, more often by observing their behavior.

Things your mother taught you (Internet humor):

1. My mother taught me to *appreciate a job well done*: "If you're going to kill each other, do it outside. I just finished cleaning."
2. My mother taught me *religion*: "You better pray that will come out of the carpet."
3. My mother taught me about *time travel*: "If you don't straighten up, I'm going to knock you into the middle of next week!"
4. My mother taught me *logic*: "Because I said so, that's why."
5. My mother taught me *more logic*: "If you fall out of that swing and break your neck, you're not going to the store with me."
6. My mother taught me *foresight*: "Make sure you wear clean underwear, in case you're in an accident."
7. My mother taught me *irony*: "Keep crying, and I'll give you something to cry about."
8. My mother taught me about the science of *osmosis*: "Shut your mouth and eat your supper."
9. My mother taught me about *contortionism*: "Will you look at that dirt on the back of your neck!"
10. My mother taught me about *stamina*: "You'll sit there until all that spinach is gone."
11. My mother taught me about *weather*: "This room of yours looks as if a tornado went through it."
12. My mother taught me about *hypocrisy*: "If I told you once, I've told you a million times. Don't exaggerate!"
13. My mother taught me the *circle of life*: "I brought you into this world, and I can take you out."
14. My mother taught me about *behavior modification*: "Stop acting like your father!"
15. My mother taught me about *envy*: "There are millions of less fortunate children in this world who don't have wonderful parents like you do."
16. My mother taught me about *anticipation*: "Just wait until we get home."
17. My mother taught me about *receiving*: "You are going to get it when you get home!"
18. My mother taught me *medical science*: "If you don't stop crossing your eyes, they are going to get stuck that way."
19. My mother taught me ESP: "Put your sweater on; don't you think I know when you are cold?"
20. My mother taught me about my *roots*: "Shut that door behind you. Do you think you were born in a barn?"

Parents also feel that their role is made more difficult by an increasingly liberal society. A sample of 2,020 Americans noted that one of the biggest problems confronting parents today is the societal influence on their children. These include drugs and alcohol; peer pressure; TV, Internet, and movies; and crime and gangs (Pew Research Center 2007).

Parents may also teach without awareness. Cui et al. (2008) noted that parents (whether together or divorced) who reported high conflict in their marriage

Parenting is being with, involving, and teaching one's children. This dad is all of these things with his daughter.

Authors

Deceive not thyself by over expecting happiness in the marriage state. Remember nightingales sing only some months in the spring, but commonly are silent when they have hatched their eggs.

Thomas Fuller, *Of Marriage*

tended to have young adults who also reported high conflict and low quality in their own romantic relationships.

4. Economic resource. New parents are also acutely aware of the costs for medical care, food, and clothes for infants, and seek ways to ensure that such resources are available to their children. Working longer hours, taking second jobs, and cutting back on leisure expenditures are attempts to ensure that money is available to meet the needs of the child. Sometimes the pursuit of money for the family has a negative consequence for children. Rapoport and Le Bourdais (2008) investigated the effects of parents' working schedules on the time they devoted to their children and confirmed that the more parents worked, the less time them spent with their children. In view of extensive work schedules, parents are under pressure to spend "quality time" with their children, and it is implied that putting children in day care robs children of this time. However, Booth et al. (2002) compared children in day care with those in home care in terms of time the mother and child spent together per week. Although the mothers of children in day care spent less time with their children than the mothers who cared for their children at home, the researchers concluded that the "groups did not differ in the quality of mother-infant interaction" and that the difference in the "quality of the mother-infant interaction may be smaller than anticipated" (p. 16).

Parents provide an economic resource for their children by providing free room and board for them. Some young adults continue to live with their parents well into adulthood and may return at other times such as following a divorce, job loss, and so on. See the following Personal Choices section, which details this issue.

PERSONAL CHOICES

Providing Housing for One's Adult Children?

Failure to Launch is a 2006 romantic comedy with Matthew McConaughey and Sarah Jessica Parker in the respective roles of Tripp and Paula. The former is 35 years old and still living with his parents. The latter has been hired by Tripp's parents to be his girlfriend and get him to move out of the house. The film reflected reality in that about 20 percent of U.S. adults age 18 and over live with their parents. About 40 percent of those adults who have lived on their own for at least four months will return to the parental home to live at least four months (Sassler et al. 2008). Over half (51.9 percent) of a sample of 1,319 university students noted that economics would be the primary reason they might live with their parents again (Knox and Zusman 2009).

Although some offspring continue to live with their parents during and after college, others have moved away but move back because of a return to school, loss of a job, or a divorce. In the case of the latter, they may bring young children back into the parental home with them. Saving money is the primary reason adult children reside with parents.

Parents vary widely in how they view, adapt to, and carry out such cohabiting. Some parents prefer that their children live with them, enjoy their company, and hope the arrangement continues indefinitely. They have no rules about their children living with them and expect nothing from them. The adult children can come and go as they please, pay for nothing, and have no responsibilities or chores. Other parents develop what is essentially a rental agreement, whereby their children are expected to pay rent, cook and clean the dishes, mow the lawn, and service the cars. No overnight guests are allowed, and a time limit is specified as to when the adult child is expected to move out.

A central issue from the points of view of young adults is whether their parents perceive them as adults or children. This perception has implications of whether they are free to come and go as well as to make their own decisions (Sassler et al. 2008). Males are generally left alone whereas females are often under more scrutiny.

Adult children also vary in terms of how they view the arrangement. Some enjoy living with their parents, volunteer to pay rent (most do not), take care of their own laundry, and participate in cooking and housekeeping. Others are depressed that they are economically forced to live with their parents, embarrassed that they do so, pay nothing, and do nothing to contribute to the maintenance of the household. In a study of thirty young adults who had returned to the parental home, two-thirds paid nothing to live there and wanted to keep it that way. Those who did pay, paid considerably less than what rent would cost on the open market. Most paid for their cell phones, long-distance charges, and personal effects like clothing and toiletries (Sassler et al. 2008).

Whether parents and adult children discuss the issues of their living together will depend on the respective parents and adult children. Although there is no best way, clarifying expectations might prevent some misunderstandings. For example, what is the norm about bringing new pets into the home? An example is a divorced son who moved in with his 6-year-old son *and* dog. His parents enjoyed being with them but were annoyed that the dog chewed on the furniture. Parental feelings eventually erupted that dismayed their adult child. He moved out, and the relationship with his parents became very strained. However about three-fourths of the respondents in the Sassler et al. (2008) study reported generally satisfactory feelings about returning to their parental home. Most looked forward to moving out again but, in the short run, were content to stay to save money.

Sources

Knox, D. and M. Zusman. (2009) Relationhsip and sexual behavior of a sample of 1,319 undergraduates. Unpublished data collected for this text. Department of Sociology, East Carolina University.

Sassler, S., D. Ciambrone, and G. Benway. 2008. Are they really mamma's boys/daddy's girls? The negotiation of adulthood upon returning home to the parental home. *Sociological Forum* 23:670–98.

5. *Protector.* Parents also feel the need to protect their children from harm. This role may begin in pregnancy. Castrucci et al. (2006) interviewed 1,451 women about their smoking behavior during pregnancy. Although 89 percent reduced their smoking during pregnancy, 24.9 percent stopped smoking during pregnancy.

Other expressions of the protective role include insisting that children wear seat belts, protecting them from violence or nudity in the media, and protecting them from strangers. Diamond et al. (2006) studied forty middle-class mothers of young children and identified fifteen strategies they used to protect their children. Their three principal strategies were to educate, control, and remove risk. The strategy used depended on the age and temperament of the child. For example, some parents feel protecting their children from certain television content is important. This ranges from families that do not allow a television in their home, to setting the V-chip on their television or allowing only G-rated movies. Research confirms that parents do find media ratings helpful (Bushman and Cantor 2003).

Some parents feel that protecting their children from harm implies appropriate discipline for inappropriate behavior. Galambos et al. (2003) noted "parents' firm behavioral control seemed to halt the upward trajectory in externalizing problems among adolescents with deviant peers." In other words, parents who intervened when they saw a negative context developing were able to help their children avoid negative peer influences. Kolko et al. (2008) compared clinically referred boys and girls (ages 6 to 11) diagnosed with **oppositional defiant disorder** (children do not comply with requests of authority figures) to a matched sample of healthy control children and found that the former had greater exposure to delinquent peers. Hence, parents who monitor the peer relationships with their children and minimize the exposure to delinquent models are making a wise time investment.

Increasingly, parents are joining the technological age and learning how to text message. In their role as protector, this allows parents to text-message their child to tell them to come home, phone home, or to work out a logistical problem—"meet me at Chick-fil-A in the mall." Children can also use text-messaging to their parents to let them know that they arrived safely at a destination, when they need to be picked up, or when they will be home.

6. *Health promotion.* The family is a major agent for health promotion. Children learn from the family context about healthy food. Indeed, one-third of U.S. children are overweight. A major cause of overweight children is parents who do not teach healthy food choices, let their children watch TV all day, and are bad models (eat junk food and don't exercise). Health promotion also involves sunburn protection, responsible use of alcohol, and safe driving skills.

7. *Ritual bearer.* To build a sense of family cohesiveness, parents often foster rituals to bind members together in emotion and in memory. Prayer at meals and before bedtime, birthday celebrations, and vacationing at the same place (beach, mountains, and so on) provide predictable times of togetherness and sharing.

The Choices Perspective of Parenting

Although both genetic and environmental factors are at work, the choices parents make have a dramatic impact on their children. In this section, we review the nature of parental choices and some of the basic choices parents make.

Nature of Parenting Choices

Parents might keep the following points in mind when they make choices about how to rear their children:

1. *Not to make a parental decision is to make a decision.* Parents are constantly making choices even when they think they are not doing so. When a child is impolite and the parent does not provide feedback and encourage polite behavior, the parent has chosen to teach the child that being impolite is acceptable. When a child makes a promise ("I'll call you when I get to my friend's house") and does not do as promised, the parent has chosen to allow the child to not take commitments seriously. Hence, parents cannot choose not to make choices in their parenting, because their inactivity is a choice that has as much impact as a deliberate decision to reinforce politeness and responsibility.

2. *All parental choices involve trade-offs.* Parents are also continually making trade-offs in the parenting choices they make. The decision to take on a second job or to work overtime to afford the larger house will come at the price of having less time to spend with one's children and being more exhausted when such time is available. The choice to enroll one's child in the highest-quality day care (which may also be the most expensive) will mean less money for family vacations. The choice to have an additional child will provide siblings for the existing children but will mean less time and fewer resources for those children. Parents should increase their awareness that no choice is without a tradeoff and should evaluate the costs and benefits in making such decisions.

3. *Reframe "regretful" parental decisions.* All parents regret a previous parental decision (for example, they should have held their child back a year in school—or not done so; they should have intervened in a bad peer relationship; they should have handled their child's drug use differently). Whatever the issue, parents chide themselves for their mistakes. Rather than berate themselves as parents, they might emphasize the positive outcome of their choices: not holding the child back made the child the "first" to experience some things among his or her peers; they made the best decision they could at the time; and so on. Children might also be encouraged to view their own decisions positively.

Five Basic Parenting Choices

The five basic choices parents make include deciding (1) whether to have a child, (2) the number of children, (3) the interval between children, (4) one's method of discipline and guidance, and (5) the degree to which one will be invested in the role of parent. Though all of these decisions are important, the relative importance one places on parenting as opposed to one's career will have implications for the parents, their children, and their children's children. Parents continually make choices in reference to their children, including whether their children will sleep with them in the "family bed" (see the following Personal Choices section).

Careful the things you say, Children will listen. Careful the things you do. Children will see. And learn.

Stephen Sondheim, *Into the Woods*

PERSONAL CHOICES

Should Children Bed-Share with Parents?

Frequency of bed-sharing of parents and children ranges from never to every night. Children most likely to sleep in their parents' bed are young (1–12 weeks) and breast-fed. Indeed, most of the infants (60 percent to 90 percent) sharing a bed with their parents do so for ease of nighttime breast-feeding. Other reasons for regular bed-sharing include that the child is sick, lack of space when traveling, or having a lot of guests in one's house.

In a longitudinal ten-year study of 493 Swiss children (Jenni et al. 2005), 10 percent slept with their parents their first year of life. This increased to 44 percent of children aged 2 to 7 who did so at least once a week. We concluded that sharing a bed with the parents was common in early childhood and that this practice should not be condemned by professionals who give advice to parents. Indeed, the child, the parents, and the context may suggest that bed-sharing should occur for the positive attachment needs of the child.

One concern about sharing a bed has been the risk of sudden infant death syndrome (SIDS). Hauck et al. (2003) studied 260 cases of SIDS and found that the usual bed-sharing in which one infant shares the bed with a parent is not associated with SIDS. However, when a parent slept on a sofa or when more than one child was in the bed, there was an increased risk of SIDS.

Sources

Hauck, F. R., S. M. Herman, M. Donovan, C. M. Moore, S. Iyasu, E. Donoghue, R. H. Kirschner, and M. Willinger. 2003. Sleep environment and the risk of sudden death syndrome in an urban population: The Chicago Infant Mortality Study. *Pediatrics* 111:1207–15.

Jenni, O. G., H. Z. Fuhrer, I. Iglowstein, L. Molinari, and R. H. Largo. 2005. A longitudinal study of bed sharing and sleep problems among Swiss children in the first ten years of life. *Pediatrics* 115:233–40.

Transition to Parenthood

The **transition to parenthood** refers to that period from the beginning of pregnancy through the first few months after the birth of a baby. The mother, father, and couple all undergo changes and adaptations during this period.

Transition to Motherhood

Of her transition to motherhood, Madonna noted a dramatic effect, "The whole idea of giving birth and being responsible for another life put me in a different place, a place I'd never been before. I feel like I'm starting life over in many ways. My daughter's birth was like a rebirth for me" (Morton 2003, 213). In effect the role of mother represents one of the most

Diversity in the United States

Parents are diverse. Amish parents rear their children in homes without electricity (no television, phones, or CD players). Charismatics (members of the conservative religious denomination) educate their children in Christian schools emphasizing a biblical and spiritual view of life and the world. More secular parents bring up their children amid cultural cutting-edge technology and encourage individualistic liberal views.

Mothers soon learn that much of the work of parenting falls to them. This mother is ensuring that her daughter practices her music lesson.

Authors

There are times when parenthood seems nothing more than feeding the hand that bites you.

Peter De Vries, American Editor and novelist

profound role changes a person ever experiences. Madonna's biographer continues:

> *The woman who once graced the front of* Playboy *is now a* Good Housekeeping *cover girl, a mother who extols the virtues of wholesome food, 'tough love,' and a ban on television. At times she sounds just like her father in her denunciation of modern vices: sex and violence on TV, junk food and the lack of a disciplined lifestyle.* (p. 211)

The Self-Assessment on page 359 examines one's view of traditional motherhood. Although childbirth is sometimes thought of as a painful ordeal, some women describe the experience as fantastic, joyful, and unsurpassed. A strong emotional bond between the mother and her baby usually develops early, and both the mother and infant resist separation.

Sociobiologists suggest that the attachment between a mother and her offspring has a biological basis (one of survival). The mother alone carries the fetus in her body for nine months, lactates to provide milk, and produces **oxytocin**—a hormone from the pituitary gland—during the expulsive stage of labor that has been associated with the onset of maternal behavior in lower animals.

Not all mothers feel joyous after childbirth. Emotional bonding may be temporarily impeded by feeling overworked, exhaustion, mild depression, irritability, crying, loss of appetite, and difficulty in sleeping. Many new mothers experience **baby blues**—transitory symptoms of depression twenty-four to forty-eight hours after the baby is born. A few, about 10 percent, experience postpartum depression—a more severe reaction than baby blues.

Postpartum depression is believed to be a result of the numerous physiological and psychological changes occurring during pregnancy, labor, and delivery. Although the woman may become depressed during pregnancy or in the hospital, she more often experiences these feelings within the first month after returning home with her baby (sometimes the woman does not experience postpartum depression until a couple of years later). Most women recover within a short time; some (between 5 percent and 10 percent) become suicidal (Pinheiro 2008).

In *Down Came the Rain*, actress Brooke Shields (2005) recounts her experience with postpartum depression, including this excerpt from the back cover:

> *I started to experience a sick sensation in my stomach; it was as if a vise were tightening around my chest. Instead of nervous anxiety that often accompanies panic; a*

Chapter 11 Parenting

The Traditional Motherhood Scale

The purpose of this survey is to assess the degree to which students possess a traditional view of motherhood. Read each item carefully and consider what you believe. There are no right or wrong answers, so please give your honest reaction and opinion. After reading each statement, select the number that best reflects your level of agreement, using the following scale:

1	2	3	4	5	6	7

Strongly
Disagree

Strongly
Agree

_____ **1.** A mother has a better relationship with her children than a father does.

_____ **2.** A mother knows more about her child than a father, thereby being the better parent.

_____ **3.** Motherhood is what brings women to their fullest potential.

_____ **4.** A good mother should stay at home with her children for the first year.

_____ **5.** Mothers should stay at home with the children.

_____ **6.** Motherhood brings much joy and contentment to a woman.

_____ **7.** A mother is needed in a child's life for nurturance and growth.

_____ **8.** Motherhood is an essential part of a female's life.

_____ **9.** I feel that all women should experience motherhood in some way.

_____ **10.** Mothers are more nurturing than fathers.

_____ **11.** Mothers have a stronger emotional bond with their children than do fathers.

_____ **12.** Mothers are more sympathetic to children who have hurt themselves than are fathers.

_____ **13.** Mothers spend more time do with their children than do fathers.

_____ **14.** Mothers are more lenient toward their children than are fathers.

_____ **15.** Mothers are more affectionate toward their children than are fathers.

_____ **16.** The presence of the mother is vital to the child during the formative years.

_____ **17.** Mothers play a larger role than fathers in raising children.

_____ **18.** Women instinctively know what a baby needs.

Scoring

After assigning a number from 1 (strongly disagree) to 7 (strongly agree), add the numbers and divide by 18. The higher your score (7 is the highest possible score), the stronger the traditional view of motherhood. The lower your score (1 is the lowest possible score), the less traditional the view of motherhood.

Norms

The norming sample of this self-assessment was based upon twenty male and eighty-six female students attending Valdosta State University. The average age of participants completing the scale was 21.72 years (SD = 2.98), and ages ranged from 18 to 34. The ethnic composition of the sample was 80.2 percent white, 15.1 percent black, 1.9 percent Asian, 0.9 percent American Indian, and 1.9 percent other. The classification of the sample was 16.0 percent freshmen, 15.1 percent sophomores, 27.4 percent juniors, 39.6 percent seniors, and 1.9 percent graduate students.

Participants responded to each of the eighteen items according to the 7-point scale. The most traditional score was 6.33; the score reflecting the least support for traditional motherhood was 1.78. The midpoint (average score) between the top and bottom score was 4.28 (SD = 1.04); thus, people scoring above this number tended to have a more traditional view of motherhood and people scoring below this number have a less traditional view of motherhood.

There was a significant difference ($p < .05$) between female participants' scores (mean = 4.19; SD = 1.08) and male participants' scores (mean = 4.68; SD = 0.73), suggesting that males had more traditional views of motherhood than females.

Source

"Attitudes Toward Motherhood Scale," 2004 by Mark Whatley, Ph.D., Department of Psychology, Valdosta State University, Valdosta, Georgia 31698-0100. Used by permission. Other uses of this scale by written permission of Dr. Whatley only (mwhatley@valdosta.edu). Information on the reliability and validity of this scale is available from Dr. Whatley.

feeling of devastation overcame me. I hardly moved. Sitting on my bed, I let out a deep, slow, guttural wail. I wasn't simply emotional or weepy. . . . this was something quite different. This was sadness of a shockingly different magnitude. It felt as if it would never go away.

To minimize baby blues and postpartum depression, antidepressants such as Paxil have been used. Brooke Shields benefited from Paxil, and the result was to give visibility to the issue of postpartum depression, its physiological basis, and the value of medication.

Postpartum psychosis, a reaction in which a woman wants to harm her baby, is experienced by only one or two women per 1,000 births (British Columbia Reproductive Mental Health Program 2005). One must recognize that having misgivings about a new infant is normal. In addition, a woman who has negative feelings about her new role as mother should elicit help with the baby from her family or other support network so that she can continue to keep up her social contacts with friends and to spend time by herself and with her partner. Regardless of the cause, a team of researchers noted that maternal depression is associated with subsequent antisocial behavior in the child (Kim-Cohen et al. 2005).

Hammarberg et al. (2008) assessed the different parenting experiences of those who had difficulty getting pregnant or who used assisted reproductive technology (ART) compared to those who did not use ART. The researchers concluded that, although the evidence is inconclusive, those couples who become pregnant via ART may possibly idealize parenthood and this might then hinder adjustment and the development of a confident parental identity. Is transition to motherhood similar for lesbian and heterosexual mothers? Not according to Cornelius-Cozzi (2002), who interviewed lesbian mothers and found that the egalitarian norm of the lesbian relationship had been altered; for example, the biological mother became the primary caregiver, and the co-parent, who often heard the biological mother refer to the child as "her child," suffered a lack of validation.

Transition to Fatherhood

Schoppe-Sullivan et al. (2008) emphasized that mothers are the "gatekeepers" of the father's involvement with his children. A father may be involved or not involved with his children to the degree that a mother encourages or discourages a father's involvement. The **gatekeeper role** is particularly pronounced in divorce where the mother ends up with custody of the children (the role of father may be severely limited). When a mother is not present, the role of the father may be enormous. Such was the case of Joe Biden's involvement with his three children. His first wife and young child were killed in an automobile accident that resulted in him becoming the sole parent until his remarriage. One of Biden's sons noted that, "Our dad had his job in Washington but his family in his heart."

The Self-Assessment on traditional fatherhood examines one's view of traditional fatherhood. The importance of the father in the lives of his children is enormous and goes beyond his economic contribution (Bronte-Tinkew et al. 2008; Flouri and Buchanan 2003; Knox 2000). Children from homes in which their fathers maintained an active involvement in their lives tend to:

Make good grades	Have higher incomes as adults
Be less involved in crime	Have higher education levels
Have good health/self-concept	Have higher cognitive functioning
Have a strong work ethic	Have stable jobs
Have durable marriages	Have fewer premarital births
Have a strong moral conscience	Have lower incidences of child sex abuse
Have higher life satisfaction	Exhibit fewer anorectic symptoms

Gavin et al. (2002) noted that parental involvement was predicted most strongly by the quality of the parents' romantic relationship. If the father was emotionally and physically involved with the mother, he was more likely to take an active role in the child's life. Fathers whose wives worked more hours than the fathers worked also reported more involvement with their children (McBride et al. 2002).

Thomas et al. (2008) noted the inadequacy of the stereotype of the "uninvolved" African American father due to data that they often do not live in the household with the mother. The researchers sought to redefine father presence in the context of feelings of closeness to the father as well as frequency of father visitation. Their findings confirmed that a considerable portion of African American nonresident fathers visit their children on a daily or weekly basis. In addition, African American

The Traditional Fatherhood Scale

The purpose of this survey is to assess the degree to which students have a traditional view of fatherhood. Read each item carefully and consider what you believe. There are no right or wrong answers, so please give your honest reaction and opinion. After reading each statement, select the number that best reflects your level of agreement, using the following scale:

1	2	3	4	5	6	7

Strongly
Disagree

Strongly
Agree

_____ 1. Fathers do not spend much time with their children.

_____ 2. Fathers should be the disciplinarians in the family.

_____ 3. Fathers should never stay at home with the children while the mother works.

_____ 4. The father's main contribution to his family is giving financially.

_____ 5. Fathers are less nurturing than mothers.

_____ 6. Fathers expect more from children than their mothers do.

_____ 7. Most men make horrible fathers.

_____ 8. Fathers punish children more than mothers do.

_____ 9. Fathers do not take a highly active role in their children's lives.

_____ 10. Fathers are very controlling.

Scoring

After assigning a number from 1 (strongly disagree) to 7 (strongly agree), add the numbers and divide by 10. The higher your score (7 is the highest possible score), the stronger the traditional view of fatherhood. The lower your score (1 is the lowest possible score), the less traditional the view of fatherhood.

Norms

The norming sample was based upon twenty-four male and sixty-nine female students attending Valdosta State University. The average age of participants completing the Traditional Fatherhood Scale was 22.15 years (SD = 4.23), and ages ranged from 18 to 47. The ethnic composition of the sample was 77.4 percent white, 19.4 percent black, 1.1 percent Hispanic, and 2.2 percent other. The classification of the sample was 16.1 percent freshmen, 11.8 percent sophomores, 23.7 percent juniors, 46.2 percent seniors, and 2.2 percent graduate students.

Participants responded to each of the ten items on the 7-point scale. The most traditional score was 5.50; the score representing the least support for traditional fatherhood was 1.00. The average score was 3.33 (SD = 1.03), suggesting a less-than-traditional view.

There was a significant difference ($p < .05$) between female participants' attitudes (mean = 3.20; SD = 1.01) and male participants' attitudes toward fatherhood (mean = 3.69; SD = 1.01), suggesting that males had more traditional views of fatherhood than females. There were no significant differences between ethnicities.

Source

"Traditional Fatherhood Scale," 2004 by Mark Whatley, Ph.D., Department of Psychology, Valdosta State University, Valdosta, Georgia 31698-0100. Used by permission. Other uses of this scale by written permission of Dr. Whatley only (mwhatley@valdosta.edu). Information on the reliability and validity of this scale is available from Dr. Whatley.

---

adult children with nonresident fathers often feel significantly closer to their fathers than do their white peers. Finally, African American adult children were more likely than their white peers to believe that their mothers supported their relationship with their father and to have positive perceptions of their parents' relationship.

Transition from a Couple to a Family

Recent research suggests that parenthood decreases marital happiness. Bost et al. (2002) interviewed 137 couples before the birth of their first child and then at 3-, 12-, and 24-month periods. The spouses consistently reported depression and adjustment through 24 months postpartum. Twenge (2003) reviewed 148 samples representing 47,692 individuals in regard to the effect children have on marital satisfaction. They found that (1) parents (both women and men) reported lower marital satisfaction than nonparents; (2) mothers of infants reported the most significant drop in marital satisfaction; (3) the higher the number of children, the lower the marital satisfaction; and (4) the factors in depressed marital satisfaction were conflict and loss of freedom. Claxton and Perry-Jenkins (2008) confirmed a decrease in marital leisure time after the birth of a baby but an increase when the wife went back to work. In addition, they noted that wives who reported high levels of prenatal joint leisure reported greater marital love and less conflict the first year after the baby's birth.

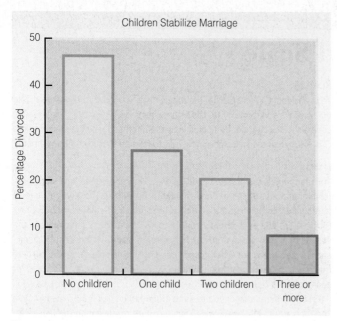

Children Stabilize Marriage

Figure 11.1
Percentage of Couples Getting Divorced by Number of Children

For parents who experience a pattern of decreased happiness, it bottoms out during the teen years. Facer and Day (2004) found that adolescent problem behavior, particularly that of a daughter, is associated with increases in marital conflict. Of even greater impact was their perception of the child's emotional state. Parents who viewed their children as "happy" were less maritally affected by their adolescent's negative behavior.

Regardless of how children affect the feelings that spouses have about their marriage, spouses report more commitment to their relationship once they have children (Stanley and Markman 1992). Figure 11.1 illustrates that the more children a couple has, the more likely the couple will stay married. A primary reason for this increased commitment is the desire on the part of both parents to provide a stable family context for their children. In addition, parents of dependent children may keep their marriage together to maintain continued access to and a higher standard of living for their children. Finally, people (especially mothers) with small children feel more pressure to stay married (if the partner provides sufficient economic resources) regardless of how unhappy they may be. Hence, though children may decrease happiness, they increase stability, because pressure exists to stay together.

Parenthood: Some Facts

The family is one of nature's masterpieces.

George Santayana, *The Life of Reason*

Parenting is only one stage in an individual's or couple's life (children typically live with an individual 30 percent of that person's life and with a couple 40 percent of their marriage). Parenting involves responding to the varying needs of children as they grow up, and parents require help from family and friends in rearing their children.

Some additional facts of parenthood follow.

Views of Children Differ Historically

Whereas children of today are thought of as dependent, playful, and adventurous, they have been historically viewed quite differently (Mayall 2002). Indeed, the concept of childhood, like gender, has been socially constructed rather than a fixed life stage. From the thirteenth through the sixteenth centuries, children were viewed as innocent, sweet, and a source of amusement for adults. From the sixteenth through the eighteenth centuries, they were viewed as in need of discipline and moral training. In the nineteenth century, whippings were routine as a means of breaking children's spirits and bringing them to submission. Although remnants of both the innocent and moralistic views of children exist today, the lives of children are greatly improved. Child labor laws protect children from early forced labor, education laws ensure a basic education, and modern medicine has been able to increase the life span of children.

Each Child Is Unique

Children differ in their genetic makeup, physiological wiring, intelligence, tolerance for stress, capacity to learn, comfort in social situations, and interests. Parents soon become aware of the uniqueness of each child—of the child's difference from every other child they know. Parents of two or more children are often amazed at how children who have the same parents can be so different.

Having a child is like throwing a hand grenade into a marriage.

Nora Ephron, writer, producer, and director

National Data

In the United States, more than 6 million children have disabilities—45 percent of these children have learning disabilities, 9 percent have mental retardation, and 8 percent have a serious emotional disturbance (*Statistical Abstract of the United States, 2009*, Table 180).

Children also differ in their mental and physical health. Mental and physical disabilities of children present emotional and financial challenges to their parents. Green (2003) discussed the potential stigma associated with disability and how parents cope with their children who are stigmatized.

Although parents often contend, "we treat our children equally," Tucker et al. (2003) found that parents treat children differently, with firstborns usually receiving more privileges than children born later. Suitor and Pillemer (2007) found that elderly mothers reported that they tended to establish a closer relationship with the firstborn child whom they are more likely to call on in later life when there is a crisis.

Birth Order Effects on Personality?

Psychologist Frank Sulloway (1996) examined how a child's birth order influenced the development of various personality characteristics. His thesis is that children with siblings develop different strategies to maximize parental investment in them. For example, children can promote parental favor directly by "helping and obeying parents" (p. 67). Sulloway identified the following personality characteristics that have their basis in a child's position in the family:

1. *Conforming or traditional*—Firstborns are the first on the scene with parents and always have the "inside track." They want to stay that way so they are traditional and conforming to their parent's expectations.

2. *Experimental or adventurous*—Children born later learn quickly that they enter an existing family constellation where everyone is bigger and stronger. They cannot depend on having established territory so must excel in ways different from the firstborn. They are open to experience, adventurousness, and trying new things because their status is not already assured.

3. *Neurotic or emotionally unstable*—Because firstborns are "dethroned" by younger children to whom parents had to divert their attention, they tend to be more jealous, anxious, and fearful. Children born later are never number one to begin with so do not experience this trauma.

As support for his ideas, Sulloway (1996) cited 196 controlled birth order studies and contended that, although there are exceptions, one's position in the family is a factor influencing personality outcomes. Nevertheless, he acknowledged that researchers disagree on the effects of birth order on the personalities of children and that birth order research is incomplete in that it does not consider the position of each child in families that vary in size, gender, and number. Indeed, Sulloway (2007) has continued to conduct research, the findings of which do not always support his prediction. For example, he examined intelligence and birth order among 241,310 Norwegian 18- and 19-year-olds and found no relationship. He recommended that researchers look to how a child was reared rather than birth order for understanding a child's IQ in the family.

Parents Are Only One Influence in a Child's Development

Although parents often take the credit—and the blame—for the way their children turn out, they are only one among many influences on child development. Although parents are the first significant influence, peer influence becomes increasingly important during adolescence. Pinquart and Silbereisen (2002) studied seventy-six dyads of mothers and their 11- to 16-year-old adolescents and observed a decrease in connectedness between the children and their mothers and a movement toward their adolescent friends.

Siblings also have an important and sometimes lasting effect on each other's development. Siblings are social mirrors and models (depending on the age) for each other. They may also be sources of competition and can be jealous of each other.

Teachers are also significant influences in the development of a child's values. Some parents send their children to religious schools to ensure that they will have teachers with conservative religious values. This may continue into the child's college and university education.

Media in the form of television—replete with MTV and "parental discretion advised" movies—are a major source of language, values, and lifestyles for children that may be different from those of the parents. Parents are also concerned about the violence to which television and movies expose their children.

Another influence of concern to parents is the Internet. Though parents may encourage their children to conduct research and write term papers using the Internet, they may fear their children are accessing pornography and related sex sites. Parental supervision of teens on the Internet and the right of the teen for privacy remain potential conflict issues (see the Social Policy on page 365).

Parenting Styles Differ

Diana Baumrind (1966) developed a typology of parenting styles that has become classic in the study of parenting. She noted that parenting behavior has two dimensions: responsiveness and demandingness. **Responsiveness** refers to the extent to which parents respond to and meet the needs of their children. In other words, how supportive are the parents? Warmth, reciprocity, person-centered communication, and attachment are all aspects of responsiveness. **Demandingness**, on the other hand, is the manner in which parents place demands on children in regard to expectations and discipline. How much control do they exert over their children? Monitoring and confrontation are also aspects of demandingness. Categorizing parents in terms of their responsiveness and their demandingness creates four categories of parenting styles: permissive (also known as indulgent), authoritarian, authoritative, and uninvolved.

1. *Permissive parents are high on responsiveness and low on demandingness.* They are very lenient and allow their children to largely regulate their own behavior.

2. *Authoritarian parents are high on demandingness and low in responsiveness.* They feel that children should obey their parents no matter what, and they provide a great deal of structure in the child's world.

3. *Authoritative parents are both demanding and responsive.* They impose appropriate limits on their children's behavior but emphasize reasoning and communication. This style offers a balance of warmth and control.

4. *Uninvolved parents are low in responsiveness and demandingness.* These parents are not invested in their children's lives.

McKinney and Renk (2008) identified the differences between maternal and paternal parenting styles, with mothers tending to be authoritative and fathers tending to be authoritarian. Mothers and fathers also use different parenting styles for their sons and daughters, with fathers being more permissive with their sons than daughters. Overall, this study emphasizes the importance of examining the different parenting styles of parents on adolescent outcome and suggests that having one authoritative parent may be a protective factor for late adolescents. Recall that the authoritative parenting style is the combination of warmth, guidelines, and discipline—"I love you but you need to be in by midnight or lose privileges of having a cell phone and a car."

In summary, parenting does not come as naturally to humans as we might hope. After many decades of exploring how to provide an optimal environment

Government or Parental Control of Internet Content for Children?

Over 40 percent (42 percent) of 10- to 17-year-olds has been exposed to Internet pornography (Preston 2007). Governmental censoring of content on the Internet is the focus of an ongoing public debate. At issue is what level of sexual content children should be exposed to—and should parents or the government make the decision? This issue has already been decided in China, where the government ensures that all major search engines filter what is made available to Internet users. In the United States, Congress passed the Communications Decency Act in 1996, which prohibited sending "indecent" messages over the Internet to people under age 18. However, the Supreme Court struck down the law in 1997, holding that it was too broadly worded and violated free speech rights by restricting too much material that adults might want to access. Other laws to restrict content access on the Internet have been passed but struck down on the basis that they violate First Amendment rights. However, The Protection of Children from Sexual Predators Act of 1998 required Internet Service Providers (ISPs) to report any knowledge of child victimization or child pornography to law enforcement.

Many object to government control of sexual content on the Internet on the grounds of First Amendment rights. Many others believe government restrictions are necessary to protect children from inappropriate sexual content. Patrick Trueman asked, "Why is the government spending tens of thousands of dollars prosecuting and incarcerating Martha Stewart rather than the criminal who spams hard-core pornography to my child?" (Krause 2008).

An overriding question is, "Should parents or the government be in control of what children are exposed to?" In a national survey of households, Mitchell et al. (2005) found that 33 percent of parents used a filtering or blocking system on their computer. The younger the child or children (ages 10–15), the more likely such a system was used.

In the United States, parents—not the government—prefer to be responsible for regulating their children's use of the Internet. Beyond exposure to sexual content, children sometimes post information about themselves on the Internet that encourages pedophiles to e-mail them. MySpace has more than 100 million profiles, with 230,000 new members signing up every day (Andrews 2006). Some of these profiles may be more revealing than intended.

Software products, such as Net Nanny, Surfwatch, CYBERsitter, CyberPatrol, and Time's Up, are being marketed to help parents control what their children view on the Internet. These software programs allow parents to block unapproved websites and categories (such as pornography), block transmission of personal data (such as address and telephone numbers), scan pages for sexual material before they are viewed, and track Internet usage. A more cumbersome solution is to require Internet users to provide passwords or identification numbers that would verify their ages before allowing access to certain websites.

Another alternative is for parents to use the Internet with their children both to monitor what their children are viewing and to teach their children values about what they believe is right and wrong on the Internet. Some parents believe that children must learn how to safely surf the Internet. Internet sites helpful in this regard are BlogSafety.com, forums for parents to discuss blogging and other aspects of social networking; NetSmartz.org service, which teaches kids 5 to 17 how to be safe on the Internet; and WiredSafety.org, which posts information on Internet safety.

One parent reported that the Internet is like a busy street, and just as you must teach your children how to safely cross in traffic, you must teach them how to avoid giving information to strangers on the Internet.

Your Opinion?

1. To what degree do you believe the government should control Internet content?
2. To what degree do you believe that parents should monitor what their children are exposed to on the Internet?
3. What can parents do to teach their children responsible use of the Internet?

Sources

Andrews, M. 2006. Decoding MySpace. *U.S. News and World Report,* Sept 18, 46.

Krause, J. 2008. The end of the NET porn wars. *ABA Journal* 94:52–57.

Mitchell, K. J., D. Finkelhor, and J. Wolak. 2005. Protecting youth online: Family use of filtering and blocking software. *Child Abuse and Neglect* 29:753–65.

Preston, C. B. 2007. Making family-friendly Internet a reality: The Internet Community Ports Act. *Brigham Young University Law Review* 2007: 1471–1534.

for the development of children, social scientists are narrowing in on the essential elements, with more emphasis now on the specific ways in which elements of effective parenting are related to specific aspects of development for children and adolescents.

Parenting Practices around the World

Every culture depends on families to rear children so that the culture continues to survive. Although parenting is necessary for the continuation of the human race, the ways of parenting vary across the globe. In this photo essay, we take a look at some parenting practices around the world.

IT TAKES A VILLAGE

In the United States, we tend to think of children as being the sole responsibility of parents. If the parents are incarcerated, abusive, or otherwise deemed unfit, grandparents or other extended family may take over the responsibility of parenting. Alternatively, the state may intervene and place a child in foster care. Aside from these atypical cases, parenthood in the United States is viewed as a relationship of ownership that emphasizes parental control over the child without interference from others, including grandparents.

However, in many cultures throughout the world, rearing children is viewed as a communal responsibility of a kin group and/or a village, hence the phrase, "it takes a village to raise a child." In Mexico and throughout Latin America, child sharing is institutionalized as godparenthood. Among the Zapotec, godparents are expected to guide the child's religious development, to help in curing a child's sickness, and to assist financially with the child's schooling in terms of books, clothes, fees, or housing. Godparents are referred to as the child's second mother and father, for they share in raising their godchild, who may live with them for a period of time.

Frans Lemmens/Alamy

BREAST-FEEDING

Among mothers in the United States, about 75 percent initiate breast-feeding. However, by the time the child is 6 months, only half of mothers are still breast-feeding their infants; by the time the child is 1 year, only a quarter of mothers still breast-feed. In many cultures throughout the world, breast-feeding is much more common and continues into toddlerhood. In most African countries, about half of infants are breast-fed at 2 years of age. In Nepal, 95 percent of 2-year-old toddlers are breast-fed.

Angus McDonald/OnAsia.com

SLEEPING ARRANGEMENTS

In the United States, parents are expected to require children to sleep in their own room throughout the night. Standard pediatric advice recommends that parents put infants in their crib and let them fall asleep alone, even if it means the infants crying themselves to sleep. Indeed, American parents are warned that "co-sleeping" (parents sleeping with their children) can have potential negative effects. For example, parents are advised that co-sleeping may interfere with a child's independence, may expose children to their parents' sexual interaction which could be frightening, and may result in the child experiencing inappropriate sexual feelings for a parent. ▶

Brit Erlanson/The Image Bank/Getty Images

However, co-sleeping is routine is most other cultures and, until the twentieth century, was the norm in the United States. A study of more than 119 societies revealed that nearly two-thirds of mothers slept in the same bed as their infants. In Japan, parent-child co-sleeping is viewed as important for the development of a child's sense of well-being and interdependence.

Kei Uesugi/Getty Images

DISCIPLINE AND PUNISHMENT

In most societies throughout the world, many parents view corporal punishment of children as an acceptable form of discipline and punishment. In Romania, for example, 84 percent of a sample of parents regarded spanking as a "normal" method of child rearing. A survey of Chinese parents of young children found that more than one-half said that they were likely to beat their children if they were being lazy in school, and more than two-thirds said that they used force to make their children obey them.

Michael Newman/PhotoEdit

In contrast, corporal punishment in the home is legally banned in more than twenty countries throughout the world. In Sweden, parents respect children as equal members of society who should not be physically punished. Swedish parents discipline children verbally through reasoning or distraction, or if that fails, through shaming.

Chad Ehlers/Photolibrary

367

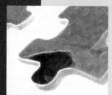

What if You and Your Partner Disagree over Parenting Styles?

Because spouses grow up in families where different parenting philosophies are operative, it is not unusual for them to disagree over how to rear or discipline their own children. The typologies previously identified, responsiveness and demandingness, which may be regarded as "loose-goosey, anything goes" and "iron discipline," will cause obvious conflicts with no easy solutions. Some parents divorce because they argue constantly over how to rear their children. One alternative is for parents to agree that the most involved parent's child-rearing style will prevail. Such an agreement is obviously a concession on the part of one parent.

Another alternative is to use the parenting philosophy that research suggests has the best outcome. As previously noted, authoritative parenting, which is a blend of compassion and discipline, seems to have the best outcome in terms of fewer problems with children and their development of high levels of social competence.

Principles of Effective Parenting

Numerous principles are involved in being effective parents. We begin with the most important of these which involves giving time/love to your children as well as praising and encouraging them.

Give Time, Love, Praise, and Encouragement

Erma Bombeck once quipped that what children need is . . . your trust, your compassion, your binding love, and your car keys. Notice the order, however: children most need to feel that they are worth spending time with and that someone loves them. Because children depend first on their parents for the development of their sense of emotional security, it is critical that parents provide a warm emotional context in which the children can develop. Feeling loved as an infant also affects one's capacity to become involved in adult love relationships.

As children mature, positive reinforcement for prosocial behavior also helps to encourage desirable behavior and a positive self-concept. Instead of focusing only on correcting or reprimanding bad behavior, parents should frequently comment on and reinforce good behavior. Comments like, "I like the way you shared your toys," "You asked so politely," and "You did such a good job cleaning your room" help to reinforce positive social behavior and may enhance a child's self-concept. However, parents need to be careful not to overpraise their children, as too much praise may lead to their children striving to please others rather than trying to please themselves.

Praise focuses on other people's judgments of a child's actions, whereas encouragement focuses more on the child's efforts. For example, telling a child who brings you his painting, "I love your picture; it is the best one that I have ever seen" is not as effective in building the child's confidence as saying, "You worked really hard on your painting. I notice that you used lots of different colors." Some parents feel that rewarding positive behavior is not a good idea (see the following Personal Choices section).

Play functions to bond children to parents and vice versa.

Buy Buy Baby: "Consumer Culture Manipulation of Parents"

Susan G. Thomas is an investigative journalist (and mother of two toddler daughters when she wrote her book) who examined how corporations use and fund child development research to sell directly to infants and toddlers. She published her findings in *Buy, Buy Baby: How Consumer Culture Manipulates Parents and Harms Young Minds*. The exposure of infants to television (including videos and DVDs) is extensive—of children from 6 to 23 months, 61 percent watch television; by age 3, 88 percent watch just under two hours a day. Parents are led to believe by "experts" (sometimes anxious to have their research funded by toy manufacturers who may turn them into celebrities) that a toy is of enormous educational value. Such value is expressed in terms of improving the cognitive development or performance of the young mind. In fact, "there is little evidence that any of these products was any more stimulating than shaking a rattle, playing with blocks, mucking around in the backyard or just hanging out, or playing with a beloved caregiver or parent" (2007, 18).

However, what advertisers found worked for baby boomer mothers (born between 1946 and 1964) would not work for Generation X mothers. The former were socialized to "fast-track" their kids; the latter were more focused on always being there emotionally for their children. Thus, "mapping the mind of the Generation X mom" became a focus of corporate America to get her to spend money on her infants. For example, Generation X moms would not hear of sticking their infant alone in a room with a gadget, toy, or video because this would be considered abandonment. So products were disguised as beneficial to the child because they taught the child to "self-soothe." As an example, Fisher-Price marketed the Slumbertime Soother with the package showing the mother "standing in the doorway holding the remote control, while her baby gazed contentedly at the mobile—apparently feeling the mother's presence but not interrupted by it" (Thomas 2007, 69).

Thomas concludes that Generation X parents should recognize that keeping children continually stimulated through structured activities, DVDs, or whatever "actually starves children's imagination, curiosity, and ability to relax. . . . All the childhood experts I spoke with said that spending time hanging out together is the best possible thing parents can do for their young children's development" (2007, 228). Indeed, she recommends that for Generation X parents to "fight for the right to do nothing with their children may be the perfect cause to celebrate" (p. 229).

More ominous is *BabyFirstTV*, available via satellite to infants as young as 6 months, which is seeking cable companies to carry its programming. The American Academy of Pediatrics recommends no television for children under 2 years. The Campaign for a Commercial-Free Childhood (CCFC) cites no evidence that television is beneficial to the cognitive development of children and has filed suit against *BabyFirstTV* for making false and deceptive marketing claims that its programs are educational for babies and toddlers.

Sources

S. G. Thomas. 2007 *Buy buy baby: How consumer culture manipulates parents and harms young minds.* Boston: Houghton Mifflin.
http://www.commercialfreechildhood.org/pressreleases/bftcable.pdf

PERSONAL CHOICES

Should Parents Reward Positive Behavior?

Most parents agree that some form of punishment is necessary to curb a child's inappropriate behavior, but parents disagree over whether positive behavior (taking out the trash, cleaning one's room, making good grades) should be rewarded by praise, extra privileges, or money. Some parents feel that children should "do the right things anyway" and that to reward them is to bribe them. One parent said, "My children are going to do what I say because I say so, not because I am going to give them something for doing it." Other parents feel that both the child and the parent benefit when the parents reward the child for good behavior. Rewarding a child for a behavior will likely result in the child's engaging in that behavior more often and developing a set of positive behaviors. The parents, in turn, feel good about the child. Behavioral family therapists emphasize the importance of parents identifying the behaviors that they want and systematically rewarding those behaviors with praise or whatever impacts the child to repeat the positive behavior (Crisp and Knox 2009).

There is also concern among some professionals that parents praise their children too much. They fear an inflated ego and not being able to cope with failure will result. Therapists recommend spacing one's praise is best since it results in move value for the praise.

The popular culture is increasingly oriented to fulfilling the X-rated fantasies and desires of adults. Child-rearing values—sacrifice, stability, dependability, maturity—seem stale and musty by comparison.

Barbara Defoe Whitehead, National Marriage Project

Be Realistic

Rid one's self about the illusions of childhood honesty. Talwar and Lee (2008) confirmed that children lie. In an experiment, 138 children (3 to 8 years) were told not to peek at a toy—82 percent peeked in the experimenter's absence, and 64 percent lied about their transgression.

Avoid Overindulgence

Look again at the opening quote for this chapter. **Overindulgence** is defined as giving children too much, too soon, too long—it is a form of child neglect in which children are not allowed to develop their own competences (see www .overindulgence.info). Children who are overindulged think they are the center of the universe, don't work to earn what they want, and have an overblown sense of entitlement. Corporate employers have discovered that Generation Y youth (79.8 million of them born between 1977 and 1995) are no longer anxious to work or appreciative to get a job. Rather, they want to know their benefits and make it clear they have no intention of working sixty hours a week. Furthermore, "when it comes to loyalty, the companies they work for are last on their list—behind their families, their friends, their communities, their co-workers and, of course, themselves" (Hira 2007).

Parents typically overindulge because they feel guilty or because they did not have certain material goods in their own youth. In a study designed to identify who overindulged, a researcher found mothers were four times more likely to overindulge as fathers (Clarke 2004). The result of overindulgence is that children grow up without consequences, and they avoid real jobs where employers expect them to show up at 8:00 A.M.

Monitor Child's Activities or Drug Use

Abundant research suggests that parents who monitor their children and teens—know where their children are, who they are with, what they are doing, and so on—are less likely to report that their adolescents receive low grades, or are engaged in early sexual activity, delinquent behavior, and drug use. Regarding drug use, Brook et al. (2008) studied the association of marijuana use during the transition from late adolescence to early adulthood with reported relationship quality with significant others. The community-based sample consisted of 534 young adults (mean age = 27) from upstate New York and was interviewed at four points in time at the mean ages 14, 16, 22, and 27 years. Marijuana use during the transition from late adolescence to early adulthood was associated with less relationship cohesion and harmony, and with more relationship conflict. The researchers concluded that marijuana use during emerging adulthood predicts diminished relationship quality with a partner in the mid- to late twenties. Hence, parents might well monitor the whereabouts of their teens.

Parents who used marijuana or other drugs themselves wonder how to go about encouraging their own children to be drug-free. Drugfree.org has some recommendations for parents, including being honest about previous drug use, making clear that you do not want your children to use drugs, and explaining that although not all drug use leads to negative consequences, staying clear of such possibilities is the best course of action.

Set Limits and Discipline Children for Inappropriate Behavior

The goal of guidance is self-control. Parents want their children to be able to control their own behavior and to make good decisions without their parents.

Guidance may involve reinforcing desired behavior or providing limits to children's behavior. This sometimes involves disciplining children for negative behavior. Unless parents provide negative consequences for lying, stealing, and hitting, children can grow up to be dishonest, to steal, and to be inappropriately aggressive.

Time-out (a noncorporal form of punishment that involves removing the child from a context of reinforcement to a place of isolation for one minute for each year of the child's age) has been shown to be an effective consequence for inappropriate behavior. Withdrawal of privileges (watching television, playing with friends), pointing out the logical consequences of the misbehavior ("you were late; we won't go"), and positive language ("I know you meant well but . . .") are also effective methods of guiding children's behavior.

Physical punishment is less effective in reducing negative behavior (see the following Personal Choices section); it teaches the child to be aggressive and encourages negative emotional feelings toward the parents. When using time-out or the withdrawal of privileges, parents should make clear to the child that they disapprove of the child's behavior, not the child. Some evidence suggests that consistent discipline has positive outcomes for children. Lengua et al. (2000) studied 231 mothers of 9- to 12-year-olds and found that inconsistent discipline was related to adjustment problems, particularly for children high in impulsivity.

Obstinacy in children is like a kite; it is kept up just as long as we pull against it.

Marlene Cox, coach/mentor

PERSONAL CHOICES

Should Parents Use Corporal Punishment?

Parents differ in the type of punishment they feel is appropriate for children. Some parents use corporal punishment as a means of disciplining their children. These parents tend to be Protestant rather than Catholic, have younger rather than older children, and are black rather than white or Latino (Grogan-Kaylor and Otis 2007).

The decision to choose a corporal or noncorporal method of punishment should be based on the consequences of use. In general, the use of time-out and withholding of privileges seems to be more effective than corporal punishment in stopping undesirable behavior (Paintal 2007). Though beatings and whippings will temporarily decrease negative verbal and nonverbal behaviors, they have major side effects. First, punishing children by inflicting violence teaches them that it is acceptable to physically hurt someone you love. Hence, parents may be inadvertently teaching their children to use violence in the family. Children who are controlled by corporal punishment grow up to be violent toward their own children, spouses, and friends (Paintal 2007). Second, parents who beat their children should be aware that they are teaching their children to fear and avoid them. The result is that children who grow up in homes where corporal punishment is used have more distant relationships with their parents (Paintal 2007). Third, children who grow up in homes in which corporal punishment is used are more likely to feel helpless, to have low self-esteem, and to withdraw (Paintal 2007). In recognition of the negative consequences of corporal punishment, the law in Sweden forbids parents to spank their children.

So, what kind of discipline is best? Parents who reason with their children and back up their reasoning with consequences report the greatest consistent behavior change. Consequences that are effective include withdrawing privileges such as use of cell phone, computer, television, and friends (for example, grounding so that the child or teen is not allowed to see friends on the weekends) (Crisp and Knox 2009). We earlier noted that the authoritative parenting style (which emphasizes a balance of structure, control, warmth, and consequences) seems to have a good outcome for children and parents.

A review of some of the alternatives to corporal punishment include the following:

1. *Be a positive role model.* Children learn behaviors by observing their parents' actions, so parents must model the ways in which they want their children to behave. If a parent yells or hits, the child is likely to do the same.

2. *Set rules and consequences.* Make rules that are fair, realistic, and appropriate to a child's level of development. Explain the rules and the consequences of not following them. If children are old enough, they can be included in establishing the rules and consequences of breaking them.

Today everybody talks about rights and privileges. Twenty-five years ago everybody talked about their obligations and responsibilities.

Lou Holtz, TV commentator

3. *Encourage and reward good behavior.* When children are behaving appropriately, give them verbal praise and occasionally reward them with tangible objects, privileges, or increased responsibility.

4. *Use charts.* Charts to monitor and reward behavior can help children learn appropriate behavior. Charts should be simple and focus on one behavior at a time, for a certain length of time.

5. *Use time-out.* "Time-out" involves removing children from a situation following a negative behavior. This can help children calm down, end an inappropriate behavior, and reenter the situation in a positive way. Explain what the inappropriate behavior is, why the time-out is needed, when it will begin, and how long it will last. Set an appropriate length of time for the time-out based on age and level of development, usually one minute for each year of the child's age (see the following Self-Assessment on Spanking versus Time-Out).

Sources

Crisp, B., and D. Knox. 2009. *Behavioral family therapy: An evidence based approach.* Durham, NC: Carolina Academic Press.

Grogan-Kaylor, A., and M. D. Otis. 2007. The predictors of parental use of corporal punishment *Family Relations* 56: 80–91.

Paintal, S. 2007. Banning corporal punishment of children. *Childhood Education* 83:410–21.

Provide Security

Predictable responses from parents, a familiar bedroom or playroom, and an established routine help to encourage a feeling of security in children. Security provides children with the needed self-assurance to venture beyond the family. If the outside world becomes too frightening or difficult, a child can return to the safety of the family for support. Knowing it is always possible to return to an accepting environment enables a child to become more involved with the world beyond the family.

As children become teenagers and young adults, they may fall victim to an abusive partner whom they protect (out of "love") so that the parents will not find out. In the case of a college student, parents might be alert to their child being isolated or cut off from them (the child calls or comes home less often), a change in their behavior (grades drop), or frequent breakups (and getting back together). Helping a child to extricate from such a relationship is difficult. Criticizing their son or daughter's partner is usually ineffective because the child may become defensive. Rather, the key may be focusing on what a good relationship is (love, mutual support) and is not (fear, guilt, anger).

Encourage Responsibility

Giving children increased responsibility encourages the autonomy and independence they need to be assertive and independent. Giving children more responsibility as they grow older can take the form of encouraging them to choose healthy snacks and letting them decide what to wear and when to return from playing with a friend (of course, the parents should praise appropriate choices).

Children who are not given any control and responsibility for their own lives remain dependent on others. Successful parents can be defined in terms of their ability to rear children who can function as independent adults. A dependent child is a vulnerable child.

Some American children remain in their parents' house into their twenties and thirties. Their doing so is primarily because it is cheaper to do so. Ward and

Spanking versus Time-Out Scale

Parents discipline their children to help them develop self-control and correct misbehavior. Some parents spank their children; others use time-out. Spanking is a disciplinary technique whereby a mild slap (that is, a "spank") is applied to the buttocks of a disobedient child. Time-out is a disciplinary technique whereby, when a child misbehaves, the child is removed from the situation. The purpose of this survey is to assess the degree to which you prefer spanking versus time-out as a method of discipline. Please read each item carefully and select a number from 1 to 7, which represents your belief. There are no right or wrong answers; please give your honest opinion.

1	2	3	4	5	6	7
Strongly Disagree						Strongly Agree

_____ 1. Spanking is a better form of discipline than time-out.

_____ 2. Time-out does not have any effect on children.

_____ 3. When I have children, I will more likely spank them than use a time-out.

_____ 4. A threat of a time-out does not stop a child from misbehaving.

_____ 5. Lessons are learned better with spanking.

_____ 6. Time-out does not give a child an understanding of what the child has done wrong.

_____ 7. Spanking teaches a child to respect authority.

_____ 8. Giving children time-outs is a waste of time.

_____ 9. Spanking has more of an impact on changing the behavior of children than time-out.

_____ 10. I do not believe "time-out" is a form of punishment.

_____ 11. Getting spanked as a child helps you become a responsible citizen.

_____ 12. Time-out is only used because parents are afraid to spank their kids.

_____ 13. Spanking can be an effective tool in disciplining a child.

_____ 14. Time-out is watered-down discipline.

Scoring

If you want to know the degree to which you approve of spanking, reverse the number you selected for all odd-numbered items (1, 3, 5, 7, 9, 11, and 13) after you have selected a number from 1 to 7 for each of the fourteen items. For example, if you selected a 1 for item 1, change this number to a 7 (1 = 7; 2 = 6; 3 = 5; 4 = 4; 5 = 3; 6 = 2; 7 = 1). Now add these seven numbers. The lower your score (7 is the lowest possible score), the lower your approval of spanking; the higher your score (49 is the highest possible score), the greater your approval of spanking. A score of 21 places you at the midpoint between being very disapproving of or very accepting of spanking as a discipline strategy.

If you want to know the degree to which you approve of using time-out as a method of discipline, reverse the number you selected for all even-numbered items (2, 4, 6, 8, 10, 12, and 14). For example, if you selected a 1 for item 2, change this number to a seven (that is, 1 = 7; 2 = 6; 3 = 5; 4 = 4; 5 = 3; 6 = 2; 7 = 1). Now add these seven numbers. The lower your score (7 is the lowest possible score), the lower your approval of time-out; the higher your score (49 is the highest possible score), the greater your approval of time-out. A score of 21 places you at the midpoint between being very disapproving of or very accepting of time-out as a discipline strategy.

Scores of Other Students Who Completed the Scale

The scale was completed by 48 male and 168 female student volunteers at East Carolina University. Their ages ranged from 18 to 34, with a mean age of 19.65 ($SD = 2.06$). The ethnic background of the sample included 73.1 percent white, 17.1 percent African American, 2.8 percent Hispanic, 0.9 percent Asian, 3.7 percent from other ethnic backgrounds; 2.3 percent did not indicate ethnicity. The college classification level of the sample included 52.8 percent freshman, 24.5 percent sophomore, 13.9 percent junior, and 8.8 percent senior. The average score on the spanking dimension was 29.73 ($SD = 10.97$), and the time-out dimension was 22.93 ($SD = 8.86$), suggesting greater acceptance of spanking than time-out.

Time-out differences. In regard to sex of the participants, female participants were more positive about using time-out as a discipline strategy ($M = 33.72$, $SD = 8.76$) than were male participants ($M = 30.81$, $SD = 8.97$; $p < .05$). In regard to ethnicity of the participants, white participants were more positive about using time-out as a discipline strategy ($M = 34.63$, $SD = 8.54$) than were nonwhite participants ($M = 28.45$, $SD = 8.55$; $p < .05$). In regard to year in school, freshmen were more positive about using spanking as a discipline strategy ($M = 34.34$, $SD = 9.23$) than were sophomores, juniors, and seniors ($M = 31.66$, $SD = 8.25$; $p < .05$).

Spanking differences. In regard to ethnicity of the participants, non-white participants were more positive about using spanking as a discipline strategy ($M = 35.09$, $SD = 10.02$) than were white participants ($M = 27.87$, $SD = 10.72$; $p < .05$). In regard to year in school, freshmen were less positive about using spanking as a discipline strategy ($M = 28.28$, $SD = 11.42$) than were sophomores, juniors, and seniors ($M = 31.34$, $SD = 10.26$; $p < .05$). There were no significant differences in regard to sex of the participants ($p > .05$) in the opinion of spanking.

Overall differences. There were no significant differences in overall attitudes to discipline in regards to sex of the participants, ethnicity, or year in school.

Source

"The Spanking vs. Time-Out Scale," 2004 by Mark Whatley, Ph.D., Department of Psychology, Valdosta State University, Valdosta, Georgia 31698-0100. Used by permission. Other uses of this scale by written permission of Dr. Whatley only (mwhatley@valdosta.edu). Information on the reliability and validity of this scale is available from Dr. Whatley.

Spitze (2007) analyzed data from the National Survey of Families and Households in regard to children aged 18 and older who lived with their parents. Findings revealed that, although disagreements between parents and children increased, the quality of parent-child or husband-wife relations did not change.

Provide Sex Education

Usher-Seriki et al. (2008) studied mother-daughter communication about sex and sexual intercourse in a sample of 274 middle- to upper-income African American adolescent girls. They found that daughters were more likely to delay sexual intercourse when they had close relationships with their mother, when they perceived that their mother disapproved of premarital sex for moral reasons, and when their mothers emphasized the negative consequences of premarital sex.

How often do parents communicate about sexual issues? Wyckoff et al. (2008) assessed the degree to which 135 African American parents communicated with their 9- to 12-year-olds about sexual issues such as the risks of sexual activity, sexual risk prevention, and so on, and found that most had communicated on such topics. Mothers and fathers were equally likely to communicate with sons whereas mothers were more likely to communicate with daughters than were fathers.

In regard to adolescent females and their first period, Lee (2008) reported that, of 155 young women, most said that their mothers were supportive and emotionally engaged with them regarding **menarche**. These emotionally connected mothers were, for the most part, able to mitigate feelings of shame and humiliation associated with the discourses of menstruation in contemporary culture.

Express Confidence

"One of the greatest mistakes a parent can make," confided one mother, "is to be anxious all the time about your child, because the child interprets this as your lack of confidence in his or her ability to function independently." Rather, this mother noted that it is best to convey to a child that you know that he will be all right and that you are not going to worry about the child because you have confidence in him. "The effect on the child," said this mother, "is a heightened sense of self-confidence." Another way to conceptualize this parental principle is to think of the self-fulfilling prophecy as a mechanism that facilitates self-confidence. If parents show a child that they have confidence in him or her, the child begins to accept these social definitions as real and becomes more self-confident.

Shellenbarger (2006) noted that some parents have become "helicopter parents" in that they are constantly hovering at school and in the workplace to ensure their child's "success." The workplace has become the new field where parents negotiate the benefits and salaries of their children, with employers they feel are out to take advantage of inexperienced workers. However, employers may not appreciate the tampering, and the parents risk hampering their child's "ability to develop self-confidence" (p. D1). Other employers are engaging parents and know that, unless the parents are convinced, the offspring won't sign on (Hira 2007).

Keep in Touch with Nature

Louv (2006) used the term **nature-deficit disorder** to denote that children today are encouraged to detach themselves from direct contact with nature—playing in the woods, wading through a stream, catching tadpoles—because they are overscheduled with "activities" such as swimming, tennis, gymnastic, soccer, and piano lessons, which leaves little time for anything else. He recommended that children need such contact with nature just as they need good nutrition and adequate sleep.

Respond to the Teen Years Creatively

Parenting teenage children presents challenges that differ from those in parenting infants and young children. The teenage years have been characterized as a time when adolescents defy authority, act rebellious, and search for their own identity. Teenagers today are no longer viewed as innocent, naive children.

Conflicts between parents and teenagers often revolve around money and independence. The desires for a cell phone, DVD player, and high-definition TV can outstrip the budget of many parents. Teens also increasingly want more freedom. However, neither of these issues needs to result in conflicts. When they do, the effect on the parent-child relationship may be inconsequential. One parent tells his children, "I'm just being the parent, and you're just being who you are; it is OK for us to disagree—but you can't go." The following suggestions can help to keep conflicts with teenagers at a low level:

Sound travels slowly. Sometimes the things you say when your kids are teenagers don't reach them till they're in their forties.

Michael Hodgkin

1. *Catch them doing what you like rather than criticizing them for what you don't like.* Adolescents are like everyone else—they don't like to be criticized but they do like to be noticed for what they do that is good.

2. *Be direct when necessary.* Though parents may want to ignore some behaviors of their children, addressing some issues directly may also be effective. Regarding the avoidance of STI or HIV infections and pregnancy, Dr. Louise Sammons (2008) tells her teenagers, "It is utterly imperative to require that any potential sex partner produce a certificate indicating no STIs or HIV infection and to require that a condom or dental dam be used before intercourse or oral sex."

3. *Provide information rather than answers.* When teens are confronted with a problem, try to avoid making a decision for them. Rather, providing information on which they may base a decision is helpful. What courses to take in high school and what college to apply for are decisions that might be made primarily by the adolescent. The role of the parent might best be that of providing information or helping the teenager to obtain information.

4. *Be tolerant of high activity levels.* Some teenagers are constantly listening to loud music, going to each other's homes, and talking on cell phones for long periods of time. Parents often want to sit in their easy chairs and be quiet. Recognizing that it is not realistic to expect teenagers to be quiet and sedentary may be helpful in tolerating their disruptions.

5. *Engage in some activity with your teenagers.* Whether renting a video, eating a pizza, or taking a camping trip, structuring some activities with your teenagers is important. Such activities permit a context in which to communicate with them.

Sometimes teenagers present challenges with which the parents feel unable to cope. Aside from monitoring their behavior closely, family therapy may be helpful. A major focus of such therapy is to increase the emotional bond between the parents and the teenagers and to encourage positive consequences for desirable behavior (for example, concert tickets for good grades) and negative consequences for undesirable behavior (for example, loss of car privileges for getting a speeding ticket).

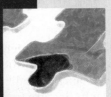

WHAT IF?

What if Your Teenager Lies to You?

Conveying to children and teens that lying is not acceptable is important. However, teens do lie about where they are, who they are with, and what they are doing. When the parent becomes aware of such a lie, the parent should confront the teen with, "We love you and only want what is best for you. Lying to us is not acceptable. You are grounded (can't go anywhere) for a week and your cell phone, television, and computer privileges are suspended. If there is a next time, it will be for a month. We need to be able to trust you and have confidence that what you tell us is true." After the week is over and the restrictions are lifted, the parents should be careful to look for examples of those times when their teen is telling them the truth and to praise the teen—"We love you and appreciate your being honest with us."

ADHD in Children

Attention-deficit/hyperactivity disorder (ADHD) is the most commonly diagnosed childhood psychiatric disorder that occurs in 3 percent to 7 percent of school-aged children. Inattentiveness, impulsiveness, forgetfulness, restlessness, and difficulty with organization are the typical symptoms that impact a child's behavior, social relationships, and schoolwork. Parents and teachers are also affected. The usual treatments are stimulant medication and behavioral therapy or a combination of the two. Psychiatrist Robert Sammons summarized the state-of-the-art thinking in regard to the use of medication for ADHD:

> *The treatment of ADHD from a biological perspective can be one of the most rewarding interventions that occur in medicine. Against the vast double-blind, placebo-controlled research supporting the existence and treatment of ADHD with medication, there are case reports and anecdotal examples of a child doing poorly on medication or medication being inappropriately prescribed or misused by the patient or his family. Some call the antagonism to medication a "faith-based belief" as it is based upon a belief after hearing one story, reading one article or focusing only on the inevitable difficulties an occasional child will have (while ignoring the irrefutable research that is in contradiction to what they want to believe).*
>
> *Many parents are concerned about having their child on medication for fear that he or she will be labeled negatively. This concern belies the fact that if their child is not treated with appropriate medication, the child will continue to do poorly in school, may flunk out, may cheat and receive a far more prejudicial label. The issue is not whether a child develops a "label" or not, but which label the child will be given. Untreated ADHD has a clearly recognized course which is certainly problematic for those who have a more disruptive condition.*
>
> *Parents also fear that in this age of substance abuse, placing a child on stimulant medication increases the child's propensity for drug abuse. That, again, is a faith-based belief because the evidence is the opposite. When children are treated for their ADHD, they are much less likely to gravitate toward, or be grouped with, children who are poor performers and begin engaging in counter-culture activities to give them success in an area.*
>
> *Researched based clinicians are not threatened by, nor antagonistic to, medical treatment of the behaviors they are trying to treat. A comprehensive whole person view is often necessary for the most robust treatment response. This is not a turf war regarding whose treatment is more powerful or more important. Rather, it is a team approach to afford the patient/client the most efficacious treatment available to him or her. The importance of a good behavioral analysis and program cannot be underestimated. (Crisp and Knox 2009)*

Single-Parenting Issues

At least half of all children will spend one-fourth of their lives in a female-headed household (Webb 2005). The stereotype of the single parent is the single, unmarried black single mother. In reality, 40 percent of single mothers are white and only 33 percent are black (Sugarman 2003).

Distinguishing between a single-parent "family" and a single-parent "household" is important. A single-parent family is one in which there is only one parent—the other parent is completely out of the child's life through death, sperm donation, or complete abandonment, and no contact is ever made with the other parent. In contrast, a single-parent household is one in which one parent typically has primary custody of the

Diversity in Other Countries

There are wide variations in the percentage of children born to unmarried mothers. Over half (64.6 percent) of the births of American Indian, Eskimo, and Aleut mothers occur when they are not married. In contrast, 16 percent of births to Asian or Pacific Islander women occur when they are not married (*Statistical Abstract of the United States, 2009*, Table 85).

child or children but the parent living out of the house is still a part of the child's family. This is also referred to as a binuclear family. In most divorce cases where the mother has primary physical custody of the child, the child lives in a single-parent household because the child is still connected to the father, who remains part of the child's family. In cases in which one parent has died, the child or children live with the surviving parent in a single-parent family because there is only one parent.

Single Mothers by Choice

Single parents enter their role though divorce or separation, widowhood, adoption, or deliberate choice to rear a child or children alone. Jodie Foster, Academy Award–winning actress, has elected to have children without a husband. She now has two children and smiles when asked, "Who's the father?" The implication is that she has a right to her private life and that choosing to have a single-parent family is a viable option. An organization for women who want children and who may or may not marry is Single Mothers by Choice.

Bock (2000) noted that single mothers by choice are, for the most part, in the middle to upper class, mature, well-employed, politically aware, and dedicated to motherhood. Interviews with twenty-six single mothers by choice revealed their struggle to avoid stigmatization and to seek legitimization for their choice. Most felt that their age (older), sense of responsibility, maturity, and fiscal capability justified their choice. Their self-concepts were those of competent, ethical, mainstream mothers.

Challenges Faced by Single Parents

The single-parent lifestyle involves numerous challenges, including some of the following issues:

   1. *Responding to the demands of parenting with limited help.* Perhaps the greatest challenge for single parents is taking care of the physical, emotional, and disciplinary needs of their children—alone. Many single parents resolve this problem by getting help from their parents or extended family.

One of the joys of single parenting is the opportunity to develop a very close bond because there is just the parent and the child.

Authors

2. *Adult emotional needs.* Single parents have emotional needs of their own that children are often incapable of satisfying. The unmet need to share an emotional relationship with an adult can weigh heavily on a single parent. One single mother said, "I'm working two jobs, taking care of my kids, and trying to go to school. Plus my mother has cancer. Who am I going to talk to about my life?" Many single women solve the dilemma with a network of friends.

3. *Adult sexual needs.* Some single parents regard their parental role as interfering with their sexual relationships. They may be concerned that their children will find out if they have a sexual encounter at home or be frustrated if they have to go away from home to enjoy a sexual relationship. Some choices with which they are confronted include, "Do I wait until my children are asleep and then ask my lover to leave before morning?" or "Do I openly acknowledge my lover's presence in my life to my children and ask them not to tell anybody?" and "Suppose my kids get attached to my lover, who may not be a permanent part of our lives?"

4. *Lack of money.* Single-parent families, particularly those headed by women, report that money is always lacking.

National Data

The median income of a single-woman householder is $26,829, much lower than that of a single-man householder ($41,844) or a married couple ($69,404) (*Statistical Abstract of the United State-s, 2009*, Table 676).

5. *Guardianship.* If the other parent is completely out of the child's life, the single parent needs to appoint a guardian to take care of the child in the event of the parent's death or disability.

6. *Prenatal care.* Single women who decide to have a child have poorer pregnancy outcomes than married women. The reason for such an association may be the lack of economic funds (no male partner with economic resources available) as well as the lack of social support for the pregnancy or the working conditions of the mothers, all of which result in less prenatal care for their babies.

7. *Absence of a father.* Another consequence for children of single-parent mothers is that they often do not have the opportunity to develop an emotionally supportive relationship with their father. Barack Obama noted in one of his campaign speeches, "I know what it is like to grow up without a father." The late Rodney Dangerfield said he spent an average of two hours a year with his father in his entire life and that he missed such love and nurturing. In contrast, Ansel Adams, the late photographer, attributed his personal and life success to his father, who was steadfastly involved in his life and guided his development.

8. *Negative life outcomes for the child in a single-parent family.* Researcher Sara McLanahan, herself a single mother, set out to prove that children reared by single parents were just as well off as those reared by two parents. McLanahan's data on 35,000 children of single parents led her to a different conclusion—children of only one parent were twice as likely as those reared by two married parents to drop out of high school, get pregnant before marriage, have drinking problems, and experience a host of other difficulties, including getting divorced themselves (McLanahan and Booth 1989; McLanahan 1991). Lack of supervision, fewer economic resources, and less extended family support were among the culprits. Other research suggests that negative outcomes are reduced or eliminated when income levels remain stable (Pong and Dong 2000).

Though the risk of negative outcomes is higher for children in single-parent homes, most are happy and well-adjusted. Benefits to single parents themselves include a sense of pride and self-esteem that results from being independent.

Approaches to Child Rearing

Professionals offer parents advice that may change over time. For example, in 1914, parents who wanted to know what to do about their child's thumb sucking were told to try to control such a bad impulse by pinning the sleeves of the child to the bed if necessary. Today, parents are told that thumb sucking meets an important psychological need for security and they should not try to prevent it. If a child's teeth become crooked as a result, an orthodontist should be consulted.

Advice may also be profit driven. As noted earlier in the Research Application section of this chapter, there is alarming information that some of what passes for "research-based advice" to provide your baby with specific toys or learning programs turns out to be child development research funded by corporations intent on selling parents merchandise for their children. In her book *Buy, Buy, Baby: How Consumer Culture Manipulates Parents and Harms Young Minds*, Thomas (2007) identified the dangerous economic and cultural shift that targets toddlers and infants to have things bought for them that may actually harm them.

There are several theoretical approaches to rearing children. A review of these approaches can be found in Table 11.1. In examining these approaches, it is important to keep in mind that no single approach is superior to another. What works for one child may not work for another. Any given approach may not even work with the same child at two different times. In addition, parents and professional caregivers of children often differ in regard to child-rearing approaches.

Table 11.1 Theories of Child Rearing

Theory	Major Contributor	Basic Perspective	Focal Concerns	Criticisms
Developmental-Maturational	Arnold Gesell	Genetic basis for child passing through predictable stages	Motor behavior Adaptive behavior Language behavior Social behavior	Overemphasis on biological clock Inadequate sample to develop norms Demanding schedule questionable Upper-middle class bias
Behavioral	B. F. Skinner B. Crisp	Behavior is learned through operant and classical conditioning	Positive reinforcement Negative reinforcement Punishment Extinction Stimulus response	De-emphasis on cognitions of child Theory too complex for parent to accurately or appropriately apply Too manipulative or controlling Difficult to know reinforcers and punishers in advance
Parent Effectiveness Training	Thomas Gordon	The child's worldview is the key to understanding the child	Change the environment before attempting to change the child's behavior Avoid hurting the child's self-esteem Avoid win-lose solutions	Parents must sometimes impose their will on the child's How to achieve win-win solutions is not specified
Socioteleological	Alfred Adler	Behavior is seen as attempt of child to secure a place in the family	Insecurity Compensation Power Revenge Social striving Natural consequences	Limited empirical support Child may be harmed taking "natural consequences"
Attachment	William Sears	Goal is to establish a firm, emotional attachment with child	Connecting with baby Responding to cues Breast-feeding Wearing the baby Sharing sleep	May result in spoiled, overly dependent child Exhausting for parents

It is important for new parents to use a cafeteria approach when examining parenting advice from health care providers, family members, friends, parenting educators, and other well-meaning individuals. Take what makes sense, works, and feels right as a parent and leave the rest behind. Parents know their own child better than anyone else and should be encouraged to combine different approaches to find what works best for them and their unique child.

Developmental-Maturational Approach

For the past sixty years, Arnold Gesell and his colleagues at the Yale Clinic of Child Development have been known for their ages and stages approach to child rearing (Gesell et al. 1995). The **developmental-maturational approach** has been widely used in the United States. The basic perspective, some considerations for child rearing, and some criticisms of the approach follow.

Basic Perspective   Gesell views what children do, think, and feel as being influenced by their genetic inheritance. Although genes dictate the gradual unfolding of a unique person, every individual passes through the same basic pattern of growth. This pattern includes four aspects of development: motor behavior (sitting, crawling, walking), adaptive behavior (picking up objects and walking around objects), language behavior (words and gestures), and personal-social behavior (cooperativeness and helpfulness). Through the observation of hundreds of normal infants and children, Gesell and his coworkers have identified norms of development. Although there may be large variations, these norms suggest the ages at which an average child displays various behaviors. For example, on the average, children begin to walk alone (although awkwardly) at age 13 months and use simple sentences between the ages of 2 and 3.

Considerations for Child Rearing   Gesell suggested that, if parents are aware of their children's developmental clock, they will avoid unreasonable expectations. For example, a child cannot walk or talk until the neurological structures necessary for those behaviors have matured. Also, the hunger of a 4-week-old must be immediately appeased by food, but at 16 to 28 weeks, the child has some capacity to wait because the hunger pains are less intense. In view of this and other developmental patterns, Gesell suggested that infants need to be cared for on a demand schedule; instead of having to submit to a schedule imposed by parents, infants are fed, changed, put to bed, and allowed to play when they want. Children are likely to be resistant to a hard-and-fast schedule because they may be developmentally unable to cope with it.

In addition, Gesell emphasized that parents should be aware of the importance of the first years of a child's life. In Gesell's view, these early years assume the greatest significance because the child's first learning experiences occur during this period.

Criticisms of the Developmental-Maturational Approach   Gesell's work has been criticized because of (1) its overemphasis on the idea of a biological clock, (2) the deficiencies of the sample he used to develop maturational norms, (3) his insistence on the merits of a demand schedule, and (4) the idea that environmental influences are weak.

Most of the children who were studied to establish the developmental norms were from the upper-middle class. Children in other social classes are exposed to different environments, which influence their development. So, norms established on upper-middle-class children may not adequately reflect the norms of children from other social classes.

Gesell's suggestion that parents do everything for the infant when the infant wants has also been criticized. Rearing an infant on the demand schedule can drastically interfere with the parents' personal and marital interests. In the

United States, with its emphasis on individualism, many parents feed their infants on a demand schedule but put them to bed to accommodate the parents' schedule.

Behavioral Approach

The **behavioral approach** to child rearing, also known as the social learning approach, is based on the work of B. F. Skinner and the theme of *Behavioral Family Therapy* (Crisp and Knox 2009). Behavioral approaches to child behavior have received the most empirical study. Public health officials and policy makers are encouraged to promote programs with empirically supported treatments. We now review the basic perspective, considerations, and criticisms of this approach to child rearing.

Basic Perspective   Behavior is learned through classical and operant conditioning. Classical conditioning involves presenting a stimulus with a reward. For example, infants learn to associate the faces of their parents with food, warmth, and comfort. Although initially only the food and feeling warm will satisfy the infant, later just the approach of the parent will soothe the infant. This may be observed when a father hands his infant to a stranger. The infant may cry because a stranger is not associated with pleasant events. However, when a stranger hands the infant back to the parent, the crying may subside because the parent represents positive events and the stimulus of the parent's face is associated with pleasurable feelings and emotional safety.

Other behaviors are learned through operant conditioning, which focuses on the consequences of behavior. Two principles of learning are basic to the operant explanation of behavior—reward and punishment. According to the reward principle, behaviors that are followed by a positive consequence will increase. If the goal is to teach the child to say "please," doing something the child likes after saying "please" will increase the use of "please" by the child. Rewards may be in the form of attention, praise, desired activities, or privileges. Whatever consequence increases the frequency of an occurrence is, by definition, a reward. If a particular consequence doesn't change the behavior in the desired way, a different reward needs to be tried.

The punishment principle is the opposite of the reward principle. A negative consequence following a behavior will decrease the frequency of that behavior; for example, the child could be isolated for five or ten minutes following an undesirable behavior. The most effective way to change behavior is to use the reward and punishment principles together to influence a specific behavior. Praise children for what you want them to do and provide negative consequences for what they do that you do not like.

Considerations for Child Rearing   Parents often ask, "Why does my child act this way, and what can I do to change it?" The behavioral approach to child rearing suggests the answer to both questions. The child's behavior has been learned through being rewarded for the behavior, and the behavior can be changed by eliminating the reward for or punishing the undesirable behavior and rewarding the desirable behavior.

The child who cries when the parents are about to leave home to go to dinner or see a movie is often reinforced for crying by the parents' staying home longer. To teach the child not to cry when the parents leave, the parents should reward the child for not crying when they are gone for progressively longer periods of time. For example, they might initially tell the child they are going outside to walk around the house and they will give the child a treat when they get back if the child plays until they return. The parents might then walk around the house and reward the child for not crying. If the child cries, they should be out of sight for only a few seconds and gradually increase the amount of time they are away. The essential point is that children learn to cry or not to cry depending on the consequences of crying. Because children learn what they are taught, parents might systematically structure learning experiences to achieve specific behavioral goals.

Criticisms of the Behavioral Approach   Professionals and parents have attacked the behavioral approach to child rearing on the basis that it is deceptively simple and does not take cognitive issues into account. Although the behavioral approach is often presented as an easy-to-use set of procedures for child management, many parents do not have the background or skill to implement the procedures effectively. What constitutes an effective reward or punishment, how it should be presented, in what situation and with what child, and to influence what behavior are all decisions that need to be made before attempting to increase or decrease the frequency of a behavior. Parents often do not know the questions to ask or lack the training to make appropriate decisions in the use of behavioral procedures. One parent locked her son in the closet for an hour to punish him for lying to her a week earlier—a gross misuse of learning principles.

Behavioral child rearing has also been said to be manipulative and controlling, thereby devaluing human dignity and individuality. Some professionals feel that humans should not be manipulated to behave in certain ways through the use of rewards and punishments. Behaviorists counter that rewards and punishments are always involved in any behavior the child engages in and parents are simply encouraged to arrange them in a way that benefits the child in terms of learning appropriate behavior.

Finally, the behavioral approach has been criticized because it de-emphasizes the influence of thought processes on behavior. Too much attention, say the critics, has been given to rewarding and punishing behavior and not enough attention has been given to how the child perceives a situation. For example, parents might think they are rewarding a child by giving the child a bicycle for good behavior. However, the child may prefer to upset the parents by rejecting the bicycle and may be more rewarded by their anger than by the gift. Behaviorists counter by emphasizing they are very much focused on cognitions and always include the perception of the child in developing a treatment program (Crisp and Knox 2009).

Children are more accepting of consequences from parents who love them and who spend time playing with them.

Parent Effectiveness Training Approach

Thomas Gordon (2000) developed the following model of child rearing based on **parent effectiveness training** (PET).

Basic Perspective Parent effectiveness training focuses on what children feel and experience—how they see the world in the here and now. The method of trying to understand what the child is experiencing is active listening, in which the parent reflects the child's feelings. For example, the parent who is told by the child, "I want to quit taking piano lessons because I don't like to practice" would reflect, "You're really bored with practicing the piano and would rather have fun doing something else." PET also focuses on the development of the child's positive self-concept.

To foster a positive self-concept in their child, parents should reflect positive images to the child—letting the child know he or she is loved, admired, and approved of.

Considerations for Child Rearing To assist in the development of a child's positive self-concept and in the self-actualization of both children and parents, Gordon (2000) recommended managing the environment rather than the child, engaging in active listening, using "I" messages, and resolving conflicts through mutual negotiation.

For example, rather than worry about how to teach children not to touch breakable knickknacks, environmental management would involve putting breakables out of reach of young children.

The use of active listening becomes increasingly important as children get older. When Joanna is upset with her teacher, it is better for the parent to reflect the child's thoughts than to take sides with the child. Saying, "You're angry that Mrs. Jones made the whole class miss play period because Becky was chewing gum" rather than saying "Mrs. Jones was unfair and should not have made the whole class miss play period" shows empathy with the child without blaming the teacher.

Gordon also suggested using "I" rather than "you" messages. Parents are encouraged to say, "I get upset when you're late and don't call" rather than "You're an insensitive, irresponsible kid for not calling me when you said you would." The former avoids damaging the child's self-concept but still expresses the parent's feelings and encourages the desired behavior.

Gordon's fourth suggestion for parenting is the no-lose method of resolving conflicts. Gordon rejects the use of power by parent or child. In the authoritarian home, the parent dictates what the child is to do and the child is expected to obey. In such a system, the parent wins and the child loses. At the other extreme is the permissive home, in which the child wins and the parent loses. The alternative, recommended by Gordon, is for the parent and the child to seek a solution that is acceptable to both and to keep trying until they find one. In this way, neither parent nor child loses and both win.

Criticisms of the Parent Effectiveness Training Approach Although much is commendable about PET, parents may have problems with two of Gordon's suggestions.

First, he recommends that, because older children have a right to their own values, parents should not interfere with their dress, career plans, and sexual behavior. Some parents may feel they do have a right (and an obligation) to "interfere." Second, the no-lose method of resolving conflict is sometimes unrealistic.

Suppose a 16-year-old wants to spend the weekend at the beach with her boyfriend and her parents do not want her to. Gordon advises negotiating until a decision is reached that is acceptable to both. However, what if neither the daughter nor the parents can suggest a compromise or shift their position? The specifics of how to resolve a particular situation are not always clear.

Socioteleological Approach

Alfred Adler, a physician and former student of Sigmund Freud, saw a parallel between psychological and physiological development. When people lose their sight, the other senses (hearing, touch, taste) become more sensitive—they compensate for the loss. According to Adler, the same phenomenon occurs in the psychological realm. When individuals feel inferior in one area, they will strive to compensate and become superior in another. Rudolf Dreikurs, a student of Adler, developed an approach to child rearing that alerts parents as to how their children might be trying to compensate for feelings of inferiority (Soltz and Dreikurs 1991). Dreikurs's **socioteleological approach** is based on Adler's theory.

Basic Perspective   According to Adler, it is understandable that most children feel they are inferior and weak. From the points of view of children, the world is filled with strong giants who tower above them. Because children feel powerless in the face of adult superiority, they try to compensate by gaining attention (making noise, becoming disruptive), exerting power (becoming aggressive, hostile), seeking revenge (becoming violent, hurting others), and acting inadequate (giving up, not trying). Adler suggested that such misbehavior is evidence that children are discouraged or feel insecure about their place in the family. The term *socioteleological* refers to social striving or seeking a social goal. In the child's case, the goal is to find a secure place within the family—the first "society" the child experiences.

Considerations for Child Rearing   When parents observe misbehavior in their children, they should recognize it as an attempt to find security. According to Dreikurs, parents should not fall into playing the child's game by, say, responding to a child's disruptiveness with anger but should encourage the child, hold regular family meetings, and let natural consequences occur. To encourage a child, the parents should be willing to let the child make mistakes. If John wants to help Dad carry logs to the fireplace, rather than saying, "You're too small to carry the logs," Dad should allow John to try and should encourage him to carry the size limb or stick that he can manage. Furthermore, Dad should praise John for his helpfulness.

As well as being constantly encouraged, the child should be included in a weekly family meeting. During this meeting, such family issues as bedtimes, the appropriateness of between-meal snacks, assignment of chores, and family fun are discussed. The meeting is democratic; each family member has a vote. Participation in family decision making is designed to enhance the self-concept of each child. By allowing each child to vote on family decisions, parents respect the child as a person as well as the child's needs and feelings.

Resolutions to conflicts with the child might also be framed in terms of choices the child can make (for example, "You can go outside and play only in the backyard or you can play in the house"). If a child strays from the backyard, the child can be brought in and told, "You can go out again later." Such a framework teaches responsibility for and consequences of one's choices.

Finally, Dreikurs suggested that the parents let natural consequences occur for their child's behavior. If a daughter misses the school bus, she walks or is charged taxi fare out of her allowance. If she won't wear a coat and boots in bad weather, she gets cold and wet. Of course, parents are to arrange logical consequences when natural consequences will not occur or would be dangerous if they did. For example, if a child leaves the television on overnight, access might be taken away for the next day or so.

Criticisms of the Socioteleological Approach   The socioteleological approach is sometimes regarded as impractical because it teaches the importance of letting children take the natural consequences for their actions. Such a principle may be interpreted to let the child develop a sore throat if she wishes to go out in the rain without a raincoat. In reality, advocates of the method would not let the child make a dangerous decision. Rather, they would give the child a choice with a logical consequence such as, "You can go outside wearing a raincoat, or you can stay inside—it is your choice."

Attachment Parenting

Dr. William Sears, along with his wife, Martha Sears, developed an approach to parenting called attachment parenting (Sears and Sears 1993). This "common-sense parenting" approach focuses on parents connecting with their baby.

Basic Perspective   The emotional attachment process between mother and child is thought to begin prior to birth and continues to be established during the next three years. Sears identified three parenting goals: to know your child, to help your child feel right, and to enjoy parenting. He also suggested five concepts or tools (identified in the following section) that comprise attachment parenting that will help parents to achieve these goals. Overall, the ultimate goal is for parents to connect with their baby. Once parents are connected, it is easy for parents to figure out what works for them and to develop a parenting style that fits them and their baby. Meeting a child's needs early in life will help the child form a secure attachment with parents. This secure attachment will help the child to gain confidence and independence while growing up. Attachment Parenting International is a nonprofit organization committed to educating society and parents about the critical emotional and psychological needs of infants and children.

Considerations for Child Rearing   The first attachment tool is for parents to connect with their baby early. The initial months of parenthood are a sensitive time for bonding with your baby and starting the process of attachment.

The second tool is to read and respond to the baby's cues. Parents should spend time getting to know their baby and learn to recognize any unique cues. Once a parent gets in tune with the baby's cues, it is easy to respond to the child's needs. Sears encourages parents to be open and responsive; responding to a baby's cries helps the baby to develop trust and encourages good communication between child and parent. Eventually, babies who are responded to will internalize their security and will not be as demanding.

The third attachment tool is for mothers to breast-feed their babies and to do this on demand rather than trying to follow a schedule. He emphasizes the important role that fathers also play in successful breast-feeding by helping to create a supportive environment.

The fourth concept of attachment parenting is for parents to wear their baby by using a baby sling or carrier. This closeness is good for the baby and makes life easier for the parent. Wearing your baby in a sling or carrier allows parents to engage in regular day-to-day activities and makes leaving the house easier.

Finally, Sears advocates that parents let the child sleep in their bed with them because this allows parents to stay connected with their child throughout the night. However, some parents and babies often sleep better if the baby is in a separate crib, and Sears recognizes that wherever parents and their baby sleep best is the best policy. Wherever you choose to have your baby sleep, Sears is clear on one thing—he feels it is never acceptable to let the baby cry when going to sleep. He believes parents need to parent their children to sleep rather than leaving them to cry.

Criticisms of Attachment Parenting   Some parents feel that responding to their baby's cries, carrying or wearing their baby, and sharing sleep with their baby will lead to a spoiled baby who is overly dependent. Some parents may feel more tied down using this parenting approach and may find getting their child on a schedule more difficult. Many women return to work after the baby is born and find some of these concepts difficult to follow. Some women choose not to breast-feed their children for a variety of reasons. Finally, the idea of sharing sleep has resulted in a lot of criticism. Some parents might be nervous that they might roll over on the child, that the child might disturb their sleep or intimacy, or that sharing a bed will mean that they will never get their child to sleep alone. However, children who grow up in an emotionally secure environment and have strong attachment report less behavioral and substance abuse problems as adolescents (Elgar et al. 2003).

SUMMARY

What are the basic roles of parents?

Parenting includes providing physical care for children, loving them, being an economic resource, providing guidance as a teacher or model, and protecting them from harm. One of the biggest problems confronting parents today is the societal influence on their children. These include drugs and alcohol; peer pressure; TV, Internet, and movies; and crime or gangs.

What is a choices perspective of parenting?

Although both genetic and environmental factors are at work, the choices parents make have a dramatic impact on their children. Parents who don't make a choice about parenting have already made one. The five basic choices parents make include deciding (1) whether to have a child, (2) the number of children, (3) the interval between children, (4) one's method of discipline and guidance, and (5) the degree to which one will be invested in the role of parent.

What is the transition to parenthood like for women, men, and couples?

Transition to parenthood refers to that period of time from the beginning of pregnancy through the first few months after the birth of a baby. The mother, father, and couple all undergo changes and adaptations during this period. Most mothers relish their new role; some may experience the transitory feelings of baby blues; a few report postpartum depression.

The father's involvement with his children is sometimes predicted by the quality of the parents' romantic relationship. If the father is emotionally and physically involved with the mother, he is more likely to take an active role in the child's life. In recent years, there has been a renewed cultural awareness of fatherhood.

A summary of almost 150 studies involving almost 50,000 respondents on the question of how children affect marital satisfaction revealed that parents (both women and men) reported lower marital satisfaction than nonparents. In addition, the higher the number of children, the lower the marital satisfaction; the factors that depressed marital satisfaction were conflict and loss of freedom.

What are several facts about parenthood?

Parenthood will involve about 40 percent of the time a couple live together, parents are only one influence on their children, each child is unique, and parenting styles differ. Research suggests that an authoritarian parenting style characterized by being both demanding and warm is associated with positive outcomes. In addition, being emotionally connected to a child, respecting the child's individuality, and monitoring the child's behavior to encourage positive contexts have positive outcomes. Birth order effects include that firstborns are the first on the scene with parents and always have the "inside track." They want to stay that way so they are traditional and conforming to their parent's expectations. Children born later learn quickly that they entered an existing family constellation where everyone is bigger and stronger. They cannot depend on having established territory so must excel in ways different from the firstborn. They are open to experience, adventurousness, and trying new things because their status is not already assured.

What are some of the principles of effective parenting?

Giving time, love, praise, and encouragement; monitoring the activities of one's child; setting limits; encouraging responsibility; and providing sexuality education are aspects of effective parenting.

How might parents respond to ADHD in their children?

Attention-deficit/hyperactivity disorder (ADHD) is the most commonly diagnosed childhood psychiatric disorder that occurs in 3 percent to 7 percent of school-aged children. Inattentiveness, impulsiveness, forgetfulness, restlessness, and difficulty with organization are the typical symptoms that impact a child's behavior, social relationships, and schoolwork. Overall, use of medication seems to have more positive outcomes than not using the medication.

What are the issues of single parenting?

About 40 percent of all children will spend one-fourth of their lives in a female-headed household. The challenges of single parenthood for the parent include taking care of the emotional and physical needs of a child alone, meeting one's own adult emotional and sexual needs, money, and rearing a child without a father (the influence of whom can be positive and beneficial).

What are five theoretical approaches to child rearing?

There are several approaches to child rearing, including the developmental-maturational approach (children are influenced by their genetic inheritance), behavioral approach (consequences influence the behaviors that children learn), socioteleological approach (children seek to gain attention from parents to overcome their feelings of powerlessness), and attachment parenting (the most important goal of parents is to become emotionally attached to their children).

KEY TERMS

ADHD (attention-deficit/ hyperactivity disorder)	developmental-maturational approach	oxytocin	responsiveness
baby blues	gatekeeper role	overindulgence	socioteleological approach
behavioral approach	menarche	parent effectiveness training	time-out
demandingness	nature-deficit disorder	parenting	transition to parenthood
	oppositional defiant disorder	postpartum depression	
		postpartum psychosis	

The Companion Website for *Choices in Relationships: An Introduction to Marriage and the Family,* Tenth Edition
www.cengage.com/sociology/knox

Supplement your review of this chapter by going to the Companion Website to take one of the tutorial quizzes, use the flash cards to master key terms, or check out the many other study aids, like crossword puzzles and self-assessments. You'll also find special features such as General Social Survey (GSS) data, Census data, and other resources to help you with that special project or to do some research on your own.

WEB LINKS

Attachment Parenting International
http://www.attachmentparenting.org/

Children, Youth, and Family Consortium
http://www.cyfc.umn.edu/

The Partnership for a Drug-Free America
http://www.drugfree.org/

The Children's Partnership Online
http://www.childrenspartnership.org

Mayberry USA (filtered Internet)
http://www.mbusa.net/

Parenthood.com
http://www.parenthoodweb.com/

REFERENCES

Baumrind, D. 1966. Effects of authoritative parental control on child behavior. *Child Development* 37:887–907.

Bock, J. D. 2000. Doing the right thing? Single mothers by choice and the struggle for legitimacy. *Gender and Society* 14:62–86.

Booth, C. L., K. A. Clarke-Stewart, D. L. Vandell, K. McCartney, and M. T. Owen. 2002. Child-care usage and mother-infant "quality time." *Journal of Marriage and the Family* 64:16–26.

Bost, K. K., M. J. Cox, M. R. Burchinal, and C. Payne. 2002. Structural and supporting changes in couples' family and friendships networks across the transition to parenthood. *Journal of Marriage and the Family* 64:517–31.

British Columbia Reproductive Mental Health Program. 2005. Reproductive mental health: Psychosis. http://www.bcrmh.com/disorders/psychosis.htm (retrieved June 15, 2005).

Brook, J. S., K. Pahl, and P. Cohen. 2008. Associations between marijuana use during emerging adulthood and aspects of the significant other relationship in young adulthood. *Journal of Child and Family Studies* 17:1–12.

Bronte-Tinkew, J., J. Carrano, A. Horowitz, and A. Kinukawa. 2008. Involvement among resident fathers and links to infant cognitive outcomes. *Journal of Family Issues* 29:1211–31.

Bushman, B. J., and J. Cantor. 2003. Media ratings for violence and sex. *American Psychologist* 58:130–41.

Castrucci, B. C., J. F. Culhane, E. K. Chung, I. Bennett, and K. F. McCollum. 2006. Smoking in pregnancy: Patient and provider risk reduction behavior. *Journal of Public Health Management & Practice* 12:68–76.

Clarke, J. I. 2004. The overindulgence research literature: Implications for family life educators. Poster at the National Council on Family Relations, Annual Meeting, November. Orlando, Florida.

Claxton, A., and M. Perry-Jenkins. 2008. No fun anymore: Leisure and marital quality across the transition to parenthood. *Journal of Marriage and the Family* 70:28–43.

Cornelius-Cozzi, T. 2002. Effects of parenthood on the relationships of lesbian couples. *PROGRESS: Family Systems Research and Therapy* 11:85–94.

Crisp, B., and D. Knox. 2009. *Behavioral family therapy: An evidence based approach.* Chapel Hill, NC: Carolina Academic Press. http://www.cap-press.com/books/1870.

Cui, M., F. D. Fincham, and B. Kay Pasley. 2008. Young adult romantic relationships: The role of parents' marital problems and relationship efficacy. *Personality and Social Psychology Bulletin* 34:1226–35.

Diamond, A., J. Bowes, and G. Robertson. 2006. Mothers' safety intervention strategies with toddlers and their relationship to child characteristics. *Early Child Development and Care* 176:271–84.

Elgar, F. J., J. Knight, G. J. Worrall, and G. Sherman. 2003. Attachment characteristics and behavioral problems in rural and urban juvenile delinquents. *Child Psychiatry and Human Development* 34:35–48.

Facer, J., and R. Day. 2004. Explaining diminished marital satisfaction when parenting adolescents. Poster at an Annual Meeting National Council on Family Relations, Orlando, Florida.

Fadiman, C., ed. 1985. *The Little, Brown book of anecdotes.* Boston: Little, Brown and Co.

Flouri, E., and A. Buchanan. 2003. The role of father involvement and mother involvement in adolescents' psychological well-being. *British Journal of Social Work* 33:399–406.

Galambos, N. L., E. T. Barker, and D. M. Almeida. 2003. Parents do matter: Trajectories of change in externalizing and internalizing problems in early adolescent. *Child Development* 74:578–95.

Gavin, L. E., M. M. Black, S. Minor, Y. Abel, and M. E. Bentley. 2002. Young, disadvantaged fathers' involvement with their infants: An ecological perspective. *Journal of Adolescent Health* 31:266–76.

Gesell, A., F. L. Ilg, and L. B. Ames. 1995. *Infant and child in the culture of today.* Northvale, NJ: Jason Aronson.

Gordon, T. 2000. *Parent effectiveness training: The parents' program for raising responsible children.* New York: Random House.

Green, S. E. 2003. "What do you mean 'what's wrong with her?'" Stigma and the lives of families of children with disabilities. *Social Science & Medicine* 57:1361–74.

Hammarberg, K., J. R. Fisher, and K. H. Wynter. 2008. Psychological and social aspects of pregnancy, childbirth and early parenting after assisted conception: A systematic review *Human Reproduction* 14:395–415.

Hauck, F. R., S. M. Herman, M. Donovan, C. M. Moore, S. Iyasu, E. Donoghue, R. H. Kirschner, and M. Willinger. 2003. Sleep environment and the risk of sudden infant death syndrome in an urban population: The Chicago Infant Mortality study. *Pediatrics* 111:1207–15.

Hira, N. A. 2007. The baby boomers' kids are marching into the workplace and look out. This crop of twentysomethings really is different. *Fortune Magazine,* May.

Jenni, O. G., H. Z. Fuhrer, I. Iglowstein, L. Molinari, and R. H. Largo. 2005. A longitudinal study of bed sharing and sleep problems among Swiss children in the first ten years of life. *Pediatrics* 115:233–40.

Kim-Cohen, J., T. E. Moffitt, A. Taylor, S. J. Pawlby, and A. Caspi. 2005. Maternal depression and children's antisocial behavior: Nature and nurture effects. *Archives of General Psychiatry* 62:173–82.

Knox, D., and K. Leggett. 2000. *The divorced dad's survival book: How to stay connected with your kids.* Reading, MA: Perseus Books.

Kolko, D. J., L. D. Dorn, O. Bukstein, and J. D. Burke. 2008. Clinically referred ODD children with or without CD and healthy controls: Comparisons across contextual domains. *Journal of Child and Family Studies* 17: 714–34.

Chapter 11 Parenting

Kouros, C. D., C. E. Merrilees, and E. M. Cummings. 2008. Marital conflict and children's emotional security in the context of parental depression. *Journal of Marriage and Family* 70:684–97.

Lee, J. 2008. "A Kotex and a smile": Mothers and daughters at menarche. *Journal of Family Issues* 29:1325–47.

Lengua, L. J., S. A. Wolchik, I. N. Sandler, and S. G. West. 2000. The additive and interactive effects of parenting and temperament in predicting problems of children of divorce. *Journal of Clinical Child Psychology* 29:232–44.

Louv, R. 2006. *Last child in the woods*. Chapel Hill: Algonquin Books.

Mayall, B. 2002. *Toward a sociology of childhood*. Philadelphia, PA: Open University Press.

McBride, B. A., S. J. Schoppe, and T. R. Rane. 2002. Child characteristics, parenting stress, and parental involvement: Fathers versus mothers. *Journal of Marriage and Family* 64:998–1011.

McKinney, C., and K. Renk 2008. Differential parenting between mothers and fathers: Implications for late adolescents. *Journal of Family Issues* 29:806–27.

McLanahan,, S. S. 1991. The long term effects of family dissolution. In *When families fail: The social costs*, ed. Brice J. Christensen, 5–26. New York: University Press of America for the Rockford Institute.

McLanahan, S. S., and K. Booth. 1989. Mother-only families: Problems, prospects, and politics. *Journal of Marriage and the Family* 51:557–80.

Morton, A. 2003. *Madonna*. New York: St. Martin's Press.

Paintal, S. 2007. Banning corporal punishment of children. *Childhood Education* 83:410–21.

Pew Research Center. 2007. Motherhood today: Tougher challenges, less success. May 2. http://pewresearch.org/pubs/468/motherhood.

Pinheiro, R. T., R. A. da Silva, P. V. S. Magalhaes, B. L. Hortam and K. A. T. Pinheiro. 2008. Two studies on suicidality in the postpartum. *Acta Psychiatrica Scandinavica* 118:160–62.

Pinquart, M., and R. K. Silbereisen. 2002. Changes in adolescents' and mothers' autonomy and connectedness in conflict discussions: An observation study. *Journal of Adolescence* 25:509–22.

Pong, S. L., and B. Dong. 2000. The effects of change in family structure and income on dropping of out of middle and high school. *Journal of Family Issues* 21:147–69.

Rapoport, B., and C. Le Bourdais. 2008. Parental time and working schedules. *Journal of Population Economics* 21:903–33.

Sammons, L. 2008. Personal communication, Grand Junction, Colorado.

Schoppe-Sullivan, S. J., G. L. Brown, E. A. Cannon, S. C. Mangelsdorf, and M. S. Sokolowski. 2008. Maternal gatekeeping, coparenting quality, and fathering behavior in families with infants. *Journal of Family Psychology* 22:389–97.

Sears, W., and M. Sears. 1993. *The baby book*. Boston: Little, Brown.

Shellenbarger, S. 2006. Helicopter parents go to work: Moms and dads are now hovering at the office. *The Wall Street Journal*, March 16, D1.

Shields, B. 2005. *Down came the rain: My journey through postpartum depression*. New York: Hyperion.

Soltz, V., and R. Dreikurs. 1991. *Children: The challenge*. New York: Penguin.

Stanley, S. M., and H. J. Markman. 1992. Assessing commitment in personal relationships. *Journal of Marriage and the Family* 54:595–608.

Statistical Abstract of the United States, 2009. 128th ed. Washington, DC: U.S. Bureau of the Census.

Sugarman, S. D. 2003. Single-parent families. In *All our families: New policies for a new century*, 2nd ed., ed. M. A. Mason, A. Skolnick, and S. D. Sugarman, 14–39. New York: Oxford University Press.

Suitor, J. J., and K. Pillemer. 2007. Mothers' favoritism in later life: The role of children's birth order. *Research on Aging* 29:32–42.

Sulloway, F. J. 1996. *Born to rebel: Birth order, family dynamics, and creative lives*. New York: Vintage Books.

Sulloway, F. J. 2007. Birth order and intelligence. *Age and Intelligence* 316:1711–21.

Talwar, V., and K. Lee. 2008. Social and cognitive correlates of children's lying behavior. *Child Development* 79:866–81.

Thomas, P. A., E. M. Krampe, and R. R. Newton. 2008. Father presence, family structure, and feelings of closeness to the father among adult African American children. *Journal of Black Studies* 38:529–41.

Thomas, S. G. 2007. *Buy, buy baby: How consumer culture manipulates parents and harms young minds*. Houghton Mifflin Publisher.

Tucker, C. J., S. M. McHale, and A. C. Crouter. 2003. Dimensions of mothers' and fathers' differential treatment of siblings: Links with adolescents' sex-typed personal qualities. *Family Relations* 52:82–89.

Twenge, J. M., W. K. Campbell, and C. A. Foster. 2003. Parenthood and marital satisfaction: A meta-analytic review. *Journal of Marriage and Family* 65:574–83.

Usher-Seriki, K. K., M. S. Bynum, and T. A. Callands. 2008. Mother–daughter communication about sex and sexual intercourse among middle- to upper-class African American girls. *Journal of Family Issues* 29:901–17.

Ward, R. A., and G. D. Spitze. 2007. Nestleaving and coresidence by young adult children: The role of family relations. *Research on Aging* 29:257–71.

Webb, F. J. 2005. The new demographics of families. In *Sourcebook of family theory & research*, ed. Vern L. Bengtson, Alan C. Acock, Katherine R. Allen, Peggye Dilworth-Anderson, and David M. Klein, 101–02. Thousand Oaks, California: Sage Publications.

Wyckoff, S. C., K. S. Miller, R. Forehand, J. J. Bau, A. Fasula1, N. Long, and L. Armistead. 2008. Patterns of sexuality communication between preadolescents and their mothers and fathers. *Journal of Child and Family Studies* 17:649–53.

chapter 12

The economy will get worse before it gets better.

Barack Obama

Family and the Economy

Authors

Contents

True or False?

1. Undergraduates in love are more likely to be in debt than those who are not in love.

2. The more a couple go into debt, the less happy they are.

3. Abundant research confirms that day care is bad for children and at least one parent should stay home with the children.

4. A woman who is unhappy in her marriage and takes a good-paying job is vulnerable to divorcing her husband.

5. The United States is one of the leading countries in providing paid leave for having children and for child care.

Answers: **1.** T **2.** T **3.** F **4.** T **5.** F

A burning issue in the lives of individuals, couples, and families is the U.S. economy. A deep recession in 2009 was reflected in job layoffs, housing foreclosures, and people fearful of their economic future. This chapter focuses on how the economy affects the health and well-being of spouses, parents, and children. We also discuss the effect of work on marriage and family life. Because debt is where most people feel stress, we begin there.

> *Money is a reality, a needed currency for every person every day of an adult life, but it is also a metaphorical currency for power, control, acknowledgment, self-worth, competence, caring, security, commitment, and feeling loved and accepted.*
>
> Margaret Shapiro, family therapist

Debt

Soaring gas prices, home foreclosures, job loss, inflation, and health care costs result in families unable to pay their bills and accumulating more debt (Zibel 2008). Dew (2008) analyzed data on 1,078 couples and found that couples in debt spend less time together and argue more over money, both of which are associated with decreases in marital satisfaction. Boushey and Weller (2008) confirmed that debt and distress are associated. Similarly, Bryant et al. (2008) studied 962 African Americans and 560 black Caribbean individuals and found that debt in both groups depressed levels of marital satisfaction (African Americans more than black Caribbean individuals).

What if You and Your Partner Feel Differently about Being in Debt?

WHAT IF?

Some individuals have always been in debt, regard it as a fixture in life, and have no anxiety about it. Others have never been in debt, view it as something to avoid, and can't sleep at night when they are in significant debt. These different philosophies may create havoc. Resolution of this dilemma usually comes through deferring to the preferences of the partner with the most anxiety. For example, the partner who can't sleep if in debt will be in greater distress and will create more stress in the relationship than the partner who can tolerate a great deal of debt. So, the least negative consequences for the couple are in favor of having minimal debt.

Money Honey: Credit Card Debt among Undergraduates

University students are not immune to being in debt. This study focused on the degree to which a sample of college students reported having credit card debt of more than a $1,000 and a profile of these undergraduates.

Sample and Findings

The data for this study were taken from a nonrandom sample of 994 undergraduates at a large southeastern university. Of these respondents, 11 percent checked "yes" to the statement, "I owe over $1,000 on one or more credit cards" in contrast to 89 percent who checked "no." Although the study showed no significant differences between women and men having such debt, three significant differences did emerge.

1. *Black individuals had more debt.* Almost a quarter (23 percent) of black individuals compared to 8 percent of the white individuals reported being over $1,000 in debt ($p < .001$). This finding is consistent with research on racial minorities and credit card debt. Black individuals tend to carry higher debt loads than white individuals, even though they have traditionally had difficulty obtaining credit cards (Grable and Joo 2006).

2. *Older undergraduates have more debt.* Almost a quarter (22.5 percent) of the undergraduates aged 20 and over compared to less than 4 percent (3.35 percent) of those younger than 19 reported having over $1,000 in debt ($p < .001$). Students' rank in college was found as a significant difference in the amount of credit card debt. In exact order, 49.2 percent of seniors, 14.8 percent of juniors, 12.5 percent of sophomores, and 3.8 percent of freshmen undergraduates reported having over $1,000 in credit card debt. Older undergraduates were less dependent on their parents for money and drifted into debt quickly when parental economic support was withdrawn. Credit card debt is even higher for graduate students. Research indicates that graduate students average seven credit cards and debt of over $5,000 (Baum and Saunders 1998). In general, the older the student, the greater the debt.

3. *Individuals in love had more debt.* Undergraduates who were emotionally involved with someone were twice as likely to report having credit card debt of over $1,000 than students who were not dating or involved with anyone (14 percent versus 7 percent; $p < .001$). Emotionally involved undergraduates tended to have greater debt because they were potentially older and had been in college longer (for example, away from parental support and supervision). Another reason is that those in relationships may spend more on each other and some of these expenditures are put on credit cards. Folklore about money in courtship suggests that either you are trying to impress your "sweetheart" or your "sweetheart" is draining your pockets.

Theoretical Perspective

College students use credit cards as a way to show others who they are and how they should be treated.

Before borrowing money from a friend, decide which you need more.

Addison Hallock, author

Income Distribution and Poverty

During the presidential debates, both candidates were asked, "What is your definition of rich?" Obama responded, "I would argue that if you are making more than $250,000, then you are in the top 3, 4 percent of this country. You are doing well." McCain responded, "I think if you're just talking about income, how about $5 million?" What are the facts? Families vary in the amount of income they have. Table 12.1 shows the percentage of families in the United States at various income levels.

Table 12.1 Distribution of Income Level in U.S. Families	
Income Level of Family	**Percentage at This Level**
Less than $15,000	8.4
$15,000–$24,999	9.2
$25,000–$34,999	10.5
$35,000–$49,999	14.5
$50,000–$74,999	19.8
$75,000–$99,999	13.5
$100,000 or more	24.2

Median family income = $52,680.
Source: *Statistical Abstract of the United States, 2009*, 128th ed. Washington, DC: U.S. Bureau of the Census, Table 673.

Credit cards are used as a way to enhance one's self-image by demonstrating class position. College students go into debt not only to pay their necessary bills, but also to buy things that they do not need. Individuals want to make themselves look better and look like they have money although the reality may be the opposite. Using Goffman's (1959) theoretical framework of dramaturgy, social life is a dramatic performance for the maintenance of the self in everyday life while in conflict with the existing social structure.

Dramatic realization of performance presupposes a notion of the "front," which translates into behaviors and attitudes that allow performers to create a desired self-image of how they want others to view them. The front stage defines the situation for those who observe the performance. In the "back stage" of the performance, individuals evaluate their public beliefs and decide if their impression of reality is true. In back stage, individuals can be themselves while at the same time exhibit a performance that might knowingly contradict the impressions they publicly present. For instance, college students may dress in expensive, name-brand clothing, but be thousands of dollars in credit card debt. They may make spending look effortless by lying about the cost of their purchases and how much debt they are truly in. The use of credit cards to boost self image is fueled and perpetuated by consumer culture.

Implications

In addition to university officials being concerned about the physical health and academic performance of their undergraduates, they should give attention to their financial well-being. Particularly noteworthy in these findings is that credit card debt tends to mount as students age, giving the university time to sensitize first-year undergraduates to be alert to credit card company enticements and to become discriminate in their purchases. Haynes and Chinadle (2007) noted that training programs for educators are already underway to educate youth on economic issues. Financial education programs have already been set up for university employees (Kim 2007) and need to be adapted for undergraduates. Because black students were almost three times as likely to report credit card debt of over $1,000, a concerted effort might be made to target this population for increasing their skills in dealing with credit card company advertisements, use of money, and so on.

Sources

Baum, S., and D. Saunders. 1998. Life after debt: Results of the National Student Loan Survey. In *Student loan debt: Problems and prospects*. Washington, DC: Institute for Higher Education Policy.

Goffman, E. 1959. *Presentation of the self in everyday life*. Garden City, NJ: Anchor.

Grable, J. E., and S. Joo. 2006. Student differences in credit card debt and financial behaviors and stress. *College Student Journal* 40:400–08.

Haynes, D. C., and N. Chinadle. 2007. Private sector/educator collaboration: Project improves financial, economic literacy of America's youth. *Journal of Family and Consumer Sciences* 99:8–11.

Kim, J. 2007. Workplace Financial Education Program: Does it have an impact on employees' personal finances? *Journal of Family and Consumer Sciences* 99:43–48.

* Abridged from C. Ross, D. Knox, and M. Zusman. 2008. Money Honey: Credit Card Debt among Undergraduates Poster, Southern Sociological Society Annual Meeting, April, 2008. Richmond, VA.

What is the definition of poverty in terms of actual dollars in the United States? Table 12.2 reflects the Department of Health and Human Services' various poverty level guidelines by size of family and where the family lives. A significant proportion of families in the United States continue to be characterized by unemployment and low wages.

You can't have everything. Where would you put it?

Steven Wright, comedian

Table 12.2 2009 HHS Poverty Guidelines			
People in Family or Household	**48 Contiguous States and D.C.**	**Alaska**	**Hawaii**
1	$10,830	$13,530	$12,460
2	14,570	18,210	16,760
3	18,310	22,890	21,060
4	22,050	27,570	25,360
5	25,790	32,250	29,660
6	29,530	36,930	33,960
7	33,270	41,610	38,260
8	37,010	46,290	42,560
For each additional person, add	3,740	4,680	4,300

Source: *Federal Register*, vol. 74, no. 14, pp. 4199–4201. January 23, 2009. http://aspe.hhs.gov/poverty/09poverty.shtml.

Poverty is no shame, but being ashamed of it is.

Benjamin Franklin, statesman

Poverty has traditionally been defined as the lack of resources necessary for material well-being—most importantly food and water, but also housing, land, and health care. This lack of resources that leads to hunger and physical deprivation is known as **absolute poverty.** In contrast, **relative poverty** refers to a deficiency in material and economic resources compared with some other group of people. Although many lower-income Americans, for example, have resources and a level of material well-being that millions of people living in absolute poverty can only dream of (for example, those in third world countries), they are relatively poor compared with the American middle and upper classes.

One of the factors driving Americans into poverty is the cost of medical care. Indeed, the primary cause of bankruptcy is the inability to pay hospital bills. Compounding the problem is the inability to afford health care insurance.

National Data

According to the U.S. Census Bureau's Current Population Survey (CPS), there were 47 million uninsured individuals in 2006, or 15.3 percent of the civilian noninstitutionalized population (U.S. Department of Health and Human Services 2008).

How much it costs to live varies by the country one lives in. In rural Mexico, the costs of food and housing are substantially below the costs in rural America. For example, lunch in the former may cost less than a dollar whereas lunch in the latter would more likely be three or four times as much. Similarly, due to the low value of the dollar in Europe, a hamburger in America may be $1.50 but could be $8.00 in Paris.

International Data

The World Bank sets a "poverty threshold" of $1 per day to compare poverty in most of the developing world, $2 per day in Latin America, $4 per day in Eastern Europe and the Commonwealth of Independent States (CIS), and $14.40 per day in industrial countries (which corresponds to the income poverty line in the United States). Another poverty measure is based on whether individuals are experiencing hunger, which is defined as consuming less than 1,960 calories a day.

Effects of Poverty on Marriages and Families

Poverty is devastating to couples and families. Those living in poverty have poorer physical and mental health, report lower personal and marital satisfaction, and die sooner. The anxiety over lack of money may result in relationship conflict. Money is the most common problem that couples report. Stanley and Einhorn (2007) suggested that the reason money is such a profound issue in marriage is its symbolic significance (for example, power and control) as well as the fact that individuals do something daily in reference to money—spend, save, or worry about it. The potential for conflict is endless. One couple in marriage therapy reported that they argued over whether to buy a new air conditioner for their car. The husband thought it necessary; the wife thought they could roll down the windows.

The stresses associated with low income also contribute to substance abuse, domestic violence, child abuse and neglect, divorce, and questionable parenting practices. For example, economic stress is associated

Diversity in Other Countries

Globally, 2.5 billion people—more than one-fourth of the world's population—live on less than $2 a day, and about 1 billion people—1 in 6 people on this planet—live on less than $1 a day (World Bank 2007). Every day, nearly one in five (18 percent) of the world's population goes hungry.

with greater marital discord, and couples with incomes less than $25,000 are 30 percent more likely to divorce than couples with incomes greater than $50,000 (Whitehead and Popenoe 2004). Child neglect is more likely to be found with poor parents who are unable to afford child care or medical expenses and leave children at home without adult supervision or fail to provide needed medical care. Poor parents are more likely than other parents to use harsh physical disciplinary techniques, and they are less likely to be nurturing and supportive of their children.

Another family problem associated with poverty is teenage pregnancy. Poor adolescent girls are more likely to have babies as teenagers or to become young single mothers. Early childbearing is associated with numerous problems, such as increased risk of having premature babies or babies of low birth weight, dropping out of school, and earning less money as a result of lack of academic achievement.

I wanted the gold, and I got it—
Came out with a fortune last fall,
Yet somehow life's not what
I thought it,
And somehow the gold isn't all.
Robert W. Service, Southern poet

Global Inequality

Global economic inequality has reached unprecedented levels. The most comprehensive study on the world distribution of household wealth offers the following facts on wealth inequality worldwide:

• The richest 1 percent of adults in the world own 40 percent of global household wealth; the richest 2 percent of adults own more than half of global wealth; and the richest 10 percent of adults own 85 percent of total global wealth.

• The poorest half of the world's adult population owns barely 1 percent of global wealth.

• Households with assets of $2,200 per adult are in the top half of the world wealth distribution; assets of $61,000 per adult places a household in the top 10 percent, and assets of more than $500,000 per adult places a household in the richest 1 percent worldwide.

• Although North America has only 6 percent of the world's adult population, it accounts for one-third (34 percent) of all household wealth worldwide. More than one-third (37 percent) of the richest 1 percent of individuals in the world resides in the United States.

• The degree of wealth inequality in the world is as if one person in a group of ten takes 99 percent of the total pie and the other nine people in the group share the remaining 1 percent. (Davies et al. 2006)

Being Wise about Credit

One way to keep from slipping deeper into debt or poverty is to use credit wisely. The "free" credit cards that college students receive in the mail are Trojan horses and can plunge them into massive debt from which recovering will take years.

You use credit when you take an item from the store today and pay for it later. The amount you pay later will depend on the arrangement you make with the seller. Suppose you want to buy a flat-panel 42-inch high-definition television that sells for $2,000. Unless you pay cash, the seller will set up one of three types of credit accounts with you: installment, revolving charge, or open charge.

Under the **installment plan,** you sign a contract to pay for the item in monthly installments. You and the seller negotiate the period of time over which the payments will be spread and the amount you will pay each month. The seller adds a finance charge to the cash price of the television set and remains the legal owner of the set until you have made your last payment. Most department stores, appliance and furniture stores, and automobile dealers offer installment credit.

Table 12.3 Calculating the Cost of Installment Credit

Amount to be financed		Cash price	$2,000
		Amount to be financed	$2,000
Amount to be paid		Monthly payments	$ 75
		X number of payments	29
Total amount to be repaid			$2,175

The total cost of buying the $2,000 high-definition TV will actually be $2,175 as shown in Table 12.3.

Instead of buying the flat-panel $2,000 high-definition television set on the installment plan, you might want to buy it on the **revolving charge** plan. Most credit cards, such as Visa and MasterCard, represent revolving charge accounts that permit you to buy on credit up to a stated amount during each month. At the end of the month, you may pay the total amount you owe, any amount over the stated minimum payment due, or the minimum payment. If you choose to pay less than the full amount, the cost of the credit on the unpaid amount is approximately 1.5 percent per month, or 18 percent per year. Avoid these finance charges by paying off the credit card monthly. You can also purchase items on an **open charge** (thirty-day) account. Under this system, you agree to pay in full within thirty days. Because this type of account has no direct service charge or interest, the television set would cost only the purchase price. For example, Sears and JCPenney offer open charge accounts. If you do not pay the full amount in thirty days, a finance charge is placed on the remaining balance. The use of both revolving charge and open charge accounts is wise if you pay off the bill before finance charges begin. In deciding which type of credit account to use, remember that credit usually costs money; the longer you take to pay for an item, the more the item will cost you.

Credit Rating and Identity Theft

When you apply for a loan, the lender will seek a credit report from credit bureaus such as Equifax, TransUnion, and Experian. In effect, you will have a "credit score"—also referred to as a NextGen score or a FICO (Fair Isaac Company) score—calculated as follows:

35 percent based on late payments, bankruptcies, judgments

30 percent based on current debts

15 percent based on how long accounts have been opened and established

10 percent based on type of credit (credit cards, loan for house or car)

10 percent based on applications for new credit or inquiries

As these percentages indicate, the way to improve your credit is to make payments on time and reduce your current debt. Your score will range from 620 to 850 (a score of excellent is 750 to 850; a score of 660 to 749 is good; a score of 620 to 659 is fair; a score of 400 to 619 is poor). The higher your score, the lower your rate of interest. For example, on a $150,000 thirty-year fixed-rate mortgage, a score above 760 would result in a 5.5 percent interest rate with a monthly payment of $852. In contrast, a score of 639 and below would result in an interest rate of 7.09 percent, with a monthly payment of $1,007 (see http://www.myfico.com/ or type in "credit report" on www.google.com). Taking all credit cards to the limit can lead to financial trouble and eventual bankruptcy.

When someone poses as you and uses your credit history to buy goods and services, that person has stolen your identity. More than 10 million Americans are victims of **identity theft,** which can destroy your credit, plunge you into debt, and keep you awake at night with lawsuits from creditors. Identity theft happens when someone gets access to personal information such as your Social Security number, credit card number, or bank account number and goes online to pose as you to buy items or services. Identity theft is the number one fraud complaint in the United States.

Safeguards include (1) never giving such information over the phone or online unless you initiate the contact, and (2) shredding bank and credit card statements and preapproved credit card offers. (A shredder can cost as little as $20.) Also, avoid paying your bills by putting an envelope in your mailbox with the flag up—use a locked box or the post office. Finally, check your credit reports, scrutinize your bank statements, and guard your personal identification number (PIN) at automatic teller machines (ATMs). If you use the Internet, protect your safety by installing firewall software.

They were always a[...]
money.

Albert Goldman, speak[...]
relationship with Pricill[...]

Discussing Debt and Money: Do It Now

Shapiro (2007) noted that sex, religion, and money are sensitive issues in polite society and that couples may shy away from discussing such details. Indeed, once partners define themselves in a serious relationship, Shapiro (a marriage and family therapist) recommended that they talk about how they feel about running up debt on their credit card, late charges, or how much they are bothered by debt. The issue becomes relevant because the debt of one partner may become the debt of the other if the relationship continues. If John thinks nothing of charging a high-definition TV on his third credit card (because the other two have been maxed out), Mary might legitimately be concerned. The following are other issues that couples might discuss:

• At the time of engagement, what do the partners feel about a ring? Should one be bought? How much should be spent on it? And what is the symbolic meaning of the "size of the ring"—does a smaller, less expensive ring mean less love and less commitment?

• When the couple has their first child, will the wife stop working? What is the implication in terms of her access to money? Does she have to ask for money, or is "his" money deposited in an account so that both have access?

• As children get older, what are the respective feelings of the spouses in regard to sending their children to college versus letting them take out student loans? What about sending money to one's parents who may need financial help with health care bills (including a nursing home for one or both sets of parents)?

• As retirement comes, does the couple save their money or travel around the world?

At each stage of the family life cycle, financial decisions can cause very deep-seated feelings about money to surface. Couples might also discuss the importance of education and its association with higher income. The "more you learn, the more you earn" slogan is true. Table 12.4 shows the increased income associated with increased education.

Table 12.4	Women's and Men's Median Income with Similar Education		
	Bachelor's	**Master's**	**Doctoral Degree**
Men	$54,403	$67,425	$90,511
Women	$35,094	$46,250	$61,091

Source: *Statistical Abstract of the United States, 2009,* 128th ed. Washington, DC: U.S. Bureau of the Census, Table 680.

Work and Marriage: Effects on Spouses

A couple's marriage is organized around the work of each. Where the couple lives is determined by where the spouses can get jobs. Jobs influence what time spouses eat, which family members eat with whom, when they go to bed, and when, where, and for how long they vacation. In this section, we examine some of the various influences of work on a couple's relationship. We begin by looking at how the income that results from work impacts the power distribution in the relationship.

Money as Power in a Couple's Relationship

Money is a central issue in relationships because of its association with power, control, and dominance. Generally, the more money a partner makes, the more power that person has in the relationship. Males make considerably more money than females and generally have more power in relationships. However, Morin and Cohn (2008) reported on a national sample and found that, although two-thirds of all husbands in dual-income families say they make more money than their wives, women are still more likely to make the decisions in more areas (42 percent versus 30 percent).

National Data

The average annual income of a male with some college who is working full-time is $48,431 compared with $35,916 for a female with the same education, also working full-time, year-round (*Statistical Abstract of the United States, 2009,* Table 681).

When a wife earns an income, her power increases in the relationship. We know of a married couple in which the wife recently began to earn an income. Before doing so, her husband's fishing boat was in the protected carport. With her new job and increased power in the relationship, she began to park her car in the carport and her husband put the fishing boat underneath the pine trees

This dual-earner married couple has their dog grooming business attached to their home.

to the side of the house. Money also provides an employed woman the power to be independent and to leave an unhappy marriage. Indeed, the higher a wife's income, the more likely she is to leave an unhappy relationship (Schoen et al. 2002). Similarly, because adults are generally the only source of money in a family, they have considerable power over children, who have no money.

To some individuals, money also means love. While admiring the engagement ring of her friend, a woman said, "What a big diamond! He must really love you." A cultural assumption is that a big diamond equals an expensive diamond and a lot of sacrifice and love. Similar assumptions are often made when gifts are given or received. People tend to spend more money on presents for the people they love, believing that the value of the gift symbolizes the depth of their love. People receiving gifts may make the same assumption. "She must love me more than I thought," mused one man. "I gave her a Blu-Ray movie for Christmas, but she gave me a Blu-Ray player. I felt embarrassed."

Success is a terrible attack on your sense of values. You get teed off because the heater of your swimming pool doesn't work.

Rod Serling, *The Twilight Zone*

PERSONAL CHOICES

Work or Relationships?

People who consistently choose their work over their relationships either have partners who have also made such choices or partners who are disenchanted. Traditionally, men have chosen their work over relationships; women have chosen their relationships over work. Most choose to balance the two to afford a lifestyle they enjoy. Professions or careers that inherently provide the opportunity for balance include elementary school teaching, where one is home by 4:00 with a couple of months off in the summer. The role of college or university teacher is even better, with greater flexibility during the day, week, and year.

Alternatively, a **momprenuer** is a woman who has a successful at-home business. She conducts her business from home, which provides her with maximum flexibility for her family. Barbie Tew is an example of a momprenuer who operates a successful "passion party" business out of her home (http://barbiespassion.com).

Some individuals require very little income and have no interest in material wealth. We have a friend who has little to no regard for material wealth. He has been homeless and now runs a homeless shelter where he daily feeds two meals a day to over 100 individuals. At night, he goes back to his $200 a month loft where he reads and paints until the next day when he feeds the homeless though private funding and donations. We asked him how his lack of concern for money affects the interest women have in establishing a long-term relationship with him. "It kills it," he noted. "They simply have no interest in being pair-bonded to someone living this vagabond existence."

Working Wives

Driven primarily by the need to provide income for the family, 69 percent of all U.S. wives are in the labor force. Most have children. The time wives are most likely to be in the labor force is when their children are teenagers (between the ages of 14 and 17), the time when food and clothing expenses are the highest (*Statistical Abstract of the United States, 2009*, Tables 578 and 579). The stereotypical family consisting of a husband who earns the income and a wife who stays at home with two or more children is no longer the norm. Only 13 percent are "traditional" in the sense of a breadwinning husband, a stay-at-home wife, and their children (Stone 2007). In contrast, most marriages may be characterized by a dual-earner couple (Amato et al. 2007).

Because women still take on more child care and household responsibilities than men, women in dual-earner marriages (marriages in which both spouses provide significant income to the family unit) are more likely than men to want to be employed part-time rather than full-time. If this is not possible, many women prefer to work only a portion of the year (the teaching profession allows employees to work about ten months and to have two months in the summer free). Although many low-wage earners need two incomes to afford basic housing and a minimal standard of living, others have two incomes to afford expensive homes, cars, vacations, and educational opportunities for their children. Whether it makes economic sense is another issue.

Some parents wonder if the money a wife earns by working outside the home is worth the sacrifices to earn it. Not only is the mother away from their children but she must also pay for strangers to care for their children. Sefton (1998) calculated that the value of a stay-at-home mother is $36,000 per year in terms of what a dual-income family spends to pay for all services that she provides (domestic cleaning, laundry, meal planning and preparation, shopping, providing transportation to activities, taking the children to the doctor, and running errands). Adjusting for changes in the consumer price index, this figure was $47,982 in 2009. A value of a househusband would be the same. However, because males typically earn higher incomes than females, the loss of income would be greater than for a female.

This estimated figure suggests that working outside the home may not be as economically advantageous as one might think—that women may work outside the home for psychological (enhanced self-concept) and social (enlarged social network) benefits. Some may also enjoy a lifestyle that is made possible by earning a significant income by outside employment. One wife noted that the only way she could afford the home she wanted was to help earn the money to pay for it.

The **mommy track** (stopping paid employment to spend time with young children) is another potential cost to those women who want to build a career. Taking time out to rear children in their formative years can derail a career. Noonan and Corcoran (2004) found that lawyers who took time out for child responsibilities were less likely to make partner and more likely to earn less money if they did make partner. Aware that executive women have found it difficult to reenter the workforce after being on the mommy track, the Harvard Business School created an executive training program for mothers to improve their technical skills and to help them return to the workforce (Rosen 2006).

Wives Who "Opt Out"

Pamela Stone (2007) published *Opting Out*, which revealed content from fifty-four interviews with women representing a broad spectrum of professions—doctors, lawyers, scientists, bankers, management consultants, editors, and teachers. **Opting out** involved women leaving their careers and returning home to take care of their children for a variety of reasons. However, two reasons stand out: (1) husbands who were unavailable or unable to "shoulder significant portions of caregiving and family responsibilities" (p. 68); and (2) employers who had a lot of policies on the books to encourage and support women parental leave "but not much in the way of making it possible for them to return or stay once they had babies" (p. 119). Part-time work didn't work out for these women because the work was not really "part-time"—the employer kept wanting more.

Keller (2008b) revealed a similar story, that career women who left work for the home found a lower salary and a demotion, and were sidelined on their return. They were, indeed, punished at work for prioritizing family. Nevertheless, women who are flexible, creative, and determined can find work that meets their needs and can be a good fit for their employer.

Michelle Obama has a law degree from Harvard. The First Lady has made it clear that the lives of her children are her priority.

Types of Dual-Career Marriages

A **dual-career marriage** is defined as one in which both spouses pursue careers and maintain a life together that may or may not include dependents. A career is different from a job in that the former usually involves advanced education or training, full-time commitment, working nights and weekends "off the clock," and a willingness to relocate. Dual-career couples operate without a person who stays home to manage the home and care for dependents.

Nevertheless, four types of dual-career marriages are those in which the husband's career takes precedence (**HIS/her**), the wife's career takes precedence (**HER/his**), both careers are regarded equally (**HIS/HER**), or both spouses share a career or work together (**THEIR career**).

When couples hold traditional gender role attitudes, the husband's career is likely to take precedence (HIS/her career). This situation translates into the wife being willing to relocate and to disrupt her career for the advancement of her husband's career. In this arrangement, the wife may also have children early, which has an effect on the development of her career. Gordon and Whelan-Berry (2005) interviewed thirty-six professional women and found that, in 22 percent of the marriages, the husband's career took precedence. The primary reasons for this arrangement were that the husband earned a higher salary, going where the husband could earn the highest income was easier because the wife could more easily find a job wherever he went (than vice versa), and ego needs (the husband needed to have the dominant career). This arrangement is sometimes at the expense of the wife's career. Mason and Goulden (2004) studied women in academia and found that those who had a child within five years of earning their PhDs were less likely to achieve tenure.

For couples who do not have traditional gender role attitudes, the wife's career may take precedence (HER/his career). Of the marriages in the Gordon and Whelan-Berry study (2005) mentioned previously, 19 percent could be categorized as giving precedence to a wife's career. In such marriages, the husband is willing to relocate and to disrupt his career for his wife's. Such a pattern is also likely to occur when a wife earns considerably more money than her husband. In some cases, the husband who is downsized or who prefers the role of full-time parent becomes "Mr. Mom." Over 100,000 husbands (and parents of at least one child under the age of 6) are married to wives who work full-time in the labor

Oh, you hate your job? Why didn't you say so? There's a support group for that. It's called EVERYBODY, and they meet at the bar.

Drew Carey, actor and comedian

This couple owned and operated a health food store for twenty years. They are now "retired" and run a bed-and-breakfast on Prince Edward Island together.

Authors

force (Tucker 2005). The incidence of Mr. Moms has increased almost 30 percent in the past ten years (Society for the Advancement of Education 2005); almost 80 percent of men in Europe report that they would be happy to stay at home with the kids (Pepper 2006). A major advantage of men assuming this role is a more lasting emotional bond with their children (Tucker 2005).

When the careers of both the wife and husband are given equal status in the relationship (HIS/HER career), they may have a commuter marriage in which they follow their respective careers wherever they lead. Alternatively, Deutsch et al. (2007) surveyed 236 undergraduate senior women to assess their views on husbands, managing children, and work. Most envisioned two egalitarian scenarios in which both spouses would cut back on their careers and/or both would arrange their schedules to devote time to child care. Still other couples may hire domestic child care help so that neither spouse functions in the role of housekeeper. In reality, equal status to HIS and HER careers is not a dominant pattern (Stone 2007).

Finally, some couples have the same career and may work together (THEIR career). Some news organizations hire both spouses to travel abroad to cover the same story. These careers are rare. In the following sections, we look at the effects on women, men, their marriage, and their children when a wife is employed outside the home.

Effects of the Wife's Employment on the Wife

Whether a wife is satisfied with her job is related to the degree to which the job takes a toll on her family life. Grandey et al. (2005) found that, when the wife's employment interfered with her family life, the wife reported less job satisfaction. Such a relationship with husbands was not found—jobs that interfered with family life did not result in decreased job satisfaction for men. Consistent with this finding, Kiecolt (2003) noted that most women with young children much prefer to be at home and view home, not work, as their primary haven of satisfaction.

Indeed, family and work become spheres to manage, and sometimes women experience **role overload**—not having the time or energy to meet the demands of their responsibilities in the roles of wife, parent, and worker. Because women have traditionally been responsible for most of the housework and child care, employed women come home from work to what Hochschild (1989) calls the second shift: the housework and child care that employed women do when they return home from their jobs. According to Hochschild, the **second shift** has the following result:

> . . . women tend to talk more intently about being overtired, sick, and "emotionally drained." Many women could not tear away from the topic of sleep. They talked about how much they could "get by on" . . . six and a half, seven, seven and a half, less, more. . . . Some apologized for how much sleep they needed. . . . They talked about how to avoid fully waking up when a child called them at night, and how to get back to sleep. These women talked about sleep the way a hungry person talks about food. (p. 9)

Another stressful aspect of employment for employed mothers in dual-earner marriages is role conflict—being confronted with incompatible role obligations. For example, the role of an employed mother is to stay late and prepare a report for the following day. However, the role of a mother is to pick up her child from day care at 5 P.M. When these roles collide, there is role conflict. Although most women resolve their role conflicts by giving preference to the mother role, some give priority to the career role and feel guilty about it. Mary Tyler Moore wrote in her biography that she spent more time with her TV son than her real son.

Role strain, the anxiety that results from being able to fulfill only a limited number of role obligations, occurs for both women and men in dual-earner marriages. No one is at home to take care of housework and children while they are working, and they feel strained at not being able to do everything.

Effects of the Wife's Employment on Her Husband

Husbands also report benefits from their wives' employment. These include being relieved of the sole responsibility for the financial support of the family and having more freedom to quit jobs, change jobs, or go to school.

Because men traditionally had no options but to work full-time, men now benefit by having a spouse with whom to share the daily rewards and stresses of employment. To the degree that women find satisfaction in their work role, men benefit by having a happier partner. Finally, men benefit from a dual-earner marriage by increasing the potential to form a closer bond with their children through active child care. Some prefer the role of househusband and stay-at-home dad. Patrick (2005) confirmed that stay-at-home dads have a stronger emotional bond with their children than traditional working dads. Though such dads are clearly the minority, their visibility is increasing.

Effects of the Wife's Employment on the Marriage

Are marriages in which both spouses earn an income more vulnerable to divorce? Not if the wife is happy; but if she is unhappy, her income will provide her a way to take care of herself when she leaves. Schoen et al. (2002) wrote, "Our results provide clear evidence that, at the individual level, women's employment does not destabilize happy marriages but increases the risk of disruption in unhappy marriages" (p. 643). Hence, employment won't affect a happy marriage but it can do in an unhappy one. Further research by Schoen et al. (2006) revealed that full-time employment of the wife is actually associated with marital stability.

Couples may be particularly vulnerable when a wife earns more money than her husband. Thirty percent of working wives earn more than their husbands (Tyre and McGinn 2003). This situation affects the couple's marital happiness in several ways. Marriages in which the spouses view the provider role as the man's responsibility, in which the husband cannot find employment, and in which the husband is jealous of his wife's employment are vulnerable to dissatisfaction. Cultural norms typically dictate that the man is supposed to earn more money than his partner and that something is wrong with him if he doesn't. Jalovaara

Today's working moms are rediscovering the joys of staying at home.

Stephanie Coontz, family historian

(2003) found that the divorce rate was higher among couples where the wife's income exceeded her husband's. On the other hand, some men want an ambitious, economically independent woman who makes a high income. Over a third of men in a national *Newsweek* poll said that they'd consider quitting their job or reducing their hours if their wife earned more money (Tyre and McGinn 2003).

Do the hours worked in terms of night or weekend make any difference? Yes. Strazdins et al. (2006) compared over 4,000 families where parents worked standard weekday times against those parents who worked nonstandard schedules and found that couples working nonstandard schedules reported worse family functioning, more depressive symptoms, and less effective parenting. Their children were also more likely to have social and emotional difficulties.

Work and Family: Effects on Children

Independent of the effect on the wife, husband, and marriage, what is the effect of the wife earning an income outside of the home on the children? Individuals disagree on the effects of maternal employment on children. The Self-Assessment section on page 405 provides a way to assess your beliefs in this regard.

Effects of the Wife's Employment on the Children

Mothers with young children are the least likely to be in the labor force. Table 12.5 reflects the percentage of employed mothers as related to the age of the child.

National Data

Data from the National Survey of America's Families indicate that most children under the age of 5 whose parents are in the workforce are in a nonparental care arrangement. For white, black, and Hispanic children, the proportions receiving such care are 87 percent, 81 percent, and 80 percent, respectively (Capizzano et al. 2006).

Dual-earner parents want to know how children are affected by maternal employment. An abundance of research has resulted in the finding of few negative effects (Perry-Jenkins et al. 2001). Hence, children do not appear to suffer cognitively or emotionally as long as positive, consistent child care alternatives are in place. Children may even benefit in terms of exercise and leisure activities. Sener et al. (2008) studied leisure activities of children as influenced by the employment patterns of parents and found that children in households with parents who are employed, and with higher income or higher education participate in structured outdoor activities at higher rates.

However, children of two-earner parents also receive less supervision. Leaving children to come home to an empty house is particularly problematic. In addition, in a study of 2,246 adults who had lived with two biological parents

Table 12.5 Percentage of Employed Mothers, by Age of Child

Age of Child, Years	Percentage of Employed Mothers
≤1	54.7
2	61.3
3	63.6
4	64.1
5	66.9
6–13	75.1
14–17	81.2

Maternal Employment Scale

Directions

Using the following scale, please mark a number on the blank next to each statement to indicate how strongly you agree or disagree.

1	2	3	4	5	6
Disagree	Disagree	Disagree	Agree	Agree	Agree
Very	Strongly	Slightly	Slightly	Strongly	Very
Strongly					Strongly

_____ 1. Children are less likely to form a warm and secure relationship with a mother who works full-time outside the home.

_____ 2. Children whose mothers work are more independent and able to do things for themselves.

_____ 3. Working mothers are more likely to have children with psychological problems than mothers who do not work outside the home.

_____ 4. Teenagers get into less trouble with the law if their mothers do not work full-time outside the home.

_____ 5. For young children, working mothers are good role models for leading busy and productive lives.

_____ 6. Boys whose mothers work are more likely to develop respect for women.

_____ 7. Young children learn more if their mothers stay at home with them.

_____ 8. Children whose mothers work learn valuable lessons about other people they can rely on.

_____ 9. Girls whose mothers work full-time outside the home develop stronger motivation to do well in school.

_____ 10. Daughters of working mothers are better prepared to combine work and motherhood if they choose to do both.

_____ 11. Children whose mothers work are more likely to be left alone and exposed to dangerous situations.

_____ 12. Children whose mothers work are more likely to pitch in and do tasks around the house.

_____ 13. Children do better in school if their mothers are not working full-time outside the home.

_____ 14. Children whose mothers work full-time outside the home develop more regard for women's intelligence and competence.

_____ 15. Children of working mothers are less well-nourished and don't eat the way they should.

_____ 16. Children whose mothers work are more likely to understand and appreciate the value of a dollar.

_____ 17. Children whose mothers work suffer because their mothers are not there when they need them.

_____ 18. Children of working mothers grow up to be less competent parents than other children because they have not had adequate parental role models.

_____ 19. Sons of working mothers are better prepared to cooperate with a wife who wants both to work and have children.

_____ 20. Children of mothers who work develop lower self-esteem because they think they are not worth devoting attention to.

_____ 21. Children whose mothers work are more likely to learn the importance of teamwork and cooperation among family members.

_____ 22. Children of working mothers are more likely than other children to experiment with alcohol, other drugs, and sex at an early age.

_____ 23. Children whose mothers work develop less stereotyped views about men's and women's roles.

_____ 24. Children whose mothers work full-time outside the home are more adaptable; they cope better with the unexpected and with changes in plans.

Scoring

Items 1, 3, 4, 7, 11, 13, 15, 17, 18, 20, and 22 refer to "costs" of maternal employment for children and yield a Costs Subscale score. High scores on the Costs Subscale reflect strong beliefs that maternal employment is costly to children. Items 2, 5, 6, 8, 9, 10, 12, 14, 16, 19, 21, 23, and 24 refer to "benefits" of maternal employment for children and yield a Benefits Subscale score. To obtain a Total Score, reverse the score of all items in the Benefits Subscale so that 1 = 6, 2 = 5, 3 = 4, 4 = 3, 5 = 2, and 6 = 1. The higher one's Total Score, the more one believes that maternal employment has negative consequences for children.

Source

E. Greenberger, W. A. Goldberg, T. J. Crawford, and J. Granger. 1988. Beliefs about the consequences of maternal employment for children. _Psychology of Women Quarterly_, Maternal Employment Scale 12:35–59. Used by permission of Blackwell Publishing.

until age 16, those whose mothers had been employed during most of their childhood reported less support and less discipline from both parents than those who had stay-at-home mothers (Nomaaguchi and Milkie 2006).

Self-Care/Latchkey Children Some dual-earner and single-parent families do not have the resources to afford child care while the parents are working. Though relatives and friends may help, children whose mothers work outside the home are vulnerable to being unsupervised by an adult for some time after school. Although these self-care, or latchkey, children often fend for themselves very well, some are at risk. Over 230,000 are between the ages of 5 and 7 and are vulnerable to a lack of care in case of an accident or emergency. Children who must spend time alone at home should know the following:

1. How to reach their parents at work (the phone number, extension number, and name of the person to talk to if the parent is not there)

2. Their home address and phone number in case information must be given to the fire department or an ambulance service

3. How to call emergency services, such as the police and fire departments

4. The name and number of a relative or neighbor to call if the parent is unavailable

5. To keep the door locked and not let anyone in

6. How to avoid telling callers their parents are not at home; instead, they should tell them their parents are busy or can't come to the phone

7. How to avoid playing with appliances, matches, or the fireplace

Parents should also consider the relationship of the children they leave alone. If the older one terrorizes the younger one, the children should not be left alone. Also, if the younger one is out of control, it is inadvisable to put the older one in the role of being responsible for the child. If something goes wrong (such as a serious accident), the older child may be unnecessarily burdened with guilt.

Quality Time

Dual-income parents struggle with having "quality time" with their children. The term *quality time* has become synonymous with good parenting. Snyder (2007) studied 220 parents from 110 dual-parent families and found that "quality time" is defined in different ways. Some parents (structured-planning parents) saw quality time as planning and executing family activities. Mormons set aside "Monday home evenings" as a time to bond, pray, and sing together (thus, quality time). Other parents (child-centered parents) noted that "quality time" occurred when they were having heart-to-heart talks with their children. Still other parents believed that all the time they were with their children was quality time. Whether they were having dinner together or riding to the post office, quality time was occurring if they were together. As might be expected, mothers assumed greater responsibity for "quality time."

Day-Care Considerations

Parents going into or returning to the workforce are intent on finding high-quality day care. Rose and Elicker (2008) surveyed the various characteristics of day care that are important to 355 employed mothers of children under 6 years of age and found that warmth of caregivers, a play-based curriculum, and educational level of caregivers emerge as the first-, second-, and third-most important factors in selecting a day-care center.

Quality of Day Care More than half of U.S. children are in center-based child-care programs. Most mothers prefer relatives for the day-care arrangement for their children. Researchers Gordon and Högnäs (2006) analyzed data from the National Institute of Child Health and Human Development Study of Early Child Care and found that nearly two-thirds of the mothers reported such a preference for relatives, including 15 percent who preferred their spouse or partner, 28 percent who preferred another relative in their home, and 22 percent who preferred another relative in another home. An additional 16 percent preferred care by a nonrelative in their own home and 11 percent preferred care by a nonrelative in another private home. Just 9 percent expressed a preference for center-based care. However, most children end up in center-based child-care programs.

Forty-two percent of 3-year-olds and 69 percent of 5-year-old children are in center-based day-care programs (*Statistical Abstract of the United States, 2009*, Table 559).

Employed parents are concerned that their children get good-quality care. Their concern is warranted. Warash et al. (2005) reviewed the literature on day-care centers and found that the average quality of such centers is mediocre—"unsafe, unsanitary, non-educational, and inadequate in regard to the teacher-child ratio for a classroom." Care for infants was particularly lacking. Of 225 infant or toddler rooms observed, 40 percent were rated "less than minimal" with regard to hygiene and safety. Because of the low pay and stress of the occupation, the rate of turnover for family child-care providers is very high (estimated at between 33 and 50 percent) (Walker 2000). However, De Schipper et al. (2008) noted that day-care workers who engage in high-frequency positive behavior engender secure attachments with the children they work with. Hence, children of such workers don't feel they are on an assembly line but bond with their caretakers. Parents concerned about the quality of day care their children receive might inquire about the availability of webcams. Some day-care centers offer full-time webcam access so that parents or grandparents can log onto their computers and see the interaction of the day-care worker with their children.

Ahnert and Lamb (2003) emphasized that attentive, sensitive, loving parents can mitigate any potential negative outcomes in day care. "Home remains the center of children's lives even when children spend considerable amounts of time in child care. . . . [A]lthough it might be desirable to limit the amount of time children spend in child care, it is much more important for children to spend as much time as possible with supportive parents" (pp. 1047–48).

Aside from quality time issues, Gordon et al. (2007) studied the effects of maternal paid work and nonmaternal child care on injuries and infectious disease for children aged 12 to 36 months. They found no statistically significant adverse effects on the incidence of infectious disease and injury. However, greater time spent by children in center-based care was associated with increased rates of respiratory problems for children aged 12 to 36 months and increased rates of ear infections for children aged 12 to 24 months.

Cost of Day Care Day-care costs are a factor in whether a low-income mother seeks employment, because the cost can absorb her paycheck. Even for dual-earner families, cost is a factor in choosing a day-care center. Day-care costs vary widely—from nothing, where friends trade off taking care of the children, to very expensive institutionalized day care in large cities. We e-mailed a dual-earner metropolitan couple (who use day care for their two children and are planning for them to enter school) to inquire about the institutional costs of day care in the Baltimore area in 2009.

The father's response follows:

There is a sliding scale of costs based on quality of provider, age of child, full-time or part-time. Full-time infant care can be hard to find in this area. Many people put their names on a waiting list as soon as they know they are pregnant. We had our first child on a waiting list for about nine months before we got him into our first choice of providers.

Infant care runs $1,250 per month for high-quality day care. That works out to $15,000 per year—and you thought college was expensive.

The cost goes down when the child turns 2—to around $900–$1,000 per month. In Maryland, this is because the required ratio of teachers to children gets bigger at age 2. This cost break doesn't last long. Preschool programs (more academic in structure than day care) begin at age 3 or 4. When our second child turned 4, he started an academic preschool in September. The school year lasts nine and a half months, and it costs about $14,000. Summer camps or summer day-care costs must *be added to this amount to get the true annual cost for the child. My wife and I have budgeted about $30,000 total for our two children to attend private school and summer camps this year.*

The news only gets worse when the children get older. A good private school for grades K–5 runs $15,000 per school year. Junior high (6–8) is about $20,000, and private high school here goes for $20,000 to $35,000 per nine-month school year.

Religious private schools run about half the costs above. However, they require that you be a member in good standing in their congregation and, of course, your child undergoes religious indoctrination.

There is always the argument of attending a good public school and thus not having to pay for private school. However, we have found that home prices in the "good school neighborhoods" were out of our price range. Some of the better-performing public schools also now have waiting lists—even if you move into that school's district.

In most urban and suburban areas, cost is secondary to admissions. Getting into any good private school is difficult. In order to get into the good high schools, it's best to be in one of the private elementary or middle schools that serves as a "feeder" school. Of course, to get into the "right" elementary school, you must be in a good feeder kindergarten. And of course to get into the right kindergarten, you have to get into the right feeder preschool. Parents have A LOT of anxiety about getting into the right preschool— because this can put your child on the path to one of the better private high schools.

Getting into a good private preschool is not just about paying your money and filling out applications. Yes, there are entrance exams. Both of our children underwent the following process to get into preschool: First you must fill out an application. Second, your child's day-care records/transcripts are forwarded for review. If your child gets through this screening, you and your child are called in for a visit. This visit with the child lasts a few hours and your child goes through evaluation for physical, emotional, and academic development. Then you wait several agonizing months to see if your child has been accepted.

Though quality day care is expensive, parents delight in the satisfaction that they are doing what they feel is best for their child.

Balancing Work and Family

Work is definitely stressful on relationships. Lavee and Ben-Ari (2007) noted that one of the effects of work stress is that spouses have greater emotional distance between them. The researchers suggested that such stress may signal a deterioration of a relationship or a way that couples minimize interaction so as to protect the relationship.

One of the major concerns of employed parents and spouses is how to juggle the demands of work and family simultaneously and achieve a sense of accomplishment and satisfaction in each area. Cinamon (2006) noted that women experience work interfering with family at higher levels. Women are more likely to resolve the conflict by giving precedence to family. Kiecolt (2003) examined national data and concluded that employed women with young children are "more likely to find home a haven, rather than finding work a haven" (p. 33). Recall the research by Stone (2007) in regard to women opting out of high-income or high-status work in favor of taking care of their children.

Nevertheless, the conflict between work and family is substantial, and various strategies are employed to cope with the stress of role overload and role conflict, including (1) the superperson strategy, (2) cognitive restructuring, (3) delegation of responsibility, (4) planning and time management, and (5) role compartmentalization (Stanfield 1998).

Superperson Strategy

The superperson strategy involves working as hard and as efficiently as possible to meet the demands of work and family. The person who uses the superperson strategy often skips lunch and cuts back on sleep and leisure to have more time available for work. Women are particularly vulnerable because they feel that if they give too much attention to child-care concerns, they will be sidelined into lower-paying jobs with no opportunities.

Hochschild (1989) noted that the terms **superwoman** or **supermom** are cultural labels that allow a woman to regard herself as very efficient, bright, and confident. However, Hochschild noted that this is a "cultural cover-up" for an overworked and frustrated woman. Not only does the woman have a job in the workplace (first shift), she comes home to another set of work demands in the form of house care and child care (second shift). Finally, she has a "third shift" (Hochschild 1997).

The **third shift** is the expense of emotional energy by a spouse or parent in dealing with various issues in family living. An example is the emotional energy needed for children who feel neglected by the absence of quality time. Although young children need time and attention, responding to conflicts and problems with teenagers also involves a great deal of emotional energy—the third shift.

Cognitive Restructuring

Another strategy used by some women and men experiencing role overload and role conflict is cognitive restructuring, which involves viewing a situation in positive terms. Exhausted dual-career earners often justify their time away from their children by focusing on the benefits of their labor—their children live in a nice house in a safe neighborhood and attend the best schools. Whether these outcomes offset the lack of "quality time" may be irrelevant—the beliefs serve simply to justify the two-earner lifestyle.

Delegation of Responsibility and Limiting Commitments

A third way couples manage the demands of work and family is to delegate responsibility to others for performing certain tasks. Because women tend to bear most of the responsibility for child care and housework, they may choose to ask their partner to contribute more or to take responsibility for these tasks. Although some husbands are involved, cooperative, and contributing, Stone (2007) revealed that fifty-three respondents in her study opted out of their careers to return home because they had a lack of available help either from husbands who were not at home or who did not do much when they were home.

Another form of delegating responsibility involves the decision to reduce one's current responsibilities and not take on additional ones. For example, women and men may give up or limit agreeing to volunteer responsibilities or commitments. One woman noted that her life was being consumed by the responsibilities of her church; she had to change churches because the demands were relentless. In the realm of paid work, women and men can choose not to become involved in professional activities beyond those that are required.

Time Management

The use of time management is another strategy for minimizing the conflicting demands of work and family. This involves prioritizing and making lists of what needs to be done each day. Time planning also involves trying to anticipate stressful periods, planning ahead for them, and dividing responsibilities with the

A generation ago, most people finished a day's work and needed a rest. Now they need exercise.

Anonymous

Government and Corporate Work-Family Policies and Programs

SOCIAL POLICY

Under the Family and Medical Leave Act, all companies with fifty or more employees are required to provide each worker with up to twelve weeks of unpaid leave for reasons of family illness, birth, or adoption of a child. In a subsequent amendment, the Family Leave Act permits states to provide unemployment pay to workers who take unpaid time off to care for a newborn child or a sick relative.

Under the Obama administration, the benefits would be available in businesses with twenty-five or more employees and workers could take leave for elder care needs. All fifty states would also be encouraged to adopt paid leave and would provide a $1.5 billion fund to assist states with start-up costs. Currently, the United States is the only industrialized country that does not provide paid child leave. Over 160 countries provide paid leave for mothers to birth their babies; forty-five countries provide the same benefits for fathers. Australia guarantees a year of leave to all new mothers (Thomas 2007). Germany provides fourteen weeks off with 100 percent salary.

Aside from government-mandated work-family policies, corporations and employers have begun to initiate policies and programs that address the family concerns of their employees. Employer-provided assistance with child care, assistance with elderly parent care, options in work schedules, and job relocation assistance are becoming more common. Widener (2008) noted that some U.S. companies have advanced strategies to balance work and life and gender equity, and that these family-friendly policies "can garner a competitive edge, attracting and retaining young, early career professionals."

However, although these programs are commendable, Stone (2007) noted that one of the reasons women opt out of the their career paths is the inflexibility of corporations. Her interviewees noted that, when a woman drops out to have or to take care of her children, her clients are assigned to someone else and, when she returns, she never seems able to get back on the same standing as those who did not drop out. She suggested family-friendly policies are simply window dressings and that, in fact, corporations view families as interfering with production. The Obama administration planned "to create a program to inform businesses about the benefits of flexible work schedules; help businesses create flexible work opportunities; and increase federal incentives for tele-commuting." Obama pledged "to make the federal government a model employer in terms of adopting flexible work schedules and permitting employees to request flexible arrangements" (Obama for America 2008).

Your Opinion?

1. Argue for and against the fact that businesses benefit from having family-friendly policies.
2. Argue for and against the theory that childfree workers should work later and on holidays so that parents can be with their children.
3. Why do you think that the United States lags behind other industrialized nations in terms of paid leave for parents?

Sources

Obama for America. 2008. Blueprint for change. Campaign booklet, 10–15. Feb 2.

Stone, P. 2007. *Opting out?* Berkley: University of California Press.

Thomas, S. G. 2007. *Buy, buy baby: How consumer culture manipulates parents and harms young minds.* Houghton Mifflin Publisher.

Widener, A. J. 2008. Family-friendly policy: Lessons from Europe-Part II Public Manager. Winter 2007/2008. 36:44–50.

spouse. Such division of labor allows each spouse to focus on an activity that needs to be done (grocery shopping, picking up children at day care) and results in a smoothly functioning unit.

Having flexible jobs and/or careers is particularly beneficial for two-earner couples. Being self-employed, telecommuting, or working in academia permits flexibility of schedule so that individuals can cooperate on what needs to be done. Alternatively, some dual-earner couples attempt to solve the problem of child care by having one parent work during the day and the other parent work at night so that one parent can always be with the children. Shift workers often experience sleep deprivation and fatigue, which may make fulfilling domestic roles as a parent or spouse difficult for them. Similarly, shift work may have a negative effect on a couple's relationship because of their limited time together.

Presser (2000) studied the work schedules of 3,476 married couples and found that recent husbands (married less than five years) who had children and who worked at night were six times more likely to divorce than husbands or parents who worked days.

Role Compartmentalization

Some spouses use **role compartmentalization**—separating the roles of work and home so that they do not think about or dwell on the problems of one when they are at the physical place of the other. Spouses unable to compartmentalize their work and home feel role strain, role conflict, and role overload, with the result that their efficiency drops in both spheres. Some families look to the government and their employers for help in balancing the demands of family and work.

Leisure is a beautiful garment, but it will not do for constant wear.

Anonymous

Balancing Work and Leisure Time

The workplace has become the home place. Because of the technology of the workplace—laptops, cell phones, wireless devices, and so on—some spouses work all the time, wherever they are. One couple noted that they are working on their laptops and talking on their cell phones when they are at home so that they rarely have any time when they are not working and communicating directly with each other. Although the family is supposed to be a place of relaxation and recovery, it has become another place where spouses work. Balance is needed.

Leisure refers to the use of time to engage in freely chosen activities perceived as enjoyable and satisfying, including exercise. Tucker et al. (2008) identified three conditions of leisure—quiet leisure at home (for example, reading a book), active leisure (for example, playing basketball), and more work. Ratings of rest, recuperation, and satisfaction were lowest in the additional work condition.

Importance of Leisure

Parents know how children impact their personal leisure and marital relationship. Indeed, having a high value for leisure is one of the reasons some women elect not to have children (McQuillan et al. 2008). Claxton and Perry-Jenkins

This self-employed businessman has a difficult time "detaching" from his work role.

Authors

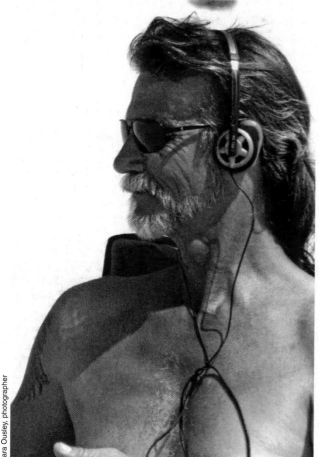

This state employee counsels undergraduates at a university forty hours a week. He notes, "I need the beach and my music to recover on weekends."

Kara Ousley, photographer

Having fun, not being in love is what keeps couples together.

Christiane Northrup, relationship guru

(2008) noted the effect of leisure on marital satisfaction of new parents. They interviewed 147 heterosexual couples across the transition to parenthood and observed a decline in leisure with the birth of a baby. However, wives who reported more shared leisure prenatally also reported more marital love and less conflict one year after the baby's birth. In contrast, husbands who did their own leisure thing prenatally reported less love and more conflict one year later. Leisure is also increasingly becoming an important cultural value among youth. Corporations are learning that individuals are no longer interested in being consumed by their work. This new work ethic is particularly operative among **millenials**, the 80 million workers born between 1980 and 1995. Having been told that they are special, that performance is not required for praise, and that fun, leisure, and lifestyle come before giving one's life to a job or career, these millenials are socializing their bosses to be more flexible or to find someone else to work for them. Indeed, corporations today are hiring consultants to socialize them how to cope with a workforce that wants a job on their own terms. They are told that they must be not just a boss but also a life coach and a shrink, and that they must motivate rather than demand. These millenials don't need the money, as one-half of college seniors will live with their parents after graduation (Textor 2007).

Functions of Leisure

Leisure fulfills important functions in our individual and interpersonal lives. Leisure activities may relieve work-related stress and pressure; facilitate social interaction and family togetherness; foster self-expression, personal growth, and skill development; and enhance overall social, physical, and emotional well-being.

National Data

In a study of leisure trips reported by households throughout the United States, 38 percent were "adults only," 31 percent were parents and children, and 31 percent were solo travelers (Travel Industry Association of America 2006).

Though leisure represents a means of family togetherness and enjoyment, it may also represent an area of stress and conflict. Some couples function best when they are busy with work and child care so that they have limited time to interact or for the relationship. Indeed, some prefer not to have a lot of time alone together.

Individual and Relationship Problems Related to Leisure

Individual or relationship problems may be involved in leisure. Excessive drinking may occur in leisure context with friends. Grekin et al. (2007) analyzed the alcohol consumption of 3,720 undergraduates (mean age 17.96) who spent spring break with either friends or parents and found that students who vacationed with friends during spring break dramatically increased their alcohol use. In contrast, students who stayed home or vacationed with parents during spring break were at low risk for excessive alcohol use.

Relationship problems may also occur in reference to leisure. In a study of 102 older couples (average age of spouses was 69), "leisure activities" was the most frequently cited problem area (accounting for 23 percent of problems) (Henry et al. 2005). The ways in which this problem expressed itself included the following:

TV watching: he wanted to watch football and she wanted to watch *American Idol.*

Travel: she wanted to stay at home and he wanted to travel, or they differed in travel preferences.

Time: both were very busy with their lives and did not take time to spend together.

The Research Application on page 414 provides another example of how leisure may affect one's relationship.

Vacation Stress

Vacations can be stressful, beginning with the preparation. A national sample identified some of the problems as taking care of one's work schedule (28 percent), arranging for pet care (23 percent), making travel plans (11 percent), and finding someone to look after one's home (11 percent) (Umminger and Parker 2005). Travel though airports has also become time-consuming and stressful.

Some people may have trouble detaching from work. An Ipsos poll of 1,000 randomly chosen adults revealed that about 40 percent of adult vacationers checked their office e-mail and messages, and 50 percent checked their voice mail via laptops and cell phones, with 20 percent taking the former and 80 percent the latter. Reasons for staying tethered to the job included worry about missing important information; feeling an expectation from bosses or coworkers that they stay connected; and enjoyment of staying involved. People most likely to use technology on vacation were under 40, white, and male (Fram 2007).

Some research suggests that males play video games to the extent that their romantic partners feel ignored.

Authors

What if Your Partner Uses Cell Phone and E-Mail Throughout Your Vacation?

WHAT IF?

Doing "business" via cell phones, e-mail, and laptops while on vacation is not unusual. Where both partners do so or the other partner is indifferent, there is no problem. However, some partners are angered that their vacation partner never detaches and is always "on." Of course, a partner legitimizes the cell phone, e-mail, and computer use as necessary "business" for income. One solution is a discussion before leaving town about the definition of the "vacation"—is it a working vacation, a pure vacation, or what? Although couples will vary about their agreements, the issue is that they have one. Otherwise, their vacation might become not only "all about business," but also about a great deal of arguing.

Coed Anger over Romantic Partner's Video Game Playing*

RESEARCH APPLICATION

Video game playing is part of the collegiate landscape. In a national study of 1,162 undergraduates in 27 colleges and universities, 65 percent reported playing video games regularly or occasionally (Jones et al. 2003). However, individual's relationships may pay a price—the focus of this study.

Sample and Methods
The data consisted of a nonrandom sample of 148 undergraduate volunteers at a large southeastern university who responded to a 45-item questionnaire on "Video Game Survey" (approved by the Institutional Review Board of the university). The objective of the study was to identify current uses and consequences of playing video games.

General Findings
Of the respondents, 97.6 percent of the men and 92.6 percent of the women reported having played a video game. *Madden Football* was the most commonly played video. Although previous researchers (Rau et al. 2006; Wan and Chiou 2006) reported the capacity of video games to become addictive, these respondents were *not* obsessed by or addicted to playing video games; they rarely skipped class nor played relentlessly for days. Indeed only two males and one female (less than 3 percent of the respondents) used the term *obsessive* to describe their video game playing. The average GPA of these students was 2.96, suggesting that their academic performance was standard for their year in school.

Significant Gender Differences
In addition to the previous general findings, three significant sex differences emerged.

1. *Women viewed video games as more experimental than recreational.* Women and men differed in why they played video games. Female respondents were significantly more likely than male respondents (33.7 percent versus 7.5 percent) to report that playing video games was experimental in the sense of curiosity, just seeing what it was like, and so on. In contrast, male respondents were significantly more likely to report that playing video games was recreational (65 percent versus 41.3 percent; $p < .000$).

   Previous researchers have examined sex differences in playing video games. Hayes (2005) found that women prefer video games that involve cooperation and interaction. They may play combat games but their focus is on learning to protect themselves and to defend themselves. Similarly, Carr (2005) studied gaming at an all-girl's state school in the United Kingdom and found that patterns of access and peer culture determined which games girls played. What emerges from the literature and this study is that playing video games for females is less about having fun or recreation and more about experimenting, connecting, interacting, and protecting.

2. *Male partners of females were more likely to play video games.* The data reflected that females were much more likely to have a partner who played video games. Of the undergraduate females in this study, 75.6 percent reported having been involved in a relationship with a partner who played video games (in contrast to 42.4 percent of male undergraduates involved with a female who played video games) ($p < .001$). In effect, the undergraduate males played video games and the undergraduate females coped with their doing so. Previous researchers have found that males report higher use of playing video games than females (57 percent versus 17 percent) (Jones et al. 2003).

3. *Females were more likely to be angry over a partner playing video games.* Of the female respondents, 32.9 percent reported that they had become upset with their partners' relentless video game playing. Of the males, only 4.5 percent reported

SUMMARY

How does debt and poverty affect relationships?

The more couples are in debt, the less time they spend together, the more they argue, and the more they are unhappy. Poverty is devastating to couples and families. Those living in poverty have poorer physical and mental health, report lower personal and marital satisfaction, and die sooner.

The stresses associated with low income also contribute to substance abuse, domestic violence, child abuse and neglect, and divorce. Couples with incomes of less than $25,000 are 30 percent more likely to divorce than those with $50,000 or higher.

having told their partner that the partner spent too much time playing video games. The difference was statistically significant ($p < .005$). We asked an undergraduate female who reported that her partner's game playing was a problem in their relationship to explain the source of her frustration:

Not only are video games expensive (not to speak of the equipment) but he hogs the TV for an entire evening and acts like I don't exist. Quality time—what is that?

Previous researchers have confirmed the deleterious effects of video game playing on relationships. Lo et al. (2005) surveyed 174 Taiwanese college students and found that the quality of their interpersonal relationships decreased as the amount of time spent playing online games increased.

Theoretical Framework

Social exchange theory is one of the more common theories for explaining human interaction (Taylor and Bagd 2005). The social exchange framework operates from a premise of utilitarianism—that individuals rationally weigh the rewards and costs associated with their involvement in relationships. Each interaction between two actors can be understood in terms of each individual seeking the most benefits at the least cost so as to have the highest "profit" and to avoid a "loss" (White and Klein 2002). The framework provides a clear understanding for the frustration of the coed who is emotionally invested in her partner and wants him to reciprocate her interest. His choosing to play video games over her translates into a "cost" and a "loss" in terms of "no profit" in the relationship. Telling her partner that he spends too much time playing video games is her way of trying to increase the benefits in the relationship to experience a "profit."

Implications

Three implications emerged from the data. First, in spite of the stereotype that video game players are geeks who are focused on machines and have no relationships, 74.5 percent of the sample reported that they were dating or involved with someone. Indeed, over half were emotionally involved, engaged, or married. Second, these respondents were neither addicted nor obsessed with playing video games. Missing class and being ensconced in their room playing video games for days on end was virtually nonexistent. Third, video game playing was a problem in relationships for about a third of the female respondents. Feeling neglected, disrespected ("doesn't care what I want to watch on TV"), and wasting money were among the dissatisfactions.

Sources

Carr, D. 2005. Contexts, gaming pleasures, and gendered preferences. *Simulation & Gaming* 36:464–82.

Hayes, E. 2005. Women, video gaming & learning: Beyond the stereotypes. *Tech Trends* 49:23–28.

Jones, S., L. N. Clarke, S. Cornish, M. Gonzales, C. Johnson, J. N. Lawson, S. Smith, et al. 2003. Let the games begin: Gaming technology and entertainment among college students. Pew Internet and American Life. July 6. www.pewinternet.org.

Lo, S. K., C. C. Wang, and W. Fang. 2005. Physical interpersonal relationships and social anxiety among online game players. *CyberPsychology & Behavior* 8:15–20.

Rau, P. L. P., S. Y. Peng, and C. C. Yang. 2006. Time distortion for expert and novice online game players. *CyberPsychology & Behavior* 9:396–403.

Taylor, A. C., and A. Bagd. 2005. The lack of explicit theory in family research: The case analysis of the *Journal of Marriage and the Family 1990–1999*. In *Sourcebook of family theory & research*, ed. Vern L. Bengtson, Alan C. Acock, Katherine R. Allen, Peggye Dilworth-Anderson, and David M. Klein, 22–25. Thousand Oaks, CA: Sage Publications.

Wan, C. S., and W. B. Chiou. 2006. Psychological motives and online games addiction: A test of flow theory and humanistic needs theory of Taiwanese adolescents. *CyberPsychology & Behavior* 9:317–24.

White, J. M., and D. M. Klein. 2002. *Family theories*, 2d ed. Thousand Oaks, CA: Sage Publications.

*Abridged from D. Knox, M. Zusman, A. White, and G. Haskins. 2009. Coed anger over romantic partner's video game playing. *Psychology Journal* 6:10–16.

How does work or money affect a couple's relationship?

Generally, the more money a partner makes, the more power that person has in the relationship. Males make considerably more money than females and generally have more power in relationships. Sixty-one percent of all U.S. wives are in the labor force. The stereotypical family consisting of a husband who earns an income and a wife who stays at home with two or more children is no longer the norm. Only 13 percent are "traditional" in the sense of a breadwinning husband, a stay-at-home wife, and their children. In contrast, most marriages may be characterized as dual-earner. Employed wives in unhappy marriages are more likely to leave the marriage than unemployed wives.

What is the effect of parents' work decisions on the children?

Children do not appear to suffer cognitively or emotionally from their parents working as long as positive, consistent child-care alternatives are in place. However, less supervision of children by parents is an outcome of having two-earner parents. Leaving children to come home to an empty house is particularly problematic.

Parents view quality time as structured, planned activities, talking with their children, or just hanging out with them. Day care is typically mediocre but any negatives are offset by consistent parental attention.

What are the various strategies for balancing the demands of work and family?

Strategies used for balancing the demands of work and family include the super-person strategy, cognitive restructuring, delegation of responsibility, planning and time management, and role compartmentalization. Government and corporations have begun to respond to the family concerns of employees by implementing work-family policies and programs. These policies are typically inadequate and cosmetic.

What is the importance of leisure and what are its functions?

Corporations are learning that the new millenials value leisure and will not let their work life end it. Leisure helps to relieve stress, facilitate social interaction and family togetherness, and foster personal growth and skill development. However, leisure time may also create conflict over how to use it. Females sometimes become angry at their romantic partners for playing video games.

KEY TERMS

absolute poverty	installment plan	poverty	second shift
dual-career marriage	leisure	relative poverty	shift work
dual-earner marriage	millenials	revolving charge	supermom
HER/his career	mommy track	role compartmentalization	superwoman
HIS/her career	momprenuer	role conflict	THEIR career
HIS/HER career	open charge	role overload	third shift
identity theft	opting out	role strain	

The Companion Website for *Choices in Relationships: An Introduction to Marriage and the Family,* Tenth Edition

www.cengage.com/sociology/knox

Supplement your review of this chapter by going to the Companion Website to take one of the tutorial quizzes, use the flash cards to master key terms, or check out the many other study aids, like crossword puzzles and self-assessments. You'll also find special features such as General Social Survey (GSS) data, Census data, and other resources to help you with that special project or to do some research on your own.

WEB LINKS

At Home Dads
http://www.angelfire.com/zine2/athomedad/index.blog

Identity Theft: Federal Trade Commission
http://www.consumer.gov/idtheft/

Identity Theft: Prevention and Survival
http://www.identitytheft.org/

Ms. Money (budgeting documents)
http://www.msmoney.com

Network on the Family and the Economy
http://www.olin.wustl.edu/macarthur/

Career.com (career planning)
http://www.career.com/

Ahnert, L., and M. E. Lamb. 2003. Shared care: Establishing a balance between home and child care settings. *Child Development* 74:1044–49.

Amato, P. R., A. Booth, D. R. Johnson, and S. F. Rogers. 2007. *Alone together: How marriage in America is changing*. Cambridge, Massachusetts: Harvard University Press.

Boushey, H., and C. E. Weller. 2008. Has growing inequality contributed to rising household economic distress? *Review of Political Economy* 20:1–2.

Bryant, C. M., R. J. Taylor, K. D. Lincoln, L. M. Chatters, and J. S. Jackson. 2008. Marital satisfaction among African Americans and Black Caribbeans: Findings from the National Survey of American Life. *Family Relations* 57:239–354.

Capizzano, J., G. Adams, and J. Ost. 2006. The child care patterns of white, black and Hispanic children. Urban Institute. http://www.urban.org/url.cfm?ID=311285 (retrieved April 2006).

Cinamon, R. G. 2006. Anticipated work-family conflict: effects of gender, self-efficacy, and family background. *Career Development Quarterly* 54:202–16.

Claxton, A., and M. Perry-Jenkins. 2008. No fun anymore: Leisure and marital quality across the transition to parenthood. *Journal of Marriage and Family* 70:28–44.

Davies, J. B., S. Sandstrom, A. Shorrocks, and E. N. Wolff. 2006. (Dec. 5). *The World Distribution of Household Wealth*. United Nations University—World Institute for Development Economics Research.

De Schipper, J. C., L. W. C. Tavecchio. and M. H Van IJzendoorn. 2008. Children's attachment relationships with day care caregivers: Associations with positive caregiving and the child's temperament. *Social Development* 17:454–65.

Deutsch, F. M., A. P. Kokot, and K. S. Binder. 2007. College women's plans for different types of egalitarian marriages. *Journal of Marriage and Family* 69:916–29.

Dew, J. 2008. Debt change and marital satisfaction change in recently married couples. *Family Relations* 57:60–72.

Fram, A. 2007. A fifth vacation with laptops. *Associated Press,* June 1.

Gordon, J. R., and K. S. Whelan-Berry. 2005. Contributions to family and household activities by the husbands of midlife professional women. *Journal of Family Studies* 26:899–923.

Gordon, R. A., R. Kaestner, and S. Korenman. 2007. The effects of maternal employment on child injuries and infectious disease. *Demography* 44:307–26.

Gordon, R. A., and R. S. Högnäs. 2006. The best laid plans: Expectations, preferences, and stability of child-care arrangements. *Journal of Marriage and Family* 68:373–93.

Grandey, A. A., B. L. Cordeiro, and A. C. Crouter. 2005. A longitudinal and multi-source test of the work-family conflict and job satisfaction. *Journal of Occupational and Organizational Psychology* 78:305–23.

Grekin, E. R., K. J. Sher, and J. L Krull. 2007. College spring break and alcohol use: Effects of spring break activity. *Journal of Studies on Alcohol and Drugs* 68:681–93.

Henry, R. G., R. B. Miller, and R. Giarrusso. 2005. Difficulties, disagreements, and disappointments in late-life marriages. *International Journal of Aging & Human Development* 61:243–65.

Hochschild, A. R. 1989. *The second shift*. New York: Viking.

———. 1997. *The time bind*. New York: Metropolitan Books.

Jalovaara, M. 2003. The joint effects of marriage partners' socioeconomic positions on the risk of divorce. *Demography* 40:67–81.

Keller, E. G. 2008b. *The comeback: Seven stories of women who went from career to family and back again*. New York: Bloomsbury.

Keller, G. 2008a. French businesses loath to end 35-hour work week. *Associated Press*. http://www.wtop.com/?nid=105&sid=1471646.

Kiecolt, K. J. 2003. Satisfaction with work and family life: No evidence of a cultural reversal. *Journal of Marriage and the Family* 65:23–35.

Kirn, W. 2007. Vacation, all I never wanted. *The New York Times Magazine,* August 5, 11–12.

Lavee, Y., and A. Ben-Ari 2007. Relationship of dyadic closeness with work-related stress: A daily diary study. *Journal of Marriage and Family* 69:1021–35.

Mason, M. A., and M. Goulden. 2004. Do babies matter? The effect of family formation on the lifelong careers of academic men and women. Annual Conference of the National Council on Family Relations, November. Orlando, Florida.

McQuillan, J., A. L. Greil, K. M. Shreffler, and V. Tichenor. 2008. The importance of motherhood among women in the contemporary United States. *Gender & Society* 22:477–92.

Morin, R., and D. Cohn. 2008. Women call the shots at home; Public mixed on gender roles in jobs, gender and power. Pew Research Center, September 25.

Nomaaguchi, K. M., and M. A. Milkie. 2006. Maternal employment in childhood and adult's retrospective reports of parenting practices. *Journal of Marriage and the Family* 68:573–91.

Noonan, M. C., and M. E. Corcoran. 2004. The mommy track and partnership: Temporary delay or dead end? *The Annals of the American Academy of Political and Social Science* 596:130–50.

Patrick, T. 2005. Stay-at-home dads. *Futurist* 39:12–13.

Pepper, T. 2006. Fatherhood: Trying to do it all. *Newsweek*, International ed., February 27.

Perry-Jenkins, M., R. L. Repetti, and A. C. Crouter. 2001. Work and family in the 1990s. In *Understanding families into the new millennium: A decade in review,* ed. R. M. Milardo, 200–17. Minneapolis: National Council on Family Relations.

Presser, H. B. 2000. Nonstandard work schedules and marital instability. *Journal of Marriage and the Family* 62:93–110.

Rose, K., and K. J. Elicker. 2008 Parental Decision Making about Child Care. *Journal of Family Issues* 29:1161–79.

Rosen, E. 2006. Derailed on the mommy track? There's help to get going again. *New York Times* 155(10):1–3.

Schoen, R., N. M. Astone, K. Rothert, N. J. Standish, and Y. J. Kim. 2002. Women's employment, marital happiness, and divorce. *Social Forces* 81:643–62.

Schoen, R., S. J. Rogers, and P. R. Amato. 2006. Wives' employment and spouses' marital happiness: Assessing the direction of influence using longitudinal couple data. *Journal of Family Issues* 27:506–28.

Sefton, B. W. 1998. The market value of the stay-at-home mother. *Mothering* 86:26–29.

Sener, I. P., R. B. Copperman, R. M. Pendyala, and C. R. Bhat. 2008. An analysis of children's leisure activity engagement: examining the day of week, location, physical activity level, and fixity dimensions. *Transportation* 35:673–97.

Shapiro, M. 2007. Money: A therapeutic tool for couples therapy. *Family Process* 46:279–91.

Snyder, K. A. 2007. A vocabulary of motives: Understanding how parents define quality time *Journal of Marriage and Family* 69:320–40.

Society for the Advancement of Education. 2005. Mr. Mom nation reaches new peak. *USA Today* August 13.

Stanfield, J. B. 1998. Couples coping with dual careers: A description of flexible and rigid coping styles. *Social Science Journal* 35:53–62.

Stanley, S. M., and L. A. Einhorn. 2007. Hitting pay dirt: Comment on "Money: A therapeutic tool for couples therapy." *Family Process* 46:293–99.

Statistical Abstract of the United States, 2009. 128th ed. Washington, DC: U.S. Bureau of the Census.

Stone, P. 2007. *Opting out?* Berkley: University of California Press.

Strazdins, L., M. S. Clements, R. J. Korda, D. H. Broom, and M. Rennie. 2006. Unsociable work? Nonstandard work schedules, family relationships, and children's well-being. *Journal of Marriage and Family* 68:394–410.

Textor, K. 2007. "The Millennials are Coming" *Sixty Minutes,* November 11. CBS Television.

Travel Industry Association of America. 2006. "Fun Alone or with the Family," report published in *USA Today,* July 7, p. 1.

Tucker, P. 2005. Stay-at-home dads. *The Futurist* 39:12–15.

Tucker, P., A. Dahlgren, T. Akerstedt, and J. Waterhouse. 2008. The impact of free-time activities on sleep, recovery and well-being. *Applied Ergonomics* 39:653–61.

Tyre, P., and D. McGinn. 2003. She works, he doesn't. *Newsweek,* May 12:45–52.

Umminger, A., and S. Parker. 2005. What hinders vacation? *USA Today,* February 18, A1.

U.S. Department of Health and Human Services. 2008. http://www.cbpp.org/8-26-08pov.htm (retrieved Nov 25, 2008).

Verbakel, E., and T. A. Diprete. 2008. The value of non-work time in cross-national quality of life comparisons: The case of the United States versus the Netherlands. *Social Forces* 87:679–712.

Walker, S. K. 2000. Making home work: Family factors related to stress in family child care providers. Poster at the Annual Conference of the National Council on Family Relations, November. Minneapolis.

Warash, B. G., C. A. Markstrom, and B. Lucci. 2005. The early childhood environment rating scale-revised as a tool to improve child care centers. *Education* 126:240–50.

Whitehead, B. D., and D. Popenoe. 2004. The state of our union: The social health of marriage in America. The National Marriage Project. Rutgers University. http://www.marriage.rutgers.edu/.

World Bank. 2007. *Global monitoring report. 2007.* Washington, DC: The World Bank.

Zibel, A. 2008. Home loan trouble break records again. *Associated Press,* Sept 5, http://news.yahoo.com/s/ap/20080905/ap_on_bi_ge/home_foreclosures.

chapter 13

*Cover up with makeup in the mirror
tell yourself, it's never gonna
happen again
you cry alone and then he
swears he loves you*

*Face down in the dirt, she said,
"This doesn't hurt", she said,
"I finally had enough."*

"Face Down," Red Jumpsuit Apparatus

Violence and Abuse in Relationships

Peterson Family/ZUMA/Corbis

Contents

True or False?

1. A primary reason women do not report abuse is the belief that the police will not help.

2. Most battered women's shelters are available to heterosexual women only. Shelters for lesbians are almost nonexistent.

3. Cybervictimization of people involved in Internet dating is minimal.

4. Women who end abusive relationships are most likely to be murdered shortly after the breakup.

5. The majority of children who observe their parents being violent toward each other do not become violent themselves.

Answers: **1.** T **2.** T **3.** T **4.** T **5.** T

On February 8, 2009, Chris Brown allegedly beat girlfriend Rihanna to the point where she called 911. He later turned himself in to the police and was released on $50,000 bail. Other examples of partner abuse are subtler than a beating. Angie is a first-year university student who is alarmed by the way her boyfriend has begun to treat her. After a year of dating, she noticed that he began to get upset when she would spend time with her friends. He would also say that she had put on weight and accuse her of "looking like a slut" when she would dress for a party. His emotionally abusive behavior resulted in her feeling hopeless to reverse his treatment of her, feeling trapped (because he threatened to kill her if she left him), and feeling depressed. She dropped out of school. Angie is not alone. This chapter focuses on abuse in relationships that happens behind closed doors. We begin by defining some terms.

Nature of Relationship Abuse

Abuse is not uncommon. The Self-Assessment Abusive Behavior Inventory on page 421 allows you to assess the degree of abuse in your current or most recent relationship.

There are several types of abuse in relationships.

Violence

Also referred to as **physical abuse, violence** may be defined as the intentional infliction of physical harm by either partner on the other. Examples of physical violence include pushing, throwing something at the partner, slapping, hitting, and forcing sex on the partner. **Intimate-partner violence** (IPV) is an all-inclusive term that refers to crimes committed against current or former spouses, boyfriends, or girlfriends. John Gottman (2007) identified two types of violence. One type is where conflict escalates over an issue and one or both partners lose control. The trigger seems to be feeling disrespected and a loss of one's dignity. The person feels threatened and seeks to defend his or her dignity by posturing and threatening the partner while in a very agitated state. Control is lost and the partner strikes out. Both partners may lose control at the same time so it is symmetrical

A second type of violence is designed to control the partner. There is a clear perpetrator and victim in this type. Gottman (2007) feels the first type of violence is preventable by recognizing the sequence of interaction leading up to violent behavior. The antidote to the second type of violence is for the victim to leave the relationship.

Abusive Behavior Inventory

Circle the number that best represents your closest estimate of how often each of the behaviors have happened in the relationship with your current or former partner during the previous six months.

1 Never
2 Rarely
3 Occasionally
4 Frequently
5 Very frequently

1. Called you a name and/or criticized you   1 2 3 4 5

2. Tried to keep you from doing something you wanted to do (for example, going out with friends or going to meetings)   1 2 3 4 5

3. Gave you angry stares or looks   1 2 3 4 5

4. Prevented you from having money for your own use   1 2 3 4 5

5. Ended a discussion and made a decision without you   1 2 3 4 5

6. Threatened to hit or throw something at you   1 2 3 4 5

7. Pushed, grabbed, or shoved you   1 2 3 4 5

8. Put down your family and friends   1 2 3 4 5

9. Accused you of paying too much attention to someone or something else   1 2 3 4 5

10. Put you on an allowance   1 2 3 4 5

11. Used your children to threaten you (for example, told you that you would lose custody or threatened to leave town with the children)   1 2 3 4 5

12. Became very upset with you because dinner, housework, or laundry was not done when or how it was wanted   1 2 3 4 5

13. Said things to scare you (for example, told you something "bad" would happen or threatened to commit suicide)   1 2 3 4 5

14. Slapped, hit, or punched you   1 2 3 4 5

15. Made you do something humiliating or degrading (for example, begging for forgiveness or having to ask permission to use the car or do something)   1 2 3 4 5

16. Checked up on you (for example, listened to your phone calls, checked the mileage on your car, or called you repeatedly at work)   1 2 3 4 5

17. Drove recklessly when you were in the car   1 2 3 4 5

18. Pressured you to have sex in a way you didn't like or want   1 2 3 4 5

19. Refused to do housework or child care   1 2 3 4 5

20. Threatened you with a knife, gun, or other weapon   1 2 3 4 5

21. Spanked you   1 2 3 4 5

22. Told you that you were a bad parent   1 2 3 4 5

23. Stopped you or tried to stop you from going to work or school   1 2 3 4 5

24. Threw, hit, kicked, or smashed something   1 2 3 4 5

25. Kicked you   1 2 3 4 5

26. Physically forced you to have sex   1 2 3 4 5

27. Threw you around   1 2 3 4 5

28. Physically attacked the sexual parts of your body   1 2 3 4 5

29. Choked or strangled you   1 2 3 4 5

30. Used a knife, gun, or other weapon against you   1 2 3 4 5

Scoring

Add the numbers you circled and divide the total by 30 to determine your score. The higher your score (five is the highest score), the more abusive your relationship.

The inventory was given to 100 men and 78 women equally divided into groups of abusers or abused and nonabusers or nonabused. The men were members of a chemical dependency treatment program in a veterans' hospital and the women were partners of these men. Abusing or abused men earned an average score of 1.8; abusing or abused women earned an average score of 2.3. Nonabusing, abused men and women earned scores of 1.3 and 1.6, respectively.

Source

M. F. Shepard and J. A. Campbell. The Abusive Behavior Inventory: A measure of psychological and physical abuse. *Journal of Interpersonal Violence* 7(3):291–305. © 1992 by Sage Publications Inc. Journals. Reproduced with permission of Sage Publications Inc. Journals in the format Other book via Copyright Clearance Center.

A syndrome related to violence is **battered-woman syndrome,** which refers to the general pattern of battering that a woman is subjected to and is defined in terms of the frequency, severity, and injury she experiences. Battering is severe if the person's injuries require medical treatment or the perpetrator could be prosecuted.

Battering may lead to murder. **Uxoricide** is the murder of a woman by a romantic partner. The murder of Laci Peterson by her convicted husband Scott Peterson is an example of uxoricide. As a prelude to murder, the man may hold his wife hostage (holding one or more people against their will with the actual or implied use of force). A typical example is an estranged spouse who reenters the house of a former spouse and holds his wife and children hostage. These situations are potentially dangerous because the perpetrator often has a weapon and may use it on the victims, himself, or both. A negotiator is usually called in to resolve the situation.

National Data

In the U.S. adult population, over 4 million women are physically harmed by their husband, boyfriend, or other intimate partner annually (Torpy et al. 2008). A great deal more abuse occurs than is reported. In a national sample of women who had been physically assaulted, almost three-fourths (73 percent) did not report the incidence to the police. The primary reason for no report was the belief that the police could not help (Dugan et al. 2003). Yet the damage is enormous. Johnson et al. (2008) emphasized that IPV is associated with post-traumatic stress disorder (PTSD) and results in social maladjustment and personal or social resource loss.

Regardless of the type, violence is not unique to heterosexual couples. Physical violence is also reported to occur in 11 percent to 12 percent of same-sex couples. Differences between violence in opposite-sex couples versus same-sex couples include that the latter is more mild, the threat of "outing" is present, and the violence is more isolated because it often occurs in a context of "being in the closet." Finally, victims of same-sex relationship abuse lack legal protections and services that are available to abuse victims in heterosexual couples. For example, most battered women's shelters do not serve lesbian women (or gay men); in nine states, legal protections for victims of domestic violence are granted only when the relationship is between a man and a woman or between spouses or former spouses (Rohrbaugh 2006).

Emotional Abuse

In addition to being physically violent, partners may also engage in **emotional abuse** (also known as **psychological abuse, verbal abuse,** or **symbolic aggression**). Whereas more than 10 percent of 1,319 undergraduates (10.7 percent) reported being involved in a physically abusive relationship, 31.6 percent reported that they "had been involved in an *emotionally* abusive relationship with a partner" (Knox and Zusman 2009). Although emotional abuse does not involve physical harm, it is designed to make the partner feel bad—to denigrate the partner, reduce the partner's status, and make the partner vulnerable to being controlled by the abuser. Although there is debate about what constitutes psychological abuse, examples of various categories of emotional abuse include the following:

Criticism and ridicule—being called obese, stupid, crazy, ugly, pitiful, and repulsive

Isolation—being prohibited by the partner from spending time with friends, siblings, and parents

Control—being told how to dress and/or accused of dressing like a slut; having one's money controlled

Silent treatment—having a partner who refuses to talk to or to touch the victim

Yelling—being yelled and screamed at by one's partner

Accusation—being told (unjustly) that one is unfaithful

Threats—being threatened by the partner with abandonment or threats of harm to one's self, family, or pets

Emotional Abuse: Victim Profile and Why Universities Should Care

The goal of the study was to identify the characteristics of emotionally abused undergraduate victims. This profile may serve to target proactive emotional abuse education programs as well as create a context for those who are emotionally abused to disclose their experiences. The latter may assist in the healing process as well as increase the visibility of emotional abusers, which may (hopefully) reduce the number of victims.

Methodology

Emotional abuse by a partner is defined as being degraded, detached from one's relationships, and being threatened. It was assessed by the response "yes" or "no" to the statement, "I have been in an emotionally abusive relationship with a partner." The data were taken from a nonrandom sample of 1,027 undergraduate volunteers at a large southeastern university. Demographics of the respondents included 77.3 percent female and 22.7 percent male students. Student age was a median of 19 (range 16 to 49). To identify the characteristics of the emotionally abused victims (as compared to those not reporting emotional abuse), cross-classification was conducted to determine any relationships, with chi-square utilized to assess statistical significance.

Results and Discussion

Of the sample, 29.1 percent reported that they had been involved in a current or past emotionally abusive relationship. When comparing the background characteristics of victims of emotional abuse in a dating context with those reporting no such abuse, the following statistically significant findings emerged:

1. *Victims were female.* Over a third of the females (33.5 percent) compared to 21 percent of the males reported involvement in an emotionally abusive relationship (p < .001). Indeed, females were 12.5 percent more likely to have experienced an abusive relationship with a dating partner.
2. *Victims tended to be seniors.* The greater the number of years in college, the more likely a student was to report involvement in an emotionally abusive relationship—almost 40 percent of seniors (37 percent) in contrast to 25.3 percent of first-year students (30 percent of sophomores and 36.6 percent of juniors also reported such abuse) (p < .02).
3. *Individuals who participate in "friends with benefits" relationships.* Undergraduates who reported previous involvement in a "friends with benefits" relationship (sex with a nonromantic friend) were significantly (p < .001) more likely to report

experience in an emotionally abusive relationship (36.2 percent versus 22.9 percent).
4. *Individuals who seek Internet partners.* Undergraduates who had looked for a partner on the Internet were significantly more likely (p < .001) to report experience in an emotionally abusive relationship with a partner (45.5 percent versus 27.5 percent). It is possible that Internet partner seekers were less discriminating in their choice of a partner or greater risk takers, both of which may result in greater vulnerability to ending up with a dependent, jealous, controlling, or emotionally abusing partner.
5. *Romantic individuals.* We defined a romantic as someone who believes in "love at first sight" and measured romanticism as a "yes" or "no" to the statement, "I believe in love at first sight." Undergraduates who believed in love at first sight were significantly more likely (p < .001) to report experience in an emotionally abusive relationship (39.0 percent versus 26.7 percent). It is possible that romantics were swept away by a wave of love into the relationship with the abuser. In effect, these romantic undergraduates were not alert to the "warning" signs and beginning levels of jealousy or control. Similarly, being a romantic may have made the individual an easy prey or vulnerable target for an abuser who found it easy to reel in the unsuspecting, trusting individual whom they could control and abuse.

Implications

There are several implications of the study.
1. Universities that sponsor rape and physical abuse prevention programs for undergraduates might consider an equal concern for undergraduate emotional abuse.
2. Victims of emotional abuse may feel less alone or isolated by being aware that others with similar characteristics may also have been emotionally abused. As a result, they may be more open to reveal their emotionally abusive experience to increase the visibility of this hidden dimension of some relationships.
3. Access to university resources (for example, counseling) may increase as a result of individuals being more willing to reveal that they have been victims of emotional abuse.
4. Perpetrators of emotional abuse may become more sensitive to the seriousness of their behavior and consider reducing it.

Source

Abowitz, D., D. Knox, and M. Zusman. Paper presented at Eastern Sociological Society, Baltimore, 2009.

Demeaning behavior—being insulted by the partner in front of others

Restricting behavior—having one's mobility restricted (for example, use of the car)

Demanding behavior—being required to do as the partner wishes (for example, have sex)

Although women may be abusers, more often abusers are men. Of 227,941 restraining orders issued to adults in California, most were for domestic violence, and most (72.2 percent) of the abusers were men, African Americans, and 25- to 34-year-olds (Shen and Sorenson 2005). Similarly, according to National Incident-Based Reporting System (NIBRS) data on intimate-partner violence, the victims tended to be young, female, and minority members (Vazquez et al. 2005).

Female Abuse of Partner

Women also abuse their partners. Swan et al. (2008) reviewed the literature on women who are violent toward their intimate partners and found that women's physical violence may be just as prevalent as men's violence but is more likely to be motivated by self-defense and fear, whereas men's physical violence is more likely than women's to be driven by control motives. Hence, women who are violent toward their partners tend to be striking back rather than throwing initial blows. An abusive female wrote the following:

> When people think of physical abuse in relationships, they get the picture of a man hitting or pushing the woman. Very few people, including myself, think about the "poor man" who is abused both physically and emotionally by his partner—but this is what I do to my boyfriend. We have been together for over a year now and things have gone from really good to terrible.
>
> The problem is that he lets me get away with taking out my anger on him. No matter what happens during the day, it's almost always his fault. It started out as kind of a joke. He would laugh and say "oh, how did I know that this was going to somehow be my fault." But then it turned into me screaming at him, and not letting him go out and be with his friends as his "punishment."
>
> Other times, I'll be talking to him or trying to understand his feelings about something that we're arguing about and he won't talk. He just shuts off and refuses to say anything but "alright." That makes me furious, so I start verbally and physically attacking him just to get a response.
>
> Or, an argument can start from just the smallest thing, like what we're going to watch on TV, and before you know it, I'm pushing him off the bed and stepping on his stomach as hard as I can and throwing the remote into the toilet. That really gets to him.

Stalking in Person

Abuse may take the form of stalking. **Stalking** is defined as unwanted following or harassment that induces fear in a target person. Stalking is a crime. A stalker is one who has been rejected by a previous lover or is obsessed with a stranger or acquaintance who fails to return the stalker's romantic overtures. In about 80 percent of cases, the stalker is a heterosexual male who follows his previous lover. Women who stalk are more likely to target a married male. Stalking is a pathological emotional or motivational state (Meloy and Fisher 2005). Over a third (33.7 percent) of 1,319 university students reported that they had been stalked (followed and harassed) (Knox and Zusman 2009). Such stalking is usually designed either to seek revenge or to win a partner back.

National Data

Between 8 percent and 15 percent of women and between 2 percent and 4 percent of men in the United States will be stalked in their lifetime (Meloy and Fisher 2005).

Stalking Online—Cybervictimization

Cybervictimization includes being sent threatening e-mail, unsolicited obscene e-mail, computer viruses, or junk mail (spamming). It may also include flaming (online verbal abuse), and leaving improper messages on message boards. Cybervictimization in reference to Internet dating is "minimal." This is the conclusion of Jerin and Dolinsky (2007) and is based on a study of 134 people who completed profiles on a variety of Internet dating sites. Cyberangels.org is a website which promotes online safety.

Prior to stalking is **obsessive relational intrusion** (ORI), the relentless pursuit of intimacy with someone who does not want it. The person becomes a nuisance but does not have the goal of harm as does the stalker. When ORI and stalking are combined, as many as 25 percent of women and 10 percent of men can expect to be pursued in unwanted ways (Spitzberg and Cupach 2007).

People who cross the line in terms of pursuing an ORI relationship or responding to being rejected (stalking) engage in a continuum of eight forms of behavior. Spitzberg and Cupach (2007) have identified these:

1. Hyperintimacy—telling a person that they are beautiful or desirable to the point of making them uncomfortable.

2. Relentless electronic contacts—flooding the person with e-mail messages, cell phone calls, text messages, or faxes.

3. Interactional contacts—showing up at the person's work or gym. The intrusion may also include joining the same volunteer groups as the pursued.

4. Surveillance—monitoring the movements of the pursued such as following the person or driving by the person's house.

5. Invasion—breaking into the person's house and stealing objects that belong to the person; identity theft; or putting Trojan horses (viruses) in the person's computer. One woman downloaded child pornography on her boyfriend's computer and called the authorities to arrest him. He is now in prison.

6. Harassment or intimidation—leaving unwanted notes on one's desk or a dead animal on one's doorstep.

7. Threat or coercion—threatening physical violence or harm to the person or one's family or friends.

8. Aggression or violence—carrying out a threat by becoming violent (for example, kidnapping or rape).

Let's go kick some ass.

George W. Bush, in response to the terrorists attack. 9/11

Stalking may occur in the form of cybervictimization, whereby a jilted person may send a lover threatening e-mails, computer viruses, or junk mail (spamming).

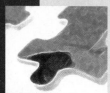
We should meet abuse by forbearance. Human nature is so constituted that if we take absolutely no notice of anger or abuse, the person indulging in it will soon weary of it and stop.

Mohandas Gandhi

Explanations for Violence and Abuse in Relationships

Research suggests that numerous factors contribute to violence and abuse in intimate relationships. These factors include those that occur at the cultural, community, and individual and family levels.

Cultural Factors

In many ways, American culture tolerates and even promotes violence. Violence in the family stems from the acceptance of violence in our society as a legitimate means of enforcing compliance and solving conflicts at interpersonal, familial, national, and international levels. Violence and abuse in the family may be linked to cultural factors, such as violence in the media, acceptance of corporal punishment, gender inequality, and the view of women and children as property. The context of stress is also conducive to violence.

Violence in the Media   One need only watch the evening news to see the violence in countries such as Iraq. In addition, feature films and TV movies regularly reflect themes of violence. In 2007, the film *No Country for Old Men* won four academy awards including Best Picture. The film is ultraviolent, depicting incessant merciless violence and murder. Its selection as Best Picture reflects a society that finds value in violence. However, media violence is only the beginning. Football is a very violent sport. Not only football players, but also males who have football players as friends, are more likely to get into fights (Kreager 2007).

Corporal Punishment of Children   **Corporal punishment** is defined as the use of physical force with the intention of causing a child to experience pain, but not injury, for the purpose of correction or control of the child's behavior. In the United States, it is legal in all fifty states for a

Diversity in Other Countries

On 1979, Sweden passed a law that effectively abolished corporal punishment as a legitimate child-rearing practice. Fifteen other countries, including Italy, Germany, and Ukraine, have banned all corporal punishment in all settings, including the home (Global Initiative to End All Corporal Punishment of Children 2005).

parent to spank, hit, belt, paddle, whip, or otherwise inflict punitive pain on a child so long as the corporal punishment does not meet the individual state's definition of child abuse. Violence has become a part of our cultural heritage through the corporal punishment of children. In a review of the literature, 94 percent of parents of toddlers reported using corporal punishment (Straus 2000). Spankers are more likely to be young parents and mothers and to have been hit when they were children (Walsh 2002). Children who are victims of corporal punishment display more antisocial behavior, are more violent, and have an increased incidence of depression as adults. Straus (2000) recommended an end to corporal punishment to reduce the risk of physical abuse and other harm to children.

Gender Inequality   Domestic violence and abuse may also stem from traditional gender roles. Nayak et al. (2003) found that individuals in countries espousing very restrictive roles for women (for example, Kuwait) tend to be more accepting of violence against women. Traditionally, men have also been taught that they are superior to women and that they may use their aggression toward women, believing that women need to be "put in their place." The greater the inequality and dependence of the woman on the man, the more likely the abuse.

Football is a very violent sport . . . but it is thought of as entertainment rather than violence.

Daniel Padavona/ 2008/ Used under license from Shutterstock.com

Some occupations lend themselves to contexts of gender inequality. In military contexts, men notoriously devalue, denigrate, and sexually harass women. In spite of the rhetoric about gender equality in the military, half of the women in the Army, Navy, and Air Force academies in a 2004 Pentagon survey reported being sexually harassed (Komarow 2005). These male perpetrators may not separate their work roles from their domestic roles. One student in our classes noted that she was the wife of a Navy Seal and that "he knew how to torment someone, and I was his victim."

Being a police officer may also be associated with abuse. Johnson et al. (2005) studied 413 officers and found that burnout, authoritarian style, alcohol use, and department withdrawal were associated with domestic violence. A team of researchers (Erwin et al. 2005) compared 106 police officers who had been charged with intimate partner violence with 105 police officers without such an offense and found that minority status, being on the force for over seven years, and being assigned to a high-crime district were associated with domestic violence. The combined data from these two studies suggest that the stress of being a police officer seems to make one vulnerable to domestic abuse.

Not surprisingly, marital violence is found to occur at a higher rate among those with less education (Verma 2003), which is another context for inequality. Similarly, women who have higher incomes than their husbands report a higher frequency of beatings by their husbands (Verma 2003).

In cultures where a man's "honor" is threatened if his wife is unfaithful, the husband's violence toward her is tolerated. In some cases, formal, legal traditions defend a man's right to beat or even to kill his wife in response to her infidelity (Vandello and Cohen 2003). Unmarried women in Jordan who have intercourse are viewed as bringing shame on their parents and

Diversity in Other Countries

The prevalence of intimate partner violence toward women varies by country. In a study of ten countries (Bangladesh, Brazil, Ethiopia, Japan, Namibia, Peru, Samoa, Serbia and Montenegro, Thailand, and Tanzania), the percentage of those who had been in a relationship who reported having experienced either sexual or physical violence, or both, ranged from 15 percent in a Japanese city to 71 percent in an Ethiopian province. In most countries, an intimate partner more commonly perpetrates violence against women than by anyone else (Ball 2007).

Diversity in Other Countries

In a study on marital power, conflict, and violence in South Korea (where the patriarchal authority power structure is in place), Kim and Emery (2003) found that violence against women who were not subservient was considered justified. They recommended that the only way to mute such abusiveness was for the roles between women and men to become more egalitarian.

siblings and may be killed; this is referred to as an **honor crime** or **honor killing.** The legal consequence is minimal to nonexistent.

View of Women and Children as Property   Prior to the late nineteenth century, a married woman was considered the property of her husband. A husband had a legal right and marital obligation to discipline and control his wife through the use of physical force.

No woman has to be a victim of physical abuse. Women have to feel like they are not alone.

Selma Hayek, actress

Stress   Our culture is also a context of stress. The stress associated with getting and holding a job, rearing children, staying out of debt, and paying bills may predispose one to lash out at others. Haskett et al. (2003) found that parenting stress was particularly predictive of child abuse. People who have learned to handle stress by being abusive toward others are vulnerable to becoming abusive partners.

Community Factors

Community factors that contribute to violence and abuse in the family include social isolation, poverty, and inaccessible or unaffordable health care, day care, eldercare, and respite care services and facilities.

Social Isolation   Living in social isolation from extended family and community members increases the risk of being abused. Spouses whose parents live nearby are least vulnerable.

Poverty   Abuse in adult relationships occurs among all socioeconomic groups. However, poverty and low socioeconomic development are associated with crime and higher incidences of violence. This violence may spill over into interpersonal relationships as well as the frustration of living in poverty.

Inaccessible or Unaffordable Community Services   Failure to provide medical care to children and elderly family members sometimes results from the lack of accessible or affordable health care services in the community. Failure to provide supervision for children and adults may result from inaccessible day-care and eldercare services. Without eldercare and respite care facilities, families living in social isolation may not have any help with the stresses of caring for elderly family members and children.

Individual Factors

Individual factors associated with domestic violence and abuse include psychopathology, personality characteristics, and alcohol or substance abuse.

Personality Factors   A number of personality characteristics have been associated with people who are abusive in their intimate relationships. Some of these characteristics follow:

   1. *Dependency.* Therapists who work with batterers have observed that they are extremely dependent on their partners. Because the thought of being left by their partners induces panic and abandonment anxiety, batterers use physical aggression and threats of suicide to keep their partners with them.

   2. *Jealousy.* Along with dependence, batterers exhibit jealousy, possessiveness, and suspicion. An abusive husband may express his possessiveness by isolating his wife from others; he may insist she stay at home, not work, and not socialize with others. His extreme, irrational jealousy may lead him to accuse his wife of infidelity and to beat her for her presumed affair. Indeed, O.J. Simpson said, "If I killed my wife it would be because I was jealous and loved her—right?"

3. *Need to control.* Abusive partners have an excessive need to exercise power over their partners and to control them. The abusers do not let their partners make independent decisions, and they want to know where they are, whom they are with, and what they are doing. They like to be in charge of all aspects of family life, including finances and recreation.

4. *Unhappiness and dissatisfaction.* Abusive partners often report being unhappy and dissatisfied with their lives, both at home and at work. Many abusers have low self-esteem and high levels of anxiety, depression, and hostility. They may expect their partner to make them happy.

5. *Anger and aggressiveness.* Abusers tend to have a history of interpersonal aggressive behavior. They have poor impulse control and can become instantly enraged and lash out at the partner. Battered women report that episodes of violence are often triggered by minor events, such as a late meal or a shirt that has not been ironed.

6. *Quick involvement.* Because of feelings of insecurity, the potential batterer will move his partner quickly into a committed relationship. If the woman tries to break off the relationship, the man will often try to make her feel guilty for not giving him and the relationship a chance.

7. *Blaming others for problems.* Abusers take little responsibility for their problems and blame everyone else. For example, when they make mistakes, they will blame their partner for upsetting them and keeping them from concentrating on their work. A man may become upset because of what his partner said, hit her because she smirked at him, and kick her in the stomach because she poured him too much alcohol.

8. *Jekyll-and-Hyde personality.* Abusers have sudden mood changes so that a partner is continually confused. One minute an abuser is nice, and the next minute angry and accusatory. Explosiveness and moodiness are typical.

9. *Isolation.* An abusive person will try to cut off a partner from all family, friends, and activities. Ties with anyone are prohibited. Isolation may reach the point at which an abuser tries to stop the victim from going to school, church, or work.

10. *Alcohol and other drug use.* Whether alcohol reduces one's inhibitions to display violence, allows one to avoid responsibility for being violent, or increases one's aggression, alcohol and substance abuse is associated with violence and abuse.

11. *Emotional deficit.* Some abusing spouses and parents may have been reared in contexts that did not provide them with the capacity to love, nurture, or be emotionally engaged. Rosenbaum and Leisring (2003) found that men who abuse women report having had limited love from their mothers, more punishment from their mothers, and less attention from their fathers than men who do not abuse their partners.

Family Factors

Family factors associated with domestic violence and abuse include being abused as a child, having parents who abused each other, and not having a father in the home.

Child Abuse in Family of Origin   Individuals who were abused as children were more likely to be abusive toward their partners as adults.

Family Conflict   Schaeffer et al. (2005) found that high conflict between spouses, parents, and children was predictive of child abuse. Fathers who were not affectionate were also more vulnerable to being abusive.

Parents Who Abused Each Other   Busby et al. (2008) reconfirmed in a study of 30,600 individuals that the family of orientation is the context where individuals

Violence is the last refuge of the incompetent.

Salvor Hardin, first mayor of Terminus

who observe their parents being violent with each other and who perpetuate the violence as children end up being more likely to be violent in their adult relationships. However, a majority of children who witness abuse do not continue the pattern. A family history of violence is only one factor out of many that may be associated with a greater probability of adult violence.

Sexual Abuse in Undergraduate Relationships

Flack et al. (2008) assessed sexual abuse among undergraduates and found that 44 percent of the women and 7 percent of the men in their sample reported at least one unwanted sexual encounter while at the university. The researchers found no evidence of the **red zone**, the first month of the first year of college when women are most likely to be victims of sexual abuse. In a sample of 1,319 undergraduates at a large southeastern university, 35 percent reported being pressured to have sex by a partner they were dating (Knox and Zusman 2009). Katz et al. (2008) noted that some women experience sexual abuse in addition to a larger pattern of physical abuse and that the combination is associated with less general satisfaction, less sexual satisfaction, more conflict, and more psychological abuse from the partner. In effect, women in these covictimization relationships are miserable.

Acquaintance and Date Rape

The word *rape* often evokes images of a stranger jumping out of the bushes or a dark alley to attack an unsuspecting victim. However, most rapes are perpetrated not by strangers but by people who have a relationship with the victim. About 85 percent of rapes are perpetrated by someone the woman knows. This type of rape is known as **acquaintance rape,** which is defined as nonconsensual sex between adults (of same or other sex) who know each other. The behaviors of sexual coercion occur on a continuum from verbal pressure and threats to the use of physical force to obtain sexual acts, such as kissing, petting, or intercourse.

Men are also raped. Chapleau et al. (2008) found that about 13 percent of men reported being raped. Rape myths abound as it is assumed that "men can't be raped," "men who are raped are gay," and that "men always want sex." Not only is there a double standard of perceptions that only women can be raped but a double standard is operative in the perception of the gender of the person

This coed is a victim of acquaintance rape, which devastated her sense of trust in men. Her new partner (also pictured) has been patient and has helped her to develop a new sense of trust.

engaging in sexual coercion. Men who rape are aggressive; women who rape are promiscuous (Oswald and Russell 2006).

One type of acquaintance rape is **date rape,** which refers to nonconsensual sex between people who are dating or on a date. Women who dress seductively, even wives, are viewed by both undergraduate men and women as partly responsible for being raped by their partners (Whatley 2005).

Women are also vulnerable to repeated sexual force. Daigle et al. (2008) noted that 14 percent to 25 percent of college women experience repeat sexual victimization during the same academic year—they are victims of rape or other unwanted sexual force more than once, often in the same month. The primary reason is that they do not change the context; they may stay in the relationship with the same person and continue to use alcohol or drugs in that context.

Both women and men may pressure a partner to have sex. Buddie and Testa (2005) studied sexual aggressiveness in women (both in and out of college) and found that women who engaged in heavy episodic drinking and who had a high number of sexual partners were most likely to be sexually aggressive and rape or attempt to rape their partners. Sexual arousal is one method a woman uses to be sexually aggressive with a male (see the following quote).

> *I locked the room door that we were in. I kissed and touched him. I removed his shirt and unzipped his pants. He asked me to stop. I didn't. Then I sat on top of him. He had had two beers but wasn't drunk.* (Struckman-Johnson et al. 2003, 84)

Although acts of sexual aggression of women on men do occur, they are less frequent than women being raped. An example provided by one of our students follows.

I Was Raped by My Boyfriend

I was 13, a freshman in high school. He was 16, a junior. We were both in band, that's where we met. We started dating and I fell head over heels in love. He was my first real boyfriend. I thought I was so cool because I was a freshman dating a junior. Everything was great for about 6 maybe 8 months and that's when it all started. He began to verbally and emotionally abuse me. He would tell me things like I was fat and ugly and stupid. It hurt me but I was young and was trying so hard to fit in that I didn't really do anything about it.

When he began to drink and smoke marijuana excessively everything got worse. I would try to talk to him about it and he would only yell at me and tell me I was stupid. He began to get physical with the abuse about this time too. He would push me around, grab me really hard, and bruise me up, things like that.

I tried to break up with him and he would tell me that if I broke up with him I would be alone because I was so ugly and fat that no one else would want me. He would say that I was lucky to have him. He began to pressure me for sex. I wasn't ready for sex. I was only 14 at that time. He told everyone that we were having sex and I never said anything different. I was scared to say anything different. It got to the point that I was trying my best to avoid being around him alone. I was afraid of him; I never knew what he would do to me.

Our school band had a competition in Myrtle Beach, South Carolina. When we were there we stayed overnight in a hotel. At the hotel he asked me to come by his room so we could go to dinner together. When I went by his room he pulled me into the room. He locked the door behind me. He pushed me into the bathroom and shut and locked the door behind us. He had his hand over my mouth and told me not to make a sound or he would hurt me. He said that it was time for him to get what everyone already thought he had.

He pushed me up against the counter where the sink was and pulled my clothes off. He put a condom on and began to rape me. I closed my eyes, tears streamed down my face. I had no idea what to do. When he was finished he cleaned himself up and turned on the shower. He pushed me into the shower and told me to take

Date Rape: Undergraduate Victim Profile*

RESEARCH APPLICATION

Methodology

The data for this study were taken from a larger nonrandom sample of 1,027 under-graduates at a large southeastern university whereby 332 or 32.7 percent "agreed or strongly agreed" with the statement, "I have been pressured to have sex by a person I was dating." These respondents were compared with the 67.3 percent who "disagreed or strongly disagreed" that they had been pressured to have sex by a dating partner. Cross-classification was conducted to determine any relationships, with chi-square utilized to assess statistical significance.

Results

Ten significant differences emerged between those who had and had not been date raped:

1. *Female.* Females were significantly (p < .008) more likely than males to report that they had been pressured to have sex by a date (35.5 percent versus 27.0 percent). Oswald and Russell (2006) reported a double standard in regard to gender differences in rape—whereas men are viewed as aggressive, women are regarded as promiscuous.

2. *Having divorced parents.* Undergraduates who reported that their biological parents were divorced were significantly (p < .008) more likely to report having been pressured by a date to have sex than those whose parents were still married (38.7 percent versus 30.0 percent). Decuzzi et al. (2004) found that undergraduates with divorced parents reported being less close to their biological father. Biological fathers may function in the role of providing greater protection for their daughter's sexuality.

3. *Living in a stepfamily.* Respondents who were living in a stepfamily were significantly (p < .03) more likely to report having been pressured by a date to have sex than those who were living in an intact family (38.6 percent versus 30.7 percent). Decuzzi et al. (2004) also confirmed that the remarriage of one's parents further alienates the daughter from the father. Such alienation may be associated with less protection of the daughter's sexuality.

4. *Previous emotional abuse.* Respondents who reported having been in an emotionally abusive relationship were significantly (p < .001) more likely to report having been pressured by a date to have sex than those who had not been in an emotionally abusive relationship (57.8 percent versus 22.3 percent). Emotional abuse may be related to vulnerability to being forced to have sex in that the person's self-esteem is lowered via emotional or verbal abuse. By not feeling good about themselves, they may feel less resistant to unwanted sexual advances: "maybe I deserve this" is the thinking.

5. *Previous physical abuse.* Similar to emotional abuse, respondents who reported having been in a physically abusive relationship were significantly (p < .001) more likely to report having been pressured by a date to have sex than those who had not been in a physically abusive relationship (57 percent versus 29.9 percent). Indeed, physically abused individuals were 27.1 percent more likely to have been date-raped. Whether the physical abuse occurred *before* or *after* the date rape is unknown. Hence, we don't know if these undergraduates had experienced being physically abused, which made abuse

---

Rape is the only crime in which the victim becomes the accused.

Freda Adler

a shower and get ready for dinner. Before he left the room he told me that if I had given in to him and had sex earlier he wouldn't have had to force me. He also told me not to tell anyone or he'd hurt me plus no one would believe me because everyone already thought we had been having sex.

I sat in the shower and cried for a while. I thought it was my fault. I didn't tell anyone about it for two years. I decided not to press charges; I didn't want to go through it again. I regret that decision still to this day. I was an emotional wreck after I was raped. I didn't know how to act. He acted normal, like nothing had happened. A few months later he broke up with me for another girl. It was a relief to me and it made me angry all at the same time. It angered me that he would rape me and then break up with me.

I didn't know what to do with myself. I started working out all the time, several hours a day, every day. After high school I didn't have the time to work out so I developed an eating disorder. This went on for almost 6 years. I am just now dealing with moving past the rape and rebuilding my self-esteem, ability to trust men, and ability to enjoy sex in a new relationship. I encourage anyone who has been raped to speak up about it. Do not let the person get away with it. I also encourage anyone who has been raped to get immediate professional help, don't try to get past it on your own.

normative so that they were less vigilant about being raped or if the date rape influenced the undergraduate to select partners who would be physically abusive. Some research suggests the latter interpretation. Lloyd and Emery (2000) noted physical abuse by a partner leads to fear, feelings of helplessness, confusion, humiliation, and anxiety.

6. *Faithfulness in relationships.* Being faithful also emerged as a characteristic associated with date rape. Respondents who reported never having cheated on a partner they had been involved with were significantly (p < .001) more likely to report having been pressured by a date to have sex than those who had cheated (43.4 percent versus 27.3 percent). These data might suggest that individuals who play by the rules (for example, being faithful) may have been blindsided by a person they did not suspect would rape them.

7. *Cohabitation.* Undergraduates who reported having lived with a person they were not married to were significantly (p < .001) more likely to report having been pressured by a date to have sex than those who had not been in a live-in relationship (44.5 percent versus 30.1 percent). These data are not surprising because previous research has shown that the more serious a relationship (from dating to living together to marriage), the greater the likelihood that abuse will occur in the relationship (Straus and Gelles 1990).

Previous research of rape victims (recall that most rapes are acquaintance rapes) has revealed various characteristics. Mohler-Kuo et al. (2004) analyzed data on over 23,000 women in 119 campuses and found that correlates associated with being raped were being under 21, being white, residing in sorority houses, having used illicit drugs, having drank heavily in high school, and having attended colleges with high rates of heavy episodic drinking. Alcohol use did not appear in the profile of the current study because no question had been asked about alcohol use.

Discussion

It is not known if some of the factors associated with the rape victims in this study occurred *before* or *after* the rape. For example, we don't know if having been involved in an emotionally abusive relationship occurred before or after the rape. Future research should analyze both (a) the time sequence of these many relationships, and (b) the suggested mechanisms, such as "self-esteem."

Sources

Decuzzi, A., D. Knox, and M. Zusman. 2004. The effect of parental divorce on relationships with parents and romantic partners of college students. Roundtable, Southern Sociological Society, Atlanta, GA.

Lloyd, S. A., and B. C. Emery. 2000. *The dark side of courtship: Physical and sexual aggression.* Thousand Oaks, CA: Sage.

Mohler-Kuo, M., G. W. Dowdall, M. P. Koss, and H. Wechsler. 2004. Correlates of rape while intoxicated in a national sample of college women. *Journal of Studies on Alcohol* 65:163–74.

Oswald, D. L., and Russell, B. L. 2006. Perceptions of sexual coercion in heterosexual dating relationships: The role of aggressor gender and tactics. *The Journal of Sex Research* 43:87–98.

Straus, M. A., and R. J. Gelles. 1990. *Physical violence in American families: Risk factors and adaptation to violence in 8,145 families.* New Brunswick, NJ: Transaction Publishers.

*Abridged from article of the same name by D. Knox, K. Vail-Smith, and M. Zusman. Research conducted for this text.

Nonagentic Sexual Experiences

Crown and Roberts (2007) identified **nonagentic sexual experiences** as those in which the partner is not a free agent and a sexual event occurs against their will. Kissing could be an example where a female feels obligated to let a guy kiss her. In a representative sample of 566 undergraduate university women, one-third reported one or more nonagentic sexual experiences (from kissing to forced intercourse) in the last ten months. More than half reported one or more such experiences during their college career. This type of rape is similar to **gray rape,** where a partner wonders if she was forceful enough in making clear that she did not want sex and wonders if it was really rape. Nevertheless, the effects of such an event were not inconsequential. Women reported intrusive thoughts, self-blame, and depression.

I was only 9 years old when I was raped by my 19-year-old cousin. He was the first of three family members to sexually molest me.

Oprah Winfrey, talk show host

Rophypnol—The Date Rape Drug

Rophypnol—also known as the date rape drug, rope, roofies, Mexican Valium, or the "forget (me) pill"—causes profound, prolonged sedation and short-term memory loss. Similar to Valium but ten times as strong, Rophypnol is a prescription drug in Europe and used as a potent sedative. It is sold in the United States for about $5, is dropped in a drink (where it is tasteless and odorless), and causes victims to lose their memory for eight to ten hours. During this time, victims may be raped yet be unaware until they notice signs of it. A former student in our classes reported being drugged ("he put something in my drink") by a "family friend" when she was 16. She noticed blood in her panties the next morning but had no memory of the previous evening. The "friend" is currently being prosecuted.

The Drug-Induced Rape Prevention and Punishment Act of 1996 makes it a crime to give a controlled substance to anyone without their knowledge and with the intent of committing a violent crime (such as rape). Violation of this law is punishable by up to twenty years in prison and a fine of $250,000.

Women are defenseless when drugged. When an assault begins when the woman is not raped, her responses may vary from pleading to resistance including "turning cold" and "running away." Gidycz et al. (2008) discussed the various responses in terms of background. Women who had been victimized as children were more likely to "freeze and turn cold."

The effect of rape, whether drug-induced or not, is negative to devastating. In addition to the loss of self-esteem, loss of trust, and ability to be sexual, Campbell and Wasco (2005) emphasized that rape also affects the family, friends, and significant others of the victim. In regard to preventing rape, Brecklin and Ullman (2005) analyzed data on 1,623 women and noted that those who had had self-defense or assertiveness training reported that their resistance stopped the offender or made him less aggressive than victims without such training. Women with the training also noted that they were less scared during the attack.

Abuse in Marriage Relationships

The chance of abuse in a relationship increases with marriage. Indeed, the longer individuals know each other and the more intimate the relationship, the greater the abuse.

General Abuse in Marriage

Abuse in marriage differs from unmarried abuse in that the husband may feel "ownership" of the wife and feel the need to "control her." The following reveals the experience of horrific marital abuse by a woman who survived it:

Twenty-Three Years in an Abusive Marriage

My name is Jane and I am a survivor (though it took me forever to get out) of a physically and mentally abusive marriage. I met my husband-to-be in high school when I was 15. He was the most charming person that I had ever met. He would see me in the halls and always made a point of coming over to speak. I remember thinking how cool it was that an older guy would be interested in a little freshman like me. He asked me out but my parents would not let me go out with him until I turned 16 so we met at the skating rink every weekend until I was old enough to go out on a date with him. Needless to say, I was in love and we didn't date other people.

When we married I remember the wedding day very well as I was on top of the world because I was marrying the man of my dreams whom I loved very much. My family (they did not like him) tried for the longest time to talk me out of marrying him. My dad always told me that something was not right with him but I did not listen. I wish to God that I had listened to my dad and walked out of the church before I said "I do."

I remember the first slap, which came six months after we had been married. I had burned the toast for his dinner. I was shocked when he slapped me, cried, and when he saw the blood coming from my lip he started crying and telling me he was sorry and that he would never do that again. But the beatings never stopped for twenty-three years. His most famous way of torturing me was to put a gun to my head while I was sleeping and wake me up and pull the trigger and say next time you might not be so lucky.

I left this man a total of seventeen times but I always went back after I got well from my beatings. At one point during this time every bone in my body had been broken with the exception of my neck and back. Some bones more than once and sometimes more than one at a time. I was pushed down a flight of stairs and still suffer from the effects of it to this day. I was stabbed several times and I had to be hospitalized a total of six times.

After our children were born I thought the beatings would stop but they didn't. When our children got older he started on them so I took many beatings for my children just so he would leave them alone. Three years ago he beat me so badly that I almost died. I remember being in the hospital wanting to die because if I did I would not hurt anymore and I would finally be safe. At that time I was thinking that death would be a blessing since I would not have to go back to live with this monster.

While I was in the hospital a therapist came to see me and told me that I had two choices—go home and be killed or fight for my life and live. Instead of going back to the monster, I moved my children in with my mother. It took me three years to get completely clear of him, and even today he harasses me but I am free. I had to learn how to think for myself and how to love again. I am now remarried to a wonderful man.

If you are in an abusive relationship there is help out there and please don't be afraid to ask for it. I can tell you this much—the first step (deciding to leave) is the hardest to take. If and when you do leave I promise your life will be better—it may take awhile but you will get there.

PERSONAL CHOICES

Would You End an Abusive Marital Relationship?

Students in our classes were asked whether they would end a marriage if the spouse hit or kicked them. Some of their comments follow.

Most said, "Don't overreact and try to work it out." Many felt that marriage was too strong a commitment to end if the abuse could be stopped.

> *I would not divorce my spouse if she hit or kicked me. I'm sure that there's always room for improvement in my behavior, although I don't think it's necessary to assault me. I recognize that under certain circumstances, it's the quickest way to draw my attention to the problems at hand. I would try to work through our difficulties with my spouse.*

***

> *The physical contact would lead to a separation. During that time, I would expect him to feel sorry for what he had done and to seek counseling. My anger would be so great, it's quite hard to know exactly what I would do.*

***

> *I wouldn't leave him right off. I would try to get him to a therapist. If we could not work through the problem, I would leave him. If there was no way we could live together, I guess divorce would be the answer.*

***

> *I would not divorce my husband, because I don't believe in breaking the sacred vows of marriage. But I would separate from him and let him suffer!*

***

> *I would tell her I was leaving but that she could keep me if she would agree for us to see a counselor to ensure that the abuse never happened again.*

Some said, "Seek a divorce." Those opting for divorce (a minority) felt they couldn't live with someone who had abused or might abuse them again.

I abhor violence of any kind, and since a marriage should be based on love, kicking is certainly unacceptable. I would lose all respect for my husband and I could never trust him again. It would be over.

Many therapists emphasize that a pattern of abuse develops and continues if such behavior is not addressed immediately. The first time abuse occurs, the couple should seek therapy. The second time it occurs, they should separate. The third time, they might consider a divorce. Later in the chapter we discussed disengaging from an abusive relationship.

Rape in Marriage

Marital rape, now recognized in all states as a crime, is forcible rape by one's spouse (Rousseve 2005). The forced sex may take the form of sexual intercourse, fellatio, or anal intercourse. Sexual violence against women in an intimate relationship is often repeated. Rand (2003) analyzed data from the National Violence Against Women Survey and noted that about half of the women raped by an intimate partner and two-thirds of the women physically assaulted by an intimate partner had been victimized multiple times.

Effects of Abuse

Abuse affects the physical and psychological well-being of victims. Abuse between parents also affects the children.

Effects of Partner Abuse on Victims

Sarkar (2008) identified the negative impact of intimate partner violence. IPV affected the woman's physical and mental health, and increased the risk for unintended pregnancy and multiple abortions. These women also reported high levels of anxiety and depression that often led to alcohol and drug abuse. Violence on pregnant women significantly increased the risk for infants of low birth weight, preterm delivery, and neonatal death. Katz and Myhr (2008) noted that 21 percent of 193 female undergraduates were experiencing verbal sexual coercion in their current relationships. The effects included feeling psychologically abused, arguing, and decreased relationship satisfaction and sexual functioning.

Effects of Partner Abuse on Children

Abuse between adult partners affects children. In the most dramatic effect, some women are abused during their pregnancy, resulting in a high rate of miscarriage and birth defects. Negative effects may also accrue to children who just witness domestic abuse. Kitzmann et al. (2003) analyzed 118 studies to identify outcomes for children who were and were not exposed to violence between their parents. The researchers found more negative outcomes (for example, arguing, withdrawing, avoidance, overt hostility) among children who had witnessed such behavior than those who had not.

Howard et al. (2002) found that adolescents who had witnessed violence reported "intrusive thoughts, distraction, and feeling a lack of belonging" (p. 455). Children who witness high levels of parental violence are also more likely to blame themselves for the violence (Grych et al. 2003), to be violent toward their parents (particularly their mother) (Ulman and Straus 2003), and to engage in aggressive delinquent behavior (Kernic et al. 2003).

Diversity in Other Countries

Parish et al. (2007) reported on a national sample of 1,127 married urban Chinese women aged 20 to 64. Almost a third (32 percent) reported experiencing unwanted spousal intercourse with about one-fifth of these events involving force. Almost three-fourths (73 percent) reported having sex only to please the husband. Wives reported lack of daily intimacy or foreplay and husband's insensitivity to wife's sexual needs. The result of the wife's unwanted sexual activity was diminished psychological well-being.

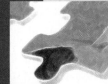

What if I'm Not Sure I Am Being Abused?

WHAT IF?

Sometimes it is not easy to know what constitutes being abused. Is a wife's PMS irritability and criticism considered abuse? Is calling a partner stupid considered abuse? Is shoving a partner an abusive act? In general, any verbal or physical behavior that is designed to denigrate and belittle the other (or take away the freedom of the other) is abuse.

How much should a person tolerate? The answer is very little, because the partner will be reinforced for being abusive and will continue to do so. In only a short time, being demeaning and pushing or shoving a partner can become routine acts considered normative in a couple's relationship. If you don't like the way your partner is treating you, it is important to register your disapproval quickly so that being abused is not an option. In Chapter 1, we discussed, "Not to decide is to decide." If you don't make a decision that you will not tolerate being abused, you have made a decision whereby you will be abused . . . and the abuse will escalate.

It is not unusual for children to observe and to become involved in adult domestic violence. One-fourth of 114 battered mothers noted that their children yelled, called for help, or intervened when an adult partner was physically abusing the mother (Edleson et al. 2003).

He [Chet Baker] would sing the tenderest love songs of romance, then beat up the woman he professed love to.

James Gavin, *Deep in a Dream: The Long Night of Chet Baker*

The Cycle of Abuse

The following reflects the cycle of abuse.

"I Got Flowers Today"

I got flowers today. It wasn't my birthday or any other special day. We had our first argument last night, and he said a lot of cruel things that really hurt me. I know he is sorry and didn't mean the things he said, because he sent me flowers today.

I got flowers today. It wasn't our anniversary or any other special day. Last night, he threw me into a wall and started to choke me. It seemed like a nightmare. I couldn't believe it was real. I woke up this morning sore and bruised all over. I know he must be sorry, because he sent me flowers today.

Last night, he beat me up again. And it was much worse than all the other times. If I leave him, what will I do? How will I take care of my kids? What about money? I'm afraid of him and scared to leave. But I know he must be sorry, because he sent me flowers today.

I got flowers today. Today was a very special day. It was the day of my funeral. Last night, he finally killed me. He beat me to death.

If only I had gathered enough courage and strength to leave him, I would not have gotten flowers today.

Author unknown

The cycle of abuse begins when a person is abused and the perpetrator feels regret, asks for forgiveness, and starts acting nice (for example, gives flowers). The victim, who perceives few options and feels guilty terminating the relationship with the partner who asks for forgiveness, feels hope for the relationship at the contriteness of the abuser and does not call the police or file charges. Forgiving the partner and taking him back usually occurs seven times before the partner leaves for good. Shakespeare (in *As You Like It*) said of such forgiveness, "Thou prun'st a rotten tree."

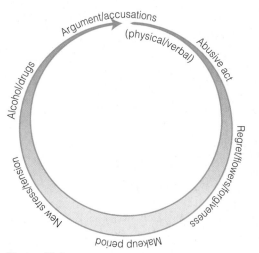

Figure 13.1
The Cycle of Abuse

After the forgiveness, couples usually experience a period of making up or honeymooning, during which the victim feels good again about the partner and is hopeful for a nonabusive future. However, stress, anxiety, and tension mount again in the relationship, which is relieved by violence toward the victim. Such violence is followed by the familiar sense of regret and pleadings for forgiveness, accompanied by being nice (a new bouquet of flowers, and so on).

As the cycle of abuse reveals, some victims do not prosecute their partners who abuse them. To deal with this problem, Los Angeles has adopted a "zero tolerance" policy toward domestic violence. Under the law, an arrested person is required to stand trial and his victim required to testify against the perpetrator. The sentence in Los Angeles County for partner abuse is up to six months in jail and a fine of $1,000.

Figure 13.1 illustrates this cycle, which occurs in clockwise fashion. In the rest of this section, we discuss reasons why people stay in an abusive relationships and how to get out of such relationships.

Why People Stay in Abusive Relationships

One of the most frequently asked questions of people who remain in abusive relationships is, "Why do you stay?" Few and Rosen (2005) interviewed twenty-five women who had been involved in abusive dating relationships from three months to nine years (average = 2.4 years) to find out why they stayed. The researchers conceptualized the women as **entrapped**—stuck in an abusive relationship and unable to extricate one's self from the abusive partner. Indeed, these women escalated their commitment to stay in hopes that doing so would eventually pay off. Among the factors of their perceived investment were the time they had already spent in the relationship, the sharing of their emotional self with their partner, and the relationships to which they were connected because of the partner. In effect, they had invested time with a partner they were in love with and wanted to turn the relationship around into a safe, nonabusive one. The following are some of the factors explaining how abused women become entrapped:

- Fear of loneliness ("I'd rather be with someone who abuses me than alone")
- Love ("I love him")
- Emotional dependency ("I need him")
- Commitment to the relationship ("I took a vow 'for better or for worse'")
- Hope ("He will stop")
- A view of violence as legitimate ("All relationships include some abuse")
- Guilt ("I can't leave a sick man")
- Fear ("He'll kill me if I leave him")
- Economic dependence ("I have no place to go")
- Isolation ("I don't know anyone who can help me")

Battered women also stay in abusive relationships because they rarely have escape routes related to educational or employment opportunities, their relatives are critical of plans to leave the partner, they do not want to disrupt the lives of their children, and they may be so emotionally devastated by the abuse (anxious, depressed, or suffering from low self-esteem) that they feel incapable of planning and executing their departure.

Diversity in Other Countries

Rivers (2005) interviewed Navajo women who had been abused by their husbands and discovered the term *hozho*, which helps to explain cultural motivations for their staying with an abuser. Hozho means beauty and harmony, and when the husband is abusive to his wife there is disharmony . . . but men and women belong together, to contribute to this ultimate beauty, so leaving the husband is not an easy consideration. Also, there is the belief that the husband is "out of balance," and the Navajo woman is less likely to leave a man who is "sick."

How One Leaves an Abusive Relationship

Leaving an abusive partner begins with the decision to do so. Such a choice often follows the belief that one will die or one's children will be harmed by staying.

A plan comes into being and the person acts (for example, moves in with a sister, mother, friend, or goes to a homeless shelter). If the alternative is better than being in the abusive context, the person will stay away. Otherwise, the person may go back and start the cycle all over. As noted previously, this leaving and returning typically happens seven times.

Sometimes the woman does not just disappear while the abuser is away but calls the police and has the man arrested for violence and abuse. While the abuser is in jail, she may move out and leave town. In either case, disengagement from the abusive relationship takes a great deal of courage. Calling the National Domestic Violence Hotline (800-799-7233 [SAFE]), available twenty-four hours, is a point of beginning. Earlier, we discussed the need to be cautious in leaving a partner because this is the time the woman is most vulnerable to being murdered.

Some women who withdraw go to abuse shelters. A team of researchers (Ham-Rowbottom et al. 2005) conducted a follow-up of eighty-one abuse victims who had escaped their situations and graduated from the abuse shelter. Although all of the women were now living independently, 43 percent and 75 percent reported clinical levels of depression and trauma symptoms, respectively. The researchers noted that earlier child sexual abuse accounted for much of the continued psychological depression and trauma.

Kress et al. (2008) noted that involvement with an intimate partner who is violent may be life-threatening. Particularly if the individual decides to leave the violent partner, the abuser may react with more violence and murder the person who has left. Indeed, a third of murders that occur in domestic violence cases occur shortly after a breakup. Specific signs that could be precursors to someone about to murder an intimate partner are stalking, strangulation, forced sex, physical abuse, perpetrator suicidality, gun ownership, and drug or alcohol use on the part of the violent partner.

Individuals in such relationships should be cautious about how they react and develop a safe plan of withdrawal. Safety plans will vary but include the following:

- Identifying a safe place an individual can go the next time she needs to leave the house. A friend or women's shelter must be set up in advance. The victim needs to stay in a protected context.
- Telling friends or neighbors about the violence and requesting that they call the police if they hear suspicious noises or witness suspicious events.
- Storing an escape kit (for example, keys, money, checks, important phone numbers, medications, Social Security cards, bank documents, birth certificates, change of clothes, and so on) somewhere safe (and usually not in the house) (Kress et al. 2008).

Above all, individuals should trust their instincts and do what they can to de-escalate the situation.

Strategies to Prevent Domestic Abuse

Family violence and abuse prevention strategies are focused at three levels: the general population, specific groups thought to be at high risk for abuse, and families who have already experienced abuse. Public education and media campaigns aimed at the general population convey the criminal nature of domestic assault, suggest ways abusers might learn to prevent abuse (seek therapy for anger, jealousy, or dependency), and identify where abuse victims and perpetrators can get help. Rothman and Silverman (2007) noted that preventative abuse programs for college students were effective in reducing violence for both men and women. However, people with a prior history of assault; who were gay, lesbian, or bisexual; or who were binge drinkers did not benefit.

Preventing or reducing family violence through education necessarily involves altering aspects of American culture that contribute to such violence. For example, violence in the media must be curbed or eliminated (although not easy

It is easier to stay out than to get out.
Mark Twain

with nightly video clips of bombing assaults in other countries and reruns of the violent *Sopranos*, it will eventually disappear), and traditional gender roles and views of women and children as property must be replaced with egalitarian gender roles and respect for women and children.

Another important cultural change is to reduce violence-provoking stress by reducing poverty and unemployment and by providing adequate housing, nutrition, medical care, and educational opportunities for everyone. Integrating families into networks of community and kin would also enhance family well-being and provide support for families under stress.

Treatment of Partner Abusers

Silvergleid and Mankowski (2006) identified learning a new way of masculinity and making a personal commitment to change as crucial to the rehabilitation of the male batterer. These new behaviors can be learned in individual or group therapy. Because alcohol or drug abuse and violence toward a partner are often related, addressing one's alcohol or substance abuse problem is often a prerequisite for treating partner abuse (Stuart 2005).

In addition, some men stop abusing their partners only when their partners no longer put up with it. One abusive male said that his wife had to leave him before he learned not to be abusive toward women. "I've never touched my second wife," he said.

This concludes our discussion of abuse in adult relationships. In the following pages, we discuss other forms of abuse, including child abuse and parent, sibling, and elder abuse.

General Child Abuse

National Data

Over 3.5 million children are alleged to have been abused and are the subjects of an abuse investigation each year by protective services (*Statistical Abstract of the United States, 2009*, Table 330). More than one thousand children die annually as a result of child abuse (Trokel et al. 2006).

Child abuse may take many forms—physical abuse, neglect, and sexual abuse.

Physical Abuse and Neglect

Horrific accounts of child abuse are not unheard of. Brenda Sullivan of Jacksonville, Florida, was sentenced to twenty years in prison in 2008, for keeping her 17-year-old adopted son in a cage. When authorities found the teenager, he weighed forty-eight pounds. "She literally starved him," said prosecutor Julie Schlax (Associated Press 2008). Worse, in his cramped cellar, 73-year-old Austrian Josef Fritzl held his own daughter prisoner, beat her and raped her, fathering seven children with her over a period that lasted nearly a quarter of a century. This was known as the "worst and most shocking case of incest in Austrian criminal history"; the retired electrical engineer also had seven other children with his own wife. He had lived a double life for twenty-four years and made a full confession (Paterson 2008).

Child abuse can be defined as any interaction or lack of interaction between children and their parents or caregiver that results in nonaccidental harm to the children's physical or psychological well-being. Child abuse includes physical abuse, such as beating and burning; verbal abuse, such as insulting or demeaning children; and neglect, such as failing to provide adequate food, hygiene, medical care, or adult supervision for children. Children can also experience emotional neglect by their parents. Children from unintended pregnancies or with poor health and developmental problems are more likely to be abused (Sidebotham et al. 2003).

The percentages of various types of child abuse in substantiated victim cases are illustrated in Figure 13.2. Notice that "neglect" is the largest category of abuse. The children most likely to be neglected are young—between infancy and age 5 (Connell-Carrick 2003). De Paul and Arruabarrena (2003) observed that these families are the most difficult to treat and are the most likely to drop out of therapy.

Although our discussion will focus on physical abuse, it is important to keep in mind that children are often not fed, are not given medical treatment, and are left to fend for themselves.

Factors Contributing to General Child Abuse

A variety of the following factors contribute to child abuse:

1. Parental psychopathology. Symptoms of parental psychopathology that may predispose a parent to abuse or neglect children include low frustration tolerance, inappropriate expression of anger, and alcohol or substance abuse.

Munchausen syndrome by proxy (MSP) is a rare form of child abuse whereby a parent (usually the mother) takes on the sick role indirectly (hence, by proxy) by inducing illness or sickness in her child. The parent may suffocate the child to the point of unconsciousness or scrub the child's skin with sandpaper to induce a rash. The goal of the caretaker (often the mother) is to find a fulfilling role, to get attention from friends and family for being heroic, or to get money from insurance companies. Sheridan (2003) analyzed 451 cases from 154 journals and found that the victims may be either males or females and are usually under 4 years of age. One-fourth of the victims' known siblings were *dead* and 61 percent of the siblings had similar illnesses. Not much is understood about MSP, and accuracy is important "to protect children from abuse and caretakers from false allegations" (p. 444). One way to assess whether MSP is operative is to separate the child from the mother. The children who return to health and show no symptoms of illness in the absence of the mother are victims of their mother's abuse (Wright 2004).

2. Unrealistic expectations. Abusive parents often have unrealistic expectations of their children's behavior. For example, a parent might view the crying of a baby as a deliberate attempt on the part of the child to irritate the parent. **Shaken baby syndrome**—whereby the caretaker, most often the father, shakes the baby to the point of causing the child to experience brain or retinal hemorrhage—most often occurs in response to a baby who won't stop crying (Ricci et al. 2003). Most victims are younger than 6 months (Smith 2003). **Abusive head trauma** (AHT) refers to nonaccidental head injury in infants and toddlers. It is estimated that over one thousand cases of AHT occur each year (Ricci et al. 2003, 279). Head injury is the leading cause of

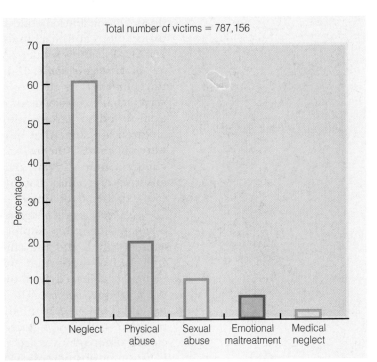

Figure 13.2
Child Abuse and Neglect Cases: 2003
Source: *Statistical Abstract of the United States, 2009.* 128th ed. Washington, DC: U.S. Bureau of the Census, Table 329.

The most prevalent form of child abuse in America today is neglect. People are working 18 hours a day, and our children are being neglected.

Laura Schlessinger, radio personality

Diversity in Other Countries

Alyahria and Goodman (2008) revealed data from caregiver and teacher reports on 1,196 Yemeni 7- to 10-year olds. More than half of the rural caregivers and about a quarter of the urban caregivers reported using harsh corporal punishment (hitting children with implements, tying them up, pinching them, or biting them). This was significantly associated with poor school performance and both behavioral and emotional difficulties.

death among abused children (Rubin et al. 2003). Managing parents' unrealistic expectations and teaching them to cope with frustration are important parts of an overall plan to reduce physical child abuse.

3. *History of abuse.* Individuals who were abused as children are more likely to report abusing their own children (Dixon et al. 2005). The researchers observed that the absence of positive parenting carries over into the next generation. Although parents who were physically or verbally abused or neglected as children are somewhat more likely to repeat that behavior than parents who were not abused, the majority of parents who were abused do *not* abuse their own children. Indeed, many parents who were abused as children are dedicated to ensuring nonviolent parenting of their own children precisely because of their own experience of abuse.

4. *Displacement of aggression.* One cartoon shows several panels consisting of a boss yelling at his employee, the employee yelling at his wife, the wife yelling at their child, and the child kicking the dog, who chases the cat up a tree. Indeed, frustration may spill over from the adults to the children, the latter being less able to defend themselves.

5. *Social isolation.* The saying, "it takes a village to raise a child," is relevant to child abuse. Unlike inhabitants of most societies of the world, many Americans rear their children in closed and isolated nuclear units. In extended kinship societies, other relatives are always present to help with the task of child rearing. Isolation means parents have no relief from the parenting role as well as no supervision by others who might interrupt observed child abuse.

6. *Fatherless homes.* Living in a home where the father is absent increases a child's risk for being abused. Some men may romance a single mother with three young daughters to get access to the daughters whom he may molest. This is largely because stepfathers and mothers' boyfriends are not constrained by the cultural incest taboo that prohibits biological fathers from having sex with their children.

7. *Disability of a child.* Jaudesa and Mackey-Bilaverb (2008) found that children who were developmentally delayed were twice as likely to be victims of abuse and neglect.

8. *Other factors.* In addition to the factors just mentioned, the following factors are also associated with child abuse and neglect:

   a. The pregnancy is premarital or unplanned, and the father or mother does not want the child.
   b. Mother-infant attachment is lacking.
   c. Child-rearing techniques are harsh, with little positive reinforcement.
   d. The parents are unemployed.
   e. Abuse between the husband and wife is present.
   f. The children are adopted or are foster children.

Effects of General Child Abuse

How does being abused in general affect a victim as a child and later as an adult? In general, the effects are negative and vary according to the intensity and frequency of the abuse. Researchers have found that children who have been abused are more likely to display the following:

1. Few close social relationships and an inability to love or trust
2. Communication problems and learning disabilities
3. Aggression, low self-esteem, depression, and low academic achievement
4. Physical injuries that may result in disfigurement, physical disability, or death
5. Increased risk of alcohol or substance abuse and suicidal tendencies as adults
6. Post-traumatic stress disorder (PTSD) (Jonzon and Lindblad 2005)

What is the relative impact of parental emotional abuse, child sexual abuse, and parental substance abuse on a child's development as an adult? Melchert (2000) studied the psychological distress of 255 college students and discovered that the largest amount of distress was explained by previous emotional abuse and neglect.

Kim (2008) compared 188 maltreated and 196 nonmaltreated children (ages 6 to 12 years) and found that religiosity provided a protective effect on negative effects (for example, depression) of maltreatment. The effects were particularly beneficial for boys.

When there is evidence of child abuse, social workers must traditionally choose between leaving children in the home or removing the children from the home and putting them in a foster care home. A new alternative is being tried in Minnesota, whereby an abusive parent is allowed to keep the children but is carefully monitored by friends and family. If parents are drug-addicted, they must agree to treatment and to being drug-tested by friends or family (Coates 2006).

Child Sexual Abuse

Child sexual abuse is often found in combination with other forms of child abuse (Dong et al. 2003). Two types are extrafamilial and intrafamilial.

Extrafamilial Child Sexual Abuse

In extrafamilial child sexual abuse, a perpetrator is someone outside the family who is not related to the child. Extrafamilial child sexual abuse received national attention with the 2002 accusation that an estimated 2,000 priests in the Catholic Church had had sex with young children; more than 3,000 children have claimed abuse (Hewitt et al. 2002). The diocese of Orange County, south of Los Angeles, agreed to pay $100 million to some ninety alleged victims of priests and other church congregants. There are still claims of another 544 alleged victims in the Orange County area alone (*The Economist* 2005).

Extrafamilial sex offenders are not just men. Strickland (2008) studied sixty incarcerated female sex offenders who had had sex with a child under the age of 18. When compared to seventy incarcerated females who were not sex offenders, the former were more likely to report considerable childhood abuse in general, sexual abuse specifically, and to be inadequate in forming adult relationships.

Intrafamilial Child Sexual Abuse

A more frequent type of child sexual abuse is intrafamilial (formerly referred to in professional literature as incest). This refers to exploitive sexual contact or attempted sexual contact between relatives before the victim is 18. Sexual contact or attempted sexual contact includes intercourse, fondling of the breasts and genitals, and oral sex. Relatives include biologically related individuals but may also include stepparents and stepsiblings.

Female children are more likely than male children to be sexually abused. Prevalence rates suggest that one out of four girls and one out of ten boys experience sex abuse (Fieldman and Crespi 2002). However, Goodman et al. (2003) suggested that nearly 40 percent of abused adults fail to report their own documented child sexual abuse. About 60 percent of sexually abused children disclose their abuse to someone within two

Some tourists go abroad to have sex with children. This poster is in an airport in Mexico and warns against this practice.

weeks after it happens—40 percent within forty-eight hours. Children who are younger, who did not feel responsible for the abuse, and who were abused by someone external to the family are more likely to disclose the abuse sooner than older children, those who felt partly responsible, and those who were abused by someone inside the family (Goodman-Brown et al. 2003).

Intrafamilial child sexual abuse involves an abuse of power and authority, particularly when the perpetrator is a parent. The following describes the experience of one woman who was forced to have sexual relations with her father over a period of years:

> *I was around 6 years old when I was sexually abused by my father. He was not drinking at that time; therefore, he had a clear mind as to what he was doing. On looking back, it seemed so well planned. For some reason, my father wanted me to go with him to the woods behind our house to help him saw wood. Once we got there, he looked around for a place to sit and wanted me to sit down with him. He said, "Susan, I want you to do something for Daddy. I want you to lie down, and we are going to play Mama and Daddy." Being a child, I said, "Okay," thinking it was going to be fun. I don't know what happened next and I can't remember if there was pain or whatever. I was threatened not to tell, and remembering how he beat my mother, I didn't want the same treatment. It happened a few more times. I remember not liking this at all.*
>
> *But what could I do? Until age 18, I was constantly on the run, hiding from him when I had to stay home alone with him, staying out of his way so he wouldn't touch me by hiding in the cornfields all day long, under the house, in the barns, and so on until my mother got back home, then getting punished by her for not doing the chores she had assigned to me that day. It was a miserable life, growing up in that environment.*

When an ex-spouse accuses her husband of child sex abuse, more often than not, the sexual abuse did occur. In a study of 9,000 families embroiled in contested divorce proceedings, 169 cases involved an allegation of child sexual abuse. Of these, only 14 percent were deliberately false allegations. Most were proven to be legitimate (Goldstein and Tyler 1998).

Conviction of a child sex abuser is rare. In one study of 323 court cases, only fifteen went to trial, and the offender was convicted in only six cases (Faller and Henry 2000).

Effects of Child Sexual Abuse

Child sexual abuse may have serious negative long-term consequences. Not only are the children violated physically, but they also lose important social support. Adult-child sexual contact is, in most cases, a child's first introduction to adult sexuality. The sexual script acquired during such relationships forms the basis on which other sexual experiences are assimilated. The negative effects include the following:

1. Early forced sex is associated with being withdrawn, anxious, and depressed, and with substance abuse (Walrath et al. 2003). Women who have experienced childhood sexual abuse are 7.75 times more likely to attempt suicide (Anderson et al. 2003). PTSD is also frequently associated with childhood sexual abuse (Koss et al. 2003).

2. Daughters of mothers who have been sexually abused are 3.6 times more likely to be sexually victimized than are daughters whose mothers have not been abused (McCloskey and Bailey 2000). It is possible that women who have been sexually abused develop an "internal working model" of sexual relationships that encompasses exploitative, coercive, and domineering behavior by men. If such a relationship "template" results from early exposure to sexual abuse, then these women might be more tolerant of men either in their households or in their social spheres who are potential abusers of their daughters (p. 1,032).

3. Spouses who were physically and sexually abused as children report lower marital satisfaction, higher individual stress, and lower family cohesion than do couples with no abuse history (Nelson and Wampler 2000).

4. Adult males who were sexually abused as children are more likely to become child molesters themselves (Lussier et al. 2005).

Successful movement beyond negative consequences of being sexually molested as a child involves disclosing the abuse to an accepting adult partner (Jonzon and Lindblad 2005). In addition, an adult who was abused as a child must accept that the adult molester (not the child) was responsible for the abuse (some children feel that they "led the adult on" and are responsible for the abuse). Nolla (2008) also noted that a substantial portion of sex abuse victims is remarkably resilient. Factors associated with such resilience include positive self-esteem, ego control, emotional support, therapy, stable home environments, and having an ability to recall and integrate past adversity into current life circumstances.

Strategies to Reduce Child Sexual Abuse

Strategies to reduce child sexual abuse include regendering cultural roles, providing specific information and training to children to be alert to inappropriate touching, improving the safety of neighborhoods, providing healthy sexuality information for both teachers and children in public schools at regular intervals, and promoting public awareness campaigns.

From a larger societal preventive perspective, Bolen (2001) recommended that child sexual abuse be viewed as a gendered problem. Indeed, "child sexual abuse is endemic within society and may be a result of the unequal power of males over females" (p. 249). Evidence for this claim includes the facts that females are at greater risk of abuse than males, males are more likely to offend, and child sexual abuse is most frequently heterosexual. The implication is that one way to discourage child sexual abuse is to change traditional notions of gender role relationships, masculinity, and male sexuality so that men respect the sexuality of women and children and take responsibility for their sexual behavior.

The public schools also help children acquire specific knowledge and skills to protect themselves from sexual abuse. A survey of 400 school districts in the United States revealed that 85 percent had offered such a prevention program in the past year (Davis and Gidyez 2000). Through various presentations in the elementary schools, children are taught how to differentiate between appropriate and inappropriate touching by adults or siblings, to understand that it is okay to feel uncomfortable if they do not like the way someone else is touching them, to say no in potentially exploitative situations, and to tell other adults if the offending behavior occurs. Boyle and Lutzker (2005) also demonstrated that even young children aged 5 and 6 years can learn to discriminate appropriate and inappropriate touching.

Finally, helping to ensure that children live in neighborhoods safe from convicted child sex offenders may reduce child sexual abuse. Protecting children from former convicted child molesters is the basis of Megan's Law (see the Social Policy section on page 446).

Parent, Sibling, and Elder Abuse

As we have seen, intimate partners and children may be victims of relationship violence and abuse. Parents, siblings, and the elderly may also be abused by family members.

Parent Abuse

Some people assume that, because parents are typically physically and socially more powerful than their children, they are immune from being abused by their children. However, parents are often targets of their children's anger, hostility, and frustration. It is not uncommon for teenage and even younger children to physically and verbally lash out at their parents. Children have been known to push

Megan's Law and Beyond

SOCIAL POLICY

In 1994, Jesse Timmendequas lured 7-year-old Megan Kanka into his Hamilton Township house in New Jersey to see a puppy. He then raped and strangled her and left her body in a nearby park. Prior to his rape of Megan, Timmendequas had two prior convictions for sexually assaulting girls. Megan's mother, Maureen Kanka, argued that she would have kept her daughter away from her neighbor if she had known about his past sex offenses. She campaigned for a law, known as **Megan's Law,** requiring that communities be notified of a neighbor's previous sex convictions. New Jersey and forty-five other states have enacted similar laws.

The 1994 Jacob Wetterling Act requires states to register individuals convicted of sex crimes against children. The law requires that convicted sexual offenders register with local police in the communities in which they live. It also requires the police to go out and notify residents and certain institutions (such as schools) that a previously convicted sex offender has moved into the area. This provision of the law has been challenged on the belief that individuals should not be punished forever for past deeds. Critics of the law argue that convicted child molesters who have been in prison have paid for their crime. To stigmatize them in communities as sex offenders may further alienate them from mainstream society and increase their vulnerability for repeat offenses.

In many states, Megan's Law is not operative because it is on appeal. Parents ask, "Would you want a convicted sex offender, even one who has completed his prison sentence, living next door to your 8-year-old daughter?" However, the reality is that little notification is afforded parents in most states. Rather, the issue is tied up in court and will likely remain so until the Supreme Court decides it. A group of concerned parents (Parents for Megan's Law) are trying to implement Megan's Law nationwide. See the Weblinks section at the end of this chapter for the group's website address.

Parents for Megan's Law have also sought to enact legislation for the "civil commitment for a specific group of the highest-risk sexual predators who freely roam our streets, unwilling or unable to obtain proper treatment. This kind of predator commitment follows a criminal sentence and generally targets repeat sex offenders who then remain in a sexual predator treatment facility until it is safe to release them to a less restrictive environment or into the community." Indeed, this group not only wants parents to be notified of criminal sex offenders but also wants the offenders to be housed in treatment centers on release from prison.

Your Opinion?

1. To what degree do you believe the Supreme Court should uphold Megan's Law?
2. To what degree do you believe that convicted child molesters who have served their prison sentence should be free to live wherever they like without neighbors being aware of their past?
3. Independent of Megan's Law, how can parents protect their children from sex abuse?

---

parents down stairs, set the house on fire while their parents are in it, and use weapons such as guns or knives to inflict serious injuries or even to kill a parent. Background characteristics of children who abuse their parents include observing parents' violence toward each other, having parents who used corporal punishment on their children as a method of discipline (Ulman and Straus 2003), and having parents who were violent toward their children (Ulman 2003).

Sibling Abuse

Observe a family with two or more children and you will likely observe some amount of sibling abuse. Even in "well-adjusted" families, some degree of fighting among children is expected. Most incidents of sibling violence consist of slaps, pushes, kicks, bites, and punches. What passes for "normal," "acceptable," or "typical" behavior between siblings would often be regarded as violent and abusive behavior outside the family context. In this regard, sibling abuse, particularly when compared to parent-child abuse, is underreported and generally of limited concern to Child Protective Services (Caffaro and Conn-Caffaro 2005).

Sibling abuse is said to be the most prevalent form of abuse. Ninety-eight percent of the females and 89 percent of the males in one study reported having received at least one type of emotionally aggressive behavior from a sibling; 88 percent of the females and 71 percent of the males reported having received at least one type of physically aggressive behavior from a sibling (Simonelli et al. 2002).

Sibling abuse may include sexual exploitation, whereby an older brother will coerce younger female siblings into nudity or sex. Though some sex between siblings is consensual, often it is not. "He did me *and* all my sisters before he was done," reported one woman. Another woman reported that, as a child and young adolescent, she performed oral sex on her brother three times a week for years because he told her that ingesting a man's semen was the only way a woman would be able to have babies as an adult. Even milder forms of sibling abuse seem to feed the cycle of abuse, as people who were abused by their siblings report abusing others in their adulthood (Simonelli et al. 2002).

In addition to physical and sexual sibling abuse, there is **sibling relationship aggression.** This is behavior of one sibling toward another sibling that is intended to induce social harm or psychic pain in the sibling. Examples include social alienation or exclusion (for example, not asking the sibling to go to a movie when a group is going), telling secrets or spreading rumors (for example, revealing a sibling's sexual or drug past), and withholding support or acceptance (for example, not acknowledging a sibling's achievements in school and sports). A team of researchers studied 185 sibling pairs—both younger siblings (mean age, 13.47 years) and older siblings (mean age, 15.95 years)—and their respective parents (married an average of 19.5 years). They found that sibling relationship aggression was more likely to occur when intimate feelings between siblings were low and their negativity toward each other was high. Family contexts in which parents are warm and involved with their children are conducive to lower levels of relationship aggression (Updegraff et al. 2005).

Elder Abuse

As increasing numbers of the elderly end up in the care of their children, abuse, though infrequent, is likely to increase.

National Data

About 6 percent of elderly American are victims of abuse each month (Cooper et al. 2008). Annually, 2.1 million elderly are abused, but only one in fourteen incidents come to the attention of the authorities (Plitnick 2008). When abuse is suspected, a nurse can ask simple questions of the patient to elicit information. This should be done in private.

Various examples of abuse include:

1. *Neglect.* Failing to buy or give the elderly needed medicine, failing to take them to receive necessary medical care, or failing to provide adequate food, clean clothes, and a clean bed are examples of neglect. Neglect is the most frequent type of domestic elder abuse; more than 70 percent of all adult protective services reports are for this reason (Fulmer et al. 2005).

2. *Physical abuse.* This includes inflicting injury or physical pain or sexual assault.

3. *Psychological abuse.* Examples of psychological abuse include verbal abuse, deprivation of mental health services, harassment, and deception.

4. *Social abuse.* Unreasonable confinement and isolation, lack of supervision, and abandonment are examples of social abuse.

5. *Legal abuse.* Improper or illegal use of an elder's resources is considered legal abuse.

Lee (2008) studied elder abuse among older adults with disabilities being cared for by their family caregivers. The sample of 1,000 primary family caregivers revealed that elder abuse was more common in those cases where the elderly was cognitively impaired, had functional disabilities, and where there was limited money. The findings suggested that psychosocial support services and programs for family caregivers are needed to prevent and reduce the prevalence of elder abuse.

Another type of elder abuse that has received recent media attention is **granny dumping.** Adult children or grandchildren who feel burdened with the care of their elderly parent or grandparent leave an elder at the entrance of a hospital with no identification. If the hospital cannot identify responsible relatives, it is required by state law to take care of the abandoned elder or transfer the person to a nursing home facility, which is paid for by state funds. Relatives of the dumped elder, hiding from financial responsibility, never visit or see the elder again.

Adult children who are most likely to dump or abuse their parents tend to be under a great deal of stress and to use alcohol or other drugs. In some cases, parent abusers are getting back at their parents for mistreating them as children. In other cases, the children are frustrated with the burden of having to care for their elderly parents. Such frustration is likely to increase. As baby boomers age, they will drain already limited resources for the elderly, and their children will be forced to care for them with little governmental support.

SUMMARY

What is the nature of relationship abuse?

Violence or physical abuse may be defined as the intentional infliction of physical harm by either partner on the other. *Intimate partner violence* (IPV) is an all-inclusive term that refers to crimes committed against current or former spouses, boyfriends, or girlfriends. Battered-woman syndrome refers to the general pattern of battering that a woman is subjected to and is defined in terms of the frequency, severity, and injury she experiences. Violence may be over an issue on which the partners disagree or a mechanism of control. Over four million women are victims of physical violence annually. IPV is associated with PTSD (post-traumatic stress disorder) and results in social maladjustment and personal or social resource loss. Uxoricide is the murder of a woman by a romantic partner. Female violence is as prevalent as male violence. The difference is that female violence is often in response to male violence whereas male violence is more often to control the partner.

Emotional abuse (also known as psychological abuse, verbal abuse, or symbolic aggression) is designed to denigrate the partner, reduce the partner's status, and make the partner vulnerable, thereby giving the abuser more control.

Stalking is unwanted following or harassment that induces fear in the target person. The stalker is most often a heterosexual male who has been rejected by someone who fails to return his advances. Stalking is typically designed either to seek revenge or to win a partner back. Cybervictimization includes being sent threatening e-mail, unsolicited obscene e-mail, computer viruses, or junk mail (spamming). It may also include flaming (online verbal abuse), and leaving improper messages on message boards designed to get back at the person. Obsessive relationship intrusion is the interjection of a person into another's life, which makes the targeted person uncomfortable. Unlike stalkers whose goals are to harm, ORI involves hyperintimacy (telling people that they are beautiful or desirable to the point of making them uncomfortable), relentless mediated contacts (flooding people with e-mail messages, cell phone messages, or faxes), or interactional contacts (showing up at work or the gym, or joining the same volunteer groups as the pursued).

What are explanations for violence in relationships?

Cultural explanations for violence include violence in the media, corporal punishment in childhood, gender inequality, and stress. Community explanations involve social isolation of individuals and spouses from extended family, poverty, inaccessible community services, and lack of violence prevention programs. Individual factors include psychopathology of the person (antisocial), personality (dependency or jealousy), and alcohol abuse. Family factors include child abuse by one's parents and observing parents who abuse each other.

How does sexual abuse in undergraduate relationships manifest itself?

Violence in dating relationships begins as early as grade school, is mutual, and escalates with emotional involvement. Violence occurs more often among couples in which the partners disagree about each other's level of emotional commitment and when the perpetrator has been drinking alcohol or using drugs. About 40 percent of undergraduates report being forced to have sex against their will. Acquaintance rape is defined as nonconsensual sex between adults who know each other.

One type of acquaintance rape is date rape, which refers to nonconsensual sex between people who are dating or on a date. Rophypnol, known as the date rape drug, causes profound sedation so that the person may not remember being raped. Most women do not report being raped by an acquaintance or date. Nonagentic sexual experiences are those in which a partner is not a free agent and a sexual event occurs against the partner's will (from unwanted kissing to sexual intercourse). Half of college students reported one or more nonagentic experiences. Gray rape is where a partner wonders if she was forceful enough in making clear that she did not want sex.

How does abuse in marriage relationships manifest itself?

Abuse in marriage is born out of the need to control the partner and may include repeated rape. About half of the women raped by an intimate partner and two-thirds of the women physically assaulted by an intimate partner have been victimized multiple times.

What are the effects of abuse?

The effects of IPV include physical harm, mental harm (depression, anxiety, low self esteem, lost of trust in others, sexual dysfunctions), unintended pregnancy, and multiple abortions. High levels of anxiety and depression often lead to alcohol and drug abuse. Violence on pregnant women significantly increased the risk for infants of low birth weight, preterm delivery, and neonatal death. Katz and Myhr (2008) noted that 21 percent of 193 female undergraduates were experiencing verbal sexual coercion in their current relationships. The effects included feeling psychologically abused, arguing, decreased relationship satisfaction, and sexual functioning.

What is the cycle of abuse and why do people stay in an abusive relationship?

The cycle of abuse begins when a person is abused and the perpetrator feels regret, asks for forgiveness, and starts acting nice (for example, gives flowers). The victim, who perceives few options and feels guilty terminating the relationship with the partner who asks for forgiveness, feels hope for the relationship at the contriteness of the abuser and does not call the police or file charges. The couple usually experiences a period of making up or honeymooning, during which the victim feels good again about the abusing partner. However, tensions mount again and are released in the form of violence. Such violence is followed by the familiar sense of regret and pleadings for forgiveness, accompanied by being nice (a new bouquet of flowers, and so on).

The reasons people stay in abusive relationships include love, emotional dependency, commitment to the relationship, hope, view of violence as legitimate, guilt, fear, economic dependency, and isolation. The catalyst for breaking free combines the sustained aversiveness of staying, the perception that they and their children will be harmed by doing so, and the awareness of an alternative path or of help in seeking one. One must be cautious in getting out of an abusive relationship because an abuser is most likely to kill his partner when she actually leaves the relationship.

What is child abuse and what factors contribute to it?

Child abuse can be defined as any interaction or lack of interaction between children and their parents or caregiver that results in nonaccidental harm to the children's physical or psychological well-being. Child abuse includes physical abuse, such as beating and burning; verbal abuse, such as insulting or demeaning the children; and neglect, such as failing to provide adequate food, hygiene, medical care, or adult supervision for children. Children can also experience emotional neglect by their parents.

Some of the factors that contribute to child abuse include parental psychopathology, a history of abuse, displacement of aggression, and social isolation.

What are the effects of general child abuse?

The negative effects of child abuse include impaired social relationships, difficulty in trusting others, aggression, low self-esteem, depression, low academic achievement, and post-traumatic stress disorder (PTSD). Physical injuries may result in disfigurement, physical disability, and even death.

One of the most devastating types of child abuse is child sexual abuse, which has serious negative long-term consequences. The effects include being withdrawn, anxious, and depressed; delinquency; suicide attempts; and substance abuse. PTSD, which means recurrent experiencing of the event, is common, as is heavy alcohol or substance abuse. Strategies to reduce child sexual abuse include regendering cultural roles, providing specific information to children on sex abuse, improving the safety of neighborhoods, providing healthy sexuality information for both teachers and children in the public schools at regular intervals, and promoting public awareness campaigns.

What is the nature of parent, sibling, and elder abuse?

Parent abuse is the deliberate harm (physical or verbal) of parents by their children. Ten percent of parents report that they have been hit, bitten, or kicked at least once by their children. About 300 parents are killed by their children annually. The Menendez brothers of California brutally murdered both parents.

Sibling abuse is the most severe prevalent form of abuse. What passes for "normal," "acceptable," or "typical" behavior between siblings would often be regarded as violent and abusive behavior outside the family context.

Elder abuse is another form of abuse in relationships. Granny dumping is a new form of abuse in which children or grandchildren who feel burdened with the care of their elderly parents or grandparents leave them at the emergency entrance of a hospital. If the relatives of the elderly patient cannot be identified, the hospital will put the patient in a nursing home at state expense.

KEY TERMS

abusive head trauma	emotional abuse	marital rape	Rophypnol
acquaintance rape	entrapped	Megan's Law	shaken baby syndrome
battered-woman syndrome	granny dumping	Munchausen syndrome by proxy	sibling relationship aggression
child abuse	gray rape	nonagentic sexual experiences	stalking
child sexual abuse	honor crime	obsessive relational intrusion	symbolic aggression
corporal punishment	honor killing	physical abuse	uxoricide
cybervictimization	intimate-partner violence	psychological abuse	verbal abuse
date rape	intrafamilial child sexual abuse	red zone	violence

The Companion Website for *Choices in Relationships: An Introduction to Marriage and the Family,* Tenth Edition
www.cengage.com/sociology/knox

Supplement your review of this chapter by going to the Companion Website to take one of the tutorial quizzes, use the flash cards to master key terms, or check out the many other study aids, like crossword puzzles and self-assessments. You'll also find special features such as General Social Survey (GSS) data, Census data, and other resources to help you with that special project or to do some research on your own.

WEB LINKS

Childabuse.com
  http://www.childabuse.com/

Male Survivor
  http://www.malesurvivor.org/

Minnesota Center against Violence and Abuse
  http://www.mincava.umn.edu

National Sex Offender Data Base
  http://www.nationalalertregistry.com

Parents for Megan's Law and the Crime Victims Center
  http://www.parentsformeganslaw.com

Rape, Abuse & Incest National Network (RAINN)
  http://www.rainn.org/

Stop It Now! The Campaign to Prevent Child Sexual Abuse
  http://www.stopitnow.com/

V-Day (movement to stop violence against women and girls)
  http://www.vday.org/

REFERENCES

Alyahria, A., and R. Goodman. 2008. Harsh corporal punishment of Yemeni children: Occurrence, type and associations. *Child Abuse and Neglect* 32:766–73.

Anderson, P. L., J. A. Tiro, A. W. Price, M. A. Bender, and N. J. Kaslow. 2003. Additive impact of childhood emotional, physical, and sexual abuse on suicide attempts among low-income African American woman. *Suicide and Life-Threatening Behavior* 32:131–38.

Associated Press. 2008. Mother keeps adopted teenager in cage. May 23.

Ball, H. 2007. Levels of intimate partner violence vary greatly according to country and rural or urban setting. *International Family Planning Perspective* 33:40–42.

Bolen, R. M. 2001. *Child sexual abuse: Its scope and our failure.* New York: Kluwer Academic/Plenum Publishers.

Boyle, C. L., and J. R. Lutzker. 2005. Teaching young children to discriminate abusive from nonabusive situations using multiple exemplars in a modified discrete trial teaching format. *Journal of Family Violence* 20:55–70.

Brecklin, L. R., and S. E. Ullman. 2005. Self-defense or assertiveness training and women's responses to sexual attacks. *Journal of Interpersonal Violence* 20:738–62.

Buddie, A. M., and M. Testa. 2005. Rates and predictors of sexual aggression among students and nonstudents. *Journal of Interpersonal Violence* 20:713–24.

Busby, D. M., T. B. Holman, and E. Walker. 2008. Pathways to relationship aggression between adult partners. *Family Relations* 57:72–83

Caffaro, J. V., and A. Conn-Caffaro. 2005. Treating sibling abuse families. *Aggression and Violent Behavior* 10:604–23.

Campbell, R., and S. M. Wasco. 2005. Understanding rape and sexual assault: 20 years of progress and future directions. *Journal of Interpersonal Violence* 20:127–31.

Chapleau, K. M., D. L. Oswald, and B. L. Russell 2008. Male rape myths: The role of gender, violence, and sexism. *Journal of Interpersonal Violence* 23:600–15.

Cooper, C., A. Selwood, and G. Livingston. 2008. The prevalence of elder abuse and neglect: a systematic review. *Age and Ageing* 37:151–61.

Coates, T. P. 2006. When parents are the threat. *Time,* May 8, Special issue.

Connell-Carrick, K. 2003. A critical review of the empirical literature: Identifying correlates of child neglect *Child and Adolescent Social Work Journal* 20:389–425.

Crown, L., and L. J. Roberts. 2007. Against their will: Young women's nonagentic sexual experiences. *Journal of Social and Personal Relationships* 24:385–405.

Daigle, L. E., B. S. Fisher, and F. T. Cullen. 2008. The violent and sexual victimization of college women: Is repeat victimization a problem? *Journal of Interpersonal Violence* 23:1296–1313.

Davis, M. K., and C. A. Gidyez. 2000. Child sexual abuse prevention programs: A meta-analysis. *Journal of Clinical Child Psychology* 29:257–66.

De Paul, J., and I. Arruabarrena. 2003. Evaluation of a treatment program for abusive and high-risk families in Spain. *Child Welfare* 82:413–42.

Dixon, L., C. Hamilton-Giachritsis, and K. Browne. 2005. Attributions and behaviors of parents abused as children: a mediational analysis of the intergenerational continuity of child maltreatment (Part II). *Journal of Child Psychology and Psychiatry and Allied Disciplines* 46:58–73.

Dong, M., R. F. Anda, S. R. Dube, W. H. Giles, and V. J. Felitti. 2003. The relationship of exposure to childhood sexual abuse to other forms of abuse, neglect, and household dysfunction during childhood. *Child Abuse and Neglect* 27:625–39.

Dugan, L., D. S. Nagin, and R. Rosenfeld. 2003. Exposure reduction or retaliation? The effects of domestic violence resources on intimate-partner homicide. *Law & Society Review* 37:169–98.

The Economist. 2005. The Orange approach. 374:31–33.

Edleson, J. L., L. F. Mbilinyi, S. K. Beeman, and A. K. Hagemeister. 2003. How children are involved in adult domestic violence. *Journal of Interpersonal Violence* 18:18–32.

Erwin, M. J., R. R. M. Gershon, M. Tiburzi, and S. Lin. 2005. Reports of intimate partner violence made against police officers. *Journal of Family Violence* 20:13–20.

Faller, K. C., and J. Henry. 2000. Child sexual abuse: A case study in community collaboration. *Child Abuse and Neglect* 24:1215–25.

Few, A. L., and K. H. Rosen 2005. Victims of chronic dating violence: How women's vulnerabilities link to their decisions to stay *Family Relations* 54:265–79.

Fieldman, J. P., and T. D. Crespi. 2002. Child sexual abuse: Offenders, disclosure, and school-based initiatives. *Adolescence* 37:151–60.

Flack, Jr., W. F., M. L. Caron, S. J. Leinen, K. G. Breitenbach, A. M. Barber, E. N. Brown, C. T. Gilbert, T. F. Harchak, M. M. Hendricks, C. E. Rector, H. T. Schatten, and H. C. Stein. 2008. "The Red Zone": Temporal risk for unwanted sex among college students. *Journal of Interpersonal Violence* 23:1177–96.

Fulmer, T., G. Paveza, C. VandeWeerd, L. Guadagno, S. Fairchild, R. Norman, V. Abraham, and M. Bolton-Blatt. 2005. Neglect assessment in urban emergency departments and confirmation by an expert clinical team. *Journals of Gerontology Series A–Biological Sciences and Medical Sciences* 60:1002–06.

Gidycz, C. A., A. V. Wynsberghe, and K. M. Edwards. 2008. Prediction of women's utilization of resistance strategies in a sexual assault situation: A prospective study. *Journal of Interpersonal Violence* 23:571–88.

Global Initiative to End All Corporal Punishment of Children. 2005. March. Legality of Corporal Punishment Worldwide. http:// www.endcorporalpunishment.org.

Goldstein, S. L., and R. P. Tyler. 1998. Frustrations of inquiry: Child sexual abuse allegations in divorce and custody cases. *FBI Law Enforcement Bulletin* 67:1–6.

Goodman, G. S., S. Ghetti, J. A. Quas, R. S. Edelstein, K. W. Alexander, A. D. Redlich, I. M. Cordon, and D. P. H. Jones. 2003. A prospective study of memory for child sexual abuse: New findings relevant to the repressed-memory controversy. *Psychological Science* 14:113–18.

Goodman-Brown, T. B., R. S. Edelstein, G. S. Goodman, D. P. H. Jones, and D. S. Gordon. 2003. Why children tell: A model of children's disclosure of sexual abuse. *Child Abuse and Neglect* 27:525–40.

Gottman, J. 2007. The mathematics of love. http://www.edge.org/3rd_culture/gottman05/gottman05_index.html (accessed August 23).

Grych, J. H., G. T. Harold, and C. J. Miles. 2003. A prospective investigation of appraisals as mediators of the link between interparental conflict and child adjustment. *Child Development* 74:1176–96.

Ham-Rowbottom, K. A., E. E. Gordon, K. L. Jarvis, and R. W. Novaco. 2005. Life constraints and psychological well-being of domestic violence shelter graduates. *Journal of Family Violence* 20:109–22.

Haskett, M. E., S. S. Scott, R. Grant, C. S. Ward, and Canby Robinson. 2003. Child-related cognitions and affective functioning of physically abusive and comparison parents. *Child Abuse and Neglect* 27:663–86.

Hewitt, B., K. Klise, L. Comander, M. Schorr, A. Hardy, T. Duffy et al. 2002. Breaking the silence. *People* 57:56.

Howard, D. E., S. Feigelman, X. Li, S. Gross, and L. Rachuba. 2002. The relationship among violence victimization, witnessing violence, and youth distress. *Journal of Adolescent Health* 31:455–62.

Jaudesa, P. K., and L. Mackey-Bilaverb. 2008. Do chronic conditions increase young children's risk of being maltreated? *Child Abuse and Neglect* 32:671–81.

Jerin, R. A., and B. Dolinsky. 2007. Cyber victimization and online dating. In *Online Matchmaking*, ed. M. T. Whitty, A. J. Baker, and J. A. Inman, 147–56. New Work: Palgrave Macmillan.

Johnson, D. W., C. Zlotnick, and S. Perez. 2008. The relative contribution of abuse severity and PTSD severity on the psychiatric and social morbidity of battered women in shelters. *Behavior Therapy* 39:232–47.

Johnson, L., M. Todd, and G. Subramanian. 2005. Violence in police families: Work-family spillover. *Journal of Family Violence* 20:3–13.

Jonzon, E., and F. Lindblad. 2005. Adult female victims of child sexual abuse: Multitype maltreatment and disclosure characteristics related to subjective health. *Journal of Interpersonal Violence* 20:651–66.

Katz, J., J. Moore, and P. May. 2008. Physical and sexual co victimization from dating partners: A distinct type of intimate abuse? *Violence Against Women* 14:961–73.

Katz, J., and L. Myhr. 2008. Perceived conflict patterns and relationship quality associated with verbal sexual coercion by male dating partners. *Journal of Interpersonal Violence* 23:798–804.

Kernic, M. A., M. E. Wolfe, V. L. Holt, B. McKnight, C. E. Huebner, and F. P. Rivara. 2003. Behavioral problems among children whose mothers are abused by an intimate partner. *Child Abuse & Neglect* 27:1231–46.

Kim, J. 2008. The protective effects of religiosity on maladjustment among maltreated and nonmaltreated children. *Child Abuse & Neglect* 32:711–20.

Kim, J., and C. Emery. 2003. Marital power: Conflict, norm consensus, and marital violence in a nationally representative sample of Korean couples. *Journal of Interpersonal Violence* 18:197–219.

Kitzmann, K. M., N. K. Gaylord, A. R. Holt, and E. D. Kenny. 2003. Child witnesses to domestic violence: A meta-analytic review. *Journal of Clinical and Consulting Psychology* 71:339–52.

Knox, D., and Zusman, M. E. 2009. Relationship and sexual behaviors of a sample of 1,319 university students. Unpublished data collected for this text. Department of Sociology, East Carolina University, Greenville, NC.

Komarow, S. 2005. Report: Military women devalued. *USA Today*, August 26.

Koss, M. P., J. A. Bailey, N. P. Yaun, V. M. Herrera, and E. L. Lichter. 2003. Depression and PTSD in survivors of male violence: Research and training initiatives to facilitate recovery. *Psychology of Women Quarterly* 27:130–42.

Kreager, D. A. 2007. Unnecessary roughness? School sports, peer networks, and male adolescent violence. *American Sociological Review* 72:705–24.

Kress, V. E., J. J. Protivnak, and L. Sadlak. 2008. Counseling clients involved with violent intimate partners: The mental health counselor's role in promoting client safety. *Journal of Mental Health Counseling* 30:200–11.

Lee, M. 2008. Caregiver stress and elder abuse among Korean family caregivers of older adults with disabilities. *Journal of Family Violence* 23:707–13.

Lussier, P., E. Beauregard, J. Proulx, and N. Alexandre. 2005. Developmental factors related to deviant sexual preferences in child molesters. *Journal of Interpersonal Violence* 20:999–1017.

McCloskey, L. A., and J. A. Bailey. 2000. The intergenerational transmission of risk for child sexual abuse. *Journal of Interpersonal Violence* 15:1019–35.

Melchert, T. P. 2000. Clarifying the effects of parental abuse, child sexual abuse, and parental care giving on adult adjustment. *Professional Psychology: Research and Practice* 31:64–69.

Meloy, J. R., and H. Fisher. 2005. Some thoughts on the neurobiology of stalking. *Journal of Forensic Science* 50:1472–80.

Nayak, M. B., C. A. Byrne, M. K. Martin, and A. G. Abraham. 2003. Attitudes toward violence against women: A cross-nation study. *Sex Roles: A Journal of Research* 49:333–43.

Nelson, B. S., and K. S. Wampler. 2000. Systemic effects of trauma in clinic couples: An exploratory study of secondary trauma resulting from childhood abuse. *Journal of Marriage and Family Counseling* 26:171–84.

Nolla, J. G. 2008. Sexual abuse of children—Unique in its effects on development? *Child Abuse and Neglect* 32:603–05.

Oswald, D. L., and B. L. Russell. 2006. Perceptions of sexual coercion in heterosexual dating relationships: the role of aggressor gender and tactics. *The Journal of Sex Research* 43:87–98.

Parish, W. L., Y. Luo, E. O. Laumann, M. Ken, and Z. Yu. 2007. Unwanted sexual activity among married women in urban China. *Journal of Sex Research* 44:158–71.

Paterson, T. 2008. Josef Fritzl, The man who haunts Austria. Associated Press, April 29.

Plitnick, K. R. 2008. Elder abuse. *Association of Operating Room Nurses Journal* 87:422–32.

Rand, M. R. 2003. The nature and extent of recurring intimate partner violence against women in the United States. *Journal of Comparative Family Studies* 34:137–46.

Ricci, L., A. Giantris, P. Merriam, S. Hodge, and T. Doyle. 2003. Abusive head trauma in Maine infants: Medical, child protective, and law enforcement analysis. *Child Abuse and Neglect* 27:271–83.

Rivers, M. J. 2005. Navajo women and abuse: The context for their troubled relationships. *Journal of Family Violence* 20:83–90.

Rohrbaugh, J. B. 2006. Domestic violence in same-gender relationships. *Family Court Review* 44:287–99.

Rosenbaum, A., and P. A. Leisring. 2003. Beyond power and control: Towards an understanding of partner abusive men. *Journal of Comparative Family Studies* 34:7–21.

Rothman, E., and J. Silverman. 2007. The effect of a college sexual assault prevention program on first year students' victimization rates. *Journal of American College Health* 55:283–90.

Rousseve, A. 2005. Domestic violence in the United States. *Georgetown Journal of Gender & the Law* 6:431–58.

Rubin, D. M., C. W. Christian, L. T. Bilaniuk, K. A. Zaxyczny, and D. R. Durbin. 2003. Occult head injury in high-risk abused children. *Pediatrics* 111:1382–86.

Sarkar, N. N. 2008. The impact of intimate partner violence on women's reproductive health and pregnancy outcome. *Journal of Obstetrics and Gynecology* 28:266–78.

Schaeffer, C. M., P. C. Alexander, K. Bethke, and L. S. Kretz. 2005. Predictors of child abuse potential among military parents: Comparing mothers and fathers. *Journal of Family Violence* 20:123–30.

Shen, H., and S. B. Sorenson. 2005. Restraining orders in California: A look at statewide data. *Violence Against Women* 11:912–33.

Sheridan, M. S. 2003. The deceit continues: An updated literature review of Munchausen syndrome by proxy. *Child Abuse & Neglect* 27:431–51.

Sidebotham, P., J. Heron, and the ALSPAC study team. 2003. Child maltreatment in the "children of the nineties:" The role of the child. *Child Abuse & Neglect* 27:337–52.

Silvergleid, C., and E. S. Mankowski. 2006. How batterer intervention programs work: Participant and facilitator accounts of processes of change. *Journal of Interpersonal Violence* 21:139–59.

Simonelli, C. J., T. Mullis, A. N. Elliott, and T. W. Pierce. 2002. Abuse by siblings and subsequent experiences of violence within the dating relationship. *Journal of Interpersonal Violence* 17:103–21.

Smith, J. 2003. Shaken baby syndrome. *Orthopaedic Nursing* 22:196–205.

Spitzberg, B. H., and W. R. Cupach. 2007. Cyberstalking as (mis)matchmaking. In *Online Matchmaking*, ed. M. T. Whitty, A J. Baker, and J. A. Inman, 127–46. New Work: Palgrave Macmillan.

Statistical Abstract of the United States, 2009. 128th ed. Washington, DC: U.S. Bureau of the Census.

Strickland, S. M. 2008. Female sex offenders: Exploring issues of personality, trauma, and cognitive distortions. *Journal of Interpersonal Violence* 23:474–89.

Struckman-Johnson, C., D. Struckman-Johnson, and P. B. Anderson. 2003. Tactics of sexual coercion: When men and women won't take no for an answer. *Journal of Sex Research* 40:76–86.

Straus, M. A. 2000. Corporal punishment and primary prevention of physical abuse. *Child Abuse and Neglect* 24:1109–14.

Stuart, G. L. 2005. Improving violence intervention outcomes by integrating alcohol treatment. *Journal of Interpersonal Violence* 20:388–93.

Swan, S. C., L. J. Gambone, J. E. Caldwell, T. P. Sullivan, and D. L Snow. 2008. A review of research on women's use of violence with male intimate partners. *Violence and Victims* 23:301–15.

Torpy, J. M., C. Lynm, and R. M Glass. 2008. Intimate partner violence. *Journal of the American Medical Association* 300:754–66.

Trokel, M., W. Anthony, J. Griffith, and R. Sege. 2006. Variation in the diagnosis of child abuse in severely injured infants. *Pediatrics* 722–29.

Ulman, A. 2003. Violence by children against mothers in relation to violence between parents and corporal punishment by parents. *Journal of Comparative Family Studies* 34:41–56.

Ulman, A., and M. A. Straus. 2003. Violence by children against mothers in relation to violence between parents and corporal punishment by parents. *Journal of Comparative Family Studies* 34:41–56.

Updegraff, K. A., S. M. Thayer, S. D. Whiteman, D. J. Denning, and S. M. McHale. 2005. Relational aggression in adolescents' sibling relationships: Links to sibling and parent-adolescent relationship quality. *Family Relations* 54:373–86.

Vandello, J. A., and D. Cohen. 2003. Male honor and female fidelity: Implicit cultural scripts that perpetuate domestic violence. *Journal of Personality and Social Psychology* 84:997–1010.

Vazquez, S., M. K. Stohr, K. Skow, and M. Purkiss. 2005. Why is a woman still not safe when she's home? Seven years of NIBRS data on victims and offenders of intimate partner violence. *Criminal Justice Studies: A Critical Journal of Crime, Law and Society* 18:125–46.

Verma, R. K. 2003. Wife beating and the link with poor sexual health and risk behavior among men in urban slums in India. *Journal of Comparative Family Studies* 34:1–61.

Walrath, C., M. Ybarra, E. W. Holden, Q. Liao, R. Santiago, and P. Leaf. 2003. Children with reported histories of sexual abuse. *Child Abuse and Neglect* 27:509–24.

Walsh, W. 2002. Spankers and nonspankers: Where they get information on spanking. *Family Relations* 51:81–88.

Whatley, M. 2005. The effect of participant sex, victim dress, and traditional attitudes on casual judgments for marital rape victims. *Journal of Family Violence* 20:191–201.

Wright, J. W., Jr. 2004. Personal communication, Monroe, LA. Dr. Wright is an attorney who has been involved in litigation of Munchausen syndrome by proxy lawsuits.

chapter 14

The problem is not that there are problems. The problem is expecting otherwise and thinking that having problems is a problem.

Theodore Rubin, psychiatrist

Stress and Crisis in Relationships

Contents

True or False?

1. National hotlines receive more calls about loneliness, and fewer calls are about depression across the lifespan.

2. Males are more likely than females to believe that love will allow them to overcome any crisis.

3. Females are more willing than males to seek marriage counseling before they get a divorce.

4. Women are more likely to become upset at emotional infidelity, and men at sexual infidelity.

5. French spouses don't confront their partner of a suspected affair; they let time pass without comment.

Answers: **1.** T **2.** T **3.** T **4.** T **5.** T

You win some, you lose some, and some get rained out, but you gotta suit up for them all.

J. Askenberg

The opening photo of this chapter is of a man in a wheelchair who became paralyzed due to a diving accident, a catastrophic life crisis. But that was long ago. He is shown in the photo with a friend last summer with whom he vacationed in Puerto Rico. Notice the rainbow above their heads. Ann Landers was once asked what she would consider the single most useful bit of advice all people could profit from. She replied, "Expect trouble as an inevitable part of life, and when it comes, hold your head high, look it squarely in the eye and say, 'I will be bigger than you.'" Life indeed brings both triumphs and tragedies. Nearly half of all adults report experiencing at least one traumatic event at some point in their lives (Ozer et al. 2003). These are often turning points that may come at any time (Leonard and Burns 2006). This chapter is about experiencing and coping with these events and the day-to-day stress we feel during the in-between time.

Personal Stress and Crisis Events

In this section, we review the definitions of crisis and stressful events, the characteristics of resilient families, and a framework for viewing a family's reaction to a crisis event.

Definitions of Stress and Crisis Events

Stress is a reaction of the body to substantial or unusual demands (physical, environmental, or interpersonal). Stress is particularly acute in the military. Duparcq (2008) wrote that "U.S. soldiers in Iraq can find stress deadlier than enemy," and cited deployments as the cause of increasing post-traumatic stress syndrome, divorce, and suicide. Stress is often accompanied by irritability, high blood pressure, and depression. Stress is a process rather than a state. For example, a person will experience different levels of stress throughout a divorce—the stress involved in acknowledging that one's marriage is over, telling the children, leaving the family residence, getting the final decree, and seeing one's ex may all result in varying levels of stress.

A **crisis** is a crucial situation that requires changes in normal patterns of behavior. A family crisis is a situation that upsets the normal functioning of the family and requires a new set of responses to the stressor. Sources of stress and crises can be external, such as Hurricane Ike that devastated the coast of Texas in 2008 or the earthquake in Italy in 2009. Other examples of an external crisis are economic recession, tornados, downsizing, or military deployment to Afghanistan. Stress and crisis events may also be induced internally (for example, alcoholism, an extramarital affair, or Alzheimer's disease of spouse or parents). Ingram et al. (2008) noted that, of 300,000 crisis calls to a national hotline over a five-year period, 73 percent were about parenting, youth, and mental health concerns. Across the lifespan, calls about loneliness increased and calls about depression decreased.

Stressors or crises may also be categorized as expected or unexpected. Examples of expected family stressors include the need to care for aging parents and the death of one's parents. Unexpected stressors include contracting human immunodeficiency virus (HIV), a miscarriage, or the suicide of one's teenager.

Both stress and crises are normal parts of family life and sometimes reflect a developmental sequence. Pregnancy, childbirth, job changes or loss, children leaving home, retirement, and widowhood are all stressful and predictable for most couples and families. Crisis events may have a cumulative effect: the greater the number in rapid succession, the greater the stress. Stress that spouses experience spills over into and negatively affects the marital relationship, with husbands being more affected by the wife's stress than vice versa (Neff and Karney 2007).

Misfortune does not always come to injure.

Robert Frost, poet

Resilient Families

Just as the types of stress and crisis events vary, individuals and families vary in their abilities to respond successfully to crisis events. **Resiliency** refers to a family's strengths and ability to respond to a crisis in a positive way. Black and Lobo (2008) defined **family resilience** as the successful coping of family members under adversity that enables them to flourish with warmth, support, and cohesion. The key factors that promote family resiliency include positive outlook, spirituality, flexibility, communication, financial management, shared family recreation, routines or rituals, and support networks. A family's ability to bounce back from a crisis (from loss of one's job to the death of a family member) reflects its level of resiliency. Resiliency may also be related to individuals' perceptions of the degree to which they are in control of their destiny. The Self-Assessment section on page 458 measures this perception.

A Family Stress Model

Various theorists have explained how individuals and families experience and respond to stressors. Kahl et al. (2007) reviewed the ABCX model of family stress, developed by Reuben Hill in the 1950s. The model can be explained as follows:

A = stressor event

B = family's management strategies, coping skills

C = family's perception, definition of the situation

X = family's adaptation to the event

A is the stressor event, which interacts with B, the family's coping ability or crisis-meeting resources. Both A and B interact with C, the family's appraisal or perception of the stressor event. X is the family's adaptation to the crisis. Thus, a family that experiences a major stressor (for example, a spouse with a spinal cord injury) but has great coping skills (for example, religion or spirituality, love, communication, and commitment) and perceives the event to be manageable will experience a moderate crisis. However, a family that experiences a less critical stressor event (for example, their child makes Cs and Ds in school) but has minimal coping skills (for example, everyone blames everyone else) and perceives the event to be catastrophic will experience an extreme crisis. Hence, how a family experiences and responds to stress depends not only on the event but

Internality, Powerful Others, and Chance Scales

People have different feelings about their vulnerability to crisis events. The following scale addresses the degree to which you feel you have control, you feel others have control, or you feel that chance has control of what happens to you.

Directions

To assess the degree to which you believe that you have control over your own life (I = Internality), the degree to which you believe that other people control events in your life (P = Powerful Others), and the degree to which you believe that chance affects your experiences or outcomes (C = Chance), read each of the following statements and select a number from −3 to +3.

−3	−2	−1	+1	+2	+3
Strongly Disagree	Slightly Disagree	Neither Disagree	Slightly Agree	Agree	Strongly Agree

Subscale

I   1. Whether or not I get to be a leader depends mostly on my ability.

C   2. To a great extent, my life is controlled by accidental happenings.

P   3. I feel like what happens in my life is mostly determined by powerful people.

I   4. Whether or not I get into a car accident depends mostly on how good a driver I am.

I   5. When I make plans, I am almost certain to make them work.

C   6. Often there is no chance of protecting my personal interests from bad luck happenings.

C   7. When I get what I want, it's usually because I'm lucky.

P   8. Although I might have good ability, I will not be given leadership responsibility without appealing to those in positions of power.

I   9. How many friends I have depends on how nice a person I am.

C   10. I have often found that what is going to happen will happen.

P   11. My life is chiefly controlled by powerful others.

C   12. Whether or not I get into a car accident is mostly a matter of luck.

P   13. People like myself have very little chance of protecting our personal interests when they conflict with those of strong pressure groups.

C   14. It's not always wise for me to plan too far ahead because many things turn out to be a matter of good or bad fortune.

P   15. Getting what I want requires pleasing those people above me.

C   16. Whether or not I get to be a leader depends on whether I'm lucky enough to be in the right place at the right time.

P   17. If important people were to decide they didn't like me, I probably wouldn't make many friends.

I   18. I can pretty much determine what will happen in my life.

I   19. I am usually able to protect my personal interests.

P   20. Whether or not I get into a car accident depends mostly on the other driver.

I   21. When I get what I want, it's usually because I worked hard for it.

P   22. To have my plans work, I make sure that they fit in with the desires of other people who have power over me.

I   23. My life is determined by my own actions.

C   24. Whether or not I have a few friends or many friends is chiefly a matter of fate.

Scoring

Each of the subscales of Internality, Powerful Others, and Chance is scored on a six-point Likert format from −3 to +3. For example, the eight Internality items are 1, 4, 5, 9, 18, 19, 21, 23. A person who has strong agreement with all eight items would score +24; strong disagreement, −24. After adding and subtracting the item scores, add 24 to the total score to eliminate negative scores. Scores for Powerful Others and Chance are similarly derived.

Norms

For the Internality subscale, means range from the low 30s to the low 40s, with 35 being the modal mean (SD values approximating 7). The Powerful Others subscale has produced means ranging from 18 through 26, with 20 being characteristic of normal college student subjects (SD = 8.5). The Chance subscale produces means between 17 and 25, with 18 being a common mean among undergraduates (SD = 8).

Source

From *Research with the Locus of Control Construct*, by Hervert M. Lefcourt, 1981, pp. 57–59. Reprinted with permission from Elsevier.

also on the family's coping resources and perceptions of the event. Kahl et al. (2007) also emphasized the importance of cognitions in perceiving a crisis event by noting that children of divorced parents are less self-assured, which impacts their marital happiness and increases their vulnerability to divorce.

The importance of how an event is perceived is crucial. In response to the recession of 2008–2009, Adolf Merckle threw himself in front of a train. He was a billionaire but had lost hundreds of millions of euros on Volkswagen shares. How many people do you know who would commit suicide if they had only a few million left?

When one door of happiness closes, another opens; but often we look so long at the closed door that we do not see the one which has opened for us.

Helen Keller, author

Positive Stress-Management Strategies

Researchers Burr and Klein (1994) administered an eighty-item questionnaire to seventy-eight adults to assess how families experiencing various stressors such as bankruptcy, infertility, a disabled child, and a troubled teen used various coping strategies and how useful they evaluated these strategies. In the following, we detail some helpful stress-management strategies.

Changing Basic Values and Perspective

The strategy that the highest percentage of respondents reported as being helpful was changing basic values as a result of the crisis situation. Survivors of Hurricane Kyle, which devastated Galveston in 2008, noted that focusing on the sparing of their lives and those close to them rather than the loss of their home or material possessions was an essential view in coping with the crisis. Sharpe and Curran (2006) confirmed that finding positive meaning in a crisis situation is associated with positive adjustment to the situation. Similarly, Waller (2008) studied new parents at two time frames (when the child was 1 and 4) and noted that whether they survived the crisis of having a child was a function of their perception. She found that "parents in stable unions framed tensions as manageable within the context of a relationship they perceived to be moving forward, whereas those in unstable unions viewed tensions as intolerable in relationships they considered volatile."

Some crisis events provide an opportunity for positive growth. In responding to the crisis of bankruptcy, people may reevaluate the importance of money and conclude that relationships are more important. In coping with unemployment, people may decide that the amount of time they spend with family members is more valuable than the amount of time they spend making money. Buddhists have the saying, "Pain is inevitable; suffering is not." This is another way of emphasizing that how one views a situation, not the situation itself, determines its impact on you.

Exercise

The Centers for Disease Control and Prevention (CDC) and the American College of Sports Medicine (ACSM) recommend that people aged 6 years and older engage regularly, preferably daily, in light to moderate physical activity for at least thirty minutes at a time. These recommendations are based on research that has shown the physical, emotional, and cognitive benefits of exercise. Tetlie et al. (2008) confirmed that a structured exercise program lasting eight to twelve weeks was associated with individuals reporting improved feelings of well-being. In addition, Taliaferro et al. (2008) noted that vigorous exercise and involvement in sports are associated with lower rates of suicide among adolescents.

Friends and Relatives

A network of relationships is associated with successful coping with various life transitions (Levitt et al. 2005). Women are more likely to feel connected to others and to feel that they can count on others in times of need (Weckwerth and Flynn 2006). News media coving hurricanes, earthquakes, and tsunamis emphasized that, as long as one's family is still together, individuals are less affected by the loss of material possessions.

This couple exercises every night after work and before dinner.

Our remedies oft in ourselves do lie.

Shakespeare, *Alls Well that Ends Well*

Love

A love relationship also helps individuals cope with stress. Being emotionally involved with another and sharing the experience with that person helps to insulate individuals from being devastated by a crisis event. Love is also viewed as helping resolve relationship problems. Over 85 percent (85.9 percent) of undergraduate males and 72.5 percent of undergraduate females agreed that, "If you love someone enough, you will be able to resolve your problems with that person" (Dotson-Blake et al. 2009).

Religion and Spirituality

Religion may be helpful in adjusting to a crisis. Park (2006) found that religion is associated with providing meaning for experiencing a crisis and for adjusting to it. In addition, religion provides a framework for being less punitive. Rather than be in a rage and seek revenge against a perceived aggressor, religious individuals might "turn the other cheek" (Unnever et al. 2005).

Humor

A sense of humor is related to lower anxiety and a happier mood. Indeed, a team of researchers compared the effects of humor, aerobic exercise, and listening to music on the reduction of anxiety and found humor to be the most effective. Just sitting quietly seemed to have no effect on reducing one's anxiety (Szabo et al. 2005).

Sleep

Getting an adequate amount of sleep is also associated with lower stress levels (Mostaghimi et al. 2005). Even midday naps are associated with positive functioning, particularly memory performance (Schabus et al. 2005). Indeed, adequate sleep helps one to respond to daily stress and to crisis events.

Biofeedback

Biofeedback is a process in which information that is relayed back to the brain enables people to change their biological functioning. Biofeedback treatment teaches a person to influence biological responses such as heart rate, nervous system arousal, muscle contractions, and even brain wave functioning. Biofeedback is used in about 1,500 clinics and treatment centers worldwide.

A typical session lasts about an hour and costs $60 to $150. The following are several types of biofeedback:

1. *Electromyographic (EMG) biofeedback.* EMG measures electrical activity created by muscle contractions, and is often used for relaxation training and for stress and pain management.

2. *Thermal or temperature biofeedback.* Because stress causes blood vessels in the fingers to constrict, reducing blood flow and leading to cooling, thermal biofeedback uses a temperature sensor to detect changes in temperature of the fingertips or toes. This trains people to quiet the nervous system arousal mechanisms that produce hand and/or foot cooling, and is often used for stress, anxiety, and pain management.

3. *Galvanic skin response (GSR) biofeedback.* GSR utilizes a finger electrode to measure sweat gland activity. This measure is very useful for relaxation and stress management training and is also used in the treatment of attention-deficit/hyperactivity disorder.

4. *Neurofeedback.* Also called *neurobiofeedback* or *EEG (electroencephalogram) biofeedback*, neurofeedback may be particularly helpful for individuals coping with a crisis. It trains people to enhance their brain-wave functioning and has been found to be effective in treating a wide range of conditions, including anxiety, stress, depression, tension and migraine headaches, addictions, and high blood pressure.

Because neurofeedback is the fastest-growing field in biofeedback, we take a closer look at this treatment modality. Neurofeedback involves a series of sessions in which a client sits in a comfortable chair facing a specialized game computer. Small sensors are placed on the scalp to detect brain-wave activity and transmit this information to the computer. The neurofeedback therapist (in the same room) also sits in front of a computer that displays the client's brain-wave patterns in the form of an electroencephalogram (EEG). After a clinical assessment of the client's functioning, the therapist determines what kinds of brain-wave patterns are optimal for the client. During neurofeedback sessions, clients learn to produce desirable brain waves by controlling a computerized game or task, similar to playing a video game, but the client's brain waves—instead of a joystick—control the game.

Neurofeedback is like an exercise of the brain, helping it to become more flexible and effective. Unlike body exercise, which will lose its benefits over time when training is stopped, brain-wave training generally does not. Once the brain is trained to function in its optimal state (which may take an average of twenty to twenty-five sessions), it generally remains in this more healthy state. Neurofeedback therapists liken the process to that of learning to ride a bicycle: once you learn to ride a bike, you can do so even if you have not in years. One neurofeedback therapist explains, "clients speak often of their disorders—panic attacks, chronic pain, etc.—as if they were stuck in a certain pattern of response. Consistently in clinical practice, EEG biofeedback helps 'unstick' people from these unhealthy response patterns" (Carlson-Catalano 2003).

Deep Muscle Relaxation

Tensing and relaxing one's muscles have been associated with an improved state of relaxation. Calling it abbreviated progressive muscle relaxation (APMR), Termini (2006) found that the cognitive benefits were particularly evident; people who tensed and relaxed various muscle groups noticed a mental relaxation more than a physical relaxation.

Education

Sometimes becoming informed about a family problem helps to cope with the problem. Friedrich et al. (2008) studied how siblings cope with the fact that a

When written in Chinese, the word 'crisis' is composed of two characters. One represents danger and the other represents opportunity.

John Fitzgerald Kennedy

brother or sister is schizophrenic. Education and family support were the primary mechanisms. Just knowing that the "parents were not to blame" resulted from becoming informed about schizophrenia.

Counseling for Children

Baggerly and Exum (2008) reviewed the value of counseling for children experiencing natural disasters such as hurricanes. Such counseling involves providing a safe context for children and having them remind themselves that they are safe (cognitive behavior therapy).

Harmful Strategies

Some coping strategies not only are ineffective for resolving family problems but also add to the family's stress by making the problems worse. Respondents in the Burr and Klein (1994) research identified several strategies they regarded as harmful to overall family functioning. These included keeping feelings inside, taking out frustrations on or blaming others, and denying or avoiding the problem.

Burr and Klein's research also suggests that women and men differ in their perceptions of the usefulness of various coping strategies. Women were more likely than men to view as helpful such strategies as sharing concerns with relatives and friends, becoming more involved in religion, and expressing emotions. Men were more likely than women to use potentially harmful strategies such as using alcohol, keeping feelings inside, or keeping others from knowing how bad the situation was.

Family Crisis Examples

Some of the more common crisis events that spouses and families face include physical illness, mental challenges, an extramarital affair, unemployment, substance abuse, and death.

Physical Illness and Disability

Absence of physical illness is important for individuals to define themselves as being healthy overall. Although approximately 60 percent of those aged 85 and older define themselves as healthy (Ostbye et al. 2006), physical problems are not unusual.

Reacting to Prostate Cancer: One Husband's Experience

For men, prostate cancer is an example of a medical issue that can rock the foundation of their personal and marital well-being. In the following section, a student described his experience with prostate cancer as follows:

> Since my father had prostate cancer, I was warned that it is genetic and to be alert as I reached age 50. At the age of 56, I noticed that I was getting up more frequently at night to urinate. My doc said it was probably just one of my usual prostate infections, and he prescribed the usual antibiotic. When the infection did not subside, a urologist did a transrectal ultrasound (TRUS) needle biopsy. The TRUS gives the urologist an image of the prostate while he takes about ten tissue samples from the prostate with a thin, hollow needle.
>
> Two weeks later I learned the bad news (I had prostate cancer) and the good news (it had not spread). Since the prostate is very close to the spinal column, failure to

act quickly can allow time for cancer cells to spread from the prostate to the bones. My urologist outlined a number of treatment options, including traditional surgery, laparoscopic surgery, radiation treatment, implantation of radioactive "seeds," cryotherapy (in which liquid nitrogen is used to freeze and kill prostate cancer cells), and hormone therapy, which blocks production of the male sex hormones that stimulate growth of prostate cancer cells. He recommended traditional surgery ("radical retropubic prostatectomy"), in which an incision is made between the belly button and the pubic bone to remove the prostate gland and nearby lymph nodes in the pelvis. This surgery is generally considered the "gold standard" when the disease is detected early. Within three weeks I had the surgery.

Every patient awakes from radical prostate surgery with urinary incontinence and impotence—which can continue for a year, two years, or forever. Such patients also awake from surgery hoping that they are cancer-free. This is determined by laboratory analysis of tissue samples taken during surgery. The patient waits for a period of about two weeks, hoping to hear the medical term "negative margins" from his doctor. That finding means that the cancer cells were confined to the prostate and did not spread past the margins of the prostate. A finding of negative margins should be accompanied by a PSA [prostate specific antigen] score of zero, confirming that the body no longer detects the presence of cancer cells. I cannot describe the feeling of relief that accompanies such a report, and I am very fortunate to have heard those words used in my case.

The psychological effects have been devastating—more for me than for my partner. I have only been intimate with one woman—my wife—and having intercourse with her was one of the greatest pleasures in my life. For a year, I was left with no erection and an inability to have an orgasm. Afterwards I was able to have an erection (via Caverject [$25], an injection) and an orgasm. Dealing with urinary incontinence (I refer to myself as Mr. Drippy) is a "wish it were otherwise" on my psyche.

When faced with the decision to live or die, the choice for most of us is clear. In my case, I am alive, cancer-free, and enjoying the love of my life (now in our 47th year together).

In addition to prostate cancer, chronic degenerative diseases (autoimmune dysfunction, rheumatoid arthritis, lupus, Crohn's disease, and chronic fatigue syndrome) can challenge a mate's and couple's ability to cope. These illnesses are particularly invasive in that conventional medicine has little to offer besides pain medication. For example, spouses with chronic fatigue syndrome may experience financial consequences ("I could no longer meet the demands of my job so I quit"), gender role loss ("I couldn't cook for my family" or "I was no longer a provider"), and changed perceptions by their children ("They have seen me sick for so long they no longer ask me to do anything"). In addition, osteoporosis is a health threat for 44 million older women and results in a decline in their ability to perform routine activities (Roberto 2005).

In those cases in which the illness is fatal, **palliative care** is helpful. This term describes the health care for the individual who has a life-threatening illness (focusing on relief of pain and suffering) and support for them and their loved ones. Such care may involve the person's physician or a palliative care specialist who works with the physician, nurse, social worker, and chaplain. Pharmacists or rehabilitation specialists may also be involved. The effects of such care are to approach the end of life with planning (how long should life be sustained on machines?) and forethought to relieve pain and provide closure.

Another physical issue with which some parents cope is that of their children being overweight. Body mass index (BMI) is calculated as weight in kilograms divided by height in meters squared; overweight is indicated by a BMI of 25.0 to 29.9, and obese by 30.0 or higher (Pyle et al. 2006). Routh and Rao (2006) studied 225 9- to 10-year-olds in primary schools and found that 20 percent were overweight; 5 percent were obese. National figures reflect that 31.5 percent are

Now, if you are going to win any battle, you have to do one thing. You have to make the mind run the body.

General George S. Patton

"Listen up people—we come in different sizes . . . get over it!"

Rosie O'Donnell, advocate for Size Acceptance Movement

Attitudes toward Overweight Children Scale

Relatively little is known about college students' attitudes toward overweight children. The purpose of this survey is to gain a better understanding of what college students think and feel about children who are overweight. Please read each item carefully and consider how you feel about each statement. There are no right or wrong answers to any of these statements, so please give your honest reactions and opinions. Please read each statement carefully and respond by using the following scale:

1	2	3	4	5	6	7
Strongly Disagree						Strongly Agree

_____ 1. Overweight children are poorer athletes.

_____ 2. Overweight children are less happy than other children.

_____ 3. Overweight children eat as much as adults.

_____ 4. Overweight children lack self-control.

_____ 5. Overweight children are lazy.

_____ 6. Overweight children have few physically active interests.

_____ 7. Children who are overweight are unhealthy.

_____ 8. Overweight children lack motivation.

Scoring

Selecting a 1 reflects the least acceptance of negative beliefs about overweight children; selecting a 7 reflects the greatest acceptance of negative beliefs about overweight children. Once you have made your responses to the eight items, add the numbers. The lower your total score (8 is the lowest possible), the less accepting you are of negative beliefs about overweight children; the higher your total score (56 is the highest possible), the greater your acceptance of negative beliefs about overweight children. A score of 24 places you at the midpoint between being very disapproving of overweight children and very accepting of overweight children.

Scores of Other Students Who Completed the Scale

The scale was completed by 143 male and 145 female student volunteers at Valdosta State University. The average score on the scale was 32.11 (standard deviation [SD] = 8.25). Their ages ranged from 18 to 45, with a mean age of 21.64 (SD = 3.20). The ethnic background of the sample was as follows: 66.0 percent white, 27.8 percent African American, 3.5 percent Hispanic, 1.0 percent Asian, 0.3 percent American Indian, and 1.4 percent other. The college classification level of the sample included 14.6 percent freshmen, 17.7 percent sophomores, 29.9 percent juniors, 32.3 percent seniors, 3.8 percent graduate students, and 1.7 percent postbaccalaureates. Male participants endorsed more negative beliefs about overweight children (mean = 33.28; SD = 7.50) than did female participants (mean = 30.96; SD = 8.80; $p < .05$). There were no significant differences in regard to race or college classification of the participants (p values $> .05$).

Source

"Attitudes Toward Overweight Children Scale" 2006 by Mark Whatley, Ph.D., Department of Psychology, Valdosta State University, Valdosta, Georgia 31698-0100. Used by permission. Other uses of this scale by written permission of Dr. Whatley only (mwhatley@valdosta.edu). Information on the reliability and validity of this scale is available from Dr. Whatley.

> _We cannot direct the wind, but we can adjust the sails._
>
> Bertha Calloway, Founder Great Plains Black History Museum

at risk for being overweight and that 16.5 percent could be classified as overweight. Minority females and individuals of lower socioeconomic status are more prone to being overweight or obese. Not only does this chronic physical health issue have medical, life-threatening implications (Pyle et al. 2006) in both industrial and developing countries (Flynn et al. 2006), but there is also prejudice and discrimination toward overweight children. The Self-Assessment section above allows you to assess your attitudes toward overweight children.

National Data

In a Gallup poll, 56 percent of Americans say they want to lose weight, including 18 percent who want to lose "a lot" of weight. Women are twice as likely to report that they want to lose a lot of weight (Moore 2006).

Mental Illness

Everyone experiences problems in living. In a national survey of 9,282 respondents, the reported psychological problems and their percentages of lifetime incidence include: anxiety (29 percent), impulse control disorder (25 percent), mood disorder (21 percent), and substance abuse (15 percent) (Mahoney 2005). Five percent of adults in the United States between the ages of 18 and 35 report being depressed (Pratt and Brody 2006).

Insel et al. (2008) noted the enormous economic costs of serious mental illness that involve a high rate of emergency room care (for example, suicide attempts), high prevalence of pulmonary disease (people with serious mental illness smoke 44 percent of all cigarettes in the United States), and early mortality (a loss of thirteen to thirty-two years).

The toll of mental illness on a relationship can be immense. A major initial attraction of partners to each other includes intellectual and emotional qualities. Butterworth and Rodgers (2008) surveyed 3,230 couples to assess the degree to which mental illness of a spouse or spouses affects divorce and found that couples in which either men or women reported mental health problems had higher rates of marital disruption than couples in which neither spouse experienced mental health problems. For couples in which both spouses reported mental health problems, rates of marital disruption reflected the additive combination of each spouse's separate risk. As an aside, mental illness is also a disadvantage for those seeking a remarriage. Teitler and Reichman (2008) found that unmarried mothers with mental illness were about two-thirds as likely as mothers without mental illness to marry.

Children may also be mentally ill. Examples include autism (three to four times more common in boys), attention-deficit/hyperactivity disorder (4 percent of children, ages 3 to 17), and antisocial behavior (*Statistical Abstract of the United States, 2009,* Table 179). These difficulties can stress spouses to the limit of their coping capacity, which may put an enormous strain on their marriage.

The reverse is also true; children must learn how to cope with the mental illness of their parents. Mordoch and Hall (2008) studied twenty-two children between 6 and 16 years of age, who were living part- or full-time with a parent with depression, schizophrenia, or bipolar illness. They found that the children learned to maintain connections with their parents by creating and keeping a safe distance between themselves and their parents so as not to be engulfed by their parents' mental illnesses.

Middle Age Crazy (Midlife Crisis)?

The stereotypical explanation for 45-year-old people who buy convertible sports cars, have affairs, marry 20-year-olds, or adopt a baby is that they are "having a midlife crisis." The label conveys that they feel old, think that life is passing them by, and seize one last great chance to do what they have always wanted. Indeed, one father (William Feather) noted, "Setting a good example for your children takes all the fun out of middle age."

However, a ten-year study of close to 8,000 U.S. adults aged 25 to 74 by the MacArthur Foundation Research Network on Successful Midlife Development revealed that, for most respondents, the middle years brought no crisis at all but a time of good health, productive activity, and community involvement. Less than a quarter (23 percent) reported a "crisis" in their lives. Those who did experience a crisis were going through a divorce. Two-thirds were accepting of getting older; one-third did feel some personal turmoil related to the fact that they were aging (Goode 1999).

Of those who initiated a divorce in midlife, 70 percent had no regrets and were confident that they did the right thing. This is the result of a study of 1,147 respondents aged 40 to 79 who experienced a divorce in their forties, fifties, or sixties. Indeed, midlife divorcers' levels of happiness or contentment were similar to those of single individuals their own age and those who remarried (Enright 2004).

Some people embrace middle age. The Red Hat Society (http://www .redhatsociety.com/) is a group of women who have decided to "greet middle age with verve, humor, and elan. We believe silliness is the comedy relief of life [and] share a bond of affection, forged by common life experiences and a genuine enthusiasm for wherever life takes us next." The society traces its beginning to

In this age, which believes that there is a short cut to everything, the greatest lesson to be learned is that the most difficult way is, in the long run, the easiest.

Henry Miller, novelist

This group of Red Hat Society women is having a grand time on an ocean cruise.

when Sue Ellen Cooper bought a bright red hat because of a poem Jenny Joseph wrote in 1961, titled the "Warning Poem." The poem says the following:

When I am an old woman I shall wear purple
With a red hat which doesn't go and doesn't suite me.

Cooper then gave red hats to friends as they turned 50. The group then wore their red hats and purple dresses out to tea, and that's how it got started. Now there are over 1 million members worldwide.

In the rest of this chapter, we examine how spouses cope with the crisis events of an extramarital affair, unemployment, drug abuse, and death. Each of these events can be viewed either as devastating and the end of meaning in one's life or as an opportunity and challenge to rise above.

Extramarital Affair (and Successful Recovery)

Extramarital affair refers to a spouse's sexual involvement with someone outside the marriage. Affairs are of different types, which may include the following:

1. *Brief encounter (situationally determined affairs).* A spouse hooks up with or meets a stranger at a conference. In this case, the spouse is usually out of town, and alcohol is involved.

2. *Periodic sexual encounters.* A spouse is sexually unsatisfied in the marriage and seeks external sex, often with a hooker (for example, former New York governor Eliot Spitzer). A married person of bisexual orientation may also seek a periodic encounter outside the marriage.

3. *Instrumental or utilitarian affair.* This is sex in exchange for a job or promotion, to get back at a spouse, to evoke jealousy, or to transition out of a marriage.

4. *Coping mechanism.* Sex can be used to enhance one's self-concept or feeling of sexual inadequacy,

compensate for failure in business, cope with the death of a family member, test out one's sexual orientation, and so on.

5. *Paraphiliac affairs.* In these, spouses act out sexual fantasies that most people would consider to be bizarre or abnormal sexual practices, such as sexual masochism, sexual sadism, or transvestite fetishism.

6. *New love.* A spouse may be in love with the new partner and may plan marriage after divorce. (Bagarozzi 2008)

In addition, the computer or Internet affair is another type of affair. Although legally an extramarital affair does not exist unless two people (one being married) have intercourse, an online computer affair can be just as disruptive to a marriage or a couple's relationship. Computer friendships may move to feelings of intimacy, involve secrecy (one's partner does not know the level of involvement), include sexual tension (even though there is no overt sex), and take time, attention, energy, and affection away from one's partner. Schneider (2000) studied ninety-one women who experienced serious adverse consequences from their partner's cybersex involvement, including loss of interest in relational sex, and feeling hurt, betrayed, rejected, abandoned, lonely, jealous, and angry over being constantly lied to. These women noted that the cyber affair was as emotionally painful as an off-line affair and that their partners' cybersex addiction was a major reason for their separation or divorce. Cramer et al. (2008) also noted that women become more upset when their man is emotionally unfaithful with another woman (although men become more upset when their partner is sexually unfaithful with another man). The Self-Assessment section is provided on page 468 to measure your attitude toward infidelity.

National Data

Of spouses in the United States, 23.2 percent of husbands and 13.18 percent of wives reported ever having had intercourse with someone to whom they were not married (Djamba et al. 2005).

Extradyadic involvement or extrarelational refers to sexual involvement of a pair-bonded individual with someone other than the partner. Extradyadic involvements are not uncommon. Of 1,319 undergraduates, 37.4 percent agreed, "I have cheated on a partner I was involved with." Over half (53 percent) agreed, "A partner I was involved with cheated on me" (Knox and Zusman 2009).

Marriage and family therapists rank an extramarital affair as the second most stressful crisis event for a couple (physical abuse is number one) (Olson et al. 2002). Characteristics associated with spouses who are more likely to have extramarital sex include male gender, a strong interest in sex, permissive sexual values, low subjective satisfaction in the existing relationship, employment outside the home, low church attendance, greater sexual opportunities, higher social status (power and money), and alcohol abuse (Hall et al. 2008; Smith 2005; Olson et al. 2002). Elmslie and Tebaldi (2008) noted that women's infidelity behavior is influenced by religiosity (less religious = more likely), city size (urban = more likely), and happiness (less happy = more likely), whereas men's infidelity behavior is affected by race (white = less likely), happiness status (happy = less likely), city size (same for women), and employment status (employed = less likely).

Reasons for Extramarital Affair. Spouses report a number of reasons why they become involved in a sexual encounter outside their marriage:

1. *Variety, novelty, and excitement.* Extradyadic sexual involvement may be motivated by the desire for variety, novelty, and excitement. One of the characteristics of sex in long-term committed relationships is the tendency for it to become routine. Early in a relationship, the partners cannot seem to have sex often enough. However, with constant availability, partners may achieve a level of

Difficulties strengthen the mind, as labor does the body.

Seneca, Roman philosopher

Attitudes toward Infidelity Scale

Infidelity can be defined as unfaithfulness in a committed monogamous relationship. Infidelity can affect anyone, regardless of race, color, or creed; it does not matter whether you are rich or attractive, where you live, or what your age. The purpose of this survey is to gain a better understanding of what people think and feel about issues associated with infidelity. There are no right or wrong answers to any of these statements; we are interested in your honest reactions and opinions. Please read each statement carefully, and respond by using the following scale:

1	2	3	4	5	6	7
Strongly Disagree						Strongly Agree

_____ 1. Being unfaithful never hurt anyone.

_____ 2. Infidelity in a marital relationship is grounds for divorce.

_____ 3. Infidelity is acceptable for retaliation of infidelity.

_____ 4. It is natural for people to be unfaithful.

_____ 5. Online/Internet behavior (for example, visiting sex chat rooms, porn sites) is an act of infidelity.

_____ 6. Infidelity is morally wrong in all circumstances, regardless of the situation.

_____ 7. Being unfaithful in a relationship is one of the most dishonorable things a person can do.

_____ 8. Infidelity is unacceptable under any circumstances if the couple is married.

_____ 9. I would not mind if my significant other had an affair as long as I did not know about it.

_____ 10. It would be acceptable for me to have an affair, but not my significant other.

_____ 11. I would have an affair if I knew my significant other would never find out.

_____ 12. If I knew my significant other was guilty of infidelity, I would confront him/her.

Scoring

Selecting a 1 reflects the least acceptance of infidelity; selecting a 7 reflects the greatest acceptance of infidelity. Before adding the numbers you selected, reverse the scores for item numbers 2, 5, 6, 7, 8, and 12. For example, if you responded to item 2 with a "6," change this number to a "2"; if you responded with a "3," change this number to "5," and so on. After making these changes, add the numbers. The lower your total score (12 is the lowest possible), the less accepting you are of infidelity; the higher your total score (84 is the highest possible), the greater your acceptance of infidelity. A score of 48 places you at the midpoint between being very disapproving and very accepting of infidelity.

Scores of Other Students Who Completed the Scale

The scale was completed by 150 male and 136 female student volunteers at Valdosta State University. The average score on the scale was 27.85 (SD = 12.02). Their ages ranged from 18 to 49, with a mean age of 23.36 (SD = 5.13). The ethnic backgrounds of the sample included 60.8 percent white, 28.3 percent African American, 2.4 percent Hispanic, 3.8 percent Asian, 0.3 percent American Indian, and 4.2 percent other. The college classification level of the sample included 11.5 percent freshmen, 18.2 percent sophomores, 20.6 percent juniors, 37.8 percent seniors, 7.7 percent graduate students, and 4.2 percent postbaccalaureate. Male participants reported more positive attitudes toward infidelity (mean = 31.53; SD = 11.86) than did female participants (mean = 23.78; SD = 10.86; $p < .05$). White participants had more negative attitudes toward infidelity (mean = 25.36; SD = 11.17) than did nonwhite participants (mean = 31.71; SD = 12.32; $p < .05$). There were no significant differences in regard to college classification.

Source

"Attitudes toward Infidelity Scale" 2006 by Mark Whatley, Ph.D., Department of Psychology, Valdosta State University, Valdosta, Georgia 31698-0100. Used by permission. Other uses of this scale by written permission of Dr. Whatley only (mwhatley@valdosta.edu). Information on the reliability and validity of this scale is available from Dr. Whatley.

satiation, and the attractiveness and excitement of sex with the primary partner seem to wane. A high-end call girl said the following of the Eliot Spitzer affair:

Almost all of my clients are married. I would say easily over 90 percent. I'm not trying to justify this business, but these are men looking for companionship. They are generally not men that couldn't have an affair [if they wanted to], but men who want this tryst with no stings attached. They're men who want to keep their lives at home intact. (Kottke 2008)

The **Coolidge effect** is a term used to describe this waning of sexual excitement and the effect of novelty and variety on sexual arousal:

One day President and Mrs. Coolidge were visiting a government farm. Soon after their arrival, they were taken off on separate tours. When Mrs. Coolidge passed the chicken pens, she paused to ask the man in charge if the rooster copulated more than once each day. "Dozens of times," was the reply. "Please tell that to the President," Mrs. Coolidge *requested. When the President passed the pens and was told about the rooster, he asked, "Same hen every time?" "Oh no, Mr. President, a different one each time." The President nodded slowly and then said, "Tell that to Mrs. Coolidge." (Bermant 1976, 76–77)*

Whether or not individuals are biologically wired for monogamy continues to be debated. Monogamy among mammals is rare (from 3 percent to 10 percent), and monogamy tends to be the exception more often than the rule (Morell 1998). Even if such biological wiring for plurality of partners does exist, it is equally debated whether such wiring justifies nonmonogamous behavior—that individuals are responsible for their decisions.

2. *Workplace friendships.* A common place for extramarital involvements to develop is the workplace. Neuman (2008) noted that four in ten of the affairs men reported began with a woman they met at work. Coworkers share the same world eight to ten hours a day and, over a period of time, may develop good feelings for each other that eventually lead to a sexual relationship. Former Democratic presidential candidate John Edwards became involved with a journalist when they were on the campaign trail together. Tabloid reports regularly reflect that romances develop between married actors making a movie together (for example, Brad Pitt and Angelina Jolie, who cohabit/have children together).

3. *Relationship dissatisfaction.* It is commonly believed that people who have affairs are not happy in their marriage. Spouses who feel misunderstood, unloved, and ignored sometimes turn to another who offers understanding, love, and attention. Djamba et al. (2005) analyzed General Social Survey data and found that unhappiness in one's marriage was the primary reason for becoming involved in an extramarital affair. Neuman (2008) confirmed that being emotionally dissatisfied in one's relationship is the primary culprit leading to an affair.

One source of relationship dissatisfaction is an unfulfilling sexual relationship. Some spouses engage in extramarital sex because their partner is not interested in sex. Others may go outside the relationship because their partners will not engage in the sexual behaviors they want and enjoy. The unwillingness of the spouse to engage in oral sex, anal intercourse, or a variety of sexual positions sometimes results in the other spouse's looking elsewhere for a more cooperative and willing sexual partner.

4. *Revenge.* Some extramarital sexual involvements are acts of revenge against one's spouse for having an affair. When partners find out that their mate has had or is having an affair, they are often hurt and angry. One response to this hurt and anger is to have an affair to get even with the unfaithful partner.

5. *Homosexual relationship.* Some individuals marry as a front for their homosexuality. Cole Porter, known for "I've Got You under My Skin," "Night and Day," and "Easy to Love," was a homosexual who feared no one would buy or publish his music if his sexual orientation were known. He married Linda Lee Porter (alleged to be a lesbian), and they had an enduring marriage for thirty years.

Other gay individuals marry as a way of denying their homosexuality. These individuals are likely to feel unfulfilled in their marriage and may seek involvement in an extramarital homosexual relationship. Other individuals may marry and then discover later in life that they desire a homosexual relationship. Such individuals may feel that (1) they have been homosexual or bisexual all along, (2) their sexual orientation has changed from heterosexual to homosexual or bisexual, (3) they are unsure of their sexual orientation and want to explore a homosexual relationship, or (4) they are predominately heterosexual but wish to experience a homosexual relationship for variety. The term **down low** refers to African American married men who have sex with men (Browder 2005).

6. *Aging.* A frequent motive for intercourse outside marriage is the desire to return to the feeling of youth. Ageism, which is discrimination against the elderly, promotes the idea that being young is good and being old is bad. Sexual attractiveness is equated with youth, and having an affair may confirm to older partners

We act as though comfort and luxury were the chief requirements of life, when all we need to make us really happy is something to be enthusiastic about.

Charles Kingsley, historian/novelist

What if You Are Tempted to Cheat on Your Partner?

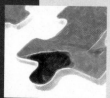

The costs of cheating on your partner will rarely be worth the anticipated gains in adventure or sex. Ask Democratic presidential candidate John Edwards if his indiscretion was worth it (his marriage was strained and his political career was devastated). To control one's temptation, it is important to control words, alcohol, and context. Flirting, alcohol, and being alone with the other person increase the chance of cheating. Being polite but scripted, avoiding alcohol or drugs, and always being in a public place with the other person will ensure that nothing sexual will happen (and negative consequences will be avoided). If you are already drifting toward an affair, it is never too late to stop and reverse your behavior.

that they are still sexually desirable. Also, people may try to recapture the love, excitement, adventure, and romance associated with youth by having an affair.

7. *Absence from partner.* One factor that may predispose a spouse to an affair is prolonged separation from the partner. Some wives whose husbands are away for military service report that the loneliness can become unbearable. Some husbands who are away say that remaining faithful is difficult. Partners in commuter relationships may also be vulnerable to extradyadic sexual relationships.

Effects of an Affair. Reactions to the knowledge that one's spouse has been unfaithful vary. For most, the revelation is difficult. The following is an example of a wife's reaction to her husband's affairs:

My husband began to have affairs within six months of our being married. Some of the feelings I experienced were disbelief, doubt, humiliation and outright heart-wrenching pain! When I confronted my husband he denied any such affair and said that I was suspicious, jealous and had no faith in him. In effect, I had the problem. He said that I should not listen to what others said because they did not want to see us happy but only wanted to cause trouble in our marriage. I was deeply in love with my husband and knew in my heart that he was guilty as sin; I lived in denial so I could continue our marriage.

Of course, my husband continued to have affairs. Some of the effects on me included:

1. I lost the inability to trust my husband and, after my divorce, other men.

2. I developed a negative self concept—the reason he was having affairs is that something was wrong with me.

3. He robbed me of the innocence and my "VIRGINITY"—clearly he did not value the opportunity to be the only man to have experienced intimacy with me.

4. I developed an intense hatred for my husband.

It took years for me to recover from this crisis. I feel that through faith and religion I have emerged "whole" again. Years after the divorce my husband made a point of apologizing and letting me know that there was nothing wrong with me, that he was just young and stupid and not ready to be serious and committed to the marriage.

Affairs may also have negative effects on children, which may result from hearing conflicts between the parents, from an absence of attention (because the father not at home), and from the breakup of the marriage (Schneider 2003).

Should You Seek a Divorce If Your Partner Has an Affair?

About 20 percent of spouses face the decision of whether to stay with a mate who has had an extramarital affair. Such an affair may be physical or online. In a study of 123 committed couples, both men and women reported more distress when there was hypothetical emotional as compared to sexual online infidelity (Henline et al. 2007). Indeed, Amy Taylor, an Englishwoman, filed for divorce in 2008, after discovering that her husband had been having an affair in the online role-playing game, *Second Life.*

Regardless of whether the indiscretion is physical or emotional, one alternative for the partner is to end the relationship immediately on the premise that trust has been broken and can never be mended. People who take this position regard fidelity as a core element of the marriage that, if violated, necessitates a divorce. College students disapprove of an extramarital affair. In a sample of 1,319 undergraduates, 68 percent said that they would "divorce a spouse who had an affair" (Knox and Zusman 2009). Americans in general tend to be unforgiving about an affair. In a national survey, 64 percent would not forgive their spouse for having an extramarital affair and almost as high a percentage (62 percent) say they would leave their spouse and get a divorce if they found out their spouse was having an affair; 31 percent would not (Jones 2008). For some, emotional betrayal is equal to sexual betrayal (Sabini and Silver 2005).

Other couples build into their relationship the fact that each will have external relationships. In Chapter 2, we discussed polyamory, in which partners are open and encouraging of multiple relationships at the same time. The term *infidelity* does not exist for polyamorous couples.

Even for traditional couples, infidelity need not be the end of a couple's marriage but the beginning of a new, enhanced, and more understanding relationship. Healing takes time; the relationship may require a commitment on the part of the straying partner not to repeat the behavior, forgiveness by the partner (and not bringing it up again), and a new focus on improving the relationship. Couples who have been through the crisis of infidelity admonish, "Don't make any quick decisions" (Olson et al. 2002, 433). In spite of the difficulty of adjusting to an affair, most spouses are reluctant to end a marriage. Not one of fifty successful couples said that they would automatically end their marriage over adultery (Wallerstein and Blakeslee 1995).

The spouse who chooses to have an affair is often judged as being unfaithful to the vows of the marriage, as being deceitful to the partner, and as inflicting enormous pain on the partner (and children). When an affair is defined in terms of giving emotional energy, time, and economic resources to something or someone outside the primary relationship, other types of "affairs" may be equally as devastating to a relationship. Spouses who choose to devote their lives to their children, careers, parents, friends, or recreational interests may deprive the partner of significant amounts of emotional energy, time, and money and create a context in which the partner may choose to become involved with a person who provides more attention and interest.

Another issue in deciding whether to take the spouse back following extramarital sex is the concern over HIV. One spouse noted that, though he was willing to forgive and try to forget his partner's indiscretion, he required that she be tested for HIV and that they use a condom for six months. She tested negative, but their use of a condom was a reminder, he said, that sex outside one's bonded relationship in today's world has a life-or-death meaning. Related to this issue is that wives are more likely to develop cervical cancer if their husbands have other sexual partners.

There is no single way to respond to a partner who has an extramarital relationship. Most partners are hurt and think of ways to work through the crisis. Some succeed.

Sources

Henline, B. H., L. K. Lamke, and M. D. Howard. 2007. Exploring perceptions of online infidelity. *Personal Relationships* 14:113–28.

Jones, J. M. 2008. Most Americans not willing to forgive unfaithful spouse. *The Gallup Poll Briefing,* March, 83. Washington.

I was married on my fifty-fourth birthday. A week later Ted [Turner] was Time *Magazine's Person of the Year. A month later I discovered he was sleeping with someone else.*

Jane Fonda *My Life So Far*

Knox, D., and M. E. Zusman. 2009. Relationship and sexual behaviors of a sample of 1,319 university students. Unpublished data collected for this text. Department of Sociology, East Carolina University, Greenville, NC.

Olson, M. M., C. S. Russell, M. Higgins-Kessler, and R. B. Miller. 2002. Emotional processes following disclosure of an extramarital affair. *Journal of Marital and Family Therapy* 28:423–34.

Wallerstein, J. S., and S. Blakeslee. 1995. *The good marriage.* Boston: Houghton Mifflin.

Successful Recovery from Infidelity.   *Sex in the City: The Movie* featured the infidelity of Steve married to Miranda. They ended up getting back together, as do most couples once an affair is discovered. Olson et al. (2002) identified three phases of successful recovery from the discovery of a partner's affair (all of these phases were beautifully illustrated in the movie). The "roller-coaster" phase involves agony at the initial discovery, which elicits an array of feelings including rage or anger, self-blame, the desire to give up, and the desire to work on the marital relationship. The second phase, "moratorium," involves less emotionality and a decision to work it out. The partners settle into a focused though tenuous commitment to get beyond the current crisis. The third phase, "trust building," involves taking responsibility for the infidelity, reassurance of commitment, increased communication, and forgiveness. Couples in this phase "reengage," "open up," and focus on problems leading up to the infidelity. Working through a discovered affair takes time, commitment to new behavior in the primary relationship, and forgiveness.

In *Sex in the City: the Movie*, Steve had an affair and told Miranda. Although she was initially devastated, she forgave him, and they renewed their relationship. Most married couples are reluctant to end their relationship over an affair.

Arnaldo Magnani/Getty Images

Bagarozzi (2008) defined forgiveness as a conscious decision on the part of the offended spouse to grant a pardon to the offending spouse, to give up feeling angry, and to relinquish the right to retaliate against the offending spouse. In exchange, offending spouses take responsibility for the affair, agree not to repeat the behavior, and grant their partner the right to check up on them to regain trust.

Positive outcomes of having experienced and worked through infidelity include a closer marital relationship, increased assertiveness, placing higher value on each other, and realizing the importance of good marital communication (Olson et al. 2002; Linquist and Negy 2005).

Spouses who remain faithful to their partners have decided to do so. They avoid intimate conversations with members of the other sex and a context (for example, where alcohol drinking and/or being alone are involved) that are conducive to physical involvement. The best antidote is to be direct, simply telling the person you are not interested.

Prevention of Infidelity.   Allen et al. (2008) identified the premarital factors predictive of future infidelity. The primary factor for both partners was a negative pattern of interaction. Partners who end up being unfaithful were in relationships where they did not connect, argued, and criticized each other. Hence, spouses least vulnerable are in loving, nurturing, communicative relationships where each affirms the other. Neuman (2008) also noted that avoiding friends who have affairs and establishing close relationships with married couples who value fidelity further insulates one from having an affair.

Unemployment

In the wake of Hurricanes Katrina and Ike, there was massive unemployment in the New Orleans and Galveston areas. The jobs of thousands were literally washed away. Coupled with these job losses, corporate America continues to downsize and outsource jobs to India and Mexico. The result is massive layoffs and insecurity in the lives of American workers. Forced unemployment or the threatened loss of one's job is a major stressor for individuals, couples, and families (Legerski et al. 2006). Also, when spouses or parents lose their jobs as a result of physical illness or disability, a family experiences a double blow—loss of income combined with high medical bills. Unless an unemployed spouse is covered by the partner's medical insurance, unemployment can also result in loss of health insurance for the family. Insurance for both health care and disability is very important to help protect a family from an economic disaster. Prolonged unemployment may result in bankruptcy (Miller 2005).

The effects of unemployment may be more severe for men than for women. Our society expects men to be the primary breadwinners in their families and equates masculine self-worth and identity with job and income. Stress, depression, suicide, alcohol abuse, and lowered self-esteem, as well as increased cigarette smoking (Falba et al. 2005), are all associated with unemployment. Macmillan and Gartner (2000) also observed that men who are unemployed are more likely to be violent toward their working wives.

Women tend to adjust more easily to unemployment than men. Women are not burdened with the cultural expectation of the provider role, and their identity is less tied to their work role. Hence, women may view unemployment as an opportunity to spend more time with their families; many enjoy doing so.

Although unemployment can be stressful, increasing numbers of workers are also experiencing job stress. With the recession, layoffs, and downsizing, workers are given the work of two and told, "we'll hire someone soon." Meanwhile, employers have learned to pay for one and get the work of two. The result is lowered morale, exhaustion, and stress that can escalate into violence.

This couple is affair proof. Fidelity is assumed, they spend all of their free time together, and enjoy taking vacations together.

Authors

Substance Abuse

Spouses, parents, and children who abuse drugs contribute to the stress and conflict experienced in their respective marriages and families. Although some individuals abuse drugs to escape from unhappy relationships or the stress of family problems, substance abuse inevitably adds to the individual's marital and family problems when it results in health and medical problems, legal problems, loss of employment, financial ruin, school failure, divorce, and even death (due to accidents or poor health). The following reflects the experience of the wife of a man addicted to crack:

> *Marriage needs a foundation of trust and open communication, but when you are married to an addict, you won't find either. When I first met "Nate," I thought he was everything I wanted in a partner—good looks, a great sense of humor, intelligence, and ambition. It didn't take me long to realize that I was extremely*

attracted to this man. Since we knew some of the same people, we ended up at several parties together. We both drank and occasionally used cocaine but it wasn't a problem. I loved being with him and whenever I wasn't with him, I was thinking about him.

After only four months of dating, we realized we were falling madly in love with each other and decided to get married. Neither of us had ever been married before but I had a five-year-old son from a previous relationship. Nate really took to my son and it seemed like we had the perfect marriage—that changed drastically and quickly. I didn't know it but my husband had been using crack cocaine the entire time we dated. I wasn't extremely familiar with this new drug and I knew even less about its addictive power. Of course, I soon found out more about it than I cared to know.

Less than three months after we married, Nate went on his first binge. After leaving work one Friday night, he never came home. I was really worried and was calling all of his friends trying to find out where he was and what was wrong. I talked to the girlfriend of one of his best friends and found out everything. She told me that Nate had been smoking crack off and on for a long time and that he was probably out using again. I didn't know what to do or where to turn. I just stayed home all weekend waiting to hear from my husband.

Finally, on Sunday afternoon, Nate came home. He looked like hell and I was mad as hell. I sent my son to play with his friends next door and as soon as he was out of hearing range, I lost it. I began screaming and crying, asking why he never came home over the weekend. He just hung his head in absolute shame. I found out later that he had spent his entire paycheck, pawned his wedding ring, and had written checks off of a closed checking account. He went through over $1,000 of "our" money in less than three days.

I was devastated and in shock. After I calmed down and my anger subsided, we discussed his addiction. He told me he loved me with all his heart and that he was so sorry for what he had done. He also swore he would never do it again. Well, this is when I became an enabler and I continued to enable my husband for three years. He would stay clean for a while and things would be great between us, then he would go on another binge. It was the roller-coaster ride from hell. Nate was on a downward spiral and he was dragging my son and me down along with him.

By the end of our third year together, we were more like roommates. Our once wonderful sex life was virtually nonexistent and what love I still had for him was quickly fading away. I knew I had to leave before my love turned to hate. It was obvious that my son had been pulling away from Nathaniel emotionally so it was a good time to end the nightmare. I packed our belongings and moved in with my sister.

Less than three months after I left, Nate went into a rehabilitation program. I was happy for him but I knew I could never go back; it was too little, too late. That was nine years ago and the last I heard, he was still struggling with his addiction, living a life of misery. I have no regrets about leaving but I am saddened by what crack cocaine had done to my once wonderful husband—it turned him into a thief and a liar and ended our marriage.

Although getting married is associated with significant reductions in cigarette smoking, heavy drinking, and marijuana use for both men and women (Merline et al. 2008), family crises involving alcohol and/or drugs are not unusual. Alcohol is also a major problem on campus (over half of 772 college students who reported drinking alcohol reported having blacked out) (White et al. 2002). The context of the most intense drinking is at a fraternity social. In a study of 306 university students, the average number of drinks at a fraternity social was 5.91 compared to 4.04 at campus parties (Miley and Frank 2006).

Some students have also grown up in homes where one or both parents abused alcohol. Haugland (2005) studied alcohol abuse by the father and found

Alcohol Abuse on Campus

Alcohol is the drug that college students most frequently use. Even in a private conservative religious college, 53.6 percent of a sample of undergraduates reported drinking an average of five or more beers at a time (Coll et al. 2008), and 43.1 percent reported drinking beer at least once a week. College students do not learn from negative consequences to their drinking. Mallett et al. (2006) found that students who threw up, made unwise sexual decisions, or experienced a hangover or blackout underestimated the amount of alcohol they could drink before they experienced negative consequences. Continuing to drink was a given.

College students who drink alcohol heavily are more likely to miss class, make lower grades, have auto accidents, have low self-esteem, and be depressed (Williams et al. 2002). Nevertheless, unless college students drink every day, they are unlikely to define themselves as having a drinking problem (Lederman et al. 2003). Alcohol is officially sanctioned at some colleges. In a study of campus policies in Minnesota and Wisconsin, 29 percent of the colleges or universities reported having bars on campus and accepted gifts from the alcohol industry (Mitchel et al. 2005).

Campus policies throughout the United States include alcohol-free dorms, alcohol bans, enforcement and sanctions, peer support, and education. A minority (around 30 percent) of colleges and universities ban alcohol or its possession (Mitchel et al. 2005). Administrators fear that students will attend other colleges where they are allowed to drink. Alumni may want to drink at football games and view such university banning as intrusive. Some attorneys think colleges and universities can be held liable for not stopping dangerous drinking patterns, but others argue that college is a place for students to learn how to behave responsibly. Should sanctions be used (for example, expelling a student or closing down a fraternity)? If police are too restrictive, drinking may go underground, where detecting may be more difficult.

For the purposes of peer education, students at the University of Buffalo in New York created a video illustrating responsible drinking and discussions by students of their own alcohol poisoning. Although such educational interventions may increase knowledge of alcohol use, subsequent reduction in alcohol is unknown (Williams et al. 2002). Rutgers regularly conducts campus focus groups and recommends replacement of the term *binge drinking* with *dangerous drinking,* because the latter emphasizes outcomes (Lederman et al. 2003).

Some universities have hired full-time alcohol education coordinators. Providing nonalcoholic ways to meet others and to socialize has also been suggested (Borsari and Bergen-Cico 2003). Policies will continue to shift in reference to parental pressure to address the issue. The latest approach is to require incoming freshmen to take an online alcohol awareness course with the right to register for classes held contingent (Lazure 2008). Other new approaches include banning "beer pong" games (Keegan 2008) and informing parents of their sons' or daughters' alcohol or drug abuse on campus. An alcohol or drug infraction is reported to the parents, who may intervene early in curbing abuse.

Your Opinion?

1. To what degree do you believe drinking on campus should be a concern of the administration?
2. What university policies do you recommend to reduce binge drinking?
3. Under what conditions should a student who abuses alcohol be expelled?

Sources

Borsari, B., and D. Bergen-Cico. 2003. Self-reported drinking-game participation of incoming college students. *Journal of American College Health* 51:149–54.

Coll, J. E., P. R. Draves, and M. E. Major. 2008. An examination of underage drinking in a sample of private university students. *College Student Journal* 42:982–85.

Keegan, R. W. 2008. Beer pong's big splash. *Time,* August 18, 46–47.

Lazure, E. P. 2008. ECU requires alcohol awareness course. *Pieces of Eight,* August 1, 16.

Lederman, L. C., L. P. Stewart, F. W. Goodhart, and L. Laitman. 2003. A case against "binge" as a term of choice: Convincing college students to personalize messages about dangerous drinking. *Journal of Health Communication* 8:79–91.

Mallett, K. A., C. M. Lee, C. Neighbors, M. E. Larimer, and R. Turrisi. 2006. Do we learn from our mistakes? An examination of the impact of negative alcohol-related consequences on college students' drinking patterns and perceptions. *Journal of Studies on Alcohol* 67:269–76.

Mitchel, R. J., T. L. Toomey, and D. Erickson. 2005. Alcohol policies on college campuses. *Journal of American College Health* 53:149–57.

Williams, D. J., A. Thomas, W. C. Buboltz, Jr., and M. McKinney. 2002. Changing the attitudes that predict underage drinking in college students: A program evaluation. *Journal of College Counseling* 5:39–49.

that a drunken father simply was not around the children during drinking episodes. University officials have attempted (mostly unsuccessfully) to curb excessive drinking (see the Social Policy section above). Miley and Frank (2006) suggested that fraternity socials might become a focus for intervention because alcohol consumption is the highest on campus.

Motives for Drinking Alcohol Scale

Read the list of reasons people sometimes give for drinking alcohol. Thinking of all the times you drink, how often would you say you drink for each of the following reasons? (Circle the appropriate number after reading each item.)

1 = almost never/never
2 = some of the time
3 = half of the time
4 = most of the time
5 = almost always

1. Because it helps me to enjoy a party 1 2 3 4 5

2. To be sociable 1 2 3 4 5

3. To make social gatherings more fun 1 2 3 4 5

4. To improve parties and celebrations 1 2 3 4 5

5. To celebrate a special occasion with friends 1 2 3 4 5

6. To forget my worries 1 2 3 4 5

7. To help my depression or nervousness 1 2 3 4 5

8. To cheer me up 1 2 3 4 5

9. To make me feel more self-confident 1 2 3 4 5

10. To help me forget about problems 1 2 3 4 5

11. Because the effects of alcohol feel good 1 2 3 4 5

12. Because it is exciting 1 2 3 4 5

13. To get high 1 2 3 4 5

14. Because it gives me a pleasant feeling 1 2 3 4 5

15. Because it is fun 1 2 3 4 5

16. Because of pressure from friends 1 2 3 4 5

17. To avoid disapproval for not drinking 1 2 3 4 5

18. To fit in with the group 1 2 3 4 5

19. To be liked 1 2 3 4 5

20. To avoid feeling left out 1 2 3 4 5

Scoring

The four basic drinking motives are social, coping, enhancement, and conformity. The items for these and the average scores from 1,243 respondents follow. The lowest score reflecting each motive would be 1 = never; the highest score reflecting each motive would be 5 = always. The most frequent motive for women and men is to be sociable. The least frequent motive for women and men is to conform. To compare your score with other respondents, add the numbers you circled for each of the following social, coping, enhancement, and conformity reasons identified. For example, to ascertain the degree to which your motivation for drinking alcohol is to be sociable, add the numbers you circled for items two and five.

Basic Reasons for drinking are social, coping, enhancement, and conformity. Items 1, 2, 3, 4, 5 pertain to social drinking; items 6, 7, 8, 9, 10 pertain to coping drinking; items 11, 12, 13, 14, 15 pertain to enhancement drinking; and items 16, 17, 18, 19, 20 pertain to conformity drinking. In this study, female respondents scored 2.29 for social drinking; 1.61 for coping drinking; 1.99 for enhancement drinking; and 1.34 for conformity drinking. Male respondents scored 2.63 for social drinking; 1.59 for coping drinking; 2.33 for enhancement drinking; and 1.43 for conformity drinking.

Source

© 1994 by the American Psychological Association. Adapted with permission. Cooper, M. Lynne. 1994 Motivations for Alcohol Use Among Adolescents: Development and Validation of a four-factor model. *Psychological Assessment* 6:117–128.

As indicated in Table 14.1, drug use is most prevalent among 18- to 25-year-olds. Drug use among teenagers under age 18 is also high. Because teenage drug use is common, it may compound the challenge parents may have with their teenagers.

The Self-Assessment above allows you to identify your motives for drinking alcohol.

Table 14.1   Drug Use by Type of Drug and Age Group

Type of Drug Used	Age 12 to 17	Age 18 to 25	Age 26 to 34
Marijuana and hashish	7.0%	16.0%	9.0%
Cocaine	.4%	2.2%	1.7%
Alcohol	17.0%	62.0%	no data
Cigarettes	10.0%	38.0%	no data

Source: Adapted from *Statistical Abstract of the United States, 2009*, 128th ed. Washington, DC: U.S. Bureau of the Census, Table 199.

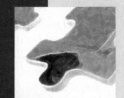
Drug Abuse Support Groups   Although treatments for alcohol abuse are varied, a combination of medications (naltrexone and acamprosate) and behavioral interventions (for example, control for social context) is a favored approach (Mattson and Litten 2005). The support group Alcoholics Anonymous (AA; www.alcoholics-anonymous.org) has also been helpful. There are over 15,000 AA chapters nationwide; one in your community can be found through the Yellow Pages. The only requirement for membership is the desire to stop drinking.

Former abusers of drugs (other than alcohol) also meet regularly in local chapters of Narcotics Anonymous (NA), to help each other continue to be drug-free. Patterned after Alcoholics Anonymous, the premise of NA is that the best person to help someone stop abusing drugs is someone who once abused drugs. NA members of all ages, social classes, and educational levels provide a sense of support for each other to remain drug-free.

Al-Anon is an organization that provides support for family members and friends of alcohol abusers. Spouses and parents of substance abusers learn how to live with and react to living with a substance abuser.

Parents who abuse drugs may also benefit from the Strengthening Families Program, which provides specific social skills training for both parents and children. After families attend a five-hour retreat, parents and children are involved in face-to-face skills training over a four-month period. A twelve-month follow-up has revealed that parenting skills remained improved and that reported heroin and cocaine use had declined.

Death of Family Member

Even more devastating than drug abuse are family crises involving death—of one's child, parent, or loved one (we discuss the death of one's spouse in Chapter 17 on Relationships in the Later Years). The crisis is particularly acute when the death is a suicide.

Death of One's Child   A parent's worst fear is the death of a child. Most people expect the death of their parents but not the death of their children. The following reflects the anguish of a father and mother who experienced the death of their daughter when she was 17.

All I know is that I am sick of living; I'm through. I'm drowned and contented on the bottom of a bottle.

Larry Slade

And yet they, who passed away long ago, still exist in us.

Rainer Maria Rilke, *Letters to a Young Poet*

Our lives changed forever when we received a phone call that our daughter was in the hospital and in critical condition. She had been on a trip to the beach with friends and was on the way home when the van flipped, crossed the divided highway and severely injured her. She then died on the side of the highway from head injuries. We discovered that the driver had put the cruise control on 70 and was playing "switch the driver" with his girlfriend, the front passenger. One of them hit the steering wheel inadvertently and our daughter (the only one of the six to die) was gone forever.

Emily was a month shy of her 17th birthday. She was a lovely child. We, as her parents, haven't been the same since her death. Even after all these years, our first thought upon awakening and last thought before we sleep is of our daughter, and how we miss her. At the time of her death, we were not alone in our grief. When we told Emily's grandfather of her death, he was overwhelmed with grief, and two weeks later died of a heart attack. To this day, we wonder if we had been protective enough. The grief goes on.

Also, our marriage has been strained due to the trauma. Since all couples have different grieving trajectories, we found one of us would be battling depression, while the other was half way level. . . . or vice versa. Her death will always remain a nightmare from which we cannot awaken. Time, therapy, support groups and the like have helped to manage our loss of our child, but we will forever continue to deal with our personal tragedy within our family . . . . we hope for peace. . . . but twelve years after her death we know our loss can only be managed.

Mothers and fathers sometimes respond to the death of their child in different ways. When they do, the respective partners may interpret these differences in negative ways, leading to relationship conflict and unhappiness. For example, after the death of their 17-year-old son, one wife accused her husband of not sharing in her grief. The husband explained that, although he was deeply grieved, he poured his grief into working more as a way of distraction. To deal with these differences, spouses might need to be patient and practice tolerance in allowing both to grieve in their own way.

Death of One's Parent Terminally ill parents may be taken care of by their children. Such care over a period of years can be emotionally stressful, financially draining, and exhausting. Hence, by the time the parent dies, a crisis has already occurred.

Reactions to the death of one's parents include depression, loss of concentration, and anger (Ellis and Granger 2002). Michael and Snyder (2005) studied college students who had experienced the death of a loved one (most often a parent) and found that their constant ruminations about the deceased correlated with a lower sense of psychological well-being. Whether the death is that of a child or a parent, Burke et al. (1999) noted that grief is not a one-time experience that people adjust to and move on. Rather, for some, there is "chronic sorrow," where grief-related feelings occur periodically throughout the lives of those left behind. The late Paul Newman was asked how he got over the death of his son who overdosed. He replied, "You never get over it." Johnny Carson, Ed McMahon, and Dean Martin also experienced the death of a child. Grief feelings may be particularly acute on the anniversary of the death or when the bereaved individual thinks of what might have been had the person lived. Burke et al. (1999) noted that 97 percent of the individuals in one study who had experienced the death of a loved one two to twenty years earlier met the criteria for chronic sorrow. Field et al. (2003) also observed bereavement-related distress five years after the death of a spouse.

Suicide of Family Member

Suicide is a devastating crisis event for families, and not that unusual. We know personally of five suicides, some of which have occurred within the family.

Annually there are 31,000 suicides (750,000 attempts), and each suicide immediately affects at least six other people in that person's life. These effects include depression (for example, grief), physical disorders (for example, shingles due to stress), and social stigma (for example, the person is viewed as weak and the family as a failure in not being able to help with the precipitating emotional problems) (De Castro and Guterman 2008). Schum (2007) identified family members who experience the suicide of a family member as having "the worst day of their lives."

People between 15 and 19, homosexual, or male, and those with a family history of suicide or mood disorder, substance abuse, or past history of child abuse and parental sex abuse are more vulnerable to suicide than others (Melhem et al. 2007). As noted earlier, Taliaferro et al. (2008) found that vigorous exercise and involvement in sports are associated with lower rates of suicide among adolescents.

Suicide is viewed as a "rational act" in that the person feels that suicide is the best option available at the time. Therapists view suicide as a "permanent solution to a temporary problem" and routinely call 911 to have people hospitalized or restrained who threaten suicide or who have been involved in an attempt.

Adjustment to the suicide of a family member takes time. The son of physician T. Schum committed suicide, which set in motion a painful adjustment for Dr. Schum. "You will never get over this but you can get through it," was a phrase Dr. Schum found helpful (Schum 2007). Survivors of Suicide is also a helpful support group. Part of the recovery process is accepting that one cannot stop the suicide of those who are adamant about taking their own life and that one is not responsible for the suicide of another. Indeed, family members often harbor the belief that they could have done something to prevent the suicide. Singer Judy Collins lost her son to suicide and began to attend a support group for people who had lost a loved to suicide. At a group she attended, one of the members in the group answered the question of whether there was something she could have done with a resounding *no*:

> *I was sitting on his bed saying, "I love you, Jim. Don't do this. How can you do this?" I had my hand on his hand, my cheek on his cheek. He said excuse me, reached his other hand around, took the gun from under the pillow, and blew his head off. My face was inches from his. If somebody wants to kill himself or herself, there is nothing you can do to stop them.* (Collins 1998, 210)

Marriage and Family Therapy

University students have a positive view of marriage therapy. In a study of 288 undergraduate and graduate students, 93 percent of the females and 82 percent of the males agreed that, "I would be willing to see a marriage counselor before I got a divorce" (Dotson-Blake et al. 2009).

Couples might consider marriage and family therapy rather than continuing to drag through dissatisfaction related to a crisis event. Signs to look for in your own relationship that suggest you might consider seeing a therapist include feeling distant and not wanting or being unable to communicate with your partner, avoiding each other, feeling depressed, drifting into a relationship with someone else or having an affair, increased drinking, and privately contemplating separation or divorce.

If you are experiencing one or more of these symptoms, it may be wise to intervene early so as to stop the spiral toward an estranged relationship before there is no motivation to do so. A relationship is like a boat. A small leak unattended can become a major problem and sink the boat. Marriage therapy sometimes serves to reverse relationship issues early by helping the partners to sort out values, make decisions, and begin new behaviors so that spouses can start feeling better about each other.

Availability of Marriage and Family Therapists

There are around 50,000 marriage and family therapists in the United States. About 40 percent are clinical members of the American Association for Marriage and Family Therapy (AAMFT). Currently there are fifty-seven masters, nineteen doctoral, and sixteen postgraduate programs accredited by the AAMFT. All but six states (Delaware, Montana, New York, North Dakota, Ohio, and West Virginia) and the District of Columbia regulate (that is, require a license) for a person to practice marriage and family therapy (Northey 2002).

Therapists holding membership in AAMFT have had graduate training in marriage and family therapy and a thousand hours of direct client contact (with 200 hours of supervision). Clients are customers and should feel comfortable with their therapists and the progress they are making. If they don't, they should switch therapists.

Marriage therapy is expensive—$100 to $125 an hour is not uncommon. Managed care has resulted in some private therapists lowering their fees so as to compete with what insurance companies will pay (about $80 per session). Some mental health centers offer marital and family therapy on a sliding-fee basis so that spouses, parents, and their children can be seen for as little as $5. Marriage therapists generally see both the husband and the wife together (called conjoint therapy); about 60 percent will involve the children as necessary but often not as active participants (Lund et al. 2002).

To what degree do spouses, parents, and children benefit from marriage and family therapy? Shadish and Baldwin (2003) synthesized twenty intervention studies on marriage and family therapy and concluded that such interventions were "clearly efficacious compared to no treatment" (p. 566).

Whether a couple in therapy remain together will depend on their motivation to do so, how long they have been in conflict, the severity of the problem, and whether one or both partners are involved in an extramarital affair. Two moderately motivated partners with numerous conflicts over several years are less likely to work out their problems than a highly motivated couple with minor conflicts of short duration. Severe depression or alcoholism on the part of either spouse is a factor that will limit positive marital and family gains. In general, these issues must be resolved individually before the spouses can profit from marital therapy.

Some couples come to therapy with the goal of separating amicably. The therapist then discusses the couple's feelings about the impending separation, the definition of the separation (temporary or permanent), the "rules" for their interaction during the period of separation (for example, see each other, date others), and whether to begin discussions with a divorce mediator or attorneys.

One alternative for enhancing one's relationship is the Association for Couples in Marriage Enrichment (ACME). This organization provides conferences for couples to enrich their marriage.

Effectiveness of Behavioral Couple Therapy versus IBCT

Members of AAMFT use more than twenty different treatment approaches (Northey 2002). Most therapists (31 percent) report that they use either a behavioral or "cognitive-behavioral" approach. A behavioral approach (also referred to as **behavioral couple therapy** or BCT) means that the therapist focuses on behaviors the respective spouses want increased or decreased, initiated or terminated, and negotiate behavioral exchanges between the partners (Crisp and Knox 2009). Following is an example of a behavioral contract that behavior therapists give to

Diversity in Other Countries

Lundblad and Hansson (2006) assessed the effectiveness of couples therapy with an initial sample of 300 Swedish couples and found that gains of improved functioning were evident at a two-year follow-up.

distressed couples. The contract assumes that the partners argue frequently, never compliment each other, no longer touch each other, and do not spend time together. The contract calls for each partner to make no negative statements to the other, give two compliments per day to the other, hug or hold each other at least once a day, and allocate Saturday night to go out to dinner alone with each other. On the contract, under each day of the week, the partners would check that they did what they agreed and return to the therapist. Partners who change their behavior toward each other often discover that the partner changes also and there is a new basis for each to feel better about each other and their relationship.

Behavior Contract for Partners*

Name of Partners _____ Date:_Week of *June 8–14*							
Behaviors each partner agrees to engage in and Days of Week							
	Mon.	Tues.	Wed.	Thurs.	Fri.	Sat.	Sun
1. No negative statements to partner	☐	☐	☐	☐	☐	☐	☐
2. Compliment partner twice each day	☐	☐	☐	☐	☐	☐	☐
3. Hug or hold partner once a day	☐	☐	☐	☐	☐	☐	☐
4. Go out to dinner with partner Saturday night	☐	☐	☐	☐	☐	☐	☐

*From B. Crisp and D. Knox. 2009. *Behavioral family therapy*. Durham, NC: Carolina Academic Press.

Sometimes clients do not like behavior contracts and say to the behavior therapist, "I want my partner to compliment me and hug me because my partner wants to, not because you wrote it down on one of these silly contracts." The behavior therapist acknowledges the desire for the behavior to come from the heart of the partner. Indeed it is, in that the partner has a choice about whether to please the partner. The partner could certainly say, "I don't care what my partner thinks or feels and I'm not doing anything to make things better. If you have to work at a relationship, it's not worth having." Of course, this position means the relationship is over (but not cooperating is unlikely because couples who come for marriage counseling are usually motivated to do things to improve the relationship).

Cognitive-behavioral therapy, also referred to as **integrative behavioral couple therapy** (IBCT), emphasizes a focus on the cognitions or assumptions of the spouses, which may have negative consequences for the relationship. For example, spouses may assume that "you have it or you don't" or "I can never trust my partner again—the marriage is over" when, indeed, both assumptions are inaccurate.

Christensen et al. (2006) provided follow-up data after two years on 130 couples who were part of a study that compared traditional couple behavior therapy (TCBT) with integrative behavioral couple therapy (IBCT). The researchers found that 60 percent of the couples who received TCBT reported significant improvement two years later compared to 69 percent of couples who received IBCT. They determined behavioral therapy involving cognitions is more effective.

Some Caveats about Marriage and Family Therapy

In spite of the potential benefits of marriage therapy, some valid reasons exist for not becoming involved in such therapy. Not all spouses who become involved in marriage therapy regard the experience positively. Some feel that their marriage is worse as a result. Reasons some spouses cite for negative outcomes include saying things a spouse can't forget, feeling hopeless at not being able to resolve a problem "even with a counselor," and feeling resentment over new demands a spouse makes in therapy.

Therapists may also give clients an unrealistic picture of loving, cooperative, and growing relationships in which partners always treat each other with respect and understanding, share intimacy, and help each other become whoever each wants to be. In creating this idealistic image of the perfect relationship, therapists may inadvertently encourage clients to focus on the shortcomings in their relationship and to expect more of their marriage than is realistic. Dr. Robert Sammons (2008) calls this his first law of therapy: "That spouses always focus on what is missing rather than what they have . . . indeed the only thing that is important to couples in therapy is that which is missing."

Couples and families in therapy must also guard against assuming that therapy will be a quick and easy fix. Changing one's way of viewing a situation (cognitions) and behavior requires a deliberate, consistent, relentless commitment to make things better. Without it, couples are wasting their time and money.

As well, couples who become involved in marriage counseling may also miss work, have to pay for child care, and be "exposed" at work if they use their employer's insurance policy to cover the cost of therapy. Though these are not reasons to decide against seeing a counselor, they are issues that concern some couples.

SUMMARY

What is stress and what is a crisis event?

Stress is a reaction of the body to substantial or unusual demands (physical, environmental, or interpersonal). Stress is a process rather than a state. A crisis is a situation that requires changes in normal patterns of behavior. A family crisis is a situation that upsets the normal functioning of the family and requires a new set of responses to the stressor. Sources of stress and crises can be external (for example, hurricane, tornado, downsizing, military separation) or internal (for example, alcoholism, extramarital affair, Alzheimer's disease).

Family resilience is when family members successfully cope of under adversity, which enables them to flourish with warmth, support, and cohesion. Key factors include positive outlook, spirituality, flexibility, communication, financial management, family shared recreation, routines or rituals, and support networks.

The ABCX model is a theoretical model of looking at family stress. *A* is the stressor event (for example, a hurricane), which interacts with *B*, the family's coping ability, or crisis-meeting resources (such as money, connections, spirituality). Both *A* and *B* interact with *C*, the family's appraisal or perception of the stressor event ("we can get through this and be better for it"). *X* is the family's adaptation to the crisis (for example, the family survives the hurricane).

What are positive stress management strategies?

Changing one's basic values and perspective is the most helpful strategy in reacting to a crisis. Viewing ill health as a challenge, bankruptcy as an opportunity to spend time with one's family, and infidelity as an opportunity to improve communication are examples. Other positive coping strategies are exercise, adequate sleep, love, religion, friends or relatives, humor, education, and counseling. Still other strategies include intervening early in a crisis, not blaming each other, keeping destructive impulses in check, and seeking opportunities for fun.

What are harmful strategies for reacting to a crisis?

Some harmful strategies include keeping feelings inside, taking out frustrations on others, and denying or avoiding the problem.

What are five of the major family crisis events?

Some of the more common crisis events that spouses and families face include physical illness, an extramarital affair, unemployment, alcohol or drug abuse, and the death of one's spouse or children. An extramarital affair is the second most stressful crisis event for a family (abuse is number one). Surviving an affair involves forgiveness on the part of the offended spouse to grant a pardon to the offending spouse, to give up feeling angry, and to relinquish the right to retaliate against the offending spouse. In exchange, an offending spouse must take responsibility for the affair, agree not to repeat the behavior, and grant the partner the right to check up on the offending partner to regain trust. The best affair prevention is a happy and fulfilling marriage as well as avoiding intimate conversations with members of the other sex and a context (for example, where alcohol is consumed and being alone), which are conducive to physical involvement. The occurrence of a "midlife crisis" is reported by less than a quarter of adults in the middle years. Those who did experience a crisis were going through a divorce.

What help is available from marriage and family therapists?

There are around 50,000 marriage and family therapists in the United States. About 40 percent are clinical members of the American Association for Marriage and Family Therapy (AAMFT). Whether a couple in therapy remain together will depend on their motivation to do so, how long they have been in conflict, the severity of the problem, and whether one or both partners are involved in an extramarital affair. Two moderately motivated partners with numerous conflicts over several years are less likely to work out their problems than a highly motivated couple with minor conflicts of short duration. Couples tend to benefit from early intervention. About 70 percent of couples involved in integrative couple behavior therapy (ICBT) (which involves behavior change and cognitions) report continued significant gains two years after the end of treatment.

KEY TERMS

Al-Anon	crisis	family resilience	resiliency
behavioral couple therapy	down low	integrative behavioral couple	stress
biofeedback	extradyadic involvement	therapy	
Coolidge effect	extramarital affair	palliative care	

The Companion Website for *Choices in Relationships: An Introduction to Marriage and the Family,* Tenth Edition
www.cengage.com/sociology/knox

Supplement your review of this chapter by going to the Companion Website to take one of the tutorial quizzes, use the flash cards to master key terms, or check out the many other study aids, like crossword puzzles and self-assessments. You'll also find special features such as General Social Survey (GSS) data, Census data, and other resources to help you with that special project or to do some research on your own.

WEB LINKS

American Association for Marriage and Family Therapy
http://www.aamft.org

Association for Applied and Therapeutic Humor
http://www.aath.org

Association for Couples in Marriage Enrichment
http://www.bettermarriages.org/

Association for Applied Psychophysiology and Biofeedback
http://www.aapb.org

Dear Peggy.com Extramarital Affairs Resource Center
http://www.vaughan-vaughan.com/

Infidelity
http://www.infidelity.com/

Red Hat Society
http://www.redhatsociety.com/

Allen, E. S., G. K. Rhoades, S. M. Stanley, H. J. Markman, et al. 2008. Premarital precursors of marital infidelity. *Family Process* 47:243–60.

Baggerly, J., and H. A Exum. 2008. Counseling children after natural disasters: Guidance for family therapists. *The American Journal of Family Therapy* 36:79–93.

Bagarozzi, D. A. 2008. Understanding and treating marital infidelity: A multidimensional model. *The American Journal of Family Therapy* 36:1–17.

Bermant, G. 1976. Sexual behavior: Hard times with the Coolidge Effect. In *Psychological research: The inside story*, ed. M. H. Siegel and H. P. Zeigler. New York: Harper and Row.

Black, K., and M. Lobo. 2008. A conceptual review of family resilience factors. *Journal of Family Nursing* 14:1–33.

Browder, B. S. 2005. *On the Up and Up: A Survival Guide for Women Living with Men on the Down Low.* New York: Kensington Publishers Corp.

Burke, M. L., G. G. Eakes, and M. A. Hainsworth. 1999. Milestones of chronic sorrow: Perspectives of chronically ill and bereaved persons and family caregivers. *Journal of Family Nursing* 5:387–84.

Burr, W. R., and S. R. Klein.1994. *Reexamining family stress: New theory and research.* Thousand Oaks, CA: Sage.

Butterworth, P., and B. Rodgers. 2008. Mental health problems and marital disruption: Is it the combination of husbands and wives' mental health problems that predicts later divorce? *Social Psychiatry and Psychiatric Epidemiology* 43:758–64.

Carlson-Catalano, J. 2003. Director of Clinical Biofeedback Services. *Health innovations.* Greenville, NC 27878. Personal communication, June 9.

Christensen, A. J. Yi, Atkins, D. C., D. H. Baucom, and W. I. George. 2006 Couple and individual adjustment for 2 years following a randomized clinical trial comparing traditional versus integrative behavioral couple therapy. *Journal of Consulting & Clinical Psychology* 74:1180–91.

Collins, J. 1998. *Singing lessons: A memoir of love, loss, hope, and healing.* New York: Pocket Books.

Cramer, R. E., R. E. Lipinski, J. D. Meteer, and J. A. Houska. 2008. Sex differences in subjective distress to unfaithfulness: Testing competing evolutionary and violation of infidelity expectations hypotheses. *The Journal of Social Psychology* 148:389–406.

Crisp, B., and Knox, D. 2009. *Behavioral family therapy.* Durham, NC: Carolina Academic Press.

De Castro, S., and J. T. Guterman. 2008. Solution-focused therapy for families with suicide. *Journal of Marital and Family Therapy* 34:93–107.

Djamba, Y. K., M. J. Crump, and A. G. Jackson. 2005. Levels and determinants of extramarital sex. Paper presented at the Southern Sociological Society, March. Charlotte, NC.

Dotson-Blake, K., D. Knox, and A. Holman. 2009. College student attitudes toward marriage, family, and sex therapy. Unpublished data from 288 undergraduate/graduate students. East Carolina University, Greenville, NC.

Druckerman, P. 2007. *Lust in translation.* New York: Penguin Group.

Duparcq, E. 2008. US soldiers in Iraq can find stress deadlier than enemy. Associated Press, October 14. http://news.yahoo.com/s/afp/20081015/wl_mideast_afp/iraqunrestus.

Ellis, R. T., and J. M. Granger. 2002. African American adults' perceptions of the effects of parental loss during adolescence. *Child and Adolescent Social Work Journal* 19:271–86.

Elmslie, B., and E. Tebaldi. 2008. So, What did you do last night? The economics of infidelity *Kyklos* 61:391–406.

Enright, E. 2004. A house divided. *AARP The Magazine,* July/August, 60.

Falba, T. M. T., J. L. Sindelar, and W. T. Gallo. 2005. The effect of involuntary job loss on smoking intensity and relapse. *Addiction* 100:1330–39.

Field, N. P., E. Gal-Oz, and G. A. Bananno. 2003. Continuing bonds and adjustment at 5 years after the death of a spouse. *Journal of Consulting and Clinical Psychology* 71:110–17.

Flynn, M. A. T., D. A. McNeil, B. Maloff, D. Matasingwa, M. Wu, C. Ford, and S. C. Tough. 2006. Reducing obesity and related chronic disease risk in children and youth: a synthesis of evidence with 'best practice' recommendations. *Obesity Reviews* 7:7–66.

Friedrich, R. M., S. Lively, and L. M Rubenstein. 2008. Siblings' coping strategies and mental health services: A national study of siblings of persons with schizophrenia *Psychiatric Services* 59:261–73.

Goode, E. 1999. New study finds middle age is prime of life. *New York Times,* July 17, D6.

Hall, J. H., W. Fals-Stewart, and F. D. Fincham. 2008. Risky sexual behavior among married alcoholic men. *Journal of Family Psychology.* 22:287–99.

Haugland, B. S. M. 2005. Recurrent disruptions of rituals and routines in families with paternal alcohol abuse. *Family Relations* 54:225–41.

Ingram, S., J. L. Ringle, K. Hallstrom, D. E. Schill, V. M. Gohr, and R. W. Thompson. 2008. Coping with crisis across the lifespan: The role of a telephone hotline. *Journal of Child and Family Studies* 17:663–75.

Insel, T. R. 2008. Assessing the economic costs of serious mental illness. *The American Journal of Psychiatry* 165:663–66.

Kahl, S. F., L. C. Steelman, L. M. Mulkey, and P. R. Koch, L. D. William, and S. Catsambis. 2007. Revisiting Reuben Hill's theory of familial response to stressors: The mediating role of mental outlook for offspring of divorce. *Family and Consumer Sciences Research Journal* 36:5–25.

Knox, D., and Zusman, M. E. 2009. Relationship and sexual behaviors of a sample of 1,319 university students. Unpublished data collected for this text. Department of Sociology, East Carolina University, Greenville, NC.

Kottke, J. 2008. The Eliot Spitzer affair and the business of sex. http://kottke.org/08/03/the-eliot-spitzer-affair-and-the-business-of-sex (retrieved December 6, 2008).

Lederman, L. C., L. P. Stewart, F. W. Goodhart, and L. Laitman. 2003. A case against "binge" as a term of choice: Convincing college students to personalize messages about dangerous drinking. *Journal of Health Communication* 8:79–91.

Legerski, E. M., M. Cornwall, and B. O'Neil. 2006 Changing locus of control: Steelworkers adjusting to forced unemployment. *Social Forces* 84:1521–37.

Leonard, R., and A. Burns. 2006. Turning points in the lives of midlife and older women: Five-year follow-up. *Australian Psychologist* 41:28–36.

Levitt, M. J., J. Levitt, G. L. Bustos, N. A. Crooks, J. D. Santos, P. Telan, J. Hodgetts, and A. Milevsky. 2005. Patterns of social support in middle childhood to early adolescent transition: Implications for adjustment. *Social Development* 14:398–420.

Linquist, L., and C. Negy. 2005. Maximizing the experiences of an extrarelational affair: An unconventional approach to a common social convention. *Journal of Clinical Psychology/In Session* 61:1421–28.

Lund, L. K., T. S. Zimmerman, and S. A. Haddock. 2002. The theory, structure, and techniques for the inclusion of children in family therapy: A literature review. *Journal of Marital and Family Therapy* 28:445–54.

Lundblad, A., and K. Hansson. 2006. Couples therapy: effectiveness of treatment and long-term follow up. *Journal of Family Therapy* 28:136–52.

Macmillan, R., and Gartner. 2000. When she brings home the bacon: Labor-force participation and the risk of spousal violence against women. *Journal of Marriage and the Family* 61:947–58.

Mahoney, D. 2005. Mental illness prevalence high, despite advances. *Clinical Psychiatry News* 33:1–2.

Mattson, M. E., and R. Z. Litten. 2005. Combining treatments for alcoholism: Why and how? *Journal of Studies on Alcohol* July:8–16.

Melhem, N. M., D. A. Brent, M. Ziegler, S. Iyengar, et al. 2007 Familial pathways to early-onset suicidal behavior: Familial and individual antecedents of suicidal behavior. *American Journal of Psychiatry* 164:1364–71.

Merline, A. C., J. E. Schulenberg, P. M. O'Malley, J. G. Bachman, and L. D. Johnston. 2008. Substance use in marital dyads: Premarital assortment and change over time. *Journal of Studies on Alcohol and Drugs* 69:352–65.

Michael, S. T., and C. R. Snyder. 2005. Getting unstuck: The roles of hope, finding meaning, and rumination in the adjustment to bereavement among college students. *Death Studies* 29:435–459.

Miley, W. M., and W. Frank. 2006. Binge and non-binge college students' perceptions of other students' drinking habits. *College Student Journal* 40:259–62.

Miller, M. 2005. Where's the outrage? *Social Policy* 35:5–8.

Mitchel, R. J., T. L. Toomey, and D. Erickson. 2005. Alcohol policies on college campuses. *Journal of American College Health* 53:149–157.

Moore, D. W. 2006. Close to 6 in 10 Americans want to lose weight. Gallup poll. March 10. http://www.gallup.com/poll/21859/Close-Americans-Want-Lose-Weight.aspx (retrieved April 20).

Morell, V. 1998. A new look at monogamy. *Science* 281:1982.

Mostaghimi, L., W. H. Obermeyer, B. Ballamudi, D. M. Gonzalez, and R. M. Benca. 2005. Effects of sleep deprivation on wound healing. *Journal of Sleep Research* 12:213–19.

Mordoch, E., and W. A. Hall. 2008. Children's perceptions of living with a parent with a mental illness: Finding the rhythm and maintaining the frame. *Qualitative Health Research* 18:1127–35.

Neff, L. A., and B. R. Karney. 2007. Stress crossover in newlywed marriage: A longitudinal and dyadic perspective. *Journal of Marriage and Family* 69:594–607.

Neuman, M. G. 2008. *The truth about cheating: Why men stray and what you can do to prevent it.* New York: John Wiley & Sons.

Northey, W. F. J. 2002. Characteristics and clinical practices of marriage and family therapists: A national survey. *Journal of Marriage and Family Therapy* 28:487–94.

Olson, M. M., C. S. Russell, M. Higgins-Kessler, and R. B. Miller. 2002. Emotional processes following disclosure of an extramarital affair. *Journal of Marital and Family Therapy* 28:423–34.

Ostbye, T., K. M. Krause, M. C. Norton, J. Tschanz, L. Sanders, K. Hayden, C. Pieper, and K. A. Welsh-Bohmer. 2006. Ten dimensions of health and their relationships with overall self-reported health and survival in a predominately religiously active elderly population: The Cache County Memory Study. *Journal of the American Geriatrics Society* 54:199–209.

Ozer, E. J., S. R. Best, T. L. Lipsey, and D. S. Weiss. 2003. Predictors of posttrauamatic stress disorder and symptoms in adults: A meta-analysis. *Psychological Bulletin* 129:52–73.

Park, C. 2006. Exploring relations among religiousness, meaning, and adjustment to lifetime and current stressful encounters in later life. *Anxiety Stress & Coping* 19:33–45.

Pratt, L. A., and D. J. Brody. 2008. Depression in the United States household population, 2005–2006. NCHS Data Brief, no. 7., September.

Pyle, S. A., J. Sharkey, G. Yetter, E. Felix, M. J. Furlog, and W. S. Poston. 2006. Fighting an epidemic: The role of schools in reducing childhood obesity. *Psychology in the Schools* 43:361–76.

Roberto, K. A. 2005. Families and policy: Health issues of older women. In *Sourcebook of family theory & research*, ed. Vern L. Bengtson, Alan C. Acock, Katherine R. Allen, Peggye Dilworth-Anderson, and David M. Klein, 547–48. Thousand Oaks, CA: Sage Publications.

Routh, K., and J. N. Rao. 2006. A simple, and potentially low-cost method for measuring the presence of childhood obesity. *Child: Care, Health & Development* 32:239–45.

Sabini, J. and M. Silver. 2005. Gender and jealousy. *Cognition and Emotion* 19:713–27.

Sammons, R. A., Jr. 2008. First law of therapy. Personal communication. Grand Junction, Colorado.

Schabus, M., K. Hodlmoser, T. Pecherstorfer, and G. Klosch. 2005. Influence of midday nap on declarative memory performance and motivation. *Somnologie* 9:148–53.

Schneider, J. P. 2000. Effects of cybersex addiction on the family: Results of a survey. *Sexual Addiction and Compulsivity* 7:31–58.

Schneider, J. P. 2003. The impact of compulsive cybersex behaviors on the family. *Sexual and Relationship Therapy* 18:329–55.

Schum, T. R. 2007. Dave's dead! Personal tragedy leading a call to action in preventing suicide. *Ambulatory Pediatrics* 7:410–12.

Shadish, W. R., and S. A. Baldwin. 2003. Metaanalysis of MTF interventions. *Journal of Marriage and the Family* 29:547–70.

Sharpe, L., and L. Curran. 2006. Understanding the process of adjustment to illness. *Social Science and Medicine* 62:1153–66.

Smith, L. R. 2005. Infidelity and emotionally focused therapy: A program design. Dissertation Abstracts. International, Section B, The Sciences and Engineering, 65(10-B):5423.

Statistical Abstract of the United States, 2009, 128th ed. Washington, DC: U.S. Bureau of the Census.

Szabo, A., S. E. Ainsworth, and P. K. Danks. 2005. Experimental comparison of the psychological benefits of aerobic exercise, humor, and music. *International Journal of Humor Research* 18:235–46.

Taliaferro, L. A., B. A. Rienzo, M. D. Miller, R. M. Pigg, and V. J. Dodd. 2008. High school youth and suicide risk: Exploring protection afforded through physical activity and sport participation. *The Journal of School Health* 78:545–56.

Teitler, J. O., and N. E Reichman. 2008. Mental illness as a barrier to marriage among unmarried mothers. *Journal of Marriage and Family* 70:772–83.

Termini, K. A. 2006. Reducing the negative psychological and physiological effects of chronic stress. 4th Annual ECU Research and Creative. Activities Symposium, April 21, East Carolina University, Greenville, NC.

Tetlie, T., N. Eik-Nes, T. Palmstierna, P. Callaghan, and J. A Nøttestad. 2008. The effect of exercise on psychological & physical health outcomes: Preliminary results from a Norwegian forensic hospital. *Journal of Psychosocial Nursing & Mental Health Services* 46:38–44.

Unnever, J. D., F. T. Cullen, B. K. Applegate. 2005. Turning the other cheek: Reassessing the impact of religion on punitive ideology. *Justice Quarterly* 22:304–39.

Waller, M. R. 2008. How do disadvantaged parents view tensions in their relationships? Insights for relationship longevity among at-risk couples. *Family Relations* 57:128–43.

Wallerstein, J. S., and S. Blakeslee. 1995. *The good marriage*. Boston: Houghton Mifflin.

Weckwerth, A. C., and D. M. Flynn. 2006. Effect of sex on perceived support and burnout in university students. *College Student Journal* 40:237–49.

White, A. M., D. W. Jamieson-Drake, and H. S. Swartzwelder. 2002. Prevalence and correlates of alcohol-induced blackouts among college students: Results of an e-mail survey. *Journal of American College Health* 51:117–32.

Williams, D. J., A. Thomas, W. C. Buboltz, Jr., and M. McKinney. 2002. Changing the attitudes that predict underage drinking in college students: A program evaluation. *Journal of College Counseling* 5:39–49.

I'm thru with love
I'll never fall again
Said adieu to love
Don't ever call again
For I must have you or no one
That's why I'm thru with love

Gus Kahn

Divorce and Ending Relationships

Contents

Oh, life is a glorious cycle of song,
A medley of extemporanea;
And love is a thing that can
never go wrong;
And I am Marie of Roumania

Dorothy Parker, poet and feminist

Just as weddings are a time of celebration and joy, divorce is a time of dismay and sadness. Divorce is the end of a dream of one living happily ever after with one's mate. Whether a divorce is the beginning of the end of one's life (some never recover) or the beginning of a new life depends on the person. College students are not unacquainted with divorce. In a sample of 1,319 undergraduates, 30.9 percent reported that their parents were divorced (Knox and Zusman 2009). In this chapter, we look at the social and individual causes of divorce, the consequences for the spouses and children, and ways to make the ending of one's marriage as painless and life-enhancing as possible. We begin by looking at how divorce rates are measured.

Ways of Measuring Divorce Prevalence

Divorce is the legal ending of a valid marriage contract. There are three ways of measuring the degree to which divorce occurs in our society.

Crude Divorce Rate

The **crude divorce rate** is a statement of how many divorces have occurred for every 1,000 people in the population. In 2003, there were 3.8 divorces per 1,000 population. In 2006, the rate dropped to 3.6 (*Statistical Abstract of the United States, 2009*, Table 77).

Refined Divorce Rate

More revealing than the crude divorce rate is the **refined divorce rate,** which is an expression of the number of divorces and annulments in a given year divided by the number of married women in the population times 1,000. For example, there are approximately 1.1 divorces and annulments per year and 63 million married women, which translates into .01746 times 1,000, or 17.5—the refined divorce rate.

Percentage of Marriages Ending in Divorce

A final way of estimating divorce is to identify the percentage of married people who eventually get divorced. The problem with this statistic is the period of time considered

Diversity in Other Countries

Compared with other countries, the United States has one of the highest divorce rates in the world. Only Belarus of Eastern Europe comes close when crude divorce rates are compared. However, one of the reasons for a high U.S. divorce rate is a very high marriage rate (Blossfeld and Muller 2002).

in identifying those who divorced. The percentage of those who divorced within five years would be lower than the percentage of those who divorced within a ten-year period. Current estimates suggest that about 40 percent of those who married in the past couple of decades will divorce (Hawkins et al. 2002). Goodwin (2003) noted that 20 percent of first marriages will end in divorce within five years, 33 percent within ten years, and 43 percent within fifteen years of marriage.

Regardless of how one measures the rate of divorce in the United States, "divorce rates have been stable or dropping for two decades" (Coltrane and Adams 2003, 363). The all-time high was in 1981 (Clarke-Stewart and Brentano 2006). The principal factor for such decline is that people are delaying marriage so that they are older at the time of marriage. According to Heaton (2002), "age at marriage plays the greatest role in accounting for trends in marital dissolution. . . . [W]omen who marry at older ages have more stable marriages." In addition, divorce rates have dropped as cohabitation rates have increased because people who live together and break up do not add to the divorce rate (Clarke-Stewart and Brentano 2006).

National Data
About 1 million divorces occur each year (*Statistical Abstract of the United States, 2009*, Table 77).

Regardless of how divorce is measured, a major question is, "why?" Both macro and micro factors help to explain why spouses divorce.

Macro Factors Contributing to Divorce

Sociologists emphasize that social context creates outcomes. This is best illustrated in the statistic that the Puritans in Massachusetts, from 1639 to 1760, averaged only one divorce per year (Morgan 1944). The social context of that era involved strong pro-family values and strict divorce laws, with the result that divorce was almost nonexistent. In contrast, divorce occurs more frequently today as a result of various structural and cultural factors, also known as macro factors (Lowenstein 2005).

Increased Economic Independence of Women
In the past, an unemployed wife was dependent on her husband for food and shelter. No matter how unhappy her marriage was, she stayed married because she was economically dependent on her husband. Her husband literally represented her lifeline. Finding gainful employment outside the home made it possible for a wife to afford to leave her husband if she wanted to. Now that about three-fourths of wives are employed, fewer wives are economically trapped in unhappy marriage relationships. As we noted earlier, a wife's employment does not increase the risk of divorce in a happy marriage. However, it does provide an avenue of escape for women in unhappy or abusive marriages (Kesselring and Bremmer 2006).

Employed wives are also more likely to require an egalitarian relationship; although some husbands prefer this role relationship, others are unsettled by it. Another effect of a wife's employment is that she may meet someone new in the workplace so that she becomes aware of an alternative to her current partner. Finally, unhappy husbands may be more likely to divorce if their wives are employed and able to be financially independent (less alimony and child support).

Changing Family Functions and Structure
Many of the protective, religious, educational, and recreational functions of the family have been largely taken over by outside agencies. Family members may now look to the police for protection, the church or synagogue for meaning, the

school for education, and commercial recreational facilities for fun rather than to each other within the family for fulfilling these needs. The result is that, although meeting emotional needs remains a primary function of the family, fewer reasons exist to keep a family together.

In addition to the changing functions of the family brought on by the Industrial Revolution, the family structure has changed from that of larger extended families in rural communities to smaller nuclear families in urban communities. In the former, individuals could turn to a lot of people in times of stress; in the latter, more stress necessarily falls on fewer shoulders. Cohen and Savaya (2003) documented an increased divorce rate among Muslim Palestinian citizens of Israel due to an increased acceptance of the modern views of marriage—increased emphasis on happiness and compatibility.

Liberal Divorce Laws

All states recognize some form of **no-fault divorce**—where neither party is identified as the guilty party or the cause of the divorce (for example, due to adultery). In effect, divorce is granted after a period of separation ranging from six weeks to twelve months. Nevada requires the shortest waiting period of six weeks. Most other states require from six to twelve months. The goal of no-fault divorce has been to try to make divorce less acrimonious. However, this has not always been successful as spouses who divorce may still fight over custody of the children, child support, spouse support, and division of property. Indeed, almost 90 percent of people who go through the divorce process report it as a negative experience (Clarke-Stewart and Brentano 2006). Although researchers disagree whether no-fault divorce is associated with more divorce (Drewianka 2008; Allen et al. 2006), a backlash has occurred and a movement is afoot to make divorce more difficult. One divorced spouse said, "I should have stayed married when the hard times hit—it was just too easy to walk out" (personal communication).

Fewer Moral and Religious Sanctions

Many priests and clergy recognize that divorce may be the best alternative in particular marital relationships and attempt to minimize the guilt that congregational members may feel at the failure of their marriage. Churches increasingly embrace single and divorced or separated individuals, as evidenced by "divorce adjustment groups."

More Divorce Models

As the number of divorced individuals in our society increases, the probability increases that a person's friends, parents, siblings, or children will be divorced. The more divorced people a person knows, the more normal divorce will seem to that person. The less deviant the person perceives divorce to be, the greater the probability the person will divorce if that person's own marriage becomes strained. Divorce has become so common that numerous websites exclusively for divorced individuals are available (for example, www.heartchoice.com/divorce).

Mobility and Anonymity

When individuals are highly mobile, they have fewer roots in a community and greater anonymity. Spouses who move away from their respective family and friends often discover that they are surrounded by strangers who don't care if they stay married or not. Divorce thrives when pro-marriage social expectations are not operative. In addition, the factors of mobility and anonymity also result in the removal of a consistent support system to help spouses deal with the difficulties they may encounter in marriage.

Diversity in Other Countries

Whether a person gets a divorce has more to do with the society in which the person lives than the "personality" of the person. Prior to 1997, there were no divorces in Ireland (Clarke-Stewart and Brentano 2006); Ireland is predominately Catholic and has been staunchly against divorce.

Race and Culture

A higher percentage of African Americans are divorced than European Americans (11.5 versus 10.4) (*Statistical Abstract of the United States, 2009*, Table 55). Contributing to this higher percentage of divorce among African Americans is the economic independence of black females and the difficulty for black males to find and keep stable jobs.

Asian Americans and Mexican Americans have lower divorce rates than European Americans or African Americans because they consider the family unit to be of greater value (familism) than their individual interests (individualism). Unlike familistic values in Asian cultures, individualistic values in American culture emphasize the goal of personal happiness in marriage. When spouses stop having fun (when individualistic goals are no longer met), they sometimes feel no reason to stay married. Of 1,319 undergraduates at a large southeastern university, only 4.5 percent agreed with the statement, "I would not divorce my spouse for any reason" (Knox and Zusman 2009). In two national samples, 36 percent agreed that "The personal happiness of an individual is more important than putting up with a bad marriage" (Amato et al. 2007). Reflecting an individualistic philosophy, Geraldo Rivera asked of his divorces, "Who cares if I've been married five times?"

Diversity in Other Countr...

Young Maasai wives of Arusha, Tanzan... do not have the option of divorce. Rat... married because divorce would result in their ret... respective homes, where they would bring shame... parents. In effect, they have no other role than tha... and mother—the role of divorcée is not an option.

A sure way to lose happiness, I found, is to want it at the expense of everything else.

Bette Davis, 1950s actress

Micro Factors Contributing to Divorce

Although macro factors may make divorce a viable cultural alternative to marital unhappiness, they are not sufficient to "cause" a divorce. One spouse must choose to divorce and initiate proceedings. Such a view is micro in that it focuses on the individual decisions and interactions within specific family units. The following subsections discuss some of the micro factors that may be operative in influencing a couple toward divorce.

Differences

As noted in the chapter on mate selection, the greater the differences between spouses, the more likely they are to divorce. Clarkwest (2007) noted that African Americans are more likely than non-Hispanic white individuals to marry someone different from themselves. Specifically, African American females are more likely to marry a man who is less supportive of gender equality, who is less religious, who wants fewer children, and who is less supportive of maternal employment than non-Hispanic white females. Earlier we noted that African Americans are more likely to divorce than European Americans. Their doing so is in reference to marring someone with significant differences.

Falling Out of Love

"Falling out of love" was a top reason for divorce that men reported (Enright 2004). Previti and Amato (2003) noted that the absence of love was also associated with both men and women being more likely to divorce. Indeed, almost half of 1,319 undergraduates reported that they would divorce a spouse they no longer loved (Knox and Zusman 2009).

Negative Behavior

Physical or emotional abuse and alcohol or drug abuse were among the top behavioral reasons identified by women who divorced in midlife (Enright 2004). Ostermann et al. (2005) confirmed that a discrepancy in the amount of alcohol spouses consume is associated with divorce. When the presence of negative behavior is coupled with the absence of positive behavior, the combination can be deadly. Shumway and Wampler (2002) emphasized that the absence of positive behaviors such as "small talk," "reminiscing about shared times together," and "encouragement" increases a couple's marital dissatisfaction.

People marry because they anticipate greater rewards from being married than from being single. During courtship, each partner engages in a high frequency of positive verbal (compliments) and nonverbal (eye contact, physical affection) behavior toward the other. The good feelings the partners experience as a result of these positive behaviors encourage them to marry to "lock in" these feelings across time. Just as love feelings are based on positive behavior from a partner, negative feelings are created when a partner engages in a high frequency of negative behavior and thoughts of divorce (to escape the negative behavior) occur.

Affair

Some extramarital affairs result in divorce (O'Leary 2005). The spouse having an affair may feel unloved at home where there is little to no sex. Involvement in an affair may bring both love and sex and speed the spouse toward divorce. Alternatively, an at-home spouse may become indignant and demand that the partner leave. Although most spouses (75 percent) do not leave their mates for a lover, an extramarital relationship may weaken the emotional tie between the spouses so that they are less inclined to stay married. Combined with a partner having an affair is the spouse who may feel betrayed and may terminate the marriage. Of 1,319 undergraduates, 67.6 percent agreed with the statement, "I would divorce a spouse who had an affair" (Knox and Zusman 2009). However, as we saw in the section on extramarital affairs in Chapter 14, Stress and Crisis in Relationships, most couples do not end a marriage because of an affair. Unmarried undergraduates say they would end a marriage, but married couples (who have invested a great deal) usually do not.

Lack of Conflict Resolution Skills

Managing differences and conflict in a relationship helps to reduce the negative feelings that develop in a relationship. Some partners respond to conflict by withdrawing emotionally from their relationship; others respond by attacking, blaming, and failing to listen to their partner's point of view. Ways to negotiate differences and reduce conflict were discussed in Chapter 4 on communication in relationships.

Value Changes

Both spouses change throughout the marriage. "He's not the same person I married" is a frequent observation of people contemplating divorce. People may undergo radical value changes after marriage. One minister married and decided seven years later that he did not like the confines of the marriage role. He left the ministry, earned a PhD, and began to drink and have affairs. His wife, who had married him when he was a minister, now found herself married to a clinical psychologist who spent his evenings at bars with other women. The couple divorced. Jane Fonda noted that she experienced a change in her assertiveness, that she was no longer willing to just go along with her mate but to specify what her needs were and to negotiate their fulfillment:

> The very thing that I feared the most—that I would gain my voice and lose my man—was actually happening. . . . The problem comes when what you need and what you see isn't seen or needed by your partner. It doesn't mean your partner is bad; it just means that he or she wants something else in life. . . . I could see Ted

[Turner] withering before my eyes. Clearly he wasn't going to be able (or willing) to make the journey with me. We agreed to separate. (Fonda 2005, 545)

Because people change throughout their lives, the person who one selects at one point in life may not be the same partner one would select at another point. Margaret Mead, the famous anthropologist, noted that her first marriage was a student marriage; her second, a professional partnership; and her third, an intellectual marriage to her soul mate, with whom she had her only child. At each of several stages in her life, she experienced a different set of needs and selected a mate who fulfilled those needs.

Satiation

Satiation, also referred to as habituation, refers to the state in which a stimulus loses its value with repeated exposure. Spouses may tire of each other. Their stories are no longer new, their sex is repetitive, and their presence no longer stimulates excitement as it did in courtship. Some people who feel trapped by the boredom of constancy divorce and seek what they believe to be more excitement by returning to singlehood and, potentially, new partners. A developmental task of marriage is for couples to enjoy being together and not demand a constant state of excitement (which is difficult over a fifty-year period). The late comedian George Carlin said, "If all of your needs are not being met, drop some of your needs." If spouses did not expect so much of marriage, maybe they would not be disappointed.

Perception That One Would Be Happier If Divorced

Brinig and Allen (2000) noted that women file two-thirds of divorce applications. Women's behavior may be based on the perception that they will achieve greater power over their own life, money (in the form of child support and/or alimony) without having the liability of dealing with an unsupportive husband on a daily basis, and greater control over their children, because women are awarded custody in 80 percent of cases. The researchers argue that "who gets the children" is by far the greatest predictor of who files for divorce, and they contend that *if* the law presumes that joint custody will follow divorce, there will be fewer women filing for divorce because women will have less to gain.

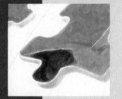

WHAT IF?

What if You Love But Get Tired of Your Partner?

Although being aware that the principle of satiation is operative in all relationships and to be realistic about one's expectations, you can also inject new ideas and activities into your relationship to experience it anew. Going new places, doing new things (taking the train, camping out), and making time for intimacy in the face of rearing children and sustaining careers become increasingly important across time for partners. Indeed, some couples discover that love feelings return when they change the context from humdrum house and work to an out-of-town bed-and-breakfast.

Mariah Carey and Nick Cannon knew each other two months before their marriage in 2008. One of the most important things a couple can do to help ensure a lasting and happy marriage is to date/know each other a MINIMUM OF TWO YEARS before getting married.

Hubert Boesl/dpa/Corbis

It destroys one's nerves to be amiable every day to the same human being.

Benjamin Disraeli

Top Twenty-Five Factors Associated with Divorce

Researchers have identified the characteristics of those most likely to divorce (Thompson 2008; Amato and Hohmann-Marriott 2007; Clarke-Stewart and Brentano 2006). Some of the more significant associations include the following:

1. Courting less than two years (partners know less about each other)

2. Having little in common (similar interests serve as a bond between people)

3. Marrying at age 17 and younger (associated with low education and income and lack of maturity)

4. Differing in race, education, religion, social class, age, values, and libido (widens the gap between spouses)

5. Not being religiously devout (less bound by traditional values)

6. Having a cohabitation history (established history of breaking social norms)

7. Having been previously married (less fearful of divorce)

8. Having no children (less reason to stay married) or female children only (male bias for male children)

9. Having limited education (associated with lower income, more stress, less happiness)

10. Living in an urban residence (more anonymity, less social control in urban environment)

11. Engaging in infidelity (broken trust, emotional reason to leave relationship)

12. Growing up with divorced parents (models for ending rather than repairing relationship; may have inherited traits such as alcoholism that are detrimental to staying married) or parents who never married and never lived together (being unmarried is normative)

13. Having poor communication skills (issues go unresolved and accumulate)

14. Husband experiencing unemployment (his self-esteem is lost, loss of respect by wife who expects breadwinner)

15. Wife obtaining employment (the wife is more independent and can afford to leave an unhappy marriage; husband feels threatened)

16. A spouse experiencing depression, anxiety disorder, alcoholism, physical illness (partners undergo grave change from earlier in relationship) as well as imprisonment (extended separation erodes relationship between the spouses) (Lopoo and Western 2005)

17. Having seriously ill child (impacts stress, finances, couple time)

18. A spouse having low self-esteem (associated with higher jealousy, less ability to love and accept love)

19. Depending on a couple's race (African Americans live under more oppressive conditions, which increases stress in the marital relationship; 55 percent of African American marriages in contrast to 42 percent of European American marriages, and 23 percent of Asian marriages will end within fifteen years) (Clarke-Stewart and Brentano 2006). African Americans also pair-bond with a mate who has more differences from them in terms of age, gender role attitudes, desired family size, and so on.

20. Going through retirement (children are gone, couple spends more time together, discovery that job was functional in keeping the spouses busy and away from each other; nothing to talk about)

Advice from Spouses Going through Divorce

What advice do spouses who are in the process of divorce have for spouses unhappy in their marriage and who are contemplating divorce?

Sample and Methods

To find out, 59 respondents (47 females and 12 males) (average age, 35) completed a 29-item Internet survey designed to reveal what they (as people going through divorce) would suggest to those still married and contemplating divorce.

Selected Findings and Conclusions

Over two-thirds of the females (68 percent) and males (67 percent) recommended that others who are considering divorce not give up on their marriage but "work it out" or "see a counselor." One interpretation of this advice is regret on the part of these spouses now on the divorce path. Females were more likely to recommend seeing a counselor than males, and males were more likely than females to recommend a "cooling-off" period before beginning divorce proceedings. Clearly, one effect of involvement in the process of separation for both genders was a reevaluation of the desirability of seeking a divorce, to the degree that they would alert others contemplating separation to rethink their situation and to attempt reconciliation.

Source

Adapted from "Work it out/See a counselor, Advice from spouses in the separation process" by D. Knox and U. Corte. *Journal of Divorce & Remarriage* 48:1, 2007, 79–90, Taylor & Francis. Reprinted by permission of Taylor & Francis Group, http://www.informaworld.com).

---

21. Experiencing rape (a spouse who has been raped before marriage is more likely to have sexual dysfunction)

22. Having premarital pregnancy or unwanted child (spouses may feel pressure to get married; stress of parenting unwanted child)

23. Having stepchildren in the household (greater conflict in household)

24. Having high debt (stress of limited income)

25. Experiencing violence or abuse (reasons to leave marriage)

The more of these factors that exist in a marriage, the more vulnerable a couple is to divorce. Regardless of the various factors associated with divorce, there is debate about the character of people who divorce. Are they selfish, amoral people who are incapable of making good on a commitment to each other and who wreck the lives of their children? Or are they individuals who care a great deal about relationships and won't settle for a bad marriage? Indeed, they may divorce precisely because they value marriage and want to rescue their children from being reared in an unhappy home. However, Foster (2008) found that narcissistic individuals tend to bail out when there is low satisfaction in a relationship.

Gone are the raptures that once we knew,
Now you are finding a new joy greater—
Well, I'll be doing the same thing, too,
Sooner or later.

Dorothy Parker, *Nocturne*

Ending an Unsatisfactory Relationship

Breaking up is never easy. Almost a third of 279 undergraduates reported that they "sometimes" remained in relationships they thought should end (31 percent) or that became "unhappy" (32.3 percent). This finding reflects the ambivalence students sometimes feel in ending an unsatisfactory relationship and their reluctance to do so (Knox et al. 2002). All relationships have difficulties, and all necessitate careful consideration of various issues before they are ended. Before you pull the plug on your relationship consider the following:

1. *Is there any desire or hope to revive and improve the relationship?* In some cases, people end relationships and later regret having done so. Setting unrealistically high standards may eliminate an array of individuals who might be superb partners, companions, and mates. If the reason for ending a relationship is conflict over an issue or set of issues, an alternative to ending the relationship is to attempt to resolve the issues through negotiating differences, compromising, and giving the relationship more time. (We do not recommend giving an abusive

The best single predictor of whether a couple is going to divorce is contempt.

John and Julie Gottman, marriage therapists

relationship more time, as abuse, once started, tends to increase in frequency and intensity. Nor do we recommend staying in a relationship in which there are great differences in interests, styles, personalities, and levels of attachment. It is often more prudent to find someone with whom you are more compatible than to try to "remake" the person in your life now.)

2. *Acknowledge and accept that terminating a relationship may be painful for both partners.* There may be no way you can stop the hurt. One person said, "I can't live with him anymore, but I don't want to hurt him either." The two feelings are incompatible. To end a relationship with someone who loves you is usually hurtful to both partners. People who end a relationship usually conclude that the pain and suffering of staying in a relationship is more than they will experience from leaving.

3. *Blame yourself for the end.* One way to end a relationship is to blame yourself by giving a reason that is specific to you ("I need more freedom," "I want to go to graduate school in another state," "I'm not ready to settle down," and so on). If you blame your partner or give your partner a way to make things better, the relationship may continue because *you* may feel obligated to give your partner a second chance if change is promised.

4. *Cut off the relationship completely.* If you are the person ending the relationship, it will probably be easier for you to continue to see the other person without feeling too hurt. However, the other person will probably have a more difficult time and will heal faster if you stay away completely. Alternatively, some people are skilled at ending love relationships and turning them into friendships. Though this is difficult and infrequent, it can be rewarding across time for the respective partners.

5. *Learn from the terminated relationship.* Included in the reasons a relationship may end are behaviors of being too controlling; being oversensitive, jealous, or too picky; cheating; fearing commitment; and being unable to compromise and negotiate conflict. Some of the benefits of terminating a relationship are recognizing one's own contribution to the breakup and working on any characteristics that might be a source of problems. Otherwise, one might repeat the process.

6. *Allow time to grieve over the end of the relationship.* Ending a love relationship is painful. It is okay to feel this pain, to hurt, to cry. Allowing yourself time to experience such grief will help you heal for the next relationship. Recovering from a serious relationship can take twelve to eighteen months.

Gender Differences in Filing for Divorce

Enright (2004) noted that two-thirds of their 1,147 respondents who filed for divorce were women. They felt that their life would be better without their husbands (few worried they would be separated from their children). Indeed, the primary reason for delay was financial and, once they could see a way to survive financially, they were on their way out of the marriage. The top advantage women reported on the other side of the divorce was feeling a sense of renewed "self-identity." Men are less likely to seek a divorce because they view the cost as separation from their children; women get primary custody of the children in 80 percent of divorces. Men who are not bonded with their children and/or those who are involved in a new relationship are more likely to seek a divorce.

Remain Unhappily Married or Divorce?

Suppose you are unhappily married. Is your best choice to stay in this relationship or take your chances and divorce? Hawkins and Booth (2005) analyzed longitudinal data of spouses in unhappy marriages over a twelve-year period and found that those who stayed unhappily married had lower life satisfaction, self-esteem, and overall health compared to those who divorced whether or not they remarried. Similarly, Gardner and Oswald (2006) found that the psychological functioning and happiness of spouses going through divorce improved after the divorce—hence divorce was good for them. However, Waite et al. (2009) compared those who were unhappily married (over a five-year period) but who stayed married against those who divorced and remarried. The researchers did not find more positive outcomes for the latter. Hence, the data are unclear if remaining unhappily married or divorcing and remarrying have a more positive outcome for the spouses.

Consequences for Spouses Who Divorce

For both women and men, divorce is often an emotional and financial disaster (see Table 15.1, which identifies stages and issues of the divorce process). In addition to the death of a spouse, separation and divorce are among the most difficult of life's crisis events.

Table 15.1   Stages and Issues of Divorce Adjustment

Stage 1: Pre-separation

Issues

Personal: Consider seeing a marriage counselor with your spouse to improve your marriage. If you must seek a divorce, get a formal and legal separation agreement drawn up and signed before you and your spouse begin to live in separate residences.

Spouse: If divorce is inevitable, adopt the perspective that you will nurture a relationship that is as positive as possible with your soon-to-be-former spouse. You, your former spouse, and your children will benefit from such a relationship.

Children: Tell your children nothing until you make a definite decision to divorce and have begun to develop a separation agreement.

Relatives: Same as for your children.

Finances: Anticipate a drop in income. Look for alternative housing. If unemployed, get a job.

Legal: Contact a divorce mediator if your relationship with your spouse is civil to develop the terms of your separation agreement. If mediation is not an option, each spouse needs to hire the best attorney he/she can afford.

Stage 2: Separation

Issues

Personal: Consider seeing a therapist alone to help you through the emotional devastation of divorce. Don't separate (move out) until you have a formal or legal signed agreement.

Spouse: Endeavor to cooperate and be civil with your former partner.

Children: Tell your children of your decision to divorce. Make clear to them that they are not to blame and that the divorce will not change your love and care for them.

Relatives: Tell your parents and friends of your decision to divorce and that you will need their support during this period of transition. Reach out to the parents of your soon-to-be former partner and tell them that, in spite of the divorce, you would like to maintain a positive relationship with them—from which your children will benefit.

Finances: Your divorce mediator or attorney will instruct you to develop an inventory of what you own. Open up a separate savings and checking account.

Legal: Complete divorce mediation with a mediator. If this is not possible, ask your attorney to develop a legal separation agreement you can live with. Be reasonable. The more you and your spouse can agree on, the more time and money you save in legal fees. Mediated divorces cost about $1,500 and take two to three months. A litigated divorce costs $18,000 and takes about three years.

Stage 3: Divorce

Issues

Personal: Nurture your relationships with friends and family who will provide support during the process of your divorce.

Spouse: Continue to nurture as civil a relationship as possible with your soon-to-be former partner.

Children: Ensure that they have frequent and regular contact with each parent. Nurture their relationship with the other parent and their grandparents on both sides.

Relatives: Continue to have regular contact with friends and family who provide emotional support.

Finances: Be frugal.

Legal: Do what your attorney tells you.

(Continued)

Table 15.1   Stages and Issues of Divorce Adjustment (*Continued*)

Stage 4: Postdivorce

Issues

Personal: Seek other relationships but go slow in terms of commitment to a new partner. Give yourself at least eighteen months before making a commitment to a new partner.

Former Spouse: Continue as civil a relationship as possible. Encourage your former partner's involvement in another relationship. Be positive about a new partner. You will want the same from your former partner some day.

Children: Spend individual time with each child. Do not require your children to like or enjoy your new partner.

Relatives: Provide both sets of grandparents access to your children.

Finances: Continue to be frugal. Move toward getting out of debt.

Legal: Make a payment plan with your attorney—begin to reduce this debt.

Adapted from The Divorce Room at Heartchoice.com. Used by permission.

Getting divorced just because you don't love a man is almost as silly as getting married just because you do.

Zsa Zsa Gabor, actress

Psychological Consequences of Divorce

Sakraida (2005) interviewed women who both initiated and were the recipients of terminated relationships and found that the person being dropped (the "dumpee") was more vulnerable to depression and ruminated more about divorce. Thuen and Rise (2006) found that perceived control was associated with positive psychological adjustment to divorce (the "dumpee" typically feels less control).

How do women and men differ in their emotional and psychological adjustment to divorce? Siegler and Costa (2000) noted that women fare better emotionally after separation or divorce than do men. They note that women are more likely than men to not only have a stronger network of supportive relationships but also to profit from divorce by developing a new sense of self-esteem and confidence, because they are thrust into more independent roles. On the other hand, men are more likely to have been dependent on their wives for domestic and emotional support and to have a weaker external emotional support system. As a result, divorced men are more likely than divorced women to date more partners sooner and to remarry more quickly. Hence, there are gender differences in adjustment to divorce, but these differences balance out over time.

We have been discussing the personal emotional consequences of divorce for the respective spouses, but the extended family and friends also feel the impact of a couple's divorce. Whereas some parents are happy and relieved that their offspring are divorcing, others grieve. Either way, the relationship with their grandchildren may be jeopardized. Friends often feel torn and divided in their loyalties. The courts divide the property and grant custody of the children. But who gets the friends? Indeed an individual going through divorce will lose an average of three friends (Clarke-Stewart and Brentano 2006).

Recovering from a Broken Heart

A sample of 410 freshmen and sophomores at a large southeastern university completed a confidential survey revealing their recovery from a previous love relationship (Knox et al. 2000). Some of the findings were as follows:

1. *Sex differences in relationship termination.* Women were significantly more likely than men to report that they initiated the breakup (50 percent versus 40 percent). Sociologists suggest that women terminating relationships more often is related to their desire to select a better father for their offspring. One female student recalled, "I got tired of his lack of ambition—I just thought I could do better. He's a nice guy but living in a trailer is not my idea of a life."

2. *Sex differences in relationship recovery.* Though recovery was not traumatic for either men or women, men reported more difficulty than women did in adjusting to

Psychological Adjustment to Separation Test*

This test is relevant to someone who has just ended a relationship. Please rate the extent to which you agree or disagree with by circling only one number for each of the following statements *for the last two weeks*.

Item	Strongly Disagree	Disagree	Neither Agree Nor Disagree	Agree	Strongly Agree
1. I find it hard to do things without a partner.	1	2	3	4	5
2. I constantly think about my former partner.	1	2	3	4	5
3. I feel isolated.	1	2	3	4	5
4. Days with special meaning for my ex-partner and I are really difficult (for example, birthdays, anniversaries).	1	2	3	4	5
5. I miss my former partner a lot.	1	2	3	4	5
6. I am used to not seeing my former partner anymore.	1	2	3	4	5
7. I wish my former partner and I could try to make the relationship work.	1	2	3	4	5
8. I don't really know why my former partner and I separated.	1	2	3	4	5
9. I find it difficult to enjoy myself.	1	2	3	4	5
10. Looking at photos and other things that remind me of my former partner is hard.	1	2	3	4	5
11. I don't have much time to see my friends.	1	2	3	4	5
12. I feel like I'm on a constant emotional roller-coaster ride.	1	2	3	4	5
13. I get angry more than I used to.	1	2	3	4	5
14. I make an effort to organize social activities.	1	2	3	4	5
15. I feel desperately lonely.	1	2	3	4	5
16. I feel like my life has less purpose in it now.	1	2	3	4	5
17. I sometimes have difficulty controlling my emotions.	1	2	3	4	5
18. I feel rejected by my former partner.	1	2	3	4	5
19. Little things seem to upset me now.	1	2	3	4	5

Scoring

To obtain a score for the two subscales on the Psychological Adjustment to Separation Test (PAST), calculate the following:

Former Partner Attachment Add together items 2, 4, 5, 6 (reverse the scores), 7, 8, 10 and 18. Scores range from 12 (no problem with the breakup or separation to 36 (great difficulty adjusting to the breakup or separation). The midpoint is 24, suggesting scores below 24 reflect more adjustment and scores above 24 reflect less adjustment. Scores up to 25 are regarded as "normal," 25 to 33 are "moderate," and above 34 are "severe," suggesting severe difficulty adjusting.

Lonely Negativity Add together items 1, 3, 9, 11, 12, 13, 14 (reverse the scores), 15, 16, 17, and 19. Scores range from 15 (not lonely or negative) to 51 (very lonely and negative). The midpoint is 33, suggesting scores below 33 reflect less loneliness and negativity, and scores above 33 reflect greater loneliness and negativity. Scores up to 31 are regarded as "normal," 32 to 41 are "moderate," and above 42 are "severe," suggesting severe loneliness and negativity.

The following is that part of the *past* that is relevant to the interaction of the divorcing parents over the care of their children. Please rate the extent to which you agree or disagree with by circling only one number for each of the following statements *for the last two weeks*.

Co-Parenting Conflict

Item	Strongly Disagree	Disagree	Neither Agree Nor Disagree	Agree	Strongly Agree
1. My former partner and I agree on the child custody arrangements.	1	2	3	4	5
2. I agree with my former partner on discipline of my child/children.	1	2	3	4	5
3. My former partner and I avoid speaking to one another.	1	2	3	4	5
4. When I speak to my former partner, we usually fight over the child/children.	1	2	3	4	5
5. My former partner and I arrange child visitation well.	1	2	3	4	5
6. I fight with my former partner over the well-being of the child/children.	1	2	3	4	5
7. My former partner and I talk in front of the child/children without fighting.	1	2	3	4	5

Scoring

Scoring of Co-Parenting Conflict Add the numbers selected for items 1 through 7 (reversing the scores for 1, 2, 5, and 7). Scores range from 7 (cooperation and low conflict) to 35 (very negative and conflictual). The midpoint is 21, suggesting scores below 21 reflect greater cooperation and scores above 21 reflect greater conflict. Scores up to 26 are regarded as "normal," 27 to 32 are "moderate," and above 33 are "severe," suggesting severely negative and conflictual.

Source

Copyright © 2006 by the American Psychological Association. Adapted with permission. Psychological Adjustment to Separation Test (PAST) (adapted) by Susie Sweeper and Kim Halford. *Journal of Family Psychology*. Vol 20(4), Dec 2006, 632–640.

Being alone after being involved in an intimate relationship is never easy . . . but over time, the cloudy sky and rough seas become a bright sky and smooth sailing.

Authors

I get along without you very well
Of course I do
Except when soft rains fall
And drip from leaves, then I recall
The thrill of being sheltered
in your arms
Of course I do
But I get along without you
very well

Hoagy Carmichael, "I Get Along Without You Very Well"

a breakup. When respondents were asked to rate their level of difficulty from "no problem" (0) to "complete devastation" (10), women scored 4.35 and men scored 4.96. In explaining why men might have more difficulty adjusting to terminated relationships, some of the female students said, "Men have such inflated egos, they can't believe that a woman would actually dump them." Others said, "Men are oblivious to what is happening in a relationship and may not have a clue that it is heading toward an abrupt end. When it does end, they are in shock."

3. *Time or new partner as factors in recovery.* The passage of time and involvement with a new partner were identified as the most helpful factors in getting over a love relationship that ended. Though the difference was not statistically significant, men more than women reported "a new partner" was more helpful in relationship recovery (34 percent versus 29 percent). Similarly, women more than men reported that "time" was more helpful in relationship recovery (34 percent versus 29 percent).

4. *Other findings.* Other factors associated with recovery for women and men were "moving to a new location" (13 percent versus 10 percent) and recalling that "the previous partner lied to me" (7 percent versus 5 percent). Men were much more likely than women to use alcohol to help them get over a previous partner (9 percent versus 2 percent). Neither men nor women reported using therapy to help them get over a partner (1 percent versus 2 percent). These data suggest that breaking up was not terribly difficult for these undergraduates (but more difficult for men than women) and that both time and a new partner enabled their recovery. These undergraduates are also young and may not view relationships at this age as permanent, making moving on easier.

Some partners seek revenge as a way of recovering from a relationship that was ended by the other partner. Breed et al. (2007) detailed one example of a former girlfriend who downloaded Internet child pornography on her partner's home computer, called the cops, and had him arrested for possession of child pornography. The penalty was fifteen months in prison per image. She loaded eighteen on his computer. He was found guilty.

PERSONAL CHOICES

Choosing to Maintain a Civil Relationship with Your Former Spouse

Spouses who divorce must choose the kind of relationship they will have with each other. This choice is crucial in that it affects not only their own but also their children's lives. Constance Ahrons (1995) identified four types of ex-spouse relationships, including "fiery foes," which 25 percent of divorcing spouses exemplified. Another 25 percent were categorized as "angry associates." Hence, half of her respondents had adversarial relationships with their former partners. Other patterns included "perfect pals" (12 percent) and "cooperative colleagues" (38 percent).

Everyone loses when the "fiery foes" and "angry associates" pattern develops and continues. The parents continue to harbor negative feelings for each other, and the children are caught in the cross fire. They aren't free to develop or express love for either parent out of fear of disapproval from the other. Ex-spouses might consider the costs to their children of continuing their hostility and do whatever is necessary to maintain a civil relationship with their former partner. We emphasize the benefits of co-parenting after divorce in Chapter 16 on remarriage.

Financial Consequences

Getting divorced affects one's finances. Both women and men experience a drop in income following divorce, but women may suffer more. Because men usually have greater financial resources, they may take all they can with them when they leave. The only money they may continue to give to an ex-wife is court-ordered child support or spousal support (alimony). Although alimony is rare, it is awarded. Former presidential candidate John McCain pays his former wife $17,000 in alimony annually. Some states, such as Texas, do not award alimony at all. However, most states do provide for an equitable distribution of property, whereby property is divided according to what seems fairest to each party, on the basis of a number of factors (like ability to earn a living, fault in breaking up the marriage, and so on).

Although 56 percent of custodial mothers are awarded child support, the amount is usually inadequate, infrequent, and not dependable, and women are forced to work (sometimes at more than one job) to take financial care of their children. A comparison of divorced mothers, single mothers by choice, and married mothers revealed that economic stability and involvement of the father were more important than family structure in determining the quality of life for the mothers (Segal-Engelchin and Wozner 2005).

Job loss is also associated with divorce. Covizzi (2008) emphasized that getting divorced is associated with losing one's job, and men are more vulnerable than women. The stress of divorce takes its toll on one's ability to function, and productivity may drop, resulting in the person being fired.

How money is divided depends on whether the couple had a prenuptial agreement or a **postnuptial agreement.** Such agreements are most likely to be upheld if an attorney insists on four conditions—full disclosure by both parties, independent representation by separate counsel, absence of coercion or duress, and terms that are fair and equitable (Abut 2005).

Fathers' Separation from Children

According to Finley (2004, F9), "... divorce transforms family power from intact patriarchy to post-divorce matriarchy," where women are typically given custody of the children and child support. Trinder (2008) emphasized that these women serve as gatekeepers for the relationship their husbands have with their children. Their patterns range from being proactive whereby they encourage such relationships and involvement to closing the gate and attempting to destroy the relationship.

As a result, about 5 million divorced dads wake up every morning in an apartment or home while their children wake up with their separated or divorced mother. These are noncustodial fathers who may find the gate to their children shut so that they are allowed to see their children only at specified times (for example, two weekends a month).

Ahrons and Tanner (2003) found that low father involvement, not divorce, has a negative impact on the father-child relationship. Fathers who stay involved in the lives of their children emotionally, physically, and economically (in spite of being a noncustodial parent, having an adversarial former spouse, and a remarriage) mitigate any negative effects on the relationship with their children. Indeed, some relationships with the father may improve because a father may spend more one-on-one time with his children.

Juby et al. (2007) found that fathers who begin a pattern of close involvement with their children during separation and early divorce tend to maintain a close pattern of involvement. Fathers who delay such involvement, become pair-bonded with a new partner, and have a child with the partner, tend to maintain minimal relationships with their nonresident children. Some fathers reduce contact with their children when their former spouse remarries and provides a stepfather for the offspring.

I've telegraphed and phoned, and sent an airmail special, too; Your answer was "Goodbye" and there was even postage due. I fell in love just once, and then it had to be you—Ev'rything happens to me.

Tom Adair and Matt Dennis, "Everything Happens to Me"

Shared Parenting Dysfunction

Shared parenting dysfunction refers to the set of behaviors on the part of each parent (embroiled in a divorce) that are focused on hurting the other parent and are counterproductive for the well-being of the children. Turkat (2002) identified the following examples:

- *A parent who forced the children to sleep in a car to prove the other parent had bankrupted them*
- *After losing a court battle over custody of the children, a noncustodial parent burned down the house of the primary residential parent*
- *One divorcing parent bought a cat for the children because the other divorcing parent was highly allergic to cats*

Finally, some of the most destructive displays of shared parenting dysfunction may include kidnapping, physical abuse, and murder (p. 390).

Parental Alienation Syndrome

Shared parenting dysfunction may lead to parental alienation syndrome. **Parental alienation syndrome** is a disturbance in which children are obsessively preoccupied with deprecation and/or criticism of a parent, denigration that is unjustified and/or exaggerated (Gardner 1998). Celebrity Alec Baldwin (2008) experienced this phenomenon firsthand after his divorce from Kim Basinger. He noted that she systematically tried to destroy the relationship he had with his daughter, and he found the court system to be of no help (he spent $3 million on the divorce and custody hearings). His plight is detailed in his book *A Promise to Ourselves: A Journey through Fatherhood and Divorce.*

Although the "alienators" are fairly evenly balanced between fathers and mothers (Gardner 1998), the custodial parent (more often the mother) has more opportunity and control to alienate the child from the other parent. A couple need not necessarily be divorcing for parental alienation syndrome to occur—this phenomenon may also occur in intact families (Baker 2006).

Several types of behavior that either parent may engage in to alienate a child from the other parent include the following:

1. Minimizing the importance of contact and the relationship with the other parent, including moving far away with the child to make regular contact difficult

2. Exhibiting excessively rigid boundaries; rudeness or refusal to speak to or inability to tolerate the presence of the other parent, even at events important to the child; refusal to allow the other parent near the home for drop-off or pick-up visitations

3. Having no concern about missed visits with the other parent

4. Showing no positive interest in the child's activities or experiences during visits with the other parent and withholding affection if the child expresses positive feelings about the absent parent

5. Granting autonomy to the point of apparent indifference ("It's up to you if you want to see your dad, I don't care.")

6. Overtly expressing dislike of a visitation ("OK, visit, but you know how I feel about it.")

Alec Baldwin's book, *A Promise to Ourselves: A Journey through Fatherhood and Divorce,* reveals how he was alienated from his child by his former wife and his perception that the courts did nothing to support his relationship with his daughter (he spent over three million dollars in litigation).

Rose Billings/Landov

7. Refusing to discuss anything about the other parent ("I don't want to hear about it.") or showing selective willingness to discuss only negative matters

8. Using innuendo and accusations against the other parent, including statements that are false, and blaming the parent for the divorce

9. Portraying the child as an actual or potential victim of the other parent's behavior

10. Demanding that the child keep secrets from the other parent

11. Destroying gifts or memorabilia of the other parent

12. Promoting loyalty conflicts (such as by offering an opportunity for a desired activity that conflicts with scheduled visitation) (Schacht 2000; Teich 2007; and Baker and Darnall 2007)

The most telling sign of children who have been alienated from a parent is the irrational behavior of the children, who for no properly explained reason say that they want nothing further to do with one of the parents. Indeed such children have a lack of ambivalence toward the alienation, lack of guilt or remorse about the alienation, and always take the alienating parent's side in the conflict (Baker and Darnall 2007).

Children who are alienated from one parent are sometimes unable to see through the alienation process and regard their negative feelings as natural. Such children are similar to those who have been brainwashed by cult leaders to view outsiders negatively. Baker (2005) interviewed thirty-eight adults who had experienced parental alienation as children and observed several areas of impact, including low self-esteem, depression, drug or alcohol abuse, lack of trust, alienation from one's own children, and divorce.

Sometimes parents intent on alienating their children from the other parent may discover that the children resent the custodial parent for such deprivation. In addition, the children may feel deceived if they are told negative things about the other parent and later learn that these were designed to foster a negative relationship with that parent. The result is often a strained and distanced relationship with the custodial parent when the children grow up—an unintended consequence. Alternatively, the negative socialization toward the other parent may create a lifelong bias against that parent.

In short, she tried to tame Penn [Sean] and he tried to domesticate her. It proved to be a recipe for emotional trauma and, ultimately divorce.

Andrew Morton, *Madonna*

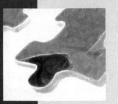

WHAT IF?

What if Your Former Spouse Tries to Turn Your Children against You?

The best antidote to parental alienation syndrome is to spend time with your children so that they can discover for themselves who you are as a parent, how you feel about them, and how much you love and value them. Regardless what your former spouse says to the children about you, the reality of how you treat them is what will determine how your children feel about you. However, should your spouse not allow you to see your children, it is imperative to hire a lawyer (and go to court if necessary) to ensure that you are awarded time with your children. You cannot have a relationship with your children if you don't spend time with them.

Effects of Divorce on Children

Over a million children annually experience the divorce of their parents. The Children's Beliefs about Parental Divorce Scale on page 505 provides a way to measure the perceived effects of divorce on children.

The well-being of children who grow up in homes where their parents remain in low-conflict marriages is clearly higher than children who have divorced parents. Children who grow up in homes where their parents are married but who constantly fight also clearly suffer in terms of their subjective well-being (Sobolewski and Amato 2007).

Gordon (2005) noted that divorce may actually benefit children. When parental conflict is very high prior to divorce, children benefit by no longer being subjected to the relentless anger and emotional abuse they observe between their parents. Indeed, when comparing children whose conflicted parents divorced with children whose parents were still together, the children were very similar. In self-reports of 158 Israeli young adults whose parents divorced when they were adolescents, Sever et al. (2007) determined that, although the children had painful feelings, almost half the participants reported more positive than negative outcomes. These included maturity and growth, empowerment, empathy, and relationship savvy. Lambert (2007) identified other advantages for children whose parents divorced as learning to be resilient, developing closer relationships with siblings, having happier parents, learning lessons about what not to do in a relationship, and receiving more attention. DeCuzzi et al. (2004) also reported that, although 26 percent of the undergraduates in their study reported that the divorce of their parents had a negative effect, 32.9 percent reported a *positive* effect. Finally, when children of divorced parents become involved in their own marriage to a supportive, well-adjusted partner, the negative effects of parental divorce are mitigated (Hetherington 2003).

Kelly and Emery (2003) reviewed the literature on the effect of divorce on children and concluded the following:

> . . . [I]t is important to emphasize that approximately 75–80% of children and young adults do not suffer from major psychological problems, including depression; have achieved their education and career goals; and retain close ties to their families. They enjoy intimate relationships, have not divorced, and do not appear to be scarred with immutable negative effects from divorce. (p. 357–58)

Indeed, Coltrane and Adams (2003) emphasized that claiming that divorce seriously damages children is a "symbolic tool used to defend a specific moral vision for families and gender roles within them" (p. 369). They go on to state that "Understanding this allows us to see divorce not as the universal moral evil depicted by divorce reformers, but as a highly individualized process that engenders different experiences and reactions among various family members . . ." (p. 370).

Nevertheless, some children experience negative fallout from their parents' divorce. Kilmann et al. (2006) compared 147 college females with intact biological parents with 157 college females whose parents had divorced. Compared to those with intact parents, females whose parents had divorced had lower self-esteem and rated both their biological fathers and mothers more negatively. Other disadvantages Lambert (2007) identified include being disrupted because of visitation arrangements, stressful holidays, not having a role model for a good relationship, feeling the divorce hurt one's siblings, financial hardships, and having no dad while growing up.

Diversity in Other Countries

A team of Norwegian researchers (Storksen et al. 2006) examined 8,984 adolescents, ages 13 to 19, comparing the levels of anxiety and depression of those in homes in which their parents were not distressed and were still together against those in which parents were distressed and divorcing. The former group of children was less likely to report anxiety or depression than those in the divorcing homes (14 percent and 30 percent, respectively).

Children's Beliefs about Parental Divorce Scale

The following are some statements about children and their separated parents. Some of the statements are true about how you think and feel, so you will want to check *yes*. Some are *not true* about how you think or feel, so you will want to check *no*. There are no right or wrong answers. Your answers will just indicate some of the things you are thinking now about your parents' separation.

1. It would upset me if other kids asked a lot of questions about my parents. ___ Yes ___ No

2. It was usually my father's fault when my parents had a fight. ___ Yes ___ No

3. I sometimes worry that both my parents will want to live without me. ___ Yes ___ No

4. When my family was unhappy, it was usually because of my mother. ___ Yes ___ No

5. My parents will always live apart. ___ Yes ___ No

6. My parents often argue with each other after I misbehave. ___ Yes ___ No

7. I like talking to my friends as much now as I used to. ___ Yes ___ No

8. My father is usually a nice person. ___ Yes ___ No

9. It's possible that both my parents will never want to see me again. ___ Yes ___ No

10. My mother is usually a nice person. ___ Yes ___ No

11. If I behave better, I might be able to bring my family back together. ___ Yes ___ No

12. My parents would probably be happier if I were never born. ___ Yes ___ No

13. I like playing with my friends as much now as I used to. ___ Yes ___ No

14. When my family was unhappy, it was usually because of something my father said or did. ___ Yes ___ No

15. I sometimes worry that I'll be left all alone. ___ Yes ___ No

16. Often I have a bad time when I'm with my mother. ___ Yes ___ No

17. My family will probably do things together just like before. ___ Yes ___ No

18. My parents probably argue more when I'm with them than when I'm gone. ___ Yes ___ No

19. I'd rather be alone than play with other kids. ___ Yes ___ No

20. My father caused most of the trouble in my family. ___ Yes ___ No

21. I feel that my parents still love me. ___ Yes ___ No

22. My mother caused most of the trouble in my family. ___ Yes ___ No

23. My parents will probably see that they have made a mistake and get back together again. ___ Yes ___ No

24. My parents are happier when I'm with them than when I'm not. ___ Yes ___ No

25. My friends and I do many things together. ___ Yes ___ No

26. There are a lot of things I like about my father. ___ Yes ___ No

27. I sometimes think that one day I may have to go live with a friend or relative. ___ Yes ___ No

28. My mother is more good than bad. ___ Yes ___ No

29. I sometimes think that my parents will one day live together again. ___ Yes ___ No

30. I can make my parents unhappy with each other by what I say or do. ___ Yes ___ No

31. My friends understand how I feel about my parents. ___ Yes ___ No

32. My father is more good than bad. ___ Yes ___ No

33. I feel my parents still like me. ___ Yes ___ No

34. There are a lot of things about my mother I like. ___ Yes ___ No

35. I sometimes think that my parents will live together again once they realize how much I want them to. ___ Yes ___ No

36. My parents would probably still be living together if it weren't for me. ___ Yes ___ No

Scoring

The Children's Beliefs about Parental Divorce Scale (CBAPS) identifies problematic responding. A *yes* response on items 1, 2, 3, 4, 6, 9, 11, 12, 14–20, 22, 23, 27, 29, 30, 35, and 36, and a *no* response on items 5, 7, 8, 10, 13, 21, 24–26, 28, and 31–34 indicate a problematic reaction to one's parents divorcing. A total score is derived by adding the number of problematic beliefs across all items, with a total score of 36. The higher the score, the more problematic the beliefs about parental divorce.

Norms: A total of 170 schoolchildren whose parents were divorced completed the scale; of the children, 84 were boys and 86 were girls, with a mean age of 11. The mean for the total score was 8.20, with a standard deviation of 4.98.

Source

Copyright © 1987 by the American Psychological Association. Adapted with permission. Kurdek, L. A., and B. Berg, 1987. Children's beliefs about parental divorce scale: Psychometric characteristics and concurrent validity. *Journal of Consulting and Clinical Psychology* 55:712–18.

Although the primary factor that determines the effect of divorce on children is the degree to which the divorcing parents are civil or adversarial (see the Personal Choices section), legal and physical custody are important issues. The following section details how judges go about making this decision.

Who Gets the Children?

Judges who are assigned to hear initial child custody cases must make a judicial determination regarding whether one or both parents will have decisional authority on major issues affecting the children (called "**legal custody**"), and the distribution of parenting time (called "visitation" or "**physical custody**"). Toward this end, judges in all states are guided by the statutory dictum called "best interests of the child." In some states (Florida, Michigan, California, New Jersey, and others), specific statutory custody factors have been enacted to guide judges in making "best interest" determinations.

In a highly contested custody case, a judge will often appoint a mental health professional to conduct a custody evaluation to assist the judge in determining what will be the best future arrangement for the child. Of course, each custody case is different because the circumstances of the children are different, but some of the frequently employed custody factors include the following:

1. The child's age, maturity, sex, and activities, including culture and religion—all relevant information about the child's life—keeping the focus of custody on the child's best interests

2. The wishes expressed by the child, particularly the older child (judges will often interview children 6 years old or older in chambers)

3. Each parent's capacity to care for and provide for the emotional, intellectual, financial, religious, and other needs of the child (including the work schedules of the parents)

4. The parents' ability to agree, communicate, and cooperate in matters relating to the child

5. The nature of the child's relationship with the parents, which considers the child's relationship with other significant people, such as members of the child's extended family

6. The need to protect the child from physical and psychological harm caused by abuse or ill treatment (focuses on the issue of domestic violence)

7. The past and present parental attitudes and behavior (dealing with issues of parenting skills and personalities)

8. The proposed plans for caring for the child (Custody is not ownership of the child, so the judge will want to know how each parent proposes to raise the child, including proposed parenting times for the other parent.) (Lewis 2008)

These and other custody factors, whether presented by the custody evaluator or by testimony, will become the basis for the judge's custody determination.

How Does Parental Divorce Affect the Romantic Relationships of College Students?

One of the greatest hopes of individuals whose parents have happy and enduring marriages is that they will also end up in such endearing relationships. Similarly, one of the greatest fears of individuals whose parents are divorced or who have unhappy and dysfunctional relationships is that they, too, will have such unhappy and unfulfilling marriages (Dennison and Koerner 2008). These hopes and fears are common emotions of offspring who contemplate their futures and wonder of the degree to which their parents' divorce will affect their own relationships.

There are about 23 million divorced individuals in the United States (*Statistical Abstract of the United States, 2009*, Table 55), 60 percent of whom have children. Earlier we noted that 31 percent of a sample of undergraduates reported that their parents had divorced. Extrapolating to the over 17.5 million college students in the United States, almost six million college students have parents who are separated or divorced (*Statistical Abstract of the United States, 2009*).

Decuzzi et al. (2004) analyzed data from 333 undergraduates, 30 percent of whom had divorced and/or remarried parents. They compared students whose parents were divorced with students whose parents were still married. The following several significant findings were revealed:

1. **Students were less happy if divorced parents had remarried.** Of those whose parents had divorced and remarried, 18 percent reported feeling less happy about life in contrast to 4 percent whose parents were still married. Hence, it seems that the happiest students were those whose parents were still together; next were those who had one parent who remarried, and lastly, those who had both parents remarry. It is commonly thought that many children whose parents divorce hold out hope that maybe their parents will get back together and they will be a "family" again. The remarriage of both parents dooms forever that possibility, which may be reflected in a lower level of happiness.

2. **Students were less close to their divorced biological father if the father had remarried.** Both divorce and remarriage weaken the relationship with one's biological father. Students from homes in which their parents divorced (in contrast to homes where the parents were still married) were less likely to agree that "I feel really close to my biological father." Of those with divorced parents, 63 percent reported a close relationship with their dad in contrast to 86 percent of students whose parents were still together.

3. **Students were less close to their divorced biological mother.** Students from homes in which their parents divorced (in contrast to homes were the parents were still married) were less likely to agree, "I feel really close to my biological mother." Of those with divorced parents, 81 percent reported a close relationship with their mother in contrast to 95 percent of students whose parents were still together.

4. **Students of divorced parents preferred long-term relationships.** Students whose parents were divorced seemed to stay in relationships longer than those whose parents were married. Of the students from divorced families, 76 percent in contrast to 57 percent of students with married parents reported that their longest relationship was more than a year. Experiencing the divorce of one's parents was possibly so traumatic that it sensitized the students to maintain their own romantic relationships.

Minimizing Negative Effects of Divorce on Children

Researchers have identified the following conditions under which a divorce has the fewest negative consequences for children:

1. **Healthy parental psychological functioning.** Children of divorced parents benefit to the degree that the parents remain psychologically fit and positive, and socialize their children to view the divorce as a "challenge to learn from." Parents who nurture self-pity, abuse alcohol or drugs, and socialize their children to view the divorce as a tragedy from which they will never recover create negative outcomes for their children. Some divorcing parents can benefit from therapy as a method for coping with their anger or depression and for making choices in the best interest of their children.

Some parents also enroll their children in the "New Beginnings Program"—"an empirically driven prevention program designed to promote child resilience during the postdivorce period" (Hipke et al. 2002, 121). The program focuses on improving the quality of the primary residential mother-child relationship, ensuring continued discipline, reducing exposure to parental conflict, and providing access to the nonresidential father. Outcome data reveal that not all children benefit, particularly those with "poor regulatory skills" and "demoralized" mothers (p. 127).

2. **A cooperative relationship between the parents.** The most important variable in a child's positive adjustment to divorce is when the child's parents continue to

maintain a cooperative relationship throughout the separation, divorce, and postdivorce period. In contrast, bitter parental conflict places the children in the middle. One daughter of divorced parents said, "My father told me, 'If you love me, you would come visit me,' but my mom told me, 'If you love me, you won't visit him.'" Baum (2003) confirmed that the longer and more conflictual the legal proceedings, the worse the co-parental relationship. Bream and Buchanan (2003) noted that children of conflictual divorcing parents are "children in need." Numerous states mandate parenting classes as part of the divorce process. Whitehurst et al. (2008) confirmed that divorcing spouses who attended a court-ordered six-session (two hours each) Cooperative Parenting and Divorce Program benefited in parenting skills improvement as well as improved relationships with their children. The finding was true for both women and men. The court-approved "Positive Parenting through Divorce" program may also be taken online (http://www.positiveparentingthroughdivorce.com/).

3. *Parental attention to the children and allowing them to grieve.* Children benefit when both the custodial and the noncustodial parent continue to spend time with them and to communicate to them that they love them and are interested in them. Parents also need to be aware that their children do not want the divorce and to allow them to grieve over the loss of their family as they knew it. Indeed, children do not want their parents to separate. Some children are devastated to the point of suicide. A team of researchers identified 15,555 suicides among 15- to 24-year-olds in thirty-four countries in a one-year period and found an association between divorce rates and suicide rates (Johnson et al. 2000).

4. *Encouragement to see noncustodial parent.* Children benefit when custodial parents (usually mothers) encourage and maintain regular and stable visitation schedules with the noncustodial parent following divorce. Cashmore et al. (2008) interviewed sixty adolescents (ages 12 through 19) and their divorced nonresident parent (usually the father) and found that overnight stays with the nonresident parent were associated with reported greater closeness and better quality relationships than was true if the parent and child had only daytime contact.

5. *Attention from the noncustodial parent.* Children benefit when they receive frequent and consistent attention from noncustodial parents, usually the fathers. Noncustodial parents who do not show up at regular intervals exacerbate their children's emotional insecurity by teaching them, once again, that parents cannot be depended on. Parents who show up often and consistently teach their children to feel loved and secure. Sometimes joint custody solves the problem of children's access to their parents. Hsu et al. (2002) noted the devastating effect on children who grow up without a father.

6. *Assertion of parental authority.* Children benefit when both parents continue to assert their parental authority and continue to support the discipline practices of each other.

7. *Regular and consistent child support payments.* Support payments (usually from the father to the mother) are associated with economic stability for the child.

8. *Stability.* Moving to a new location causes children to be cut off from their friends, neighbors, and teachers. It is important to keep their life as stable as possible during a divorce.

9. *Children in a new marriage.* Manning and Smock (2000) found that divorced noncustodial fathers who remarried and who had children in the new marriages were more likely to shift their emotional and economic resources to the new family unit than were fathers who did not have new biological children. Fathers might be alert to this potential and consider each child, regardless of when or with whom the child was born, as worthy of a father's continued love, time, and support.

10. *Age and reflection on the part of children of divorce.* Sometimes children whose parents are divorced benefit from growing older and reflecting on their parents' divorce as an adult rather than a child. Nielsen (2004) emphasized that daughters who feel distant from their fathers can benefit from examining the divorce from the viewpoint of the father (Was he alienated by the mother?), the cultural bias against fathers (they are maligned as "deadbeat dads" who "abandon their families for a younger woman"), and the facts about divorced dads (they are more likely to be depressed and suicidal following divorce than mothers). Adolescents also bear some responsibility for the postdivorce relationships with their parents. Menning et al. (2008) emphasized that adolescents are not passive recipients of their parents' divorce but may actively accelerate or decelerate having a positive or negative relationship with their parents by using a variety of relationship management strategies. For example, by deciding to shut down and disclose nothing to their parents about their lives, they increase the emotional distance between them and their parents.

11. *Divorce education program for children.* Gilman et al. (2005) found that Kid's Turn, a San Francisco area divorce education program for children, was effective in reducing the conflict between parents and children of a group of sixty 7- to 9-year-old children. However, the children also had more reconciliation fantasies.

What Divorcing Parents Might Tell Their Children: An Example

As emphasized previously, a cooperative relationship between divorcing spouses is crucial to enhancing the adjustment of children. The following are the words of a mother of two children (8 and 12) as she tells her children of the pending divorce. It assumes that both parents take some responsibility for the divorce and are willing to provide a united front to the children. The script should be adapted for one's own unique situation.

Daddy and I want to talk to you about a big decision that we have made. A while back we told you that we were having a really hard time getting along, and that we were having meetings with someone called a therapist who has been helping us talk about our feelings, and deciding what to do about them.

We also told you that the trouble we are having is not about either of you. Our trouble getting along is about our grown-up relationship with each other. That is still true. We both love you very much, and love being your parents. We want to be the best parents we can be.

Daddy and I have realized that we don't get along so much, and disagree about so many things all the time, that we want to live separately, and not be married to each other anymore. This is called getting divorced. Daddy and I care about each other but we don't love each other in the way that happily married people do. We are sad about that. We want to be happy, and want each other to be happy. So to be happy we have to be true to our feelings.

It is not your fault that we are going to get divorced. And it's not our fault. We tried for a very long time to get along living together but it just got too hard for both of us.

We are a family and will always be your family. Many things in your life will stay the same. Mommy will stay living at our house here, and Daddy will move to an apartment close by. You both will continue to live with mommy and daddy but in two different places. You will keep your same rooms here, and will have a room at Daddy's apartment. You will be with one of us every day, and sometimes we will all be together, like to celebrate somebody's birthday, special events at school, or scouts. You will still go to your same school, have the same friends, go to soccer, baseball, and so on. You will still be part of the same family and will see your aunts, uncles, and cousins.

The most important things we want you both to know are that we love you, and we will always be your mom and dad . . . nothing will change that. It's hard to understand sometimes why some people stop getting along and decide not to be friends anymore, or if they are married decide to get divorced. You will probably have lots of different feelings about this. While you can't do anything to change the decision that daddy and I have made, we both care very much about your feelings. Your feelings may change a lot. Sometimes you might feel happy and relieved that you don't have to see and feel daddy and me not getting along. Then sometimes you might feel sad, scared, or angry. Whatever you are feeling at any time is ok. Daddy and I hope you will tell us about your feelings, and it's OK to ask us about ours. This is going to take some time to get used to. You will have lots of questions in the days to come. You may have some right now. Please ask any question at any time.

Daddy and I are here for you. Today, tomorrow, and always. We love you with our heart and soul.

PERSONAL CHOICES

Is Joint Custody a Good Idea?

Traditionally, sole custody to the mother was the only option courts considered for divorcing parents. The presumption was made that the "best interests of the child" were served if they were with their mother (the parent presumed to be more involved and more caring). As men have become more involved in the nurturing of children, the courts no longer assume that "parent" means "mother." Indeed, a new **family relations doctrine** is emerging that suggests that even nonbiological parents may be awarded custody or visitation rights if they have been economically and emotionally involved in the life of the child (Holtzman 2002). A stepparent is an example.

Given that fathers are no longer routinely excluded from custody considerations, over half of the states have enacted legislation authorizing joint custody. About 16 percent of separated and divorced couples actually have a joint custody arrangement. In a typical joint physical custody arrangement, the parents continue to live in close proximity to each other. The children may spend part of each week with each parent or may spend alternating weeks with each parent.

New terminology is being introduced in the lives of divorcing spouses and in the courts. The term *joint custody,* which implies ownership, is being replaced with *shared parenting,* which implies cooperation in taking care of children.

There are several advantages of joint custody or shared parenting. Ex-spouses may fight less if they have joint custody because there is no inequity in terms of their involvement in their children's lives. Children will benefit from the resultant decrease in hostility between parents who have both "won" them. Unlike sole-parent custody, in which one parent wins (usually the mother) and the other parent loses, joint custody allows children to continue to benefit from the love and attention of both parents. Children in homes where joint custody has been awarded might also have greater financial resources available to them than children in sole-custody homes.

Joint physical custody may also be advantageous in that the stress of parenting does not fall on one parent but rather is shared. One mother who has a joint custody arrangement with her ex-husband said, "When my kids are with their dad, I get a break from the parenting role, and I have a chance to do things for myself. I love my kids, but I also love having time away from them." Another joint-parenting father said, "When you live with your kids every day, you can get very frustrated and are not always happy to be with them. But after you haven't seen them for three days, it feels good to see them again."

A disadvantage of joint custody is that it tends to put hostile ex-spouses in more frequent contact with each other, and the marital war continues. When sole custody is given to one parent, parents have minimal to no contact. One parent said that she and her ex hadn't spoken in three years . . . that they just met at McDonald's . . . one parent would walk in with the kids, see the other parent and leave. Joint custody usually means multiple contacts over a lot of issues every week.

Depending on the level of hostility between the ex-partners, their motivations for seeking sole or joint custody, and their relationship with their children, any arrangement could have positive or negative consequences for the ex-spouses as well as for the children. In those cases in which the spouses exhibit minimal hostility toward each other, have strong emotional attachments to their children, and want to remain an active influence in their children's lives, joint custody may be the best of all possible choices.

Joyal et al. (2005) interviewed both parents and children where a joint custody arrangement was in place. They found positive outcomes for the children, who were even able to adapt to half siblings.

Conditions of a "Successful" Divorce

Although acknowledging that divorce is usually an emotional and economic disaster, it is possible to have a "successful" divorce. Indeed, most people are resilient and "are able to adapt constructively to their new life situation within two to three years following divorce, a minority being defeated by the marital breakup, and a substantial group of women being enhanced" (Hetherington 2003, 318). The following are some of the behaviors spouses can engage in to achieve this:

1. ***Mediate rather than litigate the divorce.*** Divorce mediators encourage a civil, cooperative, compromising relationship while moving the couple toward an agreement on the division of property, custody, and child support. By contrast, attorneys make their money by encouraging hostility so that spouses will prolong the conflict, thus running up higher legal bills. In addition, the couple cannot divide money spent on divorce attorneys (average is $15,000 for *each* side so a litigated divorce cost will start at $30,000). Benton (2008) noted that the worse thing divorcing spouses can do is to respectively hire the "meanest, nastiest, most expensive yard dog lawyer in town" because doing so will only result in a protracted expensive divorce where neither spouse will "win." Because the greatest damage to children from a divorce is a continuing hostile and bitter relationship between their parents, some states require **divorce mediation** as a mechanism to encourage civility in working out differences and to clear the court calendar from protracted court battles. The following Social Policy section focuses on divorce mediation.

A divorce mediator is focused on getting the couple to agree. The result is a quicker, less expensive, and less contentious ending to a marriage than hiring two lawyers to fight which can end up, on average, costing the couple $30,000.

Jupiter Images

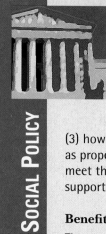

Should Divorce Mediation Be Required before Litigation?*

Divorce mediation is a process in which spouses who have decided to separate or divorce meet with a neutral third party (mediator) to negotiate the following issues: (1) how they will parent their children, which is referred to as child custody and visitation; (2) how they are going to financially support their children, referred to as child support; (3) how they are going to divide their property, known as property settlement; and (4) how each one is going to meet their financial obligations, referred to as spousal support.

Benefits of Mediation

There are enormous benefits from avoiding litigation and mediating one's divorce:

1. *Better relationship.* Spouses who choose to mediate their divorce have a better chance for a more civil relationship because they cooperate in specifying the conditions of their separation or divorce. Mediation emphasizes negotiation and cooperation between the divorcing partners. Such cooperation is particularly important if the couple has children in that it provides a positive basis for discussing issues in reference to the children and how they will be parented across time.

2. *Economic benefits. Mediation* is less expensive than litigation. The cost of hiring an attorney and going to court over issues of child custody and division of property is around $18,000. A mediated divorce costs about an average of $1,500 (six two-hour sessions at $250 per session) (Haswell 2006). A couple cannot keep as assets to later divide what they spend in legal fees.

3. *Less time-consuming process.* Whereas a litigated divorce can take two to three years, a mediated divorce takes two to three months; a "mediated settlement conference" ". . . can take place in one session from 8:00 a.m. until both parties are satisfied with the terms" (ibid.).

4. *Avoidance of public exposure.* Some spouses do not want to discuss their private lives and finances in open court. Mediation occurs in a private and confidential setting.

5. *Greater overall satisfaction.* Mediation results in an agreement developed by the spouses, not one imposed by a judge or the court system. A comparison of couples who chose mediation with couples who chose litigation found that those who mediated their own settlement were much more satisfied with the conditions of their agreement. In addition, children of mediated divorces are exposed to less marital conflict, which may facilitate their long-term adjustment to divorce.

Basic Mediation Guidelines

Divorce mediators conduct mediation sessions with certain principles in mind:

1. *Children.* What is best for a couple's children should be the major concern of the parents because they know their children far better than a judge or the mediator. Children of divorced parents adjust best under three conditions: (1) that both parents have regular and frequent access to the children; (2) that the children see the parents relating in a polite and positive way; and (3) that each parent talks positively about the other parent and neither parent talks negatively about the other to the children. Sometimes children are included in the mediation. They may be interviewed without the parents present to provide information to the mediator about their perceptions and preferences. Such involvement of the children has superior outcomes for both the parents and the children (McIntosh et al. 2008).

2. *Fairness.* It is important that the agreement be fair, with neither party being exploited or punished. It is

Lawyers are men who hire out their words and anger.

Anonymous

2. *Co-parent with your ex-spouse.* Setting aside negative feelings about your ex-spouse so as to cooperatively co-parent not only facilitates parental adjustment but also takes children out of the line of fire. Such co-parenting translates into being cooperative when one parent needs to change a child care schedule, sitting together during a performance by the children, and showing appreciation for the other parent's skill in responding to a crisis with the children.

3. *Take some responsibility for the divorce.* Because marriage is an interaction between spouses, one person is seldom totally to blame for a divorce. Rather, both spouses share reasons for the demise of the relationship. Take some responsibility for what went wrong.

4. *Learn from the divorce.* View the divorce as an opportunity to improve yourself for future relationships. What did you do that you might consider doing differently in the next relationship?

5. *Create positive thoughts.* Divorced people are susceptible to feeling as though they are failures. They see themselves as Divorced people with a capital D,

fair for both parents to contribute financially to the children and to have regular access to their children.

3. *Open disclosure.* The spouses will be asked to disclose all facts, records, and documents to ensure an informed and fair agreement regarding property, assets, and debts.

4. *Other professionals.* During mediation, spouses may be asked to consult an accountant regarding tax laws. In addition, spouses are encouraged to consult an attorney throughout the mediation and to have the attorney review the written agreements that result from the mediation. However, during the mediation sessions, all forms of legal action by the spouses against each other should be stopped.

Another term for involving a range of professionals in a divorce is **collaborative practice,** a process that brings a team of professionals (lawyer, psychologist, mediator, social worker, financial counselor) together to help a couple separate and divorce in a humane and cost-effective way.

5. *Confidentiality.* The mediator will not divulge anything spouses say during the mediation sessions without their permission. The spouses are asked to sign a document stating that, should they not complete mediation, they agree not to empower any attorney to subpoena the mediator or any records resulting from the mediation for use in any legal action.

Such an agreement is necessary for spouses to feel free to talk about all aspects of their relationship without fear of legal action against them for such disclosures.

Divorce mediation is not for every couple. It does not work where there is a history of spouse abuse, where the parties do not disclose their financial information, where one party is controlled by someone else (for example, a parent), where there is the desire for revenge, or where the mediator is biased. Mediation should be differentiated from **negotiation** (where spouses discuss and resolve the issues themselves), **arbitration** (where a third party listens to both spouses and makes a decision about custody, division of property, and so on), and **litigation** (where a judge hears arguments from lawyers representing the respective spouses and decides issues of custody, child support, division of property, and so on).

Haswell (2006) noted a continuum of consequences from negotiation to litigation.

Negotiation	Mediation	Arbitration	Litigation
Cooperative			Competitive
Low Cost			High Cost
Private			Public
Protects Relationships			Damages Relationships
Focus on the Future			Focus on the Past
Parties in Control			Parties Lose Control

Your Opinion?

1. To what degree do you believe the government should be involved in mandating divorce mediation?

2. How can divorce mediation go wrong? Why should a couple not want to mediate their divorce?

3. What are the advantages for children when parents mediate their divorce?

Source

*Appreciation is expressed to Mike Haswell for contributing to this section. See www.haswellmeditation.com.

---

a situation sometimes referred to as "hardening of the categories" disease. Improving self-esteem is important for divorced people. They can do this by systematically thinking positive thoughts about themselves. One technique is to write down twenty-one positive statements about yourself ("I am honest," "I have strong family values," "I am a good parent," and so on) and transfer them to three-by-five cards, each containing three statements. Take one of the cards with you each day and read the thoughts at three regularly spaced intervals (for example, 7:00 A.M., 1:00 P.M., and 7:00 P.M.). This ensures that you are thinking positive thoughts about yourself and are not allowing yourself to drift into a negative set of thoughts (for example, "I am a failure" or "no one wants to be with me.").

6. *Avoid alcohol and other drugs.* The stress and despair that some people feel following a divorce make them particularly vulnerable to the use of alcohol or other drugs. These should be avoided because they produce an endless negative cycle. For example, stress is relieved by alcohol; alcohol produces a hangover

Make divorce as easy, as cheap, and as private as marriage.
George Bernard Shaw

and negative feelings; the negative feelings are relieved by more alcohol, producing more negative feelings, and so on.

7. *Relax without drugs.* Deep muscle relaxation can be achieved by systematically tensing and relaxing each of the major muscle groups in the body. Alternatively, yoga, transcendental meditation, and massage can induce a state of relaxation in some people. Whatever the form, it is important to schedule a time each day for relaxation.

8. *Engage in aerobic exercise.* Exercise helps one to not only counteract stress but also to avoid it. Jogging, swimming, riding an exercise bike, or other similar exercise for thirty minutes every day increases the oxygen to the brain and helps facilitate clear thinking. In addition, aerobic exercise produces endorphins in the brain, which create a sense of euphoria ("runner's high").

9. *Engage in fun activities.* Some divorced people sit at home and brood over their "failed" relationship. This only compounds their depression. Doing what they have previously found enjoyable—swimming, horseback riding, skiing, sporting events with friends—provides an alternative to sitting on the couch alone.

10. *Continue interpersonal connections.* Adjustment to divorce is facilitated when continuing relationships with friends and family. These individuals provide emotional support and help buffer the feeling of isolation and aloneness. First Wives World (www.firstwivesworld.com) is a new interactive site to provide an Internet social network for women transitioning through divorce.

11. *Let go of the anger for your ex-partner.* Former spouses who stay negatively attached to an ex by harboring resentment and trying to get back at the ex prolong their adjustment to divorce. The old adage that you can't get ahead by getting even is relevant to divorce adjustment.

12. *Allow time to heal.* Because self-esteem usually drops after divorce, a person is often vulnerable to making commitments before working through feelings about the divorce. The time period most people need to adjust to divorce is between twelve and eighteen months. Although being available to others may help to repair one's self-esteem, getting remarried during this time should be considered cautiously. Two years between marriages is recommended.

13. *Progress through various psychological stages of divorce.* Reva Wiseman (1975) identified the various psychological stages a person goes through when getting a divorce. These include the following:

a. Denial. Marital problems are ignored or attributed to an external cause. "We are fine" or "this is normal" are ways of coping with the emotional and physical distance from the partner.

b. Loss or depression. Spouses confront the reality that they will divorce and lose their once-intimate relationship permanently, and depression sets in.

c. Anger or ambivalence. Spouses turn their anger toward each other and become critical, vindictive, and even violent. Strong negative emotions ensue during the marital separation, which is a normal response to the loss of an important attachment figure (for example, a spouse). Some spouses are not capable of detaching and maintain a negative attachment; by staying bitter and resentful, they remain attached. They may also want to hold on to the dying relationship because it feels safe.

d. New lifestyle and identify. Ex-spouses begin life as single adults and detach from marital identity. Men typically drink more alcohol. Women typically turn to girlfriends for support. Both may enter a period of being sexually indiscriminate.

e. Acceptance and integration. Individuals recognize their new status, loss of anger, and acceptance, and move on to new relationships. Some never reach this stage but harbor resentments or blame the ex for the end of the marriage.

Alternatives to Divorce

Divorce is not the only means of terminating a marriage. Others include annulment, separation (legal or informal), and desertion.

Annulment

An **annulment** returns the spouses to their premarital status. In effect, an annulment means that the marriage never existed in the first place. Celebrity Pam Anderson and Rick Soloman married October 6, 2007, and had their marriage annulled on separated December 13. In 2005, Kenny Chesney and Renee Zellweger had their three-month marriage annulled. The concept of annulment is both religious and civil. As a religious matter, annulment is a technical mechanism that allows Catholic individuals to remarry. The Roman Catholic Church views marriage as a sacrament that is indissoluble except by death. Hence, although the church does not recognize divorce, it does recognize annulment. A Catholic individual who wants to end a marriage and remain a good Catholic in the eyes of the church (be able to participate in Communion) cannot divorce but can petition for an annulment. This involves providing the right "reason" for an annulment and paying a fee. Almost all annulments are granted, even those to spouses who have been married for decades and have numerous children.

The basis used by the Catholic Church for granting an annulment is usually "lack of due discretion," which means that one or both parties lacked the ability needed to consent to the "essential obligations of matrimony." Personality or psychiatric disorders, premarital pregnancy, and problems in one's family of origin that one is trying to escape are examples of factors that the Catholic Church considers to interfere with a person's ability to fulfill the essential matrimonial obligations, such as a permanent partnership, faithfulness, and sharing.

Religious annulments are not recognized by the state in which the couple resides. Even though the church annuls a Catholic couple's marriage, the couple must still get a civil annulment (or a divorce) for the action to be legal and for the couple to legally remarry. An annulment granted by a civil court specifies that no valid marriage ever existed and returns both parties to their premarital status. Any property the couple exchanged as part of the marriage arrangement is returned to the original owner. Neither party is obligated to support the other economically.

Common reasons for granting civil annulments are bigamy, being under legal age, erectile failure, insanity, and fraud (the "reason" for Pamela Anderson's annulment from Rick Soloman and Kenny Chesney and Renee Zellweger's annulment). As an example of fraud, a university professor became involved in a relationship with one of his colleagues. During courtship, he promised her that they would rear a "houseful of babies." After the marriage, the woman discovered that the man had had a vasectomy several years earlier and had no intention of having more children. The marriage was annulled on the basis of fraud—the man misrepresented himself to the woman. Most annulments are for fraud. In the following actual annulment, Maria told Brandon that she was pregnant. After he discovered that she had tricked him, he sought an annulment on the basis of fraud.

In the District Court of El Paso County, Texas

_____ *Judicial District*

IN THE MATTER OF
THE MARRIAGE OF
Brandon Blake
AND   CASE NO. <u>2005-CN</u>
Maria DeCuzzi

1. Discovery Level

Discovery in this case is intended to be conducted under level 2 of rule 190 of the Texas Rules of Civil Procedures.

2. Parties

This suit is brought by BRANDON BLAKE, Petitioner. Respondent is MARIA DECUZZI.

3. Jurisdiction

BRANDON BLAKE is domiciled in Texas.

4. Service

No service on Respondent is necessary at this time.

5. Protective Order Statement

No protective order under title 4 of the Texas Family Code is in effect, and no application for a protective order is pending with regard to the parties to this suit.

6. Grounds

Petitioner and Respondent were married on January 5, 2008. Respondent induced Petitioner to enter into the marriage by fraud. Petitioner has not voluntarily cohabited with Respondent since learning of the fraud.

7. No Child of Marriage

No child was born or adopted of the marriage of Petitioner and Respondent, and none is expected.

8. Property

No community property was accumulated by the parties during the marriage other than personal effects, which should be awarded to the person having possession.

9. Confirmation of Name

Respondent's name before the marriage was MARIA DECUZZI, and this former name should be confirmed by the Court as her lawful name.

10. Prayer

Petitioner prays that Respondent be cited to appear and answer this petition.

Petitioner prays that the Court annul the marriage of Petitioner and Respondent.

Petitioner prays for general relief.

Respectfully submitted,
Jack Wright
Attorney At Law

Bigamy is another basis for annulment. In our society, a person is allowed to be married to only one spouse at a time. If another marriage is contracted at the time a person is already married, the new spouse can have the marriage annulled.

Most states have age requirements for marriage. When individuals younger than the minimum age marry without parental consent, the marriage may be annulled if either set of parents does not approve of the union. However, if neither set of parents or guardians disapproves of the marriage, the marriage may be regarded as legal; it is not automatically annulled.

Intercourse is a legal right of marriage. In some states, if a spouse is impotent, refuses to have intercourse, or is unable to do so for physical or psychological reasons, the other spouse can seek and may be granted an annulment.

Insanity and a lack of understanding of the marriage agreement are also reasons for annulment. Someone who is mentally deficient and incapable of understanding the meaning of a marriage ceremony can have a marriage annulled. Annulments are usually not granted if one or both of the parties is drunk at the time of the wedding ceremony or marry as a lark. However, Britney Spears and Jason Allen Alexander married in early 2004, and sought an annulment less than twelve hours after their marriage (on grounds that she "lacked understanding of her actions") (Chen 2004).

Separation

There are two types of separation—formal and informal. Typical items in a **formal separation** agreement include the following: (1) the husband and wife live separately; (2) their right to sexual intercourse with each other is ended; (3) the economic responsibilities of the spouses to each other are limited to those in the separation agreement; and (4) custody of the children is specified in the agreement, with visitation privileges granted to the noncustodial parent. The spouses may have emotional and sexual relationships with others, but neither party has the right to remarry. Although some couples live under this agreement until the death of one spouse, others draw up a separation agreement as a prelude to divorce. In some states, being legally separated for one year is a ground for divorce.

An **informal separation** (which is much more common) is similar to a legal separation except that no agreement is filed in the courthouse. The husband and wife settle the issues of custody, visitation, alimony, and child support between themselves. Because no legal papers are drawn up, the couple is still married from the state's point of view.

Attorneys advise against an informal separation (unless it is temporary) to avoid subsequent legal problems. For example, after three years of an informal separation, a mother decided that she wanted custody of her son. Although the father would have been willing earlier to sign a separation agreement that would have given her legal custody of her son, he was now unwilling to do so. Each spouse hired a lawyer, and a bitter and expensive court fight ensued.

Desertion

Desertion differs from informal separation in that the deserter walks out and breaks off all contact. Although either spouse may desert, usually the husband does so. A major reason for deserting is to escape the increasing financial demands of a family. Desertion usually results in nonsupport, which is a crime.

The sudden desertion by a husband sometimes has more severe negative consequences for the wife than an actual divorce. Unlike a divorced woman, a deserted woman is usually not free to remarry for several years. In addition, she receives no child support or alimony payments, and the children are deprived of a father.

Desertion is not unique to husbands. Although rare, wives and mothers also leave their husbands and children. Their primary reason for doing so is to escape an intolerable marriage and the sense of being trapped in the role of mother. "I'm tired of having to think about my children and my husband all the time—I want a life for myself," said one woman who deserted her family. "I want to live, too." Such desertion is not without its consequences as social norms dictate parental role responsibility, particularly for mothers. Most mothers who desert their children feel extremely guilty.

Divorce Prevention

Divorce remains stigmatized in our society, as evidenced by the term **divorcism**—the belief that divorce is a disaster. In view of this cultural attitude, a number of attempts have been made to reduce it. Marriage education workshops provide an opportunity for couples to meet with other couples and a leader who provides instruction in communication, conflict resolution, and parenting skills. Stanley et al. (2005) found positive outcomes in marital functioning for couples in marriage education classes provided for the U.S. Army.

There is so little difference between husbands you might as well keep the first.

Adela Rogers St. Johns, journalist, novelist

Another attempt at divorce prevention is **covenant marriage** (now available in Louisiana, Arizona, and Arkansas), which emphasizes the importance of staying married (Byrne and Carr 2005). In these states, couples agree to the following when they marry: (1) marriage preparation (meeting with a counselor who discusses marriage and their relationship); (2) full disclosure of all information that could reasonably affect a partner's decision to marry (for example, previous marriages, children, STIs, one's homosexuality); (3) an oath that their marriage is a lifelong commitment; (4) an agreement to consider divorce only for "serious" reasons such as abuse, adultery, and imprisonment for a felony or separation of more than two years; (5) an agreement to see a marriage counselor if problems threaten the marriage; and (6) not to divorce until after a two-year "cooling off" period (*Economist* 2005).

Although most of a sample of 1,324 adults in a telephone survey in Louisiana, Arizona, and Minnesota were positive about covenant marriage (Hawkins et al. 2002), fewer than 3 percent of marrying couples elected covenant marriages when given the opportunity to do so (Licata 2002). Although already married couples can convert their standard marriages to covenant marriages, there are no data on how many have done so (Hawkins et al. 2002).

SUMMARY

How often does divorce occur? Is it increasing?

Divorce is the legal ending of a valid marriage contract. The frequency of divorce is measured as the crude rate (the number of divorces for every 1,000 people), the refined rate (the number of divorces annually divided by the number of married women times 1,000), and percentage of married couples who eventually divorce (about 43 percent after fifteen years of marriage). Regardless of how the frequency of divorce is measured, divorce has topped out and dropping slowly. The primary reason that the divorce rate has stabilized is that individuals are waiting until their mid- to late twenties to marry. In general, the older a couple at marriage, the less likely they are to divorce.

What are macro factors contributing to divorce?

Macro factors contributing to divorce include increased economic independence of women (women can afford to leave), changing family functions (companionship is the only remaining function), liberal divorce laws (it's easier to leave), fewer religious sanctions (churches embrace single individuals), more divorce models (Hollywood models abound), and individualism (rather than familism as a cultural goal of happiness). Regarding individuals, 95 percent of 1,319 undergraduates at a large southeastern university disagreed with the statement, "I would not divorce my spouse for any reason"; hence, all but 5 percent would divorce under some circumstances.

What are micro factors contributing to divorce?

Micro factors include having numerous differences, falling out of love, negative behavior, lack of conflict resolution skills or satiation, value changes, and extramarital relationships. Being in one's teens at the time of marriage, having a courtship of less than two years, and having divorced parents are all associated with subsequent divorce.

How might one go about ending a relationship?

About 30 percent of undergraduates in one study reported that they were unhappy in their present relationship; another 30 percent reported that they knew they were in a relationship that should end. After considering that one might improve an unhappy relationship and deciding to end a relationship, telling a partner that one needs out "for one's space" without giving a specific reason helps a partner avoid feeling obligated to stay if the other partner changes. Although some couples can remain friends, others may profit from ending the relationship completely. And recovery can take time (twelve to eighteen months).

What are gender differences in filing for divorce?

Women are more likely to file for divorce because they see that, by getting divorced, they get the husband's money (via division of property or child support), the children, and the husband out of the house. Husbands are less likely to seek divorce because they more often end up without the house, with half their money, and separated from their children. Regardless of who files, over two-thirds of both women and men who are separated recommend that other couples who are contemplating divorce try to "work it out."

What are the consequences for spouses who remain unhappily married?

Spouses who remain unhappily married are less happy and healthy than spouses who divorce.

What are the consequences of divorce for spouses?

The psychological consequences for divorcing spouses depend on how unhappy the marriage was. Spouses who were miserable while in a loveless conflictual marriage often regard the divorce as a relief. Spouses who were left (for example, a spouse leaves for another partner) may be devastated and suicidal. Women tend to fare better emotionally after separation and divorce than do men. Women are more likely than men not only to have a stronger network of supportive relationships but also to profit from divorce by developing a new sense of self-esteem and confidence, because they are thrust into a more independent role.

Factors associated with a quicker adjustment on the part of both spouses include mediating rather than litigating the divorce, co-parenting their children, avoiding alcohol or other drugs, reducing stress through exercise, engaging in enjoyable activities with friends, and delaying a new marriage for two years. Recovering from a broken heart may also be expedited by recalling the negative things a partner did (for example, lied, was unfaithful, and so on).

What are the effects of divorce on children?

Although researchers agree that a civil, cooperative, co-parenting relationship between ex-spouses is the greatest predictor of a positive outcome for children, researchers disagree on the long-term negative effects of divorce on children. However, there is no disagreement that most children do not experience long-term negative effects. Divorce mediation encourages civility between divorcing spouses who negotiate the issues of division of property, custody, visitation, child support, and spousal support.

What are alternatives to divorce?

Alternatives to divorce include annulment, separation, and desertion. Annulment returns the parties to their premarital state and is both a religious and civil concept. The Catholic Church does not recognize divorce but does recognize annulment, which in effect says that the parties were never married. However, the parties are still legally married and must have their marriage legally annulled or they must get a divorce. Reasons for legal annulment include bigamy and being underage.

What are strategies to prevent divorce?

Three states (Louisiana, Arizona, and Arkansas) offer covenant marriages, in which spouses agree to divorce only for serious reasons such as imprisonment on a felony or separation of more than two years. They also agree to see a marriage counselor if problems threaten the marriage. When given the option to choose a covenant marriage, few couples do so.

The Companion Website for *Choices in Relationships: An Introduction to Marriage and the Family,* Tenth Edition

www.cengage.com/sociology/knox

Supplement your review of this chapter by going to the Companion Website to take one of the tutorial quizzes, use the flash cards to master key terms, or check out the many other study aids, like crossword puzzles and self-assessments. You'll also find special features such as General Social Survey (GSS) data, Census data, and other resources to help you with that special project or to do some research on your own.

WEB LINKS

Association for Conflict Resolution
http://www.acrnet.org

Dating after Divorce
http://heartchoice.com/divorce/index.php

Divorce Laws by State
http://www.totaldivorce.com/state-laws/default.aspx

Divorce Source (a legal resource for divorce, custody, alimony, and support)
http://www.divorcesource.com/

Divorce Support Page
http://www.divorcesupport.com/index.html

Divorce 360 (divorce advice, news, blogs, and community)
http://www.divorce360.com/

Surviving Divorce
http://www.divorceinfo.com/

DivorceBusting (solve marriage problems)
http://divorcebusting.com/

North Carolina Association of Professional Family Mediators
http://familymediators.org

The New Face of Divorce: First Wives World
www.firstwivesworld.com

A Guide to the Parental Alienation Syndrome
http://www.coeffic.demon.co.uk/pas.htm

Positive Parenting Through Divorce Online Course
http://www.positiveparentingthroughdivorce.com/

National Center for Health Statistics (marriage and divorce data)
http://www.cdc.gov/nchs/

REFERENCES

Abut, C. C. 2005. Ten common questions about postnuptial agreements. *New Jersey Law Journal,* August 15.

Ahrons, C. R. 1995. *The good divorce: Keeping your family together when your marriage comes apart.* New York: HarperCollins.

Ahrons, C. R., and J. L. Tanner. 2003. Adult children and their fathers: Relationship changes 20 years after parental divorce. *Family Relations* 52:340–51.

Allen, D. W., K. Pendakur, and W. Suen. 2006. No-fault divorce and the compression of marriage ages. *Economic Inquiry* 44:547–59.

Amato, P. R., A. Booth, D. R. Johnson, and S. F. Rogers. 2007. *Alone together: How marriage in America is changing.* Cambridge, Massachusetts: Harvard University Press.

Amato, P. R., and B. Hohmann-Marriott. 2007. A comparison of high- and low-distress marriages that end in divorce. *Journal of Marriage and Family* 69:621–38.

Baker, A. L. 2005. The long-term effects of parental alienation on adult children: A qualitative research study. *American Journal of Family Therapy* 33:289–302.

Baker, A. J. L. 2006. Patterns of Parental Alienation Syndrome: A qualitative study of adults who were alienated from a parent as a child. *American Journal of Family Therapy* 34:63–78.

Baker, A. J. L., and D. Darnall. 2007. A construct study of the eight symptoms of severe parental alienation syndrome: A survey of parental experiences. *Journal of Divorce & Remarriage* 47:55–62.

Baldwin, A. 2008. *A promise to ourselves: A journey through fatherhood and divorce.* New York: St. Martin's Press.

Baum, N. 2003. Divorce process variables and the co-parental relationship and parental role fulfillment of divorced parents. *Family Process* 42: 117–31.

Benton, S. D. 2008. Divorce mediation. Lecture, East Carolina University, November 10.

Blossfeld, H.P., and R. Muller. 2002. Union disruption in comparative perspective: The role of assertive partner choice and careers of couples. *International Journal of Sociology* 32:3–35.

Bream, V., and A. Buchanan. 2003. Distress among children whose separated or divorced parents cannot agree on arrangements for them. *British Journal of Social Work* 33: 227–38.

Breed, R., D. Knox, and M. Zusman. 2007. "Hell hath no fury" . . . Legal consequences of having Internet child pornography on one's computer. Southern Sociological Society, Atlanta.

Brinig, M. F., and D. W. Allen. 2000. "These boots are made for walking": Why most divorce filers are women. *American Law and Economic Association* 2:126–69.

Byrne, A. and D. Carr. 2005. Commentaries on: Singles in society and science. *Psychological Inquiry* 16:84–141.

Cashmore, J., P. Parkinson, and A. Taylor. 2008. Overnight stays and children's relationships with resident and nonresident parents after divorce. *Journal of Family Issues* 29:707–14.

Chen, J. 2004. Britney-Jason union wouldn't last. *USA Today*, January 5, D1.

Clarke-Stewart, A. and C. Brentano. 2006. *Divorce: Causes and consequences.* New Haven: Yale University Press.

Clarkwest, A. 2007. Spousal dissimilarity, race, and marital dissolution. *Journal of Marriage and the Family* 69:639–53.

Cohen, O., and R. Savaya. 2003. Lifestyle differences in traditionalism and modernity and reasons for divorce among Muslim Palestinian citizens of Israel. *Journal of Comparative Family Studies* 34:283–94.

Coltrane, S., and M. Adams. 2003. The social construction of the divorce "problem": Morality, child victims, and the politics of gender. *Family Relations* 52:363–72.

Covizzi, I. 2008. Does union dissolution lead to unemployment? A longitudinal study of health and risk of unemployment for women and men undergoing separation. *European Sociological Review* 24:347–62.

Decuzzi, A., D. Knox, and M. Zusman. 2004. The effect of parental divorce on relationships with parents and romantic partners of college students. Roundtable, Southern Sociological Society, Atlanta, April 17.

Dennison, R. P., and S. Koerner. 2008. A look at hopes and worries about marriage: The views of adolescents following a parental divorce. *Journal of Divorce & Remarriage* 48:91–107.

Drewianka, S. 2008. Divorce law and family formation. *Journal of Population Economics* 21:19–25.

Economist. 2005. "Yes, I really do."374:31–32.

Enright, E. 2004. A house divided. *AARP The Magazine,* July/August, 60.

Finley, G. E. 2004. Divorce inequities. *NCFR Family Focus Report* 49(3):F7.

Fonda, J. 2005. *Jane Fonda: My life so far.* New York: Random House.

Foster, J. D. 2008. Incorporating personality into the investment model: Probing commitment processes across individual differences in narcissism. *Journal of Social and Personal Relationships* 25:211–23.

Gardner, J. and A. J. Oswald. 2006. Do divorcing couples become happier by breaking up? *Journal of the Royal Statistical Society: Series A (Statistics and Society)* 169:319–36.

Gardner, R. A. 1998. *The parental alienation syndrome.* 2d ed. Cresskill, N.J.: Creative Therapeutics.

Gilman, J., D. Schneider, and R. Shulak. 2005. Children's ability to cope post-divorce: The effects of Kids' Turn intervention program on 7 to 9 year olds. *Journal of Divorce and Remarriage* 42:109–26.

Goodwin, P. Y. 2003. African American and European American women's health marital well-being. *Journal of Marriage and Family* 65:550–60.

Gordon, R. M. 2005. The doom and gloom of divorce research- Comment on Wallerstein and Lewis (2004) *Psychoanalytic Psychology* 22:450–51.

Gottman, J. M., J. S. Gottman, and J. de Claire. 2006. *Ten lesions to transform your marriage: America's lab experts share their strategies for strengthening your relationship.* New York: Random House.

Haswell, W. M. 2006. Mediation: An alternative to litigation. Presentation for the Department of Sociology, East Carolina University, April 5. www.HaswellMediation.com.

Hawkins, A. J., S. L. Nock, J. C. Wilson, L. Sanchez, and J. D. Wright. 2002. Attitudes about covenant marriage and divorce: Policy implications from a three state comparison. *Family Relations* 51:166–75.

Hawkins, D. N., and A. Booth. 2005. Unhappily ever after: Effects of long-term, low-quality marriages on well-being. *Social Forces* 84:445–65.

Heaton, T. B. 2002. Factors contributing to increasing marital stability in the United States. *Journal of Family Issues* 23:392–409.

Hetherington, E. M. 2003. Intimate pathways: Changing patterns in close personal relationships across time. *Family Relations* 52:318–31.

Hipke, K. N., S. A. Wolchik, I. N. Sandler, and S. L. Braver. 2002. Predictors of children's intervention-induced resilience in a parenting program for divorced mothers. *Family Relations* 51:121–29.

Holtzman, M. 2002. The "family relations" doctrine: Extending Supreme Court precedent to custody disputes between biological and nonbiological parents. *Family Relations* 51:335–43.

Hsu, M., D. L. Kahn, and C. Huang. 2002. No more the same: The lives of adolescents in Taiwan who have lost fathers. *Family Community Health* 25: 43–56.

Johnson, G. R., E. G. Krug, and L. B. Potter. 2000. Suicide among adolescents and young adults. A cross-national comparison of 34 countries. *Suicide and Life-Threatening Behavior* 30:74–82.

Joyal, R., A. Queniart, and H. Gijseghem. 2005. Children in joint custody: Some questions and answers. *Intervention* 122: 51–59.

Juby, H., J. Michel Billette, B. Laplante, and C. Le Bourdais. 2007. Nonresident fathers and children: Parents' new unions and frequency of contact *Journal of Family Issues* 28:1220–45.

Kelly, J. B., and R. E. Emery. 2003. Children's adjustment following divorce: Risk and resilience perspectives. *Family Relations* 52:352–62.

Kesselring, R. G., and D. Bremmer. 2006. Female income and the divorce decision: Evidence from micro data. *Applied Economics* 38:1605–17.

Kilmann, P. R., L. V. Carranza, and J. M. C. Vendemia. 2006. Recollections of parent characteristics and attachment patterns for college women of intact vs. non-intact families. *Journal of Adolescence* 29:89–102.

Knox, D., and U. Corte. 2007. "Work it out/See a counselor": Advice from spouses in the separation process. *Journal of Divorce & Remarriage* 48:79–90.

Knox, D., and M. E. Zusman. 2009. Relationship and sexual behaviors of a sample of 1,319 university students. Unpublished data collected for this text. Department of Sociology, East Carolina University, Greenville, NC.

Knox, D., M. E. Zusman, K. McGinty, and B. Davis. 2002. College student attitudes and behaviors toward ending an unsatisfactory relationship. *College Student Journal* 36:630–34.

Knox, D., M. E. Zusman, M. Kaluzny, and C. Cooper. 2000 College student recovery from a broken heart. *College Student Journal* 34:322–24.

Lambert, A. N. 2007. Perceptions of divorce- Advantages and disadvantages: A comparison of adult children experiencing one parental divorce versus multiple parental divorces. *Journal of Divorce & Remarriage* 48:55–77.

Lewis, K. (2008) Personal communication. Dr. Lewis is also the author of *Five Stages of Child Custody*. Glenside, PA: CCES Press.

Licata, N. 2002. Should premarital counseling be mandatory as a requisite to obtaining a marriage license? *Family Court Review* 40:518–32.

Lopoo, L. M., and B. Western. 2005. Incarceration and the formation and stability of marital unions. *Journal of Marriage and the Family* 67:721–35.

Lowenstein, L. F. 2005. Causes and associated factors of divorce as seen by recent research. *Journal of Divorce and Remarriage* 42:153–71.

Manning, W. D., and P. J. Smock. 2000. "Swapping" families: Serial parenting and economic support for children. *Journal of Marriage and the Family* 62:111–22.

McIntosh, J. E., Y. D. Wells, B. M. Smyth, and C. M. Long. 2008. Child-focused and child-inclusive divorce mediation: Comparative outcomes from a prospective study of post separation adjust. *Family Court Review* 46:105–15.

Menning, C. L. 2008. "I've Kept It That Way on Purpose": Adolescents' management of negative parental relationship traits after divorce and separation. *Journal of Contemporary Ethnography* 37:586–97.

Morgan, E. S. 1944. *The Puritan family*. Boston: Public Library.

Nielsen, L. 2004. *Embracing your father: How to build the relationship you always wanted with your dad*. New York: McGraw-Hill.

O'Leary, K. D. 2005. Commentary on intrapersonal, interpersonal, and contextual factors in extramarital involvement. *Clinical Psychology: Science and Practice* 12:131–33.

Ostermann, J., F. A. Sloan, and D. H. Taylor. 2005. Heavy alcohol use and marital dissolution in the USA. *Social Science and Medicine* 61:2304–20.

Previti, D., and P. R. Amato. 2003. Why stay married? Rewards, barriers, and marital stability. *Journal of Marriage and Family* 65:561–73.

Sakraida, T. 2005. Divorce transition differences of midlife women. *Issues in Mental Health Nursing* 26:225–49.

Schacht, T. E. 2000. Protection strategies to protect professionals and families involved in high-conflict divorce. *UALR Law Review* 22(3):565–92.

Segal-Engelchin, D., and Y. Wozner. 2005. Quality of life to single mothers in Israel: A comparison to single mothers and divorced mothers. *Marriage and Family Review* 37:7–28.

Sever, I., J. Guttmann, and A. Lazar. 2007. Positive consequences of parental divorce among Israeli young adults: A long-term effect model. *Marriage and Family Review* 42:7–21.

Shumway, S T., and R. S. Wampler. 2002. A behaviorally focused measure for relationships: The couple behavior report (CBR). *The American Journal of Family Therapy* 30:311–21.

Siegler, I., and P. Costa. 2000. Divorce in midlife. Paper presented at the Annual Meeting of the American Psychological Association, Boston.

Sobolewski, J. M., and P. R. Amato. 2007. Parents' discord and divorce, parent-child relationships and subjective well-being in early adulthood: Is feeling close to two parents always better than feeling close to one? *Social Forces* 1105–25.

Stanley, S. M., E. S. Allen, H. J. Markman, C. Saiz, G. Bloomstrom, R. Thomas, and W. R. Schumm. 2005. Dissemination and evaluation of marriage education in the Army. *Family Process* 44:187–201.

Statistical Abstract of the United States, 2009. 128th ed. Washington, DC: U.S. Bureau of the Census.

Storksen, I., E. Roysamb, T. L. Holmen, and K. Tambs. 2006. Adolescent adjustment and well-being: Effects of parental divorce and distress. *Scandinavian Journal of Psychology* 47:75–84.

Teich, M. 2007. A divided house. *Psychology Today* 40:96–102.

Thompson, P. 2008. Desperate Housewives? Communication difficulties and the dynamics of marital (un)happiness. *The Economic Journal* 118:1640–52.

Thuen, F., and J. Rise. 2006. Psychological adaptation after marital disruption: The effects of optimism and perceived control. *Scandinavian Journal of Psychology* 47:121–28.

Trinder, L. 2008. Maternal gate closing and gate opening in postdivorce families. *Journal of Family Issues* 29:1298–2011.

Turkat, I. D. 2002. Shared parenting dysfunction. *The American Journal of Family Therapy* 30:385–93.

Waite, L. J., Y. Luo, and A. C. Lewin. 2009. Marital happiness and marital stability: Consequences for psychological well-being. *Social Science Research* 28:201–17.

Whitehurst, D. H., S. O'Keefe, and R. A. Wilson. 2008. Divorced and separated parents in conflict: Results from a true experiment effect of a court mandated parenting education program *Journal of Divorce & Remarriage* 48:127–44.

Wiseman, R. S. 1975. Crisis theory and the process of divorce. *Social Casework* 56:205–12.

Chapter 15 Divorce and Ending Relationships

While the large number of divorces suggests that America is still the land of the free, the steady rate of marriage and remarriage suggests it is still the home of the brave.

Anonymous

Remarriage and Beginning New Relationships

Authors

Contents

True or False?

1. Most divorced individuals have been "burned by a first marriage" and do not remarry.

2. Involvement in a divorce adjustment group makes no difference in terms of one's actual divorce adjustment.

3. Marriages in which a woman brought a child into the marriage are more likely to end than if the man brought a child into the remarriage.

4. Second marriages that have lasted over 15 years are less likely to end in divorce than first marriages.

5. The biggest source of problems for kids in stepfamilies is parental conflict left over from the first marriage.

Answers: **1.** F **2.** F **3.** T **4.** T **5.** T

I don't think I'll get married again. I'll just find a woman I don't like and give her a house.

Lewis Grizzard, journalist/comic writer

"You never thought you'd be alone this far down the line" is a lyric from the Eagles song, "Wasted Time." It reflects one's shock at realizing that divorce doesn't just happen to other people and that starting over is now on one's life agenda. Most who divorce do start over. Rather than being embittered by divorce and sour on marriage, divorced individuals seem open to a new love and to starting again in a new marriage.

Indeed, a story is told of a widower who engraved on the tombstone of his former wife, "My light has gone out." As he was about to remarry, he asked Bishop Henry C. Potter whether he should have the inscription erased as he was beginning a new life. "Oh no," said the bishop, "I wouldn't have it taken off; just put underneath it, 'I have struck another match'" (Fuller 1970, 154–55). The opening photo for this chapter illustrates a remarriage. These new spouses are seen with their respective children from a former marriage (the husband's two daughters are in front of and between him and the new wife; the wife's daughter is in front of her). The parents of the respective new spouses are standing beside their son and daughter. Remarriage merges two family systems so that these children not only have new siblings but also a new stepparent and new grandparents. In this chapter, we examine the process of merging two family systems with the goal of making a happy and fulfilling transition.

Remarriage

Divorced spouses usually waste little time getting involved in a new relationship. Indeed, one-fourth date someone new before the divorce is final. Within two years, 75 percent of divorced women and 80 percent of divorced men are in a serious, exclusive relationship (Enright 2004). When comparing divorced individuals who have remarried against divorced individuals who have not remarried, the remarried individuals report greater personal and relationship happiness.

Diversity in Other Countries

Although both women and men in the United States regard getting remarried as an option, such is not the case in all societies. Divorced women living in urban centers in central India are not likely to want to remarry because they are allowed to remarry only widowers. Divorced men are allowed to remarry any single woman of their choice.

Remarriage for Divorced Individuals

Ninety percent of remarriages are of people who are divorced rather than widowed. The principle of **homogamy** is illustrated in the selection of a new spouse (never-married individuals tend to marry never-married individuals, divorced individuals tend to marry other divorced individuals, and widowed individuals tend to marry other widowed individuals). The majority of divorced people remarry for many of the same reasons as for a first marriage—love, companionship, emotional security, and a regular sex partner. Other reasons are unique to remarriage and include financial security (particularly for a wife with children), help in rearing one's children, the desire to provide a "social" father or mother for one's children, escape from the stigma associated with the label "divorced person," and legal threats regarding the custody of one's children. With regard to the latter, the courts view a parent seeking custody of a child more favorably if the parent is married.

Regardless of the reason for remarriage, it is best to proceed slowly into a remarriage. Some may benefit from involvement in a divorce adjustment program. Vukalovich and Caltabiano (2008) assessed the effectiveness of an adjustment separation or divorce program. Twenty females and ten males completed a pre- and post-questionnaire. Overall, the results indicated that participants made significant adjustment gains following participation in the program.

For others, grieving over the loss of a first spouse through divorce or death and developing a relationship with a new partner takes time. At least two years is the recommended interval between the end of a marriage and a remarriage (Marano 2000). Older divorced women (over 40) are less likely than younger divorced women to remarry. Not only are fewer men available, but also the **mating gradient** whereby men tend to marry women younger than themselves is operative. In addition, older women are more likely to be economically independent, to enjoy living alone, to value the freedom of singlehood, and to want to avoid the restrictions of marriage. Divorced people getting remarried are usually about ten years older than those marrying for the first time. People in their mid-thirties who are considering remarriage are more likely to have finished school and to be established in a job or career than individuals in their first marriages.

Courtship for previously married individuals is usually short and takes into account the individuals' respective work schedules and career commitments. Because each partner may have children, much of the couple's time together includes their children. In subsequent marriages, eating pizza at home and renting a DVD to watch with the kids often replaces the practice of going out alone on an expensive dinner date during courtship before a first marriage.

Preparation for Remarriage

Trust is a major issue for people getting remarried. Brimhall et al. (2008) interviewed sixteen remarried individuals and found that most reported that their first marriage ended over trust issues—the partner betrayed them by having an affair or by hiding or spending money without the partner's knowledge. Each was intent on ensuring a foundation of trust in the new marriage.

Some people who remarry first live together before the wedding. Teachman (2008) found that living together before a remarriage does not increase the risk of divorce in a subsequent marriage. Poortman and Lyngstad (2008) found a similar pattern.

People remarrying may also develop a prenuptial agreement. These soon-to-be remarried spouses may have assets to protect as well as wanting to ensure that their respective children get whatever portion of their estate they desire. We discussed prenuptial agreements in detail in Chapter 6. Appendix C at the end of this text provides an example of a prenuptial agreement for a couple getting remarried.

Issues of Remarriage

Several issues challenge people who remarry (Swallow 2004; Ganong and Coleman 1994; Goetting 1982).

I love to shop after a bad relationship. I don't know. I buy a new outfit and it makes me feel better. It just does. Sometimes I see a really great outfit, I'll break up with someone on purpose.

Rita Rudner

Boundary Maintenance Movement from divorce to remarriage is not a static event that is over after a brief ceremony. Rather, ghosts of the first marriage—in terms of the ex-spouse and, possibly, the children—must be dealt with. A parent must decide how to relate to an ex-spouse to maintain a good parenting relationship for the biological children while keeping an emotional distance to prevent problems from developing with a new partner. Some spouses continue to be emotionally attached to and have difficulty breaking away from an ex-spouse. These former spouses have what Masheter (1999) terms a "**negative commitment.**" Masheter says such individuals "have decided to remain [emotionally] in this relationship and to invest considerable amounts of time, money, and effort in it . . . [T]hese individuals do not take responsibility for their own feelings and actions, and often remain 'stuck,' unable to move forward in their lives" (p. 297).

One former spouse recalled a conversation with his ex from whom he had been divorced for more than seventeen years. "Her anger coming through the phone seemed like she was still feeling the divorce as though it had happened this morning," he said.

Emotional Remarriage Remarriage involves beginning to trust and love another person in a new relationship. Such feelings may come slowly as a result of negative experiences in a previous marriage.

Psychic Remarriage Divorced individuals considering remarriage may find it difficult to give up the freedom and autonomy of being single and to develop a mental set conducive to pairing. This transition may be particularly difficult for people who sought a divorce as a means to personal growth and autonomy. These individuals may fear that getting remarried will put unwanted constraints on them.

Community Remarriage This stage involves a change in focus from single friends to a new mate and other couples with whom the new pair will interact. The bonds of friendship established during the divorce period may be particularly valuable because they have given support at a time of personal crisis. Care should be taken not to drop these friendships.

Parental Remarriage Because most remarriages involve children, people must work out the nuances of living with someone else's children. Mothers are usually awarded primary physical custody, and this translates into a new stepfather

What if Your Ex-Spouse or Ex-Partner Wants to Get Back Together?

WHAT IF?

The dilemma of an ex-spouse or ex-partner wanting to get back together is not unusual and has been the subject of classic novels. Brett Butler said of getting back with Scarlett O'Hara in *Gone with the Wind*, "I'd rather remember it as best it was than try and remend it and look at the broken pieces as long as I live." His decision is worthy of duplicating. Once an intense love relationship has been seriously broken (divorce), mending it and returning it to a durable, happy relationship is not likely.

adjusting to the mother's children and vice versa. For individuals who have children from a previous marriage who do not live primarily with them, a new spouse must adjust to these children on weekends, holidays, and vacations or at other visitation times.

Economic and Legal Remarriage A second marriage may begin with economic responsibilities to a first marriage. Alimony and child support often threaten the harmony and sometimes even the economic survival of second marriages. Although the income of a new wife is not used legally to decide the amount her new husband is required to pay in child support for his children of a former marriage, his ex-wife may petition the court for more child support. The ex-wife may do so, however, on the premise that his living expenses are reduced with a new wife and that, therefore, he should be able to afford to pay more child support. Although an ex-wife is not likely to win, she can force the new wife to court and a disclosure of her income (all with considerable investment of time and legal fees for a newly remarried couple).

Economic issues in a remarriage may become evident in another way. A remarried woman who receives inadequate child support from an ex-spouse and needs money for her child's braces, for instance, might wrestle with how much money to ask her new husband for.

PERSONAL CHOICES

Consequences of a Woman Marrying a Divorced Man with Children
Women considering marriage to a divorced man with children should be cautious. In a study of 274 questionnaires of second wives—women who married men who had been married before—39 percent reported having thought about divorcing their husbands, and one in four reported that, with what she now knew, she would not have married him (Knox and Zusman 2001).

Implications of the study included the following considerations:

1. *Acknowledge that a second marriage is vulnerable.* Be realistic about the degree to which his children will accept you and/or your children. How do you really feel about his children?

2. *Delay marriage to a person who has been married before.* Over a quarter (27.4 percent) of the wives reported marrying their current husband less than a year after his divorce became final. We have previously noted the importance of knowing a person at least two years before getting married.

3. *Consider a fresh start in a new home.* Eighty-two percent of second wives reported that their new husbands had moved into their homes—homes the former husband had vacated after the prior divorce. Not one of the second wives reported that she currently lived in a newly bought or rented place with her new husband. Only 16 percent reported that the second wives had moved into their husband's home or condo.

Remarriage for Widowed Individuals

Only 10 percent of remarriages involve widows or widowers. Nevertheless, remarriage for widowed individuals is usually very different from remarriage for divorced people. Unlike divorced individuals, widowed individuals are usually much older and their children are grown. A widow or widower may marry someone of similar age or someone who is considerably older or younger. Marriages in which one spouse is considerably older than the other are referred to as May-December marriages (discussed in Chapter 7, Marriage Relationships). Here we will discuss only **December marriages,** in which both spouses are elderly.

A study of twenty-four elderly couples found that the primary motivation for remarriage was the need to escape loneliness or the need for companionship (Vinick 1978). Men reported a greater need to remarry than did the women.

Most of the spouses (75 percent) met through a mutual friend or relative and married less than a year after their partner's death (63 percent). Increasingly, elderly individuals are meeting online. Some sites cater to older individuals seeking partners, including seniorfriendfinder.com and thirdage.com.

The children of the couples in Vinick's study had mixed reactions to their parent's remarriage. Most of the children were happy that their parent was happy and felt relieved that someone would now meet the companionship needs of their elderly parent on a more regular basis. However, some children disapproved of the marriage out of concern for their inheritance rights. "If that woman marries Dad," said a woman with two children, "she'll get everything when he dies. I love him and hope he lives forever, but when he's gone, I want the house I grew up in." Though children may be less than approving of the remarriage of their widowed parent, adult friends of the couple, including the kin of the deceased spouses, are usually very approving (Ganong and Coleman 1994).

Stages of Involvement with a New Partner

After a legal separation or divorce (or being widowed), a parent who becomes involved in a new relationship passes through various transitions (see Table 16.1) (Anderson and Greene 2005). These not only affect the individuals and their relationship but any children and/or extended family.

Stability of Remarriages

National data reflect that remarriages are more likely than first marriages to end in divorce in the early years of remarriage (Clarke and Wilson 1994). Remarriages most vulnerable to divorce are those that involve a woman bringing a child into the new marriage. Teachman (2008) analyzed data on women (N = 655) from National Survey of Family Growth to examine the correlates of second marital dissolution. He found that women who brought stepchildren into their second marriage experienced an elevated risk of marital disruption. Premarital cohabitation or having a birth while cohabiting with a second husband did not raise the risk of marital dissolution, however. In addition, marrying a man who brought a child to the marriage did not increase the risk of marital disruption. One possible explanation for why a woman bringing a child into a second marriage is related to greater instability is that she may be less attentive to the new husband and more of a mother than a wife.

That second marriages, in general, are more susceptible to divorce than first marriages is because divorced individuals are less fearful of divorce than

Table 16.1 Stages of Parental Repartnering

Relationship Transition	Definition
Dating initiation	The parent begins to date.
Child introduction	The children and new dating partner meet.
Serious involvement	The parent begins to present the relationship as "serious" to the children.
Sleepover	The parent and the partner begin to spend nights together when the children are in the home.
Cohabitation	The parent and the partner combine households.
Breakup of a serious relationship	The relationship experiences a temporary or permanent disruption.
Pregnancy in the new relationship	A planned or unexpected pregnancy occurs.
Engagement	The parent announces plans to remarry.
Remarriage	The parent and partner create a legal or civil union.

Source: Stages of Parental Repartnering by E. R. Anderson and S. M. Greene. Transitions in parental repartnering after divorce. *Journal of Divorce & Remarriage.* January 8, 2007, 43:49. Reprinted by permission of the publisher (Taylor & Francis Group, http://www.informaworld.com), (http://www.haworthpress.com/web/jdr/).

The man in the photo had been married before and had a daughter from his previous marriage. The woman had not been married before and had no children, so she became a stepmother to his daughter. The couple subsequently adopted a child of their own.

individuals who have never divorced. So, rather than stay in an unhappy second marriage, the spouses leave.

Though remarried people are more vulnerable to divorce in the early years of their subsequent marriage, they are less likely to divorce after fifteen years of staying in the second marriage than those in first marriages (Clarke and Wilson 1994). Hence, these spouses are likely to remain married because they want to, not because they fear divorce. McCarthy and Ginsberg (2007) also noted that couples in functional and stable second marriages take greater pride and report higher satisfaction in their marriage than couples in their first marriage. Not only are they relieved at not having to live in their former relationships but they are older and more skilled in working out the nuances of a life together.

Families don't blend. Not like ice cream or fruit drinks, anyway. But more like patchwork quilts. Take the pieces and sew them tenderly together. Don't deny that you're two families; rejoice in those differences.

Van Chapman, researcher

Stepfamilies

Stepfamilies, also known as blended, binuclear, remarried, or reconstituted families, represent the fastest-growing type of family in the United States. Indeed, more than half of Americans are members of a blended family (Christian 2005). A **blended family** is one in which spouses in a new marriage relationship blend their children from at least one other spouse from a previous marriage. The term **binuclear** refers to a family that spans two households; when a married couple with children divorce, their family unit typically spreads into two households.

There is a movement away from the use of the term *blended* because stepfamilies really do not blend. The term **stepfamily** (sometimes referred to as **step relationships**) is the term currently in vogue. Leon and Angst (2005) reviewed American films over a thirteen-year period and found that stepfamilies and remarriages were depicted in negative or mixed ways. This section examines how stepfamilies differ from nuclear families; how they are experienced from the viewpoints of women, men, and children; and the developmental tasks that must be accomplished to make a successful stepfamily.

Definition and Types of Stepfamilies

Although there are various types of stepfamilies (Prather 2008), the most common is a family in which the partners bring children from previous relationships into the new home, where they may also have a child of their own. The couple may be married or living together, heterosexual or homosexual, and of all races. Although a stepfamily can be created when an individual who has never married or a widowed parent with children marries a person with or without children, most stepfamilies today are composed of spouses who are divorced and who bring children into a new marriage. This is different from stepfamilies characteristic of the early twentieth century, which more often were composed of spouses who had been widowed.

As noted, stepfamilies may be both heterosexual and homosexual. Lesbian stepfamilies model gender flexibility in that a biological mother and a step-mother tend to share parenting (in contrast to a traditional family, in which the mother may take primary responsibility for parenting and the father is less in-volved). This allows a biological mother some freedom from motherhood as well as support in it. In gay male stepfamilies, the gay men may also share equally in the work of parenting.

Myths of Stepfamilies

Various myths abound regarding stepfamilies, including that new family members will instantly bond emotionally, that children in stepfamilies are damaged and do not recover, that stepfamilies are not "real" families, and that stepmothers are "wicked" and "home-wreckers." The Stepfamily Association of America has identi-fied other myths, such that part-time (weekend) stepfamilies are easier than full-time stepfamilies, that it is easier or better if the biological parents withdraw, and that stepfamilies formed after the death of a parent rather than the divorce of a parent are "easier" (http://www.saafamilies.org/faqs/myths.html, 2009).

Unique Aspects of Stepfamilies

Stepfamilies differ from nuclear families in a number of ways (see Table 16.2). To begin with, children in nuclear families are biologically related to both par-ents, whereas children in stepfamilies are biologically related to only one parent. Also, in nuclear families, both biological parents live with their children, whereas only one biological parent in stepfamilies lives with the children. In some cases, the children alternate living with each parent.

Though nuclear families are not immune to loss, everyone in a stepfamily has experienced the loss of a love partner, which results in grief. About 70 per-cent of children whose parents have divorced are living without their biological father (who some children desperately hope will reappear and reunite the family). The respective spouses may also have experienced emotional disengage-ment and physical separation from a once loved partner. Stepfamily members may also experience losses because of having moved away from the house in which they lived, their familiar neighborhood, and their circle of friends.

Stepfamily members are also connected psychologically to others outside their unit. Bray and Kelly (1998) referred to these relationships as the "ghosts at the table":

> *Children are bound to absent parents, adults to past lives and past marriages. These invisible psychological bonds are the ghosts at the table and because they play on the most elemental emotions—emotions like love and loyalty and guilt and fear—they have the power to tear a marriage and stepfamily apart.* (p. 4)

Children in nuclear families have also been exposed to a relatively consistent set of beliefs, values, and behavior patterns. When children enter a stepfamily, they "inherit" a new parent, who may bring into the family unit a new set of values and beliefs and a new way of living. Likewise, a stepparent now lives with children who may rear differently from the way in which the biological parents reared the child. "His kids had never been to church," reported one frustrated stepparent.

Another unique aspect of stepfamilies is that the relationship between the biological parent and the children has existed longer than the relationship between the adults in the remarriage. Jane and her twin children have a nine-year relationship and are emotionally bonded to each other. However, Jane has known her new partner only a year, and although her children like their new stepfather, they hardly know him.

In addition, the relationship between biological parents and their children is of longer duration than that of stepparents and stepchildren. The short history of the relationship between children and stepparents is one factor that may contribute to increased conflict between these two during children's adolescence. Children may also become confused and wonder whether they are disloyal to their biological parent if they become friends with a stepparent.

Stepfamilies are also unique, in that stepchildren have two homes they may regard as theirs, unlike children in a nuclear family, who have one home they regard as theirs. In some cases of joint custody, children spend part of each week with one parent and part with the other; they live with two sets of adult parents in two separate homes.

Money, or lack of it, from an ex-spouse (usually the husband) may be a source of conflict. In some stepfamilies, an ex-spouse (usually the father) is expected to send child support payments to the parent who has custody of the children. Fewer than one-half of these fathers send any money; those who do may be irregular in their payments. Fathers who pay regular child support tend to have higher incomes, to have remarried, to live close to their children, and to visit them regularly. They are also more likely to have legal shared or joint custody, which helps to ensure that they will have access to their children.

Fathers who do not voluntarily pay child support and are delinquent by more than one month may have their wages garnisheed by the state. Some fathers change jobs frequently and move around to make it difficult for the government to keep up with them. Such dodging of the law is frustrating to custodial mothers who need the child support money. Added to the frustration is the fact that fathers are legally entitled to see their children even when they do not pay court-ordered child support. This angers mothers who must give up their children on weekends and holidays to a man who is not supporting his children financially. Such distress on the part of mothers is probably conveyed to the children.

New relationships in stepfamilies experience almost constant flux. Each member of a new stepfamily has many adjustments to make. Issues that must be dealt with include how the mate feels about the partner's children from a former marriage, how the children feel about the new stepparent, and how the newly married spouse feels about the spouse's sending alimony and child support payments to an ex-spouse. In general, families in the Bray and Kelly (1998) study did not begin to think and act like a family until the end of the second or third year. These early years are the most vulnerable, with a quarter of stepfamilies ending during that period.

Stepfamilies are also stigmatized. **Stepism** is the assumption that stepfamilies are inferior to biological families. Stepism, like racism, heterosexism, sexism, and ageism, involves prejudice and discrimination. Social changes need to be made to give support to stepfamilies. For example, if there is a graduation banquet, is this an opportunity for children to invite all four of their parents? More often, children are forced to choose, which usually results in selecting the biological parent and ignoring the stepparents. The more adults children have who love and support them (for example, both biological and stepparents), the better for the children, and our society should support this.

Stepparents also have no childfree period. Unlike newly married couples in nuclear families, who typically have their first child about two and one-half years after their wedding, many remarried couples begin their marriage with children in the house.

Profound legal differences exist between nuclear and blended families. Whereas biological parents in nuclear families are required in all states to

Table 16.2 Differences between Nuclear Families and Stepfamilies

Nuclear Families	Stepfamilies
1. Children are (usually) biologically related to both parents.	1. Children are biologically related to only one parent.
2. Both biological parents live together with children.	2. As a result of divorce or death, one biological parent does not live with the children. In the case of joint physical custody, children may live with both parents, alternating between them.
3. Beliefs and values of members tend to be similar.	3. Beliefs and values of members are more likely to be different because of different backgrounds.
4. The relationship between adults has existed longer than relationship between children and parents.	4. The relationship between children and parents has existed longer than the relationship between adults.
5. Children have one home they regard as theirs.	5. Children may have two homes they regard as theirs.
6. The family's economic resources come from within the family unit.	6. Some economic resources may come from an ex-spouse.
7. All money generated stays in the family.	7. Some money generated may leave the family in the form of alimony or child support.
8. Relationships are relatively stable.	8. Relationships are in flux: new adults adjusting to each other; children adjusting to a stepparent; a stepparent adjusting to stepchildren; stepchildren adjusting to each other.
9. No stigma is attached to nuclear family.	9. Stepfamilies are stigmatized.
10. Spouses had a childfree period.	10. Spouses had no childfree period.
11. Inheritance rights are automatic.	11. Stepchildren do not automatically inherit from stepparents.
12. Rights to custody of children are assumed if divorce occurs.	12. Rights to custody of stepchildren are usually not considered.
13. Extended family networks are smooth and comfortable.	13. Extended family networks become complex and strained.
14. Nuclear family may not have experienced loss.	14. Stepfamily has experienced loss.

The bond that links your true family is not one of blood, but of respect and joy in each other's life.

Richard Bach, American writer

support their children, only five states require stepparents to provide financial support for their stepchildren. Thus, when stepparents divorce, this and other discretionary types of economic support usually stop.

Other legal matters with regard to nuclear families versus stepfamilies involve inheritance rights and child custody. Stepchildren do not automatically inherit from their stepparents, and courts have been reluctant to give stepparents legal access to stepchildren in the event of a divorce. In general, U.S. law does not consistently recognize stepparents' roles, rights, and obligations regarding their stepchildren (Malia 2005). Without legal support to ensure such access, these relationships tend to become more distant and nonfunctional.

Finally, extended family networks in nuclear families are smooth and comfortable, whereas those in stepfamilies often become complex and strained. Table 16.2 summarizes the differences between nuclear families and stepfamilies.

Stepfamilies in Theoretical Perspective

Structural functionalists, conflict theorists, and symbolic interactionists view stepfamilies from the following different points of view:

1. *Structural-functional perspective.* To the structural functionalist, integration or stability of the system is highly valued. The very structure of the stepfamily system can be a threat to the integration and stability of a family system. The social structure of stepfamilies consists of a stepparent, a biological parent, biological children, and stepchildren. Functionalists view the stepfamily system as vulnerable to an alliance between the biological parent and the biological children who have a history together.

In 75 percent of the cases, the mother and children create an alliance. The stepfather, as an outsider, may view this alliance between the mother and her children as the mother's giving the children too much status or power in the family. Whereas a mother may relate to her children as equals, a stepfather may relate to the children as unequals whom he attempts to discipline. The result is a fragmented parental subsystem whereby the stepfather accuses the mother of being too soft and she accuses him of being too harsh.

Structural family therapists suggest that parents should have more power than children and that they should align themselves with each other. Not to do so is to give children family power, which they may use to splinter the parents off from each other and create another divorce.

2. *Conflict perspective.* Conflict theorists view conflict as normal, natural, and inevitable as well as functional in that it leads to change. Conflict in a stepfamily system is seen as desirable in that it leads to equality and individual autonomy.

Conflict is a normal part of stepfamily living. The spouses, parents, children, and stepchildren are constantly in conflict for the limited resources of space, time, and money. Space refers to territory (rooms) or property (television, CD player, or electronic games) in the house that the stepchildren may fight over. Time refers to the amount of time that the parents will spend with each other, with their biological children, and with their stepchildren. Money must be allocated in a reasonably equitable way so that each member of the family has a sense of being treated fairly.

Problems arise when space, time, and money are limited. Two new spouses who each bring a child from a former marriage into the house have a situation fraught with potential conflict. Who sleeps in which room? Who gets to watch which channel on television?

To further complicate the situation, suppose the couple have a baby. Where does the baby sleep? Because both parents may have full-time jobs, the time they have for the three children is scarce, not to speak of the fact that a baby will require a major portion of their available time. As for money, the cost of the baby's needs, such as formula and disposable diapers, will compete with the economic needs of the older children. Meanwhile, the spouses may need to spend time alone and may want to spend money as they wish. All these conflicts are functional because they increase the chance that a greater range of needs will be met within the stepfamily.

3. *Interactionist perspective.* Symbolic interactionists emphasize the meanings and interpretations that members of a stepfamily develop for events and interactions in the family. Children may blame themselves for their parents' divorce and feel that they and their stepfamily are stigmatized; parents may view stepchildren as spoiled.

Stepfamily members also nurture certain myths. Stepchildren sometimes hope that their parents will reconcile and that their nightmare of divorce and stepfamily living will end. This is the myth of reconciliation. Another is the myth of instant love, usually held by stepparents, who hope that the new partner's children will instantly love them. Although this does happen, particularly if the child is young and has no negative influences from the other parent, it is unlikely.

Stages in Becoming a Stepfamily

Just as a person must pass through various developmental stages in becoming an adult, a stepfamily goes through a number of stages as it overcomes various obstacles. Researchers such as Bray and Kelly (1998) and Papernow (1988) have identified various stages of development in stepfamilies. These stages include the following:

Stage 1: *Fantasy* Both spouses and children bring rich fantasies into a new marriage. Spouses fantasize that their new marriage will be better than the previous one. If the new spouse has adult children, they assume that these children will be open to a rewarding relationship with them. Young children have their own fantasy—they hope that their biological parents will somehow get back together and that the stepfamily will be temporary.

Stage 2: *Reality* Instead of realizing their fantasies, new spouses may find that stepchildren ignore or are rude to them. Indeed, stepparents may feel that they are outsiders in an already-functioning unit (the biological parent and child).

Stage 3: *Being Assertive* Initially a stepparent assumes a passive role and accepts the frustrations and tensions of stepfamily life. Eventually, however, resentment can reach a level where the stepparent is driven to make changes. The stepparent may make the partner aware of the frustrations and suggest that the marital relationship should have priority some of the time. The stepparent may also make specific requests, such as reducing the number of conversations the partner has with the ex-spouse, not allowing the dog on the furniture, or requiring the stepchildren to use better table manners. This stage is successful to the degree that the partner supports the recommendations for change. A crisis may ensue.

Stage 4: *Strengthening Pair Ties* During this stage, the remarried couple solidify their relationship by making it a priority. At the same time, the biological parent must back away somewhat from the parent-child relationship so that the new partner can have the opportunity to establish a relationship with the stepchildren.

This relationship is the product of small units of interaction and develops slowly across time. Many day-to-day activities, such as watching television, eating meals, and riding in the car together, provide opportunities for the stepparent-stepchild relationship to develop. It is important that the stepparent not attempt to replace the relationship that the stepchildren have with their biological parents.

Stage 5: *Recurring Change* A hallmark of all families is change, but this is even more true of stepfamilies. Bray and Kelly (1998) note that, even though a stepfamily may function well when the children are preadolescent, a new era can begin when the children become teenagers and begin to question how the family is organized and run. Such questioning by adolescents is not unique to stepchildren.

Michaels (2000) noted that spouses who become aware of the stages through which stepfamilies pass report that they feel less isolated and unique. Involvement in stepfamily discussion groups such as the Stepfamily Enrichment Program provides enormous benefits.

Strengths of Stepfamilies

Stepfamilies have both strengths and weaknesses. Strengths include children's exposure to a variety of behavior patterns, their observation of a happy remarriage, adaptation to stepsibling relationships inside the family unit, and greater objectivity on the part of the stepparent.

Exposure to a Variety of Behavior Patterns

Children in stepfamilies experience a variety of behaviors, values, and lifestyles. They have the advantage of living on the inside of two families. Although this may be confusing and challenging for children or adolescents, they are learning early how different family patterns can be. For example, one 12-year-old had never seen a couple pray at the dinner table until his mom remarried a man who was accustomed to a "blessing" before meals.

Happier Parents

Although children may want their parents to get back together, they often come to observe that their parents are happier alone than married. If a parent remarries, the children may see the parent in a new and happier relationship. Such happiness may spill over into the context of family living so that there is less tension and conflict.

Authors

Opportunity for a New Relationship with Stepsiblings

Though some children reject their new stepsiblings, others are enriched by the opportunity to live with a new person to whom they are now "related." One 14-year-old remarked, "I have never had an older brother to do things with. We both like to do the same things and I couldn't be happier about the new situation." Some stepsibling relationships are maintained throughout adulthood.

Nevertheless, there is stress associated with having stepsiblings. Tillman (2008) studied sibling relationships in stepfamilies (referring to them as "non-traditional siblings") and noted that adolescents with stepsiblings living in the same house made lower grades and had more school-related behavior problems. The researcher noted that these outcomes are related to the complexity and stress of living with stepsiblings.

More Objective Stepparents

Because of the emotional tie between a parent and a child, some parents have difficulty discussing certain issues or topics. A stepparent often has the advantage of being less emotionally involved and can relate to a child at a different level. One 13-year-old said of the relationship with his new stepmom, "She went through her own parents' divorce and knew what it was like for me to be going through my dad's divorce. She was the only one I could really talk to about this issue. Both my dad and mom were too angry about the subject to be able to talk about it."

The New Stepmother

Christian (2005) studied sixty-nine posts by stepmothers on the Stepfamily Association of America website forum (www.saafamilies.org) and noted that the stepmothers felt they were negatively stereotyped as the "wicked stepmother" and reacted to this stereotype by characterizing the biological mother as mentally unstable. Of one biological mother, a stepmother noted:

> She has chased us down and followed us to the store and places, then proceeded to cuss me out. She tried to fist fight with me at Alex's school, right in front of Alex.

The stereotype of the "wicked stepmother," which was immortalized by the Disney classic *Cinderella,* continues.

Walt Disney/Courtesy: Everett Collection

Almost every little girl grows up hoping to be a mother someday. But has there ever been one who dreamed of becoming a stepmother?

Evelyn Bassoff, psychologist

Biological mothers were also seen as incompetent:

The birth mom is an alcoholic who had hardly nothing to do with these children for several years. . .

Stepmothers also viewed themselves as martyrs for helping to save the child:

Whether BioMom likes it or not, I am more of a mother to her daughter than she is.

Specific sources of frustration for women in the role of stepmother include accepting and being accepted by their new partner's children, adjusting to alimony and child support payments made by her husband to an ex-wife, having a new partner accept her children and having her children accept him, and having another child in the new marriage.

Accepting a Partner's Children

"She'd better think a long time before she marries a guy with kids," said one 29-year-old woman who had done so. This stepmother went on to explain:

It's really difficult to love someone else's children. Particularly if the kid isn't very likable. A year after we were married, my husband's 9-year-old daughter visited us for a summer. It was a nightmare. She didn't like anything I cooked, was always dragging around making us late when we had to go somewhere, kept her room a mess, and acted like a gum-chewing smart aleck. I hated her, but felt guilty because I wanted to have feelings of love and tenderness. Instead, I was jealous of the relationship she had with her father, and I wanted to get rid of her. I began counting how many days until she would be gone.

You can hide your dislike for a while, but eventually you must tell your partner how you feel. I was lucky. My husband also thought his daughter was horrible to live with and wasn't turned off by my feelings. He told her if she couldn't act more civil, she couldn't come back. The message to every woman about to marry a guy with kids is to be aware that your man is a package deal and that the kid is in the package.

Diversity in Other Countries

Not all countries view stepmothers negatively. The French have stopped using the pejorative word for stepmother (*marâtre*) and replaced it with a new word—*belle-mère,* which literally means "beautiful mother."

Children Accepting a Stepmother

Children may blame a new stepmother for destroying the family as they knew it. Particularly if their biological mother encourages this perspective, it will be difficult for a stepmother to change this notion until the children grow up, leave home, and evaluate their stepmother independently. There is also the historical cultural view of the stepmother. This negative view of stepmothers is reflected in the prefix *step*, which in Old English referred to a family relationship caused by death. A stepchild, in essence, was an orphan child, and a stepmother was one who took care of an orphan. This view was enhanced by the structure of remarriages in early European households.

The legacy of stepmother folklore may have contributed to the fact that children have more difficulty accepting a new stepmother than a new stepfather. (It may also be that she is the more active parent, which provides greater opportunity for conflict.) In addition, a stepchild may feel the need to keep an emotional distance in the relationship with the stepmother so as not to incur the anger of the biological mother.

Lou Everett (2000), a specialist who works with stepfamilies, recommends that children remember their stepmother on Mother's Day. "The card doesn't have to say 'Mom' on it. Just something to express your appreciation . . . how great the cookies were that she baked or how happy she makes your dad. Those things mean so much to the stepmother."

Resenting Alimony and Child Support

In addition to the potential problems of not liking the partner's children, there may be problems of alimony and child support. As noted earlier, it is not unusual for a wife to become upset when her husband mails one-quarter or one-third of his income to his former wife. This amount of money is often equal to the current wife's earnings. Some wives in this position see themselves as working for their husband's ex-wife—a perception that may create negative feelings.

Her New Partner and How Her Children Accept Him

For some remarried wives, two main concerns are how her new husband accepts her children and how her children accept him. The ages of the children are important in these adjustments. If the children are young (age 3 or younger), they will usually accept any new adult in the natural parent's life. On the other hand, if the children are in adolescence, they are most likely struggling for independence from their natural parents and may not want any new authority figures in their lives.

In regard to whether a new spouse will accept and invest in her children, Hofferth and Anderson (2003) found that a new husband was more likely to do so if he did not already have and was not already supporting nonresidential children from a prior relationship. Hofferth and Anderson hypothesized that, from a biological perspective, such a father did not invest as heavily in the new family because it did not facilitate reproduction of new offspring.

Having Another Child

A national study of women in second marriages revealed that about two-thirds have a baby within six years after remarriage (Wineberg 1992). When this baby is a first biological baby, stepmothers report greater dissatisfaction with their stepchildren. Their time with their stepchildren is also diminished with the birth of a new baby (hence, stepchildren do not seem to benefit from a half-sibling) (Stewart 2005a). This same phenomenon is also true for first-time fathers and may be a function of having to choose between one's biological children and stepchildren in making certain decisions. "Evolutionary views of parental psychology suggest that stepparents have a genetic propensity to express greater solicitude toward

Child Support and Second Families

The court system is biased against men who have children in second marriages. A man who has been married before and who has children from that marriage is required to pay child support for those children at the expense of children he has in a second marriage. For example, a divorced father of two children earning $40,000 per year would normally be required to pay 25 percent of his gross income, or $10,000, annually in child support (and his ex-wife may still get the tax deduction of the children as dependents). Should he remarry and have two additional children with his new wife, the needs of those children in the second marriage are irrelevant—the man must still pay $10,000 in child support for his first two children.

Moreover, if the man's income increases or the needs of the children in his first marriage increase (excessive medical bills), the man's ex-wife can petition the court and have his child support payments increased. Again, the courts do not recognize the fact that the man has other children in his second marriage who have clothing, food, and medical needs. Indeed, "second family children are considered hardships and their needs are given consideration only after the needs of the children in the first

family are satisfied," notes Dianna Thompson. She is the founder of Second Wives Crusade, an organization for women married to men who have children from previous marriages. She discovered, to her dismay, that her husband's child support obligations to the children in his first marriage were calculated without consideration for their own children. This is the law in all fifty states. Thompson is lobbying legislators to recognize the bias against children in second marriages and encouraging them to adopt new laws to protect all children—not just those who happen to be born of first marriages.

Your Opinion?

1. To what degree do you believe a father should be financially obligated to his first children before providing money for his second set of children?
2. What laws should be passed in regard to how money is to be distributed?
3. Should the second wife's income be considered in deciding how much a father should pay for child support to his first wife?

Source

Dianna Thompson, founder of Second Wives Crusade

---

their biological children than toward stepchildren" (MacDonald and DeMaris 1996, 23).

In spite of the decreased satisfaction with one's stepchildren, having a child in a second marriage is associated with increasing the stability of the relationship and reducing the probability of divorce (Wineberg 1992). Wineberg suggested that "couples with a mutual birth may tolerate more marital stress before considering divorce than couples with no mutual children" (p. 885). Remarried spouses who have another child soon discover how biased our society is against remarriages and the children born into these marriages (see Social Policy section on top of page).

Although we have discussed the stepmother and her adjustment to her stepchildren, a biological mother has her own unique feelings and adjustments. One such mother lamented that she now had to share her daughter with a woman her husband left her for and that this was a very difficult adjustment. "I had a particularly hard time when she took my daughter shopping with her on their vacation during Christmas. . . . I wanted to share that with her. And his new wife's name was 'Star' and almost my daughter's age, to top it off" (personal correspondence).

The New Stepfather

Men in stepfamilies may or may not have children from a previous relationship. Three possible stepfamily combinations include a man with children married to a woman without children, a man with children married to a woman with children, and a man without children married to a woman with children. Men in stepfamilies are, in some ways, like men in biological families. They tend to be less involved in child care and spend less time with children than the stepmother or the biological mother (Kyungok 1994). Men in stepfamilies are also different

Parental Status Inventory*

The Parental Status Inventory (PSI) is a fourteen-item inventory that measures the degree to which respondents consider their stepfather to be a parent on an 11-point scale from 0 percent to 100 percent. Read each of the following statements and circle the percentage indicating the degree to which you regard the statement as true.

1. I think of my stepfather as my father. (0%, 10, 20, 30, 40, 50%, 60, 70, 80, 90, 100%)

2. I am comfortable when someone else refers to my stepfather as my father or dad. (0%, 10, 20, 30, 40, 50%, 60, 70, 80, 90, 100%)

3. I think of myself as his daughter/son. (0%, 10, 20, 30, 40, 50%, 60, 70, 80, 90, 100%)

4. I refer to him as my father or dad. (0%, 10, 20, 30, 40, 50%, 60, 70, 80, 90, 100%)

5. He introduces me as his son/daughter. (0%, 10, 20, 30, 40, 50%, 60, 70, 80, 90, 100%)

6. I introduce my mother and him as my parents. (0%, 10, 20, 30, 40, 50%, 60, 70, 80, 90, 100%)

7. He and I are just like father and son/daughter. (0%, 10, 20, 30, 40, 50%, 60, 70, 80, 90, 100%)

8. I introduce him as "my father" or "my dad." (0%, 10, 20, 30, 40, 50%, 60, 70, 80, 90, 100%)

9. I would feel comfortable if he and I were to attend a father-daughter/father-son function, such as a banquet, baseball game, or cookout, alone together. (0%, 10, 20, 30, 40, 50%, 60, 70, 80, 90, 100%)

10. I introduce him as "my mother's husband" or "my mother's partner." (0%, 10, 20, 30, 40, 50%, 60, 70, 80, 90, 100%)

11. When I think of my mother's house, I consider him and my mother to be parents to the same degree. (0%, 10, 20, 30, 40, 50%, 60, 70, 80, 90, 100%)

12. I consider him to be a father to me. (0%, 10, 20, 30, 40, 50%, 60, 70, 80, 90, 100%)

13. I address him by his first name. (0%, 10, 20, 30, 40, 50%, 60, 70, 80, 90, 100%)

14. If I were choosing a greeting card for him, the inclusion of the words *father* or *dad* in the inscription would prevent me from choosing the card. (0%, 10, 20, 30, 40, 50%, 60, 70, 80, 90, 100%)

Scoring

First, reverse the scores for items 10, 13, and 14. For example, if you circled a 90, change the number to 10; if you circled a 60, change the number to 40;p and so on. Add the percentages and divide by 14. A 0 percent reflects that you do not regard your stepdad as your parent at all. A 100 percent reflects that you totally regard your stepdad as your parent. The percentages between 0 percent and 100 percent show the gradations from no regard to total regard of your stepdad as parent.

Norms

Respondents in two studies (one in Canada and one in America) completed the scale. The numbers of respondents in the studies were 159 and 156, respectively, and the average score in the respective studies was 45.66 percent. Between 40 percent and 50 percent of both Canadians and Americans viewed their stepfather as their parent.

*Developed by Dr. Susan Gamache. 2000. Hycroft Medical Centre, #217, 3195 Granville Street, Vancouver, B.C., Canada, V6H 3K2 gamache@interchange .ubc.ca. Details on construction of the scale including validity and reliability are available from Dr. Gamache. The PSI Scale is used in this text the permission of Dr. Gamache and may not be used otherwise (except as in class student exercises) without written permission.

from those in nuclear families in that stepchildren often want them to respect the relationship they have with their biological dad rather than the new stepfather as a new dad (Bray and Kelly 1998).

Parental status refers to the degree to which a stepparent is considered to be a parent to a stepchild. The following Self-Assessment addresses the degree to which stepchildren view their stepfather as a parent. (Although the scale was developed for stepfathers and would not be valid for other uses, you might try it for other family relationships such as stepmothers, stepsiblings, and stepgrandparents.)

The Man with Children Who Marries a Woman without Children

Men with biological children enter stepfamilies with an appreciation for the role of parent, some skills in fathering (one would hope), and a bond with a child or children who usually live with the biological mother. The latter may mean a grieving father who not only misses his children but who also experiences a number of push-pull factors that influence how involved he is in the lives of his stepchildren.

Men with children typically want their new wife to bond with their children and actively participate in their care. Such an expectation places the new wife in

My early reaction to my new stepfamily was typical: "If I can just survive until the children leave home."

James Eckler, stepfather

the role of the "instant mother," which may backfire if his children reject her. Because a new wife in the role of new mother has typically spent limited time with her partner's children, it is important that he allow sufficient time (two years to seven years) for a relationship to develop. Although this is rare, some women may want nothing to do with their partner's children and may be jealous of the time and money he spends on them. One husband reported, "She was jealous of everything I did with my kids; our marriage ended over it."

Another concern of a father who marries a woman without children is whether she will want children of her own. Often she does (and maybe more than one), but the man who already has children may be less interested. Nevertheless, it is not unusual for men to have additional children with a new wife.

The Man with Children Who Marries a Woman with Children

A man living with children from a previous relationship is most likely to marry a woman with children (Goldscheider and Sassler 2006). Doing so not only results in multiple sets of relationships but also increases his involvement with his new wife's issue. This was the conclusion of a team of researchers who studied the family context of sixty stepfathers:

> [S]tepfathers may be drawn closer to their stepchildren, and they may have fewer negative attitudes toward them because of the strategies they adopt in striving to treat both sets of children in an equitable manner. The presence of their biological children in the household may, in effect, force them to parent to a greater extent than if they had merely been absorbed into a pre-existing family. It becomes incumbent upon them to constitute a viable living pattern and take a more active role with regard to all children in the household. This may lead them to minimize negative thoughts and feelings about their stepchildren and also to exaggerate positive attitudes about stepchildren in the interests of fairness. (Palisi et al. 1991, 102)

MacDonald and DeMaris (2002) also found that the less involved a biological father is, the more involved a stepfather will be. The more involved a stepfather is, the greater the level of reported satisfaction.

The Man without Children Who Marries a Woman with Children

A man without children is less likely to marry a woman with children than to marry a woman without children (Goldscheider and Sassler 2006). The adjustments of a never previously married, divorced, or widowed man without children who marries a woman with children are probably the most difficult and are related to her children, their acceptance of him, and his awareness that his wife is emotionally bonded to her children. Unlike childfree marital partners who are bonded only to each other, a husband entering a relationship with a woman who has children must accept her attachment with her children from the outset. New partners may view such bonding differently. One man said that such concern for her own children was a sign of a caring and nurturing person. "I wouldn't want to live with anyone who didn't care about her kids." Another said, "I felt like an outsider. . . . I couldn't stand the noise and disruption that children involve. I was used to a very quiet, ordered life—that is the exact opposite of what children in the house are like."

Lou Everett (1998) interviewed six stepfathers and identified two primary factors that contribute to a positive stepfather-stepchild relationship:

1. *Active involvement in teaching the stepchild something mutually valued.* Just spending time with a stepchild (eating meals, watching television) had no positive effect on the relationship. Teaching the stepchild (for example, how to skate, fish, fly a kite) made a stepfather feel as though he was contributing to the development of the stepchild and endeared the stepchild to the stepfather.

2. *An intense love relationship between the stepfather and the biological mother of the stepchild.* "Men who love their wives are more tolerant of their stepchildren,"

observed Dr. Everett. Marsiglio (1992) analyzed data from 195 men in stepfamilies and observed that, like the stepfathers in the Everett study, the men reported more positive relationships with stepchildren to the degree that they were happy with their partner. In addition, 55 percent reported that it was "somewhat true" or "definitely true" that "having stepchildren is just as satisfying as having your own children" (p. 204). Men who were living with their partners had perceptions of their stepfather role similar to those of married men.

The following are some questions a man without children (who is considering marriage) might ask a woman who has children:

a. *How do you expect me to relate to your children? Am I supposed to be their friend, daddy, or something else?* Men who develop a relationship first with their stepchild before they start disciplining the child report more positive outcomes (Bray and Kelly 1998).

b. *How do you feel about having another child? How many additional children are you interested in having?*

c. *How much money do you get in alimony and child support from your ex-husband? When do these payments stop?*

d. *What expenses of the children do you expect me to pay for? Who is going to pay for their college expenses?* In essence, a mother receiving child support from a biological father may create the illusion for the potential stepfather that the former husband will take care of the children's expenses. In reality, child support payments cover only a fraction of what is actually spent on a child; consequently, the new stepfather may feel burdened with more financial responsibility for his stepchildren than he bargained for. This may engender negative feelings toward the wife in a new marriage relationship.

The Stepfather and Biological Father Relationship

Marsiglio and Hinojosa (2007) interviewed forty-six stepfathers and noted an emerging new trend in stepfathers. The researchers observed engaging stepfathers whose goals are to support the biological father and co-father with him, unlike an aloof stepfather who is threatened by the biological father and who maintains a distance.

> *Some stepfathers in our diverse sample of stepfamilies shared stories illustrating how they express a cooperative style of "co-fathering" in minor as well as significant ways. They discourage others from making disparaging remarks about the father in front of children or they say nice things about the father, jump in to defend the father if circumstances call for it, give advice on how to communicate with the father, or create opportunities for the father to spend time with his child. In addition, when stepfathers are open to discussing the father or seeing representations of his existence displayed in the household (e.g., photographs, memorabilia), they foster an environment conducive to the father maintaining healthy ties with his child or the child adjusting well to the deceased/estranged father.* (p. 858)

Children in Stepfamilies

National Data

About 10 percent of all children live in stepfamilies (Furukawa 1994). Of these children, 86 percent live with their biological mother and stepfather; 14 percent live with their biological father and stepmother (Rutter 1994).

Research confirms that, of the children growing up in stepfamilies (see the previous National Data section), "80 percent . . . are doing well. Children in stable stepfamilies look very much like those reared in stable first families" (Pasley 2000, 6).

Mackay (2005) compared children from intact and nonintact homes and found that the latter were "worse off." However, the differences between the groups were not large and were moderated by loss of income following the divorce, conflict between the parents, declines in mental health of custodial mothers, and compromised parenting (reduced attentiveness of parents due to their coping with their own adult issues).

Similarly, Ruschena et al. (2005) compared longitudinal data on adolescents whose parents divorced or remarried versus those whose parents stayed married and found no significant group differences with regard to behavioral and emotional adjustment concurrently or across time, nor on academic outcomes and social competence. The researchers commented on the amazing resiliency of children as they transition through different family contexts. As noted previously, the psychological well-being of the parents who have gone through divorce or remarriage is predictive of a positive outcome for the adjustment of the children in the new stepfamily structure (Willetts and Maroules 2005). Children, particularly nonminority children, specifically benefit economically from a remarriage or cohabitation of their parents (Manning and Brown 2006).

Stepchildren have viewpoints and must make adjustments of their own when their parents remarry. They have experienced the transition from living in a family with both biological parents to either living alone with one parent (usually the mother) or alternating between the homes of both parents. When their parents remarry, they must adjust again to living with two new sets of stepparents and stepsiblings.

"The biggest source of problems for kids in stepfamilies is parental conflict left over from the first marriage," noted Rutter (1994, 32). "Study after study shows that divorce and remarriage do not harm children—parental conflict does" (p. 33). Children caught in the conflict between their parents find being loyal to both parents impossible. Children temporarily resolve conflicts by siding with one parent at the expense of the relationship with the other parent. No one wins—children feel bad for abandoning a loving parent; the parent who has been tossed aside feels deprived of the opportunity for a close parent-child relationship; and the custodial parent runs the risk that the children, as adults, may resent being prevented from developing or continuing a relationship with the other parent.

Feelings of Abandonment, Divided Loyalties, New Discipline, and Stepsiblings

Children in stepfamilies often experience problems revolving around feeling abandoned, having divided loyalties, discipline, and stepsiblings. Some stepchildren feel that they have been abandoned twice—once when their parents got divorced and again when the parents turned their attention to new marital partners. One adolescent explained:

> It hurt me when my parents got divorced and my dad moved out. I really missed him and felt he really didn't care about me. But my sister and me adjusted with just my mom, and when everything was going right again, she got involved with this new guy and we were left with baby-sitters all the time. My dad also got involved with a new woman. I feel my sister and I have lost both parents in two years.

Coping with feelings of abandonment is not easy. It is best if the parents assure the children that the divorce was not the children's fault and that both parents love them a great deal. In addition, parents should be careful to find a balance between spending time with their new partner and spending time with their children. This translates into spending some alone time with their children.

Some children experience abandonment yet again if their parents' second marriage ends in divorce. They may have established a close relationship with the new stepparent only to find the relationship disrupted. Relationships with the stepgrandparents may also become strained. Stepgrandparents may be enormous sources of emotional support for children, but a divorce can interrupt this support.

Divided loyalties represent another issue children must deal with in stepfamilies. Sometimes children develop an attachment to a stepparent that is more positive than the relationship with the natural parent of the same sex. When these feelings develop, children may feel they are in a bind. One adolescent boy explained:

> *My real dad left my mother when I was 6, and my mom remarried. My stepdad has always been good to me, and I really prefer to be with him. When my dad comes to pick me up on weekends, I have to avoid talking about my stepdad because my dad doesn't like him. I guess I love my dad, but I have a better relationship with my stepdad.*

For some adolescents, the more they care for the stepparent, the guiltier they feel, so they may try to hide their attachment. The stepparent may be aware of both positive and negative feelings coming from the child. Ideally, both the biological parent and the stepparent should encourage the child to have a close relationship with the other parent.

Discipline is another issue for stepchildren. "Adjusting to living with a new set of rules from a stepparent," "accepting discipline from a stepparent," and "dealing with the expectations of a stepparent" are situations that 80 percent of more than a hundred adolescents in stepfamilies said they had experienced (Lutz 1983). As stated earlier, at least two studies have identified that children have a more difficult time adjusting to a stepmother (Fine and Kurdek 1992), probably because the woman is more often in the role of the active parent, which increases the potential for conflict with the child. Data also suggest that stepfathers in stepfamilies are less involved in the day-to-day interaction with children than stepmothers in stepfamilies, so the opportunity for conflict with stepfathers may be less (Fisher et al. 2003). Therapists who work with stepfamilies encourage stepparents to discipline *their own* children only.

Siblings can also be a problem for stepchildren as they compete for parental approval, space, and shared materials (for example, the TV). Children who are already in a house may feel imposed upon and threatened. Children who are entering may feel out of place and that they do not belong.

Moving between Households

Other issues unique to stepchildren include moving back and forth between households. Though this is sometimes a structured transition, it may also be an issue that children use to manipulate the parents. In effect, they communicate to each parent that they will move in with the other parent if they don't get their way. Parents in conflict with each other are easy prey for this destructive ploy. They should be alert to manipulation and avoid it.

Ambiguity of the Extended Family

A final issue for children in stepfamilies is their ambiguous place in the extended family system of the new stepparent. Although some parents and siblings of the new stepparent welcome a new stepchild into the extended family system, others may ignore the child because they are busy enough with their own grandchildren and children. In other cases, a biological parent may socialize the children to not accept the new stepgrandparents and stepparents or uncles: "My mom told us not to be fooled by dad's new wife's parents and siblings—that they really didn't care about us. I now know that she was just trying to get back at my dad. She knew that our not being open to a new family would make him sad. In effect my mom deprived us of getting to know some really great people." Stewart (2005b) noted that boundary ambiguity, who is regarded as in or out of the family, is much more prevalent in stepfamilies. When stepchildren grow up, the ambiguity continues. Hans et al. (2009) noted that adult offspring feel less responsible to provide economic help to older stepparents than parents.

Stepfamily living is often difficult for everyone involved: remarried spouses, children, even ex-spouses, grandparents, and in-laws. Though some of the problems begin to level out after a few years, others may take longer. Many couples become impatient with the unanticipated problems that are slow to abate, and they divorce.

Developmental Tasks for Stepfamilies

A **developmental task** is a skill that, if mastered, allows a family to grow as a cohesive unit. Developmental tasks that are not mastered will edge the family closer to the point of disintegration. Some of the more important developmental tasks for stepfamilies are discussed in this section.

Acknowledge Losses and Changes

As noted previously, each stepfamily member has experienced the loss of a spouse or a biological parent in the home. Family members experience significant losses of an attachment figure (Marano 2000). These losses are sometimes compounded by home, school, neighborhood, and job changes. Feelings about these losses and changes should be acknowledged as important and consequential. In addition, children should not be required to love their new stepparent or stepsiblings (and vice versa). Such feelings will develop only as a consequence of positive interaction over an extended period of time. Resiliency in stepfamilies is also facilitated by having a strong marriage, support from family and friends, and good communication (Greeff and Du Toit 2009).

Preserving original relationships is helpful in reducing a child's grief over loss. It is sometimes helpful for the biological parent and child to take time to nurture their relationship apart from stepfamily activities. This will reduce the child's sense of loss and any feelings of jealousy toward new stepsiblings.

Nurture the New Marriage Relationship

It is critical to the healthy functioning of a new stepfamily that the new spouses nurture each other and form a strong unit. Indeed, the adult dyad is vulnerable because the couple had no childfree time upon which to build a common base (Pacey 2005). Once a couple develops a core relationship, they can communicate, cooperate, and compromise with regard to the various issues in their new blended family. Too often spouses become child-focused and neglect the relationship on which the rest of the family depends. Such nurturing translates into spending time alone with each other, sharing each other's lives, and having fun with each other. One remarried couple goes out to dinner at least once a week without the children. "If you don't spend time alone with your spouse, you won't have one," says one stepparent. Two researchers studied 115 stepfamily couples and found that the husbands tended to rank "spouse" as their number one role (over parent or employee), whereas wives tended to rank "parent" as their number one role (Degarmo and Forgatch 2002).

Integrate the Stepfather into the Child's Life

Stepfathers who become interested in what their stepchild does and who spend time alone with the stepchild report greater integration into the life of the stepchild and the stepfamily. The benefits to both the stepfather and the stepchild in terms of emotional bonding are enormous. In addition, the mother of the child feels closer to her new husband if he has bonded with her offspring.

Allow Time for Relationship between Partner and Children to Develop

In an effort to escape single parenthood and to live with one's beloved, some individuals rush into remarriage without getting to know each other. Not only do they have limited information about each other, but their respective children may also have spent little or no time with their future stepparent. One stepdaughter remarked, "I came home one afternoon to find a bunch of plastic bags in the living room with my soon-to-be stepdad's clothes in them. I had no idea he was moving in. It hasn't been easy." Both adults and children should have had meals together and spent some time in the same house before becoming bonded by marriage as a family. Schrodt et al. (2008) reported the positive effects of daily communication between stepparents and stepchildren. Both reported higher satisfaction when they had frequent daily communication. As noted previously, stepparents are encouraged to discipline their own children because often the stepparent and stepchild have had insufficient time to experience a relationship that allows for discipline from the stepparent.

Have Realistic Expectations

Because of the complexity of meshing the numerous relationships involved in a stepfamily, it is important to be realistic. Dreams of one big happy family often set up stepparents for disappointment, bitterness, jealousy, and guilt. As noted previously, stepfamily members often do not begin to feel comfortable with each other until the third year (Bray and Kelly 1998). Just as nuclear and single-parent families do not always run smoothly, neither do stepfamilies.

> *I've discovered that stepfamilies are kind of like salad dressing. You can shake us up and we blend really well for moments, days, months even. After a while, though, we have a tendency to settle back into original family lines and loyalties.*
>
> Natalie Nichols Gillespie,
> author of *Stepfamily Survival Guide*

WHAT IF?

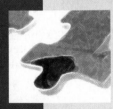

What if Your Children Will Not Accept Your New Spouse or Partner?

It never occurs to new lovers that their children will not embrace their new spouse or partner. After all, the new spouse or partner represents only joy and happiness for the recently divorced person. The children often see it otherwise. They see the new spouse or partner as the final ending of their safe and secure traditional family (mom and dad and the children in one house). Now they must be disrupted every other weekend and, when they are with their nonresident parent (usually the father), the "new woman is there."

Although most children mature and grow to accept their new stepparent, this may take years. In the meantime, the biological parent may need to lower expectations and settle for the children just being polite. The following is a script for a divorced father to give children who are barely civil: "I know the divorce is not what you wanted and you would prefer that your mom and I get back together and live in the same house again. That won't happen and we are both moving on. This means a new spouse for me and stepmother for you. Again, I know you do not want this and did not choose it. I don't require you to love and accept your new stepmother. I do require you to be polite. She will be kind to you and I expect you to be kind to her. That means "thank you" and "please." If you can't be at least polite, it is the end of your cell phone, computer/TV in your room, no friends over and no visiting friends. I will always be polite to your friends and I expect the same from you." Some divorced dads give their children *Daddy's Getting Married* (Fabrega 2006), which identifies for children the advantages of their dad's remarriage.

Accept Your Stepchildren

Rather than wishing your stepchildren were different, accepting them would be more productive. All children have positive qualities; find them and make them the focus of your thinking. Stepparents may communicate acceptance of their stepchildren through verbal praise and positive or affectionate statements and gestures. In addition, stepparents may communicate acceptance by engaging in pleasurable activities with their stepchildren and participating in daily activities such as homework, bedtime preparation, and transportation to after-school activities.

Funder (1991) studied 313 parents who had been separated for five to eight years and who had become involved with new partners. In general, the new partners were very willing to be involved in the parenting of their new spouses' children. Such involvement was highest when the children lived in the household.

Establish Your Own Family Rituals

Rituals are one of the bonding elements of nuclear families. Stepfamilies may integrate the various family members by establishing common rituals, such as summer vacations, visits to and from extended kin, and religious celebrations. These rituals are most effective if they are new and unique, not mirrors of rituals in the previous marriages and families.

Decide about Money

Money is an issue of potential conflict in stepfamilies because it can be a scarce resource, and several people may want to use it for their respective needs. For example, a father may want a new computer; the mother may want a new car; the mother's children may want bunk beds, dance lessons, and a satellite dish; the father's children may want a larger room, clothes, and a phone. How do the newly married couple and their children decide how money should be spent?

Some stepfamilies put all their resources into one bank and draw out money as necessary without regard for whose money it is or for whose child the money is being spent. Others keep their money separate; the parents have separate incomes and spend them on their respective biological children. Although no one pattern is superior to another, it is important for remarried spouses to agree on whatever financial arrangements they live by.

In addition to deciding how to allocate resources fairly in a stepfamily, remarried couples may face decisions regarding sending the children and stepchildren to college. Remarried couples may also make a will that is fair to all family members.

Give Parental Authority to Your Spouse

Adults should discuss how much authority a stepparent exercises over children before they get married. Some couples divide the authority—both spouses discipline their own children. This is the strategy we recommend. The downside is that stepchildren may test the stepparent in such an arrangement when the biological parent is not around. One stepmother said, "Joe's kids are wild when he isn't here because I'm not supposed to discipline them."

Support the Children's Relationship with Their Absent Parent

A continued relationship with both biological parents is critical to the emotional well-being of children. Ex-spouses and stepparents should encourage children to have a positive relationship with both biological parents. Respect should also be shown for the biological parent's values. Bray and Kelly (1998) note that this is "particularly difficult" to exercise. "But asking a child about an absent parent's policy on movies or curfews shows the child that, despite their differences, his/her mother and father still respect each other" (p. 92).

Cooperate with the Children's Biological Parent and Co-Parent

A cooperative, supportive, and amicable co-parenting relationship between the biological parents and stepparents is a win-win situation for the children and

Lest we forget, some remarried couples do not have children. Neither of these spouses brought children into their marriage.

parents. Otherwise, children are continually caught between the cross fire of the conflicted parental sets.

Support the Children's Relationship with Grandparents

It is important to support children's continued relationships with their natural grandparents on both sides of the family. This is one of the more stable relationships in the child's changing world of adult relationships. Regardless of how ex-spouses feel about their former in-laws, they should encourage their children to have positive feelings for their grandparents. One mother said, "Although I am uncomfortable around my ex-in-laws, I know they are good to my children, so I encourage and support my children spending time with them."

Anticipate Great Diversity

Stepfamilies are as diverse as nuclear families. It is important to let each family develop its own uniqueness. One remarried spouse said, "The kids were grown when the divorces and remarriages occurred, and none of the kids seem particularly interested in getting involved with the others" (Rutter 1994, 68). Ganong et al. (1998) also emphasized the importance of resisting the notion that stepfamilies are not "real" families and that adoption makes them a real family. Indeed, social policies need to be developed that allow for "the establishment of some legal ties between the stepparent and stepchild without relinquishing the biological parent's legal ties" (p. 69).

S U M M A R Y

What is the nature of remarriage in the United States?

Within two years, 75 percent of divorced women and 80 percent of divorced men have remarried. When comparing divorced individuals who have remarried with divorced individuals who have not remarried, the remarried report greater personal and relationship happiness. Most divorced individuals select someone who is divorced to remarry just as widowed individuals select someone who is also widowed to remarry.

Two years is the recommended time from the end of one marriage to the beginning of the next. Among those who have been previously remarried, living together does not seem to disadvantage the couple in terms of having a higher divorce rate. National data reflect that remarriages are more likely than first marriages to end in divorce in the early years of remarriage. After fifteen years, however, second marriages tend to be more stable and happier than first marriages. The reason for this is that remarried individuals tend not to be afraid of divorce and would divorce if unhappy in a second marriage. First-time married individuals may be fearful of divorce and stay married even though they are unhappy.

What is the nature of stepfamilies in the United States?

Stepfamilies represent the fastest-growing type of family in the United States. A blended family is one in which the spouses in a new marriage relationship are blended with the children of at least one of the spouses from a previous marriage.

There is a movement away from the use of the term *blended*, because stepfamilies really do not blend. Although a stepfamily can be created when a never-married or a widowed parent with children marries a person with or without children, most stepfamilies today are composed of spouses who were once divorced.

Stepfamilies differ from nuclear families: the children in nuclear families are biologically related to both parents, whereas the children in stepfamilies are biologically related to only one parent. Also, in nuclear families, both biological parents live with their children, whereas only one biological parent in stepfamilies lives with the children. In some cases, the children alternate living with each parent. Stepism is the assumption that stepfamilies are inferior to biological families. Stepism, like racism, heterosexism, sexism, and ageism, involves prejudice and discrimination.

Stepfamilies go through a set of stages. New remarried couples often expect instant bonding between the new members of the stepfamily. It does not often happen. The stages are fantasy (everyone will love everyone), reality (possible bitter conflict), assertiveness (parents speak their mind), strengthening pair ties (spouses nurture their relationship), and recurring change (stepfamily members know there will continue to be change). Involvement in stepfamily discussion groups such as the Stepfamily Enrichment Program provides enormous benefits.

What are the strengths of stepfamilies?

The strengths of stepfamilies include exposure to a variety of behavior patterns, happier parents, and greater objectivity on the part of the stepparent.

What can women do to ease their transition into stepfamily living?

A new wife must often develop skills for learning to get along with the husband's children, not being resentful of his relationship with his children, and adapting to the fact that one-third to one-half of his net income may be sent to his ex-wife as alimony or child support. The new wife may also want children with her new partner or may bring her own children into the marriage. In the latter case, she is anxious that her new husband will accept her children.

What can men do to ease their transition into stepfamily living?

New stepfathers may confront issues requiring them to get along with their wife's children, pay for many of the expenses of their stepchildren, have their new partner accept their own children, and deal with the issue of having more children.

What are the challenges for children in stepfamilies?

Children must cope with feeling abandoned and with problems of divided loyalties, discipline, and stepsiblings. They may also move between households, and their role in the extended stepfamily may be ambiguous.

What are the developmental tasks of stepfamilies?

Developmental tasks for stepfamilies include nurturing the new marriage relationship, allowing time for partners and children to get to know each other, deciding whose money will be spent on whose children, deciding who will discipline the children and how, and supporting the children's relationship with both parents and natural grandparents. Both sets of parents and stepparents should form a parenting coalition in which they cooperate and actively participate in child rearing.

KEY TERMS

binuclear	developmental task	negative commitment	stepfamily
blended family	homogamy	parental status	stepism
December marriage	mating gradient	step relationships	

The Companion Website for *Choices in Relationships: An Introduction to Marriage and the Family,* Tenth Edition
  www.cengage.com/sociology/knox

Supplement your review of this chapter by going to the Companion Website to take one of the tutorial quizzes, use the flash cards to master key terms, or check out the many other study aids, like crossword puzzles and self-assessments. You'll also find special features such as General Social Survey (GSS) data, Census data, and other resources to help you with that special project or to do some research on your own.

WEB LINKS

Bonus Families (stepfamily resources)
  http://www.bonusfamilies.com/bonus-families.php

Second Wives Club (sisterhood for stepmoms)
  http://www.secondwivesclub.com/

National Stepfamily Resource Center
  http://www.stepfam.org

Stepfamily Network
  http://www.stepfamily.net/

Online Stepfamily Magazine
  http://www.saafamilies.org/yourstepfamily/index.php

REFERENCES

Anderson, E. R. and S. M. Greene. 2005. Transitions in parental repartnering after divorce. *Journal of Divorce & Remarriage* 43:47–62.

Bray, J. H., and J. Kelly. 1998. *Stepfamilies: Love, marriage and parenting in the first decade.* New York: Broadway Books.

Brimhall, A., K. Wampler, and T. Kimball. 2008. Learning from the past, altering the future: A tentative theory of the effect of past relationships on couples who remarry. *Family Process* 47:373–408.

Christian, A. 2005. Contesting the myth of the 'Wicked stepmother': Narrative analysis of an only stepfamily support group. *Western Journal of Communication* 69:27–48.

Clarke, S. C., and B. F. Wilson. 1994. The relative stability of remarriages: A cohort approach using vital statistics. *Family Relations* 43:305–10.

Degarmo, D. S., and M. S. Forgatch. 2002. Identity salience as a moderator of psychological and marital distress in stepfather families. *Social Psychology Quarterly* 65:266–84.

Enright, E. 2004. A house divided. *AARP The Magazine,* July/August, 60.

Everett, Lou. 1998. Factors that contribute to satisfaction or dissatisfaction in stepfather-stepchild relationships. *Perspectives in Psychiatric Care* 34(2):25–35.

———. 2000. Personal communication, East Carolina University, October 12.

Fabrega, M. 2006. *Daddy's getting married.* Hauppauge, NY: Barren's Educational Series.

Fine, M. A., and L. A. Kurdek. 1992. The adjustment of adolescents in stepfather and stepmother families. *Journal of Marriage and the Family* 54:725–36.

Fisher, P. A., L. D. Leve, C. C. O'Leary, and C. Leve. 2003. Parental monitoring of children's behavior: Variation across stepmother, stepfather, and two-parent biological families. *Family Relations* 52:45–52.

Fuller, E., ed. 1970. *2500 Anecdotes for all occasions.* New York: Avenel Books.

Funder, K. 1991. New partners as co-parents. *Family Matters* April:44–46.

Furukawa, S. 1994. The diverse living arrangements of children: Summer 1991. *Current Population Reports,* series P70, no. 38. Washington, DC: U.S. Bureau of the Census.

Ganong, L. H., and M. Coleman. 1994. *Remarried family relationships.* Thousand Oaks, CA: Sage.

Ganong, L. H., M. Coleman, M. Fine, and A. K. McDaniel. 1998. Issues considered in contemplating stepchild adoption. *Family Relations* 47:63–71.

Goetting, A. 1982. The six stations of remarriage: The developmental tasks of remarriage after divorce. *The Family Coordinator* 31:213–22.

Goldscheider, F., and S. Sassler. 2006. Creating stepfamilies: Integrating children into the study of union formation. *Journal of Marriage and the Family* 68:275–91.

Greeff, A. P., and C. Du Toit. 2009. Resilience in remarried families. *The American Journal of Family Therapy* 37:114–26.

Hans, J. D., L. H Ganong, and M. Coleman. 2009. Financial responsibilities toward older parents and stepparents following divorce and remarriage. *Journal of Family and Economic Issues* 30:55–67.

Hofferth, S. L., and K. G. Anderson. 2003. Are all dads equal? Biology versus marriage as a basis for paternal investment. *Journal of Marriage and the Family* 65:213–32.

Knox, D., and M. E. Zusman. 2001. Marrying a man with "baggage": Implications for second wives. *Journal of Divorce and Remarriage* 35:67–80.

Kyungok, Huh. 1994. Father's child care time across family types. In *Families and justice: From neighborhoods to nations*. Proceedings, Annual Conference of the National Council on Family Relations, 4:22.

Leon, K., and E. Angst. 2005. Portrayals of stepfamilies in film: Using media images in remarriage education. *Family Relations* 54:3–23.

Lutz, P. 1983. The stepfamily: An adolescent perspective. *Family Relations* 32:367–75.

MacDonald, W., and A. DeMaris. 1996. Parenting stepchildren and biological children: The effects of stepparent's gender and new biological children. *Journal of Family Issues* 17:5–25.

———. 2002. Stepfather-stepchild relationship quality. *Journal of Family Issues* 23:121–37.

Mackay, R. 2005. The impact of family structure and family change on child outcomes: a personal reading of the research literature. *Social Policy Journal of New Zealand,* March 111–34.

Malia, S. E. C. 2005. Balancing family members' interests regarding stepparent rights and obligations: a social policy challenge. *Family Relations* 54:298–320.

Manning, W. D., and S. Brown. 2006. Children's economic well-being in married and cohabiting parent families. *Journal of Marriage and the Family* 68:345–62.

Marano, H. E. 2000. Divorced? Don't even think of remarrying until you read this. *Psychology Today,* March/April, 56–64.

Marsiglio, W. 1992. Stepfathers with minor children living at home. *Journal of Family Issues* 13:195–214.

Marsiglio, W., and R Hinojosa 2007. Managing the multifather family: Stepfathers as father allies. *Journal of Marriage and Family* 69:845–62.

Masheter, C. 1999. Examples of commitment in postdivorce relationships between spouses. In *Handbook of interpersonal commitment and relationship stability,* ed. J. M. Adams and W. H. Jones, 293–306. New York: Academic/Plenum Publishers.

McCarthy, B. W., and R. L. Ginsberg. 2007. Second marriages: Challenges and risks. *The Family Journal* 15:119–23.

Michaels, M. L. 2000. The stepfamily enrichment program: A preliminary evaluation using focus groups. *American Journal of Family Therapy* 28:61–73.

Pacey, S. 2005. Step change: the interplay of sexual and parenting problems when couples form stepfamilies. *Sexual & Relationship Therapy* 20:359–69.

Palisi, B. J., M. Orleans, D. Caddell, and B. Korn. 1991. Adjustment to stepfatherhood: The effects of marital history and relations with children. *Journal of Divorce and Remarriage* 14:89–106.

Papernow, P. L. 1988. Stepparent role development: From outsider to intimate. In *Relative strangers,* ed. William R. Beer, 54–82. Lanham, MD: Rowman and Littlefield.

Pasley, K. 2000. Stepfamilies doing well despite challenges. *National Council on Family Relations Report* 45:6–7.

Poortman, A., and T. H. Lyngstad. 2008. Dissolution risks in first and higher order marital and cohabiting unions. *Social Science Research* 36:1431–47.

Prather, J. E. 2008. Brave new stepfamilies: Diverse paths toward stepfamily living. *Contemporary Sociology* 37:33–35.

Ruschena, E., M. Prior, A. Sanson, and D. Smart. 2005. A longitudinal study of adolescent adjustment following family transitions. *Journal of Child Psychology & Psychiatry & Allied Disciplines* 46:353–63.

Rutter, Virginia. 1994. Lessons from stepfamilies. *Psychology Today,* May/June 27:30.

Schrodt, P., J. Soliz, and D. O. Braithwaite. 2008. A social relations model of everyday talk and relational satisfaction in stepfamilies. *Communication Monographs* 75:190–202.

Stewart, S. D. 2005a. How the birth of a child affects involvement with stepchildren. *Journal of Marriage and the Family* 67:461–73.

Stewart, S. D. 2005b. Boundary ambiguity in stepfamilies. *Journal of Family Issues* 26:1002–29.

Swallow, W. 2004. *The triumph of love over experience: A memoir of remarriage.* New York: Hyperion/Theia.

Teachman, J. 2008. Complex life course patterns and the risk of divorce in second marriages. *Journal of Marriage and Family* 70:294–306.

Tillman, K. H. 2008. "Non-traditional" siblings and the academic outcomes of adolescents *Social Science Research* 37:88–101.

Vinick, B. 1978. Remarriage in old age. *The Family Coordinator* 27:359–63.

Vukalovich, D., and N. Caltabiano 2008. The effectiveness of a community group intervention program on adjustment to separation and divorce. *Journal of Divorce & Remarriage* 48:145–68.

Willetts, M. C., and N. G. Maroules. 2005. Parental reports of adolescent well-being: Does marital status matter? *Journal of Divorce and Remarriage* 43:129–49.

Wineberg, H. 1992. Childbearing and dissolution of the second marriage. *Journal of Marriage and the Family* 54:879–87.

chapter 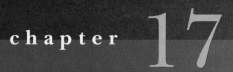 17

Life's a short trip. You'll find out.
You were seventeen yesterday.
You'll be fifty tomorrow.

Rodney Dangerfield, comedian

Relationships in the Later Years

Contents

True or False?

1. Good physical health is the single most important determinant of an elderly person's reported happiness.

2. Some researchers predict that extending life *hundreds* of years will be possible.

3. As individuals age, they become more inflexible and less tolerant.

4. Housing for the elderly is inadequate. Over sixty percent of the elderly live in housing units that are inadequate.

5. For the elderly, a drop in sexual interest and activity is associated with a decrease in marital satisfaction.

Answers: **1.** T **2.** T **3.** F **4.** F **5.** F

Age is a question of mind over matter. If you don't mind, it doesn't matter.

Satchel Paige, baseball player

Legendary screen actress Katharine Hepburn died at age 97. Her biographer, Scott Berg (2003), spent the last twenty years of Hepburn's life as a close friend. During one of their numerous after-dinner conversations, he asked her, "So what do you think it's all about? Life, I mean. What's the purpose?" Her reply . . .

> *To work hard and to love someone. And to have some fun. And if you're lucky, you keep your health and somebody loves you back.* (p. 366)

Work, loving, and being loved . . . not a bad recipe for a full life. However, the end of life comes for us all, and we have challenges as we age, including the cost of even a brief stay in the hospital, the cost of prescription medication, and care in a retirement or long-term care facility. Although most young couples marrying today rarely give a thought to their own aging, the care of their aging parents is an issue that looms ahead.

About 13 percent of the 310 million individuals in the United States are age 65 and older (*Statistical Abstract of the United States, 2009*, Table 11). This represents about 40 million "elderly." By 2030, this percentage will grow to 20 percent of the population in the United States (Willson 2007). In this chapter, we focus on the factors that confront individuals and couples as they age and the dilemma of how to care for aging parents. We begin by looking at the concept of age.

Age and Ageism

All societies have a way to categorize their members by age. And all societies provide social definitions for particular ages.

The Concept of Age

A person's **age** may be defined chronologically, physiologically, psychologically, sociologically, and culturally. Chronologically, an "old" person is defined as one who has lived a certain number of years. How many years it takes to be regarded as old varies with one's own age. Children of 12 may regard siblings of 18 as old—and their parents as "ancient." Teenagers and parents may regard themselves as "young" and reserve the label "old" for their grandparents' generation.

Chronological age has obvious practical significance in everyday life. Bureaucratic organizations and social programs identify chronological age as a criterion of certain social rights and responsibilities. One's age determines the

Table 17.1 Life Expectancy

Year	White Males	Black Males	White Females	Black Females
2010	76.5	70.2	81.3	77.2
2015	77.1	71.4	81.8	78.2
2020	77.7	72.6	82.4	79.2

Source: *Statistical Abstract of the United States, 2009*, 128th ed. Washington, DC: U.S. Bureau of the Census, 2009, Table 100.

right to drive, vote, buy alcohol or cigarettes, and receive Social Security and Medicare benefits.

Age has meaning in reference to the society and culture of the individual. In ancient Greece and Rome, where the average life expectancy was 20 years, one was old at 18; similarly, one was old at 30 in medieval Europe and at age 40 in the United States in 1850. In the United States today, however, people are usually not considered old until they reach age 65. However, our society is moving toward new chronological definitions of "old." Three groups of the elderly are the "young-old," the "middle-old," and the "old-old." The young-old are typically between the ages of 65 and 74; the middle-old, 75 to 84, and the old-old, 85 and beyond. Current life expectancy is shown in Table 17.1.

The age of a person influences that person's view of when a person becomes "old." Individuals aged 18 to 35 identify 50 as the age when the average man or woman becomes "old." However, those between the ages of 65 and 74 define "old" as 80 (Cutler 2002). Tanner (2005) noted that views of the elderly are changing from people who are needy and dependent to people who are active and resourceful. Research is underway to extend life. Dr. Aubrey de Grey of the Department of Genetics, University of Cambridge, predicted that continued research will make adding *hundreds* of years to one's life possible. Maher and Mercer (2009) noted that the most optimistic predictions are that we are two or three decades away from significant breakthroughs (Ray Kurzweil says we are forty-nine years away). Maher and Mercer (2009) also note the paths are known via genetic engineering (we must learn how to switch off the genes responsible for aging), tissue or organ replacement (knees and kidneys are already being replaced), and the merging of computer technology with human biology (hearing and seeing are now being improved). Should the human lifespan be extended hundreds of years, imagine the impact on marriage—"till death do us part"?

Some individuals have been successful in delaying the aging process. Frank Lloyd Wright, the famous architect, enjoyed the most productive period of his life between the ages 80 and 92. George Burns and Bob Hope were active into their nineties. Fitness guru Jack LaLanne remains active in his mid-nineties. Boulton-Lewis et al. (2006) found that continuing to learn was associated with the elderly continuing to feel healthy.

Physiologically, people are old when their auditory, visual, respiratory, and cognitive capabilities decline significantly. Indeed, Siedlecki (2007) confirmed that increased age is associated with increased difficulty in retrieving information. Becoming "disabled" is associated with being "old." Individuals tend to see themselves as disabled when their driver's licenses are taken away and when home health care workers come to their home to care for them (Kelley-Moore et al. 2006). Sleep changes occur for the elderly including going to bed earlier, waking up during the night, and waking up earlier in the morning, as well as issues like restless legs syndrome, snoring, and obstructive sleep apnea (Wolkove et al. 2007).

People who need full-time nursing care for eating, bathing, and taking medication properly and who are placed in nursing homes are thought of as being old. Failing health is the criterion the elderly use to define themselves as

This 85-year-old man is on an ocean cruise whooping it up.

The young know the rules, but the old know the exceptions.

Oliver Wendell Holmes, American jurist

old (O'Reilly 1997), and successful aging is typically defined as maintaining one's health, independence, and cognitive ability. Jorm et al. (1998) observed that the prevalence of successful aging declines steeply from age 70 to age 80. Garrett and Martini (2007) noted the impact on the U.S. health care system as increasing numbers of baby boomers age.

People who have certain diseases are also regarded as old. Although younger individuals may suffer from Alzheimer's, arthritis, and heart problems, these ailments are more often associated with aging. As medical science conquers more diseases, the physiological definition of aging changes so that it takes longer for people to be defined as "old."

Psychologically, a person's self-concept is important in defining how old that person is. As individuals begin to fulfill the roles associated with the elderly—retiree, grandparent, nursing home resident—they begin to see themselves as aging. Sociologically, once they occupy these roles, others begin to see them as "old." Barrett (2005) analyzed national data of 2,681 midlife respondents to assess how women and men differed in their age identity. Because women were typically pair-bonded with older partners, they typically had younger age identities than men.

Culturally, the society in which an individual lives defines when and if a person becomes old and what being old means. In U.S. society, the period from age 18 through 64 are generally subdivided into young adulthood, adulthood, and middle age. Cultures also differ in terms of how they view and take care of their elderly. Spain is particularly noteworthy in terms of care for the elderly, with eight of ten elderly people receiving care from family members and other relatives. The elderly in Spain report very high levels of satisfaction in the relationships with their children, grandchildren, and friends (Fernandez-Ballesteros 2003).

Perceptions of the Elderly by College Students

Although the elderly tend to view themselves as aging positively (until they become physically debilitated) (Pnina 2007), a team of researchers (Knox et al. 2005) examined how 441 undergraduates viewed the elderly and found gender differences in their perceptions. Significant differences included perceptions of strength (men saw less decline in strength), reaction time (women saw less decline in reaction time), and the perception of the elderly as "dangerous" drivers (women saw the elderly as less dangerous). Analyzing the same data set, Kimuna et al. (2005) found that the more exposure a student had to the elderly, the more positive the perception.

Diversity in Other Countries

Among Asians, the high status of the elderly in the extended family derives from religion. Confucian philosophy, for example, prescribes that all relationships are of the subordinate-superordinate type—husband-wife, parent-child, and teacher-pupil. For traditional Asians to abandon their elderly rather than include them in larger family units would be unthinkable. However, commitment to the elderly may be changing as a result of the Westernization of Asian countries such as China, Japan, and Korea.

Ageism

Every society has some form of **ageism**—the systematic persecution and degradation of people because they are old. Ageism is similar to sexism, racism, and heterosexism. The elderly are shunned, discriminated against in employment, and sometimes victims of abuse. Media portrayals contribute to the negative image of the elderly. They are portrayed as difficult, complaining, and burdensome and are often underrepresented in commercials and comic strips.

Negative stereotypes and media images of the elderly engender **gerontophobia**—a shared fear or dread of the elderly, which may create a self-fulfilling prophecy. For example, an elderly person forgets something and attributes the behavior to age. A younger person, however, engaging in the same behavior, is unlikely to attribute forgetfulness to age, given cultural definitions surrounding the age of the onset of senility. Individuals are also thought to become more inflexible and more conservative as they age. Analysis of national data suggests this is not true. In fact, the elderly become more tolerant (Danigelis et al. 2007).

The negative meanings associated with aging underlie the obsession of many Americans to conceal their age by altering their appearance. With the hope of holding on to youth a little bit longer, aging Americans spend billions of dollars each year on plastic surgery, exercise equipment, hair products, facial creams, and Botox injections.

The latest attempt to reset the aging clock is to have regular injections of human growth hormone (HGH), which promises to lower blood pressure, build muscles without extra exercise, increase the skin's elasticity, thicken hair, and heighten sexual potency. It is part of the regimen of clinics such as Lifespan (in Beverly Hills), which costs $1,000 a month after an initial workup of $5,000. In the absence of long-term data, many physicians remain skeptical—there is no fountain of youth.

Theories of Aging

Gerontology is the study of aging. Table 17.2 identifies several theories, the level (macro or micro) of the theory, the theorists typically associated with the theory, assumptions, and criticisms. As noted, there are diverse ways of conceptualizing the elderly. Currently popular in sociology is the life-course perspective (Willson 2007). This approach examines differences in aging across cohorts by emphasizing that "individual biography is situated within the context of social structure and historical circumstance" (p. 150).

Diversity in Other Countries

Whereas female children in the United States have the most frequent contact and are more involved in the caregiving of their elderly parents than male children, the daughters-in-law in Japan offer the most help to elderly individuals. The female child who is married gives her attention to the parents of her husband (Ikegami 1998).

Eastern cultures emphasize filial piety, which is love and respect toward their parents. **Filial piety** involves respecting parents, bringing no dishonor to parents, and taking good care of parents (Jang and Detzner 1998). Western cultures are characterized by **filial responsibility** emphasizing duty, protection, care, and financial support.

You don't stop laughing because you grow old; you grow old because you stop laughing.

Michael Pritchard, motivational speaker

Table 17.2 Theories of Aging

Name of Theory	Level of Theory	Theorists	Basic Assumptions	Criticisms
Disengagement	Macro	Elaine Cumming William Henry	The gradual and mutual withdrawal of the elderly and society from each other is a natural process. It is also necessary and functional for society that the elderly disengage so that new people can be phased in to replace them in an orderly transition.	Not all people want to disengage; some want to stay active and involved. Disengagement does not specify what happens when the elderly stay involved.
Activity	Macro	Robert Havighurst	People continue the level of activity they had in middle age into their later years. Though high levels of activity are unrelated to living longer, they are related to reporting high levels of life satisfaction.	Ill health may force people to curtail their level of activity. The older a person, the more likely the person is to curtail activity.

(Continued)

Table 17.2 Theories of Aging (*Continued*)

Name of Theory	Level of Theory	Theorists	Basic Assumptions	Criticisms
Conflict	Macro	Karl Marx Max Weber	The elderly compete with youth for jobs and social resources such as government programs (Medicare).	The elderly are presented as disadvantaged. Their power to organize and mobilize political resources such as the American Association of Retired Persons is underestimated.
Age stratification	Macro	M. W. Riley	The elderly represent a powerful cohort of individuals passing through the social system that both affect and are affected by social change.	Too much emphasis is put on age, and little recognition is given to other variables within a cohort such as gender, race, and socioeconomic differences.
Modernization	Macro	Donald Cowgill	The status of the elderly is in reference to the evolution of the society toward modernization. The elderly in premodern societies have more status because what they have to offer in the form of cultural wisdom is more valued. The elderly in modern technologically advanced societies have low status because they have little to offer.	Cultural values for the elderly, not level of modernization, dictate the status of the elderly. Japan has high respect for the elderly and yet is highly technological and modernized.
Symbolic	Micro	Arlie Hochschild	The elderly socially construct meaning in their interactions with others and society. Developing social bonds with other elderly can ward off being isolated and abandoned. Meaning is in the interpretation, not in the event.	The power of the larger social system and larger social structures to affect the lives of the elderly is minimized.
Continuity	Micro	Bernice Neugarten	The earlier habit patterns, values, and attitudes of the individual are carried forward as a person ages. The only personality change that occurs with aging is the tendency to turn one's attention and interest on the self.	Other factors than one's personality affect aging outcomes. The social structure influences the life of the elderly rather than vice versa.

Caregiving for the Frail Elderly—the "Sandwich Generation"

Elderly people are defined as **frail** if they have difficulty with at least one personal care activity or other activity related to independent living; the severely disabled are unable to complete three or more personal care activities. These personal care activities include bathing, dressing, getting in and out of bed, shopping for groceries, and taking medications. About 6.1 percent of the U.S. adult population over the age of 65 are defined as being severely disabled and are not living in nursing homes.

Only 6.8 percent of the frail elderly have long-term health care insurance (Johnson and Wiener 2006). Hence, the bulk of their care falls to the children of these elderly. The term *children* typically means female adult children. Indeed, women account for about two-thirds of all unpaid caregivers (ibid.). The adults who provide **family caregiving** to these elderly parents (and their own children simultaneously) are known as the "**sandwich generation**" because they are in the middle of taking care of the needs of both their parents and children.

Caregiving for an elderly parent has two meanings. One, caregiving refers to providing personal help with the basics of daily living such as helping the parent get in and out of bed, bathing, toileting, and eating. A second form of caregiving refers to instrumental activities such as grocery shopping, money management (including paying bills), and driving the parent to the doctor.

The typical caregiver is a middle-aged married woman who works outside the home. High levels of stress and fatigue may accompany caring for one's elders. Martire and Stephens (2003) noted even higher levels of fatigue and competing demands among women who were both employed and caring for an aging parent. Of a sample of women at midlife (most of whom had children), 55 percent reported that they were providing care to their mothers, and 34 percent were caring for their fathers (Peterson 2002). The number of individuals in the sandwich generation will increase for the following reasons:

1. *Longevity.* The over-85 age group, the segment of the population most in need of care, is the fastest-growing segment of our population.

2. *Chronic disease.* In the past, diseases took the elderly quickly. Today, diseases such as arthritis and Alzheimer's are associated not with an immediate death sentence but a lifetime of managing the illness and being cared for by others. Family caregivers of parents with Alzheimer's note the difficulty of the role: "He's not the man I married," lamented one wife. Hilgeman et al. (2007) noted that having a positive view of taking care of an Alzheimer's patient was associated with experiencing less stress in doing so.

3. *Fewer siblings to help.* The current generation of elderly had fewer children than the elderly in previous generations. Hence, the number of adult siblings to help look after parents is more limited. Only children are more likely to feel the weight of caring for elderly parents alone.

4. *Commitment to parental care.* Contrary to the myth that adult children in the United States abrogate responsibility for taking care of their elderly parents, most children institutionalize their parents only as a last resort. Furthermore, Wells (2000) identified some benefits of caregiving, including a closer relationship to the dependent person and a feeling of enhanced self-esteem. Most of Peterson's (2002) sample of women caring for their parents did not view doing so as a burden. Asian children, specifically Chinese children, are socialized to expect to take care of their elderly. Zhan and Montgomery (2003) observed, "Children were raised for the security of old age" (p. 209).

5. *Lack of support for the caregiver.* Caring for a dependent, aging parent requires a great deal of effort, sacrifice, and decision making on the part of more than 14 million adults in the United States who are challenged with this situation. The emotional toll on the caregiver may be heavy. Guilt (over not doing enough), resentment (over feeling burdened), and exhaustion (over the relentless care demands) are common feelings that are sometimes mixed. One caregiver adult child said, "I must be an awful person to begrudge taking my mother supper, but I feel that my life is consumed by the demands she makes on me, and I have no time for myself, my children, or my husband." Marks et al. (2002) noted an increase in symptoms of depression among a national sample of caregivers (of a child, parent, or spouse). Older caregivers also risk their own health in caring for their aging parents (Wallsten 2000). Caregiving can also be expensive and can devastate a family budget.

Some reduce the strain of caring for an elderly parent by arranging for home health care. This involves having a nurse go to the home of a parent and provide such services as bathing the parent and giving medication. Other services may include taking meals to the elderly (for example, through Meals on Wheels). The National Family Caregiver Support Program, enacted in 2000, provides support services for individuals (including grandparents) who provide family caregiving services. Such services might include eldercare resource and referral services, caregiver support groups, and classes on how to care for an aging parent. In addition, states are increasingly providing family caregivers a tax credit or deduction.

This daughter is preparing pills for her elderly parents.

Offspring who have no help may become overwhelmed and frustrated. Elder abuse, an expression of such frustration, is not unheard of (we discussed elder abuse in Chapter 13). Many wrestle with the decision to put their parents in a nursing home or other long-term care facility. We discuss this issue in the following Personal Choices section.

PERSONAL CHOICES

Should I Put My Parents in a Long-Term Care Facility?

Care of the frail elderly has increasingly shifted from hands-on care by adult children to the management of such care delivered by a nursing home (Willson 2007). Over 1.8 million individuals (over twice as many women as men) over the age of 65 are in a nursing home. Of those over the age of 85, 40 percent are in a nursing home (*Statistical Abstract of the United States, 2009,* Table 72). Factors relevant in deciding whether to care for an elderly parent at home, arrange for nursing home care, or provide another form of long-term care include the following.

1. *Level of care needed.* As parents age, the level of care that they need increases.

An elderly parent who cannot bathe, dress, prepare meals, or be depended on to take medication responsibly needs either full-time in-home care or a skilled nursing facility that provides 24-hour nursing supervision by registered or licensed vocational nurses. Commonly referred to as "nursing homes" or "convalescent hospitals," these facilities provide medical, nursing, dietary, pharmacy, and activity services.

An intermediate-care facility provides eight hours of nursing supervision per day. Intermediate care is less extensive and expensive and generally serves patients who are ambulatory and who do not need care throughout the night.

A skilled nursing facility for special disabilities provides a "protective" or "security" environment to people with mental disabilities. Many of these facilities have locked areas where patients reside for their own protection.

An assisted living facility is for individuals who are no longer able to live independently but who do not need the level of care that a nursing home provides. Although nurses and other health care providers are available, assistance is more typically in the form of meals and housekeeping.

Retirement communities involve a range of options, from apartments where residents live independently to skilled nursing care. These communities allow older adults to remain in one place and still receive the care they need as they age.

2. *Temperament of parent.* Some elderly parents have become paranoid, accusatory, and angry with their caregivers. Family members no longer capable of coping with the abuse may arrange for their parents to be taken care of in a nursing home or other facility.

3. *Philosophy of adult child.* Most children feel a sense of filial responsibility—a sense of personal obligation for the well-being of aging parents. Theoretical explanations for such responsibility include the norm of reciprocity (adult children reciprocate the care they received from their parents), attachment theory (caring results from positive emotions for one's parents), and a moral imperative (caring for one's elderly parents is the right thing to do).

One only child promised his dying father that he would take care of the father's spouse (the child's mother) and not put her in a nursing home. When the mother became 82 and unable to care for herself, the son bought a bed and made the living room of his home the place for his mother to spend the last days of her life. "No nursing home for my mother," he said. This man also had the same philosophy for his mother-in-law and moved her into the home with his wife when she was 94.

Whereas some adult children have the philosophy that they must care for their elderly parents themselves, others prefer to hire the help needed. Their philosophy, in combination with the amount of care needed, the amount of help from other family members, and the commitment to other responsibilities (for example, work), influences their decision.

A crisis in care for the elderly may be looming. In the past, women have taken care of their elderly parents. However, these were women who lived in traditional families where one paycheck took care of a family's economic needs. Women today work out of economic necessity, and quitting work to take care of an elderly parent is becoming less of an option. As more women enter the labor force, less free labor is available to take care of the elderly. Government programs are not in place to take care of the legions of elderly Americans. Who will care for them when both spouses are working full-time? China is facing a similar crisis. Zhan et al. (2008) noted that, due to the unavailability of adult children (for example, China has had the one-child norm), more elderly parents are ending up in nursing homes. This trend will continue.

4. *Length of time for providing care.* Offspring must also consider how long they will be in the role of caring for an aging parent. The duration of caregiving can last from less than a year to more than forty years. About 40 percent of caregivers provide assistance for five or more years; nearly a fifth provide assistance for ten or more years (Family Caregiver Alliance 2006). A team of researchers (Walz and Mitchell 2007) noted that both adult offsping and their parents underestimated the length of time both they and their parents would need full-time care as an older person.

5. *Privacy needs of caregivers.* Some spouses take care of their elderly at home but note the effect on their own marital privacy. A wife who took care of her husband's mother for twelve years in her home said that it was a relief for his mother to die and for them to get their privacy back. Chadiha et al. (2003) found that lower levels of caretaking burden were associated with higher levels of marital functioning. The impact on one's marriage needs to be considered.

6. *Cost.* For private full-time nursing home care, including room, board, medical care, and so on, count on spending $1,000 to $1,500 a week. Because women live longer than men and represent 70 percent of the older population living in poverty, they are more likely to have the need for eldercare and will not have the resources for such care unless provided by their children (Willson 2007). **Medicare**, a federal health insurance program for people 65 and older, was developed for short-term acute hospital care. Medicare generally does not pay for long-term nursing care. In

practice, adult children who arrange for their aging parent to be cared for in a nursing home end up paying for it out of the elder's own funds. After all of these economic resources are depleted, **Medicaid**, a state welfare program for low-income individuals, will pay for the cost of care. A federal law prohibits offspring from shifting the assets of an elderly parent so as to become eligible for Medicaid.

7. *Chain nursing home.* Lucas et al. (2007) found that residents of nursing homes reported higher satisfaction if they were not in a "chain nursing home." Offspring might keep this in mind when selecting a long-term care facility for their parents.

8. *Sexual orientation.* Homosexual elders may be resistant to go to a nursing home because they fear prejudice and discrimination from workers and patients at the facility. Some feel they have to "go back in the closet" (Gallanis 2002).

9. *Wishes or readiness of the elderly.* The elderly should be included in the decision to be cared for in a long-term care facility. Wielink et al. (1997) found that the more frail the elderly person, the more willing the person was to go to a nursing home. Cohen-Mansfield and Wirtz (2007) also noted that characteristics of those "ready" to go into a nursing home included advanced age, depression, and a higher number of psychiatric diagnoses. Once a decision is made for nursing home care, it is important to assess several facilities. Taking a tour of the facility, eating a meal at the facility, and meeting staff are also helpful in making a decision and a smooth transition. Because there is an acute nursing shortage, it is important to find out the ratio of registered nurses per patient. Some elderly adapt well to living in a residential facility, such as a nursing home. They enjoy the community of others of similar age, enjoy visiting others in the nursing home, and reach out to others to make new friends. In essence, they find positive meaning in the nursing home experience.

10. *Other issues.* Whether or not deciding to put one's parent (or spouse) in a nursing home, the elderly person or those with power of attorney should complete a document called an **advance directive** (also known as a **living will**), detailing the conditions under which life support measures should be used (do they want to be sustained on a respirator?). These decisions, made ahead of time, spare the adult children the responsibility of making them in crisis contexts and give clear directives to the medical staff in charge of the elderly person. For example, elderly people can direct that a feeding tube should not be used if they become unable to feed themselves. Hence, by making this decision, the children are spared the decision regarding a feeding tube. A **durable power of attorney**, which gives adult children complete authority to act on behalf of the elderly, is also advised. These documents also help to save countless legal hours, time, and money for those responsible for the elderly. Appendixes D and E present examples of the living will and durable power of attorney.

Finally, adult children may consider buying long-term care insurance (LTCI) to cover what Medicare and many private health care plans do not—"nonmedical" day-to-day care such as bathing or eating for an Alzheimer's parent, as well as nursing home costs. Costs of LTCI begin at about $1,000 a year but vary a great deal depending on the age and health of the insured individual.

As an aside, the first author's mother was 90 when she died. With a husband who had died forty-five years earlier, two adult sons who lived in other states, and no grandchildren or great-grandchildren near, she lived out the last twelve years of her life in a nursing home. There is considerable stigma about children "putting their parents in a nursing home." However, this woman's last years and days were happy ones. Both her mother and younger brother had lived out their last days in a nursing home. Life in a nursing home had become normative. She never complained, was always smiling, and grateful for each day. She loved the food, enjoyed the visits and phone calls, and commented on the helpful care she received from nurses and doctors. Her oldest son was present when she died.

*Sooner or later I am going to die,
but I am not going to retire.*

Margaret Mead, anthropologist

Sources

Cohen-Mansfield, J., and P. W. Wirtz. 2007. Characteristics of adult day care participants who enter a nursing home. *Psychology and Aging* 22:354–60.

Gallanis, T. P. 2002. Aging and the nontraditional family. The University of Memphis Law Center, 32:607–42.

Lucas, J. A., C. A. Levin, T. J. Lowe, and B. Robertson. 2007. The relationship between organizational factors and resident satisfaction with nursing home care and life. *Journal of Aging & Social Policy* 19:125–35.

Statistical Abstract of the United States, 2009. 128th ed. Washington, DC: U.S. Bureau of the Census.

Walz, H. S., and T. E. Mitchell. 2007. Adult children and their parents' expectations of future elder care needs. *Journal of Aging and Health* 19:482–91.

Wielink, G., R. Huijsman, and J. McDonnell. 1997. A study of the elders living independently in the Netherlands. *Research on Aging* 19:174–198.

Willson, A. E. 2007. The sociology of aging. In *21st century sociology: A reference handbook*, ed. Clifton D. Bryant and Dennis L. Peck, 148–55. Thousand Oaks, California: Sage.

Issues Confronting the Elderly

Numerous issues become concerns as people age. In middle age, the issues are early retirement (sometimes forced), job layoffs (recession-related cutbacks), **age discrimination** (older people are often not hired and younger workers are hired to take their place), separation or divorce from a spouse, and adjustment to children leaving home. For some in middle age, grandparenting is an issue if they become the primary caregiver for their grandchildren. As couples move from the middle to the later years, the issues become more focused on income, housing, health, retirement, and sexuality.

Income

For most individuals, the end of life is characterized by reduced income. Social Security and pension benefits, when they exist, are rarely equal to the income a retired person formerly earned.

National Data

The median income of men aged 65 and older is $23,500; women, $13,603 (*Statistical Abstract of the United States, 2009*, Table 680).

Financial planning to provide end-of-life income is important. Kemp et al. (2005) interviewed fifty-one mid- and later-life individuals about their financial planning to identify the conditions under which such planning is initiated. They found catalysts for planning were employer programs and the offering of retirement seminars. Constraints on such planning were losing one's job or unforeseen expenses (in both cases, no resources were available to plan around). Other life events that could be either catalysts or constraints were health changes, death of a spouse, divorce, or remarriage. Some adults buy long-term health care insurance. Such insurance can be costly and does not always cover needed expenses. In Chapter 12, Family and the Economy, we discussed debt management. This skill becomes particularly important for managing one's money so as to have resources for the end of life.

To be caught at the end of life without adequate resources is not unusual. Women are particularly disadvantaged because their work history has often been discontinuous, part-time, and low-paying. Social Security

Diversity in Other Countries

Loss of income is minimized among the elderly Chinese, who receive money from their children. Logan and Bian (2003) noted that money from "children accounts for nearly a third of parents' incomes" (p. 85).

and private pension plans favor those with continuous full-time work histories.

Housing

Of those over the age of 75, 78.7 percent live in and own their own home—hence, most do not live in a nursing home (*Statistical Abstract of the United States, 2009*, Table 950). Home is typically where the elderly have lived in the same neighborhood for years. Even those who do not live in their own home are likely to live in a family setting.

For the most part, the physical housing of the elderly is adequate. Indeed, only 6 percent of the housing units inhabited by the elderly are inadequate. Where deficiencies exist, the most common are inadequate plumbing and heating. However, as individuals age, they find themselves living in homes that are not "elder-friendly." Such elder-friendly homes feature bathroom doors wide enough for a wheelchair, grab bars in the bathrooms, and the absence of stairs (Nicholson 2003). The most recent trend in housing for the elderly is home health care (mentioned previously), as an alternative to nursing home care. In this situation, the elderly person lives in a single-family dwelling, and other people are hired to come in regularly to help with various needs.

Other elderly individuals live in group living or shared housing arrangements, referred to as **cohousing.** Residents essentially plan the communities in which they own a unit and have a common area where they meet for meals several times a week (they typically rotate responsibilities of cooking these meals). The upside of cohousing is companionship with others. The downside is the need to make decisions by consensus on what to do when members can no longer take care of themselves. Silver Sage Village (www.silversagevillage.com) and ElderSpirit Community (www.elderspirit.net) are two such cohousing arrangements.

Some elderly singles choose to maintain their own home even though they are in a partnered relationship. Karlsson and Borell (2005) interviewed 116 elderly men and women living in an increasingly popular arrangement: living apart together (LAT), in which partners retain their own homes although they are involved in a long-term intimate relationship. These researchers focused on the motives of the women who sought to use their homes as a way of establishing boundaries to influence their interaction with partners, friends, and kin. All the women studied seem to prioritize the possibility of keeping their various social relations separate from one another. For example, one widow involved in a new relationship insisted on keeping her house and living apart from her new boyfriend so that she could have her children visit when she wanted and for as long as she wanted. "If I lived with him, he would get upset every time they came around. I wouldn't like that," she said.

Physical Health

Our current cultural value for health is in great contrast to previous times. Film legend Clark Gable drank and smoked heavily and was told by his physicians he was on the way to a coronary. He paid no attention and died of a coronary at age 59. Dean Martin also drank and smoked himself to death.

Good physical health is the single most important determinant of an elderly person's reported happiness (Smith et al. 2002). Though health varies by social class and race, with higher social class whites reporting greater health (Willson 2007), most elderly individuals, even those of advanced years, continue to define themselves as being in good health. Ostbye et al. (2006) studied an elderly population in Cache County, Utah, and found that 80 percent to 90 percent of those aged 65 to 75 were healthy on ten dimensions of health (independent living, vision, hearing, activities of daily living, instrumental activities of daily living, absence of physical illness, cognition, healthy mood, social support and participation, and religious participation and spirituality). Prevalence of excellent and good self-reported

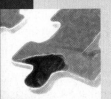
What if Your Spouse Says "No" to Your Mother Living with You?

As parents age and one spouse dies (usually the father), an older adult married child sometimes needs to take the remaining parent into his or her home. When a spouse is adamantly against such a change in living space, some alternatives should be explored: get siblings involved so that the widowed parent spends some time with each adult child, share expenses with siblings for cost of nursing home facility, or share the cost with siblings of hiring a full-time person to live in with the widowed parent. If none of these alternatives are acceptable, a marriage therapist may be needed to move past this impasse.

health decreased with age, to approximately 60 percent among those aged 85 and older. Although most (over 90 percent) of the elderly do not exercise, Morey et al. (2008) studied the elderly ages 65 to 94 and found that the greater their physical activity, the greater their ability to function physically.

Even individuals who have a chronic, debilitating illness maintain a perception of good health as long as they are able to function relatively well. However, when elders' vision, hearing, physical mobility, and strength are markedly diminished, their sense of well-being is often significantly impacted (Smith et al. 2002). For many, the ability to experience the positive side of life seems to become compromised after age 80 (ibid.). Driving accidents also increase with aging. However, unlike teenagers, who also have a high percentage of automobile accidents, the elderly are less likely to die in an accident because they are usually driving at a much slower speed (Pope 2003).

Some elderly become so physically debilitated that questions about the quality of life sometimes lead to consideration of physician-assisted suicide. Useda et al. (2007) compared a group of adults over 50 who attempted suicide versus those who had been successful in killing themselves and found that those in the latter group were more focused, planned, and organized in their movement toward ending their own life. Some debilitated elderly ask their physicians to end their lives. The debilitated elderly may also ask spouses or adult children for help in ending their life. Physician-assisted suicide is addressed in the following Social Policy section.

You gotta love livin, cause dying is a pain in the ass.
Frank Sinatra

Mental Health

Aging also affects mental processes. Elderly people (particularly those 85 and older) more often have a reduced capacity for processing information quickly, for cognitive attention to a specific task, for retention, and for motivation to focus on a task. However, judgment may not be affected, and experience and perspective are benefits to decision making. A team of researchers (Vance et al. 2005) noted that being socially active, which often leads to physical activity, is associated with keeping one's cognitive functioning. Silverstein et al. (2006) also emphasized that the elderly in rural China who live with their children and grandchildren report greater psychological well-being than the elderly who live with just their children. Hispanic elderly are also likely to live with their children, and some elderly grandparents take care of the grandchildren while the parents work outside the home.

Physician-Assisted Suicide for Terminally Ill Family Members

Euthanasia is from the Greek words meaning "good death," or dying without suffering. Euthanasia may be passive, where medical treatment is withdrawn and nothing is done to prolong the life of the patient, or active, which involves deliberate actions to end a person's life.

Adult children or spouses are often asked their recommendations about withdrawing life support (food, water, or mechanical ventilation), starting medications to end life (intravenous vasopressors), or withholding certain procedures that would prolong life (cardiopulmonary resuscitation). In the United States, 60 percent of adults in a Gallup poll reported that they approved of physician-assisted suicide (Carroll 2006).

One's aging parents may experience a significant drop in **quality of life**—defined in terms of physical functioning, independence, economic resources, social relationships, and spirituality (Willson 2007). These parents may also not want to be a burden to their children (Schaffer 2007), and may ask for death. The top reasons patients cited for wanting to end their lives are losing autonomy (84 percent), decreasing ability to participate in activities they enjoyed (84 percent), and losing control of bodily functions (47 percent) (Chan 2003).

Physician-assisted suicide (PAS) is legal in the Netherlands. Georges (2008) found that nearly half of a group of general practioners wanted to avoid physician-assisted suicide because it was against their own personal values or because it was an emotional burden for them to confront the issue. Douglas (2008) observed a "double effect" of sedatives and analgesics administered at the end of life—not only do these relieve pain but can also hasten death. Some physicians find that "slow euthanasia" is more psychologically acceptable to doctors than active voluntary euthanasia by injection.

All fifty states now have laws for living wills, permitting individuals to decide (or family members to decide on their behalf) to withhold artificial nutrition (food) and hydration (water) from a patient who is wasting away. In practice, this means not putting in a feeding tube. For elderly, frail patients who may have a stroke or heart attack, do-not-resuscitate (DNR) orders may also be put in place (Cardozo 2006). The Supreme Court has ruled that state law will apply in regard to physician-assisted suicide. In January 2006, the Supreme Court ruled that Oregon has a right to physician-assisted suicide. Its Death with Dignity Act requires that two physicians must agree that the patient is terminally ill and is expected to die within six months, the patient must ask three times for death both orally and in writing, and the patient must swallow the barbiturates themselves rather than be injected with a drug by the physician. The number of physician-assisted suicides increased from twenty-one in 2001, to thirty-eight in 2002 (an 81 percent increase). Most patients had cancer and were more likely to be white, male, and well-educated (Chan 2003).

The official position of the American Medical Association (AMA) is that physicians must respect the patient's decision to forgo life-sustaining treatment but that they should not participate in patient-assisted suicide: "PAS is fundamentally incompatible with the physician's role as healer." Rather, the AMA affirms physicians who support life. Arguments against PAS emphasize that people who want to end the life of those they feel burdened by (or worse, for money) can abuse the practice and that, because physicians make mistakes, what is diagnosed as "terminal" may not in fact be terminal.

Physician-assisted suicide has been legal in Holland for fifteen years. A concern has been the potential to misuse the law. However, a Dutch study of 5,000 requests per year of euthanasia and physician-assisted suicide in general practice over twenty-five years concluded, "Some people feared that the lives of increasing numbers of patients would end through medical intervention, without their consent and before all palliative options were exhausted. Our results, albeit based on requests only, suggest that this fear is not justified" (Marquet et al. 2003, 202).

Your Opinion?

1. Suppose your father has Alzheimer's disease and is in a nursing home. He is 88 and no longer recognizes you. He has stopped eating. Would you have a feeding tube inserted to keep him alive?
2. To what degree do you agree with the Death with Dignity policy operative in Oregon?
3. What do you think the position of the government should be in regard to physician-assisted suicide?

Sources

Carroll, J. 2006. Public continues to support right-to-die for terminally ill patients. Gallop Poll, June 19. www.galluppoll.com/content/CI=23356 (retrieved June 21).

Chan, S. 2003. Rates of assisted suicides rise sharply in Oregon. *Student BMJ* 11:137–38.

Douglas, C., I. Kerridge, and R. Ankeny. 2008. Managing intentions: End of life administration of analgesics and sedatives, and the possibility of slow euthanasia. *Bioethics* 22:388–402.

Georges, J. J. 2008. Dealing with requests for euthanasia: a qualitative study investigating the experience of general practitioners. *Journal of Medical Ethics* 34:150–63.

Marquet, R., A. Bartelds, G. J. Visser, P. Spreeuwenberg, and I. Peters. 2003. Twenty-five years of requests for euthanasia and physician assisted suicide in Dutch practice: Trend analysis. *British Medical Journal* 327:201–02.

Schaffer, M. 2007. Ethical problems in end of life decisions for elderly Norwegians. *Nursing Ethids* 14:242–57.

Willson, A. E. 2007. The sociology of aging. In *21st century sociology: A reference handbook*, ed. Clifton D. Bryant and Dennis L. Peck, 148–55. Thousand Oaks, California: Sage.

Mental health may worsen for some elderly. Mood disorders, with depression being the most frequent, are more common among the elderly. Ryan et al. (2008) analyzed detailed reproductive histories of 1,013 women aged 65 years and over and found that the prevalence of depressive symptoms was 17 percent. Women who reported menopause at an earlier age had an increased risk. Women who had taken the oral contraceptive pill for at least ten years were less likely to report depression. The elderly who abuse alcohol and who do not exercise are also more likely to report being depressed (Van Gool et al. 2007).

Regrets may also be related to depression. Elderly women who have not had children and who have not accepted their childlessness also report more mental distress than those who had children or those who have accepted their childfree status (Wu and Hart 2002). The mental health of elderly men seems unaffected by their parental status.

Regardless of the source of depression, it has a negative impact on an elderly couple's relationship. Sandberg et al. (2002) studied depression in twenty-six elderly couples and concluded, "The most striking finding was the frequent mention of marital conflict and confrontation among the depressed couples and the almost complete absence of it among the nondepressed couples" (p. 261).

National Data

Depression among the elderly may be linked to suicide. Suicide rates are among the highest for white males aged 85 or older. In 2000, 18 percent of all suicides were among individuals aged 65 and over (National Institute of Mental Health 2003).

International Data

Shah (2009) reported an increase in suicide rates among the elderly in twenty-five of twenty-seven developing countries.

Dementia, which includes Alzheimer's disease, is the mental disorder most associated with aging. Its presence is assessed in numerous ways, including clinician rating methods, questionnaire-based methods, and performance-based methods (Clare et al. 2005). In spite of the association, only 3 percent of the aged population experience severe cognitive impairment—the most common symptom is loss of memory. It can be devastating to an individual and the partner. An 87-year-old woman, who was caring for her 97-year-old demented husband, said,

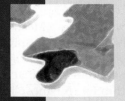

WHAT IF?

What if Your Spouse with Alzheimer's Disease Says "No" to a Nursing Home?

Advanced-stage Alzheimer's disease often results in affected people being a danger to themselves and others. Some of the symptoms of advanced Alzheimer's disease include leaving something on the stove, getting completely lost while driving or in a department store, and becoming paranoid and aggressive. When a spouse refuses to consider an alternative living arrangement, the well spouse may need to resort to deception. One spouse took her husband with Alzheimer's disease out to eat at a nursing home facility and then had security restrain her husband while she left. The experience was traumatic for both the husband and wife, but both adjusted within a month.

Alzheimer's Quiz

		True	False	Don't Know
1.	Alzheimer's disease can be contagious.	___	___	___
2.	People will almost certainly get Alzheimer's disease if they live long enough.	___	___	___
3.	Alzheimer's disease is a form of insanity.	___	___	___
4.	Alzheimer's disease is a normal part of getting older, like gray hair or wrinkles.	___	___	___
5.	There is no cure for Alzheimer's disease at present.	___	___	___
6.	A person who has Alzheimer's disease will experience both mental and physical decline.	___	___	___
7.	The primary symptom of Alzheimer's disease is memory loss.	___	___	___
8.	Among people older than age 75, forgetfulness most likely indicates the beginning of Alzheimer's disease.	___	___	___
9.	When the husband or wife of an older person dies, the surviving spouse may suffer from a kind of depression that looks like Alzheimer's disease.	___	___	___
10.	Stuttering is an inevitable part of Alzheimer's disease.	___	___	___
11.	An older man is more likely to develop Alzheimer's disease than an older woman.	___	___	___
12.	Alzheimer's disease is usually fatal.	___	___	___
13.	The vast majority of people suffering from Alzheimer's disease live in nursing homes.	___	___	___
14.	Aluminum has been identified as a significant cause of Alzheimer's disease.	___	___	___
15.	Alzheimer's disease can be diagnosed by a blood test.	___	___	___
16.	Nursing-home expenses for Alzheimer's disease patients are covered by Medicare.	___	___	___
17.	Medicine taken for high blood pressure can cause symptoms that look like Alzheimer's disease.	___	___	___

Answers: 1–4, 8, 10, 11, 13–16 False; remaining items True.

Source

Neal E. Cutler, Boettner/Gregg Professor of Financial Gerontology, Widener University. Originally published in 1987, in *Psychology Today*, 20th Anniversary Issue, "Life Flow: A Special Report—The Alzheimer's Quiz," 21(5):89, 93. Reprinted with permission from *Psychology Today* magazine, © 1987 Sussex Publishers, LLC. The scale was completed by sixty-nine undergraduates at East Carolina University in 1998. Of the respondents, 40 percent identified less than 50 percent of the items correctly.

I wouldn't swap one wrinkle of my face for all the elixirs of youth. All these wrinkles represent a smile, a grimace of pain and disappointment . . . some part of being fully alive.

Helen Hayes, actress

"After 56 years of marriage, I am waiting for him to die, so I can follow him. At this point, I feel like he'd be better off dead. I can't go before him and abandon him" (Johnson and Barer 1997, 47).

The above Self-Assessment reflects some of the misconceptions about Alzheimer's disease.

Retirement

Retirement represents a rite of passage through which most elderly pass. Some are "young" retirees who make their fortune early in life and simply stop working. More often individuals are "old" retirees who have worked thirty to forty years and retire. In 1983, Congress increased the retirement age at which individuals can receive full Social Security benefits, from 65 (for those born before 1938) to 67 (for those born after 1960). People can take early retirement at age 62, with reduced benefits. Retirement affects an individual's status, income, privileges, power, and prestige. Fabian (2007) noted that, for most of our history, the concept of retirement did not exist—older individuals were viewed as a source of wisdom and they continued to work. In the twentieth century, retirement was developed in reference to the economy, which was faced with an aging population and surplus labor (Willson 2007). Indeed, retirement is a socially programmed stage of life that is being reevaluated.

People least likely to retire are unmarried, widowed, single-parent women who need to continue working because they have no pension or even Social Security benefits—if they don't work or continue to work, they will have no income, so retirement is not an option. Some workers experience what is called **blurred retirement** rather than a clear-cut one. A blurred retirement means the individual works part-time before completely retiring or takes a "bridge job" that provides a transition between a lifelong career and full retirement. About half of all people between ages 55 and 64 who quit their primary careers take some kind of bridge job (Dychtwald and Kadlec 2005).

Individuals who have a positive attitude toward retirement are those who have a pension waiting for them, are married (and thus have social support for the transition), have planned for retirement, are in good health, and have high self-esteem. Those who regard retirement negatively have no pension waiting for them, have no spouse, gave no thought to retirement, have bad health, and have negative self-esteem (Mutran et al. 1997). Nordenmark and Stattin (2009) analyzed national data in Sweden and found that better psychosocial retirement adjustment outcomes resulted from voluntary rather than forced retirement due to health problems. Also, men whose skills were no longer needed reported a more difficult adjustment than women.

In general, most retired individuals enjoy it. Few regard continuing to work as a privilege. Although they still prefer to be active, they want to pick their own activity and pace, as they could not do when they were working. Collins and Smyer (2005) found that the loss of one's job via retirement was not a major issue, and most were very resilient in their feelings about life and self.

Retirement may have positive consequences for a marriage. Szinovacz and Schaffer (2000) analyzed national data and concluded that husbands viewed their wife's retirement as associated with a reduction in heated arguments. If both spouses were retired, they had a perceived reduction of disagreements. Webber et al. (2000) found that spouses had an easier time adjusting to retirement if they had similar retirement goals or expectations in the areas of leisure, family relationships, friendships, and finances.

Some individuals experience disenchantment during retirement; it is not enjoyable and does not live up to their expectations. Lee Iacocca, former president of Chrysler Corporation, reported that he was bored with retirement, missed "the action," and warned others "never to retire" but to stay busy and involved. Some heed his advice and either "die in harness" or go back to work. Dychtwald and Kadlec (2005) observed that some retired people benefit from volunteering—giving back their time and money to attack poverty, illiteracy, oppression, crime, and so on. Examples of volunteer organizations are the Service Corps of Retired Executives, known as SCORE (www.score.org), Experience Works (www.experienceworks.org), and Generations United (www.gu.org).

Sexuality

Levitra, Cialis, and **Viagra** (prescription drugs that help a man obtain and maintain an erection) are advertised regularly on television and have given cultural visibility to the issue of sexuality among the elderly. Though the elderly (both men and women) experience physiological changes that impact sexuality, older adults often continue their interest in sexual activity. Indeed, there is a new era of opportunity to continue sexual functioning into one's later years, which has replaced the earlier script of decline and end to sexual functioning as a natural part of aging (Potts et al. 2006).

Table 17.3 describes the physiological changes that elderly men experience during the sexual response cycle. Table 17.4 describes the physical changes elderly women experience during the sexual response cycle.

The National Institute on Aging surveyed 3,005 men and women ages 57 to 85 and found that sexual activity decreases with age (Lindau 2007). Almost

Table 17.3 Physiological Sexual Changes in Elderly Men

Phases of Sexual Response	Changes in Men
Excitement phase	As men age, getting an erection can take them longer. Although a young man may get an erection within 10 seconds, elderly men may take several minutes (10 to 30). During this time, they usually need intense stimulation (manual or oral). Unaware that the greater delay in getting erect is a normal consequence of aging, men who experience this for the first time may panic and have erectile dysfunction.
Plateau phase	The erection may be less rigid than when the man was younger, and there is usually a longer delay before ejaculation. This latter change is usually regarded as an advantage by both the man and his partner.
Orgasm phase	Orgasm in the elderly male is usually less intense, with fewer contractions and less fluid. However, orgasm remains an enjoyable experience, as over 70 percent of older men in one study reported that having a climax was very important when having a sexual experience.
Resolution phase	The elderly man loses his erection rather quickly after ejaculation. In some cases, the erection will be lost while the penis is still in the woman's vagina and she is thrusting to cause her orgasm. The refractory period is also increased. Whereas a young male needs only a short time after ejaculation to get an erection, the elderly man may need considerably longer.

Source: Adapted from W. Boskin, G. Graf, and V. Kreisworth. *Health dynamics: Attitudes and behaviors,* 1e, p. 209. © 1990. Brooks/Cole, a part of Cengage Learning, Inc. Reproduced by permission. www.cengage.com/permissions.

Table 17.4 Physiological Sexual Changes in Elderly Women

Phases of Sexual Response	Changes in Women
Excitement phase	Vaginal lubrication takes several minutes or longer, as opposed to 10 to 30 seconds when younger. Both the length and the width of the vagina decrease. Considerable decreased lubrication and vaginal size are associated with pain during intercourse. Some women report decreased sexual desire and unusual sensitivity of the clitoris.
Plateau phase	Little change occurs as the woman ages. During this phase, the vaginal orgasmic platform is formed and the uterus elevates.
Orgasm phase	Elderly women continue to experience and enjoy orgasm. Of women aged 60 to 91, almost 70 percent reported that having an orgasm made for a good sexual experience. With regard to their frequency of orgasm now as opposed to when they were younger, 65 percent said "unchanged," 20 percent "increased," and 14 percent "decreased."
Resolution phase	Defined as a return to the preexcitement state, the resolution phase of the sexual response phase happens more quickly in elderly than in younger women. Clitoral retraction and orgasmic platform disappear quickly after orgasm. This is most likely a result of less pelvic vasocongestion to begin with during the arousal phase.

Source: Adapted from W. Boskin, G. Graf, and V. Kreisworth. *Health dynamics: Attitudes and behaviors,* 1e, p. 210. © 1990. Brooks/Cole, a part of Cengage Learning, Inc. Reproduced by permission. www.cengage.com/permissions.

three-fourths (73 percent) of those 57 to 64 reported being sexually active in the last twelve months. This percentage declined to about half (53 percent) for those 65 to 74 and to about a fourth (26 percent) for those ages 75 to 80. An easy way to remember these percentages is three-fourths of those around 60, a half of those about 70 and a fourth of those around 80 report being sexually active. In general, women reported less sexual activity due to the absence of a sexual partner. Those most sexually healthy were also in good health. Diabetes and hypertension were major causes of sexual dysfunction. Only one out of seven reported using Viagra or other such medications. The most frequent sexual problem for men was erectile dysfunction; for women, the problems were low sexual desire (43 percent reporting), less vaginal lubrication (39 percent), and inability to climax (34 percent). Beckman et al. (2006) also reported that sexual interest continued for 95 percent of their sample of over 500 people in their seventies. Alford-Cooper (2006) studied the sexuality of couples married for more than fifty years and found that sexual interest, activity, and capacity declined with age but that marital satisfaction did not decrease with these changes.

Although sex may occur less often, it remains satisfying for most elderly. Winterich (2003) found that, in spite of vaginal, libido, and orgasm changes past menopause, women of both sexual orientations reported that they continued to enjoy active, enjoyable sex lives due to open communication with their partners.

The debate continues about whether menopausal women should become involved in estrogen replacement therapy and estrogen-progestin replacement therapy (collectively referred to as HRT—hormone replacement therapy). Schairer et al. (2000) studied 2,082 cases of breast cancer and concluded that the estrogen-progestin regimen increased the risk of breast cancer beyond that associated with estrogen alone. Beginning in 2003, women were no longer routinely encouraged to take HRT, and the effects of their not doing so on their physical and emotional health were minimal. A major study (Hays et al. 2003) of more than 16,608 postmenopausal women aged 50 to 79 found no significant benefits from HRT in terms of quality of life. Those with severe symptoms (for example, hot flashes, sleep disturbances, irritability) do seem to benefit without negative outcomes. Indeed, one woman reported, "I'd rather be on estrogen so my husband can stand me (and I can stand myself)." New data suggest that women who have had a hysterectomy can benefit from estrogen-alone therapy without raising their breast cancer risk.

Successful Aging

Researchers who worked on the Landmark Harvard Study of Adult Development (Valliant 2002) followed 824 men and women from their teens into their eighties and identified those factors associated with successful aging. These include not smoking (or quitting early), developing a positive view of life and life's crises, avoiding alcohol and substance abuse, maintaining healthy weight, exercising daily, continuing to educate oneself, and having a happy marriage. Indeed, those who were identified as "happy and well" were six times more likely to be in a good marriage than those who were identified as "sad and sick." Conversely, spouses with higher levels of negative marital behavior had more chronic health problems, physical disability, and poorer perceived health (Bookwala 2005). Those with negative marital interaction (particularly from lower socioeconomic backgrounds) were more likely to die of a heart attack than spouses where no such marital interaction existed (Krause 2005).

Not smoking is "probably the single most significant factor in terms of health" according to Valliant (2002), of the Landmark Harvard Study of Adult Development. Smokers who quit before age 50 were as healthy at 70 as those who had never smoked.

Exercise is one of the most beneficial activities the elderly can engage in to help them maintain good health. Yet the occurrence of exercise activities significantly decreases as a person ages. A team of researchers (Lees et al. 2005) interviewed fifty-seven adults over the age of 65 about their exercise behavior. Those who did not exercise noted fear of falling and inertia for avoiding exercise. Those who did exercise identified inertia, time constraints, and physical ailments as being the most significant barriers to exercise. Wrosch et al. (2007) studied the exercise behavior of 172 elderly adults and found that the greatest predictor of whether elderly people exercised was their having done so previously. Hence, people who exercised at year 2 of the study were likely to still be exercising at year 5 of the study. Stephenson et al. (2007) noted that community-sponsored walking programs at malls were beneficial in getting the elderly to exercise. Jack LaLanne, the health fitness guru, remarked at age 90, "I hate to exercise; I love

I don't want to get to the end of my life and find that I just lived the length of it. I want to have lived the width of it as well.

Diane Ackerman, American poet

the results." At his 90th birthday party, he challenged his well-wishers to be at his 115th birthday party.

Agahi (2008) also noted a strong positive effect of involvement in social leisure activities and successful aging among a representative sample of 1,246 men and women ages 65 to 95. Participating in only a few activities doubled mortality risk compared to those with the highest participation levels, even after controlling for age, education, walking ability, and other health indicators. Strongest benefits were found for engagement in organizational activities and study circles among women and hobby activities and gardening among men.

The elderly also benefit from a credible role model for successful aging. Horton and Deakin (2007) note that such a model is older than themselves and is "active, vigorous and illustrative of the high quality of life that is possible into very late age." Superathletic models are often not effective because they are sometimes viewed as intimidating and not realistic.

Relationships and the Elderly

Relationships continue into old age. Here we examine relationships with one's spouse, siblings, and children.

Relationships among Elderly Spouses

Marriages that survive into late life are characterized by little conflict, considerable companionship, and mutual supportiveness. All but one of the thirty-one spouses over age 85 in the Johnson and Barer (1997) study reported "high expressive rewards" from their mate. Walker and Luszcz (2009) reviewed the literature on elderly couples and found marital satisfaction related to equality of roles and marital communication. Health may be both improved by positive relationships and decreased by negative relationships.

Field and Weishaus (1992) reported interview data on seventeen couples who had been married an average of fifty-nine years and found that the husbands and wives viewed their marriages very differently. Men tended to report more marital satisfaction, more pleasure in the way their relationships had been across time, more pleasure in shared activities, and closer affectional ties. Even though club activities, including church attendance, were related to marital satisfaction, this study found that financial stability, amount of education, health, and intelligence were not. Sex was also more important to the husbands. Every man in the study reported that sex was always an important part of the relationship with his wife, but only four of the seventeen wives reported the same.

The wives, according to the researchers, presented a much more realistic view of their long-term marriage. For this generation of women, "it was never as important for them to put the best face on things" (Field and Weishaus 1992, 273). Hence, many of these wives were not unhappy; they were just more willing to report disagreements and changes in their marriages across time.

Only a small percentage (8 percent) of individuals older than 100 are married. Most married centenarians are men in their second or third marriage. Many have outlived some of their children. Marital satisfaction in these elderly marriages is related to a high frequency of expressing love feelings to one's partner. Though it is assumed that spouses who have been married for a long time should know how their partners feel, this is often not the case. Telling each other "I love you" is very important to these elderly spouses.

This couple has been married eighty-four years.

Elderly Husbands Helping Elderly Wives

Although we tend to think of elderly wives helping their husbands, sometimes this is reversed. Russell (2007) reported that elderly men who end up as caregivers of their wives—in terms of meal preparation and personal care—sometimes struggle with the meanings of such care as related to their masculinity and manhood. However, elderly men are often less avoidant of hands-on care than previously thought. Brown et al. (2009) studied 3,376 elderly married spouses and found that those spending at least fourteen hours a week providing care to a spouse predicted decreased mortality for the caregiver.

Married 84 Years, and Still Loving*

Herbert and Zelmyra Fisher of the Brownsville community in North Carolina have been married for more than eighty-four years. (see photo at top of the page) They have the world record of the longest marriage for a living couple (they have a certificate from the Guinness Book of Records) (Sawyer 2008).

Herbert was born June 10, 1905. His hearing is going but his mind is sharp. Zelmyra was born Dec. 10, 1907. She uses a walker to get around the house and yard. The two of them can still give their reasons for marrying on May 13, 1924. "He was not mean; he was not a fighter," Zelmrya said. "He was quiet and kind. He was not much to look at but he was sweet." Herbert said Zelmyra never gave him any trouble. "No, no trouble at all. We never argued, but we might have disagreed," he said.

Norma Godette, one of the couple's five children, said her parents have gotten along well through the years. "One time, mama wanted to work. Daddy told her she could not work, that he could take care of the family. She slipped down to Cherry Point and got a job as a caretaker there," Godette said. "Well, it was done; she got the job. I had to let it be," Herbert said.

Different religions did not tear the two apart. He is a member of Pilgrim Chapel Missionary Baptist Church. She is a member of Jones Chapel African Methodist Episcopal Zion Church. The churches are in James City, where they

Age does not protect you from love but love to some extent protects you from age.

Jeanne Moreau, actress

---

* This article appeared in the *New Bern Sun Journal* (New Bern, NC), Editor John Huff. Used by permission.

Difficulties, Disagreements, and Disappointments in Late-Life Marriages

RESEARCH APPLICATION

Over the last century, life expectancy in the United States has increased dramatically, from about forty-seven years in 1900 to around eighty years in 2010 (*Statistical Abstract of the United States, 2009,* Table 100). Because people are living longer, the elderly population has grown considerably and so has a number of married elderly couples. The following research study attempts to explore the difficulties, disagreements, and disappointments that husbands and wives experience in "late-life" marriages (Henry et al. 2005).

Sample and Methods

This study used data from the University of Southern California Longitudinal Study of Generations and included 105 older couples. The participants' ages ranged from 52 to 86, with the average age being 69. Total household income of participants averaged between $50,000 and $59,000. Most of the individuals in the sample (more than 86 percent) reported being in either excellent or good health, and 27 percent were in the workforce. The sample consisted of about 78 percent Caucasians and 22 percent from other groups.

The research participants were asked to write their answer to the following question: "In the last few years, what are some of the things on which you have differed, disagreed, or been disappointed about (even if not openly discussed) with your spouse?" Researchers read a total of 329 responses to this question, identified the main points or topics for each response, and condensed the main topics into ten themes.

In addition, a ten-item scale that assessed positive interaction was used to measure marital quality, and the health of the participants was measured by the question, "Compared to people your own age, how would you rate your overall physical health at the present time?" Respondents could mark *excellent, good, fair,* or *poor* to describe their health. Individuals who marked *excellent* or *good* were considered to be healthy, and those marking *fair* or *poor* were considered unhealthy.

Selected Findings and Conclusions

The average number of problems each respondent reported was 1.40. The most common theme identified as a problem in the marriage was leisure activities; 23 percent of respondents identified this as a problem. The second most common problem involved the theme of intimacy (13 percent), followed by finances (11 percent), no problems (11 percent), personality (9 percent), intergenerational relations (9 percent), household concerns (9 percent), personal habits (7 percent), health issues (6 percent), and work or retirement (2 percent). Among the 14 percent of participants who were rated as unhealthy, the most common issues were financial issues, health issues, and intergenerational relations. The following table describes each theme and presents examples of comments husbands and wives made that reflect each theme.

Theme and % Reporting	Main Topics of Theme	Examples of Comments by Spouses
Leisure (23%)	Time spent with spouse, politics, religion, hobbies or interests, traveling	"My spouse watches too much football and after forty-eight years of hearing it, I get upset." "We are both so busy with our own schedules that we neglect doing enough things together."
Intimacy (13%)	Emotional intimacy, physical intimacy	"He doesn't talk enough to me." "Sex life is nil. We are affectionate but don't 'screw.'"
Financial matters (11%)	Spending and investing	"Most disagreements are about money. She wants to eat out a lot, go to movies or plays and then can't understand why I don't have any more money."

Age puzzles me. I thought it was a quiet time. My seventies were interesting and fairly serene, but my eighties are passionate. I grow more intense as I age.

Florida Scott-Maxwell, The *Measure of My Days*

both grew up. For all of their married life, they have attended their own churches. They go their own ways on Sunday morning. She reads the Bible daily.

The two watch television together. "We separate when the baseball comes on," Zelmyra said. Herbert loves baseball, especially the Atlanta Braves. He also enjoys golf, because one of his sons-in-law plays the game.

They have no secret or sage advice as to why their marriage has lasted so long. "I didn't know I would be married this long," Herbert said. "But I lived a nice holy life and go to church every Sunday. Yes sir, anything for her."

Zelmyra said Herbert was the only boyfriend she ever had. "We got along good," she said. "There was no trouble." She said she is not tired of seeing him.

No problems (11%)	No problems in marriage	"I really can't think of anything or remember any time when we have not been able to agree on decisions . . ." "I guess we are the exception; I am very happy with my best friend."
Personality (9%)	Attitude and temperament	"He does things that bother me a great deal and his attitude is 'learn to live with it.'" "[She has an] ability to experience extreme anger over what I consider relatively minor provocations."
Intergenerational relations (9%)	Discipline of grandchildren, support of children and grandchildren, relationships	"The only thing we disagree on is how to handle grandchildren . . . like how much money to give them."
Household concerns (9%)	Where to live, home repairs	"I would like to move from [a city], but my husband likes it here." "We disagree on decorating our house or changing the landscape."
Personal habits (7%)	Grooming, driving habits, and substance use	"I wish he would take a shower every night instead of every other night." "When traveling together in the car, we sometimes disagree about directions or driving habits. . . ." "He smokes behind my back." "We disagree on what constitutes a problem with alcohol."
Health problems (6%)	General health problems, hearing and memory loss, doctor appointments, caregiving issues	"It's just a bit hard at times because [strokes] have made it harder for him to talk. . . . It can be a little lonely." "I don't think he takes care of himself. He has a poor diet and no exercise. He will try to tough it out rather than make a doctor appointment." "I need help caring for my husband now, and get virtually no assistance from his children. . . ."
Work or retirement (2%)	Current employment, retirement	"I would like my spouse to retire but he wants to keep working."

Although wives and husbands reported almost identical numbers of issues, wives were more likely than husbands to complain about personal habits (9 percent versus 5 percent) and health issues (9 percent versus 4 percent), whereas husbands were more likely than wives to report financial issues (13 percent versus 8 percent). Husbands were also more likely than wives to report that they had no problems in the marriage (15 percent versus 7 percent). Gender had no effect on how often the other themes were reported.

Not surprisingly, couples in happy marriages reported fewer problems than those in unhappy marriages, with happy couples reporting no problems 12 percent of the time and unhappy couples reporting no problems only 4 percent of the time.

Source

Difficulties, disagreements, and disappointments in late life marriages in *International Journal Of Aging & Human Development* 61(3):243–64 by Henry, R. G., R. B. Miller, and R. Giarrusso. Copyright 2005 by Baywood Publishing Company, Inc. Reproduced with permission of Baywood Publishing Company, Inc. via Copyright Clearance Center.

"I didn't think I'd be married this long. He is quiet," she said. Zelmyra said her husband had no annoying habits. They both said they shared the title of "boss." They worked hard and put all five of the children through college.

The two sit on the porch, and as a train goes by, they count the cars. They also watch the neighbors who walk by. Herbert makes his bed each day and sweeps the floor. He also checks on his wife as she rests. Between the rests, they enjoy their children, ten grandchildren, nine great-grandchildren, and nieces and nephews. Both say that if they had it to do over, they would not change their life.

Renewing an Old Love Relationship

Some widowed or divorced elderly try to find and renew an earlier love relationship. Researcher Nancy Kalish (1997) surveyed 1,001 individuals who reported that they had renewed an old love relationship. Two-thirds of those who had contacted a previous love (mostly by phone or letter) were female; one-third were male. Almost two-thirds (62 percent) reported that the person they made contact with was their first love, and 72 percent reported that they were still in love with and together with the person with whom they had renewed their relationship. An example of one reunited couple (interviewed by Kalish) follows:

> He was my first boyfriend. It was all very innocent. Mostly we were good friends. We walked home from school together, and went out a couple of times. My parents didn't like him for some reason. Neither of us remembers why we broke up.
>
> We went on to long marriages with other people. Sixty-three years passed, and we were both widowed when we went to our high school reunion. I knew as soon as we saw each other. We got to talking and nothing else mattered. It seemed like something that was destined to happen.
>
> We were married on my eightieth birthday. He's so loving and kind and caring and understanding and peaceful. He doesn't argue. He's very respectful, a perfect gentlemen. I just love everything about him. He's all I ever wanted. (p. 11)

Weintraub (2006) suggested some cautions in renewing an old love relationship. These include (1) discussing the original breakup or what went wrong—if one partner was hurt badly, the other must take responsibility or make amends; and (2) going slow in reviving the relationship. She also identified some successful couples who reunited after a long interval. Harry Kullijian contacted Carol Channing seventy years after they left high school. Carol's mother had broken up the relationship. Kullijian and Channing married in 2003.

Relationship with Siblings at Age 85 and Beyond

Relationships that the elderly have with their siblings are primarily emotional (enjoying time together) rather than functional (in which a sibling provides money or services). Earlier in the text, we noted that sibling relationships, particularly those between sisters, are the most enduring of all relationships.

Relationship with One's Own Children at Age 85 and Beyond

In regard to relationships of the elderly with their children, emotional and expressive rewards are high. Actual caregiving is rare. Only 12 percent of the Johnson and Barer (1997) sample of adults older than 85 lived with their children. Most preferred to be independent and to live in their own residence. "This independent stance is carried over to social supports; many prefer to hire help rather than bother their children. When hired help is used, children function more as mediators than regular helpers, but most are very attentive in filling the gaps in the service network" (Johnson and Barer 1997, 86).

Relationships among multiple generations will increase. Whereas three-generation families have been the norm, four- and five-generation families will increasingly become the norm. These changes have already become visible.

Grandparenthood

Another significant role for the elderly is grandparenting. Among adults aged 40 and older who had children, close to 95 percent are grandparents and most have, on average, five or six grandchildren. Grandparents may actively take care of their grandchildren full-time, provide supplemental help in a multigenerational family, help on an occasional part-time basis, or occasionally visit their grandchildren. Grandparents see themselves as caretakers, emotional and/or economic resources, teachers, and historical connections on the family tree.

Households headed by grandparents are increasing. Six million grandparents are living in homes with grandchildren; 2.5 million are rearing grandchildren alone because the parents are unavailable (for example, due to illness, drug addiction, AIDS, incarceration, Iraq war, divorce, or poverty) (Ackerman and Banks 2007). The average age of becoming a grandparent is 48; the age at which grandparents become caregivers of their grandchildren is from 53 to 59 (Landry-Meyer 2000). Fifteen percent of grandparents provide child-care services for their grandchildren while the parents work (Davies 2002).

Grandparents in a Full-Time Role of Raising Grandchildren

About 6 percent of all children are being reared full-time by their grandparents (Hayslip and Kaminski 2005). Although both grandparents may be involved, grandparenthood is primarily a "woman's issue" (Mills et al. 2005). Musil and Standing (2005) reported on the diaries of grandmothers who revealed stress in a full-time role of grandmother as they coped with their grandchildren's daily activities.

Grandfathers may also be involved in caring for grandchildren. Bullock (2005) studied twenty-one grandfathers over the age of 65 who were involved in the active care of at least one grandchild. *Powerless* was the term these grandfathers used to describe their experience. In effect, they felt overwhelmed. Hayslip and Kaminski (2005) spoke to the need for help for both grandparents and grandchildren.

Styles of Grandparenting

Grandparents also have different styles of relating to grandchildren. Whereas some grandparents are formal and rigid, others are informal and playful, and authority lines are irrelevant. Still others are surrogate parents providing considerable care for working mothers and/or single parents. Some grandparents have regular contact with their grandchildren; others are distant and show up only for special events like birthdays. E-mail is helping grandparents to stay connected to their grandchildren. Davies (2002) reported that 35 percent of grandparents use e-mail to communicate with their grandchildren.

Age seems to be a factor in determining how grandparents relate to their grandchildren. Grandparents over the age of 65 are less likely to be playful and fun-seeking than those under 65. This may be because the older grandparents are less physically able to engage in playful activities with their grandchildren. Indeed, according to Johnson and Barer (1997):

> . . . *members of the oldest generation in our study place more emphasis on their relationship with their own children over their grandchildren. This situation could stem from the fact that as grandchildren reach adulthood, they become more independent from their own parent. That parent then is freed up to strengthen the relationship with their oldest parent, at the same time they, as the middle generation, maintain a lineage bridge linking their parent to their child.* (p. 89)

This grandfather spent his last day with his granddaughter. He died unexpectedly of an aneurism. The granddaughter wrote a poem following his death called, "My Hero."

Authors

Diversity in Other Countries

In Mpumalanga (bordered by Mozambique and Swaziland in the east and Gauteng in the west), one of the nine provinces of South Africa with high unemployment and high poverty, 76 percent of older people are the sole providers for their grandchildren (Kimuna and Makiwane 2007).

Finally, the quality of the grandparent-grandchild relationship can be affected by the parents' relationship to their own parents. If a child's parents are estranged from their parents, it is unlikely that the child will have an opportunity to develop a relationship with the grandparents.

"Raging Grannies"

Patrick (2009) studied the "Raging Grannies" and noted that they are a group of feminist activists who wish to change the injustices in the world for themselves, their children and grandchildren, future generations after them, and humanity as a whole. They began in Victoria, British Columbia, Canada, in 1987, and are now represented all over Canada, the United States, and the world. They are concerned about such issues as the environment, poverty, corporate greed, racism, sexism, and any form of social and economic injustice. The Grannies are divided into gaggles, or groups, who have complete autonomy from each other. They use protests by dressing in traditional "granny" clothing and singing humorous songs about the issue.

The "Myth" of the Happy Grandmother

The stereotype of "grandmother" is that of a white-haired lady with glasses who wears an apron and bakes an apple pie for her grandchildren. The reality can be a woman who wears a stylish windbreaker as she jogs around the block or a woman who jets to New York for a corporate meeting. Although some women love their role of grandmother, the reality is sometimes different. Kulik (2007) noted the following negatives that grandmothers identify:

1. *Conflict.* Taking care of grandchildren may interfere with what grandmothers want to do. "I have a life and am involved in a new relationship," reported one grandmother.

2. *Demanding children.* Full-time care of grandchildren can be exhausting. "They wear me out after three days," one woman said of her twin grandkids.

3. *Boredom.* Not all grandmothers enjoy the activities of young children. Coloring, drawing, and playing with toys are OK for a couple of hours for some grandmothers; others get bored silly.

4. *Exploitation.* Some grandmothers feel exploited by their children. They feel that their children "dump" the kids on them and "expect" them to be a full-time mother. "I don't appreciate it," said one grandmother, but she felt guilty at not wanting to be more helpful.

5. *Ending of childbearing capacity.* Some women view grandparenting as symbolic that they are getting old and are no longer capable of having more children of their own.

Effect of Divorce on a Grandparent-Child Relationship

The degree of involvement of grandparents in the life of grandchildren is sometimes related to whether the grandparents are divorced (King 2003). "Divorced grandparents have less contact with grandchildren and participate in fewer shared activities with them" (p. 180).

In addition, grandparental involvement with grandchildren is also related to whether their own children are divorced and with whom the grandchild lives. Because mothers end up with custody in about 85 percent of custody cases, the maternal grandparents may escalate their involvement with their grandchildren. However, because divorcing fathers may have less access to their children, the paternal grandparents may find that their time with their grandchildren is radically reduced. Sometimes a custodial parent will purposefully try to sever the relationship in an attempt to seek revenge or vent hostility against a former spouse.

Indeed, when their children divorce, some grandparents are not allowed to see their grandchildren. In all fifty states, the role of the grandparent has limited legal and political support. By a vote of six to three in 2000, the Supreme Court (*Troxel v. Granville*) sided with the parents and virtually denied 60 million grandparents the right to see their grandchildren. The court viewed parents as having a fundamental right to make decisions about with whom their children could spend time. However, some grandparents have petitioned the court and won the right to see their grandchildren (Henderson 2005). Grandparents should not give up. Stepgrandparents have no legal rights to their stepgrandchildren.

Benefits to Grandchildren

Of a sample of 1,319 university students, 82.8 percent agreed with the statement, "I have a loving relationship with my grandmother" (39.9 percent reported having had a loving relationship with their grandfather) (Knox and Zusman 2009). Grandchildren report enormous benefits from having a close relationship with grandparents, including development of a sense of family ideals, moral beliefs, and a work ethic. Kennedy (1997) focused on the memories grandchildren had of their grandparents and found that "love and companionship" was identified most frequently by the grandchildren. In addition, a theme running through a fourth of the memories was that the grandchildren felt that they were regarded as "special" by a grandparent, either because of being the first or last grandchild, having personality characteristics similar to the grandparent's, or being the child of a favorite son or daughter of the grandparent. Taylor et al. (2005) surveyed seventy international college students in the Unites States regarding perceived grandparental influence and relationship satisfaction with their "closest" grandparent. These students reported that, despite distance and infrequent contact, they received significant satisfaction and influence from this relationship.

The End of One's Life

Thanatology is the examination of the social dimensions of death, dying, and bereavement (Bryant 2007). The end of one's life sometimes involves the death of one's spouse.

Death of One's Spouse

The death of one's spouse is one of the most stressful life events a person ever experiences. Because women tend to live longer than men, and because women are often younger than their husbands, women are more likely than men to experience the death of their marital partner.

If you were going to die soon and had only one phone call you could make, who would you call and what would you say? And why are you waiting?

Stephen Levine, American poet

Authors

Widows often go through a period of inconsolable grief, alone.

Although individual reactions and coping mechanisms for dealing with the death of a loved one vary, several reactions to death are common. These include shock, disbelief and denial, confusion and disorientation, grief and sadness, anger, numbness, physiological symptoms such as insomnia or lack of appetite, withdrawal from activities, immersion in activities, depression, and guilt. Eventually, surviving the death of a loved one involves the recognition that life must go on, the need to make sense out of the loss, and the establishment of a new identity. However, research is not consistent on the degree to which individuals are best served by continuing or relinquishing the emotional bonds with the deceased (Stroebe and Schut 2005).

Women and men tend to have different ways of reacting to and coping with the death of a loved one. Women are more likely than men to express and share feelings with family and friends and are also more likely to seek and accept help, such as attending support groups of other grievers. Initial responses of men are often cognitive rather than emotional. From early childhood, males are taught to be in control, to be strong and courageous under adversity, and to be able to take charge and fix things. Showing emotions is labeled weak.

Men sometimes respond to the death of their spouse in behavioral rather than emotional ways. Sometimes they immerse themselves in work or become involved in physical action in response to the loss. For example, a widower immersed himself in repairing a beach cottage he and his wife had recently bought. Later, he described this activity as crucial to getting him through those first two months. Another coping mechanism for men is the increased use of alcohol and other drugs.

Women's response to the death of their husbands may necessarily involve practical considerations. Johnson and Barer (1997) identified two major problems of widows—the economic effects of losing a spouse and the practical problems of maintaining a home alone. The latter involves such practical issues as cleaning the gutters, painting the house, and changing the air filters.

Whether a spouse dies suddenly or after a prolonged illness has an impact on the reaction of the remaining spouse. The sudden rather than prolonged death of one's spouse is associated with being less at peace with death and being more angry. The suddenness of the death provides no cognitive preparation time.

The age at which one experiences the death of a spouse is also a factor in one's adjustment. People in their eighties may be so consumed with their own health and disability concerns that they have little emotional energy left to grieve. On the other hand, a team of researchers (Hansson et al. 1999) noted that death does not end the relationship with the deceased. Some widows and widowers report a feeling that their spouses are with them at times and are watching out for them a year after the death of their beloved. They may also dream of them, talk to their photographs, and remain interested in carrying out their wishes. Such continuation of the relationship may be adaptive by providing meaning and purpose for the living or maladaptive in that it may prevent one from establishing new relationships.

Involvement with New Partners at Age 80 and Beyond

Most women who live to age 80 have lost their husbands. At age 80, only 53 men are available for every 100 women. Patterns women use to adjust to this lopsided man-woman ratio include dating younger men, romance without marriage, and "share-a-man" relationships. Most individuals in their eighties who have lost a partner do not remarry (Stevens 2002). Those who do report a need for companionship and to provide meaning in life as the primary reasons. Stevens (2002) noted "evidence of continuing loyalty to the deceased" in all the late-life partnerships she studied, suggesting that new partners do not simply "replace" former partners.

Over 3 million women are married to men who are at least ten years younger than they are. Although traditionally women were socialized to seek older, financially established men, the sheer shortage of men has encouraged many women to seek younger partners. These age-discrepant relationships were discussed in Chapter 7, Marriage Relationships.

Faced with a shortage of men but reluctant to marry those who are available, some elderly women are willing to share a man. In elderly retirement communities such as Palm Beach, Florida, women count themselves lucky to have a man who will come for lunch, take them to a movie, or be an escort to a dance. They accept the fact that the man may also have lunch, go to a movie, or go dancing with other women.

However, finding a new spouse is usually not a goal. Women in their later years have also moved away from the idea that they must remarry and have become more accepting of the idea that they can enjoy the romance of a relationship without the obligations of a marriage. Many enjoy their economic independence, their control over their life space, and their freedom not to be a nurse to an aging partner.

To avoid marriage, some elderly couples live together. Parenthood is no longer a goal, and many do not want to entangle their assets. For some, marriage would mean the end of their Social Security benefits or other pension moneys.

Preparing for One's Own Death

What is it like for those near the end of life to think about death? To what degree do they go about actually "preparing" for death? Johnson and Barer (1997) interviewed forty-eight individuals with an average age of 93 to find out their perspective on death. Most interviewees were women (77 percent); of them 56 percent lived alone, but 73 percent had some sort of support in terms of children or one or more social support services. The following findings are specific to those who died within a year after the interview.

Thoughts in the Last Year of Life   Most had thought about death and saw their life as one that would soon end. Most did so without remorse or anxiety. With their spouses and friends dead and their health failing, they accepted death as the next stage in life. Some comments follow:

> If I die tomorrow, it would be all right. I've had a beautiful life, but I'm ready to go. My husband is gone, my children are gone, and my friends are gone.

> That's what is so wonderful about living to be so old. You know death is near and you don't even care.

> I've just been diagnosed with cancer, but it's no big deal. At my age, I have to die of something. (Johnson and Barer 1997, 205)

The major fear these respondents expressed was not the fear of death but of the dying process. Dying in a nursing home after a long illness is a dreaded fear. Sadly, almost 60 percent of the respondents died after a long, progressive illness. They had become frail, fatigued, and burdened by living. They identified dying in their sleep as the ideal way to die. Some hasten their death by no longer taking their medications or wish they could terminate their own life. "I'm feeling kind of useless. I don't enjoy anything anymore. . . . What the heck am I living for? I'm ready to go anytime—straight to hell. I'd take lots of sleeping pills if I could get them" (Johnson and Barer 1997, 204). Nakashima and Canda (2005) studied sixteen hospice patients and found that having a positive death was associated with coming to terms with one's own mortality, finding meaning in death and dying, and spiritual well-being.

Behaviors in the Last Year of Life   Aware that they are going to die, most simplify their life, disengage from social relationships, and leave final instructions. In simplifying their life, they sell their home and belongings and move to smaller quarters. One 81-year-old woman sold her home, gave her car away to a friend, and moved into a nursing home. The extent of her belongings became a chair, lamp, and TV.

I went sky diving
I went Rocky Mountain climbing
I went 2.7 seconds on a bull named Fumanchu
and I loved deeper and I spoke sweeter
and I gave forgiveness I'd been denying
and he said someday I hope you get the chance
to live like you were dying.

Tim McGraw, country western singer

The end comes to us all.

Authors

*Just think some night the stars will shine
Upon a cold gray stone.
And trace a name with silver beam,
And lo, t'will be your own.*

Robert W. Service, southern poet

Disengaging from social relationships is selective. Some maintain close relationships with children and friends but others "let go." They may no longer send out Christmas cards, stop sending letters, and phone calls become the source of social connections. Some leave final instructions in the form of a will or handwritten note expressing wishes of where to be buried, handling costs associated with disposal of the body, and what to do about pets. One of Johnson and Barer's (1997) respondents left $30,000 to specific caregivers to take care of each of several pets (p. 204).

Elderly who may have counted on children to take care of them may discover that they have too few children who may have scattered because of job changes, divorce, or both (Kutza 2005). The result is that the elderly may have to fend for themselves.

One of the last legal acts of the elderly is to have a will drawn up. Stone (2008) emphasized how wills may stir up sibling rivalry (for example, one sibling may be left more than another), be used as a weapon against a second spouse (for example, by leaving all of one's possessions to one's children), or reveal a toxic secret (for example, reveal a mistress and several children who are left money).

SUMMARY

What is meant by the terms age and ageism?

Age is defined chronologically (by time), physiologically (by capacity to see, hear, and so on), psychologically (by self-concept), sociologically (by social roles), and culturally (by the value placed on elderly). Ageism is the denigration of the elderly, and gerontophobia is the dreaded fear of being elderly. Theories of aging range from disengagement (individuals and societies mutually disengage from each other) to continuity (the habit patterns of youth are continued in old age). Life course is currently the popular aging theory.

What is the "sandwich generation"?

Eldercare combined with child care is becoming common among the sandwich generation, adult children responsible for the needs of both their parents and their children. Two levels of eldercare include help with personal needs such as feeding, bathing, and toileting as well as instrumental care such as going to the grocery store, managing bank records, and so on. Members of the sandwich generation report feelings of exhaustion over the relentless demands, guilt over not doing enough, and resentment over feeling burdened.

Deciding whether to arrange for an elderly parent's care in a nursing home requires attention to a number of factors, including the level of care the parent needs, the philosophy and time availability of the adult child, and the resources of the adult children and other siblings. Full-time nursing care (not including medication) can be between $1,000–$1500 a week.

Elderly parents who are dying from terminal illnesses incur enormous medical bills. Some want to die and ask for help. Our society continues to wrestle with physician-assisted suicide and euthanasia. Only Oregon currently allows for physician-assisted suicide.

What issues confront the elderly?

Issues of concern to the elderly include housing, health, retirement, and sexuality. Most elderly live in their own homes, which they have paid for. Most elderly housing is adequate, although repair becomes a problem when people age. Health concerns are paramount for the elderly. Good health is the single most important factor associated with an elderly person's perceived life satisfaction.

Hearing and visual impairments, arthritis, heart conditions, and high blood pressure are all common to the elderly. Mental problems may also occur with mood disorders; depression is the most common.

Though the elderly are thought to be wealthy and living in luxury, most are not. The median household income of people over the age of 65 is less than half of what they earned in the prime of their lives. The most impoverished elderly are those who have lived the longest, who are widowed, and who live alone. Women are particularly disadvantaged because their work history may have been discontinuous, part-time, and low-paying. Social Security and private pension plans favor those with continuous, full-time work histories.

For most elderly women and men, sexuality involves lower reported interest, activity, and capacity. Fear of the inability to have an erection is the sexual problem elderly men most frequently (Viagra, Levitra, and Cialis have helped allay this fear). The absence of a sexual partner is the sexual problem elderly women most frequently report.

What factors are associated with successful aging?

Factors associated with successful aging include not smoking (or quitting early), developing a positive view of life and life's crises, avoiding alcohol and substance abuse, maintaining healthy weight, exercising daily, continuing to educate oneself, and having a happy marriage. Indeed, those who were identified as "happy and well" were six times more likely to be in a good marriage than those who were identified as "sad and sick." Success in one's career is also associated with successful aging.

What are relationships like for the elderly?

Marriages that survive into old age (beyond age 85) tend to have limited conflict, considerable companionship, and mutual supportiveness. Relationships with siblings are primarily emotional rather than functional. In regard to relationships of the elderly with their children, emotional and expressive rewards are high. Caregiving help is available but rare. Only 12 percent of one sample of adults older than 85 lived with their children.

What is grandparenthood like?

Among adults aged 40 and older who had children, close to 95 percent are grandparents. There is considerable variation in role definition and involvement.

Whereas some delight in seeing their lineage carried forward in their grandchildren and provide emotional and economic support, others are focused on their own lives or on their own children and relate formally and at a distance to

In a world there are no people so piteous and forlorn as those who are forced to eat the bitter bread of dependency in their old age, and find how steep are the stairs of another man's house.

Dorothy Dix, mental health advocate

their grandchildren. When grandparents are involved in their lives, grandchildren benefit in terms of positive psychological and economic benefits.

How do the elderly face the end of life?

Thanatology is the examination of the social dimensions of death, dying, and bereavement. The end of life can involve adjusting to the death of one's spouse and to the gradual decline of one's health. Most elderly are satisfied with their life, relationships, and health. Declines begin when people reach their eighties. Most fear the process of dying more than death.

KEY TERMS

advance directive	cohousing	filial responsibility	Medicaid
age	dementia	frail	Medicare
age discrimination	durable power of attorney	gerontology	quality of life
ageism	euthanasia	gerontophobia	sandwich generation
blurred retirement	family caregiving	Levitra	thanatology
Cialis	filial piety	living will	Viagra

The Companion Website for *Choices in Relationships: An Introduction to Marriage and the Family,* Tenth Edition

www.cengage.com/sociology/knox

Supplement your review of this chapter by going to the Companion Website to take one of the tutorial quizzes, use the flash cards to master key terms, or check out the many other study aids, like crossword puzzles and self-assessments. You'll also find special features such as General Social Survey (GSS) data, Census data, and other resources to help you with that special project or to do some research on your own.

WEB LINKS

AARP (American Association of Retired Persons)
   http://www.aarp.org

Calculate Your Life Expectancy
   www.livingto100.com

ElderSpirit Community
   www.elderspirit.net

ElderWeb
   http://www.elderweb.com

Family Caregiver Alliance
   http://caregiver.org/caregiver/jsp/home.jsp

Foundation for Grandparenting
   http://www.grandparenting.org/Generations United
   http://www.gu.org

GROWW (Grief Recovery Online)
   http://www.groww.com

Nolo: Law for All (wills and legal issues)
   http://www.nolo.com

Silver Sage Village
   http://www.silversagevillage.com

REFERENCES

Ackerman, R. J., and M. E. Banks. 2007. Women over 50: Caregiving issues. In *Women over fifty: Psychological perspectives,* ed. Varda Muhlbauer and Joan C. Chrisler, 147–63. New York: Springer Science and Business Media.

Agahi, N. 2008. Leisure activities and mortality: Does gender matter? *Journal of Aging and Health* 20:855–71.

Alford-Cooper, F. 2006. Where has all the sex gone? Sexual activity in lifetime marriage. Paper presented at the Southern Sociological Society, New Orleans, March 23–26.

Barrett, A. E. 2005. Gendered experiences in midlife: Implications for age identity. *Journal of Aging Studies* 19:163–83.

Beckman, N. M., M. Waern, I. Skoog, and The Sahlgrenska Academy at Goteborg University, Sweden. 2006. Determinants of sexuality in 70 year olds. *The Journal of Sex Research* 43:2–3.

Berg, A. S. 2003. *Kate remembered.* New York: G. P. Putnam's Sons.

Bookwala, J. 2005. The role of marital quality in physical health during the mature years. *Journal of Aging and Health* 17:85–97.

Boulton-Lewis, G. M., L. K. Buys, and J. Kitchin. 2006. Learning and active aging. *Educational Gerontology* 32 271–82.

Brown, S. L., D. M Smith, R. Schulz, M. U. Kabeto, et al. 2009. Caregiving behavior is associated with decreased mortality risk. *Psychological Science* 20:488–503.

Bryant, C. D. 2007. The sociology of death and dying. In *21st century sociology: A reference handbook*, ed. Clifton D. Bryant and Dennis L. Peck, 156–66. Thousand Oaks, California: Sage.

Bullock, K. 2005. Grandfathers and the impact of raising grandchildren. *Journal of Sociology and Social Welfare* 32:43–59.

Cardozo, M. 2006. What is a good death? Issues to examine in critical care. *British Journal of Nursing* 14:1056–60.

Chadiha, L., J. Rafferty, and J. Pickard. 2003. The influence of caregiving stressors, social support, and caregiving appraisal on marital function among African American wife caregivers. *Journal of Marital and Family Therapy* 29:479–90.

Chan, S. 2003. Rates of assisted suicides rise sharply in Oregon. *Student MBJ* 11:137–38.

Chen, F., and S. E. Short. 2008. Household context and subjective well-being among the oldest old in China. *Journal of Family Issues* 29:1379–88.

Clare, L., I. Markova, F. Verhey, and G. Kenny. 2005. Awareness in dementia: A review of assessment methods and measures. *Aging and Mental Health* 9:394–404.

Collins, A. L., and M. A. Smyer. 2005. The resilience of self-esteem in late adulthood. *Journal of Aging and Health* 17:471–90.

Coombes, A. 2007. What are the key ingredients to a happier old age? It's easier than you think. http://www.marketwatch.com/news/story/here-key-ingredients-staying-happy/story.aspx?guid=%7BFD3F3A18-7DF3-4BF5-A3A3-B6438317E693%7D (retrieved August 24).

Cutler, N. E. 2002. *Advising mature clients*. New York: Wiley.

Danigelis, N. L., M. Hardy, and S. J. Cutler. 2007. Population aging, intracohort aging, and sociopolitical attitudes. *American Sociological Review* 72:812–30.

Davies, C. 2002. The grandparent study 2002 report. Washington, DC: AARP.

Dychtwald, K., and D. J. Kadlec. 2005. *The power years: A user's guide to the rest of your life*. New York: Wiley.

Fabian, N. 2007. Rethinking retirement—And a footnote on diversity. *Journal of Environmental Health* 69:86–85.

Family Caregiver Alliance. http://caregiver.org/caregiver/jsp/content_node.jsp?nodeid=439 (retrieved April 10, 2006).

Fernandez-Ballesteros, R. 2003. Social support and quality of life among older people in Spain. *Journal of Social Issues* 58:645–60.

Field, D., and S. Weishaus. 1992. Marriage over half a century: A longitudinal study. In *Changing lives*, ed. M. Bloom, 269–73. Columbia, SC: University of South Carolina Press.

Gallanis, T. P. 2002. Aging and the nontraditional family. *The University of Memphis Law Review* 32:607–42.

Garrett, N., and E. M. Martini. 2007. The boomers are coming: A total cost of care model of the impact of population aging on the cost of chronic conditions in the United States. *Disease Management* 10:51–60.

Hansson, R. O., J. O. Berry, and M. E. Berry. 1999. The bereavement experience: Continuing commitment after the loss of a loved one. In *Handbook of interpersonal commitment and relationship stability*, ed. J. M. Adams and W. H. Jones, 281–91. New York: Academic/Plenum Publishers.

Hays, J., J. K. Ockene, R. L. Brunner, J. M. Kotchen, J. E. Manson, R. E. Patterson, A. K. Aragki, M. S., S. A. Shumaker, R. G. Bryzyski, et al. 2003. Effects of estrogen plus progestin on health-related quality of life. *The New England Journal of Medicine* 348:1839–54.

Hayslip, B., and P. L. Kaminski 2005. Grandparents raising their grandchildren. *Marriage and Family Review* 37:171–90.

Henderson, T. L. 2005. Grandparent visitation rights: Successful acquisition of court-ordered visitation. *Journal of Family Issues* 26:107–16.

Henry, R. G., R. B. Miller, and R. Giarrusso. 2005. Difficulties, disagreements, and disappointments in late-life marriages. *International Journal of Aging & Human Development* 61:243–265.

Hilgeman, M. M., R. S. Allen, J. DeCoster, and L. D. Burgio. 2007. Positive aspects of caregiving as a moderator of treatment outcome over 12 months. *Psychology and Aging* 22:361–71.

Horton, S., and J. Deakin. 2007. Role models for seniors and society: Seniors' perceptions of aging successfully. *Journal of Sport & Exercise Psychology* 29:14–15.

Ikegami, N. 1998. Growing old in Japan. *Age and Ageing* 27:277–78.

Jang, S., and D. F. Detzner. 1998. Filial responsibility in cross-cultural context. Poster at the Annual Conference of the National Council on Family Relations, Milwaukee, Wisconsin.

Johnson, C. L., and B. M. Barer. 1997. *Life beyond 85 years: The aura of survivorship*. New York: Springer Publishing.

Johnson, R. W., and J. M. Wiener. 2006. A profile of frail older Americans and their caregivers. Urban Institute Report. http://www.urban.org/url.cfm?ID=311284 (posted March 1).

Jorm, A. F., H. Christensen, A. S. Henderson, P. A. Jacomb, A. E. Korten, and A. Mackinnon. 1998. Factors associated with successful ageing. *Australian Journal of Ageing* 17:33–37.

Kalish, N. 1997. *Lost & found lovers: Facts and fantasies of rekindled romances*. New York: William Morrow and Company.

Karlsson, S. G., and K. Borell 2005. A home of their own. Women's boundary work in LAT-relationships. *Journal of Aging Studies* 19:73–84.

Kelley-Moore, J. A., J. G. Schumacher, E. Kahana, and B. Kahana. 2006. When do older adults become 'disabled'? Social and health antecedents of perceived disability in a panel study of the oldest old. *Journal of Health and Social Behavior* 47:126–42.

Kemp, C. L., C. J. Rosenthal, and M. Denton. 2005. Financial planning for later life: Subjective understandings of catalysts and constraints. *Journal of Aging Studies* 19:273–90.

Kennedy, G. E. 1997. Grandchildren's memories: A window into relationship meaning. Paper presented at the Annual Conference of the National Council on Family Relations, Crystal City, Virginia.

Kimuna, S., D. Knox, and M. Zusman. 2005. College students perceptions about older people and aging. *Educational Gerontology* 31:563–72.

Kimuna, S. R., and M. Makiwane. 2007. Older people as resources in South Africa: Mpumalanga households. *Journal of Aging & Social Policy* 19:97–114.

King, V. 2003. The legacy of a grandparent's divorce: Consequences for ties between grandparents and grandchildren. *Journal of Marriage and the Family* 65:170–83.

Knox, D., and Zusman, M. E. 2009. Relationship and sexual behaviors of a sample of 1319 university students. Unpublished data collected for this text. Department of Sociology, East Carolina University, Greenville, NC.

Knox, D., S. Kimuna, and M. Zusman. 2005. College student views of the elderly: Some gender differences. *College Student Journal* 39:14–16.

Krause, N. 2005. Negative interaction and heart disease in late life: Exploring variations by socio-economic status. *Journal of Aging and Health* 17:28–35.

Kulik, L. 2007. Contemporary midlife grandparenthood. In *Women over fifty: Psychological perspectives*, ed. Varda Muhlbauer and Joan C. Chrisler, 131–46. New York: Springer Science and Business Media.

Kutza, E. A. 2005. The intersection of economics and family status in later life: Implications for the future. *Marriage and Family Review* 37:3–8.

Landry-Meyer, L. 2000. Grandparents as parents: What they need to be successful. *National Council on Family Relations* 45:89.

Lees, F.D., P. G. Clark, C. R. Nigg, and P. Newman. 2005. Barriers to exercise behavior among older adults: A focus-group study. *Journal of Aging and Physical Activity* 13:23–34.

Lindau, S. T., L. P. Schumm, E. O. Laumann, W. Levinson, C. A. O'Muircheartaigh, and L. J. Waite. 2007. A study of sexuality and health among older adults in the United States. *The New England Journal of Medicine* 357:762–74.

Logan, J. R., and F. Bian. 2003. Parents' needs, family structure, and regular international financial exchange in Chinese cities. *Sociological Forum* 18:85–101.

Maher, D. and C. Mercer (editors). 2009. Introduction. *Introduction to religion and the implications of radical life extension*. New York: Palgrave Macmillan.

Marks, N. F., J. D. Lambert, and H. Choi. 2002. Transitions to caregiving, gender, and psychological well-being: A prospective U.S. national study. *Journal of Marriage and Family* 64:657–67.

Marquet, R., A. Bartelds, G. J. Visser, P. Spreeuwenberg, and I. Peters. 2003. Twenty-five years of requests for euthanasia and physician assisted suicide in Dutch practice: Trend analysis. *British Medical Journal* 327:201–02.

Martire, L. M., and M. A. P. Stephens. 2003. Juggling parent care and employment responsibilities: The dilemmas of adult daughter caregivers in the workforce. *Sex Roles: A Journal of Research* 48:167–74.

Mills, T. L., Z. Gomez-Smith, and J. M. DeLeon. 2005. Skipped generation families: Sources of psychological distress among grandmothers of grandchildren who live in homes where neither parent is present. *Marriage and Family Review* 37:191–212.

Morey, M. C., R. Sloane, C. F Pieper, and M. J. Peterson. 2008. Effect of physical activity guidelines on physical function in older adults. *Journal of the American Geriatrics Society* 56:1873–85.

Musil, C. M., and T. Standing. 2005. Grandmothers' diaries: A glimpse at daily lives *International Journal of Aging and Human Development* 60:317–29.

Mutran, E. J., D. Reitzes, and M. E. Fernandez. 1997. Factors that influence attitudes toward retirement. *Research on Aging* 19:251–73.

Nakashima, M., and E. R. Canda. 2005. Positive dying and resiliency in later life: A qualitative study. *Journal of Aging Studies* 19:109–22.

National Institute of Mental Health. 2003. Older adults: Depression and suicide facts. HIH Publication No. 03–4593. www.nimh.nih.gov/publicat/elderlydep suicide.cfm (retrieved on July 23, 2003).

Nicholson, T. 2003. Homeowners fail to prepare for aging. *AARP Bulletin* 44:7.

Nordenmark, M., and M. Stattin. 2009. Psychosocial wellbeing and reasons for retirement in Sweden. *Ageing and Society* 29:413–41.

O'Reilly, E. M. 1997. *Decoding the cultural stereotypes about aging: New perspectives on aging talk and aging issues*. New York: Garland.

Ostbye, T., K. M. Krause, M. C. Norton, J. Tschanz, L. Sanders, K. Hayden, C. Pieper, and K. A. Welsh-Bohmer. 2006. Ten dimensions of health and their relationships with overall self-reported health and survival in a predominately religiously active elderly population: *The Cache County Memory Study*. *Journal of the American Geriatrics Society* 54:199–209.

Patrick, M. 2009. A case study of the raging grannies. Poster at Eastern Sociological Society Annual Meeting, Baltimore, MD, March 20.

Peterson, B. E. 2002. Longitudinal analysis of midlife generativity, intergenerational roles, and caregiving. *Psychology and Aging* 17:161–68.

Pnina, R. 2007. Elderly people's attitudes and perceptions of aging and old age: the role of cognitive dissonance? *International Journal of Geriatric Psychiatry* 22:656–72.

Pope, E. 2003. MIT study: Older drivers know when to slow down. *AARP Bulletin* 44:11–12.

Potts, A., V. M. Grace, T. Vares, and N. Gavey. 2006. "Sex for life"? Men's counter-stories on "erectile dysfunction," male sexuality and ageing. *Sociology and Health and Illness* 28:306–29.

Russell, R. 2007. Men doing "Women's work:" Elderly men caregivers and the gendered construction of care work. *Journal of Men's Studies* 15:1–18.

Ryan, J., I. Carrière, J. Scali, K. Ritchie, and M. Ancelin. 2008. Lifetime hormonal factors may predict late-life depression in women. *International Psychogeriatrics* 20:1203–29.

Sandberg, J. G., R. B. Miller, and J. M. Harper. 2002. A qualitative study of marital process and depression in older couples. *Family Relations* 51:256–64.

Sawyer, Francine. 2008. Article is abridged from that which appeared in the *Sun Journal* of New Bern, NC, September 13, 2008. Used by permission.

Schairer, C., J. Lubin, R. Troisi, S. Sturgeon, L. Brinton, and R. Hoover. 2000. Menopausal estrogen and estrogen-progestin replacement therapy and breast cancer risk. *Journal of the American Medical Association* 283:485–91.

Shah, A. 2009. The relationship between population growth and elderly suicide rates: a cross-national study. *International Psychogeriatrics* 21:379–481.

Siedlecki, K. L. 2007. Investigating the structure and age invariance of episodic memory across the adult lifespan. *Psychology & Aging* 22:251–68.

Silverstein, M., Z. Cong, and S. Li. 2006. Intergenerational transfers and living arrangements of older people in rural China: Consequences for psychological well-being. 2006. *The Journals of Gerontology, Series B: Psychological Sciences and Social Sciences*, vol. 61B: S256–267.

Smith, J., M. Borchelt, H. Maier, and D. Jopp. 2002. Health and well-being in the young old and oldest old. *Journal of Social Issues* 58:715–33.

Statistical Abstract of the United States, 2009. 128th ed. Washington, DC: U.S. Bureau of the Census.

Stephenson, L. E., S. N. Culos-Reed, P. K. Doyle-Baker, J. A. Devonish, and J. A. Dickinson. 2007. Walking for wellness: Results from a mall walking program for the elderly. *Journal of Sport & Exercise Psychology* 29:204–14.

Stevens, N. 2002. Re-engaging: New partnerships in late-life widowhood. *Ageing International* 27:27–42.

Stone, E. 2008. The last will and testament in literature: Rupture, rivalry, and sometimes Rapprochement from Middlemarch to Lemony Snikert. *Family Process* 47:425–39.

Stroebe, M., and H. Schut. 2005. To continue or relinquish bonds: A review of consequences for the bereaved. *Death Studies* 29:477–95.

Szinovacz, M. E., and A. M. Schaffer. 2000. Effects of retirement on marital tactics. *Journal of Family Issues* 21:367–89.

Tanner, D. 2005. Promoting the well-being of older people: Messages for social workers. *Practice* 17:191–205.

Taylor, A. C., M. Robila, and L. Hae Seung. 2005. Distance, contact, and intergenerational relationships: Grandparents and adult grandchildren from an international perspective. *Journal of Adult Development* 12:33–41.

Useda, J. D., K. R. Conner, A. Beckman, N. Franus, Z. Tu, and Y. Conwell. 2007. Personality differences in attempted suicide versus suicide in adults 50 years of age or older. *Journal of Consulting and Clinical Psychology* 75:126–33.

Valliant, G. E. 2002. *Aging well: Surprising guideposts to a happier life from the Landmark Harvard study on adult development.* New York: Little, Brown.

Van Gool, C. H., G. Kempen, H. Bosma, J. Van Eijk, M. P. J. Van Boxtel, and J. Jolles. 2007. Associations between lifestyle and depressed mood: longitudinal results from the Maastricht Aging Study. *American Journal of Public Health* 97:887–94.

Vance, D. E., V. G. Wadley, K. K. Ball, D. L. Roenker, and M. Rizzo. 2005. The effects of physical activity and sedentary behavior on cognitive health in older adults. *Journal of Aging & Physical Activity* 13:294–314.

Walker, R. B., and M. A. Luszcz. 2009. The health and relationship dynamics of late-life couples: A systematic review of the literature. *Ageing and Society* 29:455–81.

Wallsten, S. S. 2000. Effects of care giving, gender, and race on the health, mutuality, and social supports of older couples. *Journal of Aging and Health* 12:90–111.

Webber, S., J. P. Scott, and R. Wampler. 2000. Perceived congruency of goals as a predictor of marital satisfaction and adjustment in retirement. Poster at the 62nd Annual Conference of the National Council on Family Relations, Minneapolis, November 12.

Weintraub, P. 2006. Guess who's back? *Psychology Today* 39(4):79–84.

Wells, Y. D. 2000. Intentions to care for spouse: Gender differences in anticipated willingness to care and expected burden. *Journal of Family Studies* 5:220–34.

Wielink, G., R. Huijsman, and J. McDonnell. 1997. A study of the elders living independently in the Netherlands. *Research on Aging* 19:174–98.

Willson, A. E. 2007. The sociology of aging. In *21st century sociology: A reference handbook*, ed. Clifton D. Bryant and Dennis L. Peck, 148–55. Thousand Oaks, California: Sage Publications.

Winterich, J. A. 2003. Sex, menopause, and culture: Sexual orientation and the meaning of menopause for women's sex lives. *Gender and Society* 17:627–42.

Wolkove, N., O. Elkholy, M. Baltzan, and M. Palayew. 2007. Sleep and aging. *Canadian Medical Association Journal* 176:1299–1304.

Wrosch, C., R. Schulz, G. E. Miller, S. Lupien, and E. Dunne. 2007. Physical health problems, depressive mood, and cortisol secretion in old age: Buffer effects of health engagement control strategies *Health Psychology* 26:341–49.

Wu, Z., and R. Hart. 2002. The mental health of the childless elderly. *Sociological Inquiry* 72:21–42.

Zhan, H. J., and R. J. V. Montgomery. 2003. Gender and elder care in China: The influence of filial piety and structural constraints. *Gender and Society* 17:209–29.

Zhan, H. J., X. Feng, and B. Luo. 2008. Placing elderly parents in institutions in urban China: A reintepretation of filial piety. *Research on Aging* 30:543–58.

The Future of Marriage and the Family

Social scientists do not have a particularly good track record of forecasting social change.

Paul Amato and colleagues, *Alone Together*

What can we predict about marriage and the family as we move toward 2015? We have no crystal ball but think it reasonable to suggest the following:

Marriage: Marriage will continue to be the lifestyle of choice for the majority (90 percent plus) of U.S. adults. Though individuals will increasingly delay getting married until their late twenties to early thirties (to complete their educations, launch their careers, and/or become economically independent), there is no evidence that they intend to avoid marriage completely. The almost 5 million who marry annually and the over 125 million already married are among the happiest, healthiest, and most sexually fulfilled in our society.

Children: Although the majority of individuals and couples will have children, they (children) will become less of a requirement for personal and marital fulfillment. Women are becoming more attentive to the sacrifices involved in child rearing and men to the restrictions children impose on their freedom. The result is that the childfree option is being met with less disapproval.

Although most children will continue to be born into married, two-parent homes, conceiving and rearing children outside legal marriage into single-parent families (both heterosexual and homosexual) will be increasingly accepted. Children born to married couples will not be immune to being reared in single-parent families because between 40 percent and 45 percent of their parents will divorce.

Singlehood: Singlehood will (in the cultural spirit of diversity) lose some of its stigma, more will choose this option, and most of those who remain unmarried will find satisfaction in this lifestyle.

Gay Marriage: Although gay marriage will remain controversial, each year, more states will legalize same-sex marriage (for example, Vermont, Massachusetts, New Hampshire, Connecticut, and Iowa will be joined by other states). However, there will continue to be no federal recognition of gay marriage, meaning that no Social Security benefits are available to survivors of deceased partners. The federal government and over half the states have enacted laws barring the recognition of gay marriages.

Cohabitation: Cohabitation has become an accepted, and for many, a predictable stage of courtship. The link between cohabitation and subsequent divorce will dissolve as more individuals elect to cohabit before marriage. Previously, only risk takers and people willing to abandon traditional norms lived together before marriage. In the future, mainstream individuals will cohabit.

Dual-Earner Relationships: The one-income family will continue to be in the minority. The prices of goods and services often requires two incomes to pay for housing, food, cars, and so on. Time with the family will continue to take precedence over work time, and job flexibility will remain an important factor in selecting a career and a job. Women will continue to give greater priority to family life than men and pay a greater cost in terms of decreased wages and career advancement.

Day Care: As more children spend more time in day care, increasing pressure will be put on the industry to provide "quality" care. However, the sheer demand will not be followed by the funds to pay for trained staff in smaller classes, with the result that more children will spend time in substandard day-care facilities. Because day care workers are predominantly women, wages will remain low and turnover high.

Violence and Abuse: Abuse in relationships will continue to occur behind closed doors. However, cultural visibility of abusive relationships, support for leaving abusive partners, and the availability of hotlines and shelters will enable increasing numbers of individuals to bravely leave these relationships.

Divorce: Divorce will continue to end more marriages than the death of a spouse. Between 40 percent and 45 percent of people beginning their lives together as spouses will end up as ex-spouses haggling over custody, child support, and visitation. Divorce mediation will become a valuable alternative to some litigated endings. The stigma of divorce will remain. At a wedding friends and family surround the bride and groom; most divorcing spouses go to court alone.

Elderly: Elderly individuals, particularly those in their late eighties, will continue to find the end of life a challenge. Health problems (and the attendant lack of health care), lower incomes, and the death of close loved ones reflect the reality for many elderly in the United States today. As our population continues to age, attention to problems of the elderly will continue and give hope to improvement of the final days.

The summary statement for the future of marriage and the family is, "Nothing endures but change" (Heraclitus). We embrace the future.

*For women the best
aphrodisiacs are words.
The G-spot is in the ears. He
who looks for it below there
is wasting his time.*

Isabel Allende

Sexual Anatomy and Physiology

Authors

Contents

If we think of the human body as a special type of machine, *anatomy* refers to that machine's parts and *physiology* refers to how the parts work. This Special Topic reviews the sexual anatomy and physiology of women and men and the reproductive process.

Female External Anatomy and Physiology

The external female genitalia are collectively known as the vulva (VUHL-vuh), a Latin term meaning "covering." The vulva consists of the mons veneris, the labia, the clitoris, and the vaginal and urethral openings (see Figure ST1.1). The female genitalia differ in size, shape, and color, resulting in considerable variability in appearance.

Terms for male genitalia (for example, *penis, testicles*) are more commonly known than are the terms for female genitalia. Some women do not even accurately name their genitals. At best, little girls are taught that they have a vagina, which becomes the word for everything "down there"; they rarely learn they also have a vulva, a clitoris, and labia.

Mons Veneris

The soft cushion of fatty tissue overlying the pubic bone is called the *mons veneris* (mahns vuh-NAIR-ihs), also known as the *mons pubis*. This area becomes covered with hair at puberty and has numerous nerve endings. The purpose of the mons veneris is to protect the pubic region during sexual intercourse.

Labia

In the sexually unstimulated state, the urethral and vaginal openings are protected by the *labia majora* (LAY-bee-uh muh-JOR-uh), or outer lips—two elongated folds of fatty tissue that extend from the mons veneris to the *perineum*, the area of skin between the opening of the vagina and the anus. Located between the labia majora are two additional hairless folds of skin, called the *labia minora* (muh-NOR-uh), or inner lips, that cover the urethral and vaginal openings and join at the top to form the hood of the clitoris. Some contend that the clitoral hood provides clitoral stimulation during intercourse. Both sets of labia—particularly the inner labia minora—have a rich supply of nerve endings that are sensitive to sexual stimulation.

Clitoris

At the top of the labia minora is the *clitoris* (KLIHT-uh-ruhs), which also has a rich supply of nerve endings. The clitoris is a very important site of sexual excitement and, like the penis, becomes erect during sexual excitation.

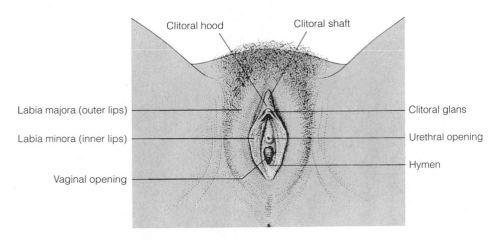

Clitoral hood
Clitoral shaft
Labia majora (outer lips)
Labia minora (inner lips)
Vaginal opening
Clitoral glans
Urethral opening
Hymen

FIGURE ST1.1
External Female Genitalia

Vaginal Opening

The area between the labia minora is called the *vestibule*. This includes the urethral opening and the vaginal opening, or *introitus* (ihn-TROH-ih-tuhs), neither of which is visible unless the labia minora are parted. Like the anus, the vaginal opening is surrounded by a ring of sphincter muscles. Although the vaginal opening can expand to accommodate the passage of a baby at childbirth, under conditions of tension these muscles can involuntarily contract, making it difficult to insert an object, including a tampon, into the vagina. The vaginal opening is sometimes covered by a *hymen*, a thin membrane.

Probably no other body part has caused as much grief to so many women as the hymen, which has been regarded throughout history as proof of virginity. A newlywed woman who was thought to be without a hymen was often returned to her parents, disgraced by exile, or even tortured and killed. It has been a common practice in many societies to parade a bloody bed sheet after the wedding night as proof of the bride's virginity. The anxieties caused by the absence of a hymen persist even today; in Japan and other countries, sexually experienced women may have a plastic surgeon reconstruct a hymen before marriage. Yet the hymen is really a poor indicator of virtue. Some women are born without a hymen or with incomplete hymens. In others, the hymen is accidentally ruptured by vigorous physical activity or insertion of a tampon. In some women, the hymen may not tear but only stretch during sexual intercourse. Even most doctors cannot easily determine whether a woman is a virgin.

Urethral Opening

Just above the vaginal opening is the urethral opening, where urine passes from the body. A short tube, the *urethra,* connects the bladder (where urine collects) with the urethral opening. Because of the shorter length of the female urethra and its close proximity to the anus, women are more susceptible than men to cystitis, a bladder inflammation.

Female Internal Anatomy and Physiology

The internal sex organs of the female include the vagina, pubococcygeus muscle, uterus, and paired fallopian tubes and ovaries (see Figure ST1.2).

FIGURE ST1.2
Internal Female Sexual and Reproductive Organs

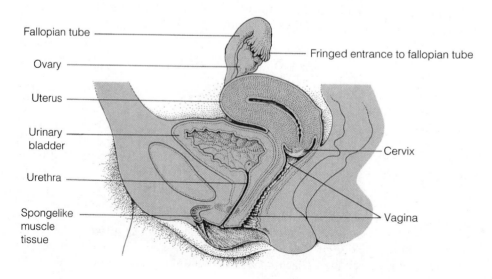

Special Topic 1 Sexual Anatomy and Physiology

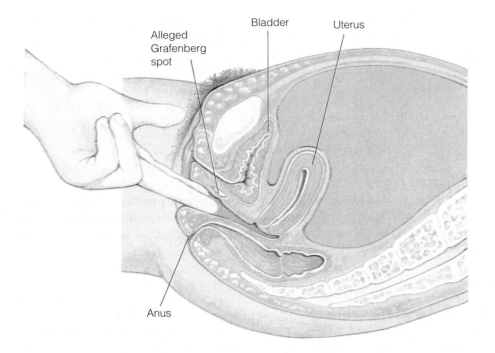

Alleged
Grafenberg
spot

Bladder

Uterus

Anus

Vagina

Some people erroneously believe that the *vagina* is a dirty part of the body. In fact, the vagina is a self-cleansing organ. The bacteria that are found naturally in the vagina help to destroy other potentially harmful bacteria. In addition, secretions from the vaginal walls help to maintain the vagina's normally acidic environment. The use of feminine hygiene sprays, as well as excessive douching, can cause irritation, allergic reactions, and, in some cases, vaginal infection by altering the normal chemical balance of the vagina.

Some researchers have reported that some women experience extreme sensitivity in an area in the front wall of the vagina one to two inches into the vaginal opening. The spot (or area) may swell during stimulation, and although a woman's initial response may be a need to urinate, continued stimulation generally leads to orgasm. The area was named the *Grafenberg spot,* or *G-spot,* for gynecologist Ernest Grafenberg, who first noticed the erotic sensitivity of this area more than forty years ago. Not all women notice a G-spot (see Figure ST1.3).

Pubococcygeus Muscle

Also called the *PC muscle,* the *pubococcygeus muscle* is one of the pelvic floor muscles that surround the vagina, the urethra, and the anus. To find her PC muscle, a woman is instructed to voluntarily stop the flow of urine after she has begun to urinate. The muscle that stops the flow is the PC muscle.

A woman can strengthen her PC muscle by performing Kegel exercises, named after the physician who devised them. The Kegel exercises involve contracting the PC muscle several times for several sessions per day. Kegel exercises are often recommended after childbirth to restore muscle tone to the PC muscle, which is stretched during the childbirth process, and to help prevent involuntary loss of urine.

Uterus

The *uterus* (YOOT-uh-ruhs), or *womb,* resembles a small, inverted pear, which measures about three inches long and three inches wide at the top in women who have not given birth. A fertilized egg becomes implanted in the wall of the uterus and continues to grow and develop until delivery. At the lower end of the uterus is the *cervix,* an opening that leads into the vagina.

All adult women should have a pelvic examination, including a Pap test, each year. A Pap test is extremely important in the detection of cervical cancer. Cancer of the cervix and uterus is the second most common form of cancer in women.

Some women may neglect to get a Pap test because they feel embarrassed or anxious about it or because they think they are too young to worry about getting cancer. For all women over age 20, however, having annual Pap tests may mean the difference between life and death.

Fallopian Tubes

The *fallopian* (ful-LOH-pee-uhn) *tubes* extend about four inches laterally from either side of the uterus to the ovaries. Fertilization normally occurs in the fallopian tubes. The tubes transport the ovum, or egg, by means of *cilia* (hairlike structures) down the tube and into the uterus.

Ovaries

The *ovaries* (OH-vuhr-eez) are two almond-shaped structures, one on either side of the uterus. The ovaries produce eggs (ova) and the female hormones estrogen and progesterone. At birth, a woman has a number of immature ova in her ovaries. Each ovum is enclosed in a thin capsule forming a follicle. Some of the follicles begin to mature at puberty; only about 400 mature ova will be released in a woman's lifetime.

Male External Anatomy and Physiology

Although they differ in appearance, many structures of the male (see Figure ST1.4) and female genitals develop from the same embryonic tissue (the penis and the clitoris, for example).

Penis

The *penis* (PEE-nihs) is the primary male sexual organ. In the unaroused state, the penis is soft and hangs between the legs. When sexually stimulated, the penis enlarges and becomes erect, enabling penetration of the vagina. The penis functions not only to deposit sperm in the female's vagina but also as a passageway from the male's bladder to eliminate urine. In a cross section, the penis can be seen to consist of three parallel cylinders of tissue containing many cavities, two *corpora cavernosa* (cavernous bodies), and a *corpus spongiosum* (spongy body) through which the urethra passes. The penis has numerous blood vessels; when stimulated, the arteries dilate and blood enters faster than it can leave. The cavities of the cavernous and spongy bodies fill with blood, and pressure against the fibrous membranes causes the penis to become erect. The head of the penis is called the glans. At birth, the glans is covered by *foreskin.*

Circumcision, the surgical procedure in which the foreskin of the male is pulled forward and cut off, has been practiced for at least 6,000 years. About 80 percent of men in the United States have been circumcised.

Circumcision is a religious rite for members of the Jewish and Muslim faiths. For Jewish people, circumcision symbolizes the covenant between God and Abraham. In the United States, the procedure is generally done within the first few days after birth. Among non-Jewish people, circumcision first became popular in the United States during the nineteenth century as a means of preventing masturbation. Such effectiveness has not been demonstrated.

Today, the primary reason for performing circumcision is to ensure proper hygiene and to maintain tradition. The smegma that can build up under the

FIGURE ST1.4
External Male Sexual Organs

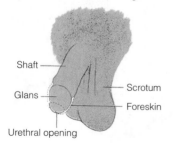

Shaft

Glans

Urethral opening

Scrotum

Foreskin

Special Topic 1 Sexual Anatomy and Physiology

foreskin is a potential breeding ground for infection. However, circumcision may be a rather drastic procedure merely to ensure proper hygiene, which can just as easily be accomplished by pulling back the foreskin and cleaning the glans during normal bathing. However, being circumcised is associated with having a lower risk of contracting penile human papillomavirus (HPV); similarly, female partners of men who engage in risky sexual behavior have a reduced likelihood of having cervical cancer if the man is circumcised (Lane and Althus 2002). Circumcision is a relatively low-risk surgical procedure. Although the male does feel pain, administering local anesthesia can minimize it.

Scrotum

The *scrotum* (SCROH-tuhm) is the sac located below the penis that contains the *testes*. Beneath the skin covering the scrotum is a thin layer of muscle fibers that contract when it is cold, helping to draw the testes (testicles) closer to the body to keep the temperature of the sperm constant. Sperm can be produced only at a temperature several degrees lower than normal body temperature; any prolonged variation can result in sterility.

Male Internal Anatomy and Physiology

The male internal organs, often referred to as the reproductive organs, include the testes, where the sperm are produced; a duct system to transport and propel the sperm out of the body; and some additional structures that produce the seminal fluid in which the sperm are mixed before ejaculation (see Figure ST1.5).

Testes

The male gonads—the paired testes, or testicles—develop from the same embryonic tissue as the female gonads (the ovaries). The two oval-shaped testicles are suspended in the scrotum by the *spermatic cord* and enclosed within a fibrous sheath. The function of the testes is to produce spermatozoa and male hormones, primarily testosterone.

Duct System

Several hundred *seminiferous tubules* come together to form a tube in each testicle called the *epididymis* (ehp-uh-DIHD-uh-muhs), the first part of the duct system that transports sperm. If uncoiled, each tube would be twenty feet long. Sperm

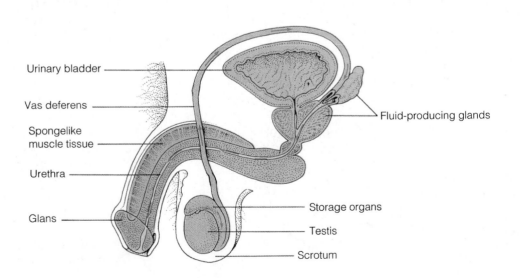

FIGURE ST1.5
Internal and External Male Sexual Organs

spend from two to six weeks traveling through the epididymis as they mature and are reabsorbed by the body if ejaculation does not occur. One ejaculation contains an average of 360 million sperm cells.

The sperm leave the scrotum through the second part of the duct system, the *vas deferens* (vas-DEF-uh-renz). These 14- to 16-inch paired ducts transport the sperm from the epididymis up and over the bladder to the prostate gland. Rhythmic contractions during ejaculation force the sperm into the paired ejaculatory ducts that run through the prostate gland. The entire length of this portion of the duct system is less than one inch. Here, the sperm mix with seminal fluid to form semen before being propelled to the outside through the urethra.

Seminal Vesicles and Prostate Gland

The *seminal vesicles* resemble two small sacs, each about two inches in length, located behind the bladder. These vesicles secrete their own fluids, which empty into the ejaculatory duct to mix with sperm and fluids from the prostate gland.

Most of the seminal fluid comes from the *prostate gland,* a chestnut-sized structure located below the bladder and in front of the rectum. The fluid is alkaline and serves to protect the sperm in the more acidic environments of the male urethra and female vagina. Males older than 45 should have a rectal examination annually to detect the presence of prostate cancer.

A small amount of clear, sticky fluid is also secreted into the urethra before ejaculation by two pea-sized *Cowper's,* or *bulbourethral,* glands located below the prostate gland. This protein-rich fluid alkalizes the urethral passage, which prolongs sperm life.

The fluid secreted by the Cowper's glands can often be noticed on the tip of the penis during sexual arousal. Because this fluid may contain sperm, withdrawal of the penis from the vagina before ejaculation is a risky method of birth control.

Couples might consider increased intimacy, rather than sexual performance, as the goal of sexual therapy.

Clark Christensen, sex therapist

Sexual Dysfunctions

Authors

Contents

Although we will discuss the various sexual dysfunctions of both women and men, it is important to keep in mind that a couple may report sexual satisfaction in their relationship despite possible sexual dysfunctions (Kleinplatz 2008). Sexual dysfunctions may be classified by time of onset, situations in which they occur, and cause. A **primary sexual dysfunction** is one that a person has always had. A **secondary sexual dysfunction** is one that a person is currently experiencing, after a period of satisfactory sexual functioning. For example, a woman who has never had an orgasm with any previous sexual partner has a primary dysfunction, whereas a woman who has been orgasmic with previous partners but not with a current partner has a secondary sexual dysfunction.

A situational dysfunction occurs in one context or setting and not in another, whereas a total dysfunction occurs in all contexts or settings. For example, a man who is unable to become erect with one partner but who can become erect with another has a situational dysfunction. Finally, a sexual dysfunction can be classified according to whether it is caused primarily by biological (organic) factors, such as insufficient hormones or physical illness, or by psychosocial or cultural factors, such as negative learning, guilt, anxiety, or an unhappy relationship.

Both women and men report experiencing sexual problems. In a study of 1,768 adults, about a third (34 percent) of the women and four in ten men (41 percent) reported having a current sexual problem (Dunn et al. 2000). Frank et al. (2008) noted that female sexual complaints occur in approximately 40 percent of women. Sexual problems often appear in tandem. Greenstein et al. (2006) assessed the degree to which 113 female partners of men with erectile dysfunction defined themselves as having a sexual dysfunction. Sixty-five percent reported having one or more sexual problems, including orgasmic disorder, low sexual desire, and low arousal. We emphasized the need to evaluate both partners when one of them has a sexual dysfunction.

Sexual problems become visible in societies where specialists (sexologists, sex therapists, and marriage and family therapists) emphasize the importance of problem-free sexual relationships and offer a therapeutic remedy (for a price). Minorities (African Americans, Hispanics, and Asian Americans), particularly women, may have a higher incidence of sexual dysfunctions than Caucasians due to cultural inducement of depression (typically associated with sexual dysfunction) (Dobkin et al. 2006).

In this Special Topics section, we examine the sexual dysfunctions common to women and to men.

The national sex study reported by Dunn et al. (2000) identified the most frequent sexual problems creating dissatisfaction in women as arousal problems (51 percent), unpleasurable sex (47 percent), and inability to achieve orgasm (39 percent). It is not unusual that women with sexual dysfunctions are also distressed over their emotional relationship with their partner.

Sexual Dysfunctions of Women

In this section we discuss the most frequent sexual problems of women.

Arousal Problems

Also referred to as hypoactive sexual desire, lack of interest in sex is the most frequent sexual problem that women in the United States report. Colson et al. (2006) also noted that diminution of sexual desire was the primary sexual complaint of 519 French women surveyed. Lack of interest and difficulty becoming aroused (Quirk et al. 2005) may be caused by one or more factors, including restrictive upbringing, nonacceptance of one's sexual orientation, learning a passive sexual role, and physical factors such as stress, illness, drug use, and fatigue. Dennerstein (2006) also noted that menopause may be related. More often, lack of interest in sex and difficulty in becoming aroused can be explained by the woman's emotional relationship with her partner. In addition to a negative emotional context, women reporting low sexual desire may have lower testosterone levels. Frank et al. (2008) noted that testosterone improves sexual function in postmenopausal women with hypoactive sexual desire disorder. However, its use is not approved in the United States, primarily because of lack of data on the side effects (Hubayter and Simon 2008).

The treatment for lack of interest in sex depends on the underlying cause or causes of the problem. The following are some of the ways in which lack of sexual desire can be treated:

1. *Improve relationship satisfaction.* Treating the relationship before treating the sexual problem is standard therapy in treating any sexual dysfunction, including lack of interest in sex. A prerequisite for being interested in sex with a partner, particularly from the viewpoint of a woman, is to be in love and feel comfortable and secure with the partner. Couples therapy focusing on a loving egalitarian relationship becomes the focus of therapy. Lau et al. (2006) also emphasized the importance of trust in one's partner as a prerequisite for positive sexual functioning.

2. *Practice sensate focus. Sensate focus* is a series of exercises developed by Masters and Johnson used to treat various sexual dysfunctions. Sensate focus may also be used by couples who are not experiencing sexual dysfunction but who want to enhance their sexual relationship. In carrying out the sensate focus exercise, the couple takes turns pleasuring each other in nongenital ways, with each taking turns giving and receiving pleasure (while getting feedback from the partner about what is and is not pleasurable). On subsequent occasions, genital touching is allowed, but orgasm is not the goal. Indeed, the goal of sensate focus is to help the partners learn to give and receive pleasure by promoting trust and communication and by reducing anxiety related to sexual performance.

3. *Be open to re-education.* Re-education involves being open to examining and reevaluating the thoughts, feelings, and attitudes learned in childhood. The goal is to redefine sexual activity so that it is viewed as a positive, desirable, healthy, and pleasurable experience. A national study of Finnish women shows dramatic changes in their reported increases in sexual satisfaction. Women from unreserved and nonreligious homes who had high education and who were sexually assertive reported the greatest pleasure in sexual intercourse (Haavio-Mannila and Kontula 1997). We suggested that increased emancipation of women would be associated with increases in the sexual pleasure women experience.

4. *Consider other treatments.* Other treatments for lack of sexual desire include rest and relaxation. This is particularly indicated where the culprit is chronic fatigue syndrome (CFS), the symptoms of which are overwhelming fatigue, low-grade fever, and sore throat. Still other treatments for lack of sexual desire include hormone treatment and changing medications (if possible) in cases where medication interferes with sexual desire. In addition, sex therapists often recommend that people who are troubled by a low level of sexual desire engage in sexual fantasies and masturbation as a means of developing positive sexual images and feelings. Meston et al. (2008) noted that ginkgo biloba extract (GBE) as a treatment for increasing sexual desire can be effective when combined with sex therapy.

In 2004, Procter and Gamble applied to the Food and Drug Administration (FDA) to market Intrinsa, a drug to treat women who experienced low libido and who wanted to feel more sexual desire. Woman would wear the patch to provide a continuous dose of testosterone. However, the fourteen-member FDA advisory committee, plus voting consultants for Reproductive Health Drugs unanimously rejected the request. The panel cited insufficient research to document the safety of the drug for premenopausal women who may be taking estrogen as well as estrogen with progesterone. There was a fear that physicians would prescribe the drug for other populations (referred to as "off label" use) if the drug were made available to surgically menopausal women. Intrinsa is available in the United Kingdom, France, and Germany. Controlled studies are yet to be published on its effectiveness.

Discrepant interests in sexual behavior can be a catastrophic problem in marriage. How couples manage this dilemma varies. Although some compromise their frequency of sex, others agree that the partner with the higher interest may have other sexual partners. One couple uniquely solved their issue, where the husband wanted sex once a day and the wife wanted it once every two weeks, by having the husband look at pornography on the Internet and masturbate nightly. The wife said, "He's still in the house, gets his nightly orgasm/ejaculation, and we don't have to get tangled up in the problems of an extramarital affair."

Unpleasurable Sex

Sex that is not pleasurable may be both painful and aversive. Pain during intercourse, or dyspareunia, occurs in about 10 percent of gynecological patients in the United States. Colson et al. (2006) noted that 15.5 percent of 519 French women identified dyspareunia as the primary sexual complaint. Dyspareunia may be caused by vaginal infection, a rigid hymen, or an improperly positioned uterus or ovary. Vaginal dryness associated with menopause is also a cause (Nelson 2008). Because the causes of dyspareunia are often medical, a physician should be consulted (for example, sometimes surgery is recommended to remove the hymen).

Dyspareunia may also be psychologically caused. Guilt, anxiety, or unresolved feelings about a previous trauma, such as rape or childhood molestation, may be operative. Therapy may be indicated.

Some women report that they find sex aversive. Sexual aversion, also known as sexual phobia and sexual panic disorder, is characterized by the individual's wanting nothing to do with genital contact with another person. The immediate cause of sexual aversion is an irrational fear of sex. Such fear may result from negative sexual attitudes acquired in childhood or sexual trauma such as rape or incest. Some cases of sexual aversion may be caused by fear of intimacy or hostility toward the other sex.

Treatment for sexual aversion involves providing insight into the possible ways in which the negative attitudes toward sexual activity developed, increasing the communication skills of the partners, and practicing sensate focus. Understanding the origins of the sexual aversion may enable an individual to view change as possible. Through communication with the partner and through sensate focus exercises, an individual may learn to associate more positive feelings with sexual behavior.

Inability to Achieve Orgasm

Orgasmic difficulty, also referred to as **inhibited female orgasm,** or orgasmic dysfunction, occurs when a woman is unable to achieve orgasm after a period of continuous stimulation. Colson et al. (2006) noted that 15.5 percent of 519 French women identified orgasm difficulty as the primary sexual complaint. Difficulty achieving orgasm can be primary, secondary, situational, or total. Situational orgasmic difficulties, in which the woman is able to experience orgasm under some circumstances but not others, are the most common. Many women are able to experience orgasm during manual or oral clitoral stimulation but are unable to experience orgasm during intercourse (that is, in the absence of manual or oral stimulation).

Biological factors associated with orgasmic dysfunction can be related to fatigue, stress, alcohol, and some medications, such as antidepressants and antihypertensives. Diseases or tumors that affect the neurological system, diabetes, and radical pelvic surgery (for example, for cancer) may also impair a woman's ability to experience orgasm.

Psychosocial and cultural factors associated with orgasmic dysfunction are similar to those related to lack of sexual desire. Causes of orgasm difficulties in women include restrictive child rearing and learning a passive female sexual role. Guilt, fear of intimacy, fear of losing control, ambivalence about commitment, and spectatoring may also interfere with the ability to experience orgasm. Other women may not achieve orgasm because of their belief in the myth that women are not supposed to enjoy sex.

Relationship factors, such as anger and lack of trust, can also produce orgasmic dysfunction. For some women, lack of information can result in orgasmic difficulties (for example, some women do not know that clitoral stimulation is important for orgasm to occur). Some women might not achieve orgasm with their partners because they do not tell their partners what they want in terms of sexual stimulation out of shame and insecurity. Or, even in those cases where the woman is open about her sexual preferences, the partner may be unwilling to provide the necessary stimulation. Hence, a cooperative partner rather than a nonorgasmic woman should be the focus for resolution.

Kelly et al. (2006) found that nonorgasmic women were more likely to be in marriages where there was poorer communication. Specifically, marriages where the wife had difficulty achieving an orgasm were characterized by greater blame and conflict.

Because the causes for primary and secondary orgasm difficulties vary, the treatment must be tailored to the particular woman. Treatment can include enhancing positive communication, rest and relaxation, testosterone injections, or limiting alcohol consumption prior to sexual activity. Sensate focus exercises might help a woman explore her sexual feelings and increase her comfort with her partner. Treatment can also involve improving relationship satisfaction and teaching the woman how to communicate her sexual needs. Teaching the woman how to masturbate is also a frequent therapeutic option. The rationale behind masturbation as a therapeutic technique for nonorgasmic women is that masturbation is the behavior that is most likely to produce orgasm and can enable women to show their partners what they need. Masturbation gives the individual complete control of the stimulation, provides direct feedback to the woman of the type of stimulation she enjoys, and eliminates the distraction of a partner.

Sexual Dysfunctions of Men

Men also report sexual problems. The national sex study reported by Dunn et al. (2000) identified erectile problems (48 percent) and premature ejaculation (43 percent) as some of the most frequent sexual problems creating dissatisfaction in men.

Erectile Dysfunction

Loss of erection, also referred to as **erectile dysfunction,** involves the man's inability to get and maintain an erection. Like other sexual dysfunctions, erectile dysfunction can be primary, secondary, situational, or total. Occasional, isolated episodes of the inability to attain or maintain an erection are not considered dysfunctional; these are regarded as normal occurrences. To be classified as an erectile dysfunction, the erection difficulty should last continuously for a period of at least three months.

Erectile dysfunction may be caused by physiological conditions. Such biological causes include blockage in the arteries, diabetes, neurological disorders, alcohol or other drug abuse, chronic disease (kidney or liver failure), pelvic surgery, and neurological disorders. Smoking is also related to erectile dysfunction; the more frequent the smoking, the more likely the erectile dysfunction.

Janssen et al. (2008) emphasized that sexual function in men is cognitive as well as physiological. Psychosocial factors associated with erectile dysfunction include depression, fear (for example, of unwanted pregnancy, intimacy, HIV infection, or other STIs), guilt, and relationship dissatisfaction. For example, a man who is having an extradyadic sexual relationship may feel guilty. This guilt may lead to difficulty in achieving or maintaining an erection in sexual interaction with the primary partner and/or the extradyadic partner.

Anxiety may also inhibit a man's ability to create and maintain an erection. One source of anxiety is performance pressure, which may be self-imposed or imposed by a partner. In self-imposed performance anxiety, the man constantly checks (mentally or visually) to see that he is erect. Such self-monitoring creates anxiety because the man fears that he may not be erect.

Partner-imposed performance pressure involves the partner's communicating to the man that he must get and stay erect to be regarded as a good lover. Such pressure usually increases the man's anxiety, thus ensuring no erection. Whether self- or partner-imposed, the anxiety associated with performance pressure results in a vicious cycle—anxiety, erectile difficulty, embarrassment, followed by anxiety, erectile difficulty, and so on.

Performance anxiety may also be related to alcohol use. After consuming more than a few drinks, a man may initiate sex but may become anxious after failing to achieve an erection (too much alcohol will interfere with erection). Although alcohol may be responsible for his initial failure, his erection difficulties continue because of his anxiety.

Treatment of erectile dysfunction (like treatment of other sexual dysfunctions) depends on the cause(s) of the problem. When psychosocial factors cause erection difficulties, treatment may include improving the relationship with the partner and/or resolving the man's fear, guilt, or anxiety (that is, performance pressure) about sexual activity. These goals may be accomplished through couple counseling, re-education, and sensate focus exercises.

A sex therapist would instruct a man and his partner to temporarily refrain from engaging in intercourse so as to remove the pressure to attain or maintain an erection. During this period, the man is encouraged to pleasure his partner in ways that do not require him to have an erection (for example, cunnilingus or manual stimulation of partner). Once the man is relieved of the pressure to perform and learns alternative ways to satisfy his partner, his erection difficulties (if caused by psychosocial factors) often disappear. Most therapists bypass the use of these exercises in favor of Viagra, Cialis, or Levitra, discussed later.

Treatment for erectile dysfunction related to biological factors can include modification of the use of medication, alcohol, or other drugs. Increasingly, physicians are prescribing sildenafil (marketed as Viagra), which increases blood flow to the penis and results in an erection when the penis is stimulated. Though a physician should be consulted before taking the medication, about 80 percent of men experiencing erectile dysfunction report restored potency as a consequence of Viagra (Sammons 2009). Two new FDA-approved drugs are Cialis and Levitra. The newer medications can be taken twelve hours prior to sex and last for twenty-four to thirty-six hours. On these medications, a man will not have a constant erection but may become erect with stimulation.

Viagra is having some unanticipated effects. Men in their eighties are beginning to take Viagra, which does produce an erection. However, in some cases, the couple may not have had intercourse in ten years, and the man's partner may no longer be interested. A reshuffling of the sexual relationship of a couple in their later years may be indicated with medications such as Viagra, Levitra, or Cialis.

Men with low libido as well as erectile dysfunction may also benefit from testosterone replacement therapy (TRT). Once a low testosterone level is confirmed by a blood test (20 percent of men over age 60 have low levels), testosterone supplements in the form of a gel, patch, or injection may be given. Karazindiyanoglu and Çayan (2008) found that symptomatic late-onset hypogonadism (SLOH), which is characterized by decreased libido and erectile dysfunction, was improved by testosterone replacement therapy of 50 to 100 milligrams taken daily for one year. Indeed, one application kicked up testosterone levels that remained stable for twenty-four hours.

Rapid Ejaculation

Also referred to as premature ejaculation, **rapid ejaculation** is defined as recurrent ejaculation with minimal sexual stimulation before, upon, or shortly after penetration and before the person wishes it. Whether a man ejaculates too soon is a matter of definition, depending on his and his partner's desires. Some partners define a rapid ejaculation in positive terms. One woman said she felt pleased that her partner was so excited by her that he "couldn't control himself." Another said, "The sooner he ejaculates, the sooner it's over with, and the sooner the better." Other women prefer that their partner delay ejaculation. Some women regard a pattern of rapid ejaculation as indicative of selfishness in their partner.

This feeling can lead to resentment and anger. Regardless of the definition, rapid ejaculation, or failing to control the timing of his ejaculation, is a man's most common sexual problem (Metz and Pryor 2000) and can lead to other sexual dysfunctions, such as female nonorgasmia, low sexual desire, and sexual aversion.

The cause of rapid ejaculation may be biological, psychogenic, or both (Metz and Pryor 2000). Some men are thought to have a constitutionally hypersensitive sympathetic nervous system that predisposes them to rapid ejaculation. Psychogenic factors include psychological distress, such as shame, or psychological constitution, such as being obsessive-compulsive. Rapid ejaculation is less of a problem for the woman than for her male partner. And, although lower sexual satisfaction for both the woman and the man is associated with rapid ejaculation, relationship satisfaction is not affected (Byers and Grenier 2003).

Treatment depends on the cause. If a hypersensitive neurological constitution seems to be the primary culprit, pharmacological intervention is used. For example, 50 milligrams of clomipramine hydrochloride taken four to six hours before sex has been found to delay orgasm in 30 percent of the cases. Where the cause is identified as psychogenic, cognitive-behavioral sex therapy is indicated. This may include the stop-start technique or frequent ejaculations.

The pause, or stop-start, involves the man's stopping penile stimulation (or signaling his partner to stop stimulation) at the point that he begins to feel the urge to ejaculate. After the period of pre-ejaculatory sensation subsides, stimulation resumes. This process may be repeated as often as desired by the partners.

Still another method of increasing the delay of ejaculation is for the man to ejaculate often. In general, the greater the number of ejaculations a man has in a period of twenty-four hours, the longer he will be able to delay each subsequent ejaculation. The man's relationship with his partner is also important. Success of the respective treatments in reference to the cause awaits further research (Metz and Pryor 2000).

Couples who decide to seek sex therapy should see only a credentialed therapist. The American Association of Sex Educators, Counselors, and Therapists (AASECT; www.aasect.org) maintains a list of certified sex therapists throughout the country.

KEY TERMS

erectile dysfunction	primary sexual dysfunction	rapid ejaculation	secondary sexual dysfunction
inhibited female orgasm			

WEB LINKS

Female Sexual Problems
http://www.aamft.org/families/Consumer_Updates/
FemaleSexualProblems.asp

Male Sexual Problems
http://www.aamft.org/families/Consumer_Updates/
MaleSexualProblems.asp

American Association of Sex Educators, Counselors, and Therapists
http://www.aasect.org

If you really loved me, you wouldn't care if I had AIDS! You'd get it from me, and we'd die together!

Chet Baker, jazz trumpet player (in his twisted drug abuse years)

Themba Hadebe/AP Photos

Human Immunodeficiency Virus and Other Sexually Transmitted Infections

Contents

This Special Topic section focuses on **sexually transmitted infections (STIs)** and the need to make choices about the level of infection risk one is willing to take. The wrong choice might lead to an early death.

Media information about the value of abstinence, safer sex, and the regular use of latex and polyurethane condoms may not translate into consistent condom use. Denial ("It won't happen to me") is the primary reason for failure to use condoms.

Human Immunodeficiency Virus Infection

Human immunodeficiency virus (HIV) attacks the white blood cells (T lymphocytes) in human blood, impairing the immune system and a person's ability to fight other diseases. Of all the diseases that can be transmitted sexually, HIV infection is the most life-threatening. Symptoms, if they occur at all, surface between two and six weeks after infection and are often dismissed because they are similar to symptoms of influenza. Antibodies may appear in the blood within two months but more often take three to six months before they reach reliable detectable levels.

International Data

Since the beginning of the HIV epidemic, more than 25 million people have died of **acquired immunodeficiency syndrome (AIDS).** Thirty-three million are living with AIDS, and almost three million people are newly infected each year (AVERT 2008).

Before HIV or its antibodies are detectable, infected individuals will test negative for the virus, making them silent carriers (this is called the "window period"). Although not all people who have HIV get AIDS (half of those infected with HIV will develop AIDS within ten years after the infection), all are infectious and are able to transmit the virus to others. Hence, even though a partner tested negative for HIV, the partner could still transmit the virus to you. If HIV progresses to AIDS, the person's body is vulnerable to opportunistic diseases that would be resisted if the immune system were not damaged. The two most common diseases associated with AIDS are a form of cancer called Kaposi's sarcoma (KS) and *Pneumocystis carinii* pneumonia (PCP), a rare form of pneumonia.

Of all HIV-related deaths, 70 percent result from PCP. HIV can also invade the brain and nervous system, producing symptoms of neurological impairment and psychiatric illness.

Modes of Transmission of HIV Infection

In the United States, HIV infection was first noted in 1981, among men who had sex with men (or MSM) who had multiple sex partners. Estimates show that male-to-male sexual contact is still the leading transmission mode of HIV infection among U.S. males. The predominant mode of transmission of HIV for women is heterosexual contact. HIV is also transmitted through sharing needles during injection drug use and, more rarely, through perinatal transmission and workplace needle contact.

Prevalence of HIV/AIDS

At the end of 2007, an estimated 551,932 people in thirty-four states reported living with HIV infection or AIDS. About 75 percent of these infected people are male, and 25 percent are female. Of those infected with HIV, 48 percent are African American, 33 percent are white, and 17 percent are Hispanic (Centers for Disease Control and Prevention 2009).

Risk group is a term that identifies a certain demographic trait associated with a higher chance of having a certain condition, such as infection with HIV. However, anyone who is exposed can become infected.

Tests for HIV Infection

Early medical detection of HIV has decided benefits, including taking medications to reduce the growth of HIV and preventing the development of some life-threatening conditions. An example of the latter is pneumonia, which is more likely to develop when one's immune system has weakened.

HIV counselors recommend that individuals who answer yes to any of the following questions should definitely seek testing:

- If you are a man, have you had sex with other men?
- Have you had sex with someone you know or suspect was infected with HIV?
- Have you had an STI?
- Have you shared needles or syringes to inject drugs or steroids?
- Did you receive a blood transfusion or blood products between 1978 and 1985?
- Have you had sex with someone who would answer yes to any of these questions?

Additionally, counselors suggest that if you have had sex with someone whose sexual history you do not know or if you have had numerous sexual partners, your risk of HIV infection is increased, and you should seriously consider being tested.

Finally, if you plan to become pregnant or are pregnant, the American Medical Association recommends being tested. Many states, such as North Carolina, passed laws in the 1990s requiring health care providers to counsel pregnant women as early in pregnancy as possible and to offer HIV testing. However, one study found that only 58 percent of surveyed women reported that they were asked by their caregivers if they wanted to be tested for HIV, and only 49 percent reported receiving pretest counseling (Sengupta and Lo 2004). The newest methods of HIV testing provide the fastest accurate results. In 1994, OraSure Technologies® released its new oral specimen collection device. This device allows for HIV testing with a shorter turnaround time for results, using a simple, two-minute collection procedure that trained health care providers can perform. In November 2002, OraSure® received approval from the U.S. Food and Drug Administration for its OraQuick® Rapid HIV-1 Antibody Test.

OraQuick became the first rapid, point-of-care test designed to detect antibodies to HIV-1 within approximately twenty minutes. This test requires taking a blood sample through a finger prick. Finally, in 2004, OraQuick® ADVANCE™ Rapid HIV-1/2 Antibody Test, a rapid test that provides accurate results for both HIV-1 and HIV-2 in twenty minutes, was introduced; it uses oral fluid, finger prick, or venipuncture whole blood or plasma specimens.

Other forms of testing may take up to two weeks for results. All three methods are 99 percent effective for detecting HIV antibodies when present.

Home HIV testing is available by calling 1-800-HIV-TEST (800-448-8378). The cost is $49. You mail in a sample of blood and call seven days later to get anonymous test results.

Treatment for HIV and Opportunistic Diseases

Although research to find a vaccine for HIV continues (no vaccine is available as of 2009), several drugs called **antiretroviral drugs** (ARVS; AZT, 3TC, indinavir, ritonavir, and saquinavir) when used in various combinations have demonstrated the most efficacy in the treatment of HIV infection. We emphasize "the most efficacy" because some of the drugs have proven to be less potent and more toxic than previously thought. Patients are not cured, but the progress of the disease is slowed and the survival rate is increased.

About twenty-five other drugs are used to treat AIDS-related illnesses. Drug therapy for AIDS and associated illnesses is expensive. The cost for just the drugs that one AIDS patient uses in one month is over $1,000.

Not all people who become HIV-infected progress to having AIDS. Indeed, about 3 percent are referred to as long-term nonprogressors—people who have not suffered any apparent damage to their immune system in twenty years.

Treatment for HIV and AIDS is not just medical. A person who is HIV-positive affects many human interaction networks, including spouses, parents, and siblings. Getting the secret out and establishing a supportive network are essential in managing the psychological trauma of being diagnosed with HIV.

The following sections consider other STIs. Researchers are increasingly giving attention the relationship of HIV infection to other STIs. HIV infection leads to altered manifestations of other STIs and thereby probably promotes their spread. Genital and some herpes ulcers normally heal within one to three weeks, but they can persist for months as highly infectious ulcers in people with HIV infection. Likewise, people with an STI are at greater risk of contracting HIV than those without.

Other Sexually Transmissible Infections

There are numerous other STIs. Young women, formerly married women, people with little education who are smokers, people with a high number of sexual partners, and people who do not use condoms regularly are more likely to be among those who contract HIV and other STIs (Lane and Althaus 2002; Capaldi et al. 2002). Some of the more common STIs include human papillomavirus (HPV) infection, chlamydia, genital herpes, gonorrhea, and syphilis.

Human Papillomavirus (HPV)

HPV infection is the most common STI. The more sexual partners an individual has, the more likely a person is to contract HPV.

There are more than seventy types of HPV. More than a dozen of these types can cause warts (called **genital warts,** or *condyloma*) or more subtle signs of infection in the genital tract. The virus infects the skin's top layers and can remain inactive for months or years before any obvious signs of infection appear. Often warts appear within three to six months after infection. However, some types of HPV produce no visible warts. Fewer than 1 percent to 2 percent of people who are infected with HPV develop symptoms. Any sexual partners of an infected individual should have a prompt medical examination.

HPV can be transmitted through vaginal or rectal intercourse, through fellatio and cunnilingus, and through other skin-to-skin contact. Genital warts are small bumps that are usually symptom-free, but they may itch. In women, genital warts most commonly develop on the vulva, in the vagina, or on the cervix. They can also appear on or near the anus. In men, the warts appear most often on the penis but can appear on the scrotum or anus or within the rectum. Incidence of infection radically increases as the number of sexual partners increases.

Health care providers disagree regarding the efficacy of treating HPV when there are no detectable warts. However, when the warts can be seen, either by visual inspection or by colposcope, providers do typically advise treatment. A number of treatment options are available. Choosing among them depends upon the number of warts and their location, availability of equipment, training of health care providers, and the preferences of the patient. Most of the treatments are at least moderately effective, but many are quite expensive. Treatments range from topical application of chemicals to laser surgery. Treatment of warts destroys infected cells, but not all of them, as HPV is present in a wider area of skin than just the precise wart location. To date, no therapy has been proven effective in eradicating HPV, and relapse is common.

A danger for women exposed to certain strains of HPV is a higher risk for cervical cancer. Just four types of HPV cause the majority of cervical cancers

(80 percent). Women who are diagnosed with HPV infection should carefully follow recommendations for cervical cancer screening and have Pap smears as directed by their health care providers.

New HPV vaccines could help reduce the risk of cervical cancer for women. Research shows that a vaccine for HPV has the potential to protect most women from cervical cancer for at least several years, but it doesn't protect completely against all strains of HPV. Merck, which makes the HPV vaccine, Gardasil, has received FDA approval. On the basis of recommendations of a federal advisory panel, the vaccine is approved for females aged 9 to 26 and is administered in three shots over a six-month period.

Not only is the HPV vaccine approved, it is recommended for the 30 million American girls and young women. Proponents argue that the vaccine, if given before sexual activity begins, can eliminate the HPV virus in these women. Those against the vaccine argue that the vaccine does not protect against all forms of cervical cancer or genital warts. Instead, young girls and women should be encouraged to have regular Pap smears.

Chlamydia trachomatis (CT) is a bacterium that can infect the genitals, eyes, and lungs. **Chlamydia** (clah-MID-ee-uh) is the most frequently occurring bacterial STI on college campuses. Indeed, it is estimated that 3 million new cases occur annually, and chlamydia is the most frequently reported infectious disease in the United States. Worldwide, chlamydial infections are even more extensive. Trachoma inclusion conjunctivitis, a chlamydial infection that occurs rarely in the United States, is the leading cause of blindness in third world countries. In women, untreated infections can progress to involve the upper reproductive tract and may result in serious complications. Around 40 percent of women with untreated chlamydia infections develop pelvic inflammatory disease, and 20 percent of those become infertile, according to the Centers for Disease Control (Burnstein et al. 2005). Other complications include spontaneous abortion and premature birth.

CT is easily transmitted directly from person to person via sexual contact or by sharing sex toys. The microorganisms are most often found in the urethra of the man, in the cervix, uterus, and fallopian tubes of the woman, and in the rectum of either men or women.

Genital-to-eye transmission of the bacteria can also occur. If a person with a genital CT infection rubs an eye or the eye of a partner after touching infected genitals, the bacteria can be transferred to the eye, and vice versa. Finally, infants can get CT as they pass through the cervix of their infected mother during delivery. CT infection rarely shows obvious symptoms—up to 70 percent of women are asymptomatic (Shih et al. 2004)—which accounts for its reputation as "the silent disease." Both women and men who are infected with CT usually do not know that they have the disease. The result is that they infect new partners unknowingly, who affect others unknowingly—unendingly.

Genital Herpes

Herpes refers to more than fifty viruses related by size, shape, internal composition, and structure. One such herpes is **genital herpes.** Although the disease has been known for at least 2,000 years, media attention to genital herpes is relatively new. Also known as **herpes simplex virus type 2** (HSV-2) infection, genital herpes is a viral infection that is almost always transmitted through sexual contact. Symptoms occur in the form of a cluster of small, painful blisters or sores at the point of infection, most often on the penis or around the anus in men. In women, the blisters usually appear around the vagina but can also develop inside the vagina, on the cervix, and sometimes on the anus. Pregnant women can transmit the herpes virus to their newborn infants, causing brain damage or death.

Another type of herpes originates in the mouth. **Herpes simplex virus type 1** (HSV-1) is a biologically different virus with which people are more familiar as cold sores on the lips. These sores can be transferred to the genitals by the fingers or by oral-genital contact. In the past, genital and oral herpes had site specificity: HSV-1 was always found on the lips or in the mouth, and HSV-2 was always found on the genitals. However, because of the increase in fellatio and cunnilingus, HSV-1 can be found in the genitals and HSV-2 can be found on the lips.

Herpes symptoms range from none at all to painful ulcers or blisters. Other symptoms that may occur include discharge, itching, or a burning sensation during urination, back pain, leg pain, stiff neck, sore throat, headache, fever, aches, swollen glands, fatigue, and heightened sensitivity of the eyes to light. The outbreaks with herpes last about ten to fourteen days on average, although they can last for as long as six weeks if not treated. "I've got herpes," said one sufferer, "and it's a very uneven discomfort. Some days I'm okay, but other days I'm miserable."

As with syphilis, the sores associated with genital herpes subside (the sores dry up, scab over, and disappear), and the person feels good again. However, the virus settles in the nerve cells in the spinal column and may cause repeated outbreaks of the symptoms in about one-third of those infected.

Stress, menstruation, sunburn, fatigue, and the presence of other infections seem to be related to the reappearance of herpes symptoms. Although such recurrences are usually milder and of shorter duration than the initial outbreak, the resurfacing of the symptoms can occur throughout the person's life. "It's not knowing when the thing is going to come back that's the bad part about herpes," said one woman.

The herpes virus is usually contagious during the time that a person has visible sores but not when the skin is healed. However, infected people may have a mild recurrence yet be unaware that they are contagious. Aside from visible sores, the itching, burning, or tingling sensations at the sore site also suggest that the person is contagious. Using a latex or polyurethane condom reduces the risk of transmitting or acquiring herpes, because the virus doesn't permeate the condom. However, if the condom doesn't cover the site of the sore, the virus may be spread through skin-to-skin contact. At the time of this writing, there is no cure for herpes. Until recently, scientists have not fully understood how HSV enters human cells, making it hard to develop drugs that could treat the virus. Researchers from the University of Michigan Medical School have now identified a receptor that appears to function as one "lock" that HSV opens to allow it to enter cells, which could be a major breakthrough for developing more effective treatments (Fuller and Wald 2005). Because it is a virus, herpes does not respond to antibiotics as do syphilis and gonorrhea. A few procedures that help to relieve the symptoms and promote healing of the sores include seeing a physician to look for and treat any other genital infections near the herpes sores, keeping the sores clean and dry, taking hot sitz baths three times a day, and wearing loose-fitting cotton underwear to enhance air circulation. Proper nutrition, adequate sleep and exercise, and avoiding physical or mental stress help people to cope better with recurrences.

Acyclovir, marketed as Zovirax, is an ointment that can be applied directly on the sores that helps to relieve pain, speed healing, and reduce the amount of time that live viruses are present in the sores. A more effective tablet form of acyclovir, which significantly reduces the rate of recurring episodes of genital herpes, is also available. Once acyclovir is stopped, the herpetic recurrences resume. Acyclovir seems to make the symptoms of first-episode genital herpes more manageable, but it is less effective during subsequent outbreaks. ImmuVir—an alternative to acyclovir—is primarily for use by people who have frequent outbreaks of genital herpes (once a month or more). This ointment is designed to reduce pain, healing time, and number of outbreaks. The drug has no known side effects.

Coping with the psychological and emotional aspects of having genital herpes is often more difficult than coping with the physical aspects of the disease.

Gonorrhea

Also known as the clap, the whites, morning drop, and the drip, **gonorrhea** is a bacterial infection that is sexually transmissible. Individuals contract gonorrhea through having sexual contact with someone who is carrying *Neisseria gonorrhoeae* bacteria. The gonorrhea bacteria, and most other STIs, cannot live long outside the human body—outside mucous membranes—so they could not survive on a toilet seat unless fluid were present, and even then they would not survive long. These bacteria thrive in warm, moist cavities, including the urinary tract, cervix, rectum, mouth, and throat. A pregnant woman can transmit gonorrhea to her infant at birth, causing eye infection. Many medical experts recommend gonorrhea testing for all pregnant women and antibiotic eye drops for all newborns.

Although some infected men show no signs, 80 percent exhibit symptoms between three and eight days after exposure. They may begin to discharge a thick, yellowish pus from the penis and to feel pain or discomfort during urination. They may also have swollen lymph glands in the groin. Women are more likely to show no signs of the infection (70 percent to 80 percent have no symptoms), but when they do, the symptoms are sometimes a yellowish discharge from the vagina along with a burning sensation or spotting between periods or after sexual intercourse. More often, a woman becomes aware of gonorrhea only after she feels extreme discomfort, which results when the untreated infection travels up into her uterus and fallopian tubes, causing pelvic inflammatory disease (PID). Salpingitis (inflammation of the fallopian tube) occurs in 10 percent to 20 percent of infected women and can cause infertility or ectopic pregnancy.

Undetected and untreated, gonorrhea can do permanent damage. Not only can the infected person pass the disease on to the next partner, but other undesirable consequences can also result. Untreated gonorrhea commonly causes long-term reproductive system complications, such as blocking and/or scarring of the urethra and possible infertility in men and PID (infection of the fallopian tubes), infertility, and damage to the uterus, fallopian tubes, and ovaries in women. In rare cases, the untreated bacteria can affect the brain, heart valves, and joints. Both men and women could develop endocarditis (an infection of the heart valves) or meningitis (inflammation of the tissues surrounding the brain and spinal column), arthritis, and sterility. Infected pregnant women could have a spontaneous abortion or a premature or stillborn infant.

A physician can detect gonorrhea by analyzing penile or cervical discharge under a microscope. A major problem with new cases of gonorrhea is the emergence of new strains of the bacteria that are resistant to penicillin. Because of high rates of resistance to penicillin and tetracycline, the current recommended treatment for gonorrhea is a single shot of ceftriaxone or a single dose of such oral medications as ofloxatin, cefixime, and ciprofloxacin.

Syphilis

Syphilis is caused by bacteria that can be transmitted through sexual contact with an infected individual. An infected pregnant woman can also transmit syphilis to her unborn baby. Although syphilis is less prevalent than gonorrhea, its effects are more devastating and include mental illness, blindness, heart disease—even death. The spirochete bacteria enter the body through mucous membranes that line various body openings. With your tongue, feel the inside of your cheek. This is a layer of mucous membrane—the substance in which spirochetes thrive. Similar membranes are in the vagina and urethra of the penis. If you kiss or have genital contact with someone harboring these bacteria, the bacteria can be absorbed into your mucous membranes and cause syphilitic infection.

Syphilis progresses through at least three stages, plus a latency stage before the final stage. In stage one (primary-stage syphilis), a small sore, or chancre, will appear at the site of the infection between ten and ninety days after exposure. The chancre, which can show up anywhere on the man's penis, or in the labia, vaginal membranes, or cervix of the woman, or in either partner's mouth or rectum, neither hurts nor itches and, if left untreated, will disappear in three to five weeks. The disappearance leads infected people to believe that they are cured—one of the tricky aspects of syphilis. In reality, the disease is still present and doing great harm, even though there are no visible signs.

During the second stage (secondary-stage syphilis), beginning from two to twelve weeks after the chancre has disappeared, other signs of syphilis appear in the form of a rash all over the body or just on the hands or feet. Welts and sores can also occur, as well as fever, headaches, sore throat, and hair loss. Syphilis has been called the great imitator because it mimics so many other diseases (for example, infectious mononucleosis, cancer, and psoriasis). Whatever the symptoms, they, too, will disappear without treatment. The person may again be tricked into believing that nothing is wrong.

Following the secondary stage is the latency stage, during which the person has no symptoms and is not infectious. However, the spirochetes are still in the body and can attack an organ at any time.

Tertiary syphilis—the third stage—can cause serious disability or even death. Heart disease, blindness, brain damage, loss of bowel and bladder control, difficulty in walking, and erectile dysfunction can result. Early detection and treatment are essential. Blood tests and examination of material from the infected site can help to verify the existence of syphilis. However, such tests are not always accurate. Blood tests reveal the presence of antibodies, not spirochetes, and it sometimes takes three months before the body produces detectable antibodies. Sometimes there is no chancre anywhere on the person's body.

Treatment for syphilis is similar to that for gonorrhea. Penicillin or other antibiotics (for those allergic to penicillin) are effective. Infected people treated in the early stages can be completely cured with no ill effects. If the syphilis has progressed into the later stages, any damage that has been done cannot be repaired.

Getting Help for HIV and Other STIs

If you are engaging in unprotected sex or are having symptoms, you should get tested for HIV and other STIs. There are different tests for different STIs.

Women must specifically ask for such tests from their gynecologist, because only a few doctors routinely perform them. If you do not know whom to call to get tested, call your local health department or the National STI Hotline at 1-800-227-8922. You will not be asked to identify yourself but will be given the name and number of local STI clinics that offer confidential, free treatment. In addition, Duke University in Durham, North Carolina, has opened an AIDS clinic to treat AIDS patients (919-684-2660). For the CDC National AIDS Hotline, call 1-800-342-2437. Students can also obtain information and assistance about HIV and STIs from their student health care facility on campus.

KEY TERMS

acquired immunodeficiency syndrome (AIDS)	genital herpes	herpes simplex virus type 2	sexually transmitted infection (STI)
antiretroviral drugs	genital warts	human immunodeficiency virus (HIV)	syphilis
chlamydia	gonorrhea		
	herpes simplex virus type 1		

WEB LINKS

American Social Health Association
http://www.ashastd.org

Centers for Disease Control and Prevention
http://www.cdc.gov/

HIV Testing Home Access
http://www.homeaccess.com

OraSure Technologies, Inc.
http://www.orasure.com/products/

Food and Drug Administration
http://www.fda.gov/bbs/topics/NEWS/NEW00503.html

The best career advice is to find a career you like and get someone to pay you to do it.

Katherine Whithorn

Careers in Marriage and the Family

Contents

Students who take courses in marriage and the family sometimes express an interest in working with people and ask what careers are available if they major in marriage and family studies. In this Special Topics section, we review some of these career alternatives, including family life education, marriage and family therapy, child and family services, and family mediation. These careers often overlap, so you might engage in more than one of these at the same time. For example, you may work in family services but participate in family life education as part of your job responsibilities.

For all the careers discussed in this section, having a bachelor's degree in a family-related field such as family science, sociology, or social work is helpful. Family science programs are the only academic programs that focus specifically on families and approach working with people from a family systems perspective. These programs have many different names, including child and family studies, human development and family studies, child development and family relations, and family and consumer sciences. Marriage and family programs are offered through sociology departments; family service programs are typically offered through departments of social work as well as through family science departments. Whereas some jobs are available at the bachelor's level, others require a master's or PhD degree. More details on the various careers available to you in marriage and the family follow.

Family Life Education

Family life education (FLE) is an educational process that focuses on prevention and on strengthening and enriching individuals and families. Family life educators empower family members by providing them with information that will help prevent problems and enrich their family well-being. This education may be offered to families in different ways: a newsletter, one-on-one, or through a class or workshop. Examples of family life education programs include parent education for parents of toddlers through a child-care center, a brown-bag lunch series on balancing work and family in a local business, a premarital or marriage enrichment program at the local church, a class on sexuality education in a high school classroom, and a workshop on family finance and budgeting at a local community center. The role as family life educator involves making presentations in a variety of settings, including schools, churches, and even prisons. Family life educators may also work with military families on military bases, within the business world with human resources or employee assistance programs, and within social service agencies or cooperative extension programs. Some family life educators develop their own business providing family life education workshops and presentations.

To become a family life educator, you need a minimum of a bachelor's degree in a family-related field such as family science, sociology, or social work. You can become a certified family life educator (CFLE) through the National Council on Family Relations (NCFR). The CFLE credential offers you credibility in the field and shows that you have competence in conducting programs in all areas of family life education. These areas are families in society, internal dynamics of the family, human growth and development, interpersonal relationships, human sexuality, parent education and guidance, family resource management, family law and public policy, and ethics. In addition, you must show competence in planning, developing, and implementing family life education programs.

Note: Appreciation is expressed to Sharon Ballard, PhD, CFLE, for the development of this Special Topic section. Dr. Ballard is an associate professor of Child Development and Family Relations at East Carolina University. She is also a certified family life educator through the National Council on Family Relations.

Your academic program at your college or university may be approved for provisional certification. In other words, if you follow a specified program of study at your school, you may be eligible for a provisional CFLE certification. Once you gain work experience, you can then apply for full certification.

Marriage and Family Therapy

Whereas family life educators help prevent the development of problems, marriage and family therapists help spouses, parents, and family members resolve existing interpersonal conflicts and problems. They treat a range of problems including communication, emotional and physical abuse, substance abuse, sexual dysfunctions, and parent-child relationships. They work in a variety of contexts, including mental health clinics, social service agencies, schools, and private practice. As of 2009, there were about 25,000 marriage and family therapists in the United States and Canada who were members of the American Association for Marriage and Family Therapy.

Currently, forty-eight states and the District of Columbia license or certify marriage and family therapists (only one province in Canada has passed license legislation). Although an undergraduate degree in sociology, family studies, or social work is a good basis for becoming a marriage and family therapist, a master's degree is required in one of these areas. Some universities offer accredited master's degree programs specific to marriage and family therapy; these involve courses in marriage and family relationships, family systems, and human sexuality, as well as numerous hours of clinical contact with couples and families under supervision. A list of graduate programs in marriage and family therapy is available at http://www.aamft.org/cgi-shl/twserver.exe?run:COALIST.

Full certification involves clinical experience, with 1,000 hours of direct client, couple, and family contact; 200 of these hours must be under the direction of a supervisor approved by the American Association of Marriage and Family Therapists (AAMFT). In addition, most states require a licensure examination. The AAMFT is the organization that certifies marriage and family therapists. A marriage and family therapist can be found at http://family-marriage-counseling.com/therapists-counselors.htm.

Child and Family Services

In addition to family life educators and marriage and family therapists, careers are available in agencies and organizations that work with families, often referred to as social service agencies. The job titles within these agencies include family interventionist, family specialist, and family services coordinator. Your job responsibilities in these roles might involve helping your clients over the telephone, coordinating services for families, conducting intake evaluations, performing home visits, facilitating a support group, or participating in grant writing activities. In addition, family life education is often a large component of child and family services. You may develop a monthly newsletter, conduct workshops or seminars on particular topics, or facilitate regular educational groups.

Some agencies or organizations focus on helping a particular group of people. If you are interested in working with children, youth, or adolescents, you might find a position with Head Start, youth development programs such as the Boys and Girls Club, after-school programs (for example, pregnant or parenting teens), child-care resource or referral agencies, or early intervention services. Child-care resource and referral agencies assist parents in finding child care, provide training for child-care workers, and serve as a general resource for parents and for child-care providers. Early intervention services focus on children with special needs. If you work in this area, you might work directly with children or you might work with the families and help to coordinate services for them.

Other agencies focus more on specific issues that confront adults or families as a whole. Domestic violence shelters, family crisis centers, and employee-assistance programs are examples of employment opportunities. In many of these positions, you will function in multiple roles. For example, at a family crisis center, you might take calls on a crisis hotline, work one-on-one with clients to help them find resources and services, and offer classes on sexual assault or dating violence to high school students.

Another focus area in which jobs are available is aging. Opportunities include those within residential facilities such as assisted-living facilities or nursing homes, senior centers, organizations such as the Alzheimer's Association, or agencies such as National Association of Area Agencies on Aging. There is also a need for eldercare resource and referral, as more and more families find that they have caregiving responsibilities for an aging family member. These families have a need for resources, support, and assistance in finding residential facilities or other services for their aging family member. Many of the available positions with these types of agencies are open to individuals with bachelor's degrees. However, if you get your master's degree in a program emphasizing the elderly, you might have increased opportunity and will be in a position to compete for various administrative positions.

Family Mediation

In Chapter 15 on divorce, we emphasized the value of divorce mediation. This is also known as family mediation and involves a neutral third party who negotiates with divorcing spouses on the issues of child custody, child support, spousal support, and division of property. The purpose of mediation is not to reconcile the partners but to help the couple make decisions about children, money, and property as amicably as possible. A mediator does not make decisions for the couple but supervises communication between the partners, offering possible solutions.

Although some family and divorce mediators are attorneys, family life professionals are becoming more common. Specific training is required that may include numerous workshops or a master's degree, offered at some universities (for example, University of Maryland). Most practitioners conduct mediation in conjunction with their role as a family life educator, marriage and family therapist, or other professional. In effect, you would be in business for yourself as a family or divorce mediator.

Students interested in any of these career paths can profit from obtaining initial experience in working with people through volunteer or internship agencies. Most communities have crisis centers, mediation centers, and domestic abuse centers that permit students to work for them and gain experience. Not only can you provide a service, but you can also assess your suitability for the "helping professions," as well as discover new interests. Talking with people already in the profession you want to enter is also a good idea for new insights. Your teacher may already be in the marriage and family profession you would like to pursue or be able to refer you to someone who is.

Resources and Organizations

ABORTION—PRO-CHOICE

Religious Coalition for Reproductive Choice
1025 Vermont Avenue NW, Suite 1130
Washington, DC 20005
Phone: 202-628-7700
 www.rcrc.org

ABORTION—PRO-LIFE

National Right to Life Committee
512 10th Street NW
Washington, DC 20004
Phone: 202-626-8820
 www.nrlc.org/Unborn_Victims/

ADOPTION

Dave Thomas Foundation for Adoption
Phone: 800-275-3832
 www.davethomasfoundationforadoption.org/

Evan B. Donaldson Adoption Institute
120 East 38th Street
New York, NY 10016
Phone: 212-925-4089
 www.adoptioninstitute.org/

AL-ANON FAMILY GROUPS

1600 Corporate Landing Parkway
Virginia Beach, VA 23454
Fax: 757-563-1655
 www.al-anon.org

CHILD ABUSE

Prevent Child Abuse
 www.preventchildabuse.org/index.shtml

CHILDREN

National Association for the Education of Young Children
1313 L St. N.W. Suite 500
Washington, DC 20005
Phone: 800-424-2460
 www.naeyc.org

COMMUNES/INTENTIONAL COMMUNITIES

Intentional Communities
 www.ic.org

Twin Oaks
138 Twin Oaks Road
Louisa, VA 23093
 www.twinoaks.org/

DIVORCE—CUSTODY OF CHILDREN

Child Custody Evaluation Services of Philadelphia, Inc.
Dr. Ken Lewis, P. O. Box 202
Glenside, PA 19038
Phone: 215-576-0177

Family Law Specialist/Divorce Mediator
Shelby Duffy Benton
130 S. John St.
P. O. Box 947
Goldsboro, NC 27533
Phone: 919-736-1830

DIVORCE RECOVERY

The divorce room
    http://heartchoice.com/divorce/index.php

American Coalition for Fathers and Children
1718 M St. NW. #187
Washington, DC 20036
Phone: 800-978-3237
    www.acfc.org

DOMESTIC VIOLENCE

National Coalition against Domestic Violence
P.O. Box 18749
1120 Lincoln Street, Suite 1603
Denver, CO 80203
Phone: 303-839-1852
    www.ncadv.org/

National Toll Free Number for Domestic Violence
Phone: 800-799-7233

FAMILY PLANNING

Planned Parenthood Federation of America
434 West 33rd Street
New York, NY 10001
    www.plannedparenthood.org

GRANDPARENTING

The Foundation for Grandparenting
108 Farnham Road
Ojai, CA 93023
    www.grandparenting.org

AARP (grandparent information center)
601 E Street NW
Washington, DC 20049
    www.aarp.org/grandparents/

HEALTHY BABY

National Healthy Mothers, Healthy Babies Coalition
2000 N. Beauregard Street 6th Floor
Alexandria, VA 22311
Phone: 703-837-4792
    www.hmhb.org

HOMOSEXUALITY

National Gay and Lesbian Task Force
1325 Massachusetts Ave. NW
Washington, DC 20005
   www.thetaskforce.org/

Parents, Families and Friends of Lesbians and Gays (PFLAG)
1726 M Street, NW Suite 400
Washington, DC 20036
   www.pflag.org

INFERTILITY

American Fertility Association
   www.theafa.org/

MARRIAGE

National Marriage Project, Rutgers, The State University of New Jersey
54 Joyce Kilmer Avenue, Lucy Stone Hall B217
Piscataway, NJ 08854-8045
Phone: 732-445-7922
   http://marriage.rutgers.edu

Marriage: Keeping It Healthy and Happy
   www.heartchoice.com/marriage/

Coalition for Marriage, Family and Couples Education
5310 Belt Road NW
Washington, DC 20015-1961
Phone: 202-362-3332
   www.smartmarriages.com/

National Healthy Marriage Resource Center
301 NW 63rd St., Suite 600
Oklahoma City, OK 73116
Phone: 866-916-4672 or 866-91-NHMRC

MARRIAGE AND FAMILY THERAPY

American Association for Marriage and Family Therapy
1133 Fifteenth Street NW, Suite 300
Washington, DC 20005
Phone: 703-838-9808
   www.aamft.org/index_nm.asp

MARRIAGE ENRICHMENT

ACME (Association for Couples in Marriage Enrichment)
56 Windsor Court
New Brighton, MN 55112
   E-mail: hamb1001@tc.umn.edu
   www.bettermarriages.org

MATE SELECTION

Right Mate
   www.heartchoice.com/rightmate

MEN'S AWARENESS

American Men's Studies Association
   www.mensstudies.org/

MOTHERHOOD

   www.mothersoughttohaveequalrights.org/

PARENTAL ALIENATION SYNDROME

www.deltabravo.net/custody/pasarchive.php

PARENTING EDUCATION

www.familyeducation.com/home/

REPRODUCTIVE HEALTH

Association of Reproductive Health Professionals
1901 L Street, NW Suite 300
Washington, DC 20036-1718
Phone: 202-466 3825
www.arhp.org

SEX ABUSE

VOICES in Action, Inc. (Victims of Incest Can Emerge Survivors)
P.O. Box 148309
Chicago, Illinois 60614
Phone: 800-7-VOICE-8
www.voices-action.org

National Clearinghouse on Marital and Date Rape
2325 Oak Street
Berkeley, California 94708-1697
Phone: 510-524-1582
www.ncmdr.org

SEX EDUCATION

Sexuality Information and Education Council of the United States
90 John St. Suite 704
New York, New York 10038
www.siecus.org

SEXUAL INTIMACY

www.heartchoice.com/sex_intimacy/

SEXUALLY TRANSMISSIBLE DISEASES

American Social Health Association (Herpes Resource Center and HPV Support Program)
P.O. Box 13827
Research Triangle Park, NC 27709
Phone: 919-361-8400
www.ashastd.org

National AIDS Hotline
Phone: 800-342-AIDS
www.thebody.com/hotlines/national.html

National Herpes Hotline
Phone: 919-361-8488 or 800-230-6039
www.ashastd.org/herpes/herpes_overview.cfm

STD Hotline
Phone: 800-227-8922
www.ashastd.org/

STD/AIDS
Phone: 919-361-8400
www.doe.state.in.us/sservices/hivaids_cdchotline.html

SINGLEHOOD

Alternatives to Marriage Project
P.O. Box 320151
Brooklyn NY, 11232
Tel: 718-788-1911
www.unmarried.org/

SINGLE PARENTHOOD

Parents without Partners
1650 South Dixie Highway, Suite 402
Boca Raton, Fl 33432
Phone: 800-637-7974
www.parentswithoutpartners.org

Single Mothers by Choice
1642 Gracie Square
Station New York, NY 10028
Phone: 212-988-0993
www.singlemothersbychoice.com

STEPFAMILIES

Stepfamily Association of America
650 J Street, Suite 205
Lincoln, NE 68508
www.saafamilies.org

Stepfamily Associates
1368 Beacon Street Suite 108
Brookline, MA 02146
Phone: 617-731-5767
www.stepfamilyboston.com

Stepfamily Foundation
333 West End Ave
New York, NY 10023
Phone: 212-877-3244
www.stepfamily.org

TRANSGENDER

Tri-Ess: The Society for the Second Self, Inc.
8880 Bellaire Blvd B2, PMB 104
Houston, TX 77036
www.tri-ess.org

WIDOWHOOD

Widowed Persons Service, American Association of Retired Persons
601 E St. NW
Washington, DC 20049
http://seniors-site.com/widowm/wps.html

WOMEN'S AWARENESS

National Organization for Women
1000 Sixteenth Street NW, Suite 700
Washington, DC 20036
Phone: 202-331-0066
www.now.org

AVERT. 2008. New AIDS Data. http://www.avert.org/worldstats.htm.

Burnstein, G., M. Snyder, D. Conley, D. Newman, C. Walsh, G. Tao, and K. Irwin. 2005. Chlamydia screening in a health plan before and after a national performance measure introduction. *Obstetrics and Gynecology* 106:327–34.

Byers, E. S., and G. Grenier. 2003. Premature or rapid ejaculation: Heterosexual couples' perceptions of men's ejaculatory behavior. *Archives of Sexual Behavior* 32:261–70.

Capaldi, D. M., J. Stoolmiller, S. Clark, and A. L. D. Owen. 2002. Heterosexual risk behaviors in at risk young men from early adolescence to young adulthood: Prevalence, prediction, and association with STD contraction. *Developmental Psychology* 38:394–406.

Centers for Disease Control and Prevention. 2009. *HIV/AIDS surveillance report, vol. 19.* Atlanta: U.S. Department of Health and Human Services, Centers for Disease Control and Prevention. http://www.cdc.gov/hiv/topics/surveillance/resources/reports/.

Colson, M., A. Lemaire, P. Pinton, K. Hamidi, and P. Klein. 2006. Sexual behaviors and mental perception, satisfaction, and expectations of sex life in men and women in France. *The Journal of Sexual Medicine* 3:121–31.

Dennerstein, L., P. Koochaki, I. Barton, and A. Graziottin. 2006. Hypoactive sexual desire disorder in menopausal women: A survey of western European women *Journal of Sexual Medicine* 3:212–22.

Dobkin, R. D., S. R. Leiblum, M. Menza, and H. Marin. 2006. Depression and sexual functioning in minority women: Current status and future directions. *Journal of Sex and Marital Therapy* 32:23–36.

Dunn, K. M., P. R. Croft, and G. I. Hackett. 2000. Satisfaction in the sex life of a general population sample. *Journal of Sex and Marital Therapy* 26:141–51.

Frank, J. E., P. Mistretta, and J. Will. 2008. Diagnosis and treatment of female sexual dysfunction. *American Family Physician* 77:635–43.

Fuller, O., and A. Wald. 2005. Session 80V, Symposium: Virus Receptors, Congress of Virology, International Union of Microbiological Societies, San Francisco, CA. *Journal of Virology* 79(12):7419–37.

Greenstein, A., L. Abramov, H. Matzkin, and J. Chen. 2006. Sexual dysfunction in women partners of men with erectile dysfunction. *International Journal of Impotence Research* 18:44–46.

Haavio-Mannila, E., and O. Kontula. 1997. Correlates of increased sexual satisfaction. *Archives of Sexual Behavior* 26:399–420.

Hubayter, Z., and J. A. Simon. 2008. Testosterone therapy for sexual dysfunction in postmenopausal women. *Climacteric* 11:181–90.

Janssen, E., K. R McBride, W. Yarber, B. J. Hill, and S. M. Butler. 2008. Factors that influence sexual arousal in men: A focus group study. *Archives of Sexual Behavior* 37:252–64.

Karazindiyanoglu, S., and S. Çayan. 2008. The effect of testosterone therapy on lower urinary tract symptoms/bladder and sexual functions in men with symptomatic late-onset hypogonadism. *Aging Male* 11:146–56.

Kelly, M., D. Strassberg, and C. Turner. 2006. Behavioral assessment of couple's communication in female orgasic disorder. *Journal of Sex and Marital Therapy* 32:81–95.

Kleinplatz, P. J. 2008. Sexuality and older people. *British Medical Journal (International Edition)* 337:121–30.

Lane, T., and F. Althus. 2002. Who engages in sexual risk behavior? *International Family Planning Perspectives* 28:185–86.

Lau, J.T.F., X. L. Yang, Q. S. Wang, Y. M. Cheng, H. Y. Tsui, L. W. H. Mui, and J. H. Kim. 2006. Gender power and marital relationship as predictors of sexual dysfunction and sexual satisfaction among young married couples in rural China. *Urology* 67:579–85.

Meston, C. M., A. H. Rellini, and M. Telch. 2008. Short and long terms effects of ginkgo biloba extract on sexual dysfunction in women. *Archives of Sexual Behavior* 37:530–48.

Metz, M. F., and J. L. Pryor. 2000. Premature ejaculation: A psychophysiological approach for assessment and management. *Journal of Sex and Marital Therapy* 26:293–320.

Nelson, H. D. 2008. Menopause. *The Lancet* 371:760–71.

Quirk, F., H. Scott, and T. Symonds. 2005. The use of the sexual function questionnaire as a screening tool for women with sexual dysfunction. *The Journal of Sexual Medicine* 2:469–77.

Sammons, R. 2009. Personal communication. Dr. Sammons is a psychiatrist in private practice in Grand Junction, Colorado.

Sengupta, S., and B. Lo. 2004. U.S. pregnant women's perceptions of universal, routine prenatal care. *AIDS & Public Policy Journal* 18(3/4; Fall/Winter):82–96.

Shih, S., S. Scholle, K. Irwin, G. Tao, C. Walsh, and W. Tun. 2004. Chlamydia screening among sexually active young female enrollees of health plans. *MMWR Morbidity and Mortality Weekly Report* 53(42):983–85.

Individual Autobiography Outline

Your instructor may ask you to write a paper that reflects the individual choices you have made that have contributed to your becoming who you are. Check with your instructor to determine what credit (if any) is available for completing this autobiography. Use the following outline to develop your paper. Some topics may be too personal, and you may choose to avoid writing about them. Your emotional comfort is important, so skip any questions you want and answer only those questions you feel comfortable responding to.

I. Choices: Free Will Versus Determinism

Specify the degree to which you feel that you are free to make your own interpersonal choices, versus the degree to which social constraints influence and determine your choices. Give an example of social influences being primarily responsible for a relationship choice and an example of you making a relationship choice where you acted contrary to the pressure you were getting from parents, siblings, and peers.

II. Relationship Beginnings

A. *Interpersonal context into which you were born.* How long had your parents been married before you were born? How many other children had been born into your family? How many followed your birth? Describe how these and other parental choices affected you before you were born and the choices you will make in regard to family planning that will affect the lives of your children.

B. *Early relationships.* What was your relationship with your mother, father, and siblings when you were growing up? What is your relationship with each of them today? Who took care of you as a baby? If this person was other than your parents or siblings (for example, a grandparent), what is your relationship with that person today? How often did your mother or father tell you that they loved you? How often did they embrace or hug you? How has this closeness or distance influenced your pattern with others today? Give other examples of how your experiences in the family in which you were reared have influenced who you are and how you behave today. How easy or difficult is it for you to make decisions and how have your parents influenced this capacity?

C. *Early self-concept.* How did you feel about yourself as a child, an adolescent, and a young adult? What significant experiences helped to shape your self-concept? How do you feel about yourself today? What choices have you made that have resulted in your feeling good about yourself? What choices have you made that have resulted in your feeling negatively about yourself?

III. Subsequent Relationships

A. *First love.* When was your first love relationship with someone outside your family? What kind of love was it? Who initiated the relationship? How long did it last? How did it end? How did it affect you and your subsequent relationships? What choices did you make in this first love relationship that you are glad you made? What choices did you make that you now feel were a mistake?

B. *Subsequent love relationships.* What other significant love relationships (if any) have you had? How long did they last and how did they end? What choices did you make in these relationships that you are glad you made? What choices did you make that you now feel were a mistake? On a ten-point scale (0 = very distant and 10 = very close), how emotionally close do you want to be to a romantic partner?

C. Subsequent relationship choices. What has been the best relationship choice you have made? What relationship choices have you regretted?

D. Lifestyle preferences. What are your preferences for remaining single, being married, or living with someone? How would you feel about living in a commune? What do you believe is the ideal lifestyle? Why?

IV. Communication Issues

A. Parental models. Describe your parents' relationship and their manner of communicating with each other. How are your interpersonal communication patterns similar to and different from theirs?

B. Relationship communication. How comfortable do you feel talking about relationship issues with your partner? How comfortable do you feel telling your partner what you like and don't like about his or her behavior? To what degree have you told your partner your feelings for him or her? To what degree have you told your partner your desires for the future?

C. Sexual communication. How comfortable do you feel giving your partner feedback about how to please you sexually? How comfortable are you discussing the need to use a condom with a potential sex partner? How would you approach this topic?

D. Sexual past. How much have you disclosed to a partner about your previous relationships? How honest were you? Do you think you made the right decision to disclose or withhold? Why?

V. Sexual Choices

A. Sex education. What did you learn about sex from your parents, peers, and teachers (both academic and religious)? What choices did your parents, peers, and teachers make about your sex education that had positive consequences? What decisions did they make that had negative consequences for you?

B. Sexual experiences. What choices have you made about your sexual experiences that had positive outcomes? What choices have you made that resulted in sexual regret?

C. Sexual values. To what degree are your sexual values absolutist, legalist, or relativistic? How have your sexual values changed since you were an adolescent?

D. Safer sex. What is the riskiest choice you have made with regard to your sexual behavior? What is the safest choice you have made with regard to your sexual behavior? What is your policy about asking your partner about previous sex history and requiring that both of you be tested for HIV and STIs before having sex? How comfortable are you buying and using condoms?

VI. Violence and Abuse Issues

A. Violent or abusive relationship. Have you been involved in a relationship in which your partner was violent or abusive toward you? Give examples of the violence or abuse (verbal and nonverbal) if you have been involved in such a relationship. How many times did you leave and return to the relationship before you left permanently?

What was the event that triggered your decision to leave the first and last time? Describe the context of your actually leaving (for example, did you leave when the partner was at work?). To what degree have you been violent or abusive toward a partner in a romantic relationship?

B. Family or sibling abuse. Have you been involved in a relationship where your parents or siblings were violent or abusive toward you? Give examples of any violence or abuse (verbal or nonverbal) if such experiences were part of your growing up. How have these experiences affected the relationship you have with the abuser today?

C. Forced sex. Have you been pressured or forced to participate in sexual activity against your will by a parent, sibling, partner, or stranger? How did you react at the time and how do you feel today? Have you pressured or forced others to participate in sexual experiences against their will?

VII. Reproductive Choices

A. Contraception. What is your choice for type of contraception? How comfortable do you feel discussing the need for contraception with a potential partner? In what percentage of your first-time intercourse experiences with a new partner did you use a condom? (If you have not had intercourse, this question will not apply.)

B. Children. How many children (if any) do you want and at what intervals? How important is it to you that your partner wants the same number of children as you do?

How do you feel about artificial insemination, sterilization, abortion, and adoption? How important is it to you that your partner feels the same way?

VIII. Childrearing Choices

A. Discipline. What are your preferences for your use of "time-out" or "spanking" as a way of disciplining your children? How important is it to you that your partner feels the same as you do on this issue?

B. Day care. What are your preferences for whether your children grow up in day care or whether one parent will stay home with and rear the children? How important is it to you that your partner feels the same as do you on this issue?

C. Education. What are your preferences for whether your children attend public or private school or are "homeschooled"? What are your preferences for whether your child attends a religious school? To what degree do you feel it is your responsibility as parents to pay for the college education of your children? How important is it to you that your partner feels the same as do you on these issues?

IX. Education or Career Choices

A. *Own educational or career choices.* What is your major in school? How important is it to you that you finish undergraduate school? How important is it to you that you earn a master's degree, PhD, MD, or law degree? In what? To what extent do you want to be a stay-at-home mom or stay-at-home dad? How important is it to you that your partner be completely supportive of your educational, career, and family aspirations?

B. *Expectations of partner.* How important is it to you that your partner has the same level of education that you have? To what degree are you willing to be supportive of your partner's educational and career aspirations? What are the career goals of you and your partner?

Family Autobiography Outline

Your instructor may want you to write a paper that reflects the influence of your family on your development. Check with your instructor to determine what credit (if any) is available for completing this family autobiography. Use the following outline to develop your paper. Some topics may be too personal, and you may choose to avoid writing about them. Your emotional comfort is important, so skip any questions you like and answer only those you feel comfortable responding to.

I. Family Background

A. Describe yourself, including age, gender, place of birth, and additional information that helps to identify you. On a scale of 0 to 10 (10 is highest), how happy are you? Explain this number in reference to the satisfaction you experience in the various roles you currently occupy (for example, offspring, sibling, partner in a relationship, employee, student, parent, roommate, friend).

B. Identify your birth position; give the names and ages of children younger and older than you. How did you feel about your "place" in the family? How do you feel now?

C. What was your relationship with and how did you feel about each parent and sibling when you were growing up?

D. What is your relationship with and how do you feel today about each of these family members?

E. Which parental figure or sibling are you most like? How? Why?

F. Who else lived in your family (for example, grandparent, spouse of sibling), and how did they impact family living?

G. Discuss the choice you made before attending college that you regard as the wisest choice you made during this time period. Discuss the choice you made prior to college that you regret.

H. Discuss the one choice you made since you began college that you regard as the wisest choice you made during this time period. Discuss the one choice you made since you began college that you regret.

II. Religion and Values

A. In what religion were you socialized as a child? Discuss the impact of religion on yourself as a child and as an adult. To what degree will you choose to teach your own children similar religious values? Why?

B. Explain what you were taught in your family in regard to each of the following values: intercourse outside of marriage, the need for economic independence, manners, honesty, importance of being married, qualities of a desirable spouse, importance of having children, alcohol and drugs, safety, elderly family members, people of other races and religions, people with disabilities, people of alternative sexual orientation, people with less or more education, people with and without "wealth," and occupational role (in regard to the latter, what occupational role were you encouraged to pursue?). To what degree will you choose to teach your own children similar values? Why?

C. What was the role relationship between your parents in terms of dominance, division of labor, communication, affection, and so on? How has your observation of the parent of the same sex and opposite sex influenced the role you display in your current relationships with intimate partners? To what degree will you choose to have a similar relationship with your own partner that your parents had with each other?

D. How close were your parents emotionally? How emotionally close were/are you with your parents? To what degree did you and your parents discuss feelings? On a scale of 0 to 10, how well do your parents know how you think and feel? To what degree will you choose to have a similar level of closeness or distance with your own partner and children?

E. Did your parents have a pet name for you? How did you feel about this?

F. How did your parents resolve conflict between themselves? How do you resolve conflict with partners in your own relationships?

III. Economics and Social Class

A. Identify your social class (lower, middle, upper); the education, jobs, or careers of your respective parents; and the economic resources of your family. How did your social class and economic well-being affect you as a child? How has the economic situation in which you were reared influence your own choices of what you want for yourself? To what degree are you economically self-sufficient?

B. How have the career choices of your parents influenced your own?

IV. Parental Plusses and Minuses

A. What is the single most important thing your mother and father, respectively, said or did that has affected your life in a positive way?

B. What is the single biggest mistake your mother and father, respectively, made in rearing you? Discuss how this impacted you negatively. To what degree does this choice still affect you?

V. Personal Crisis Events

A. Everyone experiences one or more crisis events that have a dramatic impact on life. Identify and discuss each event or events you have experienced and your reaction and adjustment to them.

B. How did your parents react to this crisis event you were experiencing? To what degree did their reaction help or hinder your adjustment? What different choice or choices (if any) could they have made to assist you in ways you would have regarded as more beneficial?

VI. Family Crisis Events

Identify and discuss each crisis event your family has experienced. How did each member of your family react and adjust to each event? An example of a family crisis event would be unemployment of a primary breadwinner, prolonged illness of a family member, aging parent coming to live with the family, death of a sibling, or alcoholism.

VII. Family Secrets

Most families have secrets. What secrets are you aware of in your family and kinship system? To what degree has it been difficult for you to be aware of this family secret?

VIII. Future

Describe yourself two, five, and ten years from now. What are your educational, occupational, marital, and family goals? How has the family in which you were reared influenced each of these goals? What choices might your parents make to assist you in achieving your goals?

Prenuptial Agreement of a Remarried Couple

Pam and Mark are of sound mind and body and have a clear understanding of the terms of this contract and of the binding nature of the agreements contained herein; they freely and in good faith choose to enter into the PRENUPTIAL AGREEMENT and MARRIAGE CONTRACT and fully intend it to be binding upon themselves.

Now, therefore, in consideration of their love and esteem for each other and in consideration of the mutual promises herein expressed, the sufficiency of which is hereby acknowledged, Pam and Mark agree as follows:

Names

Pam and Mark affirm their individuality and equality in this relationship. The parties believe in and accept the convention of the wife's accepting the husband's name, while rejecting any implied ownership.

Therefore, the parties agree that they will be known as husband and wife and will henceforth employ the titles of address Mr. and Mrs. Mark Stafford and will use the full names of Pam Hayes Stafford and Mark Robert Stafford.

Relationships with Others

Pam and Mark believe that their commitment to each other is strong enough that no restrictions are necessary with regard to relationships with others.

Therefore, the parties agree to allow each other freedom to choose and define their relationships outside this contract, and the parties further agree to maintain sexual fidelity each to the other.

Religion

Pam and Mark reaffirm their belief in God and recognize He is the source of their love. Each of the parties has his/her own religious beliefs.

Therefore, the parties agree to respect their individual preferences with respect to religion and to make no demands on each other to change such preferences.

Children

Pam and Mark both have children. Although no minor children will be involved, there are two (2) children still at home and in school and in need of financial and emotional support.

Therefore, the parties agree that they will maintain a home for and support these children as long as is needed and reasonable. They further agree that all children of both parties will be treated as one family unit, and each will be given emotional and financial support to the extent feasible and necessary as determined mutually by both parties.

Careers and Domicile

Pam and Mark value the importance and integrity of their respective careers and acknowledge the demands that their jobs place on them as individuals and on their partnership.

Both parties are well established in their respective careers and do not foresee any change or move in the future.

The parties agree, however, that if the need or desire for a move should arise, the decision to move shall be mutual and based on the following factors:

1. The overall advantage gained by one of the parties in pursuing a new opportunity shall be weighed against the disadvantages, economic and otherwise, incurred by the other.

2. The amount of income or other incentive derived from the move shall not be controlling.

3. Short-term separations as a result of such moves may be necessary.

Mark hereby waives whatever right he might have to solely determine the legal domicile of the parties.

Care and Use of Living Spaces

Pam and Mark recognize the need for autonomy and equality within the home in terms of the use of available space and allocation of household tasks. The parties reject the concept that the responsibility for housework rests with the woman in a marriage relationship whereas the duties of home maintenance and repair rest with the man.

Therefore, the parties agree to share equally in the performance of all household tasks, taking into consideration individual schedules, preferences, and abilities.

The parties agree that decisions about the use of living space in the home shall be mutually made, regardless of the parties' relative financial interests in the ownership or rental of the home, and the parties further agree to honor all requests for privacy from the other party.

Property, Debts, Living Expenses

Pam and Mark intend that the individual autonomy sought in the partnership shall be reflected in the ownership of existing and future-acquired property, in the characterization and control of income, and in the responsibility for living expenses. Pam and Mark also recognize the right of patrimony of children of their previous marriages.

Therefore, the parties agree that all things of value now held singly and/or acquired singly in the future shall be the property of the party making such acquisition. In the event that one party to this agreement shall predecease the other, property and/or other valuables shall be disposed of in accordance with an existing will or other instrument of disposal that reflects the intent of the deceased party.

Property or valuables acquired jointly shall be the property of the partnership and shall be divided, if necessary, according to the contribution of each party. If one party shall predecease the other, jointly owned property or valuables shall become the property of the surviving spouse.

Pam and Mark feel that each of the parties to this agreement should have access to monies that are not accountable to the partnership.

Therefore, the parties agree that each shall retain a mutually agreeable portion of their total income and the remainder shall be deposited in a mutually agreeable banking institution and shall be used to satisfy all jointly acquired expenses and debts.

The parties agree that beneficiaries of life insurance policies they now own shall remain as named on each policy. Future changes in beneficiaries shall be mutually agreed on after the dependency of the children of each party has been terminated. Any other benefits of any retirement plan or insurance benefits that accrue to a spouse only shall not be affected by the foregoing.

The parties recognize that in the absence of income by one of the parties, resulting from any reason, living expenses may become the sole responsibility of the employed party, and in such a situation, the employed party shall assume responsibility for the personal expenses of the other.

Both Pam and Mark intend their marriage to last as long as both shall live.

Therefore, the parties agree that, should it become necessary, due to the death of either party, the surviving spouse shall assume any last expenses in the event that no insurance exists for that purpose.

Pam hereby waives whatever right she might have to rely on Mark to provide the sole economic support for the family unit.

Evaluation of the Partnership

Pam and Mark recognize the importance of change in their relationship and intend that this CONTRACT shall be a living document and a focus for periodic evaluations of the partnership.

The parties agree that either party can initiate a review of any article of the CONTRACT at any time for amendment to reflect changes in the relationship. The parties agree to honor such requests for review with negotiations and discussions at a mutually convenient time.

The parties agree that, in any event, there shall be an annual reaffirmation of the CONTRACT on or about the anniversary date of the CONTRACT.

The parties agree that, in the case of unresolved conflicts between them over any provisions of the CONTRACT, they will seek mediation, professional or otherwise, by a third party.

Termination of the Contract

Pam and Mark believe in the sanctity of marriage; however, in the unlikely event of a decision to terminate this CONTRACT, the parties agree that neither shall contest the application for a divorce decree or the entry of such decree in the county in which the parties are both residing at the time of such application.

In the event of termination of the CONTRACT and divorce of the parties, the provisions of this and the section on "Property, Debts, Living Expenses" of the CONTRACT as amended shall serve as the final property settlement agreement between the parties. In such event, this CONTRACT is intended to effect a complete settlement of any and all claims that either party may have against the other, and a complete settlement of their respective rights as to property rights, homestead rights, inheritance rights, and all other rights of property otherwise arising out of their partnership. The parties further agree that, in the event of termination of this CONTRACT and divorce of the parties, neither party shall require the other to pay maintenance costs or alimony.

Decision Making

Pam and Mark share a commitment to a process of negotiations and compromise that will strengthen their equality in the partnership. Decisions will be made with respect for individual needs. The parties hope to maintain such mutual decision making so that the daily decisions affecting their lives will not become a struggle between the parties for power, authority, and dominance. The parties agree that such a process, although sometimes time-consuming and fatiguing, is a good investment in the future of their relationship and their continued esteem for each other.

Now, therefore, Pam and Mark make the following declarations:

1. They are responsible adults.

2. They freely adopt the spirit and the material terms of this prenuptial and marriage contract.

3. The marriage contract, entered into in conjunction with a marriage license of the State of Illinois, County of Wayne, on this 12th day of June 2004, hereby manifests their intent to define the rights and obligations of their marriage relationship as distinct from those rights and obligations defined by the laws of the State of Illinois, and affirms their right to do so.

4. They intend to be bound by this prenuptial and marriage contract and to uphold its provisions before any Court of Law in the Land.

Therefore, comes now, Pam Hayes Stafford, who applauds her development that allows her to enter into this partnership of trust, and she agrees to go forward with this marriage in the spirit of the foregoing PRENUPTIAL and MARRIAGE CONTRACT.

Therefore, comes now, Mark Robert Stafford, who celebrates his growth and independence with the signing of this contract, and he agrees to accept the responsibilities of this marriage as set forth in the foregoing PRENUPTIAL and MARRIAGE CONTRACT.

This CONTRACT AND COVENANT has been received and reviewed by the Reverend Ray Brannon, officiating.

Finally, come Vicki Whitfield and Rodney Whitfield, who certify that Pam and Mark did freely read and sign this MARRIAGE CONTRACT in their presence, on the occasion of their entry into a marriage relationship by the signing of a marriage license in the State of Illinois, County of Wayne, at which they acted as official witnesses. Further, they declare that the marriage license of the parties bears the date of the signing of this PRENUPTIAL and MARRIAGE CONTRACT. (Although this document is real, the names are fictitious to protect the real parties.)

Living Will

I, [Declarant], ("Declarant" herein), being of sound mind, and after careful consideration and thought, freely and intentionally make this revocable declaration to state that, if I should become unable to make and communicate my own decisions on life-sustaining or life-support procedures, then my dying shall not be delayed, prolonged, or extended artificially by medical science or life-sustaining medical procedures, all according to the choices and decisions I have made and which are stated here in my Living Will.

It is my intent, hope, and request that my instructions be honored and carried out by my physicians, family, and friends, as my legal right.

If I am unable to make and communicate my own decisions regarding the use of medical life-sustaining or life-support systems and/or procedures, and if I have a sickness, illness, disease, injury, or condition that has been diagnosed by two (2) licensed medical doctors or physicians who have personally examined me (or more than two (2) if required by applicable law), one of whom shall be my attending physician, as being either (1) terminal or incurable certified to be terminal, or (2) a condition from which there is no reasonable hope of my recovery to a meaningful quality of life, which may reasonably be referred to as hopeless, although not necessarily "terminal" in the medical sense, or (3) has rendered me in a persistent vegetative state, or (4) a condition of extreme mental deterioration, or (5) permanently unconscious, then in the absence of my revoking this Living Will, all medical life-sustaining or life-support systems and procedures shall be withdrawn, unless I state otherwise in the following provisions.

Unless otherwise provided in this Living Will, nothing herein shall prohibit the administering of pain-relieving drugs to me, or any other types of care purely for my comfort, even though such drugs or treatment may shorten my life, or be habit forming, or have other adverse side effects.

I am also stating the following additional instructions so that my Living Will is as clear as possible: (1) resuscitation (CPR)—I do not want to be resuscitated; (2) intravenous and tube feeding—I do not want to be kept alive via intravenous means, and I do not want a feeding tube installed if I am unable to consume food/liquids naturally; (3) Life-Sustaining Surgery—I do not want to be kept alive by any new or old life-sustaining surgery; (4) new medical developments—I do not want to become a participant in any new medical developments that would prolong my life; (5) home or hospital—I want to die wherever my family chooses, including a hospital or nursing home.

In the event that any terms or provisions of my Living Will are not enforceable or are not valid under the laws of the state of my residence, or the laws of the state where I may be located at the time, then all other provisions which are enforceable or valid shall remain in full force and effect, and all terms and provisions herein are severable.

IN WITNESS WHEREOF, I have read and understand this Living Will, and I am freely and voluntarily signing it on this the day of (month), (year) in the presence of witnesses.

Signed: [Declarant]

Street Address:

County:

City and State:

Witness:

We, the undersigned witnesses, certify by our signatures below, that we are adult (at least 18 years old), mentally competent persons; that we are not related to the Declarant by blood, marriage, or adoption; that we do not stand to inherit anything from the Declarant by any means, including will, trust, operation of law or the laws of intestate succession, or by beneficiary designation, nor do we stand to benefit in any way from the death of the Declarant; that we are not directly responsible for the health or medical care, or general welfare of the Declarant; that neither of us signed the Declarant's signature on this document; and that the Declarant is known to us.

We hereby further certify that the Declarant is over the age of 18; that the Declarant signed this document freely and voluntarily, not under any duress or coercion; and that we were both present together, and in the presence of the Declarant to witness the signing of this Living Will on this the day of (month), (year).

Witness signature:
Residing at:
Witness signature:
Residing at:
Notary Acknowledgment:
This instrument was acknowledged before me on this the day of (month), (year) by [Declarant], the Declarant herein, on oath stating that the Declarant is over the age of 18, has fully read and understands the above and foregoing Living Will, and that the Declarant's signing and execution of same is voluntary, without coercion, and is intentional.
Notary Public
My commission or appointment expires:

Durable Power of Attorney

KNOW ALL MEN BY THESE PRESENTS That I, _____ , as principal ("Principal"), a resident of the State and County aforesaid, have made, constituted, appointed and by these present do make, constitute, and appoint and, either or both of them, as my true and lawful agent or attorney-in-fact ("Agent") to do and perform each and every act, deed, matter, and thing whatsoever in and about my estate, property, and affairs as fully and effectually to all intents and purposes as I might or could do in my own proper person, if personally present, including, without limiting the generality of the foregoing, the following specifically enumerated powers which are granted in aid and exemplification of the full, complete and general power herein granted and not in limitation or definition thereof:

1. To forgive, request, demand, sue for, recover, elect, receive, hold all sums of money, debts due, commercial paper, checks, drafts, accounts, deposits, legacies, bequests, devises, notes, interest, stock of deposit, annuities, pension, profit sharing, retirement, Social Security, insurance, and all other contractual benefits and proceeds, all documents of title, all property and all property rights, and demands whatsoever, liquidated or unliquidated, now or hereafter owned by me, or due, owing, payable, or belonging to me or in which I have or may hereafter acquire an interest to have, use and take all lawful means and equitable and legal remedies and proceedings in my name for collection and recovery thereof, and to adjust, sell, compromise, and agree for the same, and to execute and deliver for me, on my behalf, and in my name all endorsements, releases, receipts, or other sufficient discharges for the same.

2. To buy, receive, lease as lessor, accept, or otherwise acquire; to sell, convey, mortgage, grant options upon, hypothecate, pledge, transfer, exchange, quitclaim, or otherwise encumber or dispose of; or to contract or agree for the acquisition, disposal, or encumbrance of any property whatsoever or any custody, possession, interest, or right therein for cash or credit and upon such terms, considerations, and conditions as Agent shall think proper, and no person dealing with Agent shall be bound to see to the application of any monies paid.

3. To take, hold, possess, invest, or otherwise manage any or all of the property or any interest therein; to eject, remove, or relieve tenants or other persons from, and recover possession of, such property by all lawful means; and to maintain, protect, preserve, insure, remove, store, transport, repair, build on, raze, rebuild, alter, modify, or improve the same or any part thereof, and/or to lease any property for me or my benefit, as lessee without option to renew, to collect, and receive any receipt for rents, issues, and profits of my property.

4. To invest and reinvest all or any part of my property in any property and undivided interest in property, wherever located, including bonds, debentures, notes secured or unsecured, stock of corporations regardless of class, interests in limited partnerships, real estate or any interest in real estate whether or not productive at the time of the investment, interest in trusts, investment trusts, whether of the open and/or closed funds types, and participation in common, collective, or pooled trust funds or annuity contracts without being limited by any statute or rule of law concerning investment by fiduciaries.

5. To make, receive, and endorse checks and drafts; deposit and withdraw funds; acquire and redeem certificates of deposit in banks, savings and loan associations, or other institutions; and execute or release such deeds of trust or other security agreements as may be necessary or proper in the exercise of the rights and powers herein granted.

6. To pay any and all indebtedness of mine in such manner and at such times as Agent may deem appropriate.

7. To borrow money for any purpose, with or without security or on mortgage or pledge of any property.

8. To conduct or participate in any lawful business of whatsoever nature for me and in my name; execute partnership agreements and amendments thereto; incorporate, reorganize, merge, consolidate, recapitalize, sell, liquidate, or dissolve any business; elect or employ officers, directors, and agents; carry out the provisions of any agreement for the sale of any business interest or stock therein; and exercise voting rights with respect to stock either in person or by proxy, and to exercise stock options.

9. To prepare, sign, and file joint or separate income tax returns or declarations of estimated tax for any year or years; to prepare, sign, and file gift tax returns with respect to gifts made by me for any year or years; to consent to any gift and to utilize any gift-splitting provision or other tax election; and to prepare, sign, and file any claims for refund of tax.

10. To have access at any time or times to any safe-deposit box rented by me, wheresoever located, and to remove all or any part of the contents thereof, and to surrender or relinquish said safety deposit box in any institution in which such safe-deposit box may be located shall not incur any liability to me or my estate as a result of permitting Agent to exercise this power.

11. To execute any and all contracts of every kind or nature.
As used herein, the term "property" includes any property, real or personal, tangible or intangible, wheresoever situated.

The execution and delivery by Agent of any conveyance paper instrument or document in my name and behalf shall be conclusive evidence of Agent's approval of the consideration therefore, and of the form and contents thereof, and that Agent deems the execution thereof in my behalf necessary or desirable.

Any person, firm, or corporation dealing with Agent under the authority of this instrument is authorized to deliver to Agent all considerations of every kind or character with respect to any transactions so entered into by Agent and shall be under no duty or obligation to see to or examine into the disposition thereof.

Third parties may rely upon the representation of Agent as to all matters relating to any power granted to Agent, and no person who may act in reliance upon the representation of Agent or the authority granted to Agent shall incur liability to me or my estate as a result of permitting Agent to exercise any power. Agent shall be entitled to reimbursement for all reasonable costs and expenses incurred and paid by Agent on my behalf pursuant to any provisions of this durable power of attorney, but Agent shall not be entitled to compensation for services rendered hereunder.

Notwithstanding any provision herein to the contrary, Agent shall not satisfy any legal obligation of Agent out of any property subject to this power of attorney, nor may Agent exercise this power in favor of Agent, Agent's estate, Agent's creditors, or the creditors of Agent's estate.

Notwithstanding any provision hereto to the contrary, Agent shall have no power or authority whatever with respect to (a) any policy of insurance owned by me on the life of Agent, and (b) any trust created by Agent as to which I am Trustee.

When used herein, the singular shall include the plural and the masculine shall include the feminine.

This power of attorney shall become effective immediately upon the execution hereof.

This is a durable power of attorney made in accordance with and pursuant to Section (this section to be completed in reference to laws of the state in which the document is executed).

This power of attorney shall not be affected by disability, incompetency, or incapacity of the principal.

Principal may revoke this durable power of attorney at any time by written instrument delivered to Agent. The guardian of Principal may revoke this instrument by written instrument delivered to Agent.

IN WITNESS WHEREOF, I have executed this durable power of attorney in three (3) counterparts, and I have directed that photostatic copies of this power be made, which shall have the same force and effect as an original.

DATED THIS THE day of (month), (year).

WITNESS:

Name of Principal here

THE STATE OF and (County)

I, a Notary Public in and for said County, in said State, hereby certify that _____, whose name is signed to the foregoing durable power of attorney, and who is known to me, acknowledged before me on this day that being informed of the contents of the durable power, executed the same voluntarily on the day the same bears date.
GIVEN under my hand and seal this day of (month), (year).
NOTARY PUBLIC

My Commission Expires:

Glossary

A

Abortion rate—the number of abortions per 1,000 women aged 15 to 44.

Abortion ratio—the number of abortions per 1,000 live births.

Absolute poverty—the lack of resources that leads to hunger and physical deprivation.

Absolutism—sexual value system based on unconditional allegiance to the authority of science, law, tradition, or religion (for example, sexual intercourse before marriage is wrong).

Abusive head trauma—nonaccidental head injury in infants and toddlers.

Accommodating style of conflict—conflict style in which the respective partners are not assertive in their positions but are cooperative. Each attempts to soothe the other and to seek a harmonious solution.

Acquaintance rape—nonconsensual sex between adults who know each other.

ADHD—attention-deficit/hyperactivity disorder is a developmental disorder affecting 3 percent to 5 percent of children before age 7. Symptoms include impulsiveness and inattention, with or without a component of hyperactivity.

Advance directive—a legal document detailing the conditions under which a person wants life-support measures to be used in the event of a medical crisis.

Agape love style—love style characterized by a focus on the well-being of the love object, with little regard for reciprocation. The love of parents for their children is agape love.

Age—term defined chronologically, physiologically, sociologically, and culturally.

Age discrimination—discriminating against a person because of age (for example, not hiring a person because he or she is old or hiring a person because he or she is young).

Ageism—systematic persecution and degradation of people because they are old.

AIDS—acquired immunodeficiency syndrome; the last stage of HIV infection, in which the immune system of a person's body is so weakened that it becomes vulnerable to disease and infection.

Al-Anon—an organization that provides support for family members and friends of alcohol abusers.

Alcohol-exposed pregnancy (AEP)—pregnancy resulting from binge drinking.

Androgyny—a blend of traits that are stereotypically associated with masculinity and femininity.

Annulment—a mechanism that returns the parties to their premarital status. An annulment states that no valid marriage contract ever existed. Annulments are both religious and civil.

Anodyspareunia—frequent and severe pain during receptive anal sex.

Antigay bias—any behavior or statement that reflects a negative attitude toward homosexual individuals.

Antinatalism—opposition to having children.

Antiretroviral drugs—drugs such as AZT, 3TC, indinavir, ritonavir, and saquinavir, which when used in various combinations, have demonstrated efficacy in the treatment of HIV infection.

Anxious jealousy—obsessive ruminations about the partner's alleged infidelity make one's life a miserable emotional torment.

Arbitration—a third party listens to both spouses and makes a decision about custody, division of property, and so on.

Arranged marriage—mate selection pattern whereby parents select the spouse of their offspring. A matchmaker may be used but the selection is someone of which the parents approve.

Artifact—concrete symbol that an event exists; in game theory, evidence that a game exists.

Asceticism—the belief that giving in to carnal lusts is wrong and that one must rise above the pursuit of sensual pleasure to a life of self-discipline and self-denial.

Asexual—absence of sexual behavior with a partner and one's self (masturbation).

Avoiding style of conflict—conflict style in which partners are neither assertive nor cooperative.

B

Baby blues—transitory symptoms of depression twenty-four to forty-eight hours after a baby is born.

Barebacking—intentional unprotected anal sex.

Battered-woman syndrome—general pattern of battering that a woman is subjected to, defined in terms of the frequency, severity, and injury she experiences.

Behavioral approach—an approach to child rearing based on the principle that behavior is learned through classical and operant conditioning.

Behavioral couple therapy (BCT)—marriage counseling approach whereby the therapist focuses on the behavior each spouse wants the other to increase or decrease, begin, or terminate with the belief that attitudes and feelings are based on behavior.

Beliefs—definitions and explanations about what is thought to be true.

Bigamy—marriage to more than one person at the same time.

Binegativity—see *Biphobia*.

Binuclear family—family in which the members live in two households. Most often one parent and offspring live in one household, and the other parent lives in a separate household. They are still a family even though the members live in separate households.

Biofeedback—in reference to stress management, a process in which information that is fed back to the brain helps a person to experience the desired brain-wave state.

Biosocial theory—emphasizes the interaction of one's biological or genetic inheritance with one's social environment to explain and predict human behavior.

Biphobia—also referred to as binegativity; refers to a parallel set of negative attitudes toward bisexuality and those identified as bisexual.

Bisexuality—a sexual orientation that involves cognitive, emotional, and sexual attraction to members of both sexes.

Blended family—a family created when two individuals marry and at least one of them brings a child or children from a previous relationship or marriage. Also referred to as a stepfamily.

Blind marriage—practiced in traditional China, a marriage in which the bride and groom were prevented from seeing each other until their wedding day.

"Blue" wedding artifact—artifact worn by bride that may be a blue ribbon symbolic of fidelity.

Blurred retirement—the process of retiring gradually so that the individual works part-time before completely retiring or takes a bridge job that provides a transition between a lifelong career and full retirement.

"Borrowed" wedding artifact—artifact worn by bride that may be a garment owned by a current happy bride.

Brainstorming—suggesting as many alternatives as possible without evaluating them.

Branching—in communication, going out on different limbs of an issue rather than staying focused on the issue.

Bride wealth—also known as bride price or bride payment, the amount of money or payment in goods (for example, cows) by the groom or his family to the wife's family for giving her up.

Bundling—a courtship custom practiced by the Puritans whereby the would-be groom slept in the future bride's bed. Both were fully clothed and had a board between them.

C

Certified family life educator (CFLE)—a credential offered through the National Council on Family Relations that provides credibility for one's competence in conducting programs in all areas of family life education.

Cervical cap—a contraceptive device that fits over the cervix.

Child abuse—emotional, physical, or sexual misuse of adult status to denigrate or harm a child.

Child sexual abuse—exploitative sexual contact or attempted sexual contact by an adult with a child before the victim is 18. Sexual contact or attempted sexual contact includes intercourse, fondling of the breasts and genitals, and oral sex.

Chlamydia—known as the silent disease, a sexually transmitted disease caused by bacteria that can be successfully treated with antibiotics.

Cialis—known as the "weekend Viagra" (effective for thirty-six hours), a medication that allows aging males (when stimulated) to get and keep an erection as desired.

Civil union—a pair-bonded relationship given legal significance in terms of rights and privileges (more than a domestic relationship and less than a marriage). New Jersey recognizes civil unions of same-sex individuals.

Clitoridectomy—cutting off the clitoris.

Closed-ended question—question that allows for a one-word answer and does not elicit much information.

Cohabitation—two unrelated adults (by blood or by law) involved in an emotional and sexual relationship who sleep in the same residence at least four nights a week.

Cohabitation effect—the research finding that couples who cohabit before marriage have greater marital instability than couples who do not cohabit.

Coitus—the sexual union of a man and woman by insertion of the penis into the vagina.

Coitus interruptus—the ineffective contraceptive practice whereby the man withdraws his penis from the vagina before he ejaculates.

Collaborating style of conflict—conflict style in which partners are both assertive and cooperative. Each expresses views and cooperates to find a solution.

Collaborative practice—a process that brings a team of professionals (lawyer, psychologist, social worker, financial counselor) together to help a couple separate and divorce in a humane and cost-effective way.

Collectivism—pattern in which one regards group values and goals as more important than one's own values and goals.

Coming out—being open and honest about one's sexual orientation and identity.

Commensality—eating with others. Most spouses eat together and negotiate who joins them.

Commitment—an intent to maintain a relationship.

Common-law marriage—a marriage by mutual agreement between a cohabiting man and woman without a marriage license or ceremony (recognized in ten states). A common-law marriage may require a legal divorce if the couple breaks up.

Commune—see *Intentional community*.

Communication—the process of exchanging information and feelings between two people.

Compersion—the "opposite of jealousy"; feeling good about and being supportive of a partner's emotional and physical involvement with and enjoyment of another person.

Competing style of conflict—conflict style in which partners are both assertive and uncooperative. Each tries to force a way on the other so that there is a winner and a loser.

Competitive birthing—a woman will want to have the same number of children as her peers. Often occurs in the upper class where affluent women may have four children.

Complementary-needs theory—mate selection theory that people with complementary needs are attracted to each other. Also known as the "opposites attract" theory.

Comprehensive program—in sex education, refers to including information about birth control and condom use rather than abstinence as the focus.

Compromising style of conflict—conflict style in which there is an intermediate solution so that both partners find a middle ground they can live with.

Conception—see *Fertilization*.

Conflict—the interaction that occurs when the behavior or desires of one person interfere with the behavior or desires of another.

Conflict framework—view that individuals in relationships compete for valuable resources.

Congruent message—one in which verbal and nonverbal behaviors match; for example the message people send is the same as that conveyed by what they do.

Conjugal love—the love between married people characterized by companionship, calmness, comfort, and security. This is in contrast to romantic love, which is characterized by excitement and passion.

Control group—group used to compare with the experimental group that is not exposed to the independent variable being studied.

Conversion therapy—see *Reparative therapy*.

Coolidge effect—term used to describe the waning of sexual excitement and the effect of novelty and variety on sexual arousal.

Corporal punishment—the use of physical force with the intention of causing a child to experience pain, but not injury, for the purpose of correction or control of the child's behavior.

Cougar—a woman, usually in her thirties and forties, who is financially stable and mentally independent and looking for a younger man with whom to have fun.

Covenant marriage—type of marriage that permits divorce only under conditions of fault (such as abuse, adultery, or imprisonment for a felony).

Crisis—a sharp change for which typical patterns of coping are not adequate and new patterns must be developed.

Cross-dresser—a generic term for individuals who may dress or present themselves in the gender of the opposite sex (for example, a heterosexual male will dress as a woman).

Crude divorce rate—the number of divorces that have occurred in a given year for every thousand people in the population.

Cryopreservation—fertilized eggs are frozen and implanted at a later time.

Cunnilingus—the oral stimulation of a woman's genitals by her partner.

Cybersex—any computer-mediated sexual experience between two people.

Cybervictimization—being sent unwanted e-mail, spam, viruses, or being threatened online.

D

Date rape—nonconsensual sex (sexual intercourse, anal sex, oral sex) between two people who are dating or on a date.

Dating—a mechanism whereby some men and women pair off for recreational purposes, which may lead to exclusive, committed relationships for the reproduction, nurturing, and socialization of children.

December marriage—a marriage in which both spouses are elderly.

Defense mechanisms—unconscious techniques that function to protect individuals from anxiety and minimize emotional hurt.

Defense of Marriage Act (DOMA)—legislation passed by Congress denying federal recognition of homosexual marriage and allowing states to ignore same-sex marriages licensed elsewhere.

Demandingness—the degree to which parents place expectations on children and use discipline to enforce the demands.

Dementia—the mental disorder most associated with aging, whereby the normal cognitive functions are slowly lost.

Depo-Provera®—also referred to as "dep," a contraceptive shot taken by the woman every six months.

Desertion—a separation in which one spouse leaves the other and breaks off all contact with him or her.

Developmental-maturational approach—an approach to child rearing that views what children do, think, and feel as being influenced by their genetic inheritance.

Developmental task—skills developed at one stage of life that are helpful at later stages.

Diaphragm—a barrier method of contraception that involves a rubber dome over the uterus to prevent sperm from moving into the uterus.

Discrimination—behavior that denies individuals or groups equality of treatment.

Disenchantment—the change in a relationship from a state of newness and high expectation to a state of mundaneness and boredom in the face of reality.

Displacement—shifting one's feelings, thoughts, or behaviors from the person who evokes them onto someone else who is a safer target.

Divorce—legal ending of a valid marriage contract.

Divorce mediation—process in which divorcing parties make agreements with a third party (mediator) about custody, visitation, child support, property settlement, and spousal support. Divorce mediation is quicker and less expensive than litigation.

Divorcism—the belief that divorce is a disaster.

Domestic partnership—a relationship in which individuals who live together are emotionally and financially interdependent and are given some kind of official recognition by a city or corporation so as to receive partner benefits (for example, health insurance).

Double standard—the idea that there is one standard for women and another for men (for example, having numerous sexual partners suggests promiscuity in a woman but manliness in a man).

Down low—African American "heterosexual" man who engages in same-sex behavior.

Dowry (also called **trousseau**)—the amount of money or valuables a woman's father pays a man's father for the man to marry his daughter. It functioned to entice the man to marry the woman because an unmarried daughter stigmatized the family of the woman's father.

Dual-career marriage—a marriage in which both spouses pursue careers and maintain a life together that may or may not include dependents.

Dual-earner marriage—both husband and wife work outside the home to provide economic support for the family.

Durable power of attorney—a legal document that gives one person the power to act on behalf of another.

E

Ecosystem—the interaction of families with their environment.

Educational homogamy—selecting a cohabitant or marital partner with similar education.

Emergency contraception—also referred to as postcoital contraception, the various types of morning-after pills that are used in three circumstances:

when a woman has unprotected intercourse, when a contraceptive method fails (such as condom breakage), and when a woman is raped.

Emotional abuse—the denigration of an individual with the purpose of reducing the victim's status and increasing the victim's vulnerability so that he or she can be more easily controlled by the abuser. Also known as verbal abuse or symbolic aggression.

Endogamous pressures—involve social approval and encouragement to select a partner within your own group (for example, race or religion).

Endogamy—in mate selection, the cultural expectation to marry within one's own social group in terms of race, religion, and social class.

Engagement—a time in which the partners are emotionally committed, are sexually monogamous, and are focused on wedding preparations.

Entrapped—stuck in an abusive relationship and unable to extricate one's self from the abusive partner.

Erectile dysfunction—a man's inability to get and maintain an erection.

Eros love style—love style characterized by passion and romance.

Escapism—the simultaneous denial and withdrawal from a problem.

Euthanasia—derived from Greek words meaning "good death," or dying without suffering or pain. Euthanasia may be passive, where medical treatment is withdrawn and nothing is done to prolong the life of the patient, or active, which involves deliberate actions to end a person's life.

Exchange theory—theory that emphasizes that relations are formed and maintained between individuals offering the greatest rewards and least costs to each other.

Exogamous pressures—involve social approval and encouragement to select a partner outside one's own group (for example, someone outside of your own family).

Exogamy—in mate selection, the social expectation that individuals marry outside their family group (for example, avoid sex and marriage with a sibling or other close relative).

Experimental group—the group exposed to the independent variable. If studying the effect of alcohol on sexual behavior, the couples drinking alcohol would be the experimental group; those not drinking alcohol would be the control group.

Extended family—the nuclear family or parts of it plus other relatives such as parents, grandparents, aunts, uncles, cousins, and siblings.

Extradyadic relationship (involvement)—emotional or sexual involvement between a member of a pair and someone other than the partner. The term *extradyadic*, external to the couple, is broader than *extramarital*, which refers specifically to spouses.

Extramarital affair—emotional or sexual involvement of a spouse with someone other than a married spouse.

F

Familism—philosophy in which decisions are made in reference to what is best for the family as a collective unit.

Family—as defined by the U.S. Census Bureau, a group of two or more people related by blood, marriage, or adoption. Broader definitions include individuals who live together who are emotionally and economically interdependent.

Family career—the various stages and events that occur within the family.

Family caregiving—activities to help the elderly, which may include daily bathing and feeding, balancing checkbooks, and transportation to the grocery store or physician.

Family life course development—the stages and process of how families change over time.

Family life cycle—stages that identify the various challenges family members face across time (for example, marriage, childbearing, preschool, school age children, teenagers, and so on).

Family of orientation—the family of origin into which a person is born.

Family of origin—the family into which an individual is born or reared, usually including a mother, father, and children.

Family of procreation—the family a person begins by getting married and having children.

Family relations doctrine—an emerging doctrine holding that even nonbiological parents may be awarded custody or visitation rights if they have been economically and emotionally involved in the life of the child.

Family resilience—the successful coping of family members under adversity that enables them to flourish with warmth, support, and cohesion.

Family systems framework—views each member of the family as part of a system and the family as a unit that develops norms of interaction.

Fellatio—the oral stimulation of a man's genitals by his partner.

Female condom—a condom that fits inside the woman's vagina to protect her from pregnancy, HIV infection, and other sexually transmitted infections.

Female genital alteration—sometimes referred to as genital cutting, mutilation, or circumcision, the cultural practice (for example, in parts of Africa and some Middle Eastern countries) of cutting off the clitoris to reduce the woman's libido and make her marriageable.

Female genital mutilation—see *Female genital alteration*.

Female genital operations—see *Female genital alteration*.

Feminist framework—views marriage and the family as contexts for inequality and oppression.

Feminization of poverty—the idea that women disproportionately experience poverty.

Feral—wild; not domesticated; refers to children who are thought to have been reared by animals.

Fertell—an at-home fertility kit that allows women to measure the level of their follicle-stimulating hormone on the third day of their menstrual cycle and the man to measure the concentration of motile sperm.

Fertilization—also known as conception, the fusion of the egg and sperm.

Filial piety—love and respect toward one's parents.

Filial responsibility—feeling a sense of duty to take care of one's elderly parents.

Formal separation—a separation between spouses based on a legal agreement drawn up by an attorney and specifying the rights and responsibilities of the parties, including custody issues.

Foster parent—also known as a family caregiver, a person who at home, either alone or with a spouse, takes care of and fosters a child taken into custody.

Frail—elderly person who has difficulty with at least one personal care activity or other activity related to independent living (for example, bathing, dressing, getting in and out of bed, grocery shopping, taking medications).

Friends with benefits—a relationship consisting of nonromantic friends who also have a sexual relationship.

Functionalists—structural functionalist theorists who view the family as an institution with values, norms, and activities meant to provide stability for the larger society.

G

Game theory—views marriage and family as a sequence of interactions in time and space.

Garriage—term for relationship of gay individuals who are married or committed.

Gatekeeper role—refers to a mother's encouragement of criticism of the father, which influences the degree to which he is involved with his children.

Gay—homosexual women or men.

Gender—the social and psychological behaviors that women and men are expected to display in society.

Gender dysphoria—the condition in which one's gender identity does not match one's biological sex.

Gender identity—the psychological state of viewing oneself as a girl or a boy, and later as a woman or a man.

Gender role ideology—the proper role relationships between women and men in a society.

Gender roles—behaviors assigned to women and men in a society.

Gender role transcendence—abandoning gender frameworks and looking at phenomena independent of traditional gender categories.

Generation Y—children of the baby boomers, typically born between 1979 and 1984. Also known as the Millennial or Internet Generation, they have been the focus of their parents' attention and expect to be nurtured and coddled by the larger society.

Genital herpes—also known as herpes simplex virus type 2 infection, a sexually transmissible viral infection. Can also be transmitted to a newborn during birth.

Genital warts—sexually transmitted lesions that commonly appear on the cervix, vulva, or penis, or in the vagina or rectum.

Gerontology—the study of aging.

Gerontophobia—fear or dread of the elderly.

GLBT—see *LGBT*.

Gonorrhea—also known as the clap, the whites, and morning drop, a bacterial infection that is sexually transmitted.

Granny dumping—a situation in which adult children or grandchildren who feel burdened with the care of their elderly parent or grandparent leave the elder at an entrance of a hospital with no identification.

Gray rape—the partner wonders if she was forceful enough in making clear she did not want sex and wonders if it was really rape.

H

Hanging out—refers to going out in groups where the agenda is to meet others and have fun.

Hedonism—sexual value system emphasizing the pursuit of pleasure and the avoidance of pain.

HER/his career—a wife's career is given precedence over a husband's career.

Hermaphrodites—(also **intersexed individuals**) people with mixed or ambiguous genitals.

Herpes simplex virus type 1 infection—a viral infection that can cause blistering, typically of the lips and mouth; it can also infect the genitals.

Herpes simplex virus type 2 infection—see *Genital herpes*.

Heterosexism—the denigration and stigmatization of any behavior, person, or relationship that is not heterosexual.

Heterosexuality—the predominance of cognitive, emotional, and sexual attraction to those of the opposite sex.

HIS/her career—a husband's career is given precedence over a wife's career.

HIS/HER career—a husband's and wife's careers are given equal precedence.

HIV—human immunodeficiency virus, which attacks the immune system and can lead to AIDS.

Homogamy—individual initiative toward sameness or "likes attract."

Homogamy theory of mate selection—tendency to be attracted to and become involved with those who are similar in characteristics such as age, race, religion, and social class.

Homonegativity—a construct that refers to antigay responses such as negative feelings (fear, disgust, anger), thoughts ("homosexuals are HIV carriers"), and behavior ("homosexuals deserve a beating").

Homophobia—used to refer to negative attitudes toward homosexuality.

Homosexuality—the predominance of cognitive, emotional, and sexual attraction to those of a person's own sex.

Honeymoon—the time following the wedding whereby the couple become isolated to recover from the wedding and to solidify their new status change from lovers to spouses.

Honor crime (also known as **honor killing**)—killing a daughter because she brought shame to the family by having sex while not married. The killing is typically overlooked by the society. Jordan is a country where honor crimes occur.

Honor killing—in countries such as Jordan, an unmarried woman who has intercourse (even by rape) brings shame on her parents so she may be killed by her brother. Prosecution is a few weeks in jail for the murder.

Hooking up—a one-time sexual encounter in which there are generally no expectations of seeing one another again. The nature of the sexual expression may be making out, oral sex, and/or sexual intercourse. The term is also used to denote getting together periodically for a sexual encounter—oral sex or sexual intercourse with no strings attached.

Human ecology framework—the study of ecosystems or the interaction of families with their environment.

Hypothesis—in research, a suggested explanation for a phenomenon (for example, "men are sexually aggressive because of higher levels of testosterone").

Hysterectomy—removal of a woman's uterus.

I

Identity theft—using the address, or Social Security and bank account numbers of another, posing as that person to make purchases.

Individualism—philosophy in which decisions are made on the basis of what is best for the individual as opposed to the family (familism).

Induced abortion—the deliberate termination of a pregnancy through chemical or surgical means.

Infatuation—emotional feelings based on little actual exposure to the love object.

Infertility—the inability to achieve a pregnancy after at least one year of regular sexual relations without birth control, or the inability to carry a pregnancy to a live birth.

Informal separation—similar to a formal separation except that no lawyer is involved in the separation agreement; the husband and wife settle issues of custody, visitation, alimony, and child support between themselves.

Inhibited female orgasm—inability to achieve an orgasm after a period of continuous stimulation.

Installment plan—taking something from the store today and paying for it over time (in installments).

Institution—established and enduring patterns of social relationships.

Integrative behavioral couple therapy—in addition to focusing on behavior change, therapists examine the assumptions and beliefs operative in a couple's relationship to ensure that they are productive.

Intentional community—group of people living together on the basis of shared values and worldview (for example, Twin Oaks in Louisa, Virginia).

Internalized homophobia—a sense of personal failure and self-hatred among lesbians and gay men resulting from social rejection and stigmatization that has been linked to increased risk for depression, substance abuse and addiction, anxiety, and suicidal thoughts.

Intersex development—refers to congenital variations in the reproductive system, sometimes resulting in ambiguous genitals.

Intersexed individuals—see *Hermaphrodite*.

Intimate-partner violence—an all-inclusive term that refers to crimes committed against current or former spouses, boyfriends, or girlfriends.

Intrafamilial child sexual abuse—sex by an adult or older family member with a child in the family.

Intrauterine device (IUD)—a small object that is inserted by a physician into a woman's uterus through the vagina and cervix for the purpose of preventing implantation of a fertilized egg in the uterine wall.

Involved Couple's Inventory—designed to help individuals in committed relationships learn more about each other by asking specific questions.

IRB approval—Institutional Review Board approval is the OK by one's college, university, or institution that the proposed research is consistent with research ethics standards and poses no undo harm to participants.

"I" statements—statements that focus on the feelings and thoughts of the communicator without making a judgment on others.

J

Jealousy—an emotional response to a perceived or real threat to an important or valued relationship.

L

Laparoscopy—a form of salpingectomy (tubal ligation) that involves a small incision through the woman's abdominal wall just below the navel.

Legal custody—decisional authority over major issues involving the child.

Leisure—the use of time to engage in freely chosen activities perceived as enjoyable and satisfying.

Lesbian—homosexual woman.

Lesbigays—collective term referring to lesbians, gays, and bisexuals.

Levitra—a medication taken by aging men to help them get and maintain an erection (an alternative to Viagra and Cialis).

LGBT—also known as GLBT, refers collectively to lesbians, gays, bisexuals, and transgendered individuals.

Litigation—a judge hears arguments from lawyers representing the respective spouses and decides issues of custody, child support, division of property, and so on, which become legally binding.

Living apart together (LAT)—a committed couple who does not live in the same home.

Living together—see *Cohabitation*.

Living will—a legal document that identifies the wishes of an individual with regard to end-of-life care.

Long distance relationship (LDR)—being separated from a love partner by at least 200 miles for a period of not less than three months.

Lose-lose solution—a solution to a conflict in which neither partner benefits.

Ludic love style—love style in which love is viewed as a game whereby the love interest is one of several partners, is never seen too often, and is kept at an emotional distance.

Lust—sexual desire.

M

Mania love style—an out-of-control love whereby the person "must have" the love object. Obsessive jealousy and controlling behavior are symptoms of manic love.

Marital rape—forcible rape (sexual intercourse, anal intercourse, oral sex) by one's spouse.

Marital success—relationship in which the partners have spent many years together and define themselves as happy and in love (hence, the factors of time and emotionality).

Marriage—a legal contract signed by a heterosexual couple with the state in which they reside that regulates their economic and sexual relationship. (The highest court in Massachusetts ruled in 2004 that homosexuals may marry.)

Marriage-resilience perspective—changes in marriage viewed as having few negative consequences for children, adults, and the wider society.

Marriage squeeze—the imbalance of the ratio of marriageable-aged men to marriageable-aged women.

Masturbation—stimulating one's own body (usually genitals) with the goal of experiencing pleasurable sexual sensations.

Mating gradient—the tendency for husbands to marry wives who are younger and have less education and less occupational success.

May-December marriage—an age-discrepant marriage in which the younger woman is in the spring of her life (May) and the man is in his later years (December).

Mediation—see *Divorce mediation*.

Medicaid—state welfare program for low-income individuals.

Medicare—federal insurance program for short-term acute hospital care and other medical benefits for people over 65.

Megan's Law—a federal law requiring that convicted sex offenders register with local police when they move into a community.

Menarche—the time of first menstruation.

Mexican American—referring to people of Mexican origin or descent who are American citizens.

Mifepristone—also known as RU-486, a synthetic steroid that effectively inhibits implantation of a fertilized egg.

Millenials—the 80 million workers born between 1980 and 1995.

Miscarriage—see *Spontaneous abortion*.

Modeling theory of mate selection—see *Role theory of mate selection*.

Modern family—the dual-earner family, in which both spouses work outside the home.

Mommy track—stopping paid employment to spend time with young children.

Momprenuer—a woman who has a successful at-home business.

Munchausen syndrome by proxy—a rare form of child abuse whereby a parent (usually the mother) takes on the sick role indirectly (hence, by proxy) by inducing illness or sickness in her child so that she can gain attention and status as a caring parent.

N

Natural family planning—a method of contraception that involves refraining from sexual intercourse when the woman is thought to be fertile.

Nature-deficit disorder—children are encouraged to detach themselves from direct contact with nature, by playing in the woods, wading through a stream, or catching tadpoles, for instance.

Negative commitment—remaining emotionally tied to a relationship that has ended. The example is the person still angry over a divorce that occurred twenty years ago.

Negotiation—divorcing spouses themselves discuss and resolve the issues of custody, child support, division of property, and spouse maintenance.

"New" wedding artifact—artifact worn by a bride that symbolizes the new life she is to begin (for example, a new, unlaundered undergarment).

No-fault divorce—a divorce that assumes that neither party is to blame.

Nonagentic sexual experiences—those in which a partner is not a free agent and a sexual event occurs against his or her will.

Nonverbal communication—the "message about the message," using gestures, eye contact, body posture, tone, volume, and rapidity of speech.

Nuclear family—family consisting of an individual, his or her spouse, and his or her children, or of an individual and his or her parents and siblings.

NuvaRing®—a soft, flexible, transparent ring approximately two inches in diameter that is worn inside the vagina and provides month-long pregnancy protection.

O

Obsessive relational intrusion—the relentless pursuit of intimacy with someone who does not want it.

Occupational sex segregation—the concentration of women in certain occupations and men in other occupations.

"Old" wedding artifact—artifact worn by a bride that symbolizes durability of the impending marriage (for example, an old gold locket).

Oophorectomy—removal of a woman's ovaries.

Open charge—taking an item from the store today and agreeing to pay the full amount for the item within thirty days.

Open-ended question—question that elicits a great deal of information (for example, "How do you feel about me?").

Open-minded—an openness to understanding alternative points of view, values, and behaviors.

Open relationship—a stable relationship in which the partners regard their own relationship as primary but agree that each may have emotional and physical relationships with others.

Oppositional defiant disorder—a condition in which children do not comply with requests of authority figures.

Opting out—when professional women leave their careers and return home to care for their children.

Ortho Evra®—a contraceptive transdermal patch that delivers hormones to a woman's body through skin absorption.

Overindulgence—giving children too much, too soon, too long is a form of child neglect in which children are not allowed to develop their own competences.

Oxytocin—a hormone released from the pituitary gland during the expulsive stage of labor that has been associated with the onset of maternal behavior in lower animals.

P

Palimony—a takeoff on the word *alimony*, referring to the amount of money one "pal" who lives with another "pal" may have to pay if the partners terminate their relationship.

Palliative care—health care focused on the relief of pain and suffering of the individual who has a life-threatening illness and support for them and their loved ones.

Pantogamy—group marriage where each member of the group is married to each other.

Parallel style of conflict—style of conflict whereby both partners deny, ignore, and retreat from addressing a problem issue (for example, "Don't talk about it, and it will go away").

Parent effectiveness training—a model of child rearing that focuses on trying to understand what a child is feeling and experiencing in the here and now.

Parental alienation syndrome—a disturbance in which children are obsessively preoccupied with deprecation or criticism of a parent (usually a noncustodial parent); the denigration is unjustified or exaggerated. Found in situations where one divorced parent has "brainwashed" the child to perceive the other parent in very negative ways.

Parental consent—individual needs permission from parent to get an abortion if individual is under age, usually 18.

Parental investment—any investment by a parent that increases the chance that the offspring will survive and thrive.

Parental notification—individual required to tell parents they are going to get an abortion if individual is under age, usually 18; but individual does not need their permission to get an abortion.

Parental status—the degree to which the stepparent is considered to be a parent to a stepchild.

Parenting—the provision by an adult or adults of physical care, emotional support, instruction, and protection from harm in an ongoing structural (home) and emotional context to one or more dependent children.

Patriarchy—"rule by the father," a norm designed to ensure that women are faithful to their husbands and remain in the home as economic assets, childbearers, and child-care workers.

Periodic abstinence—refraining from sexual intercourse during the one to two weeks each month when the woman is thought to be fertile.

Physical abuse—intentional infliction of physical harm in the form of hitting, slapping, pushing, kicking, or burning (for example, with water or cigarettes) by one individual on another.

Physical custody—also called "visitation," refers to distribution of parenting time following divorce.

Polyamory—a term meaning "many loves," whereby three or more men and women have a committed emotional and sexual relationship. The partners may rear children in this context.

Polyandry—a form of polygamy in which one wife has two or more husbands.

Polyfidelity—the expectation that those who have multiple polyamorous parters will be faithful within that group of partners.

Polygamy—a generic term referring to a marriage involving more than two spouses.

Polygyny—a form of polygamy in which one husband has two or more wives.

Pool of eligibles—the population from which a person selects an appropriate mate.

Positive androgyny—a view of androgyny that is devoid of the negative traits associated with masculinity (aggression, being hard-hearted, indifferent, selfish, showing off, and vindictive) and femininity (being passive, submissive, temperamental, and fragile).

Possessive jealousy—striking back at the partner who is perceived as being unfaithful.

POSSLQ—an acronym used by the U.S. Census Bureau that stands for "people of the opposite sex sharing living quarters."

Postmodern family—a departure from traditional models such as lesbian and gay couples and single mothers by choice, which emphasizes that a healthy family need not be heterosexual or have two parents.

Postnuptial agreement—similar to a premarital agreement (which is signed before the marriage), a postnuptial agreement specifies what is to be done with property and holdings at death or divorce.

Postpartum depression—a reaction more severe than the "baby blues" to the birth of one's baby, characterized by crying, irritability, loss of appetite, and difficulty in sleeping.

Postpartum psychosis—a reaction in which the new mother wants to harm her baby.

Poverty—the lack of resources necessary for material well-being—most important, food and water, but also housing and health care.

Power—the ability to impose one's will on another and to avoid being influenced by the partner.

Pragma love style—love style that is logical and rational. The love partner is evaluated in terms of pluses and minuses and is regarded as a good or bad "deal."

Pregnancy—a condition that begins five to seven days after conception, when the fertilized egg is implanted (typically in the uterine wall).

Prejudice—negative attitudes toward others based on differences.

Premarital education programs—both academic and religious programs are formal systematized experiences designed to provide information to individuals and to couples about how to have a good relationship.

Prenuptial agreement—a contract between intended spouses specifying which assets will belong to whom and who will be responsible for paying what in the event of a divorce.

Primary group—small, intimate, informal group. A family is a primary group.

Primary sexual dysfunction—a dysfunction that a person has always had.

Principle of least interest—principle stating that the person who has the least interest in a relationship controls the relationship.

Procreative liberty—the freedom to decide whether or not to have children.

Projection—attributing one's own thoughts, feelings, and desires to someone else while avoiding recognition that these are one's own thoughts, feelings, and desires.

Pronatalism—view that encourages having children.

Pseudohermaphroditism—refers to a condition in which an individual is born with gonads matching the sex chromosomes, but with genitals either ambiguous or resembling those of the opposite sex.

Psychological abuse—see *Emotional abuse.*

Q

Quality of life—typically associated with physical function, visual acuity, continence, being bedfast, depressed, and so on.

Quinceñera—a rite of passage for the 15-year-old Latina/Hispanic females that marks their movement from childhood to womanhood whereby they can begin to look forward to marriage and parenthood.

R

Race—group of individuals who have physical characteristics that are identified and labeled as being socially significant.

Racial homogamy—selecting a person of the same race to cohabit or marry.

Racism—the attitude that one group of people is inferior to another group on the basis of physical characteristics.

Random sample—sample in which each person in the population being studied has an equal chance of being included in the sample.

Rapid ejaculation—persistent or recurrent ejaculation with minimal sexual stimulation before, upon, or shortly after penetration and before the partner wishes it.

Rationalization—the cognitive justification for one's own behavior that unconsciously conceals one's true motives.

Reactive jealousy—feelings that the partner may be straying.

Red zone—the first month of the first year of college when women are particularly vulnerable to unwanted sexual advances.

Refined divorce rate—the number of divorces or annulments in a given year, divided by the number of married women in the population, times 1,000.

Reflective listening—paraphrasing or restating what a person has said to indicate that the listener understands.

Relative poverty—a deficiency in material and economic resources compared with some other population.

Relativism—sexual value system whereby decisions are made in the context of the situation and the relationship (for example, sexual intercourse is justified in a stable, caring, monogamous context).

Religion—a specific set of beliefs (in reference to a supreme being, and so on) and practices generally agreed upon by a number of people or sects.

Religious homogamy—when individuals seek those who share their same religious and spiritual beliefs.

Reparative therapy—therapy designed to change a person who has a homosexual orientation to a heterosexual orientation.

Resiliency—the ability of a family to respond to a crisis in a positive way.

Responsiveness—the extent to which parents respond to and meet the needs of their children. Refers to such qualities as warmth, reciprocity, person-centered communication, and attachment.

Revolving charge—the repayment plan of most credit cards whereby you may pay the total amount you owe, any amount over the stated minimum payment due, or the minimum payment.

Rite of passage—event that marks the transition from one status to another (for example, a wedding marks the rite of passage of individuals from lovers to spouses).

Role—the behavior individuals in certain status positions are expected to engage in (for example, spouses are expected to be faithful).

Role compartmentalization—separating the roles of work and home so that an individual does not dwell on the problems of one role while physically being at the place of the other role.

Role conflict—being confronted with incompatible role obligations (for example, a wife is expected to work full-time and also to be the primary caretaker of children).

Role overload—the convergence of several aspects of one's role resulting in having neither time nor energy to meet the demands of that role. For example, the role of a wife may involve coping with the demands of employee, parent, and spouse roles.

Role strain—the anxiety that results from not being able to take care of several role needs at once.

Role theory of mate selection (also known as **modeling theory of mate selection**) emphasizes that a son or daughter models after the parent of the same sex by selecting a partner similar to the one the parent selected.

Romantic love—an intense love whereby the lover believes in love at first sight, only one true love, and that love conquers all.

Rophypnol—date rape drug that renders people unconscious so that they have no memory of what happens when they are under the influence.

RU-486—see *Mifepristone*.

Rumspringa—rite of passage among Amish adolescence whereby they are released from the church and its rules to experience the world, including sex and drugs. Over 90 percent return to join the Amish church for life.

S

Salpingectomy—tubal ligation, or tying a woman's fallopian tubes, to prevent pregnancy.

Sandwich generation—individuals who attempt to meet the needs of their children and elderly parents at the same time.

Satiation—the state in which a stimulus loses its value with repeated exposure. Partners sometimes get tired of each other because they are around each other all the time.

Second-parent adoption—(also called co-parent adoption) a legal procedure that allows individuals to adopt their partner's biological or adoptive child without terminating the first parent's legal status as parent.

Second shift—the cooking, housework, and child care that employed women do when they return home from their jobs.

Secondary group—large or small group characterized by impersonal and formal interaction. A civic club is an example.

Secondary sexual dysfunction—a dysfunction that a person is currently experiencing following a period of satisfactory sexual functioning.

Secondary virginity—the conscious decision of a sexually active person to refrain from intimate encounters for a specified period of time.

Self-immolation—suicide of women by burning as an escape from mistreatment in Afghanistan and as a protest voice.

Sensate focus—an exercise whereby partners focus on pleasuring each other in nongenital ways.

Sequential ambivalence—the individual experiences one wish and then another.

Sex—the biological distinction between being female and being male (for example, having XX or XY chromosomes).

Sex roles—behaviors defined by biological constraints. Examples include wet nurse, sperm donor, and childbearer.

Sexism—an attitude, action, or institutional structure that subordinates or discriminates against an individual or group because of their biological sex (for example, women are discriminated against as national television news anchors).

Sexual double standard—see *Double standard*.

Sexual orientation—the aim and object of one's sexual interests—toward members of the same sex, the opposite sex, or both sexes.

Sexual script—shared interpretations and expected behaviors in sexual situations.

Sexual values—moral guidelines for sexual behavior.

Shaken baby syndrome—behavior in which the caretaker, most often the father, shakes the baby to the point of causing the child to experience brain or retinal hemorrhage.

Shared parenting dysfunction—the set of behaviors by both parents that are focused on hurting the other parent and are counterproductive for a child's well-being.

Shift work—having one parent work during the day and the other parent work at night so that one parent can always be with the children.

Sibling relationship aggression—behavior of one sibling toward another intended to induce social harm or psychic pain in the sibling (for example, excluding a sibling from an event, spreading a rumor).

Simultaneous ambivalence—the person experiences two conflicting wishes at the same time.

Single-parent family—family in which there is only one parent—the other parent is completely out of the child's life through death, sperm donation, or complete abandonment, and no contact is ever made with the other parent.

Single-parent household—household in which one parent typically has primary custody of the child or children but the parent living out of the house is still a part of the child's family.

Singlehood—being unmarried. Various kinds of single individuals are never married, separated or divorced, and widowed.

Social allergy—being annoyed and disgusted by a repeated behavior on the part of one's partner.

Social exchange framework—spouses exchange resources, and decisions are made on the basis of perceived profit and loss.

Social script—the identification of the roles in a social situation, the nature of the relationship between the roles, and the expected behaviors of those roles.

Socialization—the process through which we learn attitudes, values, beliefs, and behaviors appropriate to the social positions we occupy.

Sociobiology—a theory that emphasizes that there are biological explanations for social behavior.

Sociological imagination—the perspective of how powerful social structure and culture are in influencing personal decision making.

Socioteleological approach—an approach to child rearing that explains children's behavior as resulting from the attempt to compensate for feelings of inferiority.

Sodomy—oral and anal sexual acts.

Spectatoring—mentally observing one's own and one's partner's sexual performance often interferes with performance because of the associated anxiety.

Spermicide—a chemical that kills sperm.

Spontaneous abortion—an unintended termination of a pregnancy.

Stalking—unwanted following or harassment that induces fear in a target person.

Status—a social position a person occupies within a social group, such as parent, spouse, or child. The term *status* is also defined in terms of resources so that a person with high status has high education, income, or power to influence others.

STD—sexually transmitted disease that can be transmitted through sociosexual contact. Now, more often referred to as sexually transmitted infection.

Step relationships—see *Stepfamily*.

Stepfamily—a family in which at least one spouse brings at least one child into a remarriage. Also referred to as a blended family.

Stepism—the assumption that stepfamilies are inferior to biological families. Stepfamilies are stigmatized.

Sterilization—a permanent surgical procedure that prevents reproduction.

STI—sexually transmitted infection (replaces the term sexually transmitted disease).

Storge love style—a love consisting of friendship that is calm and nonsexual.

Stratification—the ranking of people according to socioeconomic status, usually indexed according to income, occupation, and educational attainment.

Stress—a nonspecific response of the body to demands made on it.

Structure function framework—emphasizes how marriage and family contribute to the larger society.

Supermom—a cultural label that allows a mother who is experiencing role overload to regard herself as particularly efficient, energetic, and confident.

Superwoman—see *Supermom*.

Symbolic aggression—see *Emotional abuse*.

Symbolic interaction framework—views marriage and families as symbolic worlds in which the various members give meaning to each other's behavior.

Syphilis—a sexually transmissible infection caused by a spirochete entering the mucous membranes that line various body openings. Can also be transmitted by a pregnant woman to her unborn child.

T

Thanatology—examination of the social dimensions of death, dying, and bereavement.

THEIR career—a career shared by a couple who travel and work together (for example, journalists).

Theoretical framework—a set of interrelated principles designed to explain a particular phenomenon and to provide a point of view.

Therapeutic abortion—an abortion performed to protect the life or health of a woman.

Third shift—the emotional energy expended by a spouse or parent in dealing with various family issues. The job and housework are the first and second shifts, respectively.

Time-out—a discipline procedure whereby a child is removed from an enjoyable context to a nonreinforcing one and left there (alone) for a minute for every year of the child's age.

Traditional family—the two-parent nuclear family with the husband as breadwinner and wife as homemaker.

Transgender—a generic term for a person of one biological sex who displays characteristics of the opposite sex.

Transgendered—individuals whose gender identities do not conform to traditional notions of masculinity and femininity.

Transgenderist—an individual who lives in a gender role that does not match his or her biological sex, but has no desire to surgically alter his or her genitalia.

Transition to parenthood—the period of time from the beginning of pregnancy through the first few months after the birth of a baby.

Transpersonal psychology framework—focuses on the transpersonal aspects of body, mind, and spirit and how these interact with and strengthen the family.

Transracial adoption—the practice of parents adopting children of another race—for example, a white couple adopting a Korean or African American child.

Transsexual—an individual who has the anatomical and genetic characteristics of one sex but the self-concept of the other.

Transvestite—a person who enjoys dressing in the clothes of the opposite sex.

True hermaphroditism—an extremely rare condition in which individuals are born with both ovarian and testicular tissue.

U

Utilitarianism—the doctrine holding that individuals rationally weigh the rewards and costs associated with behavioral choices.

Uxoricide—the murder of a woman by her romantic partner.

V

Values—standards regarding what is good and bad, right and wrong, desirable and undesirable.

Vasectomy—male sterilization involving cutting out small portions of the vas deferens.

Vees—three-person relationships in which one member is sexually connected to each of the two others.

Verbal abuse—see *Emotional abuse*.

Viagra—a medication taken by aging men to help them get and maintain an erection (the first medication of its kind—before Levitra and Cialis).

Violence—the intentional infliction of physical harm by one individual toward another.

W

Win-lose solution—a solution to a conflict in which one partner benefits at the expense of the other.

Win-win relationship—a relationship in which conflict is resolved so that each partner derives benefits from the resolution.

Withdrawal—see *Coitus interruptus*.

Y

"You statements"—statements that tend to assign blame (for example, "You made me angry") rather than "I statements" ("I got angry and blew up").

Name Index

Note: Figures are represented by an f; tables are represented by a t.

Oswalt, S. B., 284, 285
Otis, M. D., 254, 371, 372
Ott, M. A., 279
Overington, C., 315
Ovid, 176, 183
Ozer, E. J., 456

P

Pacey, S., 544
Page, S., 249
Paglia, Camille, 96
Paige, Satchel, 552
Paintal, S., 371
Palisi, B. J., 540
Palmer, R., 256
Paltrow, Gwyneth, 44
Papernow, P. L., 533
Paradis, Vanessa, 159
Parelli, S., 248
Parish, W. L., 436
Park, C., 460
Parker, Dorothy, 112, 480, 488, 495
Parker, S., 413
Parker, Sarah Jessica, 354
Parra-Cardona, J. R., 91, 221
Pasley, K., 541
Patel, S., 250
Paterson, T., 440
Patford, J. L., 118
Patrick, J., 232
Patrick, M., 576
Patrick, T., 403
Patton, George S., 465
Paul, E. L., 45
Paul, J. P., 256
Paul, M., 323, 324
Paulk, A., 17
Pawelski, J. G., 263
Pearcey, M., 257
Pelosi, Nancy, 77, 95
Pendell, G., 316
Peng, S. Y., 415
Penn, Sean, 243, 248, 269, 503
Peoples, J. G., 80
Peplau, L. A., 254
Pepper, S., 183
Pepper, T., 402
Perry-Jenkins, M., 361, 404, 411
Pescosolido, B. A., 11
Peter, Laurence, 116
Peters, J. K., 100
Peters, L., 564
Peterson, B. E., 557
Peterson, Laci, 422
Peterson, Scott, 422
Peter the Wild Boy, 27
Petri, J., 60
Picasso, Pablo, 352
Picca, L. H., 176
Picoult, Jodi, 526
Pierce, T., 152
Pillemer, K., 363
Pimentel, E. E., 198, 236
Pinello, D. R., 262
Pines, A. M., 66
Pinheiro, R. T., 358
Pinquart, M., 363

Pinsof, W., 17, 158
Pistole, M. C., 59
Pitt, Brad, 44, 326, 469
Plagnol, A. C., 237
Plato, 54, 65
Platt, L., 267
Plitnick, K. R., 447
Pnina, R., 554
Pollack, W. S., 87
Pollard, M., 229
Pong, S. L., 378
Poop, T. K., 164
Poortman, A., 525
Pope, E., 563
Popenoe, D., 395
Porche, M. V., 260
Porter, Cole, 29, 469
Porter, Linda Lee, 469
Potok, M., 248
Potter, Henry C., 524
Potts, A., 567
Povilavicius, L., 60
Powers, D. A., 127
Powers, R. S., 319
Prather, Hugh, 107
Prather, J. E., 529
Pratt, L. A., 464
Presley, Elvis, 397
Presley, Priscilla, 397
Presser, H. B., 410
Presser, L., 31
Pressinger, R. W., 322
Preston, C., 365
Preston, P., 108
Pretorius, E., 93
Previti, D., 143, 491
Pritchard, Michael, 555
Probert, B., 94
Progebin, Letty Cottin, 424
Pryor, J. H., 35, 150, 156, 260, 314
Pryor, J. L., 600
Puentes, J., 282
Punyanunt-Carter, N. N., 122
Purkett, T., 120
Purvin, D. M., 260
Pyle, S. A., 463, 464

Q

Quirk, F., 596

R

Radmacher, K., 61
Raj, A., 92
Raley, R. M., 162, 282
Ramey, M. B., 125
Rampage, A., 17
Rand, M. R., 436
Rankin, S. R., 252
Rao, J. N., 463
Rapoport, B., 354
Raso, R., 55
Rau, P. L. P., 414
Ray, J. M., 185
Rayer, A. J., 116
Regan, P., 64
Regan, P. C., 185
Regts, J. M., 186

Reichman, N. E., 465
Reid, M. J., 64
Reid, W. J., 329
Reik, Theodor, 88
Reimer, David, 80
Reiss, Ira, 57
Renk, K., 364
Renshaw, S. W., 145, 146
Rhoades, G. K., 123, 158
Ricci, L., 441
Richey, Emily, 70, 216, 279, 281, 283
Richman, J. A., 23
Ridley, Carl, 197
Riley, M. W., 555–556t17.2
Rilke, Rainer Marie, 478
Rise, J., 498
Rivadeneyraa, R., 90
Rivera, Geraldo, 491
Rivers, M. J., 438
Roach, R., 110
Robbins, C. A., 117
Robbins, Tim, 159
Roberto, K. A., 463
Roberts, L. J., 433
Robertson, B., 560
Robertson, C. C., 96
Robinson, Sylvia, 127
Rochman, B., 324
Roderick, T., 250
Rodgers, B., 465
Rodriguez, Alex, 118
Rogers, J., 279
Rohrbaugh, J. B., 422
Rolfe, A., 319
Romero, L. C., 315
Romkens, M., 312
Roopnarine, J. L., 92
Roorda, R. M., 328
Rosario, M., 245
Rose, R., 406
Rose, S., 283
Rosen, E., 400
Rosen, K. H., 438
Rosenbaum, A., 428
Rosin, H., 247
Rosof, F., 117
Ross, C. B., 61, 84, 99, 393
Ross, M., 151
Ross, R., 327
Rosten, Leo C., 578
Rothblum, E. D., 160
Rothman, E., 439
Rousseve, A., 436
Routh, K., 463
Rowland, I., 209
Royo-Vela, M., 90
Rubin, D. M., 442
Rubin, Theodore, 455
Rudner, Rita, 167, 525
Ruschena, E., 542
Russell, B. L., 431, 432
Russell, Bertrand, 50, 62
Russell, C. S., 471
Russell, Kurt, 159
Russell, R., 571
Russo, N. F., 345
Rustenbach, E., 164

Subject Index

Note: Figures are represented by an f; tables are represented by a t.

HIS/her, 401
Hispanic families, 10, 88, 154, 221–222, 311, 318
HIV. *See* Human immunodeficiency virus (HIV)
"Hold Me, Thrill Me, Kiss Me" (Carter), 277
Home health care, 557
Homogamous mating, 24t1.6
Homogamy, 176–181, 524
Homogamy theory of mate selection, 176–181
Homogenous mating, 54
Homonegativity, 249
Homophobia, 249
Homophobia: A History (Fone), 242
Homosexuality. *See also* Gays and Lesbians, 24t1.6, 244, 246
Homosexual love, 54
Honesty, 117–118
Honeymoons, 213, 217
Honor crime, 427–428
Honor killing, 427–428
Hooking up, 135, 145–146
Hopi Indians, 176, 189
Hormonal contraception, 330–333
Hormone replacement therapy (HRT), 569
Hormone therapy for fertility, 323
Hormone treatments, 597
Human ecology framework, 31
Human immunodeficiency virus (HIV), 121, 141, 256, 285, 296–298, 300, 603–605
Human papillomavirus (HPV), 605–606
Human Rights Campaign, 251, 252, 259, 268
   National Coming Out Project, 252
Humor, 460
Hunger, 394
Husbands, traditional, 187
Hypersensitivity, 186
Hypotheses, 34
Hysterectomy, 338

I

Identity, 97–98, 147
Identity theft, 396–397
Illness, 462
Immediate gratification, 6
Implanon®, 331
Impulse control, 186
Incest taboos, 176
Income, 94
Income distribution, 392–394
Income sharing, 144
Indian Medical Association, 318
Individualism, 10, 23, 24t1.6, 491
Induced abortion, 341
Industrial Revolution, 22–23, 155–156
Infatuation, 45, 48–49, 50
Infertility, 321–326
Infidelity. *See also* Extramarital affairs, 13, 472

Informal separation, 517
Inheritance, 168, 532
Inhibited female orgasm, 598–599
Insecurity, 66, 186
Installment plans, 395–396
Institute for Gay and Lesbian Strategic Studies, 247
Institute of Transpersonal Psychology, 31–32
Institutional Review Board (IRB) approval, 34–35
Insurance benefits, 201
Integrative behavioral couple therapy (IBCT), 481
Intentional communities, 141–144
Interactionist perspective, 533
Intercourse, first, 289–290
Internalized homophobia, 249
International dating, 149
International Gay and Lesbian Human Rights Commission, 257, 269
International Lesbian and Gay Association, 269
Internet. *See also* Online dating, 114, 146–148, 286–287, 364, 365
Internet Generation. *See* Generation Y
Interpersonal communication, 108–109
Interracial marriage, 52, 177, 230–231
Interreligious marriages, 232
Intersex development, 78, 100
Intersexed (middlesexed) individuals, 78, 100
Intimacy, 50–51, 98, 267
Intimate-partner violence (IPV), 420, 427
Intrafamilial child sexual abuse, 443–444
Intrauterine devices (IUD), 334–335, 337–338
Intravenous drug use, 297
In vitro fertilization (IVF), 324–325
Involved Couple's Inventory, 189, 190–192
Islam, 18, 96, 222–223
Isolation, 429, 442
ISpQ ("Eye Speak," www.ispq.com), 148
"I" statements, 115

J

Jacob Wetterling Act, 446
Jealousy, 28–29, 65–68, 428
Jekyll-and-Hyde personalities, 429
Joint custody, 493, 510–511
Journal of Marriage and Family, 37

K

Kaiser Family Foundation, 201
Kegel exercises, 591
Kid's Turn divorce education program, 509
Kissing, 287

L

Labia, 589
Labor, division of, 82

Lambda Legal, 252
Landmark Harvard Study of Adult Development, 569
Language, 32, 85
Laparoscopy, 340
Latchkey children, 405–406
Late-life marriages, 572–573
LAWbriefs, 261
Lawrence v Texas, 257
Leadership ambiguity, 113
Learning theory of love, 57
Least interest, principle of, 184
Legal changes after marriage, 217
Legal custody, 506
Leisure. *See also* Work-leisure balance, 112, 411–413
Lesbian. *See also* Gays and lesbians; Homosexuality, 244
Lesbian feminism, 31
Lesbigay population, 244
Levitra, 567, 600
LGBT, 244
Life expectancy, 97, 98, 553t17.1
Life of Reason, The (Santayana), 362
"Like a Virgin . . . Again?" (Carpenter), 280
Liking, 50
Listening to yourself, 3
Litigation, 511
Living apart together (LAT), 24t1.6, 166–168, 562
Living together. *See* Cohabitation
Living wills, 560, 629–630
Loneliness, 136
Long-acting reversible contraception (LARC), 335
Long-distance relationships, 151–152
Longevity, 557
Long-term care facilities, 558–561
Long-term care insurance (LTCI), 560
Looking-glass self, 29, 122
Lose-lose solutions, 125
Love, 14, 43–72, 207
   children and, 368
   falling out of, 51, 57, 491
   Islam and, 224
   problems in, 62–65
   stress-management and, 460
   styles of, 45–51
   summary, 71–73
   theories of, 56–59
   triangular view of, 50–51
"Love contracts," 55
Love marriages, 52
Lover, definition of, 70
Love theories, 59t2.1
   attachment, 58–59
   biochemical theories, 58
   evolutionary theory, 56–57
   learning theory, 57
   psychosexual, 58
   sociological, 57–58
Low positives, 186
Ludic love style, 45

Neglect, 441
Negotiation, 117
Neurofeedback, 461
Never-married singles, 138–139
New Beginnings Program, 507
"New" wedding artifact, 213
No Country for Old Men, 426
No-fault divorce, 490
Nonagentic sexual experiences, 433
Noncustodial parents, 508
Nonlove, 50
Nontraditional occupations, 89–90
Nonverbal communication, 108–109
Norplant, 331
Nuclear families, 20–21
NuvaRing®, 332

O

Obsessional following, 64–65
Obsessive relational intrusion
    (ORI), 425
Occupation, 97–98
Occupational sex segregation, 89
Occupations, nontraditional, 89–90
Office romances, 55
Of Marriage (Fuller), 353
Old love, renewing, 574
Old-old, 553
Old Order Amish, 225
"Old" wedding artifact, 213
On-and-off relationships, 198
One Child Policy (China), 317
Oneida community, 18
Online dating. *See also* Internet,
    146–148, 528
Oophorectomy, 338
Open adoption, 329
Open charges, 396
Open couples, 69, 256
Open-ended questions, 114
Open-mindedness, 178
Open relationships. *See also*
    Polyamory, 18
Operant conditioning, 381
Oppositonal defiant disorder, 355
Opting out, 400
Opting Out (Stone), 315, 400
Oral sex, 288–289
Orderliness, 168
Organ or tissue transplants, 297
Ortho Evra®, 332
Ovaries, 592
Overindulgence, 370
Overweight, 463–464
Ovum transfer, 325
Oxytocin, 58, 358

P

Palimony, 166
Palliative care, 463
Pantagamy, 18
Pap test, 592
Parallel style of conflict, 113–114
Parent abuse, 445–446
Parental alienation syndrome,
    502–503

Parental authority, 508, 546
Parental characteristics, 184
Parental choices, 356–357
Parental conflict, 542
Parental consent, 341
Parental disapproval, 198
Parental investment, 86
Parental leave, 92–93, 410
Parental notification, 341
Parental status, 539
Parent Effectiveness Training (PET),
    379t11.1, 383
Parenthood, 208–209, 313–314,
    357–367
Parenting, 312, 351–389
Parents, 9, 162, 193, 219–220,
    363–364, 429–430
Parents, Families, and Friends of
    Lesbians and Gays (PFLAG), 252
Parents for Megan's Law, 446
Partners
    involvement with, 149–152
    knowledge about, 161
    undergraduate interest in, 144
    ways of finding, 144–149
"Partner's night out," 218
Passion, 50–51
Past relationships, 119
Peers, 88
Penis, 592
Pension partners, 159
Perception changes, 124
Perfectionism, 186
Periodic abstinence, 336
Permissive parenting, 364
Personal changes after marriage, 217
Personal fulfillment, 208
Personality, 11, 181
Personality disorders, 64
Personality needs, fulfillment of, 58
Person-to-person commitment, 210
Pets, 19
Pew Research Center, 176, 232, 249,
    260, 262, 263, 265, 318, 353
Phantom of the Opera, The, 84
Phenylethylamine (PEA), 58
Pheromones, 294
Philadephia, 54
Philanthropia, 54
Phileo, 54
Physical abuse, 117, 420, 432
Physical appearance, 178–179
Physical care, 27
Physical custody, 506
Physician-assisted suicide, 564
Physiological androgyny, 100
Pity, 201
Pleasant behavior, 117
Polyaffective, 69
Polyamory, 18, 68–71, 471
Polyandry, 18
Polyfidelity, 69
Polygamy, 15–18
Polygeometry, 69
Polygyny, 15–17
Pool of eligibles, 176
Pornography, 284, 292

Positive androgyny, 100–101
Positive behavior in children, 369
"Positive Parenting through Divorce"
    program, 508
Positive reinforcement, 368
Positive statements, 116
Positive *versus* negative views, 5
Possessive jealousy, 66, 67
POSSLQs (people of the opposite sex
    sharing living quarters), 158
Postmodern families, 21
Postnuptial agreements, 501
Postpartum depression, 358–359
Postpartum psychosis, 360
Post-traumatic stress disorder
    (PTSD), 422
Poverty, 392–394
    feminization of, 94–95
    teen mothers and, 319, 395
    violence and, 428
Power, 28–29, 117, 219
Pragma love style, 45
Praise, 368
Pregnancy, 201, 322
Pregnancy wastage, 321
"Pregnant Man, The," 81
Prejudice, 243
Premarital education programs, 17, 193
Premature ejaculation, 601
Prenuptial agreements, 193–195, 525,
    626–628
Primary groups, 8–9
Primary infertility, 321
Primary partners, 69–70
Primary sexual dysfunction, 596
Princeton Survey Research Associates
    International, 234
Principle of least interest, 184
Priorities, 114
Procreative liberty, 315–316
Pro-Family Pediatricians, 264
Projection, 127
*Promise to Ourselves: A Journey through
    Fatherhood and Divorce*
    (Baldwin), 502
Pronatalism, 311
Prostate cancer, 462–463
Prostate gland, 594
Protestant Reformation, 224–225
Pseudohermaphroditism, 78
Psychoanalytic feminism, 31
Psychological abuse. *See*
    Emotional abuse
Psychological blackmail, 201
Psychological conditions for
    love, 60–61
Psychopathology, parental, 441
Psychosexual theory of love, 58
Pubococcygeun muscle (PC muscle),
    591
Punishment, 381
Puritan-era dating, 154–155

Q

Quads, 69
Quality time, 406